Modern Computer Algebra

Computer algebra systems are gaining more and more importance in all areas of science and engineering. This textbook gives a thorough introduction to the algorithmic basis of the mathematical engine in computer algebra systems.

It is designed to accompany one- or two-semester courses for advanced undergraduate or graduate students in computer science or mathematics. Its comprehensiveness and authority make it also an essential reference for professionals in the area.

Special features include: detailed study of algorithms including time analysis; implementation reports on several topics; complete proofs of the mathematical underpinnings; a wide variety of applications (among others, in chemistry, coding theory, cryptography, computational logic, and the design of calendars and musical scales). Some of this material has never appeared before in book form. Finally, a great deal of historical information and illustration enlivens the text.

Joachim von zur Gathen has a PhD from Universität Zürich, taught at University of Toronto from 1981 to 1994, and is now at Universität Paderborn.

Jürgen Gerhard is completing his PhD and is wissenschaftlicher Mitarbeiter at Universität Paderborn.

Modern Computer Algebra

JOACHIM VON ZUR GATHEN
and
JÜRGEN GERHARD

Universität Paderborn

CAMBRIDGE
UNIVERSITY PRESS

PUBLISHED BY THE PRESS SYNDICATE OF THE UNIVERSITY OF CAMBRIDGE
The Pitt Building, Trumpington Street, Cambridge CB2 1RP

CAMBRIDGE UNIVERSITY PRESS
The Edinburgh Building, Cambridge CB2 2RU, UK http://www.cup.cam.ac.uk
40 West 20th Street, New York, NY 10011-4211, USA http://www.cup.org
10 Stamford Road, Oakleigh, Melbourne 3166, Australia

First published 1999

© Cambridge University Press 1999

Printed in the United Kingdom at the University Press, Cambridge

British Library cataloguing in publication data available

ISBN 0 521 64176 4　　hardback

To Dorothea, Rafaela, Désirée
For endless patience

To Mercedes Cappucino

Contents

Keeping up to date

Addenda and corrigenda, comments, solutions to selected exercises, and ordering information can be found on the book's web page:

http://www-math.uni-paderborn.de/mca/

A Beggar's Book Out-worths a Noble's Blood.[1]

William Shakespeare (1613)

Some books are to be tasted, others to be swallowed,
and some few to be chewed and digested.

Francis Bacon (1597)

Les plus grands analystes eux-mêmes ont bien rarement dédaigné de se
tenir à la portée de la classe *moyenne* des lecteurs; elle est en effet la
plus nombreuse, et celle qui a le plus à profiter dans leurs écrits.[2]

Anonymous referee (1825)

It is true, we have already a great many Books of *Algebra*,
and one might even furnish a moderate Library
purely with Authors on that Subject.

Isaac Newton (1728)

فخررت هذا الكتاب و جمعت فيه جميع ما يحتاج اليه الحاسب
محترزا عن اشباع ممل و اختصار مخل [3]

Ghiyāth al-Dīn Jamshīd ben Masʿūd ben Maḥmūd al-Kāshī (1427)

---

[1] The sources for the quotations are given on pages 689–693.

[2] The greatest analysts [mathematicians] themselves have rarely shied away from keeping within the reach of the *average* class of readers; this is in fact the most numerous one, and the one that stands to profit most from their writing.

[3] I wrote this book and compiled in it everything that is necessary for the computer, avoiding both boring verbosity and misleading brevity.

Introduction

In science and engineering, a successful attack on a problem will usually lead to some equations that have to be solved. There are many types of such equations: differential equations, linear or polynomial equations or inequalities, recurrences, equations in groups, tensor equations, etc. In principle, there are two ways of solving such equations: approximately or exactly. *Numerical analysis* is a well-developed field that provides highly successful mathematical methods and computer software to compute *approximate* solutions.

Computer algebra is a more recent area of computer science, where mathematical tools and computer software are developed for the *exact* solution of equations.

Why use approximate solutions at all if we can have exact solutions? The answer is that in many cases an exact solution is not possible. This may have various reasons: for certain (simple) ordinary differential equations, one can prove that no closed form solution (of a specified type) is possible. More important are questions of efficiency: any system of linear equations, say with rational coefficients, can be solved exactly, but for the huge linear systems that arise in meteorology, nuclear physics, geology or other areas of science, only approximate solutions can be computed efficiently. The exact methods, run on a supercomputer, would not yield answers within a few days or weeks (which is not really acceptable for weather prediction).

However, within its range of exact solvability, computer algebra usually provides more interesting answers than traditional numerical methods. Given a differential equation or a system of linear equations with a parameter t, the scientist gets much more information out of a closed form solution in terms of t than from several solutions for specific values of t.

Many of today's students may not know that the *slide rule* was an indispensable tool of engineers and scientists until the 1960s. *Electronic pocket calculators* made them obsolete within a short time. In the coming years, *computer algebra systems* will similarly replace calculators for many purposes. Although still bulky and expensive (hand-held computer algebra calculators are yet a novelty), these systems can easily perform exact (or arbitrary precision) arithmetic with numbers, matrices, polynomials, etc. They will become an indispensable tool for the scientist and engineer, from students to the work place. These systems are now becoming integrated with other software, like numerical packages, CAD/CAM, and graphics.

The goal of this text is to give an introduction to the basic methods and techniques of computer algebra. Our focus is threefold:

- complete presentation of the mathematical underpinnings,
- asymptotic analysis of our algorithms, sometimes "Oh-free",
- development of asymptotically fast methods.

It is customary to give bounds on running times of algorithms (if any are given at all) in a "big-Oh" form (explained in Section 25.7), say as $O(n \log n)$ for the FFT. We often prove "Oh-free" bounds in the sense that we identify the numerical coefficient of the leading term, as $\frac{3}{2} n \log_2 n$ in the example; we may then add $O(\text{smaller terms})$. But we have not played out the game of minimizing these coefficients; the reader is encouraged to find smaller constants herself.

Many of these fast methods have been known for a quarter of a century, but their impact on computer algebra systems has been slight, partly due to an "unfortunate myth" (Bailey, Lee & Simon 1990) about their practical (ir)relevance. But their usefulness has been forcefully demonstrated in the last few years; we can now solve problems—for example, the factorization of polynomials—of a size that was unassailable a few years ago. We expect this success to expand into other areas of computer algebra, and indeed hope that this text may contribute to this development. The full treatment of these fast methods motivates the "modern" in its title. (Our title is a bit risqué, since even a "modern" text in a rapidly evolving discipline such as ours will obsolesce quickly.)

The basic objects of computer algebra are numbers and polynomials. Throughout the text, we stress the structural and algorithmic similarities between these two domains, and also where the similarities break down. We concentrate on polynomials, in particular univariate polynomials over a field, and pay special attention to finite fields.

We will consider arithmetic algorithms in some basic domains. The tasks that we will analyze include conversion between representations, addition, subtraction, multiplication, division, division with remainder, greatest common divisors, and factorization. The basic domains for computer algebra are the natural numbers, the rational numbers, finite fields, and polynomial rings.

Our three goals, as stated above, are too ambitious to keep up throughout. In some chapters, we have to content ourselves with sketches of methods and outlooks on further results. Due to space limitations, we sometimes have recourse to the lamentable device of "leaving the proof to the reader". Don't worry, be happy: solutions to the corresponding exercises are available on the book's web site.

After writing most of the material, we found that we could structure the book into five parts, each named after a mathematician that made a pioneering contribution on which some (but, of course, not all) of the modern methods in the respective part rely. In each part, we also present selected applications of some of the algorithmic methods.

The first part EUCLID examines Euclid's algorithm for calculating the gcd, and presents the subresultant theory for polynomials. Applications are numerous: modular algorithms, continued fractions, Diophantine approximation, the Chinese Remainder Algorithm, secret sharing, and the decoding of BCH codes.

The second part NEWTON presents the basics of fast arithmetic: FFT-based multiplication, division with remainder and polynomial equation solving via Newton iteration, and fast methods for the Euclidean Algorithm and the solution of systems of linear equations. The FFT originated in signal processing, and we discuss one of its applications, image compression.

The third part GAUSS deals exclusively with polynomial problems. We start with univariate factorization over finite fields, and include the modern methods that make attacks on enormously large problems feasible. Then we discuss polynomials with rational coefficients. The two basic algorithmic ingredients are Hensel lifting and short vectors in lattices. The latter has found many applications, from breaking certain cryptosystems to Diophantine approximation.

The fourth part FERMAT is devoted to two integer problems that lie at the foundation of algorithmic number theory: primality testing and factorization. The most famous modern application of these classical topics is in public key cryptography.

The fifth part HILBERT treats three different topics which are somewhat more advanced than the rest of the text, and where we can only exhibit the foundations of a rich theory. The first topic is Gröbner bases, a successful approach to deal with multivariate polynomials, in particular questions about common roots of several polynomials. The next topic is symbolic integration, where we concentrate on the basic case of integrating rational functions. The final topic is symbolic summation; we discuss polynomial and hypergeometric summation.

The text concludes with an appendix that presents some foundational material in the language we use throughout the book: The basics of groups, rings, and fields, linear algebra, probability theory, asymptotic O-notation, and complexity theory.

Each of the first three parts contains an implementation report on some of the algorithms presented in the text. As case studies, we use two special purpose packages for integer and polynomial arithmetic: NTL by Victor Shoup and BIPOLAR by the authors.

Most chapters end with some bibliographical and historical notes or supplementary remarks, and a variety of exercises. The latter are marked according to their difficulty: exercises with a * are somewhat more advanced, and the few marked with ** are more difficult or may require material not covered in the text. Laborious (but not necessarily difficult) exercises are marked by a long arrow $\longrightarrow$. The book's web page `http://www-math.uni-paderborn.de/mca/` has some hints and solutions.

This book presents foundations for the mathematical engine underlying any computer algebra system, and we give substantial coverage—often, but not always, up to the state of the art—for the material of the first three parts, dealing with Euclid's algorithm, fast arithmetic, and the factorization of polynomials. But we hasten to point out some unavoidable shortcomings. For one, we cannot cover completely even those areas that we discuss, and our treatment leaves out major interesting developments in the areas of computational linear algebra, sparse multivariate polynomials, combinatorics and computational number theory, quantifier elimination and solving polynomial equations, and differential and difference equations. Secondly, some important questions are left untouched at all; we only mention computational group theory, parallel computation, computing with transcendental functions, isolating real and complex roots of polynomials, and the combination of symbolic and numeric methods. Finally, a successful computer algebra system involves much more than just the mathematical engine: efficient data structures, a fast kernel and a large compiled or interpreted library, user interface, graphics capability, clever marketing, etc. These issues are highly technology-dependent, and there is no single good solution for them.

The present book can be used as the textbook for a one-semester or a two-semester course in computer algebra. The basic arithmetic algorithms are discussed in Chapters 2 and 3, and Sections 4.1–4.4, 5.1–5.5, 8.1–8.2, 9.1–9.4, 14.1–14.6, and 15.1–15.2. In addition, a one-semester undergraduate course might be slanted towards computational number theory (9.5, 18.1–18.4, and parts of Chapter 20), geometry (21.1–21.6), or integration (4.5, 5.11, 6.2–6.4, and Chapter 22), supplemented by fun applications from 4.6–4.8, 5.6–5.9, 6.8, 9.6, Chapter 13, and Chapters 1 and 24. A two-semester course could teach the "basics" and 6.1–6.7, 10.1–10.2, 15.4–15.6, 16.1–16.5, 18.1–18.3, 19.1–19.2, 19.4, 19.5 or 19.6–19.7, and one or two of Chapters 21–23, maybe with some applications from Chapters 17, 20, and 24. A graduate course can be more eclectic. We once taught a course on "factorization", using parts of Chapters 14–16 and 19. Another possibility is a graduate course on "fast algorithms" based on Part II. For any of these suggestions, there is enough material so that an instructor will still have plenty of choice of which areas to skip. The logical dependencies between the chapters are given in Figure 1.

The prerequisite for such a course is linear algebra and a certain level of mathematical maturity; particularly useful is a basic familiarity with algebra and analysis of algorithms. However, to allow for the large variations in students' background, we have included an appendix that presents the necessary tools. For that material, the border between the boring and the overly demanding varies too much to get it right for everyone. If those notions and tools are unfamiliar, an instructor may have to expand beyond the condensed description in the appendix. Otherwise,

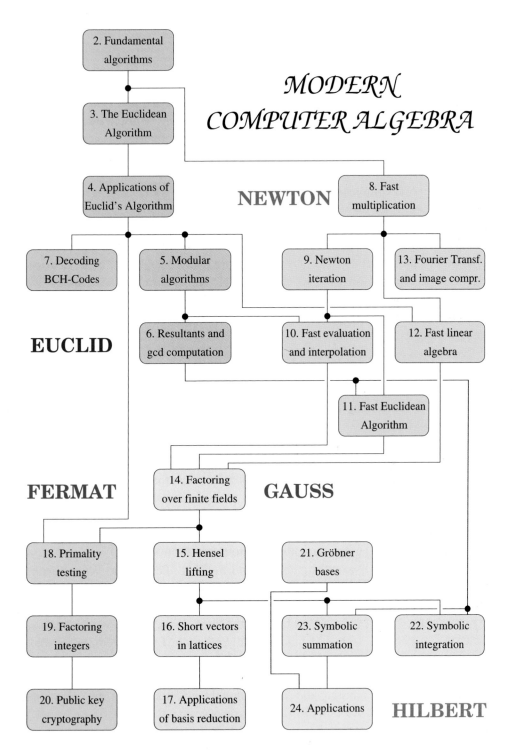

FIGURE 1: Leitfaden.

most of the presentation is self-contained, and the exceptions are clearly indicated. By their nature, some of the applications assume a background in the relevant area.

The beginning of each part presents a biographical sketch of the scientist after which it is named, and throughout the text we indicate some of the origins of our material. For lack of space and competence, this is not done in a systematic way, let alone with the goal of completeness, but we do point to some early sources, often centuries old, and quote some of the original work. Interest in such historical issues is, of course, a matter of taste. It is satisfying to see how many algorithms are based on venerable methods; our essentially "modern" aspect is the concern with asymptotic complexity and running times, faster and faster algorithms, and their computer implementation.

Acknowledgements.   This material has grown from undergraduate and graduate courses that the first author has taught over more than a decade in Toronto, Zürich, Santiago de Chile, Canberra, and Paderborn. He wants to thank above all his two teachers: Volker Strassen, who taught him mathematics, and Allan Borodin, who taught him computer science. To his friend Erich Kaltofen he is grateful for many enlightening discussions about computer algebra.

The second author wants to thank his two supervisors, Helmut Meyn and Volker Strehl, for many stimulating lectures in computer algebra.

The support and enthusiasm of two groups of people have made the courses a pleasure to teach. On the one hand, the colleagues, several of whom actually shared in the teaching: Leopoldo Bertossi, Allan Borodin, Steve Cook, Faith Fich, Shuhong Gao, John Lipson, Mike Luby, Charlie Rackoff, and Victor Shoup. On the other hand, lively groups of students took the courses, solved the exercises and tutored others about them, and some of them were the scribes for the course notes that formed the nucleus of this text. We thank particularly Paul Beame, Isabel de Correa, Wayne Eberly, Mark Giesbrecht, Rod Glover, Silke Hartlieb, Jim Hoover, Keju Ma, Jim McInnes, Pierre McKenzie, Sun Meng, Rob Morenz, Michael Nöcker, Daniel Panario, Michel Pilote, and François Pitt.

Thanks for help on various matters go to Eric Bach, Peter Blau, Wieb Bosma, Louis Bucciarelli, Désirée von zur Gathen, Keith Geddes, Dima Grigoryev, Johan Håstad, Dieter Herzog, Marek Karpinski, Wilfrid Keller, Les Klinger, Werner Krandick, Ton Levelt, János Makowsky, Ernst Mayr, François Morain, Gerry Myerson, Michael Nüsken, David Pengelley, Bill Pickering, Tomás Recio, Jeff Shallit, Igor Shparlinski, Irina Shparlinski, and Paul Zimmermann.

We thank Sandra Feisel, Carsten Keller, Thomas Lücking, Dirk Müller, and Olaf Müller for programming and the substantial task of producing the index, and Marianne Wehry for tireless help with the typing.

We are indebted to Sandra Feisel, Adalbert Kerber, Preda Mihăilescu, Michael Nöcker, Daniel Panario, Peter Paule, Daniel Reischert, Victor Shoup, and Volker Strehl for carefully proofreading parts of the draft.

It is now up to the readers to discover the remaining errors. They are encouraged to send feedback, comments, and corrections by electronic mail to the authors: {gathen,jngerhar}@uni-paderborn.de. Errata and addenda will be maintained on the book's web page http://www-math.uni-paderborn.de/mca/.

Note. We produced the postscript files for this book with the invaluable help of the following software packages: Leslie Lamport's LaTeX, based on Don Knuth's TeX, Klaus Lagally's ArabTeX, Oren Patashnik's BibTeX, Pehong Chen's MakeIndex, MAPLE, MU-PAD, Victor Shoup's NTL, Thomas Williams' and Colin Kelley's gnuplot, the Persistence of Vision Ray Tracer POV-Ray, and xfig.

Any sufficiently advanced technology is indistinguishable from magic.
Paul Theroux (1981)

L'avancement et la perfection des mathématiques
sont intimement liés à la prospérité de l'État.[1]
Napoléon I. (1812)

It must be easy [...] to bring out a *double* set of *results*, viz. —1st, the
numerical magnitudes which are the results of operations performed
on *numerical data*. [...] 2ndly, the *symbolical results* to be attached to
those numerical results, which symbolical results are not less the
necessary and logical consequences of operations performed upon
symbolical data, than are numerical results when the data are
numerical.
Augusta Ada Lovelace (1843)

There are too goddamned many machines that spew out data too fast.
Robert Ludlum (1995)

After all, the whole purpose of science is not technology—
God knows we have gadgets enough already.
Eric Temple Bell (1937)

.

.

.

.

.

---

[1] The advancement and perfection of mathematics are intimately connected with the prosperity of the State.

1
Cyclohexane, cryptography, codes, and computer algebra

Three examples in this chapter illustrate some applications of the ideas and methods of computer algebra: the spatial configurations (conformations) of the cyclohexane molecule, a chemical problem with an intriguing geometric solution; a cryptographic protocol for the secure transmission of messages; and distributed codes for sharing secrets or sending packets over a faulty network. Throughout this book you will find such sample applications in a wide variety of areas, from the design of calendars and musical scales to image compression and the intersection of algebraic curves. The last section in this chapter gives a concise overview of some computer algebra systems.

1.1. Cyclohexane conformations

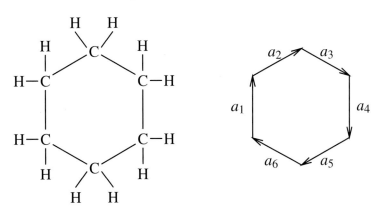

FIGURE 1.1: The structure formula for cyclohexane (C_6H_{12}), and the orientation we give to the bonds $a_1, \ldots, a_6$.

We start with an example from chemistry. It illustrates the three typical steps in mathematical applications: creating a mathematical model of the problem at hand, "solving" the model, and interpreting the solution in the original problem. Usually, none of these steps is straightforward, and one often has to go back and modify the approach.

Cyclohexane C_6H_{12} (Figure 1.1), a molecule from organic chemistry, is a hydrocarbon consisting of six carbon atoms (C) connected to each other in a cycle and twelve hydrogen atoms (H), two attached to each carbon atom. The four bonds of one carbon atom (two bonds to adjacent carbon atoms and two bonds to hydrogen atoms) are arranged in the form of a tetrahedron, with the carbon in the center and its bonds pointing to the four corners. The angle α between any two bonds is about 109 degrees (the precise value of α satisfies $\cos \alpha = -1/3$). Two adjacent carbon atoms may freely rotate around the bond between them.

Chemists have observed that cyclohexane occurs in two incongruent conformations (which are not transformable into each other by rotations and reflections), a "chair" (Figure 1.2) and a "boat" (Figure 1.3), and experiments have shown that the "chair" occurs far more frequently than the "boat". The frequency of occurrence of a conformation depends on its free energy—a general rule is that molecules try to minimize the free energy—which in turn depends on the spatial structure.

When modeling the molecule by means of plastic tubes (Figure 1.4) representing the carbon atoms and the bonds between them (omitting the hydrogen atoms for simplicity) in such a way that rotations around the bonds are possible, one observes that there is a certain amount of freedom in moving the atoms by rotations around the bonds in the "boat" conformation (we will call it the **flexible** conformation), but that the "chair" conformation is **rigid**, and that it appears to be impossible to get from the "boat" to the "chair" conformation . Can we mathematically model and, if possible, explicitly describe this behavior?

We let $a_1, \ldots, a_6 \in \mathbb{R}^3$ be the orientations of the six bonds in three-space, so that all six vectors point in the same direction around the cyclic structure (Figure 1.1), and normalize the distance between two adjacent carbon atoms to be one. By $u \star v = u_1 v_1 + u_2 v_2 + u_3 v_3$ we denote the usual inner product of two vectors $u = (u_1, u_2, u_3)$ and $v = (v_1, v_2, v_3)$ in $\mathbb{R}^3$. The cosine theorem says that $u \star v = \|u\|_2 \cdot \|v\|_2 \cdot \cos \beta$, where $\|u\|_2 = (u \star u)^{1/2}$ is the Euclidean norm and $\beta \in [0, \pi]$ is the angle between u and v, when both vectors are rooted at the origin. The above conditions then lead to the following system of equations:

$$
\begin{aligned}
a_1 \star a_1 = a_2 \star a_2 = \cdots = a_6 \star a_6 &= 1, \\
a_1 \star a_2 = a_2 \star a_3 = \cdots = a_6 \star a_1 &= \frac{1}{3}, \\
a_1 + a_2 + \cdots + a_6 &= 0.
\end{aligned}
\tag{1}
$$

The first line says that the length of each bond is 1. The second line expresses the fact that the angle between two bonds adjacent to the same carbon atom is α (the cosine is $1/3$ instead of $-1/3$ since, seen from the carbon atom, the two bonds have opposite orientation). Finally, the last line expresses the cyclic nature of the structure.

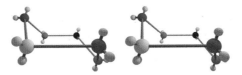

FIGURE 1.2: A stereo image of a "chair" conformation of cyclohexane. To see a three-dimensional image, hold the two pictures right in front of your eyes. Then relax your eyes and do not focus at the foreground, so that the two pictures fade away and each of them splits into two separate images (one for each eye). By further relaxing your eyes, try to match the right image that your left eye sees with the left image that your right eye sees. Now you see three images, each of the two outer ones only with one of your eyes, and the middle one with both eyes. Cautiously focus on the middle image, at the same time slowly moving the book away from your head, until the image is sharp. (This works best without wearing glasses.)

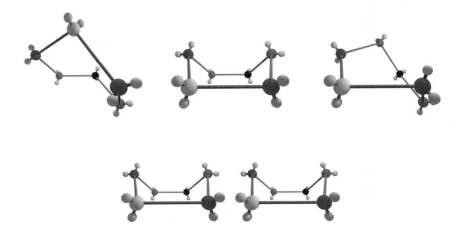

FIGURE 1.3: Three "boat" conformations of cyclohexane and a stereo image of the middle one (see Figure 1.2 for a viewing instruction).

Together, (1) comprises $6+6+3 = 15$ equations in the 18 coordinates of the points $a_1, \ldots, a_6$. The first ones are quadratic, and the last ones are linear. There is still redundancy coming from the whole structure's possibility to move and rotate around freely in three-space. One possibility to remedy this is to introduce three more equations expressing the fact that a_1 and a_2 are parallel to the x-axis respectively the x, y-plane. These equations can be solved with a computer algebra system, but the resulting description of the solutions is highly complicated and non-intuitive.

For a successful solution, we pursue a different, more symmetric approach, by taking the inner products $S_{ij} = a_i \star a_j$ for $1 \leq i, j \leq 6$ as unknowns instead of the

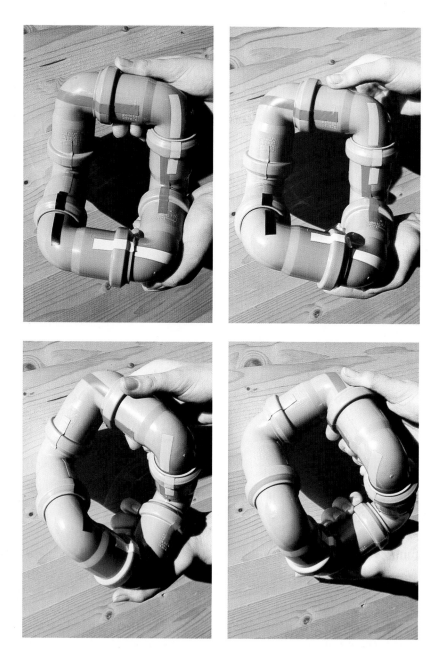

FIGURE 1.4: A plumbing knee model of cyclohexane, with nearly straight angles.

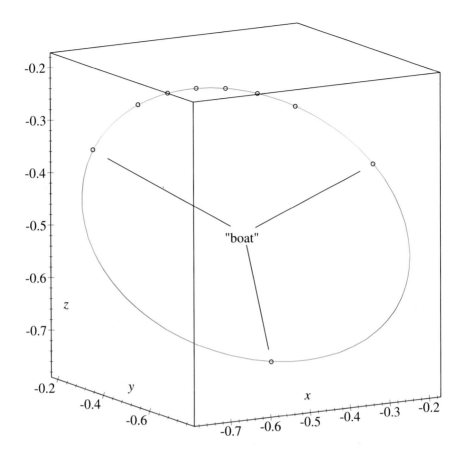

FIGURE 1.5: The curve E.

coordinates of $a_1, \ldots, a_6$. This is described in detail in Section 24.4. Under the conditions (1), S_{ij} is the cosine of the angle between a_i and a_j. It turns out that all S_{ij} depend linearly on S_{13}, S_{35}, and S_{51}, and that the triples of values $(S_{13}, S_{35}, S_{51}) \in \mathbb{R}^3$ leading to the flexible conformations are given by the space curve E in Figure 1.5. The solution makes heavy use of various computer algebra tools, such as **resultants** (Chapter 6), **polynomial factorization** (Part III), and **Gröbner bases** (Chapter 21). The three marked points $(-1/3, -1/3, -7/9)$, $(-1/3, -7/9, -1/3)$ and $(-7/9, -1/3, -1/3)$ correspond to the three "boat" conformations in Figure 1.3 (all of them are equivalent by cyclically permuting $a_1, \ldots, a_6$). Actually, some information gets lost in the transition from the a_i to the S_{ij}, and each point on the curve E corresponds to precisely two spatial conformations which are mirror images of each other. The rigid conformation corresponds to the isolated solution $S_{13} = S_{35} = S_{51} = -1/3$ not lying on the curve.

We built the simple physical "model" in Figure 1.4 of something similar to cyclohexane as follows. We bought six plastic plumbing "knees", with approximately

FIGURE 1.6: Eight flexible conformations of cyclohexane corresponding to the eight points marked in Figure 1.5. The first and the eighth ones are "boats". The point of view is such that the positions of the red, green, and blue carbon atoms are invariant for all eight pictures.

a right angle. (German plumbing knees actually have an angle of about 93 degrees, for some deep hydrodynamic reason.) This differs considerably from the 109 degrees of the carbon tetrahedron, but on the other hand, it only cost about DM 14. We stuck the six parts together and pulled an elastic cord through them to keep them from falling apart. Then one can smoothly turn the structure through the flexible conformations corresponding to the curve in Figure 1.5, physically "feeling" the curve. Pulling the whole thing forcibly apart, one can also get into the "chair" position. Now no wiggling or gentle twisting will move the structure; it is quite rigid.

1.2. The RSA cryptosystem

The basic scenario for cryptography is as follows. Bob wants to send a message to Alice in such a way that an eavesdropper (Eve) listening to the transmission channel cannot understand the message. This is done by enciphering the message so that only Alice, possessing the right **key**, can decipher it, but Eve, having no access to the key, has no chance to recover the message.

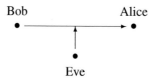

In classical **symmetric** cryptosystems, Alice and Bob use the same key for encryption and decryption. The **RSA cryptosystem**, described in detail in Section 20.2, is an **asymmetric** or **public key cryptosystem**. Alice has a **public key**

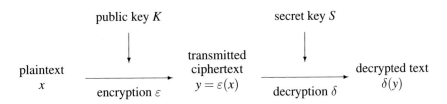

public key K secret key S

plaintext   transmitted   decrypted text

x ciphertext $\delta(y)$

$y = \varepsilon(x)$

encryption ε decryption δ

FIGURE 1.7: A public key cryptosystem.

K that she publishes in some directory, and a **secret key** S that she keeps secret. To encrypt a message, Bob uses Alice's public key, and only Alice can decrypt the ciphertext using her secret key (Figure 1.7).

The RSA system works as follows. First, Alice randomly chooses two large (150 digit, say) prime numbers $p \neq q$ and computes their product $N = pq$. Efficient probabilistic **primality tests** (Chapter 18) make it easy to find such primes and then N, but the problem of finding p and q, when just N is given (that is, factoring N), seems very hard (see Chapter 19). Then she randomly chooses another integer $e \in \{2, \ldots, \varphi(N) - 2\}$, where φ is **Euler's totient function** (Section 4.2). For our particular N, the **Chinese Remainder Theorem** 5.3 implies that $\varphi(N) = (p-1) \cdot (q-1)$. Then Alice publishes the pair $K = (N, e)$. To obtain her secret key, Alice uses the **Extended Euclidean Algorithm** 3.6 to compute $d \in \{2, \ldots, \varphi(N) - 2\}$ such that $ed \equiv 1 \bmod \varphi(N)$, and $S = (N, d)$ is her secret key. Thus $(ed - 1)/\varphi(N)$ is an integer.

Before they can exchange messages, both parties agree upon a way of encoding messages (pieces of text) as integers in the range $0, \ldots, N - 1$ (this is not part of the cryptosystem itself). For example, if messages are built from the 26 letters A through Z, we might identify A with 0, B with 1, …, Z with 25, and use the 26-ary representation for encoding. The message "CAESAR" is then encoded as

$$2 \cdot 26^0 + 0 \cdot 26^1 + 4 \cdot 26^2 + 18 \cdot 26^3 + 0 \cdot \ 6^4 + 17 \cdot 26^5 = 202\,302\,466.$$

Long messages are broken into pieces. Now Bob wants to send a message $x \in \{0, \ldots, N - 1\}$ to Alice that only she can read. He looks up her public key (N, e), computes the encryption $y = \varepsilon(x) \in \{0, \ldots, N - 1\}$ of x such that $y \equiv x^e \bmod N$, and sends y. Computing y can be done very efficiently using **repeated squaring** (Algorithm 4.8). To decrypt y, Alice uses her secret key (N, d) to compute the decryption $x^* = \delta(y) \in \{0, \ldots, N - 1\}$ of y with $x^* \equiv y^d \bmod N$. Now **Euler's theorem** (Section 18.1) says that $x^{\varphi(N)} \equiv 1 \bmod N$. Thus

$$x^* \equiv y^d \equiv x^{ed} = x \cdot \left(x^{\varphi(N)}\right)^{(ed-1)/\varphi(N)} \equiv x \bmod N,$$

and it follows that $x^* = x$ since x and x^* are both in $\{0, \ldots, N - 1\}$.

Without knowledge of d, however, it seems currently infeasible to compute x from N, e, and y. The only known way to do this is to factor N into its prime factors, and then to compute d with the Extended Euclidean Algorithm as Alice did, but **factoring integers** (Chapter 19) is extremely time-consuming: 300 digit numbers are beyond the capabilities of currently known factoring algorithms even on modern supercomputers or workstation networks.

Software packages like PGP ("Pretty Good Privacy"; see Zimmermann (1996) and http://www.pgp.com) use the RSA cryptosystem for encrypting and authenticating e-mail and data files, and for secure communication over local area networks or the internet.

1.3. Distributed data structures

We start with another problem from cryptography: **secret sharing**. Suppose that, for some positive integer n, we have n players that want to share a common secret in such a way that all of them together can reconstruct the secret but any subset of $n - 1$ of them or less cannot do so. The reader may imagine that the secret is a key in a cryptosystem or a code guarding a common bank account or inheritance, or an authorization for a financial transaction of a company which requires the signature of a certain number of managers. This can be solved by using interpolation (Section 5.2), as follows.

We choose $2n - 1$ values $f_1, \ldots, f_{n-1}, u_0, \ldots, u_{n-1}$ in a field F (say, F is $\mathbb{Q}$ or a **finite field**) such that the u_i are distinct, and let f be the polynomial $f_{n-1}x^{n-1} + \cdots + f_1 x + f_0$, where $f_0 \in F$ is the secret, encoded in an appropriate way. Then we give $v_i = f(u_i) = f_{n-1}u_i^{n-1} + \cdots + f_1 u_i + f_0$ to player i. The reconstruction of the polynomial f from its values $v_0, \ldots, v_{n-1}$ at the n distinct points $u_0, \ldots, u_{n-1}$ is called **interpolation** and may be performed, for example, by using the **Lagrange interpolation formula** (Section 5.2). The interpolating polynomial at n points of degree less than n is unique, and hence all n players together can recover f and the secret f_0, but one can show that any proper subset of them can obtain no information on the secret. More precisely, all elements of F—as potential values of f_0—are equally consistent with the knowledge of fewer than n players. We discuss the secret sharing scheme in Section 5.3.

Essentially the same scheme works for a different problem: reliable routing. Suppose that we want to send a message consisting of several packets over a network (for example, the internet) that occasionally loses packets. We want to encode a message of length n into not many more than n packets in such a way that after a loss of up to l arbitrary packets the message can still be recovered. Such a scheme is called an **erasure code**. (We briefly discuss the related **error correcting codes**, which are designed for networks that sometimes perturb packets but do not lose them, in Chapter 7.) An obvious solution would be to send the message

l times, but this increases message length and hence slows down communication speed by a factor of l and is unacceptable even for small values of l.

Again we may assume that each packet is encoded as an element of some field F, and that the whole message is the sequence of packets $f_0, \ldots, f_{n-1}$. Then we choose $k = n + l$ distinct evaluation points $u_0, \ldots, u_{k-1} \in F$ and send the k packets $f(u_0), \ldots, f(u_{k-1})$ over the net. Assuming that the sequence number i is contained in the packet header and that the recipient knows $u_0, \ldots, u_{k-1}$, she can reconstruct the original message—the (coefficients of the) polynomial f—from any n of the surviving packages by interpolation (and may discard any others).

The above scheme can also be used to distribute n data blocks (for example, records of a database) among $k = n + l$ computers in such a way that after failure of up to l of them the complete information can still be recovered. The difference between secret sharing and this scheme is that in the former the relevant piece of information is only *one* coefficient of f, while in the latter it is the whole polynomial.

The above methods can be viewed as problems in **distributed data structures**. Parallel and distributed computing is an active area of research in computer science. Developing algorithms and data structures for parallel computing is a nontrivial task, often more challenging than for sequential computing. The amount of parallelism that a particular problem admits is sometimes difficult to detect. In computer algebra, **modular algorithms** (Chapters 4 and 5) provide a "natural" parallelism for a certain class of algebraic problems. These are divided into smaller problems by reduction modulo several "primes", the subproblems can be solved independently in parallel, and the solution is put together using the **Chinese Remainder Algorithm** 5.4. An important particular case is when the "primes" are linear polynomials $x - u_i$. Then modular reduction corresponds to evaluation at u_i, and the Chinese Remainder Algorithm is just interpolation at all points u_i, as in the examples above.

If the interpolation points are **roots of unity** (Section 8.2), then there is a particularly efficient method for evaluating and interpolating at those points, the **Fast Fourier Transform** (Chapters 8 and 13). It is the starting point for efficient algorithms for polynomial (and integer) arithmetic in Part II.

1.4. Computer algebra systems

We give a short overview of the computer algebra systems available at the time of writing. We do not present much detail, nor do we aim for completeness.

The vast majority of this book's material is of a fundamental nature and technology-independent. But this short section and some other places where we discuss implementations date the book; if the rapid progress in this area continues as expected, some of this material will become obsolete in a short time.

Computer algebra systems have historically evolved in several stages. An early forerunner was Williams' (1961) PMS, which could calculate floating point polynomial gcd's. The *first generation*, beginning in the late 1960s, comprised MACSYMA from Joel Moses's MATHLAB group at MIT, SCRATCHPAD from Richard Jenks at IBM, REDUCE by Tony Hearn, and SAC-I (now SACLIB) by George Collins. MUMATH by David Stoutemyer ran on a small microprocessor; its successor DERIVE is available on the hand-held TI-92. These researchers and their teams developed systems with algebraic engines capable of doing amazing *exact* (or *formal* or *symbolic*) computations: differentiation, integration, factorization, etc. The *second generation* started with MAPLE by Keith Geddes and Gaston Gonnet from the University of Waterloo in 1985 and MATHEMATICA by Stephen Wolfram. They began to provide modern interfaces and graphic capabilities, and the hype surrounding the launching of MATHEMATICA did much to make these systems widely known. The *third generation* is on the market now: AXIOM, a successor of SCRATCHPAD, by NAG, MAGMA by John Cannon at the University of Sydney, and MUPAD by Benno Fuchssteiner at the University of Paderborn. These systems incorporate a categorical approach and operator calculations. MUPAD is designed to also work in a multiprocessor environment.

Today's research and development of computer algebra systems is driven by three goals, which sometimes conflict: wide functionality (the capability of solving a large range of different problems), ease of use (user interface, graphics display), and speed (how big a problem you can solve with a routine calculation, say in a day on a workstation). This text will concentrate on the latter goal. We will see the basics of the fastest algorithms available today, mainly for some problems in polynomial manipulation. Several groups have developed software for these basic operations: PARI by Henri Cohen in Bordeaux, LIDIA by Johannes Buchmann in Darmstadt, software by Arjen Lenstra and Mark Manasse at Bellcore, NTL by Victor Shoup, packages by Erich Kaltofen, and BIPOLAR in development at Paderborn.

A central problem is the factorization of polynomials. Enormous progress has been achieved in the last few years, in particular over finite fields. In 1991, the largest problems amenable to routine calculation were about 2 KB in size, while in 1995 Shoup's software could handle problems of about 500 KB. Almost all the progress here is due to new algorithmic ideas, and this problem will serve as a guiding light for this text.

Computer algebra systems have a wide variety of applications in fields that require computations that are tedious, lengthy and difficult to get right when done by hand. In physics, computer algebra systems are used in high energy physics, for quantum electrodynamics, quantum chromodynamics, satellite orbit and rocket trajectory computations and celestial mechanics in general. As an example, Delaunay calculated the orbit of the moon under the influence of the sun and a non-spherical earth with a tilted ecliptic. This work took twenty years to complete and was published in 1867. It was shown, in 20 hours on a small computer in 1970, to be correct to nine decimal places. Lambe & Radford (1997) present a modern application to quantum groups.

Important implementation issues for a general-purpose computer algebra system concern things like the user interface (see Kajler & Soiffer 1998 for an overview), memory management and garbage collection, and which representations and simplifications are allowed for the various algebraic objects.

Their power of visualization and of solving nontrivial examples makes computer algebra systems more and more appealing for use in education. Many topics in calculus and linear algebra can be beautifully illustrated with this technology. The eleven reports in the Special Issue of the *Journal of Symbolic Computation* (Lambe 1997) give an idea of what can be achieved. The (self-referential) use in computer algebra courses is obvious; in fact, this text grew out of courses that the first author has taught at several institutions, using MAPLE (and later other systems) since 1986.

As in most active branches of science, the *sociology* of computer algebra is shaped by its leading conferences, journals, and the researchers running these. The premier research conference is the annual International Symposium on Symbolic and Algebraic Computation (ISSAC), into which several earlier streams of meetings have been amalgamated. It is run by a Steering Committee, and national societies such as the US ACM's *Special Interest Group on Symbolic and Algebraic Manipulation* (SIGSAM), the *Fachgruppe Computeralgebra* of the German GI, and others, are heavily involved. Its venues in the 1990s have been Tokyo (1990), Bonn (1991), Berkeley (1992), Kiev (1993), Oxford (1994), Montréal (1995), Zürich (1996), Maui (1997), Rostock (1998), Vancouver (1999), and St. Andrews (2000). In addition, there are specialized meetings such as MEGA (multivariate polynomials), DISCO (distributed systems), and PASCO (parallel computation). Sometimes relevant results are presented at related conferences, such as STOC, FOCS, or AAECC. Several computer algebra systems vendors organize regular workshops or user group meetings.

The highly successful *Journal of Symbolic Computation*, created in 1985 by Bruno Buchberger, is the undisputed leader for research publications. Some high-quality journals with a different focus sometimes contain articles in the field: *computational complexity*, *Journal of the ACM*, *Mathematics of Computation*, and *SIAM Journal on Computing*. Other journals, such as *AAECC* and *Theoretical Computer Science*, have some overlap with computer algebra.

Part I
Euclid

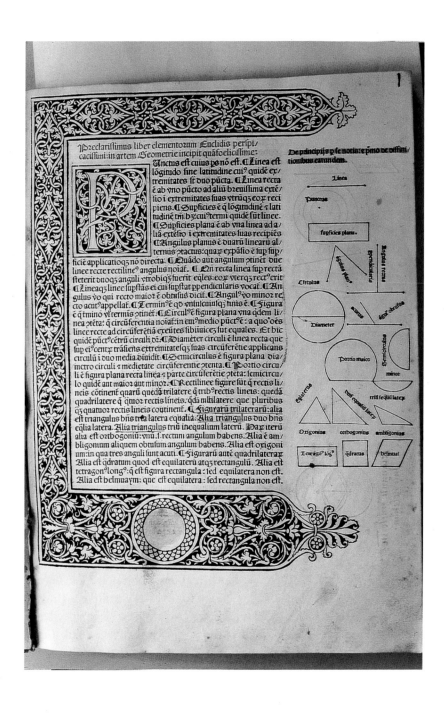

Little is known about the person of Euclid (Εὐχλείδης, c. 320–c. 275 BC). Proclus (410–485 AD) edited and commented his famous work, the *Elements* (στοιχεῖα), and summed up the meager knowledge about Euclid: *Euclid put together the* Elements, *collected many of Eudoxus' theorems, perfected many of Theaitetus', and also brought to irrefragable demonstration the things which were only somewhat loosely proved by his predecessors. This man lived in the time of the first Ptolemy. For Archimedes, who came immediately after the first (Ptolemy), makes mention of Euclid: and, further, they say that Ptolemy once asked him if there was in geometry any shorter way than that of the elements, and he answered that there was no royal road to geometry. He is then younger than the pupils of Plato but older than Eratosthenes and Archimedes; for the latter were contemporary with one another, as Eratosthenes somewhere says* (translation[1] from Heath 1925).

By interpolating between Plato's (427–347 BC) students, Archimedes (287–212 BC), and Eratosthenes (c. 275–195 BC), we can guess that Euclid lived around 300 BC; Ptolemy reigned 306–283. It is likely that Euclid learned mathematics in Athens from Plato's students. Later, he founded a school at Alexandria, and this is presumably where most of the *Elements* was written. An anecdote relates how "some one who had begun to read geometry with Euclid, when he had learned the first theorem, asked Euclid, 'But what shall I get by learning these things?' Euclid called his slave and said 'Give him threepence, since he must make gain out of what he learns.'"

In later parts of this book, we will present two giants of mathematics—Newton and Gauß—and two great mathematicians—Fermat and Hilbert. Archimedes is the third giant, in our subjective reckoning. Euclid's ticket to enter our little Hall of Fame is not a wealth of original ideas, but—besides his algorithm for the gcd—his insistence that everything must be proven from a few axioms, as he does in his systematic collection and orderly presentation of the mathematical thought of his times in the thirteen books (chapters) of his *Elements*. Probably written around 300 BC, he presents his material in the axiom-definition-lemma-theorem-proof style which—somewhat modified—has survived through the millenia. Euclid's methods go back to Aristotle's (384–322 BC) peripatetic school, and to the Eleatics.

After the Bible, the *Elements* is apparently the most often printed book, an eternal bestseller with a vastly longer half-life (before oblivion) than current-day bestsellers. It was *the* mathematical textbook for over two millenia. (In spite of their best efforts, the authors of the present text expect it to be superseded long before 4296 AD.) Even in 1908, a translator of the *Elements* exulted: *Euclid's*

---

[1] Reprinted with the kind permission of Dover Publications Inc., Mineola NY.

work will live long after all the text-books of the present day are superseded and forgotten. It is one of the noblest monuments of antiquity; no mathematician worthy of the name can afford not to know Euclid. Since the invention of non-Euclidean geometry and the new ideas of Klein and Hilbert in the 19th century, we don't take the *Elements* quite that seriously any longer.

In the Dark Ages, Europe's intellectuals were more interested in the maximal number of angels able to dance on a needle tip, and the *Elements* mainly survived in the Arabic civilization. The first translation from the Greek was done by Al-Ḥajjāj ben Yūsuf ben Maṭar (c. 786–835) for Caliph Harūn al-Rashīd (766–809). These were later translated into Latin, and Erhard Ratdolt produced in Venice the first printed edition of the *Elements* in 1482; in fact, this was the first mathematics book to be printed. On page 21 we reproduce its first page from a copy in the library of the University of Basel; the underlining is possibly by the lawyer Bonifatius Amerbach, its 16th century owner, who was a friend of Erasmus.

Most of the *Elements* deals with geometry, but Books 7, 8, and 9 treat arithmetic. Proposition 2 of Book 7 asks: "Given two numbers not prime to one another, to find their greatest common measure", and the core of the algorithm goes as follows: "Let AB, CD be the two given numbers not prime to one another [...] if CD does not measure AB, then, the lesser of the numbers AB, CD being continually subtracted from the greater, some number will be left which will measure the one before it" (translation from Heath 1925).

Numbers here are represented by line segments, and the proof that the last number left (dividing the one before it) is a common divisor and the greatest one is carried out for the case of two division steps ($\ell = 2$ in Algorithm 3.6). This is Euclid's algorithm, "the oldest nontrivial algorithm that has survived to the present day" (Knuth 1998, §4.5.2), and to whose understanding the first part of this text is devoted. In contrast to the modern version, Euclid does repeated subtraction instead of division with remainder. Since some quotient might be large, this does not give a polynomial-time algorithm, but the simple idea of removing powers of 2 whenever possible already achieves this (Exercise 3.25).

In the geometric Book 10, Euclid repeats this argument in Proposition 3 for "commensurable magnitudes", which are real numbers whose quotient is rational, and Proposition 2 states that if this process does not terminate, then the two magnitudes are incommensurable.

The other arithmetical highlight is Proposition 20 of Book 9: "Prime numbers are more than any assigned multitude of prime numbers." Hardy (1940) calls its proof "as fresh and significant as when it was discovered—two thousand years have not written a wrinkle on [it]". (For lack of notation, Euclid only illustrates his proof idea by showing how to find from three given primes a fourth one.)

It is amusing to see how after such a profound discovery comes the platitude of Proposition 21: "If as many even numbers as we please be added together, the whole is even." The *Elements* is full of such surprises, unnecessary case distinctions, and virtual repetitions. This is, to a certain extent, due to a lack of good notation. Indices came into use only in the early 19th century; a system designed by Leibniz in the 17th century did not become popular.

Euclid authored some other books, but they never hit the bestseller list, and some are forever lost.

Die ganzen Zahlen hat der liebe Gott gemacht,
alles andere ist Menschenwerk.[1]

Leopold Kronecker (1886)

"I only took the regular course." "What was that?" enquired Alice.
"Reeling and Writing, of course, to begin with," the Mock Turtle
replied: "and then the different branches of Arithmetic—Ambition,
Distraction, Uglification, and Derision."

Lewis Carroll (1865)

Computation is either perform'd by *Numbers*, as in Vulgar
Arithmetick, or by *Species* [variables][2], as usual among Algebraists.
They are both built on the same Foundations, and aim at the same End,
viz. *Arithmetick* Definitely and Particularly, *Algebra* Indefinitely and
Universally; so that almost all Expressions that are found out by this
Computation, and particularly Conclusions, may be called *Theorems*.
[…] Yet Arithmetick in all its Operations is so subservient to Algebra,
as that they seem both but to make one perfect *Science of Computing*.

Isaac Newton (1728)

It is preferable to regard the computer as a handy device
for manipulating and displaying symbols.

Stanisław Marcin Ulam (1964)

In summo apud illos honore geometria fuit, itaque nihil
mathematicis inlustrius; at nos metiendi ratiocinandique
utilitate huius artis terminauimus modum.[3]

Marcus Tullius Cicero (45 BC)

But the rest, having no such grounds [religious devotion] of hope,
fell to another pastime, that of computation.

Robert Louis Stevenson (1889)

Check your math and the amounts entered
to make sure they are correct.

State of California (1996)

---

[1] God created the integers, all else is the work of man.

[2] [Text in brackets added by the authors, also in other quotations.]

[3] Among them [the Greeks] geometry was held in highest esteem, nothing was more glorious than mathematics;
but we have restricted this science to the practical purposes of measuring and calculating.

2

Fundamental algorithms

We start by discussing the representation and fundamental arithmetic algorithms for integers and polynomials. We will keep this discussion fairly informal and avoid all the intricacies of actual computer arithmetic—that is a topic on its own. The reader must be warned that modern-day processors do *not* represent numbers and operate on them as we describe now, but to describe the tricks they use would detract us from our current goal: a simple description of how one *could*, in principle, perform basic arithmetic.

Although our straightforward approach can be improved in practice for arithmetic on small objects, say double-precision integers, it is quite appropriate for large objects, at least as a start. Much of this book deals with polynomials, and we will use some of the notions of this chapter throughout. A major goal is to find algorithmic improvements for large objects.

The algorithms in this chapter will be familiar to the reader, but she can refresh her memory of the *analysis of algorithms* with our simple examples.

2.1. Representation and addition of numbers

Algebra starts with numbers and computers work on data, so the very first issue in computer algebra is how to feed numbers as data into computers. Data are stored in pieces called **words**. Current machines use either 32- or 64-bit words; to be specific, we assume that we have a 64-bit processor. Then one machine word contains a **single precision** integer between 0 and $2^{64} - 1$.

How can we represent integers outside the range $\{0, \ldots, 2^{64} - 1\}$? Such a **multiprecision integer** is represented by an array of 64-bit words, where the first one encodes the sign of the integer and the length of the array. To be precise, we consider the 2^{64}-ary (or radix 2^{64}) representation of a nonzero integer

$$a = (-1)^s \sum_{0 \leq i \leq n} a_i \cdot 2^{64i}, \tag{1}$$

where $s \in \{0, 1\}$, $0 \leq n + 1 < 2^{63}$, and $a_i \in \{0, \ldots, 2^{64} - 1\}$ for all i are the **digits**

27

(in base 2^{64}) of a. We encode it as an array

$$s \cdot 2^{63} + n + 1, a_0, \ldots, a_n$$

of 64-bit words. This representation can be made unique by requiring that the **leading digit** a_n be nonzero if $a \neq 0$ (and using the single-entry array 0 to represent $a = 0$). We will call this the **standard representation** for a. For example, the standard representation of -1 is $2^{63} + 1, 1$. It is, however, convenient also to allow nonstandard representations with leading zero digits since this sometimes facilitates memory management, but we do not want to go into details here. The range of integers that can be represented in standard representation on a 64-bit processor is between $-2^{64 \cdot 2^{63}} + 1$ and $2^{64 \cdot 2^{63}} - 1$; each of the two boundaries requires $2^{63} + 1$ words of storage. This size limitation is quite sufficient for practical purposes: one of the larger representable numbers would fill about 10 billion 8-GB-discs.

For a nonzero integer $a \in \mathbb{Z}$, we define the **length** $\lambda(a)$ of a as

$$\lambda(a) = \lfloor \log_{2^{64}} |a| \rfloor + 1 = \left\lfloor \frac{\log_2 |a|}{64} \right\rfloor + 1,$$

where $\lfloor \cdot \rfloor$ denotes rounding down to the nearest integer (so that $\lfloor 2.7 \rfloor = 2$ and $\lfloor -2.7 \rfloor = -3$). Thus $\lambda(a) + 1 = n + 2$ is the number of words in the standard representation (1) of a (see Exercise 2.1). This is quite a cluttered expression, and it is usually sufficient to know that about $\frac{1}{64} \log_2 |a|$ words are needed, or even more succinctly $O(\log_2 |a|)$, where the **big-Oh notation** "O" hides an arbitrary constant (Section 25.7).

We assume that our hypothetical processor has at its disposal a command for the addition of two single precision integers a and b. The output of the addition command is a 64-bit word c plus the content of the **carry flag** $\gamma \in \{0, 1\}$, a special bit in the processor status word which indicates whether the result exceeds 2^{64} or not. In order to be able to perform addition of multiprecision integers more easily, the carry flag is also *input* to the addition command. More precisely, we have

$$a + b + \gamma = \gamma^* \cdot 2^{64} + c,$$

where γ is the value of the carry flag before the addition and γ^* is its value afterwards. Usually there are also processor instructions to clear and set the carry flag.

If $a = \sum_{0 \leq i \leq n} a_i 2^{64i}$ and $b = \sum_{0 \leq i \leq m} b_i 2^{64i}$ are two multiprecision integers, then their sum is

$$c = \sum_{0 \leq i \leq k} (a_i + b_i) 2^{64i},$$

where $k = \max\{n, m\}$, and if, say, $m \leq n$, then $b_{m+1}, \ldots, b_n$ are set to zero. (In other words, we may assume that $m = n$.) In general, $a_i + b_i$ may be larger than

2^{64}, and if so, then the carry has to be added to the next digit in order to get a 2^{64}-ary representation again. This process propagates from the lower order to the higher order digits, and in the worst case, a carry from the addition of a_0 and b_0 may influence the addition of a_n and b_n, as the example $a = 2^{64(n+1)} - 1$ and $b = 1$ shows. Here is an algorithm for the addition of two multiprecision integers of the same sign; see Exercise 2.3 for a subtraction algorithm.

━━ ALGORITHM 2.1 Addition of multiprecision integers. ━━━━━━━━━

Input: Multiprecision integers $a = (-1)^s \sum_{0 \le i \le n} a_i 2^{64i}$, $b = (-1)^s \sum_{0 \le i \le n} b_i 2^{64i}$, not necessarily in standard representation, with $s \in \{0, 1\}$.

Output: The multiprecision integer $c = (-1)^s \sum_{0 \le i \le n+1} c_i 2^{64i}$ such that $c = a + b$.

1. $\gamma_0 \longleftarrow 0$

2. **for** $i = 0, \ldots, n$ **do**

$\quad c_i \longleftarrow a_i + b_i + \gamma_i, \quad \gamma_{i+1} \longleftarrow 0$

$\quad$ **if** $c_i \ge 2^{64}$ **then** $c_i \longleftarrow c_i - 2^{64}, \quad \gamma_{i+1} \longleftarrow 1$

3. $c_{n+1} \longleftarrow \gamma_{n+1}$

$\quad$ **return** $(-1)^s \sum_{0 \le i \le n+1} c_i 2^{64i}$ ━━━━━━━━━━━━━━━━━━━

We use the sign $\longleftarrow$ in algorithms to denote an assignment, and indentation is used to distinguish the body of a loop.

We practise this algorithm on the addition of $a = 9438 = 9 \cdot 10^3 + 4 \cdot 10^2 + 3 \cdot 10 + 8$ and $b = 945 = 9 \cdot 10^2 + 4 \cdot 10 + 5$ and in decimal (instead of 2^{64}-ary) representation:

i	4	3	2	1	0
a_i		9	4	3	8
b_i		0	9	4	5
γ_i	1	1	0	1	0
c_i	1	0	3	8	3

How much time does this algorithm use? The basic subroutine, the addition of two single precision integers, requires some number of machine cycles, say k. This number will depend on the processor used, and the actual CPU time depends on the processor's speed. Thus the addition of two integers of length at most n takes kn machine cycles for single precision additions, plus some number of cycles for control structures, manipulating sign bits, index arithmetic, memory access, etc. We will, however, (correctly) assume that the number of machine cycles for the latter has the same order of magnitude as the cost for the single precision arithmetic operations that we count.

For the remainder of this text, it is vital to abstract from machine-dependent details as discussed above. We will then just say that the addition of two n-word integers can be done in time $O(n)$, or at cost $O(n)$, or with $O(n)$ **word operations**; the constants hidden in the big-Oh will depend on the details of the machine. We gain two advantages from this concept: a shorter and more intuitive notation, and independence of particular machines. The abstraction is justified by the fact that the *actual* performance of an algorithm often depends on compiler optimization, clever cache usage, pipelining effects, and many other things that are quite technical and nearly impossible to describe in a comparatively high-level programming language. However, experiments show that "big-Oh" statements are reflected surprisingly well by implementations on any kind of sequentially working processor: adding two multiprecision integers is a linear operation in the sense that doubling the input size also approximately doubles the running time.

One can make these statements more precise and formally satisfying. The cost measure that is widely used for algorithms dealing with integers is the number of **bit operations** which can be rigorously defined as the number of steps of a Turing or register machine (random access machine, RAM) or the number of gates of a Boolean circuit implementing the algorithm. Since the details of those computational models are rather technical, however, we will content ourselves with informal arguments and cost measures, as above.

Related data types occurring in currently available processors and mathematical software are single and multiprecision **floating point numbers**. These represent approximations of real numbers, and arithmetic operations, such as addition and multiplication, are subject to **rounding errors**, in contrast to the arithmetic operations on multiprecision integers, which are **exact**. Algorithms based on computations with floating point numbers are the main topic in *numerical analysis*, which is a theme of its own; neither it nor the recent attempts at systematically combining exact and numerical computations will be discussed in this text.

2.2. Representation and addition of polynomials

The two main data types on which our algorithms operate are **numbers** as above and **polynomials**, such as $a = 5x^3 - 4x + 3 \in \mathbb{Z}[x]$. In general, we have a commutative **ring** R, such as $\mathbb{Z}$, in which we can perform the operations of addition, subtraction, and multiplication according to the usual rules; see Section 25.2 for details. (All our rings have a multiplicative unit element 1.) If we can also divide by any nonzero element, as in the rational numbers $\mathbb{Q}$, then R is a **field**.

A polynomial $a \in R[x]$ in x over R consists of a finite sequence $(a_0, \ldots, a_n)$ of elements of R (the **coefficients** of a), for some $n \in \mathbb{N}$, and is written as

$$a = a_n x^n + a_{n-1} x^{n-1} + \cdots + a_1 x + a_0 = \sum_{0 \leq i \leq n} a_i x^i. \qquad (2)$$

If $a_n \neq 0$, then $n = \deg a$ is the **degree** of a, and $a_n = \mathrm{lc}(a)$ is its **leading coefficient**. If $\mathrm{lc}(a) = 1$, then a is **monic**. It is convenient to take $-\infty$ as the degree of the zero polynomial. We can represent a by an array whose ith element is a_i (in analogy to the integer case, we would also need some storage for the degree, but we will neglect this). This assumes that we already have a way of representing the coefficients from R. The length (the number of ring elements) of this representation is $n+1$.

For an integer $r \in \mathbb{N}_{>1}$ (in particular, for $r = 2^{64}$ as in the previous section), the representations (2) of a polynomial and the radix r representation

$$a = a_n r^n + a_{n-1} r^{n-1} + \cdots + a_1 r + a_0 = \sum_{0 \le i \le n} a_i r^i,$$

with digits $a_0, \ldots, a_n \in \{0, \ldots, r-1\}$, of an integer a are quite similar. This is particularly visible if we take polynomials over $R = \mathbb{Z}_r = \{0, \ldots, r-1\}$, the ring of integers modulo r, with addition and multiplication modulo r (Sections 4.1 and 25.2). This similarity is an important point for computer algebra; many of our algorithms apply (with small modifications) to both the integer and polynomial cases: multiplication, division with remainder, gcd and Chinese remainder computation. It is also relevant to note where this does not apply: the subresultant theory (Chapter 6) and, most importantly, the factorization problem (Parts III and IV). At the heart of this distinction lies the deceptively simple carry rule. It gives the low digits some influence on the high digits in addition of integers, and messes up the cleanly separated rules in the addition of two polynomials

$$a = \sum_{0 \le i \le n} a_i x^i \text{ and } b = \sum_{0 \le i \le m} b_i x^i \tag{3}$$

in $R[x]$. This is quite easy:

$$c = a + b = \sum_{0 \le i \le n} (a_i + b_i) x^i = \sum_{0 \le i \le n} c_i x^i,$$

where the addition $c_i = a_i + b_i$ is performed in R and, as with integers, we may assume that $m = n$.

For example, addition of the polynomials $a = 9x^3 + 4x^2 + 3x + 8$ and $b = 9x^2 + 4x + 5$ in $\mathbb{Z}[x]$ works as follows:

i	3	2	1	0
a_i	9	4	3	8
b_i	0	9	4	5
c_i	9	13	7	13

Here is the (rather trivial) algorithm in our formalism.

ALGORITHM 2.2 Addition of polynomials.

Input: $a = \sum_{0 \le i \le n} a_i x^i$, $b = \sum_{0 \le i \le n} b_i x^i$ in $R[x]$, where R is a ring.
Output: The coefficients of $c = a + b \in R[x]$.

1. **for** $i = 0, \ldots, n$ **do** $c_i \longleftarrow a_i + b_i$

2. **return** $c = \sum\limits_{0 \le i \le n} c_i x^i$

It is somewhat simpler than integer addition, with its carries. This simplicity propagates down the line for more complicated algorithms such as multiplication, division with remainder, etc. Although integers are more intuitive (we learn about them at a much earlier stage in life), their algorithms are a bit more involved, and we adopt as a general program the strategy to present mainly the simpler polynomial case which allows us to concentrate on the essentials, and often leave details in the integer cases to the exercises.

As a first example, we have seen that addition of two polynomials of degree up to n takes at most $n + 1$ or $O(n)$ arithmetic operations in R; there is no concern with machine details here. This is a much coarser cost measure than the number of word operations for integers. If, for example, $R = \mathbb{Z}$ and the coefficients are less than B in absolute value, then the cost in word operations is $O(n \log B)$, which is the same order of magnitude as the input size. Moreover, additive operations $+, -$ in R are counted at the same cost as multiplicative operations $\cdot, /$, while in most applications the latter are significantly more expensive than the former.

As a general rule, we will analyze the number of **arithmetic operations** in the ring R (additions and multiplications, and also divisions if R is a field) used by an algorithm. The number of other operations, such as index calculations or memory accesses, tends to be of the same order of magnitude. These are usually performed with machine instructions on single words, and their cost becomes negligible when the arithmetic quantities are large, say multiprecision integers. The input size is the number of ring elements that the input occupies. If the coefficients are integers or polynomials themselves, we may then consider separately the size of the coefficients involved and the cost for coefficient arithmetic.

We try to provide explicit (but not necessarily minimal) constants for the dominant term in our analyses of algorithms on polynomials when the cost measure is the number of arithmetic operations in the coefficient ring, but confine ourselves to O-estimates when counting the number of word operations for algorithms working on integers or polynomials with integral coefficients.

2.3. Multiplication

Following our program, we first consider the product $c = a \cdot b = \sum_{0 \le k \le n+m} c_k x^k$ of two polynomials a and b in $R[x]$, as in (3). Its coefficients are

$$c_k = \sum_{\substack{0 \le i \le n \\ 0 \le j \le m \\ i+j=k}} a_i b_j \tag{4}$$

for $0 \leq k \leq n+m$. We can just take this formula and turn it into a subroutine, after figuring out suitable loop variables and boundaries:

> **for** $k = 0, \ldots, n+m$ **do**
> $\quad c_k \longleftarrow 0$
> $\quad$ **for** $i = \max\{0, k-m\}, \ldots, \min\{n, k\}$ **do**
> $\quad\quad c_k \longleftarrow c_k + a_i \cdot b_{k-i}$

There are other ways to organize the loops. We learned in school the following algorithm.

▬▬ ALGORITHM 2.3 Multiplication of polynomials. ▬▬▬▬▬▬▬▬▬▬▬
Input: The coefficients of $a = \sum_{0 \leq i \leq n} a_i x^i$ and $b = \sum_{0 \leq i \leq m} b_i x^i$ in $R[x]$, where R is a (commutative) ring.
Output: The coefficients of $c = a \cdot b \in R[x]$.

1. **for** $i = 0, \ldots, n$ **do** $d_i \longleftarrow a_i x^i \cdot b$

2. **return** $c = \sum_{0 \leq i \leq m} d_i$ ▬▬▬▬▬▬▬▬▬▬▬▬▬▬▬▬▬▬▬▬▬

The multiplication $a_i x^i \cdot b$ is realized as the multiplication of each b_j by a_i plus a shift by i places. The variable x serves us just as a convenient way to write polynomials, and there is no arithmetic involved in "multiplying" by x or any power of it. Here is a small example:

$$
\begin{array}{r}
5x^2 + 2x + 1 \cdot \qquad\qquad\qquad 2x^3 \;\;+x^2\;\; +3x+5 \\
\hline
2x^3 \;\;+x^2\;\; +3x+5 \\
+4x^4 \;+2x^3\; +6x^2+10x \\
+10x^5+5x^4+15x^3+25x^2 \\
\hline
10x^5+9x^4+19x^3+32x^2+13x+5
\end{array}
$$

How much time does this take, that is, how many operations in the ground ring R? Each of the $n+1$ coefficients of a has to be multiplied with each of the $m+1$ coefficients of b, for a total of $(n+1)(m+1)$ multiplications. Then these are summed up in $n+m+1$ sums; summing s items costs $s-1$ additions. So the total number of additions is

$$(n+1)(m+1) - (n+m+1) = nm,$$

and the total cost for multiplication is $2nm + n + m + 1 \leq 2(n+1)(m+1)$ operations in R. (If b is monic, then the bound drops to $2(n+1)m$.) Thus we can say that two polynomials of degree at most n can be multiplied with $2n^2 + 2n + 1$ operations, or $2n^2 + O(n)$ operations, or $O(n^2)$ operations, or in **quadratic time**.

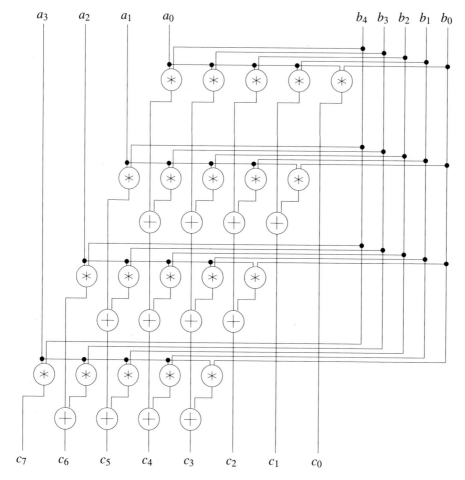

FIGURE 2.1: An arithmetic circuit for polynomial multiplication. The flow of control is directed downwards. An "electrical" view is to think of the edges as lines, where ring elements "flow", with "contact" crossings marked with a •, and no contact at the other crossings. The size of this circuit equals 32, the number of arithmetic gates in it.

The three expressions for the running time get progressively simpler but also less precise. In this book, each of the three versions has its place (and there are even more versions).

For a computer implementation, Algorithm 2.3 has the drawback of requiring us to store $n+1$ polynomials with $m+1$ coefficients each. A way around this is to interleave the final addition with the computation of the $a_i x^i b$. This takes the same time but uses only $O(n+m)$ storage and is shown in Figure 2.1 for $n = 3$ and $m = 4$. Each horizontal level corresponds to one pass through the loop body in step 1.

We will call **classical** those algorithms that take a definition of a function and implement it fairly literally, as the multiplication algorithms above implements the formula (4). One might think that this is the only way of doing it. Fortunately, there are much faster ways of multiplying, in almost linear rather than quadratic time. We will study these fast algorithms in Part II. By contrast, for the addition problem no improvement is possible, nor is it necessary: the algorithm uses only linear time.

According to our general program, we now examine the integer case. The product of two single precision integers a, b between 0 and $2^{64} - 1$ has "double precision": it lies in the interval $\{0, \ldots, 2^{128} - 2^{65} + 1\}$. We assume that our processor has a single precision multiplication instruction which returns the product in two 64-bit words c, d such that $a \cdot b = d \cdot 2^{64} + c$. Here is the integer analog of Algorithm 2.3.

▬▬ ALGORITHM 2.4 Multiplication of multiprecision integers. ▬▬▬▬▬▬▬▬▬
Input: Multiprecision integers $a = (-1)^s \sum_{0 \leq i < n} a_i 2^{64i}$, $b = (-1)^t \sum_{0 \leq i < n} b_i 2^{64i}$, not necessarily in standard representation, with $s, t \in \{0, 1\}$.
Output: The multiprecision integer ab.

1. **for** $i = 0, \ldots, n$ **do** $d_i \longleftarrow a_i 2^{64i} \cdot b$

2. **return** $c = (-1)^{s+t} \sum_{0 \leq i \leq m} d_i$ ▬▬▬▬▬▬▬▬▬▬▬▬▬▬▬

Besides the multiplication by 2^{64i}, which is just a shift in the 2^{64}-ary representation, multiplication of a multiprecision integer b by a single precision integer a_i must be implemented. The time for this is $O(m)$ (Exercise 2.5), and the total time is quadratic: $O(nm)$. In line with our general program, we omit the details for implementing this efficiently.

We conclude this section with the example multiplication of $a = 521 = 5 \cdot 10^2 + 2 \cdot 10 + 1$ and $b = 2135 = 2 \cdot 10^3 + 10^2 + 3 \cdot 10 + 5$ in decimal representation, according to Algorithm 2.4.

$$
\begin{array}{r}
521 \cdot \quad 2135 \\
\hline
2135 \\
+42700 \\
+1067500 \\
\hline
1112335
\end{array}
$$

2.4. Division with remainder

In many applications, calculations "modulo an integer" play an important role; examples from program checking, database integrity, coding theory and cryptography are discussed later in the book. But even when one is really only interested in integer problems, a "modular" approach is often computationally successful; we will see this for gcds and factorization of integer polynomials.

The basic tool for modular arithmetic is **division with remainder**: given integers a, b, with b nonzero, we want to find a **quotient** q and a **remainder** r—both integers—so that

$$a = qb + r, \quad |r| < |b|.$$

In line with our general program, we first discuss the computational aspect of this problem for polynomials. So we are given $a, b \in R[x]$, with b nonzero, and want to find $q, r \in R[x]$ so that

$$a = qb + r, \quad \deg r < \deg b. \tag{5}$$

A first problem is that such q and r do not always exist: it is impossible to divide x^2 by $2x + 1$ with remainder in $\mathbb{Z}[x]$! (See Exercise 2.8.) There is a way around this, the **pseudo-division** explained in Section 6.12. However, for the moment we simplify the problem by assuming that the leading coefficient $\mathrm{lc}(b)$ of b is a **unit** in R, so that it has an inverse $v \in R$ with $\mathrm{lc}(b)v = 1$. For $R = \mathbb{Z}$, that still only allows 1 or -1 as leading coefficient, but when R is a field, division with remainder by an arbitrary nonzero polynomial is possible.

We remind the reader of the "synthetic division" learned in high school with a small example in $\mathbb{Z}[x]$:

$$
\begin{array}{l}
3x^4 + 2x^3 \qquad\quad + x + 5 : x^2 + 2x + 3 = 3x^2 - 4x - 1 \\
\underline{-3x^4 - 6x^3 - 9x^2} \\
\qquad -4x^3 - 9x^2 \;\; + x + 5 \\
\qquad \underline{+4x^3 + 8x^2 + 12x} \\
\qquad\qquad\quad -x^2 + 13x + 5 \\
\qquad\qquad\quad \underline{+x^2 \;\; + 2x + 3} \\
\qquad\qquad\qquad\qquad 15x + 8
\end{array}
$$

Thus the coefficients of the quotient $q = 3x^2 - 4x - 1$ are determined one by one, starting at the top, by setting them equal to the corresponding coefficient of the current "remainder" (in general, one additionally has to divide by $\mathrm{lc}(b)$), which initially is $a = 3x^4 + 2x^3 + x + 5$. Then the remainder is adjusted by subtracting the appropriate multiple of $b = x^2 + 2x + 3$. The final remainder is $r = 15x + 8$. The degree of q is $\deg a - \deg b$ if $q \neq 0$. The following algorithm formalizes this familiar *classical method* for division with remainder by a polynomial whose leading coefficient is a unit.

▬▬ ALGORITHM 2.5 Polynomial division with remainder. ▬▬▬▬▬▬▬▬▬▬

Input: $a = \sum_{0 \le i \le n} a_i x^i, b = \sum_{0 \le i \le m} b_i x^i \in R[x]$, with all $a_i, b_i \in R$, where R is a ring (commutative, with 1), b_m a unit, and $n \ge m \ge 0$.

Output: $q, r \in R[x]$ with $a = qb + r$ and $\deg r < m$.

1. $r \longleftarrow a$

2. **for** $i = n-m, n-m-1, \ldots, 0$ **do**

3.   **if** $\deg r = m+i$ **then** $q_i \longleftarrow \mathrm{lc}(r)/b_m,$ $r \longleftarrow r - q_i x^i b$
        else $q_i \longleftarrow 0$

4. **return** $q = \displaystyle\sum_{0 \leq i \leq n-m} q_i x^i$ and r

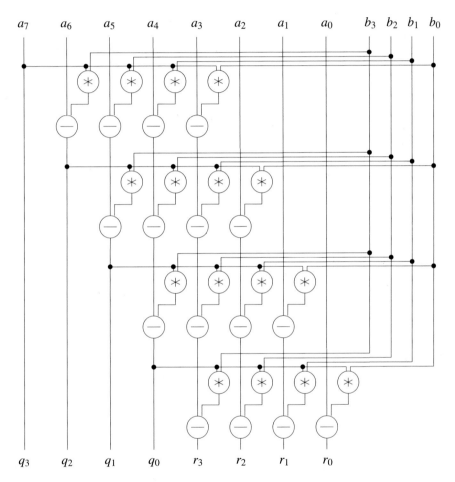

FIGURE 2.2: An arithmetic circuit for polynomial division. A subtraction node computes the difference of its left input minus its right input.

Figure 2.2 represents this algorithm for $n = 7$ and $m = 4$ when $b_m = 1$. Each horizontal level in the circuit corresponds to one pass through step 3.

As in the polynomial multiplication algorithm, the multiplication $q_i x^i b$ in step 3 is just a multiplication of each b_j by q_i, followed by a shift by i places. Thus the cost for one execution of step 3 is one division, m multiplications and m additions in R if $\deg r = m + i$. We note that the $(m+i)$th coefficient of r becomes 0 in step 3 and hence need not be computed. Together, we have a cost of at most

$$(2m+1)(n-m+1) = (2\deg b + 1)(\deg q + 1) \in O(n^2)$$

operations in R, and only at most $2\deg b(\deg q + 1)$ if b is monic. In many applications, we have $n < 2m$, and then the cost is at most $2m^2 + O(m)$ ring operations, which is essentially the same as for multiplying two polynomials of degree at most m.

It is easy to see that the quotient and remainder are uniquely determined (when $\mathrm{lc}(b)$ is a unit). Namely, another equation $a = q^*b + r^*$, with $q^*, r^* \in R[x]$ and $\deg r^* < \deg b$, yields by subtraction

$$(q^* - q)b = r - r^*.$$

The right hand side has degree less than $\deg b$, and the left hand side has degree at least $\deg b$, unless $q^* - q = 0$. Therefore the latter is true, $q = q^*$, and $r = r^*$. We write "a quo b" for the quotient q and "a rem b" for the remainder r.

What about the integer case? The analog of Algorithm 2.5 is well known from high school, at least in the decimal representation:

$$
\begin{array}{r}
32015 : 123 = 26 \\
-24600 \\
\hline
7415 \\
-7380 \\
\hline
35
\end{array}
$$

The digits of the quotient are again determined one by one, starting at the top. At each step, one has to determine how often the leading digit of b divides the one or two leading digits of the current remainder. This requires a "double-by-single-precision" division instruction. However, it may happen that this "trial" quotient digit is too large, as in the first line: the quotient of 3 on division by 1 is 3, but the leading digit of the quotient $\lfloor 32015/123 \rfloor$ is 2.

Algorithmically, in each step, the product of the shifted divisor $2^{64i}b$ with a trial quotient digit is subtracted from some integer of the same length. If the result is negative, then the trial quotient digit is too large and one has to decrement it and add $2^{64i}b$ to the remainder (repeatedly, if necessary) until the remainder is nonnegative. If things are arranged properly, then one such step can be done with $O(\lambda(b))$ word operations. The length of the quotient—the number of iterations—is at most $\lambda(a) - \lambda(b) + 1$ (Exercise 2.7), and the overall cost estimate is again $O(\lambda(b)\lambda(q))$ or $O(m(n-m))$ word operations if a and b have lengths n and m, respectively. Due to the carries, the details are somewhat more complicated than in the polynomial case; the interested reader is referred to the comprehensive discussion in Knuth (1998), §4.3.1.

In contrast to the polynomial case, the remainder r is not uniquely determined by the condition $|r| < |b|$: $13 = 2 \cdot 5 + 3 = 3 \cdot 5 + (-2)$. We will often follow the convention that the remainder be nonnegative and denote it by a rem b, and the corresponding quotient then is $\lfloor a/b \rfloor$ if $b > 0$.

Notes. Good texts on algorithms and their analysis are Brassard & Bratley (1996) and Cormen, Leiserson & Rivest (1990).

Addition and multiplication algorithms in decimal notation are explicitly described in Stevin (1585). An anonymous author (1835) presents a decimal division algorithm for hand calculation based on a "10's complement" notation. Several algorithms for computer arithmetic, such as fast (carry look-ahead and carry-save) addition, are given in Cormen, Leiserson & Rivest (1990). For information about symbolic-numeric computations see the Special Issue of the *Journal of Symbolic Computation* (Watt & Stetter 1998).

Exercises.

2.1 For an integer $r \in \mathbb{N}_{>1}$, we consider the variable-length radix r representation $(a_0, \dots, a_{l-1})$ of a positive integer a, with $a = \sum_{0 \le i < l} a_i r^i$, $a_0, \dots, a_{l-1} \in \{0, \dots, r-1\}$, and $a_{l-1} \ne 0$. Prove that its length l is $\lfloor \log_r a \rfloor + 1$.

2.2 Design a representation for integers of unlimited size on a 64-bit machine.

2.3 (i) Specify a processor instruction analogous to the addition instruction mentioned in the text which performs subtraction of two single precision integers. Use the carry flag to indicate whether the result is negative or not.

(ii) Design an algorithm similar to Algorithm 2.1 for the subtraction of two multiprecision integers a and b of equal sign and with $|a| > |b|$.

(iii) Discuss how to decide whether $|a| > |b|$ holds.

2.4 Here is a piece of code implementing Algorithm 2.1 for nonnegative multiprecision integers (that is, when $s = 0$) on a hypothetical processor. Text enclosed in /* and */ is a comment. The processor has 26 freely usable registers named A to Z. Initially, registers A and B point to the first word (the one containing the length) of the representations of a and b, respectively, and C points to a piece of memory where the representation of c shall be placed.

```
 1: LOAD N, [A]    /* load word that A points to into register N */
 2: ADD K, N, 1    /* add 1 to register N and store the result in K
                       (without affecting carry flag) */
 3: STORE [C], K   /* store K in the word that C points to */
 4: ADD A, A, 1    /* increase register A by 1 */
 5: ADD B, B, 1
 6: ADD C, C, 1
 7: LOAD I, 1      /* load the constant 1 into register I */
 8: CLEARC         /* clear carry flag */
 9: COMP I, N      /* compare contents of registers I and N ... */
10: BGT 20         /* ... and jump to line 20 if I is greater */
11: LOAD S, [A]
12: LOAD T, [B]
13: ADDC S, S, T   /* add the content of register T to register S
                       using the carry flag */
14: STORE [C], S
```

```
15: ADD A, A, 1
16: ADD B, B, 1
17: ADD C, C, 1
18: ADD I, I, 1
19: JMP 9          /* unconditionally jump to line 9 */
20: ADDC S, 0, 0   /* store carry flag in S */
21: STORE [C], S
22: RETURN
```

Suppose that our processor runs at 200 MHz and that the execution of one instruction takes one machine cycle = 5 picoseconds = $5 \cdot 10^{-9}$ seconds. Calculate the precise time, in terms of n, to run the above piece of code, and convince yourself that this is indeed $O(n)$.

2.5 Give an algorithm for multiplying a multiprecision integer b by a single precision integer a, making use of the single precision multiply instruction described in Section 2.3. Show that your algorithm uses $\lambda(b)$ single precision multiplications and the same number of single precision additions. Convert your algorithm into a machine program as in Exercise 2.4.

2.6 Prove that $\max\{\lambda(a), \lambda(b)\} \leq \lambda(a+b) \leq \max\{\lambda(a), \lambda(b)\} + 1$ and $\lambda(a) + \lambda(b) - 1 \leq \lambda(ab) \leq \lambda(a) + \lambda(b)$ hold for all $a, b \in \mathbb{N}_{>0}$.

2.7 Let $a > b \in \mathbb{N}_{>0}$, $m = \lambda(a)$, $n = \lambda(b)$ and $q = \lfloor a/b \rfloor$. Give tight upper and lower bounds for $\lambda(q)$ in terms of m and n.

2.8 Prove that in $\mathbb{Z}[x]$ one cannot divide x^2 by $2x + 1$ with remainder as in (5).

2.9* Let R be an integral domain with field of fractions K and $a, b \in R[x]$ of degree $n \geq m \geq 0$. Then we can apply the polynomial division algorithm 2.5 to compute $q, r \in K[x]$ such that $a = qb + r$ and $\deg r < \deg b$.

(i) Prove that there exist $q, r \in R[x]$ with $a = qb + r$ and $\deg r < \deg b$ if and only if $\mathrm{lc}(b) \mid \mathrm{lc}(r)$ in R every time the algorithm passes through step 3, and that they are unique in that case.

(ii) Modify Algorithm 2.5 so that on input a, b, it decides whether $q, r \in R[x]$ as in (i) exist, and if so, computes them. Show that this takes the same number of operations in R as given in the text, where one operation is either an addition or a multiplication in R, or a test which decides whether an element $c \in R$ divides another element $d \in R$, and if so, computes the quotient $d/c \in R$.

2.10 Let R be a ring (commutative, with 1) and $a = \sum_{0 \leq i \leq n} a_i x^i \in R[x]$ of degree n, with all $a_i \in R$. The **weight** $w(a)$ of a is the number of nonzero coefficients of a besides the leading coefficient:

$$w(a) = \#\{0 \leq i < n : a_i \neq 0\}.$$

Thus $w(a) \leq \deg a$, with equality if and only if all coefficients of a are nonzero. The **sparse** representation of a, which is particularly useful if a has small weight, is a list of pairs $(i, a_i)_{i \in I}$, with each $a_i \in R$ and $f = \sum_{i \in I} a_i x^i$. Then we can choose $\#I = w(a) + 1$.

(i) Show that two polynomials $a, b \in R[x]$ of weight $n = w(a)$ and $m = w(b)$ can be multiplied in the sparse representation using at most $2nm + n + m + 1$ arithmetic operations in R.

(ii) Draw an arithmetic circuit for division of a polynomial $a \in R[x]$ of degree less than 9 by $b = x^6 - 3x^4 + 2$ with remainder. Try to get its size as small as possible.

(iii) Let $n \geq m$. Show that quotient and remainder on division of a polynomial $a \in R[x]$ of degree less than n by $b \in R[x]$ of degree m, with $\mathrm{lc}(b)$ a unit, can be computed using $n - m$ divisions in R, and $w(b) \cdot (n - m)$ multiplications and subtractions in R each.

2.11 Let R be a ring and $k, m, n \in \mathbb{N}$. Show that the "classical" multiplication of two matrices $A \in R^{k \times m}$ and $B \in R^{m \times n}$ takes $(2m - 1)kn$ arithmetic operations in R.

"Immortality" may be a silly word, but probably a mathematician
has the best chance of whatever it may mean.

Godfrey Harold Hardy (1940)

The ignoraunte multitude doeth, but as it was euer wonte, enuie that
knoweledge, whiche thei can not attaine, and wishe all men ignoraunt,
like unto themself. [...] Yea, the *pointe* in *Geometrie*,
and the unitie in *Arithmetike*, though bothe be undiuisible,
doe make greater woorkes, & increase greater multitudes,
then the brutishe bande of ignoraunce is hable to withstande.

Robert Recorde (1557)

If mathematics is considered to be a science
[that is, devoted to the description of nature and its laws],
it is more fundamental than any other.

Murray Gell-Mann (1994)

I have often wished, that I had employed about the speculative part of
geometry, and the cultivation of the specious Algebra [multivariate
polynomials] I had been taught very young, a good part of that time
and industry, that I had spent about surveying and fortification (of
which I remember I once wrote an entire treatise) and other practick
parts of mathematicks. And indeed the operations of symbolical
arithmetick (or the modern Algebra) seem to me to afford men one of
the clearest exercises of reason that I ever yet met with.

Robert Boyle (1671)

The sacred writings excepted, no Greek has been so much read
and so variously translated as Euclid.

Augustus De Morgan (1837)

3

The Euclidean Algorithm

Integers and polynomials with coefficients in a field behave similarly in many respects. Often—but not always—the algorithms for both types of objects are quite similar, and sometimes one can find a common abstraction of both domains, and it is then sufficient to design one algorithm for this generalization to solve both problems in one fell swoop. In this chapter, the Euclidean domain covers the structural similarities between gcd computations for integers and polynomials. Typically, in such a situation the polynomial version is slightly simpler, and in Chapter 6, we will meet polynomial subresultants which have no integer analog at all.

3.1. Euclidean domains

The Euclidean Algorithm for the two integers 126 and 35 works as follows:

$$
\begin{aligned}
126 &= 3 \cdot 35 + 21, \\
35 &= 1 \cdot 21 + 14, \\
21 &= 1 \cdot 14 + 7, \\
14 &= 2 \cdot 7,
\end{aligned}
\tag{1}
$$

and 7 is the greatest common divisor of 126 and 35. One of the most important applications is for exact arithmetic on rational numbers, where one has to simplify $35/126$ to $5/18$ in order to keep the numbers small.

This algorithm can also be adapted to work for polynomials. It is convenient to use the following general scenario, which captures both situations under one umbrella. The reader may always think of R as being either the integers or polynomials. The algebraic terminology is explained in Chapter 25.

DEFINITION 3.1. *An integral domain R together with a function $d: R \longrightarrow \mathbb{N} \cup \{-\infty\}$ is a **Euclidean domain** if for all $a, b \in R$ with $b \neq 0$, we can divide a by b with remainder, so that*

$$
\textit{there exist } q, r \in R \textit{ such that } a = qb + r \textit{ and } d(r) < d(b).
\tag{2}
$$

We say that $q = a$ quo b is the **quotient** and $r = a$ rem b the **remainder**, although q and r need not be unique. Such a d is called a **Euclidean function** on R.

EXAMPLE 3.2.   (i) $R = \mathbb{Z}$ and $d(a) = |a| \in \mathbb{N}$. Here the quotient and the remainder can be made unique by the additional requirement that $r \geq 0$.

(ii) $R = F[x]$, where F is a field, and $d(a) = \deg a$. We define the degree of the zero polynomial to be $-\infty$. It is easy to show uniqueness of the quotient and the remainder in this case (Section 2.4).

(iii) $R = \mathbb{Z}[i] = \{a + ib : a, b \in \mathbb{Z}\}$, the ring of Gaussian integers, with $i = \sqrt{-1}$, and $d(a + ib) = a^2 + b^2$ (Exercise 3.19).

(iv) R a field, and $d(a) = 1$ if $a \neq 0$ and $d(0) = 0$. $\diamond$

The value $d(b)$ is never $-\infty$ except possibly when $b = 0$.

DEFINITION 3.3.   *Let R be a ring and $a, b, c \in R$. Then c is a **greatest common divisor** (or gcd) of a and b if*

(i) $c \mid a$ and $c \mid b$,

(ii) *if $d \mid a$ and $d \mid b$, then $d \mid c$, for all $d \in R$.*

*Similarly, c is called a **least common multiple** (or lcm) of a and b if*

(i) $a \mid c$ and $b \mid c$,

(ii) *if $a \mid d$ and $b \mid d$, then $c \mid d$, for all $d \in R$.*

*A **unit** $u \in R$ is any element with a multiplicative inverse $v \in R$, so that $uv = 1$. The elements a and b are **associate** if $a = ub$ for a unit $b \in R$; we then write $a \sim b$.*

For example, 3 is a gcd of 12 and 15, and 60 is an lcm of 12 and 15 in $\mathbb{Z}$. In general, neither the gcd nor the lcm are unique, but all gcds of a and b are precisely the associates of one of them, and similarly for the lcms. The only units in $\mathbb{Z}$ are 1 and -1, and 3 and -3 are all gcds of 12 and 15 in $\mathbb{Z}$. For $R = \mathbb{Z}$, we define $\gcd(a, b)$ as the unique nonnegative greatest common divisor and $\operatorname{lcm}(a, b)$ as the unique nonnegative least common multiple of a and b. As an example, for negative $a \in \mathbb{Z}$ we have $\gcd(a, a) = \gcd(a, 0) = -a$. More generally, $\gcd(a, a) = \gcd(a, 0) = |a|$ and $\gcd(a, 1) = 1$ for all $a \in \mathbb{Z}$. We say that two integers a, b are **coprime** (or relatively prime) if $\gcd(a, b) = 1$.

Greatest common divisors and least common multiples need not exist in an arbitrary ring; for an example, see Section 25.2. In the following section, however, we will prove that a gcd always exists in a Euclidean domain, and as a consequence an lcm also exists.

LEMMA 3.4. *The gcd in $\mathbb{Z}$ has the following properties, for all $a,b,c \in \mathbb{Z}$.*

(i) $\gcd(a,b) = |a| \iff a \mid b$,

(ii) $\gcd(a,b) = \gcd(b,a)$ *(commutativity),*

(iii) $\gcd(a,\gcd(b,c)) = \gcd(\gcd(a,b),c))$ *(associativity),*

(iv) $\gcd(c \cdot a, c \cdot b) = |c| \cdot \gcd(a,b)$ *(distributivity),*

(v) $|a| = |b| \implies \gcd(a,c) = \gcd(b,c)$.

For a proof, see Exercise 3.3. Because of the associativity, we may write

$$\gcd(a_1,\ldots,a_n) = \gcd(a_1,\gcd(a_2,\ldots,\gcd(a_{n-1},a_n)\ldots)).$$

The following algorithm computes greatest common divisors in an arbitrary Euclidean domain.

▬▬ ALGORITHM 3.5 Classical Euclidean Algorithm. ▬▬▬▬▬▬▬▬▬▬
Input: $f,g \in R$, where R is a Euclidean domain with Euclidean function d.
Output: A greatest common divisor $h \in R$ of f and g.

1. $r_0 \longleftarrow f, \quad r_1 \longleftarrow g$

2. $i \longleftarrow 1$
   while $r_i \neq 0$ **do** $r_{i+1} \longleftarrow r_{i-1}$ rem $r_i, \quad i \longleftarrow i+1$

3. **return** r_{i-1}. ▬▬▬▬▬▬▬▬▬▬▬▬▬▬▬▬▬▬▬▬

For $f = 126$ and $g = 35$, the algorithm works precisely as illustrated at the beginning of this section.

Since $\mathbb{Q}$ is a field, every nonzero rational number is a unit in $\mathbb{Q}$, and so $ua \sim a$ in $R = \mathbb{Q}[x]$ for all nonzero $u \in \mathbb{Q}$ and all $a \in R$. If we want to define a single element $\gcd(f,g) \in \mathbb{Q}[x]$, which one should we choose? In other words, how do we choose *one* representative from among all the multiples of a? A reasonable choice is the **monic** polynomial, that is, the one with leading coefficient 1. Thus if $\mathrm{lc}(a) \in \mathbb{Q} \setminus \{0\}$ is the leading coefficient of $a \in \mathbb{Q}[x]$, then we take normal$(a) = a/\mathrm{lc}(a)$ as the **normal form** of a.

To make this work in an arbitrary Euclidean domain R, we assume that we have selected some normal form normal$(a) \in R$ for every $a \in R$ so that $a \sim$ normal(a). It is natural to call the unit $u \in R$ such that $a = u \cdot$ normal(a) the **leading coefficient** $\mathrm{lc}(a)$ of a. Moreover, we set $\mathrm{lc}(0) = 1$ and normal$(0) = 0$. The following two properties are required:

○ two elements of R have the same normal form if and only if they are associate,

○ the normal form of a product is equal to the products of the normal forms.

These properties in particular imply that the normal form of any unit is 1. We say that an element a in normal form, so that $\mathrm{lc}(a) = 1$, is **normalized**.

In our two main applications, integers and polynomials over a field, we will use the following normal forms throughout. For $R = \mathbb{Z}$, $\mathrm{lc}(a) = \mathrm{sgn}(a)$ if $a \neq 0$ and $\mathrm{normal}(a) = |a|$ defines a normal form, so that an integer is normalized if and only if it is nonnegative. When $R = F[x]$ for a field F, then letting $\mathrm{lc}(a)$ be the usual leading coefficient (with the convention that $\mathrm{lc}(0) = 1$) and $\mathrm{normal}(a) = a/\mathrm{lc}(a)$ defines a normal form, and a nonzero polynomial is normalized if and only if it is monic.

Given such a normal form, we define $\gcd(a,b)$ to be the unique normalized associate of all greatest common divisors of a and b (if such exist), and similarly define $\mathrm{lcm}(a,b)$ as the normalized associate of all least common multiples of a and b. Thus $\gcd(a,b) > 0$ for $R = \mathbb{Z}$ and $\gcd(a,b)$ is monic for $R = F[x]$ if at least one of a,b is nonzero, and $\gcd(0,0) = 0$ in both cases. Lemma 3.4 then remains valid if we replace $|\cdot|$ by $\mathrm{normal}(\cdot)$.

To illustrate this, we consider two variants of the gcd calculation (1):

$$
\begin{aligned}
126 &= 4 \cdot 35 - 14, & 126 &= 4 \cdot 35 - 14, \\
35 &= (-2) \cdot (-14) + 7, & 35 &= 2 \cdot 14 + 7, \\
-14 &= (-2) \cdot 7, & 14 &= 2 \cdot 7.
\end{aligned}
$$

In the first one, we have chosen the remainder of least absolute value instead of the least nonnegative remainder (see also Exercise 3.13), and in the second one we have in addition normalized the remainder in the first step (the others are already normalized with "leading coefficient" 1).

In the polynomial case, it turns out that it is not only useful to have a normal form for the gcd, but to modify the classical Euclidean Algorithm such that *all* the remainders r_i are normalized. In Chapter 6, we will see that for $R = \mathbb{Q}[x]$ the computations of the classical Euclidean Algorithm produce remainders whose coefficients have huge numerators and denominators even for inputs of moderate size, and that the coefficients of the monic associates of the remainders are much smaller. For that reason, we will present a variant of the classical Euclidean Algorithm 3.5 in the next section which works with these monic associates. Another advantage of this variant, related to subresultants, will also appear in Chapter 6.

3.2. The Extended Euclidean Algorithm

The following variant of Algorithm 3.5, which works with normalized remainders, computes not only the gcd but also a representation of it as a linear combination of the inputs. It generalizes the representation

$$7 = 21 - 1 \cdot 14 = 21 - (35 - 1 \cdot 21) = 2 \cdot (126 - 3 \cdot 35) - 35 = 2 \cdot 126 - 7 \cdot 35,$$

which is obtained by reading the lines of (1) from the bottom up. This important method is called the **Extended Euclidean Algorithm** and works in any Euclidean domain.

ALGORITHM 3.6 Extended Euclidean Algorithm (EEA).
Input: $f, g \in R$, where R is a Euclidean domain with a normal form.
Output: $\ell \in \mathbb{N}$, $\rho_i, r_i, s_i, t_i \in R$ for $0 \le i \le \ell + 1$, and $q_i \in R$ for $1 \le i \le \ell$, as computed below.

1. $\rho_0 \longleftarrow \mathrm{lc}(f), \quad r_0 \longleftarrow \mathrm{normal}(f), \quad s_0 \longleftarrow \rho_0^{-1}, \quad t_0 \longleftarrow 0,$
   $\rho_1 \longleftarrow \mathrm{lc}(g), \quad r_1 \longleftarrow \mathrm{normal}(g), \quad s_1 \longleftarrow 0, \quad t_1 \longleftarrow \rho_1^{-1}$

2. $i \longleftarrow 1$
   while $r_i \ne 0$ **do**
   $\qquad q_i \longleftarrow r_{i-1} \text{ quo } r_i$
   $\qquad \rho_{i+1} \longleftarrow \mathrm{lc}(r_{i-1} \text{ rem } r_i)$
   $\qquad r_{i+1} \longleftarrow \mathrm{normal}(r_{i-1} \text{ rem } r_i)$
   $\qquad s_{i+1} \longleftarrow (s_{i-1} - q_i s_i)/\rho_{i+1}$
   $\qquad t_{i+1} \longleftarrow (t_{i-1} - q_i t_i)/\rho_{i+1}$
   $\qquad i \longleftarrow i + 1$

3. $\ell \longleftarrow i - 1$
   return ℓ, ρ_i, r_i, s_i, t_i for $0 \le i \le \ell + 1$, and q_i for $1 \le i \le \ell$

We note that the algorithm terminates because the $d(r_i)$ are strictly decreasing nonnegative integers, where d is the Euclidean function on R; ℓ is called the **Euclidean length** of the pair (f, g). The elements r_i for $0 \le i \le \ell + 1$ are the **remainders** and the q_i for $1 \le i \le \ell$ the **quotients** in the (Extended) Euclidean Algorithm. The elements r_i, s_i, and t_i form the *i*th row in the Extended Euclidean Algorithm, for $0 \le i \le \ell + 1$. The central property is that $s_i f + t_i g = r_i$ for all i; in particular, $s_\ell f + t_\ell g = r_\ell = \gcd(f, g)$ (see Lemma 3.8 below). The elements s_ℓ and t_ℓ are the **Bézout coefficients** of f and g.

So far, we have mainly been interested in the gcd of f and g or the Bézout coefficients. However, we will see later that in fact *all* other intermediate results computed by the algorithm are useful for various tasks in computer algebra. Before we prove some properties of the Extended Euclidean Algorithm, let us see how it works in some examples.

EXAMPLE 3.7.   (i) As in (1), we consider $R = \mathbb{Z}$, $f = 126$, $g = 35$. The following table illustrates the computation.

i	q_i	ρ_i	r_i	s_i	t_i
0		1	126	1	0
1	3	1	35	0	1
2	1	1	21	1	-3
3	1	1	14	-1	4
4	2	1	7	2	-7
5		1	0	-5	18

We can read off row 4 of the above table that $\gcd(126, 35) = 7 = 2 \cdot 126 + (-7) \cdot 35$.

(ii) $R = \mathbb{Q}[x]$, $f = 12x^3 - 28x^2 + 20x - 4$, $g = -12x^2 + 10x - 2$. Then the computation of the Extended Euclidean Algorithm goes as follows. Row $i+1$ is obtained from the two preceding ones by first computing the quotient q_i and the leading coefficient ρ_{i+1} and then for each of the three remaining columns by subtracting the quotient times the entry in row i of that column from the entry in row $i-1$ and dividing the result by ρ_{i+1}.

i	q_i	ρ_i	r_i	s_i	t_i
0		12	$x^3 - \frac{7}{3}x^2 + \frac{5}{3}x - \frac{1}{3}$	$\frac{1}{12}$	0
1	$x - \frac{3}{2}$	-12	$x^2 - \frac{5}{6}x + \frac{1}{6}$	0	$-\frac{1}{12}$
2	$x - \frac{1}{2}$	$\frac{1}{4}$	$x - \frac{1}{3}$	$\frac{1}{3}$	$\frac{1}{3}x - \frac{1}{2}$
3		1	0	$-\frac{1}{3}x + \frac{1}{6}$	$-\frac{1}{3}x^2 + \frac{2}{3}x - \frac{1}{3}$

From row 2, we find that

$$\gcd(f, g) = x - \frac{1}{3} = \frac{1}{3} \cdot (12x^3 - 28x^2 + 20x - 4) + \left(\frac{1}{3}x - \frac{1}{2}\right)(-12x^2 + 10x - 2). \ \diamond$$

For $R = \mathbb{Z}$, it is easily checked that $\rho_i = 1$ for all i if the inputs f, g are nonnegative, and we will therefore omit the ρ_i's in that case.

The computations of the Extended Euclidean Algorithm yield the following recursive equations between the r_i, s_i, and t_i.

$$\rho_2 r_2 = r_0 - q_1 r_1, \qquad \rho_2 s_2 = s_0 - q_1 s_1, \qquad \rho_2 t_2 = t_0 - q_1 t_1,$$

$$\vdots \qquad\qquad\qquad \vdots \qquad\qquad\qquad \vdots$$

$$\rho_{i+1} r_{i+1} = r_{i-1} - q_i r_i, \quad \rho_{i+1} s_{i+1} = s_{i-1} - q_i s_i, \quad \rho_{i+1} t_{i+1} = t_{i-1} - q_i t_i, \qquad (3)$$

$$\vdots \qquad\qquad\qquad \vdots \qquad\qquad\qquad \vdots$$

$$0 = r_{l-1} - q_l r_l, \quad \rho_{l+1} s_{l+1} = s_{l-1} - q_l s_l, \quad \rho_{l+1} t_{l+1} = t_{l-1} - q_l t_l.$$

For a global view of the algorithm, it is convenient to define the matrices

$$R_0 = \begin{pmatrix} s_0 & t_0 \\ s_1 & t_1 \end{pmatrix}, \quad Q_i = \begin{pmatrix} 0 & 1 \\ \rho_{i+1}^{-1} & -q_i \rho_{i+1}^{-1} \end{pmatrix} \quad \text{for } 1 \le i \le \ell$$

in $R^{2\times 2}$, and $R_i = Q_i \cdots Q_1 R_0$ for $0 \le i \le \ell$. The following lemma collects some invariants of the Extended Euclidean Algorithm.

LEMMA 3.8. *For $0 \le i \le \ell$, we have*

(i) $R_i \cdot \begin{pmatrix} f \\ g \end{pmatrix} = \begin{pmatrix} r_i \\ r_{i+1} \end{pmatrix}$,

(ii) $R_i = \begin{pmatrix} s_i & t_i \\ s_{i+1} & t_{i+1} \end{pmatrix}$,

(iii) $\gcd(f,g) = \gcd(r_i, r_{i+1}) = r_\ell$,

(iv) $s_i f + t_i g = r_i$ *(this also holds for $i = \ell + 1$),*

(v) $s_i t_{i+1} - t_i s_{i+1} = (-1)^i (\rho_0 \cdots \rho_{i+1})^{-1}$,

(vi) $\gcd(r_i, t_i) = \gcd(f, t_i)$,

(vii) $f = (-1)^i \rho_0 \cdots \rho_{i+1}(t_{i+1} r_i - t_i r_{i+1})$, $g = (-1)^{i+1} \rho_0 \cdots \rho_{i+1}(s_{i+1} r_i - s_i r_{i+1})$,

with the convention that $\rho_{\ell+1} = 1$ and $r_{\ell+1} = 0$.

PROOF. For (i) and (ii) we proceed by induction on i. The case $i = 0$ is clear from step 1 of the algorithm, and we may assume $i \ge 1$. Then

$$Q_i \begin{pmatrix} r_{i-1} \\ r_i \end{pmatrix} = \begin{pmatrix} 0 & 1 \\ \rho_{i+1}^{-1} & -q_i \rho_{i+1}^{-1} \end{pmatrix} = \begin{pmatrix} r_i \\ (r_{i-1} - q_i r_i)\rho_{i+1}^{-1} \end{pmatrix} = \begin{pmatrix} r_i \\ r_{i+1} \end{pmatrix},$$

and (i) follows from $R_i = Q_i R_{i-1}$ and the induction hypothesis. Similarly, (ii) follows from

$$Q_i \begin{pmatrix} s_{i-1} & t_{i-1} \\ s_i & t_i \end{pmatrix} = \begin{pmatrix} s_i & t_i \\ s_{i+1} & t_{i+1} \end{pmatrix}$$

and the induction hypothesis.

For (iii), let $i \in \{0, \dots, \ell\}$. We conclude from (i) that

$$\begin{pmatrix} r_\ell \\ 0 \end{pmatrix} = Q_\ell \cdots Q_{i+1} R_i \begin{pmatrix} f \\ g \end{pmatrix} = Q_\ell \cdots Q_{i+1} \begin{pmatrix} r_i \\ r_{i+1} \end{pmatrix}.$$

Comparing the first entry on both sides, we see that r_ℓ is a linear combination of r_i and r_{i+1}, and hence any common divisor of r_i and r_{i+1} divides r_ℓ. On the other hand, $\det Q_i = -\rho_{i+1}^{-1}$ is a unit in R, so that the matrix Q_i is invertible over R, with inverse

$$Q_i^{-1} = \begin{pmatrix} q_i & \rho_{i+1} \\ 1 & 0 \end{pmatrix},$$

and hence

$$\begin{pmatrix} r_i \\ r_{i+1} \end{pmatrix} = Q_{i+1}^{-1} \cdots Q_{\ell}^{-1} \begin{pmatrix} r_{\ell} \\ 0 \end{pmatrix}.$$

Thus both r_i and r_{i+1} are divisible by r_{ℓ}, and $r_{\ell} = \gcd(r_i, r_{i+1})$ since r_{ℓ} is normalized. In particular, this is true for $i = 0$, so that $\gcd(f, g) = \gcd(r_0, r_1) = r_{\ell}$.

The claim (iv) follows immediately from (i) and (ii), and (v) follows from (ii) by taking determinants:

$$s_i t_{i+1} - t_i s_{i+1} = \det \begin{pmatrix} s_i & t_i \\ s_{i+1} & t_{i+1} \end{pmatrix} = \det R_i = \det Q_i \cdots \det Q_1 \cdot \det \begin{pmatrix} s_0 & t_0 \\ s_1 & t_1 \end{pmatrix}$$
$$= (-1)^i (\rho_0 \cdots \rho_{i+1})^{-1}.$$

In particular, this implies that $\gcd(s_i, t_i) = 1$. Now let $p \in R$ be a divisor of t_i. If $p \mid f$, then clearly $p \mid s_i f + t_i g = r_i$. On the other hand, if $p \mid r_i$, then p also divides $s_i f = r_i - t_i g$, and hence p divides f since s_i and t_i are coprime. This proves (vi), and also shows that R_i is invertible.

To prove (vii), we multiply both sides of (i) by R_i^{-1} and obtain

$$\begin{pmatrix} r_0 \\ r_1 \end{pmatrix} = R_i^{-1} \begin{pmatrix} r_i \\ r_{i+1} \end{pmatrix} = (-1)^i (\rho_0 \cdots \rho_{i+1}) \begin{pmatrix} t_{i+1} & -t_i \\ -s_{i+1} & s_i \end{pmatrix} \begin{pmatrix} r_i \\ r_{i+1} \end{pmatrix},$$

using (ii) and (v), and the claim follows by writing this out as a system of linear equations. $\square$

We note that all statements of Lemma 3.8 remain valid if we set $\rho_i = 1$ for $0 \leq i \leq \ell + 1$ and $r_{i+1} = r_{i-1}$ rem r_i for $1 \leq i \leq \ell$ in Algorithm 3.6. This yields the classical Extended Euclidean Algorithm, which works over any Euclidean domain, whether there is a normal form or not.

━━ COROLLARY 3.9. ━━
Any two elements f, g of a Euclidean domain R have a gcd $h \in R$, which is expressible as a linear combination $h = sf + tg$ with $s, t \in R$. ━━━━━━━━━━━

3.3. Cost analysis for $\mathbb{Z}$ and $F[x]$

We want to analyze the cost of the Extended Euclidean Algorithm 3.6 for $f, g \in R$ with $n = d(f) \geq d(g) = m \geq 0$. The number ℓ of division steps is obviously bounded by $\ell \leq d(g) + 1$. We investigate the two important cases $R = F[x]$ and $R = \mathbb{Z}$ separately, starting with $R = F[x]$, where F is a field, and $d(a) = \deg a$ as usual.

We let $n_i = \deg r_i$ for $0 \leq i \leq \ell + 1$, with $r_{\ell+1} = 0$. Then $n_0 = n \geq n_1 = m > n_2 > \cdots > n_\ell$, and $\deg q_i = n_{i-1} - n_i$ for $1 \leq i \leq \ell$. According to Section 2.4, we can divide the polynomial r_{i-1} of degree n_{i-1} by the monic polynomial r_i of degree $n_i \leq n_{i-1}$ with remainder using at most $2n_i(n_{i-1} - n_i + 1)$ arithmetic operations in F. The cost for normalizing the remainder of degree n_i is one inversion of the leading coefficient plus n_i multiplications. Thus the total cost for the Euclidean Algorithm, that is, for computing only the ρ_i, r_i, and q_i, including the gcd of f and g, is

$$\sum_{1 \leq i \leq \ell} 2n_i(n_{i-1} - n_i + 1) + \sum_{0 \leq i \leq \ell} n_i = 2 \sum_{1 \leq i \leq \ell} n_i(n_{i-1} - n_i) + n_0 + 3 \sum_{1 \leq i \leq \ell} n_i \qquad (4)$$

additions and multiplications in F, plus $\ell + 1 \leq m + 2$ inversions. We first evaluate the above expression for the **normal** case where $n_i = n_{i-1} - 1 = \cdots = m - i + 1$ for $2 \leq i \leq \ell = m + 1$, and later show that this is the worst case. Then (4) simplifies to

$$2m(n - m) + n + 3m + 5 \sum_{2 \leq i \leq m+1} (m - i + 1)$$

$$= 2nm - 2m^2 + n + 3m + 5 \sum_{0 \leq i < m} i$$

$$= 2nm - 2m^2 + n + 3m + \frac{5}{2}(m^2 - m) \leq \frac{5}{2}nm + \frac{3}{2}n. \qquad (5)$$

We now consider the expression in (4) as a function of the integers $n_0 \geq n_1 > n_2 > \cdots > n_\ell > n_\ell \geq 0$ and show that it increases if we insert an additional integer $n_{j-1} > k > n_j$ for some $j \in \{2, \ldots, \ell\}$ or append some integer $n_\ell > k \geq 0$. It is sufficient to prove this for the first sum on the right hand side of (4), since the other two summands obviously do not decrease. So let this sum be $\sigma(n_0, n_1, \ldots, n_\ell)$. Then

$$\sigma(n_0, \ldots, n_{j-1}, k, n_j, \ldots, n_\ell) - \sigma(n_0, \ldots, n_\ell)$$

$$= 2k(n_{j-1} - k) + 2n_j(k - n_j) - 2n_j(n_{j-1} - n_j)$$

$$= 2(n_{j-1} - k)(k - n_j) > 0.$$

A similar argument works for $n_\ell > k \geq 0$. Proceeding inductively, we find that $\sigma(n_0, n_1, n_2, \ldots, n_\ell) < \sigma(n_0, n_1, n_1 - 1, \ldots, 1, 0)$, and conclude that the bound (5) is valid in any case.

It remains to determine the cost for computing s_i, t_i on the way.

LEMMA 3.10.

$$\deg s_i = \sum_{2 \leq j < i} \deg q_j = n_1 - n_{i-1} \text{ for } 2 \leq i \leq \ell + 1, \qquad (6)$$

$$\deg t_i = \sum_{1 \leq j < i} \deg q_j = n_0 - n_{i-1} \text{ for } 1 \leq i \leq \ell + 1. \qquad (7)$$

PROOF. We only prove the first equality; the second can be verified in the same way (Exercise 3.21). We show (6) and

$$\deg s_{i-1} < \deg s_i \text{ for } 2 \leq i \leq \ell + 1 \tag{8}$$

by simultaneous induction on i. For $i = 2$, we find that $s_2 = (s_0 - q_1 s_1)/\rho_2 = (1 - q_1 \cdot 0)/\rho_2 = \rho_2^{-1}$, and $\deg s_1 = -\infty < 0 = \deg s_2$. Now we assume that $i \geq 2$ and that the claims are already proven for $2 \leq j \leq i$. Then, by the induction hypothesis (8), we have

$$\deg s_{i-1} < \deg s_i < n_{i-1} - n_i + \deg s_i = \deg(q_i s_i),$$

which implies that

$$\deg s_{i+1} = \deg(s_{i-1} - q_i s_i) = \deg q_i + \deg s_i > \deg s_i,$$

and

$$\deg s_{i+1} = \deg q_i + \deg s_i = \sum_{2 \leq j < i} \deg q_j + \deg q_i = \sum_{2 \leq j < i+1} \deg q_j,$$

where we used the induction hypothesis (6). $\square$

═══ THEOREM 3.11. ═══════════════════════════════════
The Extended Euclidean Algorithm 3.6 for polynomials $f, g \in F[x]$ with $\deg f = n \geq \deg g = m$ can be performed with

- ○ *at most $m + 2$ inversions and $\frac{5}{2} nm + O(n)$ additions and multiplications in F if only the quotients q_i, the remainders r_i, and the coefficients ρ_i are needed,*

- ○ *at most $m + 2$ inversions and $\frac{13}{2} nm + O(n)$ additions and multiplications in F for computing all results.* ═══════════════════════

PROOF. We may arrange things in such a way that we compute the inverse of each ρ_i only once and then multiply by this inverse instead of dividing by ρ_i where necessary. This amounts to $\ell + 1 \leq m + 2$ inversions in total; all other operations are additions and multiplications.

It remains to analyze the cost for computing all the s_i, t_i. At each step, the computation of $t_{i+1} = (t_{i-1} - q_i t_i)\rho_{i+1}^{-1}$ requires one multiplication of the monic polynomial q_i by t_i, taking at most $2(\deg t_i + 1) \deg q_i$ field operations (Section 2.3), plus at most $2(\deg t_{i+1} + 1)$ operations for the addition and the multiplication by ρ_{i+1}^{-1}. Using Lemma 3.10, we obtain

$$\sum_{2 \leq i \leq \ell} 2((n_0 - n_{i-1} + 1)(n_{i-1} - n_i) + n_0 - n_i + 1)$$

additions and multiplications in F, plus the cost for the first iteration and step 1, which is $O(n)$. In the normal case, this simplifies to

$$2 \sum_{2 \le i \le m+1} (n-m+i-1+n-m+i) \;=\; 4(n-m)(m-1)+2 \sum_{0 \le i < m} (2i-5)$$

$$= \; 4(n-m)(m-1)+2(m^2-m)-10m$$

$$= \; 4nm-2m^2-4n-8m.$$

A similar argument as above shows that the normal case is the worst case, so that the bound is valid in general. Finally, Exercise 3.22 shows that the cost for the s_i's is at most $2m^2+O(m)$, and the claims follow from (5). $\square$

In Chapter 11, we will find a much faster algorithm for the gcd.

Now we sketch the cost analysis when $R = \mathbb{Z}$ and $d(a) = |a|$. We may assume that $f = r_0 \ge g = r_1 > r_2 \cdots > r_\ell \ge 0$, so that $\rho_i = 1$ and $q_i \ge 1$ for all i, and represent all numbers in 2^{64}-ary standard representation (Section 2.1). Then the length $\lambda(a)$ of a positive integer a is $\lambda(a) = \lfloor (\log a)/64 \rfloor + 1$, where log is the binary logarithm. But now the bound corresponding to what we used for polynomials, namely $\ell \le d(g)+1 = g+1 = (2^{64})^{(\log g)/64} + 1 \le 2^{64\lambda(g)}$, on the Euclidean length of the pair $(f,g) \in \mathbb{N}^2$ is exponential in the input size $\lambda(f)+\lambda(g)$ (if $\lambda(f)$ is not much bigger than $\lambda(g)$) and hence rather useless. We can in fact prove a polynomial upper bound on ℓ, as follows. For $1 \le i \le \ell$, we have

$$r_{i-1} = q_i r_i + r_{i+1} \ge r_i + r_{i+1} > 2r_{i+1}.$$

Thus

$$\prod_{2 \le i < \ell} r_{i-1} > 2^{\ell-2} \prod_{2 \le i < \ell} r_{i+1}$$

if $\ell \ge 2$, and $r_{\ell-1} \ge 2$ implies that

$$2^{\ell-2} < \frac{r_1 r_2}{r_{\ell-1} r_\ell} < \frac{r_1^2}{2},$$

$$\ell \le \lfloor 2\log r_1 \rfloor + 1 = \left\lfloor 128\frac{\log g}{64} \right\rfloor + 1 \le 128\left(\left\lfloor \frac{\log g}{64} \right\rfloor + 1\right) = 128\lambda(g).$$

This bound can still be improved. For $N \in \mathbb{N}$ and $f,g \in \mathbb{Z}$ with $N \ge f > g > 0$, the largest possible Euclidean length ℓ of (f,g) is the one where all the quotients are equal to 1, so that f and g are the two largest successive Fibonacci numbers up to N. As an example, the Euclidean Algorithm for $(f,g) = (13,8)$ computes

$$
\begin{aligned}
13 &= 1 \cdot 8 + 5, \\
8 &= 1 \cdot 5 + 3, \\
5 &= 1 \cdot 3 + 2, \\
3 &= 1 \cdot 2 + 1, \\
2 &= 2 \cdot 1.
\end{aligned}
$$

The nth Fibonacci number F_n (with $F_0 = 0$, $F_1 = 1$, and $F_n = F_{n-1} + F_{n-2}$ for $n \geq 2$) is approximately $\phi^n/\sqrt{5}$, where $\phi = (1+\sqrt{5})/2 \approx 1.618$ is the golden ratio (Exercise 3.28). Thus the following holds for the Euclidean length ℓ of $(f,g) = (F_{n+1}, F_n)$:

$$\ell = n - 1 \approx \log_\phi \sqrt{5}g - 1 \in 1.441 \log g + O(1). \tag{9}$$

The average Euclidean length of (f,g) when g is fixed and f varies is

$$\ell \approx \frac{12(\ln 2)^2}{\pi^2} \log g \approx 0.584 \log g.$$

Now that we have a good upper bound for the number of steps in the Euclidean Algorithm, we look at the cost for each step. First we consider the cost for one division step. Let $a > b > 0$ be integers and $a = qb + r$ with $q, r \in \mathbb{N}$ and $0 \leq r < b$. According to Section 2.4, computing q and r takes $O((\lambda(a) - \lambda(b)) \cdot \lambda(b))$ word operations, where $\lambda(a)$ and $\lambda(b)$ are the lengths of a and b in the standard representation, respectively.

Then setting $n = \lambda(f)$ and $m = \lambda(g)$, we obtain—by analogy with (5)—that the total cost for performing the Euclidean Algorithm (without computing the s_i and t_i) is $O(nm)$ word operations.

The following integer analog of Lemma 3.10 is proven in Exercise 3.23.

LEMMA 3.12. $|s_i| \leq \dfrac{g}{r_{i-1}}$ and $|t_i| \leq \dfrac{f}{r_{i-1}}$ for $1 \leq i \leq \ell + 1$.

Lemma 3.12 yields analogous bounds for the length of s_i and t_i as in the polynomial case, and we have the following theorem, which is proven in Exercise 3.24.

▬▬ THEOREM 3.13. ▬▬▬▬▬▬▬▬▬▬▬▬▬▬▬▬▬▬▬▬▬▬▬▬▬
The Extended Euclidean Algorithm 3.6 for integers $f, g \in \mathbb{N}$ with $\lambda(f) = n \geq \lambda(g) = m$ can be performed with $O(nm)$ word operations. ▬▬▬▬▬▬▬▬▬

N	c_N/N^2
10	0.63
100	0.6087
1000	0.608383
10000	0.60794971
100000	0.6079301507

TABLE 3.1: The probabilities that two random positive integers below N are coprime.

We conclude this chapter with the following question: what is the probability that two random integers are coprime? More precisely, when N gets large and

$c_N = \#\{1 \le x, y \le N : \gcd(x,y) = 1\}$, we are interested in the numerical value of c_N/N^2. Table 3.1 gives c_N/N^2 for some values of N; it seems to approach a limit which is a little larger than $3/5$. In fact, the value is

$$\frac{c_N}{N^2} \in \frac{6}{\pi^2} + O\left(\frac{\log N}{N}\right) \approx 0.6079271016 + O\left(\frac{\log N}{N}\right).$$

Interestingly, a similar approximation holds for the probability that a random integer is **squarefree**, so that it has no square divisor p^2:

$$\frac{\#\{1 \le x \le N : x \text{ is squarefree}\}}{N} \in \frac{6}{\pi^2} + O\left(\frac{1}{\sqrt{N}}\right).$$

Exercises 4.18 and 14.32 answer the corresponding questions for polynomials over a finite field.

In Figure 3.2, we see a two-dimensional coordinate system where the point $(x,y) \in \mathbb{N}^2$ for $x, y \le 200$ is colored white if $\gcd(x,y) = 1$ and gray otherwise. The intensity of a pixel is proportional to the number of prime factors in the gcd. The probability that two random integers below 200 are coprime is precisely the percentage of the area of the 200×200 pixels that is colored white. Thus about $3/5$ of all pixels are white, and about $2/5$ are gray.

If you hold the page horizontally in front of your eyes, you can see (almost) white horizontal and vertical lines corresponding to prime values of x and y, and dark lines through the origin corresponding to lines $ax = by$ with small integers a, b, the most clearly visible being the line $x = y$.

Notes. **3.1.** Allowing $-\infty$ as a value of a Euclidean function d is a bit annoying and makes our two main examples, integers and univariate polynomials over a field, look different. The proper analogy between $\mathbb{Z}$ and $F[x]$ goes as follows. We can take $d(a) = |a|$ on $\mathbb{Z}$ and $d(a) = 2^{\deg a}$ on $F[x]$, including $d(0) = 0$ in both cases. Or, equivalently, we can take $d(a) = \lfloor \log_2 |a| \rfloor$ on $\mathbb{Z}$ (Exercise 3.5) and $d(a) = \deg a$ on $F[x]$, with $d(0) = -\infty$ in both cases.

3.2. The astronomical book Āryabhaṭīya, written by Āryabhaṭa in Sanskrit near the end of the fifth century AD, contains an algorithm for computing from two coprime integers $f, g \in \mathbb{N}$ two integers s, t such that $sf + tg = 1$. This problem is also solved in Bachet (1612). The calculation of the Bézout coefficients via the EEA in general is in Euler (1748a), §70. Gauss (1863b), articles 334 and 335, does this for polynomials in $\mathbb{F}_p[x]$, where p is prime. The Euclidean Algorithm 3.6 with monic remainders appears in the 1969 edition of Knuth (1998), and in Brown (1971).

3.3. Although the polynomial version of the (Extended) Euclidean Algorithm is conceptually somewhat simpler, it is much younger (Newton 1707, p. 38) than the 2000-year old integer algorithm. One reason for this is that we have a more intuitive understanding of integers than we do of polynomials.

The fact that the Euclidean length is maximal for Fibonacci numbers is Lamé's (1844) theorem. The scholarly work of Bach & Shallit (1996) contains more complete historical information about this and many other topics in this book. The interesting paper

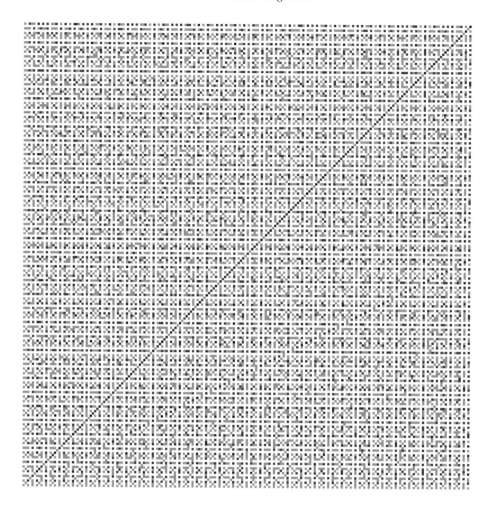

FIGURE 3.2: The greatest common divisors of x and y for $1 \leq x, y \leq 200$.

by Shallit (1994) points to three earlier analyses of the number of divisions in Euclid's algorithm: Reynaud (1824), Finck (1841), and Binet (1841); the latter allows negative remainders, as in Exercise 3.13. Finck's wording *un problème qui* [...] *a pour objet de déterminer le nombre des opérations de la recherche du p.g.c.d. de deux nombres entiers*[1] is a remarkably modern-sounding demand for the analysis of Euclid's algorithm. He gives the inequality $r_{i-1} > 2r_{i+1}$ that we used. Dupré (1846) gives the bounds of about $(\log f)/\log((1 + \sqrt{5})/2)$ for the ordinary and $(\log f)/\log(1 + \sqrt{2})$ for Binet's Euclidean algorithm (Exercise 3.30). Much earlier, Schwenter (1636), 86. Auffgab, calls the Euclidean Algorithm for $770\,020\,512\,197\,390$ and $124\,591\,930\,070\,091$, with 32 divisions, the *arithmetical labyrinth*, due to Simon Jacob von Coburg, and points to the Fibonacci numbers as requiring many divisions in the Euclidean algorithm. (The two large integers are not Fibonacci numbers, and Schwenter says that their Euclidean algorithm

---

[1] a problem that [...] has as its goal to determine the number of operations in computing the gcd of two integers

requires 54 divisions; there is a calculation or copying mistake somewhere.) We have $\gcd(F_n, F_m) = F_{\gcd(n,m)}$; see Exercise 3.31. For the the average length estimate, see Knuth (1998), §4.5.3. Ma & von zur Gathen (1990) give worst case and average case analyses of several variants of the Euclidean Algorithm for polynomials over finite fields.

The fact that two random integers are coprime with probability $6/\pi^2$ is a theorem of Dirichlet (1849). Dirichlet also proves the fact, surprising at first sight, that for fixed a in a division the remainder $r = a$ rem b, with $0 \le r < b$, is more likely to be smaller than $b/2$ than larger: If p_a denotes the probability for the former, where $1 \le b \le a$ is chosen uniformly at random, then p_a is asymptotically $2 - \ln 4 \approx 61.37\%$. For Dirichlet's theorem, and also the corresponding statement about the probability of being squarefree (due to Gegenbauer 1884), see Hardy & Wright (1985), §§18.5 and 18.6. A heuristic argument goes as follows. A prime p divides a random integer x with probability $1/p$, and neither x nor y with probability $1 - 1/p^2$. Hence $\gcd(x,y) = 1$ happens with probability $\zeta(2)^{-1} = \prod_{p \text{ prime}}(1 - 1/p^2) = 6/\pi^2$; see Notes 18.4 for a discussion of Riemann's zeta function. The value of $\zeta(2)$ was determined by Euler (1734/35b, 1743); see Apostol (1983) for a simple way of calculating this quantity.

Exercises.

3.1 Prove that two odd integers whose difference is 32 are coprime.

3.2 Let R be a ring. Show that

$$a \sim b \iff (a \mid b \text{ and } b \mid a) \iff \langle a \rangle = \langle b \rangle,$$

where $\langle a \rangle = Ra = \{ra : r \in R\}$ is the ideal generated by a.

3.3 Prove Lemma 3.4. Hint: For (iii) through (v), show that any divisor of the left hand side also divides the right hand side, and vice versa. What are the corresponding statements for the lcm? Are they also true?

3.4* Show that $\gcd(a,b) = 1$ and $\gcd(a,c) = 1$ imply that $\gcd(a,bc) = 1$.

3.5** We consider the following property of a Euclidean function on an integral domain R:

$$d(ab) \ge d(b) \text{ for all } a, b \in R \setminus \{0\}. \tag{10}$$

Our two familiar examples, the degree on $F[x]$ for a field F and the absolute value on $\mathbb{Z}$, both fulfill this property. This exercise shows that every Euclidean domain has such a Euclidean function.

(i) Show that $\delta \colon \mathbb{Z} \longrightarrow \mathbb{N}$ with $\delta(3) = 2$ and $\delta(a) = |a|$ if $a \ne 3$ is a Euclidean function on $\mathbb{Z}$ violating (10).

(ii) Suppose that R is a Euclidean domain and $D = \{\delta \colon \delta \text{ is a Euclidean function on } R\}$. Then D is nonempty, and we may define a function $d \colon R \longrightarrow \mathbb{N} \cup \{-\infty\}$ by $d(a) = \min\{\delta(a) \colon \delta \in D\}$. Show that d is a Euclidean function on R (called the **minimal Euclidean function**).

(iii) Let δ be a Euclidean function on R such that $\delta(ab) < \delta(b)$ for some $a, b \in R \setminus \{0\}$. Find another Euclidean function δ^* that is smaller than δ. Conclude that the minimal Euclidean function d satisfies (10).

(iv) Show that for all $a, b \in R \setminus \{0\}$ and a Euclidean function d satisfying (10), we have $d(0) < d(a)$, and $d(ab) = d(b)$ if and only if a is a unit.

(v) Let d be the minimal Euclidean function as in (ii). Conclude that $d(0) = -\infty$ and the group of units of R is $R^\times = \{a \in R \setminus \{0\} \colon d(a) = 0\}$.

(vi) Prove that $d(a) = \deg a$ is the minimal Euclidean function on $F[x]$ for a field F, and that $d(a) = \lfloor \log_2 |a| \rfloor$ is the minimal Euclidean function on $\mathbb{Z}$, with $d(0) = -\infty$ in both cases.

3.6* (i) Show that each two nonzero elements a,b of a UFD R have a gcd as well as a lcm. You may assume that a normal form on R is given (this is not a restriction, by Exercise 3.9). Hint: First look at the special case $R = \mathbb{Z}$, and use the factorizations of $\mathrm{normal}(a)$ and $\mathrm{normal}(b)$ into normalized primes.

(ii) Prove that $\gcd(a,b) \cdot \mathrm{lcm}(a,b) = \mathrm{normal}(a \cdot b)$.

(iii) Conclude that $\mathrm{lcm}(a_1,\ldots,a_n) = \mathrm{normal}(a_1 \cdots a_n)$ for any n nonzero elements $a_1,\ldots,a_n \in R$ that are pairwise coprime (you might need Exercise 3.4).

(iv) Is $\gcd(a_1,\ldots,a_n) \cdot \mathrm{lcm}(a_1,\ldots,a_n) = \mathrm{normal}(a_1 \cdots a_n)$ valid for arbitrary $n \in \mathbb{N}$?

3.7* Let R be a Euclidean domain, with a Euclidean function $d: R \longrightarrow \mathbb{N} \cup \{-\infty\}$ that has the additional properties

○ $d(ab) = d(a) + d(b)$,

○ $d(a+b) \leq \max\{d(a), d(b)\}$, with equality if $d(a) \neq d(b)$,

○ d is surjective,

for all $a, b \in R$. Prove that R is a polynomial ring with d as degree function. Proceed as follows:

(i) Prove that $d(a) = -\infty$ if and only if $a = 0$.

(ii) Show that $F = \{a \in R: d(a) \leq 0\}$ is a subfield of R.

(iii) Let $x \in R$ be such that $d(x) = 1$, and prove that every nonzero $a \in R$ has a unique representation

$$a = a_n x^n + a_{n-1} x^{n-1} + \cdots + a_1 x + a_0,$$

where $n = d(a)$, $a_0, \ldots, a_n \in F$, and $a_n \neq 0$.

Hint: You may find Exercise 3.5 (iv) useful.

3.8 (i) Find normal forms for $\mathbb{Z}[x]$ and for a field F.

(ii) Now let R be an integral domain with a normal form. Prove that $\mathrm{lc}(ua) = u \cdot \mathrm{lc}(a)$ holds for all units $u \in R$ and all $a \in R$. Show that a is normalized if and only if $\mathrm{normal}(a) = a$.

(iii) Prove that $\mathrm{lc}_{R[x]}(f) = \mathrm{lc}_R(f_n)$ for a polynomial $f = \sum_{0 \leq i \leq n} f_i x^i \in R[x]$ with $f_n \neq 0$ defines a normal form on $R[x]$ which extends the given normal form on R. Describe this normal form when R is a field.

(iv) Let $a = bc \in R$ with normalized a, b. Prove that c is normalized if $b \neq 0$, and conclude that $\mathrm{normal}(a/b) = \mathrm{normal}(a)/\mathrm{normal}(b)$ holds for all $a, b \in R$ such that $a \mid b$ and $b \neq 0$.

3.9* The goal of this exercise is to show that every UFD has a normal form.

(i) For a prime $p \in \mathbb{N}$, define $\mathrm{lc}(p) = 1$ if $p \neq 2$ and $\mathrm{lc}(2) = -1$. Show that "lc" can be uniquely extended to a normal form on $\mathbb{Z}$.

(ii) Now let R be an arbitrary UFD and $P \subseteq R$ a complete set of representatives for all non-associate primes of R, so that every prime of R is associate to a unique $p \in P$. (The existence of such a set is guaranteed by the axiom of choice in general.) Then every $r \in R$ can be uniquely written as $r = u \prod_{p \in S} p$ for a finite subset $S \subseteq R$ and a unit $u \in R$. Show that $\mathrm{lc}(r) = u$ defines a normal form on R.

3.10 Are there $s, t \in \mathbb{Z}$ such that $24s + 14t = 1$?

3.11 For each of the following pairs of integers, find their greatest common divisor using the Euclidean Algorithm:

(i) 34, 21;   (ii) 136, 51;   (iii) 481, 325;   (iv) 8771, 3206.

3.12 Show that $\{sf + tg: s, t \in \mathbb{Z}\} = \{k \cdot \gcd(f,g): k \in \mathbb{Z}\}$ holds for all $f, g \in \mathbb{Z}$. (In other words, the two ideals $\langle f, g \rangle$ and $\langle \gcd(f,g) \rangle$ are identical.)

3.13 The Euclidean Algorithm for integers can be slightly speeded up if it is permitted to carry out divisions with negative remainders, so that $r_{i-1} = r_i q_i + r_{i+1}$ with $-|r_i/2| < r_{i+1} \leq |r_i/2|$. Do the four examples in Exercise 3.11 using this method.

3.14 Use the Extended Euclidean Algorithm to find $\gcd(f,g)$, for $f,g \in \mathbb{Z}_p[x]$ in each of the following examples (arithmetic in $\mathbb{Z}_p = \{0,\ldots,p-1\}$ is done modulo p). In each case compute the corresponding polynomials s and t such that $\gcd(f,g) = sf + tg$.

(i) $f = x^3 + x + 1, g = x^2 + x + 1$ for $p = 2$ and $p = 3$.

(ii) $f = x^4 + x^3 + x + 1, g = x^3 + x^2 + x + 1$ for $p = 2$ and $p = 3$.

(iii) $f = x^5 + x^4 + x^3 + x + 1, g = x^4 + x^3 + x^2 + x + 1$ for $p = 5$.

(iv) $f = x^5 + x^4 + x^3 - x^2 - x + 1, g = x^3 + x^2 + x + 1$ for $p = 3$ and $p = 5$.

3.15 Show that the s_i and t_i in the Extended Euclidean Algorithm for inputs $f,g \in \mathbb{Z}$ with $f > g > 0$ alternate in sign, so that s_{2i} and t_{2i-1} are positive and s_{2i+1} and t_{2i} are negative for all admissible values of $i \geq 1$. Conclude that $0 = s_1 < 1 = s_2 \leq |s_3| < |s_4| < \cdots < |s_{\ell+1}|$ and $0 = t_0 < 1 = t_1 \leq |t_2| < |t_3| < \cdots < |t_{\ell+1}|$.

3.16 Let R be a Euclidean domain, $a,b,c \in R$, and $\gcd(a,b) = 1$. Prove the following:

(i) $a \mid bc \Longrightarrow a \mid c$,

(ii) $a \mid c$ and $b \mid c \Longrightarrow ab \mid c$.

Hint: You may want to use the fact that the Extended Euclidean Algorithm computes $s,t \in R$ such that $sa + tb = 1$.

3.17 Prove that $\mathbb{Z}[x]$ is not a Euclidean domain. Hint: If it were, then we could compute $s,t \in \mathbb{Z}[x]$ such that $s \cdot 2 + t \cdot x = \gcd(2,x)$, using the Extended Euclidean Algorithm.

3.18* Let $R = F[x]$ for a field F and

$$S = \bigcup_{\ell \geq 1} \left((F \setminus \{0\})^{\ell+1} \times (R \setminus \{0\})^2 \times \{q \in R: \deg q > 0, \ q \text{ monic}\}^{\ell-1} \right).$$

The **Euclidean representation** of a pair $(f,g) \in (R \setminus \{0\})^2$ with $\deg f \geq \deg g$ is defined as the list $(\rho_0, \ldots, \rho_\ell, r_\ell, q_1, \ldots, q_\ell) \in S$. Show that the map

$$\{(f,g) \in R^2: \deg f \geq \deg g \text{ and } g \neq 0\} \longrightarrow S$$

which maps a pair of polynomials (f,g) to its Euclidean representation is a bijection.

3.19* (i) Show that the **norm** $N: \mathbb{Z}[i] \longrightarrow \mathbb{N}$ with $N(\alpha) = \alpha\bar{\alpha}$ on the ring of Gaussian integers $\mathbb{Z}[i]$ is a Euclidean function. Hint: Consider the exact quotient of two Gaussian integers $\alpha, \beta \in \mathbb{Z}[i]$ in $\mathbb{C}$.

(ii) Show that the units in $\mathbb{Z}[i]$ are precisely the elements of norm 1 and enumerate them.

(iii) Prove that there is no multiplicative normal form on $\mathbb{Z}[i]$ which extends the usual normal form $\text{normal}(a) = |a|$ on $\mathbb{Z}$. Hint: Consider $\text{normal}((1+i)^2)$. Why is $\text{normal}(a+ib) = |a| + i|b|$ for $a,b \in \mathbb{Z}$ not a normal form?

(iv) Compute all greatest common divisors of 6 and $3+i$ in $\mathbb{Z}[i]$ and their representations as a linear combination of 6 and $3+i$.

(v) Compute a gcd of $12\,277$ and $399 + 20i$.

3.20* Let $x_1, x_2, \ldots$ be countably many indeterminates over $\mathbb{Z}$, $R = \mathbb{Z}[x_1, x_2, \ldots]$,

$$Q_i = \begin{pmatrix} 0 & 1 \\ 1 & x_i \end{pmatrix} \in R^{2 \times 2}$$

for $i \geq 1$, and $R_i = Q_1 \cdots Q_i$. We define the ith **continuant polynomial** $c_i \in R$ recursively by $c_0 = 0$, $c_1 = 1$, and $c_{i+1} = c_{i-1} + x_i c_i$ for $i \geq 1$. Then $c_i \in \mathbb{Z}[x_1, \ldots, x_{i-1}]$ for $i \geq 1$.

(i) List the first 10 continuant polynomials.

(ii) Let T be the "shift homomorphism" $Tx_i = x_{i+1}$ for $i \geq 1$. Show that $c_{i+1}(0, x_2, x_3, \ldots, x_i) = Tc_i$ for $i \geq 0$.

(iii) Show that $R_i = \begin{pmatrix} Tc_{i-1} & c_i \\ Tc_i & c_{i+1} \end{pmatrix}$ for $i \geq 1$.

(iv) Show that $\det R_i = (-1)^i$, and conclude that $\gcd(c_i, c_{i+1}) = 1$ for $i \geq 0$.

(v) Let D be a Euclidean domain and $r_i, q_i, s_i, t_i \in D$ for $0 \leq i \leq \ell$ the results of the *classical* Extended Euclidean Algorithm for r_0, r_1. Show that

$$
\begin{aligned}
s_i &= c_i(0, -q_2, \ldots, -q_{i-1}) = (-1)^i c_i(0, q_2, \ldots, q_{i-1}), \\
t_i &= c_i(-q_1, \ldots, -q_{i-1}) = (-1)^{i-1} c_i(q_1, \ldots, q_{i-1})
\end{aligned}
$$

for $1 \leq i \leq \ell$.

(vi) Write a MAPLE program that implements the classical Extended Euclidean Algorithm and additionally computes all continuants $c_i(q_{\ell-i+2}, \ldots, q_\ell)$ for $r_0 = x^{20}$ and $r_1 = x^{19} + 2x^{18} + x$ in $\mathbb{Q}[x]$, where $q_1, \ldots, q_\ell$ are the quotients in the classical Extended Euclidean Algorithm.

3.21 Prove Lemma 3.10 (7). Hint: Since q_1 may be constant, it is wise to start the induction with $i = 3$ and show the cases $i = 1$ and $i = 2$ separately.

3.22 Show that for polynomials $f, g \in F[x]$ of degrees $n \geq m$, where F is a field, computing all entries s_i in the Extended Euclidean Algorithm from the quotients q_i and the ρ_i takes at most $2m^2 + O(m)$ operations in F. Hint: Exhibit the bound for the normal case and prove that this is the worst case.

3.23 Prove Lemma 3.12. Hint: Use Lemma 3.8 and Exercise 3.15.

3.24* Prove Theorem 3.13.

3.25* We consider the following recursive algorithm for computing the gcd of two integers.

▬▬ ALGORITHM 3.14 Binary Euclidean Algorithm. ▬▬▬▬▬▬▬▬▬▬▬▬▬▬▬▬▬▬
Input: $a, b \in \mathbb{N}$ such that $a \geq b > 0$.
Output: $\gcd(a, b) \in \mathbb{N}$.

1. **if** $a = b$ **then return** a

2. **if** both a and b are even **then return** $2 \cdot \gcd(a/2, b/2)$

3. **if** exactly one of the two numbers, say a, is even **then return** $\gcd(a/2, b)$

4. **if** both a and b are odd and, say, $a > b$, **then return** $\gcd((a-b)/2, b)$ ▬▬▬▬▬▬▬▬▬▬▬

(i) Run the algorithm on the examples of Exercise 3.11.

(ii) Prove that the algorithm works correctly.

(iii) Find a "good" upper bound on the recursion depth of the algorithm, and show that it takes $O(n^2)$ word operations on inputs of length at most n.

(iv) Modify the algorithm so that it additionally computes $s, t \in \mathbb{N}$ such that $sa + tb = \gcd(a, b)$.

3.26* Adapt the algorithm from Exercise 3.25 to polynomials over a field. Hint: Start with $\mathbb{F}_2[x]$.

3.27 Let F_n and F_{n+1} be consecutive terms in the Fibonacci sequence. Show that $\gcd(F_{n+1}, F_n) = 1$.

3.28 (i) Prove the formula

$$
F_n = \frac{1}{\sqrt{5}} (\phi_+^n - \phi_-^n) \text{ for } n \in \mathbb{N} \tag{11}
$$

for the Fibonacci numbers, where $\phi_+ = (1 + \sqrt{5})/2 \approx 1.618$ is the golden ratio and $\phi_- = -1/\phi_+ = (1 - \sqrt{5})/2 \approx -0.618$. Conclude that F_n is the nearest integer to $\phi_+^n/\sqrt{5}$ for all n.

(ii) For $n \in \mathbb{N}_{>0}$, let $k_n = [1, \ldots, 1]$ be the continued fraction of length n with all entries equal to 1. Prove that $k_n = F_{n+1}/F_n$, and conclude that $\lim_{n \to \infty} k_n = \phi_+$.

3.29* This continues Exercise 3.28.

(i) Let $h = \sum_{n \geq 0} F_n x^n \in \mathbb{Q}[[x]]$ be the formal power series whose coefficients are the Fibonacci numbers. Derive a linear equation for h from the recursion formula for the Fibonacci numbers and solve it for h. (It will turn out that h is a rational function in x.)

(ii) Compute the partial fraction expansion (Section 5.11) of h and use it to prove (11) again by employing the formula $\sum_{n \geq 0} x^n = 1/(1 - x)$ for the geometric series and comparing coefficients.

3.30* In the least absolute remainder variant of the Euclidean Algorithm for integers (Exercise 3.13), all quotients q_i (with the possible exception of q_1) are at least two in absolute value. Thus the nonnegative integers with the largest possible Euclidean length in this variant, that is, the analog of the Fibonacci numbers in Lamé's theorem, are recursively defined by

$$G_0 = 0, \quad G_1 = 1, \quad G_{n+1} = 2G_n + G_{n-1} \text{ for } n \geq 1.$$

(i) Find a closed form expression similar to (11) for G_n. Hint: Proceed as in Exercise 3.29.

(ii) Derive a tight upper bound on the length ℓ of the least absolute remainder Euclidean Algorithm for two integers $f, g \in \mathbb{N}$ with $f > g$ in terms of $\log g$, and compare it to (9).

3.31* For $n \in \mathbb{N}$, let F_n be the nth Fibonacci number, with $F_0 = 0$ and $F_1 = 1$. Prove or disprove that the following properties hold for all $n, k \in \mathbb{N}$.

(i) $F_{n+k+1} = F_n F_k + F_{n+1} F_{k+1}$,

(ii) F_k divides F_{nk},

(iii) $\gcd(F_{nk+1}, F_k) = 1$ if $k \geq 1$ (hint: Exercise 3.27),

(iv) $F_n \text{ rem } F_k = F_{n \text{ rem } k}$ if $k \geq 1$,

(v) $\gcd(F_n, F_k) = \gcd(F_k, F_{n \text{ rem } k})$ if $k \geq 1$ (hint: Exercise 3.16),

(vi) $\gcd(F_n, F_k) = F_{\gcd(n,k)}$.

(vii) Conclude from (i) that F_n can be calculated with $O(\log n)$ arithmetic operations in $\mathbb{Z}$.

(viii) Generalize your answers to **Lucas sequences** $(L_n)_{n \geq 0}$ of the form $L_0 = 0, L_1 = 1$, and $L_{n+2} = aL_{n+1} + L_n$ for $n \in \mathbb{N}$, where $a \in \mathbb{Z}$ is a fixed constant.

3.32* We define the sequence $f_0, f_1, f_2, \ldots \in \mathbb{Q}[x]$ of monic polynomials by

○ $\gcd(f_n, f_{n-1}) = 1$ for $n \geq 1$,

○ for every $n \geq 1$ the Euclidean length of (f_n, f_{n-1}) is n, and all quotients in the Euclidean Algorithm are equal to x.

(i) What are the remainders in the Euclidean Algorithm for f_n and f_{n-1}? What are the ρ_i? Find a recursion for the f_n. What is the degree of f_n?

(ii) What is the connection between the f_n and the Fibonacci numbers?

(iii) State and prove a theorem saying that the pair (f_n, f_{n-1}) has maximal Euclidean length (make explicit what you mean by maximal).

Die Musik hat viel Aehnlichkeit mit der Algeber.[1]

Novalis (1799)

Ein Mathematiker, der nicht etwas Poet ist,
wird nimmer ein vollkommener Mathematiker sein.[2]

Karl Theodor Wilhelm Weierstraß (1883)

There remain, therefore, algebra and arithmetic
as the only sciences, in which we can carry on
a chain of reasoning to any degree of intricacy,
and yet preserve a perfect exactness and certainty.

David Hume (1739)

The science of algebra, independently of any of its uses, has all the
advantages which belong to mathematics in general as an object of
study, and which it is not necessary to enumerate. Viewed either as a
science of quantity, or as a language of symbols, it may be made of the
greatest service to those who are sufficiently acquainted with
arithmetic, and who have sufficient power of comprehension
to enter fairly upon its difficulties.

Augustus De Morgan (1837)

وهو تقريب لا تحقيق

ولا يقف احد علي حقيقة ذلك ولا يعلم دورها الا الله

لان الخط ليس بمستقيم فيوقف علي حقيقته

وانما قيل ذلك تقريب كما قيل في جذر الاصم

انه تقريب لا تحقيق لان جذره لا يعلمه الا الله[3]

Abū Jaʿfar Muḥammad ben Mūsā al-Khwārizmī (c. 830)

---

[1] Music has much resemblance to algebra.

[2] A mathematician who is not somewhat of a poet will never be a perfect mathematician.

[3] And this is an approximation and not a precise determination [of π]. Nobody can determine the exact value of
that and know the circumference, except God. For this curve [the circle] is not straight and cannot be determined
except approximately. That is called an approximation, just as the root of a number is an approximation and not
the exact value; nobody knows it except God.

4

Applications of the Euclidean Algorithm

This chapter presents several applications of the Extended Euclidean Algorithm: modular arithmetic, in particular modular inverses; linear Diophantine equations; and continued fractions. The latter in turn are useful for problems outside of computer algebra: devising astronomical calendars and musical scale systems.

4.1. Modular arithmetic

We start with some applications. The first one is checking programs for correctness. In Part II of this book, we will see extremely fast algorithms for multiplication of large integers. These methods are also considerably more complicated than classical multiplication, and an implementation quite error-prone. So we may want to test correctness on many inputs. We take inputs a and b, say positive integers of $10\,000$ words each, and the output c of $20\,000$ words. Can we check that $a \cdot b = c$ without using our own software?

The solution is a modular test. We take a single-precision prime p and check whether $a \cdot b \equiv c \bmod p$ (read "$a \cdot b$ and c are **congruent modulo p**"), which means that $a \cdot b - c$ is divisible by p, or equivalently, $a \cdot b$ and c have the same remainder on division by p. By (1) below, it is sufficient for this purpose to compute the remainders $a^* = a \bmod p$, $b^* = b \bmod p$, $c^* = c \bmod p$ and check whether $a^* \cdot b^* \equiv c^* \bmod p$, since $a \cdot b \equiv a^* \cdot b^* \bmod p$. If this fails to hold, then clearly somewhere there is an error. How reliable is this test?

Of course, it can happen that $ab \neq c$ and $a^*b^* \equiv c^* \bmod p$. This happens if and only if $ab - c \neq 0$ is divisible by p. If each of our primes is at least 2^{63}, then the product of k of them at least $2^{63 \cdot k}$. Now $|ab - c|$ is a number with not more than $20\,000$ words, and hence divisible by at most $\log_{2^{63}}(2^{64 \cdot 20\,000}) \leq 20318$ different primes. If we have a data base of 40636 single-precision primes and choose p at random from these, then the test will fail to detect a software error with probability at most $1/2$ (assuming that the test itself is correctly implemented). There is an abundant supply of primes: over $2 \cdot 10^{17}$ 64-bit primes, and more than 90 million 32-bit primes, by the prime number theorem 18.7 (see also Exercise 18.18).

By standard tricks, such as rerunning the test or choosing a larger data base, this probability can be made arbitrarily small.

The technique can also be used to test equalities like $f \cdot g = h$ for polynomials f, g, h, by substituting a random value, or $A \cdot B = C$ for matrices A, B, C, by evaluating at a random vector.

This **fingerprinting** method can even be applied to problems outside the algebraic realm, by "arithmetizing" combinatorial problems. Suppose that one maintains a large data base in North America and a mirror image in Europe, by performing all updates on both. Each night, one wants to check whether they indeed are identical. Sending the whole data base would take too long. So one considers the data base as a string of words, many gigabytes long, and the (large) number a whose 2^{64}-ary representation this is. Then one chooses a prime p, computes a rem p and sends this to the mirror site. The corresponding calculation is performed on the other data base, and the two results are compared. If they disagree, then the two data bases differ. If they agree, then probably the two data bases are identical, provided p was chosen appropriately. This can be set up so that the size of the transmitted message is only logarithmic in the size of the data bases. Exercise 4.3 asks you to apply this method to the more general problem of string matching.

Division with remainder of a large number by a small number is easy (Exercise 4.1), and you are familiar with one particularly simple example: the remainder of a number modulo 9 (or 3) equals the remainder of the sum of its decimal digits. In particular, the number is divisible by 9 (or 3) if and only if this sum is. Why does this work? Let $a = \sum_{0 \le i < l} a_i \cdot 10^i$ be the decimal representation of $a \in \mathbb{N}$. Since $10 \equiv 1 \bmod 9$ (and $\bmod 3$), we have $a \equiv \sum_{0 \le i < l} a_i \cdot 1^i = \sum_{0 \le i < l} a_i \bmod 9$ (and $\bmod 3$) (see Exercise 4.4 for remainders modulo 11).

Computing with remainders of arithmetic expressions modulo some nonzero integer is called **modular arithmetic**. Given an expression e involving integers and arithmetic operations $+, -, \cdot$, we can compute e modulo some number m very efficiently by first reducing all integers modulo m and then, step by step, performing an arithmetic operation in $\mathbb{Z}$ and immediately reducing the result modulo m again, as we have done in the examples above. Here is another one:

$$e = 20 \cdot (-89) + 32 \equiv 6 \cdot 2 + 4 \equiv 12 + 4 \equiv 5 + 4 \equiv 9 \equiv 2 \bmod 7.$$

In this way, the intermediate results never exceed m^2. The basic rules for computing with congruences are

$$a \equiv b \bmod m \Longrightarrow a * c \equiv b * c \bmod m, \tag{1}$$

where $a, b, c \in \mathbb{Z}$ and $*$ is one of $+, -, \cdot$. Using these rules inductively, we may replace numbers by congruent ones in any arithmetic expression involving additions, subtractions, and multiplications without changing the result modulo m. In other words, we may manipulate congruences as we are used to manipulating equations, with one important exception: we have to be careful about cancellation and division. For example, we have $0 \cdot 2 \equiv 2 \cdot 2 \equiv 0 \bmod 4$, but $0 \not\equiv 2 \bmod 4$.

We can also perform modular arithmetic with polynomials over a ring R. Here the simplest nontrivial modulus is a linear polynomial $x - u$ with $u \in R$. For any polynomial $f \in R[x]$, the polynomial $f(x) - f(u)$ has u as a zero and hence is divisible by $x - u$. If we let $q = (f(x) - f(u))/(x - u)$, then $f = q \cdot (x - u) + f(u)$, and since $f(u)$ is a constant polynomial, its degree is less than $1 = \deg(x - u)$. By the uniqueness of the remainder, $f(u)$ is the remainder of f on division by $x - u$, that is, $(f \text{ rem } (x - u)) = f(u)$ and $f \equiv f(u) \bmod (x - u)$. Thus calculating modulo $x - u$ is the same as evaluating at u.

This can be used to check equality of polynomial expressions, as follows. Suppose that we want to know whether the two polynomials $f = (x - 1)(x - 2) \cdot (x - 3)(x - 4)(x - 5) + 1$ and $g = x^5 - 15x^4 + 85x^3 - 223x^2 + 274x - 119$ are equal. To check this, we evaluate them at some number u. Let us try $u = 0$. This is easy for g, since $g \text{ rem } x = g(0) = -119$ is just its constant coefficient (this is analogous to computing $a \text{ rem } 10$ for an integer a given in decimal representation), and $f \text{ rem } x = f(0) = (-1)(-2)(-3)(-4)(-5) + 1 = -120 + 1 = -119$, so this does not hinder f from being equal to g. If we take $u = 1$, then computing $f \text{ rem } (x - 1) = f(1) = 1$ is easy, since the first summand contains the linear factor $x - 1$. Now $g \text{ rem } (x - 1) = g(1) = 1 - 15 + 85 - 223 + 274 - 119 = 3$ (this is like computing the sum of the decimal digits of an integer a; here $x \equiv 1 \bmod (x - 1)$ and hence $x^i \equiv 1^i = 1 \bmod (x - 1)$ for $i \in \mathbb{N}$), and we conclude that $f \neq g$. In fact, we would have even found this out if we had done the whole computation modulo the polynomial $x - 1$ *and* modulo the integer 5, since $g(1) \equiv 1 - 0 + 0 - 3 + 4 - 4 \equiv 3 \not\equiv 1 = f(1) \bmod 5$.

If our polynomial modulus is not linear, then things are a bit more complicated. For example, if $m = x^2 - x - 1$, then the remainder of a polynomial f on division by m is a unique polynomial of degree at most one. For $f = x^3$, we have $x^3 \equiv 2x + 1 \bmod m$, $x^2 + 2x \equiv 3x + 1 \bmod m$, and hence

$$
\begin{aligned}
(x^3 + 1)(x^2 + 2x) - x^3 &\equiv ((2x + 1) + 1)(3x + 1) - (2x + 1) \\
&= (6x^2 + 8x + 2) - (2x + 1) \equiv (14x + 8) - (2x + 1) \\
&= 12x + 7 \bmod x^2 - x - 1,
\end{aligned}
$$

since $6x^2 + 8x + 2 \equiv 14x + 8 \bmod m$.

The mathematical concept behind modular arithmetic is the **residue class ring**. If R is a ring (say $R = \mathbb{Z}$ or $R = F[x]$) and $m \in R$, then $\langle m \rangle = mR = \{mr : r \in R\}$, the set of all multiples of m, is the **ideal** generated by m, and the residue class ring $R/mR = R/\langle m \rangle = \{f \bmod n : f \in R\}$ consists of all **residue classes** $f \bmod m = \{f + mr : r \in R\}$ for $f \in R$. (The notation $f \bmod m$ for the residue class is somewhat unfortunate since it may lead to confusion with congruences like $f \equiv g \bmod m$, but it is nevertheless widely used.) For example, if we take $R = \mathbb{Z}$ and $m = 5$, then $3 \bmod 5 = \{\ldots, -12, -7, -2, 3, 8, 13, \ldots\}$ is one residue class of the residue class ring $\mathbb{Z}/5\mathbb{Z} = \{0 \bmod 5, 1 \bmod 5, 2 \bmod 5, 3 \bmod 5, 4 \bmod 5\}$. The elements of $3 \bmod 5$ can be characterized as those integers having remainder 3 on division by 5, and any two of them are congruent modulo 5. We also write $\mathbb{Z}_m$ for $\mathbb{Z}/m\mathbb{Z}$. If $R = \mathbb{Q}[x]$ and $m = x^2 - x - 1$, then $12x + 7 \bmod m$ consists of all polynomials having remainder $12x + 7$ on division by $x^2 - x - 1$, and any two of them are congruent modulo $x^2 - x - 1$.

Computationally, we work with a **system of representatives** (Section 25.2), so that the residue class $f \bmod m$ is represented by its smallest nonnegative element in the case $R = \mathbb{Z}$ and by its unique polynomial of least degree in the case $R = F[x]$; in both cases, the representative equals f rem m. In the integer case, we will often ignore the somewhat cumbersome distinction between residue classes and representatives. For example, we identify $\mathbb{Z}/5\mathbb{Z}$ and $\mathbb{Z}_5 = \{0, 1, 2, 3, 4\}$ and compute with the elements of the latter modulo 5. (The symmetric system of representatives of least absolute value is also useful, for example, $\{-2, -1, 0, 1, 2\}$ for $\mathbb{Z}/5\mathbb{Z}$.) In the polynomial case, however, we will keep this distinction.

By applying the canonical ring homomorphism $a \longmapsto a \bmod m$, congruences in R (like $4 \cdot 2 \equiv 3 \bmod 5$ in $\mathbb{Z}$ or $x^2 \cdot x \equiv 4 \bmod (x^3 - 4)$ in $\mathbb{Q}[x]$) become equalities in R/mR ($4 \cdot 2 = 3$ in $\mathbb{Z}_5$ or $\alpha^2 \cdot \alpha = 4$ in $\mathbb{Q}[x]/\langle x^3 - 4 \rangle$, where $\alpha = x \bmod x^3 - 4$), and the rules (1) guarantee that we may work freely with representatives in these equations as long as we stay within the same residue class.

As indicated above, we will often perform computations modulo polynomials *and* modulo integers, that is, in "double" residue class rings of the form $\mathbb{Z}_m[x]/\langle f \rangle$ for some polynomial $f \in \mathbb{Z}_m[x]$. Then we have two levels of computation: coefficient operations, which are performed modulo m, and polynomial operations, which are performed modulo f and are defined in terms of coefficient operations. For example,

$$(4x + 1)(3x^2 + 2x) = 12x^3 + 11x^2 + 2x \quad \text{in } \mathbb{Z}[x],$$

and hence

$$(4x + 1)(3x^2 + 2x) = 2x^3 + x^2 + 2x \quad \text{in } \mathbb{Z}_5[x].$$

Now division with remainder yields

$$\begin{aligned}
2x^3 + x^2 + 2x &= 2 \cdot (x^3 + 4x) + x^2 - 6x \quad \text{in } \mathbb{Z}[x], \\
2x^3 + x^2 + 2x &= 2 \cdot (x^3 + 4x) + x^2 + 4x \quad \text{in } \mathbb{Z}_5[x].
\end{aligned}$$

Thus

$$(4x + 1)(3x^2 + 2x) \equiv x^2 + 4x \bmod (x^3 + 4x) \quad \text{in } \mathbb{Z}_5[x],$$

or equivalently,

$$(4\alpha + 1)(3\alpha^2 + 2\alpha) = \alpha^2 + 4\alpha \quad \text{in } \mathbb{Z}_5[x]/\langle x^3 + 4x \rangle,$$

where $\alpha = (x \bmod (x^3 + 4x)) \in \mathbb{Z}_5[x]/\langle x^3 + 4x \rangle$. We have done the calculations in detail in this example to illustrate the principle; later we will suppress the details.

4.2. Modular inverses via Euclid

We have seen in the previous section how modular addition and multiplication works. What about inversion and division? Do expressions like $a^{-1} \bmod m$ and $a/b \bmod m$ make sense, and if so, how can we compute their value? The following theorem gives an answer when the underlying ring R is a Euclidean domain.

━━ THEOREM 4.1. ━━━━━━━━━━━━━━━━━━━━━━━━━━━━━━━━━━━━
Let R be a Euclidean domain, $a, m \in R$, and $S = R/mR$. Then $a \bmod m \in S$ is a unit if and only if $\gcd(a, m) = 1$. In this case, the modular inverse of $a \bmod m$ can be computed by means of the Extended Euclidean Algorithm. ━━━━━━

PROOF. We have

$$a \text{ is invertible modulo } m \iff \exists s \in R \quad sa \equiv 1 \bmod m$$
$$\iff \exists s, t \in R \quad sa + tm = 1 \implies \gcd(a, m) = 1.$$

If, on the other hand, $\gcd(a, m) = 1$, then the Extended Euclidean Algorithm provides such $s, t \in R$. □

EXAMPLE 4.2. We let $R = \mathbb{Z}$, $m = 29$, and $a = 12$. Then $\gcd(a, m) = 1$, and the Extended Euclidean Algorithm computes $5 \cdot 29 + (-12) \cdot 12 = 1$. Thus $(-12) \cdot 12 \equiv 17 \cdot 12 \equiv 1 \bmod 29$, and hence 17 is the inverse of 12 modulo 29. ◇

EXAMPLE 4.3. Let $R = \mathbb{Q}[x]$, $m = x^3 - x + 2$, and $a = x^2$. The last row in the Extended Euclidean Algorithm for m and a is

$$\left(\frac{1}{4}x + \frac{1}{2}\right)(x^3 - x + 2) + \left(-\frac{1}{4}x^2 - \frac{1}{2}x + \frac{1}{4}\right)x^2 = 1,$$

and $(-x^2 - 2x + 1)/4$ is the inverse of x^2 modulo $x^3 - x + 1$. ◇

A consequence of Theorem 4.1 is that if $S = \mathbb{Z}_p$ for a prime $p \in \mathbb{N}$ or $S = F[x]/\langle f \rangle$ for a field F and an irreducible polynomial $f \in F[x]$, then any element of $S \setminus \{0\}$ is a unit, so that S is a field. We will use the notation $\mathbb{F}_p$ for the finite field $\mathbb{Z}_p$ with p elements throughout the rest of this book. More generally, if $f \in \mathbb{Z}_p[x] = \mathbb{F}_p[x]$ is an irreducible polynomial of degree n, then $\mathbb{F}_p[x]/\langle f \rangle$ is a finite field with $q = p^n$ elements, which we will denote by $\mathbb{F}_q$. In fact, this construction works for any prime power q, namely, there exist irreducible polynomials in $\mathbb{F}_q[x]$

of any degree, and any two irreducible polynomials of the same degree lead to isomorphic fields (Section 25.4).

The following lemma says that computing modulo an irreducible polynomial f is the same as "adjoining a root of f".

LEMMA 4.4. *Let F be a field, $f \in F[x]$ a monic nonconstant irreducible polynomial, and $K = F[x]/\langle f \rangle$. Then K is an extension field of f, and $f(\alpha) = 0$ for $\alpha = (x \bmod f) \in K$.*

PROOF. K is a field according to Theorem 4.1, and

$$f(\alpha) = f(x \bmod f) = (f(x) \bmod f) = 0. \quad \square$$

EXAMPLE 4.5. Let $R = \mathbb{F}_5[x]$, $f = x^3 - x + 2$, and $a = x^2$. Then f has no zeroes in $\mathbb{F}_5$, and irreducible since its degree is 3. Thus $\mathbb{F}_{125} = \mathbb{F}_5[x]/\langle f \rangle$ is a field. The last row in the Extended Euclidean Algorithm for f and a in $\mathbb{F}_5[x]$ is

$$(-x - 2)(x^3 - x + 2) + (x^2 + 2x - 1)x^2 = 1.$$

Hence $x^2 + 2x - 1$ is the inverse of x^2 modulo $x^3 - x + 1$. If we write $\alpha = x \bmod f$ for short, then $\alpha^2 + 2\alpha - 1 = (\alpha^2)^{-1}$ in $\mathbb{F}_{125}$. ◇

The following two corollaries are a consequence of the analyses in Chapter 2 and Theorems 3.11, 3.13, and 4.1.

COROLLARY 4.6.
Let F be a field, and $f \in F[x]$ of degree $n \in \mathbb{N}$. One arithmetic operation in $F[x]/\langle f \rangle$, that is, addition, multiplication, or division by an invertible element, can be done using $O(n^2)$ arithmetic operations in F. More precisely, we have at most $4n^2 + O(n)$ operations for a multiplication modulo f and at most $\frac{13}{2}n^2 + O(n)$ operations for an inversion modulo f.

COROLLARY 4.7.
One arithmetic operation in $\mathbb{Z}_m$, where $m \in \mathbb{N}_{>0}$ and $n = \lambda(m) = \lfloor (\log_2 m)/64 \rfloor + 1$ is the length of m in the standard representation, can be done using $O(n^2)$ word operations.

If m is a positive integer, then the set $\mathbb{Z}_m^{\times}$ of those elements of $\mathbb{Z}_m$ that have multiplicative inverses is a group under multiplication, the **group of units** of the ring $\mathbb{Z}_m$ (Sections 25.1 and 25.2). Theorem 4.1 says that $\mathbb{Z}_m^{\times} = \{a \bmod m : \gcd(a, m) = 1\}$. **Euler's totient function** $\varphi : \mathbb{N}_{>0} \longrightarrow \mathbb{N}_{>0}$ counts the number of elements in $\mathbb{Z}_m^{\times}$:

$$\varphi(m) = \#\mathbb{Z}_m^{\times} = \#\{0 \le a < m : \gcd(a, m) = 1\}.$$

By convention, $\varphi(1) = 1$. If $m = p$ is a prime, then all nonzero elements of $\mathbb{Z}_p = \mathbb{F}_p$ are invertible, and hence $\varphi(p) = p - 1$. More generally, if $m = p^e$ is a prime power, with $e \geq 1$, then Theorem 4.1 implies that $a \bmod p^e$ is invertible if and only if p does not divide a. Thus there are precisely p^{e-1} nonunits in $\mathbb{Z}_{p^e}$, namely the elements $bp \bmod p^e$ with $0 \leq b < p^{e-1}$, and we obtain

$$\varphi(p^e) = p^e - p^{e-1} = (p-1)p^{e-1}. \tag{2}$$

In Section 5.4, we will derive a formula for $\varphi(m)$ when m is arbitrary from the Chinese Remainder Theorem. Exercise 4.19 discusses the analog of Euler's totient function for polynomials over a finite field.

4.3. Repeated squaring

An important tool for modular exponentiation is **repeated squaring** (or square and multiply). In fact, this technique works in any set with an associative multiplication, but we will mainly use it in residue class rings.

▬ ALGORITHM 4.8 Repeated squaring. ▬▬▬▬▬▬▬▬▬▬▬▬▬▬▬▬
Input: $a \in R$, where R is a ring with 1, and $n \in \mathbb{N}_{>0}$.
Output: $a^n \in R$.

1. { binary representation of n }
   write $n = 2^k + n_{k-1} \cdot 2^{k-1} + \cdots + n_1 \cdot 2 + n_0$, with all $n_i \in \{0, 1\}$
   $b_k \longleftarrow a$

2. **for** $i = k-1, k-2, \ldots, 0$ **do**
   if $n_i = 1$ **then** $b_i \longleftarrow b_{i-1}^2 a$ **else** $b_i \longleftarrow b_{i-1}^2$

3. **return** b_0 ▬▬▬▬▬▬▬▬▬▬▬▬▬▬▬▬▬▬▬▬▬▬

Correctness follows easily from the invariant $b_i = a^{\lfloor n/2^i \rfloor}$. This procedure uses $\lfloor \log n \rfloor$ squarings plus $w(n) - 1 \leq \lfloor \log n \rfloor$ multiplications in R, where log is the binary logarithm and $w(n)$ is the **Hamming weight** of the binary representation of n (Chapter 7), that is, the number of 1s in it. Thus the total cost is at most $2 \log n$ multiplications. For example, the binary representation of 13 is $1 \cdot 2^3 + 1 \cdot 2^2 + 0 \cdot 2 + 1$ and has Hamming weight 3. Thus a^{13} would be computed as $((a^2 \cdot a)^2)^2 \cdot a$, using three squarings and two multiplications. If $R = \mathbb{Z}_{17} = \mathbb{Z}/\langle 17 \rangle$ and $a = 8 \bmod 17$, then we compute $8^{13} \bmod 17$ as

$$\begin{aligned}
8^{13} &\equiv ((8^2 \cdot 8)^2)^2 \cdot 8 \equiv (((-4 \cdot 8)^2)^2) \cdot 8 \\
&\equiv (2^2)^2 \cdot 8 = 4^2 \cdot 8 \equiv -1 \cdot 8 = -8 \bmod 17,
\end{aligned}$$

which is much faster than first evaluating $8^{13} = 549\,755\,813\,888$ and then dividing by 17 with remainder. This method was already used by Euler (1758/59). He calculated $7^{160} \bmod 641$ by computing $7^2, 7^4, 7^8, 7^{16}, 7^{32}, 7^{64}, 7^{128}, 7^{160} = 7^{128} \cdot 7^{32}$, reducing modulo 641 after each step. (He also listed, unnecessarily, 7^3.) As another example, starting from $2^{2^3} = 2^8 = 256$, we only need two squarings modulo $5 \cdot 2^7 + 1 = 641$ to calculate $((2^8)^2)^2 = 2^{2^5} \equiv -1 \bmod 641$. This shows that 641 divides the fifth Fermat number $F_5 = 2^{2^5} + 1$, as discovered by Euler (1732/33); see Sections 18.2 and 19.1. Even if we were given the 10-digit number $2^{2^5} + 1 = 4\,294\,967\,297$, it would seem more laborious to divide it by 641 with remainder rather than to use modular repeated squaring.

There are clever ways of reducing the cost to $(1 + o(1))\log n$ multiplications (Exercise 4.21), where $o(1)$ goes to zero as n gets large. On the other hand, starting with an indeterminate x and using d multiplications or additions, one can only compute polynomials of degree at most 2^d, and thus $\lceil \log n \rceil$ multiplications are indeed necessary to obtain x^n. However, when x is not an indeterminate but from a well-structured domain, one can sometimes exploit that structure for faster exponentiation algorithms. We will see an example in the iterated Frobenius algorithm of Section 14.7. Particularly important for cryptographic applications are methods based on normal bases and Gauß periods in finite fields.

4.4. Modular inverses via Fermat

Let $p \in \mathbb{N}$ be a prime and $a, b \in \mathbb{Z}$. Then the binomial theorem implies that

$$(a+b)^p = \sum_{0 \le i \le p} \binom{p}{i} a^{p-i} b^i = a^p + p a^{p-1} b + \frac{p(p-1)}{2} a^{p-2} b^2 + \cdots + b^p.$$

If $0 < i < p$, then the binomial coefficient

$$\binom{p}{i} = \frac{p!}{i!(p-i)!}$$

is divisible by p, since the numerator is and the denominator is not. Thus we have the surprising consequence that $(a+b)^p \equiv a^p + b^p \bmod p$, or equivalently, $(\alpha + \beta)^p = \alpha^p + \beta^p$ in $\mathbb{Z}_p$, with $\alpha = a \bmod p$ and $\beta = b \bmod p$ ("the Freshman's dream"). More generally, we obtain by induction on i that

$$(a+b)^{p^i} \equiv a^{p^i} + b^{p^i} \bmod p \text{ for all } i \in \mathbb{N}. \tag{3}$$

Using this property, we obtain a pretty, elementary proof of the following famous number-theoretic theorem, which—in a more general form—will have many applications in factoring polynomials and primality testing (Chapters 14 and 18).

THEOREM 4.9 *Fermat's little theorem.*
If $p \in \mathbb{N}$ is prime and $a \in \mathbb{Z}$, then $a^p \equiv a \bmod p$ and, if $p \nmid a$, then $a^{p-1} \equiv 1 \bmod p$.

PROOF. It is sufficient to prove the claim for $a \in \{0, \dots, p-1\}$, which we do by induction on a. The case $a = 0$ is trivial, and for $a > 1$, we have

$$a^p = ((a-1)+1)^p \equiv (a-1)^p + 1^p \equiv (a-1) + 1 = a \bmod p,$$

by (3) and the induction hypothesis. If $a \neq 0$, then a is invertible modulo p, by Theorem 4.1, and the claim follows by multiplying with $a^{-1} \bmod p$. $\square$

Fermat's theorem, together with repeated squaring, gives us an alternative to compute inverses in $\mathbb{Z}_p$: since $a^{p-2}a = a^{p-1} \equiv 1 \bmod p$ for $a \in \mathbb{Z}$ with $p \nmid a$, we have $a^{-1} \equiv a^{p-2} \bmod p$. This may be computed using $O(\log p)$ multiplications and squarings modulo p, using the repeated squaring algorithm 4.8, in total $O(\log^3 p)$ word operations, by Corollary 4.7. This is cubic in the input size, while the time for modular inversion via Euclid's algorithm is only quadratic, but it may be useful for hand calculations.

4.5. Linear Diophantine equations

Another application of the Extended Euclidean Algorithm is the solution of **linear Diophantine equations**. Let $a, f, g \in \mathbb{Z}$ be given, and suppose that we are looking for all *integral* solutions $s, t \in \mathbb{Z}$ of the equation

$$sf + tg = a. \tag{4}$$

The set of all real solutions of (4) is a line in the plane $\mathbb{R}^2$, a one-dimensional object, that can be written as a sum $v + U$ of a particular solution $v \in \mathbb{R}^2$ and the set U of all solutions of the homogeneous equation

$$sf + tg = 0. \tag{5}$$

The following lemma says that this is also true for the set of integral solutions. Moreover, we can decide whether (4) is solvable over $\mathbb{Z}$, and if so, compute all solutions with the Extended Euclidean Algorithm. Since the proof is the same, we state the result for arbitrary Euclidean domains.

━━━ THEOREM 4.10. ━━━━━━━━━━━━━━━━━━━━━━━━━━━━━━━━━━━━
Let R be a Euclidean domain, $a, f, g \in R$, and $h = \gcd(f, g)$.

(i) *(4) has a solution $(s, t) \in R^2$ if and only if h divides a.*

(ii) *If $h \neq 0$ and $(s^*, t^*) \in R^2$ is a solution of (4), then the set of all solutions is $(s^*, t^*) + U$, where*

$$U = R \cdot \left(\frac{g}{h}, -\frac{f}{h} \right) \subseteq R^2$$

is the set of all solutions to the homogeneous equation (5).

(iii) If $R = F[x]$ for a field F, $h \neq 0$, (4) is solvable, and $\deg f + \deg g - \deg h > \deg a$, then there is a unique solution $(s,t) \in R^2$ of (4) such that $\deg s < \deg g - \deg h$ and $\deg t < \deg f - \deg h$. ▬▬▬▬▬▬▬

PROOF. (i) If $s,t \in R$ satisfy (4), then $\gcd(f,g)$ divides $sf + tg$ and hence a. Conversely, we assume that $h = \gcd(f,g)$ divides a. The claim is trivial if $h = 0$; otherwise we can compute $s^*, t^* \in R$ such that $s^* f + t^* g = h$, using the Extended Euclidean Algorithm, and $(s,t) = (s^*a/h, t^*a/h)$ solves (4).

(ii) For $(s,t) \in R^2$, we have, since $h \neq 0$ and f/h and g/h are coprime, that

$$(5) \iff \frac{f}{h}s = -\frac{g}{h}t \iff \exists k \in R \quad s = k\frac{g}{h} \text{ and } t = k\frac{-f}{h} \iff (s,t) \in U.$$

Then also

$$(4) \iff f(s - s^*) + g(t - t^*) = 0 \iff (s - s^*, t - t^*) \in U.$$

(iii) Let $(s^*, t^*) \in R^2$ be a solution to (4). We divide t^* by f/h with remainder and obtain $q, t \in R$ such that $t^* = qf/h + t$ and $\deg t < \deg f - \deg h$. If we let $s = s^* + qg/h$, then (ii) implies that $(s,t) = (s^*, t^*) + q(g/h, -f/h)$ solves (4). Now both $\deg(tg)$ and $\deg a$ are less than $\deg f + \deg g - \deg h$, and hence so is $\deg s + \det f = \deg(sf) = \deg(a - tg)$. This proves the existence.

Uniqueness follows from $\deg(s + kg/h) = \deg(kg/h) \geq \deg g - \deg h$ for all $k \in R \setminus \{0\}$, and hence the first component of any solution to (4) different from (s,t) has degree at least $\deg g - \deg h$. □

The situation can be generalized to higher dimensions. The following theorem is proved in Exercise 4.24.

▬▬ THEOREM 4.11. ▬▬▬▬▬▬▬▬▬▬▬▬▬▬▬▬▬▬▬▬▬▬▬▬▬▬

Let R be a Euclidean domain, $a, f_1, \ldots, f_n \in R$, with all f_i nonzero, and U the set of all solutions of the homogeneous equation $f_1 s_1 + \cdots + f_n s_n = 0$.

(i) The linear Diophantine equation

$$f_1 s_1 + \cdots + f_n s_n = a \tag{6}$$

is solvable for $s = (s_1, \ldots, s_n) \in R^n$ if and only if $\gcd(f_1, \ldots, f_n)$ divides a.

(ii) If $s \in R^n$ is a solution of (4), then the set of all integral solutions is $s + U$.

(iii) $U = Ru_2 + \cdots + Ru_n$, where

$$u_i = \left(\frac{f_i}{h_i}s_{i1}, \frac{f_i}{h_i}s_{i2}, \ldots, \frac{f_i}{h_i}s_{i,i-1}, -\frac{h_{i-1}}{h_i}, 0, \ldots, 0 \right),$$

$$h_{i-1} = \gcd(f_1, \ldots, f_{i-1}) = s_{i1}f_1 + \cdots + s_{i,i-1}f_{i-1}$$

for $2 \leq i \leq n$ and $h_n = \gcd(f_1, \ldots, f_n)$, with suitably chosen $s_{ij} \in R$. ▬▬▬

4.6. Continued fractions and Diophantine approximation

Let R be a Euclidean domain, $r_0, r_1 \in R$ and $q_i, r_i \in R$ for $1 \leq i \leq \ell$ the quotients and remainders in the *classical* Euclidean Algorithm 3.5 (where all ρ_i are 1) for r_0, r_1. Then eliminating the remainders successively, we obtain

$$\frac{r_0}{r_1} = \frac{q_1 r_1 + r_2}{r_1} = q_1 + \frac{r_2}{r_1} = q_1 + \frac{1}{\frac{r_1}{r_2}} = q_1 + \frac{1}{q_2 + \frac{r_3}{r_2}} = q_1 + \frac{1}{q_2 + \frac{1}{\frac{r_2}{r_3}}}$$

$$= q_1 + \frac{1}{q_2 + \frac{1}{q_3 + \frac{r_4}{r_3}}} = \cdots = q_1 + \frac{1}{q_2 + \frac{1}{q_3 + \frac{1}{\ddots + \frac{1}{q_\ell}}}}.$$

This is called the **continued fraction expansion** of $r_0/r_1 \in K$, where K is the field of fractions of R (Section 25.3). In general, arbitrary elements of R may occur in place of 1 in the "numerators" of a continued fraction, but when all of them are required to be 1 as above, the representation of r_0/r_1 by a continued fraction is unique and computed by the classical Euclidean Algorithm. To abbreviate, we write $[q_1, \ldots, q_\ell]$ for the continued fraction $q_1 + 1/(q_2 + 1/(\cdots + 1/q_\ell)\cdots)$.

EXAMPLE 4.12. We can rewrite the Euclidean Algorithm from page 43 for $r_0 = 126$ and $r_1 = 35$ as follows.

$$q_1 = \left\lfloor \frac{r_0}{r_1} \right\rfloor = \left\lfloor \frac{126}{35} \right\rfloor = 3, \quad \frac{r_2}{r_1} = \frac{r_0}{r_1} - q_1 = \frac{21}{35},$$

$$q_2 = \left\lfloor \frac{r_1}{r_2} \right\rfloor = \left\lfloor \frac{35}{21} \right\rfloor = 1, \quad \frac{r_3}{r_2} = \frac{r_1}{r_2} - q_2 = \frac{14}{21},$$

$$q_3 = \left\lfloor \frac{r_2}{r_3} \right\rfloor = \left\lfloor \frac{21}{14} \right\rfloor = 1, \quad \frac{r_4}{r_3} = \frac{r_2}{r_3} - q_3 = \frac{7}{14},$$

$$q_4 = \left\lfloor \frac{r_3}{r_4} \right\rfloor = \left\lfloor \frac{14}{7} \right\rfloor = 2, \quad \frac{r_5}{r_4} = \frac{r_3}{r_4} - q_4 = 0.$$

Thus the continued fraction expansion of $126/35 \in \mathbb{Q}$ is

$$\frac{126}{35} = \frac{18}{5} = [3, 1, 1, 2] = 3 + \frac{1}{1 + \frac{1}{1 + \frac{1}{2}}}. \quad \diamondsuit$$

If $R = \mathbb{Z}$, then even an element α of $\mathbb{R}$ may be represented by an (infinite) continued fraction in the sense that its initial segments converge to α with regard to the absolute value. How are these continued fractions computed? The rules (3) on page 48 for computing the quotients $q_1, q_2, \ldots$ for $(r_0, r_1) \in \mathbb{Z}^2$ can be reformulated as follows: set $\alpha_1 = r_0/r_1$, $q_1 = \lfloor \alpha_1 \rfloor$, $\beta_2 = \alpha_1 - q_1$, $\alpha_2 = 1/\beta_2$, and in general $q_i = \lfloor \alpha_i \rfloor$, $\beta_{i+1} = \alpha_i - q_i$, $\alpha_{i+1} = 1/\beta_{i+1}$. Starting with an arbitrary real number α_1, this process defines the continued fraction expansion of α_1, as in Table 4.1. We note that $0 \le \beta_i < 1$; the expansion stops when $\beta_i = 0$, which occurs if and only if α_1 is rational.

For example, when $\alpha_1 = \sqrt{3}$, we obtain

$$q_1 = \lfloor \alpha_1 \rfloor = 1, \quad \beta_2 = \alpha_1 - q_1 = -1 + \sqrt{3},$$

$$\alpha_2 = \frac{1}{\beta_2} = \frac{-1 - \sqrt{3}}{(-1 + \sqrt{3})(-1 - \sqrt{3})} = \frac{-1 - \sqrt{3}}{-2} = \frac{1}{2} + \frac{1}{2}\sqrt{3} \approx 1.366,$$

$$q_2 = \lfloor \alpha_2 \rfloor = 1, \quad \beta_3 = \alpha_2 - q_2 = -\frac{1}{2} + \frac{1}{2}\sqrt{3},$$

$$\alpha_3 = \frac{1}{\beta_3} = \frac{2}{-1 + \sqrt{3}} = 1 + \sqrt{3} \approx 2.732,$$

$$q_3 = \lfloor \alpha_3 \rfloor = 2, \quad \beta_4 = \alpha_3 - q_3 = -1 + \sqrt{3} = \beta_2,$$

and then the process repeats over and over, yielding $\sqrt{3} = [1, \overline{1, 2}, \ldots]$, where the overlined part indicates the period of this ultimately periodic sequence.

$r \in \mathbb{R}$	continued fraction expansion of r
$\frac{8}{29}$	$[0, 3, 1, 1, 1, 2]$
$\sqrt{\frac{8}{29}}$	$[0, 1, 1, 9, 2, 2, 3, 2, 2, 9, 1, 2, \overline{1, 9, 2, 2, 3, 2, 2, 9, 1, 2}, \ldots]$
$\sqrt{3}$	$[1, 1, 2, \overline{1, 2}, \ldots]$
$\sqrt[3]{2}$	$[1, 3, 1, 5, 1, 1, 4, 1, 1, 8, 1, 14, 1, 10, 2, 1, 4, 12, 2, 3, 2, 1, 3, 4, 1, 1, 2, 14, 3, 12, \ldots]$
π	$[3, 7, 15, 1, 292, 1, 1, 1, 2, 1, 3, 1, 14, 2, 1, 1, 2, 2, 2, 2, 1, 84, 2, 1, 1, 15, 3, 13, 1, 4, \ldots]$
$e = \exp(1)$	$[2, 1, 2, 1, 1, 4, 1, 1, 6, 1, 1, 8, 1, 1, 10, 1, 1, 12, 1, 1, 14, 1, 1, 16, 1, 1, 18, 1, 1, 20, \ldots]$
$\phi = \frac{1+\sqrt{5}}{2}$	$[1, 1, \overline{1}, \ldots]$
$\log_2\left(\frac{6}{5}\right)$	$[0, 3, 1, 4, 22, 4, 1, 1, 13, 137, 1, 1, 16, 6, 176, 3, 1, 1, 1, 3, 1, 2, 1, 31, 3, 1, 1, 5, \ldots]$

TABLE 4.1: Examples of continued fraction representations of real numbers.

Table 4.1 gives examples of continued fraction representations of real numbers. The continued fraction expansion of an irrational number $\alpha \in \mathbb{R}$ is an excellent tool for approximate α by rational numbers with "small" denominator. The substantial theory of Diophantine approximation deals with such questions.

The quality of approximations is best described in the form

$$\left| \alpha - \frac{p}{q} \right| \leq \frac{1}{cq^2}. \tag{7}$$

This holds for every continued fraction approximation with $c = 1$. Of three consecutive continued fraction approximations, at least one satisfies (7) with $c = \sqrt{5}$, and for any $c > \sqrt{5}$ there are real numbers α that have only finitely many rational approximations with (7); see Notes 4.6. For comparison, this is about twice as good as decimal fractions, where we restrict q to be a power of 10 and can achieve an approximation error of $1/2q$.

Polynomial analogs of (7) are discussed in Exercises 4.29 and 4.30. The latter shows that every power series f has approximations

$$f \equiv r/t \bmod x^{2n+1}$$

with polynomials r, t such that $\deg r, \deg t \leq n$, for infinitely many n. These are just certain Padé approximants (Section 5.9).

i	$[q_1, \dots, q_i]$	decimal expansion	$\pi - [q_1, \dots, q_i]$	accuracy
1	3	3.0000000000000000000	0.14159265358979323846	0 digits
2	$\dfrac{22}{7}$	3.14285714285714285714	-0.00126448926734961868	2 digits
3	$\dfrac{333}{106}$	3.14150943396226415094	0.00008321962752908752	4 digits
4	$\dfrac{355}{113}$	3.14159292035398230088	-0.00000026676418906242	6 digits
5	$\dfrac{103993}{33102}$	3.14159265301190260407	0.00000000057789063439	9 digits

TABLE 4.2: Rational approximations of π.

Table 4.2 shows the rational approximations of π that result from truncating the continued fraction expansion after the ith component for $i = 1, \dots, 5$ and the number of correct digits (after the decimal point). Throughout history, people have grappled with practical problems, in architecture, land surveying, astronomy etc., that required "squaring the circle". The Egyptian Rhind Papyrus from about 1650 BC gives the value $(16/9)^2 \approx 3.1604$. Archimedes (278–212 BC) gave a method to approximate π, in principle arbitrarily well, using polygons inscribed and circumscribed to a circle; he proved $3\frac{10}{71} < 25\,344/8069 < \pi < 29\,376/9347 < 3\frac{1}{7}$. The Chinese astronomer Tsu Ch'ung-chih (430–501) determined six decimal digits of π and deduced the approximation $355/113$, which was also found by Adrian Antoniszoon (1527–1607). Lambert (1761) proved that π is irrational, and Lindemann (1882) proved that it is transcendental. An interesting unsolved question asks whether the decimal digits of π are uniformly distributed or even random, in some sense. We do not even know to prove that the digit 1, say, occurs infinitely often!

Table 4.3 shows some steps in our knowledge about the decimal expansion of π. Of the 36 records in this century, we only list those seven where the number of decimal digits of the number of decimal digits (in the rightmost column) increased by one. The current world record is an awesome 51 billion digits, but is unlikely to stand for long.

Archimedes	c. 250 BC	2
Tsu Ch'ung-chih	5th c.	7
Al-Kāshī	1424	14
van Ceulen	1615	35
Machin	1706	100
William Shanks	1853	527
Reitwiesner	1949	2 035
Genuys	1958	10 000
Daniel Shanks & Wrench	1962	100 265
Guilloud & Bouyer	1973	1 001 250
Kanada, Yoshino & Tamura	1982	16 777 206
Kanada, Tamura *et al.*	1987	133 554 400
Kanada & Tamura	1989	1 073 740 000
Kanada & Takahashi	1997	51 539 600 000

TABLE 4.3: Computations of the decimal digits of π.

William Shanks published a book on his computation of 607 digits, but made an error at the 528th digit. With a modern computer algebra system the first 1000 digits require just a few keystrokes (DIGITS := 1000; float(PI) for example, in MuPAD), and bang! there it is on your screen. Some systems, such as MAPLE, have stored the first 10000 or so digits of π.

The computation of π to many digits is based on deep mathematics and is only possible with the help of fast algorithms for high precision integer and floating point arithmetic, based on the Fast Fourier Transform (Chapter 8) and fast division (Chapter 9). It is a good test for computer hardware, which is routinely performed on some supercomputers before shipping. Borwein, Borwein & Bailey (1989) speak from experience:

> *A large-scale calculation of* π *is entirely unforgiving; it soaks into all parts of the machine and a single bit awry leaves detectable con-sequences.*

A different large-scale number-theoretic computation discovered the famous Pentium division bug. Nicely (1996) reports in his commendably careful count of twin primes (see page 234 for records): *The first run [...] was performed on the only Pentium in the group [...] The duplicate run was completed on my wife's*

486DX-33 on 4 October 1994. It was immediately clear that their ultra-precision reciprocal sums differed. [...] Several days were then spent looking for the culprit: compiler error, memory error, system bus, etc. [... My] message and its consequences were spread worldwide over the Internet within days, and eventually Intel admitted that such errors [...] were the result of a production flaw in nearly all (over a million) of the Pentium CPUs produced to that time. [...] Intel eventually agreed to replace all such chips with corrected versions, at the company's expense. In January 1995, Intel announced (PC Week, 1995) a $475 million accounting charge to cover the cost of the episode. [...] As we tell our students—check your work!

4.7. Calendars

The **tropical year**, to which our calendar adheres, is the period of time between two successive occasions of vernal equinox, the precise point of time in spring when the sun crosses the (hypothetical) celestial equator. The length of the tropical year is about 365^d 5^h $48'$ $46''$, or 365.24220 days. (Actually, the exact value is currently diminishing by about 0.53 seconds each century, but this shall not bother us here.)

Since the dawn of civilization, people have used calendars to express the regularities of the moon's rotation around the earth and of the seasons. **Lunar calendars** divide time into months, where originally each month began with new moon. Since the length of a lunar month is between 29 and 30 days, lunar calendars are asynchronous to the year of the seasons. **Solar calendars**, however, ignore the moon phases and try to approximate the year of the seasons as closely as possible.

The early Roman calendar was of a mixed **lunisolar** type. It consisted of originally 10 and later 12 months, and occasionally one extra month was added in order to keep in step with the seasons. The **Julian calendar**, named after Julius Caesar (and which had been invented by the Egyptian Sosigenes), started on 1 January 45 BC. Since the Romans before Caesar had badly neglected the management of the calendar, the year 46 BC, the **annus confusionis**, had 445 days! Caesar used the approximation of 365.25 days for the year and introduced one additional 366th **leap day** every four years. Although this approximation is quite close to the exact length of the tropical year, the Julian calendar was fast by about three days every 400 years.

Towards the end of the 16th century, vernal equinox was on 10 March rather than on its "correct" date of 21 March. To rectify this, Pope Gregory XIII introduced the following calendar reform. First, the erroneous calendar gain was fixed by eliminating the 10 days between 4 October and 15 October 1582. Second, the leap year rule was modified by turning those years which are divisible by 100 but not by 400 into normal years; this removed three leap days in 400 years. So, for example, the years 1700, 1800, and 1900 AD were all normal years, but counting the year 2000 AD as normal would be the bug of the millennium. This **Gregorian calendar**, which is essentially still used today, corresponds to an approximation of the tropical year as

$$365 + \frac{1}{4} - \frac{3}{400} = 365\frac{97}{400} = 365.2425$$

days. It is too long by about 26 seconds a year.

approximation			difference from tropical year
$365\frac{1}{4}$	$=$	365.25000	$11' \ 14''$
$365\frac{7}{29}$	$=$	$365.24137\ldots$	$-1' \ 01''$
$365\frac{8}{33}$	$=$	$365.24242\ldots$	$19''$
$365\frac{31}{128}$	$=$	$365.24218\ldots$	$-1''$

TABLE 4.4: Continued fraction approximations of the length of the year.

Other rational approximations to the exact length of the tropical year can be obtained from its continued fraction expansion $365.24220 = [365, 4, 7, 1, 3, \ldots]$. The corresponding approximations are given by Table 4.4. The first is the one that Julius Caesar used. The third approximation is already better than the Gregorian calendar and has a considerably smaller denominator. The **binary calendar** in the last line looks appealing to computer scientists or others familiar with the binary system: a simple rule for its implementation is to have a leap day in year number n if and only if $4 \mid n$ and $128 \nmid n$.

4.8. Musical scales

Another application of continued fractions is in musical theory. A musical **interval** consists of two tones (usually of different pitch, such as G–C), and the term also denotes the sound generated from some instrument playing the two tones one after the other or simultaneously. To each interval there corresponds a unique frequency ratio of the two tones involved. Table 4.5 lists some common intervals and their frequency ratios.

frequency ratio	name	example
$r_1 = 2 : 1$	octave	c–C
$r_2 = 3 : 2$	fifth	G–C
$r_3 = 4 : 3$	fourth	F–C
$r_4 = 5 : 4$	major third	E–C
$r_5 = 6 : 5$	minor third	E♭–C
$r_6 = 9 : 8$	whole tone	D–C

TABLE 4.5: Frequency ratios of some musical intervals.

"Calculation" with intervals works as follows: combination of two intervals corresponds to multiplication of their frequency ratios. For example, the octave c–C can be regarded as combining a fifth c–F with a fourth F–C, and in fact the corresponding frequency ratios satisfy $2/1 = (3/2) \cdot (4/3)$.

The origins of musical theory date back to the early Pythagoreans, who were experimenting with the monochord, a stringed instrument with one string of fixed length that can be subdivided into two variable length parts by means of a movable bridge. They found that the tones generated by, for example, one half, two thirds, or three quarters of the string's length, together with the base tone generated by the string in its full length, give intervals that are appealing to the human ear. More generally, they postulated that this is the case if the length ratio (or equivalently, the frequency ratio) of the interval is a quotient of small positive integers.

One disadvantage of Pythagorean tuning is that transposing a piece of music written in one tonal key, say C major, into another tonal key, say D major (which corresponds to multiplying all frequencies by the ratio of the interval D–C, thus leaving all frequency ratios unchanged), is not as easily possible with a piano tuned for C major as it is for the human voice. For example, the whole tone E–D in C major has frequency ratio $(5/4)/(9/8) = 10/9$ and not $9/8$ as it would be in D major. This led to the invention of the **well-tempered scale**, which dates back to Bartolomé Ramos (1482), who gave suggestions, and to Marin Mersenne (1636), who laid the mathematical foundations. Prominent advocates of the well-tempered scale were the organist and musical scientist Andreas Werckmeister (1691) and the composer Johann Sebastian Bach. *Das Wohltemperierte Klavier*[1] by Bach (1722) promoted, in its 48 preludes and fugues, the idea that all tonal keys can be played on a well-tempered instrument (organ, harpsichord, or piano) without audible dissonances. Today, the well-tempered scale dominates the construction of instruments and the performance of music at least in the Western world.

This scale divides the octave c–C into 12 equal half-tones, corresponding to 12 neighboring keys on the piano (7 white and 5 black, see Figure 4.6). Why choose this number 12?

Suppose that we want to divide the octave into n equal parts, so that one "half-tone" has frequency ratio $2^{1/n}$, in such a way that each of the pleasant intervals can be reached with an integral number of half-tone steps. This means that for $i = 1, \ldots, 6$, the frequency ratio r_i from Table 4.5 should be close to $2^{d_i/n}$ for some integer d_i; equality would be best, but, for example, there are no integers d, n such that $r_2 = 3/2 = 2^{d/n}$ (Exercise 4.31). Taking logarithms, we have the task of finding $d_i \in \mathbb{N}$ with

$$\left| \log r_i - \frac{d_i}{n} \right| \tag{8}$$

small, where log is the binary logarithm. This is a Diophantine approximation problem and best solved by the continued fraction expansion of $\log r_i$. For $\log r_5 =$

[1] The Well-Tempered Clavier

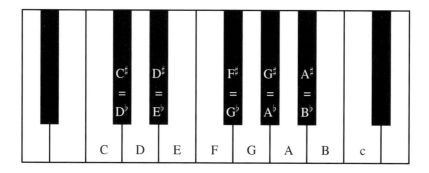

FIGURE 4.6: Part of a piano keyboard.

$\log(6/5) = 0.2630344058\ldots$, we find from the continued fraction expansion of Table 4.1 the approximations

$$\frac{1}{3} = 0.3333333333\ldots,$$

$$\frac{1}{4} = 0.2500000000,$$

$$\frac{5}{19} = 0.2631578947\ldots,$$

$$\frac{111}{422} = 0.2630331753\ldots.$$

The problem of a well-tempered scale consists in finding *one* denominator n such that with *various* numerators d_i we have (8) small. This problem of **simultaneous Diophantine approximation** is briefly discussed in Section 17.3. Here we solve it graphically: in Figure 4.7 on page 83, we have a horizontal line at $\log r_i$, for the six "pleasant intervals" shown, and the dots on the vertical line passing through $n = 6, 7, \ldots, 36$ have distance $0, 1/n, 2/n, \ldots, (n-1)/n, 1$ from the horizontal axis. Inspection reveals a reasonable fit for $n = 12$; the lower diagram depicts the quality of the approximations, defined as the sum over all i of the squares of the distance between $\log r_i$ and its closest neighbor. For $n = 12$, a whole tone is two half-tones, a minor third three, and so on. The 13 white and black keys on the piano between C and c form the **chromatic scale** built from 12 half-tone steps. The 8 white keys alone represent the **diatonic scale** (for the key of C major) with 5 whole-tone steps D–C, E–D, G–F, A–G, B–A and two half-tone steps F–E and c–B.

Another good fit is at $n = 19$. Then a whole tone is three "third-tones", a minor third is five third-tones, and so on. For example, the tones $E^\flat$ and $D^\sharp$, which are distinguished in music sheets, correspond to the same key on the piano (but are different when played on a violin, say). In a well-tempered 19-tone scale, however, the minor third $E^\flat$–C is five third-tones, while the augmented second $D^\sharp$–C is only four third-tones.

Notes. **4.1.** The fingerprinting technique was invented by Freivalds (1977); an early use was by the Persian philosopher and scientist Avicenna (980–1037), who apparently verified his calculations by checking them modulo 9. DeMillo & Lipton (1978) apply it to checking equivalence of two arithmetic circuits. Many other applications in computer science, from universal hashing to probabilistically checkable proofs, are described in Motwani & Raghavan (1995). The general topic of probabilistic algorithms is discussed in Section 6.5, and Section 18.4 presents techniques for finding prime numbers.

4.3 and 4.4. The term *repeated squaring* seems to have been standard early this century, since Pocklington (1917) uses it without further explanation (except to say that for his modular problem one divides with remainder by the modulus after each multiplication). Bürgisser, Clausen & Shokrollahi (1996) note that repeated squaring for the computation of a^n is just Horner's rule for the binary representation of the exponent n. Knuth (1998), §4.6.3, discusses at length the topic of addition chains where one tries to minimize the number of multiplications for an exponentiation. We refer to Mullin, Onyszchuk, Vanstone & Wilson (1989), Gao, von zur Gathen & Panario (1995, 1998), and von zur Gathen & Nöcker (1997) for exponentiation in finite fields.

Euler (1732/33) proved that any prime p dividing F_n satisfies $p \equiv 1 \bmod 2^{n+2}$ (Exercise 18.26). He found the factor 641 of F_5 as only the second possibility allowed by his conditions. In the same five-page paper, he also states Fermat's little theorem, but saying that he has no proof and *eo autem difficiliorem puto eius demonstrationem esse, quia non est verum, nisi $n + 1$ sit numerus primus.*[2] Our proof is from his later paper Euler (1736b).

Fermat never communicated a proof of his "little theorem". An unpublished manuscript of Leibniz from 12 September 1680 (and also Leibniz 1700) contains the first proof of Fermat's little theorem; see Mahnke (1912/13), page 38, and Vacca (1894). Mahnke considers it likely that Leibniz found the statement of the theorem himself, but it cannot be completely ruled out that he had already read Fermat's *Varia Opera*, published in 1679.

4.5. Generalizing our single linear Diophantine equation, we may consider a system of linear Diophantine equations, that is, a matrix $F \in R^{m \times n}$ and a vector $a \in R^m$, where R is a Euclidean domain, and ask for $s \in R^n$ satisfying $Fs = a$. There are variants of Gaussian elimination that allow only elementary *unimodular* row and column transformations, that is, permutations, multiplications by units of R, and additions of multiples of one row or column to another. They transform the original system into an equivalent one, for example, in **Smith** or **Hermite normal form**, in which solvability of the system and the set of solutions are easy to determine (see Exercise 16.6). Such unimodular transformations correspond to the division steps in the Euclidean Algorithm. For the case of one equation, for example, the Hermite normal form of a one-row matrix $F = (f_1, \ldots, f_n) \in R^{1 \times n}$ is $(h, 0, \ldots, 0)$, where $h = \gcd(f_1, \ldots, f_n)$, so that computing the Hermite normal form in this case is the same as computing a gcd. We will encounter a different type of unimodular "Gaussian elimination" for $R = \mathbb{Z}$ in the basis reduction of Chapter 16.

Finally, we may drop the requirement that the equations be linear and ask whether a system of polynomial equations in several variables with coefficients in R has a solution, and if so, look for an explicit description of the set of all solutions. *Hilbert's tenth problem* (see page 561) asks to determine the solvability of a Diophantine equation for $R = \mathbb{Z}$. Against Hilbert's intuition, the question turns out to be undecidable, in the sense of Turing. (See for example Sipser (1997) for the background.) This was proved by Matiyasevich

---

[2] I also assume its proof to be rather difficult because it is not true unless $n + 1$ is prime.

(1970), who showed that any recursively enumerable set $D \subseteq \mathbb{N}$ can be represented as

$$D = \{s_1 \in \mathbb{N}: \exists s_2, \dots, s_n \in \mathbb{N} \ f(s_1, \dots, s_n) = 0\}$$

for some $n \in \mathbb{N}$ and some polynomial $f \in \mathbb{Z}[x_1, \dots, x_n]$. Thus $D \neq \emptyset$ if and only if there is some $s \in \mathbb{N}^n$ such that $f(s) = 0$. By Lagrange's famous theorem, every nonnegative integer can be written as a sum of four squares, and hence $D \neq \emptyset$ if and only if $g(t) = 0$ has an integral solution $t \in \mathbb{Z}^{4n}$, where

$$g = f(y_1^2 + y_2^2 + y_3^2 + y_4^2, \dots, y_{4n-3}^4 + y_{4n-2}^2 + y_{4n-1}^2 + y_{4n}^2) \in \mathbb{Z}[y_1, \dots, y_{4n}].$$

Since nonemptiness of an arbitrary recursively enumerable set is undecidable, so is the question whether a Diophantine equation is solvable. Matiyasevich (1993) gives a nice presentation of the proof and its history.

4.6. Cataldi (1513) gives many rational approximations to square roots of integers. He derives from this rules for parading soldiers in square formations; obviously the granting agencies' pressure for "useful applications" is not a recent phenomenon. Leibniz (1701) gives the continued fraction for the golden ratio and the approximation denominators, which are the Fibonacci numbers. Hugenius (1703) treats the approximation of real numbers by fractions in the context of automata with cog wheels. Euler (1737) coined the term *fractiones continuae*, gave the first thirteen entries of the expansion for π, and showed that the continued fraction expansion is periodic for a root of an irreducible quadratic polynomial with integer coefficients; Lagrange (1770a) proved the converse. By relating continued fractions to certain differential equations, Euler (1737) derived the expansion for e. In one of his papers on continued fractions, Euler (1762/63) introduces explicit expressions for our numbers s_i and t_i and proves Lemma 3.8 (iv) and (v). Hurwitz (1891) showed the quality $1/\sqrt{5}q^2$ of rational approximations, and the optimality of $c = \sqrt{5}$ in (7). Lagrange (1798) had proven that any "best" rational approximation comes from a continued fraction. Perron's (1929) classic explains the rich and interesting theory of continued fractions in detail; for further reading and references see also Knuth (1998), §4.5.3, and Bombieri & van der Poorten (1995) give an amusing introduction.

Al-Khwārizmī gives in his *Algebra*, written around 825, three values for π: $3\frac{1}{7} \approx 3.1428$, $\sqrt{10} \approx 3.16$, and $62\,832/20\,000 = 3.1416$. Already the Indian mathematician Āryabhaṭa (c. 530) had obtained the latter. The quote at the beginning of this chapter shows that al-Khwārizmī was well aware of the inexact quality of these approximations. The word *algorithm* is derived from al-Khwārizmī's name, indicating his family's origin from the town of Khwarezm, present-day Khiva in Uzbekistan (the old-fashioned "algorism" was a better transliteration than the anagram of *logarithm*). *Algebra* comes from the word al-jabr in the title of his algebra book الكتاب المختصر في حساب الجبر و المقابلة (*al-kitāb al-muhtaṣir fī ḥisābi al-jabri wā al-muqābalati* = *The concise book on computing by moving and reducing terms*). جبر (jabara) means "to break" and refers to the technique of moving terms of an equation to the other side so that all resulting terms are positive; he did not allow negative terms. (The Spanish word *algebrista* designates both someone who does algebra or who sets broken bones, as in Cervantes (1615), chapter XV, where one of Don Quixote's companions is healed.) مقابلة (muqābalat) is probably the "reduction" of equations by subtracting equal quantities on both sides, and these are his two techniques for solving linear and quadratic equations, the topic of the first part of his book. The influence of al-Khwārizmī's work on Arab, and later medieval European, mathematics was profound.

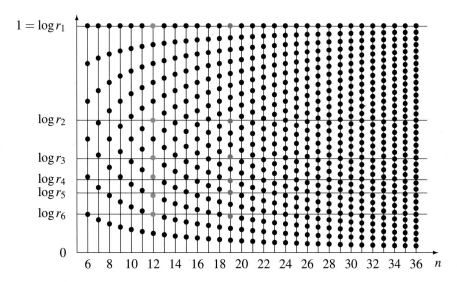

FIGURE 4.7: Diophantine approximations with denominator n to $\log r_1, \ldots, \log r_6$.

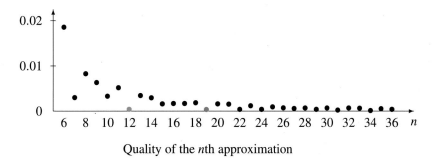

Quality of the nth approximation

Al-Kāshī was chief astronomer at Ulugh Begh's Court in Samarkand. His *Instructions on the circle's circumference*, written around 1424 (see Luckey 1953), is a remarkable achievement. He presents his calculation of π with great concern about error control, Newton iteration for square roots with just the required precision, and a conversion of his hexagesimal result to decimal notation.

Euler (1736a) introduced the symbols π (§638) and e (§171); they became standard with his *Introductio in analysin infinitorum* (Euler 1748a). π had been used by Jones (1706) and by Christian Goldbach in 1742. Ludolph van Ceulen (1540–1610) published 20 digits of π in 1596, and his tombstone is said to have recorded 35 digits. Shanks had calculated 527 digits of π by February 1853, all correct. In March and April 1853, he extended this to 607 digits, incorrectly. The current record by Kanada & Takahashi took about 25 hours on a Hitachi SR 2201 Massively Parallel Processor with 2^{10} processors and 212 GB of main memory; they used a second algorithm to verify the result. This impressive achievement is largely due to ingenious algorithms devised by the Borwein brothers, Richard Brent, and their collaborators. Hilbert's (1893) elegant paper proves the transcendence of e and π on four pages. Berggren, Borwein & Borwein (1997) present a magnificent collection of writings about π. It is a must for π gourmets, and we used their material liberally.

There are analogs of continued fractions in the polynomial case. If F is a field, then an element α of $F((x^{-1}))$ or $F((x))$, the field of formal Laurent series in x^{-1} or x, respectively, may be represented by an infinite continued fraction whose initial segments converge to α with regard to the degree valuation and the x-adic valuation (Section 9.6), respectively. This is discussed in Exercises 4.29 and 4.30.

4.7. Euler (1737) uses a year of $365^d 5^h 49' 8''$, which is $22''$ longer than our value, to calculate several calendars, including the Julian and Gregorian ones, and $365\frac{8}{33}$. Lagrange (1798), §20, finds several rational approximations to the length of the year, our four among them, via continued fractions based on a year of $365^d 5^h 48' 49''$, three seconds longer than our assumption. He ends his calculations by admonishing the astronomers to do their homework: *Comme les Astronomes sont encore partagés sur la véritable longueur de l'année, nous nous abstiendrons de prononcer sur ce sujet.*[3] We follow Lagrange's modesty.

4.8. In Example 17.1, we calculate some approximations for our musical intervals.

Exercises.

4.1 Suppose that on a 64-bit processor you are given a single precision number p with $2^{63} < p < 2^{64}$, and the words making up a positive multiprecision integer a, say of n words. Give an algorithm that computes a rem p in $O(n)$ word operations. You may assume that the processor has a double-by-single-precision division instruction, which takes as input three single precision integers a_0, a_1, p such that $a_1 < p$ and returns single precision integers q, r with $a_1 \cdot 2^{64} + a_0 = qp + r$ and $r < p$. Hint: You have to take care of the leading bit of a.

4.2 Suppose that the two data bases to be compared, as in Section 4.1, are up to 10 GB long and actually different, and that we use single-precision primes p with $2^{63} < p < 2^{64}$. There are at least 10^{17} such primes (Exercise 18.18).

(i) Modulo how many primes can they agree at most?

(ii) If we choose our prime p at random, what is the probability that our test gives an incorrect "ok"?

4.3* You are to apply the fingerprinting technique to *string matching*. Given are two strings $x = x_0 x_1 \cdots x_{m-2} x_{m-1}$ and $y = y_0 y_1 \cdots y_{n-2} y_{n-1}$, say consisting of symbols $x_i, y_i \in \{0, 1\}$ for all i, of lengths $m < n$, respectively. We want to determine whether x occurs as a substring of y. Let $z_i = y_i y_{i+1} \cdots y_{i+m-1}$ be the substring of length m of y starting at position i, for $0 \le i < n - m$. Thus the task is to determine whether $x = z_i$ for some i.

(i) Describe a simple algorithm that uses $O(mn)$ symbol comparisons.

(ii) Let $a = \sum_{0 \le j < m} x_j 2^j$ and $b_i = \sum_{0 \le j < m} y_{i+j} 2^j$ be the integers whose binary representation (with most significant bit right) is x and z_i, respectively, and $2^{63} < p < 2^{64}$ a single precision prime. Give an algorithm that computes all b_i rem p and compares them to a rem p in $O(n)$ word operations.

(iii) Any match is certainly found by your algorithm. If $m \le 63k$, $i < n - m$, and p was chosen at random among the at least 10^{17} single precision primes (Exercise 18.18), what is the probability that $x \neq y_i$ and yet $a \equiv b_i \bmod p$ (in terms of k)? What is the probability that some such false match is reported, in terms of k and n? For which k and n is the latter probability below 0.1%?

4.4 Prove that an integer $a = \sum_{0 \le i \le l} a_i \cdot 10^i \in \mathbb{N}$ is divisible by 11 if and only if the alternating sum $a_0 - a_1 + a_2 - a_3 \pm \cdots + (-1)^l a_l$ of its decimal digits is.

4.5 Show that for any integer m, congruence $\bmod\, m$ is an equivalence relation on $\mathbb{Z}$, and prove (1).

---

[3] Since the astronomers have not yet agreed on the true length of the year, we will refrain from making a recommendation on this subject.

4.6 Let $m \in \mathbb{N}$ and $f \in \mathbb{Z}_m[x]$ of degree n. Show that the residue class ring $\mathbb{Z}_m[x]/\langle f \rangle$ has m^n elements.

4.7 Is there a $b \in \mathbb{Z}$ such that $6b \equiv 1 \bmod 81$?

4.8 (i) Let $a \in \mathbb{N}$ be such that $0 \leq a < 1000$ and the three least significant digits in the decimal representation of $17a$ are 001. What is a?

(ii) Same question when the least significant digits are 209.

4.9 Let $f = x^4 + x^3 + 2x^2 + x + 1$, $g_1 = x$, and $g_2 = x^3 + x$ in $\mathbb{Q}[x]$. Compute polynomials $t_1, t_2 \in \mathbb{Q}[x]$ such that $t_i g_i \equiv 1 \bmod f$ for $i = 1, 2$, if they exist. Is $\mathbb{Q}[x]/\langle f \rangle$ a field?

4.10 Show that the polynomial $f = x^3 + x + 1 \in \mathbb{F}_2[x]$ is irreducible, and compute the inverses of all nonzero elements in $\mathbb{F}_8 = \mathbb{F}_2[x]/\langle f \rangle$ using the Extended Euclidean Algorithm.

4.11 Let $g = x^5 + x + 1 \in \mathbb{F}_2[x]$. For each of the two polynomials

(i) $f = x^3 + x + 1$, (ii) $f = x^3 + 1$

in $\mathbb{F}_2[x]$, do the following. If $f \bmod g$ is a unit in $\mathbb{F}_2[x]/\langle g \rangle$, compute its inverse $h \bmod g$. If $f \bmod g$ is a zero divisor, find a polynomial $h \in \mathbb{F}_2[x]$ of degree less than 5 such that $fh \equiv 0 \bmod g$.

4.12 Prove carefully that $\mathbb{R}[x]/\langle x^2 + 1 \rangle$ and $\mathbb{C}$ are isomorphic fields.

4.13 (i) Find a polynomial $f \in \mathbb{F}_7[x]$ of degree less than 4 solving the congruence $(x^2 - 1) \cdot f \equiv x^3 + 2x + 5 \bmod x^4 + 2x^2 + 1$ in $\mathbb{F}_7[x]$.

(ii) Show that the residue class ring $\mathbb{F}_{343} = \mathbb{F}_7[x]/\langle x^3 + x + 1 \rangle$ is a field, and compute the inverse of $x^2 \bmod x^3 + x + 1$ in $\mathbb{F}_{343}$.

4.14 (i) Let R be a Euclidean domain and $m, f \in R$. Show that $f \bmod m$ is a zero divisor in $R/\langle m \rangle$ if and only if $\gcd(f, m) \neq 1$ if and only if $f \bmod m$ is not invertible in $R/\langle m \rangle$.

(ii) Give an example of a ring containing nonzero elements that are neither units nor zero divisors.

4.15 Let R be a Euclidean domain and $a, b, c \in R$.

(i) Show that the congruence $ax \equiv b \bmod c$ has a solution $x \in R$ if and only if $g = \gcd(a, c)$ divides b. Prove that in the latter case, the congruence is equivalent to $(a/g)x \equiv (b/g)x \bmod (c/g)$.

(ii) For $R = \mathbb{Z}$ and $a = 5, 6, 7$, determine whether the congruence $ax \equiv 9 \bmod 15$ is solvable, and if so, give all solutions $x \in \{0, \ldots, 14\}$.

4.16* The **degree sequence** of a pair $(f, g) \in (F[x] \setminus \{0\})^2$ of nonzero polynomials over a field F is $(\deg r_0, \deg r_1, \ldots, \deg r_\ell) \in \mathbb{N}^{\ell+1}$, where $r_0, r_1, \ldots, r_\ell$ are the remainders in the Euclidean Algorithm for f and g. How many pairs of polynomials $(f, g) \in (\mathbb{F}_q[x] \setminus \{0\})^2$ over the finite field $\mathbb{F}_q$ with q elements have degree sequence $(4, 3, 1, 0)$? Generalize your answer for arbitrary given degree sequences $(n_0, n_1, \ldots, n_\ell) \in \mathbb{N}^{\ell+1}$ with $n_0 > n_1 > \cdots > n_\ell \geq 0$ for $\ell \geq 1$. Hint: Use Exercise 3.18. For all possible degree sequences with $n_0 = 3$ and $n_1 = 2$, list the corresponding pairs of polynomials in $(\mathbb{F}_2[x] \setminus \{0\})^2$.

4.17* This continues Exercise 4.16. Let $\mathbb{F}_q$ be a finite field with q elements and $n, m \in \mathbb{Z}$ with $n \geq m \geq 0$.

(i) For two disjoint subsets $S, T \subseteq \{0, \ldots, m-1\}$, let $p_{S,T}$ denote the probability that no degree in S and all degrees in T occur in the remainder sequence of the Euclidean Algorithm for two random polynomials in $\mathbb{F}_q[x]$ of degrees n and m, respectively. Prove that $p_{S,T} = q^{-\#S}(1 - q^{-1})^{-\#T}$.

(ii) For $0 \leq i < m$, let X_i denote the random variable that has $X_i = 1$ if i occurs in the degree sequence of the Euclidean Algorithm for two random polynomials in $\mathbb{F}_q[x]$ of degrees n and m, respectively, and $X_i = 0$ otherwise. Show that $X_0, \ldots, X_{m-1}$ are independent and $\mathrm{prob}(X_i = 0) = 1/q$ for all i.

4.18* Let q be a prime power and $n, m \in \mathbb{N}$ with $n \geq m > 0$. Use Exercise 4.17 to prove the following statements.

(i) The probability that two random polynomials of degree n and m, respectively, in $\mathbb{F}_q[x]$ are coprime is $1 - 1/q$.

(ii) The probability that $n_2 = n_1 - 1$ is $1 - 1/q$.

(iii) The probability that the degree sequence is **normal**, that is, $\ell = m + 1$ and $n_{i+1} = n_i - 1$ for $1 \leq i < \ell$, is $(1 - 1/q)^m \geq 1 - m/q$.

4.19 Let $\mathbb{F}_q$ be a finite field with q elements, $f \in \mathbb{F}_q[x]$ of degree $n > 0$, and $R = \mathbb{F}_q[x]/\langle f \rangle$ the residue class ring modulo f. Then $R^\times$, the set of elements of R that have a multiplicative inverse, is a multiplicative group, and Theorem 4.1 implies that $R^\times = \{g \bmod f : \gcd(f, g) = 1\}$. We denote its cardinality by $\Phi(f) = \#R^\times = \#\{g \in \mathbb{F}_q[x] : \deg g < n \text{ and } \gcd(f, g) = 1\}$.

(i) Prove that $\Phi(f) = q^n - 1$ if f is irreducible.

(ii) Show that $\Phi(f) = (q^d - 1)q^{n-d}$ if f is a power of an irreducible polynomial of degree d.

4.20 Devise a recursive variant of the repeated squaring algorithm 4.8, and also an iterative variant which proceeds from the low order to the high order bits of the binary representation of n. Trace all three algorithms on the computation of a^{45}.

4.21* Give a "repeated fourth powering" algorithm that uses $2\lfloor \log_4 n \rfloor$ squarings and $w_4(n) + 1$ ordinary multiplications, where $w_4(n)$ is the number of nonzero digits in the 4-ary representation of n. Trace your algorithm on the computation of a^{45}. Generalize your algorithm to a "repeated 2^kth powering" algorithm for $k \in \mathbb{N}_{>0}$.

4.22 Compute $15^{-1} \bmod 19$ via Euclid and via Fermat.

4.23 Derive $(a + b)^p \equiv a^p + b^p \bmod p$ for all $a, b \in \mathbb{Z}$ and prime p from Fermat's little theorem.

4.24* (i) Let R be a Euclidean domain, $f_1, \ldots, f_n \in R$, and $h = \gcd(f_1, \ldots, f_n)$. Prove that there exist $s_1, \ldots, s_n \in R$ such that $s_1 f_1 + \cdots + s_n f_n = h$.

(ii) Prove Theorem 4.11.

(iii) Let $l = \mathrm{lcm}(f_1, \ldots, f_n)$. Show that if $R = F[x]$ for a field F, $h \neq 0$, and $\deg a < \deg l$, then there exist $s_1, \ldots, s_n \in R$ solving (6) such that $\deg s_i < \deg l - \deg f_i$.

4.25 Compute integral solutions of the linear Diophantine equations $24s + 33t = 9$ and $6s_1 + 10s_2 + 15s_3 = 7$.

4.26 (i) Expand the rational fractions $14/3$ and $3/14$ into finite continued fractions.

(ii) Convert $[2, 1, 4]$ and $[0, 1, 1, 100]$ into rational numbers.

4.27 Expand each of the following as infinite continued fractions: $\sqrt{2}, \sqrt{2} - 1, \sqrt{2}/2, \sqrt{5}, \sqrt{7}$.

4.28 Let R be a Euclidean domain and $q_1, \ldots, q_\ell \in R \setminus 0$. Show that

$$[q_1, \ldots, q_i] = \frac{c_{i+1}(q_1, \ldots, q_i)}{c_{i+1}(0, q_2, \ldots, q_i)}$$

for $1 \leq i \leq \ell$, where c_i is the ith continuant polynomial (Exercise 3.20).

4.29** This exercise assumes familiarity with valuations and formal Laurent series. Let F be a field. The field $F((x^{-1}))$ of formal Laurent series in x^{-1} consists of expressions of the form

$$g = \sum_{-\infty < j \leq m} g_j x^j, \quad g_m, g_{m-1}, \ldots \in F$$

for some $m \in \mathbb{Z}$. We set $\deg g = \max\{j \leq m : g_j \neq 0\}$, with the convention that $\deg 0 = -\infty$. This degree function has the usual properties, as the degree of polynomials. In fact, the field $F(x)$ of rational functions is a subfield of $F((x^{-1}))$, and we have $\deg(a/b) = \deg a - \deg b$ for $a, b \in F[x]$.

For a Laurent series g, we obtain the continued fraction $[q_1, q_2, \ldots]$ of g as follows. Set $\alpha_1 = g$, and recursively define $q_i = \lfloor \alpha_i \rfloor \in F[x]$ and $\alpha_{i+1} = 1/(\alpha_i - q_i)$ for $i \in \mathbb{N}_{>0}$. Here, $\lfloor \cdot \rfloor$ extracts the polynomial part, so that $\deg(\alpha_i - q_i) < 0$.

(i) Show that $\deg q_i = \deg \alpha_i$ for all $i \in \mathbb{N}_{>0}$ and $\deg \alpha_i > 0$ if $i \geq 2$.

(ii) Prove that the continued fraction of a rational function $r_0/r_1 \in F((x^{-1}))$, with nonzero $r_0, r_1 \in F[x]$, is finite, and that the q_i are the quotients in the classical Euclidean Algorithm for r_0, r_1.

(iii) Let $s_0 = t_1 = 1$, $s_1 = t_0 = 0$, and $s_{i+1} = s_{i-1} - q_i s_i$, $t_{i+1} = t_{i-1} - q_i t_i$ for $i \geq 1$, as in the classical Extended Euclidean Algorithm (where all ρ_i are 1). Prove that the ith convergent $c_i = [q_1, \ldots, q_{i-1}]$ of g is $c_i = -t_i/s_i$, for all $i \geq 2$.

(iv) Show that $g = -(t_{i-1} - \alpha_i t_i)/(s_{i-1} - \alpha_i s_i)$, and conclude that $\deg(g - c_i) < -2 \deg s_i$ for all $i \geq 2$. Thus if $|h| = 2^{\deg h}$ is the degree valuation of a Laurent series h, then we obtain the analog $|g + t_i/s_i| < |s_i|^{-2}$ of (7).

(v) Now let $i \in \mathbb{N}_{\geq 2}$, $k \geq n = \deg s_i$, $r_0 = \lfloor x^{n+k} g \rfloor$, $r_1 = x^{n+k}$, and $r_i = s_i r_0 + t_i r_1$. Conclude from (iv) that $\deg r_i < k$, and show that $r_i/s_i \equiv r_0 \bmod x^{n+k}$ if $x \nmid s_i$. (In fact, Lemma 11.3 implies that $q_1, \ldots, q_{i-1}$ are the first $i-1$ quotients and r_i is the ith remainder in the classical Euclidean Algorithm for r_0, r_1.)

4.30[**] This exercise is an analog of Exercise 4.29, now for Laurent series in x rather than in x^{-1}. Let F be a field. The field $F((x))$ of formal Laurent series in x consists of expressions of the form

$$g = \sum_{m \leq j < \infty} g_j x^j, \quad g_m, g_{m+1}, \ldots \in F$$

for some $m \in \mathbb{Z}$. We let $v(g) = \min\{j \geq m : g_j \neq 0\}$, with the convention that $v(0) = \infty$.

For a Laurent series g, we obtain the continued fraction $[q_1, q_2, \ldots]$ of g as follows. Set $\alpha_1 = g$, and recursively define $q_i = \lfloor \alpha_i \rfloor \in F[1/x]$ and $\alpha_{i+1} = 1/(\alpha_i - q_i)$ for $i \in \mathbb{N}_{>0}$. Here, $\lfloor \cdot \rfloor$ extracts the part which is polynomial in $1/x$, so that $v(\alpha_i - q_i) > 0$, or equivalently, $x \mid (\alpha_i - q_i)$.

(i) Prove that $v(fg) = v(f) + v(g)$, $v(1/g) = -v(g)$ if $g \neq 0$, and $v(f + g) \geq \max\{v(f), v(g)\}$, with equality if $v(f) \neq v(g)$, hold for all $f, g \in F((x))$.

(ii) Let $s_0 = t_1 = 1$, $s_1 = t_0 = 0$, and $s_{i+1} = s_{i-1} - q_i s_i$, $t_{i+1} = t_{i-1} - q_i t_i$ for $i \geq 1$, as in the classical Extended Euclidean Algorithm (where all ρ_i are 1). Then the s_i, t_i are polynomials in $1/x$. Prove that the ith convergent $c_i = [q_1, \ldots, q_{i-1}]$ of g is $c_i = -t_i/s_i$, for all $i \geq 2$.

(iii) Show that $g = -(t_{i-1} - \alpha_i t_i)/(s_{i-1} - \alpha_i s_i)$, and conclude that $v(g - c_i) > -2v(s_i)$ for all $i \geq 2$. Thus if $|h| = 2^{-v(h)}$ is the x-adic valuation of a Laurent series h, then we obtain the analog $|g + t_i/s_i| < |s_i|^{-2}$ of (7).

(iv) Now assume that $g \in F[[x]]$ is a power series, let $i \in \mathbb{N}_{\geq 2}$, and $n = -v(s_i) \in \mathbb{N}$. Prove that $x^n s_i$ and $x^n t_i$ are polynomials of degree at most n, and conclude that there exist polynomials $s, t \in F[x]$ of degree not more than n such that $x \nmid s$ and $t/s \equiv g \bmod x^{2n+1}$.

4.31 Prove that there do not exist integers d, n such that $3/2 = 2^{d/n}$.

4.32[**] (Sturm 1835) Let $f \in \mathbb{R}[x]$ have no multiple roots, so that $\gcd(f, f') = 1$, and determine $f_0 = f, f_1 = f', f_2, \ldots, f_\ell, q_1, \ldots, q_\ell \in \mathbb{R}[x]$ similarly as in the classical Euclidean Algorithm, but according to the modified rule

$$q_i = f_{i-1} \text{ quo } f_i, \quad f_{i+1} = -(f_{i-1} \text{ rem } f_i)$$

for $1 \leq i \leq \ell$, with the convention that $f_{\ell+1} = 0$. The difference to the classical Euclidean Algorithm is the sign of f_{i+1}; this corresponds to taking $\rho_0 = \rho_1 = 1$ and $\rho_i = -1$ for $2 \leq i \leq \ell$ in the Extended Euclidean Algorithm 3.6. The polynomials $f_0, f_1, \ldots, f_\ell$ form the **Sturm chain** of f. For each $b \in \mathbb{R}$, let $w(b)$ be the number of sign alternations in the sequence $f_0(b), \ldots, f_\ell(b)$. Here, a sign alternation occurs when either $f_i(b) < 0$, $f_{i+1}(b) \geq 0$ or $f_i(b) > 0$, $f_{i+1}(b) \leq 0$. Prove **Sturm's theorem**, which says that for all $b, c \in \mathbb{R}$ such that $f(b) \neq 0 \neq f(c)$ and $b < c$, the number of real roots of f in the interval (b, c) is $w(b) - w(c)$. Hint: It is sufficient to prove the theorem for intervals containing at most one zero of all the f_i's. Show that w does not change at a zero of some f_i with $i > 0$, but that w drops by one at a zero of $f_0 = f$.

All is fair in war, love, and mathematics.

Eric Temple Bell (1937)

"Divide *et impera*" is as true in algebra as in statecraft;
but no less true and even more fertile is the maxim "auge *et impera*."
The more to do or to prove, the easier the doing or the proof.

James Joseph Sylvester (1878)

Quando orientur controversiae, non magis disputatione opus erit inter
duos philosophos, quam inter duos Computistas. Sufficiet enim,
calamos in manus sumere, sedereque ad abacos, et sibi mutuo (accito
si placet amico) dicere: *calculemus.*[1]

Gottfried Wilhelm Leibniz (1684)

These [results] must not be taken on trust by the student, but must be
worked by his own pen, which must never be out of his hand while
engaged in any algebraical process.

Augustus De Morgan (1831)

---

[1] When controversies arise, there will not be a greater dispute between two philosophers than between two computers. It will be sufficient for them to take pen in hand, sit down with their calculators, and (having summoned a friend, if they like) say to each other: *Let us calculate.*

5

Modular algorithms and interpolation

An important general concept in computer algebra is the idea of using various types of representation for the objects at hand. As an example, we can represent a polynomial either by a list of its coefficients or by its values at sufficiently many points. In fact, this is just computer algebra lingo for the ubiquitous quest for efficient data structures for computational problems.

One successful instantiation of the general concept are **modular algorithms**, where instead of solving an integer problem (more generally, an algebraic computation problem over a Euclidean domain R) directly one solves it modulo one or several integers m. The general principle is illustrated in Figure 5.1. There are three variants: **big prime** (Figure 5.1 with $m = p$ for a prime p), **small primes** (Figure 5.2 with $m = p_1 \cdots p_r$ for pairwise distinct primes $p_1, \ldots, p_r$), and **prime power** modular algorithms (Figure 5.3 with $m = p^l$ for a prime p). The first one is conceptually the simplest, and the basic issues are most visible in that variant. However, the other two variants are computationally superior.

In each case, two technical problems have to be addressed:

- a bound on the solution in R,

- how to find the required moduli.

The first item is sometimes easy, especially when $R = F[x]$. The second item requires the **prime number theorem** when $R = \mathbb{Z}$; for $R = F[x]$ it is easy for the small primes version, but more involved for big primes.

The small primes modular approach has the following advantages over direct computation; the first two also apply to big prime and prime power modular algorithms.

- In some applications, such as computing the greatest common divisor of two polynomials with integer coefficients, we encounter the phenomenon of **intermediate expression swell**: the coefficients of intermediate results during the computation can be much bigger than the coefficients of the final result that we are interested in. In Chapter 6, we will see that the gcd of two polynomials in

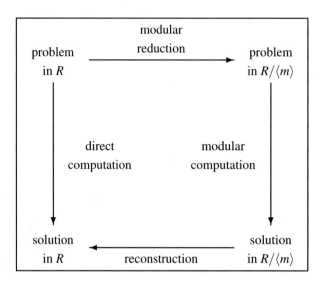

FIGURE 5.1: General scheme for modular algorithms.

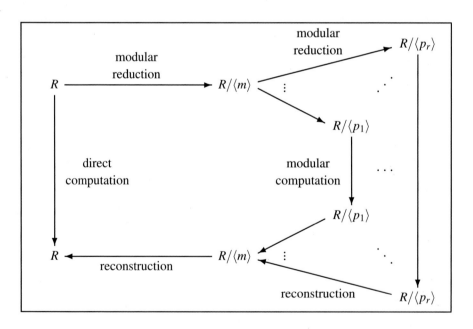

FIGURE 5.2: General scheme for small primes modular algorithms.

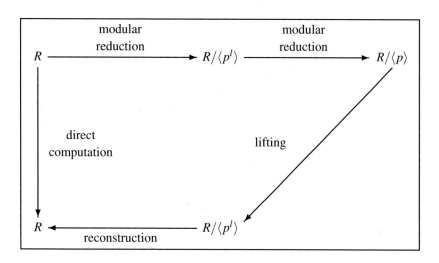

FIGURE 5.3: General scheme for prime power modular algorithms.

$\mathbb{Z}[x]$ of degree at most n has coefficients not much larger than the input polynomials, but the intermediate coefficients in Euclid's algorithm may be longer by a factor of about n than the inputs, and by a factor of about n^2 for the classical Euclidean Algorithm. When computing in a modular fashion, we may choose the moduli m_i such that their product is only slightly larger than the final result, and by reducing modulo the m_i where possible, also the intermediate results in the modular computation remain as "small" as the final result.

○ The designer of a modular algorithm is free in her choice of the moduli, as long as their product is large enough to recover the result. Thus she may choose the moduli to be **Fourier primes** which support particularly fast polynomial arithmetic; these will be discussed in Chapter 8.

○ In nearly all tasks in computer algebra, the cost for solving a problem with input size n is at least linear in n. For example, if we use the algorithms for integer and polynomial arithmetic as described in Chapters 2 and 3, then one arithmetic operation on integers of length n or on polynomials of degree n takes $O(n^2)$ operations. In such cases, it is cheaper to solve r "small" problems with inputs of size about n/r rather than one "big" problem. In the extreme case $n = r$, the cost of the modular computation becomes just $O(n)$, but this has to be balanced against the cost for the change of representation.

○ If the moduli m_i in the small primes approach fit into one machine word of the target processor, then the cost for an arithmetic operation modulo one m_i amounts to only a few machine cycles.

○ The r subtasks modulo the distinct small primes are independent of each other and can be performed in a distributed fashion using r processors or machines in parallel.

As an aside, we note that as long as the direct computation uses only additions and multiplications, but no divisions, an arbitrary modulus—or arbitrary pairwise coprime moduli in the "small primes" variant—may be chosen in a modular algorithm.

Besides the big prime method, we discuss in this chapter the theoretical underpinnings of the small primes modular algorithm, namely the **Chinese Remainder Algorithm**, and two applications: secret sharing and computing the determinant. We have to wait until Chapter 9 for the tools used in the third variant: Newton iteration and Hensel lifting. The prime power approach will play a major role in the polynomial factorization algorithm in Chapter 15. Table 15.8 on page 435 lists eleven problems for which we will have learnt modular algorithms by then.

We also discuss applications of the Extended Euclidean Algorithm and the Chinese Remainder Algorithm to various kinds of interpolation problems and to partial fraction decomposition.

5.1. Change of representation

There are two basically different types of representation for our objects. In the first, one chooses a **base** and presents data in an expansion along powers of that base. Examples for this type include the coefficient representation of polynomials (where x is the base), more generally a Taylor expansion around u (where $x - u$ is the base; see Section 5.6), and the decimal or binary representation of integers (with base 10 or 2, respectively). Even the usual floating point representation of real numbers can be considered to be in this category, with base 10^{-1}. These types of representation are the "natural" ones, and computer users like to have their input and output in this format.

Prototypical for the second type are the representations of a polynomial by its values at various points $u_0, \ldots, u_{n-1}$, or of an integer modulo different primes $p_0, \ldots, p_{n-1}$. (We number from 0 through $n - 1$ instead of 1 through n for consistency with Chapter 10.) The "bases" here are $x - u_0, \ldots, x - u_{n-1}$ and $p_0, \ldots, p_{n-1}$, respectively. Actually, a better analogy is to take

$$\frac{m}{x - u_0}, \frac{m}{x - u_1}, \ldots, \frac{m}{x - u_{n-1}},$$

where $m = (x - u_0)(x - u_1) \cdots (x - u_{n-1})$, as basis for all polynomials of degree less than n in the first case; see the Lagrange interpolation formula (3) below. Some problems, such as multiplication, are quite easy in appropriate bases of this kind, while others, like division with remainder, seem to require a representation of the first type.

For each computational problem, one should examine whether this general-purpose tool is of use. This involves two questions:

○ In which representation is the problem easiest to solve?

○ How do we convert to and from that representation?

We discuss some fundamental tools for these questions in this book: the Chinese Remainder Algorithm, the Extended Euclidean Algorithm, and Newton iteration (including Hensel lifting).

It is important to realize the similarity between evaluating a polynomial at a point u and taking the remainder of an integer modulo a prime p. The former is the same as taking the remainder modulo $x - u$, and so the latter can be thought of as "evaluating the integer at p". The inverse operation of recovering the coefficients of a polynomial from its values at several points is **interpolation**. For integers, this is afforded by the Chinese Remainder Algorithm, and it is useful to understand this as "interpolating an integer from its values at several primes".

Similar representations exist for rational functions and rational numbers. We will later discuss conversion algorithms: Cauchy interpolation and Padé approximation for rational functions (Sections 5.8 and 5.9), and rational number reconstruction (Section 5.10).

The proper choice of representation is vital when dealing with multivariate polynomials. Four important possibilities—dense, sparse, by an arithmetic circuit, or by a "black box"—are briefly discussed in Section 16.6.

An important application of the general idea of change of representation are the fast multiplication algorithms in Chapter 8 (based on the FFT). In the three major problems in Part V, namely Gröbner bases, integration, and summation, the basic task can be interpreted as transforming a general input into a representation where the problem at hand is fairly easy to solve.

5.2. Evaluation and interpolation

We start with the simplest but most important change of representation: evaluation and interpolation. Suppose that F is a field and $u_0, \dots, u_{n-1} \in F$ are pairwise distinct. A polynomial $f = \sum_{0 \leq i < n} f_i x^i \in F[x]$ can be evaluated at a single point $u \in F$ with $n - 1$ multiplications and $n - 1$ additions in F, using **Horner's rule**

$$f(u) = (\cdots (f_{n-1}u + f_{n-2})u + \cdots + f_1)u + f_0. \tag{1}$$

Thus we can evaluate F at all points u_i using $2n^2 - 2n$ operations in F. What about interpolation?

The **Lagrange interpolant**

$$l_i = \prod_{\substack{0 \leq j < n \\ j \neq i}} \frac{x - u_j}{u_i - u_j} \in F[x] \tag{2}$$

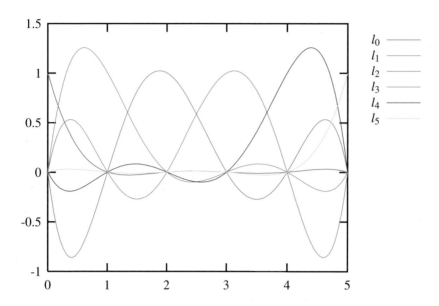

FIGURE 5.4: The Lagrange interpolants $l_0, \ldots, l_5$ when $u_i = i$ for $i = 0, \ldots, 5$.

has the property that $l_i(u_j)$ is 0 if $i \neq j$ and 1 when $i = j$; see Figure 5.4. For arbitrary $v_0, \ldots, v_{n-1} \in F$,

$$f = \sum_{0 \leq i < n} v_i l_i = \sum_{0 \leq i < n} v_i \prod_{\substack{0 \leq j < n \\ j \neq i}} \frac{x - u_j}{u_i - u_j}. \tag{3}$$

is a polynomial of degree less than n such that $f(u_i) = v_i$ for all i. The interpolating polynomial with this degree constraint is unique, since the difference of two such polynomials has degree less than n and n roots, hence is the zero polynomial.

━━━ THEOREM 5.1. ━━━━━━━━━━━━━━━━━━━━━━━━━━━━━━━━━━━
Evaluating a polynomial $f \in F[x]$ of degree less than n at n distinct points $u_0, \ldots,$
$u_{n-1} \in F$ or computing an interpolating polynomial at these points can be per-
formed with $O(n^2)$ operations in F. More precisely, evaluation takes $2n^2 - 2n$
operations, and Lagrange interpolation uses $7n^2 - 8n + 1$ operations. ━━━━━━━

PROOF. It remains to prove the claim for interpolation. Let $m_i = x - u_i$ for all i. We first compute $m_0 m_1, m_0 m_1 m_2, \ldots, m = m_0 \cdots m_{n-1}$. This amounts to multiplying a monic linear polynomial by a monic polynomial of degree i for $1 \leq i < n$, taking

$$\sum_{1 \leq i < n} (2i - 1) = n^2 - 2n + 1$$

arithmetic operations. Then for each i, we divide m by m_i, taking $2n - 2$ operations (Exercise 5.3), evaluate m/m_i at u_i, taking at most $2n - 4$ operations, and divide m/m_i by that value to obtain l_i. This amounts to $4n^2 - 5n$ operations for all i. Finally, computing the linear combination (3) takes another $2n^2 - n$ operations, and the estimate follows by adding up. $\square$

Exercise 5.11 discusses a different algorithm, **Newton interpolation**, and shows that it takes at most $\frac{5}{2}n^2$ field operations. In Chapter 10, we show that both evaluation and interpolation can be done much faster, with only $O(n \log^2 n \log \log n)$ operations.

A global view of evaluation and interpolation is the following. Given n points $u_0, \ldots, u_{n-1} \in F$, we define the evaluation map $\chi \colon F^n \longrightarrow F^n$ by

$$\chi(f_0, \ldots, f_{n-1}) = \left(\sum_{0 \leq j < n} f_j u_0^j, \ldots, \sum_{0 \leq j < n} f_j u_{n-1}^j \right) \tag{4}$$

This is just the map corresponding to evaluation of polynomials $f = \sum f_i x^i$ of degree less than n at $u_0, \ldots, u_{n-1}$; it is obviously F-linear and represented by the **Vandermonde matrix**

$$V = \mathrm{VDM}(u_0, \ldots, u_{n-1}) = \begin{pmatrix} 1 & u_0 & u_0^2 & \cdots & u_0^{n-1} \\ 1 & u_1 & u_1^2 & \cdots & u_1^{n-1} \\ 1 & u_2 & u_2^2 & \cdots & u_2^{n-1} \\ \vdots & \vdots & \vdots & & \vdots \\ 1 & u_{n-1} & u_{n-1}^2 & \cdots & u_{n-1}^{n-1} \end{pmatrix} \in F^{n \times n}.$$

If $u_i = u_j$ for some $i \neq j$, then row i and row j of V are equal, and V is singular. On the other hand, if all u_i are distinct, then the existence of a unique interpolation polynomial of degree less than n shows that χ (and hence V) is invertible, and then V^{-1} is the matrix of the interpolation map. Both evaluation and interpolation are linear maps between coefficient and value vectors, but of course not linear in $u_0, \ldots, u_{n-1}$.

5.3. Application: Secret sharing

A neat application of interpolation, which we mentioned in Section 1.3 but which will not be used later, is secret sharing: you want to give to n players a shared secret, so that together they can discover it, but no proper subset of the players can. To achieve this, you identify possible secrets with elements of the finite field $\mathbb{F}_p = \mathbb{Z}/\langle p \rangle$ for an appropriate p. Some bank cards for Automatic Teller Machine access have as their secret PIN codes four-digit decimal numbers. For such a secret, you choose a prime p just bigger than $10\,000$, say $p = 10\,007$. Then you choose $2n - 1$ random elements $f_1, \ldots, f_{n-1}, u_0, \ldots, u_{n-1} \in \mathbb{F}_p$ uniformly and independently with all u_i nonzero, call your secret f_0, set $f = f_{n-1}x^{n-1} + \cdots + f_1 x + f_0 \in \mathbb{F}_p[x]$, and give to player number i the value $f(u_i) \in \mathbb{F}_p$. (If $u_i = u_j$ for some $i \neq j$, you have to make a new random choice; this is unlikely to happen if $n \ll \sqrt{p}$.) Then together they can determine the (unique) interpolation polynomial f of degree less than n, and thus f_0. But if any smaller number of them, say $n-1$, get together, then the possible interpolation polynomials consistent with this partial knowledge are such that each value in $\mathbb{F}_p$ of f_0 is equally likely: they have no information on f_0 (Exercise 5.14).

We can extend this scheme to the situation where $k \leq n$ and each subset of k players are able to recover the secret, but no set of fewer than k players can. This is achieved by randomly and independently choosing $n + k - 1$ elements $u_0, \ldots, u_{n-1}, f_1, \ldots, f_{k-1} \in \mathbb{F}_p$ and giving $f(u_i)$ to player i, where $f = f_{k-1}x^{k-1} + \cdots + f_1 x + f_0 \in \mathbb{F}_p[x]$ and $f_0 \in \mathbb{F}_p$ is the secret as above. Again, it is required that $u_i \neq u_j$ if $i \neq j$. Since f is uniquely determined by its values at k points, each subset of k out of the n players can calculate f and thus the secret f_0, but fewer than k players together have no information on f_0.

5.4. The Chinese Remainder Algorithm

For this section, R is a Euclidean domain, and we fix the following notation:

$$m_0, \ldots, m_{r-1} \in R \text{ are pairwise coprime, so that } \gcd(m_i, m_j) = 1 \\ \text{for } 0 \leq i < j < r, \text{ and } m = m_0 \cdots m_{r-1}. \tag{5}$$

Thus $m = \operatorname{lcm}(m_0, \ldots, m_{r-1})$. For $0 \leq i < r$, we have the canonical ring homomorphism

$$\begin{aligned} \pi_i : R &\longrightarrow R/\langle m_i \rangle, \\ f &\longmapsto f \bmod m_i. \end{aligned}$$

Combining these for all i, we get the ring homomorphism

$$\begin{aligned} \chi = \pi_0 \times \cdots \times \pi_{r-1} : R &\longrightarrow R/\langle m_0 \rangle \times \ldots \times R/\langle m_{r-1} \rangle, \\ f &\longmapsto (f \bmod m_0, \ldots, f \bmod m_{r-1}). \end{aligned}$$

The following statement provides, in somewhat abstract terminology, the theoretical basis for many of our algorithms.

THEOREM 5.2.
χ *is surjective with kernel* $\langle m \rangle$.

PROOF. Let $f \in R$. Then

$$\begin{aligned} f \in \ker \chi \iff &\chi(f) = (f \bmod m_0, \ldots, f \bmod m_{r-1}) = (0, \ldots, 0) \\ \iff &m_i \mid f \text{ for } 0 \leq i < r \iff \operatorname{lcm}(m_0, \ldots, m_{r-1}) \mid f \iff m \mid f, \end{aligned}$$

and $\ker \chi = \langle m \rangle$. For the surjectivity, it is sufficient to show that a "Lagrange interpolant" $l_i \in R$ with $\chi(l_i) = e_i$ exists for $0 \le i < r$, where $e_i = (0, \ldots, 0, 1, 0, \ldots, 0) \in R/\langle m_0 \rangle \times \cdots \times R/\langle m_{r-1} \rangle$ denotes the ith unit vector. To see why this is enough, let

$$v = (v_0 \bmod m_0, \ldots, v_{r-1} \bmod m_{r-1}) \in R/\langle m_0 \rangle \times \cdots \times R/\langle m_{r-1} \rangle$$

be arbitrary, with $v_0, \ldots, v_{r-1} \in R$. Then

$$
\begin{aligned}
\chi \left(\sum_{0 \le i < r} v_i l_i \right) &= \sum_{0 \le i < r} \chi(v_i) \chi(l_i) = \sum_{0 \le i < r} (v_i \bmod m_0, \ldots, v_i \bmod m_{r-1}) \cdot e_i \\
&= \sum_{0 \le i < r} (0, \ldots, 0, v_i \bmod m_i, 0, \ldots, 0) = v.
\end{aligned}
$$

We assume $i = 0$ for simplicity. The Extended Euclidean Algorithm, when applied to $m_1 \cdots m_{r-1} = m/m_0$ and m_0, computes $s, t \in R$ with $sm/m_0 + tm_0 = 1 = \gcd(m/m_0, m_0)$. If we now let $l_0 = sm/m_0$, then obviously $l_0 \equiv 0 \bmod m_j$ for $1 \le j < r$, and

$$l_0 = s\frac{m}{m_0} \equiv s\frac{m}{m_0} + tm_0 = 1 \bmod m_0,$$

so that $\chi(l_0) = e_0$ as claimed. $\square$

COROLLARY 5.3 *Chinese Remainder Theorem (CRT).*
We have the ring isomorphism

$$R/\langle m \rangle \cong R/\langle m_0 \rangle \times \cdots \times R/\langle m_{r-1} \rangle \tag{6}$$

and the group isomorphism of the multiplicative groups

$$(R/\langle m \rangle)^\times \cong (R/\langle m_0 \rangle)^\times \times \cdots \times (R/\langle m_{r-1} \rangle)^\times.$$

PROOF. Theorem 5.2 and the homomorphism theorem for rings (Section 25.2) imply (6). For $f \in R$, we have

$$f \text{ is invertible modulo } m \iff \gcd(f, m) = 1 \iff \gcd(f, m_i) = 1 \text{ for } 0 \le i < r$$
$$\iff f \text{ is invertible modulo } m_i \text{ for } 0 \le i < r,$$

and the second claim follows. $\square$

The proof of Theorem 5.2 is constructive and yields the following algorithm.

ALGORITHM 5.4 *Chinese Remainder Algorithm (CRA).*
Input: $m_0, \ldots, m_{r-1} \in R$ pairwise coprime, $v_0, \ldots, v_{r-1} \in R$, where R is a Euclidean domain.
Output: $f \in R$ such that $f \equiv v_i \bmod m_i$ for $0 \le i < r$.

1. $m \longleftarrow m_0 \cdots m_{r-1}$

2. **for** $0 \le i < r$ **do**
    compute m/m_i
    call the Extended Euclidean Algorithm 3.6 to compute $s_i, t_i \in R$ with
    $s_i \dfrac{m}{m_i} + t_i m_i = 1 \quad c_i \longleftarrow v_i s_i$ rem m_i

3. **return** $\displaystyle\sum_{0 \le i < r} c_i \dfrac{m}{m_i}$

We recall that c_i is the remainder in R on dividing $v_i s_i$ by m_i (Section 2.4). To see that the algorithm works correctly, we observe that $c_i m/m_i \equiv 0 \bmod m_j$ for $j \ne i$ and $c_i m/m_i \equiv v_i s_i m/m_i \equiv v_i \bmod m_i$, and hence $f \equiv c_i m/m_i \equiv v_i \bmod m_i$ for $0 \le i < r$, as claimed.

EXAMPLE 5.5.   (i) We let $R = \mathbb{Z}$, $m_i = p_i^{e_i}$ for $0 \le i < r$, where the $p_i \in \mathbb{N}$ are distinct primes and $e_i \in \mathbb{N}_{>0}$ for $0 \le i < r$. Then

$$m = \prod_{0 \le i < r} p_i^{e_i}$$

is the prime decomposition of $m \in \mathbb{Z}$. The CRT tells us that

$$\mathbb{Z}/\langle m \rangle \cong \mathbb{Z}/\langle p_0^{e_0} \rangle \times \cdots \times \mathbb{Z}/\langle p_{r-1}^{e_{r-1}} \rangle,$$

and for arbitrary $v_0, \dots, v_{r-1} \in \mathbb{Z}$ the CRA computes a solution $f \in \mathbb{Z}$ of the system of congruences

$$f \equiv v_i \bmod p_i^{e_i} \text{ for } 0 \le i < r.$$

For example, we take $r = 2$, $m_0 = 11$, $m_1 = 13$, and $m = 11 \cdot 13 = 143$, and find $f \in \mathbb{Z}$ with $0 \le f < m$ and

$$f \equiv 2 \bmod 11, \quad f \equiv 7 \bmod 13.$$

There is nothing to do in step 1 of Algorithm 5.4. In step 2, we have to apply the Extended Euclidean Algorithm to 11 and 13 and get $6 \cdot 13 + (-7) \cdot 11 = 1$, that is, $s_0 = 6$ and $s_1 = -7$. The Lagrange interpolants l_0 and l_1 from Theorem 5.2, which do not occur explicitly in the algorithm, are $l_0 = 6 \cdot 13 = 78$ and $l_1 = (-7) \cdot 11 = -77$, and we check that in fact $l_0 \equiv 1 \bmod 11$, $l_0 \equiv 0 \bmod 13$, $l_1 \equiv 0 \bmod 11$, and $l_1 \equiv 1 \bmod 13$. Now

$$
\begin{aligned}
c_0 &= v_0 s_0 \text{ rem } m_0 = 2 \cdot 6 \text{ rem } 11 = 1, \\
c_1 &= v_1 s_1 \text{ rem } m_1 = 7 \cdot (-7) \text{ rem } 13 = 3.
\end{aligned}
$$

Finally, in step 3 we compute

$$f = c_0 \frac{m}{m_0} + c_1 \frac{m}{m_1} = 1 \cdot 13 + 3 \cdot 11 = 46,$$

and indeed $46 = 4 \cdot 11 + 2 = 3 \cdot 13 + 7$.

(ii) We let $R = F[x]$ for a field F and $m_i = x - u_i$ for $0 \leq i < r$, where $u_0, \ldots, u_{r-1}$ in F are pairwise distinct. Then $f \equiv f(u_i) \bmod (x - u_i)$ for $0 \leq i < r$ and arbitrary $f \in F[x]$, by Section 4.1, and hence the ring homomorphism

$$\chi: F[x] \longrightarrow F[x]/\langle x - u_0 \rangle \times \cdots \times F[x]/\langle x - u_{r-1} \rangle \cong F^r$$
$$f \longmapsto (f(u_0), \ldots, f(u_{r-1}))$$

from Theorem 5.2 is just the evaluation homomorphism (4) at $u_0, \ldots, u_{r-1}$. (The ring F^r consists of the r-tuples with entries from F, and the ring operations are done coordinatewise.) Moreover, the l_i from the proof of Theorem 5.2 satisfying

$$l_i \equiv l_i(u_i) = 1 \bmod (x - u_i),$$
$$l_i \equiv l_i(u_j) = 0 \bmod (x - u_j) \text{ for } j \neq i$$

and $\deg l_i < r$ are the Lagrange interpolants

$$l_i = \prod_{\substack{0 \leq j < r \\ j \neq i}} \frac{x - u_j}{u_i - u_j}.$$

If $v_0, \ldots, v_{r-1} \in F$ are scalars, then $f = \sum_{0 \leq i < r} v_i l_i$ is nothing but the familiar Lagrange interpolation polynomial satisfying

$$f(u_i) = v_i \text{ for } 0 \leq i < r. \tag{7}$$

Thus Chinese remaindering for r distinct monic linear polynomials is the same as interpolation at r points, and the CRT tells us once more what we already know: the interpolation polynomial is unique modulo $m = \prod_{0 \leq i < r}(x - u_i)$, so that there is exactly one polynomial $f \in F[x]$ of degree strictly less than r which solves the interpolation problem (7). In fact, it is useful to think of the CRT as a generalization of interpolation. $\diamond$

With $R = \mathbb{Z}$ and the m_i as in (i) of the above example, we obtain the following formula for Euler's totient function from (2) of Section 4.2 and the Chinese Remainder Theorem. Exercise 5.28 gives the corresponding formula for polynomials over a finite field.

═══ COROLLARY 5.6. ═══════════════════════════════════

If $m = p_0^{e_0} \cdots p_{r-1}^{e_{r-1}}$, with distinct primes $p_0, \ldots, p_{r-1} \in \mathbb{N}$ and $e_0, \ldots, e_{r-1} \in \mathbb{N}_{>0}$, then

$$\varphi(m) = (p_0 - 1)p_0^{e_0 - 1} \cdots (p_{r-1} - 1)p_{r-1}^{e_{r-1} - 1} = m \cdot \prod_{p \mid m, \, p \text{ prime}} \left(1 - \frac{1}{p}\right).$$

▬▬ THEOREM 5.7. ▬▬▬▬▬▬▬▬▬▬▬▬▬▬▬▬▬▬▬▬▬▬▬▬▬▬▬▬▬

Let $R = F[x]$ for a field F, $m_0, \ldots, m_{r-1}, m \in R$ as in (5), $d_i = \deg m_i \geq 1$ for $0 \leq i < r$, $n = \deg m = \sum_{0 \leq i < r} d_i$, and $v_i \in R$ with $\deg v_i < d_i$. Then the unique solution $f \in F[x]$ with $\deg f < n$ of the Chinese Remainder Problem

$$f \equiv v_i \bmod m_i \text{ for } 0 \leq i < r$$

for polynomials can be computed using $O(n^2)$ operations in F. ▬▬▬▬▬▬▬▬

PROOF. In step 1 of Algorithm 5.4, we first successively compute $m_0, m_0 m_1, \ldots, m_0 \cdots m_{r-1}$ with at most

$$2 \sum_{1 \leq i < r} (d_0 + \ldots + d_{i-1} + 1)(d_i + 1) = 2 \sum_{0 \leq j < i < r} d_j(d_i + 1) + 2 \sum_{1 \leq i < r} (d_i + 1)$$

$$< 2 \sum_{0 \leq i, j < r} d_j(d_i + 1) = 2 \left(\sum_{0 \leq j < r} d_j \right) \left(\sum_{0 \leq i < r} (d_i + 1) \right) = 2n(n + r) \in O(n^2)$$

operations in F (Section 2.3).

Next, we compute m/m_i for $0 \leq i < r$ in step 2. Each division takes at most $(2d_i + 1)(n - d_i + 1)$ operations, as shown in Section 2.4, and together we have

$$\sum_{0 \leq i < r} (2d_i + 1)(n - d_i + 1) \leq 2n \sum_{0 \leq i < r} (d_i + 1) = 2n(n + r) \in O(n^2)$$

operations.

We fix $i \in \{0, \ldots, r-1\}$ in step 2. The Extended Euclidean Algorithm with input m/m_i and m_i takes $O(d_i(n - d_i))$ operations (Theorem 3.11). By the degree formula for s_i (Lemma 3.10), we have $\deg s_i < \deg m_i = d_i$, and hence the multiplication of v_i and s_i, together with the subsequent division with remainder by m_i, takes $O(d_i^2)$ operations. So we have $O(d_i n)$ operations for each i, and $O(n^2)$ for step 2.

Finally, in step 3 we need $O(d_i(n - d_i))$ operations for the multiplication of c_i and m/m_i for $0 \leq i < r$, and $O(rn)$ for the addition of all the products (their degree is strictly less than n). This gives a cost of $O(n^2)$ for step 3, and also a total cost of $O(n^2)$ for the whole algorithm. □

The following is the integer analog of Theorem 5.7; see Exercise 5.29.

▬▬ THEOREM 5.8. ▬▬▬▬▬▬▬▬▬▬▬▬▬▬▬▬▬▬▬▬▬▬▬▬▬▬▬▬▬▬

Let $R = \mathbb{Z}$, $m_0, \ldots, m_{r-1}, m \in \mathbb{N}$ as in (5), $n = \lfloor \log_2 m/64 \rfloor + 1$ the word length of m, and $v_i \in \mathbb{Z}$ such that $0 \leq v_i < m_i$ for $0 \leq i < r$. Then the unique solution $f \in \mathbb{Z}$ with $0 \leq f < m$ of the Chinese Remainder Problem

$$f \equiv v_i \bmod m_i \text{ for } 0 \leq i < r$$

for integers can be computed using $O(n^2)$ word operations. ▬▬▬▬▬▬▬▬▬▬▬

5.5. Modular determinant computation

We will use our tools from Section 5.4 on an innocuous problem, namely computing the determinant $\det A \in \mathbb{Z}$ of an $n \times n$ matrix $A = (a_{ij})_{1 \leq i,j \leq n} \in \mathbb{Z}^{n \times n}$.

We know from linear algebra (Section 25.5) that this problem can be solved by means of Gaussian elimination over $\mathbb{Q}$, which costs at most $2n^3$ operations in $\mathbb{Q}$. Is this "polynomial time"? Of course $2n^3$ is polynomial in the input size, but the number of word operations that the algorithm uses will also depend on the numerators and denominators of the intermediate results. How large can these grow? We consider the kth stage during the elimination, and suppose for simplicity that A is nonsingular and that no row or column permutations are necessary.

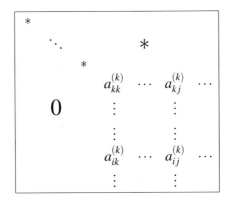

The table represents the matrix after $k-1$ pivoting stages, a "*" denotes an arbitrary rational number, and the upper diagonal entries are nonzero. The diagonal element $a_{kk}^{(k)} \neq 0$ is the new pivot element, and the entries of the kth column below the pivot element must be made zero in the kth stage by subtracting an appropriate multiple of the kth row. The entries of the matrix for $k < i \leq n$ and $k \leq j \leq n$ change according to the formula

$$a_{ij}^{(k+1)} = a_{ij}^{(k)} - \frac{a_{ik}^{(k)}}{a_{kk}^{(k)}} a_{kj}^{(k)} . \tag{8}$$

If b_k is an upper bound for the absolute value of the numerators and denominators of all $a_{ij}^{(k)}$ for $1 \leq i,j \leq n$, so that in particular $|a_{ij}| \leq b_0$ for $1 \leq i,j \leq n$, then the formula (8) gives

$$b_k \leq 2b_{k-1}^4 \leq 4b_{k-2}^{4^2} \leq \cdots \leq 2^k b_0^{4^k},$$

which is an exponentially large upper bound in the input size $n^2 \lambda(b_0) \approx n^2 \log_{2^{64}} b_0$ (see Section 2.1 for the definition of the length λ). At this point, we may wonder whether Gaussian elimination indeed uses polynomial time, if we count word operations. In fact, the length of the intermediate results and the number of word operations for Gaussian elimination over $\mathbb{Q}$ are polynomial in the input size, but the proof is nontrivial. We use an alternative approach to reach the same goal, a polynomial time algorithm for computing $\det A$. This illustrates modular computation in a simple case, and introduces some tools of more general interest.

The simplest way of obtaining a polynomial-time computation for the determinant $d = \det A$ of a matrix $A \in \mathbb{Z}^{n \times n}$ is to choose a prime p which is guaranteed to be bigger than $2|d|$, perform Gaussian elimination on $A \bmod p \in \mathbb{Z}_p^{n \times n}$ to calculate $d \bmod p$, and represent this value in the "symmetric" system

$$-\frac{p-1}{2}, \ldots, \frac{p-1}{2} \tag{9}$$

of representatives (if p is odd; see Section 4.1). If $r \in \mathbb{Z}$ is this representative, then

$$r \equiv d \bmod p, \quad -\frac{p}{2} < r < \frac{p}{2}.$$

The congruence holds since any polynomial expression like the determinant commutes with the canonical homomorphism $\mathbb{Z} \longrightarrow \mathbb{Z}_p$ (Section 25.3); so that the determinant, taken modulo p, of A equals the determinant in $\mathbb{Z}_p$ of the matrix $(A \bmod p) \in \mathbb{Z}_p^{n \times n}$ whose entries are those of A, taken modulo p. It follows that p divides $d - r$,

$$|d - r| \leq |d| + |r| < \frac{p}{2} + \frac{p}{2} = p,$$

and hence $d = r$.

We note the trivial but surprisingly useful fact that we used:

$$\text{if } a \mid b \text{ and } |b| < |a|, \text{ then } b = 0, \text{ for } a, b \in \mathbb{Z}. \tag{10}$$

The calculation of $\det(A \bmod p)$ is essentially the same as Gaussian elimination over $\mathbb{Q}$, except that when dividing by a pivot element a we have to calculate its inverse modulo p by the Extended Euclidean Algorithm 3.6. What have we gained? The big win is that we do not have to worry about the growth of the intermediate values anymore: they can always be represented in the system (9), and thus are always "small". It remains to determine a "good" a priori bound on $|\det A|$, that is, one that is only polynomially large in n and the size of the coefficients of A, and which is easy to find without actually calculating $\det A$. Such a bound is provided by **Hadamard's inequality** (Theorem 16.6) which says that $|\det A| \leq n^{n/2} B^n$, where $B = \max_{1 \leq i, j \leq n} |a_{ij}| \in \mathbb{N}$ is the maximal absolute value of an entry of A.

EXAMPLE 5.9. We let $A = \begin{pmatrix} 4 & 5 \\ 6 & -7 \end{pmatrix}$. After Gaussian elimination, the matrix has the form

$$\begin{pmatrix} 4 & 5 \\ 0 & -29/2 \end{pmatrix},$$

so that $\det A = -58$.

The Hadamard bound $|\det A| \le 2^{1}7^{2} = 98$ is reasonably close to $|\det A| = 58$. So for a modular computation, we choose a prime $p > 2 \cdot 98$, say $p = 199$, and perform Gaussian elimination modulo p. The inverse of the pivot element 4 is 50, and

$$\det(A \bmod 199) = \det \begin{pmatrix} 4 & 5 \\ 0 & 85 \end{pmatrix} = 141 = -58 \text{ in } \mathbb{Z}_{199}. \diamond$$

The word length $\lambda(C)$ of the bound $C = n^{n/2}B^{n}$ on $|\det A|$ is about $\frac{1}{64}\log_{2} C = \frac{1}{64}n(\frac{1}{2}\log_{2} n + \log_{2} B)$, and thus polynomial in the input size $n^{2}\lambda(B)$, and we will see in Section 18.4 that a prime p between, say, $2C$ and $4C$ can be found easily with a probabilistic polynomial-time algorithm. Then arithmetic modulo p can be performed in polynomial time, in fact, with $O(\log^{2} C)$ word operations. All entries of A are less than p in absolute value, and nothing happens computationally in reducing them modulo p. Thus the cost of the algorithm is $O(n^{3})$ operations modulo p, which shows that the determinant of an integer matrix can be computed with

$$O(n^{3} \cdot n^{2}(\log n + \log B)^{2}) \text{ or } O^{\sim}(n^{5}\log^{2} B) \tag{11}$$

word operations, where the $O^{\sim}$ notation ignores logarithmic factors (Section 25.7). This is polynomial time, but not cubic (in n)! Using the fast integer arithmetic of Part II, the running time can be reduced to $O^{\sim}(n^{4}\log B)$; this is softly quadratic in the input size. Well, should we call the running time of Gaussian elimination quadratic, cubic, quartic, or quintic?

The algorithm indicated above is not much progress over Gaussian elimination in $\mathbb{Q}$, except that we could easily prove that it works in polynomial time. The really big idea, however, is not to compute with a single modulus, but with several moduli at a time: **small primes modular computation**. These primes can then be chosen very small, of only logarithmic length, and the main cost of the resulting algorithm are many small Gaussian eliminations, which can be performed in a parallel or even distributed fashion. This method is much more efficient.

▬▬ ALGORITHM 5.10 Small primes modular determinant computation. ▬▬▬▬▬
Input: $A = (a_{ij})_{1 \le i,j \le n} \in \mathbb{Z}^{n \times n}$, with $|a_{ij}| \le B$ for all i, j.
Output: $\det A \in \mathbb{Z}$.

1. $C \longleftarrow n^{n/2}B^{n}, \quad r \longleftarrow \lceil \log_{2}(2C+1) \rceil$
   choose r distinct prime numbers $m_{0}, \ldots, m_{r-1} \in \mathbb{N}$

2. **for** $0 \le i < r$ compute $A \bmod m_{i}$

3. **for** $0 \le i < r$ **do**
   compute $d_{i} \in \{0, \ldots, m_{i} - 1\}$ such that $d_{i} \equiv \det A \bmod m_{i}$ using Gaussian elimination over $\mathbb{Z}_{m_{i}}$

4. **call** the Chinese Remainder Algorithm 5.4 to determine $d \in \mathbb{Z}$ of least absolute value with $d \equiv d_i \bmod m_i$ for $0 \leq i < r$

5. **return** d

Because $\det A$ is a polynomial expression in the coefficients of A, we have $\det A \equiv d_i \bmod m_i$ for $0 \leq i < r$ and hence $\det A \equiv d \bmod m$ by the Chinese Remainder Theorem, where $m = m_0 \cdots m_{r-1}$. Since $m \geq 2^r > 2n^{n/2}B^n \geq 2|d|$, we actually have $d = \det A$, as before.

EXAMPLE 5.11. We take the first four prime numbers as moduli and get

$$\det A \equiv 0 \bmod 2, \qquad \det A \equiv 2 \bmod 3,$$
$$\det A \equiv 2 \bmod 5, \qquad \det A \equiv -2 \bmod 7.$$

We have $m = 2 \cdot 3 \cdot 5 \cdot 7 = 210$, the solutions to the Chinese Remainder Problem $d \equiv d_i \bmod m_i$ for $1 \leq i \leq 4$ are $d \in -58 + 210\mathbb{Z} = \{\ldots, -268, -58, 152, 362, \ldots\}$, and the correct solution -58 is the one of least absolute value. If we had taken only the first three primes, we would have incorrectly computed $d = 2$. $\diamond$

For the cost analysis, Theorem 18.10 says that we can calculate the first r primes using $O(r\log^2 r \log\log r)$ word operations, and that $\log m_i \in O(\log r)$ for all i. (Actually, somewhat fewer than r primes are sufficient, see Exercise 18.21.) Thus $\log m = \sum_{0 \leq i < r} \log m_i \in O(r\log r)$. A single arithmetic operation modulo m_i can be done with $O(\log^2 m_i)$ or $O(\log^2 r)$ word operations, and hence the total cost of all Gaussian eliminations in step 3 is $O(n^3 r \log^2 r)$ word operations. The reduction of an entry of A modulo one modulus m_i takes $O(\lambda(m_i)\lambda(m/m_i))$ or $O(r\log^2 r)$ word operations, by Section 2.4. Therefore the reduction of all entries of A modulo $m_0, \ldots, m_{r-1}$ in step 2 takes $O(n^2 r^2 \log^2 r)$ word operations. The same estimate holds for step 4, by Theorem 5.8, and dominates the cost of step 1. The fact that $r \in O(n\log(nB))$ leads to the following theorem, which says that the small primes approach is faster by about one order of magnitude than the big prime algorithm.

THEOREM 5.12.
The determinant of a matrix $A \in \mathbb{Z}^{n \times n}$ with all entries less than B in absolute value can be computed deterministically with

$$O(n^4 \log^2(nB)(\log^2 n + (\log\log B)^2)) \text{ or } O^\sim(n^4 \log^2 B)$$

word operations.

In practice, one would precompute and store not the first r primes but r single precision primes close to the word size of the processor (say between 2^{63} and

$2^{64} - 1$ if the word size is 64). Exercise 18.18 shows that there are sufficiently many such single precision primes for all practical purposes. Then one operation modulo an m_i takes constant time, and the total cost is $O(n^3 r)$, plus $O(nr^2)$ for the initial modular reduction and the CRA, where r is about $\lambda(2C)$ or $O(n \log(nB))$. In contrast, the cost of the big prime variant is about $O(n^3 r^2)$ word operations.

Similarly to the integer case, a modular algorithm for computing determinants of matrices with entries in $F[x]$, where F is a field, can be designed. If the field is large enough, then this is even easier than the integer case (Exercise 5.32).

5.6. Hermite interpolation

Sections 5.6 through 5.11 are not essential for the rest of the text and may be skipped at first reading. In this section, we discuss an application of the Chinese Remainder Algorithm to **Hermite interpolation**. This is a generalization of polynomial interpolation where at each point not only the value of a function is prescribed, but also the values of some of the first few derivatives, or equivalently, an initial segment of the Taylor expansion.

If R is an arbitrary (commutative) ring, $f \in R[x]$ has degree at most n, and $u \in R$, then the **Taylor expansion of f around u** is

$$f = f_n \cdot (x-u)^n + \cdots + f_1 \cdot (x-u) + f_0, \tag{12}$$

where $f_n, \ldots, f_0 \in R$ are the **Taylor coefficients**. If $u = 0$, then this is just our usual way of writing polynomials. The Taylor coefficients are uniquely determined, and we have $f_n x^n + \cdots + f_1 x + f_0 = f(x+u)$, which is the polynomial f with x substituted by $x + u$. (Formally, this defines $f_n, \ldots, f_0 \in R[u]$, when we consider u as an indeterminate over R, and then (12) holds for this indeterminate and also for each value from R substituted for it.) For $R = \mathbb{Z}, \mathbb{Q}, \mathbb{R}$, or $\mathbb{C}$, the ith Taylor coefficient of f is equal to $f^{(i)}(u)/i!$, where $f^{(i)}$ is the ith derivative of f with respect to x, and (12) takes the more familiar form

$$f = \frac{f^{(n)}(u)}{n!} \cdot (x-u)^n + \cdots + \frac{f''(u)}{2} \cdot (x-u)^2 + f'(u) \cdot (x-u) + f(u).$$

Thus for $f \in \mathbb{Z}[x]$ and $n \in \mathbb{Z}$, $f^{(i)}(n)/i!$ is always an integer. For $e \leq n$, (12) implies that

$$f \equiv f_{e-1} \cdot (x-u)^{e-1} + \cdots + f_1 \cdot (x-u) + f_0 \bmod (x-u)^e. \tag{13}$$

We say that the right hand side of (13) is the **Taylor expansion of f around u of order e**.

Let F be a field, $u_0, \ldots, u_{r-1} \in F$ distinct, $e_0, \ldots, e_{r-1} \in \mathbb{N}$, and $v_0, \ldots, v_{r-1} \in F[x]$ with $\deg v_i < e_i$ for all i. The **Hermite interpolation problem** is then to compute a polynomial $f \in F[x]$ of degree less than $n = e_0 + \cdots + e_{r-1}$ such that for all i,

v_i is the Taylor expansion of f around u_i of order e_i, or equivalently, f solves the Chinese Remainder Problem

$$f \equiv v_i \bmod (x - u)^{e_i} \text{ for } 0 \le i < r. \tag{14}$$

EXAMPLE 5.13. We look for a polynomial $f \in \mathbb{Q}[x]$ of degree less than 4 such that

$$f(0) = 0, \ f'(0) = 1, \ f(1) = 1, \ f'(1) = 0, \tag{15}$$

Thus the initial segments of the Taylor expansions of f at $x = 0$ and $x = 1$ are $v_0 = f(0) + f'(0)x = x$ and $v_1 = f(1) + f'(x)(x - 1) = 1$, respectively, and the conditions (15) are equivalent to the congruences

$$f \equiv x \bmod x^2, \quad f \equiv 1 \bmod (x - 1)^2.$$

Here our moduli are $m_0 = x^2$ and $m_1 = (x - 1)^2$, and the Extended Euclidean Algorithm finds that $(-2x + 3)x^2 + (2x + 1)(x - 1)^2 = 1$. Thus $s_0 = 2x + 1$ and $s_1 = -2x + 3$ in step 2 of the Chinese Remainder Algorithm 5.4,

$$
\begin{aligned}
c_0 &= v_0 s_0 \text{ rem } m_0 = x \cdot (2x + 1) \text{ rem } x^2 = x, \\
c_1 &= v_1 s_1 \text{ rem } m_1 = 1 \cdot (-2x + 3) \text{ rem } (x - 1)^2 = -2x + 3,
\end{aligned}
$$

and finally

$$f = c_0 \frac{m}{m_0} + c_1 \frac{m}{m_1} = x(x - 1)^2 + (-2x + 3)x^2 = -x^3 + x^2 + x.$$

Thus $f' = -3x^2 + 2x + 1$, and we easily check that (15) is satisfied. $\diamond$

The Chinese Remainder Theorem 5.7 implies the following.

COROLLARY 5.14.
The Hermite interpolation problem (14) can be solved using $O(n^2)$ arithmetic operations in F.

5.7. Rational function reconstruction

In this section, we solve the problem of finding a rational function of small "degree" that is congruent to some polynomial modulo another polynomial. As a consequence, we obtain solutions for various interpolation problems, and in the most general form a "rational" Chinese Remainder Algorithm.

Let F be a field, $m \in F[x]$ of degree $n > 0$, and $f \in F[x]$ of degree less than n. For a given $k \in \{0, \dots, n\}$, we want to find a rational function $r/t \in F(x)$, with $r, t \in F[x]$, satisfying

$$\gcd(t, m) = 1 \text{ and } rt^{-1} \equiv f \bmod m, \quad \deg r < k, \quad \deg t \le n - k, \tag{16}$$

where t^{-1} is the modular inverse of t modulo m (Section 4.2). If $k = n$, then clearly $r = f$ and $t = 1$ is a solution, but it is not clear at all whether solutions exist for other values of k. The degree constraints in (16) are "natural" in the sense that, for fixed m, the input f has n coefficients, and the constraints leave exactly n "degrees of freedom" for the coefficients of r and t.

Since t is a unit modulo m, we may multiply the congruence in (16) by t to obtain an equivalent condition. When we drop the gcd requirement, we obtain

$$r \equiv tf \bmod m, \quad \deg r < k, \quad \deg t \le n - k. \tag{17}$$

Now this is a strictly weaker condition, and we will see that it can always be satisfied, but that there are (exceptional) cases where (16) has no solution.

The following lemma is in a sense the converse of Lemma 3.10, which states that the s_i, t_i in the Extended Euclidean Algorithm have small degrees. It says that any linear combination $r = sf + tg$ of f and g, where $f, g, r, s, t \in F[x]$ and the degrees of r, s, t are "small", is a multiple of some row $r_j = s_j f + t_j g$ in the EEA.

LEMMA 5.15. *Let F be a field, $f, g, r, s, t \in F[x]$ with $\deg f = n$, $r = sf + tg$ and $t \ne 0$, and suppose that*

$$\deg r + \deg t < n = \deg f.$$

Moreover, let r_i, s_i, t_i for $0 \le i \le \ell + 1$ be the rows of the Extended Euclidean Algorithm 3.6 for the pair (f, g). If we define $j \in \{1, \dots, \ell + 1\}$ by

$$\deg r_j \le \deg r < \deg r_{j-1}, \tag{18}$$

then there exists a nonzero $\alpha \in F[x]$ such that

$$r = \alpha r_j, \ s = \alpha s_j, \ t = \alpha t_j.$$

PROOF. First, we claim that $s_j t = st_j$. Suppose that the claim is false, and consider the equation

$$\begin{pmatrix} s_j & t_j \\ s & t \end{pmatrix} \begin{pmatrix} f \\ g \end{pmatrix} = \begin{pmatrix} r_j \\ r \end{pmatrix}.$$

The coefficient matrix is nonsingular, and we can solve for f in $F(x)$ using Cramer's rule (Theorem 25.6), obtaining

$$f = \frac{\det \begin{pmatrix} r_j & t_j \\ r & t \end{pmatrix}}{\det \begin{pmatrix} s_j & t_j \\ s & t \end{pmatrix}}. \tag{19}$$

The degree of the left hand side of (19) is n, while

$$
\begin{aligned}
\deg(r_j t - r t_j) \; &\leq \; \max\{\deg r_j + \deg t, \deg r + \deg t_j\} \\
&\leq \; \max\{\deg r + \deg t, \deg r + n - \deg r_{j-1}\} \\
&< \; \max\{n, \deg r_{j-1} + n - \deg r_{j-1}\} = n,
\end{aligned}
$$

by Lemma 3.10 and (18), and the degree of the right hand side of (19) is strictly less than n. Thus we have a contradiction, proving the claim.

Now, Lemma 3.8 implies that s_j and t_j are relatively prime, and from the claim we have $t_j \mid s_j t$, so that $t_j \mid t$. We write $t = \alpha t_j$, where $\alpha \in F[x]$, and $\alpha \neq 0$ since $t \neq 0$. Then we have $s t_j = s_j t = \alpha s_j t_j$, and cancelling t_j, we obtain $s = \alpha s_j$. Finally,

$$
r = sf + tg = \alpha(s_j f + t_j g) = \alpha r_j. \quad \square
$$

We now show that (17) can be solved by means of the Extended Euclidean Algorithm. We say that a rational function $r/t \in F(x)$, with $r, t \in F[x]$, is in **canonical form** if t is monic and $\gcd(r, t) = 1$. Every rational function has a unique canonical form.

▬▬ THEOREM 5.16. ▬▬
Let $m \in F[x]$ of degree $n > 0$ and $f \in F[x]$ of degree less than n. Furthermore, let $r_j, s_j, t_j \in F[x]$ be the jth row in the Extended Euclidean Algorithm for m, f, where j is minimal such that $\deg r_j < k$.

(i) *There exist polynomials $r, t \in F[x]$ satisfying (17), namely $r = r_j$ and $t = t_j$. If in addition $\gcd(r_j, t_j) = 1$, then r and t also solve (16).*

(ii) *If $r/t \in F(x)$ is a canonical form solution to (16), then $r = \tau^{-1} r_j$ and $t = \tau^{-1} t_j$, where $\tau = \mathrm{lc}(t_j) \in F \setminus \{0\}$. In particular, (16) is solvable if and only if $\gcd(r_j, t_j) = 1$.* ▬▬

PROOF. (i) We have $r_j = s_j m + t_j f \equiv t_j f \bmod m$ and

$$
\deg t_j = \deg r_0 - \deg r_{j-1} = n - \deg r_{j-1} \leq n - k,
$$

by Lemma 3.10 and the minimality of j, and hence $(r, t) = (r_j, t_j)$ satisfy (17). Here, r_{j-1} is the remainder in the EEA preceding r_j. Finally, Lemma 3.8 implies that $\gcd(m, t_j) = \gcd(r_j, t_j) = 1$, and the claim follows.

(ii) Let $s \in F[x]$ such that $r = sm + tf$. The degree constraints in (16) imply that $\deg r + \deg t < n = \deg m$. From Lemma 5.15, we conclude that $(r, t) = (\alpha r_j, \alpha t_j)$ for some nonzero $\alpha \in F[x]$. Since r and t are relatively prime and t is monic, $\alpha = \tau^{-1} \in F$ is constant and $\gcd(r_j, t_j) = 1$. $\square$

Using Theorem 3.11, we obtain the following.

━━ COROLLARY 5.17. ━━━━━━━━━━━━━━━━━━━━━━━━━━━━━
There is an algorithm which decides whether (16) is solvable, and if so, computes its unique solution using $O(n^2)$ operations in F. ━━━━━━━━━━━━━━━━━

input	moduli	polynomial output	rational function output
several values	$m_i = x - u_i$, u_i distinct	polynomial interpolation, §5.2	Cauchy interpolation, §5.8
Taylor expansion around 0	$m = x^n$		Padé approximation, §5.9
Taylor expansions around several u_i	$m_i = (x - u_i)^{e_i}$, u_i distinct	Hermite interpolation, §5.6	rational Hermite interpolation, Exercises 5.42, 5.43
remainder mod m	m arbitrary		rational function reconstruction, §5.7
remainders modulo several m_i	m_i arbitrary, pairwise coprime	CRA, §5.4	rational CRA, Exercise 5.42

TABLE 5.5: Various interpolation problems.

In the next two sections, several examples will illustrate Theorem 5.16. We will combine the Chinese Remainder Algorithm for polynomials with rational function reconstruction to solve various interpolation problems, depicted in Table 5.5. The problems will be precisely specified below. When the input consists of n items, we also have a degree constraint on the output which leaves n choices. Then the polynomial problems always have a solution, and the rational ones typically do, but not always. The next-to-last column in Table 5.5 can be considered as a special case of the last column. The third row is the "least common generalization" of the first two rows and a special case of the last row. The solution of these problems proceeds in two steps.

○ First a polynomial solution is computed, by the Chinese Remainder Algorithm. This was done in the preceding sections.

○ Then the required rational solution is calculated, via the Extended Euclidean Algorithm for the polynomial solution and a problem-specific modulus.

Like polynomial interpolation, Cauchy and Hermite interpolation and Padé approximation are well-studied problems in numerical analysis. The various designations illustrate the power of our general approach: people had found each of these problems interesting and studied them, and only in hindsight can we classify them as special instances of the single general task "rational CRA".

5.8. Cauchy interpolation

The polynomial interpolation problem is, given a collection of sample values $v_i = g(u_i) \in F$ for $0 \le i < n$ of an unknown function $g: F \longrightarrow F$ at distinct points $u_0, \ldots, u_{n-1}$ of a field F, to compute a polynomial $f \in F[x]$ of degree less than n that interpolates g at those points, so that $f(u_i) = v_i$ for all i. We saw in Section 5.2 that such a polynomial always exists uniquely and learned how to compute it using the Lagrange interpolation formula.

A more general problem is **Cauchy interpolation** or rational interpolation, where furthermore $k \in \{0, \ldots, n\}$ is given and we are looking for a rational function $r/t \in F(x)$, with $r, t \in F[x]$, such that

$$t(u_i) \ne 0 \text{ and } \frac{r(u_i)}{t(u_i)} = v_i \text{ for } 0 \le i < n, \quad \deg r < k, \quad \deg t \le n - k. \tag{20}$$

Like polynomial interpolation, Cauchy interpolation can be used to approximate real-valued functions given only by their values at a finite set of points. Empirically, it is often the case that the approximation error is smaller for rational functions than for polynomials, in particular, when the function to be approximated has singularities; we will see an example below.

Obviously $t = 1$ and $r = f$, where f is an interpolating polynomial as above, is a solution to (20) for $k = n$, but it is not clear whether solutions for other values of k exist. Multiplying (20) by $t(u_i)$ and dropping the requirement that it be nonzero, we obtain the weaker condition

$$r(u_i) = t(u_i)v_i \text{ for } 0 \le i < n, \quad \deg r < k, \quad \deg t \le n - k. \tag{21}$$

Now for any i, $r(u_i) = t(u_i)v_i = t(u_i)f(u_i)$ if and only if $r \equiv tf \mod (x - u_i)$, and by the Chinese Remainder Theorem 5.3, (21) is in turn equivalent to (17) with $m = (x - u_0) \cdots (x - u_{n-1})$. The following consequence of Theorem 5.16 on rational function reconstruction gives a complete answer on existence and uniqueness of a solution to (20).

COROLLARY 5.18.
Let F be a field, $u_0, \ldots, u_{n-1} \in F$ be distinct, $v_0, \ldots, v_{n-1} \in F$, $f \in F[x]$ of degree less than n with $f(u_i) = v_i$ for all i, and $k \in \{0, \ldots, n\}$. Furthermore, let $r_j, s_j, t_j \in F[x]$ be the jth row in the Extended Euclidean Algorithm for the polynomials $m = (x - u_0) \cdots (x - u_{n-1})$ and f, where j is minimal such that $\deg r_j < k$.

(i) There exist polynomials $r, t \in F[x]$ satisfying (21), namely $r = r_j$ and $t = t_j$. If in addition $\gcd(r_j, t_j) = 1$, then r and t also solve (20).

(ii) If $r/t \in F(x)$ is a canonical form solution to (20), then $r = \tau^{-1}r_j$ and $t = \tau^{-1}t_j$, where $\tau = \mathrm{lc}(t_j) \in F \setminus \{0\}$. In particular, (20) is solvable if and only if $\gcd(r_j, t_j) = 1$.

Thus to find a rational interpolating function as in (20), we compute the entries r_j and t_j in the jth row of the Extended Euclidean Algorithm for m, f, in the notation of the above corollary. If $\gcd(r_j, t_j) = 1$, then r_j/t_j is the unique canonical form solution to the rational interpolation problem (20). If the gcd is nontrivial, however, then also $\gcd(m, t_j) \neq 1$, by Lemma 3.8. Thus $t_j(u_i) = 0$ for some $i \in \{0, \ldots, n-1\}$, and (20) has no solution. (In numerical analysis, such a u_i is called an unreachable point.) A trivial example for the latter is when $k = 0$ and not all v_i are zero, so that $r = 0$ and $t = m$ satisfy (21) but not (20). More interesting is the following.

EXAMPLE 5.19. (i) Let $F = \mathbb{F}_5$, and suppose that we want to compute a rational function $\rho = r/t \in \mathbb{F}_5(x)$, with $r, t \in \mathbb{F}_5[x]$ of degree at most one, such that $\rho(i) = 2^i$ for $i = 0, 1, 2$. Exercise 5.4 computes the interpolating polynomial $f = 3x^2 + 3x + 1$ of degree less than 3. The Extended Euclidean Algorithm for $m = x(x-1)(x-2) = x^3 + 2x^2 + 2x$ and f computes

j	q_j	ρ_j	r_j	s_j	t_j
0		1	$x^3 + 2x^2 + 2x$	1	0
1	$x+1$	3	$x^2 + x + 2$	0	2
2	$x+4$	4	$x+2$	4	$2x+2$
3	$x+2$	4	1	$4x+1$	$2x^2+1$
4		1	0	x^2+x+2	$3x^3+x^2+x$

and from row 2 we get the desired rational function

$$\rho = \frac{r_2}{t_2} = \frac{x+2}{2x+2} = \frac{3x+1}{x+1} \in \mathbb{F}_5(x).$$

Row 3 gives another rational interpolating function, namely

$$\rho = \frac{r_3}{t_3} = \frac{1}{2x^2+1} = \frac{3}{x^2+3}.$$

Row 4 would yield $\rho = r_4/t_4 = 0$, but this is obviously not an interpolating function. We have $\gcd(r_4, t_4) = \gcd(m, t_4) = m$.

(ii) Let $F = \mathbb{Q}$, $n = 3$, $u_0 = 0$, $u_1 = 1$, $u_2 = -1$, $v_0 = 1$, $v_1 = 2$, $v_2 = 2$, and suppose that we are looking for a rational function $\rho = r/t \in \mathbb{Q}(x)$ satisfying (20) for $k = 2$. Making the ansatz $r = a_1 x + a_0$ and $t = b_1 x + b_0$ and plugging in u_0, u_1, u_2, we arrive at the linear system

$$a_0 = b_0, \quad a_1 + a_0 = 2(b_1 + b_0), \quad -a_1 + a_0 = 2(-b_1 + b_0),$$

which is equivalent to (21). It simplifies to

$$a_0 = b_0, \quad 2a_0 = 4b_0, \quad 2a_1 = 4b_1,$$

and hence $r = 2x$, $t = x$ form—up to multiplication by a constant—the unique solution of (21). However, the rational function

$$\rho = \frac{r}{t} = \frac{2x}{x} = 2$$

does not solve (20) since obviously $\rho(u_0) = \rho(0) \neq 1 = v_0$, and hence (20) has no solution.

The Extended Euclidean Algorithm for $m = x(x-1)(x+1) = x^3 - x$ and the interpolating polynomial $x^2 + 1$ yields

j	q_j	ρ_j	r_j	s_j	t_j
0		1	$x^3 - x$	1	0
1	x	1	$x^2 + 1$	0	1
2	x	-2	x	$-\frac{1}{2}$	$\frac{1}{2}x$
3	x	1	1	$\frac{1}{2}x$	$-\frac{1}{2}x^2 + 1$
4		1	0	$-\frac{1}{2}x^2 - \frac{1}{2}$	$\frac{1}{2}x^3 - \frac{1}{2}x$

We see from row 2 that $r = x$ and $t = -x/2$ solves (21), but we are not allowed to cancel the common factor x since $\rho = 2$ does not solve (20). $\diamond$

The alternative way of solving (21) via a system of linear equations, as we did above, works in general but is less efficient than the EEA.

▬ COROLLARY 5.20. ▬▬▬▬▬▬▬▬▬▬▬▬▬▬▬▬▬▬▬▬▬▬▬▬▬▬▬▬▬▬▬▬▬▬▬
There is an algorithm that either computes the canonical form solution to (20) or else certifies that (20) is unsolvable, using $O(n^2)$ arithmetic operations in F. ▬▬▬

5.9. Padé approximation

Let F be a field and $f = \sum_{i \geq 0} f_i x^i \in F[[x]]$ with all $f_i \in F$ be a formal power series (Section 25.3). A **Padé approximant** to f is a rational function $\rho = r/t \in F(x)$, with $r, t \in F[x]$ and $x \nmid t$, that "approximates" f to a sufficiently high power of x. More precisely, r/t is a $(k, n-k)$-**Padé approximant** to f if

$$x \nmid t \text{ and } \frac{r}{t} \equiv f \bmod x^n, \quad \deg r < k, \quad \deg t \leq n - k; \qquad (22)$$

the congruence is equivalent to $r \equiv tf \bmod x^n$. Obviously $r = \sum_{0 \leq i < n} f_i x^i$, the Taylor expansion of order n of f around 0, and $t = 1$ is an $(n, 0)$-Padé approximant for each $n \in \mathbb{N}$, but it is not clear whether approximants for $k < n$ exist. A more general question is to ask for Padé approximants around u of a formal power series in $x - u$ for an arbitrary $u \in F$. This may be reduced to (22) by performing the shift of variable $x \longmapsto x + u$.

In numerical analysis, one is interested in approximating arbitrary (sufficiently smooth) real-valued functions by "simple" functions such as polynomials or rational functions. Taylor expansions and Padé approximants provide such approximations in the vicinity of the origin (or any other point, after an appropriate change of variable). As in the case of interpolation, it was observed empirically that sometimes rational functions yield a much smaller approximation error, in particular when the function to be approximated has singularities; see Example 5.23 below.

The similarity with Cauchy interpolation is clear: instead of prescribing the values of ρ at n distinct points $u_0, \ldots, u_{n-1}$, we have $u_0 = \cdots = u_{n-1} = 0$ and prescribe an initial segment of the Taylor expansion of ρ at u_0. Indeed the statements of the previous section carry over almost literally if we replace $m = (x - u_0) \cdots (x - u_{n-1})$ by $m = x^n$. The following is a consequence of Theorem 5.16.

▬▬ COROLLARY 5.21. ▬▬▬▬▬▬▬▬▬▬▬▬▬▬▬▬▬▬▬▬▬▬▬▬▬▬
Let $f \in F[x]$ have degree less than $n \in \mathbb{N}$, $k \in \{0, \ldots, n\}$, and $r_j, s_j, t_j \in F[x]$ be the jth row in the Extended Euclidean Algorithm for $m = x^n$ and f, where j is minimal such that $\deg r_j < k$.

(i) *There exist polynomials $r, t \in F[x]$ satisfying*

$$r \equiv tf \bmod x^n, \quad \deg r < k, \quad \deg t \le n - k, \tag{23}$$

  namely $r = r_j$ and $t = t_j$. If in addition $\gcd(r_j, t_j) = 1$, then r and t also solve (22).

(ii) *If $r/t \in F(x)$ is a canonical form solution to (22), then $r = \tau^{-1} r_j$ and $t = \tau^{-1} t_j$, where $\tau = \mathrm{lc}(t_j) \in F \setminus \{0\}$. In particular, (22) is solvable if and only if $\gcd(r_j, t_j) = 1$.* ▬▬▬▬▬▬▬▬

EXAMPLE 5.22.   (i) Let $f = \sum_{i \ge 0}(i+1)x^i = 1 + 2x + 3x^2 + 4x^3 + \cdots \in \mathbb{F}_5[[x]]$, and suppose we want to compute a $(2,2)$-Padé approximant to f. The Extended Euclidean Algorithm 3.6 for $m = x^4$ and $4x^3 + 3x^2 + 2x + 1 \in \mathbb{F}_5[x]$ yields

j	q_j	ρ_j	r_j	s_j	t_j
0		1	x^4	1	0
1	$x+3$	4	$x^3 + 2x^2 + 3x + 4$	0	4
2	x	1	$x^2 + 2x + 3$	1	$x+3$
3	$x^2 + 2x + 3$	4	1	x	$x^2 + 3x + 1$
4		1		0	$4x^3 + 3x^2 + 2x + 1$	$4x^4$

and we can see in row 3 that

$$\frac{r_3}{t_3} = \frac{1}{x^2 + 3x + 1} = \frac{1}{(x-1)^2}$$

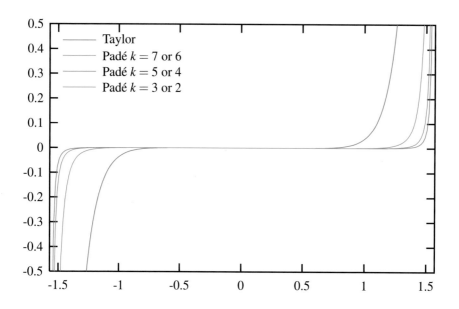

FIGURE 5.6: The difference of $\tan z$ to its Padé approximants of order 9 around the origin.

is the required solution. In fact, this is a $(k, n-k)$-Padé approximant to f for all values of $k \geq 1$ and n such that $n - k \geq 2$, since f is the formal derivative of the geometric series $1/(1-x) = \sum_{i \geq 0} x^i$, and hence $f = 1/(x-1)^2$ is the formal power series inverse of $(x-1)^2$.

The above table contains other Padé approximants to f: row 1 gives the trivial $(4,0)$ approximant $r_1/t_1 = 4x^3 + 3x^2 + 2x + 1$ and row 2 yields the $(3,1)$ approximant $r_2/t_2 = (x^2 + 2x + 3)/(x+3)$, but row 4 does not give a Padé approximant since x divides t_4, and in fact $r_4/t_4 = 0$ does not approximate f.

(ii) Let $f = x^2 + 1 \in \mathbb{Q}[[x]]$ and $n = 3$. Then there is no $(2,1)$-Padé approximant to f. To see why, we assume that there are polynomials $r, t \in \mathbb{Q}[x]$ of degree at most 1 such that $x \nmid t$ and $r \equiv tf \bmod x^3$. Let $t = ax + b$, with $a, b \in F$ and $b \neq 0$. Then

$$r \equiv (ax+b)(x^2+1) \equiv bx^2 + ax + b \bmod x^3,$$

which is impossible since $\deg r \leq 1$.

The Extended Euclidean Algorithm for $m = x^3$ and $x^2 + 1$ computes

j	q_j	ρ_j	r_j	s_j	t_j
0		1	x^3	1	0
1	x	1	x^2+1	0	1
2	x	-1	x	-1	x
3	x	1	1	x	$-x^2+1$
4		1	0	$-x^2-1$	x^3

and from row 2, we see that $r = t = x$ solve (23), but we are not allowed to divide the common factor x out of r and t, since $r/t = 1 \not\equiv x^2 + 1 \bmod x^3$. ◇

EXAMPLE 5.23. We want to approximate the tangent function in the vicinity of the origin with an approximation error of $O(z^9)$ when $z \in \mathbb{R}$ approaches 0. The Taylor series of $\tan z$ around the origin is

$$\tan z = z + \frac{1}{3}z^3 + \frac{2}{15}z^5 + \frac{17}{317}z^7 + \cdots$$

and converges for all $z \in \mathbb{C}$ such that $|z| < \pi/2$. At $z = \pm\pi/2 \approx \pm 1.57$, the tangent function has simple poles. The Taylor polynomial of order 9 is

$$f = \frac{17}{317}x^7 + \frac{2}{15}x^5 + \frac{1}{3}x^3 + x \in \mathbb{Q}[x],$$

and using rational function reconstruction, we obtain the Padé approximants of order $n = 9$ in Table 5.7. (We have not made the denominators monic.) The

	$k = 9$ or 8	$k = 7$ or 6	$k = 5$ or 4	$k = 3$ or 2
f	$\dfrac{x^5 + 45x^3 - 630x}{255x^2 - 630}$	$\dfrac{-10x^3 + 105x}{x^4 - 45x^2 + 105}$		$\dfrac{-945x}{2x^6 + 21x^4 + 315x^2 - 945}$

TABLE 5.7: The Padé approximants of order 9 to the tangent function.

approximations are so good that in a plot it is hard to tell them apart from the tangent function. Instead, Figure 5.6 on page 114 shows the difference between the tangent function and each of the four Padé approximants from Table 5.7 on the interval $(-\pi/2, \pi/2)$. It can be seen that the Padé approximant for $k = 5$ or 4 is the best one. For example, its approximation error to $\tan(1.5) \approx 14.1$ is about 0.059, while the Taylor polynomial has an approximation error of about 9.54 at that point. ◇

Corollary 5.21 yields a decision procedure for Padé approximants: Compute the appropriate results r_j and t_j of the Extended Euclidean Algorithm. If their gcd is one, then r_j/t_j is the unique $(k, n-k)$-Padé approximant as in (22), otherwise no such approximant exists.

COROLLARY 5.24.
There is an algorithm that either computes the canonical form solution to (22) or else certifies that (22) is unsolvable, using $O(n^2)$ arithmetic operations in F.

This algorithm will be put to use in Chapter 7. Using the fast Euclidean Algorithm from Chapter 11, the running time drops to $O(n \log^2 n \log\log n)$ arithmetic operations in F.

5.10. Rational number reconstruction

The integer analog of rational function reconstruction is, given integers $m > f \geq 0$ and $k \in \{1,\ldots,m\}$, to compute a rational number $r/t \in \mathbb{Q}$, with $r,t \in \mathbb{Z}$, such that

$$\gcd(t,m) = 1 \text{ and } rt^{-1} \equiv f \bmod m, \quad |r| < k, \quad 0 \leq t \leq \frac{m}{k}, \qquad (24)$$

where t^{-1} is the inverse of t modulo m. As in the polynomial case, we will see that the related problem

$$r \equiv tf \bmod m, \quad |r| < k, \quad 0 \leq t \leq \frac{m}{k}, \qquad (25)$$

is always solvable, while (24) need not have a solution. The uniqueness statements are a bit weaker than in the polynomial case, however. The following lemma is the integer analog of Lemma 5.15.

LEMMA 5.25. *Let $f,g \in \mathbb{N}$ and $r,s,t \in \mathbb{Z}$ with $r = sf + tg$, and suppose that*

$$|r| < k \text{ and } 0 < t \leq \frac{f}{k} \text{ for some } k \in \{1,\ldots,f\}.$$

We let $r_i, s_i, t_i \in \mathbb{Z}$ for $0 \leq i \leq \ell+1$ be the results of the Extended Euclidean Algorithm for f,g, so that $r_i \geq 0$ for all i, and define $j \in \{1,\ldots,\ell+1\}$ and $q \in \mathbb{N}_{\geq 1}$ by

$$r_j < k \leq r_{j-1}, \qquad (26)$$
$$r_{j-1} - qr_j < k \leq r_{j-1} - (q-1)r_j.$$

Then there exists a nonzero $\alpha \in \mathbb{Z}$ such that

$$\text{either } (r,s,t) = (\alpha r_j, \alpha s_j, \alpha t_j) \text{ or } (r,s,t) = (\alpha r_j^*, \alpha s_j^*, \alpha t_j^*),$$

where $r_j^* = r_{j-1} - qr_j$, $s_j^* = s_{j-1} - qs_j$, and $t_j^* = t_{j-1} - qt_j$.

PROOF. Multiplying $r_j = s_j f + t_j g$ by t and $r = sf + tg$ by t_j and subtracting, we obtain

$$r_j t - rt_j = s_j tf - st_j f \equiv 0 \bmod f. \qquad (27)$$

By (26), we have $0 \leq r_j t < kt \leq f$ and $|rt_j| < kf/r_{j-1} \leq f$, using Lemma 3.12. Thus either $r_j t = rt_j$ or $r_j t = rt_j + f$. In the first case, (27) implies that $s_j t = st_j$, and since $\gcd(s_j, t_j) = 1$ by Lemma 3.8, we have $t = \alpha t_j$ for some $\alpha \in \mathbb{Z}$; α is nonzero since t is. Finally, $st_j = s_j t = s_j \alpha t_j$ and $rt_j = r_j t = r_j \alpha t_j$, and hence $s = \alpha s_j$ and $r = \alpha r_j$ since $t_j \neq 0$.

Before we tackle the second case, we note that

$$r_j t_j^* - r_j^* t_j = r_j(t_{j-1} - qt_j) - (r_{j-1} - qr_j)t_j = r_j t_{j-1} - r_{j-1}t_j = (-1)^j f, \quad (28)$$
$$s_j t_j^* - s_j^* t_j = s_j(t_{j-1} - qt_j) - (s_{j-1} - qs_j)t_j = s_j t_{j-1} - s_{j-1}t_j = (-1)^j, \quad (29)$$

by Lemma 3.8. So we assume now that

$$r_j t = r t_j + f. \tag{30}$$

Then $r_j \neq 0$ and $r t_j < 0$. We claim that $r_j^* t = r t_j^*$. In analogy to (27), we have

$$r_j^* t - r t_j^* = s_j^* t f - s t_j^* f \equiv 0 \bmod f.$$

Since t_{j-1} and t_j alternate in sign (Exercise 3.15), so do t_j and t_j^*, whence $r t_j^* > 0$ and

$$r_j^* t - r t_j^* < k t - r t_j^* \leq f - r t_j^* < f.$$

On the other hand, using (30) and (28) we obtain

$$r_j(r_j^* t - r t_j^*) = r_j^*(f - r t_j) - r((-1)^j f - r_j^* t_j) = (r_j^* - (-1)^j r)f > -r_j f,$$

since $r_j^* + r_j = r_{j-1} - (q-1)r_j \geq k > |r| \geq (-1)^j r$, by the choice of q. After dividing by the positive integer r_j, we obtain $r_j^* t - r t_j^* > -f$, and the claim follows.

As in the first case, we conclude that $s_j^* t = s t_j^*$. Then equation (29) implies that $\gcd(s_j^*, t_j^*) = 1$ and $t = \alpha t_j$ for some nonzero $\alpha \in \mathbb{Z}$, and finally $s = \alpha s_j^*$ and $r = \alpha r_j^*$, as above. $\square$

The next theorem is an integer variant of Theorem 5.16. We say that a rational number $r/t \in \mathbb{Q}$, with $r, t \in \mathbb{Z}$, is in **canonical form** if $t > 0$ and $\gcd(r, t) = 1$.

▬▬ THEOREM 5.26. ▬▬▬▬▬▬▬▬▬▬▬▬▬▬▬▬▬▬▬▬▬▬▬▬▬▬▬
Let $f, m \in \mathbb{N}$ with $f < m$, $k \in \{1, \ldots, m\}$, and $r_j, s_j, t_j \in \mathbb{Z}$ be the jth row in the Extended Euclidean Algorithm for m and f, where j is minimal such that $r_j < k$.

(i) *There exist $r, t \in \mathbb{Z}$ satisfying (25), namely $(r, t) = (r_j, t_j)$ if $t_j > 0$, and $(r, t) = (-r_j, -t_j)$ otherwise. If in addition $\gcd(r, t) = \gcd(r_j, t_j) = 1$, then r and t also solve (24).*

(ii) *If $r/t \in \mathbb{Q}$ is a canonical form solution to (24), then either $(r, t) = (\tau r_j, \tau t_j)$ or $(r, t) = (\tau r_j^*, \tau t_j^*)$, where r_j^*, t_j^* are as in Lemma 5.25 and $\tau = \mathrm{sgn}(t_j)$ or $\tau = \mathrm{sgn}(t_j^*)$, respectively.*

(iii) *Equation (24) is solvable if and only if $(\gcd(r_j^*, t_j^*) = 1$ and $t_j^* \leq m/k)$ or $\gcd(r_j, t_j) = 1$.*

(iv) *There is at most one canonical form solution to (24) satisfying $|r| < k/2$.*

PROOF.   (i) We have $r_j = s_j m + t_j f \equiv t_j f \bmod m$, and conclude from Lemma 3.12 that

$$|t_j| \leq \frac{m}{r_{j-1}} \leq \frac{m}{k},$$

by the minimality of j. This proves that $(r,t) = (\pm r_j, \pm t_j)$ solve (25). The proof of the other claim is as in Theorem 5.16.

(ii) Letting $s = (r - tf)/m$, Lemma 5.25 implies that either $(r,t) = (\alpha r_j, \alpha t_j)$ or $(r,t) = (\alpha r_j^*, \alpha t_j^*)$ for some nonzero $\alpha \in \mathbb{Z}$. Furthermore, $\gcd(r,t) = 1$ implies that $\alpha = \pm 1$, and the claim follows.

(iii) By (i), $(\pm r_j, \pm t_j)$ is a canonical form solution of (24) if and only if r_j and t_j are coprime. Since $r_j^* < k$, the pair $(\pm r_j^*, \pm t_j^*)$ is a canonical form solution if and only if $t_j^* \leq m/k$ and $\gcd(r_j^*, t_j^*) = 1$. By (ii), these are the only possible solutions.

(iv) Let both r/t and r^*/t^* be canonical form solutions of (24) with $|r| < k/2$ and $|r^*| < k/2$. Since m divides $r - tf$ and $r^* - t^* f$, it also divides $t^*(r - tf) - t(r^* - t^* f) = rt^* - r^* t$. But $|r|t^* < m/2$ and $|r^*|t < m/2$, whence $rt^* = r^* t$. The claim now follows from $\gcd(r,t) = \gcd(r^*, t^*) = 1$. $\square$

We note that $t_j t_j^* < 0$ (Exercise 3.15) and $r_j, r_j^* \geq 0$, and hence the two possible solutions r_j/t_j and r_j^*/t_j^* of (24) have opposite signs (as rational numbers).

EXAMPLE 5.27.   (i) The Extended Euclidean Algorithm for $m = 29$ and $f = 12$ works as follows:

j	q_j	r_j	s_j	t_j
0		29	1	0
1	2	12	0	1
2	2	5	1	-2
3	2	2	-2	5
4	2	1	5	-12
5		0	-12	29

For $k = 10$, the smallest j such that $r_j \leq k$ is $j = 2$, and in fact $r_2/t_2 = -5/2 \equiv 12 \bmod 29$. Now $r_1 - (q-1)r_2 \geq k > r_1 - qr_2$ is satisfied for $q = 1$, whence $r_2^* = r_1 - r_2 = 7$ and $t_2^* = t_1 - t_2 = 3$. But $|t_2^*| = 3 > 29/10 = m/k$, and hence $-5/2$ is the only solution of (25) and (24).

For $k = 9$, j and q are as before, but now $|t_2^*| = 3 \leq 29/9 = m/k$, and we have a second solution $r_2^*/t_2^* = 7/3 \equiv 12 \bmod 29$ of (25) and (24).

(ii) For $m = 22$ and $f = 9$, the Extended Euclidean Algorithm gives

j	q_j	r_j	s_j	t_j
0		22	1	0
1	2	9	0	1
2	2	4	1	-2
3	4	1	-2	5
4		0	9	-22

For $k = 10$, we have $j = 1$, and $r_1/t_1 = 9/1$ is obviously a solution of (24). Now $q = 1$, $(r_1^*, t_2^*) = (r_2, t_2) = (4, -2)$, and $|t_1^*| = 2 \leq 22/10 = m/k$, whence (r_1^*, t_1^*) is a second solution of (25). But $\gcd(r_1^*, t_1^*) = 2$, and $r_1^*/t_1^* = -2$ is not a solution of (24). Thus we have two solutions of (25), but only one of them also solves (24).

For $k = 9$, we have $j = 2$, and $(r_2, t_2) = (4, -2)$ is a solution of (25), but not of (24). Here, $q = 1$ and $(r_2^*, t_2^*) = (r_1 - r_2, t_1 - t_2) = (5, 3)$, but $|t_2^*| = 3 > 22/9 = m/k$, and hence (r_2^*, t_2^*) does not solve (25), so that (25) has a unique solution and (24) is unsolvable.

If $k = 7$, however, then j and q are as before, but now $|t_2^*| = 3 \leq 22/7 = m/k$, and $r_2^*/t_2^* = 5/3$ is the only solution of (24).

(iii) Let $m = 36$ and $f = 13$. The Extended Euclidean Algorithm for m and f yields

j	q_j	r_j	s_j	t_j
0		36	1	0
1	2	13	0	1
2	1	10	1	-2
3	3	3	-1	3
4	3	1	4	-11
5		0	-13	36

and for $k = 11$ we find that $j = 2$, $(r_2, t_2) = (10, -2)$ solves (25) but not (24), $q = 1$, and $(r_2^*, t_2^*) = (r_1 - r_2, t_1 - t_2) = (3, 3)$ also solves (25) but not (24). Thus (25) has two solutions while (24) has none. ◇

Together with the Chinese Remainder Algorithm for integers, Theorem 5.26 leads to a Chinese Remainder Algorithm for rational numbers (Exercise 5.44).

5.11. Partial fraction decomposition

We discuss another one of the numerous applications of the Chinese Remainder Theorem for polynomials. It will be put to use in Chapter 22.

Let F be a field, $f_1, \ldots, f_r \in F[x]$ nonconstant monic and pairwise coprime polynomials, $e_1, \ldots, e_r \in \mathbb{N}$ positive integers, and $f = f_1^{e_1} \cdots f_r^{e_r}$. (We will see in Part III how to factor polynomials over finite fields and over $\mathbb{Q}$ into irreducible factors, but here we do not assume irreducibility of the f_i.) For another polynomial $g \in F[x]$ of degree less than $n = \deg f$, the **partial fraction decomposition** of the rational function $g/f \in F(x)$ with respect to the given factorization of the denominator f is

$$\frac{g}{f} = \frac{g_{1,1}}{f_1} + \cdots + \frac{g_{1,e_1}}{f_1^{e_1}} + \quad \cdots \quad + \frac{g_{r,1}}{f_r} + \cdots + \frac{g_{r,e_r}}{f_r^{e_r}}, \tag{31}$$

with $g_{ij} \in F[x]$ of smaller degree than f_i, for all i, j. If all f_i are linear polynomials, then the g_{ij} are just constants.

EXAMPLE 5.28. Let $F = \mathbb{Q}$, $f = x^4 - x^2$, and $g = x^3 + 4x^2 - x - 2$. The partial fraction decomposition of g/f with respect to the factorization $f = x^2(x-1)(x+1)$ of f into linear polynomials is

$$\frac{x^3 + 4x^2 - x - 2}{x^4 - x^2} = \frac{1}{x} + \frac{2}{x^2} + \frac{1}{x-1} + \frac{-1}{x+1}. \quad \diamondsuit \tag{32}$$

The following questions pose themselves: Does a decomposition as in (31) always exist uniquely, and how can we compute it? The next lemma is a first step towards an answer.

LEMMA 5.29. *There exist unique polynomials $c_i \in F[x]$ with $\deg c_i < e_i \deg f_i$ for all i such that*

$$\frac{g}{f} = \frac{c_1}{f_1^{e_1}} + \cdots + \frac{c_r}{f_r^{e_r}}. \tag{33}$$

PROOF. We multiply both sides in (34) by f and obtain the linear equation

$$g = c_1 \prod_{j \neq 1} f_j^{e_j} + \cdots + c_r \prod_{j \neq r} f_j^{e_j} \tag{34}$$

with "unknowns" $c_1, \ldots, c_r$. (We have already seen in Section 4.5 how to find polynomial solutions of such equations.) For any $i \leq r$, each summand with the possible exception of the ith one is divisible by $f_i^{e_i}$, whence $g \equiv c_i \prod_{j \neq i} f_j^{e_j} \bmod f_i^{e_i}$. Now each f_j is coprime to f_i and hence invertible modulo $f_i^{e_i}$, and we obtain

$$c_i \equiv g \prod_{j \neq i} f_j^{-e_j} \bmod f_i^{e_i}, \tag{35}$$

which together with $\deg c_i < \deg f_i^{e_i}$ uniquely determines c_i.

On the other hand, if we define $c_i \in F[x]$ of degree less than $e_i \deg f_i$ by (35), for all i, and let g^* be the right-hand side in (34), then g^* is a polynomial of degree less than n and $g^* \equiv g \bmod f_i^{e_i}$ for all i. Now the Chinese Remainder Theorem implies that $g^* \equiv g \bmod f$, and since both polynomials have degree less than n, they are equal. $\square$

It remains to say how to obtain the decomposition (31) from (33). This uses the following generalization of the Taylor expansion. Let R be a ring (commutative, with 1) and $a, p \in R[x]$ with p monic of degree $m > 0$ and a of degree less than km, for some $k, m \in \mathbb{N}$. The *p*-**adic expansion** of a is

$$a = a_{k-1} p^{k-1} + \cdots + a_1 p + a_0, \tag{36}$$

where $a_0, \ldots, a_{k-1} \in R[x]$ have degree less than m. If $p = x - u$ is a linear polynomial, then the a_j are constants, and (36) is just the Taylor expansion of a around u. If a, p are positive integers and $0 \leq a_i < p$ for all i, then (36) is the familiar radix p representation of a.

LEMMA 5.30. *The p-adic expansion exists uniquely, and it can be computed using at most* $(km)^2 - km^2$ *operations in R.*

PROOF. Dividing a by p with remainder yields $a = qp + r$, with $q, r \in R[x]$ such that $\deg r < m$. Taking $a_0 = r$ and recursively computing the p-adic expansion $q = a_{k-1}p^{k-2} + \cdots + a_1$ of q, we obtain the p-adic expansion of a. This proves the existence. For the uniqueness, let $a = a_{k-1}^* p^{k-1} + \cdots + a_1^* p + a_0^*$ be another p-adic expansion. Then a_0^* is the remainder and $a_{k-1}^* p^{k-2} + \cdots + a_1^*$ is the quotient of a on division by p. By induction, the p-adic expansion of the quotient is unique, and hence so is the p-adic expansion of a.

The cost for the first division with remainder is $2 \deg p(1 + \deg a - \deg p) \le 2m^2(k-1)$, and hence the total number of operations in R is at most

$$2m^2 \sum_{1 \le i \le k-1} i = m^2(k^2 - k). \quad \square$$

Putting it all together, we have the following theorem.

═══ THEOREM 5.31. ═══

The partial fraction decomposition (31) exists uniquely, and it can be computed using $O(n^2)$ operations in F. ════════════════════════

PROOF. The existence follows from the preceding two lemmas by taking the f_i-adic expansion $c_i = g_{i,e_i} f_i^{e_i-1} + \cdots + g_{i,2} f_i + g_{i,1}$ with $g_{ij} \in F[x]$ of degree less than $\deg f_i$ for all i, j. If

$$\frac{g}{f} = \frac{g_{1,1}^*}{f_1} + \cdots + \frac{g_{1,e_1}^*}{f_1^{e_1}} + \cdots + \frac{g_{r,1}^*}{f_r} + \cdots + \frac{g_{r,e_r}^*}{f_r^{e_r}}$$

is another partial fraction decomposition of g/f, with $g_{ij}^* \in F[x]$ of degree less than $\deg f_i$ for all i, j, then Lemma 5.29 implies that $c_i = g_{i,e_i}^* f_i^{e_i-1} + \cdots + g_{i,2} f_i + g_{i,1}^*$ for all i, and the uniqueness of the f_i-adic expansion implies that $g_{ij} = g_{ij}^*$, for all i, j.

To prove the running time bound, we let $d_i = e_i \deg f_i$ and compute $m_i = f_i^{e_i}$ and $v_i = g \operatorname{rem} f_i^{e_i}$, at a cost of $O(nd_i)$ operations in F altogether, for $1 \le i \le r$, taking in total $O(n^2)$ operations. Then we perform steps 1 and 2 of the Chinese Remainder Algorithm 5.4 with input $m_1, \ldots, m_r$ and $v_1, \ldots, v_r$ to compute $c_i \equiv v_i(f/m_i)^{-1} \equiv g(f/f_i^{e_i})^{-1}$ for all i, taking another $O(n^2)$ operations, by Theorem 5.7. Finally, we compute the f_i-adic expansion of c_i, taking $O(d_i^2)$ operations, by Lemma 5.30, for all i. This is dominated by the cost for the first step, and the claim follows. $\square$

EXAMPLE 5.28 (continued). With f and g as in Example 5.28, we have $m_1 = x^2$, $m_2 = x - 1$, $m_3 = x + 1$, and $f = m_1 m_2 m_3$. Now $v_1 = g \operatorname{rem} x^2 = -x - 2$, $v_2 = $

g rem $x - 1 = 2$, and $v_3 = g$ rem $x + 1 = 2$. Then step 2 of the Chinese Remainder Algorithm 5.4 computes

$$c_1 \equiv v_1 \left(\frac{m}{m_1} \right)^{-1} = (-x - 2)(x^2 - 1)^{-1} \equiv (-x - 2)(-1)^{-1} = x + 2 \bmod x^2,$$

$$c_2 \equiv v_2 \left(\frac{m}{m_2} \right)^{-1} = 2(x^3 + x^2)^{-1} \equiv 2 \cdot 2^{-1} = 1 \bmod x - 1,$$

$$c_3 \equiv v_3 \left(\frac{m}{m_3} \right)^{-1} = 2(x^3 - x^2)^{-1} \equiv 2 \cdot (-2)^{-1} = -1 \bmod x + 1,$$

and hence

$$\frac{x^3 + 4x^2 - x - 2}{x^4 + x} = \frac{x + 2}{x^2} + \frac{1}{x - 1} + \frac{-1}{x + 1}.$$

Using the x-adic expansion $1 \cdot x + 2$ of $x + 2$ immediately leads to (32). ◇

A different way to compute the partial fraction decomposition (31) is to plug in the g_{ij} with unknown coefficients, clear up denominators, and solve the linear system that arises from comparing coefficients on both sides. The coefficient matrix of the linear system is an $n \times n$ matrix, and its solution using Gaussian elimination takes $O(n^3)$ operations in F (Section 25.5). However, the method suggested in the above theorem is faster by one order of magnitude. Using asymptotically fast algorithms for division with remainder (Section 9.2) and Chinese remaindering (Section 10.3), the time even drops to $O(n \log^2 n \log \log n)$.

Notes.   **5.1.** A general theory of these representations and conversions for polynomials and rational functions is in von zur Gathen (1986).

5.2. The Lagrange interpolant was invented in Waring (1779) and Lagrange (1795), page 286.

5.3. The secret sharing scheme is from Shamir (1979). Asmuth & Blakley (1982) propose the use the CRA for fault-tolerant communication, and Rabin (1989) uses interpolation.

5.4. The name of the Chinese Remainder Theorem derives from the *Suan-ching* (arithmetic) of Sun-Tsŭ, written about the first century AD. He solves a particular problem (Exercise 5.15) in verse-form, using the integer versions of the "Lagrange interpolants" l_i as in the proof of Theorem 5.2; see Shen (1988) and Ku & Sun (1992). Variants of the question appear later in Chinese, Indian, and European mathematics, for example in Schwenter (1636), 3. Auffgab, with moduli 3, 5, 7, and 8. General solutions are due to Euler (1734/35a, 1747/48), Lagrange (1770b), §25, Gauß (1801), article 32, and Cauchy (1841). Euler (1760/61) proved Corollary 5.6 about his totient function, and also that $a^k \equiv 1 \bmod m$ when $\gcd(a, m) = 1$ and $k = \text{lcm}(\varphi(p_0^{e_0}), \dots, \varphi(p_{r-1}^{e_{r-1}}))$, where $m = p_0^{e_0} \cdots p_{r-1}^{e_{r-1}}$ is the prime factorization of m (see Exercise 18.13); this is also in Gauß (1801), article 92. Since Gauß (1801), article 38, the notation φ is used.

In a more general version of the Chinese Remainder Theorem, the moduli m_i are not required to be pairwise coprime, but only that $v_i \equiv v_j \bmod \gcd(m_i, m_j)$ for all i, j.

5.5. Gauß introduced his elimination method for astronomical calculations (Gauß 1809, article 182; Gauß 1810). Lagrange (1759) presented a similar procedure for 2×2 and 3×3 matrices. Edmonds (1967) and Bareiss (1968) showed that the intermediate results of Gaussian elimination over $\mathbb{Q}$ are polynomially bounded.

Early suggestions for modular computer arithmetic are in Svoboda & Valach (1955, 1957) and Garner (1959); see Szabó & Tanaka (1967) for a discussion.

5.8. Cauchy (1821) discusses his rational interpolation problem without paying attention to its solvability. Kronecker (1881a), page 544, was the first to point out the *bisher wohl noch nicht bemerkte Einschränkung der Lösbarkeit der Cauchy'schen Aufgabe*[1], namely, that (20) may have no solution (see Exercise 5.36).

5.9. The Padé approximation problem derives its name from Padé's (1892) dissertation. It is a bit of a misnomer, since Kronecker (1881a) already stated and solved the problem, also proving the necessary and sufficient conditions for solvability (Corollary 5.21). However, Kronecker's approach was purely algebraic (as is ours), while Padé also considered functions like $\exp(x)$ and brought these approximations to the attention of numerical analysts. Jacobi (1846) had given an explicit solution to (23). Frobenius (1881) describes relations between the various Padé approximants of one power series.

Baker & Graves-Morris (1996) explain in detail the theory of Padé approximants, its connection with continued fractions, and its application to root and singularity finding, convergence acceleration, and various other problems in numerical analysis and theoretical physics. They also discuss the numerical stability of different methods for computing Padé approximants.

5.10. Theorem 5.26 is essentially in Kaltofen & Rolletschek (1989). The existence of a solution to (25) in the special case where $k = \lfloor \sqrt{m} \rfloor + 1$ was shown by Thue (1902).

5.11. The partial fraction decomposition is described in Euler (1748a), §39 ff.

Exercises.

5.1 Let $m_0, \ldots, m_r \in \mathbb{N}_{\geq 2}$.

(i) Prove that every nonnegative integer $a < m_0 \cdots m_r$ has a **mixed-radix representation** of the form
$$a = a_0 + a_1 m_0 + a_2 m_0 m_1 \cdots + a_r m_0 \cdots m_{r-1},$$
with unique integers a_i satisfying $0 \leq a_i < m_i$ for all i. Relate this to the usual p-adic representation of an integer a, for an integer $p > 1$.

(ii) Compute the above representation of $a = 42$ for $m_0 = 2$, $m_1 = 3$, $m_2 = 2$, and $m_3 = 5$.

(iii) What is the analogous mixed-radix representation for polynomials?

5.2* Let $a = s/t \in \mathbb{Q}$, with coprime $s, t \in \mathbb{N}$ such that $0 < s < t$. With respect to an arbitrary base $p \in \mathbb{N}_{\geq 2}$, a has a unique periodic p-adic expansion
$$a = \sum_{i \geq 1} a_i p^{-i},$$
with all $a_i \in \{0, \ldots, p-1\}$. We say that this expansion is purely periodic if there is a positive $l \in \mathbb{N}$ such that $a_{i+l} = a_i$ for all $i \geq 1$, and the least such l is the length of the period. Moreover, we let $k \in \mathbb{N}$ be the smallest integer such that the sequence $a_{k+1}, a_{k+2}, \ldots$ is purely periodic, and call it the length of the preperiod. For example, the 10-adic representation of $1/6$ is $0.1\overline{6} = 1 \cdot 10^{-1} + \sum_{i \geq 2} 6 \cdot 10^{-i}$, with $k = l = 1$.

---
[1] *constraint on the solvability of Cauchy's problem, apparently unnoticed hitherto*

(i) Show that there exist unique $t^*, u \in \mathbb{N}$ with $t = ut^*$ such that $\gcd(p, t^*) = 1$ and every prime divisor of u divides p.

(ii) Prove that the p-adic expansion of a terminates (so that only finitely many a_i are nonzero) if and only if $t^* = 1$.

(iii) Show that the p-adic expansion of a is purely periodic if and only if p and t are coprime, and that then $l = \mathrm{ord}_t(p)$, the order of p in the multiplicative group $\mathbb{Z}_t^\times$.

(iv) Prove that $l = \mathrm{ord}_{t^*}(p)$ and $k = \min\{n \in \mathbb{N} : u \mid p^n\}$ in the general case.

(v) Conclude that $l \leq \varphi(t^*) < t$ and $k \leq \log_2 t$.

5.3 Let R be a ring (commutative, with 1) and $u \in R$. Prove that Horner's rule not only computes the remainder $f(u)$ of a polynomial $f \in R[x]$ of degree $n - 1$ on division by $x - u$ but also the coefficients of the quotient $(f - f(u))/(x - u)$.

5.4 Let $\mathbb{F}_5 = \mathbb{Z}_5$ be the finite field with 5 elements.

(i) Compute a polynomial $f \in \mathbb{F}_5[x]$ of degree at most 2 satisfying

$$f(0) = 1, \quad f(1) = 2, \quad f(2) = 4 \tag{37}$$

(ii) List all polynomials $f \in \mathbb{F}_5[x]$ of degree at most 3 satisfying (37). How many of degree at most 4 are there? Generalize your answer to solutions of degree at most n for $n \in \mathbb{N}$.

5.5 Let $\mathbb{F}_7 = \mathbb{Z}_7$ be the finite field with 7 elements and $m = x(x + 1)(x + 6) = x^3 + 6x \in \mathbb{F}_7[x]$.

(i) Let $J \subseteq \mathbb{F}_7[x]$ be the set of all polynomials $h \in \mathbb{F}_7[x]$ solving the interpolation problem

$$h(0) = 1, \quad h(1) = 5, \quad h(6) = 2.$$

Compute the unique polynomial $f \in J$ of least degree.

(ii) Find a surjective ring homomorphism $\chi : \mathbb{F}_7[x] \longrightarrow \mathbb{F}_7^3$ such that $\ker \chi = \langle m \rangle = \{rm : r \in \mathbb{F}_7[x]\}$, and compute $\chi(f)$ and $\chi(x^2 + 3x + 2)$.

(iii) Show that $J = f + \ker \chi = \{f + rm : r \in \mathbb{F}_7[x]\}$.

5.6 Let $r = x^3 + x^2 \in \mathbb{F}_5[x]$.

(i) List all polynomials $f \in \mathbb{F}_5[x]$ of degree at most 5 satisfying

$$f(a) = r(a) \text{ for all } a \in \mathbb{F}_5. \tag{38}$$

(ii) How many polynomials $f \in \mathbb{F}_5[x]$ of degree at most 6 solve (38)?

5.7 (i) Show that $\displaystyle\sum_{0 \leq i < n} l_i = 1$, where l_i are the Lagrange interpolants as in (2).

(ii) Let $u_n \in F$ be another point different from $u_0, \ldots, u_{n-1}$. Show how one can obtain the Lagrange interpolants $l_0^*, \ldots, l_{n-1}^*, l_n^*$ corresponding to $u_0, \ldots, u_n$ from $l_0, \ldots, l_{n-1}$.

5.8 Let R be an integral domain, $u_0, \ldots, u_{n-1} \in R$, and $V = \mathrm{VDM}(u_0, \ldots, u_{n-1}) \in R^{n \times n}$. Prove that

$$\det V = \prod_{1 \leq j < i \leq n} (u_i - u_j).$$

Hint: Replace u_{n-1} by an indeterminate and proceed by induction on n.

5.9 Let F be a field, $u_0, \ldots, u_{n-1} \in F$ distinct, $m = (x - u_0) \cdots (x - u_{n-1}) \in F[x]$, and $f \in F[x]$. Prove that $fm' \equiv \sum_{0 \leq i < n} f(u_i)m/(x - u_i) \bmod m$, where m' is the formal derivative of m (Section 9.3). Hint: Exercise 9.22.

5.10 Let F be a field and $f/g \in F(x)$ a rational function, with $f, g \in F[x]$ such that $g \neq 0$ is monic and $\gcd(f, g) = 1$. We say that f/g is **defined** at a point $u \in F$ if $g(u) \neq 0$, and then the value of the rational function at u is $f(u)/g(u)$. Let $f^*/g^* \in F(x)$ be another rational function, with $g^* \neq 0$ monic and $\gcd(f^*, g^*) = 1$, such that f/g and f^*/g^* are defined and their values coincide at $n = \max\{\deg f + \deg g^*, \deg f^* + \deg g\} + 1$ distinct points $u_0, \ldots, u_{n-1} \in F$. Prove that $f = f^*$ and $g = g^*$.

5.11* Another possibility to compute the interpolating polynomial of least degree is **Newton inter-polation**. Suppose that $u_0, \ldots, u_{n-1}, v_0, \ldots, v_{n-1}$ in a field F are given, with distinct $u_0, \ldots, u_{n-1}$, and let $f \in F[x]$ of degree less than n be the interpolating polynomial with $f(u_i) = v_i$ for all i. We divide f by $x - u_0$ with remainder and obtain $f = (x - u_0)g + f(u_0) = (x - u_0)g + v_0$ for some $g \in F[x]$ of degree $\deg f - 1$. For $i \geq 1$, the value of g at u_i is $g(u_i) = (v_i - v_0)/(u_i - u_0)$, and we can determine g recursively in the same fashion.

(i) Design an algorithm for Newton interpolation, prove that is works correctly, and analyze its cost. It is possible to solve the problem with at most $\frac{5}{2}n^2$ operations in F.

(ii) Trace your algorithm on the examples of Exercises 5.4 and 5.5.

(iii) What is the connection to the mixed-radix representation of f, as discussed in Exercise 5.1, when $m_i = x - u_i$ for $0 \leq i < n$?

5.12* Let F be a field, $u_0, \ldots, u_{n-1} \in F \setminus \{0\}$ with $u_i \neq \pm u_j$ for $0 \leq i < j < n$, and $v_0, \ldots, v_{n-1} \in F$.

(i) Let $f \in F[x]$ of degree less than $2n$ be such that $f(u_i) = f(-u_i)$ for $0 \leq i < n$. Prove that $f(x) = f(-x)$, so that f is **even**.

(ii) Use the Lagrange interpolation formula and (i) to show that there is a unique even interpolating polynomial $f \in F[x]$ of degree less than $2n$ such that $f(u_i) = v_i$ for $0 \leq i < n$.

(iii) Let $g \in F[x]$ be the unique polynomial of degree less than n such that $g(u_i^2) = v_i$ for $0 \leq i < n$. How is the polynomial f from (ii) related to g?

(iv) What are the statements corresponding to (i) through (iii) for odd interpolating polynomials, provided that $u_i \neq 0$ for all i?

(v) Compute an even polynomial $f_0 \in \mathbb{R}[x]$ of degree at most 4 interpolating the cosine function at $u_0 = \pi/6, u_1 = \pi/3$, and $u_2 = \pi/2$, and an odd polynomial $f_1 \in \mathbb{R}[x]$ of degree at most 5 interpolating the sine function at those points.

(Euler (1783) stated interpolation formulas for odd and even functions.)

5.13* In this exercise, we discuss bivariate interpolation.

(i) Develop an algorithm for computing $f \in F[x, y]$, F a field, where the degree of f in y is less than n and

$$f(x, u_i) = v_i \text{ for } i = 0, 1, \ldots, n-1,$$

for distinct $u_i \in F$ and arbitrary $v_i \in F[x]$. Show that f is unique.

(ii) Assuming that the degree of each v_i is less than m, what is the computing time of your algorithm (in terms of m and n)?

(iii) Compute $f \in \mathbb{F}_{11}[x, y]$ such that

$$f(x, 0) = x^2 + 7, \quad f(x, 1) = x^3 + 2x + 3, \quad f(x, 2) = x^3 + 5.$$

5.14 Let F be a field, $f \in F[x]$ of degree less than n, and $u_0, \ldots, u_{n-1} \in F \setminus \{0\}$ distinct. Determine the set of all interpolation polynomials $g \in F[x]$ of degree less than n with $g(u_i) = f(u_i)$ for $0 \leq i \leq n-2$. (In the situation of Section 5.3, this represents the knowledge of all players minus player $n-1$.) Let $c \in F$. How many of these g have constant coefficient c? (Your answer should imply that the secret sharing scheme is secure.)

5.15 What is the least nonnegative integer f with $f \equiv 2 \bmod 3$, $f \equiv 3 \bmod 5$, and $f \equiv 2 \bmod 7$?

5.16 How many common solutions $f \in \mathbb{Z}$ with $0 \leq f < 10^6$ do the following congruences possess?

$$f \equiv 2 \bmod 11, \quad f \equiv -1 \bmod 13, \quad f \equiv 10 \bmod 17.$$

5.17 Carl Friedrich, Joachim, and Jürgen met at a Sylvester party on Thursday, 31 December 1998. They agreed to play Skat (a German card game) together some day as soon as all of them find the time to do so. But they got into the usual troubles: Carl Friedrich was busy except on Fridays, Joachim had time on 7 January and then again every 9th day, and Jürgen was free on 6 January and then again every 11th day. Which date did they agree upon?

5.18 Ernie, Bert, and the Cookie Monster want to measure the length of Sesame Street. Each of them does it his own way. Ernie relates: "I made a chalk mark at the beginning of the street and then again every 7 feet. There were 2 feet between the last mark and the end of the street." Bert tells you: "Every 11 feet, there are lamp posts in the street. The first one is 5 feet from the beginning, and the last one is exactly at the end of the street." Finally, the Cookie Monster says: "Starting at the beginning of Sesame Street, I put down a cookie every 13 feet. I ran out of cookies 22 feet from the end." All three agree that the length does not exceed 1000 feet. How many feet is Sesame Street long?

5.19 (i) Find a polynomial in $\mathbb{F}_5[x]$ of degree four which is reducible but has no roots in $\mathbb{F}_5$. Are there such examples of lower degree?

(ii) Which of the following polynomials in $\mathbb{F}_5[x]$ are irreducible, which are reducible?

$$m_0 = x^2 + 2, \quad m_1 = x^2 + 3x + 4, \quad m_2 = x^3 + 2, \quad m_3 = x^3 + x + 1.$$

(iii) Conclude that the system

$$f \equiv x + 1 \bmod m_0, \quad f \equiv 3 \bmod m_1$$

has a solution $f \in \mathbb{F}_5[x]$, and compute the unique solution of least degree.

5.20 Compute a solution $f \in \mathbb{F}_5[x]$ of the system of congruences

$$f \equiv 1 \bmod x + 1, \quad x \cdot f \equiv x + 1 \bmod x^2 + 1, \quad (x+1)f \equiv x + 1 \bmod x^3 + 1$$

such that $\deg f < 5$. Hint: First bring each of the congruences into the form $f \equiv v \bmod m$ for some $v, m \in \mathbb{F}_5[x]$, using Exercise 4.15. What is the set of all solutions without the degree constraint?

5.21→ Let $m_0 = x^2 + 1$, $m_1 = x^2 - 1$, $m_2 = x^3 + x - 1$, $v_0 = -x$, $v_1 = x + 1$, and $v_2 = x^5 - x$ in $\mathbb{F}_3[x]$.

(i) How many polynomials $f \in \mathbb{F}_3[x]$ are there with $f \equiv v_i \bmod m_i$ for $i = 0, 1, 2$, and $\deg f \leq 8$? Answer this *without* solving (ii).

(ii) Give a list of all f as in (i).

5.22* Let $p_0, p_1 \in \mathbb{N}$ be distinct primes, $m = p_0 p_1$, $n \in \mathbb{N}$, and $u_0, \ldots, u_{n-1}, v_0, \ldots, v_{n-1} \in \mathbb{Z}$.

(i) Show that there exists an interpolating polynomial $f \in \mathbb{Z}[x]$ such that

$$f \text{ has coefficients in } \{0, \ldots, m-1\}, \ \deg f < n, \text{ and } f(u_i) \equiv v_i \bmod m \text{ for } 0 \leq i < n \quad (39)$$

if and only if

$$u_i \equiv u_j \bmod p_k \Longrightarrow v_i \equiv v_j \bmod p_k$$

for $0 \leq i < j < n$ and $k = 0, 1$.

(ii) Show that (39) has a unique solution if and only if $u_i \not\equiv u_j \bmod p_k$ for $0 \leq i < j < n$ and $k = 0, 1$.

(iii) Compute all interpolating polynomials $f \in \mathbb{Z}[x]$ with coefficients in $\{0, \ldots, 14\}$, $\deg f < 3$, and

$$f(1) \equiv 2 \bmod 15, \ f(2) \equiv 5 \bmod 15, \ f(4) \equiv -1 \bmod 15.$$

5.23* (i) Let R be a Euclidean domain, $m_0, m_1 \in R \setminus \{0\}$, and $v_0, v_1 \in R$. Show that

$$f \equiv v_0 \bmod m_0, \quad f \equiv v_1 \bmod m_1$$

has a solution $f \in R$ if and only if $v_0 \equiv v_1 \bmod \gcd(m_0, m_1)$. Hint: Theorem 4.10.

(ii) Compute one particular solution for $R = \mathbb{Z}$, $m_0 = 36$, $m_1 = 42$, $v_0 = 2$, $v_1 = 8$, and describe the set of all solutions.

5.24* Design and analyze a Chinese Remainder Algorithm à la "Newton interpolation" (Exercise 5.11). Trace your algorithm on the problems of Exercises 5.16 and 5.20.

5.25 Are the two rings $\mathbb{Z}_5 \times \mathbb{Z}_{12}$ and $\mathbb{Z}_3 \times \mathbb{Z}_{20}$ isomorphic?

5.26 Enumerate $\mathbb{Z}_m^\times$ and determine $\varphi(m)$ for $m = 11, 16, 33, 42$.

5.27 Make a list showing all integers m for which $\varphi(m) \leq 10$, and prove that your list is complete.

5.28 Let $\mathbb{F}_q$ be a finite field with q elements and $f = f_0^{e_0} \cdots f_{r-1}^{e_{r-1}}$ with $f_0, \ldots, f_{r-1} \in \mathbb{F}_q[x]$ irreducible and pairwise coprime and $e_0, \ldots, e_{r-1} \in \mathbb{N}_{>0}$. Let $n = \deg f$ and $n_i = \deg f_i$ for all i. Recall the analog Φ of Euler's totient function (Exercise 4.19). Prove that

$$\Phi(f) = (q^{n_0} - 1)q^{n_0(e_0 - 1)} \cdots (q^{n_{r-1}} - 1)q^{n_{r-1}(e_{r-1} - 1)} = q^n \prod_{0 \leq i < r} \left(1 - \frac{1}{q^{n_i}}\right).$$

Hint: CRT.

5.29* Prove Theorem 5.8.

5.30 Let $A_n = (i^j)_{1 \leq i, j \leq n} \in \mathbb{Z}^{n \times n}$.
(i) Compute a good upper bound on $|\det A_n|$ in terms of n using Hadamard's inequality 16.6.
(ii) Compute $\det A_3$ with the small primes modular algorithm.

5.31 Use the familiar formula $\det A = \sum_{\sigma \in S_n} \text{sgn}(\sigma) \cdot a_{1\sigma(1)} \cdots a_{n\sigma(n)}$ for the determinant of a square matrix $A \in \mathbb{Z}^{n \times n}$, where S_n is the symmetric group of all $n!$ permutations of $\{1, \ldots, n\}$ (Section 25.1), to derive an upper bound on $|\det A|$ in terms of n and $B = \max_{1 \leq i, j \leq n} |a_{ij}|$. Compare this to the Hadamard bound, and tabulate both bounds and their ratio for $1 \leq n \leq 10$.

5.32⟶ Let F be a field, $n \in \mathbb{N}_{>0}$, and $A = (a_{ij})_{1 \leq i, j \leq n} \in F[x]^{n \times n}$ a quadratic matrix with polynomial entries. Moreover, let $m = \max\{\deg a_{ij} : 1 \leq i, j \leq n\}$ for all i.
(i) Find a tight upper bound $r \in \mathbb{N}$ on $\deg(\det A)$ in terms of m and n.
(ii) Describe an algorithm for computing $\det A$ using a small primes modular approach if the field F has more than r elements. Hint: Choose linear moduli. How many operations in F does your algorithm use (in terms of n and m)?
(iii) Use your algorithm to compute the determinant of the matrix

$$A = \begin{pmatrix} -x+1 & 0 & 2 \\ x & x+1 & 2x \\ 2x & 3x+1 & x \end{pmatrix} \in \mathbb{F}_7[x]^{3 \times 3}.$$

(iv) Find a tight upper bound on $\deg(\det A)$ in terms of the maximal degrees m_i in the ith row of A for $1 \leq i \leq n$. (Sometimes, this bound or the corresponding bound arising from the maximal column degrees is better than the bound from (i).)
(v) Using the bound from (iv), compute the determinant of

$$A = \begin{pmatrix} x-1 & x-2 & x-3 \\ 2x+1 & 2x+3 & 2x-2 \\ x^2-1 & x^2+x+1 & (x-1)^2 \end{pmatrix} \in \mathbb{F}_7[x]^{3 \times 3}.$$

5.33* The goal of this exercise is to show that nonsingular linear system solving over $\mathbb{Q}$ can be done in polynomial time using a modular approach. Thus let $A \in \mathbb{Z}^{n \times n}$ and $b \in \mathbb{Z}^n$ for some $n \in \mathbb{N}$, and assume that $\det A \neq 0$. Then there is a unique solution $x \in \mathbb{Q}^n$ of the linear system $Ax = b$, namely $x = A^{-1}b$.
(i) Given a bound $B \in \mathbb{N}$ on the absolute values of the entries of A and b, show that the numerators and denominators of the coefficients of x are less than $n^{n/2}B^n$ in absolute value. Hint: Use Cramer's rule 25.6 and Hadamard's inequality 16.6.

(ii) We consider the following modular algorithm. Choose a prime $p \in \mathbb{N}$ greater than $2n^n B^{2n}$, and perform Gaussian elimination on A mod p and b mod p. Convince yourself that $p \nmid \det A$. We find a $y \in \mathbb{Z}^n$ such that y mod p is the unique solution of the modular linear system $(A \bmod p)(y \bmod p) = b \bmod p$. Now $x \equiv y \bmod p$, and we can reconstruct x from y using rational number reconstruction (Section 5.10) for each of the coefficients. Prove that this algorithm works correctly.

(iii) Show that the running time of the algorithm is $O(n^3 \log^2 p)$ word operations, or $O^{\sim}(n^5 \log^2 B)$ when p is close to $2n^n B^{2n}$.

(iv) Run your algorithm on the matrix A_3 from Example 5.30 and the vector $b = (1,1,1)^T$.

5.34* Given are a positive integer $n \in \mathbb{N}$, two polynomials $a = \sum_{0 \le i < n} a_i x^i$, $b = \sum_{0 \le i < n} b_i x^i$ in $\mathbb{Z}[x]$, and a bound $B \in \mathbb{N}$ on the coefficients such that $|a_i|, |b_i| \le B$ for $0 \le i < n$. Moreover, let $ab = c = \sum_{0 \le i < 2n} c_i x^i \in \mathbb{Z}[x]$.

(i) Find a tight common upper bound on the $|c_i|$ in terms of n and B.

(ii) Describe an algorithm for the computation of c using a small primes modular approach.

(iii) Trace your algorithm on the computation of the product of

$$a = 987x^3 + 654x^2 + 321x, \quad b = -753x^3 - 333x^2 - 202x + 815.$$

5.35$\longrightarrow$ Let $n+1$ points $u_0 < u_1 < \cdots < u_n$ in $\mathbb{R}$ be given, and $v_0, \ldots, v_n \in \mathbb{R}$ arbitrary. You are to find a continuously differentiable function $f \colon [u_0, u_n] \longrightarrow \mathbb{R}$ which takes the value v_i at point u_i and has $f'(u_0) = f''(u_0) = 0$, as follows. Construct a sequence of polynomials $f_0, \ldots, f_n \in \mathbb{R}[x]$ of degree at most 3 such that $f_0 = v_0$,

$$f_i(u_{i-1}) = f_{i-1}(u_{i-1}), \ f_i'(u_{i-1}) = f_{i-1}'(u_{i-1}), \ f_i''(u_{i-1}) = f_{i-1}''(u_{i-1}), \ f_i(u_i) = v_i,$$

for $1 \le i \le n$. This amounts to solving a Hermite interpolation problem for each interval $[u_{i-1}, u_i]$, with three conditions on f_i and its first two derivatives at the left boundary and one condition on f_i at the right boundary. Then f is defined to be equal to f_i on the interval $[u_{i-1}, u_i]$, for all i. Such an f is called a **Bézier curve**. (These curves, and also similar surfaces, were introduced in the late 1960s by Bézier at the Renault car company, and de Casteljau at Citroën; see Bézier (1970) and de Casteljau (1985).)

(i) Prove that $f_1, \ldots, f_n$ exist uniquely.

(ii) Compute and draw the Bézier curve for the data $u_i = i$ for $0 \le i \le 3$, $v_0 = v_3 = 1$, $v_2 = 0$, and $v_3 = -1$.

(iii) In (ii), give various other values to v_2, say $-5, -3, -2, -1, 1, 2, 3, 5, 7$.

5.36 (Kronecker 1881a, page 546) Let $F = \mathbb{Q}$, $n = 4$, $u_i = i + 1$ for $i = 0, \ldots, 3$, $v_0 = 6$, $v_1 = 3$, $v_2 = 2$, $v_3 = 3$. Show that for $k = 2$, (21) has a unique solution $r, t \in \mathbb{Q}[x]$ with t monic, while (20) is unsolvable.

5.37 For $1 \le k \le 5$, try to solve the Cauchy interpolation problem

$$t(i) \ne 0 \text{ and } \frac{r}{t}(i) = v_i \text{ for } 0 \le i \le 4, \quad \gcd(r,t) = 1 \qquad (40)$$

for polynomials $r, t \in \mathbb{F}_5[x]$ with $\deg r < k$ and $\deg t \le 5 - k$, where the v_i are given by the following table.

i	0	1	2	3	4
v_i	1	2	3	2	1

For which values of k does no solution exist?

5.38 Let F be a field, $u_0, \ldots, u_{n-1} \in F$ distinct, $v_0, \ldots, v_{n-1} \in F$, and $S = \{0 \le i < n : v_i = 0\}$. Show that the Cauchy interpolation problem (20) has no solution if $k \le \#S < n$.

5.39 Tabulate all $(k, n-k)$-Padé approximants to $f = x^4 + x^3 + 3x^2 + 1 \in \mathbb{F}_5[x]$ for $0 \le k \le n \le 5$. Mark the entries in the table where no approximant exists.

5.40$^{\longrightarrow}$ Give all Padé approximants in $\mathbb{Q}(x)$ to the exponential function $\exp(x) = 1 + x + x^2/2 + x^3/6 + x^4/24 + \cdots$ modulo x^5.

5.41 Let F be a field, $n \in \mathbb{N}$, $f \in F[x]$ of degree less than n, and $\ell \in \mathbb{N}_{>0}$ the Euclidean length of the pair (x^n, f).

(i) Show that there are at most ℓ distinct coprime pairs $(r, t) \in F[x]$ such that $t \neq 0$ is monic,

$$r \equiv ft \bmod x^n \text{ and } \deg r + \deg t < n.$$

Thus there are at most ℓ distinct Padé approximants to f modulo x^n.

(ii) Given the jth row $r_j = s_j x^n + t_j f$ in the Extended Euclidean Algorithm, for some $j \in \{1, \ldots, \ell\}$, and the degree sequence $n_0 = n, n_1, \ldots, n_\ell$ of (x^n, f), for which values of $k \in \{1, \ldots, n\}$ is (r_j, t_j) a solution of (23)?

5.42* This exercise discusses both Cauchy interpolation and Padé approximation from a more general point of view. We let $m_0, \ldots, m_{l-1} \in F[x]$ be nonconstant, monic, and pairwise coprime, $m = m_0 \cdots m_{l-1}$ of degree n, $v_0, \ldots, v_{l-1} \in F[x]$ such that $\deg v_i < \deg m_i$ for all i, and $0 \leq k \leq n$. (In contrast to Section 5.4, we denote the number of moduli by l.) The **rational Chinese Remainder Problem** is to compute polynomials $r, t \in F[x]$ satisfying

$$\gcd(t, m_i) = 1 \text{ and } rt^{-1} \equiv v_i \bmod m_i \text{ for } 0 \leq i < l, \deg r < k, \text{ and } \deg t \leq n - k, \tag{41}$$

where t^{-1} is the modular inverse of t modulo m_i (Section 4.2). Let $f \in F[x]$ be the polynomial solution of the system of congruences $f \equiv v_i \bmod m_i$ for all i. Furthermore, let $r_j, s_j, t_j \in F[x]$ be the jth row in the Extended Euclidean Algorithm for m and f, where j is minimal such that $\deg r_j < k$. Prove:

(i) There exist polynomials $r, t \in F[x]$ satisfying

$$r \equiv tv_i \bmod m_i \text{ for } 0 \leq i < l, \quad \deg r < k, \quad \deg t \leq n - k, \tag{42}$$

namely $r = r_j$ and $t = t_j$. If in addition $\gcd(r_j, t_j) = 1$, then r and t also solve (41).

(ii) If $r/t \in F(x)$ is a canonical form solution to (41), then $r = \tau^{-1} r_j$ and $t = \tau^{-1} t_j$, where $\tau = \mathrm{lc}(t_j) \in F \setminus \{0\}$. In particular, (41) is solvable if and only if $\gcd(r_j, t_j) = 1$.

5.43 Compute—if possible—rational functions $\rho = r/t \in \mathbb{Q}(x)$ satisfying

(i) $\rho(-1) = 1$, $\rho(0) = 2$, $\rho(1) = 1$, $\rho'(1) = -1$, with $\deg r < 3$, $\deg t \leq 1$.

(ii) $\rho(-1) = 2$, $\rho'(-1) = 1$, $\rho(1) = -1$, $\rho'(1) = 2$, with $\deg r < 1$, $\deg t \leq 3$.

5.44* Use Theorem 5.26 to formulate and prove the analog of Exercise 5.42 for integers.

5.45 Compute the partial fraction expansions of the following rational functions over $\mathbb{Q}$:

(i) $\dfrac{x+2}{(x+1)^3(x-1)^2}$, (ii) $\dfrac{x^4 + 2x - 1}{x^3(x^2 + 1)}$.

The mathematician's pattern, like a painter's or the poet's, must be
beautiful. [...] Beauty is the first test; there is no permanent place
in the world for ugly mathematics.

Godfrey Harold Hardy (1940)

Zudem ist es ein Irrtum zu glauben, daß die Strenge in der
Beweisführung die Feindin der Einfachheit sei. An zahlreichen
Beispielen finden wir im Gegenteil bestätigt, daß die strenge Methode
auch zugleich die einfachere und leichter faßliche ist. Das Streben nach
Strenge zwingt uns eben zur Auffindung einfacherer Schlußweisen.[1]

David Hilbert (1900)

Der Mathematiker ist nur in sofern vollkommen,
als er ein vollkommener Mensch ist, als er das Schöne
des Wahren in sich empfindet; dann erst wird er gründlich,
durchsichtig, umsichtig, rein, klar, anmutig, ja elegant wirken.[2]

Johann Wolfgang von Goethe (1829)

The algebraical element looked to me a pure science,
subject to mathematical law, inhuman.

Thomas Edward Lawrence (1926)

---

[1] Furthermore, it is an error to believe that rigor in proof is an enemy of simplicity. On the contrary we find it confirmed by numerous examples that the rigorous method is at the same time the simpler and the more comprehensible one. The very effort for rigor forces us to find simpler proof methods.

[2] The mathematician is perfect only in so far as he is a perfect being, in so far as he perceives the beauty of truth; only then will he appear to be thorough, transparent, comprehensive, pure, clear, gracious, and even elegant.

6

The resultant and gcd computation

We start this chapter with a typical example illustrating the growth of coefficients in the Euclidean Algorithm for polynomials over $\mathbb{Q}$. Much of the rest of this chapter is devoted to getting a handle on this growth. As an application, we obtain modular algorithms for the gcd in $\mathbb{Q}[x]$ and $F[x,y]$ for a field F; these are much more efficient than the direct computation.

Gauß' lemma in Section 6.2 illuminates the non-obvious relation between gcds of integer polynomials in $\mathbb{Z}[x]$ and $\mathbb{Q}[x]$. We then introduce the **resultant**, which gives control over the **Bézout coefficients** s and t in the presentation $sf + tg = \gcd(f,g)$. This yields a modular gcd calculation for bivariate polynomials, and, together with **Mignotte's factor bound**, also for integer polynomials. Section 6.10 discusses the more general **subresultants**, which govern the coefficient growth in the whole Extended Euclidean Algorithm, and provide a modular approach to the EEA.

In between, we digress to two applications: computing the intersection points of two plane algebraic curves, and an unexpectedly efficient way of computing the gcd of many polynomials.

6.1. Coefficient growth in the Euclidean Algorithm

Let F be a field, and $f, g \in F[x]$ with $\deg f = n \geq \deg g = m \geq 0$. We fix the notation from Section 3.2 of the results of the Extended Euclidean Algorithm for f and g:

$$
\begin{aligned}
\rho_0 r_0 &= f, & \rho_0 s_0 &= 1, & \rho_0 t_0 &= 0, \\
\rho_1 r_1 &= g, & \rho_1 s_1 &= 0, & \rho_1 t_1 &= 1, \\
\rho_2 r_2 &= r_0 - q_1 r_1, & \rho_2 s_2 &= s_0 - q_1 s_1, & \rho_2 t_2 &= t_0 - q_1 t_1, \\
&\ \ \vdots & &\ \ \vdots & &\ \ \vdots \\
\rho_{i+1} r_{i+1} &= r_{i-1} - q_i r_i, & \rho_{i+1} s_{i+1} &= s_{i-1} - q_i s_i, & \rho_{i+1} t_{i+1} &= t_{i-1} - q_i t_i, \\
&\ \ \vdots & &\ \ \vdots & &\ \ \vdots \\
0 &= r_{\ell-1} - q_\ell r_\ell, & s_{\ell+1} &= s_{\ell-1} - q_\ell s_\ell, & t_{\ell+1} &= t_{\ell-1} - q_\ell t_\ell,
\end{aligned}
\tag{1}
$$

with $\deg r_{i+1} < \deg r_i$ for all $i \geq 1$. Thus $r_{i-1} = q_i r_i + \rho_{i+1} r_{i+1}$ is the division of r_{i-1} by r_i with remainder $\rho_{i+1} r_{i+1}$; the leading coefficient ρ_{i+1} serves to have a normalized remainder r_{i+1}. A basic invariant is $r_i = s_i f + t_i g$. We define the **degree sequence** $(n_0, n_1, \ldots, n_\ell)$ by $n_i = \deg r_i$ for all i. Then

$$n = n_0 \geq n_1 > n_2 \cdots > n_\ell \geq 0.$$

It is convenient to set $\rho_{\ell+1} = 1$, $r_{\ell+1} = 0$, and $n_{\ell+1} = -\infty$. The number of arithmetic operations in F performed by the (Extended) Euclidean Algorithm for f and g is $O(nm)$ (see Chapter 3).

In order to get a bound on the number of word operations of Euclid's algorithm over $F = \mathbb{Q}$, we need to get a bound on the length of the numbers involved in the computation. We extend the definition of the **length** of an integer from Section 2.1 to rational numbers and polynomials with rational coefficients. We bring all coefficients of a polynomial $a \in \mathbb{Q}[x]$ to a common denominator, and then $\lambda(a)$ is the maximal number of words required to encode the denominator or a coefficient of the numerator of a. More precisely, we use

- $\lambda(a) = \lfloor (\log_2 |a|)/64 \rfloor + 1$, when $a \in \mathbb{Z} \setminus \{0\}$, and $\lambda(0) = 0$,
- $\lambda(a) = \max\{\lambda(b), \lambda(c)\}$, when $a = b/c \in \mathbb{Q}$ with $b, c \in \mathbb{Z}$ and $\gcd(b, c) = 1$,
- $\lambda(a) = \max(\lambda(b), \max_{0 \leq i \leq n} \lambda(a_i))$, when $a = \sum_{0 \leq i \leq n} a_i x^i / b \in \mathbb{Q}[x]$ with all $a_i \in \mathbb{Z}$ and $b_i \in \mathbb{N}_{\geq 1}$ such that $\gcd(a_0, \ldots, a_n) = 1$.

Thus a can be represented with about $\lambda(a)(2 + \deg a)$ words. Then for $a, b \in \mathbb{Z}[x]$ and $c, d \in \mathbb{Q}$, we have

$$
\begin{aligned}
\lambda(a+b) &\leq \max\{\lambda(a), \lambda(b)\} + 1, \\
\lambda(ab) &\leq \lambda(a) + \lambda(b) + \lambda(\min\{\deg a, \deg b\} + 1), \\
\lambda(cd), \lambda(c/d) &\leq \lambda(c) + \lambda(d), \\
\lambda(c+d) &\leq \lambda(c) + \lambda(d) + 1.
\end{aligned}
$$

We next consider a division with remainder $a = qb + \rho r$, where the polynomials $a = x^n + \sum_{0 \leq i < n} a_i x^i / c$, $b = x^m + \sum_{0 \leq i < m} b_i x^i / d \in \mathbb{Q}[x]$, and $r \in \mathbb{Q}[x]$ are monic, with all $a_i, b_i \in \mathbb{Z}$ and $c, d \in \mathbb{N}_{\geq 1}$, in the special case where $m = n - 1$. Then

$$
\begin{aligned}
q &= x + \frac{a_{n-1} d - b_{m-1} c}{cd}, \quad \lambda(q) \leq \lambda(a) + \lambda(b) + 1, \\
\rho r &= a - qb = \frac{acd^2 - xbcd^2 - (a_{n-1} d - b_{m-1} c) bd}{cd^2}, \\
\lambda(\rho r) &\leq \lambda(a) + 2\lambda(b) + 3,
\end{aligned}
$$

and the latter estimate also holds for $\lambda(r)$ since the cd^2 in the denominator of ρr and the numerator of $1/\rho$ cancel. Assuming that $\lambda(a) \leq \lambda(b)$, we see that the coefficient size grows at most by a factor of about 3 in one division. Some experiments with pseudorandom polynomials of degree $n = 10$ and with 10, 100, and 1000 decimal digit coefficients indicate that this is essentially sharp: the average length ratio between the remainder coefficients and those of the input was 2.92, 2.998, and 2.9999, respectively, for 10 experiments each.

In a typical execution of the Euclidean Algorithm, the degrees of all the quotient polynomials will be 1. From the above worst-case estimate, we find that $\lambda(r_\ell) \in O(3^\ell \cdot \max\{\lambda(f), \lambda(g)\})$. This looks like bad news: an exponential upper bound on the size of the gcd and the number of word operations of the Euclidean Algorithm!

In reality, however, the sizes do not grow like that at every step, and we can prove that the coefficient sizes in the Euclidean Algorithm remain polynomially bounded in the input size. To prove this non-obvious result, we need a "global view" of the Euclidean Algorithm provided by the theory of (sub-)resultants. This theory will give us explicit formulas for the coefficients that appear in the polynomials in the Euclidean Algorithm. As a bonus, this theory will allow us to compute gcds in $\mathbb{Q}[x]$ using a modular approach, yielding a much more practical algorithm.

The following example illustrates the huge coefficients that actually occur in the Euclidean Algorithm in $\mathbb{Q}[x]$. It is typical in the sense that for most pairs of polynomials, with about as many coefficient digits as the degree, a similar growth of intermediate results occurs.

EXAMPLE 6.1. The following is generated on most platforms by the MAPLE commands in typewriter font.

```
f := randpoly(x, coeffs = rand(-999 .. 999), degree = 5);
```

$$f := 824x^5 - 65x^4 - 814x^3 - 741x^2 - 979x - 764$$

```
g := randpoly(x, coeffs = rand(-999 .. 999), degree = 4);
```

$$g := 216x^4 + 663x^3 + 880x^2 + 916x + 617$$

```
rho[0] := lcoeff(f, x); r[0] := f/rho[0];
```

$$\rho_0 := 824$$

$$r_0 := x^5 - \frac{65}{824}x^4 - \frac{407}{412}x^3 - \frac{741}{824}x^2 - \frac{979}{824}x - \frac{191}{206}$$

```
rho[1] := lcoeff(g, x); r[1] := g/rho[1];
```

$$\rho_1 := 216$$

$$r_1 := x^4 + \frac{221}{72}x^3 + \frac{110}{27}x^2 + \frac{229}{54}x + \frac{617}{216}$$

```
printlevel := 2:
for i from 1 to 5 do
  q[i] := quo(r[i - 1], r[i], x, 'a[i + 1]');
  a[i + 1] := sort(a[i + 1]);
  if (a[i + 1] <> 0) then
```

```
    rho[i + 1] := lcoeff(a[i + 1], x);
    r[i + 1] := a[i + 1] / rho[i + 1];
  fi;
od;
```

$$q_1 := x - \frac{5837}{1854}$$

$$a_2 := \frac{614269}{133488}x^3 + \frac{1539085}{200232}x^2 + \frac{931745}{100116}x + \frac{3230125}{400464}$$

$$\rho_2 := \frac{614269}{133488}$$

$$r_2 := x^3 + \frac{3078170}{1842807}x^2 + \frac{3726980}{1842807}x + \frac{3230125}{1842807}$$

$$q_2 := x + \frac{61877369}{44227368}$$

$$a_3 := -\frac{1292018949205}{4527916852332}x^2 - \frac{386731352527}{1131979213083}x + \frac{914965415267}{2263958426166}$$

$$\rho_3 := \frac{-1292018949205}{4527916852332}$$

$$r_3 := x^2 + \frac{1546925410108}{1292018949205}x - \frac{1829930830534}{1292018949205}$$

$$q_3 := x + \frac{1126368994649461694}{2380941563727618435}$$

$$a_4 := \frac{4794883885762430016087234}{16693129651047923701320252}x + \frac{404451843913972189959903}{16693129651047923701320255}$$

$$\rho_4 := \frac{4794883885762430016087234}{16693129651047923701320255}$$

$$r_4 := x + \frac{731586548698031843}{867315257966502554}$$

$$q_4 := x + \frac{39644832722141411482838981017}{11205877482273441349080287695705}$$

$$a_5 := \frac{-1289900328081598608308367775585297495}{75223575670150087196145994288852291655}$$

$$\rho_5 := \frac{-1289900328081598608308367775585297495}{75223575670150087196145994288852291655}$$

$$r_5 := 1$$

$$q_5 := x + \frac{731586548698031843}{867315257966502554}$$

$$a_6 := 0$$

Thus already for comparatively small input sizes, the numerators and denominators of the intermediate results in the Euclidean Algorithm are amazingly large. The classical Euclidean Algorithm, where the remainders are not normalized at each step, is run in Section 6.11 on the same example; its intermediate results are considerably bigger than here. The example also illustrates the phenomenon of **intermediate expression swell**: The 25-digit coefficients of a_4 contract to 18 digits in its normalized version r_4. At the next step, the relation between a_5 and r_5 is even more drastic. In the normal case, where all the quotients have degree 1, this is not a serious problem: the discussion in Section 6.11 implies that then $\lambda(a_i)$ is at most about $3\lambda(r_i)$. A more important issue is that the upper bound on the size of the coefficients of the gcd is smaller by about one order of magnitude than the corresponding bound for the other remainders, even when the gcd is nonconstant. This follows from the estimates in Section 6.6 and 6.11 below. ◇

The basic question now is: does this algorithm really run in polynomial time? In other words: do the coefficients that occur have polynomially bounded length? The naive exponential upper bound and the above example may raise some doubt about this. But not to worry, all is well! Our proofs of polynomial bounds proceed in two stages: first for the computation of the gcd in Sections 6.5 and 6.6, and finally for all results of the EEA in Section 6.11.

Once we have a good bound on the final result, the basic idea to circumvent the intermediate expression swell is to use a modular approach. When the input polynomials f, g are in $\mathbb{Z}[x]$, then we may choose an appropriate prime $p \in \mathbb{N}$, compute $\gcd(f \bmod p, g \bmod p)$ in $\mathbb{F}_p[x]$, and recover the gcd from its image modulo p.

EXAMPLE 6.1 (continued). We let f, g be as in Example 6.1 and take $p = 7$. Then the Euclidean Algorithm in $\mathbb{F}_7[x]$ works as follows.

$$f := 824x^5 - 65x^4 - 814x^3 - 741x^2 - 979x - 764$$

$$g := 216x^4 + 663x^3 + 880x^2 + 916x + 617$$

```
rho[0]  := lcoeff(f, x) mod 7; r[0]  := f/rho[0] mod 7;
```

$$\rho_0 := 5$$

$$r_0 := x^5 + x^4 + x^3 + 3x^2 + 3x + 4$$

```
rho[1]  := lcoeff(g, x) mod 7; r[1]  := g/rho[1] mod 7;
```

$$\rho_1 := 6$$

$$r_1 := x^4 + 2x^3 + 2x^2 + x + 6$$

```
printlevel := 2:
for i from 1 to 5 do
  q[i]  := Quo(r[i - 1], r[i], x, 'a[i + 1]') mod 7;
  a[i + 1]  := a[i + 1];
  if (a[i + 1] <> 0) then
    rho[i + 1]  := lcoeff(a[i + 1], x);
    r[i + 1]  := a[i + 1] / rho[i + 1] mod 7;
  fi;
od;
```

$$q_1 := x+6$$
$$a_2 := x^3 +4x^2 +5x+3$$
$$p_2 := 1$$
$$r_2 := x^3 +4x^2 +5x+3$$
$$q_2 := x+5$$
$$a_3 := 5x^2 +x+5$$
$$p_3 := 5$$
$$r_3 := x^2 +3x+1$$
$$q_3 := x+1$$

$$a_4 := x+2$$
$$p_4 := 1$$
$$r_4 := x+2$$
$$q_4 := x+1$$
$$a_5 := 6$$
$$p_5 := 6$$
$$r_5 := 1$$
$$q_5 := x+2$$
$$a_6 := 0$$

Thus $\gcd(f \bmod 7, g \bmod 7) = 1$. If h is a common divisor of f and g in $\mathbb{Z}[x]$, then $h \bmod 7$ divides $f \bmod 7$ and $g \bmod 7$, which implies that $h \bmod 7$ is constant. Now $\mathrm{lc}(h)$ divides $\mathrm{lc}(f)$, and since the latter does not vanish modulo 7, we have $\deg h = \deg(h \bmod 7)$. This shows that h is constant. ◇

In the above example, the modular approach has revealed that f and g have no nonconstant common divisors in $\mathbb{Z}[x]$, but does this also imply that they have no nonconstant common divisors in $\mathbb{Q}[x]$? The answer is yes, but it requires an important tool, **Gauß' lemma**, which we will discuss in Section 6.2 below.

Besides that, the following questions have to be addressed in order to make the idea from the above example into an algorithm.

○ How big do we have to choose the modulus p so that we can recover the gcd from its image modulo p? This requires an upper bound on the size of the coefficients of the gcd, which is provided by **Mignotte's bound** 6.33 in Section 6.6. The corresponding question for polynomials with coefficients in $F[y]$ for a field F is trivial: the degree in y of the gcd is at most that of the input polynomials.

○ How do we find the denominators of the monic gcd? If the gcd is constant, as in Example 6.1, then this is not an issue, but in general a monic nonconstant gcd will have rational coefficients that are not integers. One solution is rational number reconstruction, as discussed in Section 5.10. Another possibility is to multiply the modular gcd by a known multiple of all denominators; the results of Section 6.2 will provide such a multiple.

○ Does the approach work for any prime, or are there primes where the degree of the modular gcd is too large? Unfortunately, there are such "unlucky" primes, but fortunately, not too many of them. This can be shown by using **resultants**, which we discuss in Section 6.3.

6.2. Gauß' lemma

In this chapter, we lay the groundwork for computing the gcd in rings like $\mathbb{Z}[x]$. The (Extended) Euclidean Algorithm of Chapter 3 works for polynomials in $R[x]$ only if R is a field. In fact, $\mathbb{Z}[x]$ is not a Euclidean domain (Exercise 3.17), and we first have to make sure that the gcd is well defined. One can of course apply the Euclidean Algorithm over the field of fractions K of an integral domain R such as $\mathbb{Z}$, but does that yield the gcd in $R[x]$? The answer is no: say for $f = 2x^2 + 2$, $g = 6x + 2$, we have $\gcd(f,g) = 1$ in $\mathbb{Q}[x]$, but $\gcd(f,g) = 2$ in $\mathbb{Z}[x]$. In this section, we elucidate the difference between these gcds, and will end up with an algorithm for gcds in $R[x]$. Our two standard examples are: $R = \mathbb{Z}$ and $K = \mathbb{Q}$, and $R = F[y]$ and $K = F(y)$.

We recall that two elements a, b of a Unique Factorization Domain R are **associate** if $a = ub$ for a unit $u \in R$. As in Section 3.1, we will assume that we have a multiplicative function "normal" on R such that a is associate to $\mathrm{normal}(a)$ for all $a \in R$. To avoid confusion with the leading coefficient of a polynomial in $R[x]$, we will denote the unit $u \in R$ such that $a = u \cdot \mathrm{normal}(a)$ by $\mathrm{lu}(a)$ and call it the **leading unit** of a. We will say that a is **normalized** if $\mathrm{lu}(a) = 1$, and assume that every element $b \in R$ which is associate to a has $\mathrm{normal}(b) = \mathrm{normal}(a)$. In particular, $\mathrm{normal}(a) = 1$ and $\mathrm{lu}(a) = a$ if and only if a is a unit. Then for all $a, b \in R$, $\gcd(a,b)$ is the unique normalized associate of all greatest common divisors of a and b. In our two standard examples, we take $\mathrm{lu}(a) = \mathrm{sgn}(a)$ and $\mathrm{normal}(a) = |a|$ for $R = \mathbb{Z}$, $\mathrm{lu}(a) = \mathrm{lc}(a)$ and $\mathrm{normal}(a) = a/\mathrm{lc}(a)$ for $R = F[x]$, and in both cases, $\mathrm{lu}(0) = 1$ and $\mathrm{normal}(0) = 0$.

DEFINITION 6.2. *The **content** $\mathrm{cont}(f)$ of $f = f_n x^n + \cdots + f_1 x + f_0 \in R[x]$ with $f_0, \ldots, f_n \in R$ and R a UFD is defined as $\mathrm{cont}(f) = \gcd(f_0, f_1, \ldots, f_n) \in R$. By convention, we take $\mathrm{cont}(f) = \gcd(f_0) = \mathrm{normal}(f_0)$ if $n = 0$. The polynomial f is **primitive** if $\mathrm{cont}(f) = 1$. We define the **primitive part** $\mathrm{pp}(f)$ of f by $f = \mathrm{cont}(f) \cdot \mathrm{pp}(f)$. The content and primitive part of f are unique since we have a unique gcd.*

The following examples illustrate these notions.

EXAMPLE 6.3. Let $R = \mathbb{Z}$, $K = \mathbb{Q}$,

$$f = 12x^3 - 28x^2 + 20x - 4, \; g = -12x^2 + 10x - 2 \in \mathbb{Z}[x].$$

Then

$$\begin{aligned}
\mathrm{cont}(f) &= \gcd(12, -28, 20, -4) = 4, \; \mathrm{cont}(g) = \gcd(-12, 10, -2) = 2, \\
\mathrm{pp}(f) &= 3x^3 - 7x^2 + 5x - 1, \; \mathrm{pp}(g) = -6x^2 + 5x - 1. \; \diamond
\end{aligned}$$

EXAMPLE 6.4. Let

$$
\begin{aligned}
f &= (y^3 + 3y^2 + 2y)x^3 + (y^2 + 3y + 2)x^2 + (y^3 + 3y^2 + 2y)x + (y^2 + 3y + 2), \\
g &= (2y^3 + 3y^2 + y)x^2 + (3y^2 + 4y + 1)x + (y + 1)
\end{aligned}
$$

in $\mathbb{F}_5[x, y]$. Using the Euclidean Algorithm in $R = \mathbb{F}_5[y]$ we compute

$$
\begin{aligned}
\mathrm{cont}(f) &= \gcd(y^3 + 3y^2 + 2y, y^2 + 3y + 2) = y^2 + 3y + 2, \\
\mathrm{cont}(g) &= \gcd(2y^3 + 3y^2 + y, 3y^2 + 4y + 1, y + 1) = y + 1, \\
\mathrm{pp}(f) &= yx^3 + x^2 + yx + 1, \\
\mathrm{pp}(g) &= (2y^2 + y)x^2 + (3y + 1)x + 1. \ \diamond
\end{aligned}
$$

LEMMA 6.5. *For $f \in R[x]$ and $c \in R$, $\mathrm{cont}(cf) = \mathrm{cont}(c) \cdot \mathrm{cont}(f)$ and $\mathrm{pp}(cf) = \mathrm{pp}(c) \cdot \mathrm{pp}(f)$.*

PROOF. Exercise 6.4. □

The following result, due to Gauß, is the cornerstone for unique factorization of polynomials over UFDs.

THEOREM 6.6 *Gauß' lemma.*
For a Unique Factorization Domain R, the product of two primitive polynomials in R[x] is primitive.

PROOF. Let $f, g \in R[x]$ be primitive and $p \in R$ a prime. Then $D = R/\langle p \rangle$ is an integral domain, and so is $D[x]$, since the product of the leading coefficients of two nonzero polynomials is nonzero. By assumption, $f \bmod p$ and $g \bmod p$ are both nonzero in $D[x]$, and hence $fg \bmod p$ is nonzero as well, or equivalently, $p \nmid \mathrm{cont}(fg)$. Thus $\mathrm{cont}(fg) = 1$. □

COROLLARY 6.7.
For $f, g \in R[x]$, $\mathrm{cont}(fg) = \mathrm{cont}(f)\,\mathrm{cont}(g)$ and $\mathrm{pp}(fg) = \mathrm{pp}(f)\,\mathrm{pp}(g)$.

PROOF. Let $h = \mathrm{pp}(fg)$. By Gauß' lemma, $h^* = \mathrm{pp}(f)\,\mathrm{pp}(g)$ is primitive. Then

$$
\begin{aligned}
fg &= (\mathrm{cont}(f) \cdot \mathrm{pp}(f))(\mathrm{cont}(g) \cdot \mathrm{pp}(g)) = \mathrm{cont}(f)\,\mathrm{cont}(g) \cdot h^*, \\
\mathrm{cont}(fg) &= \mathrm{cont}(\mathrm{cont}(f)\,\mathrm{cont}(g)) \cdot \mathrm{cont}(h^*) = \mathrm{cont}(f)\,\mathrm{cont}(g),
\end{aligned}
$$

by Lemma 6.5 and since $\mathrm{cont}(f)\,\mathrm{cont}(g)$ is normalized, and the claim follows. □

Lemma 6.5 is just the special case of Corollary 6.7 when $g = c$ is constant.

It is convenient to extend the definition of content and primitive part to polynomials in $K[x]$. If $f = \sum_{0 \leq i \leq n}(a_i/b)x^i \in K[x]$, with a common denominator $b \in R \setminus \{0\}$ and all $a_i \in R$, then we let $\text{cont}(f) = \gcd(a_0, \ldots, a_n)/\text{cont}(b) \in K$ and $\text{pp}(f) = f/\text{cont}(f)$. For example, we have $\text{cont}(-3x - 9/2) = 3/2 \in \mathbb{Q}$ and $\text{pp}(-3x - 9/2) = -2x - 3 \in \mathbb{Z}[x]$. Then $\text{pp}(f)$ is a primitive polynomial in $R[x]$, and Exercise 6.4 shows that Lemma 6.5 and Corollary 6.7 hold for $c \in K$ and $f, g \in K[x]$.

We recall the following notions. A nonzero nonunit p of a ring R is **prime** if $p \mid ab$ implies that $p \mid a$ or $p \mid b$, and p is **irreducible** if $p = ab$ implies that one of a and b is a unit. Multiplication by units does not change the property of being (or not being) prime or irreducible. Prime elements are irreducible, and if R is a UFD, then the two notions coincide (Section 25.2). We can now prove the following celebrated theorem of Gauß.

THEOREM 6.8 Gauß.

If R is a UFD, then $R[x]$ is a UFD.

PROOF. Since R is an integral domain, $\deg(fg) = \deg f + \deg g$ holds for any nonzero polynomials $f, g \in R[x]$. This implies that the units of $R[x]$ are precisely the units of R, and that a prime $p \in R$ is irreducible in $R[x]$.

Let $f \in R[x]$ be a nonzero nonunit. Since R is a UFD, $\text{cont}(f)$ can be written as a product of irreducibles of $R[x]$, by the above. Let K denote the field of fractions of R. Then $K[x]$ is a Euclidean domain and therefore a UFD, and $\text{pp}(f) = f_1 f_2 \cdots f_r$ in $K[x]$ with (over K) irreducible nonconstant polynomials $f_1, \ldots, f_r$. Extracting contents, Corollary 6.7 yields the factorization

$$\text{pp}(f) = \text{pp}(f_1) \cdots \text{pp}(f_r) \tag{2}$$

into primitive polynomials in $R[x]$. Since each $\text{pp}(f_i)$ is primitive (in $R[x]$) and irreducible in $K[x]$, it is irreducible in $R[x]$. This proves the existence of a factorization into irreducibles in $R[x]$.

By the additivity of the degree, every irreducible factor of a constant $f \in R$ belongs to R, and the uniqueness of the factorization of f in $R[x]$ follows from the one in R. Now we assume that $f \in R[x]$ is nonconstant, and let

$$p_1 \cdots p_k \cdot f_1 \cdots f_r = f = q_1 \cdots q_l \cdot g_1 \cdots g_s$$

be two factorizations of f into irreducibles, with normalized $p_1, \ldots, p_k, q_1, \ldots, q_l$ in R and nonconstant primitive $f_1, \ldots, f_r, g_1, \ldots, g_s \in R[x]$. Then $p_1 \cdots p_k = \text{cont}(f) = q_1 \cdots q_s$, by Corollary 6.7. Thus $k = l$ and $p_1 = q_1, \ldots, p_k = q_k$ after reordering, since R is a UFD. Furthermore,

$$f_1 \cdots f_r = \text{pp}(f) = g_1 \cdots g_s \tag{3}$$

in $R[x]$. Since any factorization in $K[x]$ of a nonconstant primitive polynomial would lead to a nontrivial factorization in $R[x]$, as in (2), these polynomials remain irreducible in $K[x]$. Thus (3) also contains two factorizations of $\mathrm{pp}(f)$ in $K[x]$ into irreducibles, and hence $r = s$ and—after a suitable renumbering—$f_i = b_i g_i$, with $b_i \in K$, for $1 \le i \le r$. Since f_i and g_i are primitive, we have

$$f_i = \mathrm{pp}(f_i) = \mathrm{pp}(b_i g_i) = \mathrm{pp}(b_i)\,\mathrm{pp}(g_i) = \mathrm{pp}(b_i) g_i$$

for $1 \le i \le r$, which concludes the proof since $\mathrm{pp}(b_i)$ is a unit in R. $\square$

In particular, since $R[x]$ is a UFD, any two elements of $R[x]$ have a gcd. In order to have a function gcd on $R[x]$, we extend "lu" to $R[x]$ via $\mathrm{lu}(f) = \mathrm{lu}(\mathrm{lc}(f))$ to define a normal form on $R[x]$. Then a polynomial in $R[x]$ is normalized precisely when its leading coefficient is, and $\gcd(f,g)$ is the unique normalized associate in $R[x]$ of all greatest common divisors of f and g, as usual.

Both 5 and $5x+1$ are primes in $\mathbb{Z}[x]$, but 5 is a unit in $\mathbb{Q}[x]$, while $5x+1$ is a prime also in $\mathbb{Q}[x]$. More generally, nonconstant polynomials are not units, so that $R^{\times} = (R[x])^{\times}$, and $\{1,-1\} = \mathbb{Z}^{\times} = (\mathbb{Z}[x])^{\times} \subset \mathbb{Q}\setminus\{0\} = \mathbb{Q}^{\times} = (\mathbb{Q}[x])^{\times}$, where $R^{\times}$ is the group of units of a ring R.

━━ COROLLARY 6.9. ━━
Let R be $\mathbb{Z}$ or a field, and $n \ge 0$. Then $R[x_1,\dots,x_n]$ is a Unique Factorization Domain. ━━━

━━ COROLLARY 6.10. ━━━
Let R be a UFD with field of fractions K, $f,g \in R[x]$, and h the normalized gcd of f and g in $R[x]$.

(i) The primes of $R[x]$ are the primes of R plus the primitive polynomials in $R[x]$ that are irreducible in $K[x]$.

(ii) $\mathrm{cont}(h) = \gcd(\mathrm{cont}(f),\mathrm{cont}(g))$ in R and $\mathrm{pp}(h) = \gcd(\mathrm{pp}(f),\mathrm{pp}(g))$ in $R[x]$. In particular, $h = \gcd(\mathrm{cont}(f),\mathrm{cont}(g)) \cdot \gcd(\mathrm{pp}(f),\mathrm{pp}(g))$, and h is primitive if one of f and g is.

(iii) $h/\mathrm{lc}(h) \in K[x]$ is the monic gcd of f and g in $K[x]$. ━━━━━━━━━━━━

PROOF. (i) Let $p \in R[x]$. We first assume that p is prime. If p is a constant, then p is prime in R. Otherwise, it is a primitive polynomial and irreducible in $K[x]$, since a factorization in $K[x]$ leads to one in $R[x]$, as in (2).

On the other hand, if p is not prime, then a factorization $p = uv$ with $u,v \notin R^{\times}$ shows that p is not prime in R, and, if p is primitive and nonconstant, that p is reducible in $K[x]$.

(ii) The polynomial h divides f, and hence cont(h) divides cont(f), and, by symmetry, it divides gcd(cont(f), cont(g)). On the other hand, this gcd is in R and a common factor of f and g, hence divides h and then also cont(h). This proves the first claim. The second one follows similarly, using the fact that pp(h) divides pp(f), by Corollary 6.7, and that pp(h) is normalized since h is (Exercise 3.8 (iv)).

(iii) Since $h/\mathrm{lc}(h)$ is a divisor of f and g in $K[x]$, it also divides their monic gcd h^*. On the other hand, $f = f^* h^*$ for some $f^* \in K[x]$, and taking contents together with Corollary 6.7 shows that pp$(h^*) \mid$ pp$(f) \mid f$ in $R[x]$, and similarly pp$(h^*) \mid g$. Thus pp(h^*) divides $h = \gcd(f, g)$ in $R[x]$, which implies that h^* and $h/\mathrm{lc}(h)$ divide each other in $K[x]$, and since both are monic, they are equal. $\square$

The following examples illustrate the difference between gcds in $R[x]$ and $K[x]$.

EXAMPLE 6.3 (continued). With the Euclidean Algorithm in $\mathbb{Q}[x]$, we find that $\gcd(f, g) = \gcd(\mathrm{pp}(f), \mathrm{pp}(g)) = x - 1/3$ in $\mathbb{Q}[x]$; see Example 3.7. Hence

$$
\begin{aligned}
\mathrm{pp}(\gcd(f, g)) &= \gcd(\mathrm{pp}(f), \mathrm{pp}(g)) = 3x - 1 \text{ in } \mathbb{Z}[x], \\
\mathrm{cont}(\gcd(f, g)) &= \gcd(\mathrm{cont}(f), \mathrm{cont}(g)) = \gcd(4, 2) = 2, \\
\gcd(f, g) &= \mathrm{cont}(\gcd(f, g)) \cdot \mathrm{pp}(\gcd(f, g)) = 6x - 2 \text{ in } \mathbb{Z}[x].
\end{aligned}
$$

The polynomials f and pp(f) are normalized in $\mathbb{Z}[x]$ since their leading coefficients are positive, but g and pp(g) are not. Both $\gcd(f, g)$ and $\gcd(\mathrm{pp}(f), \mathrm{pp}(g))$ are normalized. $\Diamond$

EXAMPLE 6.4 (continued). Since $R = \mathbb{F}_5[y]$ is a Euclidean domain and we can regard f, g as polynomials in $R[x]$, we can apply the above results to compute the greatest common divisor of f and g.

$$
\begin{aligned}
\gcd(\mathrm{cont}(f), \mathrm{cont}(g)) &= y + 1, \\
\gcd(\mathrm{pp}(f), \mathrm{pp}(g)) &= yx + 1 \text{ in } \mathbb{F}_5[y][x] = \mathbb{F}_5[x, y], \\
\gcd(f, g) &= \gcd(\mathrm{pp}(f), \mathrm{pp}(g)) = x + \frac{1}{y} \text{ in } \mathbb{F}_5(y)[x], \\
\gcd(f, g) &= \gcd(\mathrm{cont}(f), \mathrm{cont}(g)) \cdot \gcd(\mathrm{pp}(f), \mathrm{pp}(g)) \\
&= (y^2 + y)x + (y + 1) \text{ in } \mathbb{F}_5[y][x].
\end{aligned}
$$

Thus f and pp(f) are normalized in $R[x]$, while g and pp(g) are not. Both $\gcd(f, g)$ and $\gcd(\mathrm{pp}(f), \mathrm{pp}(g))$ are normalized. $\Diamond$

We obtain the following algorithm for calculating gcds in $\mathbb{Z}[x]$ and $F[x, y]$. By Corollary 6.10 (ii) we may assume that the input polynomials are primitive.

━━━ ALGORITHM 6.11 Gcd of primitive polynomials. ━━━━━━━━━━━━━━━━━
Input: Primitive $f, g \in R[x]$, where R is a UFD.
Output: $h = \gcd(f, g)$ in $R[x]$.

1. **call** the Euclidean Algorithm 3.6 to determine the monic gcd v of f and g in
   $K[x]$, where K is the field of fractions of R

2. $b \longleftarrow \gcd(\mathrm{lc}(f), \mathrm{lc}(g))$

3. **return** $\mathrm{pp}(bv) \in R[x]$ ━━━━━━━━━━━━━━━━━━━━━━━━━━━━

━━━ THEOREM 6.12. ━━━━━━━━━━━━━━━━━━━━━━━━━━━━━━━━━━━━
The algorithm works correctly as specified. ━━━━━━━━━━━━━━━━━━━

PROOF. Let h be the normalized gcd of f and g in $R[x]$. By Corollary 6.10, v as
computed in step 1 equals $h/\mathrm{lc}(h)$. Since h divides f and g in $R[x]$, $\mathrm{lc}(h)$ divides
$\mathrm{lc}(f)$ and $\mathrm{lc}(g)$ in R, hence it divides $\gcd(\mathrm{lc}(f), \mathrm{lc}(g))$, and $bv \in R[x]$. Furthermore,
$\mathrm{pp}(bv) \in R[x]$ is primitive, by definition, and normalized, since b is (Exercise 3.8),
so that $\mathrm{pp}(bv) = h$. □

To compute the gcd of arbitrary polynomials, we of course compute the gcd
of their contents in R and apply the algorithm to their primitive parts. However,
Example 6.1 indicates that Algorithm 6.11 is not the best way to do this, and the
modular algorithms of Sections 6.4 through 6.7 will be much more efficient.

6.3. The resultant

The central goal of this whole chapter is to find modular gcd algorithms for domains like $\mathbb{Z}[x]$, $\mathbb{Q}[x]$, and $F[x, y]$. Section 6.13 reports on implementations that
show how much these algorithms are superior to the "classical" one, whose prob-
lems are quite visible in Example 6.1. The simplest such approach, the **big prime
modular algorithm**, chooses a large prime p, calculates the gcd modulo p, and
recovers the true gcd from its modular image. This is quite easy, provided that the
modular gcd is indeed the image of the true gcd; this may, in fact, fail in exceptional cases.

This section provides a general tool, the **resultant**, to control modular images
of the gcd. This introduces linear algebra into our polynomial problems. We also
discuss other applications, such as curve intersection and minimal polynomials of
algebraic elements. In Section 6.10, we introduce the **subresultants**, a generalization that gives us control over all results of the EEA. But the reader should
realize clearly that for gcd calculations the resultant is purely an (indispensable)
conceptual tool and does not enter the algorithms, but only their analysis.

Now let F be a field and $f, g \in F[x]$. The following lemma says that the vanishing linear combination $(-g) \cdot f + f \cdot g = 0$ has the smallest possible coefficient degrees if and only if $\gcd(f, g) = 1$.

LEMMA 6.13. *Let $f, g \in F[x]$ be nonzero. Then $\gcd(f, g) \neq 1$ if and only if there exist $s, t \in F[x] \setminus \{0\}$ such that $sf + tg = 0$, $\deg s < \deg g$, and $\deg t < \deg f$.*

PROOF. Let $h = \gcd(f, g)$. If $h \neq 1$, then $\deg h \geq 1$, and $s = -g/h$, $t = f/h$ suffice. Conversely, let s, t be as assumed. If f and g were coprime, then $sf = -tg$ would imply that $f \mid t$, which is impossible since $t \neq 0$ and $\deg f > \deg t$. This contradiction shows that $h \neq 1$. $\square$

We now reformulate Lemma 6.13 in a different language. Given nonzero $f, g \in F[x]$ of degrees n, m, respectively, we let

$$\varphi = \varphi_{f,g} \colon \quad \begin{array}{ccc} F[x] \times F[x] & \longrightarrow & F[x] \\ (s, t) & \longmapsto & sf + tg \end{array} \tag{4}$$

be the "linear combination map". For $d \in \mathbb{N}$, we let $P_d = \{a \in F[x] \colon \deg a < d\}$, with the convention that $P_0 = \{0\}$. Then φ is a linear mapping of infinite-dimensional vector spaces over F. (It is also an $F[x]$-linear map of $F[x]$-modules, in the natural way.) The restriction of φ to $\varphi_0 \colon P_m \times P_n \longrightarrow P_{n+m}$ is an F-linear mapping between vector spaces of the same finite dimension, and Lemma 6.13 says the following.

▬ THEOREM 6.14. ▬▬▬▬▬▬▬▬▬▬▬▬▬▬▬▬▬▬▬▬▬▬
Let $f, g \in F[x]$ be nonzero of degrees n, m, respectively.

(i) $\gcd(f, g) = 1 \iff \varphi_0$ *is an isomorphism.*

(ii) *If $\gcd(f, g) = 1$, then the Bézout coefficients s_ℓ, t_ℓ computed by the EEA form the unique solution in $P_m \times P_n$ of $\varphi_0(s_\ell, t_\ell) = 1$.* ▬▬▬▬

PROOF. Lemma 6.13 says that

$$\deg \gcd(f, g) \geq 1 \iff \text{there exists a nonzero } (s, t) \in P_m \times P_n \text{ with } \varphi_0(s, t) = 0$$
$$\iff \varphi_0 \text{ is not injective.}$$

For our map φ_0 between vector spaces of equal (finite) dimension, the following three properties are equivalent:

○ φ_0 is an isomorphism,

○ φ_0 is injective (or one-to-one),

○ φ_0 is surjective (or onto).

Claim (i) now follows. For (ii), we recall from Lemma 3.10 that $(s_\ell, t_\ell) \in P_m \times P_n$. Since φ_0 is an isomorphism, the solution $\varphi_0(s_\ell, t_\ell) = 1$ is unique. □

In order to compute with the linear map φ_0, we represent it by a matrix S. We write $f = \sum_{0 \le j \le n} f_j x^j$, $g = \sum_{0 \le j \le m} g_j x^j$, with all $f_j, g_j \in F$. The natural basis for $P_m \times P_n$ consists of $(x^i, 0)$ for $i < m$ and $(0, x^j)$ for $j < n$, and for P_{n+m} we take $(x^{n+m-1}, \ldots, x^2, x, 1)$. On these bases, φ_0 is represented by the $(n+m) \times (n+m)$ matrix S with entries in F defined as

$$
S = \left(
\begin{array}{cccccccccc}
f_n & & & & & g_m & & & & \\
f_{n-1} & f_n & & & & g_{m-1} & g_m & & & \\
\vdots & \vdots & \ddots & & & \vdots & \vdots & \ddots & & \\
\vdots & \vdots & & f_n & g_1 & \vdots & & & \ddots & \\
\vdots & \vdots & & f_{n-1} & g_0 & \vdots & & & & \ddots \\
\vdots & \vdots & & \vdots & & g_0 & & & & g_m \\
f_0 & \vdots & & \vdots & & & \ddots & & & \vdots \\
& f_0 & & \vdots & & & & \ddots & & \vdots \\
& & \ddots & \vdots & & & & & \ddots & \vdots \\
& & & f_0 & & & & & & g_0
\end{array}
\right),
\tag{5}
$$

$$\underbrace{}_{m} \quad \underbrace{}_{n}$$

with m columns of f_j's and n columns of g_j's, and all entries outside the two "parallelograms" equal to zero. This means that when we write

$$
s = \sum_{0 \le j < m} y_j x^j, \quad t = \sum_{0 \le j < n} z_j x^j, \quad sf + tg = \sum_{0 \le j < n+m} u_j x^j,
$$

with all $y_j, z_j, u_j \in F$, then

$$
\begin{pmatrix} u_{n+m-1} \\ \vdots \\ \vdots \\ \vdots \\ u_0 \end{pmatrix} = S \cdot \begin{pmatrix} y_{m-1} \\ \vdots \\ y_0 \\ z_{n-1} \\ \vdots \\ z_0 \end{pmatrix}.
$$

This is the central step; we advise the reader to understand it thoroughly. Theorem 6.14 can now be restated as follows.

COROLLARY 6.15.

Let f, g, n, m be as in Theorem 6.14.

(i) $\gcd(f, g) = 1 \iff \det S \neq 0$.

(ii) If $\gcd(f, g) = 1$ and $y_0, \ldots, y_{m-1}, z_0, \ldots, z_{n-1} \in F$ satisfy

$$
S \cdot
\begin{pmatrix}
y_{m-1} \\
\vdots \\
y_0 \\
z_{n-1} \\
\vdots \\
z_0
\end{pmatrix}
=
\begin{pmatrix}
0 \\
\vdots \\
\vdots \\
0 \\
1
\end{pmatrix},
$$

then $s_\ell = \sum_{0 \leq i < m} y_i x^i$ and $t_\ell = \sum_{0 \leq i < n} z_i x^i$ are the Bézout coefficients computed by the EEA, with $s_\ell f + t_\ell g = 1$.

If R is a (commutative) ring and $f, g \in R[x]$, then $\mathrm{Syl}(f, g) = S$ is their **Sylvester matrix** (sometimes the transpose of S gets this name), and $\mathrm{res}(f, g) = \det S$ their **resultant**. If $n = m = 0$, then S is the "empty" 0×0 matrix with determinant $\mathrm{res}(f, g) = 1$, and it is convenient to define the resultant with the zero polynomial as $\mathrm{res}(f, 0) = \mathrm{res}(0, f) = 0$ if f is zero or nonconstant and $\mathrm{res}(f, 0) = \mathrm{res}(0, f) = 1$ if f is a nonzero constant. Then the resultant is defined for all pairs of polynomials, and Corollary 6.15 (i) holds in all cases.

EXAMPLE 6.16. Let $f = r_0 = x^4 - 3x^3 + 2x$ and $g = r_1 = x^3 - 1$ in $\mathbb{Q}[x]$. The quotients and remainders in the Euclidean Algorithm are

$$
\begin{aligned}
r_0 &= q_1 r_1 + \rho_2 r_2 = (x - 3) r_1 + 3(x - 1), \\
r_1 &= q_2 r_2 = (x^2 + x + 1) r_2.
\end{aligned}
$$

Thus $\gcd(f, g) = r_2 = x - 1$ (both in $\mathbb{Z}[x]$ and in $\mathbb{Q}[x]$), and the resultant is

$$
\mathrm{res}(f, g) = \det
\begin{pmatrix}
1 & 0 & 0 & 1 & 0 & 0 & 0 \\
-3 & 1 & 0 & 0 & 1 & 0 & 0 \\
0 & -3 & 1 & 0 & 0 & 1 & 0 \\
2 & 0 & -3 & -1 & 0 & 0 & 1 \\
0 & 2 & 0 & 0 & -1 & 0 & 0 \\
0 & 0 & 2 & 0 & 0 & -1 & 0 \\
0 & 0 & 0 & 0 & 0 & 0 & -1
\end{pmatrix}
= 0.
$$

If we divide out the gcd, so that $r_0 = f/(x-1) = x^3 - 2x^2 - 2x$ and $r_1 = g/(x-1) = x^2 + x + 1$, we have

$$
\begin{aligned}
r_0 &= q_1 r_1 + r_2 = (x - 3) r_1 + 3 \cdot 1, \\
r_1 &= q_2 r_2 = (x^2 + x + 1) r_2.
\end{aligned}
$$

Now r_0, r_1 are coprime and

$$\mathrm{res}(r_0, r_1) = \det \begin{pmatrix} 1 & 0 & 1 & 0 & 0 \\ -2 & 1 & 1 & 1 & 0 \\ -2 & -2 & 1 & 1 & 1 \\ 0 & -2 & 0 & 1 & 1 \\ 0 & 0 & 0 & 0 & 1 \end{pmatrix} = 9. \diamond$$

═══ COROLLARY 6.17. ═══

Let F be a field, and $f, g \in F[x]$ nonzero. Then the following are equivalent:

(i) $\gcd(f, g) = 1$,

(ii) $\mathrm{res}(f, g) = \det S \neq 0$,

(iii) *there do not exist $s, t \in F[x] \setminus \{0\}$ such that*

$$sf + tg = 0, \quad \deg s < \deg g, \quad \deg t < \deg f.$$

══

EXAMPLE 6.18. A quadratic polynomial $f = ax^2 + bx + c \in F[x]$, with $a \neq 0$, is squarefree (that is, it has no double root) if and only if its discriminant $4ac - b^2$ does not vanish. Equivalently, $\gcd(f, f') = 1$, where $f' = 2ax + b$ is the derivative of f (Section 9.3). We calculate

$$\mathrm{res}\,(f, f') = \det \begin{pmatrix} a & 2a & 0 \\ b & b & 2a \\ c & 0 & b \end{pmatrix} = a(4ac - b^2). \diamond$$

EXAMPLE 6.19. If $F \subseteq K$ are fields, $f, g \in F[x]$, and $h \in K[x]$ is nonconstant and divides f and g, then there is also a nonconstant polynomial $k \in F[x]$ dividing f and g. This is because the resultant $\mathrm{res}(f, g)$ is the same whether we consider it over F or K. By assumption, it is zero in K, hence also in F. Moreover, even the (monic) gcd of f and g is the same over F and over K. This is in contrast to the fact that a polynomial f may very well have a nontrivial factor, with degree between 1 and $\deg f - 1$, over K, but none over F, such as the irreducible $x^2 - 2 \in \mathbb{Q}[x]$, which factors as $x^2 - 2 = (x - \sqrt{2})(x + \sqrt{2})$ in $\mathbb{R}[x]$. $\diamond$

Combining Gauß' lemma 6.6 and Corollary 6.17, we obtain the following.

═══ COROLLARY 6.20. ═══

Let R be a UFD and $f, g \in R[x]$ not both zero. Then $\gcd(f, g)$ is nonconstant in $R[x]$ if and only if $\mathrm{res}(f, g) = 0$ in R. ═══════════════════════════════

═══ COROLLARY 6.21. ═══

Let R be an integral domain and $f, g \in R[x]$ nonzero. Then there exist nonzero $s, t \in R[x]$ such that $sf + tg = \mathrm{res}(f, g)$, $\deg s < \deg g$, and $\deg t < \deg f$. ═══

PROOF. Let F be the field of fractions of R. If $r = \mathrm{res}(f, g) = 0$, then Corollary 6.17 yields such $s, t \in F[x]$, and the claim follows from multiplying with a common denominator. If the resultant is nonzero, then f and g are coprime in $F[x]$, and there exist nonzero $s^*, t^* \in F[x]$ with the stated degree bounds such that $s^* f + t^* g = 1$. Now Corollary 6.48 says that the coefficients of s^* and t^* are the unique solution of a linear system with coefficient matrix $S = \mathrm{Syl}(f, g)$, and Cramer's rule 25.6 implies that each of them is the quotient of the determinant of a submatrix of S by $r = \det S$. Thus $s = r s^*$ and $t = r t^*$ are in $R[x]$. $\square$

When $f, g \in F[x, y]$, we write $\mathrm{res}_x(f, g)$ for the resultant in $F[y]$ with respect to x. Symmetrically, there is also a polynomial $\mathrm{res}_y(f, g) \in F[x]$. We have the following bound on $\deg_y \mathrm{res}_x(f, g)$, where $\deg_y$ denotes the degree with respect to the variable y (Section 25.3).

═══ THEOREM 6.22. ═══

Let $f, g \in F[x, y]$ with $n = \deg_x f \geq m = \deg_x g$, and $\deg_y f, \deg_y g \leq d$. Then

$$\deg_y \mathrm{res}_x(f, g) \leq (n + m) d.$$

PROOF. When we write the determinant $\mathrm{res}_x(f, g)$ as the familiar sum of $(n + m)!$ terms, then each nonzero term has m factors that are coefficients of f, and n factors that are coefficients of g. Hence the degree of each term is at most $md + nd$. $\square$

In Section 6.8, we discuss Bézout's theorem, which corresponds to the bound $\deg_y \mathrm{res}_x(f, g) \leq \deg f \cdot \deg g$, where $\deg$ is the total degree (see Exercise 6.11).

The following corollary gives an analogous bound on the size of the resultant, but now for integer polynomials f and g. It is an immediate consequence of Hadamard's inequality 16.6. Two expressions for the "size" of f play a role: The **2-norm** (or Euclidean norm) $\|f\|_2$ of a polynomial $f = \sum_{0 \leq i \leq n} f_i x^i \in \mathbb{Z}[x]$ is $\|f\|_2 = (\sum_{0 \leq i \leq n} f_i^2)^{1/2}$. The **max-norm** is $\|f\|_\infty = \max\{|f_i| : 0 \leq i \leq n\}$, and the relation $\|f\|_\infty \leq \|f\|_2 \leq (n+1)^{1/2} \|f\|_\infty$ shows that the two norms differ only by a small factor (Section 25.5).

═══ THEOREM 6.23. ═══

Let $f, g \in \mathbb{Z}[x]$, and $n = \deg f \geq m = \deg g \geq 1$. Then

$$|\mathrm{res}(f, g)| \leq \|f\|_2^m \|g\|_2^n \leq (n+1)^{m/2} (m+1)^{n/2} \|f\|_\infty^m \|g\|_\infty^n.$$

6.4. Modular gcd algorithms

Our goal in this and the following sections is to provide a modular gcd algorithm for $\mathbb{Z}[x]$ and $F[x,y]$. We start by investigating the relation between the modular image of the gcd and the gcd of modular images. It turns out that they are usually (essentially) equal, but this fails for the "unlucky primes" that divide an appropriate resultant.

We let $f, g \in R[x]$ for a Euclidean domain R, $p \in R$ a prime, and denote by a bar the reduction modulo p. Corollary 6.20 says that $\gcd(f,g)$ is constant if and only if $\mathrm{res}(f,g) \neq 0$. The resultant $\mathrm{res}(f,g) \in R$ is a polynomial expression in the coefficients of f and g, and one might be tempted to say: since $\mathrm{res}(f,g) = \mathrm{res}(\overline{f},\overline{g})$, $\overline{f}$ and $\overline{g}$ are coprime in $(R/\langle p \rangle)[x]$ if and only if $p \nmid \mathrm{res}(f,g)$.

EXAMPLE 6.24. To get a taste of what can go wrong without further assumptions, we let $R = \mathbb{Z}$ and $p = 2$. When $f = x + 2$ and $g = x$, then $\mathrm{res}(f,g) = -2 \neq 0$ and $\mathrm{res}(\overline{f},\overline{g}) = 0$, as expected. But when $f = 4x^3 - x$ and $g = 2x + 1$, then $\mathrm{res}(f,g) = 0$ and $\mathrm{res}(\overline{f},\overline{g}) = \mathrm{res}(x,1) = 1 \neq 0$; in particular, $\mathrm{res}(f,g) \neq \mathrm{res}(\overline{f},\overline{g})$. ◇

The reason for the unexpected behavior in the last example is that the two relevant Sylvester matrices are formed in rather different ways. Fortunately, this nuisance disappears when p does not divide at least one of the leading coefficients.

LEMMA 6.25. *We let R be a ring (commutative, with 1), $f, g \in R[x]$ nonzero, $r = \mathrm{res}(f,g) \in R$, $I \subseteq R$ an ideal, denote by a bar the reduction modulo I, and assume that $\mathrm{lc}(f) \neq 0$.*

(i) $\overline{r} = 0 \iff \mathrm{res}(\overline{f},\overline{g}) = 0$.

(ii) *If R/I is a UFD, then $\overline{r} = 0$ if and only if $\gcd(\overline{f},\overline{g})$ is nonconstant.*

PROOF. We write $f = \sum_{0 \leq j \leq n} f_j x^j$, $g = \sum_{0 \leq j \leq m} g_j x^j$, with nonzero f_n, g_m and all $f_j, g_j \in R$. If $\deg f = 0$, then both Sylvester matrices are diagonal with f on the diagonal, and the claim is clear. So let $\deg f \geq 1$. If $\overline{g} = 0$, then $\mathrm{res}(\overline{f},\overline{g}) = 0$ and each column of g_j's in the Sylvester matrix $\mathrm{Syl}(f,g)$ vanishes modulo I, so that $\overline{r} = 0$.

We now assume that $\overline{g} \neq 0$, and let i be the smallest index with $\overline{g}_{m-i} \neq 0$. Then we can partition $\mathrm{Syl}(f,g)$ as in Figure 6.1. The lower right submatrix, taken modulo I, is $\mathrm{Syl}(\overline{f},\overline{g})$. All g_j in the first i rows are zero modulo I, and repeated Laplace expansion (Section 25.5) of $r = \det \mathrm{Syl}(f,g)$ along the first row yields modulo I that $\overline{r} = \overline{f}_n^i \, \mathrm{res}(\overline{f},\overline{g})$. This proves (i), and (ii) follows from Corollary 6.20. □

The conclusion may be false when both leading coefficients vanish modulo I, as in the second case of Example 6.24.

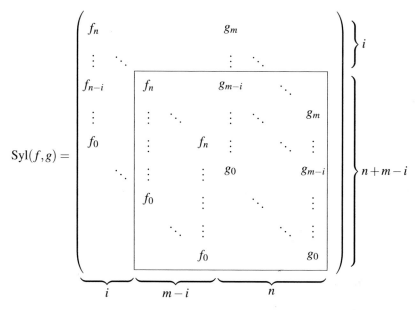

$$\mathrm{Syl}(f,g) =$$

FIGURE 6.1: The Sylvester matrix of f and g.

THEOREM 6.26.

Let R be a Euclidean domain, $p \in R$ prime, and $f, g \in R[x]$ nonzero. Furthermore, let $h = \gcd(f,g) \in R[x]$, $e = \deg h$, $\alpha = \mathrm{lc}(h)$, and assume that p does not divide $b = \gcd(\mathrm{lc}(f), \mathrm{lc}(g)) \in R$. A bar denotes reduction modulo p, and we let $e^* = \deg \gcd(\overline{f}, \overline{g})$. Then

(i) α divides b,

(ii) $e^* \geq e$,

(iii) $e = e^* \iff \overline{\alpha} \cdot \gcd(\overline{f}, \overline{g}) = \overline{h} \iff p \nmid \mathrm{res}(f/h, g/h)$ in R.

PROOF. Since h divides f and g in $R[x]$, $\mathrm{lc}(h)$ divides $\mathrm{lc}(f)$ and $\mathrm{lc}(g)$ in R, and (i) follows. Let $u = f/h$ and $v = g/h \in R[x]$. Then $\deg \overline{h} = e$ since $p \nmid b$ and by (i), and

$$\overline{u}\overline{h} = \overline{f} \quad \text{and} \quad \overline{v}\overline{h} = \overline{g} \tag{6}$$

imply that $\overline{h}$ divides $\gcd(\overline{f}, \overline{g})$, which shows (ii) and the first equivalence in (iii). (Recall that over a field such as $R/\langle p \rangle$, gcds are always taken to be monic.)

Now $p \nmid b$ implies that p divides at most one of $\mathrm{lc}(u)$ and $\mathrm{lc}(v)$, say $p \nmid \mathrm{lc}(u)$. Then Lemma 6.25 (ii) implies that p divides $\mathrm{res}(u,v)$ if and only if $\gcd(\overline{u}, \overline{v}) \neq 1$ in $R/\langle p \rangle$. From (6), we find that $\gcd(\overline{f}, \overline{g}) = \gcd(\overline{u}, \overline{v}) \cdot \overline{h}/\overline{\alpha}$, and this implies the second equivalence in (iii). □

EXAMPLE 6.3 (continued). Let $R = \mathbb{Z}$,

$$f = 12x^3 - 28x^2 + 20x - 4, \; g = -12x^2 + 10x - 2 \in \mathbb{Z}[x]$$

as in Example 6.3, and $p = 17$. Then $h = \gcd(f, g) = 6x - 2$, so that $e = 1$, and $p \nmid \mathrm{lc}(h)$. Computing $f/h = 2x^2 - 4x + 2$, $g/h = -2x + 1$, and

$$\mathrm{res}\left(\frac{f}{h}, \frac{g}{h}\right) = \det \begin{pmatrix} 2 & -2 & 0 \\ -4 & 1 & -2 \\ 2 & 0 & 1 \end{pmatrix} = 2 \not\equiv 0 \bmod 17,$$

we conclude that $\deg \gcd(\overline{f}, \overline{g}) = 1$. In fact, $\gcd(\overline{f}, \overline{g}) = x + 11 \in \mathbb{F}_{17}[x]$, and $\overline{\gcd(f, g)} = 6 \cdot \gcd(\overline{f}, \overline{g})$. ◇

EXAMPLE 6.16 (continued). Let $R = \mathbb{Z}$, $f = x^4 - 3x^3 + 2x$ and $g = x^3 - 1$ in $\mathbb{Z}[x]$. We have seen in Example 6.16 that $h = \gcd(f, g) = x - 1$, whence $e = 1$, and that $\mathrm{res}(f/h, g/h) = 9$. Thus for $p = 3$, we have $\deg \gcd(\overline{f}, \overline{g}) > 1$. Inspection reveals that $\gcd(\overline{f}, \overline{g}) = \overline{g}$ in $\mathbb{F}_3[x]$, and 3 is an "unlucky prime"; in fact, it is the only one, by Theorem 6.26. ◇

EXAMPLE 6.27. Let $R = \mathbb{F}_5[y]$,

$$f = yx^3 + x^2 + yx + 1, \quad g = (2y^2 + y)x^2 + (3y + 1)x + 1 \in R[x].$$

We have seen in Example 6.4 that $h = \gcd(f, g) = yx + 1$ in $R[x]$, and hence $e = 1$. Moreover, $f/h = x^2 + 1$, $g/h = (2y + 1)x + 1$, and

$$\mathrm{res}_x\left(\frac{f}{h}, \frac{g}{h}\right) = \det \begin{pmatrix} 1 & 2y+1 & 0 \\ 0 & 1 & 2y+1 \\ 1 & 0 & 1 \end{pmatrix} = 4y^2 + 4y + 2 = 4(y - 1)(y - 3).$$

We write res_x to indicate that we consider x as the main variable; there is also $\mathrm{res}_y(f, g) = x^2 + 1 \in \mathbb{F}_5[x]$. If we now let $\bar{a} = a(-1)$ for $a \in R$, corresponding to $p = y + 1$, then $b = \gcd(\mathrm{lc}_x(f), \mathrm{lc}_x(g)) = y$ does not vanish modulo p, $\overline{\mathrm{res}(f/h, g/h)} = \mathrm{res}(f/h, g/h)(-1) \neq 0$, and hence $\deg \gcd(\overline{f}, \overline{g}) = 1$. Actually

$$\overline{\mathrm{lc}(h)} \cdot \gcd(\overline{f}, \overline{g}) = -\gcd(-x^3 + x^2 - x + 1, x^2 - 2x + 1) = -x + 1 = h(-1) = \overline{h}.$$

On the other hand, if $\bar{a} = a(1)$ for $a \in R$, then $\bar{b} \neq 0$, $\overline{\mathrm{res}(f/h, g/h)} = 0$, and $\deg \gcd(\overline{f}, \overline{g}) > 1$. In fact, $\gcd(\overline{f}, \overline{g}) = x^2 + 3x + 2 = \overline{g}/3$. ◇

6.5. Modular gcd algorithm in $F[x,y]$

In Section 6.11, we present a modular algorithm that computes all results of the Extended Euclidean Algorithm, including the gcd and the Bézout coefficients. But if just the gcd is required, there is a better way which we now describe.

In a modular algorithm, say with a big prime p, we need two conditions to be satisfied: p has to be large enough so that the coefficients of the gcd can be recovered from their images modulo p, and p should not divide the resultant and the leading coefficient of the gcd, so that its degree does not change modulo p. When both input polynomials have degree about n and coefficients of length n, then the bound for the first condition is $O(n)$, but for the second one it is about n^2. The trick now is to choose p *randomly* so that coefficient recovery is always guaranteed, but the non-divisibility condition only with high probability.

This introduces the important method of **probabilistic algorithms**. Such an algorithm takes an input, makes some random choices (say, chooses several times a bit, either 0 or 1, each with equal probability), does some calculations, and returns an output. If one can prove that the probability of returning the correct output is at least some value greater than $1/2$, say $2/3$, then one can run the algorithm repeatedly, and will obtain the correct answer by a majority vote with probability arbitrarily close to 1. This is called a **Monte Carlo algorithm**. In some applications, as in this chapter, one can easily test the output for correctness. Then the error probability becomes zero, and only the running time is a random variable. This is called a **Las Vegas algorithm**. See Notes 6.5 and Section 25.8 for discussions.

These probabilistic algorithms actually started in computer algebra, with Berlekamp's polynomial factorization (Section 14.8) and Solovay & Strassen's primality test (Section 18.6). Their power and simplicity has made them a ubiquitous tool in many areas of computer science. We have seen examples of probabilistic modular testing in Section 4.1. These methods have an inherent uncertainty, but it can be made arbitrarily small, and thus they are like playing a highly attractive lottery: the stakes are only a tiny fraction of the jackpot (say, polynomial time vs. exponential time), but you are almost guaranteed to win!

In a probabilistic algorithm, the error probability bound has to hold no matter what the inputs are. This must not be confused with the *average-case analysis* of an algorithm, where the average cost is determined for some reasonable probability distribution of the inputs. This sometimes provides a valuable insight, but its Achilles heel is whether the inputs in a real environment actually follow the assumed distribution.

Now here is our first probabilistic algorithm. It works over a field F where sufficiently many irreducible univariate polynomials of any degree can be found. By $\mathrm{lc}_x(f)$ we denote the leading coefficient of a bivariate polynomial $f \in F[x,y]$ with respect to the variable x.

━━━ ALGORITHM 6.28 Modular bivariate gcd: big prime version. ━━━━━━━━━━━━━━━
Input: Primitive polynomials $f, g \in F[x, y] = R[x]$, where $R = F[y]$ and F is a field,
with $\deg_x f = n \geq \deg_x g \geq 1$ and $\deg_y f, \deg_y g \leq d$.
Output: $h = \gcd(f, g) \in R[x]$.

1. $b \longleftarrow \gcd(\operatorname{lc}_x(f), \operatorname{lc}_x(g))$

2. **repeat**

3.   choose a random monic irreducible polynomial $p \in R$ with $\deg p = d + 1 + \deg b$

4. $\overline{f} \longleftarrow f \bmod p, \quad \overline{g} \longleftarrow g \bmod p$
             call the Euclidean Algorithm 3.6 over $R/\langle p \rangle$ to compute the monic
             $v \in R[x]$ with $\deg_y v < \deg_y p$ and $v \bmod p = \gcd(\overline{f}, \overline{g}) \in (R/\langle p \rangle)[x]$

5.   compute $w, f^*, g^* \in R[x]$ of degrees in y less than $\deg_y p$ such that

$$w \equiv bv \bmod p, \quad f^* w \equiv bf \bmod p, \quad g^* w \equiv bg \bmod p \qquad (7)$$

6. **until** $\deg_y(f^* w) = \deg_y(bf)$ and $\deg_y(g^* w) = \deg_y(bg)$

7. **return** $\operatorname{pp}_x(w)$ ━━━

If also the cofactors f/h and g/h are needed, they can easily be obtained as
$\operatorname{pp}_x(f^*)$ and $\operatorname{pp}_x(g^*)$. Before computing f^* and g^* in step 5, one will first test
whether the constant coefficient of w divides the constant coefficients of bf and bg,
and go back to step 3 if this test fails. We may compute f^* and g^* as $f^* \equiv f/v$
$\bmod p$ and $g^* \equiv g/v \bmod p$.

To compute the gcd of non-primitive polynomials, we first compute the gcd of
their contents, then apply the algorithm to their primitive parts, and finally multiply
its result by the gcd of the contents. If the gcd of the constant coefficients of f
and g is smaller than b, then exchanging the roles of the leading and the constant
coefficients decreases the required degree of p.

The above remarks also apply to the modular gcd algorithms 6.34, 6.36, and
6.38 below.

━━━ THEOREM 6.29. ━━━
*Let f, g be an input, $h = \gcd(f, g)$ in $R[x]$, and $r = \operatorname{res}_x(f/h, g/h) \in R = F[y]$.
Then r is a nonzero polynomial of degree at most $2nd$, the halting condition in
step 6 is satisfied if and only if p does not divide r, and then the correct output is
returned in step 7. The cost for one iteration of steps 4 through 6 is no more than
$56n^2 d^2 + O(nd(n + d))$ or $O(n^2 d^2)$ operations in F. If $b = 1$, then the cost is at
most $14n^2 d^2 + O(nd(n + d))$. Steps 1 and 7 take $O(nd^2)$ operations in F.* ━━━

PROOF. Since h and f/h divide f, their degrees in y are at most $\deg_y f \le d$, and similarly for g/h, and Theorem 6.22 yields the first claim. Moreover, $\deg_y b < \deg_y p$, and hence $p \nmid b$. We first assume that $p \nmid r$, and let $\alpha = \mathrm{lc}(h) \in R$. Then Theorem 6.26 implies that $\alpha v \equiv h \bmod p$. Moreover, $\alpha \mid b$, and hence $w \equiv bv \equiv (b/\alpha)h \bmod p$. Both w and $(b/\alpha)h$ have degree in y less than $\deg_y p$, whence they are equal. Similarly, we find that $f^* = bf/w$ and $g^* = bg/w$, and the degree conditions in step 6 are satisfied since all congruences in (7) are in fact equalities. Now h is primitive, by Corollary 6.10, and the algorithm returns the correct result $\mathrm{pp}_x(w) = \mathrm{pp}_x((b/\alpha)h) = h$ in step 7 since h, α, and b are all normalized.

On the other hand, if $p \mid r$, then Theorem 6.26 implies that $\deg_y w = \deg_y v > \deg_y h$. If the degree conditions in step 6 were true, then the congruences in (7) would be equalities, and $\mathrm{pp}(w)$ would be a common divisor of f and g of higher degree in x than $\deg_x h$. This contradiction finishes the correctness proof.

Computationally, nothing happens in reducing f and g modulo p in step 4. The cost for the Euclidean Algorithm is at most $\frac{5}{2}n^2 + O(n)$ additions and multiplications in $R/\langle p \rangle$, plus at most $n+2$ modular inversions, by Theorem 3.11. The cost for one addition or multiplication in this residue class ring is at most $4(\deg p)^2 + O(\deg p)$ operations in F, by Corollary 4.6. Since $\deg p = d+1+\deg b \le 2d+1$, the total cost for step 4 is at most $40n^2d^2 + O(nd(n+d))$ operations in F (the cost for the modular inversions is subsumed by the "O" term), and only at most $10n^2d^2 + O(nd(n+d))$ if $b = 1$.

By Section 2.4, the cost for the three multiplications by leading coefficients and the two modular divisions in step 5 is at most $4\deg_x w \cdot (n - \deg_x w) + O(n)$ additions and multiplications modulo p. Since $m(n - m) \le n^2/4$ for all $m \in \mathbb{R}$, this amounts to at most $n^2 + O(n)$ modular operations or $16n^2d^2 + O(nd(n+d))$ operations in F, and only $4n^2d^2 + O(nd(n+d))$ if $b = 1$. Steps 1 and 7 use at most $n+1$ gcds and divisions of polynomials in $F[y]$ of degree at most $2d$, or $O(nd^2)$ operations in F. $\square$

We have ignored the cost for finding p in step 3. For a finite field $F = \mathbb{F}_q$, we will discuss this in Section 14.9: Corollary 14.44 implies that this can be done with an expected number of $O^\sim(d^2 \log q)$ operations in $\mathbb{F}_q$, and that the expected number of iterations of the algorithm is at most two if $d \ge 4 + 2\log_2 n$. Here the $O^\sim$ notation ignores logarithmic factors (Section 25.7).

6.6. Mignotte's factor bound and a modular gcd algorithm in $\mathbb{Z}[x]$

In order to adapt Algorithm 6.28 to $\mathbb{Z}[x]$, we need an a priori bound on the coefficient size of h. Over $F[y]$, the bound

$$\deg_y h \le \deg_y f \qquad (8)$$

is trivial and quite sufficient. Over $\mathbb{Z}$, we could use the subresultant bound of Theorem 6.52 below, but we now derive a much better bound. It actually depends only on one argument of the gcd, say f, and is valid for all factors of f. We will use this again for the factorization of f in Chapter 15.

We extend the **2-norm** to a complex polynomial $f = \sum_{0 \leq i \leq n} f_i x^i \in \mathbb{C}[x]$ by $\|f\|_2 = \left(\sum_{0 \leq i \leq n} |f_i|^2\right)^{1/2} \in \mathbb{R}$, where $|a| = (a \cdot \bar{a})^{1/2} \in \mathbb{R}$ is the norm of $a \in \mathbb{C}$ and $\bar{a}$ is the complex conjugate of a. We will derive a bound for the norm of factors of f in terms of $\|f\|_2$, that is, a bound $B \in \mathbb{R}$ such that any factor $h \in \mathbb{Z}[x]$ of f satisfies $\|h\|_2 \leq B$. One might hope that we can take $B = \|f\|_2$, but this is not the case. For example, let $f = x^n - 1$ and $h = \Phi_n \in \mathbb{Z}[x]$ be the nth cyclotomic polynomial (Section 14.10). Thus Φ_n divides $x^n - 1$, and the direct analog of (8) would say that each coefficient of Φ_n is at most 1 in absolute value, but for example Φ_{105}, of degree 48, contains the term $-2x^7$. In fact, the coefficients of Φ_n are unbounded in absolute value if $n \longrightarrow \infty$, and hence this is also true for $\|h\|_2$. Worse yet, for infinitely many integers n, Φ_n has a very large coefficient, namely larger than $\exp(\exp(\ln 2 \cdot \ln n / \ln\ln n))$, where $\ln$ is the logarithm in base e; such a coefficient has word length somewhat less than n. It is not obvious how to control the coefficients of factors at all, and it is not surprising that we have to work a little bit to establish a good bound.

LEMMA 6.30. *For $f \in \mathbb{C}[x]$ and $z \in \mathbb{C}$, we have $\|(x - z)f\|_2 = \|(\bar{z}x - 1)f\|_2$.*

PROOF. Writing $f = \sum_{0 \leq i \leq n} f_i x^i$ and letting $f_{-1} = f_{n+1} = 0$, we calculate

$$
\begin{aligned}
\|(x - z)f\|_2^2 &= \sum_{0 \leq i \leq n+1} |f_{i-1} - z f_i|^2 = \sum_{0 \leq i \leq n+1} (f_{i-1} - z f_i)(\overline{f_{i-1}} - \bar{z}\overline{f_i}) \\
&= \|f\|_2^2 (1 + |z|^2) - \sum_{0 \leq i \leq n+1} (z\overline{f_{i-1}}f_i + \bar{z}f_{i-1}\overline{f_i}) \\
&= \sum_{0 \leq i \leq n+1} (\bar{z}f_{i-1} - f_i)(z\overline{f_{i-1}} - \overline{f_i}) = \sum_{0 \leq i \leq n+1} |\bar{z}f_{i-1} - f_i|^2 \\
&= \|(\bar{z}x - 1)f\|_2^2. \quad \square
\end{aligned}
$$

Let

$$
f = \sum_{0 \leq i \leq n} f_i x^i = f_n \prod_{1 \leq i \leq n} (x - z_i),
$$

with $f_0, \ldots, f_n, z_1, \ldots, z_n \in \mathbb{C}$. We define $M(f) = |f_n| \cdot \prod_{1 \leq i \leq n} \max\{1, |z_i|\}$, and note that $M(f) \geq 1$ and $M(f) = M(g)M(h)$ if $f = gh$ for $g, h \in \mathbb{C}[x]$. The following theorem of Landau (1905) relates $M(f)$ and $\|f\|_2$.

▬▬ THEOREM 6.31 *Landau's inequality.* ▬▬▬▬▬▬▬▬▬▬▬▬▬▬▬▬
For any $f \in \mathbb{C}[x]$, we have $M(f) \leq \|f\|_2$. ▬▬▬▬▬▬▬▬▬▬▬▬▬▬

PROOF. We arrange the roots so that $|z_1|, \ldots, |z_k| > 1$ and $|z_{k+1}|, \ldots, |z_n| \leq 1$ for some $k \in \{0, \ldots, n\}$, so that $M(f) = |f_n \cdot z_1 \cdots z_k|$. Let

$$g = f_n \prod_{1 \leq i \leq k} (\overline{z_i} x - 1) \prod_{k < i \leq n} (x - z_i) = g_n x^n + \cdots + g_0 \in \mathbb{C}[x].$$

Then

$$
\begin{aligned}
M(f)^2 &= |f_n \overline{z_1} \cdots \overline{z_k}|^2 = |g_n|^2 \leq \|g\|_2^2 = \left\| \frac{g}{\overline{z_1} x - 1} (x - z_1) \right\|_2^2 = \cdots \\
&= \left\| \frac{g}{(\overline{z_1} x - 1) \cdots (\overline{z_k} x - 1)} (x - z_1) \cdots (x - z_k) \right\|_2^2 = \|f\|_2^2,
\end{aligned}
$$

using repeatedly the previous lemma, and the assertion follows. $\square$

It is convenient to use also the **1-norm** $\|f\|_1 = \sum_{0 \leq i \leq n} |f_i|$, so that $\|f\|_\infty \leq \|f\|_2 \leq \|f\|_1 \leq (n+1) \|f\|_\infty$.

THEOREM 6.32.
If $h = \sum_{0 \leq i \leq m} h_i x^i \in \mathbb{C}[x]$ *of degree* m *divides* $f = \sum_{0 \leq i \leq n} f_i x^i \in \mathbb{C}[x]$ *of degree* $n \geq m$, *then*

$$\|h\|_2 \leq \|h\|_1 \leq 2^m M(h) \leq \left| \frac{h_m}{f_n} \right| 2^m \|f\|_2.$$

PROOF. We write $h = h_m \prod_{1 \leq i \leq m} (x - u_i)$ with $u_i \in \mathbb{C}$ for $1 \leq i \leq m$, and note that each u_i equals some root z_j of f. By Viète's rule, we can express the coefficients of h in terms of its roots as

$$h_i = (-1)^{m-i} h_m \sum_{\substack{S \subseteq \{1, \ldots, m\} \\ \#S = m-i}} \prod_{j \in S} u_j,$$

where the sum is the $(m-i)$th elementary symmetric polynomial in $u_1, \ldots, u_m$, and hence

$$|h_i| \leq |h_m| \cdot \sum_S \prod_{j \in S} |u_j| \leq \binom{m}{i} M(h)$$

for $0 \leq i \leq m$. Thus

$$\|h\|_2 \leq \|h\|_1 = \sum_{0 \leq i \leq m} |h_i| \leq 2^m M(h) \leq \left| \frac{h_m}{f_n} \right| 2^m M(f) \leq \left| \frac{h_m}{f_n} \right| 2^m \|f\|_2,$$

by the sum formula for the binomial coefficients and Landau's inequality. $\square$

COROLLARY 6.33 *Mignotte's bound.*
Suppose that $f, g, h \in \mathbb{Z}[x]$ have degrees $\deg f = n \geq 1$, $\deg g = m$, $\deg h = k$, and that gh divides f (in $\mathbb{Z}[x]$). Then

(i) $\|g\|_\infty \|h\|_\infty \leq \|g\|_2 \|h\|_2 \leq \|g\|_1 \|h\|_1 \leq 2^{m+k} \|f\|_2 \leq (n+1)^{1/2} 2^{m+k} \|f\|_\infty$,

(ii) $\|h\|_\infty \leq \|h\|_2 \leq 2^k \|f\|_2 \leq 2^k \|f\|_1$ and $\|h\|_\infty \leq \|h\|_2 \leq (n+1)^{1/2} 2^k \|f\|_\infty$.

PROOF. By Theorem 6.32 and Landau's inequality, we have

$$\|g\|_1 \|h\|_1 \leq 2^{m+k} M(g) M(h) \leq 2^{m+k} M(f) \leq 2^{m+k} \|f\|_2.$$

This proves (i), and (ii) follows by taking $g = 1$. $\square$

Suppose that the polynomials $f, g \in \mathbb{Z}[x]$ have degrees $n = \deg f \geq \deg g$ and max-norm $\|f\|_\infty, \|g\|_\infty$ at most A. Then the max-norm of $\gcd(f, g) \in \mathbb{Z}[x]$ is at most $(n+1)^{1/2} 2^n A$, by Corollary 6.33. We now have the following algorithm for computing a gcd in $\mathbb{Z}[x]$, completely analogous to Algorithm 6.28.

ALGORITHM 6.34 Modular gcd in $\mathbb{Z}[x]$: big prime version.
Input: Primitive polynomials $f, g \in \mathbb{Z}[x]$ with $\deg f = n \geq \deg g \geq 1$ and max-norm $\|f\|_\infty, \|g\|_\infty \leq A$.
Output: $h = \gcd(f, g) \in \mathbb{Z}[x]$.

1. $b \longleftarrow \gcd(\mathrm{lc}(f), \mathrm{lc}(g))$, $B \longleftarrow (n+1)^{1/2} 2^n A b$

2. **repeat**

3.   choose a random prime $p \in \mathbb{N}$ with $2B < p \leq 4B$

4. $\overline{f} \longleftarrow f \bmod p$, $\overline{g} \longleftarrow g \bmod p$
      call the Euclidean Algorithm 3.6 over $\mathbb{Z}_p$ to compute the monic v in
      $\mathbb{Z}[x]$ with $\|v\|_\infty < p/2$ such that $v \bmod p = \gcd(\overline{f}, \overline{g}) \in \mathbb{Z}_p[x]$

5.   compute $w, f^*, g^* \in \mathbb{Z}[x]$ of max-norm less than $p/2$ such that

$$w \equiv bv \bmod p, \quad f^* w \equiv bf \bmod p, \quad g^* w \equiv bg \bmod p \quad (9)$$

6. **until** $\|f^*\|_1 \|w\|_1 \leq B$ and $\|g^*\|_1 \|w\|_1 \leq B$

7. **return** $\mathrm{pp}(w)$

In step 3, we need primes satisfying certain conditions. We do not yet have the tools to solve this task, and postpone its discussion to Section 18.4. The following is analogous to Theorem 6.29.

▬▬ THEOREM 6.35. ▬▬▬▬▬▬▬▬▬▬▬▬▬▬▬▬▬▬▬▬▬▬▬▬▬▬▬▬▬▬▬▬▬

Let h be the normalized gcd of f and g in $\mathbb{Z}[x]$, so that $\mathrm{lc}(h) > 0$. Then $r = \mathrm{res}(f/h, g/h)$ is a nonzero integer with $|r| \le (n+1)^n A^{2n}$, the halting condition in step 6 is true if and only if p does not divide r, and then the output in step 7 is correct. The cost for one execution of steps 4 and 5 is $O(n^2(n^2 + \log^2 A))$ word operations, and steps 1 and 7 take $O(n(n^2 + \log^2 A))$ word operations. ▬▬▬

PROOF. For the correctness, it is sufficient to see that the condition in step 6 holds if and only if $\mathrm{pp}(w) = h$. If the condition holds, then $\|f^* w\|_\infty \le \|f^* w\|_1 \le \|f^*\|_1 \|w\|_1 \le B < p/2$, and $\|bf\|_\infty < p/2$ and $f^* \equiv bf \bmod p$ imply that $f^* w = bf$. Similarly, we find $g^* w = bg$. Theorem 6.26 implies that $\deg w = \deg \gcd(bf, bg)$, and hence $\mathrm{pp}(w) = \gcd(f, g)$ since $b = \mathrm{lc}(w) > 0$. On the other hand, if $\mathrm{pp}(w) = \gcd(f, g)$ with the w calculated in step 5, then Mignotte's bound 6.33 implies the condition in step 6. We refer to Exercise 6.25 for the details.

With $k = \deg h$, we have $\|f/h\|_2, \|g/h\|_2 \le (n+1)^{1/2} 2^{n-k} A$, again by Corollary 6.33, and Theorem 6.23 gives $|r| \le 4^n(n+1)^n A^{2n}$; Exercise 6.24 yields the better bound stated in the theorem. Step 4 takes $O(n^2)$ arithmetic operations in $\mathbb{Z}_p$, and the cost for each of these is $O(\log^2 p)$ word operations. Now $\log p \le \log(4B) \in O(n + \log A)$, whence step 4 uses $O(n^2(n^2 + \log^2 A))$ word operations, and the same bound holds for the divisions in step 5. Steps 1 and 7 take $O(n)$ gcd's and divisions on integers of length $O(n + \log A)$, or $O(n(n^2 + \log^2 A))$ word operations. □

In Section 18.4, we show that we can find a random number p between $2B$ and $4B$ such that p is prime and $p \nmid r$ with probability at least $1/2$ by a probabilistic algorithm using $O^\sim(\log^3 B)$ or $O^\sim(n^3 + \log^3 A)$ word operations (Corollary 18.11). Then the expected number of iterations of the algorithm is at most two.

6.7. Small primes modular gcd algorithms

We have seen in Section 5.5 that the small primes modular approach for computing the determinant is computationally superior to the big prime scheme. The reason that we have discussed big prime modular gcd algorithms at all in the preceding sections is that they are easier and the main idea is more clearly visible than for their small prime variants that we will present now. In practice, we strongly recommend the use of the latter. We start with the algorithm for $F[x, y]$ since it is simpler to describe and analyze than the corresponding algorithm for $\mathbb{Z}[x]$.

▬▬ ALGORITHM 6.36 Modular bivariate gcd: small primes version. ▬▬▬▬▬▬▬

Input: Primitive polynomials $f, g \in F[x, y] = R[x]$ with $\deg_x f = n \ge \deg_x g \ge 1$ and $\deg_y f, \deg_y g \le d$, where $R = F[y]$ for a field F with at least $(4n+2)d + 2$ elements.

Output: $h = \gcd(f, g) \in R[x]$.

1. $b \longleftarrow \gcd(\mathrm{lc}_x(f), \mathrm{lc}_x(g)), \quad l \longleftarrow d+1+\deg_y b$

2. **repeat**

3.　　　　choose a set $S \subseteq F$ of $2l$ evaluation points

4.　　　　$S \longleftarrow \{u \in S : b(u) \neq 0\}$
　　　　for each $u \in S$ **call** the Euclidean Algorithm 3.6 over F to compute
　　　　the monic $v_u = \gcd(f(x,u), g(x,u)) \in F[x]$

5.　　　　$e \longleftarrow \min\{\deg v_u : u \in S\}, \quad S \longleftarrow \{u \in S : \deg v_u = e\}$
　　　　if $\#S \geq l$ **then** remove $\#S - l$ elements from S **else goto** 3

6.　　　　compute by interpolation each coefficient in $F[y]$ of the polynomials
　　　　$w, f^*, g^* \in R[x]$ of degrees in y less than l such that

$$w(x,u) = b(u)v_u,$$

$$f^*(x,u)w(x,u) = b(u)f(x,u), \quad g^*(x,u)w(x,u) = b(u)g(x,u)$$

　　　　for all $u \in S$

7. **until** $\deg_y(f^*w) = \deg_y(bf)$ and $\deg_y(g^*w) = \deg_y(bg)$

8. **return** $\mathrm{pp}_x(w)$

In practice, one will choose the points from F adaptively, starting with about l or even fewer elements in S, remove "unlucky" points that are detected in steps 4, 5, or 7 from S, and add some new random points to S if the condition in step 7 is violated. If the gcd is constant, then only one "lucky" point is sufficient to detect this. The analysis of the above algorithm is somewhat easier, though. These remarks also apply to Algorithm 6.38 below.

THEOREM 6.37.
Algorithm 6.36 correctly computes the gcd of f and g. One iteration of the loop uses at most $12n^2d + 36nd^2 + O((n+d)d)$ arithmetic operations in F, and only $6n^2d + 13nd^2 + O((n+d)d)$ if $b = 1$. If we choose S in step 3 as a uniform random subset with $2l$ elements of a fixed finite set $U \subseteq F$ of cardinality $\#U = (4n+2)d+2$, then the expected number of iterations is at most 2. The cost for steps 1 and 8 is at most $12nd^2 + O((n+d)d)$ operations in F, or even $3nd^2 + O((n+d)d)$ if $b = 1$.

PROOF. We have $\deg_y b \leq d$, $l \leq 2d+1$, and $\#U \geq 6d+2 \geq 2l$, which implies that enough points can be chosen in step 3. The correctness then follows as in the proof of Theorem 6.29. In step 4, the cost per u is $O(d)$ operations in F for evaluating

b at it, at most $4nd + O(n+d)$ operations in F for evaluating (all coefficients of) f and g at $y = u$, plus at most $\frac{5}{2}n^2 + O(n)$ for the gcd, by Theorem 3.11, in total $5n^2l + 8ndl + O((n+d)d)$ operations for all $u \in S$. In step 6, we first compute the modular cofactors $f(x,u)/v_u$ and $g(x,u)/v_u$ for all $u \in S$. As in the proof of Theorem 6.29, this takes at most $n^2 + O(n)$ operations in F per point u, altogether no more than $n^2l + O(nl)$ operations. Then we solve an interpolation problem at l points for each of the at most $2n+2$ coefficients of w, f^*, and g^*, taking a total of $5nl^2 + O((n+d)d)$ operations in F, by Exercise 5.11. Thus one iteration of the loop 2 takes $6n^2l + 8ndl + 5nl^2 + O((n+d)d)$ operations in F. The cost for steps 1 and 8 is at most $n+1$ gcd's of polynomials of degree at most l, plus the same number of divisions, in total no more than $3nl^2 + O((n+d)d)$ operations.

It remains to determine the expected number of iterations. The primes in the algorithm are linear polynomials $y - u$. Let $r = \mathrm{res}_x(f/h, g/h) \in F[y]$. As in the big prime approach, the halting condition in step 7 is satisfied if and only if $y - u$ does not divide the polynomial r, or equivalently, $r(u) \neq 0$, for all $u \in S$. Thus the choice of S in step 3 is successful if and only if the polynomial br does not vanish for at least l points in S. We will say that $u \in U$ is **unlucky** if $b(u)r(u) = 0$. The degree of br in y is at most $(2n+1)d$, by Theorem 6.29. Since U has at least $(4n+2)d$ elements, at most half of the points in U are unlucky. Thus the probability that at most half of the points in S in step 3 are unlucky is at least $1/2$ (Exercise 6.31). Therefore the expected number of iterations of the algorithm is at most two, and the claim follows. $\square$

By increasing the size of U, the failure probability in a single run can be reduced and the expected number of iterations of the algorithm can be brought down arbitrarily close to one. A variant of the algorithm is analyzed in Section 24.3.

The running time of the small primes modular gcd algorithm is better by about one order of magnitude than for the big prime variant when $n \approx d$. If fast polynomial arithmetic, as described in Part II, is used, then the cost even drops to $O^\sim(nd)$ (Corollary 11.9).

When F does not have sufficiently many elements, say when $F = \mathbb{F}_2$, then we have a problem in step 3. This can be circumvented by either making a suitable field extension, which increases all timings by a factor of $O(\log^2(nd))$ (Exercise 6.32), or by choosing nonlinear moduli.

Here is the analogous algorithm for $\mathbb{Z}[x]$. We denote the natural (base e) logarithm by ln.

▬▬ ALGORITHM 6.38 Modular gcd in $\mathbb{Z}[x]$: small primes version. ▬▬▬▬▬

Input: Primitive polynomials $f, g \in \mathbb{Z}[x]$ with $\deg f = n \geq \deg g \geq 1$ and max-norm $\|f\|_\infty, \|g\|_\infty \leq A$.

Output: $h = \gcd(f,g) \in \mathbb{Z}[x]$.

1. $b \longleftarrow \gcd(\mathrm{lc}(f), \mathrm{lc}(g)), \quad k \longleftarrow \left\lceil 2\log_2\left((n+1)^n b A^{2n}\right) \right\rceil$
   $B \longleftarrow (n+1)^{1/2}2^n Ab, \quad l \longleftarrow \lceil \log_2(2B+1) \rceil$

2. **repeat**

3.   choose a set S of $2l$ primes, each less than $2k \ln k$

4. $S \longleftarrow \{p \in S : p \nmid b\}$
   for each $p \in S$ **call** the Euclidean Algorithm 3.6 over $\mathbb{Z}_p$ to compute the monic $v_p \in \mathbb{Z}[x]$ with coefficients in $\{0, \ldots, p-1\}$ such that $v_p \bmod p = \gcd(\bar{f}, \bar{g}) \in \mathbb{Z}_p[x]$, where the bar indicates reduction of each coefficient modulo p

5. $e \longleftarrow \min\{\deg v_p : p \in S\}, \quad S \longleftarrow \{p \in S : \deg v_p = e\}$
   if $\#S \geq l$ **then** remove $\#S - l$ elements from S **else goto** 3

6.   **call** the Chinese Remainder Algorithm 5.4 to compute each coefficient of the unique polynomials $w, f^*, g^* \in \mathbb{Z}[x]$ with max-norms less than $(\prod_{p \in S} p)/2$ and

   $$w \equiv b v_p \bmod p, \quad f^* w \equiv bf \bmod p, \quad g^* w \equiv bg \bmod p$$

   for all $p \in S$

7. **until** $\|f^*\|_1 \|w\|_1 \leq B$ and $\|g^*\|_1 \|w\|_1 \leq B$

8. **return** $\mathrm{pp}(w)$

In step 3, we need primes satisfying certain conditions. This is discussed in Section 18.4. In practice, $2k \ln k$ will be less than the word size of the processor, and we may take (possibly precomputed) single-word primes (just under 2^{32} or 2^{64}, depending on the computer's word size).

THEOREM 6.39.
Algorithm 6.38 works correctly. One execution of steps 4 through 7 can be performed with $O(n(n^2 + \log^2 A)(\log n + \log\log A)^2)$ word operations, and the same estimate holds for steps 1 and 8.

PROOF. Correctness follows as in the proof of Theorem 6.29. For the running time estimate, we first note that $\log p \in O(\log k)$ for each prime $p \in S$. In step 4, the cost per prime p is $O(n \log A \cdot \log k)$ word operations for reducing b and all coefficients of f and g modulo p, and $O(n^2)$ operations in $\mathbb{Z}_p$ or $O(n^2 \log^2 k)$ word operations for the gcd, a total of $O(n(n \log k + \log A)l \log k)$ word operations. In step 6, we perform two divisions with remainder f/v_p and g/v_p modulo p for each $p \in S$, taking $O(n^2 \log^2 k)$ word operations, and then apply the Chinese Remainder Algorithm to each of the at most $2n + 2$ coefficients of w, f^*, and g^*. We have $\log \prod_{p \in S} p = \sum_{p \in S} \log p \in O(l \log k)$, Theorem 5.8 implies that the cost for each coefficient is $O(l^2 \log^2 k)$ word operations, and the cost for all coefficients is $O(nl^2 \log^2 k)$. The cost for steps 1 and 8 is as in Theorem 6.35. We have $l \in O(n + \log A)$ and $\log k \in O(\log n + \log \log A)$, and the claims follow. $\square$

As in the polynomial case, the cost estimate for the small primes algorithm is smaller by about one order of magnitude as for the big prime variant. If we use single precision primes, then the cost is about $O(nl(n + l))$ word operations. In Section 11.1, we will show that the cost drops to $O^{\sim}(n \log A)$ when using the fast methods for polynomial and integer arithmetic from Part II. In Section 18.4, we show that the first k primes $p_1 = 2, \ldots, p_k$ can be computed deterministically by the sieve of Eratosthenes, taking $O(k \log^2 k \log \log k)$ or $O^{\sim}(n(n + \log A))$ word operations, and that each of them is at most $2k \ln k$. The value k is an upper bound on $2 \log_2 |b \operatorname{res}(f/h, g/h)|$, by Theorem 6.35, and this guarantees that at least $k/2$ of our k primes do not divide $b \operatorname{res}(f/h, g/h)$. By Theorem 6.26, at least half of the primes $p_1, \ldots, p_k$ are "lucky". We have $2l \leq k$, and if we choose the set S as a uniform random subset with $2l$ elements of $\{p_1, \ldots, p_k\}$ in step 3, then Exercise 6.31 shows that at least l of the primes in S are lucky with probability no less than $1/2$. The product of l lucky primes exceeds $2B$, by the choice of l, and the expected number of iterations of the algorithm is at most two.

In practice, one would use an adaptive approach as described for the bivariate case, in particular since the Mignotte bound on the coefficients of h is often too large. We present running times of such an implementation in Section 6.13.

6.8. Application: intersecting plane curves

This and the following section discuss two applications of resultants which are not used later.

The historical purpose of the resultant was to solve geometric problems by elimination of variables. As an example, we want to determine the common roots of two polynomials in two variables, or, equivalently, the intersection of two plane curves. Suppose we are given $f, g \in F[x, y]$, where F is a field, and want to intersect the two plane curves

$$X = \{(a, b) \in F^2 : f(a, b) = 0\}, \quad Y = \{(a, b) \in F^2 : g(a, b) = 0\}.$$

We eliminate the variable y by considering the resultant $r = \operatorname{res}_y(f, g) \in F[x]$ with respect to y. We assume that F is **algebraically closed**, so that every nonconstant univariate polynomial over F has a root. This is often required to make general statements about geometric objects such as our curves X and Y true. The reader may imagine that $F = \mathbb{C}$. Now we let Z be the projection of $X \cap Y$ onto the x-axis. If $a \in F$ and $lc_y(f), lc_y(g)$ do not both vanish at $x = a$, then Lemma 6.25 implies that

$$
\begin{aligned}
a \in Z &\iff \exists b \in F \; (a,b) \in X \cap Y \iff \exists b \in F \; f(a,b) = g(a,b) = 0 \\
&\iff \gcd(f(a,y), g(a,y)) \neq 1 \\
&\iff r(a) = \mathrm{res}_y(f,g)(a) = 0.
\end{aligned}
$$

Thus to determine $X \cap Y$, we first compute the $(d+e) \times (d+e)$ determinant over $F[x]$ giving $r \in F[x]$, where d and e are the degrees in y of f and g, respectively, then find all roots of r, and for each such root a we find all the roots $b \in F$ of $\gcd(f(a,y), g(a,y)) \in F[y]$. The fact that $r(a) = 0$ guarantees that such b's exist if not both leading coefficients with respect to y vanish at $x = a$. In other words, Z is contained in the set of roots of r.

This means that intersecting two plane curves is reduced to finding roots of univariate polynomials, a much easier task. (For $F = \mathbb{Q}$ or a finite field, we will solve this task in Part III.) If $n = \deg f$, $m = \deg g$, where deg is the total degree, and $\gcd(f,g) = 1$ in $F[x,y]$, then $X \cap Y$ has "in general" nm points. This is called **Bézout's theorem** after the French geometer Étienne Bézout. It is valid for arbitrary algebraic varieties, provided one counts points "at infinity" and "multiple points and components" properly, and all intersection components have the "correct" dimension.

If $\gcd(f,g) = h$ for some nonconstant $h \in F[x,y]$, then all points of the curve $\{h = 0\}$ belong to $X \cap Y$, and the intersection is infinite. A trivial example is when $f = h = g$.

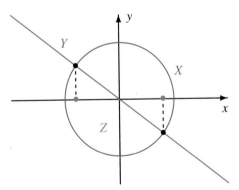

FIGURE 6.2: Intersection of the circle X with the line Y.

EXAMPLE 6.40. We start with a simple example, illustrated in Figure 6.2. Let $f = x^2 + y^2 - 1$ and $g = 3x + 4y$ in $\mathbb{C}[x]$. Then $X = \{(a,b) \in \mathbb{C}^2 : f(a,b) = 0\}$ is a circle of radius 1 centered at the origin (blue), and $Y = \{(a,b) \in \mathbb{C}^2 : g(a,b) = 0\}$ is

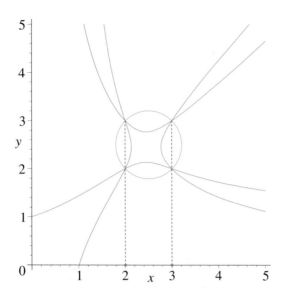

FIGURE 6.3: The three curves $f = 0$ (blue), $g = 0$ (green), and $f + g = 0$ (pink), and the projection of their intersection points to the *x*-axis (red).

a line with slope $-3/4$ through the origin (green). Bézout's theorem says that there are $\deg f \cdot \deg g = 2$ intersection points; they are depicted in Figure 6.2 (black). We might compute them by solving $g = 0$ for y and plugging this into $f = 0$, but let us proceed systematically to illustrate the resultant method. We have

$$\mathrm{res}_y(f,g) = \det \begin{pmatrix} 1 & 4 & 0 \\ 0 & 3x & 4 \\ x^2 - 1 & 0 & 3x \end{pmatrix} = 25x^2 - 16,$$

and the projection Z of $X \cap Y$ onto the x axis consists of the two zeroes $Z = \{4/5, -4/5\}$ of $\mathrm{res}_y(f,g)$ (red). We obtain the corresponding values for y by taking gcds:

$$\gcd(f(\tfrac{4}{5},y), g(\tfrac{4}{5},y)) = \gcd(y^2 - \tfrac{9}{25}, 4y + \tfrac{12}{5}) = y + \tfrac{3}{5},$$

$$\gcd(f(-\tfrac{4}{5},y), g(-\tfrac{4}{5},y)) = \gcd(y^2 - \tfrac{9}{25}, 4y - \tfrac{12}{5}) = y - \tfrac{3}{5},$$

and hence the two intersection points are

$$X \cap Y = \left\{ \left(\tfrac{4}{5}, -\tfrac{3}{5}\right), \left(-\tfrac{4}{5}, \tfrac{3}{5}\right) \right\}. \ \diamond$$

EXAMPLE 6.41. We consider the two plane curves $X, Y \subseteq \mathbb{C}^2$ given by the two polynomials

$$f = (y^2 + 6)(x - 1) - y(x^2 + 1), \quad g = (x^2 + 6)(y - 1) - x(y^2 + 1) \in \mathbb{Z}[x, y].$$

Exchanging x and y corresponds to a swap of f and g, and hence the whole situation is symmetric with respect to this exchange.

Before any calculations, let us look at a picture, in Figure 6.3 on page 163. This is easy to generate with MAPLE's `implicitplot` command. The projection Z of $X \cap Y$ onto the x-axis is readily calculated: the resultant

$$
\begin{aligned}
\mathrm{res}_y(f,g) &= 2x^6 - 22x^5 + 102x^4 - 274x^3 + 488x^2 - 552x + 288 \\
&= 2(x-2)^2(x-3)^2(x^2 - x + 4)
\end{aligned}
$$

has the four distinct roots in $Z = \{2, 3, (1 \pm \sqrt{15}i)/2\}$, where $i = \sqrt{-1}$. For each of these values for x we calculate the corresponding values for y:

$$
\begin{aligned}
\gcd(f(2,y),g(2,y)) &= \gcd(y^2 - 5y + 6, -2y^2 + 10y - 12) \\
&= y^2 - 5y + 6 = (y-2)(y-3), \\
\gcd(f(3,y),g(3,y)) &= \gcd(2y^2 - 10y + 12, -3y^2 + 15y - 18) \\
&= y^2 - 5y + 6 = (y-2)(y-3),
\end{aligned}
$$

and

$$
\gcd\left(f\left(\frac{1 \pm \sqrt{15}i}{2}, y\right), g\left(\frac{1 \pm \sqrt{15}i}{2}, y\right)\right) = \left(y - \frac{1 \mp \sqrt{15}i}{2}\right).
$$

Thus $X \cap Y$ consists of the six points

$$
\left\{(2,2),(2,3),(3,2),(3,3),\left(\frac{1+\sqrt{15}i}{2}, \frac{1-\sqrt{15}i}{2}\right), \left(\frac{1-\sqrt{15}i}{2}, \frac{1+\sqrt{15}i}{2}\right)\right\}.
$$

Only the four real points are visible in Figure 6.3. Staring a bit at the equations, one observes that in $f + g$ the terms of degree 3 cancel, and in fact $f + g = 0$ is the equation of a circle, the blue curve in Figure 6.3.

Bézout's theorem says that $X \cap Y$ consists of $3 \cdot 3 = 9$ points. We only found six of them. Where are the others? This book's margin is too narrow to contain them, because they lie at infinity! $\diamond$

EXAMPLE 6.42. As a simple example, we take our two curves to be lines: $X = \{(a,b): ua + vb + w = 0\}$, $Y = \{(a,b): pa + qb + r = 0\}$, where $u, v, w, p, q, r, \in F$ are given. The corresponding resultant is

$$
\begin{aligned}
\mathrm{res}_y(ux + vy + w, px + qy + r) &= \det\begin{pmatrix} v & q \\ ux + w & px + r \end{pmatrix} \\
&= (vp - uq)x + (vr - wq) \in F[x].
\end{aligned}
$$

This linear polynomial has a root if and only if either the leading coefficient $vp - uq$ is nonzero (then $X \cap Y$ consists of one point), or if it and $vr - wq$ both vanish (then $X = Y$). $\diamond$

The general theory of linear algebra generalizes this well-known criterion for simultaneous solvability of two linear equations in two variables. In a similar way, *geometric elimination theory* tries to generalize our curve intersection method to higher dimensions. This is a much more difficult problem, and the current algorithmic methods are feasible only for a fairly small number of variables. We give an introduction to one successful method in Chapter 21: Gröbner bases.

We give a further application of resultants from the theory of algebraic field extensions. Suppose we have two elements α, β of algebraic extensions of a field F, with minimal polynomials $f, g \in F[x]$, respectively (Section 25.3). How can we find the minimal polynomial h of $\alpha + \beta$? Since $(\alpha + \beta, \beta) \in F^2$ is a common zero of $g(y)$ and of $f(x - y)$, the resultant $r = \mathrm{res}_y(f(x - y), g(y)) \in F[x]$ is nonconstant and has $\alpha + \beta$ as a root. Thus h is a factor of r.

EXAMPLE 6.43. We let $F = \mathbb{Q}$, $\alpha = i = \sqrt{-1}$, $\beta = \sqrt{3}$. Then $f = x^2 + 1$, $g = x^2 - 3$, $f(x - y) = y^2 - 2xy + x^2 + 1$, and

$$r = \mathrm{res}_y(f(x - y), g(y)) = \det \begin{pmatrix} 1 & 0 & 1 & 0 \\ -2x & 1 & 0 & 1 \\ x^2 + 1 & -2x & -3 & 0 \\ 0 & x^2 + 1 & 0 & -3 \end{pmatrix} = x^4 - 4x^2 + 16.$$

This polynomial is irreducible in $\mathbb{Q}[x]$, as can be checked by verifying that it has no monic linear or quadratic factors in $\mathbb{Z}[x]$, and hence it is the minimal polynomial of $\alpha + \beta = i + \sqrt{3}$. Its four complex roots are $\pm i \pm \sqrt{3}$. ◇

6.9. Nonzero preservation and the gcd of several polynomials

In this section, we discuss the following problem: Given nonzero polynomials $f_1, \ldots, f_n \in F[x]$ over a field F, compute $h = \gcd(f_1, \ldots, f_n)$. Let $d \in \mathbb{N}$ be such that $\deg f_i \leq d$ for all i. We are particularly interested in the case where d is close to n. A simple approach is to set $h_1 = f_1$ and compute $h_i = \gcd(h_{i-1}, f_i)$ for $i = 2, \ldots, n$. If $\deg h$ is fairly large, say $d/10$, then this will take $n - 1$ gcd calculations of polynomials of degree at least $d/10$.

We now present a more efficient algorithm that uses only one gcd calculation. The basic tool for this probabilistic algorithm is the following useful lemma. It says that a nonzero polynomial is likely to take a nonzero value at a random point. In other words, random evaluations probably preserve nonzeroness.

LEMMA 6.44. *Let R be an integral domain, $n \in \mathbb{N}$, $S \subseteq R$ finite with $s = \#S$ elements, and $r \in R[x_1, \ldots, x_n]$ a polynomial of total degree at most $d \in \mathbb{N}$.*

(i) *If r is not the zero polynomial, then r has at most ds^{n-1} zeroes in S^n.*

(ii) *If $s > d$ and r vanishes on S^n, then $r = 0$.*

PROOF.   (i) We prove the claim by induction on n. The case $n = 1$ is clear, since a nonzero univariate polynomial of degree at most d over an integral domain has at most d zeroes (Lemma 25.4). For the induction step, we write r as a polynomial in x_n with coefficients in $x_1, \ldots, x_{n-1}$: $r = \sum_{0 \le i \le k} r_i x_n^i$ with $r_i \in R[x_1, \ldots, x_{n-1}]$ for $0 \le i \le k$ and $r_k \ne 0$. Then $\deg r_k \le d - k$, and by the induction hypothesis, r_k has at most $(d-k)s^{n-2}$ zeroes in S^{n-1}, so that there are at most $(d-k)s^{n-1}$ common zeroes of r and r_k in S^n. Furthermore, for each $a \in S^{n-1}$ with $r_k(a) \ne 0$, the univariate polynomial $r_a = \sum_{0 \le i \le k} r_i(a) x_n^i \in R[x_n]$ of degree k has at most k zeroes, so that the total number of zeroes of r in S^n is bounded by

$$(d-k)s^{n-1} + ks^{n-1} = ds^{n-1}.$$

(ii) follows immediately from (i). □

In the example $r = \prod_{1 \le i \le d}(x_n - a_i)$, where $a_1, \ldots, a_d \in S$ are distinct, the bound in (i) is achieved when $\#S \ge d$. A typical application of (i) is in the analysis of probabilistic algorithms, rewriting it as

$$\text{prob}\{r(a) = 0 : a \in S^n\} \le \frac{d}{\#S}, \qquad (10)$$

where a is chosen in S^n uniformly at random. In the applications, the tricky part is usually to show that r is nonzero. An amazing fact is that this bound on the probability is independent of the number of variables.

For the probabilistic algorithm below, we assume that we have a finite set $S \subseteq F$ and a "random element generator for S", which produces a uniform random member of S. Instead of computing many gcds, it just uses one.

ALGORITHM 6.45 Gcd of many polynomials.
Input: $f_1, \ldots, f_n \in F[x]$, where F is a field.
Output: $h \in F[x]$ monic, so that $h = \gcd(f_1, \ldots, f_n)$ is probably true.

1. choose $a_3, \ldots, a_n \in S$ independently at random

2. $g \longleftarrow f_2 + \sum_{3 \le i \le n} a_i f_i$

3. **return** $\gcd(f_1, g)$

Lemma 6.44 yields the following theorem.

THEOREM 6.46.
Suppose that $\deg f_i \le d$ for each i, and $h^* = \gcd(f_1, \ldots, f_n)$. Then the algorithm uses at most $2(n-2)(d+1) + \frac{5}{2}d^2 + O(d)$ operations in F, h^* divides h, and $\text{prob}\{h \ne h^*\} \le d/\#S$.

PROOF. The cost estimate is immediate from Theorem 3.11. Since h^* divides $f_1, \ldots, f_n$, it divides g and $\gcd(f_1, g) = h$. It remains to establish the bound on the error probability.

Dividing each f_i by h^* if necessary, we may assume that $\gcd(f_1, \ldots, f_n) = 1$, and also that $f_1 \neq 0$. Let $A_3, \ldots, A_n$ be new indeterminates over $F(x)$, $R = F[A_3, \ldots, A_n]$, $K = F(A_3, \ldots, A_n)$ the field of fractions of R, $G = f_2 + \sum_{3 \leq i \leq n} A_i f_i \in R[x]$, and $r = \operatorname{res}_x(f_1, G) \in R$. Then r is a polynomial in $A_3, \ldots, A_n$ of degree at most d, and Lemma 6.25, applied to the ideal $I = \langle A_3 - a_3, \ldots, A_n - a_n \rangle$ for which $R/I \cong F$, shows that

$$r(a_3, \ldots, a_n) \neq 0 \iff \operatorname{res}_x(f_1, g) \neq 0 \iff \gcd(f_1, g) = 1.$$

In order to apply Lemma 6.44, we have to show that r is not the zero polynomial. Let u be a common divisor of f_1 and G in $R[x]$. Since u divides f_1, its coefficients lie in the splitting field E of f_1 over F. But $E[x] \cap K[x] = F[x]$, and hence $u \in F[x]$. If we think of G as a linear polynomial in $A_3, \ldots, A_n$ with coefficients in $F[x]$, then $u \mid G$ implies that u divides the coefficients of G in that representation, so that u divides $f_1, \ldots, f_n$. Since $\gcd(f_1, \ldots, f_n) = 1$, it follows that $u \in F$. Therefore the gcd of f_1 and G in $R[x]$ is a constant. By Corollary 6.20, r is not the zero element of R, and Lemma 6.44 yields the bound on the error probability. $\square$

The $\frac{5}{2}d^2 + O(d)$ from the time bound can be replaced by $O(d \log^2 d \cdot \log\log d)$ when using the fast Euclidean Algorithm from Chapter 11. The dominating cost of about dn for Algorithm 6.45 is unavoidable, since this is the input size.

In practice, one would choose f_1 to have minimal degree among $f_1, \ldots, f_n$. To reduce the error probability to zero, we can in addition compute the remainders f_1 rem $h, \ldots, f_n$ rem h; this is somewhat cheaper than n gcds, and $h = h^*$ if and only if all remainders are zero. In the rare event that they are not, one can rerun the algorithm with h and these remainders. This is particularly useful for computing the primitive part of a bivariate polynomial with respect to one variable, since then the quotients $f_1/h^*, \ldots, f_n/h^*$ are needed anyway.

Using the Extended Euclidean Algorithm in step 3 yields a representation of h as a linear combination of $f_1, \ldots, f_n$ (Exercise 6.38). Using Algorithm 6.45, one can also compute the least common multiple of several polynomials (Exercise 6.39).

6.10. Subresultants

In this section, we extend the resultant theory—which governs the gcd—to the subresultants which cover all results of the Extended Euclidean Algorithm. As before, this leads to efficient modular methods, but now for the whole algorithm. The reader only interested in efficient gcd algorithms may skip this and proceed directly to the implementation report in Section 6.13.

So now let F be an arbitrary field, and $f, g \in F[x]$ nonzero of degrees $n \geq m$, respectively. We use the notation for the results of the Extended Euclidean Algorithm, as in (1) on page 131, and $n_i = \deg r_i$ for $0 \leq i \leq \ell + 1$, with $r_{\ell+1} = 0$ and $\deg r_{\ell+1} = -\infty$.

━━ THEOREM 6.47. ━━━━━━━━━━━━━━━━━━━━━━━━━━━━━━━━━━━

Let $0 \leq k \leq m \leq n$. Then k does not appear in the degree sequence if and only if there exist $s, t \in F[x]$ satisfying

$$t \neq 0, \quad \deg s < m - k, \quad \deg t < n - k, \quad \deg(sf + tg) < k. \qquad (11)$$

━━━

PROOF. "$\Longrightarrow$": Suppose that k does not appear in the degree sequence. Then there exists an i with $2 \leq i \leq \ell + 1$ such that $n_i < k < n_{i-1}$. We claim that $s = s_i$ and $t = t_i$ do the job. We have $sf + tg = r_i$, and $\deg r_i = n_i < k$. Furthermore, from Lemma 3.10, we have

$$\begin{aligned} \deg s &= m - n_{i-1} < m - k, \\ 0 \leq \deg t &= n - n_{i-1} < n - k. \end{aligned}$$

The case $i = \ell + 1$ gives $s = g / r_\ell$ and $t = -f / r_\ell$, where $k < n_\ell$ and $r_{\ell+1} = 0$.

"$\Longleftarrow$": Suppose there exist $s, t \in F[x]$ satisfying (11). By Lemma 5.15, there exist $i \in \{1, \ldots, \ell + 1\}$ and $\alpha \in F[x] \setminus \{0\}$ such that $t = \alpha t_i$ and $r = sf + tg = \alpha r_i$. Then from Lemma 3.10 we find

$$\begin{aligned} n - n_{i-1} &\leq \deg \alpha + n - n_{i-1} = \deg(\alpha t_i) = \deg t < n - k, \\ n_i &\leq \deg \alpha + n_i = \deg(\alpha r_i) = \deg r < k. \end{aligned}$$

Together these imply that $n_i < k < n_{i-1}$, so that k is between two consecutive remainder degrees and does not occur in the degree sequence. $\square$

As we did for the resultant, we now restate Theorem 6.47 in the language of linear algebra. The reader should keep comparing our development with the material about the resultant in Section 6.3, which is just the special case $k = 0$. For $0 \leq k \leq m$, we thus consider the restriction of the map φ from (4) to $P_{m-k} \times P_{n-k}$. These polynomials are mapped to P_{n+m-k}. But now

$$\dim(P_{m-k} \times P_{n-k}) = n + m - 2k < n + m - k = \dim P_{n+m-k},$$

if $k > 0$. In order to find an isomorphism, we need an image space of the proper dimension. It turns out that the right thing to do is to ignore the k low order coefficients of $a \in P_{n+m-k}$, so that we consider the quotient a quo x^k of a on division by x^k, and the corresponding linear map $P_{n+m-k} \longrightarrow P_{n+m-2k}$. Thus we take

$$\varphi_k : P_{m-k} \times P_{n-k} \longrightarrow P_{n+m-2k}$$
$$(s,t) \longmapsto sf + tg \text{ quo } x^k.$$

This is now a linear map between spaces of the same dimensions. Then Theorem 6.47 becomes the following.

▬▬ COROLLARY 6.48. ▬▬▬▬▬▬▬▬▬▬▬▬▬▬▬▬▬▬▬▬▬▬▬▬▬▬▬
Let $0 \le k \le m \le n$, and $0 \le i \le \ell+1$.

(i) k appears in the degree sequence $\Longleftrightarrow$ φ_k is an isomorphism.

(ii) If $k = n_i$, then the linear coefficients s_i, t_i computed in the EEA are the unique solution of $\varphi_k(s_i, t_i) = 1$. ▬▬▬▬▬▬▬▬▬▬▬▬▬▬▬▬▬▬▬▬▬▬▬▬

PROOF. From Theorem 6.47 we have

k does not appear in the degree sequence

$\qquad \Longleftrightarrow \quad$ there exists a nonzero $(s,t) \in P_{m-k} \times P_{n-k}$ with $\varphi_k(s,t) = 0$

$\qquad \Longleftrightarrow \quad \varphi_k$ is not injective.

We have used the fact that $s \ne 0$ and $\varphi_k(s,t) = 0$ implies $t \ne 0$. This proves (i). For (ii), we note that if $k = n_i$, then $s_i \in P_{m-k}$ and $t_i \in P_{n-k}$ satisfy $\varphi_k(s_i, t_i) = 1$. Since φ_k is an isomorphism, this implies the claim. $\square$

As for the resultant, it is easy to specify the matrix of φ_k. Namely, we write $f = \sum_{0 \le j \le n} f_j x^j$ and $g = \sum_{0 \le j \le m} g_j x^j$, with all $f_j, g_j \in F$. Then the $(n+m-2k) \times (n+m-2k)$ matrix S_k with entries in F defined as

$$S_k = \begin{pmatrix}
f_n & & & & g_m & & & & \\
f_{n-1} & f_n & & & g_{m-1} & g_m & & & \\
\vdots & & \ddots & & \vdots & & \ddots & & \\
f_{n-m+k+1} & \cdots & \cdots & f_n & g_{k+1} & \cdots & \cdots & g_m & \\
\vdots & & & \vdots & \vdots & & & & \ddots & \\
f_{k+1} & \cdots & \cdots & f_m & g_{m-n+k+1} & \cdots & \cdots & \cdots & \cdots & g_m \\
\vdots & & & \vdots & \vdots & & & & & \vdots \\
\vdots & & & \vdots & \vdots & & & & & \vdots \\
f_{2k-m+1} & \cdots & \cdots & f_k & g_{2k-n+1} & \cdots & \cdots & \cdots & \cdots & g_k
\end{pmatrix},$$

$$\underbrace{\qquad\qquad\qquad}_{m-k} \qquad \underbrace{\qquad\qquad\qquad}_{n-k}$$

with $m - k$ columns of f_j's and $n - k$ columns of g_j's, is the matrix of φ_k with respect to the standard bases $(x^i, 0)$ for $i < m - k$ and $(0, x^j)$ for $j < n - k$ of $P_{m-k} \times P_{n-k}$ and $(x^{n+m-2k-1}, \ldots, x^2, x, 1)$ of P_{n+m-2k}. An f_j or g_j with $j < 0$ is zero. In other words, if

$$s = \sum_{0 \le j < m-k} y_j x^j, \quad t = \sum_{0 \le j < n-k} z_j x^j, \quad sf + tg = \sum_{0 \le j < n+m-k} u_j x^j \in F[x],$$

then

$$S_k \cdot (y_{m-k-1}, \ldots, y_0, z_{n-k-1}, \ldots, z_0)^T = (u_{n+m-k-1}, \ldots, u_k)$$

where ^{T} denotes transposition. Again, the reader is advised to understand this relation carefully. We have immediately the following consequence of Corollary 6.48.

COROLLARY 6.49.
Let $0 \le k \le m \le n$, and $0 \le i \le \ell + 1$.

(i) k appears in the degree sequence $\iff \det S_k \ne 0$.

(ii) If $k = n_i$, and $y_0, \ldots, y_{m-k-1}, z_0, \ldots, z_{n-k-1} \in F$ form the unique solution to

$$S_k \cdot (y_{m-k-1}, \ldots, y_0, z_{n-k-1}, \ldots, z_0)^T = (0, \ldots, 0, 1)^T, \qquad (12)$$

then

$$s_i = \sum_{0 \le j < m-k} y_j x^j, \quad t_i = \sum_{0 \le j < n-k} z_j x^j.$$

If R is a (commutative) ring and $f, g \in R[x]$, then in Section 6.3 we called $S_0 = \mathrm{Syl}(f, g)$ their **Sylvester matrix**, and $\mathrm{res}(f, g) = \det S_0$ their **resultant**. The newly defined elements $\sigma_k = \det S_k \in R$ for $0 \le k \le \deg g$ are the **subresultants**. (In the literature and in computer algebra systems, one finds various definitions that are slightly different from ours.) In fact, S_k is a submatrix of S_i if $k > i$.

EXAMPLE 6.16 (continued). Let $f = r_0 = x^4 - 3x^3 + 2x$ and $g = r_1 = x^3 - 1$ in $\mathbb{Z}[x]$. We have seen in Example 6.16 that the degree sequence is $4, 3, 1$, and 0 and 2 do not appear. Moreover, we have calculated $\mathrm{res}(f, g) = \sigma_0 = \det S_0 = 0$. The other subresultants are

$$\sigma_1 = \det S_1 = \det \begin{pmatrix} 1 & 0 & 1 & 0 & 0 \\ -3 & 1 & 0 & 1 & 0 \\ 0 & -3 & 0 & 0 & 1 \\ 2 & 0 & -1 & 0 & 0 \\ 0 & 2 & 0 & -1 & 0 \end{pmatrix} = 9,$$

$$\sigma_2 = \det S_2 \;=\; \det \begin{pmatrix} 1 & 1 & 0 \\ -3 & 0 & 1 \\ 0 & 0 & 0 \end{pmatrix} = 0,$$

$$\sigma_3 = \det S_3 \;=\; \det \begin{pmatrix} 1 \end{pmatrix} = 1. \;\diamond$$

EXAMPLE 6.1 (continued). The following MAPLE code computes the subresultants of the two polynomials from Example 6.1.

$$f := 824x^5 - 65x^4 - 814x^3 - 741x^2 - 979x - 764$$

$$g := 216x^4 + 663x^3 + 880x^2 + 916x + 617$$

```
with(linalg):
S[0] := transpose(sylvester(f, g, x));
```

$$S_0 := \begin{bmatrix}
824 & 0 & 0 & 0 & 216 & 0 & 0 & 0 & 0 \\
-65 & 824 & 0 & 0 & 663 & 216 & 0 & 0 & 0 \\
-814 & -65 & 824 & 0 & 880 & 663 & 216 & 0 & 0 \\
-741 & -814 & -65 & 824 & 916 & 880 & 663 & 216 & 0 \\
-979 & -741 & -814 & -65 & 617 & 916 & 880 & 663 & 216 \\
-764 & -979 & -741 & -814 & 0 & 617 & 916 & 880 & 663 \\
0 & -764 & -979 & -741 & 0 & 0 & 617 & 916 & 880 \\
0 & 0 & -764 & -979 & 0 & 0 & 0 & 617 & 916 \\
0 & 0 & 0 & -764 & 0 & 0 & 0 & 0 & 617
\end{bmatrix}$$

```
S[1] := submatrix(S[0], 1 .. 7, [1, 2, 3, 5, 6, 7, 8]);
```

$$S_1 := \begin{bmatrix}
824 & 0 & 0 & 216 & 0 & 0 & 0 \\
-65 & 824 & 0 & 663 & 216 & 0 & 0 \\
-814 & -65 & 824 & 880 & 663 & 216 & 0 \\
-741 & -814 & -65 & 916 & 880 & 663 & 216 \\
-979 & -741 & -814 & 617 & 916 & 880 & 663 \\
-764 & -979 & -741 & 0 & 617 & 916 & 880 \\
0 & -764 & -979 & 0 & 0 & 617 & 916
\end{bmatrix}$$

```
S[2] := submatrix(S[1], 1 .. 5, [1, 2, 4, 5, 6]);
```

$$S_2 := \begin{bmatrix}
824 & 0 & 216 & 0 & 0 \\
-65 & 824 & 663 & 216 & 0 \\
-814 & -65 & 880 & 663 & 216 \\
-741 & -814 & 916 & 880 & 663 \\
-979 & -741 & 617 & 916 & 880
\end{bmatrix}$$

```
S[3] := submatrix(S[2], 1 .. 3, [1, 3, 4]);
```

$$S_3 := \begin{bmatrix}
824 & 216 & 0 \\
-65 & 663 & 216 \\
-814 & 880 & 663
\end{bmatrix}$$

```
S[4] := submatrix(S[3], 1..1, [1]);
```

$$S_4 := \begin{bmatrix} 824 \end{bmatrix}$$

```
for k from 0 to 4 do
  sigma[k] := det(S[k]);
od;
```

$$\sigma_0 := 3194752718140042727320764\text{8}$$

$$\sigma_1 := 27754088254928081728$$

$$\sigma_2 := -41344606374560$$

$$\sigma_3 := 176909472$$

$$\sigma_4 := 824 \ \diamond$$

Corresponding to the bound of Theorem 6.23 on the resultant, Hadamard's inequality 16.6 yields the following estimate of the subresultants.

──── THEOREM 6.50. ────

Let $f, g \in \mathbb{Z}[x]$, $n = \deg f \geq m = \deg g \geq 1$, and $0 \leq k \leq m$. Then

$$|\sigma_k| = |\det S_k| \leq \|f\|_2^{m-k}\|g\|_2^{n-k} \leq (n+1)^{n-k}\|f\|_\infty^{m-k}\|g\|_\infty^{n-k}.$$

The analogous result for bivariate polynomials reads as follows.

──── THEOREM 6.51. ────

Let $f, g \in F[x,y]$, $n = \deg_x f \geq m = \deg_x g \geq 1$, $\deg_y f, \deg_y g \leq d$, and $0 \leq k \leq m$. Then $\deg_y \sigma_k \leq (n+m-2k)d$. ────

6.11. Modular Extended Euclidean Algorithms

In this section, we use the subresultants from Section 6.10 to prove a bound on the coefficients of the Extended Euclidean Algorithm 3.6 over $\mathbb{Q}[x]$ and $F(y)[x]$, and to derive modular algorithms for the results of the EEA.

──── THEOREM 6.52. ────

Let $f, g \in \mathbb{Z}[x]$ have degrees $n \geq m$ and max-norm $\|f\|_\infty, \|g\|_\infty$ at most A, and let $\delta = \max\{n_{i-1} - n_i : 1 \leq i \leq \ell\}$ be the maximal degree difference of consecutive remainders. The results r_i, s_i, t_i of the Extended Euclidean Algorithm 3.6 for f and g in $\mathbb{Q}[x]$ have numerators and denominators (in lowest terms) absolutely bounded by $B = (n+1)^n A^{n+m}$. The corresponding bound for q_i and ρ_i is $C = (2B)^{\delta+2}$. The algorithm can be performed with $O(n^3 m \delta^2 \log^2(nA))$ word operations. ────

PROOF. Let $1 \leq i \leq \ell$ and $n_i = \deg r_i$. In the EEA, s_i and t_i form the unique solution to the system (12) of linear equations, so that $\sigma_{n_i} s_i$, $\sigma_{n_i} t_i$, and $\sigma_{n_i} r_i = \sigma_{n_i} s_i f + \sigma_{n_i} t_i g$

are in $\mathbb{Z}[x]$, and by Cramer's rule 25.6 and Hadamard's inequality 16.6 we have

$$
\begin{aligned}
|\sigma_{n_i}| &\leq \|f\|_2^{m-n_i}\|g\|_2^{n-n_i} \leq (n+1)^{n-n_i}A^{n+m-2n_i} \leq B, \\
\|\sigma_{n_i}s_i\|_\infty &\leq \|f\|_2^{m-n_i-1}\|g\|_2^{n-n_i} \leq (n+1)^{n-n_i-1/2}A^{n+m-2n_i-1} \leq B, \\
\|\sigma_{n_i}t_i\|_\infty &\leq \|f\|_2^{m-n_i}\|g\|_2^{n-n_i-1} \leq (n+1)^{n-n_i-1/2}A^{n+m-2n_i-1} \leq B, \\
\|\sigma_{n_i}r_i\|_\infty &= \|(\sigma_{n_i}s_i)f + (\sigma_{n_i}t_i)g\|_\infty \leq (n_i+1)(\|\sigma_{n_i}s_i\|_\infty \cdot \|f\|_\infty + \|\sigma_{n_i}t_i\|_\infty \cdot \|g\|_\infty) \\
&\leq (n_i+1)\cdot 2(n+1)^{n-n_i-1/2}A^{n+m-2n_i} \leq 2B.
\end{aligned}
$$

Exercise 6.45 gives the slightly better bound $\|\sigma_{n_i}r_i\|_\infty \leq B$.

Finally, we consider the division with remainder $r_{i-1} = q_i r_i + \rho_{i+1}r_{i+1}$, and let $k = \deg q = n_{i-1} - n_i$. Multiplying up, we find the pseudo-division (Section 6.12)

$$
\sigma_{n_i}^{k+1}(\sigma_{n_{i-1}}r_{i-1}) = (\sigma_{n_i}^k \sigma_{n_{i-1}}q_i)\cdot(\sigma_{n_i}r_i) + (\sigma_{n_i}^{k+1}\sigma_{n_{i-1}}\rho_{i+1}r_{i+1}), \tag{13}
$$

where the four terms in parentheses are in $\mathbb{Z}[x]$. By Exercise 6.44, we have

$$
\begin{aligned}
\|\sigma_{n_i}^k \sigma_{n_{i-1}}q_i\|_\infty &\leq \|\sigma_{n_{i-1}}r_{i-1}\|_\infty \cdot (\|\sigma_{n_i}r_i\|_\infty + |\sigma_{n_i}|)^k \leq (2B)^{k+1}, \\
\|\sigma_{n_i}^{k+1}\sigma_{n_{i-1}}\rho_{i+1}r_{i+1}\|_\infty &\leq \|\sigma_{n_{i-1}}r_{i-1}\|_\infty \cdot (\|\sigma_{n_i}r_i\|_\infty + |\sigma_{n_i}|)^{k+1} \leq (2B)^{k+2}
\end{aligned}
$$

Since $|\sigma_{n_i}^k \sigma_{n_i-1}| \leq B^{k+1}$ and $|\sigma_{n_i}^{k+1}\sigma_{n_{i-1}}| \leq B^{k+2}$, both numerators and denominators of q_i and ρ_{i+1} are absolutely bounded by $(2B)^{k+2} \leq C$.

The algorithm uses $O(nm)$ arithmetic operations (Theorem 3.11) on rational numbers with numerator and denominator absolutely bounded by C. A single such operation can be done with $O(\log^2 C)$ or $O(n^2\delta^2 \log^2(nA))$ word operations, and the claimed time bound follows. $\square$

For random inputs (say, of fixed degrees and coefficient lengths), the expected value of δ is quite small if the degrees n and m of the two inputs are close to each other (Exercise 6.46). It is conceivable that the δ in the estimates for q_i and ρ_i is an artifact and that a more careful analysis would in fact reveal that it can be replaced by 1. Lickteig & Roy (1997) discuss a variant of the EEA where this is indeed the case.

For comparison, we state the analogous bounds for the *classical EEA* 3.5, where the remainders are given by $r_{i+1}^* = r_{i-1}^* \operatorname{rem} r_i^*$ for all i, without dividing out the leading coefficient.

━━━ THEOREM 6.53. ━━━

We denote by $q_i^*, r_i^*, s_i^*, t_i^* \in \mathbb{Q}[x]$ the results of the classical Extended Euclidean Algorithm, and

$$
\alpha_i = \begin{cases} \rho_i\rho_{i-2}\cdots\rho_2\rho_0 & \text{if } i \geq 0 \text{ is even,} \\ \rho_i\rho_{i-2}\cdots\rho_3\rho_1 & \text{if } i \geq 1 \text{ is odd.} \end{cases}
$$

(i) *The length of the algorithm equals that of the monic EEA , and for all i we have*

$$q_i^* = \frac{\alpha_{i-1}}{\alpha_i} q_i, \quad r_i^* = \alpha_i r_i, \quad s_i^* = \alpha_i s_i, \quad t_i^* = \alpha_i t_i.$$

(ii) *Let n, m, δ, A, C be as in Theorem 6.52. The numerators and denominators of the coefficients of all results of the classical algorithm in $\mathbb{Q}[x]$ are bounded by C^{m+3} in absolute value, and the computing time is $O(n^3 m^3 \delta^2 \log^2(nA))$.*

Exercise 6.47 asks for a proof, and Exercise 6.49 gives a slightly better bound for the r_i^*, s_i^*, t_i^* in the classical EEA, essentially replacing δ by 1.

We compare the two bounds from Theorems 6.52 and 6.53 with Mignotte's bound, say when A is an n-digit number and $\delta = 1$. Then the "classical" bound is a number of about n^3 digits, the "monic" one has about n^2 digits, and Mignotte's only about n digits! Of course Mignotte's bound only applies to the gcd, and one cannot hope for a bound of similar quality for all results of the EEA.

Theorem 6.52 provides a clear explanation for the coefficient growth, as in Example 6.1. The results of the EEA are governed by subresultants and grow at a quadratic rate in length. But the leading coefficients α_i in the classical Euclidean Algorithm are a product of $i/2$ such entries, and thus grow at a cubic rate. This does not literally follow from Theorem 6.53, which gives only upper bounds, but there seems to be typically little cancellation in the product defining α_i. For instance, in the example below, the products of numerators and denominators in $r_5 = \alpha_5 = \rho_1 \cdot \rho_3 \cdot \rho_5$ have 50 and 48 digits, respectively, and only the 2-digit factor 24 cancels. A practical recommendation is therefore to use the monic version wherever possible.

EXAMPLE 6.1 (continued). The classical Euclidean Algorithm for the polynomials from Example 6.1 produces the following quotients and remainders; almost any (random) input will exhibit the same behavior:

$$r_0 := 824x^5 - 65x^4 - 814x^3 - 741x^2 - 979x - 764$$

$$r_1 := 216x^4 + 663x^3 + 880x^2 + 916x + 617$$

```
for i from 1 to 5 do
  q[i] := quo(r[i - 1], r[i], x, 'r[i + 1]');
  r[i + 1] := sort(r[i + 1]);
od;
```

$$q_1 := \frac{103}{27}x - \frac{5837}{486}$$

$$r_2 := \frac{614269}{162}x^3 + \frac{1539085}{243}x^2 + \frac{1863490}{243}x + \frac{3230125}{486}$$

$$q_2 := \frac{34992}{614269}x + \frac{30072401334}{377326404361}$$

$$r_3 := -\frac{23256341085690}{377326404361}x^2 - \frac{27844657381944}{377326404361}x + \frac{32938754949612}{377326404361}$$

$$q_3 := -\frac{23177991308042709}{3767527255881780}x - \frac{21250438136739791430061 2023767}{7301574909368361826957477350}$$

$$r_4 := \frac{1636304738679667846417716189 97}{15023816685943131331188225}x + \frac{27604692189910198127667206 7323}{3004763337188626266237 6450}$$

$$q_4 := -\frac{349399005257174220664364219554244000250}{6174209834848647870665812244107565124 5917}x$$
$$- \frac{53605502942609915156276524064879156029311616760832823425}{2677493197825536079181079039028534398046960224603053128600 9}$$

$$r_5 := \frac{149991809982045460866285094441835939100349686732 75}{14191920665397666794661960809129382074315418338}$$

$$q_5 := 23222307035756106796937177832200054614723837798596144 16232408\backslash$$
$$1189217602966986 \big/ 22534494575630661208071063858852539249064234\backslash$$
$$56098674898184604868575521868 75x + 19588180077596405579 15662822891\backslash$$
$$805286108190368068267554741095619477402238 4587 \big/ 22534494575630\backslash$$
$$66120807106385885253924906423456098674898184604868575521868 75$$

$$r_6 := 0$$

One can see clearly that the numerators and denominators are considerably larger than in the monic Euclidean Algorithm on page 133. ◇

The following analog of Theorems 6.52 and 6.53 for bivariate polynomials is proven in Exercise 6.48.

━━━ THEOREM 6.54. ━━

Let F be a field, $f, g \in F[x,y]$ with $n = \deg_x f \geq m = \deg_x g$ and $\deg_y f, \deg_y g \leq d$, and let $\delta = \max\{n_{i-1} - n_i \colon 1 \leq i \leq \ell\}$ be the maximal degree difference of consecutive remainders in the Euclidean Algorithm for f and g in $F(y)[x]$.

(i) *The results r_i, s_i, t_i of the Extended Euclidean Algorithm 3.6 for f and g in $F(y)[x]$ have numerators and denominators (in lowest terms) of degree in y at most $(n + m - 2n_i)d \leq (n+m)d$. The corresponding bound for the q_i and ρ_i is $(\delta + 2)(n+m)d$. The Extended Euclidean Algorithm 3.6 can be performed with $O(n^3 m \delta^2 d^2)$ operations in F.*

(ii) *For the classical EEA, the degree bound is $(m+3)(\delta+2)(n+m)d$, and the number of operations in F is $O(n^3 m^3 \delta^2 d^2)$.* ━━━

The following generalization of Theorem 6.26 will lead to modular algorithms for the EEA.

THEOREM 6.55.

Let R be a Euclidean domain with field of fractions K, $p \in R$ prime, and $f, g \in R[x]$ nonzero such that p does not divide $b = \gcd(\mathrm{lc}(f), \mathrm{lc}(g))$. Furthermore let $0 \leq i \leq \ell$ and $r_i, s_i, t_i \in K[x]$ be the results in the ith row of the monic EEA, $n_i = \deg r_i$, and $\sigma = \sigma_{n_i} \in R$ the n_ith subresultant of f, g. A bar denotes the reduction modulo p.

(i) The polynomials $\sigma r_i, \sigma s_i, \sigma t_i$ are in $R[x]$.

(ii) The remainder degree n_i occurs in the EEA for $\overline{f}, \overline{g}$ over $R/\langle p \rangle$ if and only if $p \nmid \sigma$.

(iii) If $p \nmid \sigma$, then p divides no denominator in r_i, s_i, or t_i, and $\overline{r}_i, \overline{s}_i, \overline{t}_i$ form a row in the EEA for $\overline{f}, \overline{g}$ over $R/\langle p \rangle$, with $\deg \overline{r}_i = n_i$.

PROOF. (i) follows from Cramer's rule, as in the proof of Theorem 6.52. Since $p \nmid b$, $\overline{\sigma}$ is, up to a unit modulo p, equal to the n_ith subresultant of $\overline{f}$ and $\overline{g}$, as in the proof of Lemma 6.25, and Corollary 6.49 gives (ii). For (iii), we note that the coefficients of $\overline{s}_i, \overline{t}_i$ are a solution of (12) over $R/\langle p \rangle$, and the claim follows since the solution is unique, again by Corollary 6.49. $\square$

It is interesting to note that p might divide some previous subresultants, so that some rows are "missing" modulo p, but still the correct results pop up modulo p whenever p does not divide that particular subresultant nor the leading coefficients of f and g.

EXAMPLE 6.56. Let $f = r_0 = x^4 + x^3 + x^2 + x - 4$ and $g = r_1 = x^3 - 2x^2 + x + 3$ in $\mathbb{Z}[x]$. Then the EEA in $\mathbb{Q}[x]$ computes

$$
\begin{aligned}
r_0 &= q_1 r_1 + p_2 r_2 = (x+3)r_1 + 6\left(x^2 - \frac{5}{6}x - \frac{13}{6}\right), \\
r_1 &= q_2 r_2 + p_3 r_3 = \left(x - \frac{7}{6}\right)r_2 + \frac{79}{36}\left(x + \frac{17}{79}\right), \\
r_2 &= q_3 r_3 + p_4 r_4 = \left(x - \frac{497}{474}\right)r_3 - \frac{12\,114}{6241} \cdot 1, \\
r_3 &= q_4 r_4 = r_3 r_4.
\end{aligned}
$$

Modulo $p = 3$, the computation is

$$
\begin{aligned}
r_0^* &= q_1^* r_1^* + p_2^* r_2^* = x \cdot r_1^* + 1 \cdot (x+2), \\
r_1^* &= q_2^* r_2^* = (x^2 + 2x)r_2^*.
\end{aligned}
$$

The degrees 2 and 0 are missing in the degree sequence modulo 3, but nonetheless the two remainders r_3 and r_2^* of degree 1 are equal modulo 3. $\diamond$

We obtain the following modular algorithm for the results of the EEA in $\mathbb{Q}[x]$.

━━━ ALGORITHM 6.57 Modular EEA in $\mathbb{Q}[x]$: small primes version. ━━━
Input: $f, g \in \mathbb{Z}[x]$ with $\deg f = n \geq \deg g = m \geq 1$ and $\|f\|_\infty, \|g\|_\infty \leq A$.
Output: The results r_i, s_i, t_i in $\mathbb{Q}[x]$ of the EEA for f and g.

1. $B \longleftarrow (n+1)^n A^{n+m}, \quad r \longleftarrow \lceil \log_2(2A^2 B^3 + 1) \rceil$
   choose a set $S \subseteq \mathbb{N}$ of r primes

2. $S \longleftarrow \{p \in S : p \nmid \mathrm{lc}(f)$ and $p \nmid \mathrm{lc}(g)\}$
   for each $p \in S$ **call** the Euclidean Algorithm 3.6 to compute all results in $\mathbb{Z}_p[x]$ of the EEA for f mod p and g mod p

3. Let $n_0 = n \geq n_1 = m > n_2 > \ldots > n_\ell \geq 0$ be the degrees of all remainders that were computed in step 2
   for $i = 2, \ldots, \ell$ **do**
   $\qquad S_i \longleftarrow \{p \in S : n_i$ occurs in the degree sequence of f mod p, g mod $p\}$
   $\qquad$ compute the coefficients of the monic remainder $r_i \in \mathbb{Q}[x]$ of degree
   $\qquad n_i$ and of $s_i, t_i \in \mathbb{Q}[x]$ from their images modulo the primes in S_i by
   $\qquad$ rational number reconstruction (Section 5.10)

4. **return** r_i, s_i, t_i for $2 \leq i \leq \ell$ ━━━━━━━━━━━━

━━━ THEOREM 6.58. ━━━
The algorithm returns the correct values as specified. If S in step 1 consists of the first r primes, then the algorithm uses $O(n^3 m \log^2(nA)(\log^2 n + (\log\log A)^2))$ word operations. ━━━━━━━━━━━━

PROOF. We denote by $\sigma_{m-1}, \sigma_{m-2} \ldots, \sigma_0 \in \mathbb{Z}$ the subresultants and by $m_0 = n$, $m_1 = m, m_2, \ldots, m_{\ell^*}$ the degree sequence of (f, g).

Let $0 \leq k \leq m$. Then for any prime $p \in S$, k occurs as a remainder degree, say $k = n_i$, for f mod p and g mod p if and only if $\sigma_k \not\equiv 0$ mod p. By the choice of r, we have $\prod_{p \in S} p > 2B^3 A^2$. After removing divisors of $\mathrm{lc}(f)$ and $\mathrm{lc}(g)$ from S in step 2, we still have $\prod_{p \in S} p > 2B^3$. Since $|\sigma_k| \leq B$, by Theorem 6.50, we have $\prod_{p \in S_i} p > 2B^2$ if $\sigma_k \neq 0$. (If $\sigma_k = 0$, then no modular remainder has degree k.) It follows that precisely those k with $\sigma_k \neq 0$ occur as modular remainder degrees, and $\ell^* = \ell$ and $n_i = m_i$ for $0 \leq i \leq \ell$. Theorem 6.55 says that r_i mod p, s_i mod p, t_i mod p have been computed in step 2 for the primes p in S_i. The numerators and denominators of the coefficients of the monic r_i are absolutely bounded by B, by

Theorem 6.52, and they can indeed be uniquely reconstructed from their images modulo the $p \in S_i$ (Theorem 5.26). The same holds for s_i and t_i.

For the cost analysis, Theorem 18.10 says that the first r primes can be computed in time $O(r \log^2 r \log\log r)$ in step 1, and that $\log p \in O(\log r)$ for all $p \in S$. Thus the cost per prime p in step 2 is $O(n \log A \log r)$ word operations for reducing all coefficients of f and g modulo p, a total of $O(n \log A \cdot r \log r)$ operations. The EEA modulo p takes $O(nm \log^2 r)$ word operations (Theorem 3.11 and Corollary 4.7), and $O(nmr \log^2 r)$ for all $p \in S$. Since $\log \prod_{p \in S} p = \sum_{p \in S} \log p \in O(r \log r)$, we have $O(r^2 \log^2 r)$ word operations for reconstructing one rational coefficient in step 3 from its image modulo all primes in S by means of the Chinese Remainder Algorithm 5.4 and the Extended Euclidean Algorithm 3.6 over $\mathbb{Z}$. Since all r_i, s_i, t_i together have $O(nm)$ coefficients, the total cost for step 3 is $O(nmr^2 \log^2 r)$ word operations. This dominates the cost for the other steps, and the claim follows from $r \in O(n \log(nA))$. $\square$

If also some quotient q_i and the corresponding ρ_{i+1} is required, we calculate them by one division with remainder: $r_{i-1} = q_i r_i + \rho_{i+1} r_{i+1}$.

As for the small primes modular determinant computation, actually a slightly smaller value for r is sufficient; see Exercise 18.21.

Our timing estimate is—up to logarithmic factors—the same as for direct calculation (Theorem 6.52) and for the big prime variant (Exercise 6.51). However, in many applications we are only interested in one particular row r_i, s_i, t_i of the EEA. Then the rational number reconstruction in step 3 takes only $O(nr^2 \log^2 r)$ word operations, and the overall cost drops to $O^{\sim}(n^3 \log^2 A)$, which is faster by about a factor of m than both direct calculation and the big prime version.

In practice, one would not take the first r primes but instead sufficiently many (possibly precomputed) single precision primes just below the word size, and then the cost is $O(nmr^2)$ word operations. When using fast algorithms for integer arithmetic as discussed in Part II, the cost for the algorithm drops to $O^{\sim}(n^3 \log A)$ word operations. Theorem 6.52 implies that the output size is at most about $n^2 \log_{2^{64}} B \in O^{\sim}(n^3 \log A)$ words, and hence the above time estimate is—up to logarithmic factors—optimal when the size of the output is close to the upper bound. When in addition using the fast Euclidean Algorithm from Chapter 11 in step 2, then we may compute a single row r_i, s_i, t_i in the EEA at a cost of only $O^{\sim}(n^2 \log A)$ operations (Corollary 11.11).

Here is the analogous algorithm for $F[x, y]$.

━━ ALGORITHM 6.59 Modular bivariate EEA: small primes version. ━━━━━━━━

Input: $f, g \in F[x, y] = R[x]$ of degree $n \geq m \geq 1$ in x and at most d in y, where $R = F[y]$ for a field F with at least $3(n + m + 1)d$ elements.

Output: The results r_i, s_i, t_i in $F(y)[x]$ of the EEA for f and g.

1. let $S \subseteq F$ with $\#S = 3(n+m+1)d$

2. $S \longleftarrow \{u \in S: \mathrm{lc}_x(f), \mathrm{lc}_x(g)$ do not vanish at $y = u\}$
   for each $u \in S$ **call** the Euclidean Algorithm 3.6 to compute all results in
   $F[x]$ of the EEA for $f(x,u)$ and $g(x,u)$

3. let $n_0 = n \geq n_1 = m > n_2 \cdots > n_\ell \geq 0$ be the degrees of all remainders that
   were computed in step 2
   for $i = 2, \ldots, \ell$ **do**
   $\qquad S_i \longleftarrow \{u \in S: n_i$ occurs in the degree sequence of $f(x,u), g(x,u)\}$
   $\qquad$ compute the coefficients of the monic remainder $r_i \in F(y)[x]$ and of
   $\qquad s_i, t_i \in F(y)[x]$ from their values at the points in S_i by Cauchy interpol-
   $\qquad$ ation (Section 5.8)

4. **return** r_i, s_i, t_i for $2 \leq i \leq \ell$

THEOREM 6.60.
*The algorithm returns the correct values as specified. It uses $O(n^3 m d^2)$ operations
in F.*

See Exercise 6.50 for the proof. As for the modular gcd algorithm, we make a
suitable field extension when F does not have sufficiently many elements.

The timing estimate for the small primes modular EEA is the same as for both
the big prime variant and direct calculation, and better by a factor of m if we
only want to compute a single row r_i, s_i, t_i of the EEA, as in the integer case. The
estimate drops to $O^{\sim}(n^3 d)$ when using fast arithmetic (Part II), or even to $O^{\sim}(n^2 d)$
when only one row of the EEA is required (Corollary 11.9). Both bounds are
optimal up to logarithmic factors since the output size for all results is about $n^3 d$,
and for one row about $n^2 d$, at least in a generic sense.

Our purpose in studying subresultants has been to gain a conceptual understanding of Euclid's algorithm and a bound on the coefficients occurring in it. One
might be tempted to actually execute Euclid's algorithm by calculating subresultants via Gaussian elimination. This would be highly inefficient; in Section 11.2
we show how to calculate subresultants efficiently from the ρ_i in the Euclidean Algorithm. They may then be used to replace the rational number reconstruction and
the Cauchy interpolation, respectively, in step 3 of the modular EEA algorithms,
by a (computationally easier) polynomial Chinese remainder or interpolation algorithm, after multiplying all modular images by the corresponding subresultant.

The same modular techniques also apply to gcds of multivariate polynomials
over $\mathbb{Q}$ or a finite field. The rational case is reduced to the finite field case by computing modulo small prime numbers, and the computation of multivariate polynomial gcds over finite fields is reduced to univariate gcd computations by evaluating
one of the variables at distinct points and proceeding recursively.

6.12. Pseudo-division and primitive Euclidean Algorithms

Gauß' lemma 6.6 suggests another way of computing the gcd of two primitive polynomials $f, g \in \mathbb{Z}[x]$: use the primitive versions of the remainders r_i, that is, an integral multiple $\alpha_i r_i \in \mathbb{Z}[x]$ which is primitive. This corresponds to taking essentially the primitive part of a polynomial as its normal form in $\mathbb{Q}[x]$; see Exercise 6.5. It is convenient to replace the usual division with remainder by a **pseudo-division** computing $q, r \in \mathbb{Z}[x]$ from $a, b \in \mathbb{Z}[x]$ with

$$\mathrm{lc}(b)^{1+\deg a - \deg b} a = qb + r, \quad \deg r < \deg b$$

(assuming $b \neq 0$). The integer factor multiplied to a ensures that the division can be carried out in $\mathbb{Z}[x]$ (see also Exercise 2.9). This works with any integral domain R instead of $\mathbb{Z}$, and is useful when R is a ring of multivariate polynomials over an integral domain.

ALGORITHM 6.61 Primitive Euclidean Algorithm.
Input: Primitive polynomials $f, g \in R[x]$, where R is a UFD, of degrees $n \geq m$.
Output: $h = \gcd(f, g) \in R[x]$.

1. $r_0 \longleftarrow f, \quad r_1 \longleftarrow g, \quad n_0 \longleftarrow n, \quad n_1 \longleftarrow m$

2. $i \longleftarrow 1$
   while $r_i \neq 0$ **do**
       { Pseudo-division }
       $a_{i-1} \longleftarrow \mathrm{lc}(r_i)^{1+n_{i-1}-n_i} r_{i-1}, \quad q_i \longleftarrow a_{i-1} \; \mathrm{quo} \; r_i,$
       $r_{i+1} \longleftarrow \mathrm{pp}(a_{i-1} \; \mathrm{rem} \; r_i), \quad n_{i+1} \longleftarrow \deg r_{i+1}$
       $i \longleftarrow i+1$

3. $\ell \longleftarrow i-1$
   return $\mathrm{normal}(r_\ell)$

THEOREM 6.62.
The algorithm correctly computes the gcd as specified. We let $\delta = \max\{n_{i-1} - n_i: 1 \leq i \leq \ell\}$ *be the maximal quotient degree.*

(i) *If* $R = \mathbb{Z}$ *and* $\|f\|_\infty, \|g\|_\infty \leq A$, *then the max-norm of the intermediate results is at most* $(2(n+1)^n A^{n+m})^{\delta+2}$, *and the algorithm uses* $O(n^3 m \delta^2 \log^2(nA))$ *word operations.*

(ii) *If* $R = F[y]$ *for a field* F *and* $\deg_y f, \deg_y g \leq d$, *then the degree in* y *of all intermediate results is at most* $(\delta+2)(n+m)d$, *and the time is* $O(n^3 m \delta^2 d^2)$ *operations in* F.

PROOF. Let $\alpha_i = \mathrm{lc}(r_i) \in R$ for all i, and K be the field of fractions of R. As in Exercise 6.47, we find that $r_i/\alpha_i \in K[x]$ is the ith remainder in the Euclidean Algorithm for f, g. In particular, r_ℓ is a primitive multiple of the monic gcd, and hence $\mathrm{normal}(r_\ell) = h$.

We only prove the claim (i) for $R = \mathbb{Z}$; the bivariate case is left as Exercise 6.53, which also discusses a primitive *Extended* Euclidean Algorithm. For $1 \leq i \leq \ell$, the number r_i is a primitive multiple of the corresponding monic remainder, and thus α_i divides the subresultant σ_{n_i} of f and g, by Theorem 6.55. Let $B = (n+1)^n A^{n+m}$. Then Theorem 6.52 implies that $|\alpha_i|, \|r_i\|_\infty \leq B$. Thus

$$\|a_{i-1}\|_\infty = |\alpha_i|^{n_{i-1}-n_i+1} \|r_{i-1}\|_\infty \leq B^{\delta+2},$$

and Exercise 6.44 implies that

$$\|q_i\|_\infty, \|a_{i-1} \text{ rem } r_i\|_\infty \leq \|r_{i-1}\|_\infty (\|r_i\|_\infty + |\alpha_i|)^{n_{i-1}-n_i+1} \leq (2B)^{\delta+2}.$$

The latter number bounds all integers in the algorithm. The number of operations in $\mathbb{Z}$ is $O(nm)$, and the estimate follows from $\log B \in O(n \log(nA))$. $\square$

The time estimate for the primitive Euclidean Algorithm is the same as for the monic variant; Exercise 6.53 gives a slightly better bound. Its main advantage over the monic algorithm is that it avoids rational numbers or functions completely. Experiments with $R = \mathbb{Z}$ in Section 6.13 show that the primitive algorithm clearly beats the monic algorithm in practice, but it is still slower than the modular algorithms.

We can profitably use Algorithm 6.45 for computing the content and the primitive part of a_{i-1} rem r_i in step 2 when $R = F[y]$. This content is usually quite large: Exercise 6.54 shows that its degree is about $(n_{i-1} - n_i + 1)(n+m-2n_i)d - 2(n_{i-1}-n_{i+1})d \geq 2(n+m-2n_i-2)d$.

EXAMPLE 6.1 (continued). We run the primitive Euclidean Algorithm 6.61 on the polynomials from Example 6.1 in MAPLE.

$$r_0 := 824x^5 - 65x^4 - 814x^3 - 741x^2 - 979x - 764$$

$$r_1 := 216x^4 + 663x^3 + 880x^2 + 916x + 617$$

```
for i from 1 to 5 do
   a[i - 1] := r[i - 1] * lcoeff(r[i], x)
      ^ (degree(r[i - 1], x) - degree(r[i], x) + 1);
   q[i]  := quo(a[i - 1], r[i], x, 'r[i + 1]');
   r[i + 1] := sort(primpart(r[i + 1], x));
od;
```

$$a_0 := 38444544\,x^5 - 3032640\,x^4 - 37977984\,x^3 - 34572096\,x^2 - 45676224\,x$$
$$- 35645184$$

$$q_1 := 177984\,x - 560352$$

$$r_2 := 1842807\,x^3 + 3078170\,x^2 + 3726980\,x + 3230125$$

$$a_1 := 733522530077784\,x^4 + 2251506654822087\,x^3 + 2988425122539120\,x^2$$
$$+ 3110678877552084\,x + 2095293523416633$$

$$q_2 := 398046312\,x + 556896321$$

$$r_3 := -1292018949205\,x^2 - 1546925410108\,x + 1829930830534$$

$$a_2 := 3076221617285867113225886594175\,x^3$$
$$+ 5138429089796618729969295394250\,x^2$$
$$+ 6221496034686259067634654534500\,x$$
$$+ 5392089541409117454572707253125$$

$$q_3 := -2380941563727618435\,x - 1126368994649461694$$

$$r_4 := 867315257966502554\,x + 731586548698031843$$

$$a_3 := -9719028519279011934380367226685286903848824 81780\,x^2$$
$$- 11636526064333709456981010205232425699596 56034928\,x$$
$$+ 137653940301814944695275958692916694665237 1517144$$

$$q_4 := -11205877482273441349080287695 70\,x - 396448327221414114828389881017$$

$$r_5 := 1$$

$$a_4 := 867315257966502554\,x + 731586548698031843$$

$$q_5 := 867315257966502554\,x + 731586548698031843$$

$$r_6 := 0$$

In the example, the leading coefficients of the remainders agree—up to sign—with the numerators of the corresponding coefficients in the monic Euclidean Algorithm. ◇

6.13. Implementations

Table 6.4 gives an overview of the different variants of the Euclidean Algorithm for computing gcds in $\mathbb{Z}[x]$ and $F[x, y]$ that we have discussed in this chapter.

We have implemented all algorithms discussed in this chapter for computing the gcd of two polynomials with integral coefficients in C++, using Victor Shoup's "Number Theory Library" NTL 1.5 for integer and polynomial arithmetic (see http://www.cs.wisc.edu/~shoup/ntl/); we will describe parts of it in Section 9.7. The running times are given in Figures 6.5 and 6.6 for various degrees and coefficient sizes. The integer arithmetic of NTL uses Karatsuba's multiplication algorithm (Section 8.1) which is asymptotically faster than classical multiplication, so that, for example, the running time of the big prime gcd algorithm is

Algorithm	for $\mathbb{Z}[x]$	for $F[x,y]$	time
classical	Algorithm 3.5		n^8
monic	Algorithm 3.6		n^6
primitive	Algorithm 6.61		n^6
big prime modular EEA	Exercise 6.51		n^6
small primes modular EEA	Algorithm 6.57	Algorithm 6.59	n^6
small primes modular EEA, single row	Algorithm 6.57	Algorithm 6.59	n^5
"heuristic gcd"	Exercise 6.27	Exercise 6.28	n^4
big prime modular gcd	Algorithm 6.34	Algorithm 6.28	n^4
small primes modular gcd	Algorithm 6.38	Algorithm 6.36	n^3

TABLE 6.4: Comparison of various Euclidean Algorithms in $\mathbb{Z}[x]$ and $F[x,y]$. The time (word and field operations, respectively) is for polynomials of degree at most n in x and with coefficients of length or degree at most n, respectively, with a normal degree sequence, and ignores logarithmic factors.

only about $n^{3.18}$. All timings are the averages over 10 pseudorandom inputs. The software ran on a Sun Sparc Ultra 1 clocked at 167 MHz.

The experiments were as follows. For each choice of n and k, we pseudorandomly and independently chose three polynomials $a,b,c \in \mathbb{Z}[x]$ of degree $n-1$ and with nonnegative coefficients less than 2^k, and computed the gcd of ac and bc in $\mathbb{Z}[x]$. Thus the degree of the gcd was at least $n-1$; in fact, it was equal to $n-1$ in all cases when $n \geq 3$.

In these cases where the gcd is essentially c, the Mignotte bound for the length of the coefficients of the gcd is too large by a factor of about 2^{2n}, which discriminates against our implementation of the big prime algorithm. For that reason we also ran a variant of the big prime method using the known bound 2^n on the coefficients of c, and it computed the correct gcd in all cases, in time faster than the original big prime algorithm but still slower than the small primes algorithm. The standard deviations in the experiments with the big prime algorithm are considerably higher than for the other algorithms. The reason is that there were enormous differences in the time spent for finding a big prime with the routines of NTL that implement the probabilistic primality testing algorithms of Chapter 18. Figure 6.5 also shows the timings for the big prime algorithm with bound 2^n and *without* the cost of the prime search; one can see that the corresponding curves are much smoother.

We implemented two variants of the "heuristic" gcd algorithm (Exercise 6.27). In the first variant, the two input polynomials are evaluated at a random point, and the evaluation point is a power of two in the second variant. The most time consuming part in both variants is the gcd calculation of two integers with about n^2 bits.

We give timings for two variants of the small primes algorithm: our implementation and the built-in routine of NTL. Both routines differ from Algorithm 6.38 in that they work in an adaptive fashion. They do not compute the Mignotte bound

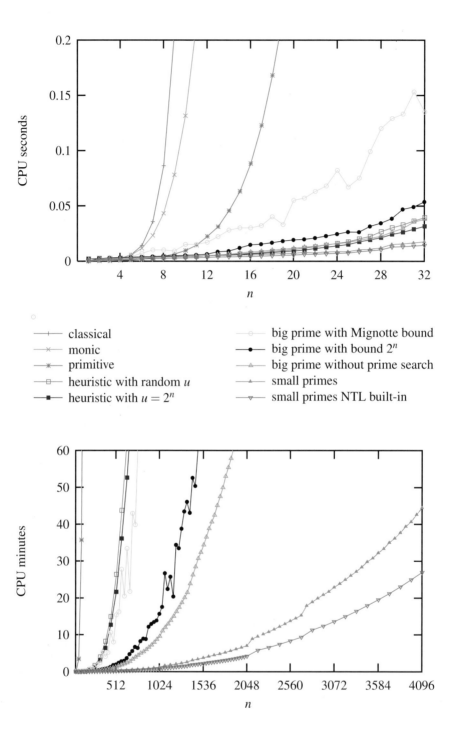

FIGURE 6.5: Various gcd algorithms in $\mathbb{Z}[x]$ for pseudorandom polynomials of degree $n-1$ with nonnegative coefficients less than 2^n, for $1 \leq n \leq 32$ and for $32 \leq n \leq 4096$.

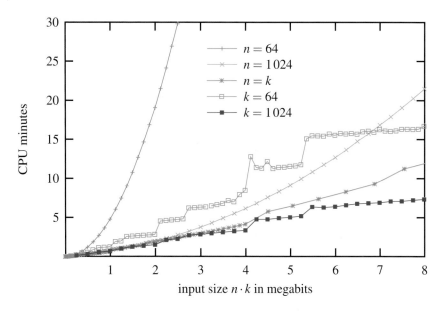

FIGURE 6.6: The small primes modular gcd algorithm in $\mathbb{Z}[x]$ of NTL for various pseudorandom polynomials of degree $n - 1$ with k-bit coefficients.

at all, but take only as many single precision primes as needed to recover the coefficients of the gcd. This is achieved by deterministically adding one new prime each time, discarding the "unlucky" ones which lead to a modular gcd of too large degree, and performing a divisibility test after each new "lucky" prime, starting with the divisibility check for the constant coefficients.

We did not try to optimize our routines and merely implemented them as described in the text, using low-level routines of NTL. The one exception is the small primes algorithm where we employed the adaptivity. By their nature, such comparisons depend on the effort spent on the various subroutines and hence contain an element of unfairness. In particular, the different types of integer and polynomial arithmetic of NTL favor some algorithms and disfavor others.

Nevertheless, the timings confirm the ranking that the theoretical bounds of Table 6.4 suggest, in particular, the efficiency of small primes modular algorithms. Moreover, they show a clear distinction between the monic and the primitive Euclidean Algorithm, which is probably caused by the absence of arithmetic with rational numbers in the latter, and between the big prime and the small primes modular algorithm, which is partly due to the adaptivity and partly reflects our intuition that it is cheaper to solve many "small" problems than one "big" problem of the same total size. In summary, an adaptive small primes modular algorithm appears to be the most favorable method to implement.

Notes. **6.1.** When researchers started experimenting in the late 1960s with the first computer algebra systems (often built by themselves), they observed an unpleasant phenomenon: the rapid coefficient growth in the classical Euclidean Algorithm, say in $\mathbb{Q}[x]$, as in Example 6.1 on page 174 (and almost any random example). One even finds variants of the Euclidean Algorithm having exponential coefficient growth; as long as each rational number is reduced to lowest terms, Theorem 6.52 guarantees that all coefficient lengths in the (monic) Extended Euclidean Algorithm 3.6 are polynomially bounded. This was discovered by Collins (1966, 1967), and led to several new variants of the classical Euclidean Algorithm: using the monic versions, as discussed in Chapter 3, or the primitive versions (Section 6.12) of the remainders, and, most importantly, modular algorithms.

6.2. Gauss (1863b) shows in article 340 that $\mathbb{F}_p[x]$ is a UFD, for a prime p.

6.3. Leibniz (1683) drafted a letter to Tschirnhaus, but never mailed it. He describes how to calculate the resultant of two polynomials of degree five by Euclid's Algorithm, and says that its vanishing means that the two polynomials have a nontrivial gcd. After earlier work of Newton and Maclaurin, Euler (1748c) and Bézout (1764) introduced the resultant; the name comes perhaps from Bézout's *équation resultante de l'élimination*. Bézout obtains the resultant as the determinant of a matrix, today called *Bézout's matrix*, with only $\min\{n,m\}$ rows and columns (Exercise 6.14). He describes how to calculate an $k \times k$ determinant as the familiar sum of $k!$ terms, and gives the linear equations describing the Bézout coefficients s,t with $sf + tg =$ constant, tacitly assuming the gcd to be trivial.

Later algebraic geometers generalized the resultant to more than two variables and polynomials: Euler (1764), Sylvester (1840, 1853), Cayley (1848), Macaulay (1902, 1916, 1922), and many others. The basics of the subresultant theory for univariate polynomials, as presented here, were developed by Jacobi (1836, 1846), Cayley (1848), Kronecker (1873, 1878, 1881b), and Frobenius (1881). Jacobi (1836), § 4, shows that the resultant is irreducible (as a polynomial in indeterminate coefficients of the two input polynomials) and proves Lemma 5.15 in his §15. (He only considers the normal case.) He performs Euclid's algorithm with pseudo-division, and obtains the description $s_i f + t_i g = r_i$ of the remainders. Cauchy (1840) discusses various elimination methods, Euler's and Bézout's among them, proves irreducibility of the resultant, and writes down explicitly the 5×5 Sylvester matrix for two polynomials of degrees 2 and 3, respectively. Cauchy presents an early use of indices: he writes "$f = a_0 x^n + \cdots + a_n$". The lack of such a notation had made earlier work cumbersome. Kronecker (1881b) contains many of the (non-computational) results of this section, including Theorem 6.47. A "modern" presentation along these lines is in von zur Gathen (1984b), where the goal is parallel algorithms for the results of the Extended Euclidean Algorithm—not a topic of this text.

The general notion of a field emerged only towards the end of the 19th century; before that, results were proven separately for various cases. As an example, Sylvester (1881) wrote a note saying that Corollary 6.17 is also valid for polynomials with integer coefficients modulo a prime number.

Sylvester (1840) contains an explicit description of the resultant and of subresultants, as determinants of his matrix and its submatrices, and how to compute the remainders in the Euclidean Algorithm—which he calls derivation—from them. Apparently ignorant of Gauß' elimination method, he calculates $n \times n$ determinants as a sum of $n!$ terms, and ends on the following hopeful note: *"Through the well-known ingenuity and kindly preferred [sic!] help of a distinguished friend, I trust to be able to get a machine made for working Sturm's theorem, and indeed all problems of derivation, after the method here expounded;*

on which subject I have a great deal more yet to say, than can be inferred from this or my preceding papers." It seems that his "Euclidean engine" was never built.

6.5. Ulam invented probabilistic *Monte Carlo algorithms* to estimate the success probability in a solitaire card game; it was much used in the 1940s to approximate multidimensional integrals in high-energy physics at Los Alamos; see Metropolis & Ulam (1949), and Halton (1970) for a survey. Berlekamp's (1970) algorithm (Section 14.8) was the first to use them in computer science, but the breakthrough came in the wake of Solovay & Strassen's (1977) primality test (Section 18.6). Babai (1979) coined the term *Las Vegas algorithms*. Gill (1977) set up the corresponding complexity classes (Section 25.8), and since then they found applications in many areas of computer science: testing (see Section 4.1), sorting, hashing, routing on networks, geometric algorithms such as triangulations or convex hulls, counting problems, online algorithms, and many more. Motwani & Raghavan (1995) give a nice survey of the numerous areas of application.

Early probabilistic algorithms are in Legendre (1785) (see Notes 14.2 and 14.3), Galois (1830) (see Notes 14.9), and Pocklington (1917) who finds a nonsquare modulo a prime by trial, but calls this *a defect in the method*. Buffon gave in 1777 a probabilistic method for approximating π by dropping a needle of length l randomly over an array of equidistant parallel lines with distance $d > l$. The probability of hitting a line is $2l/\pi d$.

6.6. The lower bound on some cyclotomic coefficients is from Vaughan (1974). Theorem 6.32 and Corollary 6.33 are due to Mignotte (1974). For a variety of bounds for factors, see Mignotte (1982, 1988), Mignotte (1989), §IV.3, and Mignotte & Glesser (1994). Since $|g_m| \leq |f_n|$, Mignotte's bound implies that $\|g\|_2 \leq \alpha \|f\|_2$ with $\alpha = 2^m$. Granville (1990) shows that one can use $\alpha = \phi^n$, where $\phi = (1 + \sqrt{5})/2 \approx 1.61803\ldots$ is the golden ratio. Mignotte (1989), Proposition 4.9, proves that for all $m \in \mathbb{N}$ there exist polynomials $f, g \in \mathbb{Z}[x]$ with $\deg g = m$ and $\deg f = \lfloor (m^2 \ln m)/c \rfloor$ such that $\|f\|_1 \geq c2^m (m^2 \ln m)^{-1/2} \|g\|_2$, for an absolute constant $c \in \mathbb{R}_{>0}$.

6.7. Modular gcd algorithms for (multivariate) polynomials over a UFD were discovered by Collins and Brown and stated and analyzed in Brown (1971). Moses & Yun (1973) state a prime power modular algorithm for multivariate polynomials based on Hensel lifting (Chapter 15). It is particularly useful for sparse multivariate polynomials.

6.8. Bézout stated his theorem in 1779; for conics this was already in a book by the Greek mathematician Apollonius, and it was also given by Maclaurin in 1720 and in Cramer (1750), §46. Euler (1748b, §4, 1748c, §3, 1764) states Bézout's theorem correctly: two plane curves of degrees n and m without common components meet in at most nm points. His proof uses his product representation of the resultant (Exercise 6.12). For a proof that the resultant has degree at most nm, in a similar spirit, see Exercise 6.11. General versions of Bézout's theorem for higher-dimensional varieties were first proven in the modern sense by van der Waerden in the 1920s and by Weil in 1946.

6.9. Lemma 6.44 was discovered independently by DeMillo & Lipton (1978), Zippel (1979), and Schwartz (1980). Von zur Gathen, Karpinski & Shparlinski (1996) and Díaz & Kaltofen (1995), Theorem 6.2 and "Note Added in Proof", analyze Algorithm 6.45, the latter also for multivariate polynomials. Chen & Kao (1997) and Lewin & Vadhan (1998) use algebraic field extensions to reduce the amount of randomness for zero testing of polynomials. A method similar to Algorithm 6.45 also works to calculate the gcd of many integers. It is particularly useful to calculate the content of a polynomial in $\mathbb{Z}[x]$, but its analysis is considerably more complicated (Cooperman, Feisel, von zur Gathen & Havas 1998).

6.10. Subresultants were introduced into computer algebra by Collins (1966, 1967, 1973); see also Brown (1971, 1978) and Brown & Traub (1971). In fact, they work with a slightly different notion of "subresultant"; in our presentation, both definitions and theorems take a somewhat simpler form. Their "subresultants" are constant multiples of the remainders of the Euclidean Algorithm, rather than just constants. Mulders (1997) describes an error in software implementations of an integration algorithm in which these subresultants occur.

Subresultants are treated in Gordan's (1885) textbook, §132 ff. Habicht (1948) studies subresultants systematically in the generic case where the coefficients of the input polynomials are indeterminates. He calls our subresultants *Nebenresultanten*[1] and also gives explicit formulas for the s_i, t_i in the EEA in terms of determinants of submatrices of the Sylvester matrix. Von zur Gathen (1984b) discusses the relation between the monic and the classical Euclidean Algorithm. The "primitive polynomial remainder sequence" discussed in Section 6.12 was introduced by Collins (1967). Two further algorithms, based on the so-called "reduced polynomial remainder sequence" and the "subresultant polynomial remainder sequence", were invented by Collins (1967) and Brown & Traub (1971). Both avoid rational arithmetic by using pseudo-division, but in contrast to the primitive Euclidean Algorithm, they do not divide out the complete content but a divisor of it which can be computed without gcd calculations. The "reduced" algorithm appears to use exponential time in the worst case (Brown 1971, page 485). This is not the case for the "subresultant" algorithm: Brown (1978) gives an estimate for its running time which is essentially the same as the bound for the primitive Euclidean Algorithm from Exercise 6.53. Lickteig & Roy (1997) present a clever variant of the "subresultant" algorithm that eliminates the factor δ from the time bound of Exercise 6.53.

Exercises.

6.1 Give a sharp estimate for $\lambda(ab)$ when $a, b \in \mathbb{Q}[x]$.

6.2 Let $a = qb + r$ be a division with remainder, with $a, b, q, r \in \mathbb{Q}[x]$, $-1 + \deg a = \deg b > \deg r$, and $\lambda(a), \lambda(b) \leq l \in \mathbb{N}$. Give estimates for $\lambda(q)$ and $\lambda(r)$ in terms of l (a and b need not be monic).

6.3 Let $f \in R[x]$ for a Unique Factorization Domain R. Show that $f = \mathrm{pp}(f)$ if and only if f is primitive.

6.4 Prove that Lemma 6.5 and Corollary 6.7 hold when $c \in K$ and $f, g \in K[x]$, where K is the field of fractions of R.

6.5 Let R be a UFD on which a normal form lu_R in the sense of Section 3.1 is given, and let K be the field of fractions of R. We extend cont and pp to $K[x]$ as described in Section 6.2. Prove that taking $\mathrm{lu}_{K[x]}(f) = \mathrm{lu}_R(\mathrm{lc}(\mathrm{pp}(f)))\,\mathrm{cont}(f)$ defines a normal form for $K[x]$. Hint: Exercise 3.8. Why is $\mathrm{lu}_{K[x]}(f) = \mathrm{cont}(f)$ *not* a normal form?

6.6 Let $f \in \mathbb{Z}[x]$ be monic, and $\alpha \in \mathbb{Q}$ be a root of f. Show that $\alpha \in \mathbb{Z}$.

6.7 Let p be a prime and $\varphi\colon \mathbb{Z}[x] \longrightarrow \mathbb{Z}_p[x]$ be defined by taking coefficients modulo p. Show that when $f \in \mathbb{Z}[x]$, $p \nmid \mathrm{lc}(f)$, and $\varphi(f)$ is irreducible in $\mathbb{Z}_p[x]$, then f is irreducible in $\mathbb{Q}[x]$.

6.8 Show that the probability for two random polynomials in $\mathbb{Z}[x]$ of degree at most n and max-norm at most A to be coprime in $\mathbb{Q}[x]$ is at least $1 - 1/(2A + 1)$. Hint: Exercise 4.18.

6.9 Consider the ring $R = \mathbb{Z}[1/2] = \{a/2^n : a \in \mathbb{Z}, n \in \mathbb{N}\}$ of binary rationals.
  (i) Prove that R is the smallest subring of $\mathbb{Q}$ containing $\mathbb{Z}$ and $1/2$.

---

[1] minor resultants

(ii) What are the units of R?

(iii) You may use the fact that R is a UFD and that any two elements of R have a gcd which is unique up to associates. Find a normal form on R and use this to define a gcd function on R.

(iv) Determine the content and primitive part of the polynomial $f = 2x^2 + 6x - 4$ with respect to the three rings $\mathbb{Z}$, R, and $\mathbb{Q}$. Is f primitive with respect to R?

6.10 Let $f, g \in \mathbb{Z}[x]$, $r = \mathrm{res}(f, g) \in \mathbb{Z}$, and $u \in \mathbb{Z}$. Prove that $\gcd(f(u), g(u))$ divides r. Hint: Corollary 6.21.

6.11 Let F be a field and $f = \sum_{0 \le i \le n} f_i x^i$ and $g = \sum_{0 \le i \le m} g_i x^i$ in $F[x, y]$ have total degrees n and m, respectively, so that each $f_i, g_i \in F[y]$ with $\deg_y f_i \le n - i$, $\deg_y g_i \le m - i$. Let $r = \mathrm{res}_x(f, g) \in F[y]$. Show that each of the $(n + m)!$ summands contributing to r has degree at most nm, and hence $\deg_y r \le nm$.

6.12* Let R be a UFD with field of fractions F, $f, g \in R[x]$ nonzero of degrees n, m, respectively, and $\alpha_1, \ldots, \alpha_n$ and $\beta_1, \ldots, \beta_m$ the roots of f and g, respectively, in an extension field of F, counted with multiplicities.

(i) Prove:

$$\mathrm{res}(f, g) = \mathrm{lc}(f)^m \prod_{1 \le i \le n} g(\alpha_i) = (-1)^{nm} \mathrm{lc}(g)^n \prod_{1 \le j \le m} f(\beta_j) = \mathrm{lc}(f)^m \mathrm{lc}(g)^n \prod_{\substack{1 \le i \le n \\ 1 \le j \le m}} (\alpha_i - \beta_j).$$

Hint: First prove the claim in the case where the roots are considered to be indeterminates. Then apply the ring homomorphism which maps them to the actual roots.

(ii) Conclude that $\mathrm{res}(f, gh) = \mathrm{res}(f, g)\,\mathrm{res}(f, h)$ for all $f, g, h \in R[x]$.

6.13 This exercise provides an alternative proof of Corollaries 6.20 and 6.21. Let R be a UFD and $f, g \in R[x]$ nonzero of degrees n, m, respectively.

(i) Prove that

$$(x^{n+m-1}, \ldots, x, 1) \cdot \mathrm{Syl}(f, g) = (x^{m-1} f, \ldots, f, x^{n-1} g, \ldots, g) \text{ in } R[x]^{n+m},$$

and conclude that there exist nonzero $s, t \in R[x]$ with $\deg s < m$ and $\deg t < n$ such that $sf + tg = \mathrm{res}(f, g)$. Hint: Cramer's rule.

(ii) Conclude that $\mathrm{res}(f, g) = 0$ if and only if $\gcd(f, g)$ is nonconstant.

6.14* Let $f = \sum_{0 \le i \le n} f_i x^i$, $g = \sum_{0 \le i \le n} g_i x^i \in F[x]$, with a field F and $f_0 \ne 0$. For $0 \le k < n$, cross-multiply each polynomial by the leading $k + 1$ terms of the other polynomial and subtract:

$$b_k = f \cdot \sum_{0 \le j \le k} g_{n-k+j} x^j - g \cdot \sum_{0 \le j \le k} f_{n-k+j} x^j = \sum_{0 \le l} b_{kl} x^l.$$

(i) Show that $\deg b_k < n$ for all k.

(ii) Let $B = (b_{kl})_{0 \le k, l < n} \in F^{n \times n}$ be the **Bézout matrix** made up from these coefficients. Prove that $\det B = 0$ if $\gcd(f, g) \ne 1$. Hint: If $\gcd(f, g) \ne 1$, then there exists a common root of f and g in some extension field of F.

6.15* The aim of this exercise is to show that Corollaries 6.17 and 6.21 remain essentially true over arbitrary (commutative) coefficient rings R. Let $f, g \in R[x]$ nonzero of degrees n, m, respectively, such that $r = \mathrm{res}(f, g) \in R$ is nonzero.

(i) Show that there exist polynomials $s, t \in R[x]$ such that $sf + tg = \mathrm{res}(f, g)$. Hint: Apply Corollary 6.21 to the generic case where the coefficients of f and g are indeterminates, and then map them to the actual coefficients in R.

(ii) Now assume that f and g are monic. Prove that there exist polynomials $s, t \in R[x]$ with $\deg s < \deg g$ and $\deg t < \deg f$ satisfying $sf + tg = 1$ if and only if $\mathrm{res}(f, g)$ is a unit in R.

6.16* This exercise generalizes Lemma 6.13. Let F be a field, $f,g \in F[x]$ nonzero of degrees n and m, respectively, and $h = \gcd(f,g) \in F[x]$ of degree d.

(i) Prove that there exists a nonzero pair $(s,t) \in P_{m-i} \times P_{n-i}$ with $\varphi_0(s,t) = 0$ if and only if $i < d$.

(ii) Give d pairs $(s_1,t_1),\ldots,(s_d,t_d) \in P_m \times P_n$ such that $\varphi_0(s_i,t_i) = 0$ and s_i is monic of degree $m - i$ for all i.

(iii) Suppose that $(s,t) \in P_m \times P_n$ is linearly independent of all pairs from (ii) and $\varphi_0(s,t) = 0$. Show that there is a nonzero pair $(s^*,t^*) \in P_{m-d-1} \times P_{n-d-1}$ with $\varphi_0(s^*,t^*) = 0$, contradicting (i).

(iv) Conclude that $\dim \ker \mathrm{Syl}(f,g) = \deg \gcd(f,g)$.

6.17 Why are the results of `gcd(x^2+1,x+1) mod 2` and `Gcd(x^2+1,x+1) mod 2` in MAPLE different?

6.18 Let $f = x^4 - 13x^3 - 62x^2 - 78x - 408$ and $g = x^3 + 6x^2 - x - 30$ be polynomials with integral coefficients.

(i) Set up the Sylvester matrix of f and g and compute $\mathrm{res}(f,g)$.

(ii) Let $p_1 = 5$, $p_2 = 7$, $p_3 = 11$, and $p_4 = 13$. Compute $h = \gcd(f,g)$ in $\mathbb{Q}[x]$. For which of the primes is the modular image of h equal to the gcd modulo that prime, and why? Answer the latter question without actually computing the modular gcd's, then check your answer.

6.19 Let $\alpha \in \mathbb{R}$ be a parameter and $f, g_\alpha \in \mathbb{R}[x]$ monic polynomials with $\mathrm{res}(f,g_\alpha) = \alpha^3 + \alpha^2 + \alpha + 1$. Determine all values of α for which $\gcd(f,g_\alpha) \neq 1$.

6.20 Let F be a field, $f,g \in F[x,y]$ nonzero with $\deg_x f, \deg_x g \leq n$, $\deg_y f, \deg_y g \leq d$, and $\mathrm{lc}_x(f) = \mathrm{lc}_x(g) = 1$. Suppose that $\gcd(f(x,u),g(x,u)) \neq 1$ for at least $2nd + 1$ values $u \in F$. Conclude that $\deg_x \gcd(f,g) > 0$.

6.21 Let $\mathbb{F}_q$ be a finite field with q elements. What is wrong in the following argument: Exercise 4.18 shows that the probability that two random nonconstant polynomials in $\mathbb{F}_q[x]$ are coprime is $1 - 1/q \geq 1/2$. Thus there is a probabilistic algorithm for computing gcds in $\mathbb{F}_q[x]$ which always outputs 1, independently of the inputs, and errs with probability at most $1/2$.

6.22 Let $f = x^n - 1$ and $g = \Phi_n \in \mathbb{Z}[x]$ be the nth cyclotomic polynomial, of degree $\varphi(n) \leq n - 1$. Compare Vaughan's lower bound on $\|\Phi_n\|_\infty$ (valid for certain, but not all, values of n) to Mignotte's upper bound 6.33.

6.23* (i) Let $f = \sum_{0 \leq i \leq n} f_i x^i \in \mathbb{C}[x]$ of degree $n > 0$ and $\alpha \in \mathbb{C}$ a root of f. Prove that $|\alpha| \leq 2b$, where $b = \max_{0 \leq i < n} |f_i/f_n|^{1/(n-i)}$. Hint: Start with the case $f_n = 1$, and assume that $|\alpha| > b$.

(ii) Conclude that $|\alpha| \leq 2\|f\|_\infty$ if $f \in \mathbb{Z}[x]$, and compare this to Mignotte's bound for $|\alpha|$ that you obtain from Theorem 6.32.

(iii) Show that in fact $|\alpha| \leq \|f\|_\infty$ if $f \in \mathbb{Z}[x]$ and $\alpha \in \mathbb{Z}$.

6.24* (i) Let R be a UFD and $f,g,h \in R[x]$ nonzero of degrees n,m,k, respectively, such that h divides f and g, and $f^* = f/h$ and $g^* = g/h$. Moreover, let $S = \mathrm{Syl}(f^*,g^*) \in R^{(n+m-2k) \times (n+m-2k)}$, $r = \det S = \mathrm{res}(f^*,g^*) \in R$, and

$$H = \begin{pmatrix} h_k & 0 & 0 & \cdots & 0 \\ h_{k-1} & h_k & 0 & \cdots & 0 \\ h_{k-2} & h_{k-1} & h_k & \cdots & 0 \\ \vdots & \vdots & \vdots & \ddots & \vdots \\ \vdots & \vdots & \vdots & \cdots & h_k \end{pmatrix} \in R^{(n+m-2k) \times (n+m-2k)}$$

the Toeplitz matrix whose rows are shifts of the coefficient sequence $h_0, \ldots, h_k \in R$ of h. Prove that $T = HS$ is a matrix whose first $m - k$ columns are shifts of the coefficient sequence of f and whose last $n - k$ columns are shifts of the coefficient sequence of g, and show that $\det T = \mathrm{lc}(h)^{n+m-2k} r$. (In fact, $\det T$ is the kth subresultant of f and g.)

(ii) Let $R = \mathbb{Z}$, $m \leq n$, and $\|f\|_\infty, \|g\|_\infty \leq A$. Show that $|r| \leq (n+1)^n A^{2(n-k)}$.

6.25 Work out the details in the proof of Theorem 6.35.

6.26 Let F be a field. This exercise discusses the task to decide whether a polynomial $g \in F[x,y]$ divides another polynomial $f \in F[x,y]$, and if so, to compute the quotient $f/g \in F[x,y]$, using a modular approach. Suppose that $\deg_x g \leq \deg_x f = n$ and $\deg_y g \leq \deg_y f = d$, and let $p \in F[y]$ be nonconstant and coprime to $\mathrm{lc}_x(g)$.

(i) Convince yourself that $g \bmod p$ divides $f \bmod p$ in $(F[y]/\langle p \rangle)[x]$ if g divides f in $F[x,y]$.

(ii) Now assume that $g \bmod p$ divides $f \bmod p$. One might be tempted to assume that $\deg_y p > d$ is sufficient to conclude that g divides f. Prove that this is wrong in general by considering the example $f = x^n + (y^d + y^{d-1})x^{n-2}$, $g = x - y^d$, and $p = y^{d+1} + y + 1$ for $n \geq 2$ and $d \geq 1$.

(iii) Assume that $g \bmod p$ divides $f \bmod p$ and $\deg_y p > d$, and let $h \in F[x,y]$ be the modular quotient, with $\deg_x f \geq \deg_x g + \deg_x h$, $\deg_y h < \deg_y p$, and $f \equiv gh \bmod p$. Prove that $f = gh$ if $\deg_y f \geq \deg_y g + \deg_y h$. Given p, what is the running time of this method? Compute h in the example of (ii).

(iv) Find and prove analogs of (ii) and (iii) for $f, g \in \mathbb{Z}[x]$ and $p \in \mathbb{Z}$. Hint: Use Mignotte's bound 6.33 and look at the proof of Theorem 6.35.

6.27* This exercise discusses a modular gcd algorithm for $\mathbb{Z}[x]$ by Char, Geddes & Gonnet (1989) (who in fact give an algorithm for multivariate polynomials over $\mathbb{Z}$; they call it "heuristic gcd") and Schönhage (1985, 1988). The modulus is not a prime but a linear polynomial $x - u$. Let $f, g \in \mathbb{Z}[x]$ be nonzero and primitive of degree at most n and with max-norm at most A, $h = \gcd(f, g) \in \mathbb{Z}[x]$, and $u \in \mathbb{N}$ such that $u > 4A$.

(i) Prove that $h(u) \mid c = \gcd(f(u), g(u))$ in $\mathbb{Z}$ and that $h(u) \neq 0$.

(ii) Let $v \in \mathbb{Z}[x]$ whose coefficients v_i satisfy $-u/2 < v_i \leq u/2$, and $v(u) = c$. Give an algorithm for computing v from c.

(iii) Now assume that $\mathrm{pp}(v) \mid f$ and $\mathrm{pp}(v) \mid g$. Writing $h = \mathrm{pp}(v)w$ with a primitive $w \in \mathbb{Z}[x]$, prove that $w(u) \mid \mathrm{cont}(v)$. Use Exercise 6.23 to show that $u/2 \geq |w(u)| \geq |\mathrm{lc}(w)| \cdot (u - 2A)^{\deg w} > (u/2)^{\deg w}$ if w is nonconstant, and conclude that $h = \pm \mathrm{pp}(v)$.

(iv) Compute $\gcd(3x^4 + 6x^3 + 5x^2 - 2x - 2, x^3 + 4x^2 + 6x + 4)$ by the above method. Find out the smallest evaluation point where the method works, and compare it to your choice of u.

Schönhage (1988) proves that for $u > 4(n+1)^n A^{2n}$ the divisibility conditions assumed in (iii) are always satisfied, so that the method always terminates. He also discusses a probabilistic variant where u is chosen at random from a "small" interval and the length of u is dynamically increased (say, doubled) on failure, and proves that the expected length of a successful u is only $O^\sim(n)$, in contrast to $O^\sim(n \log A)$ for the deterministic algorithm.

6.28* Find an analog of Exercise 6.27 for bivariate polynomials.

6.29→ Compute (with explanation) the gcd over $\mathbb{Z}[x]$ of the polynomials $36x^4 + 72x^3 + 68x^2 + 104x + 60$ and $36x^5 + 24x^4 + 116x^3 + 126x^2 + 150x + 150$ with the small primes modular algorithm.

6.30→ (Newton 1707, page 46) Compute the gcd of $x^4 - 3ax^3 - 8a^2x^2 + 18a^3x - 8a^4$ and $x^3 - ax^2 - 8a^2x + 6a^3$ in $\mathbb{Q}[x,a]$ using the small primes modular algorithm.

6.31* A bin contains w white balls, labeled $1, \ldots, w$, and $0 < b \leq w$ black balls. Consider choosing l balls without replacement, where $0 < l \leq 2b$, and show that the probability that at least $\lceil l/2 \rceil$ balls are white is at least $1/2$. Hint: Use induction on w, starting with $w = b$, and for the induction step from w to $w + 1$, distinguish the two cases whether the white ball number $w + 1$ has been chosen or not.

6.32* Let $\mathbb{F}_q$ be a finite field with q elements and $f, g \in \mathbb{F}_q[x,y]$ of degree at most n in x and at most d in y.

(i) Determine the smallest value $t \in \mathbb{N}$ such that $\mathbb{F}_{q^t}$ has at least $(4n+2)d+2$ elements and conclude that the modular gcd algorithm 6.36 with $F = \mathbb{F}_{q^t}$ correctly computes the gcd over $\mathbb{F}_q$ (hint: Example 6.19) and takes $O(nd(n+d)\log^2(nd))$ operations in $\mathbb{F}_q$.

(ii) Let $f = x^2 + y^2 + xy + x + y$ and $g = x^2y + xy^2 + xy$ in $\mathbb{F}_2[x,y]$. Check that $t = 5$, and that $\gcd(f \bmod p, g \bmod p) \neq 1$ for the linear moduli $x, x+1, y, y+1$. Compute $\gcd(f(x,\alpha), g(x,\alpha))$ in $\mathbb{F}_4[x]$, where $\mathbb{F}_4 = \mathbb{F}_2[z]/\langle z^2 + z + 1 \rangle$ and $\alpha = z \bmod z^2 + z + 1 \in \mathbb{F}_4$, and conclude that $\gcd(f,g) = 1$. The construction of the field extension $\mathbb{F}_{q^t}$, that is, of an irreducible polynomial of degree t over $\mathbb{F}_q$, is discussed in Section 14.9.

6.33 $\longrightarrow$ We consider the plane curves

$$\begin{aligned} X &= \{(a,b) \in \mathbb{R}^2 : b - a^3 + 7a - 5 = 0\}, \\ Y &= \{(a,b) \in \mathbb{R}^2 : 20a^2 - 5ab - 4b^2 + 35a + 35b - 21 = 0\} \end{aligned}$$

in $\mathbb{R}^2$. Determine the intersection of X and Y in two ways: by projecting it to the first coordinate, and by projecting it to the second coordinate. Comment on the differences. Plot the two curves and mark their intersection points.

6.34 Compute the minimal polynomial $f \in \mathbb{Q}[x]$ of $\sqrt{2} + \sqrt{3}$ over $\mathbb{Q}$. Let $\mathbb{F}_{19^2} = \mathbb{F}_{19}[z]/\langle z^2 - 2 \rangle$ and $\alpha = z \bmod x^2 - 2 \in \mathbb{F}_{19^2}$ a square root of 2. Check that 7α is a square root of 3, and compute the minimal polynomial of $\alpha + 7\alpha$ over $\mathbb{F}_{19}$. How is it related to f?

6.35* Let α, β be two nonzero algebraic numbers, with (monic) minimal polynomials $f, g \in \mathbb{Q}[x]$ of degrees n, m, respectively.

(i) Prove that the reversal $\mathrm{rev}(f) = x^n f(x^{-1})$ of f is the minimal polynomial of α^{-1}.

(ii) Let $r = \mathrm{res}_y(\mathrm{rev}(f)(y), g(xy)) \in \mathbb{Q}[x]$. Show that $\deg_x r = nm$ and $r(\alpha\beta) = 0$ (hint: Exercise 6.12), and conclude that r is the minimal polynomial of $\alpha\beta$ if it is irreducible.

(iii) Find multiples of degree nm of the minimal polynomials of $a\alpha + b\beta$, where $a, b \in \mathbb{Q} \setminus \{0\}$ are arbitrary, and of α/β.

(iv) Compute the minimal polynomials of $\sqrt{2} - 2\sqrt{3}$ over $\mathbb{Q}$ and of $\sqrt{2}\sqrt[3]{3}$ over $\mathbb{Q}$ and over $\mathbb{F}_{13}$.

6.36* Let α be an algebraic number and $f, g \in \mathbb{Q}[x]$ of degrees $n, m \in \mathbb{N}_{\geq 1}$ such that f is the minimal polynomial of α. We want to compute the minimal polynomial of $g(\alpha)$ and therefore may assume that $n > m$.

(i) Let $r = \mathrm{res}_y(f(y), x - g(y)) \in \mathbb{Q}[y]$. Show that $\deg_x r = n$ and that the minimal polynomial of $g(\alpha)$ divides r (hint: Exercise 6.12). (In fact, r is a power of the minimal polynomial of $g(\alpha)$, which equals $r/\gcd(r, r')$.)

(ii) Compute the minimal polynomials of $\sqrt{3} + 1$ and $2^{2/3} + 2^{1/3} + 1$ over $\mathbb{Q}$. A different algorithm is given in Exercise 12.10.

6.37 This exercise discusses a variant of Lemma 6.44, due to Zippel (1993). Let R be an integral domain, $n \in \mathbb{N}$, $S \subseteq R$ finite with $s = \#S$ elements, and $r \in R[x_1, \ldots, x_n]$ a polynomial of degree at most $d_i \leq s$ in the variable x_i.

(i) Show that r has at most $s^n - (s - d_1) \cdots (s - d_n) \leq (d_1 + \cdots + d_n)s^{n-1}$ zeroes in S^n if it is not the zero polynomial. Hint: Prove inductively that the number of elements of S that are not zeroes of r is at least $(s - d_1) \cdots (s - d_n)$.

(ii) Let $u_1, \ldots, u_s$ be the elements of S. Prove that the polynomial

$$r = \prod_{1 \leq i \leq n} \prod_{1 \leq j \leq d_i} (x_i - u_j)$$

achieves the first bound from (i) exactly.

6.38 Modify Algorithm 6.45 so as to also produce $s_1, \ldots, s_n \in F[x]$ of degree less than d such that $s_1 f_1 + \cdots + s_n f_n = h$, taking at most $3(n-2)(d+1) + O(d^2)$ operations in F.

6.39 Let R be a Unique Factorization Domain, $f_1, \ldots, f_n \in R$, $m = f_1 \cdots f_n$, and $g_i = m/f_i$ for $1 \leq i \leq n$. Show that $\mathrm{lcm}(f_1, \ldots, f_n) = m/\gcd(g_1, \ldots, g_n)$. Derive a probabilistic algorithm for computing $\mathrm{lcm}(f_1, \ldots, f_n)$ if $R = F[x]$ for a field F, and analyze its cost and success probability.

6.40 For each $n \in \mathbb{N}$, find polynomials $f_1, \ldots, f_n \in \mathbb{Q}[x]$ such that $\gcd(f_1, \ldots, f_n) = 1$ and any proper subset of them has a nonconstant gcd.

6.41 Let R be a UFD and $f, g \in R[x]$ nonzero with $\deg g \leq \deg f$. Prove that for $0 \leq k \leq \deg g$, $\gcd(\mathrm{lc}(f), \mathrm{lc}(g))$ divides the kth subresultant of f and g.

6.42→ Let $f = x^8 + x^6 - 3x^4 - 3x^3 + 8x^2 + 2x - 5$ and $g = 3x^6 + 5x^4 - 4x^2 - 9x + 21$ be polynomials in $\mathbb{Z}[x]$ and $S_k \in \mathbb{Z}^{(14-2k) \times (14-2k)}$ be the submatrix of the Sylvester matrix of f and g whose determinant is the kth subresultant σ_k, as in Section 6.10, for $0 \leq k \leq 6$.

(i) Trace the Extended Euclidean Algorithm 3.6 for f and g over $\mathbb{Q}$, and check that $s_i f + t_i g = r_i$ for $2 \leq i \leq \ell$. Compute the degree sequence $n_0 = 8, n_1 = 6, n_2, \ldots, n_\ell$.

(ii) Set up the matrices S_k and compute σ_k for $0 \leq k \leq 6$. Explain which of the S_k are singular and what this has to do with the remainders in the EEA.

(iii) Let $2 \leq i \leq \ell$ and $u_{n_i} \in \mathbb{Q}^{14-2n_i}$ such that its last entry is 1 and all other coefficients are zero. Say why the linear system $S_{n_i} v = u_{n_i}$ has a unique solution $v \in \mathbb{Q}^{14-2n_i}$ and state the coefficients of the solution *without calculation*. Then check your answer by actually computing $S_{n_i} v$.

(iv) For those $k \in \{0, \ldots, 5\}$ where $\sigma_k = 0$, find a nonzero vector $v \in \mathbb{Q}^{14-2k}$ such that $S_k v = 0$ *without calculation*. Then check your answer by actually computing $S_k v$.

6.43 Let F be a field, $m, n \in \mathbb{N}$ with $m < n$, and $f = \sum_{0 \leq i \leq m} f_i x^i \in F[x]$ of degree m. For $0 \leq h \leq m$, we define square matrices $A_h = (f_{h-i+j})_{0 \leq i,j < n-h} \in F^{(n-h) \times (n-h)}$ and $B_h = (f_{h-i+j})_{0 \leq i,j < n-h-1} \in F^{(n-h-1) \times (n-h-1)}$, so that B_h is the leading principal submatrix of A_h of order $n - h - 1$.

(i) Prove that the hth subresultant of x^n and f is $\sigma_h = \det A_h$, for $0 \leq h \leq m$.

(ii) Let $0 \leq h \leq m$ be such that $\sigma_h \neq 0$ and $r, s, t \in F[x]$ the row in the EEA for (x^n, f) that has $\deg r = h$. Prove that the constant coefficient of t is $\det B_h / \det A_h$. Hint: Theorem 6.48 and Cramer's rule.

(iii) Let $0 \leq h < k \leq m$ be such that h is maximal with $\sigma_h \neq 0$. Conclude from (ii) that there exists a $(k, n-k)$-Padé approximant to f if and only if $\det B_h \neq 0$. Hint: Corollary 5.21.

6.44* You are to estimate the coefficient size of quotient and remainder in a pseudo-division and its cost. Let $a, b \in \mathbb{Z}[x]$, with $n = \deg a \geq m = \deg b > 0$, $k = n - m$, and $c = \mathrm{lc}(b) \in \mathbb{Z}$. Furthermore, let $q = \sum_{0 \leq i \leq k} q_i x^i$, $r = \sum_{0 \leq i < m} r_i x^i \in \mathbb{Z}[x]$ be such that $a_0 = c^{k+1} a = qb + r$ and $\deg r < m$, and $a_i \in \mathbb{Z}[x]$ be the remainder in the ith iteration of the polynomial division algorithm 2.5 applied to a_0 and b (see also Exercise 2.9).

(i) Let $\|a\|_\infty \leq A$, $\|b\|_\infty \leq B$, and $|c| \leq C$. Prove that we have $|q_{k-i}| \leq A(B+C)^i C^{k-i}$ and $|a_i| \leq A(B+C)^i C^{k+1-i}$ for $0 \leq i \leq k$, and $\|r\|_\infty \leq A(B+C)^{k+1}$.

(ii) Conclude that the cost for computing q, r from a, b is $O(mk^2 \log^2 B)$ word operations if $A \leq B$.

(iii) Let $A, B, C \in \mathbb{N}_{>0}$, and assume that a has positive coefficients not smaller than A, and that $b = Cx^m - b^*$ for a polynomial $b^* \in \mathbb{Z}[x]$ with $\deg b^* < m$ and positive coefficients greater or equal to B. Show that $q_{k-i} \geq A(B+C)^i C^{k-i}$ for $0 \leq i \leq k$ and $r_i \geq A(B+C)^{k+1}$ for $0 \leq i < m$. (Thus the bound from (i) is essentially sharp.)

(iv) Give statements analogous to (i) and (ii) for pseudo-division of bivariate polynomials.

6.45 Let F be a field, $f, g \in F[x]$ nonzero of degree $n \geq m$ and with max-norm $\|f\|_\infty, \|g\|_\infty \leq A$, $r_i, s_i, t_i \in F[x]$ the ith row in the EEA for f, g and some $i \geq 1$, $n_i = \deg r_i$, S the n_ith submatrix of the Sylvester matrix of f and g, and $\sigma = \det S$ the n_ith subresultant.

(i) We have shown in Theorem 6.52 that the coefficients of σs_i and σt_i are determinants of submatrices of S of order $n + m - 2n_i - 1$. Let U, V be the matrices that arise from S by replacing the last row by $(x^{m-n_i-1}, \ldots, x, 1, 0, \ldots, 0)$ and $(0, \ldots, 0, x^{n-n_i-1}, \ldots, x, 1)$, respectively. Prove that $\sigma s_i = \det U$ and $\sigma t_i = \det V$.

(ii) Let W be the matrix S with its last row replaced by $(x^{m-n_i-1}f,\ldots,xf,f,x^{n-n_i-1}g,\ldots,xg,g)$. Conclude from (i) that $\sigma r_i = \det W$.

(iii) Prove that every coefficient of σr_i has absolute value at most $(n+1)^{n-n_i}A^{n+m-2n_i}$. Hint: The coefficient of x^j in σr_i is obtained by taking only terms containing x^j in the last row of W.

6.46* Let $\mathbb{F}_q$ be a finite field with q elements and $n, m \in \mathbb{Z}$ with $n \geq m \geq 0$.

(i) Let $X_0,\ldots,X_{m-1}$ be independent random variables with $\mathrm{prob}(X_i = 0) = q^{-1}$ for all i, and ρ the random variable that counts the longest run of zeroes in $X_0,\ldots,X_{m-1}$:

$$\rho = \max\{0 \leq i \leq m \colon \exists j \leq m-i \quad X_j = X_{j+1} = \cdots = X_{j+i-1} = 0\}.$$

Prove that $\mathrm{prob}(\rho \geq d) \leq (m-d+1)q^{-d}$ for $1 \leq d \leq m$, and conclude that the expected value

$$\mathcal{E}(\rho) = \sum_{0 \leq d \leq m} d\,\mathrm{prob}(\rho = d) = \sum_{0 \leq d \leq m} \mathrm{prob}(\rho \geq d)$$

of ρ is at most $1 + m/(q-1)$. (In fact, the better bound $\mathcal{E}(\rho) \in O(\log m)$ holds; see Guibas & Odlyzko (1980) for a proof and references.)

(ii) For two uniform random polynomials $f, g \in \mathbb{F}_q[x]$ of degrees n and m, respectively, let δ denote the maximal degree difference of two consecutive remainders in the Euclidean Algorithm for f, g, with $\delta(f,g) = 0$ if $g \mid f$ (the first difference $\deg f - \deg g$ is not counted). Use Exercise 4.17 to conclude that $\mathcal{E}(\delta) \in O(\log m)$.

(iii) Let $A \geq 1$. Derive the same upper bound on the expected value of δ for random $f, g \in \mathbb{Z}[x]$ of degrees n and m, respectively, and with $\|f\|_\infty, \|g\|_\infty \leq A$.

6.47* Prove Theorem 6.53.

6.48* Prove Theorem 6.54.

6.49* The aim of this exercise, which follows Shoup (1991), is to prove a bound on the coefficients of the results r_i^*, s_i^*, t_i^* of the classical EEA for two nonzero elements f, g of $\mathbb{Z}[x]$ or $F[x,y]$, where F is a field, that is independent of the value δ from Theorems 6.53 and 6.54. So let $\alpha_i = \mathrm{lc}(r_i^*)$ and $n_i = \deg r_i^*$ for $0 \leq i \leq \ell$, σ_k the kth subresultant, and S_k the submatrix of the Sylvester matrix $\mathrm{Syl}(f,g)$ whose determinant is σ_k, for $0 \leq k \leq n_1$, as usual.

(i) Let κ_i, λ_i be the constant coefficients of $s_i = \alpha_i^{-1}s_i^*$ and $t_i = \alpha_i^{-1}t_i^*$, respectively, for $2 \leq i \leq \ell$. By Theorem 6.48 and Cramer's rule, we have

$$\kappa_i = \frac{\det Y_i}{\sigma_{n_i}}, \quad \lambda_i = \frac{\det Z_i}{\sigma_{n_i}} \quad \text{for } 2 \leq i \leq \ell,$$

where Y_i, Z_i are matrices that result from S_{n_i} by replacing a certain column by a unit vector. Let

$$\gamma_2 = \det Y_2, \quad \gamma_i = \det Y_{i-1} \cdot \det Z_i - \det Z_{i-1} \cdot \det Y_i \quad \text{for } 3 \leq i \leq \ell,$$

and prove that

$$\alpha_2 = \frac{\sigma_{n_2}}{\gamma_2}, \quad \alpha_i = \frac{(-1)^{i-1}\sigma_{n_i}\sigma_{n_{i-1}}}{\gamma_i \alpha_{i-1}} \quad \text{for } 3 \leq i \leq \ell.$$

Hint: Lemma 3.8 and Theorem 6.53. Conclude that

$$\alpha_i = (-1)^{(i+1)(i+2)/2}\sigma_{n_i} \prod_{2 \leq j \leq i} \gamma_j^{(-1)^{i+j-1}} \quad \text{for } 2 \leq i \leq \ell.$$

(ii) Let $f, g \in \mathbb{Z}[x]$ with max-norm at most A, $n = n_0 \geq m = n_1$, $B = (n+1)^n A^{n+m}$, as in Theorem 6.52, and $2 \leq i \leq \ell$. Prove that the numerator and denominator of α_i are absolutely at most $(2B)^i$. Using the bounds from Theorem 6.52 on the coefficients of the results $r_i = \alpha_i^{-1}r_i^*, s_i, t_i$ of the monic EEA, show that the numerators and denominators of r_i^*, s_i^*, t_i^* are absolutely bounded by $(2B)^{i+1}$. Conclude that their length is $O(nm\log(nA))$.

(iii) Let $f, g \in F[x, y]$ of degrees at most d in y, $n = n_0 \geq m = n_1$, and $2 \leq i \leq \ell$. Prove that the numerator and denominator of α_i has degree in y at most $i(n+m)d$. Using the bounds from Theorem 6.54 on the coefficients of the results r_i, s_i, t_i of the monic EEA, conclude that the numerators and denominators of r_i^*, s_i^*, t_i^* have degree at most $(i+1)(n+m)d$.

6.50* Prove Theorem 6.60 and try to find a "small" constant $c \in \mathbb{Q}$ such that the running time is at most $cn^3md^2 + O(n^3d(n+d))$ arithmetic operations in F in the normal case where $\deg r_{i+1} = \deg r_i - 1$ for $1 \leq i < \ell = m+1$.

6.51* Design big prime modular algorithms for the monic EEA in $\mathbb{Z}[x]$ and $F[x, y]$, where F is a field. Prove that your algorithms are correct and on input f, g of degree $n \geq m$ in x take $O(n^3m\log^2(nA))$ word operations if $\|f\|_\infty, \|g\|_\infty \leq A$ and $O(n^3md^2)$ field operations if $\deg_y f, \deg_y g \leq d$, respectively. You may ignore the cost for finding a big prime or irreducible polynomial.

6.52 Let f, g be primitive polynomials in $R[x]$, where R is a UFD, and let $\text{prem}(f, g)$ be the remainder in the pseudo-division of f by g. Show that $\gcd(f, g) = \gcd(g, \text{prem}(f, g))$.

6.53* (i) Prove the running time estimate of Theorem 6.62 for the primitive Euclidean Algorithm 6.61 for bivariate polynomials.

(ii) Modify the primitive Euclidean Algorithm 6.61 so as to also compute $s_i, t_i \in R[x]$ with $r_i = s_i f + t_i g$ for $0 \leq i \leq \ell$, and prove that the time estimate from Theorem 6.62 is still valid for the modified algorithm.

(iii) Use Exercise 6.44 to show that Algorithm 6.61 can be executed using only $O(n^3m\delta\log^2(nA))$ word operations for $R = \mathbb{Z}$ and only $O(n^3m\delta d^2)$ operations in F when $R = F[y]$ for a field F.

6.54* Let F be a field and $f, g \in F[x, y]$ with $\deg_x f = n \geq \deg_x g = m$ and $\deg_y f, \deg_y g \leq d$. Assuming that all coefficients of the remainders r_i in the primitive Euclidean Algorithm 6.61 for f, g achieve the degree bounds from Theorem 6.54 on the numerators of the corresponding coefficients in the monic Euclidean Algorithm exactly, and also the degree bounds for the pseudo-division of r_{i-1} by r_i according to Exercise 6.44 are in fact equalities, prove that $\deg_y \text{cont}_x(a_{i-1} \text{ rem } r_i) = (n_{i-1} - n_i + 1)(n+m-2n_i)d - 2(n_{i-1} - n_{i+1})d$.

6.55$^\longrightarrow$ You are to compare five methods for computing gcds in $\mathbb{Z}[x]$ in your favorite computer algebra system. The first method is simply to call its appropriate routine. Try to find out which algorithm it uses. The other methods are the primitive Euclidean Algorithm 6.61, the big primes modular algorithm 6.34, the small primes modular algorithm 6.38, and the "heuristic" algorithm from Exercise 6.27. Implement and run your algorithms on several examples. Choose examples of increasing complexity; construct examples so that the resulting gcds have several different degrees, including cases where the gcd is 1. Measure running times and see if you can draw any conclusions about relative merits of the algorithms.

I would have my son mind and understand Business,
read a little History, study the Mathematics and Cosmography:
—these are good, with subordination to the things of God.
[...] These fit for Public services, for which man is born.

Oliver Cromwell (1649)

They that are ignorant of Algebra cannot imagine
the wonders in this kind are to be done by it: and what
further improvements and helps advantageous to other parts
of knowledge the sagacious mind of man may yet find out,
it is not easy to determine.

John Locke (1690)

What kind of world do we live in where 11 and 7 equal 2?

John Cougar Mellencamp (1989)

Scientists pretended that history didn't matter,
because the errors of the past were now corrected
by modern discoveries. But of course their forebears
had believed exactly the same thing in the past, too.

Michael Crichton (1995)

Bei dem Kinde aber muss man im Unterrichte allmälig
das Wissen und Können zu verbinden suchen. Unter allen
Wissenschaften scheint die Mathematik die einzige der Art zu seyn,
die diesen Endzweck am besten befriedigt.[1]

Immanuel Kant (1803)

---

[1] The instruction of children should aim gradually to combine knowing and doing. Among all sciences mathematics seems to be the only one that satisfies this purpose best.

7

Application: Decoding BCH codes

Coding theory deals with the detection and correction of transmission errors. The scenario is that a message m is sent over a transmission channel, and due to noise on the channel some of the symbols in the received message r are different from those in m. How can we correct them?

$$m \qquad \text{channel} \qquad r$$

A simple strategy is to send m three or five times and take a majority vote on each symbol. If errors occur too frequently, then this may not help much, but the usual assumption is that errors occur only with fairly small probability, and then this strategy will give an erroneous result only with much smaller probability than accepting r as is.

However, the cost ($=$ length) of transmission has increased by a factor of three or five. The fundamental task of coding theory is to see whether small error probability can be achieved at reasonable cost. The basic framework of this theory was established in the pioneering work of Shannon (1948). Error correcting codes are employed in numerous situations, from computer networks to satellite TV, digital telephony, and the technology that make CDs so remarkably resistant against scratches. They must not be confused with *cryptography*, the art of sending secret messages that only the intended receiver can read (see Section 20).

It turns out that the tools of algebra provide many useful codes. We describe a particular class of such codes. Let $\mathbb{F}_q$ be a finite field with q elements, $n, k \in \mathbb{N}$, and $C \subseteq \mathbb{F}_q^n$ a k-dimensional linear subspace. C is called a **linear code** over $\mathbb{F}_q$. Any basis of C provides an isomorphism $\mathbb{F}_q^k \longrightarrow C$, and $\varepsilon \colon \mathbb{F}_q^k \longrightarrow C \subseteq \mathbb{F}_q^n$ is the **encoding map**. The number n is the **length** of C, k is its **dimension**, and the ratio $k/n \leq 1$ is the **rate** of C.

To transmit a message m, we first identify it with an element of $\mathbb{F}_q^k$. If, say, $q = 2$ and $k = 64$, and we want to transmit messages in ASCII, then each ASCII letter can be identified with an 8-bit string, and a block of 8 letters with a "word" in $\mathbb{F}_2^{64}$. Now the simple code which sends each "word" three times has length 192, dimension 64, and rate $1/3$.

For an element $a = (a_1, \ldots, a_n) \in \mathbb{F}_q^n$, we denote by

$$w(a) = \#\{i : 1 \le i \le n, a_i \ne 0\}$$

its **Hamming weight**, and by

$$d(C) = \min\{w(a) : a \in C \setminus \{0\}\}$$

the **minimal distance** of C. Since C is a linear subspace, $w(a - b) \ge d(C)$ for all distinct $a, b \in C$. Our triple repetition code is $C = \{(a,a,a) \in \mathbb{F}_2^{192} : a \in \mathbb{F}_2^{64}\}$ and has minimal distance $d(C) = 3$.

On receiving a word $r \in \mathbb{F}_q^n$, it is decoded as $c \in C$ with $d(r - c)$ minimal. Since fewer errors are more probable, this is called **maximum likelihood decoding**. If less than $d(C)/2$ errors occurred in transmitting the word, then this will work correctly. If a single letter in $\mathbb{F}_q$ is received incorrectly with probability $\varepsilon \ll 1$, and errors occur independently, then this decoding procedure makes a mistake with probability no more than

$$\sum_{d(C)/2 \le j \le n} \binom{n}{j} \varepsilon^j (1 - \varepsilon)^{n-j}.$$

One of the goals in coding theory is to make this probability small without decreasing the rate too much.

For example, $\varepsilon \approx 10^{-4}$ seems to be a reasonable value for transmissions over copper wires. In Table 7.1 below, we have a code C over $\mathbb{F}_2$ with dimension 8, length 15, and minimal distance 5. Then this error probability becomes $\approx 5 \cdot 10^{-8}$: a tremendous gain, at the cost of not even halving the transmission rate. This is much better than the triple repetition code mentioned above, which has error probability of about 10^{-5} and transmission rate $1/3$.

We now describe a popular class of codes, the BCH codes, together with an efficient way of implementing the decoding procedure.

Let $\mathbb{F}_q$ be a finite field and $f \in \mathbb{F}_q[x]$ be irreducible and monic with $\deg f = m$. Then $\mathbb{F}_{q^m} = \mathbb{F}_q[x]/\langle f \rangle$, and $\alpha = x \bmod f \in \mathbb{F}_{q^m}$ is a root of f (Lemma 4.4). Since $f(x^q) = f(x)^q$ for each $f \in \mathbb{F}_q[x]$, the elements $\alpha^q, \alpha^{q^2}, \ldots, \alpha^{q^{m-1}} \in \mathbb{F}_{q^m}$ are also roots of f. Furthermore, the α^{q^i} for $0 \le i < m$ are all distinct (we will prove this in Section 14.10 when α is a primitive root of unity). Hence they are all roots of f, and $f = (x - \alpha)(x - \alpha^q) \cdots (x - \alpha^{q^{m-1}})$. The minimal polynomial of an element $\beta \in \mathbb{F}_{q^m}$ is the monic (nonzero) polynomial $f \in \mathbb{F}_q[x]$ of least degree such that $f(\beta) = 0$. It exists and is unique, and for all $g \in \mathbb{F}_q[x]$, we have $g(\beta) = 0$ if and only if $f \mid g$. These basic facts about finite fields are explained in Section 25.4.

EXAMPLE 7.1. (i) If $m = 1$, then the minimal polynomial of β is $f = x - \beta$.

(ii) The minimal polynomial of $\beta = x \bmod f \in \mathbb{F}_{q^m} = \mathbb{F}_q[x]/\langle f \rangle$ over $\mathbb{F}_q$ is f.

(iii) The polynomial $f = x^4 + x + 1 \in \mathbb{F}_2[x]$ is irreducible, and $\mathbb{F}_{16} = \mathbb{F}_2[x]/\langle f \rangle$ is a field with 16 elements. By (ii), the minimal polynomial of $\beta = x \bmod f \in \mathbb{F}_{16}$ is $x^4 + x + 1$. $\diamond$

DEFINITION 7.2. *An element $\beta \in \mathbb{F}_{q^m}$ is called a* **primitive nth root of unity** *if* $\gcd(n, q) = 1$ *and*

(i) $\beta^n = 1$, *and*

(ii) $\beta^k \neq 1$ *for* $0 < k < n$.

Thus a primitive nth root of unity is just an element of order n (Section 25.1) in the multiplicative group $\mathbb{F}_{q^m}^\times = \mathbb{F}_{q^m} \setminus \{0\}$. Such roots of unity will play a major role for the Fast Fourier Transform in Section 8.2. We are now in a position to say what a BCH code is.

DEFINITION 7.3. *Let $q = p^r$ for some prime p and let $n, \delta \geq 1$, β a primitive nth root of unity in some extension $\mathbb{F}_{q^m}$ of $\mathbb{F}_q$, and $g \in \mathbb{F}_q[x]$ the monic lcm of the minimal polynomials of $\beta, \beta^2, \ldots, \beta^{\delta-1}$. Then the vector space*

$$C = \sum_{0 \leq i < n - \deg g} x^i \bar{g} \cdot \mathbb{F}_q \subseteq \mathbb{F}_q[x]/\langle x^n - 1 \rangle = R \cong \mathbb{F}_q^n$$

is a **BCH code**, *denoted by* $\mathrm{BCH}(q, n, \delta)$. *Here $\bar{g} = (g \bmod x^n - 1) \in R$, and C is the ideal generated by $\bar{g}$ in R. The code C has length n and dimension $n - \deg g$, and g is its* **generator polynomial**.

The notation $\mathrm{BCH}(q, n, \delta)$ does not reflect the fact that the code depends on the choice of the primitive nth root of unity β, but the properties of the code (in particular, its minimal distance) are essentially independent of β. We will discuss in Section 14.10 how to construct BCH codes in general, and only give an example here.

EXAMPLE 7.4. We will construct all BCH codes of length 15 over $\mathbb{F}_2$. The factorization of $x^{15} - 1$ over $\mathbb{F}_2$ into irreducible factors is

$$x^{15} + 1 = \underbrace{(x + 1)}_{f_1} \underbrace{(x^2 + x + 1)}_{f_2} \underbrace{(x^4 + x^3 + x^2 + x + 1)}_{f_3} \underbrace{(x^4 + x^3 + 1)}_{f_4} \underbrace{(x^4 + x + 1)}_{f_5}.$$

From the factorization of the **cyclotomic polynomials** Φ_k in $\mathbb{Z}[x]$ (Section 14.10) we find that $x^{15} - 1 = \Phi_1 \Phi_3 \Phi_5 \Phi_{15}$, where $\Phi_1 \equiv f_1$, $\Phi_3 \equiv f_2$, $\Phi_5 \equiv f_3$, and $\Phi_{15} \equiv$

$f_4 f_5$ mod 2. We take $\mathbb{F}_{16} = \mathbb{F}_2[x]/\langle f_5 \rangle$, as in Example 7.1 (iii). For $\beta = x$ mod $f_5 \in \mathbb{F}_{16}$, the elements $\beta^3, \beta^2, \beta, 1$ form a basis of $\mathbb{F}_{16}$ over $\mathbb{F}_2$, and

$$\mathbb{F}_{16} = \{a_3\beta^3 + a_2\beta^2 + a_1 + a_0 : a_3, a_2, a_1, a_0 \in \mathbb{F}_2\}.$$

We see that $\beta^3 \neq 1, \beta^5 = \beta^2 + \beta \neq 1$, and $\beta^{15} = 1$. This means that β is a primitive 15th root of unity. We only have to check the divisors of 15, because the order of β is a divisor of the order 15 of the multiplicative group $\mathbb{F}_{16}^\times$ of $\mathbb{F}_{16}$, by Lagrange's theorem.

Table 7.1 gives all BCH codes of length 15 over $\mathbb{F}_2$. $\diamond$

δ	generator polynomial g	exponents i with $g(\beta^i) = 0$	$\dim C$	$d(C)$
1	1	$\varnothing$	15	1
2,3	f_5	$1,2,4,8$	11	3
4,5	$f_3 f_5$	$1,2,3,4,6,8,9,12$	8	5
6,7	$f_2 f_3 f_5$	$1,2,3,4,5,6,8,9,10,12$	5	7
$8,\dots,15$	$f_2 f_3 f_4 f_5$	$1,\dots,14$	1	15

TABLE 7.1: The BCH codes of length 15 over $\mathbb{F}_2$.

The parameter δ is called the **designed distance** of the BCH code. The next theorem shows that the minimal distance is at least as great.

THEOREM 7.5.
The minimal distance $d(C)$ of the code $C = \mathrm{BCH}(q, n, \delta)$ is at least δ.

PROOF. We identify $\mathbb{F}_q^n$ with $R = \mathbb{F}_q[x]/\langle x^n - 1 \rangle$ via

$$(a_{n-1}, \dots, a_0) \longleftrightarrow a_{n-1}x^{n-1} + \cdots + a_1 x + a_0 \bmod x^n - 1.$$

Furthermore we have a primitive nth root of unity $\beta \in \mathbb{F}_{q^m}$ for some $m \geq 1$, and for $a \in R$ we have

$$a \in C \iff a(\beta^i) = 0 \text{ for } 1 \leq i < \delta$$

$$\iff \begin{pmatrix} \beta^{n-1} & \cdots & \beta^2 & \beta & 1 \\ \beta^{2(n-1)} & \cdots & \beta^4 & \beta^2 & 1 \\ \vdots & & \vdots & \vdots & \vdots \\ \beta^{(\delta-1)(n-1)} & \cdots & \beta^{2(\delta-1)} & \beta^{\delta-1} & 1 \end{pmatrix} \begin{pmatrix} a_{n-1} \\ \vdots \\ a_1 \\ a_0 \end{pmatrix} = 0.$$

We denote the $(\delta - 1) \times n$-matrix above by B, and show that each $(\delta - 1) \times (\delta - 1)$ submatrix of B is nonsingular. From this the claim follows, because then for each $a \in C$ with $a \neq 0$ and $w(a) \leq \delta - 1$ we have $Ba \neq 0$.

For $0 \leq i < n$, the $(n-i-1)$st column of B is

$$
\begin{pmatrix}
\beta^i \\
\beta^{2i} \\
\vdots \\
\beta^{(\delta-1)i}
\end{pmatrix}.
$$

If we divide it by β^i, we obtain

$$
\begin{pmatrix}
1 \\
\beta^i \\
\vdots \\
\beta^{(\delta-2)i}
\end{pmatrix},
$$

which is a column of a Vandermonde matrix (Section 5.2). Hence each $(\delta-1) \times (\delta-1)$ submatrix of B is a Vandermonde matrix, where the columns are multiplied by some power of β. Since the β^i are pairwise distinct for $0 \leq i < n$ and any power of β is nonzero, all such submatrices are nonsingular. $\square$

Table 7.1 shows that the minimal distance of a BCH code can be strictly larger than the designed distance.

Now we will see how the decoding of a BCH code works. Let $C = \mathrm{BCH}(q,n,\delta)$ be given via β, and let δ be odd. Suppose that $c \in C$ is the transmitted and r the received word. We want to correct up to $t = (\delta-1)/2$ errors. Let

$$
e = r - c = e_{n-1}x^{n-1} + \cdots + e_1 x + e_0 \bmod x^n - 1 \longleftrightarrow (e_{n-1}, \ldots, e_1, e_0)
$$

be the error vector. Our assumption is that $w(e) \leq t$. We define:

$$
\begin{aligned}
M &= \{i : e_i \neq 0\}, \text{ the positions where an error occurs,} \\
u &= \prod_{i \in M}(1 - \beta^i y) \in \mathbb{F}_q[y], \text{ the \textbf{error locator polynomial}, and} \\
v &= \sum_{i \in M} e_i \beta^i y \prod_{j \in M \setminus \{i\}}(1 - \beta^j y) \in \mathbb{F}_q[y].
\end{aligned}
$$

Then $\#M \leq t$, $\deg u \leq t$, and $\deg v \leq t$. If we know u and v, then the errors can be corrected in the following way. By evaluating u at $1, \beta^{-1}, \beta^{-2}, \ldots, \beta^{-n+1}$, we obtain M. If $i \in M$, then we use the following observations to calculate e_i (this is only necessary, of course, if $q > 2$). The formal derivative u' of u with respect to y (Section 9.3) is

$$
u' = \sum_{i \in M}(-\beta^i) \prod_{j \in M \setminus \{i\}}(1 - \beta^j y).
$$

Thus

$$v(\beta^{-i}) = e_i \prod_{j \in M \setminus \{i\}} (1 - \beta^{j-i}) = -e_i \beta^{-i} u'(\beta^{-i}),$$

and hence

$$e_i = \frac{-v(\beta^{-i})\beta^i}{u'(\beta^{-i})}.$$

To compute u and v, we define

$$w = \frac{v}{u} = \sum_{i \in M} \frac{e_i \beta^i y}{1 - \beta^i y} = \sum_{i \in M} \sum_{k \geq 1} e_i (\beta^i y)^k = \sum_{k \geq 1} y^k \sum_{i \in M} e_i \beta^{ki} = \sum_{k \geq 1} y^k e(\beta^k).$$

Since $c(\beta^k) = 0$ for $1 \leq k \leq \delta - 1$, we have $e(\beta^k) = r(\beta^k)$ for $1 \leq k \leq \delta - 1$. We can compute these values, because r is the received word, and hence compute w rem y^δ. So we have to solve the following problem: Given w rem y^δ, compute u and v.

It is possible to formulate this problem as a system of linear equations. On the other hand, v/u is just a $(t+1, t)$-Padé approximant to w. It is unique and can be computed with the Extended Euclidean Algorithm, as described in Section 5.9. The computation can be done with $O(\delta^2)$ operations in $\mathbb{F}_{q^m}$, and with $O^\sim(\delta)$ operations using the fast algorithms from Part II.

EXAMPLE 7.4 (continued). Let $g = f_5 = x^4 + x + 1 \in \mathbb{F}_2[x]$ from Example 7.4 be the generator polynomial of the code $C = \mathrm{BCH}(2, 15, 3)$ when we take $\beta = (x \bmod x^4 + x + 1) \in \mathbb{F}_{16} = \mathbb{F}_2[x]/\langle x^4 + x + 1 \rangle$. Table 7.1 shows that $d(C) = 3$, and we can correct one error. Suppose that we have received

$$r = x^5 + x^4 + 1 \bmod x^{15} - 1 \in \mathbb{F}_2[x]/\langle x^{15} - 1 \rangle.$$

Using $\beta^4 = \beta + 1$, we have

$$r(\beta) = \beta^5 + \beta^4 + 1 = \beta^2, \quad r(\beta^2) = \beta^{10} + \beta^8 + 1 = \beta + 1,$$

and hence

$$w = \sum_{k \geq 1} e(\beta^k) y^k = \sum_{k \geq 1} r(\beta^k) y^k \equiv (\beta + 1)y^2 + \beta^2 y \bmod y^3. \tag{1}$$

Exercise 7.2 shows that the $(2, 1)$-Padé approximant of w is

$$\frac{u}{v} = \frac{(\beta^3 + \beta^2 + \beta)y}{(\beta^3 + \beta^2 + \beta)y + \beta^3 + \beta} = \frac{\beta^2 y}{\beta^2 y + 1},$$

so that $v = \beta^2 y$ and $u = \beta^2 y + 1$ in $\mathbb{F}_{16}[y]$. The only zero of u is at $y = \beta^{-2}$, and if we assume that at most one error has occurred, then this happened at position $i = 2$, and the original codeword was

$$c = x^5 + x^4 + x^2 + 1 \bmod x^{15} - 1.$$

In fact, we have $c = (x+1)g \bmod x^{15} - 1 \in C$. Expressing everything in terms of bit strings, the original message is $m = 00000000011$ of length eleven, encoded as $c^* = 000000000110101$ of length 15, using the isomorphism $\mathbb{F}_2^{11} \longrightarrow C$ given by the basis $x^{10}g, x^9g, \ldots, g$ of C. The received word is 000000000110001, and the decoding procedure discovers and corrects the error in the third last position, giving the receiver the correct word c^*, which then has to be converted back to the original message m. $\diamond$

Notes. Coding theory was founded by Shannon (1948). There are many good texts available, among them Berlekamp (1984), MacWilliams & Sloane (1977), and van Lint (1982). The coding technology for CDs is described in detail in Hoffman, Leonard, Lindner, Phelps, Rodger & Wall (1991).

For arbitrary codes, it is not clear how to decode them efficiently, and, in fact, a sufficiently general version of this problem is $\mathcal{NP}$-complete (Berlekamp, McEliece & van Tilborg 1978). BCH codes were discovered by Bose & Ray-Chaudhuri (1960) and independently by Hocquenghem (1959). Berlekamp (1984), already in the 1968 edition, and Massey (1965) discovered the decoding procedure for BCH codes, in a different formalism, and Dornstetter (1987) pointed out the relation to the Euclidean Algorithm.

Rabin (1989), Albanese, Blömer, Edmonds, Luby & Sudan (1994), and Alon, Edmonds & Luby (1995) describe *erasure codes*, a related class of codes which is used for communication over faulty networks that occasionally lose (or delay) packets (but do not change them).

Exercises.

7.1 Let F be a field, $k < n$ positive integers, and $u_1, \ldots, u_n \in F$ distinct. For $f \in F[x]$, let $\chi(f) = (f(u_1), \ldots, f(u_n)) \in F^n$, that is, χ is the evaluation map at $u_1, \ldots, u_n$. We define the linear code $C \subseteq F^n$ by $C = \{\chi(f) : f \in F[x], \deg f \leq k\}$. Show that C has minimal distance $n - k$.

7.2 Compute the $(2,1)$-Padé approximant to w from (1).

7.3 Determine generator polynomials and minimal distances of all BCH codes for $q = 2$ and $n = 7$. Hint: The polynomial $x^7 - 1 \in \mathbb{F}_2[x]$ factors into three irreducible polynomials

$$x^7 - 1 = (x+1)(x^3 + x + 1)(x^3 + x^2 + 1),$$

and $\beta = x \bmod x^3 + x + 1 \in \mathbb{F}_8 = \mathbb{F}_2[x]/\langle x^3 + x + 1 \rangle$ is a primitive 7th root of unity.

7.4 Let $C = \mathrm{BCH}(2,7,3)$ be generated by $g = x^3 + x + 1 \in \mathbb{F}_2[x]$, and $\beta = x \bmod g$ be as in Exercise 7.3. Assuming that at most one error has occurred, decode the received words

$$r_1 = x^6 + x^5 + x^3 + 1 \bmod x^7 - 1, \quad r_2 = x^6 + x + 1 \bmod x^7 - 1.$$

Find a codeword $c \in C$ such that $d(r_2 - c) = 2$.

7.5$^{\longrightarrow}$ Let $q = 11$ and $n = 10$.
 (i) Prove that $\beta = 2 \in \mathbb{F}_q$ is a primitive nth root of unity.
 (ii) Show that the polynomial $x^{10} - 1$ splits into linear factors over $\mathbb{F}_q$.
 (iii) Tabulate generator polynomials and minimal distances of all BCH codes for the above values of q, n, and β.
 (iv) Let $C = \mathrm{BCH}(11, 10, 5)$. Check that the generator polynomial for C is $g = x^4 + 3x^3 + 5x^2 + 8x + 1$. Assuming that at most two errors have occurred, decode the received word

$$r = x^6 + 7x + 4 \bmod x^{10} - 1 \in \mathbb{F}_{11}[x]/\langle x^{10} - 1 \rangle.$$

Part II
Newton

Isaac Newton (1642–1727) had a rather tough childhood. His father died during his mother's pregnancy and his mother remarried when he was three years old—and left little Isaac in the care of his grandmother.

In 1661, Newton entered Trinity College in Cambridge, and graduated with a BA in 1664, after an unimpressive student career. But then the university shut down for two years because of the Great Plague, and Newton, back in his native Woolsthorpe, laid the ground for much of his future work in the *anni mirabiles* 1664–1666. He invented calculus (his method of *fluxions*) and the law of gravitation, and showed by experiment the prismatic composition of white light. All this before he turned 25. (*Inventing calculus* means that he developed a widely applicable theory; its roots go back, of course, to the work of many people, Archimedes and Fermat among them.)

Back at Cambridge, Newton became Lucasian Professor of Mathematics, at the age of 26. His former teacher, Isaac Barrow, resigned from that position to make way for the greater scientist (and to prepare his own move into a better position as chaplain to King Charles II). At that time, Newton was the prototype of the "forgetful professor", rather negligent about trifles such as his appearance. His nephew Humphrey Newton wrote: *He very rarely went to Dine in ye Hall unless upon some Publick Dayes, & then, if He has not been minded, would go very carelesly, wth Shooes down at Heels, Stockins unty'd, surplice on, & his Head scarcely comb'd.*

Newton did not publish his early results; this was later to work against him in disputes over priority. This was partly due to the publishers who were reluctant to invest in a money pit like a mathematical monograph. A 1672 paper on optics was so heavily criticized by overbearing referees (against whose beliefs his new and correct theory ran) that he withdrew it in the end.

Finally, he published in 1687 his masterpiece *Philosophiae Naturalis Principia Mathematica*, containing his discoveries in mechanics and astronomy.

In the summer of 1669, Newton had finished his *De Analysi per Æquationes Numero Terminorum Infinitas*. It circulated among English mathematicians and also abroad (Scotland and France), but appeared in print only in 1711. Among other things, he describes what is now called *Newton's method* (or Newton iteration) for approximating real roots of polynomial equations. He takes $\varphi = y^3 - 2y - 5 \in \mathbb{Q}[y]$ as an example, and proceeds as follows:

> Let the Equation $y^3 - 2y - 5 = 0$ be proposed to be resolved: and let
> 2 be a number which differs from the Root sought, by less than a
> tenth Part of itself. Then I put $2 + p = y$, and I substitute this Value in
> Place of it in the Equation, and thence a new Equation arises, viz.
> $p^3 + 6p^2 + 10p - 1 = 0$, whose Root p is to be sought for, that it may

be added to the Quotient: viz. thus (neglecting $p^3 + 6p^2$ upon the Account of their smallness) $10p - 1 = 0$, or $p = 0.1$ is near the Truth; therefore I write 0.1 in the Quotient, and then suppose $0.1 + q = p$, and this it's value I substitute, as formerly, whence results $q^3 + 6.3q^2 + 11.23q + 0.061 = 0$.

And since $11.23q + 0.061 = 0$ comes near to the Truth, or since q is almost equal to -0.0054 (viz. by dividing until as many Figures arise as there are places betwixt the first Figures of this and the principal Quotient) I write -0.0054 in the lower Part of the Quotient, since it is negative.

His choice of the starting point 2 is justified by the fact that $\varphi(2) = -1 < 0 < 16 = \varphi(3)$, so that there is a root of φ between 2 and 3. This example later became a standard test for root finding methods. Joseph Raphson (1690) discussed this approach, acknowledging Newton as the originator, and it is sometimes called the Newton–Raphson method. Newton himself calls it "an improved version of the procedure, expounded by Viète and simplified by Oughtred". We will use Newton iteration in Chapters 9 and 15.

After many years of studying religious subjects (in particular, the Biblical chronology), Newton turned to public office, serving as Member of (powerless) Parliament until its dissolution in 1690. In 1699, he was awarded the moderately prestigious office of *Warden of the Mint*. Bell (1937) writes scathingly about this elevation: "The crowning imbecility of the Anglo-Saxon breed is its dumb belief in public office or an administrative position as the supreme honour for a man of intellect."—is that restricted to one "breed"?

The "universal genius" Leibniz, in Hannover, invented calculus independently, probably in the mid-1670s, and published this in 1684, before Newton published his ideas, almost two decades old by then. At first, the two men seem to have had mutual respect for each other's achievements. But fueled by the nationalism of the day (so, what else is new?), this degenerated into one of the bitterest controversies about priority in the history of science, an embarrassment for all persons involved.

Sir Isaac Newton, knighted by Queen Anne in 1705, was President of the Royal Society until his death at the age of 85.

Classical in this context came to mean something like make-believe.

Richard Phillips Feynman (1984)

We shall not build a new world
until we have got rid of the mentalities of the old.

John le Carré (1989)

Rule 8: The development of fast algorithms is slow!

Arnold Schönhage (1994)

Jede mathematische Aufgabe könnte durch direktes Zählen gelöst
werden. Es gibt aber Zähloperationen, die gegenwärtig in wenigen
Minuten vollführt werden, welche aber ohne Methode vorzunehmen
die Lebensdauer eines Menschen bei weitem nicht reichen würde.[1]

Ernst Mach (1896)

---

[1] Any mathematical task could, in principle, be solved by direct counting. However, there are counting problems that can presently be solved in a few minutes, but for which without mathematical method a lifetime would not be sufficient.

8

Fast multiplication

In this chapter, we introduce fast methods for multiplying integers and polynomials. We start with a simple method due to Karatsuba which reduces the cost from the classical $O(n^2)$ for polynomials of degree n to $O(n^{1.59})$. The Discrete Fourier Transform and its efficient implementation, the Fast Fourier Transform, are the backbone of the fastest algorithms. These work only when appropriate **roots of unity** are present, but Schönhage & Strassen (1971) showed how to create "virtual" roots that lead to a multiplication cost of only $O(n \log n \log \log n)$. In Chapter 9, Newton iteration will help us extend this to fast division with remainder.

General-purpose computer algebra systems typically only implement the classical method, and sometimes Karatsuba's. This is quite sufficient as long as one deals with fairly small numbers or polynomials, but for many high-performance tasks fast arithmetic is indispensable. Examples include factoring large polynomials (Section 15.7), finding primes and prime twins (Indlekofer & Járai 1998), and computing billions of digits of π (Section 4.6) or billions of roots of Riemann's zeta function (Notes 18.4).

Asymptotically fast methods are standard tools in many areas of computer science, where, say, $O(n \log n)$ sorting algorithms like quicksort or mergesort are widely used and experiments show that they outperform the "classical" $O(n^2)$ sorting algorithms like bubble sort or insertion sort already for values of n below 100. In contrast, the asymptotically fast algorithms for polynomial and integer arithmetic, in particular for multiplication, have received comparatively little attention in the computer algebra world since their invention around 1970. (At the time of writing, MAGMA V2.4 is the only general purpose computer algebra system implementing FFT multiplication that the authors are aware of.) Some of the reasons may be that the fast algorithms are often considerably more complicated than the classical ones, and that the crossover points between these algorithms may be disappointingly high when the algorithms are implemented "literally" as described in textbooks, without any further optimization. On the other hand, experiments with highly optimized software, such as those described in Section 9.7, show that Karatsuba's algorithm has a fairly small crossover with the classical algorithm, and that even faster multiplication algorithms already come into play for moderately sized inputs. Designers of a computer algebra system should carefully determine the crossover points and then, depending on the size of the problems their system is intended to solve, decide which algorithms to offer.

Last but not least there is the intellectual beauty of asymptotic analysis. Complexity theory provides a precise framework in which to compare algorithms via their asymptotic running time (or some other measure, such as memory or parallel time). For our problems, both *Boolean* and *arithmetic complexity theory* play a role; Bürgisser, Clausen & Shokrollahi (1996) give an overview of the impressive results of the latter. It provides tools for proving *lower bounds*, saying that every conceivable algorithm must use at least so and so many operations, and in lucky cases even that some algorithms are *optimal*. Furthermore, this crystal-clear framework allows for a precise statement that "this new method makes progress" and, if incorrect, its refutation. Practical results, such as the experiments reported in this book, are also important, but often open to dispute as they take place in the muddy waters of difficult-to-compare computing environments, difference of opinion on the "important cases and examples", and difficulty to reproduce. The latter is extremely laborious or virtually impossible for a large implementation effort. As an example, improving the $O(n \log n \log \log n)$ multiplication algorithm of Schönhage & Strassen (1971) has been a well-defined challenge for over a quarter century; it is difficult to imagine this status for an experimental problem. Some areas have an accepted set of concrete benchmark problems, such as the "most wanted" Cunningham numbers for integer factorization (see Chapter 19). But even there, asymptotic progress is the holy grail.

The lower table on the inside front cover lists the problems in polynomial algebra for which we will achieve almost linear-time algorithms in the following chapters. The algorithms work over an arbitrary ring or field, and fast polynomial multiplication is crucial for them. For all these problems, the input size is about n, and the classical algorithms from Part I take quadratic time. All algorithms have integer analogs, which—as always—are more complicated due to the carries, with about the same running time in word operations when the input consists of n words.

8.1. Karatsuba's multiplication algorithm

We start with the multiplication of two polynomials $f, g \in R[x]$ of degree less than n over a ring R. As usual, "ring" means a commutative ring with 1. If $f_i, g_j, h_k \in R$ are the coefficients of f, g and $h = fg$, respectively, the classical multiplication algorithm uses $O(n^2)$ operations in R to compute the h_k from the f_i and g_j: n^2 multiplications $f_i g_j$ plus $(n-1)^2$ additions for all $h_k = \sum_{i+j=k} f_i g_j$ (Section 2.3). For instance, multiplying $(ax+b)(cx+d) = acx^2 + (ad+bc)x + bd$ uses four multiplications ac, ad, bc, bd, and one addition $ad + bc$.

Surprisingly, there is an easy method of doing better. We compute ac, bd,

$u = (a + b)(c + d)$, and $ad + bc = u - ac - bd$, with three multiplications and four additions and subtractions. The total has increased to seven operations, but a recursive application will drastically reduce the overall cost (see Figure 8.2). To explain the general approach, we assume that $n = 2^k$ for some $k \in \mathbb{N}$, set $m = n/2$, and rewrite f and g in the form $f = F_1 x^m + F_0$ with $F_0, F_1 \in R[x]$ of degree less than m and similarly $g = G_1 x^m + G_0$. (If $\deg f < n - 1$, then some of the top coefficients are zero.) Now $fg = F_1 G_1 x^n + (F_0 G_1 + F_1 G_0) x^m + F_0 G_0$. In this form, multiplication of f and g has been reduced to four multiplications of polynomials of degree less than m. Multiplication by a power of x does not count as a multiplication, since it corresponds merely to a shift of the coefficients.

So far we have not really achieved anything. But the method by Karatsuba in Karatsuba & Ofman (1962), explained for $n = 1$ above, shows how this expression for fg can be rearranged to reduce the number of multiplications of the smaller polynomials at the expense of increasing the number of additions. Since multiplication is slower than addition, a saving is obtained when n is sufficiently large. We rewrite the product as $fg = F_1 G_1 x^n + ((F_0 + F_1)(G_0 + G_1) - F_0 G_0 - F_1 G_1) x^m + F_0 G_0$. This expression shows that multiplication of f and g requires only three multiplications of polynomials of degree less than m and some additions. The same method is now applied recursively to the smaller multiplications. If $T(n)$ denotes the time necessary to multiply two polynomials of degree less than n, then $T(2n) \leq 3T(n) + cn$, for some constant c. The linear term comes from the observation that addition of two polynomials of degree less than d can be done with d operations in R.

Here is the corresponding algorithm.

▬ ALGORITHM 8.1 Karatsuba's polynomial multiplication algorithm. ▬▬▬▬
Input: $f, g \in R[x]$ of degrees less than n, where R is a ring (commutative, with 1) and n a power of 2.
Output: $fg \in R[x]$.

1. **if** $n = 1$ **then return** $f \cdot g \in R$

2. let $f = F_1 x^{n/2} + F_0$ and $g = G_1 x^{n/2} + G_0$, with $F_0, F_1, G_0, G_1 \in R[x]$ of degrees less than $n/2$

3. compute $F_0 G_0$, $F_1 G_1$, and $(F_0 + F_1)(G_0 + G_1)$ by a recursive call

4. **return** $F_1 G_1 x^n + ((F_0 + F_1)(G_0 + G_1) - F_0 G_0 - F_1 G_1) x^{n/2} + F_0 G_0$ ▬

Figure 8.1 visualizes this algorithm in the form of an arithmetic circuit for $n = 4$.

We first need a lemma which will be helpful in the analysis of several recursive algorithms. $T(n)$ will be the cost on input size n of the algorithm, which consists

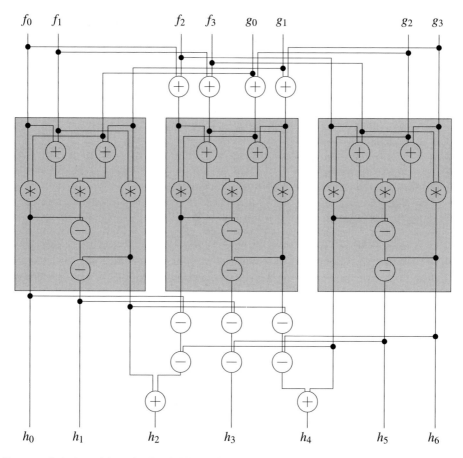

FIGURE 8.1: An arithmetic circuit illustrating Karatsuba's algorithm for $n = 4$. The shaded boxes are Karatsuba circuits for $n = 2$. A subtraction node computes the difference of its left input minus its right input.

of b recursive calls with inputs of size $n/2$, plus some cost denoted by $S(n)$. We denote by log the binary logarithm.

LEMMA 8.2. *Let* $b, d \in \mathbb{N}$ *with* $b > 0$, $S, T \colon \mathbb{N} \longrightarrow \mathbb{N}$ *be functions with* $S(2n) \geq 2S(n)$ *and* $S(n) \geq n$ *for all* $n \in \mathbb{N}$, *and*

$$T(1) = d, \quad T(n) \leq bT(n/2) + S(n) \text{ for } n = 2^i \text{ and } i \in \mathbb{N}_{\geq 1}.$$

Then for $i \in \mathbb{N}$ *and* $n = 2^i$ *we have*

$$T(n) \leq \begin{cases} (2 - 2/n)S(n) + d \in O(S(n)) & \text{if } b = 1, \\ S(n)\log n + dn \in O(S(n)\log n) & \text{if } b = 2, \\ \frac{2}{b-2}(n^{\log b - 1} - 1)S(n) + dn^{\log b} \in O(S(n)n^{\log b - 1}) & \text{if } b \geq 3. \end{cases}$$

PROOF. Unraveling the recursion, we obtain inductively

$$
\begin{aligned}
T(2^i) &\leq bT(2^{i-1}) + S(2^i) \leq b(bT(2^{i-2}) + S(2^{i-1})) + S(2^i) \\
&= b^2 T(2^{i-2}) + bS(2^{i-1}) + S(2^i) \leq \cdots \\
&\leq b^i T(1) + \sum_{0 \leq j < i} b^j S(2^{i-j}) \leq d2^{i \log b} + S(2^i) \sum_{0 \leq j < i} \left(\frac{b}{2}\right)^j,
\end{aligned}
$$

where we have used that $S(2^{i-j}) \leq 2^{-j} S(2^i)$ in the last inequality. If $b = 2$, then the last sum simplifies to $S(2^i) \cdot i$. If $b \neq 2$, then we have a geometric sum

$$
\sum_{0 \leq j < i} \left(\frac{b}{2}\right)^j = \frac{(\frac{b}{2})^i - 1}{\frac{b}{2} - 1} = \frac{2}{b-2}(2^{i(\log b - 1)} - 1),
$$

and the claim follows. $\square$

THEOREM 8.3.

Karatsuba's algorithm 8.1 for multiplying polynomials of degree less than a power n of 2 over a ring can be done with at most $9n^{\log 3}$ or $O(n^{1.59})$ ring operations.

PROOF. In step 3, we have n additions for computing $F_0 + F_1$ and $G_0 + G_1$. The computation of $F_1 G_1 x^n + F_0 G_0$ in step 4 is just a concatenation of coefficients. The computation of $((F_0 + F_1)(G_0 + G_1) - F_0 G_0 - F_1 G_1)x^{n/2}$ takes $2n$ subtractions, and we have another n additions for adding the result to $F_1 G_1 x^n + F_0 G_0$. Thus we may choose $b = 3$, $d = 1$, and $S(n) = 4n$ in Lemma 8.2 and obtain a total cost of $9 \cdot n^{\log 3} - 8n$ operations. The claim follows from $\log 3 < 1.59$. $\square$

This is a substantial improvement over the classical method, since $\log 3 < 2$. The savings are visualized in Figure 8.2.

If n is not a power of 2, then there are two ways to proceed. The first one is to apply the algorithm for the least power of 2 that is greater than n, that is, for $2^{\lceil \log n \rceil}$. This is easy to analyze, but introduces an additional factor of 3 in the running time, which is annoying if n is only slightly greater than a power of 2. The second possibility is to split the polynomials into blocks of about half the degree each time in the recursive process. This leads to an algorithm that performs better than the first variant, but the analysis is somewhat more involved; see Exercise 8.5.

The same method applies to multiplication of two (positive) integers a and b in r-ary representation, say with $r = 2^{64}$ (see Section 2.1). When they have length at most n, the classical integer multiplication algorithm requires $O(n^2)$ word operations (Section 2.3). Karatsuba's algorithm for integers writes $a = A_1 2^{64m} + A_0$ and $b = B_1 2^{64m} + B_0$, where $A_0, A_1, B_0, B_1 < 2^{64m}$ and $n = 2m$ is assumed to be a power of 2. Then $ab = A_1 B_1 2^{64n} + ((A_0 + A_1)(B_0 + B_1) - A_0 B_0 - A_1 B_1)2^{64m} + A_0 B_0$. As

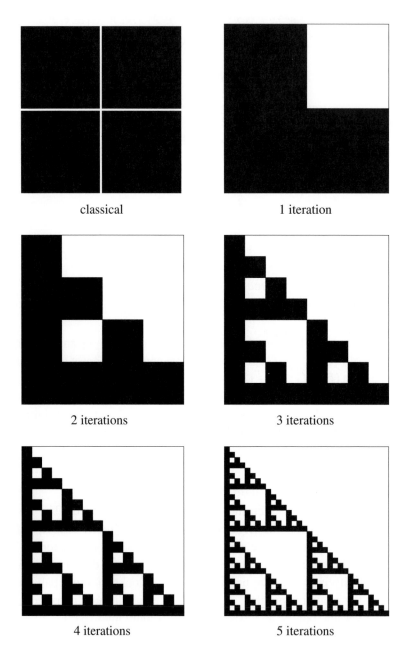

classical   1 iteration

2 iterations   3 iterations

4 iterations   5 iterations

FIGURE 8.2: Cost (= black area) of Karatsuba's algorithm for increasing recursion depths. The image approaches a fractal of dimension $\log 3 \approx 1.59$.

in the polynomial case, multiplication of two integers has been reduced to multiplication of three integers of at most half the size plus $O(n)$ word operations (if $A_0 + A_1$ or $B_0 + B_1$ exceed 2^{64n}, then one has to take extra care of the leading bits, or alternatively computes $A_0 B_1 + A_1 B_0 = A_0 B_0 + A_1 B_1 - (A_0 - A_1)(B_0 - B_1)$). This leads to the following theorem.

▬▬ THEOREM 8.4. ▬▬▬▬▬▬▬▬▬▬▬▬▬▬▬▬▬▬▬▬▬▬▬▬▬▬▬
Multiplication of two integers of length at most n words can be done with $O(n^{\log 3})$ or $O(n^{1.59})$ word operations using Karatsuba's algorithm. ▬▬▬▬▬▬▬▬

Karatsuba's algorithm is used in computer algebra systems like MAPLE. The classical method is faster for polynomials of small degree and integers of small length; see Exercises 8.4 and 8.6.

8.2. The Discrete Fourier Transform and the Fast Fourier Transform

In this section, we discuss a polynomial multiplication algorithm which works in nearly linear time. It requires that the coefficient ring contain certain roots of unity. We recall that an element a of a ring R is a **zero divisor** if there exists a $b \in R$ with $ab = 0$. In particular, 0 is a zero divisor.

DEFINITION 8.5. *Let R be a ring, $n \in \mathbb{N}_{\geq 1}$, and $\omega \in R$.*

(i) ω *is an **nth root of unity** if $\omega^n = 1$.*

(ii) ω *is a **primitive nth root of unity** (or root of unity of order n) if it is an nth root of unity, $n \in R$ is a unit in R, and $\omega^{n/t} - 1$ is not a zero divisor for any prime divisor t of n.*

Here n has two meanings: in "ω^n" it is an integer used as a counter to express the n-fold product of ω with itself, and in "$n \in R$" it stands for the ring element $n \cdot 1_R \in R$ (Section 25.3).

EXAMPLE 8.6. (i) $\omega = e^{2\pi i/8} \in R = \mathbb{C}$ is a primitive 8th root of unity; see Figure 8.3.

(ii) $\mathbb{Z}_8$ has no primitive square root of unity, despite the fact that $3^2 \equiv 1$, since 2 is not a unit.

(iii) For the "Fermat prime" $2^4 + 1 = 17$, the element 3 is a primitive 16th root of unity in $\mathbb{Z}_{17}$, and 2 is not. ◇

The following lemma extends the property of Definition 8.5 (ii) for $\omega^\ell - 1$ from $\ell = n/t$ to all ℓ that are not divisible by n.

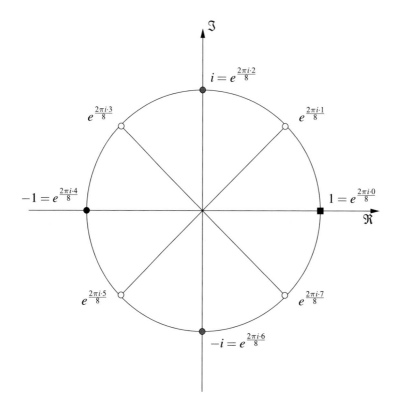

FIGURE 8.3: The 8th roots of unity in $\mathbb{C}$. The black square has order 1, the black circle order 2, the two gray circles order 4, and the four white circles are the primitive 8th roots of unity.

LEMMA 8.7. *Let R be a ring, $\ell, n \in \mathbb{N}_{\geq 1}$ such that $1 < \ell < n$, and $\omega \in R$ a primitive nth root of unity. Then*

  (i) $\omega^{\ell} - 1$ *is not a zero divisor in R,*

  (ii) $\sum_{0 \leq j < n} \omega^{\ell j} = 0$.

PROOF. We will make repeated use of the formula

$$(c - 1) \sum_{0 \leq j < m} c^{j} = c^{m} - 1, \tag{1}$$

which holds for all $m \in \mathbb{N}$ and $c \in R$ (in fact, even for an indeterminate c).

  (i) Let $g = \gcd(\ell, n)$ and $s, t \in \mathbb{Z}$ so that $s\ell + tn = g$. Since $1 \leq g < n$, we can choose a prime divisor t of n so that g divides n/t. Letting $c = \omega^{g}$ and $m = nt/g$ in (1), we obtain $a \cdot (\omega^{g} - 1) = \omega^{n/t} - 1$ for some $a \in R$. If $b \in R$ satisfies $b \cdot (\omega^{g} - 1) = 0$, then also $b \cdot (\omega^{n/t} - 1) = 0$, and hence $b = 0$ since $\omega^{n/t} - 1$ is not a zero divisor. Thus $\omega^{g} - 1$ is not a zero divisor either.

Furthermore, (1) with $c = \omega^\ell$ and $m = s$ implies that $\omega^\ell - 1$ divides $\omega^{s\ell} - 1 = \omega^{s\ell}\omega^{tn} - 1 = \omega^g - 1$. The same argument as above implies that $\omega^\ell - 1$ is not a zero divisor.

(ii) By letting $c = \omega^\ell$ and $m = n$ in (1), we see that

$$(\omega^\ell - 1) \sum_{0 \leq j < n} (\omega^\ell)^j = \omega^{\ell n} - 1 = 0.$$

Thus $\sum_{0 \leq j < n} \omega^{\ell j} = 0$, since $\omega^\ell - 1$ is not a zero divisor, by (i). $\square$

When R is an integral domain (for example, a field), then (i) simply says $\omega^\ell \neq 1$, and it is sufficient to check this for $\ell = n/t$, with t running through the prime divisors of n, for the last property required of a primitive nth root of unity.

The following lemma, proven in Exercise 8.18, says when primitive roots of unity exist in finite fields.

LEMMA 8.8. *For a prime power q and $n \in \mathbb{N}$ with $\gcd(q,n) = 1$, a finite field $\mathbb{F}_q$ with q elements contains a primitive nth root of unity if and only if n divides $q - 1$.*

Let R be a ring, $n \in \mathbb{N}_{\geq 1}$, and $\omega \in R$ be a primitive nth root of unity. In what follows, we identify a polynomial $f = \sum_{0 \leq i < n} f_i x^i \in R[x]$ of degree less than n with its coefficient vector $(f_0, \ldots, f_{n-1}) \in R^n$.

DEFINITION 8.9.   (i) *The R-linear map*

$$\mathrm{DFT}_\omega \colon \begin{cases} R^n & \longrightarrow & R^n \\ f & \longmapsto & \Big(f(1), f(\omega), f(\omega^2), \ldots, f(\omega^{n-1}) \Big) \end{cases}$$

*which evaluates a polynomial at the powers of ω is called the **Discrete Fourier Transform (DFT)**.*

(ii) *The **convolution** of two polynomials $f = \sum_{0 \leq i < n} f_i x^i$ and $g = \sum_{0 \leq j < n} g_j x^j$ in $R[x]$ is the polynomial*

$$h = f *_n g = \sum_{0 \leq k < n} h_k x^k \in R[x],$$

where

$$h_k = \sum_{i + j \equiv k \bmod n} f_i g_j = \sum_{0 \leq i < n} f_i g_{k-i} \text{ for } 0 \leq k < n,$$

*with index arithmetic modulo n. If n is clear from the context, we will simply write $*$ for $*_n$. If we regard the coefficients as vectors in R^n, then c is called the **cyclic convolution** of the vectors f and g.*

This notion of convolution is equivalent to polynomial multiplication in the ring $R[x]/\langle x^n - 1\rangle$. The kth coefficient of the product polynomial $f \cdot g$ is $\sum_{i+j=k} f_i g_j$, and hence $f *_n g \equiv fg \bmod x^n - 1$. We will exploit this relationship between convolution and multiplication to obtain fast polynomial multiplication algorithms.

EXAMPLE 8.10. Let $R = \mathbb{F}_5$, $n = 4$, $u \in \mathbb{F}_5$, and suppose we want to multiply $f = x^3 + 1$, $g = 2x^3 + 3x^2 + x + 1$ in $\mathbb{F}_5[x]$ modulo $x^4 - u$. Then

$$
\begin{aligned}
fg &= 2x^6 + 3x^5 + x^4 + 3x^3 + 3x^2 + x + 1 \\
&= (2x^2 + 3x + 1)(x^4 - u) + 3x^3 + 3x^2 + x + 1 + (2x^2 + 3x + 1)u \\
&= (2x^2 + 3x + 1)(x^4 - u) + 3x^3 + (3 + 2u)x^2 + (1 + 3u)x + (1 + u).
\end{aligned}
$$

The special form of the binomial $x^4 - u$ makes division with remainder particularly easy: the quotient is the upper part of fg, and the remainder is the lower part of fg plus u times the upper part. In particular, for $u = 1$ we have $fg \equiv 3x^3 + 4x + 2 \bmod x^4 - 1$, or equivalently, $f *_4 g = 3x^2 + 4x + 2$. A similar phenomenon will help us in the FFT algorithm below. $\diamond$

LEMMA 8.11. *For polynomials $f, g \in R[x]$ of degree less than n, we have*

$$
\mathrm{DFT}_\omega(f * g) = \mathrm{DFT}_\omega(f) \cdot \mathrm{DFT}_\omega(g),
$$

where $\cdot$ denotes the pointwise multiplication of vectors.

PROOF. We have $f * g = fg + q \cdot (x^n - 1)$ for some $q \in R[x]$, so that

$$
(f * g)(\omega^i) = f(\omega^i)g(\omega^i) + q(\omega^i)(\omega^{in} - 1) = f(\omega^i)g(\omega^i) \text{ for } 0 \leq i < n. \ \square
$$

We may also consider the map $F[x] \longrightarrow R^n$ that evaluates f at $\omega^0, \ldots, \omega^{n-1}$. Its kernel is $\langle x^n - 1\rangle$, and the lemma says that $\mathrm{DFT}_\omega \colon R[x]/\langle x^n - 1\rangle \longrightarrow R^n$ is a homomorphism of R-algebras, where multiplication in R^n is pointwise multiplication of vectors. The following commutative diagram illustrates this:

$$
\begin{array}{ccc}
\left(R[x]/\langle x^n - 1\rangle\right)^2 & \xrightarrow{\ \mathrm{DFT}_\omega \times \mathrm{DFT}_\omega\ } & R^n \times R^n \\
{\scriptstyle \text{cyclic}} \downarrow {\scriptstyle \text{convolution}} & & \downarrow {\scriptstyle \text{pointwise multiplication}} \qquad (2) \\
R[x]/\langle x^n - 1\rangle & \xrightarrow[\ \mathrm{DFT}_\omega\ ]{} & R^n
\end{array}
$$

In fact, DFT_ω is an isomorphism. If R is a field, then this the special case of the Chinese Remainder Theorem 5.3, where $m_i = x - \omega^i$ for $0 \leq i < n$. We discussed in Section 5.1 the general principle of **change of representation** and will now see how the particular example (2) gives rise to a fast multiplication algorithm.

In the following, polynomials of degree less than n over an integral domain R are—besides the usual **dense** representation by their coefficient vectors—represented by their values at n distinct points $u_0, \ldots, u_{n-1} \in R$, namely the powers $u_i = \omega^i$ for $0 \le i < n$ of a primitive nth root of unity $\omega \in R$. The reason for considering the value representation is that multiplication in that representation is easy: If $f(u_0), \ldots, f(u_{n-1})$ and $g(u_0), \ldots, g(u_{n-1})$ are the values of two polynomials f and g with $\deg(fg) < n$ at n distinct points, then the values of the product polynomial fg at those points are $f(u_0) \cdot g(u_0), \ldots, f(u_{n-1}) \cdot g(u_{n-1})$. Hence the cost of polynomial multiplication in the value representation is linear in the degree, while we do not know how to multiply polynomials in the dense representation in linear time. Thus a fast way of doing multipoint evaluation and interpolation leads to a fast polynomial multiplication algorithm: evaluate the two input polynomials, multiply the results pointwise, and finally interpolate to get the product polynomial.

The Discrete Fourier Transform is a special multipoint evaluation at the powers $1, \omega, \ldots, \omega^{n-1}$ of a primitive nth root of unity ω, and we will now show that both the DFT and its inverse, the interpolation at the powers of ω, can be computed with $O(n \log n)$ operations in R, and thus obtain an $O(n \log n)$ multiplication algorithm for polynomials. In Chapter 10, we will see a fast algorithm for evaluation and interpolation at arbitrary points.

First we show that interpolation at the powers of ω is essentially again a Discrete Fourier Transform. The Vandermonde matrix

$$V_\omega = \text{VDM}(1, \omega, \ldots, \omega^{n-1}) = \begin{pmatrix} 1 & 1 & 1 & \cdots & 1 \\ 1 & \omega & \omega^2 & \cdots & \omega^{n-1} \\ 1 & \omega^2 & \omega^4 & \cdots & \omega^{2(n-1)} \\ \vdots & \vdots & \vdots & \ddots & \vdots \\ 1 & \omega^{n-1} & \omega^{2(n-1)} & \cdots & \omega^{(n-1)^2} \end{pmatrix}$$

$$= (\omega^{ij})_{0 \le i, j < n} \in R^{n \times n}$$

is the matrix of the multipoint evaluation map DFT_ω (Section 5.2).

EXAMPLE 8.12. For the primitive 4th root of unity $\omega = i = \sqrt{-1} \in \mathbb{C}$, we have

$$V_i = \text{VDM}(1, i, -1, -i) = \begin{pmatrix} 1 & 1 & 1 & 1 \\ 1 & i & -1 & -i \\ 1 & -1 & 1 & -1 \\ 1 & -i & -1 & i \end{pmatrix}. \quad \diamond$$

Since $1, \omega, \ldots, \omega^{n-1}$ are distinct, V_ω is invertible if R is a field (Section 5.2), and its inverse is the matrix of the interpolation map at the n points. The following theorem says that this is true for arbitrary rings.

▬▬ THEOREM 8.13. ▬▬▬▬▬▬▬▬▬▬▬▬▬▬▬▬▬▬▬▬▬▬▬▬▬▬▬▬▬▬▬▬

Let R be a ring (commutative, with 1), $n \in \mathbb{N}_{\geq 1}$, and $\omega \in R$ be a primitive nth root of unity. Then ω^{-1} is a primitive nth root of unity and $V_\omega \cdot V_{\omega^{-1}} = nI$, where I is the $n \times n$ identity matrix. ▬▬▬▬▬▬▬▬▬▬▬▬▬▬▬▬▬▬▬▬▬▬▬▬▬▬▬▬▬▬

PROOF. Exercise 8.13 shows that ω^{-1} is a primitive nth root of unity. Let $0 \leq i, k < n$, and

$$u = (V_\omega \cdot V_{\omega^{-1}})_{ik} = \sum_{0 \leq j < n} (V_\omega)_{ij}(V_{\omega^{-1}})_{jk} = \sum_{0 \leq j < n} \omega^{ij}\omega^{-jk} = \sum_{0 \leq j < n} (\omega^{i-k})^j.$$

If $i = k$, then $u = \sum_{0 \leq j < n} 1 = n$. If $i \neq k$, then $u = \sum_{0 \leq j < n} \omega^{(i-k)j} = 0$, by Lemma 8.7. $\square$

In particular, the theorem implies that $(V_\omega)^{-1} = n^{-1}V_{\omega^{-1}}$, so that computing the inverse is fairly easy.

EXAMPLE 8.12 (continued). $V_i^{-1} = \dfrac{1}{4} \begin{pmatrix} 1 & 1 & 1 & 1 \\ 1 & -i & -1 & i \\ 1 & -1 & 1 & -1 \\ 1 & i & -1 & -i \end{pmatrix}.$ ◇

We next discuss an important algorithm—the **Fast Fourier Transform**, or FFT for short—that computes the DFT quickly. It was (re)discovered by Cooley and Tukey in 1965, and is possibly the second most important nontrivial algorithm in practice. (Contender for first place is fast sorting.) The inverse DFT can then also be computed quickly, by Theorem 8.13.

Let $n \in \mathbb{N}_{\geq 1}$ be even, $\omega \in R$ a primitive nth root of unity, and $f \in R[x]$ of degree less than n. To evaluate f at the powers $1, \omega, \omega^2, \ldots, \omega^{n-1}$, we divide f by $x^{n/2} - 1$ and $x^{n/2} + 1$ with remainder:

$$f = q_0(x^{n/2} - 1) + r_0 = q_1(x^{n/2} + 1) + r_1, \tag{3}$$

for some $q_0, r_0, q_1, r_1 \in R[x]$ of degree less than $n/2$. Due to the special form of the divisor polynomials, the computation of the remainders r_0 and r_1 (we do not actually need the quotients) can be done by adding the upper $n/2$ coefficients of f to, respectively subtracting them from, the lower $n/2$ coefficients, as in Example 8.10, at a total cost of n operations in R. In other words, if $f = F_1 x^{n/2} + F_0$

with $\deg F_0, \deg F_1 < n/2$, then $x^{n/2} - 1$ divides $f - F_0 - F_1$, and hence $r_0 = F_0 + F_1$; similarly $r_1 = F_0 - F_1$. If we plug in a power of w for x in (3), we find

$$
\begin{aligned}
f(w^{2i}) &= q_0(w^{2i})(w^{ni} - 1) + r_0(w^{2i}) = r_0(w^{2i}), \\
f(w^{2i+1}) &= q_1(w^{2i+1})(w^{ni}w^{n/2} + 1) + r_1(w^{2i+1}) = r_1(w^{2i+1})
\end{aligned}
$$

for all $0 \le i < n/2$. We have used the facts that $w^{ni} = 1$ and $w^{n/2} = -1$, since

$$
0 = w^n - 1 = (w^{n/2} - 1)(w^{n/2} + 1)
$$

and $w^{n/2} - 1$ is not a zero divisor. It remains to evaluate r_0 at the even powers of w and r_1 at the odd powers. Now w^2 is a primitive $(n/2)$th root of unity (Exercise 8.13), and hence the first task is a DFT of order $n/2$. But also the evaluation of r_1 can be reduced to a DFT of order $n/2$ by noting that $r_1(w^{2i+1}) = r_1^*(w^{2i})$ for $r_1^* = r_1(wx)$. The computation of the coefficients of r_1^* uses $n/2$ multiplications by powers of w. If n is a power of 2, we can proceed recursively to evaluate r_0 and r_1^* at the powers $1, w^2, \ldots, w^{2n-2}$ of w^2, and obtain the following algorithm.

━━━ ALGORITHM 8.14 Fast Fourier Transform (FFT). ━━━━━━━━━
Input: $n = 2^k \in \mathbb{N}$ with $k \in \mathbb{N}$, $f = \sum_{0 \le i < n} f_i x^i \in R[x]$, and the powers $w, w^2, \ldots, w^{n-1}$ of a primitive nth root of unity $w \in R$.
Output: $\mathrm{DFT}_w(f) = (f(1), f(w), \ldots, f(w^{n-1})) \in R^n$.

1. **if** $n = 1$ **then return** (f_0)

2. $r_0 \longleftarrow \displaystyle\sum_{0 \le j < n/2} (f_j + f_{j+n/2}) x^j, \quad r_1^* \longleftarrow \displaystyle\sum_{0 \le j < n/2} (f_j - f_{j+n/2}) w^j x^j$

3. **call** the algorithm recursively to evaluate r_0 and r_1^* at the powers of w^2

4. **return** $\left(r_0(1), r_1^*(1), r_0(w^2), r_1^*(w^2), \ldots, r_0(w^{n-2}), r_1^*(w^{n-2}) \right)$ ━━━━

━━━ THEOREM 8.15. ━━━━━━━━━━━━━━━━━━━━━━━━━━━━━
Let n be a power of 2 and $w \in R$ be a primitive nth root of unity. Then Algorithm 8.14 correctly computes DFT_w using $n \log n$ additions in R and $(n/2) \log n$ multiplications by powers of w, in total $\frac{3}{2} n \log n$ ring operations. ━━━

PROOF. We prove correctness by induction on k. If $k = 0$, then $f = f_0$ is constant and the algorithm returns the correct result. If $k > 1$, we have to show that $f(w^{2i}) = r_0(w^{2i})$ and $f(w^{2i+1}) = r_1^*(w^{2i})$ for all $0 \le i < n/2$, and then the claim follows from the induction hypothesis. Retracing the calculations above, we find

$$
\begin{aligned}
r_0(w^{2i}) &= \sum_{0 \le j < n/2} (f_j + f_{j+n/2}) w^{2ij} = \sum_{0 \le j < n/2} f_j w^{2ij} + \sum_{0 \le j < n/2} f_{j+n/2} w^{2ij} w^{in} \\
&= \sum_{0 \le j < n} f_j w^{2ij} = f(w^{2i}),
\end{aligned}
$$

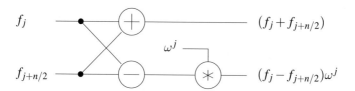

f_j ──────●────⊕────────── $(f_j + f_{j+n/2})$

ω^j

$f_{j+n/2}$ ──●────⊖──────⊛── $(f_j - f_{j+n/2})\omega^j$

FIGURE 8.4: A butterfly operation. Flow of control is from left to right, and a subtraction node computes the difference of its upper input minus its lower input.

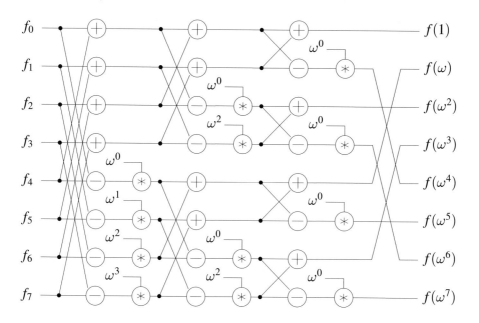

FIGURE 8.5: An arithmetic circuit computing the FFT for $n = 8$

$$
\begin{aligned}
r_1^*(\omega^{2i}) &= \sum_{0 \le j < n/2} (f_j - f_{j+n/2}) \omega^j \omega^{2ij} \\
&= \sum_{0 \le j < n/2} f_j \omega^{(2i+1)j} + \sum_{0 \le j < n/2} f_{j+n/2} \omega^{(2i+1)j} \omega^{in} \omega^{n/2} \\
&= \sum_{0 \le j < n} f_j \omega^{(2i+1)j} = f(\omega^{2i+1}).
\end{aligned}
$$

Let $S(n)$ and $T(n)$ denote the number of additions and multiplications in R, respectively, that the algorithm uses for input size n. The cost for the individual steps is: 0 in steps 1 and 4, n additions and $n/2$ multiplications in step 2, and $2S(n/2)$ additions and $2T(n/2)$ multiplications in step 3. This yields $S(1) = T(1) = 0$, $S(n) = 2S(n/2) + n$, and $T(n) = 2T(n/2) + n/2$, and by unfolding the recursions we find that $S(n) = n \log n$ and $T(n) = \frac{1}{2} n \log n$. □

The FFT can be nicely illustrated in form of an arithmetic circuit. It is built from elementary blocks that execute step 2 of the above algorithm for one particular value of j, called a **butterfly operation**. One such building block is shown in Figure 8.4, and the entire circuit for $n = 8$ in Figure 8.5.

Figure 8.6 illustrates the cost of Algorithm 8.14 if the recursion is stopped at depths $0, 1, \ldots, 5$ and the remaining subproblems are computed by Horner's rule. The diagonal lines visualize the linear cost at each recursive step which—in contrast to Karatsuba's method—contributes to the overall cost. Now we use the FFT to compute convolutions and products of polynomials quickly.

▬▬ ALGORITHM 8.16 Fast convolution. ▬▬▬▬▬▬▬▬▬▬▬▬▬▬▬▬▬
Input: $f, g \in R[x]$ of degree less than $n = 2^k$ with $k \in \mathbb{N}$, and a primitive nth root of unity $\omega \in R$.
Output: $f * g \in R[x]$.

1. compute $\omega^2, \ldots, \omega^{n-1}$

2. $\alpha \longleftarrow \mathrm{DFT}_\omega(f), \quad \beta \longleftarrow \mathrm{DFT}_\omega(g)$

3. $\gamma \longleftarrow \alpha \cdot \beta \quad \{$ pointwise product $\}$

4. **return** $\mathrm{DFT}_\omega{}^{-1}(\gamma) = \dfrac{1}{n}\mathrm{DFT}_{\omega^{-1}}(\gamma)$ ▬▬▬▬▬▬▬▬▬▬

DEFINITION 8.17. *We say that a (commutative) ring R **supports the FFT** if R has a primitive 2^kth root of unity for any $k \in \mathbb{N}$.*

An example of a ring supporting the FFT is $R = \mathbb{C}$.

▬▬ THEOREM 8.18. ▬▬▬▬▬▬▬▬▬▬▬▬▬▬▬▬▬▬▬▬▬▬
Let R be a ring that supports the FFT, and $n = 2^k$ for some $k \in \mathbb{N}$. Then convolution in $R[x]/\langle x^n - 1 \rangle$ and multiplication of polynomials $f, g \in R[x]$ with $\deg(fg) < n$ can be performed using $3n \log n$ additions in R, $\frac{3}{2}n \log n + n - 2$ multiplications by powers of ω, n multiplications in R, and n divisions by n, in total $\frac{9}{2}n \log n + O(n)$ arithmetic operations. ▬▬▬▬▬▬▬▬▬▬▬▬▬▬▬▬▬▬▬▬

PROOF. Let $f, g \in R[x]$ of degree less than n and $h = f * g$. Then h is uniquely determined by its values at n distinct points. Since the convolution satisfies

$$\mathrm{DFT}_\omega(h) = \mathrm{DFT}_\omega(f) \cdot \mathrm{DFT}_\omega(g),$$

by Lemma 8.11, where the multiplication is the componentwise product, we conclude that Algorithm 8.16 correctly computes the convolution of f and g. In particular, the output does not depend on the choice of the primitive root of unity ω. If furthermore $\deg(fg) < n$, then $f * g \equiv fg \bmod (x^n - 1)$ implies that $fg = f * g$.

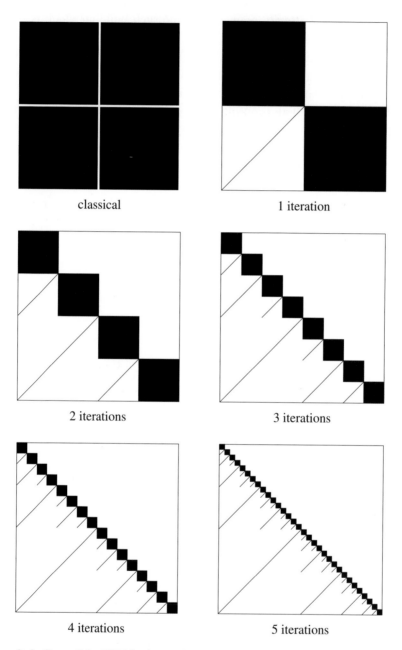

FIGURE 8.6: Cost of the FFT for increasing recursion depths. The black area is proportional to the total work.

The cost for the individual steps is

1. $n-2$ multiplications by ω,

2. $2n\log n$ additions and $n\log n$ multiplications by powers of ω,

3. n multiplications,

4. $n\log n$ additions, $\frac{1}{2}n\log n$ multiplications by powers of ω, and n divisions by n,

and the claim follows. $\square$

To multiply two arbitrary polynomials of degree less than $n \in \mathbb{N}$, we only need a primitive 2^kth root of unity, where $2^{k-1} < 2n \leq 2^k$. Then we have decreased the cost of about $2n^2$ of the classical algorithm to $O(n\log n)$.

━━ COROLLARY 8.19. ━━━━━━━━━━━━━━━━━━
If R supports the FFT, then polynomials in $R[x]$ of degree less than n can be multiplied with $18n\log n + O(n)$ operations in R. ━━━━━━━━━━━━━

8.3. Schönhage and Strassen's multiplication algorithm

In the previous section we have discussed an asymptotically fast FFT-based polynomial multiplication algorithm over rings containing certain primitive roots of unity. If the underlying coefficient ring R is arbitrary, an FFT-based approach will not work directly. In this section, we will show how to make it work by adjoining "virtual" roots of unity.

Let R be a ring such that 2 is a unit in R, $n = 2^k$ for some $k \in \mathbb{N}$, and $D = R[x]/\langle x^n + 1 \rangle$. D is generally not a field, even if R is, as the example $R = \mathbb{C}$ and $n = 2$ shows. The congruences

$$x^n \equiv -1 \bmod (x^n + 1), \quad x^{2n} = (x^n)^2 \equiv 1 \bmod (x^n + 1)$$

imply that $\omega = x \bmod (x^n + 1) \in D$ is a $2n$th root of unity. Moreover, $\omega^n - 1 = (-1) - 1 = -2$ is a unit in R since 2 is, and ω is a primitive $2n$th root of unity.

To multiply two polynomials $f, g \in R[x]$ with $\deg(fg) < n = 2^k \in \mathbb{N}$, it is clearly sufficient to compute fg modulo $x^n + 1$. This is called the **negative wrapped convolution of f and g**. We let $m = 2^{\lfloor k/2 \rfloor}$, $t = n/m = 2^{\lceil k/2 \rceil}$, and partition the coefficients of f and g into t blocks of size m, that is, we write

$$f = \sum_{0 \leq i < t} f_i x^{mi}, \quad g = \sum_{0 \leq i < t} g_i x^{mi},$$

with $f_i, g_i \in R[x]$ of degree less than m for $0 \le i < t$. With $f' = \sum_{0 \le i < t} f_i y^i$, $g' = \sum_{0 \le i < t} g_i y^i \in R[x,y]$, we then have $f = f'(x,x^m)$ and $g = g'(x,x^m)$. It is sufficient to compute $f'g'$ modulo $y^t + 1$, since

$$f'g' = h' + q'(y^t + 1) \equiv h' \mod (y^t + 1) \tag{4}$$

for some $h', q' \in R[x,y]$ implies that

$$fg = h'(x,x^m) + q'(x,x^m)(x^{tm} + 1) \equiv h'(x,x^m) \mod (x^n + 1).$$

We now take the primitive $4m$th root of unity

$$\xi = x \mod (x^{2m} + 1) \in D = R[x]/\langle x^{2m} + 1 \rangle.$$

We want to compute $h' \in R[x,y]$ with $\deg_y h' < t$ satisfying (4) (this uniquely determines h'; see Section 2.4). Comparing coefficients of y^i for $i \ge t$, we see that $\deg_x q' \le \deg_x(f'g') < 2m$ and conclude that

$$\deg_x h' \le \max\{\deg_x(f'g'), \deg_x q'\} < 2m. \tag{5}$$

With $f^* = f' \mod (x^{2m} + 1)$, $g^* = g' \mod (x^{2m} + 1)$, and $h^* = h' \mod (x^{2m} + 1)$ in $D[y]$, (4) implies

$$f^*g^* \equiv h^* \mod (y^t + 1) \text{ in } D[y]. \tag{6}$$

Since the three polynomials have degrees in x less than $2m$, by (5), reducing them modulo $x^{2m} + 1$ is just taking a different algebraic meaning of the same coefficient array. In particular, the coefficients of $h' \in R[x][y]$ can be read off the coefficients of $h^* \in D[y]$.

The following picture illustrates the relations between h, h' and h^*; the arrows are ring homomorphisms.

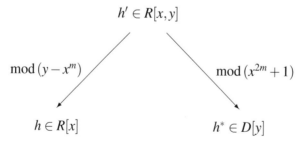

For example, let $h = 4x^3 + 3x^2 + 2x + 1 \in \mathbb{Q}[x]$, $m = 2$, and $\xi = x \mod (x^4 + 1) \in D = \mathbb{Q}[x]/\langle x^4 + 1 \rangle$. Then $h' = (4x+3)y + (2x+1) \in \mathbb{Q}[x,y]$ and $h^* = (4\xi+3)y + (2\xi+1) \in D[y]$.

Computationally, "nothing happens" in mapping h' to h^*, but we are now in a situation where we can apply the machinery of the FFT to compute (6), as follows.

Since t equals either m or $2m$, D contains a primitive $2t$th root of unity η, namely $\eta = \xi$ if $t = 2m$ and $\eta = \xi^2$ if $t = m$. Then (6) is equivalent to

$$f^*(\eta y)g^*(\eta y) \equiv h^*(\eta y) \bmod \left((\eta y)^t + 1 \right),$$

or

$$f^*(\eta y)g^*(\eta y) \equiv h^*(\eta y) \bmod (y^t - 1), \qquad (7)$$

since $\eta^t = -1$. Given $f^*(\eta y)$ and $g^*(\eta y)$ in $D[y]$, Algorithm 8.16 computes $h^*(\eta y)$ with $O(t \log t)$ operations in D, using essentially three t-point FFTs. A multiplication of two elements in D is again a negative wrapped convolution over R which can be handled recursively. Putting things together, we obtain the following algorithm.

▬ ALGORITHM 8.20 Fast negative wrapped convolution. ▬▬▬▬▬▬▬▬
Input: Two polynomials $f, g \in R[x]$ of degree less than $n = 2^k$ for some $k \in \mathbb{N}$, where R is a (commutative) ring such that 2 is a unit in R.
Output: $h \in R[x]$ such that $fg \equiv h \bmod (x^n + 1)$ and $\deg h < n$.

1. **if** $k \leq 2$ **then**
      call the classical algorithm 2.3 (or Karatsuba's algorithm 8.1) to compute $f \cdot g$
      return fg rem $x^n + 1$

2. $m \longleftarrow 2^{\lfloor k/2 \rfloor}, \quad t \longleftarrow n/m$
   let $f', g' \in R[x, y]$ with $\deg_x f', \deg_x g' < m$ such that $f = f'(x, x^m)$ and $g = g'(x, x^m)$

3. let $D = R[x]/\langle x^{2m} + 1 \rangle$
   if $t = 2m$ **then** $\eta \longleftarrow x \bmod (x^{2m} + 1)$ **else** $\eta \longleftarrow x^2 \bmod (x^{2m} + 1)$
   { η is a primitive $2t$th root of unity }
   $f^* \longleftarrow f' \bmod (x^{2m} + 1), \quad g^* \longleftarrow g' \bmod (x^{2m} + 1)$
   call the fast convolution algorithm 8.16 with $\omega = \eta^2$ to compute $h^* \in D[y]$
   of degree less than t such that

   $$f^*(\eta y)g^*(\eta y) \equiv h^*(\eta y) \bmod (y^t - 1),$$

   using Algorithm 8.20 recursively for the multiplications in D

4. let $h' \in R[x, y]$ with $\deg_x h' < 2m$ such that $h^* = h' \bmod (x^{2m} + 1)$
   $h \longleftarrow h'(x, x^m)$ rem $(x^n + 1)$
   return h ▬▬▬▬▬▬▬▬▬▬▬▬▬▬▬▬▬▬▬▬▬

EXAMPLE 8.21. Let $R = \mathbb{F}_5$, $f = x^4 + 2x + 3$ and $g = 2x^3 + x^2 + 4x + 2$ in $\mathbb{F}_5[x]$. Then we can compute $fg \in \mathbb{F}_5[x]$ using Algorithm 8.20 with $k = 3$, as follows. In step 2, we calculate $m = 2$, $t = 4$, $f' = y^2 + 2x + 3$ and $g' = (2x+1)y + 4x + 2$. In step 3, we have $\eta = x \bmod (x^4 + 1)$,

$$
\begin{aligned}
f^* &= y^2 + 2\eta + 3, & g^* &= (2\eta + 1)y + 4\eta + 2, \\
f^*(\eta y) &= \eta^2 y^2 + 2\eta + 3, & g^*(\eta y) &= (2\eta^2 + \eta)y + 4\eta + 2.
\end{aligned}
$$

Now Algorithm 8.16 (or, in this case, a direct calculation of $f^*(\eta y)g^*(\eta y)$) yields

$$
\begin{aligned}
h^*(\eta y) &= (2\eta^4 + \eta^3)y^3 + (4\eta^3 + 2\eta^2)y^2 + (4\eta^3 + 3\eta^2 + 3\eta)y + 3\eta^2 + \eta + 1, \\
h^* &= h^*(\eta(\eta^{-1}y)) \\
&= (2\eta + 1)y^3 + (4\eta + 2)y^2 + (4\eta^2 + 3\eta + 3)y + 3\eta^2 + \eta + 1.
\end{aligned}
$$

Finally, in step 4 we have

$$
\begin{aligned}
h' &= (2x+1)y^3 + (4x+2)y^2 + (4x^2 + 3x + 3)y + (3x^2 + x + 1), \\
h'(x, x^2) &= 2x^7 + x^6 + 4x^5 + x^4 + 3x^3 + x^2 + x + 1 \equiv fg \bmod (x^8 + 1),
\end{aligned}
$$

and in fact equality holds in the second line since the degrees of both sides are less than 8. ◇

━━━ THEOREM 8.22. ━━

Algorithm 8.20 works correctly and uses $\frac{9}{2}n\log n\log\log n + O(n\log n)$ operations in R. ━━━

PROOF. Correctness follows from the discussion preceding the algorithm. Let $T(k)$ denote the number of arithmetic operations in R that the algorithm uses on inputs of size $n = 2^k$. The cost for step 1 is $O(1)$. In step 2, no arithmetic operations in R are performed. By Theorem 8.18, Algorithm 8.16 uses $3t\log t$ additions in D and $\frac{3}{2}t\log t$ multiplications by powers of $\omega = \eta^2$ in the FFT-steps, plus t divisions by $t \in R$ and t "essential" multiplications of two arbitrary elements of D (the powers of ω in step 1 of Algorithm 8.16 need not be computed). One addition in D costs $2m$ additions in R, one division by t costs $2m$ divisions in R, and one multiplication of $a = \sum_{0 \le i < 2m} a_i x^i \bmod (x^{2m} + 1)$ by a power of η corresponds to a cyclic shift of the coordinates a_i and a sign inversion of the "wrapped around" coordinates, using at most $2m$ operations in R. Each essential multiplication in D is done recursively, using $T(\lfloor k/2 \rfloor + 1)$ operations in R. The computation of $f^*(\eta y), g^*(\eta y)$ from f^*, g^* and of $h^* = h^*(\eta(\eta^{-1}y))$ from $h^*(\eta y)$ amounts to $3t$ multiplications by powers of η. Thus the total cost of step 3 is at most $9mt\log t + 8mt + t \cdot T(\lfloor k/2 \rfloor + 1)$. In step 4, the only cost is at most $n = mt$ additions for the computation of h from h'. Together, we have

$$
T(k) \le 2^{\lceil k/2 \rceil} T\left(\left\lfloor \frac{k}{2} \right\rfloor + 1\right) + 9 \cdot 2^k \left(\left\lceil \frac{k}{2} \right\rceil + 1\right)
$$

if $k > 2$. Thus

$$2^{-k}T(k+1)+45 \leq 2^{\lceil(k+1)/2\rceil-k}T\left(\left\lfloor\frac{k+1}{2}\right\rfloor+1\right)+90+18\left(\left\lceil\frac{k+1}{2}\right\rceil+1\right)-45$$

$$= 2\left(2^{-\lceil k/2\rceil}T\left(\left\lceil\frac{k}{2}\right\rceil+1\right)+45\right)+18\left(\left\lfloor\frac{k}{2}\right\rfloor-\frac{1}{2}\right)$$

if $k > 1$, where we used $\lfloor(k+1)/2\rfloor = \lceil k/2\rceil$ and $\lceil(k+1)/2\rceil = \lfloor k/2\rfloor+1$. Writing $S(k) = (2^{-k}T(k+1)+45)/(k-1)$, we obtain

$$S(k) \leq \frac{2(\lceil k/2\rceil-1)}{k-1}S\left(\left\lceil\frac{k}{2}\right\rceil\right)+9\frac{2(\lfloor k/2\rfloor-1/2)}{k-1}$$

$$\leq S\left(\left\lceil\frac{k}{2}\right\rceil\right)+9\leq\cdots\leq S(2)+9(\lceil\log k\rceil-1)$$

for $k > 1$, by induction, and hence

$$T(k) = 2^{k-1}\left((k-2)S(k-1)-45\right)$$

$$\leq \frac{9}{2}2^k(k-2)(\lceil\log(k-1)\rceil-1)+\frac{S(2)}{2}2^k(k-2)-\frac{45}{2}2^k$$

$$\in \frac{9}{2}2^k k\log k+O(2^k k)=\frac{9}{2}n\log n\log\log n+O(n\log n). \quad\square$$

In an implementation, one has to carefully determine the "crossover" threshold for k in step 1 below which one uses a different algorithm.

We note that the value of m in step 2 and also the value of n need not be powers of 2; it is sufficient that t be a power of 2 dividing $2m$. This allows for choices of n such as $n = 3\cdot 2^k$ or $n = 5\cdot 3^k$, which have the advantage that fewer zeroes have to be padded when $\deg(fg)$ is just below such a number. For example, if $\deg(fg) = 3\cdot 2^{2l-1}-1$ for some $l \in \mathbb{N}$, then the literal approach would use $n = 2^{2l+1}$ and $m = 2^l$, $t = 2^{l+1}$ in step 2, while it seems better to choose $n = 3\cdot 2^{2l-1}$, with $m = 3\cdot 2^{l-1}$ and $t = 2^l$ in step 2.

Exercise 8.30 discusses the analog of Algorithm 8.20 when 3 is a unit in R, using a 3-adic FFT. In particular, this covers the case when R is a field of characteristic 2. What about arbitrary rings R? All divisions in Algorithm 8.16 are by powers of two. We replace the last line by

4. **return** $n\cdot\mathrm{DFT}_\omega^{-1}(\gamma)=\mathrm{DFT}_{\omega^{-1}}(\gamma)$

Then it uses only additions and multiplications, but no divisions in R, and returns $n\cdot(a*b)$ instead of $a*b$. If we use this modified algorithm in step 3 of Algorithm 8.20, then Exercise 8.31 shows that the modified algorithm works over any (commutative) ring and returns $2^\kappa\cdot h$ for some $\kappa\in\mathbb{N}$. Similar modifications of the 3-adic FFT algorithm from Exercise 8.30 lead to an algorithm that computes $3^\lambda \cdot h$ for some $\lambda \in \mathbb{N}$.

If we now want to compute the product of two polynomials $f, g \in R[x]$ of degree less than n, we choose $k, l \in \mathbb{N}$ such that $2^{k-2} < n \le 2^{k-1}$ and $3^{l-1} < n \le 3^l$ and call both the modified 2-adic and the modified 3-adic algorithm to compute $2^\kappa fg$ and $3^\lambda fg$. Using the Extended Euclidean Algorithm, we find $s, t \in \mathbb{Z}$ such that $s2^\kappa + t3^\lambda = 1$, and obtain $s2^\kappa fg + t3^\lambda fg = fg$. Thus we have the following result.

━━━ THEOREM 8.23. ━━

Over any commutative ring R, polynomials of degree less than n can be multiplied using at most $(18 + 72\log_3 2) n \log n \log\log n + O(n \log n)$ or $63.43 n \log n \log\log n + O(n \log n)$ arithmetic operations in R. ━━━━━━━━━━━━━━━━━━━━━

PROOF. Let $k, l \in \mathbb{N}$ be as above. By Theorem 8.22, computing $2^\kappa fg$ modulo $x^{2^k} + 1$ takes $\frac{9}{2} 2^k k \log k + O(k \log k)$ or $18 n \log n \log\log n + O(n \log n)$ operations, since $2^k < 4n$. Similarly, $2^\lambda fg$ modulo $x^{2 \cdot 3^k} + x^{3^k} + 1$ can be computed using $24 \cdot 3^k k \log k + O(k \log k)$ or $72 n \log_3 n \log\log n + O(n \log n)$ operations, by Exercise 8.30 and the fact that $3^k < 3n$. Computing $s2^\kappa fg + t3^\lambda fg$ takes at most $6n$ operations, and the claim follows by noting that $\log_3 n = \log_3 2 \log n$ and $72 \log_3 2 < 45.43$. □

The constant 63.43 is probably not the best possible, and the reader is encouraged to figure out a smaller constant herself.

Can this method be extended to integer multiplication? The following result introduced the FFT into algebraic complexity theory and high-performance computing.

━━━ THEOREM 8.24 *Schönhage & Strassen (1971).* ━━━━━━━━━━━━━━━━━━━━━━━━━━━━

Multiplication of integers of length n can be performed with $O(n \log n \log\log n)$ word operations. ━━━

We do not present the details of this algorithm (it is partly described in Exercise 8.36), but rather a different approach for fast integer multiplication which only works for integers of bounded length but seems sufficient for most practical purposes (inputs up to millions of gigabytes). Let $a = \sum_{0 \le i < l} a_i 2^{64i}$, $b = \sum_{0 \le j < l} b_j 2^{64j}$ in 64-adic representation, and $A = \sum_{0 \le i < l} a_i x^i$, $B = \sum_{0 \le j < l} b_j x^j$ in $\mathbb{Z}[x]$, so that $a = A(2^{64})$ and $b = B(2^{64})$. If $C = AB = \sum_{0 \le k < 2l-1} c_k x^k \in \mathbb{Z}[x]$, then we obtain $ab = C(2^{64})$. Now $0 \le c_k = \sum_{i+j=k} a_i b_j < \sum_{i+j=k} 2^{128} \le l \cdot 2^{128}$ for all k. We assume that $l < 2^{61}$, take three single precision primes p_1, p_2, p_3 between 2^{63} and 2^{64}, and multiply A and B modulo each p_i. Then the Chinese Remainder Theorem guarantees that we can reconstruct AB from its images modulo the three primes.

For the three modular multiplications, we want to use the FFT multiplication algorithm 8.16, and this requires that each $p_i - 1$ be divisible by a sufficiently high power of 2; we will call such a prime a **Fourier prime**. More precisely, if $t = \lceil \log(2l - 1) \rceil$ and 2^t divides $p_i - 1$ for $i = 1, 2, 3$, then $\mathbb{F}_{p_i}$ contains a primitive tth root of unity, by Lemma 8.8, and we may use Algorithm 8.16 with $R = \mathbb{F}_{p_i}$ to compute $AB \bmod p_i$. If l is not too large, then three such primes can be found by successively testing $2^t + 1, \; 2 \cdot 2^t + 1, \; 3 \cdot 2^t + 1, \ldots$ for primality, using the algorithms from Chapter 18. (Exercise 18.16 shows how to find a primitive 2^tth root of unity modulo such a prime.) For example, for each of the six pairs

k	29	71	75	95	108	123
ω	21	287	149	55	64	493

$p = k \cdot 2^{57} + 1$ is prime and ω is the least positive primitive 2^{57}th root of unity modulo p. In fact, these are all primes p below 2^{64} such that 2^{57} divides $p - 1$, and all but the first one are greater than 2^{63}. (For $p = 108 \cdot 2^{57} + 1$, $p - 1$ is even divisible by 2^{59}; it is the only prime below 2^{64} with that property, and there is no prime p below 2^{64} such that $p - 1$ is divisible by a higher power of 2.) Three such pairs may be precomputed once and for all. Here is the corresponding algorithm.

━━ ALGORITHM 8.25 Three primes FFT integer multiplication. ━━━━━━━
Input: Two integers $a, b \in \mathbb{N}$ in 64-adic representation such that $a, b < 2^{64 \cdot 2^{s-1}}$, where $s \leq 62$.
Output: $ab \in \mathbb{N}$.

{ we assume three precomputed pairs (p_1, ω_1), (p_2, ω_2), (p_2, ω_3) of single precision integers such that each $p_i \in \{2^{63}, \ldots, 2^{64} - 1\}$ is prime and each $\omega_i \in \{1, \ldots, p_i - 1\}$ is a primitive 2^sth root of unity in $\mathbb{F}_{p_i}$ }

1. let $A, B \in \mathbb{Z}[x]$, with all coefficients nonnegative and less than 2^{64}, such that $a = A(2^{64})$ and $b = B(2^{64})$
   $t \longleftarrow \lceil \log_2(1 + \deg(AB)) \rceil$

2. **for** $i = 1, 2, 3$ **call** the fast convolution algorithm 8.16 over $R = \mathbb{F}_{p_i}$ with $\omega \equiv \omega_i^{2^{s-t}} \bmod p_i$ to compute $C_i = AB \operatorname{rem} p_i$

3. **call** the Chinese Remainder Algorithm 5.4 to compute $C \in \mathbb{Z}[x]$ with nonnegative coefficients less than $p_1 p_2 p_3$ such that $C \equiv C_i \bmod p_i$ for $i = 1, 2, 3$

4. **return** $C(2^{64})$ ━━━━━━━━━━━━━━━━━━━━━━━━━━━━━━━━━

The number s in the algorithm is an implementation dependent constant; it limits the size of the numbers that can be multiplied. By the discussion preceding the algorithm, with primes up to 2^{64} the maximal possible value is $s = 57$, and then the largest integers that can be multiplied by this method have $64 \cdot 2^{56}$ bits or $536\,870\,912$ gigabytes. The analogous algorithm for 32-bit processors allows factors of 256 megabytes each (Exercise 18.16).

The number $t \leq s$ corresponds to the size of the inputs; the sum of the lengths of a and b in the 2^{64}-ary representation is close to 2^t. The cost for Algorithm 8.25 amounts to essentially nine 2^t-point FFT's of polynomials with single precision coefficients, in total $O(t2^t)$ word operations.

Throughout this text, we discuss algorithms for many problems in computer algebra based on fast polynomial and integer multiplication. In order to abstract from the underlying multiplication algorithm in our cost analyses, we introduce the following notation.

DEFINITION 8.26. *Let R be a ring (commutative, with 1). We call a function $\mathsf{M} \colon \mathbb{N}_{>0} \longrightarrow \mathbb{R}_{>0}$ a **multiplication time for $R[x]$** if polynomials in $R[x]$ of degree less than n can be multiplied using at most $\mathsf{M}(n)$ operations in R. Similarly, a function M as above is called a **multiplication time for $\mathbb{Z}$** if two integers of length n can be multiplied using at most $\mathsf{M}(n)$ word operations.*

Algorithm	$\mathsf{M}(n)$
classical	$2n^2$
Karatsuba (Karatsuba & Ofman 1962)	$O(n^{1.59})$
FFT multiplication (provided that R supports the FFT)	$O(n \log n)$
Schönhage & Strassen (1971), Schönhage (1977) Cantor & Kaltofen (1991); FFT based	$O(n \log n \log\log n)$

TABLE 8.7: Various polynomial multiplication algorithms and their running times.

In principle, any multiplication algorithm leads to a multiplication time. Table 8.7 summarizes the multiplication times for the algorithms that we discuss. You find a similar table for quick reference on the inside front cover. In the remainder of this text, we will assume that the multiplication time satisfies

$$\mathsf{M}(n)/n \geq \mathsf{M}(m)/m \text{ if } n \geq m, \quad \mathsf{M}(mn) \leq m^2 \mathsf{M}(n), \tag{8}$$

for all $n, m \in \mathbb{N}_{>0}$. The first inequality yields the superlinearity properties

$$\mathsf{M}(mn) \geq m \cdot \mathsf{M}(n), \quad \mathsf{M}(n+m) \geq \mathsf{M}(n) + \mathsf{M}(m), \text{ and } \mathsf{M}(n) \geq n \tag{9}$$

for all $m, n \in \mathbb{N}_{>0}$ (Exercise 8.33). The last property in (8) says that M is "at most quadratic" and implies that $\mathsf{M}(cn) \in O(\mathsf{M}(n))$ for all positive constants c. Theorem 8.23 implies that we may take

$$\mathsf{M}(n) \in 63.43\, n \log n \log\log n + O(n \log n)$$

for an arbitrary commutative ring R, and we will mainly use this result.

8.4. Multiplication in $\mathbb{Z}[x]$ and $R[x,y]$

Let $f, g \in \mathbb{Z}[x]$ be of degree less than n. Theorem 8.23 tells us that f and g can be multiplied using $O(n \log n \log \log n)$ additions and multiplications in $\mathbb{Z}$. If we want to determine the number of word operations for their multiplication, we need a bound on the coefficients of the intermediate results. A more detailed analysis of Algorithm 8.20 would provide such an estimate, but we choose a different approach here: **Kronecker substitution**.

Let $f = \sum_{0 \le i < n} f_i x^i$ and $g = \sum_{0 \le j < n} g_j x^j$, with all $f_i, g_j \in \mathbb{Z}$ of length at most l in the 64-adic representation, and $h = fg = \sum_{0 \le k \le 2n-2} h_k x^k$, where $h_k = \sum_{i+j=k} f_i g_j$. To simplify our discussion, we assume that all f_i, g_j are nonnegative (this can be achieved, for example, by splitting f and g into their positive and negative parts if necessary). Then

$$0 \le h_k < \sum_{i+j=k} 2^{128l} \le n2^{128l}$$

for $0 \le k \le 2n-2$. If we choose $t \in \mathbb{N}$ so that $n2^{128l} < 2^{64t}$, then the coefficients of h can be read off the 64-adic representation of the number $h(2^{64t}) = f(2^{64t})g(2^{64t})$; this corresponds to calculating modulo $x - 2^{64t}$. Thus $t = 2l + \lfloor (\log n)/64 \rfloor + 1 \in O(l + \log n)$ suffices, and then $f(2^{64t})$ and $g(2^{64t})$ have length $O(n(l + \log n))$. Theorem 8.24 now implies the following.

═══ COROLLARY 8.27. ═══
Polynomials in $\mathbb{Z}[x]$ of degree less than n with coefficients of length at most l can be multiplied using $O(\mathsf{M}(n(l + \log n)))$ or $O^{\sim}(nl)$ word operations. ═══

The $O^{\sim}$ notation ignores logarithmic factors; see Section 25.7.

The above result is not easy to implement efficiently. In practice, other modular approaches have proven useful. A method using Fermat numbers is discussed in Exercise 8.36, and we now present a different approach, similar to the three primes FFT algorithm. We choose a collection of distinct single precision primes $p_1, \ldots, p_r \in \mathbb{N}$ such that their product exceeds $n2^{128l+1}$, compute $fg \bmod p_1 \in \mathbb{F}_{p_1}[x], \ldots, fg \bmod p_r \in \mathbb{F}_{p_r}[x]$, and finally recover fg by applying the Chinese Remainder Algorithm 5.4 to each of its coefficients (Exercise 5.34). If furthermore $2n \le 2^k$ for some $k \in \mathbb{N}$ and we let the p_i be Fourier primes such that $2^k \mid (p_i - 1)$ for all i, then each $\mathbb{F}_{p_i}$ contains a primitive 2^kth root of unity (Lemma 8.8), and $fg \bmod p_i$ can be computed using Algorithm 8.16 directly, without constructing any "virtual" primitive roots of unity. Each p_i fits into one machine word of the target processor, and coefficient arithmetic in $\mathbb{F}_{p_i}$ amounts to just a few machine instructions. The primes p_i and appropriate primitive roots of unity in $\mathbb{F}_{p_i}$ (Exercise 18.16), as well as the "Lagrange interpolants" in the Chinese Remainder Algorithm, which only depend on the p_i, may be precomputed and stored if many polynomial multiplications of the same size have to be performed.

Of course, this approach limits the degree and the coefficient size of the polynomials that can be handled, but it appears to be highly sufficient for practical
applications. An implementation by Shoup (1995) and an implementation of the
Fermat number approach are described in Section 9.7, and the timings indicate that
the former is well suited for small coefficients, while the latter is better when the
coefficients get large.

Kronecker substitution also applies to multiplication of bivariate polynomials
over a ring R. Let $f = \sum_{0 \le i < n} f_i x^i, g = \sum_{0 \le i < n} g_i x^i \in R[y][x]$ be two polynomials,
with $f_i, g_i \in R[y]$ of degree less than d for all i. Then $h = fg = \sum_{0 \le i < 2n-2} h_i x^i$,
with $h_i \in R[y]$ of degree at most $2d - 2$ for all i. Substituting $x = y^{2d-1}$ (that is,
calculating modulo $x - y^{2d-1}$), we obtain

$$f \cdot g \equiv f(y^{2d-1}, y) \cdot g(y^{2d-1}, y) = h(y^{2d-2}, y) = \sum_{0 \le i \le 2n-2} h_i y^{2d-1} \equiv h \bmod x - y^{2d-1},$$

and we see that the coefficients of h can be read off the image of fg modulo
$x - y^{2d-1}$, which in turn can be computed using fast multiplication of univariate
polynomials in $R[y]$. Since the degrees of $f(y^{2d-1}, y)$ and $g(y^{2d-1}, y)$ are at most
$(n-1)(2d-1) + d - 1 = 2nd - n - d$, we have the following result.

COROLLARY 8.28.

*Polynomials in $R[x,y]$, where R is a ring (commutative, with 1), of degree less
than n in x and less than d in y can be multiplied using $O(\mathsf{M}(nd))$ or $O^\sim(nd)$ ring
operations.*

Notes. Indlekofer & Járai (1998) found the largest twin primes known at the time of
writing: $242\,206\,083 \cdot 2^{38\,880} \pm 1$; see Indlekofer & Járai (1996) for the previous record.
Their software uses finely tuned fast arithmetic in an essential way.

8.2. Cooley & Tukey (1965) discovered the FFT for computer science, causing a revolution in digital signal processing methods. Its original invention goes back a century and a
half: Gauß found it around 1805, but it appeared only posthumously (Gauß 1866). Gauß
also discovered the usual Fourier Transform, before Fourier did so in 1807 (published in
Fourier 1822). The algorithm was rediscovered several times over the years. The fascinating history of the FFT is described in Cooley (1987, 1990) and Heideman, Johnson &
Burrus (1984).

8.3. Algorithm 8.20 is an adaption to polynomials of Schönhage & Strassen's (1971) integer multiplication algorithm, where 2 plays the role of our x; Schönhage (1977) solved
the additional complication that occurs in characteristic 2 by using a 3-adic FFT (Exercise 8.30). These two papers, and also Cantor & Kaltofen (1991), showed Theorem 8.23.
Before Schönhage & Strassen's breakthrough, Toom (1963), Cook (1966), Schönhage
(1966), and Strassen (1968, unpublished) had found $n^{1+o(1)}$ multiplication algorithms for
integers of length n, but Schönhage & Strassen set the world record that still stands a
quarter century later. Gentleman & Sande (1966) had earlier proposed to use the FFT for
polynomial multiplication. See Knuth (1998), §4.3.3, for a description of some of these

methods. An alternative, also briefly discussed there, is to employ the FFT over the complex numbers, with approximations to sufficiently high precision of the complex roots of unity. This is used in calculating π to record accuracy; FFT multiplication uses 90% of the CPU time for such high precision calculations (Kanada (1988); see Section 4.6). Bernstein (1997) gives an exhaustive discussion of fast multiplication routines.

Pollard (1971) presents an FFT-based multiplication algorithm for polynomials over finite fields, over $\mathbb{Z}$, and for integers, including an implementation report, but without asymptotic analysis or a general construction of the required primitive roots of unity. He also gives the three primes FFT algorithm 8.25; see also Lipson (1981), §IX.2.2. Moenck (1976) presents an early implementation report.

For some of the multiplication times that we use, the required properties (8) may fail to hold for $n \leq 2$. We will ignore this systematically.

8.4. Kronecker (1882), §4, invented his substitution for multivariate polynomials; its effect is to keep distinct coefficients "apart" after the substitution. The algorithm for multiplying in $\mathbb{Z}[x]$ modulo several small primes appears in Pollard (1971).

Exercises.

8.1 Given the real and imaginary parts $a_0, a_1, b_0, b_1 \in \mathbb{R}$ of two nonzero complex numbers $z_1 = a_0 + a_1 i$ and $z_2 = b_0 + b_1 i$, show how to compute the real and imaginary parts of the quotient $z_1/z_2 \in \mathbb{C}$ using at most 7 multiplications and divisions in $\mathbb{R}$. Draw an arithmetic circuit illustrating your algorithm. Can you find an algorithm using at most 6 real multiplications and divisions?

8.2 Let R be a ring (commutative, with 1) and $f, g \in R[x, y]$, and assume that f and g have degrees less than m in y and less than n in x. Let $h = f \cdot g$.

(i) Using classical univariate polynomial multiplication and viewing $R[x, y]$ as $R[y][x]$, bound the number of arithmetic operations in R to compute h.

(ii) Using Karatsuba's algorithm bound the number of operations in R to compute h.

(iii) Generalize parts (i) and (ii) to polynomials in an arbitrary number of variables.

8.3 With notation as in Lemma 8.2, assume that in addition S and T are monotonically increasing and $S(2n) \leq 4S(n)$ for all $n \in \mathbb{N}_{>0}$. Derive a tight upper bound on $T(n)$ that is valid for *all* $n \in \mathbb{N}_{>0}$ and not only for powers of two. Hint: n lies in some interval $[2^{k-1} + 1, 2^k]$.

8.4 We have seen in Section 2.3 that the classical multiplication method for polynomials of degree less than n requires $2n^2 - 2n + 1$ ring operations. For which values of $n = 2^k$ is this larger than the $9 \cdot 3^k - 8 \cdot 2^k$ for Karatsuba's algorithm?

8.5* Let R be a ring (commutative, with 1) and $f, g \in R[x]$ of degrees less than n. You are to analyze two variants of Karatsuba's algorithm 8.1 when n is not a power of two.

(i) The first variant is to call Algorithm 8.1 with $2^{\lceil \log n \rceil}$ instead of n. Show that this takes at most $9 \cdot 3^{\lceil \log n \rceil} \leq 27 n^{\log 3}$ operations in R.

(ii) Let $m = \lceil n/2 \rceil$, and modify Algorithm 8.1 so that it divides f and g into blocks of degree less than m. If $T(n)$ denotes the cost of this algorithm, show that $T(1) = 1$ and $T(n) \leq 3T(\lceil n/2 \rceil) + 4n$.

(iii) Show that $T(2^k) \leq 9 \cdot 3^k - 8 \cdot 2^k$ and $T(2^{k-1} + 1) \leq 6 \cdot 3^k - 4 \cdot 2^k - 2$ for all $k \in \mathbb{N}_{>0}$, and compare this to (i) for $n = 2^k$ and $n = 2^{k-1} + 1$. Plot the curves of the two running time bounds from (i) and (ii) for $n \leq 50$.

(iv) Implement both algorithms for $R = \mathbb{Z}$. Experiment with various values of n, say $2 \leq n \leq 50$ and $n = 100, 200, \ldots, 1000$. Use random polynomials with one-digit coefficients, and also with n-digit coefficients.

8.6* Karatsuba's algorithm is slower for small inputs than classical multiplication. You are to investigate a hybrid algorithm which recursively does Karatsuba until the degrees get smaller than some
bound $2^d \in \mathbb{N}$ and then switches to classical multiplication, that is, we replace line 1 of Karatsuba's
algorithm 8.1 by

> 1. **if** $n \leq 2^d$ **then call** Algorithm 2.3 to compute $fg \in R[x]$

Algorithm 8.1 then corresponds to $d = 0$. Let $T(n)$ denote the cost of this algorithm when $n = 2^k$ for
some $k \in \mathbb{N}$, and prove that $T(n) \leq \gamma(d)n\log n - 8n$ holds for $n \geq 2^d$, where $\gamma(d)$ depends only on d.
Find the value of $d \in \mathbb{N}$ which minimizes $\gamma(d)$, and compare the result to the running time bound of
Theorem 8.3.

8.7 Karatsuba's method for polynomial multiplication can be generalized as follows. Let F be a
field, $m, n \in \mathbb{N}_{>0}$, and $f = \sum_{0 \leq i < n} f_i x^i$, $g = \sum_{0 \leq i < n} g_i x^i$ in $F[x]$. To multiply f and g, we divide each
of them into $m \geq 2$ blocks of size $k = \lceil n/m \rceil$:

$$f = \sum_{0 \leq i < m} F_i x^{ki}, \quad g = \sum_{0 \leq i < m} G_i x^{ki},$$

with all $F_i, G_i \in F[x]$ of degree less than k. Then $fg = \sum_{0 \leq i < 2m-1} H_i x^{ki}$, where $H_i = \sum_{0 \leq j \leq i} F_j G_{i-j}$
for $0 \leq i < 2m - 1$ and we assume that $F_j, G_j = 0$ if $j \geq m$.

 (i) Find a way to compute $H_0, \ldots, H_4$ when $m = 3$ using at most 6 multiplications of polynomials
of degree less than k. Use this method to construct a recursive algorithm à la Karatsuba and analyze
its cost when n is a power of 3.

 (ii) Suppose that you have found a scheme to compute $H_0, \ldots, H_{2m-2}$ using d multiplications of
polynomials of degree less than k, and made this scheme into a recursive algorithm as in (i). How
large may d be at most such that your algorithm is asymptotically faster than Karatsuba's? Compare
with your result from (i).

8.8** This continues Exercise 8.7.

 (i) You are to show that $d = 2m - 1$ can be achieved provided that the cardinality of F is at least
$2m - 1$. Let $K = F(\alpha_0, \ldots, \alpha_{m-1}, \beta_0, \ldots, \beta_{m-1})$ be the field of rational functions in $2m$ indetermin-
ates, $\alpha = \sum_{0 \leq i < n} \alpha_i x^i$ and $\beta = \sum_{0 \leq i < n} \beta_i x^i$ in $K[x]$, $u_0, \ldots, u_{2m-2} \in F$ distinct, and $v_j = \alpha(u_j)\beta(u_j)$
for $0 \leq j \leq 2m - 2$. If

$$l_j = \prod_{\substack{0 \leq k \leq 2m-2 \\ k \neq j}} \frac{x - u_j}{u_k - u_j} \in F[x]$$

are the Lagrange interpolants at $u_0, \ldots, u_{2m-2}$ for $0 \leq j \leq 2m - 2$, then

$$\alpha\beta = \sum_{0 \leq j \leq 2m-2} v_j l_j = \sum_{0 \leq i \leq 2m-2} \gamma_i x^i \in K[x],$$

since $\deg(\alpha\beta) < 2m - 1$ and the interpolating polynomial is unique, and each $\gamma_i \in K$ is an F-linear
combination

$$\gamma_i = \sum_{0 \leq j \leq 2m-2} c_{ij} v_j$$

of $v_0, \ldots, v_{2m-2}$, with $c_{ij} \in F$ for $0 \leq i, j \leq 2m - 2$. (In fact, the matrix $(c_{ij})_{0 \leq i,j \leq 2m-2}$ is the inverse
of the Vandermonde matrix $(u_i^j)_{0 \leq i,j \leq 2m-2}$ in $F^{(2m-1) \times (2m-1)}$.) This yields the following scheme for
computing $H_0, \ldots, H_{2m-2}$. We assume that the values u_i^j and c_{ij} for $0 \leq i, j \leq 2m - 2$ are precomputed
and stored.

 1. Set $P_i = \sum_{0 \leq j < m} F_j u_i^j$ and $Q_i = \sum_{0 \leq j < m} G_j u_i^j$ for $0 \leq i \leq 2m - 2$.

 2. Compute $R_i = P_i Q_i$ for $0 \leq i \leq 2m - 2$.

 3. Set $H_i = \sum_{0 \leq j \leq 2m-2} c_{ij} R_j$ for $0 \leq i \leq 2m - 2$.

Prove that this scheme works correctly (hint: first consider $k = 1$) and figure out the precise number of additions and multiplications in F that steps 1 and 3 take.

(ii) Calculate the values of u_i^j and c_{ij} for $F = \mathbb{F}_5$, $m = 3$, and $u_i = i \bmod 5$ for $0 \le i \le 4$.

(iii) Use the scheme from (i) to construct a recursive algorithm for polynomial multiplication, and determine its asymptotic cost when n is a power of m. Conclude that if F is infinite, then for each positive $\varepsilon \in \mathbb{R}$ there is an algorithm for multiplying polynomials of degree less than n in $F[x]$ taking $O(n^{1+\varepsilon})$ operations in F.

8.9 Let $F = \mathbb{F}_{29}$.

(i) Find a primitive 4th root of unity $\omega \in F$, and compute its inverse $\omega^{-1} \in F$.

(ii) Find the matrices for DFT_ω and DFT_ω^{-1}, and check that their product is $4I$.

8.10$\longrightarrow$ Let $F = \mathbb{F}_{17}$ and $f = 5x^3 + 3x^2 - 4x + 3$, $g = 2x^3 - 5x^2 + 7x - 2$ in $F[x]$.

(i) Show that $\omega = 2$ is a primitive 8th root of unity in F, and compute the inverse $2^{-1} \bmod 17$ of ω in F.

(ii) Compute $h = f \cdot g \in F[x]$.

(iii) For $0 \le i < 8$, compute $\alpha_i = f(\omega^i)$, $\beta_i = g(\omega^i)$, and $\gamma_i = \alpha_i \cdot \beta_i$. Compare γ_i to $h(\omega^i)$.

(iv) Show the two matrices $V_1 = V_\omega$ and $V_2 = 8^{-1} V_{\omega^{-1}}$, and compute their product. Compute the matrix–vector products $V_1\alpha, V_1\beta$, and $V_2\gamma$, with vectors $\alpha = (\alpha_i)_{0 \le i < 8}$, $\beta = (\beta_i)_{0 \le i < 8}$, and $\gamma = (\gamma_i)_{0 \le i < 8}$ as computed. Comment.

(v) Trace the FFT multiplication algorithm 8.16 to multiply f and g, with ω as above.

8.11$\longrightarrow$ Let $F = \mathbb{F}_{41}$.

(i) Prove that $\omega = 14 \in F$ is a primitive 8th root of unity. Compute all powers of ω, and mark the ones that are primitive 8th roots of unity.

(ii) Let $\eta = \omega^2$, and $f = x^7 + 2x^6 + 3x^4 + 2x + 6 \in F[x]$. Give an explicit calculation of $\alpha = \mathrm{DFT}_\omega(f)$, using the FFT. You only have to do one recursive step, and then can use direct evaluation at powers of η.

(iii) Let $g = x^7 + 12x^5 + 35^3 + 1 \in F[x]$. Compute $\beta = \mathrm{DFT}_\omega(g)$, $\gamma = \alpha \cdot \beta$ with coordinate–wise product, and $h = \mathrm{DFT}_{\omega^{-1}}(\gamma)$.

(iv) Compute $f \cdot g$ in $F[x]$ and $f *_8 g$. Compare with your result from (iii).

8.12$\longrightarrow$ The complex number $\omega = \exp(2\pi i/8) \in \mathbb{C}$ is a primitive 8th root of unity. Let $f = 5x^3 + 3x^2 - 4x + 3$ and $g = 2x^3 - 5x^2 + 7x - 2$ in $\mathbb{C}[x]$, and run the fast convolution algorithm 8.16 on this example to calculate the coefficients of the product $f \cdot g$. (Of course, on such a small example the "fast" algorithm is more tedious than the school method. But, who knows, you may want to multiply polynomials of degree $1\,000\,000$ one day ....) Multiply linear polynomials by the "classical" method. Use ω only symbolically, with the fact that $\omega^4 = -1$.

8.13 Let R be a ring, $n \in \mathbb{N}_{\ge 1}$, and $\omega \in R$ be a primitive nth root of unity.

(i) Show that ω^{-1} is a primitive nth root of unity.

(ii) If n is even, then show that ω^2 is a primitive $(n/2)$th root of unity. If n is odd, then show that ω^2 is a primitive nth root of unity.

(iii) Let $k \in \mathbb{Z}$ and $d = n/\gcd(n,k)$. Show that ω^k is a primitive dth root of unity; this generalizes both (i) and (ii).

8.14 Let R be a ring, $n \in \mathbb{N}_{\ge 2}$, $\omega \in R$ a primitive nth root of unity, and $\eta \in R$ with $\eta^2 = \omega$. Under what conditions is η a primitive $2n$th root of unity?

8.15* Let $n \in \mathbb{N}_{>0}$ and R be an integral domain of characteristic coprime to n.

(i) Show that the set R_n of all nth roots of unity is a subgroup of the multiplicative group $R^\times$.

(ii) Prove that the following are equivalent for an nth root of unity $\omega \in R$:

(a) ω is a primitive nth root of unity,

(b) $\omega^l \neq 1$ for $0 < l < n$ (that is, ω has order n in R),

(c) $\omega^l \neq 1$ for all $0 < l < n$ with $l \mid n$,

(d) $\omega^{n/p} \neq 1$ for all prime divisors p of n.

We now assume that R contains a primitive nth root of unity ω.

(iii) Draw all 12th roots of unity for $R = \mathbb{C}$ and mark the primitive ones.

(iv) Show that R_n is cyclic and isomorphic to the additive group $\mathbb{Z}_n$ of integers modulo n (so in particular, $\#R_n = n$).

(v) Prove that there are precisely $\varphi(n)$ primitive nth roots of unity, where φ is Euler's totient function.

8.16* Let q be a prime power, $\mathbb{F}_q$ a finite field with q elements, and $t \in \mathbb{N}$ a divisor of $q - 1$, with prime factorization $t = p_1^{e_1} \cdots p_r^{e_r}$. For $a \in \mathbb{F}_q^\times$, we denote by $\mathrm{ord}(a)$ the order of a in the multiplicative group $\mathbb{F}_q^\times$. Prove:

(i) $\mathrm{ord}(a) = t$ if and only if $a^t = 1$ and $a^{t/p_i} \neq 1$ for $1 \leq i \leq r$.

(ii) $\mathbb{F}_q^\times$ contains an element b_i of order $p_i^{e_i}$, for $1 \leq i \leq r$. Hint: Consider an element of $\mathbb{F}_q^\times$ which is not a root of the polynomial $x^{(q-1)/p_i} - 1$.

(iii) If $a, b \in \mathbb{F}_q^\times$ are elements of coprime orders, then $\mathrm{ord}(ab) = \mathrm{ord}(a)\,\mathrm{ord}(b)$. Hint: Prove that $a^{\mathrm{ord}(ab)} \in U = \langle a \rangle \cap \langle b \rangle$, and show that $U = \{1\}$.

(iv) $\mathbb{F}_q^\times$ contains an element of order t.

(v) $\mathbb{F}_q^\times$ is cyclic.

8.17 (i) For all $a \in \mathbb{F}_{19}^\times$, determine the powers a^k with $k \mid 18$, and derive $\mathrm{ord}(a)$ from this data only.

(ii) Determine all $n \in \mathbb{N}_{>0}$ for which $\mathbb{F}_{19}$ contains a primitive nth root of unity, and for each such n, list all primitive nth roots of unity.

8.18 Prove Lemma 8.8. Hint: Exercises 8.15 and 8.16.

8.19* Let $p, q \in \mathbb{N}$ be distinct odd primes, $n = pq$, and $k, l \in \mathbb{N}$.

(i) Given a primitive kth root of unity in $\mathbb{Z}_p^\times$ and a primitive lth root of unity in $\mathbb{Z}_q^\times$, how can you construct a primitive mth root of unity in $\mathbb{Z}_n^\times$, where $m = \mathrm{lcm}(k, l)$?

(ii) Show that $\mathbb{Z}_n^\times$ contains a primitive kth root of unity if and only if $k \mid \mathrm{lcm}(p - 1, q - 1)$.

(iii) Find primitive 16th roots of unity in $\mathbb{Z}_{17}^\times$ and in $\mathbb{Z}_{97}^\times$, and construct a primitive 16th root of unity in $\mathbb{Z}_{1649}^\times$.

8.20* (i) Let $x, m, n \in \mathbb{N}_{>0}$, $x \geq 2$, $r = n$ rem m, and $g = \gcd(n, m)$. Prove that $x^n - 1$ rem $x^m - 1 = x^r - 1$, and conclude that $\gcd(x^n - 1, x^m - 1) = x^g - 1$. Answer the same questions when x is an indeterminate.

(ii) Let $n \in \mathbb{N}_{\geq 2}$. The integer $M_n = 2^n - 1$ is the nth **Mersenne number**. Use (i) and Exercise 4.14 to prove that 2 is a primitive nth root of unity in $\mathbb{Z}/\langle M_n \rangle$ if and only if n is prime. Hint: Use Fermat's little theorem 4.9.

8.21 Let F be a field supporting the FFT, and $a, b, q, r \in F[x]$ such that $a = qb + r$ and $\deg r < \deg b \leq \deg a < n$ for a power n of 2. We assume that b is coprime to $x^n - 1$. Give an algorithm which on input a, b decides whether $r = 0$, and if so, computes the quotient q using essentially three n-point FFTs.

8.22 Let R be a (commutative) ring supporting the FFT, $f_1, \ldots, f_r, g_1, \ldots, g_r \in R[x]$ polynomials, and $h = \sum_{1 \leq i \leq r} f_i g_i \in R[x]$, of degree less than a power $n \in \mathbb{N}$ of 2. Prove that h can be computed using $2r + 1$ FFTs of order n plus $O(rn)$ operations in R. Determine the constant hidden in the "O". Compare this result to the time for multiplying each f_i by g_i using the fast convolution algorithm 8.16 and then adding up the products.

8.23$\overset{\rightarrow}{}$ Let $p = 66537 = 2^{2^4} + 1$ be the fourth Fermat prime and $\omega = 3$.

(i) Check that $\omega \in \mathbb{F}_p^\times$ is a primitive 2^{16}th root of unity.

(ii) Program classical polynomial multiplication, Karatsuba's algorithm, and the FFT multiplication algorithm 8.16 in $\mathbb{F}_p[x]$ in a computer algebra system of your choice. The inputs and outputs of your program should be the coefficient arrays of two polynomials of degree less than 2^{15} and their product, respectively.

(iii) Design a suitable test series of polynomials with degrees increasing up to 32767 and determine the crossover points between your implementations of the three algorithms. Compare your timings also to the built-in multiplication routine of the computer algebra system. Create a plot of your timings. Comment on your results.

8.24* We may interleave Algorithms 8.14 and 8.16, as follows. Instead of evaluating f and g at all powers of ω, we reduce the multiplication of f and g modulo $x^n - 1$ to two multiplications modulo $x^{n/2} - 1$. Here is the algorithm:

▬ ALGORITHM 8.29 Fast convolution. ▬▬▬▬▬▬▬▬▬▬▬▬▬▬▬▬▬▬▬▬
Input: $f, g \in R[x]$ of degree less than $n = 2^k$ with $k \in \mathbb{N}$, and the powers $\omega, \omega^2, \ldots, \omega^{n/2} - 1$ of a primitive nth root of unity $\omega \in R$.
Output: $f * g \in R[x]$.

1. **if** $k = 0$ **then return** $f \cdot g \in R$

2. $f_0 \longleftarrow f$ rem $x^{n/2} - 1$, $\quad f_1 \longleftarrow f$ rem $x^{n/2} + 1$,
   $g_0 \longleftarrow g$ rem $x^{n/2} - 1$, $\quad g_1 \longleftarrow g$ rem $x^{n/2} + 1$

3. **call** the algorithm recursively to compute $h_0, h_1 \in R[x]$ of degrees less than $n/2$ such that

$$h_0(x) \equiv f_0(x) \cdot g_0(x) \bmod x^{n/2} - 1, \quad h_1(\omega x) \equiv f_1(\omega x) \cdot g_1(\omega x) \bmod x^{n/2} - 1$$

4. **return** $\dfrac{1}{2}((h_0 - h_1)x^{n/2} + h_0 + h_1)$ ▬▬▬▬▬▬▬▬▬▬▬▬▬▬

(i) Prove that the algorithm works correctly and takes $\frac{11}{2} n \log n$ operations in R.

(ii) For small inputs, it is faster to use classical multiplication (or Karatsuba's algorithm and a subsequent reduction modulo $x^n - 1$ to compute the result. Replace the first line of the above algorithm by

1. **if** $k \leq d$ **then call** Algorithm 2.3 to compute $fg \in R[x]$ and **return** fg rem $x^n - 1$

The above algorithm corresponds to $d = 0$. Let $T(n)$ denote the cost of the hybrid algorithm when $n = 2^k$ for some $k \in \mathbb{N}$, and prove that $T(n) = \frac{11}{2} n \log n + \gamma(d) n$ holds for $n \geq 2^d$, where $\gamma(d)$ depends only on d. Find the value of $d \in \mathbb{N}$ which minimizes $\gamma(d)$, and compare the result to (i).

8.25* Algorithm 8.14 computes DFT_ω over a (commutative) ring R by dividing the input polynomial $f \in R[x]$ of degree less than n by $x^{n/2} - 1$ and $x^{n/2} + 1$ with remainder. A different approach is to split f into its odd and even parts, that is, to write $f = f_0(x^2) + x f_1(x^2)$ with $f_0, f_1 \in R[x]$ of degree less than $n/2$, and then to compute $\mathrm{DFT}_{\omega^2}(f_0)$ and $\mathrm{DFT}_{\omega^2}(f_1)$ recursively. Work out the details and prove that your algorithm uses $cn \log n$ operations in R for some positive constant $c \in \mathbb{Q}$ when n is a power of 2. Modify, if necessary, your algorithm so that $c = 3/2$, as in Theorem 8.15. Hint: Use $\omega^{n/2} = -1$. Draw an arithmetic circuit illustrating your algorithm for $n = 8$, and compare it to the circuit in Figure 8.5.

8.26* Let R be a ring (commutative, with 1) containing a primitive 3^kth root of unity for any $k \in \mathbb{N}$.

(i) Design a 3-adic FFT algorithm, taking as input $k \in \mathbb{N}$, a polynomial $f \in R[x]$ of degree less than $n = 3^k$, and a list of powers $1, \omega, \omega^2, \ldots, \omega^{n-1}$ of a primitive nth root of unity $\omega \in R$, and returning $f(1), f(\omega), f(\omega^2), \ldots, f(\omega^{n-1})$. Prove the correctness of your algorithm. Hint: Consider dividing f with remainder by $x^{n/3} - 1$, $x^{n/3} - \omega^{n/3}$, and $x^{n/3} - \omega^{2n/3}$.

(ii) Draw an arithmetic circuit illustrating your algorithm for $n = 9$.

(iii) Let $T(n)$ denote the cost of your algorithm in operations in R when $n = 3^k$ for some $k \in \mathbb{N}$. Set up a recursion for $T(n)$ (don't forget the initial condition) and solve it.

(iv) Assuming that R contains primitive nth root of unity for any $n \in \mathbb{N}$, generalize the above to an m-adic FFT algorithm for arbitrary $m \in \mathbb{N}_{\geq 2}$.

(v) Formulate an alternative m-adic FFT algorithm as in Exercise 8.25.

8.27 Let F be a field containing a primitive 2^kth root of unity for all $k \in \mathbb{N}$. Algorithm 8.16 shows that the convolution $*_n$ in $F[x]$ can be computed with $O(n \log n)$ operations in F if n is a power of 2. The goal of this exercise is to generalize this to arbitrary $n \in \mathbb{N}$. So let $f, g \in F[x]$ and $m \in \mathbb{N}$ be a power of 2 such that $m/2 < 2n \leq m$, and set $a = f \cdot (x^{m-n} + 1)$ and $b = g$. Show how to obtain the coefficients of $f *_n g$ from those of $a *_m b$, and derive the claim from this.

8.28 Show that $\omega = x \bmod (x^n - 1) \in R = F[x]/\langle x^n - 1 \rangle$, where F is a field of characteristic not dividing n, is *not* a primitive nth root of unity for $n \geq 2$.

8.29* Let R be a ring (commutative, with 1).

(i) For $p \in \mathbb{N}_{\geq 2}$, determine the quotient and remainder on division of $f_p = x^{p-1} + x^{p-2} + \cdots + x + 1$ by $x - 1$ in $R[x]$. Conclude that $x - 1$ is invertible modulo f_p if p is a unit in R and that $x - 1$ is a zero divisor modulo f_p if p is a zero divisor in R.

(ii) Assume that 3 is a unit in R, and let $n = 3^k$ for some $k \in \mathbb{N}$, $D = R[x]/\langle x^{2n} + x^n + 1 \rangle$, and $\omega = x \bmod x^{2n} + x^n + 1 \in D$. Prove that $\omega^{3n} = 1$ and $\omega^n - 1$ is a unit. Hint: Calculate $(\omega^n + 2)(\omega^n - 1)$. Conclude that ω is a primitive $3n$th root of unity.

(iii) Let $p \in \mathbb{N}$ be prime and a unit in R, $n = p^k$ for some $k \in \mathbb{N}$, $\Phi_{pn} = f_p(x^n) = x^{(p-1)n} + x^{(p-2)n} + \cdots + x^n + 1 \in R[x]$ the pnth cyclotomic polynomial, $D = R[x]/\langle \Phi_{pn} \rangle$, and $\omega = x \bmod \Phi_{pn} \in D$. Prove that $\omega^{pn} = 1$ and $\omega^n - 1$ is a unit. Hint: Calculate $(\omega^{(p-2)n} + 2\omega^{(p-3)n} + \cdots + (p-2)\omega^n + (p-1)) \cdot (\omega^n - 1)$. Conclude that ω is a primitive pnth root of unity.

8.30** In this exercise, we discuss Schönhage's (1977) 3-adic variant of Algorithm 8.20. It works over any (commutative) ring R such that 3 is a unit in R, so in particular over a field of characteristic 2.

━━━ ALGORITHM 8.30 Schönhage's algorithm. ━━━━━━━━━━━━━━━━━━━━━━━
Input: Two polynomials $f, g \in R[x]$ of degree less than $2n = 2 \cdot 3^k$ for some $k \in \mathbb{N}$, where R is a (commutative) ring and 3 is a unit in R.
Output: $h \in R[x]$ such that $fg \equiv h \bmod (x^{2n} + x^n + 1)$ and $\deg h < 2n$.

    1. **if** $k \leq 2$ **then**
           call the classical algorithm 2.3 (or Karatsuba's algorithm 8.1) to compute $f \cdot g$
           return fg rem $x^{2n} + x^n + 1$

    2. $m \longleftarrow 3^{\lceil k/2 \rceil}, \quad t \longleftarrow n/m$
       let $f, g \in R[x, y]$ with $\deg_x f, \deg_x g < m$ such that $f = f'(x, x^m)$ and $g = g'(x, x^m)$

    3. let $D = R[x]/\langle x^{2m} + x^m + 1 \rangle$
       if $m = t$ **then** $\eta \longleftarrow x \bmod (x^{2m} + x^m + 1)$ **else** $\eta \longleftarrow x^3 \bmod (x^{2m} + x^m + 1)$
       { η is a primitive $3t$th root of unity }
       $f^* \longleftarrow f' \bmod (x^{2m} + x^m + 1), \quad g^* \longleftarrow g' \bmod (x^{2m} + x^m + 1)$

    4. **for** $i = 1, 2$ **do**
           $f_i^* \longleftarrow f^*$ rem $y^t - \eta^{it}, \quad g_i^* \longleftarrow g^*$ rem $y^t - \eta^{it}$
           call the fast convolution algorithm 8.16 with $\omega = \eta^3$ to compute $h_i^* \in D[y]$ of degrees less than t such that

$$f^*(\eta^i y) g^*(\eta^i y) \equiv h_i^*(\eta^i y) \bmod y^t - 1$$

    { the DFTs are performed by the 3-adic FFT algorithm from Exercise 8.26, and Algorithm 8.30 is used recursively for multiplications in D }

5. $h^* \longleftarrow \dfrac{1}{3}(y^t(h_2 - h_1) + \eta^{2t}h_1 - \eta^t h_2)(2\eta^t + 1)$

    let $h' \in R[x, y]$ with $\deg_x h' < 2m$ such that $h^* = h' \bmod (x^{2m} + x^m + 1)$

    $h \longleftarrow h'(x, x^m) \operatorname{rem} (x^{2n} + x^n + 1)$

    return h

(i) Use Exercise 8.29 to prove that the algorithm works correctly.

(ii) Let $T(k)$ denote the cost of the algorithm for $n = 3^k$. Prove that $T(k) \leq 2 \cdot 3^{\lfloor k/2 \rfloor} T(\lceil k/2 \rceil) + (c + 48(\lfloor k/2 \rfloor + 1/2))3^k$ for $k > 2$ and some constant $c \in \mathbb{N}$, and conclude that $T(k)$ is at most $24 \cdot 3^k \cdot k \cdot \log k + O(3^k \cdot k) = 24n \log_3 n \log_2 \log_3 n + O(n \log n)$. Hint: Consider the function $S(k) = (3^{-k}T(k) + c)/(k-1)$, and prove that $S(k) \leq S(\lceil k/2 \rceil) + 24$ if $k > 2$.

8.31*   (i) Let R be a (commutative) ring, $n \in \mathbb{N}_{\geq 2}$ a power of two, and $\omega = (x \bmod x^{n/2} + 1) \in R[x]/\langle x^{n/2} + 1 \rangle$. Show that the conclusion $V_\omega \cdot V_{\omega^{-1}} = nI$ of Theorem 8.13 holds even when n is not a unit in R. Hint: Show first that $\omega^{nj/2} + 1 = 0$ for all odd $j \in \mathbb{N}$ and use the factorization

$$\sum_{0 \leq i < n} x^i = (x+1)(x^2+1)(x^4+1) \cdots (x^{n/2}+1)$$

in $R[x]$. Generalize this to the case when n is an arbitrary prime power.

(ii) Let $e(k)$ be such that the division-free variant of Algorithm 8.20 described in the text returns $2^{e(k)}h$ on input $n = 2^k$ for $k \geq 2$. Prove that $e(k+1) = e(\lceil k/2 \rceil + 1) + \lfloor k/2 \rfloor + 1$ for $k \geq 2$, and conclude that $e(k) = k - 2 + \lceil \log(k-1) \rceil$.

8.32* Prove that for $n \in \mathbb{N}_{\geq 1}$, $\omega = 2$ is a primitive $2n$th root of unity modulo $2^n + 1$ if and only if n is a power of 2.

8.33 Prove (9).

8.34 Let M be a multiplication time for polynomials. Prove that $\mathsf{M}(n+1) \leq \mathsf{M}(n) + 4n$ for all n.

8.35 Let $k, n \in \mathbb{N}$.

(i) Prove that a polynomial of degree less than n can be multiplied by a polynomial of degree less than kn in time $k\mathsf{M}(n) + O(kn)$. Determine a "small" value for the constant in the "O".

(ii) Now let n and k be powers of 2. For which values of k is your method from (i) faster than the naive $\mathsf{M}(kn)$? Answer the latter question for the classical $\mathsf{M}(n) = 2n^2$, Karatsuba's $\mathsf{M}(n) = 9n^{\log 3}$, and $\mathsf{M}(n) = \frac{9}{2}n \log n$ from Theorem 8.18.

8.36* Let $k, l \in \mathbb{N}$ and $f, g \in \mathbb{Z}[x]$ with $\deg(fg) < n = 2^k$ and max-norm $\|f\|_\infty, \|g\|_\infty \leq 2^l$.

(i) We assume that $2l + 1 \leq n - k$. Show that $\|fg\|_\infty < 2^{n-1}$.

(ii) Use Exercise 8.32 (i) and the fast convolution algorithm 8.16 over $R = \mathbb{Z}/\langle 2^n + 1 \rangle$ to compute $fg \in \mathbb{Z}[x]$, and show that this takes $O(n^2 \log n \log\log n)$ word operations. (This is the essential part of Schönhage & Strassen's (1971) fast integer multiplication algorithm; they call the algorithm recursively for the coefficient multiplications.)

8.37* Adapt Exercise 8.36 to bivariate polynomials.

8.38 Generalize the Kronecker substitution to reduce multiplication of r-variable polynomials to multiplication of univariate polynomials, and analyze its cost, including the dependency on r.

What we know is a drop, what we don't know, an ocean.

Isaac Newton

Mit Ausnahme der paar von Hand gefertigten Möbel, Kleider, Schuhe
und der Kinder erhalten wir alles unter Einschaltung mathematischer
Berechnungen. Dieses ganze Dasein, das um uns läuft, rennt, steht, ist
nicht nur für seine Einsehbarkeit von der Mathematik abhängig,
sondern ist effektiv durch sie entstanden.[1]

Robert Musil (1913)

Hat man diesen Gegenstand [*die imaginären Grössen*] bisher aus
einem falschen Gesichtspunkt betrachtet und eine geheimnissvolle
Dunkelheit dabei gefunden, so ist diess grossentheils den wenig
schicklichen Benennungen zuzuschreiben. Hätte man $+1, -1, \sqrt{-1}$
nicht positive, negative, imaginäre (oder gar unmögliche) Einheit,
sondern etwa directe, inverse, laterale Einheit genannt, so hätte von
einer solchen Dunkelheit kaum die Rede sein können.[2]

Carl Friedrich Gauß (1831)

Before the introduction of the Arabic notation, multiplication was
difficult, and the division even of integers called into play the highest
mathematical faculties. Probably nothing in the modern world could
have more astonished a Greek mathematician than to learn that [...]
a large proportion of the population of Western Europe could
perform the operation of division for the largest numbers.

Alfred North Whitehead (1911)

Dixit Alchoarizmi: [...] Hec sunt igitur universa, que necessaria sunt
hominibus ex divisione et multiplicatione in integro numero
et in ceteris, que secuntur. His peractis incipiemus narrare
multiplicationem fractionum et divisionem earum sive radices,
si deus voluerit.[3]

Abū Jaʿfar Muḥammad ben Mūsā al-Khwārizmī (c. 830)

---

[1] Except for a few hand-made pieces of furniture, clothes, shoes, and our children we obtain everything by using mathematical computations. The whole world we live in, everything which walks, runs, stands around us, depends not only for our understanding on mathematics, but has effectively been created by it.

[2] That this subject [*the imaginary magnitudes*] has hitherto been considered from the wrong point of view and surrounded by a mysterious obscurity, is to be attributed largely to an unfortunate notation. If $+1, -1, \sqrt{-1}$ had not been called positive, negative, and imaginary (or even impossible) unit, but rather direct, inverse, and lateral unit, then such an obscurity would probably not have arisen.

[3] Thus spake Al-Khwārizmī: [...] So this is everything that is necessary for men concerning the division and multiplication with an integer, and the other things that are connected with it. Having completed this, we now begin to discuss the multiplication of fractions and their division, and the extraction of roots, if God so wills.

9

Newton iteration

We mentioned on pages 206–207 Newton's method for approximating roots of polynomials. It has become a staple of numerical computation, and seen many generalizations and improvements over the years. But what does this decidedly *continuous, approximative* method, computing values that are closer and closer to some real root, have to do with the *discrete, exact* calculations prevalent in computer algebra? There is a somewhat counter-intuitive notion of *closeness* for integers (and polynomials), corresponding to divisibility by higher and higher powers of a fixed prime. Newton iteration works just beautifully in this purely algebraic setting.

We start by using it to find a division algorithm that is about as fast as multiplication, and then describe its use for finding roots of polynomials. Finally, we describe a common framework—valuations—into which both the analytical method over the real numbers and our symbolic version fit. In Chapter 15, we will apply Newton's method to the factorization of polynomials; it is then called Hensel lifting.

9.1. Division with remainder using Newton iteration

Integers and polynomials over a field form a Euclidean domain when the absolute value and the polynomial degree, respectively, is used as the Euclidean function. This means that for all a, b with $b \neq 0$ there exist unique q, r such that $a = qb + r$ where $0 \leq r < |b|$ in the integer case and $\deg r < \deg b$ in the polynomial case. The division problem is then to find q, r, given a, b.

The "classical" (or "synthetic") division algorithm 2.5 requires $O(n^2)$ (word or field) operations for inputs of size n. We will now see how this can be improved to $O(\mathsf{M}(n))$, where M is a multiplication time. We only discuss the polynomial case since it is somewhat easier, and then briefly indicate the ideas in the integer case. Let D be a ring (commutative, with 1) and $a, b \in D[x]$ two polynomials of degree n and m, respectively. We assume that $m \leq n$ and that b is monic. We wish to find polynomials q and r in $D[x]$ satisfying $a = qb + r$ with $\deg r < \deg b$ (where, as

243

usual, we assume that the zero polynomial has degree $-\infty$). Since b is monic, such q, r exist uniquely even if D is not a field (Section 2.4).

Substituting $1/x$ for the variable x and multiplying by x^n, we obtain

$$x^n a\left(\frac{1}{x}\right) = \left(x^{n-m} q\left(\frac{1}{x}\right)\right) \cdot \left(x^m b\left(\frac{1}{x}\right)\right) + x^{n-m+1}\left(x^{m-1} r\left(\frac{1}{x}\right)\right). \tag{1}$$

We define the **reversal** of a as $\mathrm{rev}_k(a) = x^k a(1/x)$. When $k = n$, this is the polynomial with the coefficients of a reversed, that is, if $a = a_n x^n + a_{n-1} x^{n-1} + \cdots + a_1 x + a_0$, then

$$\mathrm{rev}_n(a) = a_0 x^n + a_1 x^{n-1} + \cdots + a_{n-1} x + a_n.$$

Equation (1) now reads

$$\mathrm{rev}_n(a) = \mathrm{rev}_{n-m}(q) \cdot \mathrm{rev}_m(b) + x^{n-m+1}\,\mathrm{rev}_{m-1}(r),$$

and therefore,

$$\mathrm{rev}_n(a) \equiv \mathrm{rev}_{n-m}(q) \cdot \mathrm{rev}_m(b) \bmod x^{n-m+1}.$$

We note that $\mathrm{rev}_m(b)$ has constant coefficient 1 and thus is invertible modulo x^{n-m+1}, by Theorem 4.1. Hence we find

$$\mathrm{rev}_{n-m}(q) \equiv \mathrm{rev}_n(a) \cdot \mathrm{rev}_m(b)^{-1} \bmod x^{n-m+1}, \tag{2}$$

and obtain $q = \mathrm{rev}_{n-m}(\mathrm{rev}_{n-m}(q))$ and $r = a - q \cdot b$.

EXAMPLE 9.1. Let $a = 5x^5 + 4x^4 + 3x^3 + 2x^2 + x$ and $b = x^2 + 2x + 3$ be polynomials in $\mathbb{F}_7[x]$. Then

$$\mathrm{rev}_5(a) = x^4 + 2x^3 + 3x^2 + 4x + 5, \quad \mathrm{rev}_2(b) = 3x^2 + 2x + 1.$$

We claim that $\mathrm{rev}_2(b)^{-1} \equiv 4x^3 + x^2 + 5x + 1 \bmod x^4$ in $\mathbb{F}_7[x]$, and indeed

$$(3x^2 + 2x + 1)(4x^3 + x^2 + 5x + 1) = 5x^5 + 4x^4 + 1 \equiv 1 \bmod x^4.$$

It follows that

$$\mathrm{rev}_3(q) \equiv (x^4 + 2x^3 + 3x^2 + 4x + 5)(4x^3 + x^2 + 5x + 1) \equiv 6x^3 + x + 5 \bmod x^4.$$

Thus $q = 5x^3 + x^2 + 6$ and

$$r = a - qb = 5x^5 + 4x^4 + 3x^3 + 2x^2 + x - (5x^3 + x^2 + 6)(x^2 + 2x + 3) = 3x + 3. \ \Diamond$$

So now we have to solve the problem of finding, from a given $f \in D[x]$ and $l \in \mathbb{N}$ with $f(0) = 1$, a $g \in D[x]$ satisfying $fg \equiv 1 \bmod x^l$.

From numerical analysis, we recall that Newton iteration involves computing successive approximations to solutions of $\varphi(g) = 0$. From a suitable initial approximation g_0, subsequent approximations are computed using

$$g_{i+1} = g_i - \frac{\varphi(g_i)}{\varphi'(g_i)}, \tag{3}$$

where φ' is the derivative of φ. This corresponds to intersecting the tangent with an axis, as illustrated in Figure 9.1, or in other words, to replacing φ by its "linearization" at that point. For the task at hand, we want to find (or approximate) a root

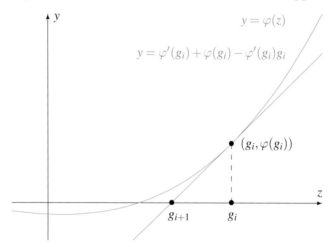

FIGURE 9.1: Newton iteration over the reals.

of $1/g - f = 0$. The Newton iteration step is

$$g_{i+1} = g_i - \frac{1/g_i - f}{-1/g_i^2} = 2g_i - fg_i^2.$$

The following theorem tells us a good initial approximation and shows us that this method converges "quickly" to a solution also in our algebraic setting.

THEOREM 9.2.
Let D be a ring (commutative, with 1), $f, g_0, g_1, \ldots \in D[x]$, with $f(0) = 1$, $g_0 = 1$, and $g_{i+1} \equiv 2g_i - fg_i^2 \bmod x^{2^{i+1}}$, for all i. Then $fg_i \equiv 1 \bmod x^{2^i}$ for all $i \geq 0$.

PROOF. The proof is by induction on i. For $i = 0$ we have

$$fg_0 \equiv f(0)g_0 \equiv 1 \cdot 1 \equiv 1 \bmod x^{2^0}.$$

For the induction step, we find

$$1 - fg_{i+1} \equiv 1 - f(2g_i - fg_i^2) \equiv 1 - 2fg_i + f^2g_i^2 \equiv (1 - fg_i)^2 \equiv 0 \bmod x^{2^{i+1}}. \quad \square$$

We obtain the following algorithm to compute the inverse of $f \bmod x^l$. We denote by log the binary logarithm.

ALGORITHM 9.3 Inversion using Newton iteration.
Input: $f \in D[x]$ with $f(0) = 1$, and $l \in \mathbb{N}$.
Output: $g \in D[x]$ satisfying $fg \equiv 1 \bmod x^l$.

1. $g_0 \longleftarrow 1, \quad r \longleftarrow \lceil \log l \rceil$

2. **for** $i = 1, \ldots, r$ **do** $g_i \longleftarrow (2g_{i-1} - fg_{i-1}^2) \operatorname{rem} x^{2^i}$

3. **return** g_r

If we want to compute the inverse of a polynomial $f \in D[x]$ with $f(0)$ a unit different from 1, then we set $g_0 = f(0)^{-1}$ in step 1. If $f(0)$ is not a unit, then no inverse of f modulo x^l exists, since $fg \equiv 1 \bmod x^l$ implies that $f(0) \cdot g(0) = 1$.

EXAMPLE 9.1 (continued). Let $f = 3x^2 + 2x + 1 \in \mathbb{F}_7[x]$ and $l = 4$. Then Algorithm 9.3 computes $g_0 = 1, r = 2$, and

$$
\begin{aligned}
g_1 &\equiv 2g_0 - fg_0^2 = 2 - (3x^2 + 2x + 1) \equiv 5x + 1 \bmod x^2, \\
g &\equiv 2g_1 - fg_1^2 = 2(5x + 1) - (3x^2 + 2x + 1)(5x + 1)^2 \\
&= 2x^4 + 4x^3 + x^2 + 5x + 1 \equiv 4x^3 + x^2 + 5x + 1 \bmod x^4.
\end{aligned}
$$

We have already checked in Example 9.1 that indeed $fg \equiv 1 \bmod x^4$. $\diamond$

THEOREM 9.4.
Algorithm 9.3 correctly computes the inverse of f modulo x^l. If $l = 2^r$ is a power of 2, then it uses at most $3\mathsf{M}(l) + l \in O(\mathsf{M}(l))$ arithmetic operations in D.

PROOF. Correctness follows from Theorem 9.2 and the fact that x^l divides x^{2^r}. In step 2, all powers of x up to 2^i can be dropped, and since $g_i \equiv g_{i-1} \cdot (2 - fg_i) \equiv g_{i-1} \bmod x^{2^{i-1}}$, also the powers of x less than 2^{i-1}. The cost for one iteration of step 2 is $\mathsf{M}(2^{i-1})$ for the computation of g_{i-1}^2, $\mathsf{M}(2^i)$ for the product $fg_{i-1}^2 \bmod x^{2^i}$, and then the negative of the upper half of fg_{i-1}^2 modulo x^{2^i} is the upper half of g_i, taking 2^{i-1} operations. Thus we have $\mathsf{M}(2^i) + \mathsf{M}(2^{i-1}) + 2^{i-1} \le \frac{3}{2}\mathsf{M}(2^i) + 2^{i-1}$ in step 2, and the total running time is

$$
\sum_{1 \le i \le r} \left(\frac{3}{2}\mathsf{M}(2^i) + 2^{i-1} \right) \le \left(\frac{3}{2}\mathsf{M}(2^r) + 2^{r-1} \right) \sum_{1 \le i \le r} 2^{i-r} < 3\mathsf{M}(2^r) + 2^r = 3\mathsf{M}(l) + l,
$$

where we have used $2\mathsf{M}(n) \le \mathsf{M}(2n)$ for all $n \in \mathbb{N}$. $\square$

If l is not a power of 2, then the above algorithm computes too many coefficients of the inverse. Exercise 9.6 gives a better algorithm with essentially the same running time bound in this general case.

▬▬ ALGORITHM 9.5 Fast division with remainder. ▬▬▬▬▬▬▬▬▬▬▬▬▬
Input: $a, b \in D[x]$, where D is a ring (commutative, with 1) and $b \neq 0$ is monic.
Output: $q, r \in D[x]$ such that $a = qb + r$ and $\deg r < \deg b$.

    1. **if** $\deg a < \deg b$ **then return** $q = 0$ and $r = a$

    2. $m \longleftarrow \deg a - \deg b$
       call Algorithm 9.3 to compute the inverse of $\mathrm{rev}_{\deg b}(b) \in D[x]$ modulo x^{m+1}

    3. $q^* \longleftarrow \mathrm{rev}_{\deg a}(a) \cdot \mathrm{rev}_{\deg b}(b)^{-1}$ rem x^{m+1}

    4. **return** $q = \mathrm{rev}_m(q^*)$ and $r = a - bq$ ▬▬▬▬▬▬▬

▬▬ THEOREM 9.6. ▬▬▬▬▬▬▬▬▬▬▬▬▬▬▬▬▬▬▬▬▬▬▬▬
Let D be a ring (commutative, with 1). Division with remainder of a polynomial $a \in D[x]$ of degree $n + m$ by a monic polynomial $b \in D[x]$ of degree n, where $n \geq m \in \mathbb{N}$, can be done using $4\mathsf{M}(m) + \mathsf{M}(n) + O(n)$ ring operations. ▬▬▬▬

PROOF. Let $a = qb + r$, with $q, r \in D[x]$ such that $\deg r < n$. Then we have $\deg q = \deg a - \deg b = m$. The correctness of Algorithm 9.5 follows from the discussion at the beginning of the section. Using Exercises 8.34 and 9.6, we have at most $3\mathsf{M}(m) + O(m)$ operations in step 2 of Algorithm 9.5, $\mathsf{M}(m) + O(m)$ in step 3, and finally $\mathsf{M}(n) + O(n)$ in step 4; only the lower part of $a - qb$ has to be computed since $\deg r < \deg b$. $\square$

It may seem circular to use an algorithm that uses the rem operation to perform division. However, we are only using the rem operation to truncate the polynomial. It is similar to finding the quotient and remainder of a large number written in base 10 when divided by 10000. Division in this special case costs no operations.

What is the number of word operations for division with remainder in $\mathbb{Z}[x]$? If b is monic and a, b have max-norm $\|a\|_\infty, \|b\|_\infty < 2^l$, then Exercise 6.44 shows that $\|q\|_\infty, \|r\|_\infty < 2^{nl}$. Exercise 9.15 shows that all intermediate results in Algorithm 9.3 have coefficients of length $O(nl)$, and hence the cost for division using Newton inversion is $O(\mathsf{M}(n)\mathsf{M}(nl))$ or $O^\sim(n^2 l)$ word operations. Since the output size is $O(n^2 l)$ and Exercise 6.44 also shows that this bound can be achieved, the running time is—up to logarithmic factors—asymptotically optimal. A similar statement also holds for division with remainder in $F[y][x]$ for a field F.

Exercises 8.21 and 9.14 discuss slightly faster algorithms for **exact division**, where the remainder is known to be zero in advance.

▭ COROLLARY 9.7. ▭

Let D be a ring (commutative, with 1) and $f \in D[x]$ monic of degree n. Then one multiplication in the residue class ring $D[x]/\langle f \rangle$ can be done using $6\mathsf{M}(n) + O(n)$ or $O(\mathsf{M}(n))$ arithmetic operations in D. ▭

If several divisions by or multiplications modulo the same f have to be performed, then we may precompute $f^* = \operatorname{rev}_n(f)^{-1} \operatorname{rem} x^n$ and store it, and the time for one division or one modular multiplication drops to at most $2\mathsf{M}(n) + O(n)$ and $3\mathsf{M}(n) + O(n)$, respectively. When using FFT multiplication, then also $\mathrm{DFT}_\omega(f)$ and $\mathrm{DFT}_\omega(f^*)$, where ω is an appropriate root of unity, may be precomputed and stored, thus further saving two FFTs per modular multiplication.

Now we want to divide with remainder an integer a by a nonzero integer b. Taking reversals with respect to the binary representation does not work here because of the carries. Instead, *numerical* Newton iteration over $\mathbb{R}$ is used to compute an approximation g to $1/b \in \mathbb{Q}$ with sufficient accuracy, then q is obtained by rounding ag to the nearest integer, and finally $r = a - qb$. The quotient may need to be adjusted by ± 1 if $r \geq b$ or $r < 0$. To avoid fractions, things are scaled appropriately by multiplying by powers of 2.

▭ THEOREM 9.8. ▭

Division with remainder of integers of length n can be done with $O(\mathsf{M}(n))$ word operations. ▭

▭ COROLLARY 9.9. ▭

For an integer $m \in \mathbb{N}$ of length n, one multiplication in the residue class ring $\mathbb{Z}_m$ can be performed using $O(\mathsf{M}(n))$ word operations. ▭

Algorithm 9.3 can be generalized to compute inverses modulo p^l for an element p in an arbitrary ring R. One minor difference is that we need an initial inverse modulo p, which is trivial to compute if $p = x$ and $R = D[x]$, and for a Euclidean domain R can be computed with the Extended Euclidean Algorithm in R.

▭ ALGORITHM 9.10 *p-adic inversion using Newton iteration.* ▭

Input: $f, g_0 \in R$ with $fg_0 \equiv 1 \bmod p$, where R is a ring (commutative, with 1) and $p \in R$ arbitrary, and $l \in \mathbb{N}$.
Output: $g \in R$ satisfying $fg \equiv 1 \bmod p^l$.

1. $r \longleftarrow \lceil \log l \rceil$

2. **for** $i = 1, \ldots, r$ compute $g_i \in R$ such that $g_i \equiv (2g_{i-1} - fg_{i-1}^2) \bmod p^{2^i}$

3. **return** g_r ▭

EXAMPLE 9.11. We let $R = \mathbb{Z}$, and wish to compute the inverse of 5 modulo 81. We begin with $g_0 = -1$, since $-1 \cdot 5 \equiv 1 \bmod 3$. Then

$$g_1 \equiv 2g_0 - 5g_0^2 \equiv 2 \bmod 9, \quad g_2 \equiv 2g_1 - 5g_1^2 \equiv -16 \bmod 81,$$

and indeed $-16 \cdot 5 = -80 \equiv 1 \bmod 81$. $\Diamond$

THEOREM 9.12.

Algorithm 9.10 correctly computes the inverse of f mod p^l. It uses $O(\mathsf{M}(l \log p))$ word operations if $R = \mathbb{Z}$, $p > 1$, and $|f| < p^l$, and $O(\mathsf{M}(l \deg p))$ operations in D if $R = D[x]$ for a (commutative) ring D, p is monic, and $\deg p < l \deg p$.

See Exercise 9.8 for a proof.

In step 2, there are in general many g_i's satisfying the congruence. But in our applications such as integers or polynomials we have a unique "smallest" such g_i, namely from the standard system of representatives for $R/\langle p^{2^i}\rangle$ (see Section 25.2).

We have already seen in Section 4.2 that modular inverses can be computed using the Extended Euclidean Algorithm. If the modulus is a perfect power p^l with $l \in \mathbb{N}$ not too small and we use $\mathsf{M}(n) \in O(n \log n \log\log n)$, then the above theorem tells us that using the Extended Euclidean Algorithm to compute an inverse modulo p and then applying Algorithm 9.10 is asymptotically faster for our two main applications $R = \mathbb{Z}$ and $R = F[x]$, where F is a field, than using the Extended Euclidean Algorithm to compute the inverse modulo p^l. This is still true if we have an asymptotically fast Euclidean Algorithm like the one that will be discussed in Chapter 11.

Let R be a Euclidean domain, $p, f \in R$, and $l \in \mathbb{N}_{>0}$. Theorem 4.1 implies that

$$f \text{ is invertible modulo } p^l \iff \gcd(p^l, f) = 1 \iff \gcd(p, f) = 1$$
$$\iff f \text{ is invertible modulo } p.$$

(For $R = F[x]$ for a field F and $p = x$, this is equivalent to $f(0) \neq 0$, as we have seen before.) The following corollary says that this is true for arbitrary rings.

COROLLARY 9.13.

Let R be a ring (commutative, with 1), $p \in R$, and $l \in \mathbb{N}_{>0}$. An element $f \in R$ is invertible modulo p^l if and only if it is invertible modulo p.

PROOF. If f has an inverse modulo p, then Algorithm 9.10 computes an inverse of f modulo p^l. Conversely, if $g \in R$ is such that $fg \equiv 1 \bmod p^l$, then it follows from $l \geq 1$ that $fg \equiv 1 \bmod p$. $\square$

9.2. Generalized Taylor expansion and radix conversion

We now use fast division with remainder to compute quickly the **p-adic expansion** (or generalized Taylor expansion) of a polynomial a: given $a, p \in R[x]$ of degrees n, m, respectively, where R is a ring and p is monic, we want the unique $a_0, \ldots, a_{k-1} \in R[x]$ such that

$$a = \sum_{0 \le i < k} a_i p^i, \quad \deg a_i < m \text{ for } 0 \le i < k, \tag{4}$$

where $k = \lfloor n/m \rfloor + 1$ (see Section 5.11). This will be used in the integration algorithm of Chapter 22; the reader may skip the present section at first reading.

A special case is the usual coefficient sequence when $p = x$, or, more generally, the Taylor expansion of a around u for $p = x - u$ (Section 5.6). We have seen in Section 5.11 that the p-adic expansion can be computed using $O(n^2)$ operations in R, and we will now see how to do this in softly linear time.

━━━ ALGORITHM 9.14 Generalized Taylor expansion. ━━━━━━━━━━━━━━━━━
Input: $a, p \in R[x]$ with $\deg p = m$ and $\deg a < km$, where R is a ring (commutative, with 1), p is monic, and $k \in \mathbb{N}_{\ge 1}$ is a power of 2.
Output: $a_0, \ldots, a_{k-1} \in R[x]$ such that (4) holds.

1. **if** $k = 1$ **then return** $a_0 = a$

2. $t \longleftarrow k/2$
    call the repeated squaring algorithm 4.8 to compute $p^t \in R[x]$

3. $q \longleftarrow a \text{ quo } p^t, \quad r \longleftarrow a \text{ rem } p^t$

4. **call** the algorithm recursively to compute the generalized Taylor expansions
    $r = \sum_{0 \le i < t} a_i p^i$ and $q = \sum_{0 \le i < t} a_{t+i} p^i$

5. **return** $a_0, \ldots, a_{k-1}$ ━━━━━━━━━━━━━━━━━━━━━━━━━━━━

━━━ THEOREM 9.15. ━━━━━━━━━━━━━━━━━━━━━━━━━━━━━━━━━━
Algorithm 9.14 correctly computes the p-adic expansion of a and uses at most $(3\mathsf{M}(km) + O(km)) \log k$ *or* $O(\mathsf{M}(km) \log k)$ *operations in R.* ━━━━━━━━━━

PROOF. Correctness is clear when $k = 1$. If $k > 1$, then

$$a = qp^t + r = \sum_{0 \le i < t} a_{i+t} p^i p^t + \sum_{0 \le i < t} a_i p^i = \sum_{0 \le i < k} a_i p^i.$$

Let $T(k)$ denote the cost of the algorithm. Step 1 is for free, and hence $T(1) = 0$. By treating leading coefficients in polynomial multiplication separately, we have

$M(n+1) \le M(n) + 5n$ if $n \ge 1$ (Exercise 8.34). Thus the cost for step 2 is

$$M(m+1) + M(2m+1) + \cdots + M\left(\frac{km}{4} + 1\right)$$

$$\le \ M\left(m + 2m + \cdots + \frac{km}{4}\right) + 5\left(m + 2m + \cdots + \frac{km}{4}\right)$$

$$\le \ M\left(\frac{km}{2}\right) + \frac{5}{2}km \in \frac{1}{2}M(km) + O(km).$$

The cost for step 3 is at most $5M(km/2) + O(km)$ or $\frac{5}{2}M(km) + O(km)$, by Theorem 9.6, and step 4 costs $2T(k/2)$. Thus we have the recursive inequality $T(k) \le 2T(k/2) + 3M(km) + ckm$, for some constant $c \in \mathbb{R}$, and Lemma 8.2 implies that $T(k)$ is at most $(3M(km) + O(km)) \log k$. $\square$

One may also take $k = \lfloor(\deg f)/m\rfloor + 1$, not necessarily a power of 2, and $t = \lfloor k/2 \rfloor$ in step 2. The effect is a more "balanced" binary splitting in steps 3 and 4, possibly resulting in a slightly faster algorithm, but the analysis is more involved. If k is a power of 2, however, one may precompute $p^2, p^4, \ldots, p^{k/4}, p^{k/2}$, thus performing repeated squaring only once instead of every time the algorithm passes through step 2 in the recursive process.

Exercise 9.20 shows that the "reverse" task of computing the coefficients of a from its p-adic expansion (4) can also be done in time $O(M(mk) \log k)$.

COROLLARY 9.16.
Let $n \in \mathbb{N}$ be a power of 2. The Taylor expansion of a polynomial $a \in R[x]$ of degree n around $u \in R$ can be computed using at most $(3M(n) + O(n)) \log n$ or $O(M(n) \log n)$ operations in R.

The analog of Algorithm 9.14 for integers can be used to convert an integer from the 2^{64}-ary representation to an expansion with respect to the powers of an arbitrary base $p \in \mathbb{N}_{>1}$ in softly linear time. The following theorem is proven in Exercise 9.21.

THEOREM 9.17.
Given $a, p \in \mathbb{N}$ with p of length m and a of length at most km for some $k, m \in \mathbb{N}$, we can compute the p-adic expansion of a using $O(M(km) \log k)$ word operations.

9.3. Formal derivatives and Taylor expansion

In the next section, we solve the problem of finding a root g in a ring R of $\varphi(g) \equiv 0 \bmod p^l$, where $\varphi \in R[y]$ and $p \in R$. As in the case of inversion modulo p^l, Newton iteration will lead to a fast algorithm—provided we have a starting solution modulo p. But first we need to adapt some well known tools from calculus to our purely algebraic setting.

DEFINITION 9.18. *Let R be an arbitrary ring (commutative, with 1). For $\varphi = \sum_{0 \le i \le n} \varphi_i y^i \in R[y]$ we define the **formal derivative** of φ by*

$$\varphi' = \sum_{0 \le i \le n} i \varphi_i y^{i-1}.$$

For $R = \mathbb{R}$, this is the familiar notion usually defined by a limit process. But in general, say over a finite field, there is no concept like a "limit". We note that i plays two different roles here: as a summation index, where it is really just a convenient notation for the vector $(\varphi_0, \dots, \varphi_n) \in R^{n+1}$ of coefficients, and the ring element $i = 1 + \cdots + 1 \in R$.

The formal derivative has some familiar properties.

LEMMA 9.19.   (i) $'$ *is R-linear,*

(ii) $'$ *satisfies the Leibniz (or product) rule $(\varphi \psi)' = \varphi' \psi + \psi' \varphi$,*

(iii) $'$ *satisfies the chain rule $(\varphi(\psi))' = \varphi'(\psi) \psi'$.*

PROOF.   (i) Let $\varphi, \psi \in R[y]$, $\varphi = \sum_{0 \le i \le n} \varphi_i y^i$, $\psi = \sum_{0 \le i \le n} \psi_i y^i$, and $a, b \in R$. Then

$$\begin{aligned}
(a\varphi + b\psi)' &= (\sum_{0 \le i \le n} (a\varphi_i + b\psi_i)y^i)' = \sum_{0 \le i \le n} i(a\varphi_i + b\psi_i)y^{i-1} \\
&= a \sum_{0 \le i \le n} i\varphi_i y^{i-1} + b \sum_{0 \le i \le n} i\psi_i y^{i-1} = a\varphi' + b\psi'.
\end{aligned}$$

(ii) Because of linearity, it is enough to show the claim for powers of y. So let $n, m \in \mathbb{N}$.

$$\begin{aligned}
(y^n y^m)' &= (y^{n+m})' = (n+m)y^{n+m-1} = ny^{n-1}y^m + my^{m-1}y^n \\
&= (y^n)' y^m + (y^m)' y^n.
\end{aligned}$$

(iii) Again, it is sufficient to show the claim for φ being a power of y, $\varphi = y^n$ for $n \in \mathbb{N}$ say. But then the claim reduces to $(\psi^n)' = n\psi^{n-1}\psi'$, which is easily proven using the Leibniz rule and induction on n. $\square$

We note one difference from the usual derivatives, say over $\mathbb{R}$. Over $\mathbb{F}_p$ (or, more generally, any field of characteristic $p > 0$) any pth derivative is zero. For example, $\varphi'' = 0$ for all $\varphi \in \mathbb{F}_2[y]$.

LEMMA 9.20. *Let* $\varphi = \sum_{0 \le i \le n} \varphi_i y^i \in R[y]$ *and* $g \in R$. *Then*

$$\varphi = \varphi(g) + \varphi'(g)(y - g) + \psi \cdot (y - g)^2$$

for some $\psi \in R[y]$.

PROOF. We have seen in Section 5.6 that φ has the Taylor expansion

$$\varphi = \sum_{0 \le i \le n} \varphi_i \cdot (y - g)^i = \varphi_0 + \varphi_1 \cdot (y - g) + \psi \cdot (y - g)^2,$$

around g, with unique $\varphi_i \in R$ and $\psi = \sum_{2 \le i \le n} \varphi_i y^{i-2} \in R[y]$. Substituting $y = g$ yields $\varphi_0 = \varphi(g)$. Now we take derivatives:

$$\varphi' = \varphi_1 + \psi' \cdot (y - g)^2 + \psi \cdot 2(y - g).$$

Again substituting $y = g$ yields $\varphi_1 = \varphi'(g)$, and the claim follows. $\square$

This is the Taylor expansion of order 2 of φ around g. In fact, we can even consider g to be a new indeterminate, and then the lemma is true with $\psi \in R[y, g]$.

9.4. Solving polynomial equations via Newton iteration

Now we are ready to state the main result for the Newton iteration algorithm. Let R be an arbitrary ring and $p \in R$. The algorithm corresponding to (5) below computes better and better approximations, that is, modulo higher and higher powers of p, to a root of a polynomial, just as the Newton iteration (3) does over the real numbers.

LEMMA 9.21. *(Quadratic convergence of Newton iteration) Let* $\varphi \in R[y]$, $g, h \in R$ *with* $\varphi(g) \equiv 0 \bmod p^k$ *for some* $k \in \mathbb{N}_{>0}$ *and* $\varphi'(g)$ *invertible modulo* p, *and suppose that Newton's formula holds "approximately":*

$$h \equiv g - \varphi(g)\varphi'(g)^{-1} \bmod p^{2k}. \tag{5}$$

Then $\varphi(h) \equiv 0 \bmod p^{2k}$, $h \equiv g \bmod p^k$, *and* $\varphi'(h)$ *is invertible modulo* p.

Intuitively, if g is a "good" approximation to a zero of φ, then h is a "better" approximation, at least "twice as accurate".

PROOF. By Corollary 9.13, $\varphi'(g)$ is invertible modulo p^k, and hence the right hand side of (5) is well defined; Algorithm 9.10 computes $\varphi'(g)^{-1} \bmod p^{2k}$ given $\varphi'(g)^{-1} \bmod p$. Since $p^k \mid p^{2k}$, the congruence (5) also holds modulo p^k, and

$$h \equiv g - \varphi(g)\varphi'(g)^{-1} \equiv g \bmod p^k$$

because $\varphi(g)$ vanishes modulo p^k. This proves the second assertion.

For the first one, we make use of the Taylor expansion given by Lemma 9.20 of φ around g by substituting h for y:

$$\begin{aligned} \varphi(h) &= \varphi(g) + \varphi'(g)(h-g) + \psi(h-g) \cdot (h-g)^2 \\ &\equiv \varphi(g) + \varphi'(g)(h-g) \equiv \varphi(g) + \varphi'(g) \cdot (-\varphi(g)\varphi'(g)^{-1}) \equiv 0 \bmod p^{2k}. \end{aligned}$$

Here, we use the fact that $p^{2k} \mid (h-g)^2$ by the second assertion, and $\psi(h-g)$ is, of course, ψ with $h-g$ substituted for y.

The last claim is a simple consequence of the second one: since $h \equiv g \bmod p^k$, we have $h \equiv g \bmod p$, which in turn implies $\psi(h) \equiv \psi(g) \bmod p$ for any $\psi \in R[y]$, in particular for $\psi = \varphi'$. This is just a special case of a general principle: Since the reduction map modulo p is a ring homomorphism, it commutes with the ring operations $+$ and $\cdot$, and hence with any polynomial over R. $\square$

For a prime element p in a Euclidean domain R, the condition that $\varphi'(g)$ be invertible modulo p is equivalent to $\varphi'(g) \not\equiv 0 \bmod p$.

Note the similarities of the p-adic Newton iteration below to the Newton iteration for inversion (Algorithm 9.10).

ALGORITHM 9.22 p-adic Newton iteration.
Input: $\varphi \in R[y]$, where R is a ring (commutative, with 1), $p \in R$, $l \in \mathbb{N}_{>0}$, $g_0 \in R$ a starting solution, with $\varphi(g_0) \equiv 0 \bmod p$ and $\varphi'(g_0)$ invertible modulo p, and a modular inverse s_0 of $\varphi'(g_0)$ modulo p.
Output: $g \in R$ with $\varphi(g) \equiv 0 \bmod p^l$ and $g \equiv g_0 \bmod p$.

1. $r \longleftarrow \lceil \log l \rceil$

2. **for** $1 \le i < r$ compute $g_i, s_i \in R$ such that

$$g_i \equiv g_{i-1} - \varphi(g_{i-1})s_{i-1} \bmod p^{2^i}, \quad s_i \equiv 2s_{i-1} - \varphi'(g_i)s_{i-1}^2 \bmod p^{2^i}$$

{ The second computation is the ith execution of step 2 in the Newton iteration of Algorithm 9.10 for the inversion of $\varphi'(g_i)$ }

3. compute $g \in R$ with $g \equiv g_{r-1} - \varphi(g_{r-1})s_{r-1} \bmod p^l$
   return g

THEOREM 9.23.
Algorithm 9.22 works correctly.

PROOF. Let $g_r \equiv g_{r-1} - \varphi(g_{r-1})s_{r-1} \bmod p^{2^r}$. Then $g \equiv g_r \bmod p^l$, and it is sufficient to show the invariants

$$g_i \equiv g_0 \bmod p, \quad \varphi(g_i) \equiv 0 \bmod p^{2^i}, \quad s_i \equiv \varphi'(g_i)^{-1} \bmod p^{2^i} \text{ if } i < r$$

for $0 \le i \le r$ by induction on i. The case $i = 0$ is clear, and we assume that $i > 0$. Then the induction hypotheses imply that $p^{2^{i-1}}$ divides both $\varphi(g_{i-1})$ and $s_{i-1} - \varphi'(g_{i-1})^{-1}$, and hence p^{2^i} divides their product. Thus

$$g_i \equiv g_{i-1} - \varphi(g_{i-1})s_{i-1} \equiv g_{i-1} - \varphi(g_{i-1})\varphi'(g_{i-1})^{-1} \bmod p^{2^i},$$

and the first two invariants follow from Lemma 9.21 with $g = g_{i-1}$, $h = g_i$, and $k = 2^{i-1}$. If $i < r$, then $g_i \equiv g_{i-1} \bmod p^{2^{i-1}}$ implies that

$$\varphi'(g_i)^{-1} \equiv \varphi'(g_{i-1})^{-1} \equiv s_{i-1} \bmod p^{2^{i-1}}.$$

Now s_i is obtained by one Newton step for inversion, as in Algorithm 9.3, and the third invariant follows. $\square$

When $R = \mathbb{Z}$ or $R = F[x]$ for a field F and $p \in R$ is prime or irreducible, respectively, then finding a starting solution means computing a root of a polynomial in the field $K = R/\langle p \rangle$. We discuss this problem when K is finite or $K = \mathbb{Q}$ in Part III of this book.

EXAMPLE 9.24. (i) We take $R = \mathbb{Z}$ and $p = 5$, and determine a nontrivial solution (different from ± 1) of the equation $g^4 \equiv 1 \bmod 625$, so that $\varphi = y^4 - 1$. For a starting solution we can use $g_0 = 2$, since $\varphi(2) \equiv 0 \bmod 5$ (for example, by Fermat's little theorem) and $\varphi'(2) = 4 \cdot 2^3 \equiv 2 \not\equiv 0 \bmod 5$. Thus $s_0 \equiv 2^{-1} \equiv 3 \bmod 5$,

$$
\begin{aligned}
g_1 &\equiv g_0 - \varphi(g_0)s_0 = 2 - 15 \cdot 3 \equiv 7 \bmod 25, \\
s_1 &\equiv 2s_0 - \varphi'(g_1)s_0^2 = 2 \cdot 3 - 1372 \cdot 3^2 \equiv 8 \bmod 25, \\
g &\equiv g_1 - \varphi(g_1)s_1 \equiv 7 - 2400 \cdot 8 \equiv 182 \bmod 625,
\end{aligned}
$$

and indeed $182^4 = 1 + 1755519 \cdot 625$.

(ii) We take $R = \mathbb{F}_3[x]$ and $p = x$, and determine a square root g of the polynomial $f = x + 1$ modulo x^4 that satisfies $g(0) = -1$. Here $\varphi = y^2 - f \in \mathbb{F}_3[x][y]$, and $g_0 = -1$ can serve as a starting solution, since $g_0(0) = -1$, $\varphi(g_0) = -x \equiv 0 \bmod x$, and $\varphi'(g_0) = 2g_0 = 1 \not\equiv 0 \bmod x$. Thus $s_0 = 1$,

$$
\begin{aligned}
g_1 &\equiv g_0 - \varphi(g_0)s_0 = -1 - (-x) \cdot 1 = x - 1 \bmod x^2, \\
s_1 &\equiv 2s_0 - \varphi'(g_1)s_0^2 = 2 \cdot 1 - 2(x - 1) \cdot 1^2 = x + 1, \\
g &\equiv g_1 - \varphi(g_1)s_1 = x - 1 - x^2(x + 1) = -x^3 - x^2 + x - 1 \bmod x^4,
\end{aligned}
$$

and a calculation shows $(-x^3 - x^2 + x - 1)^2 = (x + 1) + x^4(x^2 - x - 1)$. $\Diamond$

THEOREM 9.25.

When $R = D[x]$ for a ring D (commutative, with 1), $p = x$, $g_0 \in D$, $l \in \mathbb{N}$ is a power of 2, and $\varphi \in R[y]$ with $\deg_y \varphi = n$ and $\deg_x \varphi < l$, then Algorithm 9.22 takes $(3n + 3/2)\mathsf{M}(l) + O(nl)$ operations in D.

PROOF. Reducing modulo x^{2^i} where possible, we may assume that the degrees of s_i and g_i are less than 2^i for all i. At first, we compute φ', taking $nl = n2^r$ operations in D. In step 2, we compute $\varphi(g_{i-1})$ and $\varphi'(g_i)$ modulo x^{2^i} using Horner's rule, at a total cost of $2n-1$ multiplications and the same number of additions modulo x^{2^i}, or $(2n-1)(\mathsf{M}(2^i)+2^i)$ operations in D. Computing g_i from g_{i-1}, s_{i-1}, and $\varphi(g_{i-1})$ can be done using at most $\mathsf{M}(2^{i-1})+2^{i-1} \leq \frac{1}{2}\mathsf{M}(2^i)+2^{i-1}$ operations in D: since the lower part of $\varphi(g_{i-1})$ is zero, we only need to multiply its upper part by s_{i-1} and take the negative of the lower part of the result as the upper part of g_i. Similarly, computing s_i from s_{i-1} and $\varphi'(g_i)$ takes $\mathsf{M}(2^i)+\mathsf{M}(2^{i-1})+2^{i-1} \leq \frac{3}{2}\mathsf{M}(2^i)+2^{i-1}$ operations, as in the proof of Theorem 9.4. Thus the cost for the ith iteration of step 2 is at most $(2n+1)\mathsf{M}(2^i)+2n\cdot 2^i$ operations in D, and similarly we have $(n+1/2)(\mathsf{M}(2^r)+2^r)$ operations in step 3. Now

$$\sum_{1\leq i<r}\left((2n+1)\mathsf{M}(2^i)+2n\cdot 2^i\right) \leq \left((2n+1)\mathsf{M}(2^r)+2n\cdot 2^r\right)\sum_{1\leq i<r}2^{i-r}$$
$$\leq (2n+1)\mathsf{M}(2^r)+2n\cdot 2^r,$$

and the total cost is at most

$$(3n+\frac{3}{2})\mathsf{M}(2^r)+(4n+\frac{1}{2})2^r = (3n+\frac{3}{2})\mathsf{M}(l)+(4n+\frac{1}{2})l. \quad \square$$

The more general statement when p is an arbitrary polynomial is discussed in Exercise 9.31, and the following integer analog is proven in Exercise 9.32.

▬▬ THEOREM 9.26. ▬▬▬▬▬▬▬▬▬▬▬▬▬▬▬▬▬▬▬▬▬▬▬▬▬▬▬▬▬▬▬▬▬
When $R = \mathbb{Z}$, $0 \leq g_0 < p$, and φ has degree n and coefficients absolutely less than p^l, then Algorithm 9.22 takes $O(n\mathsf{M}(l\log p))$ word operations. ▬▬▬▬▬▬▬▬

When calculating by hand, one may perform all computations in Algorithm 9.22 in the p-adic representation, since then reductions modulo powers of p are for free.

One question that did not come up with the Newton iteration algorithm for inversion is that of uniqueness of the solution. Inverses modulo p^l are unique, but solutions of an arbitrary polynomial equation $\varphi(y) = 0$ modulo p^l generally are not, because there may already be several solutions modulo p. The following theorem implies that for any $l \in \mathbb{N}_{>0}$, every starting solution gives rise to exactly one solution modulo p^l, so that there are as many solutions modulo p^l as there are modulo p (with nonvanishing φ').

▬▬ THEOREM 9.27 Uniqueness of Newton iteration. ▬▬▬▬▬▬▬▬▬▬▬▬▬▬▬▬
Let $\varphi \in R[y]$, $g \in R$ with $\varphi(g) \equiv 0 \bmod p$ and $\varphi'(g)$ invertible modulo p a starting solution, and $l \in \mathbb{N}_{>0}$. If $h, h^* \in R$ are solutions modulo p^l with $h \equiv g \equiv h^* \bmod p$ and $\varphi(h) \equiv 0 \equiv \varphi(h^*) \bmod p^l$, then $h \equiv h^* \bmod p^l$. ▬▬▬▬▬▬▬▬▬▬

PROOF. Again, we make use of the Taylor expansion of φ and get

$$\varphi(h^*) = \varphi(h) + \varphi'(h)(h^* - h) + c \cdot (h^* - h)^2$$

for some $c \in R$, or equivalently

$$\varphi(h^*) - \varphi(h) = (h^* - h)(\varphi'(h) + c \cdot (h^* - h)). \qquad (6)$$

Now

$$
\begin{aligned}
\varphi'(h) + c \cdot (h^* - h) &\equiv \varphi'(h) \bmod p && \text{(since } h^* - h \equiv 0 \bmod p) \\
&\equiv \varphi'(g) \bmod p && \text{(since } h \equiv g \bmod p).
\end{aligned}
$$

By Corollary 9.13, there exist some $s, t \in R$ such that $s \cdot (\varphi'(h) + c \cdot (h^* - h)) = 1 + tp^l$, and (6) implies that

$$s \cdot (\varphi(h^*) - \varphi(h)) - tp^l(h^* - h) = h^* - h.$$

The left hand side of this equation vanishes modulo p^l, and the claim follows. □

The conclusion of Theorem 9.27 need no longer be true if g violates the second condition for a starting solution, namely if $\varphi'(g)$ is not invertible modulo p. For example, the equation $y^4 = 0$ has only one solution $g \equiv 0$ modulo 5, but five solutions $h \equiv 0, 5, 10, 15, 20$ modulo 25 that are all congruent to 0 modulo 5. Here $\varphi = y^4$ and $\varphi'(0) \equiv 0 \bmod 5$, so that 0 is not a proper starting solution.

We will meet Newton iteration again in Chapter 15, under the name of Hensel lifting, which is used for (approximate) factorizations of polynomials.

9.5. Computing integer roots

In this section, we illustrate the prime power modular approach for solving problems over the integers with the example of computing roots of positive integers. We have introduced the concept in Chapter 5, but only now have the tool to fill in the details: Newton iteration.

Suppose that we are given positive $a, n \in \mathbb{N}$ and want to decide whether a is an nth power of an integer, and if so, we want to compute $\sqrt[n]{a} \in \mathbb{N}$. We might use numerical Newton iteration, applied to the equation $y^n - a = 0$, stop when the precision is sufficiently high, and then round to the nearest integer. A different approach is p-adic Newton iteration, where the precision management is somewhat easier.

For simplicity, we assume that n is odd (see Exercise 9.43 for square roots) and a is odd, by extracting the largest power of 2 dividing a and computing its nth root separately; if it does not have one, then a does not either. Then $1^n - a \equiv 0 \bmod 2$, and $g_0 = 1$ is a valid starting solution for the 2-adic Newton iteration to solve $\varphi(y) = y^n - a = 0$, as in Algorithm 9.22, since $\varphi'(1) = n \cdot 1^{n-1} \equiv 1 \not\equiv 0 \bmod 2$. We choose $k \in \mathbb{N}$ minimal such that $2^{nk} > a$, and after $r = \lceil \log k \rceil$ steps Algorithm 9.22 has computed $g \in \mathbb{N}$ with $\varphi(g) = g^n - a \equiv 0 \bmod 2^k$. If now $g^n = a$ in $\mathbb{Z}$, then $g = \sqrt[n]{a}$. Otherwise, we claim that a is not an nth power in $\mathbb{Z}$. To see why, we assume that we have $b \in \mathbb{N}$ with $b^n = a$. Then b is odd, $b \equiv g_0 \equiv g \bmod 2$, $0 \leq b < 2^k$, and

$$\varphi(b) = b^n - a = 0 \equiv g^n - a = \varphi(g) \bmod 2^k.$$

Now the uniqueness of Newton iteration (Theorem 9.27) yields $b \equiv g \bmod 2^k$, and since both sides are nonnegative and less than 2^k, they are equal.

In order to save computing time, we set $t_0 = 1$ in step 1 and additionally compute $t_i = g_i^{n-1} \text{ rem } 2^{2^{i+1}}$ in step 2. In the ith iteration of step 2 in Algorithm 9.22, we then calculate

$$g_i \equiv g_{i-1} - \varphi(g_{i-1})s_{i-1} \equiv g_{i-1} - (g_{i-1}t_{i-1} - a)s_{i-1} \bmod 2^{2^i}$$

with two multiplications and two additions modulo 2^{2^i}. Then we compute t_i and

$$s_i \equiv 2s_{i-1} - \varphi'(g_i)s_{i-1}^2 \equiv 2s_{i-1} - nt_i s_{i-1}^2 \bmod 2^{2^i},$$

taking three multiplications and two additions modulo 2^{2^i}. For the computation of t_i, we use repeated squaring (Section 4.3), at a cost of at most $2\log n$ multiplications modulo $2^{2^{i+1}}$. Thus the total cost for the ith iteration of step 2 is $O(\mathsf{M}(2^i)\log n)$ word operations. In the 2^{64}-ary representation, reduction modulo 2^{2^i} is essentially free.

═══ THEOREM 9.28. ═══

Let $a, n \in \mathbb{N}$ be odd, $a < 2^l$, and $3 \leq n < l$. Then the above algorithm either computes the unique positive integer $\sqrt[n]{a} \in \mathbb{N}$, or certifies that a is not an nth power in $\mathbb{Z}$, using $O(\mathsf{M}(l))$ word operations. ═══════

PROOF. Correctness is clear from the above discussion. Let $c \in \mathbb{R}_{>0}$ such that the cost for the ith iteration of step 2 of the Newton iteration algorithm 9.22 is at most $c\,\mathsf{M}(2^i)\log n$ word operations and the cost for step 3 is at most $c\,\mathsf{M}(k)\log n$. With $r = \lceil \log k \rceil$ as above, the total cost is no more than

$$c\log n\left(\mathsf{M}(k) + \sum_{1 \leq i < r} \mathsf{M}(2^i)\right) \leq c\log n\left(\mathsf{M}(k) + \mathsf{M}\left(\sum_{1 \leq i < r} 2^i\right)\right)$$

$$\leq c\log n(\mathsf{M}(k) + 2\mathsf{M}(2^{r-1})) \leq 3c\,\mathsf{M}(k)\log n.$$

Now $2^{n(k-1)} \leq a < 2^l$, by the minimality of k, and hence $k - 1 < l/n$ and $\mathsf{M}(k) \in O(\mathsf{M}(\lfloor l/n \rfloor))$. Finally, we check whether $g^n = a$ using repeated squaring, at a cost of $O(\mathsf{M}(l))$ (Exercise 9.39), which dominates the cost for the other steps. □

EXAMPLE 9.29. Let us compute $\sqrt[3]{2197}$. We may choose $k = 4$, since $2^{3 \cdot 4} = 2^{12} = 4096 > 2197$. Now $g_0 = s_0 = t_0 = 1$ and

$$
\begin{aligned}
g_1 &\equiv g_0 - (t_0 g_0 - 2197)s_0 \equiv 1 - (1-1) \equiv 1 \bmod 4, \\
t_1 &\equiv g_1^2 = 1 \bmod 16, \quad s_1 \equiv 2s_0 - 3t_1 s_0^2 = 2 - 3 \equiv 3 \bmod 4, \\
g &\equiv g_1 - (t_1 g_1 - 2197)s_1 = 1 - (1-5) \cdot 3 \equiv 13 \bmod 16,
\end{aligned}
$$

and in fact $2197 = 13^3$. ◇

In Exercise 9.44, we use this to test whether $a \in \mathbb{N}$ is a perfect power. In Sections 14.4 and 15.6, we discuss algorithms for computing integer roots of arbitrary polynomials.

9.6. Valuations, Newton iteration, and Julia sets

This section gives a general framework for Newton iteration, and presents some of the similarities and differences with the method over the real numbers. These results are not needed later. The real (or complex) iteration makes basic use of the notion of convergence. This can be carried over to numbers and polynomials, by saying that two elements are close together if their difference is divided by a large power of our prime p.

DEFINITION 9.30. A **valuation** on an integral domain R is a *map* $v: R \longrightarrow \mathbb{R}$ *which is multiplicative, subadditive, and positive definite, so that it satisfies for all* $a, b \in R$

(i) $v(ab) = v(a)v(b)$,

(ii) $v(a+b) \le v(a) + v(b)$,

(iii) $v(a) \ge 0$ *and* $v(a) = 0$ *if and only if* $a = 0$.

The following are some commonly used valuations on integers and polynomials. A ring may, of course, have more than one valuation.

EXAMPLE 9.31. (i) Let $R = \mathbb{Z}$, and $v(a) = |a|$, the **absolute value**.
(ii) With $R = \mathbb{Z}$ and p prime, let

$$
v_p(a) = \begin{cases} 0, & \text{if } a = 0, \\ p^{-n}, & \text{if } p^n \mid a \text{ and } p^{n+1} \nmid a. \end{cases}
$$

This is the **p-adic valuation**.

(iii) With $R = F[x]$, F a field, let

$$v(a) = \begin{cases} 0, & \text{if } a = 0, \\ 2^{-n}, & \text{if } x^n \mid a \text{ and } x^{n+1} \nmid a. \end{cases} \tag{7}$$

This is the **x-adic valuation**. Similarly, if $p \in F[x]$ is irreducible, we get the p-adic valuation if x is replaced by p in (7).

(iv) With $R = F[x]$, F a field, let

$$v(a) = \begin{cases} 0, & \text{if } a = 0, \\ 2^{\deg(a)}, & \text{if } a \neq 0. \end{cases}$$

This is the **degree valuation**. ◇

A similar p-adic valuation can be defined for any prime p in a UFD.

The notion of being "close together" can be expressed in terms of a valuation. In the polynomial case with valuation (iii), we use the intuition that a polynomial a is small if $x^n \mid a$ for some large n. Two polynomials a, b are close if their distance $d(a, b) = v(a - b)$ is small.

EXAMPLE 9.32. $v_3(54) = 3^{-3} = \dfrac{1}{27}$, $\quad v_3(55) = 1$, $\quad v_3(54\,000\,000) = \dfrac{1}{27}$. ◇

DEFINITION 9.33. *A **non-Archimedean valuation** is a valuation with the property of subadditivity replaced by the stronger condition that for all $a, b \in R$*

$$v(a + b) \leq \max\{v(a), v(b)\}.$$

*This is the **ultrametric inequality**.*

The p-adic valuation for integers is non-Archimedean, while the absolute value for integers is Archimedean. The Newton iteration of Algorithm 9.22 for solving polynomial equations approximately can be carried over to any non-Archimedean valuation. Lemma 9.21 reads as follows in this generality.

LEMMA 9.34. *Let v be a non-Archimedean valuation on R, with $v(a) \leq 1$ for all $a \in R$, $\varphi \in R[y]$, $0 < \varepsilon < 1$, and $g, h \in R$ with $v(\varphi(g)) \leq \varepsilon$ and $v(\varphi'(g)) = 1$, and suppose that*

$$v(h - (g - \varphi(g)/\varphi'(g))) \leq \varepsilon^2.$$

Then $v(\varphi(h)) \leq \varepsilon^2$, $v(h - g) \leq \varepsilon$, and $v(\varphi'(h)) = 1$.

PROOF. We only show the first two bounds, using the Taylor expansion (Lemma 9.20) of φ around g:

$$v(h-g) = v\left(h-g+\frac{\varphi(g)}{\varphi'(g)}-\frac{\varphi(g)}{\varphi'(g)}\right) \le \max\left\{v\left(h-g+\frac{\varphi(g)}{\varphi'(g)}\right), v\left(\frac{\varphi(g)}{\varphi'(g)}\right)\right\}$$

$$= \max\{\varepsilon^2, \varepsilon\} = \varepsilon,$$

$$v(\varphi(h)) = v(\varphi(g)+\varphi'(g)(h-g)+\psi(h-g)\cdot(h-g)^2)$$

$$= v\left(\varphi(g)-\varphi'(g)\frac{\varphi(g)}{\varphi'(g)}+\varphi'(g)\left(h-g+\frac{\varphi(g)}{\varphi'(g)}\right)+\psi(h-g)\cdot(h-g)^2\right)$$

$$\le \max\left\{v(\varphi'(g))\cdot v\left(h-g+\frac{\varphi(g)}{\varphi'(g)}\right), v(\psi(h-g))\cdot v(h-g)^2\right\}$$

$$\le \max\{1\cdot\varepsilon^2, 1\cdot\varepsilon^2\} = \varepsilon^2. \ \square$$

The division by $\varphi'(g)$ in the above formulas leads, in principle, out of the ring R. There are three ways of dealing with this problem: we can replace $\varphi'(g)^{-1}$ by a sufficiently good approximation in R, as computed by Algorithm 9.10, or we can extend v to the field of fractions of R, by setting $v(a/b) = v(a)/v(b)$ if $b \ne 0$, or we can multiply by $\varphi'(g)$, where necessary, and conclude from $v(\varphi'(g)) = 1$ that the valuations do not change.

Newton iteration in $R = \mathbb{Q}$ for solving $y^2 - 2 = 0$ and starting with $g_0 = 2$ leads to better and better rational approximations to the root. But $\sqrt{2}$ itself is not a rational number; in order to capture such an exact root, the domain has to be enlarged, say to $\mathbb{R}$.

A similar phenomenon happens with the p-adic valuations on $\mathbb{Z}$ or $F[x]$. One can enlarge these rings to their **completions**, namely to the ring $\mathbb{Z}_{(p)}$ of p-adic integers or the ring $F[[x]]$ of formal power series (for the x-adic valuation), and in these larger rings Newton iteration converges to an exact root. We do not go into details, since these quantities cannot be represented in a finite manner, and these rings are mainly of conceptual interest to computer algebra. One can finitely represent initial segments of them, say $a \bmod p^l$ for $a \in \mathbb{Z}_{(p)}$, but that is essentially the same as some integer modulo p^l.

Newton iteration for inversion tells us what the units are in these rings. An element $a = a_0 + a_1 p + a_2 p^2 + \cdots \in \mathbb{Z}_{(p)}$, with $a_0, a_1, a_2, \ldots \in \{0, \ldots, p-1\}$, is a unit if and only if $a_0 \bmod p$ is a unit in $\mathbb{Z}_p$, that is, if and only if $a_0 \ne 0$. The power series $a = a_0 + a_1 x + a_2 x^2 + \cdots \in F[[x]]$, with $a_0, a_1, a_2, \ldots \in F$ is a unit in $F[[x]]$ if and only if $a_0 \ne 0$. As an example, $1 - x \in F[[x]]$ is a unit, with inverse $1 + x + x^2 + \cdots$.

Although derived from the real Newton iteration, with the absolute value on $\mathbb{Q}$ or $\mathbb{R}$ or $\mathbb{C}$, the integer and polynomial variants are more powerful in one sense. Namely, as a starting condition, it suffices to have a rough approximation g with $v(\varphi(g)) < 1$ or $\varphi(g) \equiv 0 \bmod p$ plus a condition on $\varphi'(g)$; in fact this is necessary and sufficient. In $\mathbb{R}$ or $\mathbb{C}$, no such simple and general conditions are known. Indeed, the problem of "good" starting points is difficult, as seen in the simple case of finding the three roots $1, e^{2\pi i/3}, e^{4\pi i/3} \in \mathbb{C}$ of $\varphi = y^3 - 1$.

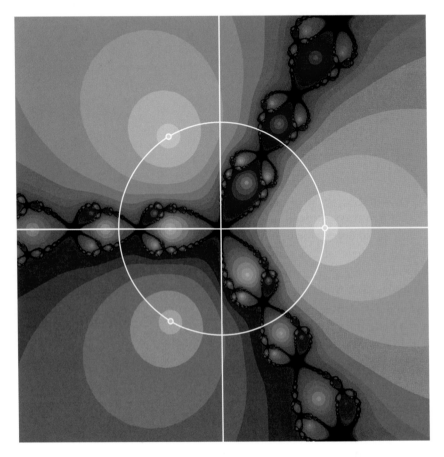

FIGURE 9.2: Convergence of Newton iteration to solve $y^3 = 1$ over $\mathbb{C}$.

In Figure 9.2, the three roots are marked in red, green, and blue, and also each point converging to them via the Newton iteration. Brightness corresponds to the "convergence speed": the brighter the color of a point, the earlier does Newton iteration starting at that point approach its final limit. The intricacy of the picture illustrates the difficulty of finding a simple rule guaranteeing convergence.

This problem is part of a larger question: given an iteration function $g_{i+1} = \psi(g_i)$, determine the behavior for any starting value g_0. For example, for which g_0 does this converge at all? The set of all these g_0 is called the **Julia set** of ψ, after the French mathematician Gaston Julia who first studied it. These sets are highly complicated and provide stunning pictures. Their study is mainly a part of *dynamical systems theory*. The beautiful mathematical theory of chaos and fractals

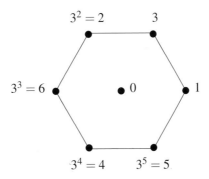

FIGURE 9.3: Representation of $\mathbb{Z}_7$ in Figure 9.4.

is described and richly illustrated in Mandelbrot (1977) and Peitgen, Jürgens & Saupe (1992).

In Figure 9.4, we see the analog of Figure 9.2 over $\mathbb{Z}_{(7)}$, the set of 7-adic integers. The seven elements of $\mathbb{Z}_7$ are arranged as in Figure 9.3, and $\mathbb{Z}_{(7)}$ can be represented by the fractal composed of infinitely many recursive compositions of this centered hexagon. The white points are not roots of φ modulo 7 and hence do not converge to a root of $\varphi = x^3 - 1$. All other points converge to the root of f of their color, and brightness corresponds to convergence speed. The three roots of φ in $\mathbb{Z}_{(7)}$, whose sum equals 0, are $1, 2 + 4 \cdot 7 + 6 \cdot 7^2 + 3 \cdot 7^3 + \cdots$, and $4 + 2 \cdot 6 + 0 \cdot 7^2 + 3 \cdot 7^3 + \cdots$.

9.7. Implementations of fast arithmetic

In this book you can learn some of the fundamental algorithms in computer algebra, with an emphasis on the modern fast methods that one needs to solve large problems. The enterprising reader might now say to herself: "Ok, so let's do it. Let's build a computer algebra system." But that is a tall order. Not only does it require an enormous effort of dozens (or hundreds) of woman-years, but it also needs many tools that cannot even be mentioned in this book. Some of them become apparent as soon as you start up your favorite system on your own machine.

Nevertheless, we present in this section some notes on implementations, mainly a case study of two software packages, one designed by Victor Shoup and the other one by the authors. These packages are rather limited in scope; Shoup's basically provides fast arithmetic for polynomials and matrices over finite fields and the integers, and ours only works over $\mathbb{F}_2$. The fact that even the latter modest goal requires about $10\,000$ lines of code indicates the amount of effort necessary to implement carefully the basic algorithms.

The framework for determining the (arithmetic) cost of our algorithms is *asymptotic analysis*, with a typical statement like "$O(n \log n \log \log n)$ operations" for multiplication. This is a powerful, reliable, and universal tool for comparing algorithms. For any new algorithm, an improvement of the previously known asym-

FIGURE 9.4: Convergence of Newton iteration to solve $y^3 = 1$ over the 7-adic integers.

ptotic estimates is sufficient justification of its relevance; however, such improvements are hard to come by for well-studied problems. This section describes some of the additional efforts that have to supplement the asymptotic analysis for any practical implementation.

By its nature, the flavor of this section is rather different from the rest of the book (except that in Section 15.7 we continue this report on implementations). Many of our algorithms are (hopefully) of long-lasting interest, but the computer timings reported now will be out of date before the book goes to press.

The first lesson in implementing a software package for fast integer or polynomial arithmetic is that a large variety of algorithms have to be coded and tested to determine the **crossover points**. These are the input sizes at which one algorithm beats another one. A typical experience is that, say for multiplication, the classical method is best for small inputs, Karatsuba's algorithm takes over for intermediate sizes, and a fast, for example, an FFT-based method, excels for large problems.

The second lesson is that just casting the algorithms "from the book" into software will not work well. One has to understand the algorithmic ideas in depth and use a multitude of tricks and special relations to make things go at lightning speed. Only a few of these methods can be explained here; fortunately, there is no limit to the ingenuity of the programmer (except for having to complete the project in some reasonable time frame).

Several factors determine whether a software package for (integer or polynomial) arithmetic is fast in practice. Besides choosing the algorithms and determining the crossover points between various methods, one has to design suitable data types, exploit fast hardware arithmetic whenever possible, and customize for specific types and sizes of problems.

Currently, there are—besides implementations in any general purpose computer algebra system—several libraries available for arbitrary precision integer arithmetic and univariate polynomial arithmetic over finite fields, $\mathbb{Z}$, $\mathbb{Q}$, algebraic number fields, $\mathbb{R}$, and $\mathbb{C}$ (among others GNU MP, PARI, LIDIA), but only few that implement the fast algorithms presented in Chapters 8 through 11. Among them are LIP by Arjen Lenstra and Paul Leyland (the library and a description can be obtained via anonymous ftp from `ftp.ox.ac.uk/pub/math/freelip`), the package of Schönhage, Grotefeld & Vetter (1994) (see also Reischert 1995), NTL by Shoup (an early version is described in Shoup 1995), and BIPOLAR (Binary Polynomial Arithmetic) by von zur Gathen & Gerhard (1996). The last two of these will be described below.

The C++ library BIPOLAR was designed and optimized for univariate polynomial factorization over $\mathbb{F}_2$. This is a very narrow focus, but we use it to explain some general principles. The first question when writing the package was the choice of *data types*. When programming on top of an existing package, one may not have much choice. Experience has shown that for high performance code, one should represent algebraic data as compactly as possible, since all linear operations like addition or copying take time proportional to the length of the representation (that is, the number of machine words it occupies in memory). Thus, on a machine with a word size of 32 bit, we represent polynomials over $\mathbb{F}_2$ as arrays of 32 bit words; each word contains 32 consecutive coefficients. In this representation, all linear-time operations are straightforward to implement, and the next task is to tackle the nontrivial arithmetic operations, starting with multiplication.

We have five methods at our disposal:

○ table lookup,

○ classical multiplication,

○ Karatsuba's algorithm,

○ an algorithm by Cantor (1989),

○ FFT-based algorithms.

We did not experiment with the last one. As explained above, each method typically has its range of input sizes where it beats the other methods. One has to implement many variations of these approaches and test them to determine the best one for each range, starting with the small ranges. A typical outcome then is a **hybrid** algorithm where one performs, say, first a few Karatsuba steps and then classical multiplication on small arguments. As an example, for **single precision** polynomials of degree less than 32 we found the following to work best: two stages of Karatsuba's algorithm plus table lookup for the 9 resulting multiplications at degrees less than 8; the size of the table is $2^8 \cdot 2^8 \cdot 16$ bits or 128 kilobytes. (Unfortunately, there is no hardware support for multiplication in $\mathbb{F}_2[x]$ on general purpose microprocessors—there is no possibility to sever the "carry" line—and one has to implement the single precision multiplication in software.) On top of this, both the classical algorithm 2.3 and Karatsuba's algorithm 8.1 are implemented at machine word level, that is, with base x^{32} instead of x; the block sizes are multiples of 32 and recursion in the latter algorithm stops as soon as the polynomials are of degree less than 32.

We also implemented an algorithm by Cantor (1989) for multiplication in $\mathbb{F}_2[x]$, which uses evaluation and interpolation at linear subspaces of $\mathbb{F}_{2^m}$ for some $m \in \mathbb{N}$ and is similar to the FFT based methods from Chapter 8. Its running time is $O(n(\log n)^{1.59})$ arithmetic operations in $\mathbb{F}_2$. For practical purposes, we may take $m = 32$, so that one element of $\mathbb{F}_{2^m}$ fits precisely into a machine word. Here the single precision operations are multiplications in $\mathbb{F}_{2^{16}}$ and $\mathbb{F}_{2^{32}}$. Again, we might have implemented these by doing one polynomial multiplication in the way described above and one subsequent division with remainder, but we have chosen a different approach using tables based on the multiplicative structure of finite fields, as in Pollard (1971) and Montgomery (1991). We take a fixed generator g of the multiplicative group $\mathbb{F}_{2^{16}}^{\times}$, and compute two tables for the exponentiation map $\{0, \ldots, 2^{16} - 2\} \longrightarrow \mathbb{F}_{2^{16}}^{\times}$, with $a \longmapsto g^a$, and its inverse. Two nonzero elements $c, d \in \mathbb{F}_{2^{16}}$ are multiplied by determining $a, b \in \{0, \ldots, 2^{16} - 2\}$ such that $c = g^a$ and $d = g^b$, and computing $cd = g^{a+b}$. This amounts to essentially one addition modulo $2^{16} - 1$ and three table lookups; the size of each table is $2^{16} \cdot 16$ bits or 128 KB. Inversion in $\mathbb{F}_{2^{16}}^{\times}$ is done similarly. One multiplication in $\mathbb{F}_{2^{32}}$ is reduced to three multiplications in $\mathbb{F}_{2^{16}}$ à la Karatsuba; this requires a change of basis.

After determining the best (that is, the fastest) routines for single precision arithmetic, we implemented the three multiplication algorithms mentioned above for multiprecision polynomials. An important aspect here is space considerations: due to the overhead involved in dynamic storage management, one should try to limit dynamic allocation whenever possible. When starting with two polynomials of length at most 2^k machine words each, one can implement Karatsuba's algorithm so as to use at most 2^{k+2} words of work space. In our implementation, we preallocate this amount of storage and free it again at the end of the computation. Both the multipoint evaluation and the interpolation in Cantor's algorithm can be implemented **in place**, which means that the output is returned in the space of the input, and no additional work space (besides a constant number of registers) is

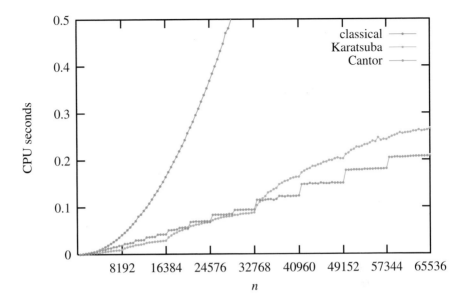

FIGURE 9.5: Multiplication of polynomials in $\mathbb{F}_2[x]$ of degree $n-1$ in BIPOLAR.

required (the same is true for the FFT; see Figure 8.5). Figure 9.5 gives running times for the three multiplication algorithms. The experiments in this section were run on a Sparc Ultra 1 with 167 MHz. The timings shown are the average of 10 pseudorandom inputs; the relative standard deviation was less than 10% (except in some cases where the time was less than 0.01 seconds).

The recursive algorithms work particularly well at degrees just below a power of 2, and a direct implementation gives a picture with large steps at these powers of 2. In Figure 9.5 you can see the effect of several tricks that have made the behavior of Karatsuba's algorithm quite smooth, and for Cantor's algorithm have broken the big step between $2^{15}-1$ and 2^{15} (to $2^{16}-1$) into five smaller steps.

The crossover points between the algorithms are near degree 500 for Karatsuba's algorithm, and near degree 33 000 for Cantor's algorithm (see Figure 9.5). After determining these, we have built a hybrid multiplication algorithm which compares the degrees of the input polynomials to the two crossover degrees and then decides which of the three algorithms to use. Its performance can be seen in Table 9.6.

We have to stress that here (and in all our implementation discussions) the timings and crossover points depend on *our* efforts and on *our* computing environment. We expect our software to perform quite well on other similar processors, but for example to use the power of true 64 bit machines one would have to start all over again—at least for the single precision arithmetic. The one universal truth is that a well-done implementation is very labor-intensive and requires close familiarity with the algorithmics.

n	CPU seconds
512	0.0004
1024	0.0006
2048	0.0014
4096	0.0038
8192	0.0110
16 384	0.0329
32 768	0.0971
65 536	0.2135
131 072	0.4666
262 144	1.0218
524 288	2.2330
1 048 576	4.9560

TABLE 9.6: Multiplication of polynomials in $\mathbb{F}_2[x]$ of degree $n-1$ in BIPOLAR using the hybrid algorithm.

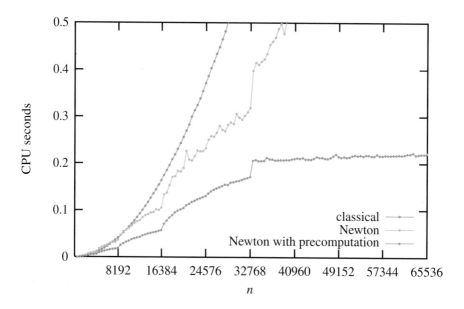

FIGURE 9.7: Division of a polynomial in $\mathbb{F}_2[x]$ of degree $2n-2$ by a polynomial of degree $n-1$ with remainder in BIPOLAR.

For division with remainder in $\mathbb{F}_2[x]$, we first wrote single precision routines for both the classical algorithm and Newton inversion, working at the bit level. On top of these, we implemented multiprecision versions working at machine word level (Algorithm 2.5 with base x^{32} instead of x, and Algorithm 9.3 followed by essentially two polynomial multiplications). The asymptotically fast division algorithm uses the hybrid multiplication algorithm as a subroutine. Figure 9.7 shows some experiments; the crossover point between the two algorithms (the top two curves) is near degree 10 000.

In some applications, in particular in modular arithmetic and polynomial factorization, many remainder computations modulo a fixed divisor $f \in \mathbb{F}_2[x]$ have to be performed. In that case, $\text{rev}(f)^{-1} \bmod x^{\deg f}$ can be precomputed using Algorithm 9.3 and stored, and then one remainder computation amounts to essentially two polynomial multiplications of degree about $\deg f$. When counting only the latter, the crossover point drops to about 4000 (Figure 9.7). Further optimization is possible when $\deg f$ is above the crossover degree for Cantor multiplication, which reduces the time for one remainder computation modulo f to essentially the time for a polynomial multiplication of the same size. Similar optimizations are possible when many modular multiplications $gh \text{ rem } f$ with both f and h fixed are performed.

BIPOLAR also implements the Extended Euclidean Algorithm and polynomial factorization routines for $\mathbb{F}_2[x]$; the latter will be discussed in Section 15.7.

The integer arithmetic of Shoup's NTL is highly optimized. On a processor with a word length of 32 bits, arbitrary precision integers are represented as arrays of machine words, where—depending on the underlying hardware—between 26 and 30 consecutive bits of the binary representation are packed into one machine word. Multiplication and division of such single precision integers is done by cleverly employing the hardware floating point arithmetic, which in most currently available microprocessors is considerably faster than hardware integer arithmetic.

NTL uses classical integer multiplication for integers of size up to about 500 bits, and Karatsuba's algorithm for larger integers. Other arithmetic operations like division with remainder and the Extended Euclidean Algorithm are all done in the classical way.

We have implemented the classical algorithm 2.4, Karatsuba's algorithm 8.1, the three primes FFT algorithm 8.25, and the algorithm of Schönhage & Strassen (1971) for integer multiplication using low-level routines of NTL version 1.5. Figure 9.8 gives running times for our implementations and the built-in routine of NTL. We have not invested much effort into optimizing our routines, and the timings of our Karatsuba implementation are at most twice as large as those of NTL's routine. The graphs for the algorithms which are not FFT-based are quite smooth, while we have large steps near powers of 2 for the three primes FFT and Schönhage & Strassen's algorithm. These steps may be smoothed with some additional effort, but we have not tried this.

For multiplying polynomials over $\mathbb{Z}$ and $\mathbb{Z}_m$ with $m \in \mathbb{Z}$, NTL implements the classical algorithm for small degrees and coefficient sizes, Karatsuba's algorithm for polynomials of medium degree, and the FFT-based modular approach described in Section 8.4 and a variant of Algorithm 8.20 using FFT modulo Fermat numbers (Exercise 8.36) for larger polynomials. Figures 9.9 through 9.11 show running times for various degrees and coefficient sizes in NTL. For division with remainder, NTL uses the classical algorithm for polynomials of small degree, and Newton inversion (Algorithm 9.3) for higher degree polynomials.

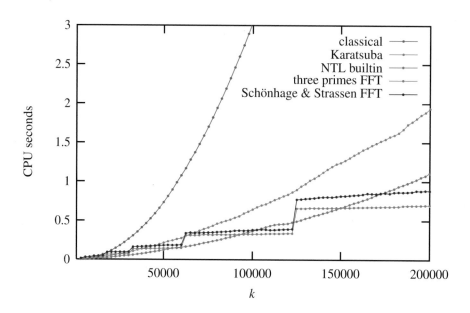

FIGURE 9.8: Multiplication of *k*-bit integers in NTL.

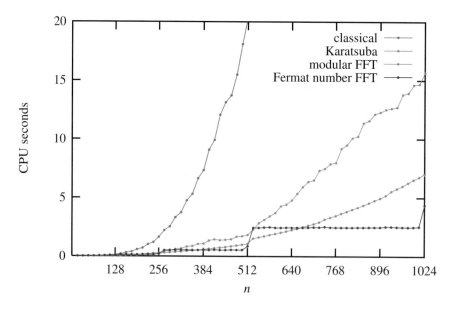

FIGURE 9.9: Multiplication of polynomials of degree $n - 1$ with n bit integer coefficients in NTL.

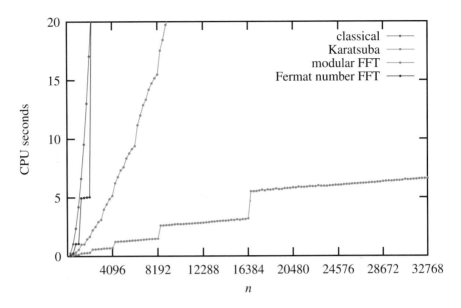

FIGURE 9.10: Multiplication of polynomials of degree $n - 1$ with 64 bit integer coefficients in NTL.

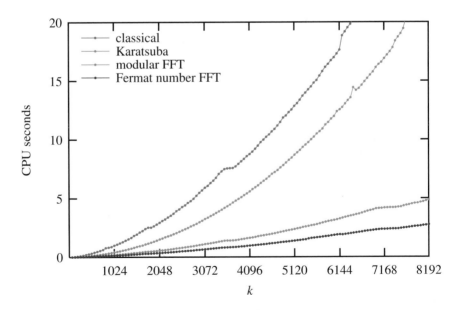

FIGURE 9.11: Multiplication of polynomials of degree 63 with k bit integer coefficients in NTL.

Besides basic arithmetic for multiprecision integers, floating point numbers, finite fields, and univariate polynomials and matrices over these domains, the recent version 3.1 of NTL includes routines for primality testing (Chapter 18), Chinese remaindering (Chapters 5 and 10), computing greatest common divisors (Chapters 3 and 6), factorization of univariate polynomials (Part III), computing reduced bases in lattices over $\mathbb{Z}$ (Chapter 16), and much more. The polynomial factorization routines will be discussed in Section 15.7. NTL is a C++ library and can be downloaded from Victor Shoup's homepage http://www.cs.wisc.edu/~shoup/. We recommend this package to anybody who is not ready to reinvent the wheel.

Notes.   9.1. Cook (1966) devised a division algorithm for integers that costs the same number of word operations as a multiplication, up to a constant factor. Sieveking (1972), Strassen (1973a), Kung (1974), and Borodin & Moenck (1974) gave analogous algorithms for polynomials. For the details of the division method for integers, see Knuth (1998), Algorithm 4.3.3 R, and Aho, Hopcroft & Ullman (1974), §8.2. Schönhage has given a method for division with remainder of polynomials of degree n with $3.75\,M(n)$ operations, at least in the so-called nonscalar model (see Kalorkoti 1993 and Bürgisser, Clausen & Shokrollahi 1996, Corollary 2.26 and Notes 2.8).

9.2. Algorithm 9.14 is from von zur Gathen (1990a).

9.3. The Taylor expansion goes back to Taylor (1715) and Maclaurin (1742), and is already in Newton (1710) for $\varphi = y^n$.

9.4 and 9.5. The formulas of Newton's iteration for square and cube roots were known by the Babylonians, and appear in the 6th century Indian text Āryabhaṭīya. Muhammad al-Khwārizmī described the Newton iteration for square roots around 830 (see Folkerts 1997). Jamshīd Al-Kāshī, who lived in Samarkand in the early 15th century, had used a single Newton step for root finding. Both one- and two-dimensional Newton iteration is explicitly described in Waring (1770). The history of Newton's method is traced in Goldstine (1977), §2.4. Cauchy (1847) describes the arithmetic Newton iteration for finding, from a root of an integer polynomial modulo m, roots modulo m^2, m^3, ... Bach & Sorenson (1993) and Bernstein (1998b) present efficient tests whether an integer is a perfect power.

9.7. Von zur Gathen & Gerhard (1996) describe an extension of Cantor's (1989) algorithm. Montgomery (1992) discusses algorithms and implementation results for fast integer arithmetic, in the context of factoring with the elliptic curve method.

Exercises.

9.1 Use Newton iteration to compute $f^{-1} \bmod x^8$ for $f = x^2 - 2x + 1 \in \mathbb{Q}[x]$.

9.2 Compute $94^{-1} \bmod 6561$ using Newton iteration.

9.3 Let $a = x^7 + 2x^4 - 1$ and $b = x^3 + 2x^2 - 3x - 1$ in $\mathbb{Q}[x]$. Compute the quotient and remainder of the division of a by b. Trace by hand the "fast" algorithm for division with remainder on this example.

9.4$\longrightarrow$ Let $a = 30x^7 + 31x^6 + 32x^5 + 33x^4 + 34x^3 + 35x^2 + 36x + 37$ and $b = 17x^3 + 18x^2 + 19x + 20$ in $\mathbb{F}_{101}[x]$, and $f \in \mathbb{F}_{101}[x]$ the reversal of b.

  (i) Compute $f^{-1} \bmod x^4$.

  (ii) Use (i) to find $q, r \in \mathbb{F}_{101}[x]$ with $a = qb + r$ and $\deg r < 3$.

(iii) Use the Extended Euclidean Algorithm to find a^{-1} mod b, that is, a polynomial $c \in \mathbb{F}_{101}[x]$ of degree less than 3 with $ac \equiv 1$ mod b.

(iv) Use Newton iteration to find a^{-1} mod b^4.

9.5 Let D be a ring (commutative, with 1) and $f, g \in D[x]$ monic of degree $n > 0$.

(i) Prove that $\text{rev}(fg)^{-1}$ rem x^{2n} can be computed from $\text{rev}(f)^{-1}$ rem x^n, $\text{rev}(g)^{-1}$ rem x^n, and fg using $2\mathsf{M}(n) + \mathsf{M}(2n) + O(n)$ arithmetic operations in D.

(ii) Prove that $\text{rev}(f)^{-1}$ rem x^n can be computed from $\text{rev}(fg)^{-1}$ rem x^{2n} using $\mathsf{M}(n) + O(n)$ operations in D.

9.6* Consider the following variant of the Newton inversion algorithm 9.3. Instead of computing f^{-1} mod x^{2^i} for $i = 1, 2, \ldots$, compute the inverse modulo $x^{\lceil l/2^r \rceil}, x^{\lceil l/2^{r-1} \rceil}, \ldots, x^{\lceil l/2 \rceil}, x^l$. Show that the cost of this algorithm is at most $l + \sum_{1 \le j \le r}(\mathsf{M}(\lceil l2^{-j} \rceil) + \mathsf{M}(\lceil l2^{-j-1} \rceil))$. Use $\lceil l2^{-j} \rceil \le \lfloor l2^{-j} \rfloor + 1$ for all j and Exercise 8.34 to conclude that the overall cost is at most $3\mathsf{M}(l) + O(l)$.

9.7 Let D be a ring (commutative, with 1), $R = D[x]$, $p \in R$ monic nonconstant, $r \in \mathbb{N}$, and $f \in R$ of degree less than $n = 2^r \deg p$.

(i) Show that $p^2, p^4, \ldots, p^{2^r}$ can be computed with $\mathsf{M}(n) + O(n)$ ring operations in D.

(ii) Prove that given the polynomials from (i), $\text{rev}(p)^{-1}$ rem $x^{\deg p}$, $\text{rev}(p^2)^{-1}$ rem $x^{2\deg p}$, $\ldots$, $\text{rev}(p^{2^r})^{-1}$ rem x^n can be computed using at most $4\mathsf{M}(n) + O(n)$ operations in D. Hint: Exercise 9.5.

(iii) Given the data from (i) and (ii), show that f rem $p^{2^{r-1}}$, f rem $p^{2^{r-2}}, \ldots, f$ rem p^2, f rem p can be computed with $2\mathsf{M}(n) + O(n)$ operations in D.

(iv) Show that when $R = \mathbb{Z}$ and $f, p \in \mathbb{N}$ with $f < 2^r p$, you can compute $p^2, p^4, \ldots, p^{2^r}$ and f rem $p^{2^{r-1}}$, f rem $p^{2^{r-2}}, \ldots, f$ rem p^2, f rem p using $O(\mathsf{M}(2^r \log p))$ word operations.

9.8 (i) Prove that the Newton inversion algorithm 9.3 works correctly as specified.

(ii) Use Exercise 9.7 to show that the algorithm takes $14\mathsf{M}(l \deg p) + O(l \deg p)$ ring operations in D if $R = D[x]$ for a (commutative) ring D, p is monic, l is a power of 2, and $\deg f < l \deg p$, and $O(\mathsf{M}(l \log p))$ word operations if $R = \mathbb{Z}$ and $|f| < p^l$.

9.9 We consider the linear variant of the Newton inversion algorithm 9.3, where the inverse is computed successively modulo $x^2, x^3, x^4, \ldots, x^l$. If g_i is the inverse modulo x^i, give an explicit formula for the coefficient of x^i in g_{i+1} in terms of the coefficients of g_i and the first $i + 1$ coefficients of f. Show that this algorithm takes $O(l^2)$ ring operations.

9.10 Show that the cost of the Newton inversion algorithm 9.3 drops to at most $2\mathsf{M}(l)$ arithmetic operations if char $D = 2$.

9.11* Let D be a (commutative) ring, $k \in \mathbb{N}_{>0}$, and $f, g \in D[x]$ with $f(0) = 1$ and $fg \equiv 1$ mod x^k.

(i) Let $d \in \mathbb{N}$, $e = 1 - fg$, and $h = g \cdot (e^{d-1} + e^{d-2} + \cdots + e + 1)$. Prove that $fh \equiv 1$ mod x^{dk}.

(ii) Letting $d = 2$ gives precisely Algorithm 9.3. State an algorithm for Newton inversion modulo x^l with cubic convergence (that is, $d = 3$), and analyze its cost when l is a power of 3.

9.12* This exercise discusses an alternative to the fast division algorithm 9.5 for computing in residue class rings. It is an adaption of Montgomery's (1985) integer algorithm to polynomials. We let F be a field and $f, r \in F[x]$ such that f is nonconstant, $\deg r < \deg f = n$, and f and r are coprime. For $a \in F[x]$, we represent the residue class a mod $f \in R = F[x]/\langle f \rangle$ by the polynomial $a^* = ra$ rem $f \in F[x]$. This is particularly useful when performing a long computation in R, for example, a modular exponentiation.

(i) Show that $(a + b)^* = a^* + b^*$ and $(ab)^* \equiv r^{-1} a^* b^*$ mod f for all $a, b \in F[x]$.

(ii) Let $s \in F[x]$ of degree less than n be the inverse of r modulo f, so that $sr \equiv 1$ mod f. Consider the following algorithm for computing $(ab)^*$ from a^* and b^*.

▬▬ Algorithm 9.35 Montgomery multiplication. ▬▬▬▬▬▬▬▬
Input: $a^*, b^* \in F[x]$ of degrees less than n.
Output: $(ab)^* \in F[x]$.

1. $u \longleftarrow a^* b^*, \quad v \longleftarrow u \text{ rem } r$

2. $w \longleftarrow vs \text{ rem } r, \quad c^* \longleftarrow (u - wf)/r$

3. **return** c^* ▬▬

Prove that r divides $u - wf$ in step 2. Conclude that the algorithm works correctly, so that $\deg c^* < n$ and $c^* \equiv r^{-1} a^* b^* \bmod f$, if $\deg r = n - 1$.

(iii) Now let $r = x^{n-1}$ and show that the algorithm can be executed with $3\mathsf{M}(n) + n$ operations in F. You may ignore the cost for computing s. Compare this to using Newton iteration with precomputation.

(iv) Let $a \in F[x]$ of degree less than n and r as in (iii). Employ the above algorithm to show that a can be computed from a^* using $2\mathsf{M}(n) + n$ operations in F, and that conversely a^* can be computed from a using $3\mathsf{M}(n) + n$ operations if r^* is precomputed.

9.13 Let F be a field of characteristic different from 2, and $\mathsf{M}(n), \mathsf{I}(n), \mathsf{D}(n), \mathsf{S}(n)$ be the computing times for multiplying two polynomials of degree less than n, computing the inverse of a polynomial modulo x^n, division of a polynomial of degree less than $2n$ by a polynomial of degree n, and squaring a polynomial of degree less than n, respectively. Theorems 9.4 and 9.6 show that $\mathsf{I} \in O(\mathsf{M})$ and $\mathsf{D} \in O(\mathsf{M})$. The purpose of this exercise is to show that all four functions are of the same order of magnitude.

(i) Prove the identity $y^2 = \left(y^{-1} - (y+1)^{-1}\right)^{-1} - y$, and conclude that $\mathsf{S} \in O(\mathsf{I})$.

(ii) Show that $\mathsf{M} \in O(\mathsf{S})$, using the identity $fg = ((f+g)^2 - f^2 - g^2)/2$.

(iii) For a polynomial $b \in R[x]$ of degree n, relate $\text{rev}_n(b)^{-1} \bmod x^n$ to the quotient of x^{2n-1} on division by b, and conclude that $\mathsf{I} \in O(\mathsf{D})$. Conclude that $O(\mathsf{M}) = O(\mathsf{I}) = O(\mathsf{D}) = O(\mathsf{S})$.

9.14* Let $a, b, q \in \mathbb{Z}[x]$ such that $a = qb$, $\deg a = n$, and $\|a\|_\infty \leq A$. Use Mignotte's bound 6.33 and a big prime modular approach to show that q can be computed from a and b using $O^\sim(n(n + \log A))$ word operations. You may ignore the cost for finding a big prime. Use Corollary 11.10 for modular arithmetic. See also Exercises 6.26 and 10.21; the latter discusses the small primes variant.

9.15* Let $a, b \in \mathbb{Z}[x]$ such that $n = \deg a = m + \deg b$, with $n, m \in \mathbb{N}$, b is monic, and $\|a\|_\infty, \|b\|_\infty < 2^l$.

(i) Let $f = \text{rev}_{\deg b}(b) \in \mathbb{Z}[x]$. Prove that $\|g_i\|_\infty < 2^{2(i-1)+l}\|g_{i-1}\|_\infty^2$ for $1 \leq i \leq r$ in the Newton inversion algorithm 9.3.

(ii) Prove that $\sum_{0 \leq j < i} j 2^{-j} \leq 2$ for all $i \in \mathbb{N}$. Hint: Consider the formal derivative of the polynomial $\sum_{0 \leq j < i} x^j = (1 - x^i)/(1 - x) \in \mathbb{Z}[x]$.

(iii) Let $S(i) = \log \|g_i\|_\infty$ for $0 \leq i \leq r$. Conclude from (i) and (ii) that $S(i) \leq (2 + l)2^i \in O(nl)$ for all i.

(iv) Perform a similar analysis when $a, b \in R[y][x]$ are bivariate polynomials over a (commutative) ring R and b is monic with respect to x.

9.16 This exercise discusses division with remainder when the degrees of the divisor and the quotient differ significantly. Let $k, m \in \mathbb{N}$ be positive. We consider univariate polynomials over an arbitrary ring (commutative, with 1, as usual).

(i) Prove that division with remainder of a polynomial a of degree less than km by a monic polynomial b of degree m can be done in time $(2k + 1)\mathsf{M}(m) + O(km)$. Hint: Partition the dividend a into blocks of size m, and compute $\text{rev}_m(b)^{-1} \bmod x^m$ only once.

(ii) Prove that dividing a polynomial of degree $n < km$ by a monic polynomial of degree $n - m$ takes at most $(k + 3)\mathsf{M}(m) + O(km)$ ring operations. Hint: Exercise 8.35.

Determine a small value for the constant in the "O" in both cases.

9.17 Trace the generalized Taylor expansion algorithm 9.14 on computing the $(x^2 + 1)$-adic expansion of x^{15} in $\mathbb{Q}[x]$.

9.18 Use the integer variant of Algorithm 9.14 to convert the decimal integer 64 180 into hexadecimal.

9.19 This exercise discusses a divide-and-conquer variant of Horner's rule for computing Taylor expansions. Let R be a ring (commutative, with 1), $u \in R$, $n = 2^k \in \mathbb{N}$ a power of 2, and $a \in R[x]$ of degree less than n. By writing $a = a_1 x^{n/2} + a_0$ with $a_0, a_1 \in R[x]$ of degree less than $n/2$, devise a recursive algorithm which computes $a(x+u)$ and $(x+u)^n$ and takes at most $(cM(n) + O(n)) \log n$ ring operations for some constant c. (The coefficients of $a(x+u)$ are the coefficients in the Taylor expansion of a around u, by Section 5.6.) Determine a small value for c, and compare your result to Corollary 9.16.

9.20 Let R be a ring (commutative, with 1) and $a, p \in R[x]$ with $\deg p = m$ and $\deg a < km$ for some $k, m \in \mathbb{N}$. Prove that the coefficients of a can be computed from its p-adic expansion (4) using at most $(\frac{1}{2}M(km) + O(km))(1 + \log k)$ ring operations when k is a power of 2.

9.21 Prove Theorem 9.17.

9.22 Let R be a ring (commutative, with 1), $f \in R[x]$, $u \in R$ a root of f, and $g = f/(x-u)$. Prove that $f'(u) = g(u)$.

9.23 Let R be a ring (commutative, with 1), $f \in R[x]$, and $m \in R$. Prove that $(f \bmod m)' = f' \bmod m$.

9.24 Let R be a ring (commutative, with 1), $f, g \in R[x]$, and $n \in \mathbb{N}$. Prove that $f \equiv g \bmod x^{n+1}$ implies $f' \equiv g' \bmod x^n$, and give an example where $f' \equiv g' \bmod x^{n+1}$ does not hold.

9.25 Let $n \in \mathbb{N}$, R be a ring such that $n!$ is a unit in R, $f \in R[x]$ of degree n, and $f = \sum_{0 \leq i \leq n} f_i \cdot (x-u)^i$ its Taylor expansion around some $u \in R$. Prove that $f_i = f^{(i)}(u)/i!$ for all i, where $f^{(i)}$ is the ith derivative of f.

9.26 Let R be a ring (commutative, with 1, as usual). For $k \in \mathbb{N}$, the kth **Hasse–Teichmüller derivative** $f^{[k]}$ of a polynomial $\sum_{0 \leq i \leq n} f_i x^i \in R[x]$ is defined as

$$f^{[k]} = \sum_{k \leq i \leq n} f_i \binom{i}{k} x^{i-k} \in R[x].$$

Let y be another indeterminate. Show that f has the Taylor expansion $f(x) = \sum_{0 \leq i \leq n} f^{[i]}(y) \cdot (x-y)^i$ around y.

9.27 Let R be a ring (commutative, with 1), $f_1, \ldots, f_r \in R[x]$ and $e_1, \ldots, e_r, n \in \mathbb{N}_{\geq 1}$. You are to prove three generalizations of the Leibniz rule.

(i) $(f_1 f_2)^{(n)} = \sum_{0 \leq i \leq n} \binom{n}{i} f_1^{(i)} f_2^{(n-i)}$, where $^{(i)}$ denotes the ith derivative,

(ii) $(f_1 \cdots f_r)' = \sum_{1 \leq i \leq r} f_i' \prod_{j \neq i} f_j$,

(iii) $(f_1^{e_1} \cdots f_r^{e_r})' = \sum_{1 \leq i \leq r} e_i f_i' f_i^{e_i - 1} \prod_{j \neq i} f_j^{e_j}$.

(iv) Conclude from (ii) that

$$\frac{f'}{f} = \frac{f_1'}{f_1} + \cdots + \frac{f_r'}{f_r}$$

is the partial fraction decomposition of f'/f, for $f = f_1 \cdots f_r$.

9.28 Compute the first 16 decimal digits of the real root of $y^3 - 2y - 5$ using Newton iteration and $y_0 = 2$ as your starting value. Compare your results with Newton's (page 207). What are the other two roots?

9.29 Under which condition does the Newton iteration algorithm 9.22 work for a rational function $\varphi \in R(y)$? The Newton formula for $\varphi = 1/y - f \in R(y)$ gives exactly the inversion procedure from Theorem 9.2. Why does the polynomial $\varphi = fy - 1 \in R[y]$ not work directly?

9.30 Let $\varphi = x^4 + 25x^3 + 129x^2 + 60x + 108 \in \mathbb{Z}[x]$ and $p = 5$.

(i) Determine all roots of φ mod p in $\mathbb{F}_p$.

(ii) Find an a priori bound B such that every root $a \in \mathbb{Z}$ of φ has $|a| \leq B$.

(iii) Choose $l \in \mathbb{N}$ such that $2B < p^l$, and apply p-adic Newton iteration to all modular roots of φ from (i).

(iv) Use the results from (iii) to find all roots of φ in $\mathbb{Z}$.

9.31* Let $R = D[x]$ for a (commutative) ring D, and φ, p, l, g_0 be inputs to the p-adic Newton iteration 9.22 with p monic nonconstant, $\deg g_0 < \deg p$, $\deg_x \varphi < l \deg p$, and $\deg_y \varphi = n$. Show that Algorithm 9.22 takes $O(n\mathsf{M}(l \deg p))$ operations in D. Hint: Exercise 9.7.

9.32* Prove Theorem 9.26. Hint: Exercise 9.7.

9.33* In this exercise, we consider the **linearly convergent Newton iteration**. Let R be a ring (commutative, with 1), $p \in R$, $\varphi \in R[y]$, and $s, g \in R$ such that $\varphi(g) \equiv 0$ mod p^k for some $k \in \mathbb{N}$ and $s\varphi'(g) \equiv 1$ mod p. We define $h \in R$ by the Newton formula

$$h \equiv g - s \cdot \varphi(g) \text{ mod } p^{k+1}.$$

Prove that $\varphi(h) \equiv 0$ mod p^{k+1}, $h \equiv g$ mod p^k, and $s\varphi'(h) \equiv 1$ mod p. Derive a linearly convergent analog of Algorithm 9.22 from this, and show that when $R = D[x]$ for a ring D and $p = x$, it takes $O(nl^2)$ operations in D. This is slower than the quadratically convergent variant, but has the advantage that the inverse of the derivative need not be updated.

9.34 Derive the formula

$$g_{i+1} = \frac{1}{2}\left(g_i + \frac{a}{g_i}\right)$$

for $i \geq 0$, which was already known to the Babylonians, and is the Newton iteration for approximating the square root of a. Using this formula, compute a square root of 2 modulo 3^8. What is the corresponding formula for computing an nth root of a?

9.35 Find the Newton formula for approximating $1/\sqrt{a}$. What is the remarkable difference to the Newton formula for $\sqrt{a}$?

9.36 Compute a square root $g \in \mathbb{Q}[x]$ of $f = 1 + 4x \in \mathbb{Q}[x]$ modulo x^8 such that $g(0) = 1$, using Newton iteration.

9.37 Compute a cube root of 2 modulo 625, that is, $g \in \{0, \ldots, 624\}$ such that $g^3 \equiv 2$ mod 625. How many such g are there?

9.38 Consider the three prime numbers $p = 5, 7$, and 17. We want to calculate p-adic approximations to $\sqrt{2}$.

(i) For which of the three p does 2 have a square root modulo arbitrary powers of p?

(ii) For those p where possible, compute all square roots of 2 modulo p^6.

9.39 Let $a \in \mathbb{N}_{>0}$ be of word length l, such that $a < 2^{64l}$. For $n \in \mathbb{N}$, we denote by $T(n)$ the number of word operations to compute a^n using repeated squaring. Prove that $T(n) \leq T(\lfloor n/2 \rfloor) + O(\mathsf{M}(nl))$ if $n > 1$, and conclude that $T(n) \in O(\mathsf{M}(nl))$. What is the corresponding result when a is a univariate polynomial over a (commutative) ring R?

9.40$\overrightarrow{}$ For $n \in \mathbb{N}_{\geq 2}$ and $a \in \mathbb{Z}$ let $S_n(a)$ be the number of solutions $g \in \{0, \ldots, n-1\}$ of the quadratic congruence $g^2 \equiv a$ mod n.

(i) Which values for $S_p(a)$ are possible when p is prime? Distinguish the three cases $p = 2$, $p \mid a$ and $2 \neq p \nmid a$.

(ii) Let $p \neq 2$ be prime and $e \in \mathbb{N}_{>0}$. Show that $S_{p^e}(a) = S_p(a)$ if $p \nmid a$, and give a counterexample when $p \mid a$.

(iii) Now let n be an odd integer and $n = p_1^{e_1} \cdot \ldots \cdot p_r^{e_r}$ its prime factorization, with distinct primes $p_1, \ldots, p_r \in \mathbb{N}$ and positive integers $e_1, \ldots, e_r$. Find a formula expressing $S_n(a)$ in terms of $S_{p_1}(a), \ldots, S_{p_r}(a)$ in the case where a and n are coprime. Hint: Chinese Remainder Theorem. Conclude that $S_n(1) = 2^r$.

(iv) Which of the numbers $10001, 42814, 31027, 17329$ have square roots modulo 50625?

(v) Compute all square roots of 91 modulo 2025 and of 1 modulo 50625.

9.41* For $n \in \mathbb{N}_{\geq 2}$ and $a \in \mathbb{Z}$ let $C_n(a)$ be the number of solutions $g \in \{0, \ldots, n-1\}$ of the cubic congruence $g^3 \equiv a \bmod n$.

(i) Show that the following hold for an odd prime p:

○ $C_p(a) \leq 3$,

○ $C_p(a) = 1$ if $p \mid a$ or $p = 3$,

○ $C_p(a) \neq 2$, and for any value $C \in \{0, 1, 3\}$ there is an odd prime p and an integer a such that $3 \neq p \nmid a$ and $C_p(a) = C$.

(ii) Let $p > 3$ be a prime and $e \in \mathbb{N}_{>0}$. Show that $C_{p^e}(a) = C_p(a)$ if $p \nmid a$, and give a counterexample when $p \mid a$.

(iii) Now let $n \in \mathbb{N}$ such that $\gcd(n, 6) = 1$, and let $n = p_1^{e_1} \cdot \ldots \cdot p_r^{e_r}$ be its prime factorization, with distinct primes $p_1, \ldots, p_r \in \mathbb{N}$ and positive integers $e_1, \ldots, e_r$. Find a formula expressing $C_n(a)$ in terms of $C_{p_1}(a), \ldots, C_{p_r}(a)$ in the case where a and n are coprime.

(iv) Compute all cube roots of 11 modulo 225625.

9.42 Let $n \in \mathbb{N}_{>0}$. How many cube roots $g \in \mathbb{F}_7[x]$ modulo x^n of degree less than n does $f = -x^3 + x^2 - x + 1 \in \mathbb{F}_7[x]$ have, and how can they be computed? Compute one for $n = 4$.

9.43* Modify the algorithm for computing nth roots in $\mathbb{Z}$ so as to work when n is a power of 2, by using a 3-adic Newton iteration. Prove that your algorithm is correct, and show that is uses $O(\mathsf{M}(l))$ word operations on inputs of length l. Apply your algorithm to compute $\sqrt[4]{2313441}$.

9.44* Design a test whether $a \in \mathbb{N}$ is a perfect power. Your test should output $b, d, e, r \in \mathbb{N}$ such that $a = 2^d 3^e b^r$, $\gcd(b, 6) = 1$, and r is maximal, using $O(\log a \cdot \mathsf{M}(\log a))$ word operations.

9.45 Let R be a ring (commutative, with 1) with a valuation v, with the special property that $v(a) \leq 1$ for all $a \in R$. Show that if $a \in R$ is a unit, then $v(a) = 1$.

9.46 Let R be an integral domain with a valuation v, and K the field of fractions of R. Show that $w(a/b) = v(a)/v(b)$ defines a valuation w on K.

9.47 Conclude the proof of Lemma 9.34.

9.48* Let F be a field, and $v \colon F[[x]] \longrightarrow \mathbb{R}$ be the x-adic valuation on the ring $F[[x]]$ of formal power series.

(i) For $n \in \mathbb{N}$, let $f_n = 1 + x + \cdots + x^{2n} - x^{2n+1} \in F[[x]]$. Show that $f_0, f_1, \cdots$ is a Cauchy sequence, so that

$$\forall \varepsilon > 0 \quad \exists N \in \mathbb{N} \quad \forall n, m > N \quad v(f_n - f_m) \leq \varepsilon.$$

(ii) Prove that the sequence has a limit in $F[[x]]$, so that there exists $f \in F[[x]]$ with

$$\forall \varepsilon > 0 \quad \exists N \in \mathbb{N} \quad \forall n > N \quad v(f - f_n) \leq \varepsilon.$$

(iii) Prove that every Cauchy sequence in $F[[x]]$ has a limit in $F[[x]]$, so that $F[[x]]$ is **complete**. Show that $F[x]$ with the x-adic valuation does not have this property. (In fact, $F[[x]]$ can be obtained from $F[x]$ by the same process of "completion" by which one obtains $\mathbb{R}$ from $\mathbb{Q}$ with respect to the absolute value.)

(iv) Let $f = a_0 + a_1 x + \cdots \in F[[x]]$, and $a_0 = 0$. Prove that f does not have an inverse in $F[[x]]$.

(v) Let $f = a_0 + a_1 x + \cdots \in F[[x]]$, and $a_0 \neq 0$. Use Newton iteration to prove that f has an inverse in $F[[x]]$.

The second concept is the asymptotic behavior of the number of operations. This was not significant for small N so the importance of early forms of the FFT algorithms was not noticed even where they would have been very useful.

James William Cooley (1987)

Il y a une imagination étonnante dans les mathématiques. [...]
Il y avait beaucoup plus d'imagination dans la tête d'Archimède
que dans celle d'Homère.[1]

Voltaire (1771)

Leibnitz [sic!] crut voir l'image de la création, dans son arithmétique
binaire où il n'employait que les deux caractères zéro et l'unité.
Il imagina que l'unité pouvait représenter Dieu, et zéro le néant; et que
l'Être suprême avait tiré du néant tous les êtres, comme l'unité avec le
zéro exprime tous les nombres dans ce système d'arithmétique.[2]

Pierre Simon Laplace (1812)

Guided by an instinctive sense of the beautiful and fitting, in a happy
moment I have succeeded in grasping this much wished for
representation, with which I propose now and for ever to take my
farewell of this long and deeply excogitated theorem.

James Joseph Sylvester (1853)

---

[1] There is an astonishing imagination in mathematics. [...] There was far more imagination in the head of Archimedes than in that of Homer.

[2] Leibniz believed he saw the image of creation in his binary arithmetic in which he employed only the two characters, zero and unity. He imagined that unity can represent God, and zero nothing; and that the Supreme Being might have drawn all beings from nothing, just as unity with zero expresses in this binary arithmetic all numbers.

10

Fast polynomial evaluation and interpolation

In the preceding chapters, we have seen extremely fast algorithms for multiplication and division with remainder. We now tackle the next set of problems: evaluation of a polynomial at many points, its inverse problem, interpolation, and a substantial generalization, the Chinese Remainder Algorithm.

10.1. Fast multipoint evaluation

We consider the following situation: R is a ring (commutative, with 1, as always), $n \in \mathbb{N}$, $u_0, \ldots, u_{n-1} \in R$, $m_i = x - u_i \in R[x]$, and $m = \prod_{0 \leq i < n}(x - u_i)$. Then the evaluation map

$$\chi: R[x]/\langle m \rangle \longrightarrow R^n$$
$$f \longmapsto (f(u_0), \ldots, f(u_{n-1}))$$

is a ring homomorphism. If R is a field, then $R[x]$ and R^n are vector spaces over R, thus R-algebras, and χ is in fact an isomorphism of R-algebras if $u_0, \ldots, u_{n-1}$ are distinct. This is a special case of the Chinese Remainder Theorem 5.3.

In this and the next section, we want to solve the following two problems. For simplicity, we assume that the number n of points is a power of 2.

PROBLEM 10.1. *(Multipoint evaluation) Given $n = 2^k$ for some $k \in \mathbb{N}$, $f \in R[x]$ of degree less than n, and $u_0, \ldots, u_{n-1} \in R$, compute*

$$\chi(f) = (f(u_0), \ldots, f(u_{n-1})).$$

PROBLEM 10.2. *(Interpolation) Given $n = 2^k$ for some $k \in \mathbb{N}$, $u_0, \ldots, u_{n-1} \in R$ such that $u_i - u_j$ is a unit for $i \neq j$, and $v_0, \ldots, v_{n-1} \in R$, compute $f \in R[x]$ of degree less than n with*

$$\chi(f) = (f(u_0), \ldots, f(u_{n-1})) = (v_0, \ldots, v_{n-1}).$$

We have already discussed these problems for a field R and presented algorithms taking time $O(n^2)$ in Chapter 5. The methods of this chapter are *only* of interest in connection with subquadratic multiplication routines, as those from Chapter 8. There we have seen that the evaluation and interpolation problems can be solved with $O(n \log n)$ operations in R if R supports the FFT and $u_i = \omega^i$, where ω is a primitive nth root of unity. Our goal now is a similar bound for the general case.

For arbitrary points $u_0, \ldots, u_{n-1}$, multipoint evaluation can be done with $O(n^2)$ operations in R by using Horner's rule n times. In fact, it can be proved that one evaluation requires at least n multiplications. One might be tempted to think that then n evaluations require at least n^2 multiplications. This is false, and our goal in this section is to see that mass-production of evaluations can be done much cheaper. In the next section, we show the same bound for interpolation.

The idea of the evaluation algorithm is to split the point set $\{u_0, \ldots, u_{n-1}\}$ into two halves of equal cardinality and to proceed recursively with each of the two halves. This leads to a binary tree of depth $\log n$ with root $\{u_0, \ldots, u_{n-1}\}$ and the singletons $\{u_i\}$ for $0 \le i < n$ at the leaves (see Figure 10.1), where log is the binary logarithm.

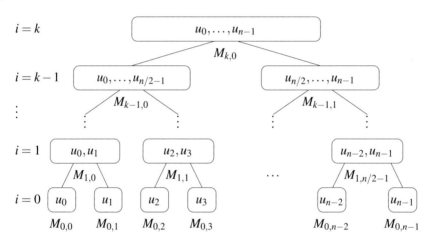

FIGURE 10.1: Subproduct tree for the multipoint evaluation algorithm.

We let $m_i = x - u_i$ as above, and define

$$M_{i,j} = m_{j \cdot 2^i} \cdot m_{j \cdot 2^i + 1} \cdots m_{j \cdot 2^i + (2^i - 1)} = \prod_{0 \le l < 2^i} m_{j \cdot 2^i + l} \qquad (1)$$

for $0 \le i \le k = \log n$ and $0 \le j < 2^{k-i}$. Thus each $M_{i,j}$ is a subproduct with 2^i factors of $m = \prod_{0 \le l < n} m_l = M_{k,0}$ and satisfies for each i, j the recursive equations

$$M_{0,j} = m_j, \qquad M_{i+1,j} = M_{i,2j} \cdot M_{i,2j+1}. \qquad (2)$$

If R is an integral domain and $u_0, \ldots, u_{n-1}$ are distinct, then $M_{i,j}$ is the monic squarefree polynomial whose zero set is the jth node from the left at level i of the tree in Figure 10.1.

The following algorithm solves the more general problem of computing the sub-products $M_{i,j}$ for *arbitrary* moduli $m_0, \ldots, m_{r-1}$. It proceeds from the leaves to the root of the subproduct tree in Figure 10.1.

━━ ALGORITHM 10.3 Building up the subproduct tree. ━━━━━━━━━━━
Input: $m_0, \ldots, m_{r-1} \in R[x]$, where $r = 2^k$ for some $k \in \mathbb{N}$.
Output: The polynomials $M_{i,j}$ as in (1) for $0 \le i \le k$ and $0 \le j < 2^{k-i}$.

1. **for** $0 \le j < r$ **do** $M_{0,j} \longleftarrow m_j$

2. **for** $1 \le i \le k$ **do**

3.   **for** $0 \le j < 2^{k-i}$ **do** $M_{i,j} \longleftarrow M_{i-1,2j} \cdot M_{i-1,2j+1}$ ━━━━━━━━

We recall the multiplication time M (see inside front cover).

LEMMA 10.4. *Algorithm 10.3 correctly computes all subproducts $M_{i,j} \in R[x]$ and takes at most $\mathsf{M}(n) \log r$ operations in R, where $n = \sum_{0 \le i < r} \deg m_i$.*

PROOF. Correctness is clear from (2). Let $d_{i,j} = \deg M_{i,j}$ for all i and j. Step 1 uses no arithmetic operations, and the cost for the ith iteration of step 3 is at most

$$\sum_{0 \le j < 2^{k-i}} \mathsf{M}(d_{i,j}) \le \mathsf{M}\left(\sum_{0 \le j < 2^{k-i}} d_{i,j} \right) = \mathsf{M}(n)$$

operations in R, since $\sum_{0 \le j < 2^{k-i}} d_{i,j} = n$. The time estimate follows, since there are $k = \log r$ iterations. $\square$

Exercise 10.8 proves an analogous result for integers. If all m_i have the same degree, then Exercise 10.3 proves the better timing estimate $(\frac{1}{2}\mathsf{M}(n) + O(n)) \log r$. If the degrees of the m_i differ considerably from each other, then the tree in Figure 10.1 is quite unbalanced with respect to the degree. In fact, it is possible to prove a slightly better bound on the arithmetic cost for that case. If $p_0, \ldots, p_{r-1} \in \mathbb{R}$ are positive probabilities that sum to 1, then

$$H(p_0, \ldots, p_{r-1}) = - \sum_{0 \le i < r} p_i \log p_i$$

is known from information theory as the **entropy** of $p_0, \ldots, p_{r-1}$. Exercise 10.4 shows that $0 < H(p_0, \ldots, p_{r-1}) \le \log r$, and $H(p_0, \ldots, p_{r-1}) = \log r$ if and only if $p_0 = \cdots = p_{r-1} = 1/r$. If we organize the subproduct tree in such a way that at each node the total degree of the left and of the right subtree are about the same, then the running time bound for computing $m = m_0 \cdots m_{r-1}$ drops to at most $\mathsf{M}(n)(H(\deg m_0/n, \ldots, \deg m_{r-1}/n) + 1)$ (Exercise 10.7); the case where all $\deg m_i$ are equal to n/r yields the bound from Lemma 10.4. The same also applies to the other algorithms in Sections 10.1 through 10.3.

The computation of all the subproducts $M_{i,j}$ can be regarded as a precomputation stage for the fast multipoint evaluation algorithm that we are going to present now. If several polynomials have to be evaluated at the same points $u_0, \ldots, u_{n-1}$, it is sufficient to carry out the precomputation stage only once in advance.

For $n \in \mathbb{N}$, we let $\mathsf{D}(n)$ denote the number of operations in R for dividing a polynomial of degree less than $2n$ by a monic polynomial of degree n in $R[x]$, and assume that $\mathsf{D}(n+m) \geq \mathsf{D}(n) + \mathsf{D}(m)$ and $\mathsf{D}(n) \geq n$ for all $n, m \in \mathbb{N}$. By Theorem 9.6, $\mathsf{D}(n)$ is at most $5\mathsf{M}(n) + O(n)$.

We now present a divide-and-conquer algorithm that, given all subproducts $M_{i,j}$, proceeds top down along the tree in Figure 10.1.

━━ ALGORITHM 10.5 Going down the subproduct tree. ━━━━━━━━━━━━━━━
Input: $f \in R[x]$ of degree less than $n = 2^k$ for some $k \in \mathbb{N}$, $u_0, \ldots, u_{n-1} \in R$, and the subproducts $M_{i,j}$ from (1).
Output: $f(u_0), \ldots, f(u_{n-1}) \in R$.

1. **if** $n = 1$ **then return** f

2. $r_0 \longleftarrow f$ rem $M_{k-1,0}$, $r_1 \longleftarrow f$ rem $M_{k-1,1}$

3. **call** the algorithm recursively to compute $r_0(u_0), \ldots, r_0(u_{n/2-1})$

4. **call** the algorithm recursively to compute $r_1(u_{n/2}), \ldots, r_1(u_n - 1)$

5. **return** $r_0(u_0), \ldots, r_0(u_{n/2-1}), r_1(u_{n/2}), \ldots, r_1(u_{n-1})$ ━━━━━━━━

━━ THEOREM 10.6. ━━━━━━━━━━━━━━━━━━━━━━━━━━━━━━━
Algorithm 10.5 works correctly and takes at most $\mathsf{D}(n)\log n$ *operations in* R, *which is at most* $(5\mathsf{M}(n) + O(n))\log n$ *or* $O(\mathsf{M}(n)\log n)$. ━━━━

PROOF. We prove the correctness by induction on k. If $k = 0$, then f is constant, and the algorithm outputs the correct value in step 1. Otherwise, if $k \geq 1$, we may inductively assume that the results of steps 3 and 4 are correct. Let $q_0 = f$ quo $M_{k-1,0}$ and $q_1 = f$ quo $M_{k-1,1}$. Then

$$f(u_i) = \begin{cases} q_0(u_i)M_{k-1,0}(u_i) + r_0(u_i) = r_0(u_i) & \text{if } 0 \leq i < \dfrac{n}{2}, \\ q_1(u_i)M_{k-1,1}(u_i) + r_1(u_i) = r_1(u_i) & \text{if } \dfrac{n}{2} \leq i < n. \end{cases}$$

Let $T(n) = T(2^k)$ denote the cost for the recursive process. Then $T(1) = 0$ and

$$T(2^k) = 2T(2^{k-1}) + 2\mathsf{D}(2^{k-1})$$

for $k \geq 1$, so that $T(2^k) \leq 2k \cdot \mathsf{D}(2^{k-1}) \leq \mathsf{D}(n) \log n$, by Lemma 8.2, and the claim follows from Theorem 9.6. □

Putting things together, we obtain the following algorithm for fast multipoint evaluation.

ALGORITHM 10.7 Fast multipoint evaluation.
Input: $f \in R[x]$ of degree less than $n = 2^k$ for some $k \in \mathbb{N}$ and $u_0, \ldots, u_{n-1} \in R$.
Output: $f(u_0), \ldots, f(u_{n-1}) \in R$.

1. **call** Algorithm 10.3 with input $(x - u_0), \ldots, (x - u_{n-1})$ to compute the subproducts $M_{i,j}$ as in (1)

2. **call** Algorithm 10.5 with input f, the points u_i, and the subproducts $M_{i,j}$
   return its results

COROLLARY 10.8.
Evaluation of a polynomial in $R[x]$ of degree less than n at n points in R can be performed using at most $(\frac{11}{2}\mathsf{M}(n) + O(n)) \log n$ or $O(\mathsf{M}(n) \log n)$ operations in R.

The time bound follows from Exercise 10.3 and Theorem 10.6. Exercise 10.9 proves the smaller bound $(1 + \frac{7}{2} \log n)(\mathsf{M}(n) + O(n))$. Exercise 10.11 shows that if many evaluations at the same set of points have to be performed, then all data depending only on the evaluation points may be precomputed and stored, and the cost drops to essentially $(2\mathsf{M}(n) + O(n)) \log n$.

10.2. Fast interpolation

We recall the Lagrange interpolation formula from Chapter 5. Given distinct $u_0, \ldots, u_{n-1}$ in a field F and arbitrary $v_0, \ldots, v_{n-1} \in F$, the unique polynomial $f \in F[x]$ of degree less than n that takes the value v_i at the point u_i for all i is $f = \sum_{0 \leq i < n} v_i s_i m / (x - u_i)$, where $m = (x - u_0) \cdots (x - u_{n-1})$, as before, and

$$s_i = \prod_{j \neq i} \frac{1}{u_i - u_j}. \tag{3}$$

Over a ring R, this is still valid if we demand that $u_i - u_j$ is a unit for $i \neq j$. Theorem 10.13 below shows that this condition is also necessary in the general case.

We first explain an idea to compute the s_i fast. The formal derivative m is $m' = \sum_{0 \leq j < n} m/(x - u_j)$, and since $m/(x - u_i)$ vanishes at all points u_j with $j \neq i$, we have

$$m'(u_i) = \left. \frac{m}{x - u_i} \right|_{x = u_i} = \frac{1}{s_i}. \tag{4}$$

Given m, the computation of all the s_i amounts to one evaluation of m' at n points, at a cost of $O(\mathsf{M}(n) \log n)$ operations in R, plus n inversions.

The following divide-and-conquer algorithm is the core of the fast interpolation algorithm. It proceeds from the leaves to the root of the tree in Figure 10.1.

ALGORITHM 10.9 Linear combination for linear moduli.

Input: $u_0, \ldots, u_{n-1}, c_0, \ldots, c_{n-1} \in R$, where $n = 2^k$ for some $k \in \mathbb{N}$, and the polynomials $M_{i,j}$ as in (1).

Output: $\displaystyle\sum_{0 \leq i < n} c_i \frac{m}{x - u_i} \in R[x]$, where $m = (x - u_0) \cdots (x - u_{n-1})$.

1. **if** $n = 1$ **then return** c_0

2. **call** the algorithm recursively to compute $r_0 = \displaystyle\sum_{0 \leq i < n/2} c_i \frac{M_{k-1,0}}{x - u_i}$

3. **call** the algorithm recursively to compute $r_1 = \displaystyle\sum_{n/2 \leq i < n} c_i \frac{M_{k-1,1}}{x - u_i}$

4. **return** $M_{k-1,1} r_0 + M_{k-1,0} r_1$

THEOREM 10.10.
Algorithm 10.9 takes at most $(\mathsf{M}(n) + O(n)) \log n$ or $O(\mathsf{M}(n) \log n)$ arithmetic operations in R to correctly compute the result.

PROOF. As usual, we prove the correctness by induction on k. If $k = 0$, then $m = x - u_0$, and the output in step 1 is correct. If $k \geq 1$, then the results of the recursive calls in steps 2 and 3 are correct by the induction hypothesis, and the algorithm outputs the correct result in step 4 since $m = M_{k-1,0} \cdot M_{k-1,1}$.

Let $T(n) = T(2^k)$ denote the cost of the algorithm. The cost for the individual steps is 0 for step 1, $T(n/2)$ for each of the steps 2 and 3, and at most $2\mathsf{M}(n/2 + 1) + n \in \mathsf{M}(n) + O(n)$ (Exercise 8.34) for step 4. (The "+1" comes from our convention that $\mathsf{M}(n)$ is the time to multiply polynomials of degree less than n.) Thus $T(1) = 0$ and $T(n) \leq 2T(n/2) + \mathsf{M}(n) + cn$ for $n > 1$ and some constant $c \in \mathbb{R}$, and Lemma 8.2 yields the claim. $\square$

Putting things together, we have the following fast interpolation algorithm.

━━ ALGORITHM 10.11 Fast interpolation. ━━━━━━━━━━━━━━

Input: $u_0, \ldots, u_{n-1} \in R$ such that $u_i - u_j$ is a unit for $i \neq j$, and $v_0, \ldots, v_{n-1} \in R$, where $n = 2^k$ for some $k \in \mathbb{N}$.

Output: The unique polynomial $f \in R[x]$ of degree less than n such that $f(u_i) = v_i$ for $0 \leq i < n$.

1. **call** Algorithm 10.3 with input $u_0, \ldots, u_{n-1}$ to compute the polynomials $M_{i,j}$ as in (1)

2. $m \longleftarrow M_{k,0}$
   call Algorithm 10.5 with input $u_0, \ldots, u_{n-1}$ and the $M_{i,j}$ to evaluate m' at $u_0, \ldots, u_{n-1}$
   for $0 \leq i < n$ **do** $s_i \longleftarrow \dfrac{1}{m'(u_i)}$

3. **call** Algorithm 10.9 with input $u_0, \ldots, u_{n-1}, v_0 s_0, \ldots, v_{n-1} s_{n-1}$, and the $M_{i,j}$
   return its result ━━━━━━━━━━━━━

━━ COROLLARY 10.12. ━━━━━━━━━━━━━━━━━━

Algorithm 10.11 solves the interpolation problem 10.2 over a (commutative) ring R using at most $\left(\frac{13}{2} \mathsf{M}(n) + O(n)\right) \log n$ or $O(\mathsf{M}(n) \log n)$ operations in R. ━━━

PROOF. The cost for step 1 is at most $\left(\frac{1}{2}\mathsf{M}(n) + O(n)\right) \log n$, by Exercise 10.3. The cost for step 2 is at most $(5\mathsf{M}(n) + O(n)) \log n$ operations, by Theorem 10.6, including the computation of m' and the final modular inversions. Finally, step 3 takes no more than $(\mathsf{M}(n) + O(n)) \log n$ operations, by Theorem 10.10. $\square$

Exercise 10.11 shows that if many interpolations at the same set of points have to be performed, then all data depending only on the interpolation points may be precomputed and stored, and the cost drops to essentially $(\mathsf{M}(n) + O(n)) \log n$.

10.3. Fast Chinese remaindering

The ideas and algorithms of the previous sections carry over to monic moduli of arbitrary degree in $R[x]$ and to $\mathbb{Z}$. We only discuss the polynomial case in detail and refer to the exercises for the integer analog.

Let R be a field, $m_0, \ldots, m_{r-1} \in R[x]$ nonconstant and pairwise coprime, $m = m_0 \cdots m_{r-1}$, and $n = \deg m$. Then evaluation and interpolation correspond to computing the Chinese Remainder isomorphism

$$\begin{aligned} \chi : R[x]/\langle m \rangle &\longrightarrow R[x]/\langle m_0 \rangle \times \ldots \times R[x]/\langle m_{r-1} \rangle, \\ f \bmod m &\longmapsto (f \bmod m_0, \ldots, f \bmod m_{r-1}), \end{aligned} \tag{5}$$

and its inverse. For arbitrary coefficient rings, we have the following variant of the Chinese Remainder Theorem 5.3; Exercise 10.13 asks for a proof.

▬ THEOREM 10.13. ▬

Let $r \geq 1$, R be a ring (commutative, with 1, as always), $m_0, \ldots, m_{r-1} \in R[x]$ monic and nonconstant, and $m = m_0 \cdots m_{r-1}$. Then the following are equivalent.

(i) *The ring homomorphism χ in (5) is an isomorphism.*

(ii) *There exist polynomials $s_0, \ldots, s_{r-1} \in R[x]$ such that $\sum_{0 \leq i < r} s_i m / m_i = 1$.*

(iii) *For $i \neq j$ there exist polynomials $s_{ij}, t_{ij} \in R[x]$ such that $s_{ij} m_j + t_{ij} m_i = 1$.*

(iv) $\mathrm{res}(m_i, m_j) \in R^\times$ *for $i \neq j$.* ▬

If each $m_i = x - u_i$ is linear, with $u_i \in R$, then

$$\mathrm{res}(m_i, m_j) = \det \begin{pmatrix} 1 & 1 \\ -u_i & -u_j \end{pmatrix} = u_i - u_j,$$

and (iv) is equivalent to $u_i - u_j \in R^\times$ for $i \neq j$.

Let us assume for simplicity that $r = 2^k$ is a power of 2 for some $k \in \mathbb{N}$. For the moment, we also drop the requirement that $\mathrm{res}(m_i, m_j) \in R^\times$ for $i \neq j$. We build the subproduct tree with $M_{i,j} \in F[x]$ as in (1). The following algorithm generalizes Algorithm 10.5.

▬ ALGORITHM 10.14 Fast simultaneous reduction with precomputation. ▬
Input: Monic nonconstant moduli $m_0, \ldots, m_{r-1} \in R[x]$, where $r = 2^k$ with $k \in \mathbb{N}$, $f \in R[x]$ of degree less than $n = \sum_{0 \leq i < r} \deg m_i$, and the polynomials $M_{i,j}$ from (1).
Output: f rem $m_0, \ldots, f$ rem $m_{r-1} \in R[x]$.

1. **if** $r = 1$ **then return** f

2. $r_0 \longleftarrow f$ rem $M_{k-1,0}$, $\quad r_1 \longleftarrow f$ rem $M_{k-1,1}$

3. **call** the algorithm recursively to compute r_0 rem $m_0, \ldots, r_0$ rem $m_{r/2-1}$

4. **call** the algorithm recursively to compute r_1 rem $m_{r/2}, \ldots, r_1$ rem $m_r - 1$

5. **return** r_0 rem $m_0, \ldots, r_0$ rem $m_{r/2-1}, r_1$ rem $m_{r/2}, \ldots, r_1$ rem m_{r-1} ▬

▬ THEOREM 10.15. ▬
Algorithm 10.14 works correctly and takes no more than $(10\mathsf{M}(n) + O(n)) \log r$ or $O(\mathsf{M}(n) \log r)$ operations in R. ▬

PROOF. The correctness proof is similar to that of Theorem 10.6 and left as Exercise 10.15. For the cost analysis, we see that the algorithm works from the root to the leaves along the binary tree formed by the subproducts $M_{i,j}$. The cost for a vertex $M_{i,j}$ with $i \geq 1$ is the cost for dividing a polynomial of smaller degree than $\deg M_{i,j}$ by $M_{i-1,2j}$ and $M_{i-1,2j+1}$ with remainder, using at most $2\mathsf{D}(\deg M_{i,j})$ ring operations. The total cost at level i is then at most $2\sum_{0 \leq j < 2^i} \mathsf{D}(\deg M_{i,j}) \leq 2\mathsf{D}(n)$, as in the proof of Lemma 10.4, and the claim follows from Theorem 9.6 and the fact that there are $\log r$ levels. $\square$

━━ ALGORITHM 10.16 Fast simultaneous modular reduction. ━━━━━━━━━━
Input: Monic nonconstant moduli $m_0, \ldots, m_{r-1} \in R[x]$, where $r = 2^k$ with $k \in \mathbb{N}$, and $f \in R[x]$ of degree less than $n = \sum_{0 \leq i < r} \deg m_i$.
Output: f rem $m_0, \ldots, f$ rem $m_{r-1} \in R[x]$.

1. **call** Algorithm 10.3 with input $m_0, \ldots, m_{r-1}$ to compute the subproducts $M_{i,j}$ as in (1)

2. **call** Algorithm 10.14 with input $m_0, \ldots, m_{r-1}$, f, and the subproducts $M_{i,j}$
   return its results ━━━━━━━━

━━ COROLLARY 10.17. ━━━━━━━━━━━━━━━━━━━━━━━━━━━━
Given monic nonconstant polynomials $m_0, \ldots, m_{r-1} \in R[x]$, where $r \in \mathbb{N}$ is a power of 2, and $f \in R[x]$ of degree less than $n = \sum_{0 \leq i < r} \deg m_i$, Algorithm 10.16 computes f rem $m_0, \ldots, f$ rem m_{r-1} using at most $(11\mathsf{M}(n) + O(n)) \log r$ or $O(\mathsf{M}(n) \log r)$ operations in R. ━━━━━━━━━━━

Exercise 10.17 gives a better analysis of Algorithm 10.16 when all moduli have the same degree.

For the fast Chinese Remainder Algorithm, we recall the generalization of Lagrange's formula from Chapter 5. Given pairwise distinct and nonconstant moduli $m_0, \ldots, m_{r-1} \in F[x]$ for a field F and polynomials $v_0, \ldots, v_{r-1} \in F[x]$ with $\deg v_i < \deg m_i$ for all i, there is a unique polynomial $f \in F[x]$ of degree less than $n = \sum_{0 \leq i < r} \deg m_i$ satisfying $f \equiv v_i \bmod m_i$ for all i, and it is given by $f = \sum_{0 \leq i < r} (v_i s_i \text{ rem } m_i) m/m_i$, where $m = m_0 \cdots m_{r-1}$ and $s_i \in F[x]$ is an inverse of m/m_i modulo m_i. Theorem 10.13 implies that this is true for arbitrary coefficient rings R if we require $\text{res}(m_i, m_j) \in R^\times$ for $i \neq j$.

As in the case of interpolation, we first address the task of computing the s_i. This need be done only once if several computations with the same set of moduli are to be executed.

━━ ALGORITHM 10.18 Simultaneous inverse computation. ━━━━━━━━━
Input: $m_0, \ldots, m_{r-1} \in R[x]$ monic and nonconstant such that $\text{res}(m_i, m_j) \in R^\times$ for $i \neq j$, where $r = 2^k$ for some $k \in \mathbb{N}$, and $m = m_0 \cdots m_{r-1}$.
Output: $s_0, \ldots, s_{r-1} \in R[x]$ with $s_i \dfrac{m}{m_i} \equiv 1 \bmod m_i$ and $\deg s_i < \deg m_i$ for all i.

1. **call** Algorithm 10.16 to compute m rem m_i^2 for all i

2. **for** $0 \leq i < r$ compute $\dfrac{m}{m_i}$ rem m_i

3. **for** $0 \leq i < r$ compute $s_i \in R[x]$ with $\deg s_i < \deg m_i$ and $s_i \cdot \left(\dfrac{m}{m_i} \text{ rem } m_i \right) \equiv 1 \bmod m_i$, using the Extended Euclidean Algorithm if R is a field and Exercise 6.15 otherwise

4. **return** $s_0, \ldots, s_{r-1}$ ▬▬▬▬▬▬▬▬▬▬▬▬▬▬▬▬▬▬▬▬▬▬▬▬▬▬▬

LEMMA 10.19. *Algorithm 10.18 works correctly. If R is a field, then it takes $O(\mathsf{M}(n) \log n)$ operations in R for $n = \deg m$.*

PROOF. Let R be a field and $d_i = \deg m_i$ for $0 \leq i < r$. The cost for step 1 is $O(\mathsf{M}(2n) \log r)$ ring operations, including the cost for computing all m_i^2. Step 2 costs $\mathsf{D}(d_i) \in O(\mathsf{M}(d_i))$ for m_i. In Chapter 11, we will see that step 3 can be done with $O(\mathsf{M}(d_i) \log d_i)$ operations in R for each i. Using

$$\sum_{0 \leq i < r} \mathsf{M}(d_i) \leq \mathsf{M}\left(\sum_{0 \leq i < r} d_i \right) = \mathsf{M}(n),$$

we have a cost of $O(\mathsf{M}(n))$ and $O(\mathsf{M}(n) \log n)$ for steps 2 and 3, respectively, and the claim follows. $\square$

Here is the corresponding generalization of Algorithm 10.9.

▬▬▬ ALGORITHM 10.20 Linear combination. ▬▬▬▬▬▬▬▬▬▬▬▬▬▬
Input: $m_0, \ldots, m_{r-1} \in R[x]$ monic and nonconstant, where $r = 2^k$ for some $k \in \mathbb{N}$, $c_0, \ldots, c_{r-1} \in R[x]$ with $\deg c_i < \deg m_i$ for all i, and the polynomials $M_{i,j}$ as in (1).
Output: The polynomial $f = \displaystyle\sum_{0 \leq i < r} c_i \frac{m}{m_i} \in R[x]$, where $m = m_0 \cdots m_{r-1}$.

1. **if** $r = 1$ **then return** c_0

2. **call** the algorithm recursively to compute $r_0 = \displaystyle\sum_{0 \leq i < r/2} c_i \frac{M_{k-1,0}}{m_i}$

3. **call** the algorithm recursively to compute $r_1 = \displaystyle\sum_{r/2 \leq i < r} c_i \frac{M_{k-1,1}}{m_i}$

4. **return** $M_{k-1,1} r_0 + M_{k-1,0} r_1$ ▬▬▬▬▬▬▬▬▬▬▬▬▬▬▬▬▬▬▬▬

▬ THEOREM 10.21. ▬

Algorithm 10.20 works correctly. If $\sum_{0 \leq i < r} \deg m_i < n$, then it takes no more than $(2M(n) + O(n)) \log r$ or $O(M(n) \log r)$ arithmetic operations in R. ▬

The correctness proof is analogous to the proof of Theorem 10.10 and the running time bound can be obtained by considering the same binary tree as in the proof of Theorem 10.15. The details can be found in Exercise 10.16.

▬ ALGORITHM 10.22 Fast Chinese Remainder Algorithm. ▬

Input: $m_0, \ldots, m_{r-1} \in R[x]$ such that $\text{res}(m_i, m_j) \in R^\times$ for $i \neq j$, where R is a ring (commutative, with 1), $r = 2^k$ for some $k \in \mathbb{N}$, and $v_0, \ldots, v_{r-1} \in R[x]$ with $\deg v_i < \deg m_i$ for all i.

Output: The unique polynomial $f \in R[x]$ of degree less than $n = \sum_{0 \leq i < r} \deg m_i$ such that $f \equiv v_i \bmod m_i$ for $0 \leq i < n$.

1. **call** Algorithm 10.3 with input $m_0, \ldots, m_{r-1}$ to compute the polynomials $M_{i,j}$ as in (1)

2. **call** Algorithm 10.18 with input $m_0, \ldots, m_{r-1}$ and $m = M_{k,0}$ to compute polynomials $s_i \in R[x]$ with $s_i \dfrac{m}{m_i} \equiv 1 \bmod m_i$ and $\deg s_i < \deg m_i$ for all i

3. **call** Algorithm 10.9 with input $m_0, \ldots, m_{r-1}$, $v_0 s_0 \text{ rem } m_0, \ldots, v_{r-1} s_{r-1} \text{ rem } m_{r-1}$, and the polynomials $M_{i,j}$
   return its result ▬

▬ COROLLARY 10.23. ▬

Given $m_0, \ldots, m_{r-1} \in F[x]$ monic and pairwise coprime, where F is a field, and $v_0, \ldots, v_{r-1} \in F[x]$ with $\deg v_i < \deg m_i$ for all i, we can compute the unique solution $f \in F[x]$ of degree less than $n = \sum_{0 \leq i < r} \deg m_i$ of the Chinese Remainder Problem

$$f \equiv v_i \bmod m_i \text{ for } 0 \leq i < r$$

using $O(M(n) \log n)$ operations in F. ▬

Exercise 10.17 gives an explicit constant for the leading cost term of Algorithm 10.22 when all moduli have the same degree.

We only state the corresponding results for the integer case. Algorithms 10.14 and 10.20 carry over almost literally; the details are left as an exercise.

▬ THEOREM 10.24. ▬

Given $m_0, \ldots, m_{r-1} \in \mathbb{N}_{\geq 2}$ and $f \in \mathbb{N}$ less than $m = \prod_{0 \leq i < r} m_i$, we can compute $f \text{ rem } m_0, \ldots, f \text{ rem } m_{r-1}$ using $O(M(\log m) \log r)$ word operations. ▬

━━━ THEOREM 10.25. ━━

Given pairwise coprime integers $m_0, \dots, m_{r-1} \in \mathbb{N}_{\geq 2}$ and $v_0, \dots, v_{r-1} \in \mathbb{N}$ such that $v_i < m_i$ for all i, we can compute the unique solution $f \in \mathbb{N}$ with $f < m = \prod_{0 \leq i < r} m_i$ of the Chinese Remainder Problem $f \equiv v_i \bmod m_i$ for $0 \leq i < r$, at a cost of $O(\mathsf{M}(\log m) \log\log m)$ operations in F. ━━━

Notes.   Pan (1966) proved the optimality of Horner's rule. The results in Sections 10.1 through 10.3 are based on Lipson (1971), Fiduccia (1972a), Horowitz (1972), Moenck & Borodin (1972), and Borodin & Moenck (1974). Borodin & Munro (1975) give a comprehensive treatment.

Exercises.

10.1 Let $f = 8x^7 + 7x^6 + 6x^5 + 5x^4 + 4x^3 + 3x^2 + 2x + 1 \in \mathbb{Q}[x]$. Trace Algorithm 10.7 to evaluate f at the eight integer points $-3, -2, \cdots, 4$. In the recursive algorithm 10.5, you need only execute the last recursive step and may compute its inputs directly.

10.2 Let R be a ring (commutative, with 1), $n \in \mathbb{N}$ a power of 2, and $k \in \mathbb{N}$. Show that you can evaluate a polynomial of degree less than kn at n points from R using $(2k + 1 + \frac{11}{2}\log n)\mathsf{M}(n) + O((k + \log n)n)$ additions and multiplications in R. Hint: Exercise 9.16.

10.3 Let R be a ring (commutative, with 1), $m_0, \dots, m_{r-1} \in R[x]$ of degree $d > 0$, and $n = rd$ for a power of two r. Using Exercise 8.34, prove that Algorithm 10.3 takes only $(\mathsf{M}(n/2) + O(n))\log r$ or $(\frac{1}{2}\mathsf{M}(n) + O(n))\log r$ ring operations.

10.4* Let $n \in \mathbb{N}$ and $p_1, \dots, p_n \in \mathbb{R}_{>0}$ such that $\sum_{1 \leq i \leq n} p_i = 1$.
  (i) Prove that $H(p_1, \dots, p_n) \geq 0$, with equality if and only if $n = 1$.
  (ii) Prove that $H(p_1, \dots, p_n) \leq \log n$, with equality if and only if $p_1 = \cdots = p_n = 1/n$. Hint: Use $\ln x \leq x - 1$ for all $x \in \mathbb{R}$, with equality if and only if $x = 1$, and apply this to the expression $\sum_{1 \leq i \leq n} p_i \ln(1/p_i n)/\ln 2$.

10.5** A **mobile** is a complete binary tree with additive node weights, so that each node has either no child (it is a **leaf**) or two children (it is an **internal node**), and a positive real number, its **weight**. The weight of an internal node is the sum of the weights of its two children. By induction, the weight of any node in a mobile is the sum of the weights of all leaves in the subtree rooted at that node, and in particular, the weight of the root is the sum of the weights of all leaves. A **stochastic mobile** is a mobile with root weight 1; it is useful to imagine all weights to be probabilities. Any mobile can be turned into a stochastic mobile by dividing all weights by the root weight. The **depth** of a node in a mobile is the length of the path from the root to that node. The **average depth** of a stochastic mobile with n leaves is $\sum_{1 \leq i \leq n} p_i d_i$, where p_i is the weight and d_i is the depth of leaf i. For given stochastic leaf weights, we are interested in mobiles whose average depth is as small as possible. The following figure shows a stochastic mobile with five leaves and average depth $9/4$.

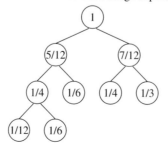

(i) Prove that the average depth of any stochastic mobile with leaf weights $p_1, \ldots, p_n$ is at least $H(p_1, \ldots, p_n)$. Hint: Induction on n.

(ii) For given $p_1, \ldots, p_n \in \mathbb{R}_{>0}$ such that $\sum_{1 \le i \le n} p_i = 1$, let $l_i = -\lfloor \log p_i \rfloor > 0$ for $1 \le i \le n$, $l = \max\{l_i : 1 \le i \le n\}$, and n_j be the number of indices i such that $l_i = j$, for $1 \le j \le l$. Prove that $\sum_{1 \le j \le l} n_j 2^{-j} \le 1$.

(iii) Consider the following algorithm, which uses ideas by Shannon (1948), Fano (1949, 1961), and Kraft (1949) for constructing a stochastic mobile of small average depth.

▬▬ ALGORITHM 10.26 Building a mobile. ▬▬▬▬▬▬▬▬▬▬▬▬▬▬▬▬▬▬▬▬
Input: $p_1, \ldots, p_n \in \mathbb{R}_{>0}$ such that $\sum_{1 \le i \le n} p_i = 1$.
Output: A stochastic mobile with leaf weights $p_1, \ldots, p_n$.

1. let $l_1, \ldots, l_n, l, n_1, \ldots, n_l$ be as in (ii), and create a full binary tree t (that is, a complete binary tree with 2^l leaves of depth l) with all node weights equal to zero

2. **for** $j = 1, \ldots, l$ **do**

3.   assign those weights p_i with $l_i = j$ to the first n_j of the nodes of depth j in t and remove the subtree of each such node with positive weight from t

4. **for** $j = l, l-1, \ldots, 1$ remove the leaves of depth j with zero weight in t

5. **while** the tree t is not complete, so that there exists a node with a single child, identify that node with its child and remove the edge between them

6. compute the weights of the inner nodes in t, proceeding from the leaves to the root
   return t ▬▬▬▬▬▬▬▬▬▬▬▬▬▬▬▬▬▬▬▬▬▬▬▬▬▬▬▬▬▬

Use (ii) to show that before the jth pass through step 3, there are precisely $2^j - n_1 2^{j-1} - n_2 2^{j-2} - \cdots - n_{j-1} \cdot 2 \ge n_j$ nodes of depth j left in t, and conclude that the algorithm works correctly.

(iv) Prove that the average depth of t after step 4 is less than $H(p_1, \ldots, p_n) + 1$, and conclude that this is true as well for the tree returned in step 6.

(v) Run the algorithm with $p_1 = p_3 = p_7 = p_8 = 1/17$, $p_2 = 5/17$, $p_4 = p_5 = 2/17$, and $p_6 = 4/17$.

10.6* This exercise discusses Huffman (1952) codes, a tool for data compression. suppose that we want to encode a piece of text over a finite alphabet $\Sigma = \{\sigma_1, \ldots, \sigma_n\}$ in binary using as few bits as possible. If we know nothing more than the size of Σ, then there seems to be no better way than to choose some encoding of the elements Σ as bit strings of fixed length $\lceil \log n \rceil$. Suppose now that for each element σ_i, we know the frequency p_i with which it occurs in our text. The idea of the Huffman code is then to use a variable-length encoding which encodes letters that occur frequently by shorter bit strings than letters that only rarely occur. Huffman codes are **instantaneous codes**, so that no codeword is a prefix of another codeword, and can be represented by binary trees.

Here is an algorithm which dynamically builds a stochastic mobile (Exercise 10.5) with leaf weights $p_1, \ldots, p_n$, the **Huffman tree**, which has minimal average depth.

▬▬ ALGORITHM 10.27 Building a Huffman tree. ▬▬▬▬▬▬▬▬▬▬▬▬▬▬
Input: $p_1, \ldots, p_n \in \mathbb{R}_{>0}$ such that $p_1 + \cdots + p_n = 1$.
Output: A Huffman tree for $p_1, \ldots, p_n$.

1. create n nodes $t_1, \ldots, t_n$, such that t_i has weight p_i,
   $T \longleftarrow \{t_1, \ldots, t_n\}$

2. **repeat**

3.   choose two trees $t^*, t^{**} \in T$ with root weights p^*, p^{**}, such that $p^* \le p^{**}$ and the roots of all other trees in T have weight at least p^{**}

4.   create a new tree t with root weight $p^* + p^{**}$ and children t^* and t^{**}

5. $T \longleftarrow (T \setminus \{t^*, t^{**}\}) \cup \{t\}$

6. **until** $\#T = 1$

7. **return** the single tree in T ▭▭▭▭▭▭▭▭▭▭▭▭▭▭▭▭▭▭

(i) Build a Huffman tree for "MISSISSIPPI_RIVER" over the alphabet $\Sigma = \{E, I, M, P, R, S, V, \_\}$. (There is some non-determinism in step 3 if there are several trees with minimal root weights, so the Huffman tree is not unique.)

(ii) To encode a piece of text, the two edges from a node to its two children in the Huffman tree are labeled 0 and 1, and the encoding of σ_i is obtained by concatenating the edge labels on the path from the root to leaf i of weight p_i. The average length of a codeword is then the average depth of the tree. Encode the text from (i), both with the Huffman tree and with the tree from Exercise 10.5, and compare the length of the resulting bit string to the length when using a fixed-length 3 bit code.

It is possible to show that the Huffman tree has minimal average depth (see, for example, Hamming (1986), §4.8, or Knuth (1997), §2.3.4.5), and Exercise 10.5 implies that its average depth is less than $H(p_1, \ldots, p_n) + 1$.

10.7* Let R be a ring (commutative, with 1), $m_0, \ldots, m_{r-1} \in R[x]$ nonconstant, $m = m_0 \cdots m_{r-1}$ of degree n, and $p_i = (\deg m_i)/n$ for all i. Let t be a stochastic mobile for $p_0, \ldots, p_{r-1}$ with average depth d, as in Exercise 10.5.

(i) Prove that $d + 1 = \sum_v p(v)$, where the sum is over all nodes of t and $p(v)$ is the weight of node v. Conclude that d is the sum of the weights of all internal nodes in t.

(ii) Show that computing m along the tree t, with m_i at the leaf of weight p_i, takes at most $d\,\mathsf{M}(n)$ operations in R. You may assume that $\mathsf{M}(n) = n S(n)$ for a monotonic function S. Conclude that m can be computed with less than $\mathsf{M}(n)(H(p_0, \ldots, p_{r-1}) + 1)$ operations.

(iii) Now assume that $\deg m_0 = 1$ and $\deg m_i = 2^{i-1}$ for $1 \leq i < r$. Show that $H(p_0, \ldots, p_{r-1}) = 2$ and find a stochastic mobile for $p_0, \ldots, p_{r-1}$ of average depth 2. Conclude that you can compute m using at most $2\mathsf{M}(n)$ operations in R, and compare this to the bound from Lemma 10.4. Using Exercise 8.34, reduce the bound to $\mathsf{M}(n) + O(n)$.

10.8 Let $r = 2^k$ for some $k \in \mathbb{N}$, $m_0, \ldots, m_{r-1}$ positive integers of length $\lambda(m_i) \leq l$ (see Section 2.1), and $M_{ij} \in \mathbb{N}$ for $0 \leq i \leq k$ and $0 \leq j < 2^{k-i}$ as in (1).

(i) Find a close upper bound on the length of $M_{i,j}$ depending only on i and l.

(ii) Prove that all $M_{i,j}$ can be computed using $O(\mathsf{M}(rl) \log r)$ word operations.

10.9 (Montgomery 1992) Let R be a ring (commutative, with 1), $m_0, \ldots, m_{r-1} \in R[x]$ monic of degree $d > 0$, the subproducts M_{ij} as in (1) for all i, j, and $n = rd$ for a power $r = 2^k$ of 2.

(i) Use Exercise 9.5 to show that all $\mathrm{rev}(M_{ij})^{-1}$ rem $x^{2^i d}$ for $i < k$ can be computed with $(k+1) \cdot (\mathsf{M}(n) + O(n))$ ring operations.

(ii) Conclude from Exercise 10.3 and (i) that the fast multipoint evaluation algorithm 10.7 can be modified so as to use only $(1 + \frac{7}{2}\log n)(\mathsf{M}(n) + O(n))$ arithmetic operations in R.

10.10 Trace Algorithm 10.11 on computing the interpolating polynomial $f \in \mathbb{Q}[x]$ of degree less than 4 such that $f(u) = 2^u$ for $u = 0, 1, 2, 3$.

10.11 In this exercise, you are to examine the cost for several evaluations and interpolations at the same set of points. Show that one evaluation can be done with at most $(2\mathsf{M}(n) + O(n)) \log n$ operations in R and one interpolation with at most $(\mathsf{M}(n) + O(n)) \log n$ operations if the cost for precomputing data depending only on the points is ignored. Hint: Some preconditioning on the divisors in the "going down" is possible; see Section 9.1.

10.12* Let $n = 2^k$ be a power of 2, F a field, $u_0, \ldots, u_{n-1} \in F$ distinct, and $v_0, \ldots, v_{n-1} \in F$. You are to design an interpolation algorithm with running time $O(\mathsf{M}(n) \log^2 n)$.

(i) Let $m_1, m_2 \in F[x]$ of degree n be monic and coprime and $v_1, v_2 \in F[x]$ of degree less than n. Using Theorem 11.7, give an algorithm that computes a solution $f \in F[x]$ of degree less than $2n$ of the congruences $f \equiv v_1 \bmod m_1$ and $f \equiv v_2 \bmod m_2$, taking $O(\mathsf{M}(n) \log n)$ operations in F.

(ii) Use (i) to design a divide-and-conquer algorithm computing the interpolating polynomial $f \in F[x]$ of degree less than n such that $f(u_i) = v_i$ for all i, and show that it takes $O(\mathsf{M}(n) \log^2 n)$ operations in F.

(iii) Trace your algorithm on the example from Exercise 10.10.

10.13* Prove Theorem 10.13. Hint: Exercise 6.15.

10.14* Prove the following generalized version of the Chinese Remainder Theorem. Let R be a ring (commutative, with 1), $I_0, \ldots, I_{r-1}$ ideals, and $I = I_0 \cap \cdots \cap I_{r-1}$. If $I_i + I_j = R$ for $i \neq j$, then the map

$$\begin{aligned} \chi : R/I &\longrightarrow R/I_0 \times \ldots \times R/I_{r-1}, \\ f \bmod I &\longmapsto (f \bmod I_0, \ldots, f \bmod I_{r-1}) \end{aligned}$$

is an isomorphism.

10.15 Prove that Algorithm 10.14 works correctly.

10.16* Prove Theorem 10.21.

10.17* (i) Prove that when all moduli have the same degree, then the fast modular reduction algorithm 10.16 takes only $(11\mathsf{M}(n/2) + O(n)) \log r$ or $(\frac{11}{2}\mathsf{M}(n) + O(n)) \log r$ ring operations and Algorithm 10.20 takes only $(\mathsf{M}(n) + O(n)) \log r$ operations.

(ii) Show that Algorithm 10.18 takes at most $(11 \log r + 24 \log(n/r) + 5)\mathsf{M}(n) + O(n \log n)$ arithmetic operations if R is a field and all moduli have the same degree, using (i) and Theorem 11.7.

(iii) Conclude that the fast Chinese Remainder Algorithm 10.22 takes at most $(24\mathsf{M}(n) + O(n)) \cdot \log n$ arithmetic operations if R is a field and all moduli have the same degree.

You may find Exercise 10.3 useful.

10.18 Let F be a field, $f_1, \ldots, f_r \in F[x]$ pairwise coprime, $e_1, \ldots, e_r \in \mathbb{N}_{>0}$, $f = f_1^{e_1} \cdots f_r^{e_r}$, and $g \in F[x]$ of degree less than $\deg f$. Show that the partial fraction decomposition of g/f with respect to the given factorization of f (see Section 5.11) can be computed with $O(\mathsf{M}(n) \log n)$ field operations.

10.19* Work out the details for the integer versions of Algorithms 10.14 and 10.20, and prove Theorems 10.24 and 10.25.

10.20$^\rightarrow$ You are to trace the integer analog of Algorithms 10.14 and 10.20. The point is to see how the algorithm works, not just to compute the final result. Let $m_0 = 23, m_1 = 24, m_2 = 25$, and $m_3 = 29$.

(i) Check that the moduli are pairwise coprime.

(ii) Compute the binary tree of products.

(iii) Compute $300\,000 \bmod m_i$ for $0 \leq i < 3$, using Algorithm 10.14.

(iv) Let $v_0 = 5, v_1 = 3, v_2 = 1$, and $v_3 = 22$. Use the fast Chinese Remainder Algorithm to compute $f \in \mathbb{Z}$ such that $f \equiv v_i \bmod m_i$ for $0 \leq i < 4$.

10.21* Let $a, b \in \mathbb{Z}[x]$ nonzero such that $\deg b < \deg a = n$ and $\|a\|_\infty \leq A$. You are to design a small primes modular algorithm that decides whether $b \mid a$, and if so, computes the quotient $q = a/b \in \mathbb{Z}[x]$. By Mignotte's bound 6.33, we have $\|b\|_1 \|q\|_1 \leq B = (n+1)^{1/2} 2^n A$ in the latter case. The algorithm should choose a collection of distinct primes $p_1, \ldots, p_r < 2r \log r$ not dividing $\mathrm{lc}(b)$, with r chosen appropriately such that their product exceeds $2B$, calculate $(a \bmod p_i)/(b \bmod p_i)$ for all i (if this is not possible, then certainly $b \nmid a$), compute a trial quotient q by Chinese remaindering, and finally check whether $\|b\|_1 \|q\|_1 \leq B$. Work out the details, prove that this procedure works correctly, and show that it takes $O((\mathsf{M}(n) + \log\log\log B) \log B \cdot \mathsf{M}(\log\log B) + n\mathsf{M}(\log B \log\log B) \log\log B)$ or $O^\sim(n^2 + n \log A)$ word operations. You may ignore the cost of $O(\log B (\log\log B)^2 \log\log\log B)$ word operations for finding the small primes (Theorem 18.10). Use Corollary 11.10 for arithmetic in $\mathbb{F}_{p_i}$. See also Exercises 6.26 and 9.14.

The mathematically sophisticated will know how to skip formulæ.
This skill is easy to practice for others also.

Leslie G. Valiant (1994)

Thus it appears that whatever may be the number of digits
the Analytical Engine is capable of holding, if it is required to
make all the computations with k times that number of digits,
then it can be executed by the same Engine,
but in an amount of time equal to k^2 times the former.

Charles Babbage (1864)

Τόδε ἤδη ἐπεσκέψω, ὡς οἵ τε φύσει λογιστικοὶ εἰς πάντα τὰ
μαθήματα ὡς ἔπος εἰπεῖν ὀξεῖς φύονται, οἵ τε βραδεῖσ, ἄν ἐν τούτω
παιδευθῶσι καὶ γυμνάσωνται, κἄν μηδὲν ἄλλο ὠφεληθῶσιν, ὅμως
εἴς γε τὸ ὀξύτεροι αὐτοὶ αὑτῶν γίγνεσθαι πάντες ἐπιδιδόασιν.[1]

Plato (c. 375 BC)

---

[1] Have you [Glaukon] ever noticed that those who have a talent for mathematics are, almost without exception, talented in all sciences? And that mentally slow people, if they be trained and exercised in this study, become invariably quicker than they were before, even if they draw no other profit from it?

11

Fast Euclidean Algorithm

The main result of this chapter is a fast algorithm for the quotients in the Euclidean Algorithm for univariate polynomials over a field, using $O(\mathsf{M}(n)\log n)$ field operations for inputs of degree at most n. One can also compute a single remainder r_i together with the corresponding s_i and t_i, at the same cost, but this is not possible for all remainders together. The last section shows how one can also calculate subresultants in softly linear time.

11.1. A fast Euclidean Algorithm for polynomials

Let F be a field, $r_0, r_1 \in F[x] \setminus \{0\}$ monic with $\deg r_0 \geq \deg r_1$, $s_0 = t_1 = 1$, $s_1 = t_0 = 0$, and

$$\rho_2 r_2 \; = \; r_0 - q_1 r_1, \qquad \rho_2 s_2 = s_0 - q_1 s_1, \qquad \rho_2 t_2 = t_0 - q_1 t_1,$$

$$\vdots$$

$$\rho_{i+1} r_{i+1} \; = \; r_{i-1} - q_i r_i, \qquad \rho_{i+1} s_{i+1} = s_{i-1} - q_i s_i, \qquad \rho_{i+1} t_{i+1} = t_{i-1} - q_i t_i,$$

$$\vdots$$

$$0 \; = \; r_{\ell-1} - q_\ell r_\ell, \qquad \rho_{l+1} s_{l+1} = s_{l-1} - q_l s_l, \qquad \rho_{l+1} t_{l+1} = t_{l-1} - q_l t_l$$

be the results of the Extended Euclidean Algorithm for r_0, r_1, where $\deg r_{i+1} < \deg r_i$ for $1 \leq i < \ell$, as introduced in (3) of Section 3.2. We will assume that $\rho_{\ell+1} = 1$, $r_{\ell+1} = 0$, and $\deg r_{\ell+1} = -\infty$. Then Lemma 3.8 says that

$$\begin{pmatrix} r_i \\ r_{i+1} \end{pmatrix} = \begin{pmatrix} 0 & 1 \\ \rho_{i+1}^{-1} & -q_i \rho_{i+1}^{-1} \end{pmatrix} \begin{pmatrix} r_{i-1} \\ r_i \end{pmatrix} = Q_i \begin{pmatrix} r_{i-1} \\ r_i \end{pmatrix} = Q_i \cdots Q_1 \begin{pmatrix} r_0 \\ r_1 \end{pmatrix},$$

where

$$Q_i = \begin{pmatrix} 0 & 1 \\ \rho_{i+1}^{-1} & -q_i \rho_{i+1}^{-1} \end{pmatrix} \in F[x]^{2 \times 2} \quad \text{and} \quad R_i = Q_i \cdots Q_1 = \begin{pmatrix} s_i & t_i \\ s_{i+1} & t_{i+1} \end{pmatrix}. \quad (1)$$

Let $n_i = \deg r_i$ for $0 \leq i \leq \ell$ and $m_i = \deg q_i = n_{i-1} - n_i$ for $1 \leq i \leq \ell$. The sequence $(n_0, n_1, \ldots, n_\ell)$ is the **degree sequence** in the Extended Euclidean Algorithm for r_0, r_1. If $F = \mathbb{F}_q$ is the finite field with q elements, $n_0 > n_1$, and

$r_0, r_1 \in \mathbb{F}_q[x]$ with $\deg r_0 = n_0$ and $\deg r_1 = n_1$ are uniform random polynomials, then

$$\text{prob}(\deg r_2 < n_1 - 1) = \frac{1}{q}$$

(Exercise 4.18), which is rather small for large q. So typically one can expect that the degree of each quotient is 1, or equivalently, that $n_{i+1} = n_i - 1$ for $1 \leq i < \ell$. In that case, we call the degree sequence $(n_0, \ldots, n_\ell)$ **normal**.

The basic idea leading to a fast gcd algorithm is that the first quotients q_i only depend on the highest coefficients of r_0 and r_1. To express this idea formally, we introduce the following notation.

Let $f = f_n x^n + f_{n-1} x^{n-1} + \cdots + f_0 \in F[x]$ with leading coefficient $f_n \neq 0$, and $k \in \mathbb{Z}$. Then we define the truncated polynomial

$$f \upharpoonright k = f_n x^k + f_{n-1} x^{k-1} + \cdots + f_{n-k},$$

where we set $f_i = 0$ for $i < 0$. So for $k \geq 0$, $f \upharpoonright k$ is a polynomial of degree k whose coefficients are the $k+1$ highest coefficients of f, and $f \upharpoonright k = 0$ for $k < 0$. For all $i \geq 0$ we have that $(fx^i) \upharpoonright k = f \upharpoonright k$.

Now let $f, g, f^*, g^* \in F[x] \setminus \{0\}$ with $\deg f \geq \deg g$ and $\deg f^* \geq \deg g^*$, and $k \in \mathbb{Z}$. Then (f, g) **and** (f^*, g^*) **coincide up to** k if

$$
\begin{aligned}
f \upharpoonright k &= f^* \upharpoonright k, \\
g \upharpoonright (k - (\deg f - \deg g)) &= g^* \upharpoonright (k - (\deg f^* - \deg g^*)).
\end{aligned}
$$

This defines an equivalence relation on $F[x] \times F[x]$ (Exercise 11.1). If (f, g) and (f^*, g^*) coincide up to k and $k \geq \deg f - \deg g$, then $\deg f - \deg g = \deg f^* - \deg g^*$.

We consider one division step in the Euclidean Algorithm.

LEMMA 11.1. *Let $k \in \mathbb{Z}$, (f, g) and (f^*, g^*) in $(F[x] \setminus \{0\})^2$ coincide up to $2k$, and $k \geq \deg f - \deg g \geq 0$. Define $q, r, q^*, r^* \in F[x]$ by division with remainder:*

$$
\begin{aligned}
f &= qg + r, & \deg r &< \deg g, \\
f^* &= q^* g^* + r^*, & \deg r^* &< \deg g^*.
\end{aligned}
$$

Then $q = q^*$, and either (g, r) and (g^*, r^*) coincide up to $2(k - \deg q)$ or $r = 0$ or $k - \deg q < \deg g - \deg r$.

PROOF. By multiplying (f, g) and (f^*, g^*) with appropriate powers of x if necessary, we may assume that $\deg f = \deg f^* > 2k$ holds. Then $\deg g = \deg g^*$, $k \geq \deg q = \deg f - \deg g = \deg f^* - \deg g^* = \deg q^*$,

$$
\begin{aligned}
\deg(f - f^*) &< \deg f - 2k \leq \deg g - k, \\
\deg(g - g^*) &< \deg g - (2k - (\deg f - \deg g)) = \deg f - 2k \\
&\leq \deg g - k \leq \deg g - \deg q, \\
\deg(r - r^*) &\leq \max\{\deg r, \deg r^*\} < \deg g,
\end{aligned}
\tag{2}
$$

and

$$f - f^* = q(g - g^*) + (q - q^*)g^* + (r - r^*). \tag{3}$$

The polynomials $f - f^*$, $q(g - g^*)$ and $r - r^*$ all have degree less than $\deg g$ by (2), hence also $\deg((q - q^*)g^*) < \deg g = \deg g^*$, which implies that $q = q^*$.

Now we assume that $r \neq 0$ and $k - \deg q \geq \deg g - \deg r$. We have to show that

$$
\begin{aligned}
g \upharpoonright (2(k - \deg q)) &= g^* \upharpoonright (2(k - \deg q)), \\
r \upharpoonright (2(k - \deg q) - (\deg g - \deg r)) &= r^* \upharpoonright (2(k - \deg q) - (\deg g^* - \deg r^*)).
\end{aligned}
$$

The first assertion follows from the coincidence up to $2k$ of (f, g) and (f^*, g^*). Furthermore we have

$$
\begin{aligned}
\deg(r - r^*) &\leq \max\{\deg(f - f^*), \deg q + \deg(g - g^*)\} \\
&< \deg q + \deg f - 2k = \deg g - 2(k - \deg q) \tag{4} \\
&= \deg r - (2(k - \deg q) - (\deg g - \deg r)),
\end{aligned}
$$

by (3) and (2), and by the above assumption

$$\deg r \geq \deg q + \deg g - k \geq \deg q + \deg f - 2k,$$

so that $\deg r = \deg r^*$. Now the second assertion follows from the second inequality in (4). $\square$

EXAMPLE 11.2. Let

$$
\begin{aligned}
f &= x^8 + 5x^7 + 3x^6 + 5x^4 + 5x^3 + 5x^2 + 2x + 2, \\
g &= x^7 + 4x^6 + 4x^5 + 2x^4 + x^3 + 5x^2 + x + 3
\end{aligned}
$$

be polynomials over $\mathbb{F}_7$, and

$$f \upharpoonright 4 = x^4 + 5x^3 + 3x + 5, \quad g \upharpoonright 3 = x^3 + 4x^2 + 4x + 2.$$

Then (f, g) and $(f \upharpoonright 4, g \upharpoonright 3)$ coincide up to $2 \cdot 2 = 4$, so that $k = 2$. In the proof of Lemma 11.1, we multiply the second pair with x^4 and obtain

$$f^* = x^8 + 5x^7 + 3x^5 + 5x^4, \quad g^* = x^7 + 4x^6 + 4x^5 + 2x^4.$$

Then

$$
\begin{aligned}
q &= x + 1, & r &= 2x^6 + x^5 + 2x^4 + 6x^3 + 6x^2 + 5x + 6, \\
q^* &= x + 1, & r^* &= 2x^6 + x^5 + 3x^4.
\end{aligned}
$$

We see that $q = q^*$ and $r \upharpoonright 1 = r^* \upharpoonright 1$, and since $g \upharpoonright 2 = g^* \upharpoonright 2$, we have that (g, r) and (g^*, r^*) coincide up to $2 = 2(k - \deg q)$. Now $r^*/x^4 = (f \upharpoonright 4)$ rem $(g \upharpoonright 3)$, and we find that also (g, r) and $(g \upharpoonright 3, (f \upharpoonright 4)$ rem $(g \upharpoonright 3))$ coincide up to $2(k - \deg q)$, as stated in the lemma. $\diamond$

Lemma 11.1 gives only sufficient conditions for the quotients to be equal. Often less information is necessary; in the above example, the constant coefficient of f^* may be altered without changing the quotient.

Next we consider the Euclidean Algorithm for two pairs r_0, r_1 and r_0^*, r_1^* of monic polynomials with $\deg r_0 > \deg r_1$ and $\deg r_0^* > \deg r_1^*$:

$$
\begin{array}{rclcrcl}
r_0 &=& q_1 r_1 + p_2 r_2, & & r_0^* &=& q_1^* r_1^* + p_2^* r_2^*, \\
&\vdots& & & &\vdots& \\
r_{i-1} &=& q_i r_i + p_{i+1} r_{i+1}, & & r_{i-1}^* &=& q_i^* r_i^* + p_{i+1}^* r_{i+1}^*, \\
&\vdots& & & &\vdots& \\
& & & & r_{\ell^*-1}^* &=& q_{\ell^*}^* r_{\ell^*}^*, \\
r_{\ell-1} &=& q_\ell r_\ell
\end{array}
$$

of length ℓ and ℓ^*, respectively, and let $m_i = \deg q_i$ for $1 \le i \le \ell$ and $m_i^* = \deg q_i^*$ for $1 \le i \le \ell^*$. As usual, we let $n_i = \deg r_i = n_0 - m_1 - \cdots - m_i$ for $0 \le i \le \ell$ and $n_{\ell+1} = -\infty$.

We define for any $k \in \mathbb{N}$ the number $\eta(k) \in \mathbb{N}$ by

$$
\eta(k) = \max\{0 \le j \le \ell : \sum_{1 \le i \le j} m_i \le k\},
$$

so that

$$
n_0 - n_{\eta(k)} = \sum_{1 \le i \le \eta(k)} m_i \le k < \sum_{1 \le i \le \eta(k)+1} m_i = n_0 - n_{\eta(k)+1}, \tag{5}
$$

where the second inequality only holds if $\eta(k) < \ell$, and $\eta(k)$ is uniquely determined by (5). In other words, the number $n_0 - k$ is sandwiched between the two consecutive remainder degrees $\deg r_{\eta(k)}$ and $\deg r_{\eta(k)+1}$ in the Euclidean Algorithm. In particular, $\eta(k) \le k$ since $m_i \ge 1$ for $1 \le i \le \ell$. We define $\eta^*(k)$ analogously. The following lemma says, in a precise way, that the first results in the Euclidean Algorithm only depend on the top part of the inputs.

LEMMA 11.3. *Let* $k \in \mathbb{N}$, $h = \eta(k)$, *and* $h^* = \eta^*(k)$. *If* (r_0, r_1) *and* (r_0^*, r_1^*) *coincide up to* $2k$, *then* $h = h^*$, $q_i = q_i^*$ *and* $p_{i+1} = p_{i+1}^*$ *for* $1 \le i \le h$.

PROOF. We show by induction on j that the following holds for $0 \le j \le h$.

$j \le h^*$, $q_i = q_i^*$ and $p_{i+1} = p_{i+1}^*$ for $1 \le i \le j$, and either $j = h$ or (r_j, r_{j+1}) and (r_j^*, r_{j+1}^*) coincide up to $2(k - \sum_{1 \le i \le j} m_i)$.

The assertion of the lemma follows from this and the symmetric statement.

There is nothing to prove for $j = 0$, and the induction step follows from the induction hypothesis with one application of Lemma 11.1 and a subsequent normalization. The assertion $j \leq h^*$ is true because

$$\sum_{1 \leq i \leq j} \deg q_i^* = \sum_{1 \leq i \leq j} \deg q_i \leq \sum_{1 \leq i \leq h} \deg q_i \leq k,$$

and hence $j \leq \eta^*(k) = h^*$. $\square$

We use this lemma to construct a divide-and-conquer algorithm for a single row in the Extended Euclidean Algorithm, say the last one. One has to be careful in dividing the problem into two subproblems of about the same size. An appealing idea is to first compute the first $\ell/2$ of the quotients q_i and then the second half, where ℓ is the Euclidean length as usual, but this is not the best way because in general the quotients may have very different degrees. It is better to divide the sequence of the quotients into two parts such that the sum of the degrees in the first part is about the same as in the second part. In the case of a normal degree sequence, this will of course yield the same result as the first idea.

The following algorithm uses this strategy. For simplicity, it does not return the quotients, but instead returns the product of the corresponding Q-matrices. We recall that a nonzero polynomial is normalized if it is monic, and the zero polynomial is normalized.

━━ ALGORITHM 11.4 Fast Extended Euclidean Algorithm. ━━━━━━━━
Input: $r_0, r_1 \in F[x]$ normalized, $n = n_0 = \deg r_0 > n_1 = \deg r_1$, and $k \in \mathbb{N}$ with $0 \leq k \leq n$.
Output: $h = \eta(k) \in \mathbb{N}$ as defined above and $R_h \in F[x]^{2 \times 2}$ as in (1).

1. **if** $r_1 = 0$ or $k < n_0 - n_1$ **then return** 0 and $\begin{pmatrix} 1 & 0 \\ 0 & 1 \end{pmatrix}$

2. $d \longleftarrow \lfloor k/2 \rfloor$

3. **call** the algorithm recursively with input $r_0 \upharpoonright 2d$, $r_1 \upharpoonright (2d - (n_0 - n_1))$ and d, returning $j - 1 = \eta(d)$ and $R = Q_{j-1} \cdots Q_1$

4. $\begin{pmatrix} r_{j-1} \\ r_j \end{pmatrix} \longleftarrow R \begin{pmatrix} r_0 \\ r_1 \end{pmatrix}$, $\begin{pmatrix} n_{j-1} \\ n_j \end{pmatrix} \longleftarrow \begin{pmatrix} \deg r_{j-1} \\ \deg r_j \end{pmatrix}$

5. **if** $r_j = 0$ or $k < n_0 - n_j$ **then return** $j - 1$ and R

6. $q_j \longleftarrow r_{j-1}$ quo r_j, $\quad \rho_{j+1} \longleftarrow \mathrm{lc}(r_{j-1}$ rem $r_j)$,
   $r_{j+1} \longleftarrow \mathrm{normal}(r_{j-1}$ rem $r_j)$, $\quad n_{j+1} \longleftarrow \deg r_{j+1}$

7. $d^* \longleftarrow k - (n_0 - n_j)$

8. **call** the algorithm recursively with input $r_j \upharpoonright 2d^*$, $r_{j+1} \upharpoonright (2d^* - (n_j - n_{j+1}))$
   and d^*, returning $h - j = \eta(d^*)$ and $S = Q_h \cdots Q_{j+1}$

9. $Q_j \longleftarrow \begin{pmatrix} 0 & 1 \\ \rho_{j+1}^{-1} & -q_j\rho_{j+1}^{-1} \end{pmatrix}$
   return h and SQ_jR ▬▬▬▬▬▬▬▬▬▬▬▬▬

The restriction that $\deg r_0$ be strictly larger than $\deg r_1$ can be circumvented by interchanging r_0 and r_1 if $\deg r_0 < \deg r_1$, and by calling the algorithm with r_1 and normal$(r_0 - r_1)$ if $\deg r_0 = \deg r_1$. The subtraction, normalization, and the corresponding correction of R_h cost only $O(n)$ field operations and hence do not affect the asymptotic running time. Similarly, if we are given two arbitrary, not necessarily monic, polynomials $f, g \in F[x]$, then of course we run the algorithm on $r_0 = f / \mathrm{lc}(f)$ and $r_1 = g / \mathrm{lc}(g)$ and divide the first and the second column of the result R_h by $\mathrm{lc}(f)$ and $\mathrm{lc}(g)$, respectively, taking only $O(n)$ additional operations.

Before proving the correctness of the above algorithm, let us see how it works in the above example.

EXAMPLE 11.2 (continued). Let $r_0 = f$ and $r_1 = g$, where f and g are as in Example 11.2, and $k = 4$. The quotients in the Euclidean Algorithm for r_0 and r_1 are

$$q_1 = x + 1, \quad q_2 = x, \quad q_3 = x + 2, \quad q_4 = x^3 + 2$$

of degrees $m_1 = 1$, $m_2 = 1$, $m_3 = 1$, and $m_4 = 3$, the length is $\ell = 4$, and the ρ_i are $\rho_2 = \rho_4 = 2$, $\rho_3 = 3$, and $\rho_5 = 1$. The algorithm proceeds as follows.

2. $d = \lfloor 4/2 \rfloor = 2$.

3. The recursive call with $r_0 \upharpoonright (2 \cdot 2) = x^4 + 5x^3 + 3x + 5$, $r_1 \upharpoonright (2 \cdot 2 - (8 - 7)) = x^3 + 4x^2 + 4x + 2$ and $d = 2$ yields $j = 3$ and

$$R = Q_2Q_1 = \begin{pmatrix} 0 & 1 \\ 5 & 2x \end{pmatrix} \begin{pmatrix} 0 & 1 \\ 4 & 3x+3 \end{pmatrix}$$

$$= \begin{pmatrix} 4 & 3x+3 \\ x & 6x^2+6x+5 \end{pmatrix} = \begin{pmatrix} s_2 & t_2 \\ s_3 & t_3 \end{pmatrix}.$$

4. $\begin{pmatrix} r_2 \\ r_3 \end{pmatrix} = R \begin{pmatrix} r_0 \\ r_1 \end{pmatrix} = \begin{pmatrix} x^6 + 4x^5 + x^4 + 3x^3 + 3x^2 + 6x + 3 \\ x^5 + 2x^4 + 4x^3 + 2x^2 + 4x + 1 \end{pmatrix}.$

6. Here q_3, ρ_4, and $r_4 = x^2 + 2x + 4$ are computed.

7. $d^* = 4 - (8 - 5) = 1$.

8. The recursive call with $r_3 \lceil (2 \cdot 1) = x^2 + 2x + 4$, $r_4 \lceil (2 \cdot 1 - (5 - 2)) = 0$ and $d^* = 1$ yields $h = j$ and $S = \begin{pmatrix} 1 & 0 \\ 0 & 1 \end{pmatrix}$.

9. The matrix

$$
\begin{aligned}
SQ_3R &= \begin{pmatrix} 1 & 0 \\ 0 & 1 \end{pmatrix} \begin{pmatrix} 0 & 1 \\ 4 & 3x+6 \end{pmatrix} \begin{pmatrix} 4 & 3x+3 \\ x & 6x^2+6x+5 \end{pmatrix} \\
&= \begin{pmatrix} x & 6x^2+6x+5 \\ 3x^2+6x+2 & 4x^3+5x^2 \end{pmatrix} = \begin{pmatrix} s_3 & t_3 \\ s_4 & t_4 \end{pmatrix}
\end{aligned}
$$

and $h = \eta(4) = 3$ are returned, which is correct because

$$
\sum_{1 \le i \le 3} m_i = 3 \le 4 < 6 = \sum_{1 \le i \le 4} m_i. \quad \diamond
$$

We denote by log the binary logarithm.

━━━ THEOREM 11.5. ━━━

Algorithm 11.4 works correctly and uses no more than $(24M(k) + O(k)) \log k$ additions and multiplications plus k inversions, in total $O(M(k) \log k)$ operations in F if $n \le 2k$. The bound on the number of additions and multiplications drops to $(12M(k) + O(k)) \log k$ if the degree sequence is normal. ━━━

PROOF. Let ℓ be the Euclidean length of (r_0, r_1), $n_i = \deg r_i$ for $0 \le i \le \ell$, and $m_i = \deg q_i$ for $1 \le i \le \ell$ as usual. If $r_1 = 0$ or $k < n_0 - n_1$, then $\eta(k) = 0$, and the algorithm correctly returns the identity matrix in step 1 (note that the empty product is defined to be the multiplicative neutral element). Otherwise, we see by induction on k and Lemma 11.3 that the results of the recursive call in step 3 are correct. In particular, $n_0 - n_{j-1} \le d \le k$ by (5) and the definition of d. If now $r_j = 0$ or $k < n_0 - n_j$ in step 5, then $\eta(k) = j - 1$ and the algorithm returns the correct result. Otherwise, again by induction and Lemma 11.3, the results of the recursive call in step 8 are correct, and

$$
n_j - n_h = \sum_{j+1 \le i \le h} m_i \le d^* < \sum_{j+1 \le i \le h+1} m_i = n_j - n_{h+1} \tag{6}
$$

or $h = \ell$. It remains to show that $h = \eta(k)$. By (6) we have

$$
\begin{aligned}
n_0 - n_h &= (n_0 - n_j) + (n_j - n_h) \le (n_0 - n_j) + d^* \\
&< (n_0 - n_j) + (n_j - n_{h+1}) = n_0 - n_{h+1}
\end{aligned}
$$

or $h = \ell$. But this implies $h = \eta(n_0 - n_j + d^*) = \eta(k)$ by (5) and the definition of d^*, and hence the final results in step 9 are correct.

We may arrange things in such a way that the only inversions in F take place in step 6, and that ρ_{j+1}^{-1} is computed only once. During the recursive process, the number of times step 6 is executed is at most k.

Let $T(k)$ denote the number of additions and multiplications that the algorithm uses on input k. Steps 3 and 8 take $T(d) = T(\lfloor k/2 \rfloor)$ and $T(d^*)$ operations for solving a subproblem of the same kind, together at most $2T(\lfloor k/2 \rfloor)$ since $d^* = k - (n_0 - n_j) < k - d = \lceil k/2 \rceil$, by (5). We now analyze the cost for the polynomial multiplications, divisions, and additions in steps 4, 6 and 9.

In step 4, the entries of R are $s_{j-1}, t_{j-1}, s_j, t_j$, by Lemma 3.8, and their degrees are $n_1 - n_{j-2}, n_0 - n_{j-2}, n_1 - n_{j-1}, n_0 - n_{j-1}$, by Lemma 3.10. All four degrees are at most $n_0 - n_{j-1} \leq d = \lfloor k/2 \rfloor$. We have four multiplications of polynomials of degree at most $\lfloor k/2 \rfloor$ by polynomials of degree at most $2k$, plus some additions. Dividing the larger polynomials into blocks of degree at most $\lfloor k/2 \rfloor$ (Exercise 8.35), the cost for step 4 is $16M(\lfloor k/2 \rfloor) + O(k)$, or $8M(k) + O(k)$.

In step 6 we have $k \geq n_0 - n_j > d$. Thus

$$0 \leq n_0 - k \leq n_j < n_{j-1} \leq n_0 \leq 2k$$

and $0 < n_{j-1} - n_j \leq n_0 - (n_0 - k) = k$. Therefore computing the quotient of degree $n_{j-1} - n_j$ of the division of r_{j-1} by r_j takes $4M(k) + O(k)$ operations, by Theorem 9.6. By partitioning the divisor r_j into two blocks of size at most k, as in Exercise 8.35, the remainder can be computed using at most another $2M(k) + O(k)$ operations, together no more than $6M(k) + O(k)$, including the cost for the normalization. When the degree sequence is normal, then $n_{j-1} = n_j + 1$, and the time for the division is only $O(k)$.

In step 9, we first compute $Q_j R$, or equivalently, $s_{j+1} = (s_{j-1} - q_j s_j)\rho_{i+1}^{-1}$ and $t_{j+1} = (t_{j-1} - q_j t_j)\rho_{i+1}^{-1}$. This amounts to two multiplications of the quotient q_j of degree $n_{j-1} - n_j \leq n_0$ by a polynomial of degree at most $n_0 - n_{j-1} \leq \lfloor k/2 \rfloor$ plus some additions and multiplications, taking at most $8M(\lfloor k/2 \rfloor) + O(k)$ or $4M(k) + O(k)$. In the normal case, we have again only $O(k)$.

The degrees of s_{j+1} and t_{j+1}, the lower row of $Q_j R$, are at most $n_0 - n_j \leq k$. The entries of S have degrees $n_{j+1} - n_{h-1}, n_j - n_{h-1}, n_{j+1} - n_h, n_j - n_h$, all at most $n_j - n_h \leq d^* < k - d = \lceil k/2 \rceil$. Thus the computation of $S \cdot Q_j R$ takes at most another $4M(\lfloor k/2 \rfloor) + 4M(k) + O(k)$ or $6M(k) + O(k)$ operations. In the normal case, we have $n_0 - n_j = n_0 - n_{j-1} + 1 \leq \lfloor k/2 \rfloor + 1$, and an application of Exercise 8.34 shows that the bound drops to $8M(\lfloor k/2 \rfloor) + O(k)$ or $4M(k) + O(k)$.

Putting things together, we have a cost of at most $24M(k) + O(k)$. Thus T satisfies the recursive inequalities

$$T(0) = 0, \quad T(k) \leq 2T(\lfloor k/2 \rfloor) + 24M(k) + ck \text{ for } k > 0,$$

for some constant $c \in \mathbb{R}$, and hence $T(k)$ is at most $(24M(k) + O(k))\log k$, by Lemma 8.2. In the normal case, the bound drops to $(12M(k) + O(k))\log k$. $\square$

We have not attempted to determine the smallest possible constant in the place of 24. We note that if $\deg r_0 > 2k$, then it suffices to call the algorithm with input $r_0 \upharpoonright 2k$ and $r_1 \upharpoonright (2k - \deg r_0 + \deg r_1)$, by Lemma 11.3.

In fact, it is possible to prove a slightly better bound on the arithmetic cost for the "non-normal" case where not all the quotients have small degree. Strassen (1983) showed that in the nonscalar model of computation, where additions and multiplications by scalars are not counted and an interpolation algorithm proves (over an infinite field) that $M(n) \in O(n)$, the cost for Algorithm 11.4 when $k = n$ can be bounded by $O(n \cdot H(m_1/m, \ldots, m_\ell/m))$, where $m = \sum_{1 \le i \le \ell} m_i$ and H is the entropy function, as in Section 10.1. This coincides with the bound of Theorem 11.5 in the normal case, since then $m_i/m = 1/n$ for $1 \le i \le \ell = n$.

Strassen also showed that the computation of all quotients of the Euclidean Algorithm in the nonscalar model requires at least about $n \cdot H(m_1/m, \ldots, m_\ell/m)$ field operations for almost all pairs of polynomials with quotient degrees $m_1, \ldots, m_\ell$. This lower bound shows that Algorithm 11.4 is *uniformly optimal* in the nonscalar model.

Taking $M(n) \in O(n \log n \log \log n)$, Theorem 11.5 implies that all the quotients q_i in the Euclidean Algorithm can be computed in time $O^\sim(n)$. Can we also compute all the remainders r_i together in softly linear time? The answer is: no. In the normal case, where always $\deg r_i = n - i$, the number of coefficients of $r_0, \ldots, r_\ell$ is

$$\sum_{0 \le i \le \ell} (\deg r_i + 1) = \sum_{0 \le i \le n} (n - i + 1) = (n^2 + 3n + 2)/2.$$

But this means that the output size is quadratic in the input size $2n$, and hence any algorithm that computes $r_0, \ldots, r_\ell$ requires at least $n^2/2$ field operations, since in some examples all output values are different (if the field is large enough), and therefore each requires at least one operation.

Algorithm 11.4 computes the product $R_{\eta(k)}$ of the Q-matrices in the Euclidean Algorithm such that the sum of the degrees of the corresponding quotients is roughly k. Given $f = \rho_0 r_0$ and $g = \rho_1 r_1$, with nonzero $\rho_0, \rho_1 \in F$ and monic $r_0, r_1 \in F[x]$, it is easy to compute the gcd r_ℓ of f and g and the Bézout coefficients s_ℓ, t_ℓ from this matrix, by letting $k = n$. Then $\eta(k) = \ell$, s_ℓ and t_ℓ constitute the first row of the matrix R_ℓ, and

$$r_\ell = s_\ell r_0 + t_\ell r_1 = (s_\ell \rho_0^{-1}) f + (t_\ell \rho_1^{-1}) g.$$

Moreover, it is possible (as is with classical Extended Euclidean Algorithm) to compute any *single* row r_h, s_h, t_h for some $h \in \{1, \ldots, \ell\}$ when h is specified by a lower bound on $\deg r_h$, or equivalently, an upper bound on $\sum_{1 \le i \le h} \deg q_i$, so that a number $k \in \mathbb{N}$ is given and h is determined as $h = \eta(k)$. This has applications in computer algebra and coding theory beyond the sole computation of gcds. Examples are: rational function reconstruction (Section 5.7), Padé approximation

(Section 5.9), Cauchy interpolation (Section 5.8), decoding of BCH codes (the Berlekamp–Massey algorithm in Chapter 7), and fast sparse linear system solving (Chapter 12).

▬ COROLLARY 11.6. ▬▬▬▬▬▬▬▬▬▬▬▬▬▬▬▬▬▬▬▬▬▬▬▬▬▬▬▬▬▬
For polynomials $f, g \in F[x]$ of degree at most n, each of the following can be computed with $O(M(n) \log n)$ additions and multiplications plus at most $n + 2$ inversions, or $O^{\sim}(n)$ operations in F:

○ *$r_\ell = \gcd(f, g)$,*

○ *$s, t \in F[x]$ with $sf + tg = r_\ell$,*

○ *the entries $r_h, s_h, t_h \in F[x]$ of an arbitrary row in the Extended Euclidean Algorithm for f, g.* ▬▬▬▬▬▬▬▬▬▬▬▬▬▬▬▬▬▬▬▬▬▬▬▬▬▬▬▬▬

We give explicit constants for the first two statements of the above corollary.

▬ THEOREM 11.7. ▬▬▬▬▬▬▬▬▬▬▬▬▬▬▬▬▬▬▬▬▬▬▬▬▬▬▬▬▬▬▬
Let $f, g \in F[x]$ with $\deg g \le \deg f \le n$.

(i) *With at most $(24M(n) + O(n)) \log n$ additions and multiplications plus $n + 2$ inversions in F, we can decide whether f and g are coprime, and if so, compute the Bézout coefficients $s, t \in F[x]$ such that $sf + tg = 1$.*

(ii) *If the degree sequence is normal, then we can compute $\gcd(f, g)$ and the Bézout coefficients $s, t \in F[x]$ such that $sf + tg = \gcd(f, g)$ using at most $12M(n) \log n + 2M(n) + O(n \log n)$ additions and multiplications plus $n + 2$ inversions.* ▬▬▬▬▬▬▬▬▬▬▬▬▬▬▬▬▬▬▬▬▬▬▬▬▬▬▬▬▬

PROOF. By the discussion following Algorithm 11.4, we may assume that $\deg g < \deg f$, and call the algorithm with input $r_0 = f / \mathrm{lc}(f)$, $r_1 = g / \mathrm{lc}(g)$, and $k = \deg f$. It returns $\eta(k) = \ell$ and

$$R_\ell = \begin{pmatrix} s_\ell & t_\ell \\ s_{\ell+1} & t_{\ell+1} \end{pmatrix}.$$

Computing r_0 and r_1 takes 2 inversions and $O(n)$ multiplications.

(i) We see from Lemma 3.10 that the gcd is constant if and only if $\deg s_{\ell+1} = \deg g$ and $\deg t_{\ell+1} = \deg f$. If so, then we return $s = s_\ell / \mathrm{lc}(f)$ and $t = t_\ell / \mathrm{lc}(f)$. The additional cost is $O(n)$ multiplications, and the claim follows from $k \le n$ and Theorem 11.5.

(ii) The degrees of s_ℓ and t_ℓ are less than n, by Lemma 3.10, and hence computing $r_\ell = s_\ell r_0 + t_\ell r_1$ amounts to $2M(n) + O(n)$ arithmetic operations. □

Exercise 11.7 shows that a slight modification of Algorithm 11.4 leads to a bound of at most $10\mathsf{M}(n) + O(n\log n)$ for (ii) in the above theorem.

━━━ COROLLARY 11.8. ━━━

Let $f \in F[x]$ of degree n. A multiplication in the residue class ring $F[x]/\langle f\rangle$ can be computed with $6\mathsf{M}(n) + O(n)$ arithmetic operations in F, and an inverse with no more than $(24\mathsf{M}(n) + O(n))\log n$ operations. Thus one arithmetic operation in $F[x]/\langle f\rangle$ takes $O^{\sim}(n)$ arithmetic operations in F. ━━━

Applying Corollaries 10.17, 10.12, 11.6, and 11.8 to the analysis of the modular Extended Euclidean Algorithms 6.36 and 6.59, we obtain the following result.

━━━ COROLLARY 11.9. ━━━

Let F be a field with at least $(6n+3)d$ elements and $f, g \in F[y][x]$ of degree at most n in x and at most d in y.

(i) *With an expected number of $O(d\,\mathsf{M}(n)\log n + n\mathsf{M}(d)\log d)$ or $O^{\sim}(nd)$ arithmetic operations in F, we can compute the gcd of f and g.*

(ii) *A single row of the EEA for f, g can be computed with $O(n\mathsf{M}(nd)\log(nd))$ or $O^{\sim}(n^2 d)$ operations in F.* ━━━

The Euclidean Algorithm for integers. The method also works for integers, although there are some complications due to the carries. But Corollary 11.6 is true also for integers when the cost measure is the number of word operations instead of field operations. We state the following result without proof.

━━━ COROLLARY 11.10. ━━━

For an integer $m \in \mathbb{N}$ of length n, one arithmetic operation in the residue class ring $\mathbb{Z}_m$ can be performed using $O^{\sim}(n)$ word operations. More precisely, the cost is $O(n)$ for an addition, $O(\mathsf{M}(n))$ for a multiplication, and $O(\mathsf{M}(n)\log n)$ for an inversion or division. ━━━

The following is the analog of Corollary 11.9 for integer polynomials.

━━━ COROLLARY 11.11. ━━━

Let $f, g \in \mathbb{Z}[x]$ of degree at most n and with max-norm at most A.

(i) *The gcd of f and g can be computed using an expected number of*

$$O\Big(\mathsf{M}(n)\log n \cdot (n + \log A) \cdot \mathsf{M}(\log(n\log(nA))) \cdot \log\log(n\log(nA))$$
$$+ n\mathsf{M}((n + \log A)\log(n\log(nA))) \cdot (\log n + \log\log A)\Big)$$

or $O^{\sim}(n^2 + n\log A)$ word operations.

(ii) A single row in the EEA of f, g can be computed taking

$$O(\mathsf{M}(n)\log n \cdot \mathsf{M}(n\log(nA))) \cdot \log(n\log(nA))) \text{ or } O^{\sim}(n^2 \log A)$$

word operations. ▬▬▬▬▬▬▬▬▬▬▬▬▬▬▬▬▬▬▬▬▬▬▬▬▬▬▬

11.2. Subresultants via Euclid's algorithm

We have seen in Section 6.10 how to express each result of the Extended Euclidean Algorithm for polynomials via subresultants. Now we turn this question around: can we express subresultants, in particular the resultant, via the results of the Euclidean Algorithm? The answer is yes.

This section may be skipped at first reading. The main application of its result, a variant of the so-called *fundamental theorem on subresultants*, is to make the fast Euclidean Algorithm of this chapter also work for resultants, which appear in Section 6.8 and Chapters 15, 22, and 23.

We start by relating the two subresultants corresponding to one division step. We write $S_k(f,g)$ for the kth submatrix of $\mathrm{Syl}(f,g)$, as in Section 6.10, and $\sigma_k(f,g) = \det S_k(f,g)$.

LEMMA 11.12. *Let $f, g, r \in F[x]$ be monic polynomials with degrees n, m, d, respectively, $n \geq m$, $\rho r = f$ rem g with a nonzero $\rho \in F$, and $0 \leq k \leq d$. Then*

$$\sigma_k(f,g) = (-1)^{(n-k)(m-k)} \rho^{m-k} \sigma_k(g,r).$$

PROOF. There exists $q \in F[x]$ of degree $n-m$ such that $f = qg + \rho r$. Denoting by f_j, g_j, q_j, r_j the coefficients of f, g, q, r, respectively, we can rewrite this as

$$
\begin{pmatrix} 1 \\ f_{n-1} \\ \vdots \\ \vdots \\ \vdots \\ \vdots \\ \vdots \\ f_0 \end{pmatrix}
-
\underbrace{\begin{pmatrix} 1 & & & \\ g_{m-1} & 1 & & \\ \vdots & & \ddots & \\ \vdots & & & 1 \\ g_0 & & & \vdots \\ & \ddots & & \vdots \\ & & \ddots & \vdots \\ & & & g_0 \end{pmatrix}}_{n-m+1}
\begin{pmatrix} q_{n-m} \\ \vdots \\ \vdots \\ \vdots \\ q_0 \end{pmatrix}
=
\begin{pmatrix} 0 \\ \vdots \\ \vdots \\ \vdots \\ 0 \\ \rho r_d \\ \vdots \\ \rho r_0 \end{pmatrix}. \tag{7}
$$

The first column of $S_k(f,g) \in F^{(n+m-2k)\times(n+m-2k)}$, defined on page 169, is

$$(1, f_{n-1}, \ldots, f_{2k-m+1})^T, \tag{8}$$

where ^{T} denotes transposition, and the second summand on the left hand side of (7), extended by zeroes or truncated—as necessary—to length $n+m-2k$, is a linear combination of the columns in the right part of $S_k(f,g)$. Thus the column $(0,\ldots,0,\rho r_d,\ldots,\rho r_{2k-m+1})^T$ is a linear combination of columns $S_k(f,g)$, with coefficient 1 at the column (8), and we may substitute it for the column (8) in $S_k(f,g)$ without changing the value of the determinant; as usual, coefficients out of range are set to zero.

Similarly, we may replace each other column of f_j's in $S_k(f,g)$ by the corresponding column of ρr_j's. Next, we move the columns of ρr_j's in order to the right side of their matrix. This changes the sign of the determinant $(n-k)(m-k)$ times. Together we find

$$\sigma_k(f,g) = \det S_k(f,g)$$

$$= (-1)^{(n-k)(m-k)} \det \begin{pmatrix} 1 & & & & & & \\ g_{m-1} & & \ddots & & \rho r_d & & \\ \vdots & & & 1 & \vdots & & \ddots \\ \vdots & & & & \vdots & \vdots & & \rho r_d \\ \vdots & & & & \vdots & \vdots & & \vdots \\ g_{2k-n+1} & \cdots & g_k & \rho r_{2k-m+1} & \cdots & \rho r_k \end{pmatrix}.$$

$$\underbrace{\qquad\qquad}_{n-k} \quad \underbrace{\qquad\qquad}_{m-k}$$

This matrix is of block form

$$\begin{pmatrix} D & 0 \\ * & S_k(g,\rho r) \end{pmatrix},$$

$$\underbrace{}_{n-d} \quad \underbrace{}_{m+d-2k}$$

where D is a lower triangular $(n-d) \times (n-d)$ matrix with diagonal entries equal to 1. Thus

$$\sigma_k(f,g) = (-1)^{(n-k)(m-k)}\sigma_k(g,\rho r) = (-1)^{(n-k)(m-k)}\rho^{m-k}\sigma_k(g,r). \qquad \square$$

We recall the degree sequence $(n_0,\ldots,n_\ell)$, with $n_i = \deg r_i$ for all i. The following result, when formulated in terms of the classical Euclidean Algorithm, is known as the *fundamental theorem on subresultants*.

THEOREM 11.13.

Let $f = \rho_0 r_0, g = \rho_1 r_1 \in F[x]$ of degree n,m, respectively, with nonzero $\rho_0, \rho_1 \in F$ and monic r_0, r_1, and n_i and ρ_i the degrees and "leading coefficients" from the Euclidean Algorithm 3.6 for $0 \le i \le \ell$.

(i) For $0 \le k \le m$, the kth subresultant of (f,g) is

$$\sigma_k = \det S_k = \begin{cases} (-1)^{\tau_i} \rho_0^{m-n_i} \prod_{1 \le j \le i} \rho_j^{n_{j-1}-n_i} & \text{if } k = n_i \text{ for some } i \le \ell, \\ 0 & \text{otherwise}, \end{cases}$$

where $\tau_i = \sum_{1 \le j < i} (n_{j-1} - n_i)(n_j - n_i)$.

(ii) The subresultants satisfy for $1 \le i < \ell$ the recursive formulas

$$\sigma_m = \rho_1^{n-m}, \quad \sigma_{n_{i+1}} = (-1)^{(n_i - n_{i+1})(n - n_{i+1} + i + 1)} (\rho_0 \cdots \rho_{i+1})^{n_i - n_{i+1}} \sigma_{n_i}.$$

PROOF.   (i) We know from Theorem 6.48 that σ_k vanishes in the second case. So we may assume that $k = n_i$ for some $i \le \ell$. This i is unique, so that the expressions in the claim are well defined.

Induction on h for $0 \le h \le i$, using Lemma 11.12, shows that

$$\sigma_k(r_0, r_1) = \sigma_k(r_h, r_{h+1}) \prod_{1 \le j \le h} (-1)^{(n_{j-1}-k)(n_j-k)} \rho_{j+1}^{n_j - k}.$$

The claim follows from the case $k = n_i$ and $h = i - 1$, together with $\sigma_{n_i}(r_{i-1}, r_i) = 1$ and $\sigma_k(f, g) = \rho_0^{m-k} \rho_1^{n-k} \sigma_k(r_0, r_1)$.

(ii) follows from (i) by calculating $\tau_{i+1} - \tau_i$ modulo 2. $\square$

We illustrate the theorem with an example.

EXAMPLE 11.14.   Let $f = x^3 + 2x^2 + 3x + 4$ and $g = 3x^2 + 2x + 1$ in $\mathbb{Q}[x]$. Then the Euclidean Algorithm computes $f = \rho_0 r_0 = 1 \cdot f$, $g = \rho_1 r_1 = 3(x^2 + \frac{2}{3}x + \frac{1}{3})$,

$$r_0 = q_1 r_1 + \rho_2 r_2 = \left(x + \frac{4}{3}\right) r_1 + \frac{16}{9}(x+2),$$

$$r_1 = q_2 r_2 + \rho_3 r_3 = \left(x - \frac{4}{3}\right) r_2 + 3 \cdot 1,$$

$$r_2 = q_3 r_3 = (x+2) r_3.$$

The subresultants of (f,g) are

$$\sigma_2 = \sigma_{n_1} = \det(3) = 3 = \rho_1,$$

$$\sigma_1 = \sigma_{n_2} = \det \begin{pmatrix} 1 & 3 & 0 \\ 2 & 2 & 3 \\ 3 & 1 & 2 \end{pmatrix} = 16 = (-1)^{\tau_2} \rho_0 \rho_1^2 \rho_2,$$

$$\sigma_0 = \sigma_{n_3} = \det \begin{pmatrix} 1 & 0 & 3 & 0 & 0 \\ 2 & 1 & 2 & 3 & 0 \\ 3 & 2 & 1 & 2 & 3 \\ 4 & 3 & 0 & 1 & 2 \\ 0 & 4 & 0 & 0 & 1 \end{pmatrix} = 256 = (-1)^{\tau_3} \rho_0^2 \rho_1^3 \rho_2^2 \rho_3. \diamond$$

Theorem 11.5 implies the following.

═══ COROLLARY 11.15. ═══

Let $f, g \in F[x]$ have degrees $n = n_0 \geq n_1$, and $0 \leq k \leq n_1$. Then all subresultants σ_j for $n_1 \geq j \geq (n - k)$ of (f, g) can be calculated with at most $(24\mathsf{M}(k) + O(k)) \log k$ operations in F.

PROOF. Algorithm 11.4 may be easily modified so as to also return the ρ_i at no additional cost. We may compute the subresultants up to σ_{n-k} along the recursion formula (ii) from Theorem 11.13 in tandem with the values $\rho_0 \cdots \rho_i$. This takes $O(k)$ additional multiplications, and Theorem 11.5 implies the claim. $\square$

Because of its importance, we highlight the case $n = k$.

═══ COROLLARY 11.16. ═══

Let $f, g \in F[x]$ of degrees n_0, n_1, respectively, with $n = n_0 \geq n_1$, let $n_2, \ldots, n_\ell$ be the degrees of the remainders in the Euclidean Algorithm for (f, g), and $\rho_0, \ldots, \rho_\ell$ the "leading coefficients".

If $\deg \gcd(f, g) \geq 1$, then $\mathrm{res}(f, g) = 0$. Otherwise,

$$\mathrm{res}(f, g) = (-1)^\tau \rho_0^{n_1} \prod_{1 \leq j \leq \ell} \rho_j^{n_{j-1}},$$

where $\tau = \sum_{1 \leq j < \ell} n_{j-1} n_j$. This resultant can be calculated using no more than $(24\mathsf{M}(n) + O(n)) \log n$ operations in F.

Corollary 11.15 implies that in fact all subresultants can be computed within the same time bound. This can be used to replace the rational number reconstruction (or Cauchy interpolation) in the modular EEA algorithms of Section 6.11, as follows. We multiply the modular images of the ith row r_i, s_i, t_i of the EEA with the modular image of the subresultant σ_{n_i}, for all "lucky" primes, and reconstruct $\sigma_{n_i} r_i, \sigma_{n_i} s_i, \sigma_{n_i} t_i$, which have integral (or polynomial) coefficients, by the fast Chinese Remainder Algorithm (or fast interpolation), for all i.

═══ COROLLARY 11.17. ═══

We can compute all subresultants of two polynomials $f, g \in \mathbb{Z}[x]$ of degree at most n and with max-norm at most A using $O(\mathsf{M}(n) \log n \cdot \mathsf{M}(n \log(nA)) \log(n \log(nA)))$ or $O^\sim(n^2 \log A)$ word operations.

PROOF. We modify the small primes modular EEA of Section 6.11 so that it in addition computes all subresultants modulo each small prime, using the values ρ_i

from the fast Euclidean Algorithm, and recover them from their modular images by Chinese remaindering. By Corollary 11.15, the additional cost is negligible, and Corollary 11.11 implies the claim. □

The proof of the following result for bivariate polynomials is analogous.

━━ COROLLARY 11.18. ━━━━━━━━━━━━━━━━━━━━━━━━━━━━━━━━
We can compute all subresultants of two polynomials $f, g \in F[y][x]$ of degree at most n in x and at most d in y, where F is a field, using $O(n\,\mathsf{M}(nd)\log(nd))$ or $O^\sim(n^2 d)$ arithmetic operations in F. ━━━━━━━━━━━━━━━━━━━━━━

Since all subresultants together have about $n^2 d$ coefficients, at least in a generic sense, the above result is—up to logarithmic factors—optimal. However, this is no longer true if we are only interested in a particular subresultant, for example, the resultant, and it is not clear to us whether an $O^\sim(nd)$ algorithm exists. Similar remarks apply to the integer case.

Notes. **11.1.** The idea for a fast gcd algorithm is due to Lehmer (1938); later work includes Knuth (1970), Schönhage (1971), Moenck (1973), Aho, Hopcroft & Ullman (1974), §8.9, Schwartz (1980), Brent, Gustavson & Yun (1980), and Strassen (1983); the first three papers actually deal with integers. Brent, Gustavson & Yun apply their algorithm to computing Padé approximants and solving Toeplitz (or Hankel) systems of linear equations, and show that the two problems are equivalent. They also note that the "HGCD" algorithm from Aho, Hopcroft & Ullman does not always return the correct result in non-normal cases where not all quotients have degree 1. The concept of and notation for "coinciding" is from Strassen's paper. Pan (1997) gives a (sometimes) faster computation for Padé approximants and the decoding of BCH codes.

11.2. Lemma 11.12 for the resultant is in Gordan (1885), §145 and Haskell (1891/92). When $|\rho| = 1$, as in the classical and in Sturm's variant of the Euclidean Algorithm (Exercise 4.32), then the (sub)resultants of consecutive entries are all identical, up to sign. The fundamental theorem on subresultants is in Collins (1967) and Brown & Traub (1971); for our development, it takes a back seat compared to the results of Chapter 6. Exercise 11.8 provides a simple proof of the special case $k = 0$ of Lemma 11.12.

Lickteig & Roy (1997) and Reischert (1997) give non-modular algorithms for computing resultants of polynomials in $\mathbb{Z}[x]$ or $F[y,x]$ and prove running time estimates which are—up to logarithmic factors—within the bounds from Corollaries 11.17 and 11.18.

Exercises.

11.1 Prove that for a ring R and each $k \in \mathbb{N}$, "coinciding up to k" is an equivalence relation on $(R[x] \setminus \{0\})^2$.

11.2 Let F be a field supporting the FFT. In the text, we have given fast $O(n\log n)$ and $O(n\log^2 n)$ algorithms, respectively, for the following six problems for polynomials in one variable of degree less than n over F: multiplication, division with remainder, inverse modulo x^n, evaluation at n points, interpolation at n points, and greatest common divisor. For each of these problems, describe with one sentence of at most 20 words how the algorithm for it depends on the FFT and the algorithms for the other problems, and what method is used for the "dependency".

11.3 Let F be a field, $k \in \mathbb{N}$, and $f, g, f^*, g^* \in F[x]$ nonzero. Prove or disprove the following "converse" of Lemma 11.1: If $g \upharpoonright k = g^* \upharpoonright k$ and f quo $g = f^*$ quo g^* has degree k, then $f \upharpoonright 2k = f^* \upharpoonright 2k$.

11.4 Let F be a field, $f \in F[x]$ of degree n, and $m_1, \ldots, m_r \in F[x]$ such that $\sum_{1 \le i \le r} \deg m_i \le n$. Prove that $\gcd(f, m_1), \ldots, \gcd(f, m_r)$ can be computed with $O(\mathsf{M}(n) \log n)$ operations in F. Hint: Corollary 10.17.

11.5* Let $F = \mathbb{Q}$. Modify the fast Euclidean Algorithm 11.4 so as to work with primitive remainders $r_i^* \in \mathbb{Z}[x]$ (see Section 6.12). You may assume that the input polynomials are primitive, and your algorithm should output $Q_h^* \cdots Q_1^*$, where $Q_i^* \in F[x]^{2 \times 2}$ is such that $Q_i^* \left(\begin{smallmatrix} r_{i-1}^* \\ r_i^* \end{smallmatrix} \right) = \left(\begin{smallmatrix} r_i^* \\ r_{i+1}^* \end{smallmatrix} \right)$ for all i. Hint: Exercise 6.53.

11.6 In this exercise, you are to show how the fast Euclidean Algorithm 11.4 can be speeded up if FFT-multiplication is used. Suppose that F is a field that supports the FFT. We know that the entries of SQ_jR in step 9 are of degree at most $n_0 - n_h \le k$, and it is sufficient to compute all of them modulo $x^\kappa - 1$, where $\kappa \in \mathbb{N}$ is the least power of 2 strictly larger than k. Then the product matrix can be computed by evaluating all entries of S, Q_j, R at the primitive κth roots of unity, performing the matrix products pointwise, and interpolating to obtain the result. Count the number of κ-point FFTs computed, and compare your result to the number of κ-point FFTs that the usual approach of computing all polynomial products separately takes.

11.7* You are to analyze a variant of the fast Euclidean Algorithm 11.4 which in addition outputs the two remainders $\left(\begin{smallmatrix} r_h \\ r_{h+1} \end{smallmatrix} \right) = R_h \left(\begin{smallmatrix} r_0 \\ r_1 \end{smallmatrix} \right)$. You may assume that $n_0 \le 2k$ and the degree sequence is normal. Prove that the cost of the modified algorithm is at most $(10\mathsf{M}(k) + O(k)) \log k$ field operations. Hint: In step 4, you only have to compute $R \left(\begin{smallmatrix} r_0^* \\ r_1^* \end{smallmatrix} \right)$, where r_0^*, r_1^* are the "lower parts" of r_0, r_1, in order to obtain r_{j-1} and r_j, and a similar computation in step 9 gives r_h, r_{h+1}. Trace your algorithm on the data of Example 11.2.

11.8 Give an alternative proof of Lemma 11.12 for $k = 0$ using Exercise 6.12.

Research problems.

11.9 Determine the smallest possible constant $c \le 24$ such that your favorite fast Euclidean Algorithm works in time $(c\mathsf{M}(k) + O(k)) \log k$.

11.10 Can you find an algorithm for computing the resultant of two polynomials $f, g \in F[x, y]$ of degree at most n in x and at most d in y taking $O^\sim(nd)$ operations in the field F?

11.11 Implement carefully fast algorithms for large instances of the problems discussed in this book.

Общеизвестно, что задача обращения матриц [...]
является одной из центральных и трудных задач теории
матриц. [...] К сожалению, несмотря
на обширную литературу, посвященную этому вопросу,
проблема во многих её аспектах требует
дальнейшего углублённого исследования.[1]

Iosif Semenovich Iohvidov (1974)

For what is the theory of determinants? It is an algebra upon algebra; a
calculus which enables us to combine and foretell the results of
algebraical operations, in the same way as algebra itself enables us to
dispense with the performance of the special operations of arithmetic.
All analysis must ultimately clothe itself under this form.

James Joseph Sylvester (1851)

Lorsqu'il n'est pas en notre pouvoir de discerner les plus vraies
opinions, nous devons suivre les plus probables.[2]

René Descartes (1637)

---

[1] It is commonly known that the problem of the inversion of matrices [...] is one of the central and difficult
problems in matrix theory. [...] Unfortunately, in spite of extensive literature dealing with this question, the
problem requires in many of its aspects a further and profound investigation.

[2] When it is not in our power to tell the most correct opinions apart, we ought to follow the most probable ones.

12

Fast linear algebra

The "classical" algorithms for problems in linear algebra, such as matrix multiplication, computing the determinant, or solving systems of linear equations, all take
$O(n^3)$ arithmetic operations for inputs of size $n \times n$. In this chapter, we discuss
two totally different approaches to improving this. The first is a general method
whose most powerful variant leads to $O(n^{2.376})$ operations, but whose practical
use may be limited. The second one uses a radically different model of linear
algebra: instead of writing down the matrix ("explicit linear algebra"), we only
use a (fast) mechanism for evaluating the matrix at a vector ("black box linear algebra"). This is only applicable with profit to restricted classes of matrices, but
many problems arising in practice fall into this category: Sylvester, Vandermonde,
and Toeplitz matrices, the Berlekamp matrix in Berlekamp's polynomial factorization algorithm 14.31, and large sparse matrices over $\mathbb{F}_2$ in integer factorization
algorithms (Algorithm 19.12).

12.1. Strassen's matrix multiplication

Let R be a ring and $A, B \in R^{n \times n}$ two square matrices. The classical algorithm for
computing the product matrix AB by computing n^2 row-by-column products uses
n^3 multiplications and $n^3 - n^2$ additions in R. After having seen in Chapter 8 that
we can multiply polynomials faster than by the obvious method, a natural question
is whether something similar applies to matrix multiplication.

A few years after Karatsuba's polynomial and integer multiplication algorithm,
Strassen (1969) found such an algorithm. The input matrices are divided into four
$n/2 \times n/2$ blocks, and the computation of AB is reduced to seven multiplications
and 18 additions of $n/2 \times n/2$ matrices, in comparison to eight multiplications and
four additions for the classical algorithm. Like in the polynomial case, the multiplications are handled recursively, and the saving of one (costly) multiplication
at the expense of 14 (cheap) additions leads to an asymptotically smaller running
time of $O(n^{\log_2 7})$ operations in R, where the exponent is $\log_2 7 = 2.807354922\dots$

We present a slightly different version, also using seven multiplications of $n/2 \times n/2$ matrices, but only 15 additions.

ALGORITHM 12.1 Matrix multiplication.
Input: $A, B \in R^{n \times n}$, where R is a ring and $n = 2^k$ for some $k \in \mathbb{N}$.
Output: The product matrix $AB \in R^{n \times n}$.

1. **if** $n = 1$ **then** let $A = (a)$, $B = (b)$ for some $a, b \in R$ and **return** (ab)

2. write $A = \begin{pmatrix} A_{11} & A_{12} \\ A_{21} & A_{22} \end{pmatrix}$, $B = \begin{pmatrix} B_{11} & B_{12} \\ B_{21} & B_{22} \end{pmatrix}$, with all $A_{ij}, B_{ij} \in R^{(n/2) \times (n/2)}$

3. $\begin{aligned}
S_1 &\leftarrow A_{21} + A_{22}, & T_1 &\leftarrow B_{12} - B_{11} \\
S_2 &\leftarrow S_1 - A_{11}, & T_2 &\leftarrow B_{22} - T_1 \\
S_3 &\leftarrow A_{11} - A_{21}, & T_3 &\leftarrow B_{22} - B_{12} \\
S_4 &\leftarrow A_{12} - S_2, & T_4 &\leftarrow T_2 - B_{21}
\end{aligned}$

4. **call** the algorithm recursively to compute

$$\begin{aligned}
P_1 &= A_{11}B_{11}, & P_5 &= S_1 T_1, \\
P_2 &= A_{12}B_{21}, & P_6 &= S_2 T_2, \\
P_3 &= S_4 B_{22}, & P_7 &= S_3 T_3. \\
P_4 &= A_{22} T_4,
\end{aligned}$$

5. $\begin{aligned}
U_1 &\leftarrow P_1 + P_2, & U_5 &\leftarrow U_4 + P_3 \\
U_2 &\leftarrow P_1 + P_6, & U_6 &\leftarrow U_3 - P_4 \\
U_3 &\leftarrow U_2 + P_7, & U_7 &\leftarrow U_3 + P_5 \\
U_4 &\leftarrow U_2 + P_5
\end{aligned}$

6. **return** $\begin{pmatrix} U_1 & U_5 \\ U_6 & U_7 \end{pmatrix}$

THEOREM 12.2.
Algorithm 12.1 correctly computes the product matrix and uses at most $6n^{\log_2 7}$ additions and multiplications in R. For arbitrary $n \in \mathbb{N}$, an $n \times n$ matrix product can be computed with $42n^{\log_2 7} \in O(n^{\log_2 7})$ ring operations.

PROOF. The correctness is left as Exercise 12.1. For $n = 2^k \in \mathbb{N}$, let $T(n)$ denote the number of arithmetic operations in R that the algorithm performs on inputs of size $n \times n$. Then $T(1) = 1$ and $T(2^k) = 15 \cdot 2^{2k-2} + 7T(2^{k-1})$ for $k \geq 1$, and Lemma 8.2 implies the first claim. For arbitrary n, we pad the matrices with zeroes, thereby at most doubling the dimension. □

Strassen's (1969) discovery was the starting signal for the development of fast algorithms. Although subquadratic integer multiplication algorithms had been around for a while (Section 8.1), it was the surprise of realizing that the "obvious" cubic algorithm for matrix multiplication could be improved that kicked this development into high gear and inspired, within the following five years, the many new ideas for almost all the fast algorithms discussed in Part II of this book.

On a more technical level, Strassen's result spawned three lines of research:

o faster matrix multiplication,

o other problems from linear algebra,

o bilinear complexity.

For a field F, a number $\omega \in \mathbb{R}$ is a **feasible matrix multiplication exponent** if two $n \times n$ matrices over F can be multiplied with $O(n^{\omega})$ operations in F. The classical algorithm shows that $\omega = 3$ is feasible, and Strassen's that $\omega = \log_2 7$ is. The **matrix multiplication exponent** μ (for F) is the infimum of all feasible ones. Thus

$$2 \leq \mu \leq \omega$$

for all feasible ω's. This μ is the same for all fields of a fixed characteristic, and all feasible exponents discovered so far work for all fields.

The fascinating history of the smallest exponents known is in the Notes 12.1; the current world record is $\omega < 2.376$. It seems natural to conjecture that $\mu = 2$; there is currently no method in sight that might prove or disprove this.

How practical are these algorithms? Bailey, Lee & Simon (1990) deplore "an unfortunate myth [...] regarding the *crossover* point for Strassen's algorithm", and show that for the Sun–4 "Strassen is faster for matrices as small as 16×16. For Cray systems the crossover point is roughly 128". They conclude that "it appears that Strassen's algorithm can indeed be used to accelerate practical-sized linear algebra calculations." Besides a Cray library implementation (SGEMMS) of fast matrix multiplication, there is also one, the ESSL library, for IBM 3090 machines. Higham (1990) reports on a set of FORTRAN 77 routines (level 3 BLAS) using "Strassen's method for fast matrix multiplication, which is now recognized to be a practically useful technique once matrix dimensions exceed about 100". In all these experiments, the coefficients are floating point numbers of a fixed precision.

A further avenue to explore with Strassen's algorithm is that its recursive partition employs data access that is essentially different from classical multiplication. This may make it attractive for machines with a hierarchical memory structure and for large matrices stored in secondary memory, possibly reducing data transfer (paging) time.

Further computational problems in linear algebra include matrix inversion, computing the determinant, the characteristic polynomial, or the LR-decomposition of a matrix, and, for $F = \mathbb{C}$, the QR-decomposition and unitary transformation to upper Hessenberg form. It turns out that all these problems have the same asymptotic complexity as matrix multiplication (up to constant factors), so that a fast algorithm for one of them immediately gives fast algorithms for all of them.

The exponent η for solving systems of linear equations satisfies $\eta \leq \omega$ for all feasible ω. It is not known whether $\eta = \mu$.

The most fundamental consequence of Strassen's breakthrough was the development of *bilinear complexity theory*, a deep and rich area that is concerned with good and optimal algorithms for functions that depend linearly on each of two sets of variables, just like the entries of the product of two matrices (or polynomials) do. Bürgisser, Clausen & Shokrollahi (1996) give a detailed account of the achievements in this theory, which is part of *algebraic complexity theory*.

12.2. Application: fast modular composition of polynomials

As an application of fast matrix multiplication, we now discuss a fast algorithm for **modular composition** of polynomials. The problem is, given three polynomials $f, g, h \in R[x]$ with $\deg g, \deg h < \deg f = n$, where R is a (commutative) ring and $f \neq 0$ is monic, to compute $g(h)$ rem f, that is, the remainder of the composition of g and h modulo f. Using Horner's rule, this can be done with at most n multiplications and additions modulo f, at a cost of $O(n\mathsf{M}(n))$ operations in R. The surprising fact is that we can do better if we use not only fast polynomial arithmetic but also fast matrix arithmetic.

▬ ALGORITHM 12.3 Fast modular composition. ▬▬▬▬▬▬▬▬▬▬▬▬▬▬▬▬
Input: $f, g, h \in R[x]$ with $\deg g, \deg h < \deg f = n$ and $f \neq 0$ monic.
Output: $g(h)$ rem $f \in R[x]$.

1. $m \longleftarrow \lceil n^{1/2} \rceil$
   let $g = \sum_{0 \leq i < m} g_i x^{mi}$, with $g_0, \ldots, g_{m-1} \in R[x]$ of degree less than m

2. **for** $2 \leq i \leq m$ compute h^i rem f

3. let $A \in R^{m \times n}$ be the matrix whose rows are the coefficients of 1, h rem f, h^2 rem $f, \ldots, h^{m-1}$ rem f, and $B \in R^{m \times m}$ the matrix whose rows are the coefficients of $g_0, g_1, \ldots, g_{m-1}$, and compute $BA \in R^{m \times n}$ via $\lceil n/m \rceil \leq m$ matrix multiplications of size $m \times m$

4. **for** $0 \leq i < m$ **do**
   let $r_i \in R[x]$ be the polynomial whose coefficients form the ith row of BA, and compute $b = \sum_{0 \leq i < m} r_i \cdot (h^m)^i$ rem f using Horner's rule

5. **return** b ▬▬▬▬▬▬▬▬▬▬▬▬▬▬▬▬▬▬▬▬▬▬▬▬▬▬▬▬▬▬▬▬▬▬

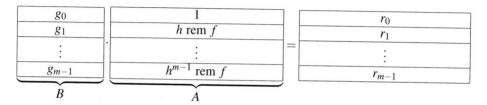

FIGURE 12.1: The matrix product in the modular composition algorithm 12.3.

<hr>

THEOREM 12.4.

Algorithm 12.3 works correctly and uses at most $\lceil n^{1/2} \rceil$ matrix multiplications of size $\lceil n^{1/2} \rceil \times \lceil n^{1/2} \rceil$, plus no more than $6n^{1/2}(\mathsf{M}(n) + O(n))$ additions and multiplications in R.

<hr>

PROOF. Let $i < m$, and $g_i = \sum_{0 \le j < m} g_{ij} x^j$ with all $g_{ij} \in R$. Then $r_i = \sum_{0 \le j < m} g_{ij} \cdot (h^j \text{ rem } f) = g_i(h) \text{ rem } f$ (see Figure 12.1), and

$$b \equiv \sum_{0 \le i < m} r_i \cdot (h^m)^i \equiv \sum_{0 \le i < m} g_i(h) \cdot h^{mi} = g(h) \bmod f.$$

The cost for step 2 is $m - 1$ multiplications modulo f. We may precompute $\text{rev}_n(f)^{-1} \bmod x^n$ for the fast division algorithm, at a cost of $3\mathsf{M}(n) + O(n)$, and then step 2 takes $3n^{1/2}\mathsf{M}(n) + O(n^{3/2})$ ring operations, by Corollary 9.7 and the discussion following it. Step 3 may be done by computing about m products of pairs of $m \times m$ matrices. Finally, step 4 costs at most m multiplications and additions modulo h, with about the same cost as for step 2. □

Taking $\mathsf{M}(n) \in O(n \log n \log\log n)$ and $\omega < 2.376$, we obtain the following.

<hr>

COROLLARY 12.5.

The modular composition $g(h) \text{ rem } f$ for three polynomials $f, g, h \in R[x]$ with $\deg g, \deg h < \deg f = n$ and $f \ne 0$ monic can be computed using $O(n^{1.688})$ operations in R.

<hr>

12.3. Linearly recurrent sequences

In this and the following section, we introduce a new way, called **black box linear algebra**, of solving linear equations. So the task is, for a given matrix $A \in F^{n \times m}$ and a vector $b \in F^n$ over a field F, to find one (or a description of all) solution $y \in F^m$ to the equation $Ay = b$. From basic linear algebra, we know that Gaussian elimination solves the problem with $O(\max\{n, m\}^3)$ operations in F (Section 25.5).

In some applications, such as polynomial factorization (Section 14.8) and integer factorization (Section 19.5), linear systems have to be solved where the coefficient matrix has a special form, for example, it is sparse. Wiedemann (1986) presented an algorithm that is asymptotically faster than Gaussian elimination for sparse matrices. Kaltofen & Saunders (1991) gave a more general variant of Wiedemann's algorithm that is particularly well suited for a much larger class of matrices, namely those where multiplication of the matrix by an arbitrary vector is cheap. A square matrix $A \in F^{n \times n}$ is not given by its $n \times n$ array of entries, but by a black box for evaluating A, that is, a procedure which on input of a vector $v \in F^n$ produces $Av \in F^n$. We denote by $c(A)$ the arithmetic cost for evaluating A at a vector. Then the cost of Kaltofen & Saunders' version of Wiedemann's algorithm is essentially $O(n \cdot c(A))$. If A is arbitrary and we use the classical algorithm for computing Av, then $c(A)$ is about $2n^2$, and Wiedemann's algorithm provides no asymptotic gain over Gaussian elimination, but it does if A is special such that $c(A) \in o(n^2)$. Table 12.2 collects the evaluation costs for some important classes of matrices.

class of matrices	$c(A)$
general	$2n^2 - n$
Sylvester matrix	$O(\mathsf{M}(n))$
DFT_ω, ω a primitive 2^kth root of unity	$O(n \log n)$
Vandermonde matrix	$O(\mathsf{M}(n) \log n)$
Berlekamp matrix over $\mathbb{F}_q$	$O(\mathsf{M}(n) \log q)$
sparse, with $\leq s$ nonzero entries	$\leq 2s$
random squares integer factorization	$O(n \log^2 n)$

TABLE 12.2: Evaluation cost for some matrix classes.

For matrices with "small" evaluation cost we also have "fast" matrix multiplication, in that the product with an arbitrary (explicitly given) $n \times n$ matrix can be calculated with $n \cdot c(A)$ arithmetic operations. The *transposition principle* (see Notes 12.3) says that for the evaluation cost, it does not matter whether we multiply by a vector from the right or the left, or whether we consider a matrix or its transpose.

Before we can present the algorithm, we need some facts about linearly recurrent sequences. Let F be a field and $V \neq \{0\}$ a vector space over F. Then $V^{\mathbb{N}}$ is the (infinite-dimensional) vector space of infinite sequences $(a_i)_{i \in \mathbb{N}}$, with all $a_i \in V$.

DEFINITION 12.6. *A sequence $a = (a_i)_{i \in \mathbb{N}} \in V^{\mathbb{N}}$ is **linearly recurrent (over F)** if there exist $n \in \mathbb{N}$ and $f_0, \ldots, f_n \in F$ with $f_n \neq 0$ such that*

$$\sum_{0 \leq j \leq n} f_j a_{i+j} = f_n a_{i+n} + \cdots + f_1 a_{i+1} + f_0 a_i = 0.$$

for all $i \in \mathbb{N}$. The polynomial $f = \sum_{0 \le j \le n} f_j x^j \in F[x]$ of degree n is called a **characteristic** (or annihilating, or generating) **polynomial** of a.

EXAMPLE 12.7. (i) $V = F$, $a_i = 0$ for all $i \in \mathbb{N}$. This sequence is linearly recurrent, and *any* nonzero polynomial f is a characteristic polynomial.

(ii) $V = F = \mathbb{Q}$, $a_0 = 0$, $a_1 = 1$, $a_{i+2} = a_{i+1} + a_i$ for all $j \ge 2$. Then $a = (a_i)_{i \ge 0}$ is the **Fibonacci sequence**, and $f = x^2 - x - 1$ is a characteristic polynomial of a.

(iii) $V = F^{n \times n}$, $A \in F^{n \times n}$ arbitrary. Then $a = (A^i)_{i \ge 0}$ is linearly recurrent, and the characteristic polynomial $\chi_A \in F[x]$ is a characteristic polynomial of a, by the Cayley–Hamilton theorem (Section 25.5).

(iv) $V = F^n$, $A \in F^{n \times n}$ and $b \in F^n$ arbitrary. Then $a = (A^i b)_{i \in \mathbb{N}}$ is linearly recurrent, and any characteristic polynomial of $(A^i)_{i \in \mathbb{N}}$ also annihilates a. The subspace of F^n spanned by the entries of a is called the **Krylov subspace of A and b**.

(v) $V = F$, $A \in F^{n \times n}$, $b, u \in F^n$ arbitrary. Then $a = (u^T A^i b)_{i \in \mathbb{N}}$ is linearly recurrent, and any characteristic polynomial of $(A^i b)_{i \in \mathbb{N}}$ also annihilates a.

(vi) This generalizes the two previous examples. If V and W are vector spaces over F, $\varphi \colon V \longrightarrow W$ is F-linear, and $a = (a_i)_{i \in \mathbb{N}} \in V^{\mathbb{N}}$ is linearly recurrent with characteristic polynomial $f \in F[x]$, then so is $\varphi(a) = (\varphi(a_i))_{i \in \mathbb{N}} \in W^{\mathbb{N}}$. ◇

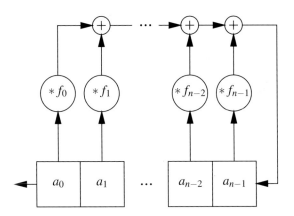

FIGURE 12.3: Initial state of a linear feedback shift register for the sequence $a = (a_i)_{i \in \mathbb{N}}$ with characteristic polynomial $f = x^n - f_{n-1} x^{n-1} - f_{n-2} x^{n-2} - \cdots - f_1 x - f_0$.

A linearly recurrent sequence $a = (a_i)_{i \in \mathbb{N}} \in V^{\mathbb{N}}$ with characteristic polynomial $f = \sum_{0 \le j \le n} f_j x^j \in F[x]$ of degree n is completely determined by the n initial values $a_0, \ldots, a_{n-1}$. The ith entry of a can be computed in linear time with space for n elements of F, independent of i, using a **linear feedback shift register** (see Figure 12.3). It consists of a shift register with n places, holding n consecutive entries $a_i, \ldots, a_{i+n-1}$ of a at a time, plus n gates for multiplication by the c_j and $n + 1$ addition gates. The shift register is regulated by an external clock. At the

ith clock tick, the entries of the shift register are shifted one place to the left, the leftmost entry a_i is output, and the next entry $a_{i+n} = \sum_{0 \leq j < n} c_j a_{i+j}$ of the sequence is computed by the part of the circuit consisting of arithmetic gates, and fed into the rightmost place of the shift register. Initially, the shift register is loaded with $a_0, \ldots, a_{n-1}$.

It is convenient to define a multiplication of sequences by polynomials. For $f = \sum_{0 \leq j \leq n} f_j x^j \in F[x]$ and $a = (a_i)_{i \in \mathbb{N}} \in V^{\mathbb{N}}$, we set

$$f \bullet a = \left(\sum_{0 \leq j \leq n} f_j a_{i+j} \right)_{i \in \mathbb{N}} \in V^{\mathbb{N}}.$$

The constants $f \in F$ act on sequences in the usual way, and the indeterminate x acts as a shift operator:

$$x \bullet a = (a_{i+1})_{i \in \mathbb{N}}.$$

This makes $V^{\mathbb{N}}$, together with $\bullet$, into an $F[x]$-module. A module is something similar to a vector space, with the only difference that the "scalars" may be elements of an arbitrary (commutative) ring instead of a field. In particular, $\bullet$ has the following properties:

$$
\begin{align}
f \bullet (a+b) &= f \bullet a + f \bullet b, \tag{1} \\
f \bullet 0 &= 0, \tag{2} \\
(f+g) \bullet a &= f \bullet a + g \bullet a, \tag{3} \\
(fg) \bullet a &= f \bullet (g \bullet a) = g \bullet (f \bullet a), \tag{4} \\
0 \bullet a &= 0, \tag{5} \\
1 \bullet a &= a, \tag{6}
\end{align}
$$

for all $f, g \in F[x]$ and $a, b \in V^{\mathbb{N}}$, where $0 = (0)_{i \in \mathbb{N}}$ is the zero sequence. Their proof is in Exercise 12.5. For example, every commutative group G is a $\mathbb{Z}$-module by letting $f \bullet a = a^f$ for $a \in G$ and $f \in \mathbb{Z}$.

We can express the property of being a characteristic polynomial in terms of the operation $\bullet$: $f \in F[x] \setminus \{0\}$ is a characteristic polynomial of $a \in V^{\mathbb{N}}$ if and only if $f \bullet a = 0$. The set of all characteristic polynomials of a sequence $a \in V^{\mathbb{N}}$, together with the zero polynomial, is an ideal in $F[x]$: if f, g are both characteristic polynomials or zero, then so is $f + g$, and if $r \in F[x]$ is arbitrary, then rf is either zero or a characteristic polynomial, by (2), (3), and (4). This ideal is called the **annihilator** of a and denoted by $\text{Ann}(a)$. Since any ideal in $F[x]$ is generated by a single polynomial (Section 25.3), either $\text{Ann}(a) = \{0\}$ or there is a unique monic polynomial $m \in \text{Ann}(a)$ of least degree such that $\langle m \rangle = \{rm : r \in F[x]\} = \text{Ann}(a)$. This polynomial is called the **minimal polynomial** of a and divides any other characteristic polynomial of a. We denote it by m_a. If a is not linearly recurrent, then $\text{Ann}(a) = \{0\}$, and we set $m_a = 0$. The degree of m_a is called the **recursion**

order of a. Summarizing, we have the following equivalences for $f \in F[x]$ and $a \in V^{\mathbb{N}}$:

$$f = 0 \text{ or } f \text{ is a characteristic polynomial of } a \iff f \bullet a = 0$$
$$\iff f \in \mathrm{Ann}(a) \iff m_a \mid f,$$
$$a \in V^{\mathbb{N}} \text{ is linearly recurrent} \iff \exists f \in F[x] \setminus \{0\} \quad f \bullet a = 0$$
$$\iff \mathrm{Ann}(a) \neq \{0\} \iff m_a \neq 0.$$

EXAMPLE 12.7 (continued). (i) Any polynomial annihilates the zero sequence, by (2). Thus $\mathrm{Ann}(\mathbf{0}) = F[x]$ and $m_{\mathbf{0}} = 1$.

(ii) The minimal polynomial of the Fibonacci sequence is $m_a = x^2 - x - 1$. This is because the polynomial is irreducible over $\mathbb{Q}$ (its roots $(1 \pm \sqrt{5})/2$ are irrational), and hence no proper divisor of m_a annihilates a (1 obviously does not).

(iii) The minimal polynomial of the matrix A is also the minimal polynomial of the sequence $(A^i)_{i \in \mathbb{N}}$.

(iv) m_a divides the minimal polynomial of A.

(v) m_a divides the minimal polynomial of $(A^i b)_{i \in \mathbb{N}}$.

(vi) $\mathrm{Ann}(a) \subseteq \mathrm{Ann}(\varphi(a))$ and $m_{\varphi(a)} \mid m_a$.

(vii) Let V be an algebraic field extension of F, $\alpha \in V$, and $a = (\alpha^i)_{i \geq 0}$. Then a is linearly recurrent, and the minimal polynomial of a is the minimal polynomial of α over F. $\diamond$

We now indicate how to compute the minimal polynomial of a given sequence $a = (a_i)_{i \in \mathbb{N}} \in F^{\mathbb{N}}$, provided that we know an upper bound $n \in \mathbb{N}$ on the recursion order. We recall from Section 9.1 the reversal of a polynomial: for $f = f_d x^d + \cdots + f_0 \in F[x]$ of degree d, we have

$$\mathrm{rev}(f) = \mathrm{rev}_d(f) = x^d f(x^{-1}) = f_0 x^d + f_1 x^{d-1} + \cdots + f_d \in F[x].$$

LEMMA 12.8. *Let* $a = (a_i)_{i \in \mathbb{N}} \in F^{\mathbb{N}}$ *be linearly recurrent,* $h = \sum_{i \in \mathbb{N}} a_i x^i \in F[[x]]$, *the formal power series whose coefficients are the coefficients of the sequence* a, $f \in F[x] \setminus \{0\}$ *of degree* d, *and* $r = \mathrm{rev}(f)$ *its reversal.*

(i) *The following are equivalent.*

    (a) f *is a characteristic polynomial of* a,

    (b) $r \cdot h$ *is a polynomial of degree less than* d,

    (c) $h = g/r$ *for some* $g \in F[x]$ *with* $\deg g < d$.

(ii) *If* f *is the minimal polynomial of* a, *then* $d = \max\{1 + \deg g, \deg r\}$ *and* $\gcd(g, r) = 1$ *in* (i).

PROOF. For the proof of (i), see Exercise 12.7. For (ii), we note that $\deg r \leq d$, with equality if and only if $x \nmid f$, and hence $d \geq \max\{1 + \deg g, \deg r\}$ in (i). Now let $f = m_a$, and suppose that $d > \max\{1 + \deg g, \deg r\}$. Then x divides f, $r = \mathrm{rev}(f/x)$, and f/x is a characteristic polynomial of a of degree $d - 1$, by (i), contradicting the minimality of m_a. Thus $d = \max\{1 + \deg g, \deg r\}$.

Let $u = \gcd(g, r)$. Then $f^* = f/\mathrm{rev}(u)$ is a polynomial of degree $d - \deg u$, $r/u = \mathrm{rev}(f^*)$, and $(r/u)h = (g/u)$ is a polynomial of degree less than $d - \deg u$. Hence f^* is a characteristic polynomial of a, again by (i), and the minimality of d implies that $\deg u = 0$. $\square$

If $n \in \mathbb{N}$ is an upper bound on the recursion order of a, then we may compute m_a by solving the Padé approximation problem

$$h \equiv \frac{s}{t} \bmod x^{2n}, \quad x \nmid t, \quad \deg s < n, \quad \deg t \leq n, \quad \gcd(s, t) = 1, \qquad (7)$$

since Lemma 12.8 (ii) implies that $(s, t) = (g, r)$ is a solution to (7) (note that $x \nmid r$, by the definition of rev). We have seen in Section 5.9 that the solution to (7) is unique (up to multiplication by constants) and can be computed with the Extended Euclidean Algorithm, using $O(n^2)$ arithmetic operations in F. This leads to the following algorithm.

═══ ALGORITHM 12.9 Minimal polynomial for $F^{\mathbb{N}}$. ═══
Input: An upper bound $n \in \mathbb{N}$ on the recursion order and the first $2n$ entries $a_0, \ldots,$ $a_{2n-1} \in F$ of a linearly recurrent sequence $a \in F^{\mathbb{N}}$.
Output: The minimal polynomial $m_a \in F[x]$ of a.

1. $h \longleftarrow a_{2n-1}x^{2n-1} + \cdots + a_1 x + a_0$
   call the Extended Euclidean Algorithm to compute $s, t \in F[x]$ such that $t(0) = 1$ and (7) holds, as described in Section 5.9

2. $d \longleftarrow \max\{1 + \deg s, \deg t\}$, **return** $\mathrm{rev}_d(t)$ ═══

═══ THEOREM 12.10. ═══
Algorithm 12.9 correctly computes the minimal polynomial of a linearly recurrent sequence $(a_i)_{i \in \mathbb{N}}$ of recursion order at most n and uses $O(n^2)$ operations in F. ═══

PROOF. Let $f \in F[x]$ be the minimal polynomial of a. The discussion preceding the algorithm implies that $(g, r) = (s, t)$, where g, r are as in Lemma 12.8 (i). Finally, $f = \mathrm{rev}_k(r)$ for some $k \in \mathbb{N}$, and Lemma 12.8 (ii) implies that $k = d$. $\square$

Using the fast Euclidean Algorithm from Chapter 11, the minimal polynomial can actually be computed with $O(\mathsf{M}(n) \log n)$ field operations, but this does not help in our intended application.

EXAMPLE 12.11. (i) Let $F = \mathbb{F}_5$ and $a = (3,0,4,2,3,0,\ldots) \in \mathbb{F}_5^{\mathbb{N}}$ be linearly recurrent of recursion order at most 3. Then $h = 3x^4 + 2x^3 + 4x^2 + 3$ in step 1 of Algorithm 12.9, and the relevant results of the Extended Euclidean Algorithm for x^6 and h are

j	q_{j-1}	a_j	t_j
0		x^6	0
1		$3x^4 + 2x^3 + 4x^2 + 3$	1
2	$2x^2 + 2x + 1$	$4x + 2$	$3x^2 + 3x + 4$
3	$2x^3 + 2x^2$	3	$4x^5 + 3x^4 + x^3 + 2x^2 + 1$
4	$3x + 4$	0	$3x^6$

We read off row 2 that

$$h \equiv \frac{4x + 2}{3x^2 + 3x + 4} = \frac{x + 3}{2x^2 + 2x + 1} \mod x^6,$$

whence $s = x + 3$ and $t = 2x^2 + 2x + 1$. Finally, in step 2 we have $d = 2$ and $m_a = \operatorname{rev}_2(t) = x^2 + 2x + 2$. We check that indeed $a_{i+2} + 2a_{i+1} + 2a_i = 0$ in $\mathbb{F}_5$ for $i = 0, 1, 2, 3$. Thus the series continues as $(3,0,4,2,3,0,4,2,3,0,\ldots)$.

(ii) Let $a = (0,0,1,0,1,0,\ldots) \in F^{\mathbb{N}}$ of recursion order at most 3. Then $h = x^4 + x^2$, the Extended Euclidean Algorithm for x^6 and h computes

j	q_{j-1}	a_j	t_j
0		x^6	0
1		$x^4 + x^2$	1
2	$x^2 - 1$	x^2	$-x^2 + 1$
3	$x^2 + 1$	0	x^4

so that $s = x^2$ and $t = -x^2 + 1$. Here $d = 3$ and $m_a = \operatorname{rev}_3(t) = x^3 - x$. Thus $a_{i+3} = a_{i+1}$ for all $i \geq 0$, $a_i = 0$ if i is odd, and $a_i = 1$ if $i > 0$ is even. Hence $(a_1, a_2, a_3, \ldots)$ is periodic with period 2, and a has a **preperiod** of length 1. $\Diamond$

12.4. Wiedemann's algorithm and black box linear algebra

The main idea of Wiedemann's (1986) algorithm for solving linear equations is as follows. For simplicity, we assume that $A \in F^{n \times n}$ is a nonsingular square matrix. Then for any $b \in F^n$, $y = A^{-1}b \in F^n$ is the unique solution of $Ay = b$. Suppose that $m = m_a = \sum_{0 \leq j \leq d} m_j x^j \in F[x]$ is the minimal polynomial of the linearly recurrent sequence $a = (A^i b)_{i \in \mathbb{N}}$, that is, the unique monic polynomial of least degree such that $m \bullet a = 0$. Then in particular the first entry of $m \bullet a$ is zero, and

$$m(A)b = \sum_{0 \leq j \leq d} m_j A^j b = 0 \text{ in } F^n. \tag{8}$$

Now m is a divisor of the minimal polynomial of A, which in turn divides χ_A, the characteristic polynomial of A, according to Example 12.7 (iii). The constant coefficient of χ_A is $\det A \neq 0$, since A is nonsingular, and hence also the constant coefficient $m_0 = m(0)$ of m is nonzero. Thus

$$A \cdot (-m_0^{-1}) \sum_{1 \leq j \leq d} m_j A^{j-1} b = -m_0^{-1} \sum_{1 \leq j \leq d} m_j A^j b = b,$$

and $y = -m_0^{-1} \sum_{1 \leq j \leq d} m_j A^{j-1} b \in F^n$ is the required solution and can be computed in a Horner-like fashion (Section 5.2), using $d - 1 < n$ evaluations of A at a vector plus $O(n^2)$ field operations for additions of vectors and multiplications by scalars. We note that y belongs to the Krylov subspace of A and b.

This leads to the following algorithm.

───── ALGORITHM 12.12 Solving a nonsingular square linear system. ═══════
Input: A nonsingular matrix $A \in F^{n \times n}$ and a vector $b \in F^n$.
Output: $y = A^{-1}b \in F^n$.

1. compute the minimal polynomial $m \in F[x]$ of the linearly recurrent sequence $(A^i b)_{i \in \mathbb{N}} \in (F^n)^{\mathbb{N}}$

2. $h \longleftarrow -\dfrac{m - m(0)}{m(0) \cdot x} \in F[x],$ compute $y = h(A)b$ in a Horner-like fashion

3. **return** y ══

Thus we have reduced our original problem of solving $Ay = b$ to computing the minimal polynomial m_a of $a = (A^i b)_{i \in \mathbb{N}}$; any small multiple of m_a would also do. We have seen at the end of the previous section how to compute minimal polynomials for sequences whose entries are field elements, but there is no obvious analog of that procedure when the sequence entries are n-dimensional vectors. The idea now is to choose vectors $u \in F^n$ randomly, compute the minimal polynomial $m \in F[x]$ of the linearly recurrent sequence $(u^T A^i b)_{i \in \mathbb{N}} \in F^{\mathbb{N}}$, using Algorithm 12.9, and then check whether m is actually the minimal polynomial of a (in general, it divides m_a) by computing $m(A)b \in F^n$. If p is the probability of success, then the algorithm will be successful after $O(1/p)$ expected trials (Section 25.6).

The following algorithm even works for singular square matrices.

───── ALGORITHM 12.13 Minimal polynomial for Krylov subspaces. ═══════
Input: A matrix $A \in F^{n \times n}$ and a vector $b \in F^n$.
Output: The minimal polynomial $m \in F[x]$ of the sequence $(A^i b)_{i \in \mathbb{N}}$.

1. **if** $b = 0$ **then return** 1

2. let $U \subseteq F$ be finite

3. choose $u \in U^n$ uniformly at random and compute $u^T A^i b \in F$ for $0 \leq i < 2n$

4. **call** Algorithm 12.9 to compute the minimal polynomial $m \in F[x]$ of the linearly recurrent sequence $(u^T A^i b)_{i \in \mathbb{N}} \in F^{\mathbb{N}}$, with recursion bound n

5. **if** $m(A)b = 0$ in F^n **then return** m **else goto** 3

EXAMPLE 12.14. Let $F = \mathbb{F}_5$,

$$A = \begin{pmatrix} 1 & 4 & 4 \\ 4 & 0 & 3 \\ 1 & 2 & 4 \end{pmatrix} \text{ and } b = \begin{pmatrix} 3 \\ 1 \\ 2 \end{pmatrix},$$

and suppose that we want to find $y \in F^3$ such that $Ay = b$. We have

$$Ab = \begin{pmatrix} 0 \\ 3 \\ 3 \end{pmatrix}, \quad A^2 b = A(Ab) = \begin{pmatrix} 4 \\ 4 \\ 3 \end{pmatrix}, \quad A^3 b = A(A^2 b) = \begin{pmatrix} 2 \\ 0 \\ 4 \end{pmatrix},$$

$$A^4 b = A(A^3 b) = \begin{pmatrix} 3 \\ 0 \\ 3 \end{pmatrix}, \quad A^5 b = A(A^4 b) = \begin{pmatrix} 0 \\ 1 \\ 0 \end{pmatrix}.$$

In step 3 of Algorithm 12.13, we choose $u = (1,0,0)^T \in F^3$, and obtain

$$(u^T A^i b)_{i \in \mathbb{N}} = (3,0,4,2,3,0,\ldots).$$

We have already seen in Example 12.11 that the minimal polynomial of this sequence is $m = x^2 + 2x + 2$. In step 5 of Algorithm 12.13, we calculate

$$m(A)b = A^2 b + 2Ab + 2b = \begin{pmatrix} 0 \\ 2 \\ 3 \end{pmatrix},$$

so that m is not the minimal polynomial of $(A^i b)_{i \in \mathbb{N}}$. We go back to step 3 and choose $u = (1,2,0)^T$ this time. Then $(u^T A^i b)_{i \in \mathbb{N}} = (0,1,2,2,3,2,\ldots)$, and Algorithm 12.9 yields the minimal polynomial $m = x^3 + 3x + 1$. Since the minimal polynomial of $(A^i b)_{i \in \mathbb{N}}$ is a monic multiple of m of degree at most 3, it equals m. We check this by calculating

$$m(A)b = A^3 b + 3Ab + b = \begin{pmatrix} 0 \\ 0 \\ 0 \end{pmatrix}.$$

Finally, in step 2 of Algorithm 12.12, we compute

$$h = -\frac{m - m(0)}{m(0)x} = 4x^2 + 2, \quad y = h(A)b = 4A^2b + 2b = \begin{pmatrix} 2 \\ 3 \\ 1 \end{pmatrix},$$

and in fact $Ay = b$. $\diamond$

THEOREM 12.15.
An output returned by Algorithm 12.13 is correct. If it returns after k iterations, the cost is at most $2kn(c(A) + O(n))$ operations in F.

PROOF. Let $a = (A^ib)_{i\in\mathbb{N}}$. Correctness is clear if $b = 0$, and we assume that b is nonzero. The polynomial m computed in step 4 of the algorithm is a divisor of m_a, according to Example 12.7 (v) on page 319. If the algorithm returns m in step 5, then $m(A)b = 0$, so that m is a characteristic polynomial of a and hence a multiple of m_a. Since both m and m_a are monic, we have $m = m_a$.

Steps 3 and 5 can be done in a Horner-like way, using $2n$ applications of A to a vector if the n vectors $b, Ab, \ldots, A^{n-1}b \in F^n$ are stored in step 3, and $3n$ evaluations of A otherwise, plus $O(n^2)$ field operations for additions of vectors, inner products, and multiplications by scalars. The cost for step 4 is $O(n^2)$. $\square$

It remains to prove that the condition in step 5 is true with reasonable probability, so that we expect to get an output after a small number of iterations. Thus we have to find a lower bound on the probability that for random $u \in U^n$, the polynomial m computed in step 4 of Algorithm 12.13 is the minimal polynomial of $(A^ib)_{i\in\mathbb{N}}$.

For a nonzero $f \in F[x]$ of degree d, we consider the set $M_f \subseteq F^\mathbb{N}$ of all sequences $a \in F^\mathbb{N}$ that are annihilated by f. For example, M_{x^d-1} is the set of all periodic sequences with period d. M_f is an $F[x]$-submodule of $F^\mathbb{N}$, since $a + b$ and $g \bullet a$ are annihilated by f if a and b are and $g \in F[x]$ is arbitrary, by (1), (2), and (4). Since any sequence in M_f is completely determined by its d initial values, M_f is d-dimensional as a vector space over F, and a basis is formed by the d shifts

$$
\begin{aligned}
x^0 \bullet c &= (0, 0, \ldots, 0, 0, 1, c_d, c_{d+1}, \ldots), \\
x^1 \bullet c &= (0, 0, \ldots, 0, 1, c_d, c_{d+1}, c_{d+2} \ldots), \\
&\;\;\vdots \\
x^{d-1} \bullet c &= (1, c_d, \ldots, c_{2d-4}, c_{2d-3}, c_{2d-2}, c_{2d-1}, c_{2d}, \ldots)
\end{aligned}
$$

of the **impulse response sequence** $c = (c_i)_{i\in\mathbb{N}}$ for f, whose d initial values are $0, 0, \ldots, 0, 1$, and whose remaining values are determined by the recurrence relation $f \bullet c = 0$. Hence M_f is the **cyclic** $F[x]$-module $F[x] \bullet c$ generated by c: if $a = \sum_{0 \le j < d} g_j(x^j \bullet c) \in M_f$ is arbitrary and $g = \sum_{0 \le j < d} g_j x^j \in F[x]$, then $a = g \bullet c$.

A cyclic module $M = R \bullet c$ over a ring R is isomorphic to $R/\text{Ann}(c)$. This follows from the fact that $\lambda: R \longrightarrow M$ with $\lambda(g) = g \bullet c$ is a surjective homomorphism of R-modules with kernel $\text{Ann}(c)$, and by the homomorphism theorem for R-modules, the map $\varphi: R/\text{Ann}(c) \longrightarrow M$ given by $\varphi(g \bmod \text{Ann}(c)) = g \bullet c$ is an isomorphism (see the latest edition of van der Waerden 1931, §86). This may be familiar to the reader in the case of commutative groups, where $R = \mathbb{Z}$, M is a finite cyclic group of order $n \in \mathbb{N}$, and the module operation is $g \bullet a = a^g$ for $g \in \mathbb{Z}$ and $a \in M$. Then, for any generator c of M, we have $M = \mathbb{Z} \bullet c$, $\text{Ann}(c) = n\mathbb{Z}$, and in fact $\varphi: \mathbb{Z}/n\mathbb{Z} \longrightarrow M$ with $\varphi(g \bmod n) = c^g$ is an isomorphism of $\mathbb{Z}$-modules.

In our situation, $\text{Ann}(c) = \langle f \rangle$. This is because clearly f annihilates c, and on the other hand no nonzero $g \in F[x]$ of degree $k < d$ satisfies $g \bullet c = \mathbf{0}$, since the $(d-1-k)$th coefficient of $g \bullet c$ is the leading coefficient of g. Thus M_f and $F[x]/\langle f \rangle$ are isomorphic as $F[x]$-modules, where the module operation on $F[x]/\langle f \rangle$ is defined by $g \bullet (h \bmod f) = (g \bmod f)(h \bmod f) = gh \bmod f$, and

$$\varphi: F[x]/\langle f \rangle \longrightarrow M_f, \quad g \bmod f \longmapsto g \bullet c \qquad (9)$$

is an isomorphism.

LEMMA 12.16. *Let $A \in F^{n \times n}$, $b \in F^n \setminus \{0\}$, and $f \in F[x]$ be the minimal polynomial of the sequence $(A^i b)_{i \in \mathbb{N}} \in (F^n)^{\mathbb{N}}$. There is a surjective F–linear map $\psi: F^n \longrightarrow F[x]/\langle f \rangle$ such that for all $u \in F^n$ we have*

$$f \text{ is the minimal polynomial of } (u^T A^i b)_{i \in \mathbb{N}} \in F^n \iff \psi(u) \text{ is a unit.} \qquad (10)$$

PROOF. We have $d = \deg f \le n$. We define the F–linear map $\psi^*: F^n \longrightarrow F^{\mathbb{N}}$ by $\psi^*(u) = (u^T A^i b)_{i \in \mathbb{N}}$. Then $\psi^*(u)$ is linearly recurrent with characteristic polynomial f for all $u \in F^n$, so that $\psi^*(u) \in M_f$. On the other hand, the d vectors $b, Ab, \ldots, A^{d-1} b \in F^n$ are linearly independent over F, by the minimality of f. Hence for any sequence $a = (a_i)_{i \in \mathbb{N}} \in M_f$ there exists a $u \in F^n$ with $u^T A^i b = a_i$ for $0 \le i < d$, and $\psi^*(u) = a$ since the first d entries of both sequences agree and both are annihilated by f. This shows that we can regard ψ^* as a surjective map from F^n onto M_f. We now set $\psi = \varphi^{-1} \circ \psi^*$, where $\varphi: F[x]/\langle f \rangle \longrightarrow M_f$ is the isomorphism (9) of cyclic $F[x]$-modules. Then ψ is surjective,

$$g \bullet \psi^*(u) = g \bullet (\varphi \circ \psi(u)) = \varphi(g \bullet \psi(u)) = \varphi((g \bmod f) \cdot \psi(u))$$

for all $g \in F[x]$ and $u \in F^n$, and

$$
\begin{aligned}
f = m_{\psi^*(u)} &\iff \forall g \in F[x] \quad (g \bullet \psi^*(u) = \mathbf{0} \iff f \mid g) \\
&\iff \forall g \in F[x] \quad ((g \bmod f) \cdot \psi(u) = 0 \iff g \bmod f = 0) \\
&\iff \forall h \in F[x]/\langle f \rangle \quad (h \cdot \psi(u) = 0 \iff h = 0) \\
&\iff \psi(u) \text{ is a unit,}
\end{aligned}
$$

since $d \ge 1$ and any nonunit is a zero divisor in $F[x]/\langle f \rangle$ (Exercise 4.14). $\square$

LEMMA 12.17. *Let $U \subseteq F$ be finite, $A \in F^{n \times n}$, $b \in F^n \setminus \{0\}$, f be the minimal polynomial of $(A^i b)_{i \in \mathbb{N}} \in (F^n)^{\mathbb{N}}$, and $d = \deg f$. Then the probability p that f is the minimal polynomial of the sequence $(u^T A^i b)_{i \in \mathbb{N}}$ for a $u \in U^n$ chosen uniformly at random satisfies $p \geq 1 - d/\#U$.*

PROOF. Let $\psi: F^n \longrightarrow F[x]/\langle f \rangle$ be as in Lemma 12.16, $e_j \in F^n$ the jth unit vector for $1 \leq j \leq n$, and $u = (u_1, \ldots, u_n)^T = u_1 e_1 + \cdots + u_n e_n \in F^n$ be an arbitrary vector. Since ψ is F–linear, we have

$$\psi(u) = u_1 \psi(e_1) + u_1 \psi(e_1) + \cdots + u_n \psi(e_n) = (u_1 h_1 + \cdots + u_n h_n) \bmod f,$$

with $h_1, \ldots, h_n \in F[x]$ of degree less than d and $\psi(e_j) = h_j \bmod f$ for all j. Let $y_1, \ldots, y_n$ be new indeterminates over $F[x]$ and $r = \mathrm{res}_x(y_1 h_1 + \cdots + y_n h_n, f) \in F[y_1, \ldots, y_n]$. Then the total degree of r is at most d, and by Lemma 6.25

$$\psi(u) \text{ is a unit} \iff \gcd(u_1 h_1 + \cdots + u_n h_n, f) = 1 \iff r(u_1, \ldots, u_n) \neq 0. \quad (11)$$

Since ψ is surjective and $d \geq 1$, there exists some $u \in F^n$ such that $\psi(u) = 1$ is a unit, and hence r is not the zero polynomial. By (10) and (11), p is the probability that $r(u_1, \ldots, u_n) \neq 0$ for $u_1, \ldots, u_n \in U$ chosen uniformly at random and independently, and the assertion follows from Lemma 6.44. □

Lemma 12.17 gives a good lower bound on the success probability of Algorithm 12.13 for fields of sufficiently large cardinality, say at least $2n$.

THEOREM 12.18.
The expected cost of Algorithms 12.12 and 12.13 is at most $4nc(A) + O(n^2)$ field operations if F has at least $2n$ elements.

PROOF. From Lemmas 12.16 and 12.17, we conclude that the expected number of iterations of Algorithm 12.13 is at most 2 if we take any subset $U \subseteq F$ of cardinality at least $2n$. We may assume that the vectors $Ab, A^2 b, \ldots, A^{n-1} b$ computed in step 3 of Algorithm 12.13 are stored, and then the cost for step 2 of Algorithm 12.12 is only another $O(n^2)$ field operations for vector additions and scalar multiplications. The claim now follows from Theorem 12.15. □

For "small" finite fields $\mathbb{F}_q$, we might make a suitable field extension (Exercise 12.16), which would add a factor of $O(\mathsf{M}(\log_q n))$ to the timings from Theorem 12.18. Wiedemann (1986) shows that this factor can be replaced by 2 (Exercise 12.18), by computing the least common multiple of the minimal polynomials of $(u^T A^i b)_{i \in \mathbb{N}}$ for several independently chosen uniformly random $u \in F^n$.

Wiedemann (1986) also addresses the singular and nonsquare case. A different variant in the singular case is from Kaltofen & Saunders (1991). They prove the following theorem.

▬▬ THEOREM 12.19. ▬▬

Let F be a field, $n \in \mathbb{N}_{>0}$, $A \in F^{n \times n}$ of rank $r \leq n$ with leading principal $r \times r$ submatrix nonsingular, and $b \in F^n$ such that the linear system $Ay = b$ is solvable. Then for any vector $v \in F^n$ there is a unique $v^* \in F^n$ such that $A \cdot (v^* - v) = b$ and the lower $n - r$ coordinates of v^* are zero. Moreover, $v^* - v$ is a uniform random vector in the solution space $\{y \in F^n : Ay = b\}$ if v is a uniform random vector in F^n.

Thus given A, b as in the theorem, we choose a random vector v and apply Wiedemann's algorithm 12.12 to the linear system $A_r y_r = b_r$, where $A_r \in F^{r \times r}$ is the leading principal submatrix of A, the vector $b_r \in F^r$ consists of the upper r coordinates of $b + Av$, and $y_r \in F^r$ is to be computed. If we let $v^* \in F^n$ be the vector whose upper part is y_r and whose lower part is zero, then the theorem implies that $y = v^* - v$ is a uniform random solution of the linear system $Ay = b$. (This works, in particular, for $b = 0$.) Since we may apply A_r to a vector $v_r \in F^r$ by applying A to the vector whose upper r coordinates are those of v_r and whose lower $n - r$ ones are zero and taking the upper r coordinates of the result, the cost for the method described above is $O(n(c(A) + n))$ operations in F.

Kaltofen & Saunders also give a probabilistic algorithm which transforms an arbitrary matrix $C \in F^{n \times n}$ into the form required in Theorem 12.19, thereby preserving the black box property, and determines its rank. If the field has at least $3(n^2 + n)$ elements, then their algorithm uses $O(n(c(C) + \mathsf{M}(n)))$ field operations and returns the correct result with probability at least $1/2$. To find a solution of the linear system with coefficient matrix C, the above method is applied to the transformed matrix, and a uniform random solution of the original linear system can be computed within the same time bound. The cost for one application of the transformed matrix to a vector is $c(C) + 2\mathsf{M}(n)$, and the overall cost is $O(n(c(C) + \mathsf{M}(n)))$ operations.

An important aspect of Wiedemann's algorithm is that the only use of the matrix A is to evaluate it at vectors. Thus instead of storing an array of n^2 entries, all we need is a "black box" for the evaluation of A, that is, a subroutine which on input $v \in F^n$ returns $Av \in F^n$. This leads to a new way of doing linear algebra, **black box linear algebra** (or implicit linear algebra), in contrast to the traditional explicit linear algebra, where all entries of A are explicitly stored. A somewhat intermediate concept is **sparse linear algebra**, where A is stored in a sparse format, listing only those (i, j, a_{ij}) with $a_{ij} \neq 0$; this is appropriate for Wiedemann's original application to integer factorization (Chapter 19).

As an example, let $\omega \in F$ be a primitive nth root of unity and suppose that $A = \text{VDM}(1, \omega, \omega^2, \ldots, \omega^{n-1})$ is the matrix of the Discrete Fourier Transform DFT_ω (Section 8.2). Thus solving $Av = b$ for v corresponds to interpolating at the powers of ω with values determined by b, and evaluation of A at v corresponds to computing the Discrete Fourier Transform of the polynomial corresponding to v, which can be done at a cost of $O(n \log n)$ arithmetic operations. Actually, this does not yield improved algorithms here, since DFT_ω^{-1} can be computed with $O(n \log n)$ operations, while the black box linear algebra approach takes $O(n^2 \log n)$, but it does when applied to the Berlekamp matrix for factoring polynomials (Section 14.8).

Notes.   **12.1.** Algorithm 12.1 is due to Winograd (1971), and the current world record $\omega < 2.376$ is from Coppersmith & Winograd (1990). The entries of the following table indicate the approximate date of discovery of new feasible matrix multiplication exponents in history; publication was often years later.

Strassen 1968	2.808	Pan 1979	2.522
Pan 1978	2.781	Coppersmith & Winograd 1980	2.498
Bini *et al.* 1979	2.780	Strassen 1986	2.479
Schönhage 1979	2.609	Coppersmith & Winograd 1986	2.376

The details of these algorithms are beyond the scope of this text. The most comprehensive treatment is in Bürgisser, Clausen & Shokrollahi (1996); we also refer to the books by Pan (1984) and de Groote (1987), and the survey articles of Strassen (1984, 1990) and von zur Gathen (1988) for details and references. Also for the rest of this section, we refer the reader to those texts.

Fast algorithms (or reductions) for the problems at the end of the section are in van der Waerden (1938), Strassen (1969, 1973a), Bunch & Hopcroft (1974), Baur & Strassen (1983), and Keller-Gehrig (1985). Chou, Deng, Li & Wang (1995) report on a successful parallel implementation of Strassen's matrix multiplication.

12.2. Algorithm 12.3 is from Brent & Kung (1978). It can be slightly speeded up by using faster algorithms for *rectangular matrix multiplication*. The direct approach for multiplying an $n \times n$ matrix by an $n \times n^2$ matrix using $\omega < 2.376$ takes $O(n^{3.376})$ ring operations. Huang & Pan (1998) have improved the exponent for this particular rectangular problem to less than 3.334, and then the $n^{1.688}$ in Corollary 12.5 drops to $n^{1.667}$. In the special case $f = x^n$, Brent & Kung give a $O(\mathsf{M}(n)(n \log n)^{1/2})$ solution (Exercise 12.4). Bernstein (1998a) presents a faster algorithm for rings of small characteristic.

12.3. Linearly recurrent sequences were already studied by de Moivre, and the equivalence between finding recurrence relations and computing Padé approximants (Lemma 12.8) was known to Kronecker (1881a), page 566. The problem is also intimately connected to solving Toeplitz (or Hankel) systems of equations. Krylov (1931) invented his method in the context of solving differential equations for oscillation problems. The *transposition principle* says that for a given square matrix A, the cost of computing Av or wA, for input vectors v and w, are essentially the same (Fiduccia 1972b, 1973, Kaminski, Kirkpatrick & Bshouty 1988). Kaltofen (1998) proposes as an open problem the task to relate these two costs more precisely. The connection between these two problems is well-studied in digital filter design; see Antoniou (1979), §4.7.

12.4. The *block Wiedemann* method, proposed by Coppersmith (1994) and analyzed and improved by Kaltofen (1995b) and Villard (1997), reduces the number of evaluations of A from $2n$ to $(1+\varepsilon)n$ for any $\varepsilon > 0$. It is particularly well suited for $F = \mathbb{F}_2$ and also leads to efficient parallel algorithms over arbitrary fields.

A different black box method, based on inner products, for solving linear systems is due to Lanczos (1952). LaMacchia & Odlyzko (1990) introduced the algorithm into computer algebra by employing it for integer factorization. Block variants were given by Copper-smith (1993) and Montgomery (1995), and Eberly & Kaltofen (1997) analyze randomized Lanczos algorithms. Giesbrecht, Lobo & Saunders (1998) solve the problem of certifying inconsistency over the integers of a system of linear equations by the Wiedemann method.

Exercises.

12.1 Prove that Algorithm 12.1 works correctly.

12.2 Let $g = h = x^3 + 2x^2 + 3x + 4$ and $f = x^4 - 1$ in $\mathbb{F}_5[x]$. Trace Algorithm 12.3 on computing $g(h)$ rem f.

12.3 Let R be a ring (commutative, with 1), $f, g, h \in R[x]$ with $\deg f = n$, $\deg g < d$, and $\deg h < m$, such that f is monic and d is a power of 2. Devise a divide-and-conquer algorithm for computing $g(h)$ rem f by splitting g into two blocks of size $d/2$. Prove that your algorithm takes $O(\mathsf{M}(n) \log n)$ operations in R if $dm \leq n$, and $O((dm/n)\mathsf{M}(n) \log n)$ in general.

12.4* Let $n, m \in \mathbb{N}$, R be a (commutative) ring such that $n!$ is a unit in R, and $g, h \in R[x]$ of degrees less than n. We let $k = \lceil n/m \rceil$ and write $h = h_1 + h_0$, with $h_0, h_1 \in R[x]$ such that $\deg h_0 < m$ and x^m divides h_1.

(i) Prove that the following Taylor expansion holds:

$$g(h) \equiv g(h_0) + g'(h_0)h_1 + \cdots + \frac{g^{(k)}(h_0)}{k!}h_1^k \bmod x^n.$$

(ii) The chain rule implies that $g^{(i+1)}(h_0) \cdot h_0' = (g^{(i)}(h_0))'$ for all $i \in \mathbb{N}$. Assuming that $h_0'(0)$ is nonzero, show that $g^{(i+1)}(h_0)$ rem $x^{n+k-i-1}$ can be computed from $g^{(i)}(h_0)$ rem x^{n+k-i} using $O(\mathsf{M}(n))$ operations in R, for $0 \leq i < k$.

(iii) Consider Brent & Kung's (1978) algorithm for computing $g(h) \bmod x^n$.

━━━ ALGORITHM 12.20 Composition modulo powers of x. ━━━━━━━━━
Input: $n \in \mathbb{N}$ and $g, h \in R[x]$ of degrees less than n such that $h'(0) \neq 0$.
Output: $g(h)$ rem $x^n \in R[x]$.

    1. write $h = h_1 + h_0$ as above
       for $2 \leq i \leq k$ compute $h_1^i / i!$ rem x^n

    2. **call** the algorithm from Exercise 12.3 to compute $g(h_0)$ rem x^{n+k}

    3. **for** $1 \leq i \leq k$ compute $g^{(i)}(h_0)$ rem x^{n+k-i}

    4. **return** $\displaystyle\sum_{0 \leq i \leq k} g^{(i)}(h_0)\frac{h_1^i}{i!}$ rem x^n ━━━━━━━━━━━

Its correctness follows from (i). Use (ii) to prove that the algorithm takes $O((k + m \log n)\mathsf{M}(n))$ operations in R.

(iv) Which choice of m minimizes the running time?

(v) Can you remove the restriction that $h'(0)$ be nonzero, using essentially the same time bound?

12.5 Prove properties (1) through (6) of a module operation $\bullet$.

12.6 Let V be a vector space over a field F.

(i) What is the minimal polynomial of the sequence $(a_i)_{i \in \mathbb{N}} \in F^{\mathbb{N}}$ defined by $a_i = 1$ for $0 \leq i < n$ and $a_i = 0$ otherwise?

(ii) How are m_a and $m_{x^n \bullet a}$ for $a \in V^{\mathbb{N}}$ and $n \in \mathbb{N}$ related?

12.7 Prove Lemma 12.8 (i).

12.8 Determine a recurrence relation and sufficiently many initial values of the sequence $(a_i)_{i \in \mathbb{N}} \in \mathbb{Q}^{\mathbb{N}}$ if $h = \sum_{i \geq 0} a_i x^i \in \mathbb{Q}[[x]]$ is

(i) $h = \dfrac{x^2 + x}{x^3 - x - 1}$, (ii) $h = \dfrac{x^2 - x}{x^4 - x^2 - x}$, (iii) $h = \dfrac{x^4 + x}{x^3 - x - 1}$.

12.9 Compute the minimal polynomial of the sequence $1, 3, 4, 7, 11, 18, 29, 47, \ldots$ of rational numbers using Algorithm 12.9. You may assume that the recursion order is at most four. Give the next 12 elements of the sequence.

12.10* Let F be a field, $f \in F[x]$ an irreducible polynomial of degree n, $E = F[x]/\langle f \rangle$, $\alpha = x \bmod f \in E$, and $\beta = g(\alpha) \in E$ for some nonzero polynomial $g \in F[x]$ of degree less than n.

(i) Prove that the minimal polynomial $m \in F[x]$ of β is equal to the minimal polynomial of the sequence $(\beta^i)_{i \in \mathbb{N}} \subseteq E^{\mathbb{N}}$.

(ii) Let $\tau : E \longrightarrow F$ be the linear map with $\tau(\sum_{0 \leq i < n} c_i \alpha^i) = c_0$ for all $c_0, \ldots, c_{n-1} \in F$. Prove that m is the minimal polynomial of the sequence $(\tau(\beta^i))_{i \in \mathbb{N}} \subseteq F^{\mathbb{N}}$. Hint: m is irreducible.

(iii) Show that m can be computed using $O(n \mathsf{M}(n))$ operations in F.

(iv) Compute the minimal polynomial of $2^{2/3} + 2^{1/3} + 1$ over $\mathbb{Q}$.

12.11 Let F be a field, $A \in F^{n \times n}$, $u, b \in F^n$, and define sequences $a = (A^i)_{i \in \mathbb{N}}$ and $a^* = (A^i b)_{i \in \mathbb{N}}$.

(i) Prove that $f \in F[x]$ is a characteristic polynomial of a if and only if $f(A) = 0$ in $F^{n \times n}$.

(ii) Prove that $f \in F[x]$ is a characteristic polynomial of a^* if and only if $f(A)b = 0$ in F^n.

12.12* This continues Exercise 12.11. Let $a^{**} = (u^T A^i b)_{i \in \mathbb{N}}$. Find a situation where $u^T f(A)b = 0$, but f is not a characteristic polynomial of a^{**}. Can you determine a stronger condition such that a similar equivalence as in Exercise 12.11 holds? Hint: Consider the condition that $u^T f(A)$ be orthogonal to the Krylov subspace $\langle A^i b : i \in \mathbb{N} \rangle$ of F^n generated by b.

12.13$\longrightarrow$ Let

$$ A = \begin{pmatrix} 1 & 2 & 3 \\ 4 & 0 & 1 \\ 1 & 3 & 1 \end{pmatrix} \in \mathbb{F}_5^{3 \times 3}, \quad b = \begin{pmatrix} 0 \\ 1 \\ 2 \end{pmatrix} \in \mathbb{F}_5^3, $$

and compute $A^{-1}b$ using Wiedemann's algorithm 12.12.

12.14* Let F be a field, $n \in \mathbb{N}$, $A \in F^{n \times n}$, and $e_i \in F^n$ be the ith unit vector, that is, the column vector with 1 in coordinate i and 0 everywhere else, for $1 \leq i \leq n$. Prove that if $f, f_1, \ldots, f_n \in F[x]$ are the minimal polynomials of A, $(A^i e_1)_{i \in \mathbb{N}}, \ldots, (A^i e_n)_{i \in \mathbb{N}}$, respectively, then $f = \mathrm{lcm}\{f_1, \ldots, f_n\}$. Generalize this to arbitrary bases $e_1, \ldots, e_n$ of F^n.

12.15* Let F be a field.

(i) Design an algorithm that, given a matrix $A \in F^{n \times n}$, computes its minimal polynomial by randomly choosing $u, b \in F^n$, computing the minimal polynomial of $(u^T A^i b)_{i \in \mathbb{N}}$, and checking whether it is actually the minimal polynomial of A. Prove that your algorithm is correct if it halts.

(ii) Let $f \in F[x]$ be the minimal polynomial of A. Show that there is a surjective bilinear map $\psi : F^n \times F^n \longrightarrow F[x]/\langle f \rangle$ (bilinear means that ψ is linear with respect to both arguments) such that

$$ f \text{ is the minimal polynomial of } (u^T A^i b)_{i \in \mathbb{N}} \in F^n \iff \psi(u, b) \text{ is a unit} $$

for all $u, b \in F^n$. Hint: Proceed as in Lemma 12.16.

(iii) Use (ii) to show that the probability for f being the minimal polynomial of $(u^T A^i b)_{i \in \mathbb{N}}$, when the entries of u and b are chosen uniformly at random and independently from a fixed finite subset $U \subseteq F$, is at least $1 - 2 \deg f / \#U$. Hint: Proceed as in the proof of Lemma 12.17.

12.16 Let $F \subseteq E$ be fields, $n \in \mathbb{N}$, $V = F^n$, $b \in V$, and $A \in F^{n \times n}$.

(i) Let $a = (A^i b)_{i \in \mathbb{N}} \in V^{\mathbb{N}}$. Prove that the recursion order of a is the smallest $r \in \mathbb{N}$ such that $b, Ab, \ldots, A^r b$ are linearly dependent in F^n.

(ii) Let $r \leq n$, and prove that vectors $b_0, \ldots, b_{r-1} \in F^n$ are linearly dependent in F^n if and only if they are linearly dependent in E^n. Hint: Gaussian elimination. Conclude that the minimal polynomial of a over F is the same as over E.

12.17* Let $n \in \mathbb{N}$, F be a field of cardinality at least $4n$, and $A \in F^{n \times n}$. Give a probabilistic "black box" algorithm taking $O(c(A)n + n^2)$ field operations that decides whether A is singular, such that the answer is always correct when A is nonsingular and correct with probability at least $1/2$ when A is singular. Hint: Exercise 12.15.

12.18** Let F be a field, $n \in \mathbb{N}$, $A \in F^{n \times n}$, and $b \in F^n$. This exercise discusses a modification of Algorithm 12.12, due to Wiedemann (1986), which proves that the time bound from Theorem 12.18 can be achieved within a factor of 2 when F is a small finite field.

(i) Let V be a vector space over F, $f \in F[x]$ the minimal polynomial of a linearly recurrent sequence $a \in V^{\mathbb{N}}$, and $g \in F[x]$. Prove that $g \bullet a$ has minimal polynomial $f / \gcd(f, g)$.

(ii) Replace steps 1, 2, and 5 of Algorithm 12.13 by

    1. let $U \subseteq F$ be finite, $g \longleftarrow 1$

    2. **if** $b = 0$ **then return** g

    5. $g \longleftarrow gm$, $b \longleftarrow m(A)b$,   **goto** 2

Prove that the modified algorithm works correctly.

(iii) Let $u_k \in F[x]$ be the value of u chosen in the kth iteration and $g_k \in F[x]$ the minimal polynomial of the sequence $a^{(k)} = (u_k^T A^i b^*)_{i \in \mathbb{N}}$, where $b^* \in F^n$ is the initial value of b. Prove that the invariant $m = g_k / \gcd(g, g_k)$ holds after the kth pass through step 3, and conclude that $g = \mathrm{lcm}(g_1, \ldots, g_k)$ holds before the kth pass through step 2.

(iv) Let $U = F = \mathbb{F}_q$ be a finite field with q elements and $f \in F[x]$. Prove that for k polynomials $h_1, \ldots, h_k \in F[x]$ of degree less than $\deg f$ chosen uniformly at random and independently, the probability that $\gcd(h_1, \ldots, h_k, f) = 1$ is $p_k = \prod_{1 \leq j \leq r}(1 - q^{-k \deg f_j})$, where $f_1, \ldots, f_r \in F[x]$ are the distinct monic irreducible factors of f.

(v) Now let f be the minimal polynomial of $(A^i b^*)_{i \in \mathbb{N}}$. Prove the following generalization of Lemma 12.16 (with b replaced by b^*): If $\psi(u) = h \bmod f$ with $h \in F[x]$, then $m_{\psi^*(u)} = f / \gcd(f, h)$. Conclude that p_k from (iv) is the probability that the above algorithm terminates after at most k iterations.

(vi) Let $n_i = \#\{1 \leq j \leq r: \deg f_j = i\}$ for all i. Prove that

$$\prod_{1 \leq j \leq r}(1 - q^{-k \deg f_j}) \geq 1 - \sum_{1 \leq j \leq r} q^{-k \deg f_j} = 1 - \sum_{i \geq 1} n_i q^{-ki}.$$

Use that $n_i \leq q^i / i$, by Lemma 14.38, to show that $p_k \geq 1 - 2q^{1-k}$ if $k \geq 2$. Conclude that the expected number $\sum_{k \geq 0}(1 - p_k)$ of iterations of the algorithm is at most 4.

Research problem.

12.19 Can you improve the cost for modular composition of polynomials of degrees at most n to, say, $O^\sim(n^{1.5})$ or better?

Völker, hört die Signale![1]

Emil Luckhardt (c. 1890)

L'étude approfondie de la nature est la source la plus féconde des
découvertes mathématiques. Non seulement cette étude,
en offrant aux recherches un but déterminé, a l'avantage d'exclure
les questions vagues et les calculs sans issue: elle est encore
un moyen assuré de former l'Analyse elle-même, et d'en découvrir
les éléments qu'il nous importe le plus de connaître,
et que cette science doit toujours conserver.[2]

Jean Baptiste Joseph Fourier (1822)

Unsere Allergrößten, wie Archimedes, Newton, Gauß,
haben stets Theorie und Anwendungen gleichmäßig umfaßt.[3]

Felix Klein (1908)

Die Mathematiker sind eine Art Franzosen, redet man zu ihnen,
so übersetzen sie es in ihre Sprache
und dann ist es alsobald ganz etwas anders.[4]

Johann Wolfgang von Goethe (1829)

He said he would rather decline two drinks
than one German adjective.

Mark Twain (1879)

---

[1] Peoples, hear the signals!

[2] The deep study of nature is the most fruitful source of mathematical discoveries. By offering a well-defined goal for research, this study not only has the advantage of excluding vague questions and useless calculations, but is also a sure means of performing the analysis itself and of discovering the elements which are most important to know, and which this science ought always to conserve.

[3] Our greatest mathematicians, as Archimedes, Newton, and Gauß, always united theory and applications in equal measure.

[4] Mathematicians are like Frenchmen; if you talk to them, they translate it into their own language, and right away it is something entirely different.

13

Fourier Transform and image compression

In this chapter, we discuss the background of the Fourier Transform from electrical engineering and signal processing. Its fundamental property of transforming a (discrete or continuous) signal from its description in the time domain to an equivalent characterization in the frequency domain is used to describe and analyze the contributions of different frequencies to a signal. Furthermore, we present an application of the Fourier Transform in image processing.

13.1. The Continuous and the Discrete Fourier Transform

DEFINITION 13.1. *A **continuous signal** (or **analog signal**) is a function*

$$f : D \longrightarrow \mathbb{R}^n, \; \text{where } D \subseteq \mathbb{R}^m \text{ and } m, n \in \mathbb{N}.$$

*A **discrete(-time) signal** is a function*

$$f : D \longrightarrow \mathbb{R}^n, \; \text{where } D \subseteq \mathbb{Z}^m \text{ and } m, n \in \mathbb{N}.$$

*If in addition $f(D) \subseteq \mathbb{Z}^n$, then f is called a **digital signal**.*

Sound is a continuous signal that varies over time and has range loudness. It is an example of a signal $f : \mathbb{R} \longrightarrow \mathbb{R}$. In the case of gray-scale pixels on a screen, the signal associates to each point an intensity value, so that $f : D \subseteq \mathbb{Z}^2 \longrightarrow \mathbb{R}$. When color is represented by the constituent amounts of three basic colors (RGB) or four basic colors (CMYK), we have a signal mapping into $\mathbb{R}^3$ or $\mathbb{R}^4$, respectively.

A discrete signal is often obtained by sampling a continuous signal at discrete intervals. This is illustrated in Figure 13.1, where a continuous signal is sampled at regularly spaced points.

Discrete signals find applications in areas such as biomedical engineering, seismology, acoustics, sonar and radar imaging, speech communication, data communication, television satellite communication, satellite images, and many more. Speech and telephone signals are examples of signals with only one dimensional

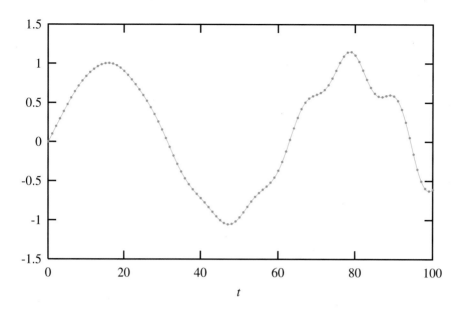

FIGURE 13.1: The analog signal $f(t) = \sin(t/10) + t^2 \sin(t/2)/40000$ (red), and the corresponding discrete signal (blue).

domains, while radar imaging, satellite images, and lunar images are processed with two dimensional domains. When modeling complicated problems, such as those that appear in seismology, the domain can have many dimensions.

It is important to perform certain operations on signals to extract relevant information from them, or to transform the signal to make it easier to use. For instance one may wish to extract some important parameters from the data such as danger alerts from an electrocardiogram or electroencephalogram. One may want to compress the data contained in a telephone signal or recognize the words associated with speech signals. A common problem is to extract relevant information from masses of data associated with such things as television transmission or satellite images. Another application of signal processing in signal transmission is to try to remove signal interference contributed by transmission noise, fading or channel distortion.

Of particular importance are the sine signal $f: \mathbb{R} \longrightarrow \mathbb{R}$ with $f(t) = \sin t$, and its complex variant $f: \mathbb{R} \longrightarrow \mathbb{R}^2 \cong \mathbb{C}$ with $f(t) = e^{it} = \cos t + i \sin t$, where $i = \sqrt{-1}$. More generally, we have the signal $f: \mathbb{R} \longrightarrow \mathbb{C}$ with $f(t) = a \cdot e^{ikt}$, with **amplitude** a, corresponding to the intensity of the signal (for example, loudness of an audio signal or luminance of a video signal), and **frequency** k (corresponding to pitch or color, respectively). All those signals are examples of **periodic** signals: there exists a **period** $T \in \mathbb{R}_{>0}$ such that $f(t+T) = f(t)$ for all $t \in \mathbb{R}$. Applying the transformation $t \longmapsto 2\pi t/T$, we may assume that $T = 2\pi$. For the sinusoidal signal $f(t) = a \cdot e^{ikt}$, the smallest such period T is the wavelength and related to

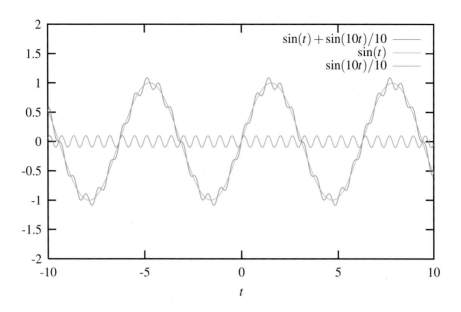

FIGURE 13.2: A 2π-periodic signal and its harmonics.

the frequency k by $T = 2\pi/k$. Similarly, a discrete signal is periodic with period $N \in \mathbb{N}_{>0}$ if $f(n+N) = f(n)$ for all $n \in \mathbb{Z}$.

Other popular examples of 2π-periodic functions are obtained by taking a function defined on a bounded interval, normalizing the interval to be $[0, 2\pi]$, and extending the function by periodicity. Examples are given in Exercise 13.4. In the following, we assume without further mention that our functions are sufficiently "smooth", so that, for example, the required integrals and sums are well defined.

DEFINITION 13.2. *The **(Continuous) Fourier Transform** of a 2π-periodic signal $f: \mathbb{R} \longrightarrow \mathbb{C}$ is $\widehat{f}: \mathbb{Z} \longrightarrow \mathbb{C}$ with*

$$\widehat{f}(k) = \int_0^{2\pi} f(t)e^{-ikt}\,dt \text{ for } k \in \mathbb{Z},$$

where $i = \sqrt{-1} \in \mathbb{C}$ as usual.

The following inversion formula expresses the function f in terms of its Fourier Transform:

$$f(t) = \frac{1}{2\pi} \sum_{k \in \mathbb{Z}} \widehat{f}(k)e^{ikt}. \tag{1}$$

This holds for all $t \in \mathbb{R}$; the series converges uniformly to f. This series is called the **Fourier series** of f, and the numbers $\beta_k = \frac{1}{2\pi}\widehat{f}(k) = \frac{1}{2\pi}\int_0^{2\pi} f(t)e^{-ikt}\,dt$ for

$k \in \mathbb{Z}$ are the **Fourier coefficients** of f. The inversion formula says that the function f is uniquely determined by the sequence of its Fourier coefficients $(\beta_k)_{k \in \mathbb{Z}}$. The special functions e^{ikt}, for $k \in \mathbb{Z}$, are a "basis" for the complex vector space of all 2π-periodic functions; however, there are in general infinitely many nonzero coefficients.

While the original signal f is described in the time domain by assigning to each time $t \in [0, 2\pi]$ the value $f(t)$ of the signal at that time, the Fourier Transform $\widehat{f}$ is an equivalent characterization of f in the frequency domain. It associates to each frequency $k \in \mathbb{Z}$ the contribution $\widehat{f}(k)$ of that frequency, namely of the signal $\exp(ikt)/2\pi$, to f, as given by the inversion formula (1). It compresses the "continuously" many values $f(t)$ into the countably many values $\widehat{f}(k)$. For $k \in \mathbb{N}_{>0}$, the signal $(\widehat{f}(k)\exp(ikt) + \widehat{f}(-k)\exp(-ikt))/2\pi$ is called the kth **harmonic** of f.

EXAMPLE 13.3. Consider the 2π-periodic signal $f : \mathbb{R} \longrightarrow \mathbb{R}$ defined by $f(t) = \sin(t) + \sin(10t)/10$, which is plotted in green in Figure 13.2. We may think of f as consisting of a low frequency part $\sin(t)$ with a large amplitude plus a high frequency part $\sin(10t)/10$ with a small amplitude; these are the blue and red curves in Figure 13.2. The Fourier Transform decomposes f into its harmonics: Exercise 13.3 shows that

$$\widehat{f}(1) = -2\pi i = -\widehat{f}(-1), \quad \widehat{f}(10) = -\frac{1}{5}\pi i = -\widehat{f}(-10),$$

and $\widehat{f}(k) = 0$ for $k \neq \pm 1, \pm 10$. Thus the first harmonic of f is $(\widehat{f}(1)\exp(it) + \widehat{f}(-1)\exp(-it))/2\pi = \sin(t)$, the 10th harmonic is $\sin(10t)/10$, and all other harmonics are zero. $\diamond$

The **Discrete Fourier Transform** is the analog of the Continuous Fourier Transform for discrete periodic signals. If $f : \mathbb{Z} \longrightarrow \mathbb{C}$ is a discrete signal with period $N \in \mathbb{N}_{>0}$, its Discrete Fourier Transform $\widehat{f} : \mathbb{Z} \longrightarrow \mathbb{C}$ is defined by

$$\widehat{f}(k) = \sum_{0 \leq n < N} f(n)e^{-2\pi ikn/N} = \sum_{0 \leq n < N} f(n)\omega^{kn} \text{ for } k \in \mathbb{Z},$$

where $\omega = e^{-2\pi i/N} \in \mathbb{C}$ is a primitive Nth root of unity. If we start with a continuous 2π-periodic signal g and sample it at regularly spaced points $2\pi n/N$ for $0 \leq n < N$ to obtain f, then the Discrete Fourier Transform of f is just one of the common approximations to the integral defining the Continuous Fourier Transform of g. In contrast to the continuous case, $\widehat{f}$ is again periodic with period N. The analog of the inversion formula (1) is

$$f(n) = \frac{1}{N} \sum_{0 \leq k < N} \widehat{f}(k)e^{2\pi ikn/N} = \frac{1}{N} \sum_{0 \leq k < N} \widehat{f}(k)\omega^{-kn}. \qquad (2)$$

The connection to Section 8.2 is as follows. If we associate to a polynomial $f \in \mathbb{C}[x]$ of degree less than n a discrete signal $g\colon \mathbb{Z} \longrightarrow \mathbb{C}$ of period n mapping $\{0, \ldots, n-1\}$ to the coefficients of f, then $\mathrm{DFT}_\omega(f)$ with $\omega = \exp(-2\pi i/n)$ is the Discrete Fourier Transform of g, and Theorem 8.13 is the analog of the inversion formula (2).

In digital signal processing, continuous signals such as sounds or images are sampled. The analysis or modification of the corresponding discrete signals (for example, noise reduction or contrast amplification) on digital hardware or software systems usually involves the computation of Discrete Fourier Transforms for large amounts of data, and the use of the Fast Fourier Transform is indispensable.

13.2. Audio and video compression

The Fourier Transform and its inverse can be considered as a change of representation between the time domain and the frequency domain. If f is a (continuous or discrete) signal and $\widehat{f}$ its Fourier Transform, then $f(t)$ is the value of the signal at time t, while $\widehat{f}(k)$ is the contribution of the frequency k to the signal. Both are equivalent characterizations of a signal. Often audio and video data intended for reception by humans tend to vary "slowly" in the time domain, so that their high frequency contributions are "small". In the frequency domain, this means that $|\widehat{f}(k)|$ is small for large values of k. The idea for data compression is now to discard the values of $\widehat{f}(k)$ that are "close to zero" and to only store the rest. Since the perceptive faculty of the human ear or eye is much better for low frequencies than for high ones, the listener or observer hardly notices this loss of information, and considerable compression rates can be achieved.

Audio and video data are real-valued signals, and often a variant of the Fourier Transform is used that maps real-valued signals again to real-valued signals, as follows. Let $f\colon \{0, \ldots, N-1\} \longrightarrow \mathbb{R}$ be a discrete real-valued signal of finite duration $N \in \mathbb{N}$, for example, a sampled piece of music or one row of a digital screen image. We may think of f as being extended to a periodic signal on $\mathbb{Z}$ by letting $f(n) = f(n \text{ rem } N)$ for all $n \in \mathbb{Z}$. If we let

$$\mathrm{DCT}(f)(k) = \frac{1}{\sqrt{N}} c(k) \sum_{0 \le n < N} f(n) \cos \frac{\pi k(2n+1)}{2N} \quad \text{for } 0 \le k < N,$$

$$\mathrm{IDCT}(f)(n) = \frac{1}{\sqrt{N}} \sum_{0 \le k < N} c(k) f(k) \cos \frac{\pi k(2n+1)}{2N} \quad \text{for } 0 \le n < N,$$

where $c(k) = 1$ if $k = 0$ and $c(k) = \sqrt{2}$ otherwise, then DCT and IDCT are inverse operators mapping real-valued signals of finite duration N to signals of the same kind (Exercise 13.6). $\mathrm{DCT}(f)$ is the **Discrete Cosine Transform (DCT)** of f. Exercise 13.6 also shows that computing this transform or its inverse can be reduced

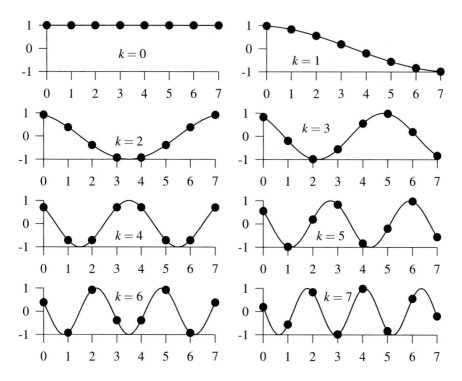

FIGURE 13.3: The discrete cosine signals γ_k for $0 \leq k < 8$.

to computing a Discrete Fourier Transform, which can be done efficiently via the FFT if N is a power of 2, using $O(N \log N)$ operations in $\mathbb{R}$.

The inversion formula

$$f(n) = (\text{IDCT} \circ \text{DCT})(f)(n) = \frac{1}{\sqrt{N}} \sum_{0 \leq k < N} c(k) \text{DCT}(f)(k) \cos \frac{\pi k (2n+1)}{2N}$$

for $0 \leq n < N$ shows that the Discrete Cosine Transform leads to a representation of the original signal f as a linear combination of periodic signals γ_k, where $\gamma_k(n) = \cos(\pi k(2n+1)/2N)$, with coefficients $c(k)\text{DCT}(f)(k)/\sqrt{N}$. Figure 13.3 depicts the signals γ_k on the interval $0, \ldots, N-1$ for $N = 8$. Larger values of k correspond to a more rapid variation of γ_k.

A possible image data compression algorithm works as follows. For each row $f: \{0, \ldots, N-1\} \longrightarrow \mathbb{R}$ of the image, where $f(n)$ is the luminance of the nth pixel in that row, compute $\text{DCT}(f)(k)$ for $0 \leq k < N$ (if the image is a color image, then, for example, apply this separately for the intensities of each of the three colors red, green, and blue). Then choose a quantizing parameter $q \in \mathbb{R}_{\geq 1}$, divide all values of $\text{DCT}(f)$ by q, and round to the nearest integer. The effect of quantization is that those values of $\text{DCT}(f)(k)$ that are close to zero in absolute value (which

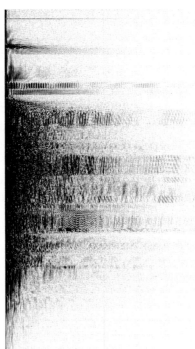

FIGURE 13.4: A grayscale image of Schloß Neuhaus at Paderborn, and the absolute values of its row-wise Discrete Cosine Transform. The color white corresponds to zero, and frequency increases from left to right.

in general will be the case for the high frequency parts, that is, for large k) vanish completely. Thus large values of q correspond to high compression rates but also to worse image quality. Finally a combination of lossless data compression techniques, such as run length encoding and **Huffman encoding**, is applied to the quantized values. **Run length encoding** compresses each consecutive sequence (= run) of zeroes to two integers: a zero marking the position of the run, followed by the length of the run. For example, the sequence

$$1,2,3,0,0,0,0,4,0,5,-6,0,0,0,1,2$$

is compressed to

$$1,2,3,0,4,4,0,1,5,-6,0,3,1,2$$

thereby decreasing the length by two. We note that "runs" of zeroes of length 1 actually increase the size, like the single zero between 4 and 5 in the above example. In order to reconstruct the image, we proceed in the opposite direction: after decoding the compressed values, we multiply them by q and apply the Discrete Cosine Transform row by row.

Figure 13.4 shows at left a grayscale image with 1088 rows, 728 columns, and luminance values between 0 (= black) and 255 (= white). Hence the size of the image is $1088 \cdot 728 = 792\,064$ bytes in a dense encoding, where the luminance value of each pixel is stored in one byte. At right, we see the absolute values of the row-wise Discrete Cosine Transforms of that image. The luminance of the kth pixel from the left in row f_i corresponds to the absolute value of $\mathrm{DCT}(f_i)(k)$ (for better visibility, white represents 0 in this image and all values are multiplied by 10), and one can observe that the DCT coefficients get smaller as the frequency increases. Finally, Figure 13.5 shows the same image after quantizing and dequantizing with parameter q (that is, rounding the DCT coefficients to integral multiples of q) and row-wise application of IDCT, for $q = 10$ and $q = 100$. The image at right in Figure 13.4 illustrates why these compression methods are successful. Light gray areas are "rounded down" to 0, and the darker values are similarly simplified. The larger q is, the more rounding occurs.

FIGURE 13.5: The image from Figure 13.4 after quantizing with $q = 10$ and $q = 100$, using a row-wise Discrete Cosine Transform.

Table 13.6 lists the compression rates—the size ratio of the compressed and the original image—for the image from Figure 13.4 with various quantizing parameters q and different lossless data compression techniques. For example, the size of the file after quantizing with $q = 10$ and using both run length and Huffman encoding is $108\,377$ bytes, which is about 13.68% of the original size, and this compression rate is the entry in the last row of the column with head 10 in Table 13.6. For comparison, Huffman encoding applied to the image itself (in-

q	1	2	5	10	20	50	100
Huffman	56.00	44.11	29.47	22.69	18.32	14.96	13.66
Run length	91.82	75.04	43.29	28.56	18.58	9.06	4.71
Run length + Huffman	52.94	40.01	22.36	13.68	8.29	3.92	1.99

TABLE 13.6: Compression rates in % for the image from Figure 13.4 with the row-wise Discrete Cosine Transform and different encoding schemes.

q	1	2	5	10	20	50	100
Huffman	42.53	30.53	20.70	17.27	15.51	14.22	13.60
Run length	83.40	57.88	24.63	12.93	8.18	5.38	4.23
Run length + Huffman	37.22	25.29	11.76	6.32	3.74	2.10	1.34

TABLE 13.7: Compression rates in % for the image from Figure 13.4 with the Discrete Cosine Transform for 8×8 squares and different encoding schemes.

FIGURE 13.8: The image from Figure 13.4 after quantizing with $q = 10$ and $q = 100$, using the Discrete Cosine Transform for 8×8 squares.

stead of its Discrete Cosine Transform) yields a compression rate of 81.13%, and the GIF graphics format achieves a lossless compression to 60.00% of the original size.

The method described above has the disadvantage that quantization leads to perturbations in the whole row, as can be seen in Figure 13.5 for $q = 100$. Thus the *local* structure of an image (for example, slow variation of the luminance in the sky parts of Figure 13.4) cannot be exploited. This can be circumvented by dividing the image into smaller parts of a fixed size (instead of complete rows) and applying the above compression technique to each part separately.

In the JPEG still image compression standard, for example, the original image is divided into squares of 8×8 pixels, and the two-dimensional Discrete Cosine Transform of each square (which is a combination of a row-wise and a column-wise one-dimensional Discrete Cosine Transform) is computed. Then the DCT coefficients of all squares are quantized, run length encoded and finally Huffman encoded. While the one-dimensional row-wise Discrete Cosine Transform takes only horizontal dependencies into account, its two-dimensional variant covers horizontal and vertical dependencies simultaneously. This together with the improved adaptivity to the local structure of an image leads to significantly higher compression rates than the above row-wise approach (Table 13.7).

Figure 13.8 shows the image from Figure 13.4 after compression and decompression with the Discrete Cosine Transform for 8×8 squares and quantization factors $q = 10, 100$. For $q = 10$, for example, one hardly notices any differences between the images in Figures 13.5 and 13.8, but the compression rate of the former is about 13.68%, while the latter compresses down to 6.32%.

Notes.   **13.1.** Good references for (digital) signal processing are Oppenheim & Schafer (1975) and Oppenheim, Willsky & Young (1983).
13.2. For a description of the Huffman code, see Huffman (1952), Cormen, Leiserson & Rivest (1990), §17.3, and Exercise 10.6. The JPEG standard is described in Wallace (1991) and Pennebaker & Mitchell (1993).

Exercises.

13.1 Show that for any discrete or continuous periodic signal $f: \mathbb{Z} \longrightarrow \mathbb{C}$ or $f: \mathbb{R} \longrightarrow \mathbb{C}$, respectively, there is a least period (called the **fundamental period**) $T \in \mathbb{N}_{>0}$ or $T \in \mathbb{R}_{>0}$ such that any other period of f is an integral multiple of T.

13.2 Let $f, g: \mathbb{R} \longrightarrow \mathbb{C}$ be two 2π-periodic signals. If f, g are sufficiently smooth, then the **convolution**

$$(f * g)(t) = \int_0^{2\pi} f(s)g(t-s)ds$$

exists for all $t \in R$. Prove that $f * g$ is again 2π-periodic, and that the convolution property $\widehat{f * g} = \widehat{f} \cdot \widehat{g}$ holds, so that

$$(\widehat{f * g})(k) = \widehat{f}(k) \cdot \widehat{g}(k) \text{ for all } k \in \mathbb{Z}.$$

(Thus the Fourier Transform converts convolution into pointwise multiplication.) You may assume that all occurring integrals exist.

13.3 Let $f(t) = \sin(t) + \sin(10t)/10$. Compute $\widehat{f}(k)$ for $k \in \mathbb{Z}$.

13.4→ (i) Compute the Fourier coefficients of $f(t) = e^{int}$ for a fixed $n \in \mathbb{Z}$.

(ii) Compute the Fourier coefficients of the 2π-periodic square wave which has $f(t) = -1$ for $-\pi \le t < 0$ and $f(t) = 1$ for $0 \le t < \pi$.

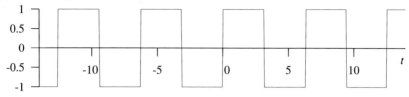

(iii) Compute the Fourier coefficients of the 2π-periodic triangular wave which has $f(t) = t/\pi$ for $-\pi \le t < \pi$.

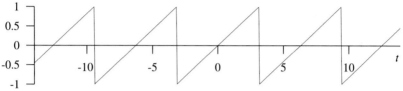

13.5 Let $f: \mathbb{Z} \longrightarrow \mathbb{C}$ be a discrete signal of period $N \in \mathbb{N}_{>0}$. Show that $\Re \widehat{f}(k) = 0$ for all k if f is odd, so that $f(t) = -f(-t)$ for all t, and that $\Im \widehat{f}(k) = 0$ for all k if f is even, so that $f(t) = f(-t)$ for all t.

13.6* Let $f: \{0, \ldots, N-1\} \longrightarrow \mathbb{R}$ be a discrete signal of finite duration N. We associate to f a signal $g: \mathbb{Z} \longrightarrow \mathbb{R}$ of period $4N$, by letting

$$
\begin{aligned}
g(2n+1) &= g(4N - 2n - 1) = f(n) \text{ for } 0 \le n < N, \\
g(2n) &= 0 \text{ for } 0 \le n < 2N,
\end{aligned}
\tag{3}
$$

and periodically extending g to a function that is defined for all integers. This corresponds to gluing f and a reflected copy of f together and interleaving the result with zeroes. Obviously g is even and $g(n)$ vanishes if n is even.

(i) Prove that the Discrete Fourier Transform $\widehat{g}$ is real-valued of period $4N$ and has the symmetry properties

$$\widehat{g}(k) = \widehat{g}(4N - k) = -\widehat{g}(2N + k) = -\widehat{g}(2N - k) \text{ for } k \in \mathbb{Z}.$$

(ii) Show that the inversion formula

$$f(n) = g(2n+1) = \frac{1}{N}\left(\frac{\widehat{g}(0)}{2} + \sum_{1 \le k < N} \widehat{g}(k) \cos \frac{\pi k(2n+1)}{2N} \right)$$

holds for $0 \le n < N$.

(iii) Conclude that DCT and IDCT are inverse operators.

Part III
Gauß

Carl Friedrich Gauß (1777–1855), the *Prince of Mathematicians*, was the latest, after Archimedes and Newton, in this trio of great men whose ideas shaped mathematics for centuries after their work (and two of whom figure prominently in this book).

Born on April 30, 1777, and registered as Johann Friderich Carl Gauß, he grew up in a poor bricklayer's family in Braunschweig. His father, an honest but tough and simple-minded person, did not succeed in keeping his son as uneducated as himself, mainly because of the efforts of Gauß' mother Dorothea and his uncle Friederich.

Gauß loved to tell the story of how—at ten years of age—one of the first flashes of his genius surprised his unsuspecting teacher Büttner. The class had been given the task to sum the first hundred terms of an arithmetic series. (What a useless task!) Gauß figured out the corresponding summation formula (see Section 23.1), wrote down the correct answer almost immediately, and waited while the other boys took the full hour to get their answers—all wrong. (Such stupid things have not vanished from German schools: the first author had a high-school geography teacher who would set similarly useless tasks in order to have some time for serious study—of the current *Playboy* issue.)

Luckily for Gauß, this teacher and others recognized his genius, and Duke Ferdinand of Braunschweig funded his high-school education and then university studies at Göttingen. This feudal generosity may have contributed to Gauß' absence of political involvement, although his were turbulent times: the French Revolution, Napoleonic Wars, and the revolutions of 1830 and 1848.

His student years 1795–1798 were incredibly productive. He found the ruler-and-compass construction of the regular 17–gon (and the determination, without proof, of which regular polygons can be constructed in this way), proved the law of quadratic reciprocity (where Euler's and Legendre's efforts had failed), discovered the method of least squares, classified binary quadratic forms, established the normal error distribution in probability theory (*Gauß' bell curve*), gave the first rigorous proof of the factorization of real polynomials into linear and quadratic factors (the *fundamental theorem of algebra*, his doctoral thesis in 1799), and much more.

He finished his masterpiece *Disquisitiones Arithmeticae* in 1798, at the age of 21 (Gauß 1801). Written in a terse style, according to Gauß' motto *pauca sed matura*[1], it was heavy going for the mathematicians of his age, but its wealth of ideas paved the way for new directions. Its publication was funded by the Duke; to limit the cost, Gauß had to leave out the last of eight planned parts, containing methods for the factorization of polynomials (see the Notes to Chapters 14

---

[1] few but mature

and 15). This material was published posthumously from his handwritten notes (Gauss 1863b).

Gauß married Johanna Osthoff, younger by three years, in 1805. They had three children, but Johanna died after the last birth. Less than a year later, Gauß married her friend Minna Waldeck, eleven years younger, and they also had three children.

Gauß' influence permeates many parts of this book. His study of roots of unity and their subdivision according to subgroups of the relevant Galois group, the *Gauß periods*, can be seen as a precursor of the Fast Fourier Transform in Section 8.2. (These periods are also instrumental for modern fast algorithms for exponentiation in finite fields.) He proved the basic facts about factoring polynomials and the relation between factoring over $\mathbb{Z}$ and over $\mathbb{Q}$ (Section 6.2), found (but did not publish) the distinct-degree factorization method over finite fields (Section 14.2) and Hensel lifting (Section 15.4), guessed the prime number theorem (but did not prove it; see Notes 18.4), and studied hypergeometric series (Section 23.4). His *Gaussian elimination* is a staple of linear algebra (Sections 5.5 and 14.8).

Perhaps as important as his monumental contributions to so many fields is the fact that he championed the idea of mathematical rigor and watertight proof. This was often absent in 18th century mathematics, which lacked a precise understanding of things like limits and infinite sums. (Later, people such as Cauchy, Weierstraß, and Hilbert perfected Gauß' approach.)

According to himself, Gauß' work was only motivated by his inner urge for mathematical discoveries, and not his desire to publish or impress others. This manifested itself in markedly weak public relations. He did not educate a school of eager young disciples to spread his gospel, but he had a few brilliant students: Bernhard Riemann was his only pupil in the usual sense; Ferdinand Eisenstein and Richard Dedekind were his students in a wider sense. Many of Gauß' discoveries were not published during his lifetime: his insights on the arithmetic–geometric mean, elliptic functions and their double periodicity (with which Abel and Jacobi struggled later), the fundamental theorem on analytic functions (vanishing of closed curve integrals, rediscovered by Cauchy), quaternions (found by William Hamilton on 16 October 1843, when Gauß' notes had already slumbered in his drawers for thirty years), and his 1816 discovery of non-Euclidean geometry (given to the world by Nikolas Lobachevsky in 1829, and the son Johann Bolyai de Bolya of Gauß' friend Wolfgang Bolyai in 1832).

His appointment at the university of Göttingen in 1807 was as professor of astronomy. On 1 January 1801, Guiseppe Piazzi had discovered the asteroid Ceres—and it vanished in February. The astronomers could not find it again. Gauß used his newly devised computational methods in astronomy to calculate the orbit, and thanks to this, Ceres was rediscovered in December. This brought world-wide fame to him instantly. During his 48 years as professor, he gave 181 courses and seminars; of these, 128 were on astronomy, and only one on number theory.

One highly unusual aspect of Gauß' work is his uncanny mixture of theory and practice, with either profiting from the other. (Archimedes had a similar talent, while Newton's theoretical determination of improved ship hull cross-sections failed in practice.) This gave his scientific achievements a much wider audience than usual, and, after the low ebb of natural science (as opposed to literature, music, and philosophy) in Germany during the 18th century, he helped create an atmosphere in which bright young men were attracted to mathematics and science in the 19th century.

Gauß led, over many years, a geodetical survey of the Kingdom of Hannover. A private goal was to determine, in view of his discovery of non-Euclidean geometry, whether physical triangles really have an angle sum of 180 degrees—a question that astronomers still work on today with high-precision instruments. This work stimulated his research in differential geometry, leading to the important concept of Gaussian curvature and the Gauß–Bonnet theorem. He constructed, with Wilhelm Weber, an electric telegraph in 1833, with a 2-km-long wire, destroyed by lightning in 1845. He worked, also with Weber, on earth magnetism, and the unit of the magnetic force is called a *gauß*. At the Senate's request, he reorganized the University Widow's Fund, and on the way created the basis for modern life insurance calculations.

Gauß died in 1855, at age 77, and was buried in St. Albani's cemetery in Göttingen; today this is a pleasant park.

Polynomial factorization is perhaps one of the
most striking successes of symbolic computation.

Zhuojun Liu and Paul S. Wang (1994)

La question de factorisation, que GAUSS considérait
avec raison comme *fondamentale*, est traitée dans notre ouvrage
avec une abondance de détails qu'on ne trouve pas
habituellement dans un livre d'étude, et certaines notions
y sont développées pour la première fois. [...]
Il ne nous appartient pas de nous prononcer sur la valeur scientifique
de notre exposé, mais nous avons la conviction
de n'avoir épargné, ni notre travail, ni notre temps,
pour élucider cette question importante.[1]

Maurice Kraïtchik (1926)

Le plus souvent, cependant, il sera aisé de trouver par le tâtonnement
une congruence irréductible d'un degré donné ν.[2]

Évariste Galois (1830)

In den meisten Wissenschaften pflegt eine Generation das
niederzureißen, was die andere gebaut, und was jene gesetzt,
hebt diese auf. In der Mathematik allein setzt jede Generation
ein neues Stockwerk auf den alten Unterbau.[3]

Hermann Hankel (1869)

Two bombs each. Every bomb had a 95 percent probability of hitting
[...] Even the paper probability was less than half a percent chance
of a double miss, but that times ten targets meant a five percent chance
that one missile would survive.

Tom Clancy (1994)

---

[1] The question of factorization, which GAUSS rightly considered as fundamental, is treated in our work with an abundance of details that one does not find usually in a textbook, and some notions are developed there for the first time. [...] It is not appropriate for us to make statements about the scientific value of our exposition, but we have the conviction that we have spared neither effort nor time in order to elucidate this important question.

[2] Most often, however, it will be easy to find by trial an irreducible polynomial [modulo a prime number] of a given degree ν.

[3] In most sciences one generation tears down what another has built and what one has established another undoes. In mathematics alone each generation builds a new storey on top of the old structure.

14

Factoring polynomials over finite fields

In this chapter, we present several algorithms for the factorization of univariate polynomials over finite fields. The two central steps are distinct-degree factorization, where irreducible factors of distinct degrees are separated from each other, and equal-degree factorization, where all irreducible factors of the input polynomial have the same degree. The reader who is happy with the basic result of probabilistic polynomial-time factorization only has to go up to Section 14.4. The remaining sections discuss root finding (14.5), squarefree factorization (14.6), faster algorithms (14.7), methods using a different approach based on linear algebra (14.8), and the construction of irreducible polynomials and BCH codes (14.9 and 14.10). The implementations, briefly described in Section 15.7, show that this is an area where computer algebra has been tremendously successful: we can now factor enormously large polynomials.

14.1. Factorization of polynomials

The **fundamental theorem of number theory** states that every integer can be (essentially uniquely) factored as a product of primes. Similarly, for any field F the polynomials in $F[x_1,\ldots,x_n]$ can be (essentially uniquely) factored into a product of irreducible polynomials. In other words, $\mathbb{Z}$ and $F[x_1,\ldots,x_n]$ are **Unique Factorization Domains** (Sections 6.2, 25.2).

The "essentially uniquely" says that such a factorization is unique up to the order of the factors and multiplication by units, that is, by 1 or -1 in $\mathbb{Z}$ and by nonzero constants from F in $F[x_1,\ldots,x_n]$. As an example, $x^2-1=(x-1)(x+1)=(-x-1)(-x+1)$. A polynomial $f \in F[x_1,\ldots,x_n]$ is **irreducible** if and only if $f \notin F$ and for any $g,h \in F[x_1,\ldots,x_n]$ with $f=gh$ we have $g \in F$ or $h \in F$. We say that f is **squarefree** if it has no proper quadratic divisor, so that for any $g \in F[x_1,\ldots,x_n]$ with g^2 dividing f we have $g \in F$.

The problem of univariate polynomial factorization is, given a polynomial f in $F[x]$ for a field F, to determine pairwise distinct monic irreducible polynomials $f_1,\ldots,f_r \in F[x]$ and positive integers $e_1,\ldots,e_r \in \mathbb{N}$ such that $f = \mathrm{lc}(f)f_1^{e_1}\cdots f_r^{e_r}$.

It seems computationally difficult to factor large integers (Chapter 19). However, computer algebra systems can routinely factor reasonably large polynomials; this is a task where the usual computational analogies between integers and polynomials break down. The irreducible factors of a univariate polynomial of degree n have degree at most n, and over a finite field $\mathbb{F}_q$ with q elements (Section 25.4) there are only finitely many such polynomials. But an exhaustive search might consume roughly $q^{n/2}$ trials, and this is exponential both in n and the bit size $\log_2 q$ of the representation of a field element.

We will describe in detail probabilistic algorithms that factor a univariate polynomial of degree n over a finite field $\mathbb{F}_q$ in time polynomial in n and $\log q$, in fact, with about $n^2 + n \log q$ operations in $\mathbb{F}_q$. An interesting effect of having the two independent input size parameters n and $\log q$ is that today there are several asymptotically best algorithms, depending on the relation between the two parameters (Figure 14.9). More general questions include factoring polynomials in

o $\mathbb{Z}[x]$ and $\mathbb{Q}[x]$,

o $\mathbb{Q}(\alpha)[x]$, where $\mathbb{Q}(\alpha)$ is an algebraic number field (a finite algebraic extension of $\mathbb{Q}$),

o $\mathbb{Z}_m[x]$, where $m \in \mathbb{N}$ is a positive integer,

o $\mathbb{R}[x]$ and $\mathbb{C}[x]$,

o and multivariate polynomials.

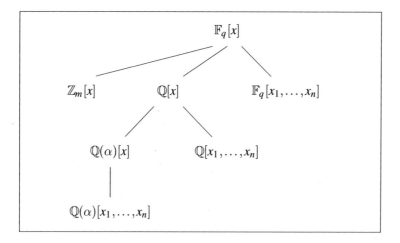

FIGURE 14.1: Polynomial factorization in various domains.

The dependencies between some of these are shown in Figure 14.1. It turns out that factoring univariate polynomials over finite fields is a basic task used in many other factoring algorithms. Factoring in $\mathbb{Q}[x]$ is the topic of Chapters 15 and 16.

Some algorithms for finite fields proceed in three stages:

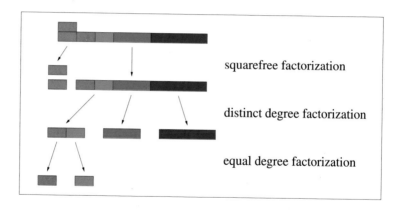

FIGURE 14.2: The stages of univariate polynomial factorization over finite fields.

1. squarefree factorization,

2. distinct-degree factorization,

3. equal-degree factorization.

Squarefree factorization gets rid of multiple factors, distinct-degree factorization splits irreducible factors according to their degrees, and equal-degree factorization solves the remaining problem, where all irreducible factors are distinct and of the same degree. In Figure 14.2, we see how the three stages work. The width of a box represents the degree of the corresponding polynomial; different colors stand for different irreducible factors. In the example, the original polynomial consists of four factors of degree 2 (two of them equal), one factor of degree 4, and one of degree 6.

The first stage is quite easy, both in theory and in practice. When the input is a large random polynomial, then the third stage is likely to be needed only for very small polynomials, and the second stage consumes the bulk of the computing time (more than 99% in our experiments described in Section 15.7).

In the next three sections we present in detail a conceptually simple complete factorization algorithm. The procedure indicated in Figure 14.2 is actually simplified by merging the "squarefree" and "distinct-degree" stages.

An fundamental tool for our algorithms is the following theorem (see Section 25.4 for a proof), which generalizes Theorem 4.9.

THEOREM 14.1 *Fermat's little theorem.*
For nonzero $a \in \mathbb{F}_q$, we have $a^{q-1} = 1$, and for all $a \in \mathbb{F}_q$, we have $a^q = a$, and

$$x^q - x = \prod_{a \in \mathbb{F}_q} (x - a) \text{ in } \mathbb{F}_q[x].$$

The reader must be thoroughly familiar with the material of Section 25.4 on finite fields, of which we make substantial use. The notation $\mathbb{F}_q$ and Fermat's little theorem in $\mathbb{F}_q$ are used over and over again. We will also use the fact that if $f \in \mathbb{F}_q[x]$ is irreducible of degree n, then $\mathbb{F}_{q^n} = \mathbb{F}_q[x]/\langle f \rangle$ is a field with q^n elements (Section 4.2).

The possible sizes of finite fields are precisely the prime powers, and in the following, q always denotes a prime power. The reader may think of q being a prime number. However, most statements or proofs do not become simpler for this special case, so that we may as well work in full generality.

14.2. Distinct-degree factorization

In this section, we describe the distinct-degree factorization stage for squarefree polynomials, deferring the question of how to deal with other polynomials until Section 14.4.

Fermat's little theorem is the special case $d = 1$ of the following result.

▬▬▬ THEOREM 14.2. ▬▬▬▬▬▬▬▬▬▬▬▬▬▬▬▬▬▬▬▬▬▬▬▬▬▬▬▬▬
For any $d \geq 1$, $x^{q^d} - x \in \mathbb{F}_q[x]$ is the product of all monic irreducible polynomials in $\mathbb{F}_q[x]$ whose degree divides d. ▬▬▬▬▬▬▬▬▬

PROOF. By Fermat's little theorem 14.1, applied to $\mathbb{F}_{q^d}$, $h = x^{q^d} - x$ is the product of all $x - a$ with $a \in \mathbb{F}_{q^d}$. If g^2 divides h (over $\mathbb{F}_q$) with $g \in \mathbb{F}_q[x] \setminus \mathbb{F}_q$, then some $x - a$ divides g and $(x - a)^2$ divides h. Since this is impossible, no such g exists, and $x^{q^d} - x$ is squarefree. It is sufficient to show for any monic irreducible polynomial $f \in \mathbb{F}_q[x]$ of degree n that

$$f \text{ divides } x^{q^d} - x \iff n \text{ divides } d.$$

We consider the field extension $\mathbb{F}_q \subseteq \mathbb{F}_{q^d}$. If f divides $x^{q^d} - x$, then from Theorem 14.1, applied to $\mathbb{F}_{q^d}$, we get a set $A \subseteq \mathbb{F}_{q^d}$ with $f = \prod_{a \in A}(x - a)$. We choose some $a \in A$, and let $\mathbb{F}_q[x]/\langle f \rangle \cong \mathbb{F}_q(a) \subseteq \mathbb{F}_{q^d}$, where $\mathbb{F}_q(a)$ is the smallest subfield of $\mathbb{F}_{q^d}$ containing a (Section 25.3). This is a field with q^n elements, and $\mathbb{F}_{q^d}$ is an extension of $\mathbb{F}_q(a)$, so that $q^d = (q^n)^e$ for some integer $e \geq 1$. Hence n divides d.

Now suppose that n divides d, let $\mathbb{F}_{q^n} = \mathbb{F}_q[x]/\langle f \rangle$, and $a = (x \bmod f) \in \mathbb{F}_{q^n}$ be a root of f. Theorem 14.1 says that $a^{q^n} = a$. Since $q^n - 1$ divides $q^d - 1 = (q^n - 1) \cdot e$ with $e = q^{d-n} + q^{d-2n} + \cdots + 1$, also $x^{q^n - 1} - 1$ divides

$$x^{q^d - 1} - 1 = (x^{q^n - 1} - 1)(x^{(q^n - 1)(e - 1)} + \cdots + 1).$$

Multiplying by x, we find that $x^{q^n} - x$ divides $x^{q^d} - x$, and hence

$$(x - a) \mid (x^{q^n} - x) \mid (x^{q^d} - x),$$

so that $x - a$ divides $\gcd(f, x^{q^d} - x)$ in $\mathbb{F}_{q^n}[x]$. But the gcd of two polynomials with coefficients in $\mathbb{F}_q$ also has coefficients in $\mathbb{F}_q$ (Example 6.19), and since it is nonconstant and f is irreducible, $\gcd(f, x^{q^d} - x) = f$, or, equivalently, f divides $x^{q^d} - x$. $\square$

The **distinct-degree decomposition** of a nonconstant polynomial $f \in \mathbb{F}_q[x]$ is the sequence $(g_1, \ldots, g_s)$ of polynomials, where g_i is the product of all monic irreducible polynomials in $\mathbb{F}_q[x]$ of degree i that divide f and $g_s \neq 1$ (but some g_i for $i < s$ may be 1). As an example, $(x^2 + x, x^4 + x^3 + x + 2)$ is the distinct-degree decomposition of $f = x(x + 1)(x^2 + 1)(x^2 + x + 2) \in \mathbb{F}_3[x]$; the two quadratic factors are irreducible since they have no zeroes in $\mathbb{F}_3$.

━━ ALGORITHM 14.3 Distinct-degree factorization. ━━━━━━━━━
Input: A squarefree monic polynomial $f \in \mathbb{F}_q[x]$ of degree $n > 0$.
Output: The distinct-degree decomposition $(g_1, \ldots, g_s)$ of f.

1. $h_0 \longleftarrow x$, $\quad f_0 \longleftarrow f$, $\quad i \longleftarrow 0$
   repeat

2. $\quad\quad i \longleftarrow i + 1$
   $\quad\quad$ **call** the repeated squaring algorithm 4.8 in $R = \mathbb{F}_q[x]/\langle f \rangle$ to compute
   $\quad\quad h_i = h_{i-1}^q$ rem f

3. $\quad\quad g_i \longleftarrow \gcd(h_i - x, f_{i-1})$, $\quad f_i \longleftarrow \dfrac{f_{i-1}}{g_i}$

4. **until** $f_i = 1$

5. $s \longleftarrow i$
   return $(g_1, \cdots, g_s)$ ━━━━━━━━━━━━━━━

The distinct-degree decomposition is a sequence of polynomials, and **distinct-degree factorization** is the process of computing this sequence.

In our cost analyses, we use a multiplication time M as on the inside front cover.

━━ THEOREM 14.4. ━━━━━━━━━━━━━━━━━━━━━━━━━
The distinct-degree factorization algorithm works correctly as specified. It takes $O(s\,\mathsf{M}(n)\log(nq))$ or $O^\sim(n^2 \log q)$ operations in $\mathbb{F}_q$, where s is the largest degree of an irreducible factor of f. ━━━━━━━━━━━━━

PROOF. Let $(G_1, \ldots, G_t)$ be the distinct-degree decomposition of f, with $G_t \neq 1$. For the correctness, it is sufficient to show by induction on $i \geq 0$ that

$$h_i \equiv x^{q^i} \bmod f, \quad f_i = G_{i+1} \cdots G_t, \quad g_i = G_i \text{ if } i \geq 1.$$

The first two claims are clear for $i = 0$. For $i \geq 1$, we have $h_i \equiv h_{i-1}^q \equiv (x^{q^{i-1}})^q = x^{q^i} \bmod f$, so that $h_i - x \equiv x^{q^i} - x \bmod f$ and

$$g_i = \gcd(h_i - x, f_{i-1}) = \gcd(x^{q^i} - x, f_{i-1}).$$

By Theorem 14.2, g_i is the product of all monic irreducible polynomials in $\mathbb{F}_q[x]$ of degree dividing i that divide $f_{i-1} = G_i \cdots G_n$, hence $g_i = G_i$. Furthermore, $f_i = G_i \cdots G_n / g_i = G_{i+1} \cdots G_n$. This finishes the inductive step and also shows that $s = t$.

The cost for computing h_i in step 2 is $O(\log q)$ multiplications modulo f in step 2, or $O(\mathsf{M}(n) \log q)$ operations in $\mathbb{F}_q$, by Corollary 11.8. Similarly, the cost for computing g_i and f_i is $O(\mathsf{M}(n) \log n)$ operations. $\square$

Algorithm 14.3 may be stopped as soon as $\deg f_i < 2(i+1)$, since all irreducible factors of f_i have degree at least $i+1$, and hence f_i is irreducible in that case. This is called **early abort** and guarantees that the algorithm stops after $i = \max\{m_1/2, m_2\} \leq n/2$, where m_1 and m_2 are the degrees of the largest and the second largest irreducible factor of f, respectively. In step 2, h_i is actually only needed modulo f_{i-1}.

EXAMPLE 14.5. We let $q = 3$ and trace Algorithm 14.3 on the squarefree polynomial $f = x^8 + x^7 - x^6 + x^5 - x^3 - x^2 - x \in \mathbb{F}_3[x]$. Then

$$h_1 = h_0^3 \text{ rem } f = x^3 \text{ rem } f = x^3,$$
$$g_1 = \gcd(h_1 - x, f_0) = \gcd(x^3 - x, f) = x,$$
$$f_1 = \frac{f_0}{g_1} = \frac{f}{x} = x^7 + x^6 - x^5 + x^4 - x^2 - x - 1,$$
$$h_2 = h_1^3 \text{ rem } f = x^9 \text{ rem } f = -x^7 + x^6 + x^5 + x^4 - x,$$
$$g_2 = \gcd(h_2 - x, f_1) = \gcd(-x^7 + x^6 + x^5 + x^4 + x, f_1) = x^4 + x^3 + x - 1,$$
$$f_2 = \frac{f_1}{g_2} = \frac{x^7 + x^6 - x^5 + x^4 - x^2 - x - 1}{x^4 + x^3 + x - 1} = x^3 - x + 1.$$

At this point, Algorithm 14.3 would perform one further iteration, but the early abort rule condition $\deg f_2 < 2(2+1) = 6$ says that this is not necessary since f_2 is already irreducible. Thus f has one linear factor, two distinct irreducible quadratic factors (which we do not know yet), and one irreducible cubic factor. The trace is illustrated in Figure 14.3. $\diamond$

14.3. Equal-degree factorization: Cantor and Zassenhaus' algorithm

The remaining task is **equal-degree factorization**: to factor one of the polynomials that are produced by the previous distinct-degree factorization. Our algorithm works only for an *odd* prime power q; a method for characteristic 2 is described in Exercise 14.16.

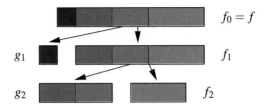

FIGURE 14.3: Sample distinct-degree factorization.

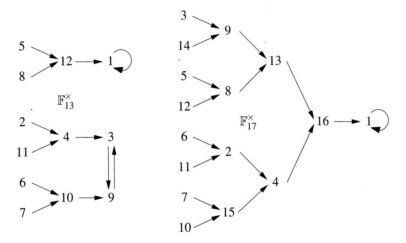

FIGURE 14.4: Squaring in $\mathbb{F}_{13}^{\times}$ and $\mathbb{F}_{17}^{\times}$.

We first collect some facts about the squaring map $\sigma\colon \mathbb{F}_q^{\times} \longrightarrow \mathbb{F}_q^{\times}$, with $\sigma(a) = a^2$. As an example, the effect of σ on the elements of $\mathbb{F}_{13}^{\times}$ and of $\mathbb{F}_{17}^{\times}$ is given in Figure 14.4. An arrow from a number i to a number j indicates that $j = \sigma(i)$. Each element has either two or zero arrows pointing to it; the first ones are the **squares**, the second ones the **nonsquares**. Both sets contain exactly half of the elements. Lemma 14.7 below, which is the special case $k = 2$ of the following lemma, says that this is always the case.

LEMMA 14.6. *Let q be a prime power, k a divisor of $q - 1$, and $S = \{b^k : b \in \mathbb{F}_q^{\times}\}$ the set of kth powers in $\mathbb{F}_q^{\times}$.*

   (i) *S is a subgroup of order $(q - 1)/k$.*

   (ii) *$S = \{a \in \mathbb{F}_q^{\times} : a^{(q-1)/k} = 1\}$.*

PROOF. S is the image of the kth power homomorphism $\sigma_k\colon \mathbb{F}_q^{\times} \longrightarrow \mathbb{F}_q^{\times}$ with $\sigma_k(b) = b^k$ and hence a subgroup of $\mathbb{F}_q^{\times}$. The kernel of σ_k is

$$\ker \sigma_k = \{a \in \mathbb{F}_q^{\times} : \sigma_k(a) = 1\} = \{a \in \mathbb{F}_q^{\times} : a^k = 1\}, \qquad (1)$$

the set of kth roots of unity. Since $\mathbb{F}_q$ is a field, the polynomial $x^k - 1 \in \mathbb{F}_q[x]$ has at most k roots in $\mathbb{F}_q[x]$ (Lemma 25.4), and hence $\#\ker \sigma_k \leq k$.

Since $(b^k)^{(q-1)/k} = b^{q-1} = 1$ for all $b \in \mathbb{F}_q^\times$, by Fermat's little theorem 14.1, we have $S \subseteq \ker \sigma_{(q-1)/k}$. By the same reasoning as above, this implies that $\#S \leq (q-1)/k$. Now

$$q - 1 = \#\mathbb{F}_q^\times = \#\ker \sigma_k \cdot \#\operatorname{im} \sigma_k = \#\ker \sigma_k \cdot \#S \leq k \cdot (q-1)/k = q - 1,$$

by the homomorphism theorem for groups, and this implies that $\#\ker \sigma_k = k$, $\#S = (q-1)/k$, and $S = \ker \sigma_{(q-1)/k}$. $\square$

Applying the lemma for $k = 2$ and $k = (q-1)/2$, we obtain the following.

LEMMA 14.7. *Let q be an odd prime power and*

$$S = \{a \in \mathbb{F}_q^\times : \exists b \in \mathbb{F}_q^\times \; a = b^2\}$$

be the set of squares in $\mathbb{F}_q^\times$. Then

(i) $S \subseteq \mathbb{F}_q^\times$ is a (multiplicative) subgroup of order $(q-1)/2$,

(ii) $S = \{a \in \mathbb{F}_q^\times : a^{(q-1)/2} = 1\}$,

(iii) $a^{(q-1)/2} \in \{1, -1\}$ for all $a \in \mathbb{F}_q^\times$.

Now we want to factor a monic polynomial $f \in \mathbb{F}_q[x]$ with $\deg f = n$, and have a divisor $d \in \mathbb{N}$ of n so that each irreducible factor of f has degree d. There are $r = n/d$ such factors, and we can write $f = f_1 \cdots f_r$ with distinct monic irreducible $f_1, \ldots, f_r \in \mathbb{F}_q[x]$. We may assume that $r \geq 2$; otherwise, we know that f is irreducible. Since $\gcd(f_i, f_j) = 1$ for $i \neq j$, we have the ring isomorphism of the Chinese Remainder Theorem 5.3:

$$\chi : R = \mathbb{F}_q[x]/\langle f \rangle \longrightarrow \mathbb{F}_q[x]/\langle f_1 \rangle \times \cdots \times \mathbb{F}_q[x]/\langle f_r \rangle = R_1 \times \cdots \times R_r.$$

Each R_i is a field with q^d elements and an algebraic extension of $\mathbb{F}_q$ of degree d:

$$\mathbb{F}_{q^d} \cong R_i = \mathbb{F}_q[x]/\langle f_i \rangle \supseteq \mathbb{F}_q.$$

We use the convention that for $a \in \mathbb{F}_q[x]$, we have $a \bmod f \in R$ and $\chi(a \bmod f) = (a \bmod f_1, \ldots, a \bmod f_r) = (\chi_1(a), \ldots, \chi_r(a))$, where $\chi_i(a) = a \bmod f_i \in R_i$. For $a \in \mathbb{F}_q[x]$ and $i \leq r$, we have that f_i divides a if and only if $\chi_i(a) = 0$. If we obtain an $a \in \mathbb{F}_q[x]$ with some $\chi_i(a)$ equal to zero and others nonzero, then $\gcd(a, f)$ is a nontrivial divisor of f. We now describe a probabilistic procedure to find such a **splitting polynomial** a.

We assume that q is odd, and write $e = (q^d - 1)/2$. For any $\beta \in R_i^\times = \mathbb{F}_{q^d}^\times$, we have $\beta^e \in \{1, -1\}$, and both possibilities occur equally often, by Lemma 14.7 with q^d instead of q. If we choose $a \in \mathbb{F}_q[x]$ with $\deg a < n$ and $\gcd(a, f) = 1$ uniformly at random, then $\chi_1(a), \ldots, \chi_r(a)$ are independent uniformly distributed elements of $\mathbb{F}_{q^d}^\times$, and $\varepsilon_i = \chi_i(a^e) \in R_i$ is 1 or -1, each with probability $1/2$. Therefore

$$\chi(a^e - 1) = (\varepsilon_1 - 1, \ldots, \varepsilon_r - 1),$$

and $a^e - 1$ is a splitting polynomial unless $\varepsilon_1 = \cdots = \varepsilon_r$. The latter occurs with probability $2 \cdot (1/2)^r = 2^{-r+1} \leq 1/2$.

━━━ ALGORITHM 14.8 Equal-degree splitting. ━━━━━━━━━━━━━
Input: A squarefree monic polynomial $f \in \mathbb{F}_q[x]$ of degree $n > 0$, where q is an odd prime power, and a divisor $d < n$ of n, so that all irreducible factors of f have degree d.
Output: A proper monic factor $g \in \mathbb{F}_q[x]$ of f, or "failure".

1. choose $a \in \mathbb{F}_q[x]$ with $\deg a < n$ at random
   if $a \in F$ **then return** "failure"

2. $g_1 \longleftarrow \gcd(a, f)$
   if $g_1 \neq 1$ **then return** g_1

3. **call** the repeated squaring algorithm 4.8 in $R = \mathbb{F}_q[x]/\langle f \rangle$ to compute $b = a^{(q^d - 1)/2}$ rem f

4. $g_2 \longleftarrow \gcd(b - 1, f)$
   if $g_2 \neq 1$ **and** $g_2 \neq f$ **then return** g_2 **else return** "failure" ━━━━━

━━━ THEOREM 14.9. ━━━━━━━━━━━━━━━━━━━━━━━━━━━
Algorithm 14.8 works correctly as specified. It returns "failure" with probability less than $2^{1-r} \leq 1/2$, where $r = n/d \geq 2$, and takes an expected number of $O((d \log q + \log n)\mathsf{M}(n))$ or $O^\sim(n^2 \log q)$ operations in $\mathbb{F}_q$. ━━━━━

PROOF. The failure probability has been given above as 2^{1-r} if $\gcd(a, f) = 1$. For general a, where step 2 might find a factor, the failure probability is less than 2^{1-r}. The cost for the gcds in steps 2 and 4 is $O(\mathsf{M}(n) \log n)$, and computing b in step 3 takes at most $2 \log_2(q^d) \in O(d \log q)$ multiplications modulo f or $O(\mathsf{M}(n)d \log q)$ operations in $\mathbb{F}_q$. $\square$

The usual trick of running the algorithm k times makes the failure probability less than $2^{(1-r)k} \leq 2^{-k}$.

EXAMPLE 14.5 (continued). We run Algorithm 14.8 on the remaining unfactored polynomial $f = x^4 + x^3 + x - 1 \in \mathbb{F}_3[x]$ from Example 14.5. We know that this polynomial factors into $r = 2$ irreducible polynomials of degree $d = 4/r = 2$. If our first choice in step 1 happens to be $a = x + 1$, then

$$
\begin{aligned}
g_1 &= \gcd(a, f) = \gcd(x + 1, x^4 + x^3 + x - 1) = 1, \\
b &= a^4 \text{ rem } f = (x + 1)^4 \text{ rem } x^4 + x^3 + x - 1 = -1, \\
g_2 &= \gcd(b - 1, f) = \gcd(1, f) = 1,
\end{aligned}
$$

and this choice is unlucky. Our next random choice might be $a = x$. Then

$$
\begin{aligned}
g_1 &= \gcd(a, f) = \gcd(x, x^4 + x^3 + x - 1) = 1, \\
b &= a^4 \text{ rem } f = x^4 \text{ rem } x^4 + x^3 + x - 1 = -x^3 - x + 1, \\
g_2 &= \gcd(b - 1, f) = \gcd(-x^3 - x, x^4 + x^3 + x^2 - 1) = x^2 + 1.
\end{aligned}
$$

The latter is one irreducible factor of f, and the other one is $f/(x^2 + 1) = x^2 + x - 1$.

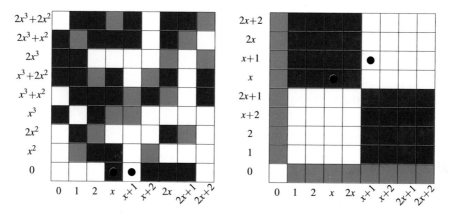

FIGURE 14.5: The lucky and unlucky choices for factoring $x^4 + x^3 + x - 1 \in \mathbb{F}_3[x]$.

Figure 14.5 illustrates the situation. On the left hand side, we have $R = F[x]/\langle f \rangle$, consisting of the 81 polynomials $a_3 x^3 + a_2 x^2 + a_1 x + a_0 \bmod f$, with all $a_i \in \mathbb{F}_3$. The possible values for $a_1 x + a_0$ are along the horizontal axis, and similarly $a_3 x^3 + a_2 x^2$ along the vertical axis. Our two choices are marked by a $\bullet$.

We have $R \cong \mathbb{F}_3[x]/\langle x^2 + 1 \rangle \times \mathbb{F}_3[x]/\langle x^2 + x - 1 \rangle \cong \mathbb{F}_9 \times \mathbb{F}_9$ on the right hand side, with the nine elements of the first factor on the horizontal axis, and the second factor on the vertical axis. We have arranged our two copies of $\mathbb{F}_9$ in an isomorphic way; in particular, mapping $x \bmod x^2 + 1$ to $x + 2 \bmod x^2 + x - 1$ gives an isomorphism, since $(x + 2)^2 + 1 \equiv 0 \bmod x^2 + x - 1$. On both axes, we first have 0, then the four nonzero squares, and then the four nonsquares.

The lucky choices of a are colored, the unlucky ones white. At right, it is clear what happens: the 16 light blue elements with exactly one coordinate 0 give a factorization in step 2, and the 32 dark blue elements of type square/nonsquare or nonsquare/square are splitting polynomials. The $1 + 32 = 33$ other elements are unlucky. In general, only $2q^d - 2$ of the q^{rd} elements of R are "light blue", so that for larger values of q^d it is very unlikely that the algorithm hits upon one of them by chance.

The representation at left is the one we can compute with. The magic of an isomorphism transforms this chaotic conglomerate into the disciplined diagram at right, about which we can easily reason, derive algorithms and prove their properties; these algorithms then are executed in the messy real world at left. ◇

Algorithm 14.8 gives a factorization into two factors. If we need just one irreducible factor, we can apply the algorithm recursively to the smaller factor (Exercise 14.15). However, we will usually want all r factors, and this can be done by running the algorithm recursively on each factor.

▬▬ ALGORITHM 14.10 Equal-degree factorization. ▬▬▬▬▬▬▬▬▬▬▬
Input: A squarefree monic polynomial $f \in \mathbb{F}_q[x]$ of degree $n > 0$, for an odd prime power q, and a divisor d of n, so that all irreducible factors of f have degree d.
Output: The monic irreducible factors of f in $\mathbb{F}_q[x]$.

1. **if** $n = d$ **then return** f

2. **call** the equal-degree splitting algorithm 14.8 with input f and d repeatedly until it returns a proper factor $g \in \mathbb{F}_q[x]$ of f

3. **call** the algorithm recursively with input g and with input f/g
   return the results of the two recursive calls ▬▬▬▬▬▬▬▬▬▬▬

▬▬ THEOREM 14.11. ▬▬▬▬▬▬▬▬▬▬▬▬▬▬▬▬▬▬▬▬
A squarefree polynomial of degree $n = rd$ with r irreducible factors of degree d can be completely factored with an expected number of $O((d \log q + \log n)\mathsf{M}(n) \log r)$ or $O^{\sim}(n^2 \log q)$ operations in $\mathbb{F}_q$. ▬▬▬▬▬▬▬▬▬▬▬▬▬

PROOF. The workings of Algorithm 14.10 can be illustrated by means of a labeled tree (see Figure 14.6 for an example). The node labels are factors of f, with f at the root and the irreducible factors of f at the leaves. If the call to Algorithm 14.8 in step 2 returns "failure" at a particular node, then the corresponding node has precisely one child with the same label. Otherwise, it has two children labeled g and f/g. The product over all labels at one level of the tree is a divisor of f, and hence the total degree over all nodes at each level is at most n. The cost at a node of degree m is $O((d \log q + \log m)\mathsf{M}(m))$ operations in $\mathbb{F}_q$, by Theorem 14.9, and by the subadditivity of M (Section 8.3), the total cost at each level of the tree is $O((d \log q + \log n)\mathsf{M}(n))$ operations.

We now show that the expected depth of the tree is $O(\log r)$, which together with $r \leq n$ implies the claims. Let $1 \leq i < j \leq r$ be fixed. Then in Algorithm 14.8, the probability that $a \bmod g_i$ and $a \bmod g_j$ are neither both squares nor both non-squares is at least $1/2$, by the Chinese Remainder Theorem. Thus for each level of the tree, the probability that a call to Algorithm 14.8 separates g_i and g_j at that level is at least $1/2$ (if they were not already separated before). Hence the probability that g_i and g_j are not yet separated at depth k is at most 2^{-k}. This is true for any pair of irreducible factors of f, and since there are $(r^2 - r)/2 \leq r^2$ such pairs, the probability p_k that not all irreducible factors are separated at depth k is at most $r^2 2^{-k}$. This is the probability that the depth of the tree is greater than k, and $p_{k-1} - p_k$ is the probability that the depth is exactly k. Let $s = \lceil 2 \log_2 r \rceil$. Then the expected depth of the tree is

$$
\begin{aligned}
\sum_{k \geq 1} k(p_{k-1} - p_k) &= \sum_{k \geq 0} p_k = \sum_{0 \leq k < s} p_k + \sum_{k \geq s} p_k \leq \sum_{0 \leq k < s} 1 + \sum_{k \geq s} r^2 2^{-k} \\
&= s + r^2 2^{-s} \sum_{k \geq 0} 2^{-k} \leq s + 2 \in O(\log r). \quad \square
\end{aligned}
$$

EXAMPLE 14.12. Suppose that we want to find all the irreducible factors f_i of $f = f_0 \cdots f_9 \in \mathbb{F}_q[x]$, where the f_i are monic, irreducible, pairwise distinct, and have the same degree d.

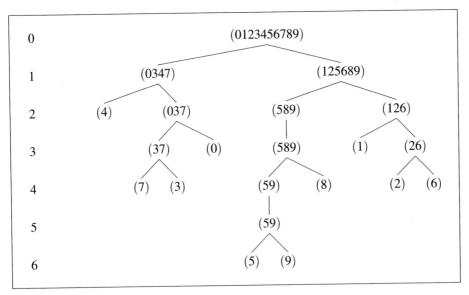

FIGURE 14.6: The workings of the equal-degree factorization algorithm 14.10 in Example 14.12.

Figure 14.6 illustrates the process of a typical execution of Algorithm 14.10 in the form of a tree. The leaves correspond to the isolated irreducible factors. The labels are the indices of the irreducible factors of the polynomial at that node. The numbers in the left column are the levels. For example, the rightmost label at level 2 corresponds to the factor $f_1 f_2 f_6$ of f. The depth 6 is less than our upper bound $\lceil 2\log_2 10\rceil + 2 = 9$ on the average value. $\diamond$

When q is large enough, there is a way to replace almost all powerings with exponent $(q^d - 1)/2$ in step 3 of Algorithm 14.8 by cheaper powerings with exponent $(q-1)/2$, leading to an expected time of $O(d\,\mathsf{M}(n)\log q + \mathsf{M}(n)\log(qn)\log r)$ operations in $\mathbb{F}_q$ for a variant of Algorithm 14.10 (Exercise 14.17).

14.4. A complete factoring algorithm

It remains to deal with polynomials that are not squarefree. Section 14.6 describes the squarefree factorization stage in detail, but we now discuss a simpler approach by modifying the distinct-degree factorization stage.

The algorithm proceeds as follows. For $i = 1, 2, \ldots$, the (squarefree) product g of all irreducible factors of f of degree i is computed, via one distinct-degree factorization step. Then g is factored into irreducibles, by calling the equal-degree factorization algorithm. For each irreducible factor g_j obtained, we determine its multiplicity e in f by trial division, and then remove g_j^e.

━━ ALGORITHM 14.13 Polynomial factorization over finite fields. ━━━━
Input: A nonconstant polynomial $f \in \mathbb{F}_q[x]$, where q is a prime power.
Output: The monic irreducible factors of f and their multiplicities.

1. $h_0 \longleftarrow x, \quad v_0 \longleftarrow \dfrac{f}{\mathrm{lc}(f)}, \quad i \longleftarrow 0, \quad U \longleftarrow \varnothing$
   repeat

2. $\quad i \longleftarrow i + 1$
   { one distinct-degree factorization step }
   call the repeated squaring algorithm 4.8 in $R = \mathbb{F}_q[x]/\langle f\rangle$ to compute
   $h_i = h_{i-1}^q \text{ rem } f$
   $g \longleftarrow \gcd(h_i - x, v_{i-1})$

3. $\quad$ **if** $g \neq 1$ **then**
   { equal-degree factorization }
   call Algorithm 14.10 to compute the monic irreducible factors
   $g_1, \ldots, g_s \in \mathbb{F}_q[x]$ of g

4. $\quad v_i \longleftarrow v_{i-1}$
   { determine multiplicities }

for $j = 1, \ldots, s$ **do**

$\qquad e \longleftarrow 0$

$\qquad$ **while** $g_j \mid v_i$ **do** $v_i \longleftarrow \dfrac{v_i}{g_j}, \quad e \longleftarrow e+1$

$\qquad U \longleftarrow U \cup \{(g_j, e)\}$

5. **until** $v_i = 1$

6. **return** U

As in the distinct-degree factorization algorithm 14.3, the algorithm may be aborted as soon as $\deg v_i < 2(i+1)$, and h_i need only be computed modulo v_{i-1} in step 2.

THEOREM 14.14.

Algorithm 14.13 correctly computes the irreducible factorization of f. If $\deg f = n$, then it takes an expected number of $O(n\,\mathsf{M}(n)\log(qn))$ or $O^{\sim}(n^2\log q)$ arithmetic operations in $\mathbb{F}_q$.

PROOF. Let $f = \mathrm{lc}(f)\prod_{1 \le i \le k} f_i^{e_i}$ be the irreducible factorization of f, with distinct monic irreducible polynomials $f_1, \ldots, f_k \in \mathbb{F}_q[x]$ and positive integers $e_1, \ldots, e_k$. We prove that the invariants

$$h_i \equiv x^{q^i} \bmod f, \quad v_i = \mathrm{lc}(f)\prod_{\deg f_k > i} f_k^{e_k}$$

hold each time before the algorithm passes through step 2. The first invariant is shown as in the proof of Theorem 14.4. The second one is clear for $i = 0$, and we may assume that $i \ge 1$. By Theorem 14.2, $x^{q^i} - x$ is the product of all distinct monic irreducible polynomials in $\mathbb{F}_q[x]$ of degree dividing i, and hence in particular it is squarefree. Thus, since $v_{i-1} \mid f$ and by the induction hypothesis, the polynomial

$$g = \gcd(h_i - x, v_{i-1}) = \gcd(x^{q^i} - x, v_{i-1}) = \prod_{\deg f_k = i} f_k$$

is a squarefree polynomial with irreducible factors of degree i only, and $g_1, \ldots, g_s$ are in fact the irreducible factors of g at the end of step 3 if $g \ne 1$. These are then removed with the correct multiplicity from v_i in step 4, and the invariants hold again before the next pass through step 2.

The cost for one execution of step 2 is $O(\mathsf{M}(n)\log(qn))$ operations in $\mathbb{F}_q$. There are at most n iterations of the outer loop, and hence the overall cost for step 2 is $O(n\,\mathsf{M}(n)\log(nq))$ operations. If $m_i = \deg g$, then step 3, the only probabilistic part of the algorithm, takes an expected number of $O((i\log q + \log m_i)\mathsf{M}(m_i)\log(m_i/i))$ operations, by Theorem 14.11. Now

$$i\log(m_i/i) = m_i \frac{\log(m_i/i)}{m_i/i} \le m_i,$$

$$\sum_i (i \log q + \log m_i) \mathsf{M}(m_i) \log(m_i/i) \leq \sum_i (m_i \log q + \log^2 m_i) \mathsf{M}(n)$$

$$\in O(n \mathsf{M}(n) \log q),$$

where we have used $\sum_i m_i \leq n$ and log is the binary logarithm. If e_j denotes the multiplicity of g_j in f, then one execution of the body of the **for** loop in step 4 takes $O(e_j \mathsf{M}(n))$ operations in $\mathbb{F}_q$, and the overall cost for step 4 is $O(n \mathsf{M}(n))$ operations, since the sum of the multiplicities of all irreducible factors of f is at most n. The timing estimate for step 2 is dominant, and the claim follows. $\square$

We note that this is the same time bound as for the distinct-degree factorization algorithm 14.3 with a squarefree input.

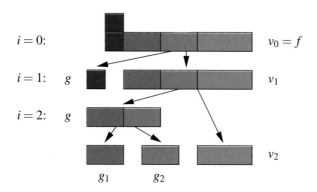

FIGURE 14.7: Sample polynomial factorization.

EXAMPLE 14.5 (continued). Let $q = 3$ and $f = x^9 + x^8 - x^7 + x^6 - x^4 - x^3 - x^2 \in \mathbb{F}_3[x]$ be the polynomial from Example 14.5 multiplied by x. Then Algorithm 14.13 computes $v_0 = f$ in step 1, and $h_1 = h_0^3 \text{ rem } f = x^3 \text{ rem } f = x^3$ and $g = \gcd(h_1 - x, f) = \gcd(x^3 - x, f) = x$ in step 2. The latter is obviously irreducible, so that $s = 1$ and $g_1 = g$ in step 3, and in step 4 we find that x divides f precisely twice, so that $(x, 2)$ is adjoined to U and $v_1 = x^7 + x^6 - x^5 + x^4 - x^2 - x - 1$ at the end of step 4. For $i = 2$, we compute in step 2 that

$$h_2 = h_1^3 \text{ rem } f = x^9 \text{ rem } f = -x^8 + x^7 - x^6 + x^4 + x^3 + x^2,$$
$$g = \gcd(h_2 - x, v_1) = x^4 + x^3 + x - 1.$$

In step 3, we find, as before, that the irreducible factors of g are $g_1 = x^2 + 1$ and $g_2 = x^2 + x - 1$. In step 4, we find that each of them has multiplicity one, adjoin $(g_1, 1)$ and $(g_2, 1)$ to U, and are left with $v_2 = x^3 - x + 1$. The algorithm would now continue for one further iteration, but the early abort condition $\deg v_2 < 2(2 + 1) = 6$ tells us that v_2 is already irreducible, and we are done. The trace is illustrated in Figure 14.7. $\diamond$

We now have the central result of this chapter: a complete factorization algorithm over finite fields in polynomial time. In the next sections, we study the problem in greater depth, discussing different (and faster) algorithms and various applications.

14.5. Application: root finding

If we are looking for all zeroes of a given polynomial $f \in \mathbb{F}_q[x]$, so that we want to determine all the linear factors of f, it is clearly sufficient to first compute $g = \gcd(x^q - x, f)$ and then apply the equal-degree factorization algorithm to g, so that we need not compute the *whole* distinct-degree decomposition of f.

ALGORITHM 14.15 Root finding over finite fields.
Input: A nonconstant polynomial $f \in \mathbb{F}_q[x]$.
Output: The distinct roots of f in $\mathbb{F}_q$.

1. **call** the repeated squaring algorithm 4.8 in $R = \mathbb{F}_q[x]/\langle f \rangle$ to compute $h = x^q$ rem f

2. $g \longleftarrow \gcd(h - x, f)$, $r \longleftarrow \deg g$
   if $r = 0$ **then return** $\emptyset$

3. **call** the equal-degree factorization algorithm 14.10 to compute the irreducible factors $x - u_1, \ldots, x - u_r$ of g

4. **return** $u_1, \ldots, u_r$

COROLLARY 14.16.
Given $f \in \mathbb{F}_q[x]$ of degree n, we can find all roots of f in $\mathbb{F}_q$ using an expected number of $O(\mathsf{M}(n) \log n \log(nq))$ or $O^\sim(n \log q)$ operations in $\mathbb{F}_q$.

Algorithm 14.15 can be used to find all integral roots of a polynomial $f \in \mathbb{Z}[x]$ in a modular fashion, as follows.

ALGORITHM 14.17 Root finding over $\mathbb{Z}$ (big prime version).
Input: A nonconstant polynomial $f \in \mathbb{Z}[x]$ of degree n with max-norm $\|f\|_\infty = A$.
Output: The distinct roots of f in $\mathbb{Z}$.

1. $B \longleftarrow 2n(A^2 + A)$
   let $p \in \mathbb{N}$ be an odd prime between $B + 1$ and $2B$

2. **call** Algorithm 14.15 to find all distinct roots $\{u_1 \bmod p, \ldots, u_r \bmod p\}$ in $\mathbb{F}_p$ of $f \bmod p$, with $u_i \in \mathbb{Z}$ and $|u_i| < p/2$ for all i

3. **for** $1 \leq i \leq r$ compute $v_i \in \mathbb{Z}[x]$ of degree $n-1$ and with max-norm less than $p/2$ such that $f \equiv (x - u_i)v_i \bmod p$

4. **return** $\{u_i \colon 1 \leq i \leq r, \ |u_i| \leq A \text{ and } \|v_i\|_\infty \leq nA\}$

THEOREM 14.18.

Algorithm 14.17 correctly computes all integral roots of f. The cost for step 2 is

$$O(\mathsf{M}(n)\log n \log(nA)\, \mathsf{M}(\log(nA))\log\log(nA))$$

or $O^\sim(n \log^2 A)$ word operations, and the cost for step 3 per u_i is $O(n\mathsf{M}(\log(nA)))$ or $O^\sim(n\log A)$ word operations.

PROOF. Dividing out powers of x if necessary, we may assume that $f(0) \neq 0$. If $f(u) = 0$ for some $u \in \mathbb{Z}$, then $(x - u) \mid f$ and u divides the constant coefficient of f, so that $|u| \leq A < p/2$. Thus all distinct roots of f can be uniquely recovered from their images modulo p. We show that $f(u_i) = 0$ if and only if $|u_i| \leq A$ and $\|v_i\|_\infty \leq nA$, for all i. If $f(u_i) = 0$, then $|u_i| \leq A$, by the above, and $\|f/(x - u_i)\|_\infty \leq nA < p/2$, by Exercise 14.21. But $f/(x - u_i) \equiv v_i \bmod p$, and since both sides have coefficients less than $p/2$ in absolute value, they are equal. On the other hand, if $|u_i| \leq A$ and $\|v_i\|_\infty \leq nA$, then $\|(x - u_i)v_i\|_\infty \leq (1 + A)nA < p/2$, and the congruence $f \equiv (x - u_i)v_i \bmod p$ is in fact an equality.

We have $\log p \in O(\log(nA))$, and the cost estimate for step 2 follows from Corollaries 14.16 and 11.10. The cost for each u_i in step 3 is $O(n)$ additions and multiplications in $\mathbb{F}_p$ or $O(n\mathsf{M}(\log(nA)))$ word operations. $\square$

The cost for finding p is discussed in Section 18.4. In Section 15.6, we will discuss a faster algorithm for computing integer roots.

14.6. Squarefree factorization

For the moment, we let F be an arbitrary field. We will show how to reduce the problem of factoring arbitrary polynomials to that of factoring squarefree polynomials. Polynomial factorization software usually performs this reduction first; it is not quite clear when the (small) advantage one gains outweighs the (small) cost of the reduction. Our purpose in skipping it was to describe, with Algorithm 14.13, a factorization method that is conceptionally as simple as possible. In Section 9.3, we defined the derivative f' of a polynomial $f = \sum_{0 \leq i \leq n} a_i x^i \in F[x]$ as $f' = \partial f/\partial x = \sum_{0 \leq i \leq n} i a_i x^{i-1}$.

Suppose that f is not squarefree, so that $f = g^2 h$ for some $g, h \in F[x]$ and $g \notin F$. Then $f' = g \cdot (2g'h + gh')$, so that g divides $u = \gcd(f, f')$. If the characteristic (Section 25.3) of F is zero, then $f' \neq 0$ and $\deg f' < \deg f = n$, so that u is a proper divisor of f.

Now let $f = \prod_{1 \le i \le r} f_i^{e_i}$ be the irreducible factorization of the monic polynomial $f \in F[x]$, with distinct monic irreducible $f_1, \ldots, f_r$ and positive $e_1, \ldots, e_r \in \mathbb{N}$. We define the **squarefree part of** f to be $\prod_{1 \le i \le r} f_i$. Then

$$f' = \sum_{1 \le i \le r} e_i \frac{f}{f_i} f_i' \tag{2}$$

(Exercise 14.22). In order to compute the squarefree part, let us determine $u = \gcd(f, f')$. The only possible divisors are powers of $f_1, \ldots, f_r$. But what is the multiplicity of f_i in f'? Each summand in (2) but the ith is divisible by $f_i^{e_i}$, and the ith equals $e_i f_i' \cdot f/f_i$ and is divisible by $f_i^{e_i-1}$. Thus $f_i^{e_i-1}$ divides f'. Can $f_i^{e_i}$ divide it? This happens if and only if it divides $e_i f_i' \cdot f/f_i$. Certainly f_i divides none of the other factors in f/f_i, except $f_i^{e_i-1}$, but can it divide $e_i f_i'$? This is a polynomial of degree smaller than $\deg f_i$, and one might think that it cannot be divisible by f_i. But indeed it can, namely when (and only when) $e_i f_i' = 0$. We leave this situation to Exercises 14.27 and 14.30, and now put together our current knowledge in the case where this cannot happen, namely when the characteristic is zero.

▬▬ ALGORITHM 14.19 Squarefree part in characteristic zero. ▬▬▬▬▬
Input: $f \in F[x]$ monic of degree $n > 0$, where F is a field of characteristic zero.
Output: The squarefree part of f, that is, the product of all distinct monic irreducible factors of f.

   1. $u \longleftarrow \gcd(f, f')$

   2. **return** $v = \dfrac{f}{u}$. ▬▬▬▬▬▬▬▬▬▬▬▬▬▬▬▬▬▬.

▬▬ THEOREM 14.20. ▬▬▬▬▬▬▬▬▬▬▬▬▬▬▬▬▬▬▬▬▬▬▬
Algorithm 14.19 works correctly as specified and takes $O(\mathsf{M}(n) \log n)$ operations in F. ▬▬▬▬▬▬▬▬▬▬▬▬▬▬▬▬▬▬▬▬▬▬▬▬▬▬▬▬▬▬

PROOF. For the correctness, we note that each $e_i f_i'$ is nonzero, and by the above

$$u = \prod_{1 \le i \le r} f_i^{e_i-1}, \qquad v = \prod_{1 \le i \le r} f_i.$$

The running time estimate follows from Theorems 9.6 and 11.5. $\square$

The **squarefree decomposition** provides more information than the squarefree part. For a nonconstant monic polynomial $f \in F[x]$, this is the unique sequence of monic squarefree pairwise coprime polynomials $(g_1, \ldots, g_m)$ with

$$f = g_1 g_2^2 g_3^3 \cdots g_m^m$$

and $g_m \neq 1$. For example, the squarefree decomposition of $x^4(x+1)^2(x-1)^2 \cdot (x^2+1)^2(x^2+x+1) \in \mathbb{Q}[x]$ is $(x^2+x+1, x^4-1, 1, 1, x)$. Thus g_i is the product of those monic irreducible polynomials that divide f exactly i times. The squarefree part of f is $g_1 \cdots g_m$. The process of computing the squarefree decomposition is called **squarefree factorization**.

We now present algorithms for computing the squarefree decomposition. This decomposition will be used in an integration algorithm in Chapter 22. For simplicity, we assume characteristic zero. A simple idea is to call Algorithm 14.19, compute $g_1 = v/\gcd(u,v)$, and proceed recursively with f replaced by u. This takes $O(m\mathsf{M}(n)\log n)$ field operations. The following method is faster by one order of magnitude.

▬▬ ALGORITHM 14.21 Yun's squarefree factorization in characteristic zero. ▬▬
Input: A monic polynomial $f \in F[x]$ of degree $n \geq 1$, where F is a field of characteristic zero.
Output: The squarefree decomposition of f.

1. $u \longleftarrow \gcd(f, f'), \quad v_1 \longleftarrow \dfrac{f}{u}, \quad w_1 \longleftarrow \dfrac{f'}{u}$

2. $i \longleftarrow 1$
   repeat
   $$h_i \longleftarrow \gcd(v_i, w_i - v_i'), \quad v_{i+1} \longleftarrow \dfrac{v_i}{h_i}, \quad w_{i+1} \longleftarrow \dfrac{w_i - v_i'}{h_i}$$
   $i \longleftarrow i+1$
   until $v_i = 1$
   $k \longleftarrow i-1$

3. **return** $(h_1, \ldots, h_k)$ ▬▬▬▬▬▬▬▬▬▬▬▬▬▬▬▬▬▬▬▬▬

The correctness of the algorithm depends on the following lemma.

LEMMA 14.22. *Let F be a field of characteristic zero, $g_1, \ldots, g_m \in F[x]$ monic squarefree and pairwise coprime, $g = g_1 \cdots g_m$, and $h = \sum_{1 \leq i \leq m} c_i g_i' g/g_i$, for some constants $c_i \in F$. Then $\gcd(g, h - cg') = \prod_{c_j = c} g_j$ for all $c \in F$.*

PROOF. We have $g' = \sum_{1 \leq i \leq m} g_i' g/g_i$, by Exercise 9.27, and hence

$$h - cg' = \sum_{1 \leq i \leq m} (c_i - c) g_i' \frac{g}{g_i}.$$

Now g_j divides each summand with $i \neq j$, and $\gcd(g_j, g_j') = \gcd(g_j, g/g_j) = 1$ since F has characteristic zero and g_j and g are squarefree. Thus the claim follows from

$$\gcd(g_j, h - cg') = \gcd\left(g_j, (c_j - c) g_j' \frac{g}{g_j}\right) = \gcd(g_j, c_j - c). \quad \square$$

▬▬ THEOREM 14.23. ▬▬

The algorithm uses $O(\mathsf{M}(n)\log n)$ operations in F and it computes correctly the squarefree decomposition of f. ▬▬

PROOF. Let $(g_1,\dots,g_m)$ be the squarefree decomposition of f. Then we have $u = g_2 g_3^2 \cdots g_m^{m-1}$, and we prove by induction on i that

$$h_i = g_i \text{ if } i \geq 1, \quad v_{i+1} = \prod_{i<j\leq m} g_j, \quad w_{i+1} = \sum_{i<j\leq m} (j-i)g_j' \frac{v_{i+1}}{g_j}$$

for $0 \leq i \leq m$. This is clear for v_1, and the claim for w_1 follows from

$$f' = \sum_{1\leq j\leq m} \frac{f}{g_j} \cdot jg_j' = u \sum_{1\leq j\leq m} j\frac{v_1}{g_j}g_j'.$$

For $i \geq 1$, Lemma 14.22 gives $h_i = g_i$. Then $v_{i+1} = \prod_{i<j\leq m} g_j$ is clear, and

$$
\begin{aligned}
w_{i+1} &= \left(\sum_{i\leq j\leq m} (j-(i-1))g_j' \frac{v_i}{g_j} - \sum_{i\leq j\leq m} g_j' \frac{v_i}{g_j} \right) / g_i \\
&= \sum_{i<j\leq m} (j-i)g_j' \frac{v_i}{g_j g_i} = \sum_{i<j\leq m} (j-i)g_j' \frac{v_{i+1}}{g_j}.
\end{aligned}
$$

For the cost estimate, let $d_j = \deg g_j$ for $1 \leq j \leq m$. Step 1 takes $O(\mathsf{M}(n)\log n)$ arithmetic operations. Moreover, $\deg v_i = \sum_{i<j\leq m} d_j$, $\deg w_i = (\deg v_i) - 1$, the gcd computation in the ith loop takes $O(\mathsf{M}(\deg v_i)\log n)$, and the two division steps $O(\mathsf{M}(\deg v_i))$ operations in F. Using the subadditivity of M, we find

$$
\begin{aligned}
\sum_{1\leq i\leq m} \mathsf{M}(\deg v_i) &\leq \mathsf{M}\left(\sum_{1\leq i\leq m} \deg v_i \right) = \mathsf{M}\left(\sum_{1\leq i\leq j\leq m} d_j \right) \\
&= \mathsf{M}\left(\sum_{1\leq i\leq m} id_i \right) = \mathsf{M}(n). \ \square
\end{aligned}
$$

EXAMPLE 14.24. Suppose that $f = abc^2d^4$ for monic distinct irreducible polynomials $a,b,c,d \in F[x]$. Then Algorithm 14.21 computes $u = \gcd(f,f') = cd^3$,

$$
\begin{aligned}
v_1 &= f/u = abcd, \quad w_1 = f'/u = a'bcd + ab'cd + 2abc'd + 4abcd', \\
h_1 &= \gcd(abcd, abc'd + 3abcd') = ab, \\
v_2 &= abcd/ab = cd, \quad w_2 = (abc'd + 3abcd')/ab = c'd + 3cd', \\
h_2 &= \gcd(cd, 2cd') = c, \quad v_3 = cd/c = d, \quad w_3 = 2cd'/c = 2d', \\
h_3 &= \gcd(d,d') = 1, \quad v_4 = d/1 = d, \quad w_4 = d'/1 = d', \\
h_4 &= \gcd(d,0) = d, \quad v_5 = d/d = 1, \quad w_5 = 0/d = 0.
\end{aligned}
$$

Thus the correct squarefree decomposition $(ab,c,1,d)$ is returned. $\Diamond$

An interesting possibility may occur if char $F = p$ for a prime p, which does not happen if char $F = 0$: $f = \sum_{0 \le i \le n} a_i x^i \notin F$ and $f' = 0$. This happens if and only if each i with $a_i \ne 0$ is divisible by p; then the summand $i a_i x^{i-1}$ is zero in $F[x]$. If $F = \mathbb{F}_p$, then we can write

$$f = \sum_{0 \le i \le n/p} a_{ip} x^{ip} = \left(\sum_{0 \le i \le n/p} a_{ip} x^i \right)^p, \tag{3}$$

since $(g + h)^p = g^p + h^p$ for all $g, h \in \mathbb{F}_p[x]$ and $a_{ip}^p = a_{ip}$ for all $a_{ip} \in \mathbb{F}_p$ (Section 25.4). For example, $(x^4 + x^2 + 1)' = 0$ in $\mathbb{F}_2[x]$, and $x^4 + x^2 + 1 = (x^2 + x + 1)^2$.

Similarly, if $F = \mathbb{F}_q$ for a prime power $q = p^s$ and $s \ge 1$, then Fermat's little theorem 14.1 says that $a^q = a$ for all $a \in \mathbb{F}_q$, and hence $a^{p^{s-1}} = a^{q/p}$ is a pth root of a. Then for $g = \sum_{0 \le i \le n/p} a_{ip}^{q/p} x^i$, we have $f = g^p$, in analogy to (3). On the other hand, if $f = g^p$, then $f' = p g^{p-1} g' = 0$, and thus

$$\forall f \in \mathbb{F}_q[x] \quad f' = 0 \iff f \text{ is a } p\text{th power in } \mathbb{F}_q[x]. \tag{4}$$

Let $f = f_1^{e_1} \cdots f_r^{e_r}$ be the irreducible factorization of f. For $1 \le i \le r$, $f_i' = 0$ would imply that f_i is a pth power, in contradiction to the irreducibility of f_i. In the language of field theory, any irreducible polynomial has a nonzero derivative and thus is **separable**, and therefore finite fields and fields of characteristic zero are **perfect**. The field $F = \mathbb{F}_p(y)$ of rational functions in y is not perfect, since for example $f = x^p - y \in F[x]$ is irreducible with $f' = 0$ (Exercise 14.33). The reason for this is that the "constant" $y \in F$ has no pth root in F. Thus $f_i' \ne 0$ over a finite field, and $\deg f_i' < \deg f_i$ implies that the $\gcd(f_i', f_i)$ is not f_i and hence 1, by the irreducibility of f_i. But it can still happen that $e_i f_i' = 0$, namely when the nonzero integer e_i is divisible by p. In that case, (2) implies that $f_i^{e_i}$ divides f'.

COROLLARY 14.25.

Let F be a finite field or a field of characteristic zero and $f \in F[x]$ nonconstant. Then f is squarefree if and only if $\gcd(f, f') = 1$.

Exercises 14.27 and 14.30 discuss squarefree factorization over finite fields.

14.7. The iterated Frobenius algorithm

We now sketch a faster algorithm for our problem of polynomial factorization. A central role is played by the **Frobenius automorphism**

$$\sigma: \begin{cases} \mathbb{F}_{q^n} & \longrightarrow \mathbb{F}_{q^n}, \\ a & \longmapsto a^q. \end{cases}$$

In the language of Galois theory, the field extension $\mathbb{F}_{q^n}/\mathbb{F}_q$ is normal, σ generates its Galois group $\{\mathrm{id},\sigma,\ldots,\sigma^{n-1}\}$, and $\sigma^n = \mathrm{id}$, by Fermat's little theorem 14.1.

For a squarefree monic polynomial $f \in \mathbb{F}_q[x]$ of degree n, we now consider the residue class ring $R = \mathbb{F}_q[x]/\langle f \rangle$ and the map

$$\sigma: \begin{cases} R & \longrightarrow & R, \\ a & \longmapsto & a^q, \end{cases}$$

which is also called the **Frobenius automorphism** of R (it is in fact an automorphism since f is squarefree). It generalizes the above notion, where $R = \mathbb{F}_{q^n}$ if f is irreducible, and satisfies the following rules for all $a, b \in R$:

$$\sigma(a+b) = \sigma(a) + \sigma(b), \quad \sigma(ab) = \sigma(a)\sigma(b), \quad \sigma(a) = a \iff a \in \mathbb{F}_q.$$

The last one is Fermat's little theorem, where we identify $\mathbb{F}_q$ with the subfield of R consisting of the residue classes of the constant polynomials modulo f. These rules imply in particular that $g(a^q) = g(a)^q$ for any $a \in R$ and any polynomial $g \in \mathbb{F}_q[x]$.

Let $\xi = (x \bmod f) \in R$. Then the powers $1, \xi, \cdots, \xi^{n-1}$ of ξ form an $\mathbb{F}_q$-basis of R, and any element $\alpha \in R$ can be written as

$$\alpha = a_{n-1}\xi^{n-1} + \cdots + a_1\xi + a_0 = a(\xi) = (a \bmod f),$$

with unique $a_{n-1}, \ldots, 0 \in \mathbb{F}_q$, where $a = a_{n-1}x^{n-1} + a_1x + a_0 \in \mathbb{F}_q[x]$ is the canonical representative in $\mathbb{F}_q[x]$ of degree less than n for the residue class α. We will write $\check{a}$ for a in what follows, so that

$$\check{a}(\xi) = \check{a} \bmod f = \alpha. \tag{5}$$

In software, there is no need to distinguish between α and $\check{a}$, or, equivalently, between $(a \bmod f)$ and a. Both will be represented by an array $[a_0, \ldots, a_{n-1}]$ of coefficients. But conceptually, one has to make the distinction; for example, it does not make sense to "evaluate α at ξ^q", but we can (and will) evaluate $\check{a}$ at ξ^q.

If $\alpha \in R$ is arbitrary and $a = \check{a} \in \mathbb{F}_q[x]$ as above, we can compute the image of α under the Frobenius map as

$$\alpha^q = a(\xi)^q = a(\xi^q) = \check{a}(\xi^q). \tag{6}$$

This is called the **polynomial representation** of the Frobenius map and is the basis for the following algorithm.

▬▬ ALGORITHM 14.26 Iterated Frobenius. ▬▬▬▬▬▬▬▬▬▬▬▬▬▬
Input: $f \in \mathbb{F}_q[x]$ squarefree of degree n, $d \in \mathbb{N}$ with $d \le n$, $\xi^q \in R = \mathbb{F}_q[x]/\langle f \rangle$, where $\xi = x \bmod f \in R$, and $\alpha \in R$.
Output: $\alpha, \alpha^q, \ldots, \alpha^{q^d} \in R$.

1. $\gamma_0 \longleftarrow \xi, \quad \gamma_1 \longleftarrow \xi^q, \quad l \longleftarrow \lceil \log_2 d \rceil$

2. **for** $1 \le i \le l$ **do**

    call the fast multipoint evaluation algorithm 10.7 over R to compute
    $\gamma_{2^{i-1}+j} = \check{\gamma}_{2^{i-1}}(\gamma_j)$ for $1 \le j \le 2^{i-1}$

3. **call** the fast multipoint evaluation algorithm 10.7 over R to compute $\delta_k = \check{\alpha}(\gamma_k)$ for $0 \le k \le d$

4. **return** $\delta_0, \ldots, \delta_d$

We note that the input ξ^q is not required for the correctness of the algorithm, but we need it for the running time bound.

THEOREM 14.27.
Algorithm 14.26 works correctly as specified and uses $O(\mathsf{M}(n)^2 \log n \log d)$ or $O^{\sim}(n^2)$ operations in $\mathbb{F}_q$.

PROOF. For the correctness, we prove the invariant

$$\gamma_k = \xi^{q^k} \text{ for } 0 \le k \le 2^i$$

by induction on i. The case $i = 0$ is clear from step 1. For the inductive step, it is sufficient to prove the claim for $k > 2^{i-1}$. For $1 \le j \le 2^{i-1}$, we have that

$$\gamma_{2^{i-1}+j} = \check{\gamma}_{2^{i-1}}(\gamma_j) = \check{\gamma}_{2^{i-1}}(\xi^{q^j}) = (\check{\gamma}_{2^{i-1}}(\xi))^{q^j} = \gamma_{2^{i-1}}^{q^j} = \left(\xi^{q^{2^{i-1}}} \right)^{q^j} = \xi^{q^{2^{i-1}+j}},$$

by step 2, (5), (6), and the induction hypothesis. Finally, in step 3 we correctly compute

$$\delta_k = \check{\alpha}(\gamma_k) = \check{\alpha}(\xi^{q^k}) = \check{\alpha}(\xi)^{q^k} = \alpha^{q^k}$$

for $0 \le k \le d$.

By Corollary 10.8, the polynomials $\check{\gamma}_{2^{i-1}}$ and $\check{\alpha}$ in $R[x]$ of degree less than n can be evaluated at no more than n ring elements using at most $(\frac{11}{2}\mathsf{M}(n) + O(n)) \log_2 n$ multiplications and additions in R. In steps 2 and 3 of Algorithm 14.26, we solve $l + 1 \in O(\log d)$ such multipoint evaluation problems, at a total cost of $O(\mathsf{M}(n) \log n \log d)$ in R, or $O(\mathsf{M}(n)^2 \log n \log d)$ operations in $\mathbb{F}_q$. $\square$

Exercise 14.35 asks for a better O-free timing estimate. In fact, it can be shown that $O((n/d)\mathsf{M}(nd) \log d)$ operations in $\mathbb{F}_q$ are sufficient, but since this saves only factors $\log n$ when $d = n$, we omit the proof.

The process of the iterated Frobenius algorithm can be illustrated as follows:

$$\xi^{q^1} \quad \underbrace{\xi^{q^2}}_{i=1} \quad \underbrace{\xi^{q^3} \; \xi^{q^4}}_{i=2} \quad \underbrace{\xi^{q^5} \; \xi^{q^6} \; \xi^{q^7} \; \xi^{q^8}}_{i=3} \quad \underbrace{\xi^{q^9} \; \xi^{q^{10}} \; \xi^{q^{11}} \; \xi^{q^{12}} \; \xi^{q^{13}} \; \xi^{q^{14}} \; \xi^{q^{15}} \; \xi^{q^{16}}}_{i=4} \quad \cdots$$

The ith brace encloses those powers of ξ that are newly computed in the ith iteration of step 2. The advantage of the iterated Frobenius algorithm over the naïve successive computation of the ξ^{q^k} might be compared to the advantage of repeated squaring for the computation of one power a^n over repeated multiplication.

Algorithm 14.26 can be used for distinct-degree factorization as well as for equal-degree factorization. Remember that in Algorithm 14.3, we had to compute

$$x^{q^i} - x \bmod f = \xi^{q^i} - \xi = \gamma_i - \xi$$

for $1 \leq i \leq n$. This can be done by first computing ξ^q using repeated squaring and then applying steps 1 and 2 of the iterated Frobenius algorithm with $d = n$. The cost for the other steps in the distinct-degree factorization algorithm is dominated by the cost for the iterated Frobenius, and so we have the following corollary.

━━ COROLLARY 14.28. ━━━━━━━━━━━━━━━━━━━━━━━━━━━━━━━━━━━
The distinct-degree decomposition of a squarefree polynomial $f \in \mathbb{F}_q[x]$ of degree n can be computed using $O(\mathsf{M}(n^2)\log n + \mathsf{M}(n)\log q)$ or $O^\sim(n^2 + n\log q)$ operations in $\mathbb{F}_q$. ━━

In the equal-degree factorization of Algorithm 14.8, we compute $\alpha^{(q^d-1)/2}$ for a uniform random element $\alpha \in R = \mathbb{F}_q[x]/\langle f \rangle$, where d is the degree of any of the irreducible factors of f. The exponent can be written as

$$\frac{q^d - 1}{2} = (q^{d-1} + q^{d-2} + \cdots + q + 1)\frac{q-1}{2},$$

and hence

$$\alpha^{(q^d-1)/2} = (\alpha^{q^{d-1}} \cdots \alpha^q \cdot \alpha)^{(q-1)/2} = (\delta_{d-1} \cdots \delta_1 \cdot \delta_0)^{(q-1)/2},$$

which can be computed using the iterated Frobenius algorithm, and repeated squaring for the computation of the initial power ξ^q and the final $\frac{q-1}{2}$th power.

━━ COROLLARY 14.29. ━━━━━━━━━━━━━━━━━━━━━━━━━━━━━━━━━━━
The complete factorization of a squarefree polynomial $f \in \mathbb{F}_q[x]$ of degree $n = rd$ with r irreducible factors of degree d can be computed using an expected number of $O((\mathsf{M}(nd)r\log d + \mathsf{M}(n)\log q)\log r)$ or $O^\sim(n^2 + n\log q)$ operations in $\mathbb{F}_q$. ━━━

Similarly as for the equal-degree factoring algorithm 14.10, one finds a slightly better estimate of $O(\mathsf{M}(nd)r\log d + \mathsf{M}(n)\log r\log q)$ arithmetic operations in $\mathbb{F}_q$ (Exercise 14.17), or even $O(\mathsf{M}(nd)r + \mathsf{M}(n)\log q)$ for finding only one irreducible factor. By replacing steps 2 and 3 in Algorithm 14.13 with the two algorithms for distinct-degree and equal-degree factorization presented above, we obtain the following result.

▬ COROLLARY 14.30. ▬

A polynomial $f \in \mathbb{F}_q[x]$ of degree n can be completely factored with an expected number of $O(\mathsf{M}(n^2)\log n + \mathsf{M}(n)\log n \log q)$ or $O^\sim(n^2 + n \log q)$ operations in $\mathbb{F}_q$.

A single operation in $\mathbb{F}_q$ can be done with $O(\mathsf{M}(\log q)\log\log q)$ or $O^\sim(\log q)$ word operations. Factorization thus takes $O^\sim(n^2 \log q + n \log^2 q)$ word operations, which is softly quadratic in the input size of about $n \log_{264} q$ words. In the Notes 14.8 we mention subquadratic algorithms by Kaltofen & Shoup (1998) in the case of small characteristic.

14.8. Algorithms based on linear algebra

The earliest factoring algorithm over finite fields running in polynomial time is due to Berlekamp (1967, 1970). Instead of performing a distinct-degree factorization, he takes a linear algebra approach to split the polynomial, as follows. Let $f \in \mathbb{F}_q[x]$ be a squarefree monic polynomial of degree $n > 0$ and $R = \mathbb{F}_q[x]/\langle f \rangle$. Then R is a vector space of dimension n over $\mathbb{F}_q$ (in fact, it is even an $\mathbb{F}_q$-algebra), and the map $\beta = \sigma - \mathrm{id} \colon R \longrightarrow R$ with $\beta(a) = a^q - a$ is $\mathbb{F}_q$-linear. Let us determine its kernel. If $f = f_1 \cdots f_r$ is the factorization of f into distinct monic irreducible polynomials $f_1, \ldots, f_r \in \mathbb{F}_q[x]$, then we have the Chinese remainder decomposition

$$R \cong \mathbb{F}_q[x]/\langle f_1 \rangle \times \cdots \times \mathbb{F}_q[x]/\langle f_r \rangle. \tag{7}$$

As in Section 14.3, each $\mathbb{F}_q[x]/\langle f_i \rangle$ is a finite field with $q^{\deg f_i}$ elements and contains $\mathbb{F}_q$ as a subfield (the constant polynomials modulo f_i). Now for $a \in \mathbb{F}_q[x]$, we have

$$a \bmod f \in \ker\beta \iff a^q \equiv a \bmod f \iff a^q \equiv a \bmod f_i \text{ for } 1 \le i \le r$$
$$\iff a \bmod f_i \in \mathbb{F}_q \text{ for } 1 \le i \le r,$$

by Fermat's little theorem 14.1. Thus $\mathcal{B} = \ker\beta$ is the subspace corresponding to $\mathbb{F}_q \times \cdots \times \mathbb{F}_q = \mathbb{F}_q^r$ in (7), as illustrated in Figure 14.8. In fact, $\mathcal{B}$ is an $\mathbb{F}_q$-subalgebra of R, called the **Berlekamp subalgebra**. If χ is the isomorphism in (7), then $a \bmod f \in \mathcal{B}$ if and only if $\chi(a \bmod f) = (a_1 \bmod f_1, \ldots, a_r \bmod f_r)$ for some constants $a_1, \ldots, a_r \in \mathbb{F}_q$.

The matrix $Q \in \mathbb{F}_q^{n \times n}$ representing the Frobenius map σ with respect to the polynomials basis $x^{n-1} \bmod f, \ldots, x \bmod f, 1 \bmod f$ of R was first used in Petr (1937) for distinct-degree factorization, and has been a staple of computer algebra since Berlekamp's work. We will call it the **Petr-Berlekamp matrix** of f. Now Berlekamp's algorithm first determines a basis $b_1 \bmod f, \ldots, b_r \bmod f$ of $\mathcal{B}$ using Gaussian elimination on $Q - I$. We note that

$$f \text{ is irreducible} \iff r = 1 \iff \mathrm{rank}(Q - I) = n - 1. \tag{8}$$

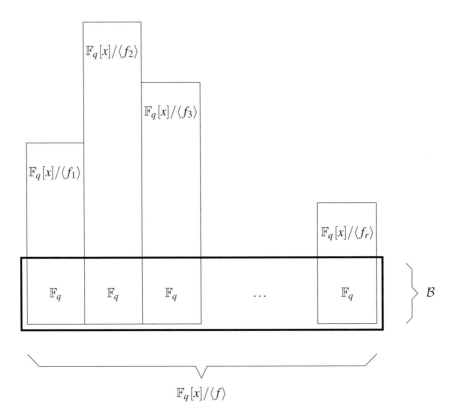

FIGURE 14.8: The Berlekamp subalgebra $\mathcal{B}$ of $R = \mathbb{F}_q[x]/\langle f \rangle$.

Now we assume for simplicity that q is odd (see Exercise 14.16 for characteristic 2), and let $b = c_1 b_1 + \cdots + c_r b_r$ be a uniformly random linear combination of basis elements, with $c_1, \ldots, c_r \in \mathbb{F}_q$ chosen independently, so that $b \bmod f$ is a uniform random element of $\mathcal{B}$. We now employ the same $(q-1)/2$ trick as in the equal-degree factorization. The $b \bmod f_i$ are uniformly and independently distributed random elements of $\mathbb{F}_q$ for $1 \leq i \leq r$. Hence, if no f_i divides b, then $b^{(q-1)/2} \equiv \pm 1 \bmod f_i$, and both possibilities occur with probability $1/2$ and independently for all i, by Lemma 14.7. This yields the following Las Vegas algorithm.

━━ ALGORITHM 14.31 Berlekamp's algorithm. ━━━━━━━━━━━━━
Input: A monic squarefree polynomial $f \in \mathbb{F}_q[x]$ of degree $n > 0$, where q is an odd prime power.
Output: Either an irreducible factor g of f, or "failure".

1. **call** the repeated squaring algorithm 4.8 in $\mathbb{F}_q[x]/\langle f \rangle$ to compute x^q rem f

2. **for** $0 \leq i < n$ compute x^{qi} rem $f = \sum_{0 \leq j < n} q_{ij} x^j$
   $Q \longleftarrow (q_{ij})_{0 \leq i,j < n}$

3. use Gaussian elimination on $Q - I \in \mathbb{F}_q^{n \times n}$, where I is the $n \times n$ identity matrix, to compute the dimension $r \in \mathbb{N}$ and a basis $b_1 \bmod f, \ldots, b_r \bmod f$ of the Berlekamp algebra $\mathcal{B}$, with $b_1, \ldots, b_r \in \mathbb{F}_q[x]$ of degree less than n
if $r = 1$ **then return** f

4. choose independent uniformly random elements $c_1, \ldots, c_r \in \mathbb{F}_q$
$a \longleftarrow c_1 b_1 + \cdots + c_r b_r$

5. $g_1 \longleftarrow \gcd(a, f)$
if $g_1 \neq 1$ **then return** g_1

6. **call** the repeated squaring algorithm 4.8 in $R = \mathbb{F}_q[x]/\langle f \rangle$ to compute $b = a^{(q-1)/2} \bmod f$

7. $g_2 \longleftarrow \gcd(b - 1, f)$
if $g_2 \neq 1$ and $g_2 \neq f$ **then return** g_2 **else return** "failure"

The Gaussian elimination in step 3 can be done with $O(n^3)$ operations in $\mathbb{F}_q$. In Section 12.1 we have seen faster methods, and we may use any feasible matrix multiplication exponent ω, so that $n \times n$ matrices can be multiplied with $O(n^\omega)$ operations. The reader may very well think of the classical $\omega = 3$.

▬ THEOREM 14.32. ▬▬▬▬▬▬▬▬▬▬▬▬▬▬▬▬▬▬▬▬▬▬▬▬▬▬
Algorithm 14.31 works correctly as specified and fails with probability at most $1/2$*. It uses* $O(n^\omega + \mathsf{M}(n) \log q)$ *operations in* $\mathbb{F}_q$ *if* $\omega > 2$. ▬▬▬▬▬▬▬

PROOF. Correctness is clear from the discussion preceding the algorithm. If $g_1 = 1$ in step 5, then g_2 is trivial (that is, 1 or f) in step 7 if and only if either $b^{(q-1)/2} \equiv -1 \bmod f_i$ for all i or $b^{(q-1)/2} \equiv 1 \bmod f_i$ for all i, and each case occurs with probability 2^{-r}. Hence the probability of success is at least $1 - 2 \cdot 2^{-r} \geq 1/2$ since $r \geq 2$.

The cost for step 1 is $O(\mathsf{M}(n) \log q)$ field operations. Step 2 uses $n - 2$ multiplications modulo f, or $O(n\mathsf{M}(n))$ operations in $\mathbb{F}_q$. The cost for step 3 is $O(n^\omega)$, by Section 12.1. This dominates the cost for step 2, the $O(nr)$ field operations for step 4, and the $O(\mathsf{M}(n) \log n)$ for the gcds in steps 5 and 7. Finally, step 6 uses another $O(\mathsf{M}(n) \log q)$ field operations. $\square$

When we want the complete factorization of f, it is sufficient to compute the basis of $\mathcal{B}$ only once and to apply the splitting process of steps 4 through 7 recursively to g and f/g, as in the equal-degree factorization algorithm 14.10. Then an analysis similar to that of Theorem 14.11 implies that all irreducible factors of f can be computed in expected time $O(n^\omega + \mathsf{M}(n) \log r \log q)$.

When $\log q$ is small in comparison to n, then the dominant cost of Algorithm 14.31 is the nullspace computation in step 2. Since evaluating the matrix $Q - I$ at a vector corresponds to computing $\beta(a) = a^q - a$ for some $a \in R$, at a cost of $O(\mathsf{M}(n)\log q)$ field operations, it looks promising to try the black box linear algebra approach from Section 12.4. By combining the algorithm of Kaltofen & Saunders (1991) (see Theorem 12.19 and the discussion following it) with Berlekamp's algorithm in a straightforward manner, we would obtain an $O^\sim(n^2 \log q)$ factoring algorithm. Exploiting the special properties of the Frobenius automorphism, Kaltofen & Lobo (1994) have taken the following more sophisticated approach which leads to an $O^\sim(n^2 + n\log q)$ algorithm.

━━ ALGORITHM 14.33 Kaltofen & Lobo's algorithm. ━━━━━━━━━━━
Input: A monic squarefree polynomial $f \in \mathbb{F}_q[x]$ of degree $n > 0$.
Output: If f is reducible, then a proper factor of f, otherwise f itself, or "failure".

{ $Q \in \mathbb{F}_q^{n \times n}$ denotes the Petr-Berlekamp matrix of f }

1. randomly choose two row vectors $u, v \in \mathbb{F}_q^n$
   call the iterated Frobenius algorithm 14.26 to compute $Q^i v$ for $0 \le i < 2n$
   call Algorithm 12.9 with input $u^T Q^i v$ for $0 \le i < 2n$ to compute the minimal polynomial $m \in \mathbb{F}_q[x]$ of the sequence $(u^T Q^i v)_{i \ge 0} \in \mathbb{F}_q^{\mathbb{N}}$
   { with "high" probability, m is the minimal polynomial of Q; see Exercise 12.15 }

2. **if** $m = x^n - 1$ **return** f **else if** $m(1) \ne 0$ **return** "failure"

3. $h \longleftarrow \dfrac{m(x+1)}{x}$
   choose another random vector $w \in \mathbb{F}_q^n$
   call the iterated Frobenius algorithm 14.26 to compute $Q^i w$ for $0 \le i \le \deg h$
   compute the polynomial $a \in \mathbb{F}_q[x]$ with coefficient vector $h(Q) \cdot w$

4. $g_1 \longleftarrow \gcd(a, f)$
   if $g_1 \ne 1$ and $g_1 \ne f$ **then return** g_1

5. **call** the repeated squaring algorithm 4.8 in $R = \mathbb{F}_q[x]/\langle f \rangle$ to compute $b = a^{(q-1)/2}$ rem f

6. $g_2 \longleftarrow \gcd(b-1, f)$
   if $g_2 \ne 1$ and $g_2 \ne f$ **then return** g_2 **else return** "failure" ━━━━━━━

The analyses in Kaltofen & Lobo (1994) and Kaltofen & Shoup (1998) imply the following.

━━━ THEOREM 14.34. ━━━━━━━━━━━━━━━━━━━━━━━━━━━━━━━━━━

Algorithm 14.33 works correctly as specified, returns "failure" with probability at most $1/2$ if $q \geq 4n$, and takes $O(\mathsf{M}(n^2)\log n + \mathsf{M}(n)\log q)$ operations in $\mathbb{F}_q$. If the algorithm is used recursively to factor f completely, then the expected recursion depth is $O(\log_p n \cdot \log r)$, where $p = \operatorname{char}\mathbb{F}_q$ and r is the number of irreducible factors of f. ━━━━━━━━━━━━━━━━━━━━━━━━━━━━━━━━

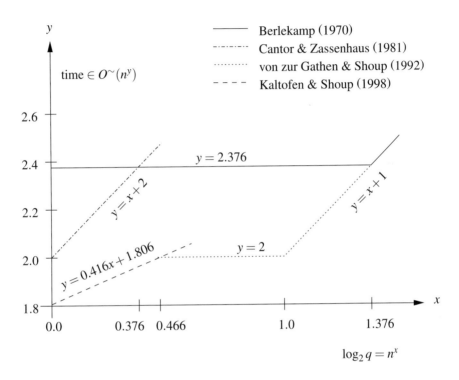

FIGURE 14.9: Asymptotic running times of various factoring algorithms.

Figure 14.9 illustrates how the asymptotic running times of four factorization algorithms depend on the relation between the two independent parameters n, the degree of the input polynomial, and $\log_2 q$. The figure, based on a similar one in Kaltofen & Shoup (1998), abstracts a three-dimensional picture of the running time as a function of n and $\log_2 q$ into a two-dimensional figure with two logarithmic axes x and y, where $\log_2 q$ and the time are about n^x and n^y, respectively. The figure pictures Berlekamp's classical algorithm 14.31, the method of Cantor & Zassenhaus (Algorithms 14.3 and 14.10), the iterated Frobenius algorithm of von zur Gathen & Shoup (Corollary 14.30), and the subquadratic algorithm of Kaltofen & Shoup (1998), incorporating Huang & Pan's (1998) fast rectangular matrix multiplication. A derivation of the (rounded) numerical value in Figure 14.9 for the latter is given in Notes 14.9. Huang & Pan (1998) present another algorithm whose running time, corresponding to $x + 1.80535$, beats the others for $x \leq 0.00173$; its graph is virtually indistinguishable for these small values from the lower left segment. Each of these five algorithms is asymptotically faster than previously known methods for some choices of n and q.

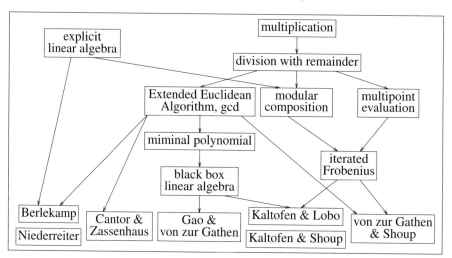

FIGURE 14.10: Algorithms in computer algebra used for polynomial factorization over finite fields.

Computationally, (fast) polynomial factorization over a finite field is a much more advanced task than, for example, multiplication or even gcd computation. Before implementing a particular algorithm, one has to implement carefully many other routines for basic polynomial arithmetic, and designing a polynomial factorization package usually requires several woman-years. Figure 14.10 gives an overview of various factorization algorithms for univariate polynomials over finite fields and the polynomial arithmetic they are based on. The arrows indicate dependencies.

14.9. Testing irreducibility and constructing irreducible polynomials

Any factorization algorithm can be used as an irreducibility test. For example, in the distinct-degree factorization algorithm 14.3 we can stop when we either find a proper factor or reach degree more than $n/2$ without having found a factor. An alternative is provided by the following corollary.

COROLLARY 14.35.

A polynomial $f \in \mathbb{F}_q[x]$ of degree $n \geq 1$ is irreducible if and only if

(i) *f divides $x^{q^n} - x$, and*

(ii) *$\gcd(x^{q^{n/t}} - x, f) = 1$ for all prime divisors t of n.*

PROOF. It follows immediately from Theorem 14.2 that f satisfies the two conditions if it is irreducible. Conversely, if (i) holds, then Theorem 14.2 implies that the degree of any irreducible factor of f divides n. Let g be such an irreducible factor, and suppose that $d = \deg g < n$. Then d divides n/t for some prime factor t of n, and hence $g \mid x^{q^{n/t}} - x$. This contradicts (ii), and we conclude that $d = n$ and f is irreducible. $\square$

━━ ALGORITHM 14.36 Irreducibility test over finite fields. ━━
Input: $f \in \mathbb{F}_q[x]$ of degree n.
Output: "irreducible" or "reducible".

    1. **call** the repeated squaring algorithm 4.8 to compute x^q rem f
       use the modular composition algorithm 12.3 to compute $a = x^{q^n}$ rem f
       if $a \neq x$ **then return** "reducible"

    2. **for** all prime divisors t of n **do**

    3.   use the modular composition algorithm 12.3 to compute $b = x^{q^{n/t}}$ rem f
          if $\gcd(b - x, f) \neq 1$ **then return** "reducible"

    4. **return** "irreducible" ━━━━━━━━━━━━━━━━━━━━━━━━━━━

For an integer $n \geq 1$, we denote by $\delta(n)$ the number of distinct prime divisors of n. Since 2 is the smallest prime, we have the trivial upper bound $\delta(n) \leq \log_2 n$. In fact, $\delta(n) \leq \ln n / \ln \ln n$, and $\delta(n)$ is $O(\log\log n)$ on average.

━━ THEOREM 14.37. ━━━━━━━━━━━━━━━━━━━━━━━━━━━
Algorithm 14.36 correctly decides whether the input polynomial is irreducible. It can be implemented so as to use $O(\mathsf{M}(n)\log q + (n^{(\omega+1)/2} + n^{1/2}\mathsf{M}(n))\delta(n)\log n)$ or $O^\sim(n^{(\omega+1)/2} + n\log q)$ operations in $\mathbb{F}_q$. ━━━━━━━━━━━━━

PROOF. Correctness follows from Corollary 14.35. The cost for computing x^q rem f in step 1 is $O(\mathsf{M}(n)\log q)$ field operations. To compute $s_m = x^{q^m}$ rem f for some $m \in \mathbb{N}$, we employ the polynomial representation (6) of the Frobenius map, noting that

$$x^{q^{i+j}} \bmod f = \left(\xi^{q^i}\right)^{q^j} = s_i(\xi)^{q^j} = s_i(\xi^{q^j}) = s_i(s_j(\xi)) = s_i(s_j) \bmod f$$

for all i, j. Thus x^{q^m} rem f can be computed from x^q rem f in a "repeated squaring" fashion along the binary representation of m, taking $O(\log m)$ modular composition steps of the form $s_i(s_j)$ rem f. By Theorem 12.4, this can be done at a total cost of $O((n^{(\omega+1)/2} + n^{1/2}\mathsf{M}(n))\log m)$ operations in $\mathbb{F}_q$, dominating the cost for the gcd in step 3. The total number of times we have to compute some s_m is $1 + \delta(n)$, and the claim follows since $m \leq n$ in all those cases. $\square$

With the current world record $\omega < 2.376$ (Section 12.1), we have $(\omega + 1)/2 < 1.688$. The iterated Frobenius algorithm for distinct-degree factorization can be used for testing irreducibility and takes $O^{\sim}(n^2 + n \log q)$ operations in $\mathbb{F}_q$ (Corollary 14.28). A third irreducibility test (for a squarefree polynomial) is given by (8); it is sufficient to compute the rank of $Q - I$, taking $O(n^\omega + \mathsf{M}(n) \log q)$ field operations.

Comparing the three tests and using classical matrix arithmetic, where $\omega = 3$, the first two give the same soft-Oh estimate $n^2 + n \log q$, but the Oh-bound shows that the test 14.36 is faster: $n^2 \delta(n) \log n$ versus $\mathsf{M}(n^2) \log n$, for small q. The n^3 estimate for the third method is in a different league. When we take $\omega < 3$, say $\omega = 2.376$ (Section 12.1), then the estimate for Algorithm 14.36 shrinks to only $O^{\sim}(n^{1.688} + n \log q)$.

Now that we know how to test a polynomial for irreducibility, it is natural to ask how to find irreducible polynomials. This is used to construct finite extension fields of finite fields and in modular algorithms. The following result tells us how frequently irreducible polynomials occur among arbitrary polynomials.

LEMMA 14.38. *Let q be a prime power and $n \in \mathbb{N}_{\geq 1}$. Then the number $I(n,q)$ of monic irreducible polynomials of degree n in $\mathbb{F}_q[x]$ satisfies*

$$\frac{q^n - 2q^{n/2}}{n} \leq I(n,q) \leq \frac{q^n}{n}.$$

In particular, if $q^n \geq 16$, then the probability p_n for a uniformly random monic polynomial of degree n to be irreducible satisfies

$$\frac{1}{2n} \leq \frac{1}{n}\left(1 - \frac{2}{q^{n/2}}\right) \leq p_n \leq \frac{1}{n}.$$

PROOF. Let f_n be the product of all monic irreducible polynomials of degree n in $\mathbb{F}_q[x]$. Thus $\deg f_n = n \cdot I(n,q)$. Theorem 14.2 can then be reformulated as

$$x^{q^n} - x = \prod_{d \mid n} f_d = f_n \cdot \prod_{d \mid n, d < n} f_d.$$

Taking degrees on both sides, we obtain

$$q^n = \deg f_n + \sum_{d \mid n, d < n} \deg f_d,$$

and hence

$$q^n \geq \deg f_n = n \cdot I(n,q). \tag{9}$$

This proves the upper bound. Now

$$\sum_{d \mid n, d < n} \deg f_d \leq \sum_{1 \leq d \leq n/2} \deg f_d \leq \sum_{1 \leq d \leq n/2} q^d < \frac{q^{n/2+1} - 1}{q - 1} \leq 2q^{n/2},$$

by (9) with d instead of n and the fact that $q \geq 2$, and hence

$$n \cdot I(n,q) = \deg f_n = q^n - \sum_{d \mid n, d < n} \deg f_d \geq q^n - 2q^{n/2},$$

which establishes the lower bound.

There are q^n monic polynomials of degree n in $\mathbb{F}_q[x]$, and hence

$$\frac{1}{n} \geq \frac{I(n,q)}{q^n} \geq \frac{1}{n}(1 - 2q^{-n/2}) \geq \frac{1}{2n}$$

if $q^n \geq 16$. This proves the last assertion. $\square$

In fact, the probability is close to $1/n$ when q^n is not too small. The precise formula

$$n \cdot I(n,q) = \sum_{d \mid n} \mu\left(\frac{n}{d}\right) q^d$$

can be found by using a well-known number theoretic tool called **Möbius inversion** (Exercise 14.46). Here

$$\mu(n) = \begin{cases} 1 & \text{if } n = 1, \\ (-1)^k & \text{if } n \text{ is the product of } k \text{ distinct primes}, \\ 0 & \text{if } n \text{ is not squarefree}, \end{cases} \tag{10}$$

is the **Möbius function**, defined for positive integers n. The first few values of μ are listed in Section 17.4. Table 14.11 tabulates the values of $I(n,q)$ for some small values of n and q.

n	$q = 2$	$q = 3$	$q = 4$	$q = 5$	$q = 7$	$q = 8$	$q = 9$
2	1	3	6	10	21	28	36
3	2	8	20	40	112	168	240
4	3	18	60	150	588	1008	1620
5	6	48	204	624	3360	6552	11 808
6	9	116	670	2580	19 544	43 596	88 440
7	18	312	2340	11 160	117 648	299 592	683 280
8	30	810	8160	48 750	720 300	2 096 640	5 380 020
9	56	2184	29 120	217 000	4 483 696	14 913 024	43 046 640
10	99	5880	104 754	976 248	28 245 840	107 370 900	348 672 528

TABLE 14.11: The number $I(n,q)$ of irreducible polynomials for $2 \leq n \leq 10$ and $q \leq 9$.

A simple idea to find a random irreducible polynomial of a given degree n is now to repeatedly and independently choose random polynomials of degree n and test them for irreducibility. Using Algorithm 14.36, this leads to the following result.

━━ COROLLARY 14.39. ━━

For a prime power q and $n \in \mathbb{N}_{>0}$, one can find a uniformly random irreducible polynomial of degree n in $\mathbb{F}_q[x]$ using an expected number of

$$O(n\mathsf{M}(n)\log q + (n^{(\omega+3)/2} + n^{3/2}\mathsf{M}(n))\delta(n)\log n) \text{ or } O^{\sim}(n^{(\omega+3)/2} + n^2\log q)$$

operations in $\mathbb{F}_q$. ━━━

The exponent $(\omega+3)/2$ is less than 2.688 for the smallest currently known ω. The following alternative method is somewhat faster.

━━ ALGORITHM 14.40 Ben-Or's generation of irreducible polynomials. ━━━━━━
Input: A prime power q and $n \in \mathbb{N}_{>0}$.
Output: A uniformly random monic irreducible polynomial of degree n in $\mathbb{F}_q[x]$.

1. randomly choose a monic polynomial $f \in \mathbb{F}_q[x]$ of degree n

2. **for** $i = 1, \ldots, \lfloor n/2 \rfloor$ **do**
   $$g_i \longleftarrow \gcd(x^{q^i} - x, f), \quad \text{**if** } g_i \neq 1 \text{ **then goto** } 1$$

3. **return** f ━━

By Theorem 14.4, step 2 can be performed with $O^{\sim}(n^2\log q)$ field operations, and Lemma 14.38 would imply a total cost of $O^{\sim}(n^3\log q)$, but the following analysis shows that the actual cost is lower by about one order of magnitude. We state the following property without proof.

LEMMA 14.41. *Let q be a prime power and $n \in \mathbb{N}_{>0}$. The expected value of the degree of the smallest irreducible factor of a uniformly random polynomial of degree n in $\mathbb{F}_q[x]$ is $O(\log n)$.*

━━ THEOREM 14.42. ━━

Ben-Or's algorithm 14.40 works correctly as specified and takes an expected number of $O(n\mathsf{M}(n)\log n\log(nq))$ or $O^{\sim}(n^2\log q)$ operations in $\mathbb{F}_q$. ━━━━

PROOF. A reducible polynomial has an irreducible factor of degree at most $n/2$, which divides some g_i, by Theorem 14.2. This proves the correctness.

The test for a single value of i takes $O(\mathsf{M}(n)\log(nq))$ operations in $\mathbb{F}_q$, and the expected number of operations for step 2 for a single f is $O(\mathsf{M}(n)\log n\log(nq))$, by Lemma 14.41. The expected number of trials is $O(n)$, by Lemma 14.38. □

In practice, it may be advantageous to use a hybrid algorithm which switches from the distinct-degree factorization in step 2 of Algorithm 14.40 to Algorithm 14.36 as soon as the former has certified that the polynomial in question has no irreducible factors below a certain bound, say $\log_2 n$. A random polynomial of degree n without factors of degree up to $m \in O(\log n)$ is irreducible with probability about cm/n, for some constant c. Experiments for $q = 2$ in Section 15.7, where variants of the distinct-degree factorization algorithm and of Algorithm 14.36 were run in parallel, indicate that this is useful even when classical matrix multiplication with $\omega = 3$ is used.

COROLLARY 14.43.

For a prime power q and $n \in \mathbb{N}$, we can construct the extension field $\mathbb{F}_{q^n}$ of $\mathbb{F}_q$ using an expected number of $O(n\mathsf{M}(n)\log n\log(nq))$ or $O^{\sim}(n^2\log q)$ operations in $\mathbb{F}_q$.

For the big prime modular gcd algorithm 6.28 in $\mathbb{F}_q[x,y]$, we have to find an irreducible polynomial which does not divide some unknown resultant $r \in \mathbb{F}_q[y]$, on which only a degree bound $\deg r \leq m$ is known.

COROLLARY 14.44.

Let $n \in \mathbb{N}$, q be a prime power, and $r \in \mathbb{F}_q[y]$ nonzero of degree at most m. Then we can compute a uniform random irreducible polynomial $f \in \mathbb{F}_q[y]$ of degree n taking $O(n\mathsf{M}(n)\log n\log(nq))$ or $O^{\sim}(n^2\log q)$ operations in $\mathbb{F}_q$, and f does not divide r with probability at least $1/2$ if $q^n \geq 2m$.

PROOF. The cost estimate is from Theorem 14.42. There are $I(n,q)$ irreducible polynomials of degree n, and at most $\lfloor m/n \rfloor$ of them divide r. Thus the probability that f does not divide r is

$$\frac{I(n,q) - \left\lfloor \dfrac{m}{n} \right\rfloor}{I(n,q)} \geq 1 - \frac{m}{n} \cdot \frac{n}{q^n} = 1 - \frac{m}{q^n},$$

and the claim follows. $\square$

In fact, the probability is close to 1 when q^n is not too small.

14.10. Cyclotomic polynomials and constructing BCH codes

We recall from Section 8.2 that an element ω in a field F is an **nth root of unity** if $\omega^n = 1$, and a **primitive nth root of unity** if in addition $\operatorname{char} F \nmid n$ and $\omega^k \neq 1$ for $1 \leq k < n$, or equivalently, ω has multiplicative order n in $F^{\times}$.

DEFINITION 14.45. *The polynomial*

$$\Phi_n = \prod_{\substack{\omega \in \mathbb{C} \text{ primitive} \\ n\text{th root of unity}}} (x - \omega) = \prod_{\substack{1 \leq k < n \\ \gcd(k,n)=1}} (x - e^{2\pi i k/n}) \in \mathbb{C}[x]$$

*is called the nth **cyclotomic polynomial**.*

Lemma 14.47 below implies that Φ_n has coefficients in $\mathbb{Z}$. Table 14.12 lists the first 20 cyclotomic polynomials. We have $\deg \Phi_n = \varphi(n)$, where φ is Euler's totient function (Section 4.2).

n	Φ_n	n	Φ_n
1	$x - 1$	11	$x^{10} + x^9 + \cdots + x + 1$
2	$x + 1$	12	$x^4 - x^2 + 1$
3	$x^2 + x + 1$	13	$x^{12} + x^{11} + \cdots + x + 1$
4	$x^2 + 1$	14	$x^6 - x^5 + x^4 - x^3 + x^2 - x + 1$
5	$x^4 + x^3 + x^2 + x + 1$	15	$x^8 - x^7 + x^5 - x^4 + x^3 - x + 1$
6	$x^2 - x + 1$	16	$x^8 + 1$
7	$x^6 + x^5 + x^4 + x^3 + x^2 + x + 1$	17	$x^{16} + x^{15} + \cdots + x + 1$
8	$x^4 + 1$	18	$x^6 - x^3 + 1$
9	$x^6 + x^3 + 1$	19	$x^{18} + x^{17} + \cdots + x + 1$
10	$x^4 - x^3 + x^2 - x + 1$	20	$x^8 - x^6 + x^4 - x^2 + 1$

TABLE 14.12: The first 20 cyclotomic polynomials.

LEMMA 14.46. *For a positive integer n, we have the factorization*

$$x^n - 1 = \prod_{d \mid n} \Phi_d. \tag{11}$$

PROOF. Let $\omega \in \mathbb{C}$ be a zero of $x^n - 1$, that is, an nth root of unity. Then $\mathrm{ord}(\omega) = d$ for some divisor d of n, by Lagrange's theorem (Section 25.1). But this means that ω is a primitive dth root of unity, and hence $\Phi_d(\omega) = 0$. Conversely, if $\omega \in \mathbb{C}$ is a primitive dth root of unity for some divisor d of n, then $\omega^d = 1$, and hence also $\omega^n = 1$. This shows that both polynomials in (11) have the same roots in $\mathbb{C}$.

Now $(x^n - 1)' = nx^{n-1}$ is coprime to $x^n - 1$, which implies that $x^n - 1$ is square-free. By definition, Φ_d is squarefree for all d, and Φ_d and Φ_e have no roots in common unless $d = e$. This proves that also the polynomial on the right hand side is squarefree, and since both polynomials are monic, they are equal. $\square$

As examples, we have

$$\begin{aligned}
x^6 - 1 &= (x^2 - x + 1)(x^2 + x + 1)(x + 1)(x - 1) = \Phi_6 \Phi_3 \Phi_2 \Phi_1, \\
x^8 - 1 &= (x^4 + 1)(x^2 + 1)(x + 1)(x - 1) = \Phi_8 \Phi_4 \Phi_2 \Phi_1.
\end{aligned}$$

Using Möbius inversion, Lemma 14.46 yields the formula

$$\Phi_n = \prod_{d \mid n} (x^d - 1)^{\mu(n/d)}$$

for the cyclotomic polynomials. For example, we have

$$\Phi_6 = x^2 - x + 1 = \frac{(x^6 - 1)(x - 1)}{(x^3 - 1)(x^2 - 1)}.$$

The following lemma, which is proven in Exercise 14.45, yields an alternative method for computing Φ_n.

LEMMA 14.47. *Let $n, k \in \mathbb{N}_{>0}$. Then*

(i) $\Phi_n = x^{n-1} + x^{n-2} + \cdots + x + 1$ *if n is prime,*

(ii) $\Phi_{2n} = \Phi_n(-x)$ *if n is odd,*

(iii) $\Phi_{kn}\Phi_n = \Phi_n(x^k)$ *if k and n are coprime,*

(iv) $\Phi_{kn} = \Phi_n(x^k)$ *if every prime divisor of k divides n.*

▬▬ ALGORITHM 14.48 Cyclotomic polynomial computation. ▬▬▬▬
Input: $n \in \mathbb{N}_{>0}$ and the distinct prime divisors $p_1, \ldots, p_r$ of n.
Output: $\Phi_n \in \mathbb{Z}[x]$.

1. $f_0 \longleftarrow x - 1$

2. **for** $i = 1, \ldots, r$ **do** $f_i \longleftarrow \dfrac{f_{i-1}(x^{p_i})}{f_{i-1}}$

3. **return** $f_r\big(x^{n/(p_1 \cdots p_r)}\big)$ ▬▬▬▬▬▬▬▬▬▬

▬▬ THEOREM 14.49. ▬▬▬▬
Algorithm 14.48 uses $O(\mathsf{M}(n)\log n)$ arithmetic operations in $\mathbb{Z}$ and correctly computes the nth cyclotomic polynomial. ▬▬▬▬▬▬

PROOF. We claim that $f_i = \Phi_{p_1 \cdots p_i}$ for $0 \le i \le r$. This is clear if $i = 0$ and follows inductively from Lemma 14.47 (iii). Now let $m = p_1 \cdots p_r$ be the squarefree part of n. Then

$$f_r(x^{n/m})/f_r = \Phi_m(x^{n/m})/\Phi_m = \Phi_n,$$

by Lemma 14.47 (iv), since every prime divisor of n/m divides m.

The only arithmetic operations occur in step 2, where the ith operation is a division of a polynomial of degree $(p_1 - 1) \cdots (p_{i-1} - 1)p_i$ by a polynomial of degree $(p_1 - 1) \cdots (p_{i-1} - 1)$. Roughly, this takes $O(\mathsf{M}(n))$ additions and multiplications in $\mathbb{Z}$ (since the divisor is monic), and the claim follows since $r \le \log_2 n$. $\square$

Now let F be an arbitrary field and $n \in \mathbb{N}$. We may consider Φ_n as a polynomial in $F[x]$ by reducing its coefficients modulo the characteristic p of F. Then (11), Lemma 14.47, and Algorithm 14.48 are still valid. In Galois theory, it is shown that if p does not divide n, then

$$\Phi_n = \prod_{\substack{\omega \in E \text{ primitive} \\ n\text{th root of unity}}} (x - \omega)$$

holds over any extension E of F containing a primitive nth root of unity, and that Φ_n is irreducible over $\mathbb{Q}$ (so that (11) is the irreducible factorization of $x^n - 1$ over $\mathbb{Q}$). The following lemma says that the latter is not true over finite fields.

LEMMA 14.50. *Let* $n \in \mathbb{N}_{>0}$, $\mathbb{F}_q$ *be a finite field of characteristic* p *not dividing* n, *and* $d = \text{ord}_n(q)$ *the multiplicative order of* q *in* $\mathbb{Z}_n^\times$. *Then* Φ_n *factors in* $\mathbb{F}_q[x]$ *into a product of* $\varphi(n)/d$ *irreducible polynomials of degree* d *each. In particular, the degree of the minimal polynomial of any primitive* nth *root of unity over* $\mathbb{F}_q$ *is* d.

PROOF. First we note that $d \mid \varphi(n) = \#\mathbb{Z}_n^\times$, by Lagrange's theorem. Now n divides $q^d - 1 = \#\mathbb{F}_{q^d}^\times$, and hence $\mathbb{F}_{q^d}$ contains a primitive nth root of unity ω (Lemma 8.8). We choose such an ω, and let $f \in \mathbb{F}_q[x]$ be the unique irreducible factor of Φ_n that has ω as a root. Since $f(x^q) = f(x)^q$, the element ω^{q^i} is a root of f for all $i \in \mathbb{N}$. Now $1, q, q^2, \dots, q^{d-1}$ are distinct modulo n, the order of ω in $\mathbb{F}_{q^d}^\times$, and hence $\{\omega, \omega^q, \omega^{q^2}, \dots, \omega^{q^{d-1}}\}$ are d distinct roots of f. Thus $\deg f \geq d$. On the other hand, we have $\mathbb{F}_q[x]/\langle f \rangle \cong \mathbb{F}_q(\omega) \subseteq \mathbb{F}_{q^d}$ (Section 25.3), whence $\deg f \leq d$. Thus $\deg f = d$, and since the choice of ω was arbitrary, this is true for all irreducible factors of Φ_n. $\square$

For example, the order of 3 modulo 8 is 2, and in fact Φ_8 splits into two irreducible factors of degree 2 over $\mathbb{F}_3$: $x^4 + 1 = (x^2 + x - 1)(x^2 - x - 1)$.

EXAMPLE 14.51. We take $q = 2$ and $n = 15$. Then $d = \text{ord}_{15}(2) = 4$. The polynomial $x^{15} - 1$ factors in $\mathbb{F}_2[x]$ as

$$\begin{aligned}
x^{15} - 1 &= \Phi_{15}\Phi_5\Phi_3\Phi_1 \\
&= (x^8 - x^7 + x^5 - x^4 + x^3 - x + 1)(x^4 + x^3 + x^2 + x + 1)(x^2 + x + 1)(x - 1) \\
&= (x^4 + x + 1)(x^4 + x^3 + 1)(x^4 + x^3 + x^2 + x + 1)(x^2 + 2 + 1)(x + 1).
\end{aligned}$$

As predicted by Lemma 14.50, Φ_{15} splits into two irreducible factors of degree 4, and Φ_5, Φ_3, and Φ_1 remain irreducible. Let $\beta \in \mathbb{F}_{q^4}$ be a root of $x^4 + x + 1$. Then β is a primitive 15th root of unity. The roots of the minimal polynomial $x^4 + x + 1$ of β are $\beta, \beta^2, \beta^4, \beta^8$.

For $i \in \mathbb{Z}$, β^i is a primitive lth root of unity, where $l = \mathrm{ord}(\beta^i) = n/\gcd(n,i)$ (Exercise 8.13). We have $\mathrm{ord}(\beta^3) = 15/\gcd(3,15) = 5$, so that β^3 is a primitive 5th root of unity. Now $\mathrm{ord}_5(2) = 4$, so that the minimal polynomial of β^3 has precisely the four roots $\beta^3, \beta^6, \beta^{12}, \beta^{24} = \beta^9$. Similarly, $\mathrm{ord}(\beta^5) = 3$ and $\mathrm{ord}_3(2) = 2$, whence β^5 is a primitive third root of unity and its minimal polynomial only has the two roots β^5, β^{10}. $\diamond$

We define an equivalence relation $\sim$ on $\mathbb{Z}_n$ by

$$i \sim j \iff \exists i \in \mathbb{Z} \ iq^l = j. \tag{12}$$

If $i \in \mathbb{Z}_n^\times$, then the equivalence class of i is precisely the coset $i \cdot \langle q \rangle$ of the cyclic subgroup $\langle q \rangle$ of $\mathbb{Z}_n^\times$. If $d = \mathrm{ord}_n(q)$ and $\beta \in \mathbb{F}_{q^d}$ is a primitive nth root of unity, then the powers β^i and β^j have the same minimal polynomial if and only if $i \sim j$, as in the example.

Lemma 14.50 implies that cyclotomic polynomials can be directly factored over finite fields using equal-degree factorization, without performing either squarefree or distinct-degree factorization. The cost is $O^\sim(n^2 + n\log q)$ operations in $\mathbb{F}_q$ or $O^\sim(n^2 \log q + n\log^2 q)$ word operations if $p \nmid n$. Exercise 14.47 yields an even faster algorithm for factoring $x^n - 1$, taking only $O^\sim(n\log^2 q)$ word operations, which can be modified so as to work for Φ_n as well. When p divides n, we have $\Phi_n = \Phi_{n/p}^p$ in $\mathbb{F}_q[x]$.

In Chapter 7, we discussed a class of cyclic codes that are of importance in modern coding theory, the **BCH codes**. For a finite field $\mathbb{F}_q$, a primitive nth root of unity $\beta \in \mathbb{F}_{q^d}$ in some extension field of $\mathbb{F}_q$, and a positive integer δ, $\mathrm{BCH}(q,n,\delta)$ is the cyclic code (that is, the ideal) in $\mathbb{F}_q[x]/\langle x^n - 1 \rangle$ generated by $g \bmod x^n - 1$, where $g \in \mathbb{F}_q[x]$ is the least common multiple of the minimal polynomials of $\beta, \beta^2, \ldots, \beta^{\delta-1}$ over $\mathbb{F}_q$. We now show how to compute such a generator polynomial g.

━━ ALGORITHM 14.52 Construction of BCH codes. ━━━━━━━━
Input: A prime power q and positive integers $n \geq \delta$ with $\gcd(n,q) = 1$.
Output: A generator polynomial $g \in \mathbb{F}_q[x]$ of a $\mathrm{BCH}(q,n,\delta)$ code.

1. let $p_1, \ldots, p_r \in \mathbb{N}$ be the distinct prime divisors of n
   call Algorithm 14.48 over $\mathbb{F}_q$ to compute Φ_n

2. use equal-degree factorization to find one irreducible factor $f \in \mathbb{F}_q[x]$ of Φ_n
   $\beta \longleftarrow x \bmod f$

3. determine the distinct $\sim$ equivalence classes $S_1, \ldots, S_t \subseteq \mathbb{Z}_n$ of $1, \ldots, \delta - 1$

4. compute $\beta^2, \beta^3, \ldots, \beta^{\delta-1}$

5. **for** $k = 1, \ldots, t$ **do**

     $i \longleftarrow \min S_k, \quad m \longleftarrow \# S_k$

     compute $\beta^{2i}, \ldots, \beta^{(2m-1)i}$

     use Exercise 12.10 to compute the minimal polynomial $g_k \in \mathbb{F}_q[x]$
     of β^i

6. **return** $g_1 \cdots g_t$

Before analyzing the algorithm, we give an example. Let $1 \leq i < \delta$ and $l = \mathrm{ord}(\beta^i)$. By Lemma 14.50, the degree of the minimal polynomial of β^i over $\mathbb{F}_q$ is $m = \mathrm{ord}_l(q)$ and its roots are precisely $\beta^i, \beta^{iq}, \ldots, \beta^{iq^{m-1}}$, and $\{i, iq, \ldots, iq^{m-1}\}$ is the $\sim$ equivalence class of i in step 3.

EXAMPLE 14.51 (continued). We take $\delta = 7$, corresponding to the fourth row in Table 7.1. The distinct $\sim$ equivalence classes of $1, \ldots, 6$ are

$$S_1 = \{1, 2, 4, 8\}, \quad S_2 = \{3, 6, 9, 12\}, \quad S_3 = \{5, 10\}.$$

Suppose that we have $f = x^4 + x + 1$ in step 2. Then $g_1 = f$ in step 5, $g_2 = \Phi_5$ ($\beta^3, \beta^6, \beta^9, \beta^{12}$ are precisely the primitive 5th roots of unity), and $g_3 = \Phi_3$ (β^5, β^{10} are the primitive 3rd roots of unity). Thus

$$g = g_1 g_2 g_3 = x^{10} + x^8 + x^5 + x^4 + x^2 + x + 1 \in \mathbb{F}_2[x]$$

generates a $\mathrm{BCH}(2, 15, 6)$ code. Its minimal distance is 7. $\diamond$

THEOREM 14.53.

Algorithm 14.52 works correctly as specified and takes $O(\mathsf{M}(nd)(n/d)\log n + \mathsf{M}(n)\log q)$ or $O^{\sim}(n^2 + n\log q)$ operations in $\mathbb{F}_q$, where $d = \mathrm{ord}_n(q)$.

PROOF. Since β is a root of Φ_n, it is a primitive nth root of unity. For $1 \leq j < \delta$, the minimal polynomial of β^j is equal to g_k for the unique $k \in \{1, \ldots, t\}$ such that $j \in S_k$, and hence the least common multiple of the minimal polynomials of all β^j for $1 \leq j < \delta$ is $g_1 \cdots g_t$. This proves correctness.

The cost for step 1 is $O(\mathsf{M}(n)\log n)$ operations in $\mathbb{F}_q$, by Theorem 14.49. Step 2 can be done with $O(\mathsf{M}(nd)(n/d)\log n + \mathsf{M}(n)\log q)$ operations, by the discussion following Corollary 14.29. All powers of β needed in steps 4 and 5 may be computed with at most $\min\{\delta - 2 + t(2d - 2), n - 2\}$ multiplications in $\mathbb{F}_{q^d}$, or $O(\min\{\delta d, n\}\mathsf{M}(d))$ operations in $\mathbb{F}_q$, since $t \leq \delta - 1$. The cost for one minimal polynomial computation in step 5 is $O(\mathsf{M}(m)\log m)$ operations in $\mathbb{F}_q$, by Exercise 12.10. The total cost for steps 4 and 5 is $O(\min\{\delta d, n\}\mathsf{M}(d) + \delta\mathsf{M}(d)\log d)$, since $m \leq d$ in step 5. Finally, multiplying the g_k together may be done with $O(\mathsf{M}(n)\log t)$ operations, by Lemma 10.4. The total cost is dominated by the cost for step 2 since $d \leq \varphi(n) < n$ and $\delta \leq n$. $\square$

Notes. The pioneering works for this area of computer algebra are those of Berlekamp (1967, 1970), Zassenhaus (1969), and Cantor & Zassenhaus (1981).

14.2 and 14.3. The distinct-degree factorization of Section 14.2 appears in Zassenhaus (1969), Kempfert (1969), Knuth (1998), already in the 1969 edition, Berlekamp (1970), and Cantor & Zassenhaus (1981); the latter also contains the equal-degree factorization of Section 14.3.

Actually the basic algorithms go back almost two centuries. Gauß' *Disquisitiones Generales de Congruentiis* were to appear as Part 8 of his *Disquisitiones Arithmeticae*, but did not make it (see page 348). Written in 1797 or 1798, but not quite polished to the Master's usual high gloss, his hand-written notes were published in his Nachlass (Gauß 1863a, 1863b). In article 370, Gauß writes: *Sit itaque X functio, quae nullos amplius divisores aequales involvit. Supra vidimus, $x^p - x$ esse productum ex omnibus functionibus primis unius dimensionis. Sit ξ divisor communis maximae dimensionis functionum X et $x^p - x$, erit ξ productum ex omnibus divisoribus ipsius X unius dimensionis et $\frac{X}{\xi}$ huiusmodi divisores non amplius habebit. Quodsi autem inveniatur, functiones X et $x^p - x$ esse inter se primas, X nullum divisorem unius dimensionis habebit adeoque congruentia $X \equiv 0$ radices reales non habebit. Porro quoniam $x^{pp} - x$ est productum ex omnibus functionibus primis duarum dimensionum uniusque, divisor communis maximae dimensionis functionum $x^{pp} - x$ et $\frac{X}{\xi}, \xi'$ involvet omnes divisores ipsius X, qui sunt duarum dimensionum. Hinc ulterius progrediendo perspicitur, X hoc modo in factores ξ, ξ', ξ'' etc. resolvi, qui continent respective omnes divisores unius, duarum, trium etc. dimensionum*[1].

The algorithm was found independently and first published by Galois (1830) (who forgot to say that the gcd has to be removed before the next step and the possibility that f' might be zero). Serret's (1866) book contains a correct version of Galois's algorithm. Arwin's (1918) paper contains many of the modern ideas on factorization, including this algorithm. Since Cantor & Zassenhaus (1981) it is a staple of modern computer algebra.

Theorem 14.2 is in Gauss (1863b), article 353, for a prime q. Galois (1830) also discovered and was the first to publish it. In his article 372, Gauß begins with the simplest case of equal-degree factorization, where all factors are linear. He points out the analogy with factoring integers, but ends on a somewhat helpless note: *Sed huic rei inhaerere nolumus, nam calculator exercitatus principia probe assecutus, quando opus est, facile artificia particularia reperiet*[2].

Legendre (1785) already knew the basics of the probabilistic root finding method, via Algorithm 14.10. He suggests (§§25–28) splitting f via $\gcd(f, x^{(A-1)/2} \pm 1)$, where A is a prime, and to translate the variable x if necessary: *On cherchera [...] la valeur de $x^{\frac{A-1}{2}}$ exprimée en puissances de x inférieures à x^n, & on égalera cette valeur à $+1$ & -1 successivement. [...] Toutes les fois que l'équation proposée aura des racines de deux espèces,*

---

[1] Let X be a polynomial that has no further multiple divisors. We have seen above that $x^p - x$ is the product of all irreducible polynomials of degree one. If ξ is the greatest common divisor of the polynomials X and $x^p - x$, then ξ will be the product of all divisors of X of degree one, and X/ξ will not have such factors any more. But if it is found that the polynomials X and $x^p - x$ are coprime, then X will have no divisor of degree one and hence the congruence $X \equiv 0$ will have no real [integer] roots. Moreover, since $x^{p^2} - x$ is the product of all irreducible polynomials of degrees two or one, the greatest common divisor ξ' of $x^{p^2} - x$ and X/ξ will contain all divisors of X of degree two. Continuing from here, one sees that X will be factored in this manner into factors ξ, ξ', ξ'' etc., which contain all [irreducible] divisors of degree one, two, three etc., respectively.

[2] We do not want to expand on this question, since a skilled calculator, well versed in these principles, will easily find special tricks when needed.

les unes au nombre de p, donnant $x^{\frac{A-1}{2}} = 1$, *les autres au nombre de q, donnant* $x^{\frac{A-1}{2}} = -1$; *la séparation en sera faite par la méthode précédente.* [...] *On peut faire* $x = y \pm k, k$ *étant à volonté, & résoudre l'équation en y par les mêmes principes.*[3] Euler (1758/59) proved Lemma 14.6 (ii), and Euler (1754/55) showed Lemma 14.7 (i), both in the case where q is prime. He introduced the terminology of *residuum* and *non-residuum*; sometimes even in the modern literature one finds the unfortunate *nonresidue* for a *nonsquare*. Legendre (1798) also proves Lemma 14.6 (ii) (Théorème 134, page 196).

The history of factorization algorithms involves many more people; see the references in the surveys of Kaltofen (1982, 1990, 1992) and von zur Gathen & Panario (1999), and in Shparlinski's (1992, 1999) treatises. Other early algorithms are by Prange (1959), Lloyd (1964), Lloyd & Remmers (1966), and Willett (1978). The survey by Slisenko (1981) mentions unpublished algorithms by Skopin and Faddeev, apparently found in the late 1960s.

If each $\deg g_i$ in Algorithm 14.3 is 0 or i, then the distinct-degree factorization is already the complete factorization of f. How often does this happen? We consider monic random polynomials in $\mathbb{F}_q[x]$ of degree n. Then, when n is fixed and $q \longrightarrow \infty$, the probability goes to $e^{-\gamma} \approx 56\%$ for large n, and for q fixed and $n \longrightarrow \infty$, this probability tends to a limit $L(q)$, with $66.56\% \approx L(2) > L(q) > e^{-\gamma}$ for all $q \geq 3$. This was shown by Flajolet, Gourdon & Panario (1996), who give further results on the distribution of factor degrees of random polynomials and the average case analysis of factoring algorithms. Similar and related results are in Knopfmacher & Knopfmacher (1993), Knopfmacher (1995), Knopfmacher & Warlimont (1995), Gourdon (1996), Gao & Panario (1997), Panario (1997), Panario, Gourdon & Flajolet (1998), Panario & Richmond (1998), and Panario & Viola (1998).

Gourdon (1996), Panario (1997), and Panario, Gourdon & Flajolet (1998) give results about the distributions of the degrees of the largest and the second largest irreducible factor of a random polynomial in $\mathbb{F}_q[x]$.

In general, an isomorphism between finite fields $\mathbb{F}_q \cong \mathbb{F}_p[x]/\langle f \rangle$ and $\mathbb{F}_q \cong \mathbb{F}_p[x]/\langle g \rangle$, where $f, g \in \mathbb{F}_p[x]$ are irreducible of degree n and $q = p^n$, can be obtained by mapping $x \bmod f$ to a root of f in $\mathbb{F}_p[x]/\langle g \rangle$. Lenstra (1991) shows that such an isomorphism can even be constructed in deterministic polynomial time.

Instead of the norm $N(\alpha) = \alpha^{q^{d-1}+q^{d-2}+\cdots+1}$, one can also use the trace $T(\alpha) = \alpha^{q^{d-1}} + \alpha^{q^{d-2}} + \cdots + \alpha$ in equal-degree factorization; see McEliece (1969), Berlekamp (1970), Camion (1981, 1982, 1983), and von zur Gathen & Shoup (1992). Both functions have the crucial property that $N(\alpha), T(\alpha) \in \mathbb{F}_q$ for all $\alpha \in \mathbb{F}_{q^d}$. The trace also works in characteristic 2 (Exercise 14.16) where it is more tricky to apply the norm for factoring.

14.6. Gauss (1863b), article 368, basically describes the squarefree part algorithm 14.19, but does not deal with the difficulty when the characteristic divides all exponents (and the editor Dedekind repeats the incorrect statement). Lagrange (1769), §15, notes that $f / \gcd(f, f')$ has the same roots as f, but each with multiplicity one (over $\mathbb{C}$).

Algorithm 14.21 is from Yun (1976). For a random polynomial in $\mathbb{F}_q[x]$ of degree n, the expected degree of the squarefree part is asymptotically about $n - 1/q$ (Flajolet, Gourdon & Panario 1996).

---

[3] One expands [...] $x^{(A-1)/2}$ in powers of x less than x^n, and sets this value equal to 1 and to -1. [...] Whenever the original equation has roots of both types [both squares and nonsquares], say p of the first type, satisfying $x^{(A-1)/2} = 1$ and q of the other type, satisfying $x^{(A-1)/2} = -1$, the separation of these types is achieved by the preceding method. [...] One can set $x = y \pm k$, k being arbitrary, and solve the equation in y by the same principles.

We have already noted that (4), saying that a polynomial with vanishing derivative over a finite field of characteristic $p > 0$ is a pth power, is not true for arbitrary fields of characteristic p. In fact, over sufficiently bizarre (but still "computable") fields it is undecidable—in the sense of Turing—whether a polynomial is squarefree or not (von zur Gathen (1984a), based on van der Waerden (1930a) and Fröhlich & Shepherdson (1955–56)). Van der Waerden's result is of particular interest because he has to assume explicitly that an undecidable problem—an "ignorabimus"—exists (this was proven by Turing later in 1937) and because Hilbert's (1930) article in the same volume of the *Mathematische Annalen* ends with Hilbert's credo: *In der Mathematik gibt es kein ignorabimus.*[4]

14.7. The iterated Frobenius algorithm is from von zur Gathen & Shoup (1992). Using fast modular composition as in the irreducibility test 14.36, equal-degree factorization can actually be done with $O(n^{(\omega+1)/2} + \mathsf{M}(n)\log r \log q)$ operations in $\mathbb{F}_q$. Huang & Pan's (1998) fast rectangular matrix multiplication method reduces the first summand from $n^{1.688}$ to $n^{1.667}$; see Notes 12.2.

14.8. The first pioneering random polynomial-time algorithms, based on linear algebra, are due to Berlekamp (1967, 1970). The matrix Q was already used by Petr (1937) who determined the characteristic polynomial of $Q - I$ and gave a distinct-degree factorization method using Q as representing the Frobenius automorphism. Schwarz (1939, 1940, 1956, 1960, 1961) and Butler (1954) used Q in various algorithms, for example to compute the number of factors of a given degree. Camion (1980) coined the term *Berlekamp algebra* for the kernel of β.

Berlekamp (1970) introduced the $(q - 1)/2$ trick into modern polynomial factorization; Legendre already stated it in 1785.

A different linear algebra based method for factoring polynomials in $\mathbb{F}_q[x]$ was developed by Niederreiter (1993a, 1993b, 1994a), Göttfert (1994), and Niederreiter & Göttfert (1993, 1995); see Niederreiter (1994b) for an overview. The method turned out to be closely related to Berlekamp's algorithm. Gao & von zur Gathen (1994) showed how to combine it with Wiedemann's method. The special case where q is prime is discussed in Exercise 14.42.

Kaltofen & Shoup (1998) have found clever improvements to the factorization methods in this chapter that yield algorithms whose dependence on the degree of the polynomial to be factored is less than quadratic, namely $O(n^{1.815}(\log q)^{0.407})$ operations in $\mathbb{F}_q$. For practical purposes, they recommend a $O^{\sim}(n^{2.5} + n \log q)$ version of their method.

As Kaltofen and Shoup say in their "Note added in proof", their estimates can be improved slightly by combining them with the fast rectangular matrix multiplication algorithm of Huang & Pan (1998). This does not require any new algorithmic idea. As it is not in the literature, we briefly explain such an improvement, assuming familiarity with both papers. Theorem 10.2 of Huang & Pan gives an upper bound on $\omega(1, 1, r)$, which is defined so that an $n \times n$ times $n \times n^r$ matrix product can be calculated with $O(n^{\omega(1,1,r)})$ arithmetic operations. This bound contains two parameters l and b. We set $l = 7$ and $b = -0.00191r + 0.03551$ in their bound and obtain a function $\varphi(r)$ with $\omega(1, 1, r) \leq \varphi(r)$. Then one verifies that $\varphi(r) \leq 0.95732r + 1.42261$ for $1.36437 \leq r \leq 1.67555$. In Lemma 3 of Kaltofen & Shoup (1998), the dominating cost is a $t \times t$ times $t \times t^r$ matrix multiplication (more exactly, its transpose) with $t = n^{1/r}$ and $r = 1/(1 - \beta/2)$, for a parameter β. The cost for their algorithm is then $O^{\sim}(n^{\omega(1,1,r)/r} + n^{1+\beta+x})$, where $x = \log_n \log_2 q$, as in

---

[4] There is no undecidable problem in mathematics.

Figure 14.9. Using fast square matrix multiplication and the Coppersmith & Winograd exponent, we have $\omega(1,1,r) \leq r - 1 + \omega(1,1,1) \leq r + 1.375477$. Equating the two exponents of n yields the value of β which minimizes the cost and provides the upper bound of $0.407x + 1.815$ given in Kaltofen & Shoup (1998). Substituting the better linear bound on $\omega(1,1,r)$ for fast rectangular matrix multiplication from above and equating exponents, we find the upper bound $0.41565x + 1.80636$, as in Figure 14.9. The required values of r all lie within the interval given above.

This estimate is not the best that one can get from the methods of Kaltofen & Shoup and Huang & Pan, but it is not clear to us how to obtain a simple explicit description of the running time that results from combining these methods in an optimal way. We do not claim that calculations as the above are of much value for practical purposes.

For large fields of small characteristic, say $\mathbb{F}_{2^k}$, Kaltofen & Shoup (1997) present even faster solutions by applying variants of the iterated Frobenius algorithm 14.26 over the prime field. The natural cost measure now is to count word operations; as an example, they achieve $O(n(\log q)^{1.688})$ word operations when $k = \lceil n^{1.5} \rceil$.

14.9. The worst-case and average upper bounds on $\delta(n)$ are in Hardy & Wright (1985), §22.10. An exact formula for $I(n,q)$ and the approximation q^n/n are in Gauss (1863b), articles 344–347; the slightly sharper bound

$$\frac{q^n}{n} - \frac{q(q^{n/2} - 1)}{(q-1)n} \leq I(n,q) \leq \frac{q^n - q}{n}$$

for $n \geq 2$ is in Lidl & Niederreiter (1997), Theorem 3.25 and Exercises 3.26 and 3.27. Algorithm 14.36 is due to Rabin (1980b), and Algorithm 14.40 to Ben-Or (1981). Lemma 14.41 was stated in Ben-Or (1981) and is proven in the solution to Exercise 7.32 of Bach & Shallit (1996). Panario & Richmond (1998) give a precise analysis of the implied constant. The expected minimal degree has a large variance, namely about cn for some constant $c \approx 0.5568$. Shepp & Lloyd (1966) proved a similar result about permutations, namely that the expected length of the shortest cycle of a random permutation on n letters is $O(\log n)$. Panario & Viola (1998) give an analysis of Rabin's algorithm. The estimate of the probability that a random polynomial over a finite field with no small factors is irreducible is from Gao & Panario (1997).

Galois (1830) proposed a probabilistic approach to finding irreducible polynomials over finite fields; see the quote at the beginning of this chapter. The asymptotically fastest method for computing irreducible polynomials is in Shoup (1994), using $O^\sim(n^2 + n\log q)$ operations in $\mathbb{F}_q$.

Further notes. The central open question in the theory of factoring polynomials over finite fields is: can this be done in deterministic polynomial time? We recall that the distinct-degree algorithm 14.3 is deterministic, but the equal-degree algorithm 14.10 is probabilistic. Thus we may assume $f \in \mathbb{F}_q[x]$ to be equal-degree. Berlekamp (1970) significantly simplified the problem: we may assume that q is a prime, and that f has only linear factors (see Exercise 14.40). Thus the question is the following:

> Given $f \in \mathbb{F}_p[x]$, of degree $n \leq p$, which is known to have n distinct roots in $\mathbb{F}_p$, and where p is prime, can we find these roots with a number of operations that is polynomial in n and $\log p$?

Several special cases have been solved: when $p - 1$ has only small prime factors (so that $p - 1$ is **smooth**, see Section 19.5) (Moenck 1977a, von zur Gathen 1987, Mignotte &

Schnorr 1988), when $\Phi_k(p)$ is smooth for some cyclotomic polynomial $\Phi_k \in \mathbb{Z}[y]$ (Bach, von zur Gathen & Lenstra 1998), when f is cyclotomic when considered in $\mathbb{Q}[x]$ or, more generally, has commutative Galois group (Huang 1985, Rónyai 1989), or when n is small (Rónyai 1988). The most general result is Evdokimov's (1994) algorithm with an almost polynomial number of word operations $(n^{\log n} \log p)^{O(1)}$. All these results assume the Extended Riemann Hypothesis (ERH; see Notes 18.4). Irreducible polynomials can be computed in deterministic polynomial time under the ERH (Adleman & Lenstra 1986).

We stress that a solution of this interesting problem is unlikely to affect the practice of factoring, since there the probabilistic algorithms are just fine.

Exercises.

14.1 (i) Let $\mathbb{F}_q$ be a finite field with q elements. Prove **Wilson's theorem** $\prod_{a \in \mathbb{F}_q^\times} a = -1$. Hint: Every $a \in \mathbb{F}_q^\times$ different from ± 1 has $a^{-1} \neq a$.
(ii) Prove a converse of Wilson's theorem: If n is an integer such that $(n-1)! \equiv -1 \bmod n$, then n is prime.

14.2 Suppose $p \geq 5$ is a prime, $f \in \mathbb{F}_p[x]$ has degree 4, and $\gcd(x^p - x, f) = \gcd(x^{p^2} - x, f) = 1$. What can you say about the factorization of f in $\mathbb{F}_p[x]$?

14.3 Trace Algorithm 14.3 on computing the distinct-degree decomposition of the squarefree polynomial

$$f = x^{17} + 2x^{15} + 4x^{13} + x^{12} + 2x^{11} + 2x^{10} + 3x^9 + 4x^8 + 4x^4 + 3x^3 + 2x^2 + 4x \in \mathbb{F}_5[x].$$

Tell from the output only how many irreducible factors of degree i the polynomial f has, for all i.

14.4 Let $q \in \mathbb{N}$ be a prime power.
(i) Use Theorem 14.2 to prove that if r is a prime number, then there are $(q^r - q)/r$ distinct monic irreducible polynomials of degree r in $\mathbb{F}_q[x]$. (Observe that, by Fermat's little theorem 4.9, $(q^r - q)/r$ is an integer.)
(ii) Now suppose that r is a prime power. Find a simple formula for the number of monic irreducible polynomials of degree r over $\mathbb{F}_q$.

14.5 Let $p \in \mathbb{N}$ be a prime and $f \in \mathbb{Z}[x]$ monic of degree n. Prove that the congruence $f(a) \equiv 0 \bmod p$ has n solutions $a \in \mathbb{Z}_p$ if and only $f \bmod p$ is a factor of $x^p - x$; that is, if and only if $x^p - x = fq + pr$, where q and r have integral coefficients, and where r is a polynomial of degree less than n.

14.6* Let q be a prime power and $f \in \mathbb{F}_q[x]$ squarefree of degree n.
(i) Prove that for $1 \leq a \leq b \leq n$, the polynomial

$$\gcd\left(\prod_{a \leq d < b} x^{q^d} - x, f \right)$$

is the product of all monic irreducible factors of f whose degree divides some number in the interval $\{a, a+1, \ldots, b-1\}$.
(ii) Determine $\gcd\left(\prod_{a \leq d < b} x^{q^b} - x^{q^{b-d}}, f \right)$.
(iii) Consider the following **blocking strategy** for distinct degree factorization. We partition the set $\{1, \ldots, n\}$ of possible degrees of irreducible factors of f into k intervals $I_1 = \{c_0 = 1, 2, \ldots, c_1 - 1\}$, $I_2 = \{c_1, c_1 + 1, \ldots, c_2 - 1\}$, $\ldots$, $I_k = \{c_{k-1}, c_{k-1} + 2, \ldots, c_k - 1 = n\}$, with integers $1 = c_0 < c_1 < c_2 < \cdots < c_k = n+1$. Describe an algorithm which, on input f, computes the polynomials $g_1, \ldots, g_k$ such that g_j is the product of all monic irreducible factors of f with degree in the interval I_j, for $1 \leq j \leq k$.

14.7 Show that -1 is a square in $\mathbb{F}_q^{\times}$ for an odd prime power q if and only if $q \equiv 1 \bmod 4$.

14.8 Let $\mathbb{F}_q$ be a finite field with q elements and $a, b \in \mathbb{F}_q^{\times}$ two nonsquares. Prove that ab is a square. Hint: Lemma 14.7.

14.9 If G is a group and $a, b \in G$, then b is a square root of a if $b^2 = a$.

(i) Prove that every element of a cyclic group G has at most two square roots.

(ii) Find a counterexample to (i) when G is not cyclic.

14.10 We consider $\mathbb{F}_{41}$.

(i) Draw the "squaring graph" in $\mathbb{F}_{41}^{\times}$, the directed graph on vertices $1, \ldots, 40$ with the edge (i, j) present if and only if $i^2 \equiv j \bmod p$, for $1 \leq i, j \leq 40$. Arrange your drawing so that the structure of the graph is easy to see.

(ii) Draw the "cubing graph" ($i^3 \equiv j \bmod p$).

(iii) Draw the "fifth power graph" ($i^5 \equiv j \bmod p$).

(iv) Can you see the qualitative differences in the three graphs above? Can you explain them?

(v) Let q be a prime larger than $1\,000\,000$. What can you say about the "qth power graph" on $\mathbb{F}_{41}^{\times}$?

(vi) How many elements of $\mathbb{F}_{41}^{\times}$ are squares? How many are nonsquares? Same question for cubes and fifth powers.

14.11 This exercise generalizes Lemma 14.6. Let $\mathbb{F}_q$ be a finite field with q elements, and $k \in \mathbb{N}$.

(i) For $q = 13$ and $q = 17$, draw the graph of the cubing map $a \longmapsto a^3$ on $\mathbb{F}_q$, with the elements of $\mathbb{F}_q$ as vertices and an edge $a \longrightarrow b$ present if and only if $a^3 = b$.

(ii) Show that $\operatorname{ord}(a^k) = \operatorname{ord} a / \gcd(k, \operatorname{ord} a)$ for all $a \in \mathbb{F}_q^{\times}$.

(iii) Show that the kth power group homomorphism $\sigma_k \colon \mathbb{F}_q^{\times} \longrightarrow \mathbb{F}_q^{\times}$ is an automorphism if and only if $\gcd(k, q-1) = 1$.

(iv) Conclude that $\ker \sigma_k = \ker \sigma_g$ and $\operatorname{im} \sigma_k = \operatorname{im} \sigma_g$, where $g = \gcd(k, q-1)$.

14.12 The squarefree polynomial

$$
\begin{aligned}
f \;=\; & x^{18} - 7x^{17} + 4x^{16} + 2x^{15} - x^{13} - 7x^{12} + 4x^{11} + 7x^{10} + 4x^9 \\
& - 3x^8 - 3x^7 + 7x^6 - 7x^5 + 7x^4 + 7x^3 - 3x^2 + 5x + 5 \in \mathbb{F}_{17}[x]
\end{aligned}
$$

splits into 3 irreducible factors of degree 6.

(i) How would you check the above statement without factoring f, by computing at most three gcd's? (You need not actually compute the gcd's.)

(ii) Trace the equal-degree factorization algorithm 14.10 on computing these factors.

14.13 Write an efficient probabilistic algorithm that, given a prime p and an $a \in \mathbb{Z}_p^{\times}$, computes the square roots of $a \bmod p$—provided they exist. Apply your algorithm to $p = 2591$ and $a = 1005$.

14.14* This exercise discusses how to find primitive 2^kth roots of unity in $\mathbb{F}_q$, where $q \in \mathbb{N}$ is a prime power such that $2^k \mid q-1$. This is needed for the Fast Fourier Transform over $\mathbb{F}_q$, as discussed in Chapter 8 when q is prime. Since -1 is the only primitive square root of unity, we may assume that $q - 1 = 2^k u$ with $k \geq 2$ and $u \in \mathbb{N}$.

(i) Let $S \subseteq \mathbb{F}_q^{\times}$ be the subgroup of 2^kth roots of unity. What is the order of S, and how many primitive 2^kth roots of unity are there?

(ii) Show that $a^u \in S$ for all $a \in \mathbb{F}_q^{\times}$, and that $b = a^u$ is a primitive 2^kth root of unity with probability $1/2$ if a is chosen uniformly at random.

(iii) Prove that b is a primitive 2^kth root of unity if and only if $b^{2^{k-1}} = -1$.

(iv) Derive a probabilistic algorithm for finding a primitive 2^kth root of unity, and show that it uses an expected number of $O(\log q)$ operations in $\mathbb{F}_q$, or $O(\log q \cdot \mathsf{M}(\log q))$ word operations. Use your algorithm to find a primitive 2^{59}th root of unity for $q = 27 \cdot 2^{59} + 1$. Hint: You may find Exercise 14.11 helpful.

14.15* Show that recursively applying the equal-degree splitting algorithm 14.8 to the smaller factor leads to an algorithm for finding *one* irreducible factor of the input polynomial with an expected running time of $O((d\log q + \log n)\mathsf{M}(n))$ operations in $\mathbb{F}_q$.

14.16* This exercise discusses variants of Algorithms 14.8 and 14.31 for finite fields of characteristic two. For $m \in \mathbb{N}$, we define the mth **trace polynomial** over $\mathbb{F}_2$ by $T_m = x^{2^{m-1}} + x^{2^{m-2}} + \cdots + x^4 + x^2 + x \in \mathbb{F}_2[x]$. Let $q = 2^k$ for some $k \in \mathbb{N}_{>0}$, $f \in \mathbb{F}_q[x]$ squarefree of degree n, with $r \geq 2$ irreducible factors $f_1, \ldots, f_r \in \mathbb{F}_q[x]$, $R = \mathbb{F}_q[x]/\langle f\rangle$, and $R_i = \mathbb{F}_q[x]/\langle f_i\rangle$ and $\chi_i: R \longrightarrow R_i$ with $\chi_i(a \bmod f) = a \bmod f_i$, for all i.

(i) Prove that $x^{2^m} + x = T_m \cdot (T_m + 1)$. Conclude that $T_m(\alpha) \in \mathbb{F}_2$ for any $\alpha \in \mathbb{F}_{2^m}$, and that both $T(\alpha) = 0$ and $T(\alpha) = 1$ occur with probability $1/2$ when α is chosen uniformly at random. Hint: The map induced by T_m is $\mathbb{F}_2$-linear.

(ii) Suppose that all irreducible factors of f have the same degree d. Show that $\chi_i(T_{kd}(\alpha)) \in \mathbb{F}_2$ for all $\alpha \in R$, and conclude that for a uniformly random $\alpha \in R$, we have $T_{kd}(\alpha) \in \mathbb{F}_2$ with probability $2^{1-r} \leq 1/2$.

(iii) Modify the equal-degree splitting algorithm 14.8 so as to work for $q = 2^k$, by computing $b = T_{kd}(a) \bmod f$ in step 3. Prove that the modified algorithm fails with probability at most $1/2$, and that its running time is the same as that of the original algorithm.

(iv) Now let the degrees of the f_i be arbitrary again and $\mathcal{B} \subseteq R$ the Berlekamp subalgebra of R. Show that $\chi_i(T_k(\alpha)) \in \mathbb{F}_2$ for all $\alpha \in \mathcal{B}$, and conclude that for a uniformly random $\alpha \in \mathcal{B}$, we have $T_k(\alpha) \in \mathbb{F}_2$ with probability $2^{1-r} \leq 1/2$.

(v) Modify Berlekamp's algorithm 14.31 so as to work for $q = 2^k$, by computing $b = T_k(a) \bmod f$ in step 6. Prove that the modified algorithm fails with probability at most $1/2$, and that its running time is the same as that of the original algorithm.

14.17** Let q be a prime power and $f \in \mathbb{F}_q[x]$ squarefree of degree n with $r \geq 2$ irreducible factors $f_1, \ldots, f_r$ of degree $d = n/r$. We let $R, R_1, \ldots, R_r$ and the Chinese remainder isomorphism $\chi = \chi_1 \times \cdots \times \chi_r: R \longrightarrow R_1 \times \cdots \times R_r$ be as in Section 14.3. The **norm** on $R_i \cong \mathbb{F}_{q^d}$ is defined by $N(\alpha) = \alpha\alpha^q\alpha^{q^2}\cdots\alpha^{q^{d-1}} = \alpha^{(q^d-1)/(q-1)}$, and we use the same formula to define the norm on R.

(i) Let $\alpha \in R^\times$ be a uniform random element, $\beta = N(\alpha)$, and $1 \leq i \leq r$. Show that $\chi_i(\beta)$ is a root of $x^{q-1} - 1$, and conclude that $\chi_i(\beta)$ is a uniform random element in $\mathbb{F}_q^\times$. Hint: N is a homomorphism of multiplicative groups.

(ii) Provided that $q > r$, what is the probability that the $\chi_i(\beta)$ are distinct for $1 \leq i \leq r$? Prove that this probability is at least $1/2$ if $q - 1 \geq 2(r-1)^2$.

(iii) Let $u, v \in \mathbb{F}_q$ be distinct. Prove that with probability at least $1/2$, $u+t$ is a square and $v+t$ is a nonsquare or vice versa, for a uniformly random $t \in \mathbb{F}_q$. Hint: The map $t \longmapsto (u+t)/(v+t)$ if $t \neq -v$ and $-v \longmapsto 1$ is a bijection of $\mathbb{F}_q$.

(iv) Consider the following variant of Algorithm 14.8, due to Rabin (1980b).

▬▬ ALGORITHM 14.54 Equal-degree splitting. ▬▬▬▬▬▬▬▬▬▬▬▬▬▬▬▬▬
Input: A squarefree monic reducible polynomial $f \in \mathbb{F}_q[x]$ of degree n, where q is an odd prime power, a divisor $d < n$ of n, so that all irreducible factors of f have degree d, and $a \in \mathbb{F}_q[x]$ of degree less than n with $\chi_i(a) \in \mathbb{F}_q$ for all i.
Output: A proper monic factor $g \in \mathbb{F}_q[x]$ of f, or "failure".

1. $g_1 \longleftarrow \gcd(a, f)$
   if $g_1 \neq 1$ and $g_1 \neq f$ **then return** g_1

2. choose $t \in \mathbb{F}_q$ at random

3. **call** the repeated squaring algorithm 4.8 in $R = \mathbb{F}_q[x]/\langle f\rangle$ to compute $b = (a+t)^{(q-1)/2} \bmod f$

4. $g_2 \longleftarrow \gcd(b - 1, f)$
   if $g_2 \neq 1$ and $g_2 \neq f$ **then return** g_2 **else return** "failure" ▬▬▬▬▬

Use (iii) to prove that the failure probability of the algorithm is at most $1/2$ if $a \notin \mathbb{F}_q$.

(v) Use the algorithm from (iv) as a subroutine to create a recursive algorithm for equal-degree factorization, which has the same input specification as the above algorithm and outputs all irreducible factors of f. Prove that the algorithm never halts if $\chi_i(a) = \chi_j(a)$ for some $i \neq j$, and that otherwise, if all $\chi_i(a)$ are distinct elements of $\mathbb{F}_q$, the probability for its recursion depth being more than $k = 1 + \lceil 2\log_2 r \rceil$ is at most $1/2$. Conclude that in the latter case, the number of operations in $\mathbb{F}_q$ is $O(\mathsf{M}(n)\log(qn)\log r)$.

(vi) Now we first compute $a = c^{(q^d-1)/(q-1)}$ rem f for a uniform random polynomial $c \in \mathbb{F}_q[x]$ of degree less than n, and then call the algorithm from (v) for that value of a and stop the recursion at depth k. Prove that with probability at least $1/4$ if $q - 1 \geq 2(r-1)^2$, this method yields the r irreducible factors of f in time $O(d\mathsf{M}(n)\log q + \mathsf{M}(n)\log(qn)\log r)$.

14.18$\longrightarrow$ Use Algorithm 14.13 to factor the polynomial $x^6 + x^3 + x^2 + x + 1 \in \mathbb{F}_2[x]$ into irreducible factors. Show all your steps.

14.19 Let F be a field and $f \in F[x]$ with $f(0) \neq 0$. We recall $\mathrm{rev}(f) = f^* = x^{\deg f}f(1/x)$, the **reversal** (or reciprocal polynomial) of f (Section 9.1). We say that f is **self-reciprocal** if $f = f^*$.

(i) Show that * is multiplicative, so that $(fg)^* = f^*g^*$ for all $g \in F[x]$ with $g(0) \neq 0$.

(ii) Prove that $f(\alpha^{-1}) = 0 \Longleftrightarrow f^*(\alpha) = 0$, for all $\alpha \in F$. Conclude that the set of zeroes of f is closed under inversion if f is self-reciprocal.

(iii) Show that every self-reciprocal polynomial f of odd degree satisfies $f(-1) = 0$.

(iv) Let $f \in F[x]$ with $f(0) \neq 0$ be self-reciprocal and $g \in F[x]$ an irreducible factor of f. Then also g^* is an irreducible factor of f.

(v) The squarefree polynomial $f = (x^{21} + 1)/(x+1) \in \mathbb{F}_2[x]$ has—among others—the following irreducible factors: $x^2 + x + 1$, $x^3 + x + 1$, and $x^6 + x^4 + x^2 + x + 1$. What are the others?

14.20* Let $f \in \mathbb{F}_q[x]$ of degree n be given, and for $a \in \mathbb{F}_q$, let $B_a = \{b \in \mathbb{F}_q : f(b) = a\}$ be the set of preimages of a under the mapping $b \longmapsto f(b)$ induced by f.

(i) Given a, show how to compute $\prod_{b \in B_a}(y - b) \in \mathbb{F}_q[y]$ with $O(\mathsf{M}(n)\log(qn))$ operations in $\mathbb{F}_q$.

(ii) Given a, show how to compute probabilistically B_a with $O(\mathsf{M}(n)\log n\log(qn))$ operations in $\mathbb{F}_q$.

(iii) If the function corresponding to f is bijective (so that $\#B_a = 1$ for all $a \in \mathbb{F}_q$), then f is called a **permutation polynomial**. Use Exercise 14.11 to derive a criterion when $f = x^n$ is a permutation polynomial.

(iv) If f is not a permutation polynomial, then in fact

$$\#\{a : B_a \neq \emptyset\} = \#\mathrm{im}f \leq q\left(1 - \frac{1}{n}\right)$$

(Wan 1993; a weaker result is in von zur Gathen 1991b). Use this fact to derive a probabilistic (Monte Carlo) test for permutation polynomials, taking $O(n\mathsf{M}(n)\log(qn))$ operations in $\mathbb{F}_q$.

14.21 Let $f \in \mathbb{Z}[x]$ be of degree n and max-norm $\|f\|_\infty = A$, and $f = (ux + v)g$, with nonzero $u, v \in \mathbb{Z}$ and $g = \sum_{0 \leq i < n} g_i x^i \in \mathbb{Z}[x]$.

(i) Prove that $|g_i| \leq (i+1)A/|v|$ for $0 \leq i < n - 1$ if $|u| = |v|$, and conclude that then $\|g\|_\infty \leq nA$.

(ii) Now assume that $\alpha = |u/v| < 1$. Show that $|g_i| \leq A(1 - \alpha^{i+1})/(1 - \alpha)|v|$ for $0 \leq i < n - 1$, and conclude that $\|g\|_\infty \leq A$. Prove that the latter also holds if $|u/v| > 1$.

14.22 (i) Use the Leibniz rule to prove (2).

(ii) Conclude that $f/\gcd(f, f') = \prod_{e_i f_i' \neq 0} f_i$.

14.23 Prove or disprove:

(i) The polynomial $x^{1000} + 2 \in \mathbb{F}_5[x]$ is squarefree.

(ii) Let F be a field and $f, g \in F[x]$. Then the squarefree part of fg is the product of the squarefree parts of f and of g.

14.24 (Yun 1977b) Over a field F of characteristic zero, Algorithm 14.19 reduces the problem of computing the squarefree part of a polynomial to a gcd computation.

(i) Show that conversely computing a gcd of two squarefree polynomials $f, g \in F[x]$ can be reduced to computing the squarefree part of a certain polynomial.

(ii) Let $f, g \in F[x]$ be monic nonconstant, with squarefree decompositions $f = \prod_{1 \leq i \leq m} f_i^i$ and $g = \prod_{1 \leq i \leq k} g_i^i$. Show that $\gcd(f, g) = \prod_{1 \leq i \leq \min\{m,k\}} \gcd(f_i \cdots f_m, g_i \cdots g_k)$, and conclude from (i) that computing gcd's can be reduced to computing squarefree decompositions.

14.25 Test the following polynomials for multiple factors in $\mathbb{Q}[x]$.

(i) $x^3 - 3x^2 + 4$,   (ii) $x^3 - 2x^2 - x + 2$.

14.26 Let F be a field of characteristic zero, $f \in F[x]$ monic nonconstant, $g_1, \ldots, g_m \in F[x]$ its squarefree decomposition, $v = f/\gcd(f, f')$, and $w = f'/\gcd(f, f')$.

(i) Prove that $g_i = \gcd(v, w - iv')$ for $1 \leq i \leq m$.

(ii) State and analyze the squarefree factorization algorithm resulting from (i).

14.27* Let $\mathbb{F}_q$ be a finite field of characteristic p, and $f = f_1^{e_1} \cdots f_r^{e_r} \in \mathbb{F}_q[x]$ of degree n, with irreducible and pairwise coprime polynomials $f_1, \ldots, f_r \in \mathbb{F}_q[x]$ and positive $e_1, \ldots, e_r \in \mathbb{N}$.

(i) Show that Algorithm 14.19 returns $v = \prod_{p \nmid e_i} f_i$.

(ii) Prove that $w = \gcd(u, v^n) = \prod_{p \mid e_i} f_i^{e_i}$, and show how to compute it at a cost of $O(\mathsf{M}(n) \log n)$ operations in $\mathbb{F}_q$.

(iii) Derive an algorithm for computing the squarefree part over $\mathbb{F}_q$ by computing a pth root of w and proceeding recursively. Show that this algorithm uses $O(\mathsf{M}(n) \log n + n \log(q/p))$ operations in $\mathbb{F}_q$.

(iv) Let $f = ab^2c^2d^6e^8 \in \mathbb{F}_2[x]$, with irreducible and pairwise coprime polynomials $a, b, c, d, e \in \mathbb{F}_2[x]$. Use your algorithm from (iii) to compute its squarefree part.

14.28 Prove that the squarefree decomposition of a monic polynomial is unique.

14.29 Compute the squarefree decomposition of the following polynomials in $\mathbb{Q}[x]$ and in $\mathbb{F}_3[x]$.

(i) $x^6 - x^5 - 4x^4 + 2x^3 + 5x^2 - x - 2$,

(ii) $x^6 - 3x^5 + 6x^3 - 3x^2 - 3x + 2$,

(iii) $x^5 - 2x^4 - 2x^3 + 4x^2 + x - 2$,

(iv) $x^6 - 2x^5 - 4x^4 + 6x^3 + 7x^2 - 4x - 4$,

(v) $x^6 - 6x^5 + 12x^4 - 6x^3 - 9x^2 + 12x - 4$.

14.30* Let $\mathbb{F}_q$ be a finite field of characteristic p, and $f \in \mathbb{F}_q[x]$ monic and nonconstant with squarefree decomposition $(g_1, \ldots, g_m)$.

(i) Show that Yun's algorithm 14.21 returns the correct result if $m < p$.

(ii) Let $m \geq p$ and show that Algorithm 14.21 when applied to f computes $h_i = \prod_{j \equiv i \bmod p} g_j$ for $1 \leq i < p$ and $h_i = 1$ for $i \geq p$.

(iii) Modify Algorithm 14.21 so as to work correctly also for $m \geq p$. Hint: $f h_1^{-1} h_2^{-2} \cdots h_{p-1}^{-p+1}$ is a pth power. Show that the modified algorithm takes $O(\mathsf{M}(n) \log n + n \log(q/p))$ operations in $\mathbb{F}_q$. Trace the algorithm on the example polynomial from Exercise 14.27.

14.31 Let F be a field, and let $f, g_1, \ldots, g_m \in F[x]$ be monic nonconstant polynomials. Recall that $(g_1, \ldots, g_m)$ is the squarefree decomposition of f if $f = g_1 g_2^2 \cdots g_m^m$, each g_i is squarefree, the g_i are pairwise coprime, and $g_m \neq 1$.

(i) Prove that there is a unique decomposition $f = h_1 \cdots h_m$ such that each h_i is monic, nonconstant, and squarefree, $h_i \mid h_{i-1}$ for $2 \leq i \leq m$, and $h_m \neq 1$.

(ii) Give both decompositions for $f = x^4(x+1)^3$.

(iii) Express the h_i in terms of the g_i and vice versa, and show that both conversions can be computed in time $O(\mathsf{M}(n))$ if $n = \deg f$.

14.32 You are to show that for a prime power q and a positive integer $n \geq 2$, the probability for a random polynomial in $\mathbb{F}_q[x]$ of degree n to be squarefree is $1 - 1/q$. Let s_n denote the number of monic squarefree polynomials of degree n in $\mathbb{F}_q[x]$. Then $s_0 = 1$ and $s_1 = q$.

(i) Prove the recursive formula $\sum_{0 \leq 2k \leq n} q^k s_{n-2k} = q^n$. Hint: Every polynomial $f \in \mathbb{F}_q[x]$ can be uniquely written as $f = g^2 h$ with a squarefree polynomial h.

(ii) Conclude that $s_n = q^n - q^{n-1}$ if $n \geq 2$ by subtracting a suitable multiple of the above formula for $n - 2$ from the formula itself.

14.33 Let F be a field of positive characteristic p and $a \in F$ such that a has no pth root in F. Prove that $x^p - a \in F[x]$ is irreducible. Hint: $f = (x - a^{1/p})^p$ over its splitting field $F(a^{1/p})$. Look at the coefficient of x^{n-1} of a hypothetical factor $g \in F[x]$ of degree n of f.

14.34 Let $\mathbb{F}_q$ be a finite field with q elements, $f \in \mathbb{F}_q[x]$ nonconstant, and $\xi = x^q \bmod f \in R = \mathbb{F}_q[x]/\langle f \rangle$. Prove or disprove that $\alpha^q = \check{\xi}(\alpha)$ for all $\alpha \in R$.

14.35* Find "small" constants $c_1, c_2 \in \mathbb{Q}$ such that the running time of the iterated Frobenius algorithm 14.26 is at most $(c_1 n/d + c_2)\mathsf{M}(d)\log_2 d + O(n\log d)$ additions and multiplications in R when n and d are powers of 2. Hint: Exercise 10.2.

14.36* Let q be a prime power, $f \in \mathbb{F}_q[x]$ of degree n, and $R = \mathbb{F}_q[x]/\langle f \rangle$.

(i) Consider the following algorithm for computing the norm $N_d(\alpha) = \alpha \alpha^q \cdots \alpha^{q^{d-1}}$ for $\alpha \in R$ and a power of two $d < n$.

━━━ ALGORITHM 14.55 Norm computation. ━━━━━━━━━━━━━━━━━━━━━━━━━━

Input: $f \in \mathbb{F}_q[x]$ of degree n, a power of two $d \in \mathbb{N}$ with $d \leq n$, $\xi^q \in R = \mathbb{F}_q[x]/\langle f \rangle$, where $\xi = x \bmod f \in R$, and $\alpha \in R$.

Output: $N_d(\alpha) \in R$.

1. $\gamma_0 \longleftarrow \xi^q, \quad \delta_0 \longleftarrow \xi, \quad l \longleftarrow \log_2 d$

2. **for** $1 \leq i \leq l$ **do**

           call the modular composition algorithm 12.3 to compute $\gamma_i = \check{\gamma}_{i-1}(\gamma_{i-1})$ and $\check{\delta}_{i-1}(\gamma_{i-1})$

           $\delta_i \longleftarrow \delta_{i-1} \cdot \check{\delta}_{i-1}(\gamma_{i-1})$

3. **return** δ_l ━━

Prove that the algorithm works correctly and takes $O((n^{(\omega+1)/2} + n^{1/2}\mathsf{M}(n))\log d)$ operations in $\mathbb{F}_q$. Compare this to the time for computing the norm by employing the iterated Frobenius algorithm 14.26.

(ii) Modify the algorithm so as to also work when d is not necessarily a power of two.

(iii) Design a similar algorithm for computing the trace $T_d(\alpha) = \alpha + \alpha^q + \cdots + \alpha^{q^{d-1}}$ of $\alpha \in R$.

14.37 Let q be a prime power, $f = f_1 \cdots f_r \in \mathbb{F}_q[x]$ squarefree, with monic irreducible and pairwise coprime $f_1, \ldots, f_r \in \mathbb{F}_q[x]$, and $\mathcal{B} \subseteq \mathbb{F}_q[x]/\langle f \rangle$ the Berlekamp algebra of f. Prove that the "Lagrange interpolants" $l_1, \ldots, l_r \in \mathbb{F}_q[x]$ of degree less than $\deg f$ and with $l_i \equiv 0 \bmod f_j$ if $j \neq i$ and $l_i \equiv 1 \bmod f_i$ are a basis of $\mathcal{B}$.

14.38* Let $f = f_1 \cdots f_r \in \mathbb{F}_2[x]$ be squarefree of degree n, with $f_1, \ldots, f_r \in \mathbb{F}_2[x]$ monic irreducible and pairwise coprime, $\mathcal{B} \subseteq \mathbb{F}_2[x]/\langle f \rangle$ its Berlekamp algebra, and $b_1 \bmod f, \ldots, b_r \bmod f$ a basis of $\mathcal{B}$, with all $b_i \in \mathbb{F}_2[x]$ of degree less than n.

(i) Show that for $1 \leq i \leq r$, there exist indices j, k such that $f_i \mid b_j$ and $f_i \nmid b_k$.

(ii) Let $f = g_1 \cdots g_s$ be a partial factorization of f, with all g_j monic nonconstant and pairwise coprime, and $1 \leq i \leq r$. Use Exercise 11.4 to show that

$$\gcd(b_i, g_1), \frac{g_1}{\gcd(b_i, g_1)}, \ldots, \gcd(b_i, g_s), \frac{g_s}{\gcd(b_i, g_s)}$$

can be computed using $O(\mathsf{M}(n) \log n)$ operations in $\mathbb{F}_2$ (we call this a refinement with b_i).

(iii) Show that by successively refining partial factorizations of f with $b_1, \ldots, b_r$, starting with the trivial factorization $f = f$, we obtain all irreducible factors of f in time $O(r \cdot \mathsf{M}(n) \log n)$.

14.39* Let $p \in \mathbb{N}$ be prime and $q = p^k$ for some positive $k \in \mathbb{N}$, $f \in \mathbb{F}_q[x]$ monic squarefree of degree n, and $R = \mathbb{F}_q[x]/\langle f \rangle$. We may replace the Frobenius endomorphism $\alpha \longmapsto \alpha^q$ of R over $\mathbb{F}_q$ in Berlekamp's algorithm 14.31 by the **absolute Frobenius endomorphism** $\alpha \longmapsto \alpha^p$ of R over the prime field $\mathbb{F}_p$. Analyze this variant and compare its expected running time to that of the original algorithm.

14.40* It is clear that finding roots of polynomials is a special case of factoring polynomials. This exercise shows conversely how factoring over a finite field can be reduced to root finding over the prime field. Let $q = p^k$ be a prime power for some positive $k \in \mathbb{N}$, $f \in \mathbb{F}_q[x]$ monic squarefree of degree n, $R = \mathbb{F}_q[x]/\langle f \rangle$, and $\mathcal{B} = \{a \bmod f \in R : a^p \equiv a \bmod f\} \subseteq R$ the absolute Berlekamp subalgebra (see Exercise 14.39).

(i) Let $b \in \mathbb{F}_q[x]$ such that $b \bmod f \in \mathcal{B}$. Prove that $f = \prod_{a \in \mathbb{F}_p} \gcd(f, b - a)$.

(ii) Let y be a new indeterminate and $r = \mathrm{res}_x(f, b - y) \in \mathbb{F}_q[y]$. Show that r has some roots in $\mathbb{F}_p$, and that any root of r in $\mathbb{F}_p$ leads to a nontrivial factor of f if $b \notin \mathbb{F}_p$.

(iii) Make this to a deterministic polynomial-time reduction from factoring in $\mathbb{F}_q[x]$ to root finding in $\mathbb{F}_p[x]$.

14.41* Let q be a prime power, $f \in \mathbb{F}_q[x]$ monic squarefree of degree n, and $R = \mathbb{F}_q[x]/\langle f \rangle$, as usual.

(i) Show that if f splits into r irreducible factors of degrees $d_1, \ldots, d_r$, then $\mathrm{lcm}\{x^{d_i} - 1 : 1 \leq i \leq r\}$ is the minimal polynomial of the matrix Q representing the Frobenius endomorphism $\alpha \longmapsto \alpha^q$ on R. Hint: Start with $r = 1$. Conclude that f is irreducible if and only if the minimal polynomial of Q is $x^n - 1$.

(ii) Use (i) and Exercise 12.15 to design a Monte Carlo test whether f is irreducible. Your test should take $O(n \cdot \mathsf{M}(n) \log q)$ operations in $\mathbb{F}_q$ if q is "large enough".

14.42** This exercise discusses the easiest case of another factoring method based on linear algebra, due to Niederreiter (see Notes 14.8). Let $p \in \mathbb{N}$ be prime.

(i) Prove that for all rational functions $y \in \mathbb{F}_p(x)$, the $(p-1)$st derivative $y^{(p-1)}$ is a pth power.

(ii) Show that for any polynomial $h \in \mathbb{F}_p[x]$, the rational function $y = h'/h$ is a solution of the differential equation

$$y^{(p-1)} + y^p = 0. \tag{13}$$

Hint: Use the Leibniz rule and Wilson's theorem (Exercise 14.1).

(iii) Prove that if $y = g/h \in \mathbb{F}_p(x)$ satisfies (13), with nonzero coprime $g, h \in \mathbb{F}_p[x]$ and h monic, then $\deg g < \deg h$ and h is squarefree.

(iv) Let g, h be as in (iii) and E the splitting field of h over $\mathbb{F}_p$. By partial fraction decomposition, there exist $d_1, \ldots, d_n \in E$ such that

$$\frac{g}{h} = \sum_{1 \leq i \leq n} \frac{d_i}{x - \lambda_i},$$

where $\lambda_1, \ldots, \lambda_n \in E$ are the (distinct) roots of h. Show that $y = d_i/(x - \lambda_i)$ solves (13) for $1 \leq i \leq n$. Hint: Uniqueness of partial fraction decomposition. Prove that $d_i = d_j \in \mathbb{F}_p$ if λ_i, λ_j are roots of the same irreducible factor of h, and conclude that

$$\frac{g}{h} = \sum_{1 \leq j \leq r} c_j \frac{h'_j}{h_j}$$

for some $c_1, \ldots, c_r \in \mathbb{F}_p$, where $h_1, \ldots, h_r$ are the distinct monic irreducible factors of h.

(v) Let $f \in \mathbb{F}_p[x]$ be monic of degree n and

$$\mathcal{N} = \{g \in \mathbb{F}_p[x] : \deg g < n \text{ and } y = \frac{g}{f} \text{ solves (13)}\}.$$

Prove that $f_1'/f_1, \ldots, f_r'/f_r$ is a basis of $\mathcal{N}$ if $f = f_1^{e_1} \cdots f_r^{e_r}$ is the factorization of f into irreducible polynomials.

(vi) Now let f be squarefree and $\mathcal{B} \subseteq \mathbb{F}_q[x]/\langle f \rangle$ the Berlekamp algebra of f. Prove that the map $\varphi : \mathcal{N} \longrightarrow \mathcal{B}$ with $\varphi(g) = gf'^{-1} \bmod f$ is a vector space isomorphism. Hint: Consider $\varphi(g) \bmod f_i$ for all i.

(vii) Assume that $p > 2$. Let f as in (vi), $g = \sum_{1 \leq i \leq r} c_i f f_i'/f_i \in \mathcal{N}$, and $S \subseteq \mathbb{F}_p^\times$ the set of squares. Show that

$$\gcd(g^{(p-1)/2} - (f')^{(p-1)/2}, f) = \prod_{c_i \in S} f_i,$$

and conclude that this gcd is nontrivial with probability at least $1/2$ if $c_1, \ldots, c_r$ are chosen uniformly at random in $\mathbb{F}_p$ and $\gcd(g, f) = 1$.

14.43** This exercise turns the theory from Exercise 14.42 into an algorithm for $p = 2$. Let $f = \sum_{0 \leq i \leq n} f_i x^i \in \mathbb{F}_2[x]$ be monic squarefree of degree n.

(i) Prove that $\mathcal{N} = \{g \in \mathbb{F}_2[x] : \deg g < n \text{ and } (fg)' = g^2\}$.

(ii) Let $N \in \mathbb{F}_2^{n \times n}$ be the matrix of the linear operator $g \longmapsto \left((fg)'\right)^{1/2}$ on the vector space of all polynomials in $\mathbb{F}_2[x]$ of degree less than n with respect to the polynomial basis $x^{n-1}, x^{n-2}, \ldots, x, 1$, so that

$$\left(f \sum_{0 \leq i < n} g_i x^i\right)' = \left(\sum_{0 \leq i < n} h_i x^i\right)^2 \iff N \cdot \begin{pmatrix} g_{n-1} \\ \vdots \\ g_0 \end{pmatrix} = \begin{pmatrix} h_{n-1} \\ \vdots \\ h_0 \end{pmatrix}.$$

Prove that

$$N = \begin{pmatrix} f_n & 0 & 0 & 0 & 0 & 0 & \cdots \\ f_{n-2} & f_{n-1} & f_n & 0 & 0 & 0 & \cdots \\ f_{n-4} & f_{n-3} & f_{n-2} & f_{n-1} & f_n & 0 & \cdots \\ \vdots & & & & & \vdots \end{pmatrix}.$$

(iii) Design an algorithm for factoring f by determining a basis of $\mathcal{N} - I$, where I is the $n \times n$ identity matrix, and using an analog of Exercise 14.38. Prove that it takes $O(n^\omega)$ operations in $\mathbb{F}_2$, like Berlekamp's algorithm.

14.44* Let q be a prime power, $t \in \mathbb{N}$ a prime divisor of $q - 1$, and $a \in \mathbb{F}_q^\times$.

(i) Show that the polynomial $x^t - a \in \mathbb{F}_q[x]$ splits into linear factors if a is a tth power Hint: Use Lemma 8.8.

(ii) Show that $x^t - a$ is irreducible if a is not a tth power Hint: Use (i) for the splitting field of $x^t - a$ and consider the constant coefficient of a hypothetical factor $f \in \mathbb{F}_q[x]$ of $x^t - a$.

(iii) Derive a formula for the probability that a random binomial $x^t - a$ (that is, for random $a \in \mathbb{F}_q^\times$) is irreducible, and compare it to the probability that a random polynomial of degree t in $\mathbb{F}_q[x]$ is irreducible.

14.45 Prove Lemma 14.47.

14.46 This exercise discusses a useful tool from number theory: **Möbius inversion**. Let the Möbius function μ be defined as in (10).

(i) Prove that μ is multiplicative, so that $\mu(mn) = \mu(m)\mu(n)$ whenever $m, n \in \mathbb{N}_{>0}$ are coprime.

(ii) Show that $\sum_{d | n} \mu(d) = 0$ if $n > 1$, where the sum is over all positive divisors of n.

(iii) Let R be an arbitrary ring (commutative, with 1) and $f, g \colon \mathbb{N}_{>0} \longrightarrow R$ be two functions such that

$$f(n) = \sum_{d \mid n} g(d) \text{ for } n \in \mathbb{N}_{>0}.$$

Prove that

$$g(n) = \sum_{d \mid n} \mu\left(\frac{n}{d}\right) f(d) = \sum_{d \mid n} \mu(d) f\left(\frac{n}{d}\right) \text{ for } n \in \mathbb{N}_{>0}.$$

(iv) Now assume that

$$f(n) = \prod_{d \mid n} g(d) \text{ for } n \in \mathbb{N}_{>0}.$$

Give a similar formula for g in terms of μ and f as in (iii).

(v) Let $d(n)$ denote the number of positive divisors of $n \in \mathbb{N}_{>0}$. Prove that $\sum_{e \mid n} \mu(n/e) d(e) = 1$ for all positive integers n.

14.47* (Prange 1959) Let $q \in \mathbb{N}$ be a prime power coprime to $n \in \mathbb{N}$. We use the equivalence relation $\sim$ as in (12). Let $S_1, \ldots, S_r$ be the distinct equivalence classes of $\mathbb{Z}_n$ with respect to $\sim$, and $b_i = \sum_{j \in S_i} x^j \in \mathbb{F}_q[x]$ for $1 \leq i \leq r$.

(i) Show that a basis of the Berlekamp algebra $\mathcal{B} \subseteq \mathbb{F}_q[x]/\langle x^n - 1 \rangle$ belonging to the polynomial $x^n - 1$ is given by $b_1 \bmod x^n - 1, \ldots, b_r \bmod x^n - 1$.

(ii) Give an algorithm which computes all irreducible factors of the polynomial $x^n - 1$ in $\mathbb{F}_q[x]$ using $O(\log q \log n + n\mathsf{M}(\log n))$ word operations and an expected number of $O(\mathsf{M}(n)\log(qn)\log r)$ field operations in $\mathbb{F}_q$, in total $O^\sim(n\log^2 q)$ word operations. Hint: Use the method of Exercise 11.4 to split factors already found and perform a similar analysis as in the proof of Theorem 14.11.

Research problem.

14.48 Find a deterministic polynomial-time algorithm for computing a root of a squarefree polynomial $f \in \mathbb{F}_p[x]$ which divides $x^p - x$, where p is a prime number. (Exercise 14.40 implies that then the general problem of factoring polynomials can be solved in deterministic polynomial time.)

The operation of factoring [polynomials]
must be performed by inspection.

Charles Davies (1867)

Tous les effets de la nature ne sont que les résultats
mathématiques d'un petit nombre de lois immuables.[1]

Pierre Simon Laplace (1812)

---

[1] All the effects of nature are only mathematical results of a small number of immutable laws.

15

Hensel lifting and factoring polynomials

In this chapter, we present two modular algorithms for factoring in $\mathbb{Q}[x]$ and $F[x,y]$ for a field F. The first one uses factorization modulo a "big" prime and is conceptually easier, and the second one uses factorization modulo a "small" prime and then "lifts" it to a factorization modulo a power of that prime. The latter is computationally faster and comprises our most powerful employment of the prime power modular approach introduced in Chapter 5.

15.1. Factoring in $\mathbb{Z}[x]$ and $\mathbb{Q}[x]$: the basic idea

Our first goal is to understand the difference between "factoring in $\mathbb{Z}[x]$" and "factoring a polynomial with integer coefficients in $\mathbb{Q}[x]$". The basic fact is that the latter corresponds to factoring primitive polynomials in $\mathbb{Z}[x]$, while the former requires in addition the factoring of an integer, namely the polynomial's content. We rely on the following notions which were introduced in Section 6.2.

Let R be a Unique Factorization Domain (our two main applications are, as usual, $R = \mathbb{Z}$ and $R = F[y]$ for a field F). The **content** $\operatorname{cont}(f)$ of a polynomial $f \in R[x]$ is the greatest common divisor of its coefficients (with the convention that the gcd is positive if $R = \mathbb{Z}$ and monic if $R = F[y]$). The **primitive part** $\operatorname{pp}(f)$ of f is $f/\operatorname{cont}(f) \in R[x]$, and f is **primitive** if $\operatorname{cont}(f) = 1$. Corollary 6.7, a consequence of Gauß' lemma, says that for any $f, g \in R[x]$, we have $\operatorname{cont}(fg) = \operatorname{cont}(f)\operatorname{cont}(g)$ and $\operatorname{pp}(fg) = \operatorname{pp}(f)\operatorname{pp}(g)$. In particular, if f and g are primitive, then so is fg. As a consequence, $R[x]$ is a Unique Factorization Domain, and its primes are the primes of R plus the primitive polynomials in $R[x]$ that are irreducible in $K[x]$, where K is the field of fractions of R.

Thus the relation between factoring polynomials over $\mathbb{Q}$ and over $\mathbb{Z}$ is as follows. If $f \in \mathbb{Z}[x]$ is primitive, then a factorization $f = f_1 \cdots f_k$ into irreducible $f_i \in \mathbb{Q}[x]$ yields a factorization $f = f_1^* \cdots f_k^*$ into irreducible $f_i^* \in \mathbb{Z}[x]$ by multiplying up denominators and then removing contents. On the other hand, any irreducible factorization in $\mathbb{Z}[x]$ is also one in $\mathbb{Q}[x]$. For an arbitrary f the factorization of f is the factorization of the content of f together with the factorization of the primitive part of f. Thus

$$\text{factoring in } \mathbb{Z}[x] \longleftrightarrow \text{factoring in } \mathbb{Q}[x] \text{ plus factoring in } \mathbb{Z}.$$

The best known algorithms for factoring in $\mathbb{Z}$ (Chapter 19) are much less efficient than those for $\mathbb{Q}[x]$ that we present in this and the next chapter. From now on, "factoring in $\mathbb{Z}[x]$" will usually refer to primitive polynomials, for which the part "factoring in $\mathbb{Z}$" is trivial.

The basic idea of the factoring algorithm is as follows. Let $f \in \mathbb{Z}[x]$ be a primitive polynomial to be factored. Using the squarefree part algorithm 14.19 if necessary, we may assume that f is squarefree. We take a "big" prime $p \in \mathbb{Z}$ not dividing the leading coefficient of f and such that $f \bmod p \in \mathbb{F}_p[x]$ is squarefree (we will make precise later what "big" means). Using one of the (probabilistic) algorithms in Chapter 14, we factor f modulo p. If $g \in \mathbb{Z}[x]$ is a factor of f and $g_1, \ldots, g_s$ are the irreducible factors of g modulo p, then we can recover g from them. If f factors as $f = f_1 \cdots f_k$ in $\mathbb{Z}[x]$, then also $\overline{f} = \overline{f_1} \cdots \overline{f_k}$ in $\mathbb{Z}_p[x]$, where the bar means taking each coefficient modulo p. But if the true factor f_1 is irreducible, then $\overline{f_1}$ need not be irreducible, and our factorization modulo p will return all the irreducible modular factors of all f_i, but we will not immediately know which of them belong together (see Figure 15.2).

The following questions arise if we want to turn this sketch into an algorithm.

○ How large do we have to choose p so that we can recover the coefficients of any factor from its image modulo p? The answer has already been given by **Mignotte's bound** 6.33 in Section 6.6.

○ In what range do we have to choose a random p so that $f \bmod p$ is squarefree with sufficiently high probability? The answer to this question is provided by the **resultant theory** from Chapter 6 and the **prime number theorem** in Chapter 18.

○ Finally, the trickiest question is: how can we find the modular factors of $f \bmod p$ that correspond to a true factor of f in $\mathbb{Z}[x]$? Very easy: we simply try all possible **factor combinations**. Unfortunately, this leads to an exponential algorithm in the worst case; examples are given by the **Swinnerton-Dyer polynomials** in Section 15.3. In Chapter 16, we present a method to circumvent this: **short vectors in lattices**.

Our algorithms consist of two stages: a modular factorization stage, where we take either a single big prime or a prime power as modulus, and a second stage where we try to find true factors from modular ones, either by factor combination or with the aid of short vectors in lattices. This is illustrated in Figure 15.1; each of the two variants in the top row may be freely combined with each of the two methods in the bottom row. The next section describes the "big prime" and "factor combination" stages, Sections 15.4 and 15.5 the "prime power" approach, and "short vectors" are treated in Chapter 16.

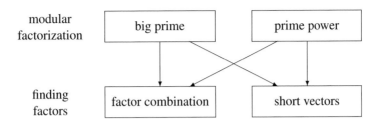

FIGURE 15.1: The building blocks of factoring algorithms for $\mathbb{Z}[x]$.

15.2. A factoring algorithm

Let $f \in \mathbb{Z}[x]$ be squarefree. We first have to understand for which primes p the polynomial $\overline{f} = f \bmod p \in \mathbb{Z}_p[x]$ is squarefree, where the bar denotes the reduction modulo p. We abbreviate the **discriminant** of f as $\mathrm{disc}(f) = \mathrm{res}(f, f')$, where $'$ is the formal derivative. (In the literature, there are other definitions of the discriminant which differ slightly from ours.) Thus Corollary 14.25 says that $\overline{f}$ is squarefree if and only if $\mathrm{disc}(\overline{f}) \neq 0$. From Lemma 6.25 and the fact that $\overline{f'} = \overline{f}'$ (Exercise 9.23), we obtain the following.

LEMMA 15.1. *Let $f \in \mathbb{Z}[x]$ be a nonzero squarefree polynomial, $p \in \mathbb{N}$ a prime not dividing $\mathrm{lc}(f)$, and denote by a bar the reduction modulo p. Then $\overline{f}$ is squarefree if and only if $p \nmid \mathrm{disc}(f)$.*

A closer look at the Sylvester matrix shows that $\mathrm{lc}(f)$ divides $\mathrm{res}(f, f')$ (Exercise 6.41). Hence $\overline{f}$ is squarefree if p does not divide $\mathrm{res}(f, f') \in \mathbb{Z} \setminus \{0\}$; the resultant is nonzero because f is squarefree.

FIGURE 15.2: Factorization patterns in $\mathbb{Z}[x]$ and $\mathbb{F}_p[x]$.

Now let $f = f_1 \cdots f_k$ be the factorization of f into (primitive) irreducible polynomials $f_1, \ldots, f_k$ in $\mathbb{Z}[x]$. Then

$$\overline{f} = \overline{f_1} \cdots \overline{f_k} = \overline{\mathrm{lc}(f)} g_1 \cdots g_r$$

in $\mathbb{F}_p[x]$, where $g_1, \ldots, g_r$ are the monic irreducible factors of $\overline{f}$ in $\mathbb{F}_p[x]$. This is illustrated in Figure 15.2 for $k = 3$ and $r = 7$: the boxes represent irreducible factors, the width of a box corresponds to the degree, and a box in the upper row splits modulo p into the boxes in the lower row of the same color. Suppose that by factoring f modulo p, we have computed all the g_i. Let f_1 be an irreducible factor of f (say, the gray box in the upper row of Figure 15.2). Modulo p some of the g_i's divide f_1 (the gray boxes in the lower row). We let $S \subseteq \{1,\ldots,r\}$ be the set of indices of the irreducible factors of $\overline{f_1}$ (which we do not know). Then

$$\frac{\mathrm{lc}(f)}{\mathrm{lc}(f_1)} f_1 \equiv \mathrm{lc}(f) \prod_{i \in S} g_i \bmod p. \tag{1}$$

If $p/2$ is larger than the Mignotte bound $(n+1)^{1/2} 2^n |\mathrm{lc}(f)| \cdot \|f\|_\infty$, then the coefficients of $\mathrm{lc}(f) f_1 / \mathrm{lc}(f_1)$ are integers less than $p/2$ in absolute value, by Corollary 6.33, and the polynomials in (1) are equal if we use symmetric representatives between $-(p-1)/2$ and $(p-1)/2$ for the elements of $\mathbb{F}_p$. Therefore we can construct f_1 from the g_i's and S.

Unfortunately, there seems to be no easy way to find the set S: in Figure 15.2, we are only given the boxes in the lower row, but do not know which ones have the same color. Trying all subsets of $\{1,\ldots,r\}$ leads to the following algorithm. For compatibility with later algorithms, it has no step numbered 4. We recall the max-norm $\|f\|_\infty = \max_i |f_i|$ and the one-norm $\|f\|_1 = \sum_i |f_i|$ of a polynomial $f = \sum_i f_i x^i \in \mathbb{Z}[x]$.

━━ ALGORITHM 15.2 Factorization in $\mathbb{Z}[x]$ (big prime version). ━━━━━━
Input: A squarefree primitive polynomial $f \in \mathbb{Z}[x]$ of degree $n \geq 1$ with $\mathrm{lc}(f) > 0$ and max-norm $\|f\|_\infty = A$.
Output: The irreducible factors $\{f_1,\ldots,f_k\} \subseteq \mathbb{Z}[x]$ of f.

1. **if** $n = 1$ **then return** $\{f\}$
   $b \longleftarrow \mathrm{lc}(f), \quad B \longleftarrow (n+1)^{1/2} 2^n A b$

2. **repeat**
          choose a random odd prime number p with $2B < p < 4B$
          $\overline{f} \longleftarrow f \bmod p$
   until $\gcd(\overline{f}, \overline{f}') = 1$ in $\mathbb{F}_p[x]$

3. { Modular factorization }
   compute $g_1,\ldots,g_r \in \mathbb{Z}[x]$ of max-norm less than $p/2$ that are nonconstant, monic, and irreducible modulo p, such that $f \equiv bg_1 \cdots g_r \bmod p$

5. { initialize the index set T of modular factors still to be treated, the set G of found factors, and the polynomial f^* still to be factored }
   $T \longleftarrow \{1,\ldots,r\}, \quad s \longleftarrow 1, \quad G \longleftarrow \emptyset, \quad f^* \longleftarrow f$

6. { Factor combination }
   while $2s \leq \#T$ **do**

7.   **for** all subsets $S \subseteq T$ of cardinality $\#S = s$ **do**

8.   compute $g^*, h^* \in \mathbb{Z}[x]$ with max-norm less than $p/2$ satisfying $g^* \equiv b \prod_{i \in S} g_i \bmod p$ and $h^* \equiv b \prod_{i \in T \setminus S} g_i \bmod p$

9.   **if** $\|g^*\|_1 \|h^*\|_1 \leq B$ **then**
$$T \longleftarrow T \setminus S, \quad G \longleftarrow G \cup \{pp(g^*)\},$$
$$f^* \longleftarrow pp(h^*), \quad b \longleftarrow lc(f^*)$$
break the loop 7 and **goto** 6

10. $s \longleftarrow s + 1$

11. **return** $G \cup \{f^*\}$

We recall the multiplication time M (see inside front cover).

THEOREM 15.3.

Algorithm 15.2 works correctly. If $\beta = \log B$, then $\beta \in O(n + \log A)$, and the expected cost of steps 2 and 3 is

$$O\left(\beta^2 \mathsf{M}(\beta) \log \beta + (\mathsf{M}(n^2) + \mathsf{M}(n)\beta) \log n \cdot \mathsf{M}(\beta) \log \beta\right) \text{ or } O^{\sim}(n^3 + \log^3 A)$$

word operations. One execution of steps 8 and 9 takes

$$O((\mathsf{M}(n) \log n + n \log \beta) \mathsf{M}(\beta)) \text{ or } O^{\sim}(n^2 + n \log A)$$

word operations, and there are at most 2^{n+1} iterations.

PROOF. By Lemma 15.1, $f \bmod p$ is squarefree in step 3, since $p > B$ implies that $p \nmid b$.

We show first that the condition in step 9 is true if and only if $g^* h^* = bf^*$. If the latter holds, then $\|g^*\|_1 \|h^*\|_1 \leq B$, by Corollary 6.33. Conversely, let g^* and h^* be as in step 8. Then $g^* h^* \equiv bf^* \bmod p$. Now $\|g^* h^*\|_\infty \leq \|g^* h^*\|_1 \leq \|g^*\|_1 \|h^*\|_1 \leq B < p/2$ implies that both sides of the congruence have coefficients less than $p/2$ in absolute value, and hence they are equal.

For a factor $u \in \mathbb{Z}[x]$ of f, we denote by $\mu(u)$ the number of monic irreducible factors which divide u modulo p; since $\mathbb{F}_p[x]$ is a UFD, these factors form a subset of $\{g_1, \ldots, g_r\}$. We show by induction that the invariants

$$f^* \equiv b \prod_{i \in T} g_i \bmod p, \quad b = lc(f^*), \quad f = f^* \prod_{g \in G} g,$$
each polynomial in G is irreducible, $\qquad\qquad\qquad\qquad$ (2)
f^* is primitive and each of its irreducible factors $u \in \mathbb{Z}[x]$ has $\mu(u) \geq s$

hold each time the algorithm passes through step 6. This is clear initially. So we assume that the invariants hold before step 8, and that the condition in step 9 is true for some subset $S \subseteq T$ of cardinality s. Then $g^* h^* = bf^*$, by the above, and by Gauß' lemma, $pp(g^*)$ is a factor of $pp(bf^*) = f^*$. Since $\mu(g^*) = s$ and $\mu(u) \geq s$ for each irreducible factor u of f^*, $pp(g^*)$ is an irreducible factor of f. The actions taken in step 9 then ensure that the invariants hold the next time through step 6. Now we assume that the condition in step 9 is false for all subsets $S \subseteq T$ of cardinality s, but that f^* has an irreducible factor $g \in \mathbb{Z}[x]$ with $\mu(g) = s$. Then there is a subset $S \subseteq T$ of cardinality s such that $g \equiv lc(g) \prod_{i \in S} g_i \bmod p$, since $\mathbb{F}_p[x]$ is a UFD. We set $h = f^*/g \in \mathbb{Z}[x]$. Then $lc(g) lc(h) = lc(f^*) = b$,

$$lc(h)g \equiv b \prod_{i \in S} g_i \equiv g^* \bmod p, \text{ and } lc(g)h \equiv b \prod_{i \in T \setminus S} g_i \equiv h^* \bmod p.$$

By Mignotte's bound 6.33, the coefficients of $lc(h)g$ and $lc(g)h$ are at most $B < p/2$ in absolute value. Since also $\|g^*\|_\infty, \|h^*\|_\infty < p/2$, we have $lc(h)g = g^*$, $lc(g)h = h^*$, $g^* h^* = bf^*$, and the condition in step 9 is true for that particular subset S of T. This contradiction shows that f^* has no irreducible factor g with $\mu(g) = s$, and step 10 guarantees that the invariants hold again at the next pass through step 6.

It remains to show that f^* is irreducible if $2s > \#T$ in step 6. Let $g \in \mathbb{Z}[x]$ be an irreducible factor of f^* and $h = f^*/g$. By (2), we have $s \leq \mu(g), \mu(h) \leq \#T$ if h is nonconstant. But $\mu(g) + \mu(h) = \#T$, and $s > \#T/2$ implies that $h = \pm 1$ and $f^* = \pm g$ is irreducible.

For the running time estimate, we first note that $b \leq \|f\|_\infty = A$, and hence $\beta \in O(n + \log A)$. In Section 18.4, we show that a random prime as required in step 2 can be found by a probabilistic algorithm using $O(\beta^2 M(\beta) \log \beta)$ word operations, and that $p \nmid disc(f)$ with probability at least $1/2$ (Corollary 18.12). Hence the expected number of iterations of step 2 is at most two. The cost for the gcd is $O(M(n) \log n)$ arithmetic operations in $\mathbb{F}_p$ or $O(M(n) \log n M(\beta) \log \beta)$ word operations. Thus the expected cost of step 2 is $O((\beta^2 + M(n) \log n \log \beta) M(\beta))$ word operations. By Corollary 14.30, step 3 can be done with $O((M(n^2) + M(n)\beta) \log n)$ arithmetic operations in $\mathbb{F}_p$. Each of these in turn takes $O(M(\beta) \log \beta)$ word operations, by Corollary 11.10, and the expected number of word operations for step 3 is $O((M(n^2) + M(n)\beta) \log n \cdot M(\beta) \log \beta)$.

Computing g^* and h^* in step 8 can be done with $O(M(n) \log n)$ additions and multiplications modulo p, by Lemma 10.4, or $O(M(n) \log n M(\beta))$ word operations. The primitive parts in step 9 can be computed with at most n gcds of integers absolutely bounded by B, or $O(n M(\beta) \log \beta)$ word operations. Between two subsequent times that the condition in step 9 is true, there are at most $2^{\#T}$ executions of steps 8 and 9. Now $\#T$ decreases by at least one if the condition is true, and hence the total number of iterations of steps 8 and 9 is at most

$$\sum_{1 \leq i \leq r} 2^i \leq 2^{r+1} \leq 2^{n+1}. \quad \square$$

EXAMPLE 15.4. Let $f = 6x^4 + 5x^3 + 15x^2 + 5x + 4 \in \mathbb{Z}[x]$. Then f is primitive, $n = 4$, $A = 15$, $b = \mathrm{lc}(f) = 6$, and we have $f' = 24x^3 + 15x^2 + 30x + 5$ and $\mathrm{disc}(f) = 19\,250\,814$, so that f is squarefree, and $B = (n+1)^{1/2}2^n Ab = 1440\sqrt{5} \approx 3219.9$. Suppose that we choose $p = 6473 > 2B$ in step 2. Then $p \nmid b$, and f and f' are coprime modulo p. In fact, the only "unlucky" primes for f, with $p \mid \mathrm{lc}(f)$ or $f \bmod p$ not squarefree, are the prime divisors $2, 3, 11, 31$, and 97 of $\mathrm{disc}(f)$.

In step 3, we obtain the modular factorization

$$f \equiv bg_1 g_2 g_3 g_4 = 6(x - 819)(x + 605)(x + 2632)(x + 2977) \bmod p.$$

We now trace steps 8 and 9 for two specific subsets $S \subseteq \{1, \ldots, 4\}$. It turns out that the condition in step 9 is false for all subsets $S \subseteq \{1, \ldots 4\}$ of cardinality $s = 1$, and $f^* = f$ has no linear factor. For $s = 2$ and $S = \{1, 2\}$, we compute

$$
\begin{aligned}
g^* &\equiv bg_1 g_2 = 6(x - 819)(x + 605) \equiv 6x^2 - 1284x - 1863 \bmod p, \\
h^* &\equiv bg_3 g_4 = 6(x + 2632)(x + 2977) \equiv 6x^2 + 1289x - 615 \bmod p
\end{aligned}
$$

in step 8. Obviously $\|g^*\|_1 \|h^*\|_1 \geq \|g^*\|_\infty \|h^*\|_\infty = 1863 \cdot 1289 > B$ in step 9, and in fact $g^* h^* \neq bf^*$, which can be seen by comparing the constant coefficients

$$g^*(0)h^*(0) = (-1863) \cdot (-615) \neq 24 = 6 \cdot 4 = bf^*(0).$$

On the other hand, if we take $S = \{1, 4\}$, then

$$
\begin{aligned}
g^* &\equiv bg_1 g_4 = 6(x - 819)(x + 2977) \equiv 6x^2 + 2x + 2 \bmod p, \\
h^* &\equiv bg_2 g_3 = 6(x + 605)(x + 2632) \equiv 6x^2 + 3x + 12 \bmod p
\end{aligned}
$$

in step 8, $\|g^*\|_1 \|h^*\|_1 = 10 \cdot 21 < B$ in step 9, and in fact $g^* h^* = bf^*$, so that $\mathrm{pp}(g^*) = 3x^2 + x + 1$ and $\mathrm{pp}(h^*) = 2x^2 + x + 4$ are the irreducible factors of f in $\mathbb{Z}[x]$. $\diamond$

Before computing g^* and h^* in step 8, one will test first whether the constant coefficients of $g^* h^*$ and bf^* are equal (unless $f(0) = 0$, which can be ruled out in advance), as in Example 15.4. They can be computed with at most r multiplications of integers of absolute value at most B or $O(r \cdot \mathsf{M}(n + \log A))$ word operations, which is much faster than the worst case bound for steps 8 and 9 in the theorem. In practice, most unsuccessful g^* and h^* already fail this simple test. Instead of multiplying with b, we might also compute the monic associates of g^* and h^* by rational number reconstruction (Section 5.10). If the constant coefficient of f is smaller than b, then exchanging the roles of the leading and the constant coefficient decreases the required size of p. These remarks also apply to the prime power algorithms 15.19 and 15.22 below and the corresponding algorithms in Chapter 16.

To factor an arbitrary polynomial $f \in \mathbb{Z}[x]$, we might apply Algorithm 15.2 to the squarefree part $h/\gcd(h, h') \in \mathbb{Z}[x]$ of $h = \mathrm{pp}(f)$ and afterwards determine the multiplicities. We use an alternative approach, where we apply it to the polynomials in the squarefree decomposition of h (Section 14.6). Here is the algorithm for factoring in $\mathbb{Q}[x]$ arbitrary polynomials with integer coefficients.

ALGORITHM 15.5 Polynomial factorization in $\mathbb{Q}[x]$.

Input: A polynomial $f \in \mathbb{Z}[x]$ with $\deg f = n \geq 1$ and max-norm $\|f\|_\infty = A$.
Output: A constant $c \in \mathbb{Z}$ and a set of pairs $\{(f_1, e_1), \ldots, (f_k, e_k)\}$ such that the $f_i \in \mathbb{Z}[x]$ are irreducible and pairwise coprime, the $e_i \in \mathbb{N}$ are positive, and $f = c f_1^{e_1} \cdots f_r^{e_r}$.

1. $c \longleftarrow \text{cont}(f), \quad g \longleftarrow \text{pp}(f)$
   if $\text{lc}(f) < 0$ **then** $c \longleftarrow -c, \quad g \longleftarrow -g$

2. **call** Yun's algorithm 14.21 to compute the squarefree decomposition $g = \prod_{1 \leq i \leq s} g_i^i$ of g, with squarefree and pairwise coprime polynomials $g_1, \ldots, g_s$ in $\mathbb{Z}[x]$ such that $\text{lc}(g_i) > 0$ for all i and g_s is nonconstant.

3. $G \longleftarrow \emptyset$
   for $1 \leq i \leq s$ **do**

4.   **call** Algorithm 15.2 to compute all irreducible factors $h_1, \ldots, h_t \in \mathbb{Z}[x]$ of g_i
         $G \longleftarrow G \cup \{(h_1, i), \ldots, (h_t, i)\}$

5. **return** c and G

If we use Algorithm 14.21 literally in step 2, then it computes monic polynomials with rational coefficients. We obtain the squarefree decomposition into primitive polynomials in $\mathbb{Z}[x]$ by multiplying with a common denominator, or by performing all gcd computations in Algorithm 14.21 in $\mathbb{Z}[x]$ instead of $\mathbb{Q}[x]$, or by using a modular approach (Exercises 15.26 and 15.27).

We forego a cost analysis, because Algorithms 15.2 and 15.5 have exponential running time in the worst case. This does not follow from the upper bound of Theorem 15.3, but we will see in Section 15.3 that there are polynomials for which the algorithm takes exponentially many steps. In Chapter 16, we will present and analyze a polynomial-time algorithm for factoring in $\mathbb{Q}[x]$.

Algorithm 15.2 can be easily adapted to bivariate polynomials over a field F, provided that we know how to factor univariate polynomials over algebraic extensions of F. We have solved this problem over finite fields, but the prime power algorithm in Section 15.6 below only requires univariate factorization over F itself, and thus also applies to $F = \mathbb{Q}$. For this reason, we forego the details of the adaptation mentioned above.

15.3. Frobenius' and Chebotarev's density theorems

We briefly explain how the factorization of $f \in \mathbb{Z}[x]$ is related to factorizations of $f \bmod p \in \mathbb{F}_p[x]$ for various primes $p \in \mathbb{Z}$. This section requires some familiarity with basic Galois theory. It is not required later and may be skipped at first reading.

We may assume that f is primitive and $p \nmid \mathrm{lc}(f)$, and let $f = f_1 \cdots f_k$ be its factorization, with $f_1, \ldots, f_k \in \mathbb{Z}[x]$ irreducible. Then of course

$$f \bmod p = (f_1 \bmod p) \cdots (f_k \bmod p)$$

in $\mathbb{F}_p[x]$. The computational difficulty is that some $f_i \bmod p$ may not be irreducible in $\mathbb{F}_p[x]$, and that the factor combination stage may have to try exponentially many combinations of the irreducible factors that were computed modulo p.

An example of a "bad" polynomial is the ith **Swinnerton-Dyer polynomial**

$$f = \prod (x \pm \sqrt{2} \pm \sqrt{3} \pm \sqrt{5} \pm \cdots \pm \sqrt{p_i}) \in \mathbb{Z}[x],$$

where p_i is the ith prime and the product runs over all 2^i possible combinations of $+$ and $-$ signs. It follows from Galois theory that f is an irreducible polynomial of degree 2^i in $\mathbb{Z}[x]$. But since for any prime p, $\mathbb{F}_{p^2}$ contains all the square roots $\sqrt{2} \bmod p, \ldots, \sqrt{p_i} \bmod p$, the reduction of f modulo p splits into linear factors over $\mathbb{F}_{p^2}$. Hence the irreducible factors of $f \bmod p$ in $\mathbb{F}_p[x]$ are either all linear (namely, if $2, 3, \ldots, p_i$ are squares modulo p) or all quadratic (Exercise 15.8), and there are at least $2^{i-1} = n/2$ of them, where $n = 2^i$ is the degree of f. Then the factorization algorithm 15.2 will run through about $2^{n/4}$ sets S before it is finally able to decide that f is irreducible. Other examples of "bad" polynomials are the cyclotomic polynomials Φ_n, which are irreducible over $\mathbb{Q}$ but split modulo each prime for most n (Exercise 15.7).

The Swinnerton-Dyer polynomials and the cyclotomic polynomials make the factor combination stage work really hard. But is that typical? For example, we have used the fact that squarefree polynomials "usually" remain squarefree modulo a prime. Can we hope that "usually" an irreducible polynomial in $\mathbb{Z}[x]$ remains irreducible modulo a prime? The answer is no, and the powerful theorems of Frobenius (1896) and Chebotarev (1926) give precise information. Their explanation requires some concepts not used elsewhere in this text; the background and a proof can be found in Stevenhagen & Lenstra (1996).

So we have a primitive polynomial $f \in \mathbb{Z}[x]$ of degree n, irreducible over $\mathbb{Q}$. We let G be the Galois group of the splitting field of f over $\mathbb{Q}$. Each automorphism in G is a permutation of the n roots of f and has a unique decomposition into disjoint cycles, say of lengths $\lambda_1, \ldots, \lambda_r$. Then $\lambda_1 + \cdots + \lambda_r = n$, so that $\lambda = (\lambda_1, \ldots, \lambda_r)$ is a partition of n. For an arbitrary partition λ of n, we let $H_\lambda \subseteq G$ be the set of those automorphisms that have cycle decomposition λ. Thus $\mu(\lambda) = \#H_\lambda / \#G$ is the relative frequency with which the cycle type λ occurs in G.

EXAMPLE 15.6. We consider the three irreducible polynomials of degree $n = 4$

$$
\begin{aligned}
f_1 &= x^4 - 6x^3 - 5x^2 + 8, \\
f_2 &= x^4 + x^3 + x^2 + x + 1, \\
f_3 &= x^4 - 10x^2 + 1 = \prod(x \pm \sqrt{2} \pm \sqrt{3})
\end{aligned}
$$

in $\mathbb{Q}[x]$. The first one f_1 was chosen at random from the monic polynomials in $\mathbb{Z}[x]$ with coefficients absolutely less than 10, $f_2 = \Phi_5$ is the 5th cyclotomic polynomial, and f_3 is a Swinnerton-Dyer polynomial. With appropriate numberings of the roots of f_1, f_2, f_3, their Galois groups are $\mathrm{Gal}(f_1) = S_4$, the full symmetric group on four letters, $\mathrm{Gal}(f_2) = \langle(1234)\rangle \cong \mathbb{Z}_4$, the cyclic group with four elements, and $\mathrm{Gal}(f_3)$ is **Klein's group** $V_4 \cong \mathbb{Z}_2 \times \mathbb{Z}_2$. The partitions of 4, that is, the possible cycle types of automorphisms of f_1, f_2, f_3, are $(1,1,1,1)$, $(2,1,1)$, $(2,2)$, $(3,1)$, and (4). For each of the three polynomials and each cycle type λ, Table 15.3 lists the automorphisms of type λ in the Galois group. The fractions in bold are the relative frequencies. $\diamond$

cycle type	f_1		f_2		f_3	
$(1,1,1,1)$	id	$\dfrac{1}{24}$	id	$\dfrac{1}{4}$	id	$\dfrac{1}{4}$
$(2,1,1)$	(12), (13), (14), (23), (24), (34)	$\dfrac{6}{24}$				
$(2,2)$	(12)(34), (13)(24), (14)(23)	$\dfrac{3}{24}$	(13)(24)	$\dfrac{1}{4}$	(12)(34), (13)(24), (14)(23)	$\dfrac{3}{4}$
$(3,1)$	(123), (124), (132), (134), (142), (143), (234), (243)	$\dfrac{8}{24}$				
(4)	(1234), (1243), (1324), (1342), (1423), (1432)	$\dfrac{6}{24}$	(1234), (1432)	$\dfrac{2}{4}$		

TABLE 15.3: Cycle types of the Galois groups of f_1, f_2, f_3 and their relative frequencies.

If we factor f modulo a prime p that does not divide $\mathrm{res}(f, f')$, then the degrees $\lambda_1, \ldots, \lambda_r$ of the irreducible factors also form a partition of n, the **factorization pattern** $\lambda = (\lambda_1, \ldots, \lambda_r)$ of f modulo p. For any partition λ, we can consider the set P_λ of those primes where λ is this factorization pattern. Then **Frobenius' density theorem** says that P_λ has density $\mu(\lambda)$, so that a randomly chosen prime is in P_λ with probability $\mu(\lambda)$. Chebotarev proved a stronger version of this result, and **Chebotarev's density theorem** has become much better known than Frobenius' theorem. For practical purposes, we would like to use this kind of estimate for the primes in our algorithms. Unfortunately, nothing much can be proved about this, because even the best versions of Chebotarev's theorem (Lagarias & Odlyzko

1977, Oesterlé 1979) do not allow us to conclude that the asymptotic density of P_λ already applies to the fairly small values of p that we use (or of any size that leads to practical algorithms). However, case studies like Example 15.6 give rise to the hope that more may be true than what can be proved today.

pattern	f_1	f_2	f_3
$(1,1,1,1)$	3.96%	24.84%	24.78%
$(2,1,1)$	25.30%		
$(2,2)$	12.70%	24.91%	75.22%
$(3,1)$	33.18%		
(4)	24.86%	50.25%	

TABLE 15.4: Factorization patterns of f_1, f_2, f_3 modulo the first 10000 primes not dividing the discriminant.

EXAMPLE 15.6 (continued). For each of the three polynomials f_1, f_2, f_3 from Example 15.6, Table 15.4 shows the frequencies of factorization patterns modulo the first 10000 primes where the polynomial is squarefree. One can see that these approximate the relative frequencies of the conjugacy classes quite well. For example, the partition $(2,2)$, corresponding to a factorization into two irreducible quadratic factors, occurs in 12.70% of all cases for f_1, which is close to the frequency 12.5% of the cycle type $(2,2)$ in $\mathrm{Gal}(f_1)$. For f_2, this factorization pattern occurs about twice as often, in 24.91% of all cases, and 25% of the four elements of its Galois group have cycle type $(2,2)$. ◇

Now f is irreducible modulo p if and only if $p \in P_{(n)}$. For a Swinnerton-Dyer polynomial of degree $n = 2^i$, the Galois group is isomorphic to $\mathbb{Z}_2^i$, and $\mu((n)) = 0$. If $G = S_n$ (which is the case for almost all random polynomials of degree n), then $\mu((n)) = 1/n$, so that f remains irreducible modulo p for a fraction of only about $1/n$ of all primes. Moreover, the average number of cycles of a random permutation in S_n is $O(\log n)$ (see Notes 15.3), and Chebotarev's theorem implies that this is also the average number of factors of f modulo a random prime p.

The reader who has absorbed the technique of modular algorithms may have wondered why we do not use several small primes and Chinese remaindering to factor polynomials. The reason is that the irreducible factors in $\mathbb{Z}[x]$ split independently modulo different primes, obeying Frobenius' rule, and it would be even harder to fit them together than combining factors modulo a single prime. As a more practical approach, we might factor modulo several primes, choose one of them as the p in the factor combination step, and for each possible combination $S \subseteq \{1, \ldots, r\}$ check whether the degree $\deg \prod_{i \in S} g_i$ is compatible with all other modular factorizations.

EXAMPLE 15.7. Suppose that $f \in \mathbb{Z}[x]$ of degree 8 is squarefree modulo $2, 3, 5$ and has the factorization patterns $(3,3,2)$ modulo 2, $(5,2,1)$ modulo 3, and $(4,3,1)$

modulo 5. From the factorization modulo 2, we can conclude that the possible degrees of factors of f in $\mathbb{Z}[x]$ are $D_2 = \{2,3,5,6,8\}$. Similarly, from the factorizations modulo 3 and 5, we obtain $D_3 = \{1,2,3,5,6,7,8\}$ and $D_5 = \{1,3,4,5,7,8\}$. Taking the intersection $D_2 \cap D_3 \cap D_5 = \{3,5,8\}$, we conclude that every nonconstant factor of $f \in \mathbb{Z}[x]$ has degree $3, 5$, or 8, so that f is either irreducible or it splits into two irreducible factors of degree 3 and 5. $\diamond$

15.4. Hensel lifting

In Chapter 9, we employed Newton iteration for computing inverses and solving polynomial equations modulo p^l over a ring R, where an initial solution modulo $p \in R$ is given. Hensel (1918) invented a similar method to compute factorizations of polynomials modulo p^l, which Zassenhaus (1969) introduced into modern factorization algorithms, and which—no surprise—had been known to Gauß.

This is the third of the modular algorithms mentioned at the beginning of Chapter 5. In the big prime version, we took a large enough prime, and in the small primes version, we took small prime numbers $m_1, \ldots, m_l$ so that $m_1 \cdots m_l$ is large enough. Now we take a single small prime p and an integer l so that p^l is large enough.

We start with the simplest idea and then add more technical details. Let R be a ring (commutative, with 1, as usual, our two main examples being $R = \mathbb{Z}$ and $R = F[y]$ for a field F), $f, g, h \in R[x]$, and $m \in R$ such that $f \equiv gh \bmod m$. We want to "lift" this to a factorization $f \equiv \hat{g}\hat{h} \bmod m^2$. We assume that we have $s, t \in R[x]$ with $sg + th \equiv 1 \bmod m$, and think of g and h as being coprime modulo m. When $R/\langle m \rangle$ is a field, we can find these via the Extended Euclidean Algorithm in $(R/\langle m \rangle)[x]$. We now calculate

$$e = f - gh, \quad \hat{g} = g + te, \quad \hat{h} = h + se, \tag{3}$$

and find

$$
\begin{aligned}
f - \hat{g}\hat{h} &= f - gh - gse - hte - ste^2 = f - gh - (sg + th)e - ste^2 \\
&= (1 - sg - th)e - ste^2 \equiv 0 \bmod m^2,
\end{aligned}
$$

since $e \equiv 0 \bmod m$ and $1 - sg - th \equiv 0 \bmod m$. Hence $f \equiv \hat{g}\hat{h} \bmod m^2$, so that $\hat{g}\hat{h}$ is a factorization of f modulo m^2. Starting with a prime p for m and proceeding inductively (and simultaneously lifting the congruence $sg + th \equiv 1$), we can lift the factorization modulo arbitrary powers of p.

EXAMPLE 15.8. In Example 9.24, we computed a nontrivial solution to $x^4 - 1 \equiv 0 \bmod 625$ using Newton iteration with the starting value $x = 2$ modulo 5. This can also be regarded as lifting the factorization

$$x^4 - 1 \equiv (x - 2)(x^3 + 2x^2 - x - 2) \bmod 5$$

to a factorization modulo 625. In the above setting, we then have $f = x^4 - 1$, $p = 5$, $g = x^3 + 2x^2 - x - 2$, and $h = x - 2$. The polynomials g and h are coprime modulo 5, and with the Extended Euclidean Algorithm in $\mathbb{F}_5[x]$, we get $s = -2$ and $t = 2x^2 - 2x - 1$ such that $sg + th \equiv 1 \bmod 5$. With $m = p$, we obtain

$$
\begin{aligned}
e &= f - gh = 5x^2 - 5, \\
\hat{g} &= g + te = 10x^4 - 9x^3 - 13x^2 + 9x + 3, \\
\hat{h} &= h + se = -10x^2 + x + 8,
\end{aligned}
$$

and in fact

$$
f - \hat{g}\hat{h} = 25 \cdot (4x^6 - 4x^5 - 8x^4 + 7x^3 + 5x^2 - 3x - 1) \equiv 0 \bmod 25,
$$

so that $f \equiv \hat{g}\hat{h} \bmod 25$. ◇

The above example shows one drawback to our first approach: the degrees of $\hat{g}$ and $\hat{h}$ are higher than those of g and h, in particular their sum exceeds the degree of f. This may happen because the multiples of m are zero divisors modulo m^2, and hence the product of the leading coefficients of two polynomials may vanish modulo m^2.

To overcome this problem, we use division with remainder in $R[x]$. Since R is not a field, this is not always possible. The following lemma states that division with remainder by monic polynomials always works.

LEMMA 15.9.   (i) *Let $f, g \in R[x]$, with g nonzero and monic. Then there exist unique polynomials $q, r \in R[x]$ with $f = qg + r$ and $\deg r < \deg g$.*

(ii) *If f, g, q, r are as in (i) and $f \equiv 0 \bmod m$ for some $m \in R$, then $q \equiv r \equiv 0 \bmod m$.*

Part (i) has been proven in Section 2.4, and the proof of (ii) is Exercise 15.12. We do not need the coefficients of the new polynomials exactly, but only modulo m^2. This means that over a Euclidean domain R we can reduce them accordingly and keep their sizes small. Here are the formulas that work.

━━ ALGORITHM 15.10 Hensel step. ━━━━━━━━━━━━━━━
Input: An element m in a (commutative) ring R, and polynomials $f, g, h, s, t \in R[x]$ such that

$$
f \equiv gh \bmod m \text{ and } sg + th \equiv 1 \bmod m,
$$

h is monic, $\deg f = n = \deg g + \deg h$, $\deg s < \deg h$, and $\deg t < \deg g$.

Output: Polynomials $g^*, h^*, s^*, t^* \in R[x]$ such that

$$f \equiv g^* h^* \bmod m^2 \text{ and } s^* t^* + t^* h^* \equiv 1 \bmod m^2,$$

h^* is monic, $g^* \equiv g \bmod m$, $h^* \equiv h \bmod m$, $s^* \equiv s \bmod m$, $t^* \equiv t \bmod m$, $\deg g^* = \deg g$, $\deg h^* = \deg h$, $\deg s^* < \deg h^*$, and $\deg t^* < \deg g^*$.

1. compute $e, q, r, g^*, h^* \in R[x]$ such that $\deg r < \deg h$ and

$$
\begin{aligned}
e &\equiv f - gh \bmod m^2, & se &\equiv qh + r \bmod m^2, \\
g^* &\equiv g + te + qg \bmod m^2, & h^* &\equiv h + r \bmod m^2
\end{aligned}
\tag{4}
$$

2. compute $b, c, d, s^*, t^* \in R[x]$ such that $\deg d < \deg h^*$ and

$$
\begin{aligned}
b &\equiv sg^* + th^* - 1 \bmod m^2, & sb &\equiv ch^* + d \bmod m^2, \\
s^* &\equiv s - d \bmod m^2, & t^* &\equiv t - tb - cg^* \bmod m^2
\end{aligned}
\tag{5}
$$

3. **return** g^*, h^*, s^*, t^* ▬▬▬▬▬▬▬▬▬▬▬▬▬▬▬▬▬▬▬▬▬▬▬▬▬▬▬▬▬▬

EXAMPLE 15.8 (continued). We let $m = 5$ and f, g, h, s, t, e in $\mathbb{Z}[x]$ be as in Example 15.8. Division of se by h with remainder yields $q = -10x + 5$ and $r = -5$ with $se \equiv qh + r \bmod 25$. Moreover, we compute

$$g^* \equiv g + te + qg \equiv x^3 + 7x^2 - x - 7 \bmod 25, \quad h^* \equiv h + r \equiv x - 7 \bmod 25.$$

Then $f \equiv g^* h^* \bmod 25$, and the degrees of g^*, h^* are the same as those of g and h; the polynomials are simpler than $\hat{g}, \hat{h}$ as calculated before. As in Example 9.24, we obtain that 7 is a solution to $x^4 - 1 \equiv 0 \bmod 25$ that is congruent to the starting solution 2 modulo 5.

To obtain s^*, t^*, which we need for the next iteration, we compute

$$b \equiv sg^* + th^* - 1 \equiv 5x^3 + 10x^2 + 5x \bmod 25.$$

Polynomial division yields $c = -5$ and $d = -10x^3 + 10x + 10$ with $sb \equiv ch^* + d$ mod 25. Now

$$s^* \equiv s - d \equiv 8 \bmod 25, \quad t^* \equiv t - tb - cg^* \equiv -8x^2 - 12x - 1 \bmod 25.$$

Then indeed $s^* g^* + t^* h^* \equiv 1 \bmod 25$, and the degrees of s^*, t^* agree with those of s, t, respectively. ◇

▬▬ THEOREM 15.11. ▬▬▬▬▬▬▬▬▬▬▬▬▬▬▬▬▬▬▬▬▬▬▬▬▬▬▬▬▬▬

Algorithm 15.10 works correctly as specified. It uses $O(\mathsf{M}(n)\mathsf{M}(\log m))$ word operations if $R = \mathbb{Z}$, $m > 1$, and all inputs have max-norm less than m^2, and $O(\mathsf{M}(n)\mathsf{M}(\deg_y m))$ operations in the field F if $R = F[y]$ and the degree in y of all inputs is less than $2 \deg_y m$. ▬▬▬▬▬▬▬▬▬▬▬▬▬▬▬▬▬▬▬▬▬▬▬

PROOF. For the correctness, we only prove the claims about g^*, h^*; those for s^*, t^* are left as Exercise 15.17. We calculate

$$
\begin{aligned}
f - g^* h^* &\equiv f - (g + te + qg)(h + se - qh) \\
&= f - gh - (sg + th)e - ste^2 - (sg - th)qe + ghq^2 \\
&\equiv (1 - sg - th)e - ste^2 - (sg - th)qe + ghq^2 \equiv 0 \bmod m^2,
\end{aligned}
$$

since we have $1 - sg - th \equiv e \equiv 0 \bmod m$, by assumption, and $q \equiv 0 \bmod m$, by Lemma 15.9. These also imply that $g^* \equiv g \bmod m$ and $h^* \equiv h \bmod m$. Now $\deg r < \deg h$ by construction, and thus h^* is also monic and of the same degree as h. Finally, $f \equiv g^* h^* \bmod m^2$ and h^* monic imply that $\deg g^* = \deg f - \deg h^* = \deg f - \deg h = \deg g$.

We note that for any arithmetic operation (addition, multiplication, division with remainder) of polynomials in $\mathbb{Z}[x]$ occurring in the algorithm, their degrees are at most n, and their coefficients are less than m^4, with length in $O(\log m)$. Thus the cost for one arithmetical operation in $\mathbb{Z}$ is $O(\mathsf{M}(\log m))$ word operations. The number of arithmetic operations in $\mathbb{Z}$ for one polynomial addition, multiplication, or division with remainder by a monic polynomial is $O(\mathsf{M}(n))$. The estimate for $R = F[y]$ goes analogously. $\square$

▬▬ THEOREM 15.12 *Hensel's lemma.* ▬▬▬▬▬▬▬▬▬▬▬▬▬▬▬▬▬▬▬▬
Given $l \in \mathbb{N}_{>0}$ and assuming the input specification of Algorithm 15.10, we can compute polynomials as in the output specification, but with m^2 replaced by m^l.

PROOF. Apply the Hensel step inductively with m replaced by $m, m^2, m^4, \ldots$. $\square$

EXAMPLE 15.8 (continued). Let $m = 5$ and $f, g_1 = g^*, h_1 = h^*, s_1 = s^*, t_1 = t^*$ in $\mathbb{Z}[x]$ as in Example 15.8. Then $f \equiv g_1 h_1 \bmod 25$ and $s_1 g_1 + t_1 h_1 \equiv 1 \bmod 25$, and another execution of Algorithm 15.10 yields

$$
\begin{aligned}
e_2 &\equiv 50x^2 - 50 \bmod 625, \\
q_2 &\equiv -225x + 300 \bmod 625, \quad r_2 \equiv -175 \bmod 625, \\
g_2 &\equiv x^3 + 182x^2 - x - 182 \bmod 625, \quad h_2 \equiv x - 182 \bmod 625, \\
b_2 &\equiv -225x^2 + 300x - 25 \bmod 625, \\
c_2 &\equiv 75x - 200 \bmod 625, \quad d_2 \equiv 275 \bmod 625, \\
s_2 &\equiv -267 \bmod 625, \quad t_2 \equiv 267x^2 - 312x - 176 \bmod 625.
\end{aligned}
$$

Then $s_2 g_2 + t_2 h_2 \equiv 1 \bmod 625$, which we don't actually need if we are only interested in a factorization modulo m^4, $f \equiv g_2 h_2 \bmod 625$, and as in Example 9.24, we see that 182 is the fourth root of 1 modulo 625 that is congruent to the starting solution 2 modulo 5. ◇

EXAMPLE 15.13. Let $m = 3$, $f = x^4 - 2x^3 - 11x^2 + 4x + 3 \in \mathbb{Z}[x]$. Then $f \equiv x(x+1)(x^2+1) \bmod 3$, and with $g_0 = x^2 + x$ and $h_0 = x^2 + 1$, we compute $s_0 = x + 1$ and $t_0 = -x + 1$ such that $s_0 g_0 + t_0 h_0 \equiv 1 \bmod 3$. Two Hensel steps yield

$$e_1 \equiv -3x^3 - 3x^2 + 3x + 3 \bmod 9,$$
$$q_1 \equiv -3x^2 + 3x + 3 \bmod 9, \quad r_1 \equiv 3x \bmod 9,$$
$$g_1 \equiv x^2 + 4x + 3 \bmod 9, \quad h_1 \equiv x^2 + 3x + 1 \bmod 9,$$
$$b_1 \equiv 3x^2 + 3 \bmod 9,$$
$$c_1 \equiv 3x + 3 \bmod 9, \quad d_1 \equiv 0 \bmod 9,$$
$$s_1 \equiv x + 1 \bmod 9, \quad t_1 \equiv -x - 2 \bmod 9,$$
$$e_2 \equiv -9x^3 - 27x^2 - 9x \bmod 81,$$
$$q_2 \equiv -9x^2 - 9x \bmod 81, \quad r_2 \equiv 0 \bmod 81,$$
$$g_2 \equiv x^2 - 5x + 3 \bmod 81, \quad h_2 \equiv x^2 + 3x + 1 \bmod 81,$$
$$b_2 \equiv -9x^2 - 9x \bmod 81,$$
$$c_2 \equiv -9x + 9 \bmod 81, \quad d_2 \equiv -27x - 9 \bmod 81,$$
$$s_2 \equiv 28x + 10 \bmod 81, \quad t_2 \equiv -28x - 29 \bmod 81.$$

In fact, $f = g_2 h_2$ is the irreducible factorization of f in $\mathbb{Z}[x]$. ◇

The following result corresponds to the uniqueness of Newton iteration (Theorem 9.27). It says essentially that two liftings modulo m^l of the same factorization modulo m coincide modulo m^l.

▬▬ THEOREM 15.14 Uniqueness of Hensel lifting. ▬▬▬▬▬▬▬▬
Let R be a ring (commutative, with 1), $m \in R$ not a zero divisor, $l \in \mathbb{N}_{\geq 1}$, and $g, h, g^*, h^*, s, t \in R[x]$ nonzero such that $sg + th \equiv 1 \bmod m$, the leading coefficients $\mathrm{lc}(g), \mathrm{lc}(h)$ are not zero divisors modulo m, the polynomials g and g^* have the same leading coefficient and the same degree, and coincide modulo m, and similarly for h and h^*. If $gh \equiv g^* h^* \bmod m^l$, then $g \equiv g^* \bmod m^l$ and $h \equiv h^* \bmod m^l$. ▬▬▬

PROOF. We assume to the contrary that $g \not\equiv g^* \bmod m^l$ or $h \not\equiv h^* \bmod m^l$, and let $1 \leq i < l$ be maximal such that m^i divides both $g^* - g$ and $h^* - h$. Thus $g^* - g = um^i$ and $h^* - h = vm^i$ for some $u, v \in R[x]$ such that $m \nmid u$ or $m \nmid v$. We may assume that $m \nmid u$. Now

$$0 \equiv g^* h^* - gh = g^*(h^* - h) + h(g^* - g) = (g^* v + hu)m^i \bmod m^l.$$

Since m is not a zero divisor, we have $m \mid m^{l-i} \mid (g^* v + hu)$. We denote by a bar the reduction modulo m. Then $\overline{sg} + \overline{th} = 1$, $\overline{g^*} = \overline{g}$, and $\overline{g^* v} + \overline{hu} = 0$. Thus

$$0 = \overline{t}(\overline{g^* v} + \overline{hu}) = \overline{t}\overline{gv} + (1 - \overline{sg})\overline{u} = (\overline{tv} - \overline{su})\overline{g} + \overline{u},$$

and hence $\bar{g} \mid \bar{u}$. Since $\mathrm{lc}(g) = \mathrm{lc}(g^*)$ and $\deg g = \deg g^*$, we have $\deg \bar{u} < \deg \bar{g}$. Since $\mathrm{lc}(\bar{g}) = \overline{\mathrm{lc}(g)}$ is not a zero divisor, neither is $\bar{g}$, and $\bar{u}$ is the zero polynomial. This contradicts our assumption that $m \nmid u$, and the claim is proved. $\square$

The following consequence will be used in Section 16.5.

▬▬ COROLLARY 15.15. ▬▬▬▬▬▬▬▬▬▬▬▬▬▬▬▬▬▬▬▬▬▬

Let R be a Euclidean domain, $p \in R$ prime, $l \in \mathbb{N}_{>0}$, $f, g, u \in R[x]$ nonzero such that $p \nmid \mathrm{lc}(f)$, $f \bmod p$ is squarefree, g divides f in $R[x]$, and u is monic, nonconstant, and divides f modulo p^l and g modulo p. Then u divides g modulo p^l. ▬▬

PROOF. Let $h, v, w \in R[x]$ such that $f = gh \equiv uw \bmod p^l$ and $g \equiv uv \bmod p$. Since $f \bmod p$ is squarefree, so is $g \bmod p$, and $\gcd(u \bmod p, v \bmod p) = 1$ in $\mathbb{F}_p[x]$. Then Hensel's lemma 15.12 yields $u^*, v^* \in R[x]$ such that $u^* \equiv u \bmod p$, $v^* \equiv v$ $\bmod p$, and $g \equiv u^* v^* \bmod p^l$. Now $uvh \equiv gh \equiv uw \bmod p$ implies $vh \equiv w \bmod p$. Thus $v^* h \equiv vh \equiv w \bmod p$ and $u^* \cdot (v^* h) \equiv gh = f \equiv uw \bmod p^l$. Together with the fact that u and v are coprime modulo p, Theorem 15.14 gives $u \equiv u^* \bmod p^l$, and finally $g \equiv uv^* \bmod p^l$. $\square$

There is also an infinite version of Hensel's lemma. Let $p \in R$ be prime and $R_{(p)}$ the **p-adic completion** of R (Section 9.6). If $R = \mathbb{Z}$, then this is the ring $\mathbb{Z}_{(p)}$ of **p-adic integers**, whose elements can be represented by "power series in p" of the form $\sum_{i \geq 0} a_i p^i$ with $0 \leq a_i < p$ for all $i \in \mathbb{N}$. If $R = F[y]$ for a field F and $p = y$, then $R_{(p)} = F[[y]]$ is the ring of formal power series in y with coefficients in F.

▬▬ THEOREM 15.16 *Hensel's lemma, infinite version.* ▬▬▬▬▬▬▬▬
Assuming the input specification of Algorithm 15.10 for a prime $m = p \in R$, there exist polynomials as in the output specification, but with all congruences modulo m^2 replaced by equalities in $R_{(p)}$. ▬▬▬▬▬▬▬▬▬▬▬▬▬▬

The general multivariate Newton iteration works as follows. One has n functions $\varphi = (\varphi_1, \ldots, \varphi_n)$ in n variables $y_1, \ldots, y_n$, and from an approximation $a \in R^n$ to a common root of $\varphi_1, \ldots, \varphi_n$ obtains a better one a^* as

$$a^* = a - J^{-1}(a) f(a),$$

where $J = (\partial \varphi_i / \partial y_j)_{1 \leq i, j \leq n} \in R[y_1, \ldots, y_n]^{n \times n}$ is the **Jacobian** of φ.

We have seen in Example 15.8 that Hensel lifting generalizes Newton iteration. But Hensel lifting can also be considered as a special case of multivariate Newton iteration, as follows. We regard the coefficients of g and h in a factorization $f = gh$ as indeterminates. Comparing the coefficients of $x^{n-1}, \ldots, x, 1$ on both sides, we obtain n equations for the n unknown coefficients, and a common solution to those equations corresponds to a factorization of f. Invertibility of J is equivalent to coprimality of g and h (Exercise 15.21).

15.5. Multifactor Hensel lifting

In this section, we will employ the Hensel step algorithm 15.10 to lift a factorization into arbitrarily many factors.

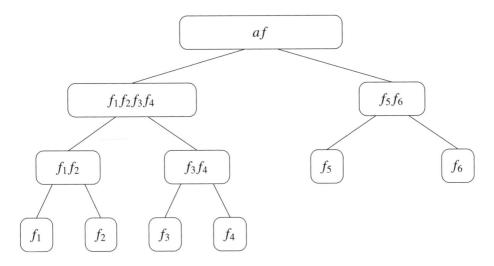

FIGURE 15.5: A factor tree.

Let R be a ring, $m \in R$, and $f, f_1, \ldots, f_r \in R[x]$ such that $\mathrm{lc}(f)$ is a unit modulo m, $f_1, \ldots, f_r$ are monic, and $f \equiv \mathrm{lc}(f) f_1 \cdots f_r \bmod m^i$. Then there is some $a \in R$ such that $a \cdot \mathrm{lc}(f) \equiv 1 \bmod m$. We arrange the monic factors v of f modulo m as a binary tree τ of depth $d = \lceil \log_2 r \rceil$, with leaves $f_1, \ldots, f_r$, root af, and such that each internal node is the product of its two children modulo m. Many different such arrangements are possible, and Figure 15.5 illustrates one such tree for $r = 6$. Furthermore, at each internal node $v \in R[x]$ with children $g_v, h_v \in R[x]$, we need $s_v, t_v \in R[x]$ such that $\deg s_v < \deg h_v$, $\deg t_v < \deg g_v$, and $s_v g_v + t_v h_v \equiv 1 \bmod m$ (this says that $f \bmod m$ is "squarefree"). We call such a tree τ, including the s_v, t_v, a **factor tree of f modulo m**. We obtain a factor tree modulo m^2 from τ by essentially applying Algorithm 15.10 to each node of τ, proceeding from the root to the leaves. If $R/\langle m \rangle$ is a field, then we obtain the initial s_v, t_v by means of the Extended Euclidean Algorithm.

The following algorithm lifts a factor tree modulo m to one modulo an arbitrary power of m. The graph-theoretic structure of the tree remains unchanged throughout the algorithm, only the data associated to the vertices changes.

ALGORITHM 15.17 Multifactor Hensel lifting.

Input: An element m in a ring R (commutative, with 1), $f \in R[x]$ of degree n, $a_0 \in R$ such that $a_0 \, \mathrm{lc}(f) \equiv 1 \bmod m$, $l \in \mathbb{N}$, and a factor tree τ of f modulo m, with root $a_0 f$ and r leaves.

Output: An inverse $a^* \in R$ of $\mathrm{lc}(f)$ modulo m^l and a factor tree τ^* of f modulo m^l with root $a^* f$ such that each node $v^* \in R[x]$ of τ^* is congruent modulo m to the corresponding node $v \in R[x]$ of τ.

1. $d \longleftarrow \lceil \log_2 l \rceil, \quad \tau_0 \longleftarrow \tau$

2. **for** $j = 1, \ldots, d$ **do**

3.   { lift inverse of $\mathrm{lc}(f)$ }
    compute $a_j \in R$ such that $a_j \equiv 2a_{j-1} - \mathrm{lc}(f)a_{j-1}^2 \bmod m^{2^j}$
    $\tau_j \longleftarrow \tau_{j-1}$
    replace the root of τ_j by $a_j f$

4.   { lift tree }
    for each internal node $v \in R[x]$ of τ_j, proceeding from the root to the leaves **do**

5.   **call** the Hensel step algorithm 15.10 with m replaced by $m^{2^{j-1}}$ to lift the congruences $v \equiv g_v h_v$ and $s_v g_v + t_v h_v \equiv 1$ modulo $m^{2^{j-1}}$ to congruences modulo m^{2^j}

6. **return** a_d and τ_d

THEOREM 15.18.

Algorithm 15.17 works correctly as specified. It takes $O(\mathsf{M}(n) \log r \, \mathsf{M}(l \log m))$ word operations if $R = \mathbb{Z}$, $m > 1$, and all inputs have max-norm less than m^l, and $O(\mathsf{M}(n) \log r \, \mathsf{M}(l \deg_y m))$ operations in F if $R = F[y]$ for a field F and the degree in y of all inputs is less than $l \deg_y m$.

PROOF. The Newton iteration in step 3 works correctly, according to Theorem 9.2, so that the root of each τ_j is the monic scalar multiple of f modulo m^{2^j}. We now show by induction on j that τ_j is a factor tree of f modulo m^{2^j}, and that each vertex of τ_j is congruent modulo m to the corresponding vertex of τ.

The case $j = 0$ is trivial, and we assume that $j \geq 1$. Now we know that the root of τ_j is a factor as required, and the claim about τ_j follows from the correctness of Algorithm 15.10 by topological induction along the tree τ_j. Finally, since $l \leq 2^d$, τ_d is also a factor tree of f modulo m^l, which concludes the correctness proof.

We only show the running time estimate for the case $R = \mathbb{Z}$; the case $R = F[y]$ is similar and left as Exercise 15.22. By Exercise 9.7, we can reduce all coefficients of f modulo $m, m^2, m^4, \ldots, m^{2^{d-1}}$ with $O(n \mathsf{M}(l \log m))$ word operations. Theorem

15.11 implies that the cost for one execution of step 5 is $O(\mathsf{M}(\deg v)\mathsf{M}(2^j \log m))$ word operations. At one fixed level of the tree τ_j, the sum of the degrees of all nodes is at most n, and the cost for this level is at most $O(\mathsf{M}(n)\mathsf{M}(2^j \log m))$ word operations, by the subadditivity of M (Section 8.3). There are $d \in O(\log r)$ levels, and the total cost of steps 4 and 5 for a fixed value of j is $O(\mathsf{M}(n)\log r\,\mathsf{M}(2^j \log m))$ word operations. This dominates the cost for step 3, and the estimate for the whole algorithm follows again from the subadditivity of M and from the geometric sum $\sum_{1 \le j \le d} 2^j \le 4l$. $\square$

By balancing the factor tree with respect to the degree, as discussed in Section 10.1, the factor $\log r$ in the timing estimate may be replaced by the entropy $H(n_1/n, \dots, n_r/n)$, where $n_i = \deg f_i$ for $1 \le i \le r$.

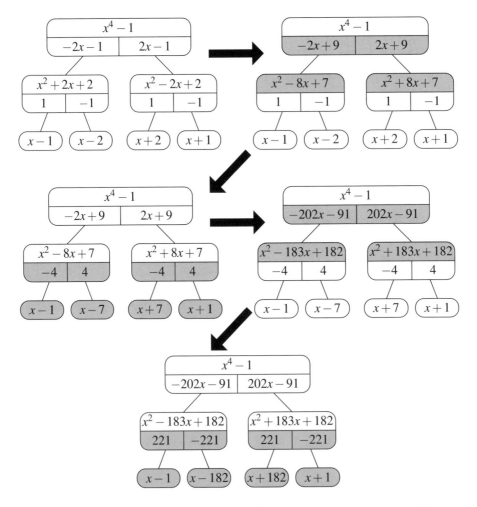

FIGURE 15.6: Lifting a factor tree of $x^4 - 1$ modulo 5 to one modulo 5^4.

Figure 15.6 illustrates five steps of multifactor lifting in the example $x^4 - 1 \equiv (x-1)(x-2)(x+2)(x+1)$ mod 5 which is lifted to a factorization modulo 625. An inner vertex contains three data items: a monic factor v of $x^4 - 1$ in the upper half, and two polynomials s_v and t_v in the lower half such that $s_v g_v + t_v h_v \equiv 1$, where g_v and h_v are the left and right children of v, respectively. The shaded boxes contain those elements that are lifted from the previous tree. The first, third, and last trees are factor trees modulo 5, 25, and 625, respectively; the second and fourth represent intermediate stages of the computation.

15.6. Factoring using Hensel lifting: Zassenhaus' algorithm

Let $R = \mathbb{Z}$ and $f \in \mathbb{Z}[x]$ be a squarefree primitive polynomial of degree n. We will now replace step 3 of the big prime algorithm 15.2 by factoring modulo a "small" prime $p \in \mathbb{N}$ and subsequent Hensel lifting. As in Algorithm 15.2, we will choose p in such a way that $f \bmod p$ is squarefree and of the same degree as f, so that p does not divide $\mathrm{res}(f, f')$. The bound on the resultant from Theorem 6.23 implies that this is an easy task; the details are given later in Corollary 18.12.

━━ ALGORITHM 15.19 Factorization in $\mathbb{Z}[x]$ (prime power version). ▬▬▬▬▬▬
Input: A squarefree primitive polynomial $f \in \mathbb{Z}[x]$ of degree $n \geq 1$ with $\mathrm{lc}(f) > 0$ and max-norm $\|f\|_\infty = A$.
Output: The irreducible factors $\{f_1, \ldots, f_k\} \subseteq \mathbb{Z}[x]$ of f.

1. **if** $n = 1$ **then return** $\{f\}$
   $b \longleftarrow \mathrm{lc}(f), \quad B \longleftarrow (n+1)^{1/2} 2^n A b,$
   $C \longleftarrow (n+1)^{2n} A^{2n-1}, \quad \gamma \longleftarrow \lceil 2 \log_2 C \rceil$

2. **repeat** choose a prime $p \leq 2\gamma \ln \gamma, \quad \overline{f} \longleftarrow f \bmod p$
   until $p \nmid b$ and $\gcd(\overline{f}, \overline{f}') = 1$ in $\mathbb{F}_p[x]$
   $l \longleftarrow \lceil \log_p(2B+1) \rceil$

3. { Modular factorization }
   compute $h_1, \ldots, h_r \in \mathbb{Z}[x]$ of max-norm at most $p/2$ that are nonconstant, monic, and irreducible modulo p, such that $f \equiv b h_1 \cdots h_r \bmod p$

4. { Hensel lifting }
   $a \longleftarrow b^{-1} \bmod p$
   use the Extended Euclidean Algorithm 3.6 in $\mathbb{F}_p[x]$ to set up a factor tree of f modulo p with leaves $h_1, \ldots, h_r$
   call Algorithm 15.17 to compute a factorization $f \equiv b g_1 \cdots g_r \bmod p^l$ with monic polynomials $g_1, \ldots, g_r \in \mathbb{Z}[x]$ of max-norm at most $p^l/2$ such that $g_i \equiv h_i \bmod p$ for $1 \leq i \leq r$

5. { initialize the index set T of modular factors still to be treated, the set G of
　　 found factors, and the polynomial f^* still to be factored }
　　 $T \longleftarrow \{1,\dots,r\}, \quad s \longleftarrow 1, \quad G \longleftarrow \emptyset, \quad f^* \longleftarrow f$

6. { Factor combination }
　 while $2s \leq \#T$ **do**

7.　　　　 **for** all subsets $S \subseteq T$ of cardinality $\#S = s$ **do**

8.　　　　　　 compute $g^*, h^* \in \mathbb{Z}[x]$ with max-norm at most $p^l/2$ satisfying
　　　　　　 $g^* \equiv b \prod_{i \in S} g_i \bmod p^l$ and $h^* \equiv b \prod_{i \in T \setminus S} g_i \bmod p^l$

9.　　　　　　 **if** $\|g^*\|_1 \|h^*\|_1 \leq B$ **then**
　　　　　　　　 $T \longleftarrow T \setminus S, \quad G \longleftarrow G \cup \{\mathrm{pp}(g^*)\},$
　　　　　　　　 $f^* \longleftarrow \mathrm{pp}(h^*), \quad b \longleftarrow \mathrm{lc}(f^*)$
　　　　　　　　 break the loop 7 and **goto** 6

10.　　　 $s \longleftarrow s + 1$

11. **return** $G \cup \{f^*\}$

There are several ways to find suitable primes in step 2: we might try the small
primes $2, 3, 5, \dots$ one after the other, or we might use a single precision prime just
below the processor's word length from a precalculated list. Both approaches work
well in practice, but do not yield a generally valid result since for some particular input all primes from any fixed list might divide the discriminant. Another
alternative which provably works is to choose p randomly; the required number
theoretic arguments will be discussed in Section 18.4.

THEOREM 15.20.
*Algorithm 15.19 works correctly. We have $\gamma \in O(n \log(nA))$, and the expected
cost of steps 2 and 3 is*

$$O\left(\gamma \log^2 \gamma \log\log \gamma + n\, M(\log A) + (M(n^2) + M(n) \log \gamma) \log n \cdot M(\log \gamma) \log\log \gamma\right)$$

*or $O^{\sim}(n^2 + n \log A)$ word operations. Step 4 takes $O(M(n)M(n + \log A)\log n)$ or
$O^{\sim}(n^2 + n \log A)$ word operations. The cost for one execution of steps 8 and 9 is*

$$O((M(n)\log n + n \log(n + \log A))M(n + \log A)) \text{ or } O^{\sim}(n^2 + n \log A)$$

word operations, and there are at most 2^{n+1} iterations.

PROOF. The correctness proof of Theorem 15.3 carries over with the following
modifications. We replace the congruence in (2) by $f^* \equiv b \prod_{i \in T} g_i \bmod p^l$. In

one part of that proof we assume that the condition in step 9 is false for all subsets $S \subseteq T$ of cardinality s, but that f^* has an irreducible factor $g \in \mathbb{Z}[x]$ with $\mu(g) = s$, and the fact that $\mathbb{F}_p[x]$ is a UFD yields a set $S \subseteq T$ of cardinality s such that the condition in step 9 is true for that particular subset. Now $\mathbb{Z}_{p^l}[x]$ is not a UFD in general (it even has nonzero zero divisors), and we have to replace the argument by unique factorization in $\mathbb{F}_p[x]$ plus an appeal to the uniqueness of Hensel lifting (Theorem 15.14). Namely, let $h = f^*/g$ and $S \subseteq T$ with $\#S = s$ be such that $\mathrm{lc}(h)g \equiv b\prod_{i \in S} h_i \bmod p$ and $\mathrm{lc}(g)h \equiv b\prod_{i \in T \setminus S} h_i \bmod p$. Now for that same subset S, let $g^* \equiv b\prod_{i \in S} g_i \bmod p^l$ and $h^* \equiv b\prod_{i \in T \setminus S} g_i \bmod p^l$. Thus $bf^* \equiv \mathrm{lc}(h)g \cdot \mathrm{lc}(g)h \bmod p^l$ and $bf^* \equiv g^*h^* \bmod p^l$ are both liftings of the same factorization of bf^* modulo p, and the uniqueness of Hensel lifting (Theorem 15.14) implies that $\mathrm{lc}(h)g \equiv g^* \bmod p^l$ and $\mathrm{lc}(g)h \equiv h^* \bmod p^l$. Now $B < p^l/2$, by the choice of l, and as in the proof of Theorem 15.3, we arrive at the contradiction that $\|g^*\|_1 \|h^*\|_1 \leq B$ holds in step 9.

Corollary 18.12 says that with $O(\gamma \log^2 \gamma \log\log \gamma)$ word operations, we can find a random p in step 2, and that p divides $\mathrm{disc}(f)$ with probability at most $1/2$. Now $b \mid \mathrm{disc}(f)$, by Exercise 6.41, and Lemma 15.1 implies that the expected number of iterations of step 2 is at most two. The length of p is in $O(\log \gamma)$, the cost for reducing all coefficients of f modulo p is $O(n\mathsf{M}(\log A))$ word operations, and the gcd takes $O(\mathsf{M}(n) \log n \cdot \mathsf{M}(\log \gamma) \log\log \gamma)$ word operations. The cost for computing $a^{-1} \bmod p$ in step 4 is negligible, and the cost for setting up the factor tree, that is, for computing the polynomials s_v, t_v, is $O(\mathsf{M}(\deg v) \log(\deg v))$ arithmetic operations in $\mathbb{F}_p$ per vertex v. Now the sum of the degrees over all vertices at one level of the tree is at most n, there are $O(\log n)$ levels, and the properties of M imply that the setup cost for the whole tree is $O(\mathsf{M}(n) \log^2 n)$ arithmetic operations in $\mathbb{F}_p$ or $O(\mathsf{M}(n) \log^2 n \mathsf{M}(\log \gamma) \log\log \gamma)$ word operations. Now the cost estimate for step 4 follows from Theorem 15.18, and the rest of the analysis is as in the proof of Theorem 15.3. $\square$

EXAMPLE 15.4 (continued). Let $f = 6x^4 + 5x^3 + 15x^2 + 5x + 4 \in \mathbb{Z}[x]$ be as in Example 15.4, and suppose that we choose $p = 5$ in step 2, so that p divides neither the leading coefficient nor the discriminant of f. Then $l = \lceil \log_5(2B+1) \rceil = 6$. In step 3, we obtain the modular factorization

$$f \equiv bh_1 h_2 h_3 h_4 = 1 \cdot (x-1)(x+1)(x-2)(x+2) \bmod 5.$$

In step 4, we set up a factor tree of f modulo 5, and Algorithm 15.17 lifts it to a factor tree of f modulo 5^6; both trees are visualized in Figure 15.7 (we have omitted the inverse of $\mathrm{lc}(f)$).

Among the subsets $S \subseteq \{1,2,3,4\}$ of cardinality $s = 1$, none leads to a factorization. For $S = \{1,3\}$ we compute

$$g^* \equiv bg_1 g_3 = 6(x - 5136)(x - 72) \equiv 6x^2 + 2x + 2 \bmod 5^6,$$

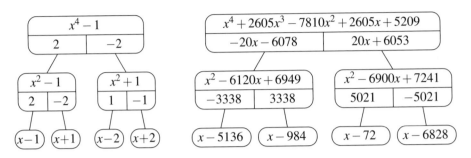

FIGURE 15.7: Factor trees modulo 5 and 5^6 for the polynomial f from Example 15.4.

$$h^* \equiv bg_2g_4 = 6(x-984)(x-6828) \equiv 6x^2 + 3x + 12 \bmod 5^6,$$

in step 8 and obtain $\|g^*\|_1\|h^*\|_1 \le B$ and $g^*h^* = bf^*$ in step 9. Thus $\mathrm{pp}(g^*) = 3x^2 + x + 1$ and $\mathrm{pp}(h^*) = 2x^2 + x + 4$ are the irreducible factors of f in $\mathbb{Z}[x]$, as in Example 15.4. $\diamond$

Steps 2 and 3 of the big prime algorithm 15.2 take about $O^{\sim}(n^3 + \log^3 A)$ word operations, while the cost for the corresponding steps 2 through 4 in the prime power algorithm 15.19 is only about $O^{\sim}(n^2 + n\log A)$ word operations. If $n \approx \log A$, then the former is roughly cubic in n, while the latter is only quadratic. Like Algorithm 15.2, Zassenhaus' algorithm has exponential running time in the worst case. Nevertheless, the algorithm works well in practice and should be used in the complete factorization algorithm 15.5; this is confirmed by experiments in Section 15.7. Collins (1979) showed, under a plausible but unproven hypothesis, that the algorithm uses polynomial time "on the average".

There is one further advantage of Zassenhaus' algorithm over the big prime approach: since the Mignotte bound determining l is usually far too large, we may interleave Hensel lifting and factor combination, as follows. We first lift the factorization modulo p^{l^*} for some $l^* < l$, then check whether some of the modular factors are true factors in $\mathbb{Z}[x]$, remove these from f, and then lift the remaining factorization modulo some higher power of p. This is iterated until all factors of f are found, which—if we are lucky—may happen before p^l is reached. A natural choice for these l^* are consecutive powers of 2, starting with the smallest such l^* which is at least $\|f\|_\infty$.

If we are only interested in computing all integral or rational roots of a given polynomial $f \in \mathbb{Z}[x]$, then we can greatly simplify Zassenhaus' algorithm 15.19. We have already discussed an approach via factoring modulo a big prime in Section 14.5. For the prime power approach, we modify Algorithm 15.19 in the following respects. Firstly, since we are only interested in linear factors, we may replace the bound $2B$ by $2nb(A^2 + A)$ if the latter is smaller, as in the big prime algorithm 14.17. Secondly, we need only compute the linear factors of f modulo

p in step 3 (executing the distinct-degree and equal-degree factorization only for degree 1), and finally—and most importantly—the whole factor combination stage may be replaced by a simple check whether the linear factors modulo p^l are linear factors in $\mathbb{Z}[x]$.

▬▬ THEOREM 15.21. ▬▬▬▬▬▬▬▬▬▬▬▬▬▬▬▬▬▬▬▬▬▬▬▬▬▬▬
Given a nonconstant squarefree primitive polynomial $f \in \mathbb{Z}[x]$, we can compute all its rational roots with an expected number of

$$O\left(n\log(nA)(\log^2 n\log\log n + (\log\log A)^2\log\log\log A) + n^2\mathsf{M}(\log(nA)))\right)$$

or $O^{\sim}(n^2\log A)$ word operations. ▬▬▬▬▬▬▬▬▬▬▬▬▬▬▬▬▬▬▬▬▬▬

PROOF. Let $\gamma = \log C \in O(n\log(nA))$. The expected cost for step 2 of Algorithm 15.19, modified as described above, is

$$O(\gamma\log^2\gamma\log\log\gamma + n\mathsf{M}(\log A) + \mathsf{M}(n)\log n \cdot \mathsf{M}(\log\gamma)\log\log\gamma)$$

word operations, as in the proof of Theorem 15.20. The expected cost for computing all (monic) linear factors of f mod p in step 3 is $O(\mathsf{M}(n)\log n\log(n\log\gamma))$ arithmetic operations in $\mathbb{F}_p$, by Corollary 14.16, or

$$O(\mathsf{M}(n)\log n\log(n\log\gamma)\mathsf{M}(\log\gamma)\log\log\gamma)$$

word operations. For the Hensel lifting in step 4, we take all monic linear factors plus the remaining monic cofactor of f mod p as leaves of the factor tree. The cost for step 4 is $O(\mathsf{M}(n)\log n(\log n\mathsf{M}(\log\gamma)\log\log\gamma + \mathsf{M}(\log(nA))))$ word operations, as in the proof of Theorem 15.20. For each linear factor $bx - c \in \mathbb{Z}[x]$ dividing f modulo p^l, with $b = \mathrm{lc}(f)$, we compute the corresponding cofactor $v \in \mathbb{Z}[x]$ such that $(bx - c)v \equiv bf \bmod p^l$ in step 8, at a cost of $O(n\mathsf{M}(\log(nA)))$ word operations, as in the proof of Theorem 14.18. There are at most n modular factors, and hence the total cost for checking all of them is $O(n^2\mathsf{M}(\log(nA)))$ word operations. Using $\log\gamma \in O(\log n + \log\log A)$, we obtain an overall cost of $O(\gamma\log^2\gamma\log\log\gamma + n^2\mathsf{M}(\log(nA)))$ word operations, and the claim follows. □

Due to the checking in the last step, the overall asymptotic running time of the prime power algorithm for root finding is about the same as for the big prime variant (Algorithm 14.17). However, the modular factorization stage of the former takes about $O^{\sim}(n\log^2 A)$ word operations, while the cost for the modular factorization stage, including Hensel lifting, is only about $O^{\sim}(n\log A)$ for the prime power algorithm. In practice, one would expect that most of the "false" roots exceed the trailing coefficient in absolute value, and would test the remaining trial roots modulo some other small primes first; this should rule out most of those which are not roots in $\mathbb{Q}$. The hope is that then there remain only few false roots.

With minor changes, Zassenhaus' algorithm 15.19 can be adapted to factor bivariate polynomials over a field F with **effective univariate factorization**, so that we know how to factor univariate polynomials over F (for example, $F = \mathbb{Q}$ or $F = \mathbb{F}_q$ for a prime power q). The degree in y of a polynomial $f \in F[x, y]$ plays the role of the max-norm, and a bound for possible factors of f is much simpler than in the integer case: divisors of f never have larger degree than f does. "Primitive" now is with respect to the variable x, so that $\mathrm{cont}_x(f) = 1$. Moreover, we require f to have a trivial gcd with its derivative with respect to x. This implies that f is squarefree. The converse is true in characteristic zero; see Exercise 15.25 for a counterexample in positive characteristic.

▬▬ ALGORITHM 15.22 Bivariate factorization (prime power version). ▬▬▬▬▬
Input: A primitive polynomial $f \in R[x] = F[x, y]$, where $R = F[y]$ for a field F with at least $4nd$ elements and effective univariate factorization, such that $\deg_x f = n \geq 1$, $\deg_y f = d$, and $\gcd(f, \partial f / \partial x) = 1$ in $F(y)[x]$.
Output: The irreducible factors $\{f_1, \ldots, f_k\} \subseteq F[x, y]$ of f.

1. **if** $n = 1$ **then return** f
   $b \longleftarrow \mathrm{lc}_x(f)$
   choose $U \subseteq F$ of cardinality $\#U = 4nd$

2. **repeat** randomly choose an element $u \in U$, $\quad \overline{f} \longleftarrow f(x, u)$
   until $b(u) \neq 0$ and $\gcd(\overline{f}, \overline{f}') = 1$ in $F[x]$
   $l \longleftarrow d + 1 + \deg b$

3. { Modular factorization }
   use the univariate factorization algorithm to compute a factorization $f \equiv bh_1 \cdots h_r \bmod (y - u)$ in $(F[y]/\langle y - u \rangle)[x] \cong F[x]$ with distinct monic irreducible $h_1, \ldots, h_r \in F[x]$

4. { Hensel lifting }
   $a \longleftarrow b(u)^{-1}$
   use the Extended Euclidean Algorithm 3.6 in $F[x]$ to set up a factor tree of f modulo $y - u$ with leaves $h_1, \ldots, h_r$
   call Algorithm 15.17 to compute a factorization $f \equiv bg_1 \cdots g_r \bmod (y - u)^l$ with polynomials $g_1, \ldots, g_r \in F[x, y]$ that are monic with respect to x such that $\deg_y g_i < l$ and $g_i(x, u) = h_i$ for $1 \leq i \leq r$

5. { initialize the index set T of modular factors still to be treated, the set G of found factors, and the polynomial f^* still to be factored }
   $T \longleftarrow \{1, \ldots, r\}, \quad s \longleftarrow 1, \quad G \longleftarrow \emptyset, \quad f^* \longleftarrow f$

6. { Factor combination }
   while $2s \leq \#T$ **do**

7.   **for** all subsets $S \subseteq T$ of cardinality $\#S = s$ **do**

8.   compute $g^*, h^* \in F[x,y]$ of degree less than l in y satisfying
            $g^* \equiv b \prod_{i \in S} g_i \bmod (y-u)^l$ and $h^* \equiv b \prod_{i \in T \setminus S} g_i \bmod (y-u)^l$

9.   **if** $\deg(g^* h^*) = \deg(bf^*)$ **then**
            $$T \longleftarrow T \setminus S, \quad G \longleftarrow G \cup \{\mathrm{pp}_x(g^*)\},$$
            $$f^* \longleftarrow \mathrm{pp}_x(h^*), \quad b \longleftarrow \mathrm{lc}_x(f^*)$$
            break the loop 7 and **goto** 6

10. $s \longleftarrow s+1$

11. **return** $G \cup \{f^*\}$

The following analysis of the algorithm is in Exercise 15.24.

THEOREM 15.23.
Algorithm 15.22 works correctly. The expected cost of step 2 is $O(nd + \mathsf{M}(n)\log n)$ or $O^{\sim}(nd)$ arithmetic operations in F, and step 4 takes $O(\mathsf{M}(n)\log n(\log n + \mathsf{M}(d))$ or $O^{\sim}(nd)$ operations. The number of field operations for one iteration of steps 8 and 9 is $O((n\log d + \mathsf{M}(n)\log n)\mathsf{M}(d))$ or $O^{\sim}(nd)$, and there are at most 2^{n+1} iterations. If $F = \mathbb{F}_q$ is a finite field with q elements, then the expected number of operations in $\mathbb{F}_q$ for step 3 is $O(\mathsf{M}(n^2)\log n + \mathsf{M}(n)\log n \log q)$ or $O^{\sim}(n^2 + n\log q)$.

When $F = \mathbb{F}_q$ is a "small" finite field, then we have a problem in step 1. There are several ways to circumvent this. We may employ a big prime algorithm, with a worse cost estimate for the modular factorization stage. Or we may factor f modulo a nonlinear irreducible $m \in \mathbb{F}_q[y]$ of degree $O(\log(nd))$ in step 3 instead of modulo $y - u$, and lift this to a factorization modulo a sufficiently high power of m in step 4. This increases the timings of steps 2 and 3 by a factor of at most $O^{\sim}(\log^2(nd))$. Or we perform a field extension of degree $O(\log(nd))$ and employ the algorithm over the larger field, thereby multiplying a factor of $O^{\sim}(\log^2(nd))$ to all timings. However, irreducible factors of f in $\mathbb{F}_q[x,y]$ may split over the larger field. In some applications, such a finer factorization may be advantageous, but if factors over $\mathbb{F}_q$ are needed, one has to take care of this separately if necessary. For example, if $g \in \mathbb{F}_{q^l}[x,y]$ is an irreducible factor of f over the larger field $\mathbb{F}_{q^l}$, then $g^{(q^l-1)/(q-1)} \in \mathbb{F}_q[x,y]$ (the norm of g) is a power of an irreducible factor of f over $\mathbb{F}_q$.

To factor an arbitrary polynomial $f \in F[x,y]$, we proceed similarly as described after Algorithm 15.2, with one notable difference: If $F = \mathbb{F}_q$ is a finite field, then $\mathbb{F}_q(y)$ is not a perfect field, and we cannot literally use the algorithms of Section 14.6 for squarefree factorization. For example, if $p = \mathrm{char}\,\mathbb{F}_q$, then the polynomial

$f = x^p - y$ is irreducible, but has derivative $\partial f/\partial x = 0$. If we exchange the roles of x and y, then $\partial f/\partial y = -1$ and $\gcd(f, \partial f/\partial y) = 1$ in $\mathbb{F}_q(x)[y]$, and the algorithm can be applied. If both partial derivatives $\partial f/\partial x$ and $\partial f/\partial y$ vanish, as for $f = x^p - y^p$, then f is a pth power, as in the univariate case (here $f = (x-y)^p$), and it is sufficient to factor $f^{1/p}$. Here is the analog of Algorithm 15.5; see Exercise 15.25 for a correctness proof.

▬▬ ALGORITHM 15.24 Bivariate polynomial factorization. ▬▬▬▬▬▬▬▬▬▬
Input: A nonconstant polynomial $f \in F[x,y]$ with $\deg_x f = n$ and $\deg_y f = d$, where F is a field with effective univariate factorization.
Output: A constant $a \in F$ and a set of pairs $\{(f_1, e_1), \ldots, (f_k, e_k)\}$ such that the $f_i \in F[x,y]$ are irreducible and distinct, the $e_i \in \mathbb{N}$ are positive, and $f = a f_1^{e_1} \cdots f_r^{e_r}$.

1. $G \longleftarrow \emptyset, \quad c_x \longleftarrow \mathrm{cont}_x(f), \quad c_y \longleftarrow \mathrm{cont}_y(f), \quad g \longleftarrow \dfrac{f}{c_x c_y}$

2. compute the irreducible factorizations of c_x and c_y in $F[y]$ and $F[x]$, respectively, and add them to G

3. $g_x \longleftarrow \partial g/\partial x, \quad u \longleftarrow \dfrac{g}{\gcd(g, g_x)}$
   $g_y \longleftarrow \partial g/\partial y, \quad v \longleftarrow \dfrac{g}{\gcd(g, g_y)}, \quad w \longleftarrow \dfrac{u}{\gcd(u, v)}$
   { gcd denotes the greatest common divisor in $F[x,y]$ }

4. **call** Algorithm 15.22 with the roles of x and y exchanged to compute the set $V \subseteq F[x,y]$ of all irreducible factors of v
   call Algorithm 15.22 to compute the set $W \subseteq F[x,y]$ of all irreducible factors of w

5. **for** all $v \in V \cup W$ **do**
       determine the multiplicity e of v in g by trial division
       $G \longleftarrow G \cup \{(v, e)\}, \quad g \longleftarrow \dfrac{g}{v^e}$

6. **if** F is finite of characteristic p and $g \notin F$ **then**
       call the algorithm recursively with input $g^{1/p}$, yielding $a \in F$ and a set of pairs H
       $a \longleftarrow a^p$
       for each pair $(g, e) \in H$ **do** $G \longleftarrow G \cup \{(g, ep)\}$
     else $a \longleftarrow g$

7. **return** a and G ▬▬▬▬▬▬▬▬▬▬▬▬▬▬▬▬▬▬▬▬▬▬▬

We conclude this section with a recapitulation of the algorithms considered so far which employ one of our three modular computation schemes: big prime, small primes, or prime power modular algorithms. They are given in Table 15.8.

computation problem	big prime	small primes	prime power
determinant	Section 5.5	Algorithm 5.10, Exercise 5.32	
linear system solving	Exercise 5.33		
polynomial gcd	Algorithms 6.28, 6.34	Algorithms 6.36, 6.38	EZ-GCD (Notes 15.6)
polynomial EEA		Algorithms 6.57, 6.59	
integer multiplication	Exercise 8.36	Algorithm 8.25	
polynomial multiplication		Algorithms 8.16, 8.20, Exercise 5.34	
polynomial division	Exercise 9.14	Exercise 10.21	Algorithm 9.3
roots of integers			Section 9.5
squarefree decomposition		Exercise 15.26	Exercise 15.27
polynomial factorization	Algorithm 15.2		Algorithms 15.19, 15.22, 16.22

TABLE 15.8: Modular algorithms.

For all problems listed, there exist big prime algorithms, and in most cases also small primes and prime power algorithms, although we did not discuss all of them. Usually the small primes or prime power variants are more efficient, both in theory and in practice, than either the big prime approach or a direct computation. To apply the prime power approach, the computational problem needs to be described in terms of "equations" which are then lifted. Some problems are badly suited for the small primes approach, such as polynomial factorization.

15.7. Implementations

In this section, we continue the description of NTL and BIPOLAR from Section 9.7, the focus now being on polynomial factorization. All experiments with NTL were done in version 1.5.

BIPOLAR is a C++ library for polynomial factorization in $\mathbb{F}_2[x]$. It contains algorithms for squarefree decomposition (Section 14.6), distinct-degree factorization (Section 14.2), and equal-degree factorization (Section 14.3). Experiments show that for random polynomials, the distinct-degree factorization stage is by far the dominant part of the whole computation.

Both in theory and in practice, a gcd computation is more costly than a multiplication or a division with remainder. Since a polynomial of degree n does not have irreducible factors of all degrees between 1 and n (on average, the number

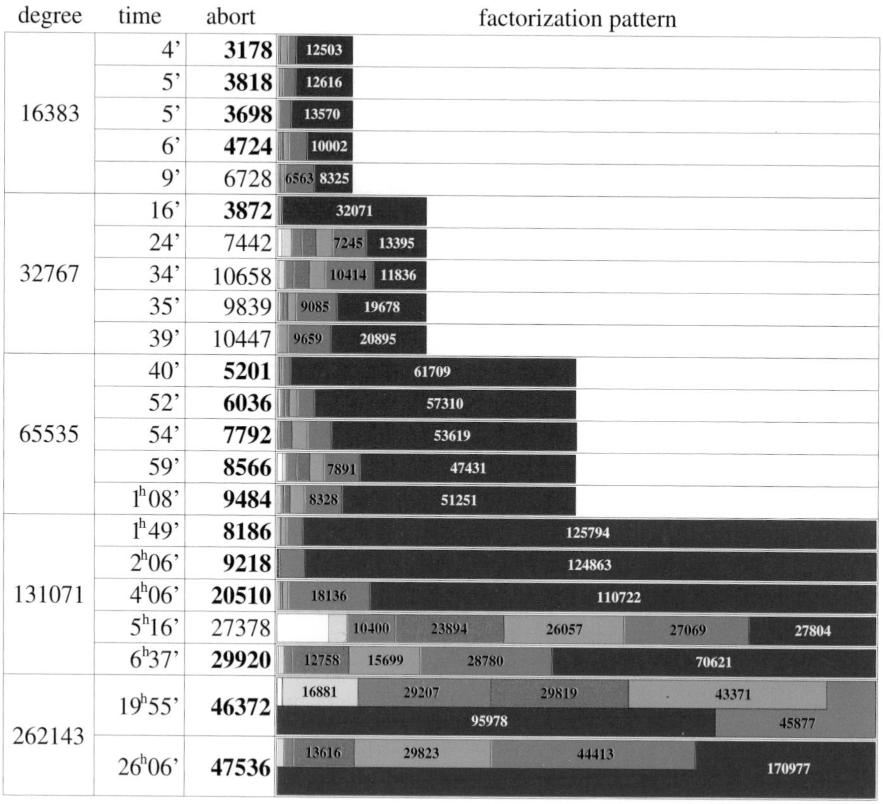

degree	time	abort	factorization pattern
16383	4'	**3178**	12503
	5'	**3818**	12616
	5'	**3698**	13570
	6'	**4724**	10002
	9'	6728	6563 8325
32767	16'	**3872**	32071
	24'	7442	7245 13395
	34'	10658	10414 11836
	35'	9839	9085 19678
	39'	10447	9659 20895
65535	40'	**5201**	61709
	52'	**6036**	57310
	54'	**7792**	53619
	59'	**8566**	7891 47431
	1^{h}08'	**9484**	8328 51251
131071	1^{h}49'	**8186**	125794
	2^{h}06'	**9218**	124863
	4^{h}06'	**20510**	18136 110722
	5^{h}16'	27378	10400 23894 26057 27069 27804
	6^{h}37'	**29920**	12758 15699 28780 70621
262143	19^{h}55'	**46372**	16881 29207 29819 43371 / 95978 45877
	26^{h}06'	**47536**	13616 29823 44413 170977

FIGURE 15.9: Factoring polynomials in $\mathbb{F}_2[x]$ with BIPOLAR.

of irreducible factors is $O(\log n)$; see Notes 15.7), most gcds in the distinct-degree factorization algorithm 14.3 are equal to 1. BIPOLAR uses a blocking strategy to reduce the number of gcds, at the expense of additional—but cheaper—modular multiplications. The range $\{1,\dots,n\}$ of possible degrees for the irreducible factors of f is partitioned into disjoint intervals, and then for each interval I—proceeding from lower to higher degrees—the product of all irreducible factors with degree in I is obtained as $\gcd\left(f, \prod_{i \in I}(x^{q^i} - x)\right)$ and removed from f (Exercise 14.6). If we are lucky, then each of these polynomials is already irreducible; otherwise a fine distinct-degree factorization à la Algorithm 14.3 is performed. Experiments with random polynomials show that on average, this is only necessary for small degrees. In BIPOLAR, the intervals grow linearly in size; this takes into account the fact that random polynomials tend to have many small but few large factors.

Every time a factor is split off, an irreducibility test (similar to Algorithm 14.36) for the remaining polynomial is started up on a second processor. Much of the data required for this test has already been computed in the distinct-degree factorization phase.

Figure 15.9 gives some running times with BIPOLAR on two Sun Sparc Ultra 1 computers rated at 167 MHz each; one running the distinct-degree algorithm described above, and the second one performing the irreducibility test in parallel. The timings are the maximum of the CPU times on both machines.

The abort degree is the degree to which the distinct-degree factorization had progressed when the computation was finished. It is printed in bold if the irreducibility test won; otherwise the distinct-degree factorization terminated when degree about $\max\{m_1/2, m_2\}$ was reached, where m_1, m_2 are the degrees of the largest and the second largest factor of the input polynomial, respectively.

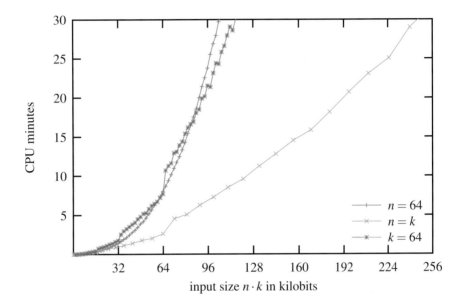

FIGURE 15.10: Factoring polynomials of degree $n-1$ modulo k-bit primes in NTL.

For factoring in $\mathbb{F}_p[x]$ for a prime p and in $\mathbb{Q}[x]$, NTL first computes the square-free decomposition. Over finite prime fields, both the algorithms of Berlekamp (1967,1970) and Shoup (1995) (who also does distinct- and equal-degree factorization) are implemented. For efficiency reasons, there are special factoring subroutines for "small" primes p that fit into one machine word. Figure 15.10 shows some running times in NTL for various primes and degrees. The timings are averages for 10 pseudorandomly chosen inputs.

To factor a squarefree polynomial with integral coefficients in $\mathbb{Q}[x]$, NTL first computes—after extracting its content—its irreducible factorizations modulo several "small" primes, thus (hopefully) gaining some information about the factorization pattern in $\mathbb{Q}[x]$, as described at the end of Section 15.3. Then one of these primes is selected and the factorization is lifted using Algorithm 15.17. For each product in the factor combination stage, the divisibility test is only executed after checking that the degree of the product is compatible with all modular factorization

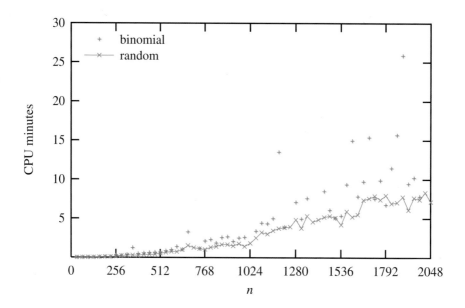

FIGURE 15.11: Factoring $x^{n-1} - 1$ in $\mathbb{Z}[x]$ in NTL (green crosses). The timings depend highly on the factorization of $n - 1$. The test series is for $n = 32, 64, 96, \ldots, 2048$. The running times for the seven values $n = 704, 1024, 1248, 1376, 1408, 2016$, and 2048 were above four hours, in five of these cases even over one day. For comparison, we have included the average timings for 10 pseudorandom polynomials of degree $n - 1$ with coefficients in $\{-1, 0, 1\}$ (blue curve).

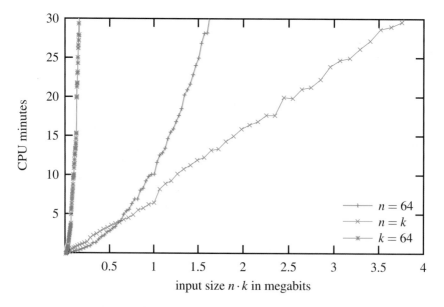

FIGURE 15.12: Factoring products of two pseudorandom polynomials of degree $(n/2) - 1$ with about $k/2$-bit integer coefficients in NTL.

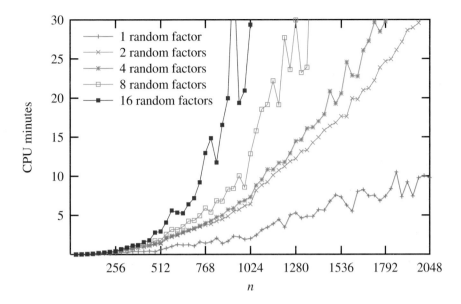

FIGURE 15.13: Factoring polynomials of degree about n with about n-bit integer coefficients in NTL. The green curve is for pseudorandom polynomials, the blue curve for products of two pseudorandom polynomials of degree $(n/2) - 1$ with about $n/2$-bit coefficients, and so on.

patterns, and then performing the constant coefficient test. Figures 15.11 through 15.13 give some running times in NTL for pseudorandom polynomials with various degrees, coefficient sizes, and factorization patterns. The timings are averaged over 10 pseudorandomly chosen inputs. Since random polynomials are irreducible with high probability (see Notes 15.3), we also took polynomials with a designed number of pseudorandom factors of the same degree as input; in fact, these were the irreducible factors in almost all cases.

Figure 15.13 indicates that the algorithms take longer if there are more factors, as expected. For a fixed input size $n \cdot k$, the "diagonal" case $n = k$ appears to be the most favorable to the implementation, as in Figure 15.12. A comparison to Figure 15.10 indicates that the software factors random polynomials with k-bit coefficients over the integers much faster than modulo k-bit primes. (A major difference between the two factorization tasks is that random polynomials of degree n are irreducible over $\mathbb{Q}$ with high probability, but modulo a prime only with probability about $1/n$.) Presumably the reason is that the modular factorization stage, which takes about $O^\sim(n^2 \log p + n \log^2 p)$ word operations, uses a small prime p with only about $\log_2 k$ bits when factoring over $\mathbb{Z}$ by Hensel lifting.

We also tested NTL on Swinnerton-Dyer polynomials; it factored the 5th such polynomial (of degree 32) in about 1.7 seconds, but it took more than two days of CPU time for the 6th polynomial (of degree 64).

Notes.   **15.1.** The first factoring algorithms for $\mathbb{Z}[x]$ are due to von Schubert (1793) and Kronecker (1882, 1883). In our terminology, they use a "small primes approach" with linear moduli $x - u_i$ for small integers u_i, plus factor combination. It involves the factorization of large integers.

15.2. Algorithm 15.2 appears in Musser (1971). Our algorithms become somewhat simpler when the input is monic. One can reduce the general case to this, replacing $f \in \mathbb{Z}[x]$ by $lc(f)^{n-1} f(x/lc(f))$, but this is computationally disadvantageous.

In our approach, factors are selected according to the number of irreducible modular factors that they comprise. One might also consider selecting them according to their degree, but Collins (1979) argues that this is disadvantageous. Collins & Encarnación (1996) propose some heuristic techniques for the factor combination stage.

Arjen Lenstra (1984, 1987) gives algorithms for factoring polynomials over algebraic number fields.

15.3. The Swinnerton-Dyer polynomials were suggested by H. P. F. Swinnerton-Dyer, as Berlekamp (1970) mentions. Kaltofen, Musser & Saunders (1983) investigate generalizations and also give bounds on the coefficient sizes.

Frobenius (1896) had found his theorem in 1880, and Chebotarev (1926) generalized it in the following way, as already conjectured by Frobenius. In the full symmetric group S_n, all permutations with the same cycle structure form a conjugacy class, but this may not be true in other Galois groups. As an example, the two 4-cycles in the Galois group of f_2 in Table 15.3 are not conjugate within that group. But still each set of permutations with the same cycle structure is a union of conjugacy classes. While Frobenius' theorem refers to cycle structure (and primes with that factorization pattern), Chebotarev's result proves the corresponding density estimate for the finer division into conjugacy classes (and primes whose Frobenius automorphism lies within that conjugacy class).

Van der Waerden (1933/34) proved that random integer polynomials have the full symmetric group as their Galois group with probability 1. In particular, they are probably irreducible. Wilf (1994), §4.1, proves that the average number of cycles of a random permutation on n letters is $H_n \in \ln n + O(1)$, where $H_n = 1 + \frac{1}{2} + \cdots + \frac{1}{n}$ is the nth harmonic number (Section 23.2).

15.4. Legendre (1785) factors some integer polynomials by a p-adic method. One of his examples is in Exercise 15.11. Another example gives two cubic factors of a polynomial of degree six. But he does not state a general method, and cautions the reader (pages 506/507): *Ces méthodes sont fort imparfaites, mais l'utilité de leur objet nous a engagés à les insérer ici, quelque petit que soit le nombre des cas où on peut s'en servir avec succès.*[1]

Hensel (1918) introduced the p-adic numbers, and his factoring method *Hensel lifting* was first used in a computer algebra context by Zassenhaus (1969); see also Kempfert (1969). As with so many topics of this book, Gauß had preempted them all. In his Nachlass (Gauß 1863a, 1863b, see page 348) we find in articles 373 and 374 an explicit description of the lifting procedure modulo prime powers, and Gauß concludes *si functio X aequales non habeat divisores secundum modulum p, eam secundum modulum p^k similiter in factores discerpi posse, uti secundum modulum p. At si X divisores aequales habeat, res fit multo magis complicata neque adeo ex principiis praecedentibus prorsus exhauriri*

---

[1] These methods are quite imperfect, but the importance of their goal induced us to insert them here, however small the number of cases may be where they can be used successfully.

potest.[2] He then even considers the case where multiple factors modulo p may occur, but the calculations in his manuscript end dramatically in the middle of an equation.

Indeed, an integer polynomial f that is squarefree modulo a prime p has a unique factorization modulo any power p^k, and this is easily computed by Hensel lifting. But when f is not squarefree modulo p, this factorization is quite tricky. Hensel lifting reduces the problem to the case where f is a power of an irreducible polynomial modulo p. There may be exponentially (in $\deg f$) many irreducible factors, but a representation of them can still be computed in polynomial time (in $\deg f, \log p$, and k) if the discriminant is nonzero modulo p^k (von zur Gathen & Hartlieb 1998). This is based on the polynomial-time factoring algorithm over the p-adic integers $\mathbb{Z}_{(p)}$ by Chistov (1990). Exercise 15.18 shows how factoring the innocuous polynomial x modulo a composite number is a nontrivial task.

15.5. The idea of the "tree lifting" is from Victor Shoup, who has implemented it in NTL. A different approach to lift factors simultaneously is in von zur Gathen (1984a).

15.6. The prime power factorization algorithm 15.19, based on Hensel lifting, is essentially due to Zassenhaus (1969). Loos (1983) gives an algorithm based on Hensel lifting for computing all rational roots of an integer polynomial.

A conceptually simple way to factor bivariate polynomials over small finite fields is to make an extension of prime degree larger than $\deg(f)$; then all factors over the extension are actually in the ground field (von zur Gathen 1985). However, this approach is computationally inferior to the other solutions presented.

Trager (1976) shows that if $F \subseteq E$ is a finite Galois extension of fields, $f \in F[x]$ is irreducible, and $g \in E[x]$ is an irreducible factor of f, then the norm of g is a power of f.

Moses & Yun (1973) propose the EZ-GCD algorithm for computing gcds in $\mathbb{Z}[x]$ and rings of multivariate polynomials via Hensel lifting. Yun (1976) gives a similar algorithm for computing the squarefree decomposition of a multivariate polynomial.

15.7. The blocking strategy was introduced by von zur Gathen & Shoup (1992). The average number of irreducible factors of a random polynomial with coefficients in a finite field appears in Berlekamp (1984), exercise 3.6 (already in the 1968 edition).

Figure 15.9 is from von zur Gathen & Gerhard (1996). The running time depends very much on the factorization pattern, not just on the degree. A similar phenomenon happened with our factorizations in $\mathbb{Z}[x]$. Among the ten inputs leading to one data point in Figures 15.11 through 15.13, the standard deviation was, in some cases, about as large as the average value.

In our factoring experiments with products of pseudorandom polynomials in $\mathbb{Z}[x]$, the pseudorandom factors were almost always irreducible; exceptions occurred up to degree 7 with 7-bit coefficients, and also for higher degrees with coefficients in $\{-1, 0, 1\}$.

Exercises.

15.1   (i) Prove **Eisenstein's theorem**: If $f \in \mathbb{Z}[x]$ and $p \in \mathbb{N}$ is a prime number such that $p \nmid \mathrm{lc}(f)$, p divides all other coefficients of f, and $p^2 \nmid f(0)$, then f is irreducible in $\mathbb{Q}[x]$.

  (ii) Conclude that for any $n \in \mathbb{N}$, the polynomial $x^n - p$ is irreducible in $\mathbb{Q}[x]$.

---

[2] If the polynomial X is squarefree modulo p, then it factors modulo p^k in the same way as modulo p. But if X has multiple factors, the task is much more complicated and cannot even be solved by the preceding principles in a straightforward manner.

15.2 Trace Algorithm 15.2 on factoring $f = 30x^5 + 39x^4 + 35x^3 + 25x^2 + 9x + 2 \in \mathbb{Z}[x]$. Choose the prime $p = 5003$ in step 2.

15.3 Here are the irreducible factorizations of $f \in \mathbb{Z}[x]$ of degree 6 modulo some small primes:

$$
\begin{array}{rcl}
f &=& (x+1)^2 \cdot (x^2 + x + 1) \cdot (x^4 + x^3 + x^2 + x + 1) \in \mathbb{F}_2[x] \\
f &=& (x+3) \cdot (x^3 + 3) \cdot (x^4 + 4x^3 + 2x^2 + x + 4) \in \mathbb{F}_7[x] \\
f &=& (x+9) \cdot (x^2 + 2x + 4) \cdot (x^5 + 5) \in \mathbb{F}_{11}[x]
\end{array}
$$

What can you say about the degrees of the irreducible factors of f in $\mathbb{Z}[x]$?

15.4$^{\longrightarrow}$ Compute the coefficients of the Swinnerton-Dyer polynomial

$$f = (x + \sqrt{-1} + \sqrt{2})(x + \sqrt{-1} - \sqrt{2})(x - \sqrt{-1} + \sqrt{2})(x - \sqrt{-1} - \sqrt{2}) \in \mathbb{Z}[x]$$

and its factorizations modulo $p = 2, 3, 5$. Prove that f is irreducible.

15.5 We have discussed big prime and prime power approaches to factoring in $\mathbb{Z}[x]$. Use Chebotarev's theorem to explain why a *small primes* approach is not promising.

15.6 Construct two polynomials which have factorization patterns modulo $2, 3, 5$ as in Example 15.7, such that the first one is irreducible in $\mathbb{Z}[x]$ and the second one splits into two irreducible factors of degrees 3 and 5.

15.7* Let $n = p_1 p_2$, where $p_1, p_2 \in \mathbb{N}$ are distinct odd primes. The nth cyclotomic polynomial Φ_n is irreducible in $\mathbb{Z}[x]$. Prove that it splits modulo any prime p into at least two factors. Hint: Lemma 14.50. Show that the number of factors is at least $p_1 - 1$ if $(p_1 - 1) \mid (p_2 - 1)$.

15.8** Let $p \in \mathbb{N}$ be prime. Prove that any Swinnerton-Dyer polynomial splits modulo p either completely into linear factors or completely into irreducible quadratic factors.

15.9** Let $\mathbb{F}_q$ be a finite field with q elements, for an odd prime power q, let x, y be indeterminates over $\mathbb{F}_q$, and

$$f = (x + \sqrt{y} + \sqrt{y+1})(x + \sqrt{y} - \sqrt{y+1})(x - \sqrt{y} + \sqrt{y+1})(x - \sqrt{y} - \sqrt{y+1}).$$

Show that $f \in \mathbb{F}_q[x, y]$ and that f is irreducible, but that $f(x, u) \in \mathbb{F}_q[x]$ splits into at least two factors for all $u \in \mathbb{F}_q$.

15.10* A **partition** of a positive integer n is a sequence $\lambda = (\lambda_1, \ldots, \lambda_r)$ of positive integers such that $\lambda_1 \geq \cdots \geq \lambda_r$ and $n = \lambda_1 + \cdots + \lambda_r$; r is the length of the partition. For example, if F is a field and $f \in F[x]$ of degree n, then the factorization pattern of f, with the degrees of the factors in descending order, is a partition of n.

If $\lambda = (\lambda_1, \ldots, \lambda_r)$ and $\mu = (\mu_1, \ldots, \mu_s)$ are two partitions of n, then we say that λ is finer than μ and write $\lambda \preccurlyeq \mu$ if there is a surjective map $\sigma: \{1, \ldots, r\} \longrightarrow \{1, \ldots, s\}$ such that $\mu_i = \sum_{\sigma(j)=i} \lambda_j$ for all $i \leq s$. For example, $\lambda = (4, 2, 1, 1)$ is finer than $\mu = (5, 3)$, as furnished by $\sigma(1) = \sigma(3) = 1$ and $\sigma(2) = \sigma(4) = 2$. (The function σ need not be unique.) In particular, (n) is the coarsest and $(1, 1, \ldots, 1)$ is the finest partition of n.

(i) Prove that if $f \in \mathbb{Z}[x]$ has degree n and $p \in \mathbb{N}$ is prime, μ is the factorization pattern of f in $\mathbb{Q}[x]$, and λ is the factorization pattern of $f \bmod p$ in $\mathbb{F}_p[x]$, then $\mu \succcurlyeq \lambda$.

(ii) Show that $\lambda \preccurlyeq \lambda$, $\lambda \preccurlyeq \mu \Longrightarrow \neg(\mu \preccurlyeq \lambda)$, and $\lambda \preccurlyeq \mu \preccurlyeq \nu \Longrightarrow \lambda \preccurlyeq \nu$ holds for all partitions λ, μ, ν of n, so that $\preccurlyeq$ is a partial order on the set of all partitions of n.

(iii) Enumerate all partitions of $n = 8$, and draw them in form of a directed graph, with an edge from λ to μ if μ is a direct successor of λ with respect to the order $\preccurlyeq$, so that $\lambda \preccurlyeq \mu$, $\lambda \neq \mu$, and $\lambda \preccurlyeq \nu \preccurlyeq \mu \Longrightarrow \lambda = \nu$ or $\nu = \mu$ for all partitions ν.

(iv) Use (iii) to show that there exist partitions λ, μ of 8 that do not have a supremum with respect to $\preccurlyeq$. (Thus the partitions do not form a "lattice" in the sense of order theory, not to be confused with the $\mathbb{Z}$-module lattices in Chapter 16.)

(v) Let $a_{n,r}$ denote the number of partitions of n of length r. Thus $a_{n,1} = a_{n,n} = 1$ and $a_{nr} = 0$ for $1 \leq n < r$. Prove the recursion formula $a_{n,r} = \sum_{1 \leq j \leq r} a_{n-r,j}$ for $1 \leq r < n$. Calculate $a_{n,r}$ for $1 \leq k \leq n \leq 8$, and compare with your results from (iii).

15.11 (Legendre 1785, p. 490) Let $f = x^3 - 292x^2 - 2\,170\,221x + 6\,656\,000 \in \mathbb{Z}[x]$. Find 13-adic linear factors $x - a_i$ with f rem $x - a_i \equiv 0$ mod 13^{2^i} for $i = 0, 1, 2$, starting with $a_0 = 0$.

15.12 Prove Lemma 15.9 (ii).

15.13 Suppose that $f \in \mathbb{Z}[x]$ has degree 8, and p is a prime so that f mod $p = g_1 g_2 g_3$ factors into three irreducible and pairwise coprime polynomials $g_1, g_2, g_3 \in \mathbb{F}_p[x]$ with $\deg g_1 = 1$, $\deg g_2 = 2$, and $\deg g_3 = 5$.

(i) What can you say about the possible factorizations of f modulo p^{100}?

(ii) What can you say about the possible factorizations of f in $\mathbb{Q}[x]$?

(iii) Suppose q is another prime for which f mod $q = h_1 h_2$ with $h_1, h_2 \in \mathbb{F}_q[x]$ irreducible and $\deg h_1 = \deg h_2 = 4$. What can you say about the possible factorizations of f in $\mathbb{Q}[x]$, using all this information?

15.14 Let $f = x^{15} - 1 \in \mathbb{Z}[x]$. Take a nontrivial factorization $f \equiv gh$ mod 2 with $g, h \in \mathbb{Z}[x]$ monic and of degree at least 2. Compute $g^*, h^* \in \mathbb{Z}[x]$ such that

$$f \equiv g^* h^* \text{ mod } 16, \quad \deg g^* = \deg g, \quad g^* \equiv g \text{ mod } 2.$$

Show your intermediate results. Can you guess some factors of f in $\mathbb{Z}[x]$?

15.15 Let $f = 14x^4 + 15x^3 + 42x^2 + 3x + 1 \in \mathbb{Z}[x]$.

(i) Find a suitable prime $p \in \mathbb{N}$ such that f mod p is squarefree and has degree 4.

(ii) Compute the irreducible factorization of f mod p in $\mathbb{F}_p[x]$. Choose two factors $g, h \in \mathbb{Z}[x]$ that are coprime modulo p such that h is monic and irreducible modulo p and $f \equiv gh$ mod p. Determine $s, t \in \mathbb{Z}[x]$ with $sg + th \equiv 1$ mod p.

(iii) Execute two successive Hensel steps (Algorithm 15.10 for $m = p$ and $m = p^2$) to obtain a factorization $f \equiv g^* h^*$ mod p^4 with $g \equiv g^*$ mod p and $h \equiv h^*$ mod p. Can you derive a factorization of f in $\mathbb{Q}[x]$ from it?

15.16$^{\longrightarrow}$ Consider the polynomial

$$
\begin{aligned}
f \ = \ & x^5 + \left(3y^3 + 39y^2 + 50y + 28\right)x^4 + \left(36y^5 + 2y^4 + 47y^3 + 63y^2 + 49y + 58\right)x^3 \\
& + \left(91y^6 + 18y^5 + 81y^4 + 37y^3 + 36y^2 + 53y + 64\right)x^2 \\
& + \left(74y^7 + 54y^6 + 24y^5 + 39y^4 + 71y^3 + 18y^2 + 93y + 53\right)x \\
& + \left(62y^6 + 72y^5 + 87y^4 + 27y^3 + 19y^2 + 61y\right) \in \mathbb{F}_{97}[x, y].
\end{aligned}
$$

(i) Compute a factorization $f \equiv gh$ mod y with coprime nonconstant polynomials $g, h \in \mathbb{F}_{97}[x]$, and polynomials $s, t \in \mathbb{F}_{97}[x]$ with $sg + th = 1$.

(ii) Execute two successive Hensel steps (Algorithm 15.10 with $m = y$ and $m = y^2$) to obtain polynomials $g^*, h^* \in \mathbb{F}_{97}[x, y]$ such that $f \equiv gh$ mod y^4, $g^* \equiv g$ mod y, and $h^* \equiv h$ mod y.

15.17 Complete the proof of Theorem 15.11.

15.18 (Shamir 1993) Let $N = p \cdot q$ be the product of two distinct primes p, q.

(i) Show that $u = p^2 + q^2$ is a unit in $\mathbb{Z}_N^\times$.

(ii) Verify the factorization $x \equiv u^{-1}(px+q)(qx+p) \bmod N$.

(iii) Prove that the two linear factors in (ii) are irreducible in $\mathbb{Z}_N[x]$. Hint: CRT.

15.19* Let $N = p_1 \cdots p_s$ be a product of s distinct primes, and $f \in \mathbb{Z}_N[x]$ be monic and squarefree.

(i) Let $g_1 \in \mathbb{Z}_{p_1}[x]$ be irreducible, and $g \in \mathbb{Z}_N[x]$ with $g \equiv g_1 \bmod p_1$ and $g \equiv 1 \bmod p_i$ for $i \geq 2$. Prove that g is irreducible in $\mathbb{Z}_N[x]$.

(ii) Assume that we have factored f modulo each p_i. Determine the factorization of f into irreducible polynomials in $\mathbb{Z}_N[x]$. How many irreducible factors are there, in terms of the numbers of irreducible factors modulo each p_i?

(iii) How many irreducible factors does $x^3 - x$ have modulo 105? Find four of them.

15.20 This exercise discusses a variant of Hensel lifting with linear convergence.

(i) One step works as follows. In Algorithm 15.10, we have an additional input $p \in R$, and the congruence $sg + th \equiv 1$ should hold modulo p instead of m. In step 1, we perform all computations modulo mp instead of m^2, and step 2 is omitted completely. Prove that then the output specifications of Algorithm 15.10 for f, g^*, h^* hold if m^2 is replaced by mp.

(ii) Now we start with a factorization of f, including the polynomials s, t, as specified in Algorithm 15.10 for $m = p$, and want to compute a factorization modulo p^l for some $l \in \mathbb{N}$. Show that for $R = \mathbb{Z}$, this takes $O(\mathsf{M}(n)\mathsf{M}(l \log p) \log l)$ word operations when using the quadratic lifting algorithm 15.10 for $m = p, p^2, p^4, p^8, \ldots$, and $O(\mathsf{M}(n)\mathsf{M}(l \log p)l)$ word operations when using the linear lifting algorithm from (i) for $m = p, p^2, p^3, p^4, \ldots$.

In fact, by employing fast lazy multiplication techniques (van der Hoeven 1997), the cost for linear Hensel lifting can be reduced to $O^\sim(nl \log p)$ as well (Bernardin 1998, private communication).

15.21 Let R be a ring (commutative, with 1) and $f \in R[x], g = \sum_{0 \leq i \leq m} g_i x^i, h = \sum_{0 \leq i \leq k} h_i x^i$ be polynomials such that $n = \deg f = m + k$ and $\mathrm{lc}(f) = g_m h_k$. Regarding the n coefficients $g_0, \ldots, g_{m-1}$, $h_0, \ldots, h_{k-1}$ as indeterminates, we define n polynomials $\varphi_0, \ldots, \varphi_{n-1}$ in these indeterminates by letting φ_i be the coefficient of x^i in $f - gh$ for $0 \leq i < n$.

(i) Prove that the Jacobian $J \in R[g_0, \ldots, g_{m-1}, h_0, \ldots, h_{n-1}]^{n \times n}$, whose ith row comprises the partial derivatives $\partial \varphi_i / \partial h_j$ and $\partial \varphi_i / \partial g_j$, is precisely the Sylvester matrix of g and h.

(ii) Conclude that for specific values of the coefficients of g, h and a given $m \in R$, there exist $s, t \in R[x]$ such that $sg + th \equiv 1 \bmod m$ if and only if J is invertible modulo m. Hint: Exercise 6.15.

15.22 Prove the running time estimate of Theorem 15.18 for the case $R = F[y]$.

15.23 Let $f = 6x^5 + 23x^4 + 51x^3 + 65x^2 + 65x + 42 \in \mathbb{Z}[x]$ and $p = 11$.

(i) Compute the irreducible factorization of $f/6 \bmod p$, and set up a factor tree of f modulo p.

(ii) Use Algorithm 15.17 to compute a factor tree of f modulo p^4.

(iii) Try to find nontrivial factors of f in $\mathbb{Z}[x]$ via factor combination.

15.24* Prove Theorem 15.23.

15.25* (i) Show that the bivariate polynomial factorization algorithm 15.24 works correctly when F is a field of characteristic zero. First convince yourself that $u = v$ is the squarefree part of g.

(ii) Let $\mathbb{F}_q$ be a finite field of characteristic p and $h \in \mathbb{F}_q[x, y]$. Prove that h is a pth power if and only if $\partial h / \partial x = \partial h / \partial y = 0$.

(iii) Show that h is squarefree if and only if it is coprime to one of $\partial h / \partial x$ or $\partial h / \partial y$. Hint: Exercise 14.22.

(iv) Prove that in step 3 of Algorithm 15.24, $\gcd(u, \partial u / \partial x) = \gcd(w, \partial w / \partial x) = 1$ in $\mathbb{F}_q(y)[x]$ and $\gcd(v, \partial v / \partial y) = 1$ in $\mathbb{F}_q(x)[y]$, and conclude that u, v, w are squarefree.

(v) Now assume that h is an irreducible factor of g with multiplicity e in step 3 of Algorithm 15.24. Conclude from the above that if $p \nmid e$, then $h \mid vw$ in step 3 and $h \nmid g$ in step 8, and that h^e still divides g in step 8 if $p \mid e$.

(vi) Prove that Algorithm 15.24 works correctly when $F = \mathbb{F}_q$.

15.26* (Gerhard 1999) This exercise discusses a small primes modular algorithm for computing the squarefree decomposition of a primitive polynomial $f \in \mathbb{Z}[x]$.

(i) We may assume that f is nonconstant and $\mathrm{lc}(f) > 0$. Prove that there exist unique primitive squarefree and pairwise coprime polynomials $g_1, \ldots, g_m \in \mathbb{Z}[x]$ such that $\mathrm{lc}(g_i) > 0$ for all i, g_m is nonconstant, and $f = g_1 g_2^2 \cdots g_m^m$.

(ii) Now let p be a prime not dividing $\mathrm{lc}(f)$ and $f \equiv \mathrm{lc}(f) h_1 h_2^2 \cdots h_k^k \bmod p$ be the squarefree decomposition of f modulo p, with monic nonconstant $h_1, \ldots, h_k \in \mathbb{Z}[x]$ that are squarefree and pairwise coprime modulo p. Show that $k \geq m$ and the modular squarefree part $h_1 \cdots h_k$ divides modulo p the squarefree part $g = g_1 \cdots g_m$ of f. Prove that $k = m$ and $g_i \equiv \mathrm{lc}(g_i) h_i \bmod p$ for all i if p does not divide the (nonzero) discriminant $\mathrm{res}(g, g') \in \mathbb{Z}$ of g.

(iii) Design a small primes modular algorithm for computing the squarefree decomposition of f, in analogy to the small primes modular gcd algorithm 6.38. Your algorithm should check that the result is correct, so that it is Las Vegas, and use $O^\sim(n^2 + n \log A)$ word operations if $A = \|f\|_\infty$.

15.27* Using Exercise 15.26, design a prime power modular algorithm for computing the squarefree decomposition of a primitive polynomial $f \in \mathbb{Z}[x]$. Your algorithm should check that the result is correct, so that it is Las Vegas, and use $O^\sim(n^2 + n \log A)$ word operations if $n = \deg f$ and $A = \|f\|_\infty$.

15.28 We have indicated in Section 15.7 that factoring a random polynomial with k-bit coefficients over the integers is computationally faster than factoring the same polynomial modulo a k-bit prime. This suggests a factoring algorithm over finite prime fields which first factors the input polynomial over the integers and then calls the factoring algorithm over finite fields for its (in $\mathbb{Z}[x]$) irreducible factors. Explain why this is not of much help for random polynomials.

Research problem.

15.29 Let $f \in \mathbb{Z}[x]$, p be a prime, and $k \in \mathbb{N}$. Can you find all factorizations of f into irreducible factors modulo p^k in time polynomial in $\deg f$ and $k \log p$? An apparently difficult case is when the discriminant $\mathrm{res}(f, f')$ is zero.

La clarté est, en effet, d'autant plus nécessaire,
qu'on a dessein d'entraîner le lecteur plus loin
des routes battues et dans des contrées plus arides.[1]

Joseph Liouville (1846)

Mathematics was orderly and it made sense. The answers were
always there if you worked carefully enough, or that's what she said.

Sue Grafton (1982)

A good idea, but not as simple in life as it is in theory.

Philip Friedman (1992)

---

[1] Clarity is all the more necessary when one intends to guide the reader further away from the beaten track and
into more arid countryside.

16

Short vectors in lattices

In this chapter, we present a polynomial-time algorithm for factoring univariate polynomials with integer coefficients. We will also indicate how the algorithm can be modified so as to also work for bivariate polynomials over a field where we have univariate factorization, such as $\mathbb{Q}$ or a finite field. The main technical ingredient, short vectors in lattices, will be the central topic of this chapter.

16.1. Lattices

The methods we discuss in this chapter deal with computational aspects of the *geometry of numbers*, a mathematical theory initiated by Hermann Minkowski in the 1890s. This theory produces many results about Diophantine approximation, convex bodies, embeddings of algebraic number fields in $\mathbb{C}$, and the ellipsoid method for rational linear programming.

Let $f = (f_1, \ldots, f_n) \in \mathbb{R}^n$. In this chapter, we use the **norm** (or 2-norm, or Euclidean norm) of f, given by

$$\|f\| = \|f\|_2 = \left(\sum_{1 \leq i \leq n} f_i^2 \right)^{1/2} = (f \star f)^{1/2} \in \mathbb{R},$$

where $f \star g = \sum_{1 \leq i \leq n} f_i g_i \in \mathbb{R}$ is the usual **inner product** of two vectors f and $g = (g_1, \ldots, g_n)$ in $\mathbb{R}^n$ (often written as (f, g), or $\langle f, g \rangle$, or $f \cdot g^T$ in the literature). The vectors f and g are **orthogonal** if $f \star g = 0$.

DEFINITION 16.1. *Let $n \in \mathbb{N}$ and $f_1, \ldots, f_n \in \mathbb{R}^n$ with $f_i = (f_{i1}, \ldots, f_{in})$. Then*

$$L = \sum_{1 \leq i \leq n} \mathbb{Z} f_i = \{ \sum_{1 \leq i \leq n} r_i f_i : r_1, \ldots, r_n \in \mathbb{Z} \}$$

*is the **lattice** or $\mathbb{Z}$-module generated by $f_1, \ldots, f_n$. The vectors $f_1, \ldots, f_n$ are a **basis** of L. The **norm of L** is $|L| = |\det(f_{ij})_{1 \leq i, j \leq n}| \in \mathbb{R}$. Lemma 16.2 below implies that it is well defined, in other words, that the norm is independent of the choice of the generators of L.*

LEMMA 16.2. *Let $N \subseteq M \subseteq \mathbb{R}^n$ be lattices, generated by $g_1, \ldots, g_n$ and $f_1, \ldots, f_n$, respectively, where $f_i = (f_{i1}, \ldots, f_{in})$ and $g_i = (g_{i1}, \ldots, g_{in})$. Then $\det(f_{ij})_{1 \le i,j \le n}$ divides $\det(g_{ij})_{1 \le i,j \le n}$.*

PROOF. For $1 \le i, j \le n$ there exist $a_{ij} \in \mathbb{Z}$ such that $g_i = \sum_{1 \le j \le n} a_{ij} f_j$. Hence $|\det(g_{ij})| = |\det(a_{ij})| \cdot |\det(f_{ij})|$, and the claim follows. $\square$

If we let $N = M$ in the above lemma, so that $f_1, \ldots, f_n$ and $g_1, \ldots, g_n$ both generate the same lattice, we see that $|\det(f_{ij})| = |\det(g_{ij})|$. Hence the norm is indeed independent of the choice of basis of L. Geometrically, $|L|$ is the volume of the parallelepiped spanned by $f_1, \ldots, f_n$, and Hadamard's inequality (Theorem 16.6) says that $|L| \le \|f_1\| \cdots \|f_n\|$ holds.

EXAMPLE 16.3. We let $n = 2$, $f_1 = (12, 2)$, $f_2 = (13, 4)$ and $L = \mathbb{Z}f_1 + \mathbb{Z}f_2$. Figure 16.1 shows some lattice points of L near the origin of the plane $\mathbb{R}^2$. The norm of L is

$$|L| = \left| \det \begin{pmatrix} 12 & 2 \\ 13 & 4 \end{pmatrix} \right| = 22$$

and equals the area of the blue parallelogram in Figure 16.1. Another basis of L is $g_1 = (1, 2)$ and $g_2 = (11, 0)$, and g_1 is a shortest vector in L with respect to the Euclidean norm $\|\cdot\|$. $\diamondsuit$

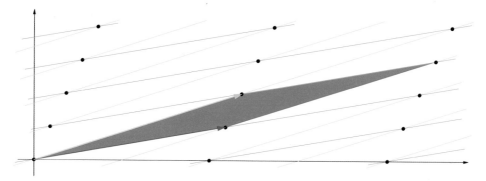

FIGURE 16.1: The lattice in $\mathbb{R}^2$ generated by $(12, 2)$ (red) and $(13, 4)$ (yellow).

A natural question is to compute a shortest vector in a given lattice. An exciting recent development, reported in Section 20.7, shows that this problem is "$\mathcal{NP}$-hard", and there is no hope for efficient algorithms. But for our current application, the factorization of polynomials with integer coefficients, it will be sufficient to compute a "relatively short" vector, a problem for which Lenstra, Lenstra & Lovász (1982) first gave a polynomial time algorithm. Their "short vector" is guaranteed to be off by not more than a specified factor, which depends on the dimension but not the lattice itself.

16.2. Lenstra, Lenstra and Lovász' basis reduction algorithm

We briefly review the Gram-Schmidt orthogonalization procedure from linear algebra. Given an arbitrary basis $(f_1, \ldots, f_n)$ of $\mathbb{R}^n$, it computes an orthogonal basis $(f_1^*, \ldots, f_n^*)$ of $\mathbb{R}^n$ by essentially performing Gaussian elimination on the **Gramian matrix** $(f_i \star f_j)_{1 \le i, j \le n} \in \mathbb{R}^{n \times n}$ (Section 25.5). The f_i^* are defined inductively as follows.

$$f_i^* = f_i - \sum_{1 \le j < i} \mu_{ij} f_j^*, \quad \text{where } \mu_{ij} = \frac{f_i \star f_j^*}{f_j^* \star f_j^*} = \frac{f_i \star f_j^*}{\|f_j^*\|^2} \text{ for } 1 \le j < i. \tag{1}$$

In particular, $f_1^* = f_1$. We will call $(f_1^*, \ldots, f_n^*)$ the **Gram-Schmidt orthogonal basis** of $(f_1, \ldots, f_n)$, and the f_i^* together with the μ_{ij} form the **Gram-Schmidt orthogonalization** (or GSO for short) of $f_1, \ldots, f_n$. The GSO has rational coefficients if $f_1, \ldots, f_n$ have, and then the cost for computing the GSO is $O(n^3)$ arithmetic operations in $\mathbb{Q}$.

We consider the f_i and f_i^* to be row vectors in $\mathbb{R}^n$, and define three $n \times n$ matrices F, F^*, and M in $\mathbb{R}^{n \times n}$:

$$F = \begin{pmatrix} f_1 \\ \vdots \\ f_n \end{pmatrix}, \quad F^* = \begin{pmatrix} f_1^* \\ \vdots \\ f_n^* \end{pmatrix}, \quad M = (\mu_{ij})_{1 \le i, j \le n},$$

where $\mu_{ii} = 1$ for $i \le n$, and $\mu_{ij} = 0$ for $1 \le i < j \le n$. Then M is lower triangular with ones on the diagonal, and (1) reads:

$$F = \begin{pmatrix} f_1 \\ \vdots \\ f_n \end{pmatrix} = \begin{pmatrix} 1 & & 0 \\ \vdots & \ddots & \\ \mu_{n1} & \cdots & 1 \end{pmatrix} \begin{pmatrix} f_1^* \\ \vdots \\ f_n^* \end{pmatrix} = M \cdot F^*. \tag{2}$$

EXAMPLE 16.4. We let $n = 3$, $f_1 = (1,1,0)$, $f_2 = (1,0,1)$, $f_3 = (0,1,1)$, and calculate $f_1^* = f_1 = (1,1,0)$,

$$\mu_{21} = \frac{f_2 \star f_1^*}{f_1^* \star f_1^*} = \frac{1}{2}, \quad f_2^* = f_2 - \mu_{21} f_1^* = \left(\frac{1}{2}, -\frac{1}{2}, 1\right),$$

$$\mu_{31} = \frac{f_3 \star f_1^*}{f_1^* \star f_1^*} = \frac{1}{2}, \quad \mu_{32} = \frac{f_3 \star f_2^*}{f_2^* \star f_2^*} = \frac{1}{3}, \quad f_3^* = f_3 - \mu_{31} f_1^* - \mu_{32} f_2^* = \left(-\frac{2}{3}, \frac{2}{3}, \frac{2}{3}\right),$$

$$F = \begin{pmatrix} 1 & 1 & 0 \\ 1 & 0 & 1 \\ 0 & 1 & 1 \end{pmatrix} = \begin{pmatrix} 1 & 0 & 0 \\ \frac{1}{2} & 1 & 0 \\ \frac{1}{2} & \frac{1}{3} & 1 \end{pmatrix} \cdot \begin{pmatrix} 1 & 1 & 0 \\ \frac{1}{2} & -\frac{1}{2} & 1 \\ -\frac{2}{3} & \frac{2}{3} & \frac{2}{3} \end{pmatrix} = M \cdot F^*.$$

We have $\|f_1\|^2 = \|f_2\|^2 = \|f_3\|^2 = 2$ and $\|f_1^*\|^2 = 2$, $\|f_2^*\|^2 = 3/2$, $\|f_3^*\|^2 = 4/3$. ◇

The following theorem collects the properties of the Gram-Schmidt orthogonalization that we will need. The proof is left as Exercise 16.2.

▰▰▰ THEOREM 16.5. ▰▰▰▰▰▰▰▰▰▰▰▰▰▰▰▰▰▰▰▰▰▰▰▰▰▰▰▰▰▰▰▰▰

Let $f_1,\ldots,f_n \in \mathbb{R}^n$ be linearly independent, and $f_1^*,\ldots,f_n^*$ their Gram-Schmidt orthogonal basis. Let $0 \leq k \leq n$, and let $U_k = \sum_{1 \leq i \leq k} \mathbb{R} f_i \subseteq \mathbb{R}^n$ be the $\mathbb{R}$-subspace spanned by $f_1,\ldots,f_k$.

(i) $\sum_{1 \leq i \leq k} \mathbb{R} f_i^* = U_k$.

(ii) f_k^* is the projection of f_k onto the orthogonal complement

$$U_{k-1}^{\perp} = \{f \in \mathbb{R}^n : f \star u = 0 \text{ for all } u \in U_{k-1}\}$$

of U_{k-1}, and hence in particular $\|f_k^*\| \leq \|f_k\|$.

(iii) $f_1^*,\ldots,f_n^*$ are pairwise orthogonal, that is, $f_i^* \star f_j^* = 0$ if $i \neq j$.

(iv) $\det \begin{pmatrix} f_1 \\ \vdots \\ f_n \end{pmatrix} = \det \begin{pmatrix} f_1^* \\ \vdots \\ f_n^* \end{pmatrix}.$ ▰▰▰▰▰▰▰▰▰▰▰▰▰▰▰▰▰▰▰▰

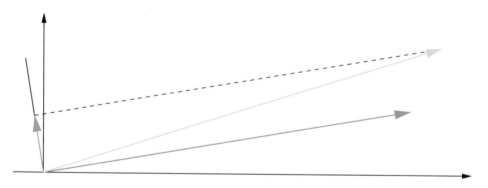

FIGURE 16.2: The Gram-Schmidt orthogonal basis of $(12,2)$ and $(13,4)$.

EXAMPLE 16.3 (continued). We have $f_1^* = f_1 = (12,2)$,

$$\mu_{21} = \frac{f_2 \star f_1^*}{f_1^* \star f_1^*} = \frac{41}{37}, \quad f_2^* = f_2 - \mu_{21} f_1^* = \left(-\frac{11}{37}, \frac{66}{37}\right).$$

This is illustrated in Figure 16.2: the vector f_2^* (pink) is the projection of f_2 (yellow) onto the orthogonal complement of f_1 (red). ◇

An immediate consequence of Theorem 16.5 is the following famous inequality.

▬▬ THEOREM 16.6 *Hadamard's inequality.* ▬▬▬▬▬▬▬▬▬▬▬▬▬▬▬▬

Let $A \in \mathbb{R}^{n \times n}$, with row vectors $f_1, \ldots, f_n \in \mathbb{R}^{1 \times n}$, and $B \in \mathbb{R}$ such that all entries of A are at most B in absolute value. Then

$$|\det A| \leq \|f_1\| \cdots \|f_n\| \leq n^{n/2} B^n.$$

PROOF. We may assume that A is nonsingular and the f_i are linearly independent. If $(f_1^*, \ldots, f_n^*)$ is their Gram-Schmidt orthogonal basis, then Theorem 16.5 implies that

$$\det \begin{pmatrix} f_1 \\ \vdots \\ f_n \end{pmatrix} = \det \begin{pmatrix} f_1^* \\ \vdots \\ f_n^* \end{pmatrix} = \|f_1^*\| \cdots \|f_n^*\| \leq \|f_1\| \cdots \|f_n\|.$$

The second inequality follows from noting that $\|f_i\| \leq n^{1/2} B$ for all i. □

Of course, the theorem also holds for the column vectors of A.

The next lemma exhibits the connection between the Gram-Schmidt orthogonal basis and short vectors.

LEMMA 16.7. *Let $L \subseteq \mathbb{R}^n$ be a lattice with basis $(f_1, \ldots, f_n)$, and let $(f_1^*, \ldots, f_n^*)$ be its Gram-Schmidt orthogonal basis. Then for any $f \in L \setminus \{0\}$ we have*

$$\|f\| \geq \min\{\|f_1^*\|, \ldots, \|f_n^*\|\}.$$

PROOF. Let $f = \sum_{1 \leq i \leq n} \lambda_i f_i \in L \setminus \{0\}$ be arbitrary, with all $\lambda_i \in \mathbb{Z}$, and let k be the highest index such that $\lambda_k \neq 0$. Substituting $\sum_{1 \leq j \leq i} \mu_{ij} f_j^*$ for f_i yields

$$f = \sum_{1 \leq i \leq k} \lambda_i \sum_{1 \leq j \leq i} \mu_{ij} f_j^* = \lambda_k f_k^* + \sum_{1 \leq i < k} \nu_i f_i^*$$

for some appropriate $\nu_i \in \mathbb{R}$. Then

$$
\begin{aligned}
\|f\|^2 &= f \star f = \left(\lambda_k f_k^* + \sum_{1 \leq i < k} \nu_i f_i^* \right) \star \left(\lambda_k f_k^* + \sum_{1 \leq i < k} \nu_i f_i^* \right) \\
&= \lambda_k^2 (f_k^* \star f_k^*) + \sum_{1 \leq i < k} \nu_i^2 (f_i^* \star f_i^*) \geq \lambda_k^2 \cdot \|f_k^*\|^2 \\
&\geq \|f_k^*\|^2 \geq \min\{\|f_1^*\|^2, \ldots, \|f_n^*\|^2\},
\end{aligned}
$$

where we used the pairwise orthogonality of the f_i^* and that $\lambda_k \in \mathbb{Z} \setminus \{0\}$. □

Our goal is to compute a short vector in L. If the Gram-Schmidt orthogonal basis of $(f_1, \ldots, f_n)$ is a basis for the lattice L generated by $f_1, \ldots, f_n$, then the lemma says that one of the f_i^* is a shortest vector. But usually the f_i^* are not even in L, as in Example 16.4. This problem motivates the following definition of a reduced basis as an "almost orthogonal" basis of L.

DEFINITION 16.8. Let $f_1, \ldots, f_n \in \mathbb{R}^n$ be *linearly independent* and $(f_1^*, \ldots, f_n^*)$ *the corresponding Gram-Schmidt orthogonal basis. Then* $(f_1, \ldots, f_n)$ *is* **reduced** *if* $\|f_i^*\|^2 \leq 2\|f_{i+1}^*\|^2$ *for* $1 \leq i < n$.

The basis in Example 16.4 is reduced. Lemma 16.7 provided a lower bound on the length of nonzero vectors in L, in terms of the GSO. With a reduced basis, we get a similar, though somewhat weaker, bound in terms of the original basis.

THEOREM 16.9.
Let $(f_1, \ldots, f_n)$ *be a reduced basis of the lattice* $L \subseteq \mathbb{R}^n$ *and* $f \in L \setminus \{0\}$. *Then* $\|f_1\| \leq 2^{(n-1)/2} \cdot \|f\|$.

PROOF. We have $\|f_1\|^2 = \|f_1^*\|^2 \leq 2\|f_2^*\|^2 \leq 2^2\|f_3^*\|^2 \leq \cdots \leq 2^{n-1}\|f_n^*\|^2$. Thus $\|f\| \geq \min\{\|f_1^*\|, \ldots, \|f_n^*\|\} \geq 2^{-(n-1)/2}\|f_1\|$, using Lemma 16.7. $\square$

We now present an algorithm that computes a reduced basis of a lattice $L \subseteq \mathbb{Z}^n$ from an arbitrary basis. One can use this to find a reduced basis of a lattice in $\mathbb{Q}^n$, by multiplying with a common denominator of the given basis vectors. For $\mu \in \mathbb{R}$, we write $\lceil \mu \rfloor = \lfloor \mu + 1/2 \rfloor$ for the integer nearest to μ.

ALGORITHM 16.10 Basis reduction.
Input: Linearly independent row vectors $f_1, \ldots, f_n \in \mathbb{Z}^n$.
Output: A reduced basis $(g_1, \ldots, g_n)$ of the lattice $L = \sum_{1 \leq i \leq n} \mathbb{Z} f_i \subseteq \mathbb{Z}^n$.

1. **for** $i = 1, \ldots, n$ **do** $g_i \longleftarrow f_i$
   compute the GSO $G^*, M \in \mathbb{Q}^{n \times n}$, as in (1) and (2), $\quad i \longleftarrow 2$

2. **while** $i \leq n$ **do**

3. $\qquad$ **for** $j = i - 1, i - 2, \ldots, 1$ **do**

4. $\qquad\qquad g_i \longleftarrow g_i - \lceil \mu_{ij} \rfloor g_j$, $\quad$ update the GSO $\quad$ { replacement step }

5. $\qquad$ **if** $i > 1$ **and** $\|g_{i-1}^*\|^2 > 2\|g_i^*\|^2$
   $\qquad$ **then** exchange g_{i-1} and g_i and update the GSO, $\quad i \longleftarrow i - 1$
   $\qquad$ **else** $i \longleftarrow i + 1$

6. **return** $g_1, \ldots, g_n$

step	$\begin{pmatrix} g_1 \\ g_2 \end{pmatrix}$	M	$\begin{pmatrix} g_1^* \\ g_2^* \end{pmatrix}$	action
4	$\begin{pmatrix} 12 & 2 \\ 13 & 4 \end{pmatrix}$	$\begin{pmatrix} 1 & 0 \\ \frac{41}{37} & 1 \end{pmatrix}$	$\begin{pmatrix} 12 & 2 \\ -\frac{11}{37} & \frac{66}{37} \end{pmatrix}$	row 2 ⟵ row 2 + row 1
5	$\begin{pmatrix} 12 & 2 \\ 1 & 2 \end{pmatrix}$	$\begin{pmatrix} 1 & 0 \\ \frac{4}{37} & 1 \end{pmatrix}$	$\begin{pmatrix} 12 & 2 \\ -\frac{11}{37} & \frac{66}{37} \end{pmatrix}$	exchange rows 1 and 2
4	$\begin{pmatrix} 1 & 2 \\ 12 & 2 \end{pmatrix}$	$\begin{pmatrix} 1 & 0 \\ \frac{16}{5} & 1 \end{pmatrix}$	$\begin{pmatrix} 1 & 2 \\ \frac{44}{5} & -\frac{22}{5} \end{pmatrix}$	row 2 ⟵ row 2 − row 1
6	$\begin{pmatrix} 1 & 2 \\ 9 & -4 \end{pmatrix}$	$\begin{pmatrix} 1 & 0 \\ \frac{1}{5} & 1 \end{pmatrix}$	$\begin{pmatrix} 1 & 2 \\ \frac{44}{5} & -\frac{22}{5} \end{pmatrix}$	

TABLE 16.3: Trace of the basis reduction algorithm 16.10 on the lattice of Example 16.3.

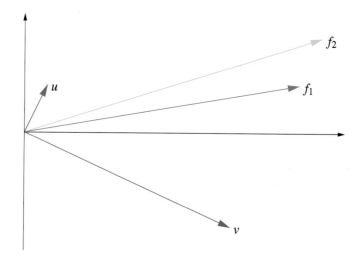

FIGURE 16.4: The vectors computed by the basis reduction algorithm 16.10 for the lattice of Example 16.3.

EXAMPLE 16.3 (continued). Table 16.3 traces the algorithm on the lattice of Example 16.3, later.) and Figure 16.4 depicts the vectors g_i in the computation. We start with $g_1 = f_1 = (12,2)$ (red) and $g_2 = f_2 = (13,4)$ (yellow). In the second row of Table 16.3, g_2 is replaced by $u = g_2 - \lceil 41/37 \rfloor g_1 = (1,2)$ (green). Then g_1 and g_2 are exchanged in the third row. In the last row, $v = g_2 - \lceil 16/5 \rfloor g_1 = f_1 - 3u = (9,-4)$ (blue) is computed, and the algorithm returns the reduced basis $u = (1,2)$ and $v = (9,-4)$. We can see clearly in Figure 16.4 that the final $g_1 = u$ (the green vector) is much shorter than the two input vectors f_1, f_2, and that the computed basis u, v (the green and the blue vector) is nearly orthogonal. ◇

In the above example, the final g_1 is actually a *shortest* vector. This seems to happen quite often, but Theorem 16.9 only guarantees that the norm of the first vector in the computed basis is bigger by a factor of at most $2^{(n-1)/2}$ than the norm of a shortest vector, where n is the dimension of the lattice.

16.3. Cost estimate for basis reduction

THEOREM 16.11.
Algorithm 16.10 correctly computes a reduced basis of L and runs in polynomial time. It uses $O(n^4 \log A)$ arithmetic operations on integers whose length is $O(n \log A)$, where $A = \max_{1 \le i \le n} \|f_i\|$.

The idea of the estimate on the number of arithmetic operations is as follows. Each execution of steps 4 or 5 has polynomial cost, and it is sufficient to bound the number of passes through step 5 with an exchange. In fact, at first glance it is not obvious that the algorithm terminates at all, since the decrease and increase of i in step 5 might continue forever. The crucial point then is to exhibit a value D with the following properties: It is always a positive integer, reasonably small in the beginning, and does not change in the algorithm except that at each exchange step it decreases (at least) by a factor of $3/4$. Therefore only few exchange steps can happen.

To structure the somewhat lengthy proof, we first investigate in the following two lemmas how the GSO of $(g_1, \ldots, g_n)$ changes in steps 4 and 5.

LEMMA 16.12.   (i) *We consider one execution of step 4, and let* $\lambda = \lceil \mu_{ij} \rfloor$ *for short. Let* G, G^*, M *and* H, H^*, N *in* $\mathbb{Q}^{n \times n}$ *be the matrices of the* g_k, g_k^*, μ_{kl} *before and after the replacement, respectively, and* $E = (e_{kl}) \in \mathbb{Z}^{n \times n}$ *the matrix which has* $e_{kk} = 1$ *for all* k, $e_{ij} = -\lambda$, *and* $e_{kl} = 0$ *otherwise. Then*

$$H = EG, \quad N = EM, \text{ and } H^* = G^*.$$

(ii) *The following invariant holds before each execution of step 4:*

$$|\mu_{il}| \le \frac{1}{2} \text{ for } j < l < i.$$

(iii) *The Gram-Schmidt orthogonal basis* $g_1^*, \ldots, g_n^*$ *does not change in step 4, and after the loop in step 3 we have* $|\mu_{il}| \le 1/2$ *for* $1 \le l < i$.

PROOF.   (i) The equality $H = EG$ is just another way of saying that g_i is replaced by $g_i - \lambda g_j$ and all other g_k remain unchanged. Since $j < i$, for any $k \le n$ the space spanned by $g_1, \ldots, g_k$ remains the same, and hence the orthogonal vectors $g_1^*, \ldots, g_n^*$

are not changed, which means that $G^* = H^*$. Now the third claim follows from the equations analogous to (2),

$$EMG^* = EG = H = NH^* = NG^*,$$

and the fact that G^* is invertible.

(ii) The invariant is trivial at the beginning of the loop, and we suppose that it holds before step 4. Now the multiplication by E subtracts λ times row j from row i of M, which does not affect the μ_{il} with $j < l$. Finally, μ_{ij} is replaced by $\mu_{ij} - \lambda\mu_{ij}$, which has absolute value at most $1/2$, by the choice of λ, and the invariant holds again before the next execution of step 4.

(iii) is immediate from (i) and (ii). $\square$

$$\begin{pmatrix}
1 & 0 & \cdots & \cdots & \cdots & \cdots & \cdots & 0 \\
\cdot & 1 & \ddots & & & & & \vdots \\
\cdot & \cdot & 1 & \ddots & & & & \vdots \\
\cdot & \cdot & \cdot & 1 & \ddots & & & \vdots \\
\cdot & \cdot & \cdot & \cdot & 1 & \ddots & & \vdots \\
\circ & \circ & \bullet & \cdot & \cdot & 1 & \ddots & \vdots \\
* & * & * & * & * & * & 1 & 0 \\
* & * & * & * & * & * & * & 1
\end{pmatrix}$$

FIGURE 16.5: The effect of one replacement step on the μ_{ij}.

The effect of one replacement step 4 is illustrated in Figure 16.5 for $n = 8$, $i = 6$, and $j = 3$. Each $\cdot$ represents a number which is absolutely less that $1/2$; it is not modified in the current or any later replacement in the loop 3. Each $\circ$ represents a number that is changed in step 4, and the $\bullet$ is μ_{63}, which is reduced to not more than $1/2$ in absolute value by it. (This is also the position of the lonely nonzero off-diagonal entry of E.) The values of $*$ are arbitrary and not changed by the current or any later replacement in the loop 3.

LEMMA 16.13. *Suppose that g_{i-1} and g_i are exchanged in step 5, and denote by h_k and h_k^* the vectors and their Gram-Schmidt orthogonal basis after the exchange, respectively. Then*

(i) $h_k^* = g_k^*$ *for $k \in \{1,\dots,n\} \setminus \{i-1,i\}$,*

(ii) $\|h_{i-1}^*\|^2 < \frac{3}{4}\|g_{i-1}^*\|^2$,

(iii) $\|h_i^*\| \le \|g_{i-1}^*\|$.

PROOF.   (i) For such k, we have $g_k = h_k$ and $\Sigma_{1 \leq l < k} \mathbb{R} g_l = \Sigma_{1 \leq l < k} \mathbb{R} h_l$, and so Theorem 16.5 (ii) implies that $h_k^* = g_k^*$.

(ii) The vector h_{i-1}^* is the component of g_i orthogonal to $\Sigma_{1 \leq l < i-1} \mathbb{R} g_l$. Since $g_i = g_i^* + \Sigma_{1 \leq l \leq i-1} \mu_{i,l} g_l^*$, we have $h_{i-1}^* = g_i^* + \mu_{i,i-1} g_{i-1}^*$ and

$$\|h_{i-1}^*\|^2 = \|g_i^*\|^2 + \mu_{i,i-1}^2 \|g_{i-1}^*\|^2 \leq \frac{1}{2} \|g_{i-1}^*\|^2 + \frac{1}{4} \|g_{i-1}^*\|^2 = \frac{3}{4} \|g_{i-1}^*\|^2,$$

by the condition for the exchange, the orthogonality of g_i^* and g_{i-1}^*, and the fact that $|\mu_{i,i-1}| \leq 1/2$, by the previous lemma.

(iii) We let $u = \Sigma_{1 \leq l < i-1} \mu_{i-1,l} g_l^*$ and $U = \Sigma_{1 \leq l < i-1} \mathbb{R} g_l$ for short. Then the vector h_i^* is the component of $g_{i-1} = g_{i-1}^* + u$ orthogonal to $U + \mathbb{R} g_i$. Now Theorem 16.5 implies that $u \in U \subseteq U + \mathbb{R} g_i$. Thus h_i^* is the component of g_{i-1}^* orthogonal to $U + \mathbb{R} g_i$, and hence $\|h_i^*\| \leq \|g_{i-1}^*\|$. $\square$

LEMMA 16.14.   *At the beginning of each iteration of the loop in step 2, the following invariants hold:*

$$|\mu_{kl}| \leq \frac{1}{2} \text{ for } 1 \leq l < k < i, \quad \|g_{k-1}^*\|^2 \leq 2\|g_k^*\|^2 \text{ for } 1 \leq k < i.$$

PROOF.   The claim is trivial at the beginning of the algorithm. So we assume that the invariants hold at the beginning of step 3 and prove that they hold again at the end of step 5. Lemma 16.12 implies that the first invariant also holds for $k = i$ immediately before step 5, and since an exchange does not affect the μ_{kl} for $k < i - 1$, the first invariant holds after step 5 in any case. Again by Lemma 16.12, the g_k^* do not change in steps 3 and 4, and the second invariant is still valid immediately before step 5. Now an exchange in step 5 does not affect the g_k^* for $k \notin \{i-1, i\}$, by Lemma 16.13, and the second invariant holds again after step 5 in any case as well. $\square$

In particular, the above lemma implies that the basis $g_1, \ldots, g_n$ is reduced upon termination of the algorithm, and it remains to bound the number of iterations of the loop in step 2. At any stage in the algorithm and for $1 \leq k \leq n$, we consider the matrix

$$G_k = \begin{pmatrix} g_1 \\ \vdots \\ g_k \end{pmatrix} \in \mathbb{Z}^{k \times n}$$

comprising the first k vectors, their Gramian matrix $G_k \cdot G_k^T = (g_j \star g_l)_{1 \leq j,l \leq k} \in \mathbb{Z}^{k \times k}$, and the **Gramian determinant** $d_k = \det(G_k \cdot G_k^T) \in \mathbb{Z}$. For convenience, we let $d_0 = 1$.

LEMMA 16.15. *For* $1 \leq k \leq n$, *we have* $d_k = \prod_{1 \leq l \leq k} \|g_l^*\|^2 > 0$.

PROOF. Let $1 \leq k \leq n$, M_k the upper left $k \times k$ submatrix of the transition matrix M, and

$$G_k^* = \begin{pmatrix} g_1^* \\ \vdots \\ g_k^* \end{pmatrix} \in \mathbb{R}^{k \times n}.$$

Then $\det M_k = 1$, $G_k^* \cdot (G_k^*)^T \in \mathbb{R}^{k \times k}$ is a diagonal matrix with diagonal entries $\|g_1^*\|^2, \ldots, \|g_k^*\|^2$, $G_k = M_k G_k^*$, and

$$\begin{aligned} d_k &= \det(G_k G_k^T) = \det(M_k G_k^* (G_k^*)^T (M_k)^T) \\ &= \det(M_k) \cdot \det(G_k^* (G_k^*)^T) \cdot \det(M_k^T) = \prod_{1 \leq l \leq k} \|g_k^*\|^2. \quad \square \end{aligned}$$

LEMMA 16.16.   (i) *In steps 3 and 4, none of the d_k changes.*

(ii) *If g_{i-1} and g_i are exchanged in step 5 and d_k^* denotes the new value of d_k, for any k, then $d_k^* = d_k$ for $k \neq i-1$ and $d_{i-1}^* \leq \frac{3}{4} d_{i-1}$.*

PROOF.   (i) follows from Lemmas 16.12 and 16.15.

(ii) For $k \neq i-1$ the effect of the exchange on the matrix G_k is a multiplication by a $k \times k$ permutation matrix, whose determinant is 1 or -1. Thus $d_k^* = d_k$. Lemma 16.15 says that $d_{i-1} = \prod_{1 \leq l < i} \|g_l^*\|^2$, and Lemma 16.13 yields $d_{i-1}^* \leq \frac{3}{4} d_{i-1}$. $\square$

So now we have found our desired loop variant $D = \prod_{1 \leq k < n} d_k$, and can bound the number of arithmetic operations. Step 1 takes $O(n^3)$ operations in $\mathbb{Z}$. With the notation as in Lemma 16.12, one execution of step 4 amounts to computing the matrix products EG and EM, at a cost of $O(n)$ operations. Thus the number of operations in $\mathbb{Z}$ used in the loop in step 3 is $O(n^2)$. If an exchange happens in step 5, then only g_{i-1}^*, g_i^*, and rows and columns $i-1$ and i of the transition matrix M change, and they can be updated using $O(n)$ operations, which is dominated by the cost for the loop 3. We always have $1 \leq D \in \mathbb{Z}$, and its initial value D_0, at the start of the algorithm, satisfies

$$D_0 = \|f_1^*\|^{n-1} \|f_2^*\|^{n-2} \cdots \|f_{n-1}^*\| \leq \|f_1\|^{n-1} \|f_2\|^{n-2} \cdots \|f_{n-1}\| \leq A^{n(n-1)/2},$$

since f_i^* is a projection of f_i for all i. By Lemma 16.16, D does not change in steps 3 and 4, and decreases at least by a factor of $3/4$ if an exchange happens in step 5, so that the number of such exchange steps is bounded by $\log_{4/3} D_0 \in O(n^2 \log A)$. At any stage in the algorithm, let $e \in \mathbb{N}$ denote the number of exchange steps performed so far and e^* the number of times where the else-branch in step 5 has been taken. Since i is decreased by one in an exchange step and increased by one otherwise, the number $i + e - e^*$ is constant throughout the loop of step 2. Initially, it equals 2, and hence $n + 1 + e - e^* = 2$ at termination. Thus the total number of iterations of the loop in step 2 is $e + e^* = 2e + n - 1 \in O(n^2 \log A)$, and we get a total of $O(n^4 \log A)$ operations in $\mathbb{Z}$, as claimed in Theorem 16.11.

step	$\begin{pmatrix} g_1 \\ g_2 \\ g_3 \end{pmatrix}$	$\begin{pmatrix} \mu_{21} & \\ \mu_{31} & \mu_{32} \end{pmatrix}$	$\begin{pmatrix} \|g_1^*\|^2 \\ \|g_2^*\|^2 \\ \|g_3^*\|^2 \end{pmatrix}$	$\begin{matrix} d_1, d_2 \\ D \end{matrix}$	action
4	$\begin{pmatrix} 1 & 1 & 1 \\ -1 & 0 & 2 \\ 3 & 5 & 6 \end{pmatrix}$	$\begin{pmatrix} \frac{1}{3} & \\ \frac{14}{3} & \frac{13}{14} \end{pmatrix}$	$\begin{pmatrix} 3 \\ \frac{14}{3} \\ \frac{9}{14} \end{pmatrix}$	$\begin{matrix} 3, 14 \\ 42 \end{matrix}$	$\text{rep}(3,2)$
4	$\begin{pmatrix} 1 & 1 & 1 \\ -1 & 0 & 2 \\ 4 & 5 & 4 \end{pmatrix}$	$\begin{pmatrix} \frac{1}{3} & \\ \frac{13}{3} & \frac{-1}{14} \end{pmatrix}$	$\begin{pmatrix} 3 \\ \frac{14}{3} \\ \frac{9}{14} \end{pmatrix}$	$\begin{matrix} 3, 14 \\ 42 \end{matrix}$	$\text{rep}(3,1)$
5	$\begin{pmatrix} 1 & 1 & 1 \\ -1 & 0 & 2 \\ 0 & 1 & 0 \end{pmatrix}$	$\begin{pmatrix} \frac{1}{3} & \\ \frac{1}{3} & \frac{-1}{14} \end{pmatrix}$	$\begin{pmatrix} 3 \\ \frac{14}{3} \\ \frac{9}{14} \end{pmatrix}$	$\begin{matrix} 3, 14 \\ 42 \end{matrix}$	$\text{ex}(3,2)$
5	$\begin{pmatrix} 1 & 1 & 1 \\ 0 & 1 & 0 \\ -1 & 0 & 2 \end{pmatrix}$	$\begin{pmatrix} \frac{1}{3} & \\ \frac{1}{3} & \frac{-1}{2} \end{pmatrix}$	$\begin{pmatrix} 3 \\ \frac{2}{3} \\ \frac{9}{2} \end{pmatrix}$	$\begin{matrix} 3, 2 \\ 6 \end{matrix}$	$\text{ex}(2,1)$
4	$\begin{pmatrix} 0 & 1 & 0 \\ 1 & 1 & 1 \\ -1 & 0 & 2 \end{pmatrix}$	$\begin{pmatrix} 1 & \\ 0 & \frac{1}{2} \end{pmatrix}$	$\begin{pmatrix} 1 \\ 2 \\ \frac{9}{2} \end{pmatrix}$	$\begin{matrix} 1, 2 \\ 2 \end{matrix}$	$\text{rep}(2,1)$
6	$\begin{pmatrix} 0 & 1 & 0 \\ 1 & 0 & 1 \\ -1 & 0 & 2 \end{pmatrix}$	$\begin{pmatrix} 0 & \\ 0 & \frac{1}{2} \end{pmatrix}$	$\begin{pmatrix} 1 \\ 2 \\ \frac{9}{2} \end{pmatrix}$	$\begin{matrix} 1, 2 \\ 2 \end{matrix}$	

TABLE 16.6: Trace of the basis reduction algorithm 16.10 on the lattice $L = \mathbb{Z}(1,1,1) + \mathbb{Z}(-1,0,2) + \mathbb{Z}(3,5,6)$. We have $d_1 = \|g_1^*\|^2$, $d_2 = \|g_1^*\|^2 \|g_2^*\|^2$, $D = d_1 d_2$, and $(\det L)^2 = d_3 = \|g_1^*\|^2 \|g_2^*\|^2 \|g_3^*\|^2 = 9$ throughout. Only the relevant values of the μ_{ij} and the squares of the norms of the g_i^* are given, and we have abbreviated a replacement $g_i \longleftarrow g_i - \lceil \mu_{ij} \rfloor g_j$ by $\text{rep}(i,j)$ and an exchange of g_i and g_{i-1} by $\text{ex}(i, i-1)$ in the "action" column.

Table 16.6 traces Algorithm 16.10 and the values of the Gramian determinants d_k and of their product D on a three-dimensional lattice.

We still have the task of bounding the size of (the numerators and denominators of) the rational numbers that occur in the algorithm. The following lemma gives general bounds on the Gram-Schmidt orthogonalization at any stage in the algorithm.

LEMMA 16.17. *Let* $g_1, \ldots, g_n \in \mathbb{Z}^n$, *let* G^* *and* M *be its Gram-Schmidt orthogonalization, and* $1 \leq l < k \leq n$. *Then*

(i) $d_{k-1} g_k^* \in \mathbb{Z}^n$,

(ii) $d_l \mu_{kl} \in \mathbb{Z}$,

(iii) $|\mu_{kl}| \leq d_{l-1}^{1/2} \|g_k\|$.

PROOF. (i) We can write $g_k^* = g_k - \sum_{1 \leq l < k} \lambda_{kl} g_l$, with some $\lambda_{kl} \in \mathbb{R}$. (In fact, the λ_{kl} are the coefficients of M^{-1} below the diagonal.) We take the inner product with g_j for some $j < k$. Then $g_k^* \star g_j = 0$, and

$$g_k \star g_j = \sum_{1 \leq l < k} \lambda_{kl} (g_l \star g_j).$$

Thus $\lambda_{k1}, \ldots, \lambda_{k,k-1}$ form the solution of a $(k-1) \times (k-1)$ system of linear equations. The coefficient matrix is $G_{k-1} \cdot G_{k-1}^T$, its determinant is d_{k-1}, and by Cramer's rule (Theorem 25.6), $d_{k-1} \lambda_{kl} \in \mathbb{Z}$ for each l. Hence $d_{k-1} g_k^* \in \mathbb{Z}^n$.

(ii) $d_l \mu_{kl} = d_l \dfrac{g_k \star g_l^*}{\|g_l^*\|^2} = d_l \dfrac{g_k \star g_l^*}{d_l / d_{l-1}} = d_{l-1}(g_k \star g_l^*) = g_k \star (d_{l-1} g_l^*) \in \mathbb{Z}$, by (i).

(iii) By Lemma 16.15, we have $\|g_l^*\|^2 = d_l / d_{l-1} \geq 1/d_{l-1}$. Using Cauchy's inequality (Exercise 16.10), we find

$$|\mu_{kl}| = \frac{|g_k \star g_l^*|}{\|g_l^*\|^2} \leq \frac{\|g_k\| \|g_l^*\|}{\|g_l^*\|^2} = \frac{\|g_k\|}{\|g_l^*\|} \leq d_{l-1}^{1/2} \|g_k\|. \quad \square$$

We have assumed that $\|f_k\| \leq A$ for all k. Then A is also an upper bound on the initial Gram-Schmidt orthogonal basis: $\|f_k^*\| \leq A$ for all k. Lemmas 16.12 and 16.13 guarantee that the value of $\max\{\|g_k^*\| : 1 \leq k \leq n\}$ never increases during the algorithm, so that at any stage and for all k, we have

$$\|g_k^*\| \leq A \text{ and } d_k = \prod_{1 \leq l \leq k} \|g_l^*\|^2 \leq A^{2k}. \tag{3}$$

LEMMA 16.18. *Let* $1 \leq k \leq n$.

(i) *At any stage in the algorithm, except possibly in steps 3 and 4 when* $k = i$, *we have* $\|g_k\| \leq n^{1/2} A$.

(ii) *During each execution of step 4,* $\|g_i\| \leq n(2A)^n$.

PROOF. Initially, we have $\|g_k\| \le A$ for all k. Step 5 does not change the $\|g_k\|$, and it is sufficient to examine what happens in steps 3 and 4. So we assume that the claims are true immediately before step 3. The vectors g_k for $k \ne i$ are not affected by step 4. Let $m_i = \max\{|\mu_{il}| : 1 \le l \le i\}$ be the maximal absolute value in the ith row of M. From $g_i = \sum_{1 \le l \le i} \mu_{il} g_l^*$ and the orthogonality of the g_l^*'s, we find

$$\|g_i\|^2 = \sum_{1 \le l \le i} \mu_{il}^2 \|g_l^*\|^2 \le nm_i^2 A^2, \text{ and } \|g_i\| \le n^{1/2} m_i A. \tag{4}$$

At the end of loop 3, we have $m_i = 1$, by Lemma 16.12; this concludes the proof of (i).

Lemma 16.17 and (i) imply that at the beginning of loop 3, we have

$$m_i \le \max\{d_{l-1}^{1/2} : 1 \le l < i\} \cdot \|g_i\| \le A^{n-2} \cdot n^{1/2} A = n^{1/2} A^{n-1}. \tag{5}$$

We now consider the replacement in step 4. Since $m_i \ge 1$ and $|\mu_{jl}| \le 1/2$ for $1 \le l < j$, by Lemma 16.14, we have

$$|\mu_{il} - \lceil \mu_{ij} \rfloor \mu_{jl}| \le |\mu_{il}| + |\lceil \mu_{ij} \rfloor| \cdot |\mu_{jl}| \le m_i + \left(m_i + \frac{1}{2}\right) \cdot \frac{1}{2} = \frac{3}{2} m_i + \frac{1}{4} \le 2m_i$$

for $1 \le l < j$. For $l = j$, the new value of μ_{ij} is absolutely at most $1/2$, by construction, and also the values of μ_{il} for $l > j$, by Lemma 16.12. Together we find that for each value of j, the value of m_i doubles at most, so that during the loop 3 the value of m_i increases at most by a factor $2^{i-1} \le 2^{n-1}$. Together with (5), this shows that $m_i \le n^{1/2}(2A)^{n-1}$ at all times. Using (4), we have

$$\|g_i\| \le n^{1/2} m_i A \le n(2A)^n. \quad \square$$

We now put things together for the final result.

PROOF of Theorem 16.11. We have already shown the correctness, and that the number of arithmetic operations in $\mathbb{Z}$ is $O(n^4 \log A)$. The denominators d_l of the rational numbers computed in the algorithm are at most A^{2n}, and their length is $O(n \log A)$. The numerators are absolutely at most

○ $\|g_k\|_\infty \le \|g_k\| \le n(2A)^n$ for g_k, by Lemma 16.18,

○ $\|d_{k-1}g_k^*\|_\infty \le \|d_{k-1}g_k^*\| \le A^{2k-2}A \le A^{2n}$ for g_k^*, by Lemma 16.17 and (3),

○ $|d_l\mu_{kl}| \le d_l d_{l-1}^{1/2}\|g_l\| \le A^{2l}A^{l-1}n(2A)^n \le n(2A^4)^n$ for μ_{kl}, by Lemmas 16.17 and 16.18,

and hence their length is $O(n \log A)$ as well. $\square$

▬▬ COROLLARY 16.19. ▬▬▬

Given linearly independent vectors $f_1, \ldots, f_n \in \mathbb{Z}^n$ with $\max_{1 \leq i \leq n} \|f_i\| = A$, we can compute a "short" nonzero vector $u \in L = \sum_{1 \leq i \leq n} \mathbb{Z} f_i$ with

$$\|u\| \leq 2^{(n-1)/2} \min\{\|f\| : 0 \neq f \in L\}$$

using $O((n^4 \log A) \mathsf{M}(n \log A) \log(n \log A))$ or $O^\sim(n^5 \log^2 A)$ word operations. ▬▬▬

PROOF. The claim follows immediately from Theorem 16.11, noting that one arithmetic operation in $\mathbb{Z}$ (addition, multiplication, division with remainder, or gcd) on integers of length m can be performed with $O(\mathsf{M}(m) \log m)$ or $O^\sim(m)$ word operations. □

We note that $A \leq n^{1/2} B$ when B is an upper bound on the absolute value of the coefficients of the f_i, and hence $n^5 \log^2 A \in O^\sim(n^5 \log^2 B)$, which is indeed polynomial in the input size of about $n^2 \log_{2^{64}} B$ words.

16.4. From short vectors to factors

We identify a polynomial $f \in \mathbb{Z}[x]$ of degree n with its coefficient vector in $\mathbb{Z}^{n+1}$, and let $\|f\|$ denote the Euclidean norm of this coefficient vector.

The following lemma states that if two polynomials in $\mathbb{Z}[x]$ have a nonconstant common divisor modulo m for some $m \in \mathbb{N}$ and m is absolutely larger than their resultant, then they have a nonconstant common factor in $\mathbb{Z}[x]$. For a prime m, it is a consequence of Lemma 6.25.

LEMMA 16.20. *Let $f, g \in \mathbb{Z}[x]$ have positive degrees n, k, respectively, and suppose that $u \in \mathbb{Z}[x]$ is nonconstant, monic, and divides both f and g modulo m for some $m \in \mathbb{N}$ with $\|f\|^k \|g\|^n < m$. Then $\gcd(f, g) \in \mathbb{Z}[x]$ is nonconstant.*

PROOF. Suppose that $\gcd(f, g) = 1$ in $\mathbb{Q}[x]$. Then there exist $s, t \in \mathbb{Z}[x]$ such that $sf + tg \equiv \operatorname{res}(f, g) \bmod m$, by Corollary 6.21. Since u divides both f and g modulo m, it divides $\operatorname{res}(f, g)$ modulo m. But u is monic and nonconstant, and thus $\operatorname{res}(f, g) \equiv 0 \bmod m$. Since $|\operatorname{res}(f, g)| \leq \|f\|^k \|g\|^n < m$, by Theorem 6.23, it follows that $\operatorname{res}(f, g)$ is zero. This contradiction to our assumption shows that $\gcd(f, g) \in \mathbb{Q}[x]$ is nonconstant. By Corollary 6.10, the gcd of f and g in $\mathbb{Z}[x]$ is also nonconstant. □

The idea of the factoring algorithm is as follows. Suppose that we are given a squarefree primitive polynomial $f \in \mathbb{Z}[x]$ of degree n and have computed a monic polynomial $u \in \mathbb{Z}[x]$ of degree $d < n$ that divides f modulo m for some $m \in \mathbb{N}$.

Then we find a "short" polynomial $g \in \mathbb{Z}[x]$, meaning that $\|g\|^n < m\|f\|^{-d}$, that is also divisible by u modulo m. Then the above lemma gives us a nontrivial factor of f in $\mathbb{Z}[x]$.

To find such a g of degree less than some bound j, we consider the lattice $L \subseteq \mathbb{Z}^j$ generated by (the coefficient vectors of)

$$\{ux^i : 0 \leq i < j - d\} \cup \{mx^i : 0 \leq i < d\}.$$

An element g of L has the form

$$g = qu + rm \text{ with } q, r \in \mathbb{Z}[x], \quad \deg q < j - d, \quad \deg r < d, \qquad (6)$$

and degree less than j. In particular, u divides g modulo m. If, on the other hand, some $g \in \mathbb{Z}[x]$ is of degree less than j and divisible by u modulo m, then we have $g = q^*u + r^*m$ for some $q^*, r^* \in \mathbb{Z}[x]$. Division with remainder by the monic polynomial u yields $q^{**}, r^{**} \in \mathbb{Z}[x]$ with $q^* = q^{**}u + r^{**}$ and $\deg r^{**} < \deg u$. Letting $q = q^* + mq^{**}$ and $r = r^{**}$, we see that g has the form (6), and conclude that

$$g \in L \iff \deg g < j \text{ and } u \text{ divides } g \text{ modulo } m. \qquad (7)$$

Thus we can use basis reduction to find a "short" vector $g \in L$ with the desired properties.

EXAMPLE 16.21. We let $f = x^3 - 1 \in \mathbb{Z}[x]$ and $m = 7^6 = 117\,649$. Using factorization over finite fields and Hensel lifting, we find that $f \equiv (x - 1)(x - 2)(x + 3)$ mod 7 and $f \equiv (x - 1)(x - 34\,967)(x + 34\,968)$ mod 7^6. Taking $u = x - 34\,967$ and $j = 3$, we consider the lattice $L \subseteq \mathbb{Z}^3$ generated by the coefficient vectors of $ux = x^2 - 34\,967x$, u, and m, namely

$$(1, -34\,967, 0), \quad (0, 1, -34\,967), \quad (0, 0, 117\,649).$$

Since this lattice contains the coefficient vectors of all polynomials in $\mathbb{Z}[x]$ of degree at most two that are divisible by u modulo m, it contains in particular the irreducible factor f_1 of f that is divisible by u modulo m, provided that $\deg f_1 < 3$. By Mignotte's bound 6.33, we then have $\|f_1\| \leq 2^{\deg f}\|f\| = 8\sqrt{2}$, and Theorem 16.9 guarantees that the basis reduction algorithm 16.10 will find a polynomial $g \in \mathbb{Z}[x]$ of degree at most two with $\|g\| \leq 2^{(3-1)/2}\|f_1\| \leq 16\sqrt{2}$. Then

$$\|f\|^{\deg g}\|g\|^{\deg f} \leq \sqrt{2}^2 (16\sqrt{2})^3 = 16384\sqrt{2} < m,$$

and Lemma 16.20 implies that f and g have a common divisor in $\mathbb{Z}[x]$. Indeed, Algorithm 16.10 finds that the three vectors

$$(1, 1, 1), \quad (132, 95, -228), \quad (228, -132, -95)$$

form a reduced basis of L, and if we take $g = x^2 + x + 1$, corresponding to the first vector, then $\gcd(f, g) = g$. $\diamond$

16.5. A polynomial-time factoring algorithm for $\mathbb{Q}[x]$

Now we are ready to state a polynomial-time factoring algorithm for $\mathbb{Q}[x]$. The first four steps are identical to Zassenhaus' algorithm 15.19, with the exception of the values of B in step 1 and of l in step 2, and the factor combination is replaced by the short vector computation.

▬▬ ALGORITHM 16.22 Polynomial-time factorization in $\mathbb{Z}[x]$. ▬▬▬▬▬▬▬▬▬▬▬▬

Input: A squarefree primitive polynomial $f \in \mathbb{Z}[x]$ of degree $n \geq 1$ with $\mathrm{lc}(f) > 0$ and max-norm $\|f\|_\infty = A$.

Output: The irreducible factors $\{f_1, \ldots, f_k\} \subseteq \mathbb{Z}[x]$ of f.

1. **if** $n = 1$ **then return** $\{f\}$
   $b \longleftarrow \mathrm{lc}(f), \quad B \longleftarrow (n+1)^{1/2} 2^n A$
   $C \longleftarrow (n+1)^{2n} A^{2n-1}, \quad \gamma \longleftarrow \lceil 2 \log_2 C \rceil$

2. **repeat** choose a prime $p \leq 2\gamma \ln \gamma, \quad \overline{f} \longleftarrow f \bmod p$
   until $p \nmid b$ and $\gcd(\overline{f}, \overline{f}') = 1$ in $\mathbb{F}_p[x]$
   $l \longleftarrow \lceil \log_p(2^{n^2} B^{2n}) \rceil$

3. { Modular factorization }
   compute $h_1, \ldots, h_r \in \mathbb{Z}[x]$ of max-norm at most $p/2$ that are nonconstant, monic, and irreducible modulo p, such that $f \equiv b h_1 \cdots h_r \bmod p$

4. { Hensel lifting }
   $a \longleftarrow b^{-1} \bmod p$
   use the Extended Euclidean Algorithm 3.6 in $\mathbb{F}_p[x]$ to set up a factor tree of f modulo p with leaves $h_1, \ldots, h_r$
   call Algorithm 15.17 to compute a factorization $f \equiv b g_1 \cdots g_r \bmod p^l$ with monic polynomials $g_1, \ldots, g_r \in \mathbb{Z}[x]$ of max-norm at most $p^l/2$ such that $g_i \equiv h_i \bmod p$ for $1 \leq i \leq r$

5. { initialize the index set T of modular factors still to be treated, the set G of found factors, and the polynomial f^* still to be factored }
   $T \longleftarrow \{1, \ldots, r\}, \quad G \longleftarrow \varnothing, \quad f^* \longleftarrow f$

6. **while** $T \neq \varnothing$ **do**

7.   choose u among $\{g_t : t \in T\}$ of maximal degree
        $d \longleftarrow \deg u, \quad n^* \longleftarrow \deg f^*$
        { Find the irreducible factor of f^* that is divisible by u modulo p }
        for $d < j \leq n^*$ **do**

8.　　　　　　　　{ Short vector computation }
　　　　　　　　call Algorithm 16.10 to compute a "short" vector g^* in the lattice $L \subseteq \mathbb{Z}^j$ generated by the coefficient vectors of

$$\{ux^i : 0 \leq i < j - d\} \cup \{p^l x^i : 0 \leq i < d\},$$

　　　　　　　　and denote the corresponding polynomial also by g^*

9.　　　　　　　　determine by trial division the set $S \subseteq T$ of indices i for which h_i divides g^* modulo p
　　　　　　　　compute $h^* \in \mathbb{Z}[x]$ with max-norm at most $p^l/2$ satisfying $h^* \equiv b \prod_{i \in T \setminus S} g_i \bmod p^l$
　　　　　　　　if $\| \mathrm{pp}(g^*) \|_1 \| \mathrm{pp}(h^*) \|_1 \leq B$ **then**
　　　　　　　　　　{ $\mathrm{pp}(g^*)$ is the irreducible factor of f^* that is divisible by u modulo p }
　　　　　　　　　　$T \longleftarrow T \setminus S, \quad G \longleftarrow G \cup \{\mathrm{pp}(g^*)\},$
　　　　　　　　　　$f^* \longleftarrow \mathrm{pp}(h^*), \quad b \longleftarrow \mathrm{lc}(f^*)$
　　　　　　　　　　break the loop 7 and **goto** 6

10.　　　　　$T \longleftarrow \emptyset, \quad G \longleftarrow G \cup \{f^*\}$

11. **return** G

To detect whether u in step 7 is already a true factor, we would check whether $u^* \mid bf$ in step 7, where $u^* \equiv bu \bmod p^l$ and $\|u^*\|_\infty \leq p^l/2$, before performing any short vector computations in step 8.

▬▬ THEOREM 16.23. ▬▬
The algorithm works correctly, and its expected cost in word operations is

$$O\!\left(n^6 (n + \log A) \mathsf{M}(n^2 (n + \log A))(\log n + \log\log A)\right) \text{ or } O^\sim(n^{10} + n^8 \log^2 A).$$

PROOF. For the correctness proof, we show that the invariants

$$f^* \equiv b \prod_{i \in T} g_i \bmod p^l, \quad b = \mathrm{lc}(f^*), \quad f = \pm f^* \prod_{g \in G} g, \tag{8}$$
$$\text{each polynomial in } G \text{ is irreducible}$$

hold each time the algorithm passes through step 6. This is clear initially, and we may assume that they hold before step 7. Let $g \in \mathbb{Z}[x]$ be the irreducible factor of f^* that u divides modulo p. Then (8) and Corollary 15.15 imply that u divides g modulo p^l as well. Conversely, if $v \in \mathbb{Z}[x]$ is a divisor of f which is divisible by u modulo p, then g divides v in $\mathbb{Z}[x]$. As in the proof of Theorem 15.3, the condition in step 9 is satisfied if and only if $\mathrm{pp}(g^*)\mathrm{pp}(h^*) = \pm f^*$, and since $\deg g^* < j$ in step 8, we conclude that the condition is false as long as $j \leq \deg g$. In particular, step 10 guarantees that the invariant (8) holds at the end of the algorithm if $\#T = 1$ and $g = f^*$ is irreducible.

Now we assume that $\deg g < n^*$ and let $j = 1 + \deg g$. Then the coefficient vector of g is in L, by (7), and Theorem 16.9 and Mignotte's bound 6.33 imply that $\|g^*\| \leq 2^{(j-1)/2}\|g\| < 2^n B$. By the choice of l, we have

$$\|g^*\|^{j-1}\|g\|^{\deg g^*} < (2^n B)^n B^n \leq p^l,$$

and Lemma 16.20 says that $\gcd(g, g^*)$ is nonconstant in $\mathbb{Z}[x]$. Since g is irreducible and $\deg g^* \leq j - 1 = \deg g$, we have $g = \pm\operatorname{pp}(g^*)$.

We let $h = f^*/g$ and $S \subseteq T$ be as in step 9. As in the proof of Theorem 15.20, the uniqueness of Hensel lifting (Theorem 15.14) implies that $\operatorname{lc}(g)h \equiv h^* \bmod p^l$ in step 9. Since $p^l/2$ is larger than the Mignotte bound bB on $\|bh\|_\infty$, we have $\operatorname{lc}(g)h = h^*$, $h = \operatorname{pp}(h^*)$, and $f^* = \pm\operatorname{pp}(g^*)\operatorname{pp}(h^*)$, and Corollary 6.33 implies that the condition in step 9 is true. The actions taken in the **then** clause ensure that the invariants (8) hold at the next pass through step 6. This proves that the algorithm will indeed return the factor g of f.

The cost of the algorithm is dominated by the cost for the short vector computations in step 7. We have $\|v\| \leq j^{1/2}\|v\|_\infty \leq n^{1/2}p^l$ for all generators v of L in step 7. Letting $\delta = \log(n^{1/2}p^l) \in O(n^2 + n\log B) = O(n^2 + n\log A)$, Corollary 16.19 implies that one short vector computation takes $O(j^4\delta\,\mathsf{M}(j\delta)\log(j\delta))$ word operations. Let $f_1, \ldots, f_k \in \mathbb{Z}[x]$ be the irreducible factors of f. By what we have shown above, the value j in step 7 runs through $j = 2, \ldots, 1 + \deg f_i$ for each irreducible factor f_i. Now $\sum_{1 \leq i \leq k}(1 + \deg f_i) = k + n \leq 2n$, and hence

$$\sum_{1 \leq i \leq k} \sum_{2 \leq j \leq 1 + \deg f_i} j^4\delta\,\mathsf{M}(j\delta)\log(j\delta)$$

$$\leq \sum_{1 \leq i \leq k} (1 + \deg f_i)^5\delta\,\mathsf{M}((1 + \deg f_i)\delta)\log((1 + \deg f_i)\delta)$$

$$\in O(n^5\delta\,\mathsf{M}(n\delta)\log(n\delta)),$$

by the subadditivity properties of M (Section 8.3). This establishes the time estimate. $\square$

We might also replace steps 1 through 4 of Algorithm 16.22 by the first three steps of the big prime algorithm 15.2, yielding an algorithm with the same asymptotic time bound.

EXAMPLE 16.24. Let $f = 6x^4 + 5x^3 + 15x^2 + 5x + 4 \in \mathbb{Z}[x]$, as in Example 15.4. Choosing $p = 5$ in step 2 of Algorithm 16.22, we would find $l = 39$. Since the coefficients in the algorithm become fairly large with that value of l, we take $l = 6$

for illustration. We skip steps 3 and 4, since we have already found that $f \equiv 6g_1g_2g_3g_4 \bmod 5^6$ in Example 15.4, where

$$g_1 = x - 5136, \quad g_2 = x - 984, \quad g_3 = x - 72, \quad g_4 = x - 6828.$$

Thus $r = 4$. In step 7, we choose $u = g_1 = x - 5136$, and then $d = \deg u = 1$ and $n^* = \deg f^* = 4$. We start the loop in step 7 with $j = 2$. Then the lattice in step 8 is generated by the coefficient vectors $(1, -5136)$ and $(0, 15625)$ of the two polynomials u and p^l. Algorithm 16.10 finds the reduced basis consisting of the two vectors $(73, 72)$ and $(-143, 73)$, and the polynomial g^* in step 8 is $g^* = 73x + 72$. In step 9, we find that only $g_1 \bmod 5 = x - 1$ divides $g^* \bmod 5$, whence $S = \{1\}$ and

$$h^* \equiv 6g_2g_3g_4 \equiv 6x^3 - 420x^2 - 840x - 1728 \bmod 5^6.$$

Now both g^* and h^* are primitive, $\| \mathrm{pp}(g^*) \|_1 \| \mathrm{pp}(h^*) \|_1 \geq \| \mathrm{pp}(g^*) \|_\infty \| \mathrm{pp}(h^*) \|_\infty > B \approx 3219.9$, and in fact $f \neq \pm \mathrm{pp}(g^*) \mathrm{pp}(h^*)$, which can also seen by comparing leading coefficients, and we continue the loop 7 with $j = 3$.

So now we consider the lattice generated by the vectors

$$(1, -5136, 0), \quad (0, 1, -5136), \quad (0, 0, 15625).$$

Exercise 16.6 shows that a "short" vector in this lattice is $(3, 1, 1) \in \mathbb{Z}^3$, and hence $g^* = 3x^2 + x + 1$ in step 8. Now both $g_1 \bmod 5 = x - 1$ and $g_3 \bmod 5 = x - 2$ divide $g^* \bmod 5$, so that $S = \{1, 3\}$, $h^* \equiv 6g_2g_4 \equiv 6x^2 + 3x + 12 \bmod 5^6$, $\mathrm{pp}(g^*) = g^*$, and $\mathrm{pp}(h^*) = 2x^2 + x + 4$ in step 9. In fact, we have $f = \mathrm{pp}(g^*) \mathrm{pp}(h^*)$, g^* is an irreducible factor of f (although we started with a smaller value for l as required), and the assignments in the **if** clause yield $T = \{2, 4\}$, $G = \{x - 984, x - 6828\}$, $f^* = 2x^2 + x + 4$, and $b = 2$. The next iteration of the **while** loop 6 would reveal that f^* is irreducible, as we have already seen in Example 15.4. $\diamond$

One might run factor combination and the short vector algorithm concurrently (on one or, even better, on two processors) after Hensel lifting, and take the result from whoever finishes first. This hybrid algorithm is reasonably fast on all inputs, at a cost of at most doubling the overall running time.

COROLLARY 16.25.
A polynomial $f \in \mathbb{Z}[x]$ of degree $n \geq 1$ and with max-norm $\|f\|_\infty = A$ can be completely factored in $\mathbb{Q}[x]$ with an expected number of

$$O\left(n^6(n + \log A)\mathsf{M}(n^2(n + \log A))(\log n + \log \log A)\right) \text{ or } O^\sim(n^{10} + n^8 \log^2 A)$$

word operations.

PROOF. We replace the call to Algorithm 15.19 (using factor combination) by a call to Algorithm 16.22 (using basis reduction) in step 4 of the complete factorization algorithm 15.5. The dominant cost is for the calls to Algorithm 16.22 in step 4 for the polynomials $g_1, \ldots, g_s$ in the squarefree decomposition of $pp(f)$. For $1 \le i \le s$, let $n_i = \deg g_i$ and $A_i = \|g_i\|_\infty \le (n_i + 1)^{1/2} 2^{n_i} A$, using Mignotte's bound 6.33, so that $\log A_i \in O(n_i + \log A)$. Then Theorem 16.23 implies that the cost for the ith call is

$$O(n_i^6 (n_i + \log A) \mathsf{M}(n_i^2(n_i + \log A))(\log n_i + \log\log A))$$

word operations, and the claim follows from $n_1 + \cdots + n_s \le n$ and the subadditivity of M. $\square$

Polynomial-time factoring in $F[x,y]$. Algorithm 16.22 can be adapted to the factorization of polynomials in $F[x,y]$, where F is a field with effective univariate factorization. This is the case, for example, when F is a finite field (Chapter 14), or when $F = \mathbb{Q}$, by the above. The variant of Algorithm 16.22 is then merely a (deterministic) polynomial time **reduction** from bivariate to univariate polynomial factorization.

The main difference is that basis reduction is much easier over $F[y]$ than over $\mathbb{Z}$. The appropriate norm is the **maximum norm** $\|f\|_\infty = \max_{1 \le i \le n} \deg f_i$ for a vector $f = (f_1, \ldots, f_n) \in F[y]^n$. In this case, one can always find a *shortest* vector in an n-dimensional lattice in $F[y]^n$ in polynomial time (Exercise 16.12).

16.6. Factoring multivariate polynomials

We have discussed at length the factorization of univariate polynomials over finite fields and over the rational numbers, and briefly indicated a method for bivariate polynomials. What about more variables? This section tells the story of this exciting subject; a precise description of the algorithms and relevant theorems is beyond the scope of this book.

The first issue that distinguishes this problem from the univariate and bivariate cases is that of the appropriate *data structure* or *representation*. We assume we have a polynomial $f \in F[x, \ldots, x_t]$ of total degree n. In the **dense representation**, we write down every term of total degree at most n. For the Fermat polynomial

$$f = x^3 + y^3 - z^3 \in \mathbb{Q}[x,y,z] \tag{9}$$

this reads:

$$
\begin{aligned}
f = \ & 1 \cdot x^3 + 0 \cdot x^2 y + 0 \cdot x^2 z + 0 \cdot x^2 + 0 \cdot xy^2 + 0 \cdot xyz + 0 \cdot xz^2 \\
& + 0 \cdot xy + 0 \cdot xz + 0 \cdot x + 1 \cdot y^3 + 0 \cdot y^2 z + 0 \cdot y^2 \\
& + 0 \cdot yz^2 + 0 \cdot yz + 0 \cdot y + (-1) \cdot z^3 + 0 \cdot z^2 + 0 \cdot z + 0 \cdot 1
\end{aligned}
\tag{10}
$$

Throughout this book, we have assumed (at least implicitly) this representation for univariate and bivariate polynomials as inputs to algorithms, such as gcd computations or factorization. (In examples, the format like (9) is used.) Multivariate polynomials can be factored in random polynomial time in the length of this dense representation over the usual fields of relevance to computer algebra, such as finite fields, the rational numbers, and finite algebraic and transcendental extensions of these. In fact, it is not hard to adapt the gcd algorithms of Chapter 6 and the bivariate factorization in the previous section to this situation. Is the problem then completely solved? Obviously not, because the drawback of this representation is already visible in the small Example (10) above: it is much too large. It has

$$\alpha_{t,n} = \binom{t+n}{n}$$

terms; in the example, $\alpha_{3,3} = 20$. This number grows exponentially with t and n, and our objects become unmanageable even for reasonable values of t and n. Exercise 16.16 describes a factoring algorithm, based on the **Kronecker substitution**.

It seems clear what to do. The **sparse representation** as in (9) is much more concise and readable than (10). In general, it consists of a list of coefficients and exponents $(a_k, i_{k1}, \ldots, i_{kt})$ so that

$$f = \sum_k a_k \cdot x_1^{i_{k1}} \cdots x_t^{i_{kt}}.$$

If the list consists of s entries, then clearly the length is at least s. But this is not enough; we have to bring the degree into play, since otherwise arbitrarily large degrees might occur. So we consider the length of a list entry $(a_k, i_{k1}, \ldots, i_{kt})$ to be $1 + i_{k1} + \cdots + i_{kt}$; if we count word operations, say over $\mathbb{Q}$, then the summand 1 has to be replaced by the length of a_k. This convention for the length can be expressed by saying that the individual degrees $i_{k1}, \ldots$ are encoded in unary. One might think that the binary encoding for the exponents is more natural. But then the degree may be exponential in the length, and even univariate polynomials become unmanageable. For very simple questions no polynomial-time answer is known for this ultra-concise encoding; for example: given two polynomials in this representation, does the first one divide the second one?

This sparse representation is the natural mathematical notation, and the user of a computer algebra system will want to see her input and output in that format. For a "random" polynomial (with a fixed number of variables and fixed degree), almost all possible coefficients will be nonzero, and there will not be much difference between the sparse and the dense representations. However, natural problems given to a computer algebra system tend to be sparse; see the cyclohexane example in Section 24.4.

Unfortunately, no algorithm for factoring is known that runs in time polynomial in the length of the sparse representation. There are even examples where the output size is more than polynomial in the input size. But even if one allows time polynomial in the combined input plus output size, no solution is known.

The key to get over this hurdle is to consider even more concise representations. At first sight, the problem becomes even harder, since the input size (for a fixed polynomial) might be even smaller. But the gain is that the output might also be smaller, and, above all, that new computational methods may be used.

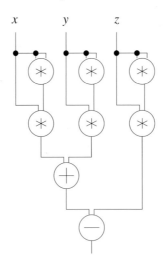

FIGURE 16.7: An arithmetic circuit for $x^3 + y^3 - z^3$.

The first new idea is the **arithmetic circuit representation**, where a polynomial is represented by an arithmetic circuit, as illustrated in Chapters 2 and 8, that computes f using $x_1, \dots, x_t$ and constants from F as inputs and only addition and multiplication gates. (There is an efficient way to remove division gates if they are also present.) For (9), this looks like Figure 16.7. Equivalently, an arithmetic circuit may be represented by a **straight-line program** such as

$$g_1 \longleftarrow x * x$$
$$g_2 \longleftarrow g_1 * x$$
$$g_3 \longleftarrow y * y$$
$$g_4 \longleftarrow g_3 * y$$
$$g_5 \longleftarrow z * z$$
$$g_6 \longleftarrow g_5 * z$$
$$g_7 \longleftarrow g_2 + g_4$$
$$g_8 \longleftarrow g_6 - g_7$$

This approach culminated in Kaltofen's (1989) celebrated result of random polynomial-time factorization in the arithmetic circuit representation.

The technical key ingredient is an efficient version of *Hilbert's irreducibility theorem*. In Hilbert's (1892) version (see page 560), it says that an irreducible polynomial $f \in \mathbb{Q}[x,y]$ usually yields an irreducible polynomial $f(x,a) \in \mathbb{Q}[x]$ if an integer a is substituted for y. (This is not true for polynomials over finite fields or the complex numbers.) Although there are many generalizations and improvements of this in the literature, none of them is strong enough to derive a (probabilistic) polynomial-time algorithm.

However, the situation can be saved by leaving one more variable and considering more general substitutions of the form $ax_1 + bx_2 + c$ for the variables, where a,b,c are chosen randomly from a (sufficiently large) finite subset of the ground field. Then for an irreducible polynomial in $F[x_1,\ldots,x_n]$, the substituted polynomial in $F[x_1,x_2]$ will be irreducible for almost all random choices. An arbitrary polynomial can be mapped to two variables by such a substitution, then the bivariate factoring technology can be applied, and finally Hensel lifting to get back to the original multivariate situation. The role of the efficient Hilbert irreducibility theorem is to insure that one (probably) does not have to worry about irreducible polynomials splitting after the substitution. This phenomenon required factor combination or a short vector computation for substitutions $\mathbb{Z}[x] \longrightarrow \mathbb{Z}_p[x]$ or $F[x,y] \longrightarrow F[x]$, but such methods would not lead to polynomial-time methods in the multivariate case.

An even more powerful technique is the **black box representation**. A polynomial $f \in F[x_1,\ldots,x_n]$ is now given by a "black box" subroutine which on input $a_1,\ldots,a_n \in F$ returns the value $f(a_1,\ldots,a_n) \in F$. We have discussed this type of representation for matrices in Section 12.4. Initially, a polynomial will often be given in some other representation, say the sparse one. It is then easy to build a black box for it. The power of the method is that now these black boxes can be handled efficiently; Kaltofen & Trager (1990) give random polynomial-time algorithms for several problems, including factorization. Finally, the black box representation has to be converted back to human-readable output. There are several interpolation algorithms for achieving this. Now an output polynomial with a few hundred terms is rather useless for the human reader (but possibly useful as input to another procedure). One interpolation method has the beautiful feature that one can tell it to print only about a dozen (or about a hundred) terms (and to say that there are more if that is so).

The black box technology has also been successfully applied to other problems such as the gcd of two multivariate polynomials.

Notes. **16.1.** Minkowski (1910) describes the *geometry of numbers* that he invented. Grötschel, Lovász & Schrijver (1993) is a good textbook in this area, and Kannan (1987) present an overview on computational aspects of this theory, including basis reduction and several applications.

16.2 and 16.3. The Gram-Schmidt orthogonalization procedure is from Schmidt (1907), §3, who states that Gram (1883) has given essentially the same formulas. Hadamard (1893) proved Theorem 16.6. The geometrical idea is that the volume $|\det A|$ of the polytope spanned by $f_1, \ldots, f_n \in \mathbb{R}^n$ is maximal when these vectors are mutually orthogonal; in this case it precisely equal to $\|f_1\| \cdots \|f_n\|$.

Basis reduction (sometimes called the LLL algorithm) was introduced in the important paper of Lenstra, Lenstra & Lovász (1982), who used it to factor integer polynomials in polynomial time. Their definition of a reduced basis is slightly different from ours. We are grateful to Victor Shoup for his permission to use unpublished lecture notes of his.

Odlyzko (1990) notes that basis reduction *turns out to be fast in practice, and usually finds a reduced basis in which the first vector is much shorter than is guaranteed* [by Theorem 16.9]. *(In low dimensions, it has been observed empirically that this algorithm usually finds the shortest nonzero vector in a lattice.)*

Improvements both on the algorithm and its analysis are from Kaltofen (1983), Schönhage (1984), whose algorithm takes only $O^\sim(n^4 \log^2 A)$ word operations for a slightly different notion of reduced basis, Schnorr (1987, 1988), who proves a bound of $O^\sim(n^5 \log A + n^4 \log^2 A)$ word operations for his algorithm and approximation quality $(1 + \varepsilon)^n \|f\|$ for any $\varepsilon > 0$ in Theorem 16.9 by employing floating point arithmetic, and Schnorr & Euchner (1991), who also give efficient implementations. The current record is due to Storjohann (1996), who achieves $O^\sim(n^{3.381} \log^2 A)$ word operations with a modular approach and by employing fast matrix multiplication. De Weger (1989) and Storjohann (1996) give fraction-free variants of Algorithm 16.10. Gauß (1801), article 171, describes basis reduction in two dimensions. An exciting recent (at the time of writing) development on the complexity of computing shortest vectors and applications to cryptography is discussed in Section 20.7.

16.5. For a unified discussion of the factoring algorithms over $\mathbb{Z}$ and $F[y]$, we refer to von zur Gathen (1984a). By performing a binary search on the degree of f^* instead of the linear search in step 7 of Algorithm 16.22, Lenstra, Lenstra & Lovász (1982) achieve a time bound of $O^\sim(n^9 + n^7 \log^2 A)$ word operations.

Schönhage (1984) gives an algorithm with only $O^\sim(n^6 + n^4 \log^2 A)$ word operations. His approach is numerical: modular factorization and Hensel lifting are replaced by the computation of a complex root of f to a sufficiently high precision, and Diophantine approximation based on basis reduction (see Section 17.3) is used to find the irreducible factor of f with that root.

16.6. The polynomial-time solution for dense multivariate factorization was given by Kaltofen (1985a). An algorithm for sparse factorization is in von zur Gathen & Kaltofen (1985); that paper also has the example with very large factors. Open questions such as the divisibility problem (for exponentially large degrees), are discussed in von zur Gathen (1991a). For the circuit representation, the solution is again by Kaltofen (1989); von zur Gathen (1985) has an irreducibility test in the same data structure. The latter paper introduced this representation into the factorization business, but it has its origins in Strassen (1972, 1973a, 1973b); see also Heintz & Sieveking (1981).

The generic determinant polynomial for $n \times n$ matrices is an example where the length of the sparse representation, which is essentially $n!$, is exponential in the length of the arithmetic circuit representation, since there is an arithmetic circuit (with divisions) of size $O(n^3)$ performing Gaussian elimination.

Lang (1983), chapter 9, describes Hilbert's irreducibility theorem and the theory of *Hilbertian fields* for which this theorem holds. Results on specific substitutions that conserve irreducibility are in Sprindžuk (1981, 1983) and Dèbes (1996). Efficient probabilistic versions of Hilbert irreducibility, valid over any field but reducing only to two variables, can be found in Kaltofen (1985b), von zur Gathen (1985), and Kaltofen (1995a). Huang & Wong (1998) give a similar result for more general polynomial ideals.

The important paper of Kaltofen & Trager (1990) introduced the black box method and gave several algorithms discussed above. A seminal idea for sparse interpolation is due to Zippel (1979); several other papers deal with various aspects of interpolation: Ben-Or & Tiwari (1988), Kaltofen & Lakshman (1988), Borodin & Tiwari (1990), Grigoriev, Karpinski & Singer (1990), Clausen, Dress, Grabmeier & Karpinski (1991), Grigoriev, Karpinski & Singer (1994). Freeman, Imirzian, Kaltofen & Lakshman (1988) and Díaz & Kaltofen (1998) describe implementations of the straight-line and the black box technologies, respectively.

Exercises.

16.1 Let $F \in \mathbb{R}^{n \times n}$ be nonsingular. Show that the GSO M, F^* of F is uniquely determined by the conditions that $F = MF^*$, M be lower triangular with ones on the diagonal, and $F^*(F^*)^T$ be diagonal.

16.2* Prove Theorem 16.5.

16.3 We define an inner product $\star$ on the vector space V of continuous real-valued functions on the real interval $[-1, 1]$ by $(f \star g)(x) = \int_{-1}^{1} f(y)g(y)\sqrt{1 - y^2}dy$.
   (i) Convince yourself that $\star$ is in fact an inner product.
   (ii) Compute the Gram-Schmidt orthogonal basis of f_0, f_1, f_2, f_3, where $f_i(x) = x^i$ for $-1 \leq x \leq 1$. (The resulting polynomials are the first four **Chebyshev polynomials**).

16.4* Let $g_1, \dots, g_n \in \mathbb{R}^n$ be linearly independent and $L = \sum_{1 \leq i \leq n} \mathbb{Z}g_i$ the lattice that they generate. Prove that for each vector $x \in \mathbb{R}^n$ there is a vector $g \in L$ such that

$$\|x - g\|^2 \leq \frac{1}{4}(\|g_1\|^2 + \dots + \|g_n\|^2).$$

Hint: Induction on n. For the induction step, determine a suitable $\lambda \in \mathbb{Z}$ such that the vector $x - \lambda g_n$ has minimal distance to the hyperplane spanned by $g_1, \dots, g_{n-1}$.

16.5 (i) Compute the GSO of $(22, 11, 5)$, $(13, 6, 3)$, $(-5, -2, -1) \in \mathbb{R}^3$.
   (ii) Trace Algorithm 16.10 on computing a reduced basis of the lattice in $\mathbb{Z}^3$ spanned by the vectors from (i). Trace also the values of the d_i and of D, and compare the number of exchange steps to the theoretical upper bound from Section 16.3.

16.6$^{\longrightarrow}$ Compute a "short" vector in the lattice in $\mathbb{Z}^3$ spanned by $(1, -5136, 0)$, $(0, 1, -5136)$, and $(0, 0, 15625)$.

16.7* A nonsingular matrix $W \in \mathbb{Z}^{n \times n}$, for a positive integer n, is in **Hermite normal form** if all entries above the diagonal are zero. The following algorithm takes an arbitrary nonsingular matrix $V \in \mathbb{Z}^{n \times n}$ and computes a Hermite normal form W of V, such that $W = UV$ for a matrix $U \in \mathbb{Z}^{n \times n}$ which is **unimodular**, so that $\det U = \pm 1$.

▬▬ ALGORITHM 16.26 Hermite normal form. ▬▬▬▬▬▬▬▬▬▬▬▬▬▬▬▬▬▬▬▬
Input: A matrix $V \in \mathbb{Z}^{n \times n}$ with $\det V \neq 0$.
Output: A matrix $W \in \mathbb{Z}^{n \times n}$ in Hermite normal form such that $W = UV$ for a unimodular matrix $U \in \mathbb{Z}^{n \times n}$.

   1. $W \longleftarrow V$, $\quad m \longleftarrow n$

   2. **if** $m = 1$ **then goto** 8

   3. choose a row index k with $1 \leq k \leq m$ such that $|w_{km}| = \min\{|w_{im}| : 1 \leq i \leq m \text{ and } w_{im} \neq 0\}$
      exchange rows k and m of W

4. **if** $w_{mm} \mid w_{lm}$ for $1 \le l \le m$ **then goto** 7

5. choose a column index l with $1 \le l < m$ and $w_{mm} \nmid w_{lm}$
   compute $q \in \mathbb{Z}$ with $|w_{lm} - q w_{mm}| \le |w_{mm}|/2$ by division with remainder

6. subtract q times row m from row l of W,   **goto** 3

7. **for** $l = 1, \ldots, m-1$ subtract w_{lm}/w_{mm} times row m from row l in W
   $m \longleftarrow m - 1$,   **goto** 2

8. **return** W

(i) Trace the algorithm on input

$$V = \begin{pmatrix} 5 & 2 & -4 & 7 \\ 3 & 6 & 0 & -3 \\ 1 & 2 & -2 & 4 \\ 7 & 1 & 5 & 6 \end{pmatrix} \in \mathbb{Z}^{n \times n}.$$

(ii) Prove that the algorithm works correctly, using the invariant that before each execution of step 2, $W = UV$ for some unimodular matrix U and $w_{ij} = 0$ and $w_{jj} \ne 0$ for $m < j \le n$ and $1 \le i < j$. Conclude from the invariant and from the fact that $\deg V \ne 0$ that the minimum in step 3 always exists.

(iii) Show that at most $\log_2 u$ executions of steps 3 through 6 lie between two executions of step 2, where $u = \min\{|w_{im}| : 1 \le i \le m$ and $w_{im} \ne 0\}$ at the previous execution of step 2. Conclude that the algorithm terminates.

(iv) Let $a_1, \ldots, a_n \in \mathbb{Q}^n$ be linearly independent, $L = \sum_{1 \le i \le n} \mathbb{Z} a_i$ the lattice that they generate, and $b_1, \ldots, b_n \in L$ be linearly independent as well. Then $M = \sum_{1 \le i \le n} \mathbb{Z} b_i \subseteq L$ is a **sublattice** of L. Prove that there exists a basis $c_1, \ldots, c_n$ of M which has the form

$$
\begin{aligned}
c_1 &= w_{11} a_1, \\
c_2 &= w_{21} a_1 + w_{22} a_2, \\
&\vdots \\
c_n &= w_{n1} a_1 + w_{n2} a_2 + \cdots + w_{nn} a_n,
\end{aligned}
\tag{11}
$$

with $w_{ij} \in \mathbb{Z}$ and $w_{ii} \ne 0$ for $1 \le j \le i \le n$.

An asymptotically fast algorithm for computing the Hermite normal form is by Storjohann & Labahn 1996.

16.8 Modify the basis reduction algorithm 16.10 so as to work for arbitrary inputs $f_1, \ldots, f_m \in \mathbb{Z}^n$, not necessarily linearly independent, and with arbitrary $m \in \mathbb{N}$.

16.9 With notation as in Lemma 16.13, prove the formula

$$h_i^* = \frac{\|g_i^*\|^2 g_{i-1}^* - \mu_{i,i-1} \|g_{i-1}^*\|^2 g_i^*}{\|h_{i-1}^*\|^2}.$$

Hint: h_i^* is the projection of h_i onto $(\mathbb{R} h_1 + \cdots + \mathbb{R} h_{n-1})^{\perp}$.

16.10 Let $x, y \in \mathbb{C}^n$.

(i) Prove the **Cauchy-Schwarz inequality** $|x \star y| \le \|x\|_2 \|y\|_2$. Hint: Assume that $\|x\|_2 \|y\|_2 > 0$, and consider $(\|y\|_2 x + \|x\|_2 y) \star (\|y\|_2 x + \|x\|_2 y)$.

(ii) Use (i) to prove the triangle inequality $\|x + y\|_2 \le \|x\|_2 + \|y\|_2$.

16.11* Lemma 16.17 shows that at any stage in the basis reduction algorithm 16.10, $d_l \mu_{kl}$ and $d_{k-1} g_k^*$ have integral coefficients for $1 \leq l < k \leq n$. By multiplying the entries of the GSO by (and, where possible, dividing out) appropriate d_l's, convert Algorithm 16.10 into a fraction-free algorithm, so that all intermediate coefficients are in $\mathbb{Z}$.

16.12* This exercises discusses basis reduction for polynomials. Let F be a field, $R = F[y]$, and $n \in \mathbb{N}_{>0}$. The **max-norm** of a vector $f = (f_1, \ldots, f_n) \in R^n$ is $\|f\| = \|f\|_\infty = \max\{\deg f_i \colon 1 \leq i \leq n\}$. For vectors $f_1, \ldots, f_m \in R$ which are linearly independent over $F(y)$, the field of fractions of R, the **R-module** spanned by $f_1, \ldots, f_m$ is $M = \sum_{1 \leq i \leq m} R f_i$, and $(f_1, \ldots, f_m)$ is a **basis** of M.

(i) Let $f_1, \ldots, f_m \in R^n$ be linearly independent, with $f_i = (f_{i1}, \ldots, f_{in})$ for $1 \leq i \leq m$. We say that the sequence $(f_1, \ldots, f_m)$ is **reduced** if

○ $\|f_1\| \leq \|f_2\| \leq \cdots \leq \|f_m\|$, and

○ $\deg f_{ij} \leq \deg f_{ii}$ for $1 \leq j \leq n$, with strict inequality if $j < i$, for $1 \leq i \leq m$.

In particular, we have $\|f_i\| = \deg f_{ii}$ for $1 \leq i \leq m$. Prove that f_1 is a **shortest vector** in the R-module $M = \sum_{1 \leq i \leq m} R f_i$, so that $\|f_1\| \leq \|f\|$ for all nonzero $f \in M$.

(ii) Consider the following algorithm, from von zur Gathen (1984a).

▬▬▬ ALGORITHM 16.27 Basis reduction for polynomials. ▬▬▬▬▬▬▬
Input: $f_1, \ldots, f_m \in R^n$, where $R = F[y]$ for a field F, with $\|f_i\| < d$ for $1 \leq i \leq m$.
Output: Row vectors $g_1, \ldots, g_m \in R^n$ and a permutation matrix $A \in R^{n \times n}$ such that $(g_1 A, \ldots, g_m A)$ is a reduced basis of $M = \sum_{1 \leq i \leq m} R f_i$.

1. **for** $1 \leq i \leq m$ **do** $g_i \longleftarrow f_i$
   $A \longleftarrow$ id, $k \longleftarrow 1$

2. **while** $k \leq m$ **do**

3.   { $(g_1 A, \ldots, g_{k-1} A)$ is already reduced }
   $u \longleftarrow \|g_k\|$

4.   **for** $i = 1, \ldots, k-1$ **do**

5. $q \longleftarrow g_{ki}$ quo g_{ii}, $g_k \longleftarrow g_k - q g_i$

6.   **if** $\|g_k\| < u$ **then** $k \longleftarrow \min\{i \colon i = k$ or $(1 \leq i < k$ and $\|g_i\| > \|g_k\|)\}$,   **goto 2**

7. $l \longleftarrow \min\{k \leq j \leq n \colon \deg g_{kj} = u\}$
   let $B \in R^{n \times n}$ be the permutation matrix for the exchange of columns k and l
   for $1 \leq i \leq m$ **do** $g_i \longleftarrow g_i B$
   $A \longleftarrow BA$, $k \longleftarrow k+1$

8. **return** $g_1, \ldots, g_m$ and A ▬▬▬▬▬▬▬▬▬▬▬▬▬▬▬▬▬▬▬▬

Show that $M = \sum_{1 \leq i \leq m} R \cdot g_i A$ holds throughout the algorithm.

(iii) Prove the invariant $\|g_k\| \leq u$ and $\deg g_{kj} < u$ for $1 \leq j < i$ of the loop 4, and conclude that $\|g_i\| < d$ for $1 \leq i \leq m$ holds throughout the algorithm.

(iv) Show that $(g_1 A, \ldots, g_{k-1} A)$ is reduced each time before the algorithm passes through step 3. Conclude that it works correctly if it halts in step 8.

(v) Prove that the cost for one execution of steps 3 through 7 is $O(mn)$ arithmetic operations (additions, multiplications, and divisions with remainder) in R or $O(mn \mathsf{M}(d))$ operations in F.

(vi) Show that the function $s(g_1, \ldots, g_m) = \sum_{1 \leq i \leq m} \|g_i\|$ never increases in the algorithm and strictly decreases if the condition in step 6 is true. Conclude that the number of times when the latter happens is at most md and that the number of iterations of the loop 2 is at most $m^2 d$.

(vii) Putting everything together, show that the running time of the algorithm is $O(nm^3 d \mathsf{M}(d))$ arithmetic operations in F.

(viii) Trace the algorithm on the $\mathbb{F}_{97}[y]$-module generated by

$$\left(5y^3 + 44y^2 + 37y + 91,\ 8y^3 + 86y^2 + 91y + 89,\ 16y^3 + 65y^2 + 20y + 76\right),$$
$$\left(8y^3 + 70y + 37,\ 16y^3 + 7y^2 + 54y + 38,\ 32y^3 + 23y^2 + 80y + 77\right),$$
$$\left(16y^2 + 84y + 63,\ 32y^2 + 15y + 19,\ 64y^2 + 48y + 51\right) \in \mathbb{F}_{97}[y]^3.$$

16.13 State and prove the analog of Lemma 16.20 for polynomials in $F[x,y]$ for a field F when $\|\cdot\|_2$ is replaced by $\|f\|_\infty = \deg_y f$.

16.14* Use Exercises 16.12 and 16.13 to adapt Algorithm 16.22 to bivariate polynomials over a field. Prove that your algorithm works correctly and analyze its running time. You may assume that F has effective univariate factorization and is "large enough", so that the modulus p may be chosen linear.

16.15 Let F be a field and $n \in \mathbb{N}$. What is the size of the sparse representation of the polynomial $\prod_{0 \le i < n}(x + y^{2^i}) \in F[x,y]$? Find an arithmetic circuit representation of size $3n - 2$.

16.16* You are to design an algorithm for factoring multivariate polynomials over a field F with efficient univariate factorization. Suppose that $f \in F[x_1,\ldots,x_t]$ has degree less than n in each variable, and consider the **Kronecker substitution** $\sigma \colon F[x_1,\ldots,x_t] \longrightarrow F[x]$ which maps x_i to $x^{n^{i-1}}$ for $1 \le i \le t$. This is a ring homomorphism.

(i) Show that polynomials with degree less than n in each variable can be uniquely recovered from their image under σ. More precisely, let $U \subseteq F[x_1,\ldots,x_t]$ be the vector space of all these polynomials, and $V = \{g \in F[x] \colon \deg g < n^t\}$. Show that σ gives a vector space isomorphism between U and V.

(ii) Prove that the following procedure correctly factors f: Factor $\sigma(f)$ into irreducible factors $g_1,\ldots,g_r \in F[x]$, and test for each factor combination h of them whether its inverse $\sigma^{-1}(h)$, in the sense of (i), divides f.

(iii) Analyze the cost of your algorithm from (ii). You will first have to estimate the cost for multivariate multiplication (Exercise 8.38). Ignore the time for univariate factorization in this analysis.

(iv) Trace your algorithm on the example $f = -x^4y + x^3z + xz^2 + yz^2 \in \mathbb{F}_3[x,y,z]$.

Research problem.

16.17 Can one compute the gcd of two multivariate polynomials in random polynomial time in the length of the sparse representation plus the degree? Is the output length always polynomial in the input length? (If not, one might consider the combined input plus output lengths in the first question.)

Il faut bien distinguer entre la géométrie utile et la géométrie curieuse.
L'utile est le compas de proportion inventé par Galilée [...]
Presque tous les autres problèmes peuvent éclairer l'esprit et le
fortifier; bien peu seront d'une utilité sensible au genre humain.[1]

Voltaire (1771)

Partager une nuit entre une jolie femme et un beau ciel,
le jour à rapprocher ses observations et les calculs,
me paraît être le bonheur sur la terre.[2]

Napoléon I. (1812)

But yet one commoditie moare [...] I can not omitte. That is the
filyng, sharpenyng, and quickenyng of the witte, that by practice of
Arithmetike doeth insue. It teacheth menne and accustometh them, so
certainly to remember thynges paste: So circumspectly to consider
thynges presente: And so prouidently to forsee thynges that followe:
that it maie truelie bee called the *File of witte.*

Robert Recorde (1557)

---

[1] One has to distinguish carefully between practical geometry and theoretical geometry. Practical is the rule of proportions invented by Galileo [...] Almost all other problems can enlighten the mind and strengthen it; rather few will be of any reasonable usefulness to mankind.

[2] To share a night between a beautiful woman and a clear sky, the day in seeking agreement between one's observations and calculations, seems to me happiness on earth.

17

Applications of basis reduction

This chapter presents four applications of basis reduction: breaking certain cryptosystems and linear congruential pseudorandom generators, finding simultaneous Diophantine approximations, and a refutation of Mertens' conjecture. We can only give the basic ideas; technical details can be found in the references, provided in the notes. The first two sections assume familiarity with the basics of cryptography, as explained in Chapter 20.

17.1. Breaking knapsack-type cryptosystems

The **subset sum problem** seeks to answer the following.

Given $a_1, \ldots, a_n, s \in \mathbb{N}$, are there $x_1, \ldots, x_n \in \{0, 1\}$ with $\sum_{1 \le i \le n} a_i x_i = s$? \hfill (1)

For example, an instance is to ask whether there exist $x_1, \ldots, x_6 \in \{0, 1\}$ such that $366x_1 + 385x_2 + 392x_3 + 401x_4 + 422x_5 + 437x_6 = 1215$.

This problem is $\mathcal{NP}$-complete, as is a slight generalization of it, called the **knapsack problem**. After Diffie & Hellman (1976) invented public key cryptography, Merkle & Hellman (1978) proposed a public key cryptosystem based on the subset sum problem. The computations in this system were much less voluminous than for other systems such as RSA (Section 20.2), and its higher throughput seemed to promise a bright future. Several other such systems were proposed, based on versions of the knapsack problem. But the roof fell in when Shamir (1984) broke the Merkle & Hellman system, and almost all subsequently proposed improved schemes have suffered the same fate. Basis reduction has played a major role in some of these cryptanalyses.

In the notation of Section 20.1, Alice publishes her public key $a_1, \ldots, a_n$ for such a **knapsack cryptosystem**. When Bob wants to send her n bits $x_1, \ldots, x_n$ secretly, he encodes them as $s = \sum_{1 \le i \le n} a_i x_i$ and sends s. Decoding a general such problem is $\mathcal{NP}$-complete and hence infeasible, but the idea now is to use a special type of problem for which decoding is easy with some secret additional knowledge, but hopefully hard without the secret. These special subset sum problems start with "superincreasing" $b_1 \ll b_2 \ll \cdots \ll b_n$ as the summands; a trivial example is $b_i = 2^{i-1}$, where the solution $(x_1,\dots,x_n)$ is just the binary representation of s. More generally, it is sufficient to have $b_i > \sum_{1 \leq j < i} b_j$ for all i; the solution is then unique and easy to calculate. The "easiness" is then hidden by multiplying the b_i's with a random number c modulo another random number m to obtain the public a_i's. Alice's secret key c, m allows her to multiply s by c^{-1} modulo m and then solve an easy subset sum problem. At first sight, the a_i look like a general subset sum problem, but the cryptanalysts' work then showed that this hiding does not work. Of course, the breaking of these schemes does *not* mean that large instances of an $\mathcal{NP}$-complete problem can be solved routinely; the "superincreasing" subset sum problem is just too special.

The connection between the subset sum problem and short vectors is given by the fact that a solution of (1) yields a short vector in the lattice $L \subseteq \mathbb{Z}^{n+1}$ generated by the rows $r_1, \dots, r_{n+1} \in \mathbb{Z}^{n+1}$ of the matrix

$$\begin{pmatrix} 1 & 0 & \cdots & 0 & -a_1 \\ 0 & 1 & \cdots & 0 & -a_2 \\ \vdots & \vdots & \ddots & \vdots & \vdots \\ 0 & 0 & \cdots & 1 & -a_n \\ 0 & 0 & \cdots & 0 & s \end{pmatrix} \in \mathbb{Z}^{(n+1) \times (n+1)}.$$

To see this, let $(x_1, \dots, x_n) \in \{0,1\}^n$ be a solution of (1). Then

$$v = \sum_{1 \leq i \leq n} x_i r_i + r_{n+1} = (x_1, \dots, x_n, 0) \in L$$

is a vector with $\|v\|_2 \leq \sqrt{n}$, which is very small since the a_i are typically very large numbers. The approach to breaking such a cryptosystem is to compute a reduced basis of L and to hope that the resulting short vector is (essentially) v. Of course, this does not work too well for general subset sum problems, but it does work for **low-density subset sums**, where the ratio $n / (\max_i \log_2 a_i)$ of information bits to transmitted bits is small. This number is about $1/n$ for Merkle & Hellman's original scheme, and then this attack is very successful. In the example, the density $6 / \log_2 437 \approx 0.684$ is high.

For example, with $a_1, \dots, a_6$ as in the beginning, we consider the lattice $L \subseteq \mathbb{Z}^7$ generated by the rows of the matrix

$$\begin{pmatrix} 1 & 0 & 0 & 0 & 0 & 0 & -366 \\ 0 & 1 & 0 & 0 & 0 & 0 & -385 \\ 0 & 0 & 1 & 0 & 0 & 0 & -392 \\ 0 & 0 & 0 & 1 & 0 & 0 & -401 \\ 0 & 0 & 0 & 0 & 1 & 0 & -422 \\ 0 & 0 & 0 & 0 & 0 & 1 & -437 \\ 0 & 0 & 0 & 0 & 0 & 0 & 1215 \end{pmatrix} \in \mathbb{Z}^{7 \times 7}.$$

Algorithm 16.10 then computes the short vector $v = (0,0,1,1,1,0,0) \in L$, and indeed $1215 = 366 \cdot 0 + 385 \cdot 0 + 392 \cdot 1 + 401 \cdot 1 + 422 \cdot 1 + 437 \cdot 0$.

17.2. Pseudorandom numbers

The simplest version of a **linear congruential pseudorandom number generator** is given by three parameters $a, b, m \in \mathbb{N}$, and for any seed $x_0 \in \{0, \dots, m-1\}$ successively computes the elements $x_i \in \{0, \dots, m-1\}$ defined by $x_{i+1} \equiv a x_i + b$ mod m for $i \in \mathbb{N}$. Pseudorandom numbers are used in many situations; the `rand` function in most computer systems is based on some form of these generators. These work just fine for computer algebra applications in modular algorithms or in the factorization of polynomials or integers. In cryptography, one would like to use them for the generation of keys. Therefore it is necessary that the numbers x_i are not only (almost) uniformly distributed but that it is practically impossible or computationally hard to infer x_i from $x_0, \dots, x_{i-1}$, and to break a pseudorandom number generator means exactly to do this with a reasonable amount of time.

Boyar (1989) broke the simple generator given above by noting that

$$x_{n+1} - x_n \equiv a(x_n - x_{n-1}) \bmod m, \quad x_{n+2} - x_{n+1} \equiv a(x_{n+1} - x_n) \bmod m$$

imply that m divides $(x_{n+1} - x_n)^2 - (x_n - x_{n-1})(x_{n+2} - x_{n+1})$, provided that a and m are coprime. This yields guesses for m, a, and b. She uses these guesses to predict the sequence. If a prediction ever turns out to be wrong, this leads to a new, improved guess. She proves that in polynomial-time one arrives at a permanently correct prediction.

Frieze, Hastad, Kannan, Lagarias & Shamir (1988) considered a generator, which they attribute to the 1981 edition of Knuth (1998), where not the whole of x_i, but only the top half of the bits of x_i are used. They broke this using basis reduction, assuming that the generator m, a, b is known, but not the seed x_0.

The methods of both Boyar and Frieze *et al.* apply to much more general generators than explained here, and all these generators are useless for cryptographic purposes.

17.3. Simultaneous Diophantine approximation

We are given real numbers $\alpha_1, \dots, \alpha_n$ and want to find $p_1, \dots, p_n, q \in \mathbb{Z}$ such that $|\alpha_i - (p_i/q)|$ is "small" for all i and q is not too large. We can simply take q to be a power of 10 and p_i an appropriate initial segment of the decimal expansion of α_i. However, we look for much better solutions, with q much smaller than (the inverse of) the approximation error.

For $n = 1$, this is the classical Diophantine approximation problem, discussed in Section 4.6: the "best" approximations can be computed with the Extended Euclidean Algorithm and yield $|\alpha_1 - p_1/q| < 5^{-1/2} q^{-2}$.

For general n, Dirichlet (1842) showed that there are infinitely many approximations with $|\alpha_i - p_i/q| \leq q^{-(1+1/n)}$ for all i. Lenstra, Lenstra & Lovász (1982) expressed this as a short vector problem, as follows. Given individual rational approximations $\alpha_i \approx \beta_i = u_i/v_i$ with $u_i, v_i \in \mathbb{Z}$ for $1 \leq i \leq n$ (but not necessarily the same denominator as demanded for a simultaneous approximation), and a rational ε with $0 < \varepsilon < 1$, we take $Q = \varepsilon^{-n}$ as an approximate bound on the denominator q. We set $w = 2^{-n(n+1)/4}\varepsilon^{n+1}$, and let $L \subseteq \mathbb{Q}^{n+1}$ be the lattice generated by the rows $f_0, \ldots, f_n \in \mathbb{Q}^{n+1}$ of the matrix

$$\begin{pmatrix} w & \beta_1 & \beta_2 & \cdots & \beta_n \\ 0 & -1 & 0 & \cdots & 0 \\ 0 & 0 & -1 & \cdots & 0 \\ \vdots & \vdots & \vdots & \ddots & \vdots \\ 0 & 0 & 0 & \cdots & -1 \end{pmatrix} \in \mathbb{Q}^{(n+1)\times(n+1)}.$$

In our treatment, we always assumed the vectors generating the lattice to have integral coefficients, but basis reduction also works for rational coefficients, as we have them here. It will produce in polynomial time a reduced basis for $L = \sum_{0 \leq i \leq n} \mathbb{Z}f_i$. By multiplying together the $n+1$ inequalities in the proof of Theorem 16.9, we find that its first vector g satisfies

$$\|g\|^{2(n+1)} \leq \|f_0^*\|^2 \cdot 2\|f_1^*\|^2 \cdots 2^n\|f_n^*\|^2 = 2^{n(n+1)/2}\|f_0^*\|^2 \cdots \|f_n^*\|^2.$$

Since $f_0^*, \ldots, f_n^*$ are orthogonal, we find from Theorem 16.5 (iv)

$$\|g\| \leq 2^{n/4}(\|f_0^*\| \cdots \|f_n^*\|)^{1/(n+1)} = 2^{n/4}\left|\det\begin{pmatrix} f_0^* \\ \vdots \\ f_n^* \end{pmatrix}\right|^{1/(n+1)}$$

$$= 2^{n/4}\left|\det\begin{pmatrix} f_0 \\ \vdots \\ f_n \end{pmatrix}\right|^{1/(n+1)} = \varepsilon < 1.$$

Since $g \in L$, there exist $q, p_1, \ldots, p_n \in \mathbb{Z}$ so that

$$g = qf_0 + \sum_{1 \leq i \leq n} p_i f_i = (qw, q\beta_1 - p_1, \ldots, q\beta_n - p_n).$$

If $q \leq 0$, we replace g by $-g$, so that $q \geq 0$, and $\|g\| < 1$ implies that $q \geq 1$. Then $|\beta_i - p_i/q| \leq \|g\|/q \leq \varepsilon/q = q^{-1}Q^{-1/n}$ for all i, and $1 \leq q \leq \varepsilon/w = 2^{n(n+1)/4}\varepsilon^{-n} = 2^{n(n+1)/4}Q$. This is about as good as guaranteed by Dirichlet's theorem, except for the factor $2^{n(n+1)/4}$; the latter does not depend on the sizes of the β_i, but only on their number.

Lagarias (1985) gave the following all-integer variant. Input is the vector

$$\beta = (u_1/v_1, \ldots, u_n/v_n) \in \mathbb{Q}^n.$$

For any nonzero $q \in \mathbb{N}$, we write

$$\{\{\beta q\}\} = \min_{p_1, \ldots, p_n \in \mathbb{Z}} \max_{1 \le i \le n} \left\{ \left| \frac{u_i}{v_i} - \frac{p_i}{q} \right| \right\}$$

for the best approximation quality with denominator q. For p_i, one simply takes the integer nearest to $u_i q / v_i$. A further input is a bound Q on the denominator. If a simultaneous approximation denominator q^* exists with $1 \le q^* \le Q$ and $\varepsilon = \{\{\beta q^*\}\}$, say as guaranteed by Dirichlet's theorem but unknown, then the algorithm produces an approximation q which is almost as good:

$$1 \le q \le 2^{n/2} QV, \text{ and } \{\{\beta q\}\} \le \sqrt{5n}\, 2^{(n-1)/2} \varepsilon. \tag{2}$$

We let $V = v_1 \cdots v_n$, and assume that $\varepsilon > 0$. For all $j \in \{0, \ldots, n + \log_2(QV)\}$, we consider the lattice $L_j \subseteq \mathbb{Z}^{n+1}$ spanned by the rows of the matrix

$$\begin{pmatrix} 2^j & QV\dfrac{u_1}{v_1} & QV\dfrac{u_2}{v_2} & & QV\dfrac{u_n}{v_n} \\ 0 & QV & 0 & \cdots & 0 \\ 0 & 0 & QV & \cdots & 0 \\ \vdots & \vdots & \vdots & & \vdots \\ 0 & 0 & 0 & \cdots & QV \end{pmatrix} \in \mathbb{Z}^{(n+1) \times (n+1)}.$$

The lower n vectors have only one nonzero entry each. We run the basis reduction algorithm 16.10 on this basis, and let $x^{(j)} = (x_0^{(j)}, \ldots, x_n^{(j)}) \in \mathbb{Z}^{n+1}$ be the short vector returned. Lagarias shows that for some value of j, the denominator $q = x_0^{(j)}$ provides an approximation satisfying (2), and that the whole algorithm runs in polynomial time.

EXAMPLE 17.1. We try Lagarias' method on the binary logarithms of the musical intervals $2, 3/2, 4/3, 5/4, 6/5, 9/8$ from Section 4.8. Since $\log_2 2 = 1$ and $\log_2(3/2) + \log_2(4/3) = 1$, it suffices to find simultaneous Diophantine approximations for $\alpha_1 = \log_2(4/3) \approx 0.42$, $\alpha_2 = \log_2(5/4) \approx 0.32$, $\alpha_3 = \log_2(6/5) \approx 0.26$, and $\alpha_4 = \log_2(9/8) \approx 0.17$. We take as initial approximation u_i/v_i the decimal expansion of α_i rounded to two digits, so that we start with a simultaneous Diophantine approximation with common denominator $V = 100$ (instead of the product required above). Letting $Q = 1$ and $j = 0$, we obtain the lattice $L \subseteq \mathbb{Z}^5$ generated by the rows of the matrix

$$\begin{pmatrix} 1 & 42 & 32 & 26 & 17 \\ 0 & 100 & 0 & 0 & 0 \\ 0 & 0 & 100 & 0 & 0 \\ 0 & 0 & 0 & 100 & 0 \\ 0 & 0 & 0 & 0 & 100 \end{pmatrix}.$$

Then Algorithm 16.10 computes the matrix

$$\begin{pmatrix} 12 & 4 & -16 & 12 & 4 \\ -19 & 2 & -8 & 6 & -23 \\ 1 & 42 & 32 & 26 & 17 \\ 16 & -28 & 12 & 16 & -28 \\ 22 & 24 & 4 & -28 & -26 \end{pmatrix},$$

whose rows form a reduced basis of L. Indeed, the leftmost entries of the first two rows yield our familiar common denominator 12 and the next best choice 19. $\diamond$

17.4. Disproof of Mertens' conjecture

We defined the **Möbius function** $\mu(n)$ for $n \in \mathbb{N}$ in Section 14.9, equation (10). Its summation $M \colon \mathbb{N} \longrightarrow \mathbb{N}$ is given by $M(x) = \sum_{n \leq x} \mu(n)$. Table 17.1 lists the first fifteen values of μ and M.

n	1	2	3	4	5	6	7	8	9	10	11	12	13	14	15
$\mu(n)$	1	-1	-1	0	-1	1	-1	0	0	1	-1	0	-1	1	1
$M(n)$	1	0	-1	-1	-2	-1	-2	-2	-2	-1	-2	-2	-3	-2	-1

TABLE 17.1: The values of $\mu(n)$ and $M(n)$ for $n \leq 15$.

Mertens (1897) contains a table of values up to $10\,000$, and he conjectured that $|M(x)| \leq \sqrt{x}$ for all $x \in \mathbb{N}$; a similar conjecture had been made in 1885 by Stieltjes.

The conjecture may seem to come out of the blue, but in analytic number theory one studies various functions that take values $0, 1, -1$ (or other complex values with absolute value 0 or 1) such as the Jacobi symbol (Section 18.6) and proves that their sum up to x is absolutely bounded by $O(\sqrt{x})$. The same is true for the absolute value of the sum of a random sequence of 1 and -1 (Exercise 19.18; the sum itself has mean 0); in fact, the quotient $M(x)/x$ goes to zero if and only if μ takes the values 1 and -1 roughly equally often. This principle will motivate the bound on the size of elliptic curves (Hasse's theorem 19.20).

Mertens proved that his conjecture implies the famous Riemann Hypothesis (Notes 18.4). Furthermore, it was known that it implies the unsolvability of a certain (inhomogeneous) simultaneous Diophantine approximation problem, as in the previous section, involving roots of Riemann's zeta function. However, Odlyzko & te Riele (1985) used basis reduction in a lattice in $\mathbb{R}^{70}$ to show that this approximation problem does have a solution, and thus disproved Mertens' conjecture. Their account is eminently readable also for the non-specialist, and their method suggests that a counterexample might exist for an x of order $\exp(10^{65})$, but current algorithmics do not allow us to calculate M for such huge arguments. So we know that an x with $M(x) > 1.065\sqrt{x}$ exists, but we do not know any such x.

Notes. **17.1.** The subset sum problem was proven to be $\mathcal{NP}$-complete by Karp (1972); see problem SP13 of Garey & Johnson (1979). The original successful attack on the Merkle & Hellman system was by Shamir (1984). Lagarias & Odlyzko (1985) described the short vector attack, and Odlyzko (1990) gives a nice overview of the problem. Other subset sum cryptosystems were proposed by Graham & Shamir (see Shamir & Zippel (1980) for a description), Lu & Lee (1979), Niederreiter (1986), Goodman & McAuley (1984), Ong, Schnorr & Shamir (1984). Most of them were broken in the 1980s using basis reduction, among others by Adleman (1983) and Brickell (1984, 1985). The only knapsack type cryptosystem withstanding all attacks up to now is the Chor & Rivest (1988) scheme.

17.2. Lagarias (1990), §8, surveys pseudorandom number generators in cryptography.

17.3. Dirichlet (1842) showed that there exist simultaneous Diophantine approximations with absolute error bound $q^{-(1+1/n)}$, and Lagarias (1982a, 1982b) presents many results concerning best approximations. Lagarias (1985) discusses the computational complexity of various such problems, which, depending on the specification, ranges from polynomial-time to $\mathcal{NP}$-complete. As an example, the following is $\mathcal{NP}$-complete: given $\beta \in \mathbb{Q}^n$, as in Section 17.3, and integers Q, s, t, is there an approximation denominator q with $1 \le q \le Q$ and $\{\{\beta q\}\} \le s/t$?

Exercises.

17.1$^{\longrightarrow}$ We consider the following knapsack cryptosystem. The pairs $AA, AB, \ldots, AZ, BA, BB, \ldots,$ $BZ, \ldots, ZA, ZB, \ldots, ZZ$ of letters are identified with the binary representations of the numbers $0, \ldots,$ $26^2 - 1 = 675$. For example, the pair SO corresponds to the bit string $x_9 x_8 \cdots x_0 = 0111100010$. Longer messages are broken into two-letter blocks and each block is treated separately.

1. The secret key is $c_9, \ldots, c_0, m, w \in \mathbb{N}$ with $c_{i+1} \ge 2c_i$ for $0 \le i \le 8$, $m > \sum_{0 \le i \le 9} c_i$, and $\gcd(w, m) = 1$.

2. The public key is $a_i = (wc_i \text{ rem } m) \in \mathbb{N}$ for $i = 0, \ldots, 9$.

3. A bit string $x = x_9 x_8 \cdots x_0$ is encrypted as $s = \sum_{0 \le i \le 9} x_i a_i \in \mathbb{N}$.

4. To decrypt a ciphertext s, you compute $t \in \mathbb{N}$ such that $t \equiv w^{-1} s \mod m$ and $0 \le t < m$. Then $t = \sum_{0 \le i \le 9} x_i c_i \in \mathbb{N}$, and you can reconstruct $x_9, x_8, \ldots, x_0$ from t.

(i) Write procedures for encryption and decryption, and check them with the key $c_0 = 1$ and $c_{i+1} = 2c_i + 1$ for $0 \le i \le 8$, $m = 9973$, and $w = 2001$, on the message "ALGEBRAISFUN".

(ii) Prove that $t = \sum_{0 \le i \le 9} x_i c_i$ actually holds in step 4.

(iii) Now you are an eavesdropper who knows the public key

i	9	8	7	6	5	4	3	2	1	0
a_i	3208	8694	3335	1964	5982	2991	6199	5741	1698	8194

and has intercepted the following ciphertext consisting of the eight blocks

$$25\,323, \, 11\,402, \, 18\,182, \, 25\,330, \, 24\,037, \, 11\,105, \, 30\,405, \, 34\,024$$

(in decimal representation). Try basis reduction to find the original message. This need not work for all blocks.

Part IV
Fermat

Pierre Fermat (c. 1601–1665) has been called the greatest amateur mathematician. After growing up in Beaumont-de-Lomagne in Gascony (where his home now houses an interesting museum**), he studied in Orléans and Toulouse, became "commissioner of requests" in 1631, and *conseiller du roi* in the local *parlement*, through which any petitions to the king had to pass. He died in Castres, where he was in the commission implementing the *Édit de Nantes*, which gave some protection to the persecuted protestant Huguenots. Fermat never left the area, never published a paper, and still became the second-best mathematician of his century (after Newton). Fermat communicated his mathematical discoveries in numerous letters, usually without proof and often in the form of challenges, to his contemporaries. (Among them was René Descartes, who could only be reached through his friend Marin Mersenne in Paris, because for many years he lived in Holland without a fixed address—a Flying Dutchman of mathematics, like the modern-day late Pál Erdős.)

Fermat was a pioneer in several areas. His method for drawing a tangent to certain plane curves was a step in the invention of calculus— later came Newton and Leibniz. He invented probability theory, in extensive correspondence with Blaise Pascal around 1654. He determined extrema of functions as zeroes of their derivative, and used this to calculate the path of light through different media according to the "principle of least time". There was a controversy between him and Descartes about the discovery of analytical geometry; certainly Fermat was the first to use it in three dimensions.

But Fermat's greatest contributions—and those of interest for computer algebra—were in number theory. He was fascinated by perfect and amicable numbers, and the Pell–Fermat equation $x^2 - ny^2 = 1$. Fermat discovered that primes of the form $4n + 1$ can be represented (in exactly one way) as a sum of two squares; for example, $29 = 5^2 + 2^2$. (It is easy to show that numbers of the form $4n - 1$ are never sums of two squares; see Exercise 18.1.) His "method of infinite descent" can determine the (un)solvability of many Diophantine equations.

** worth the detour

486

Fermat wrote to Bernard Frénicle de Bessy around August 1640 that the numbers $2^{2^0} + 1 = 3, 2^{2^1} + 1 = 5, 2^{2^2} + 1 = 17, 2^{2^3} + 1 = 257$, and $2^{2^4} + 1 = 65\,537$ are primes; he conjectured that all these **Fermat numbers** $F_n = 2^{2^n} + 1$ were prime. He was wrong; the next values of F_n, at least up to $n = 23$, are not prime; see Section 4.3. Not much harm done; he pointed out that he did not have a proof of his conjecture. We come across Fermat numbers in Chapter 8, where they are used in the integer Fourier Transform, and Chapter 18. Weil (1984) presents Fermat's achievements in detail.

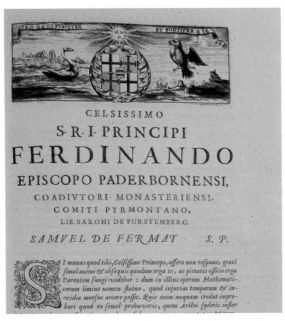

CELSISSIMO

S·R·I·PRINCIPI

FERDINANDO

EPISCOPO PADERBORNENSI,

CO·ADIVTORI·MONASTERIENSI,
COMITI·PYRMONTANO,
LIB. BARONI DE FURSTENBERG.

SAMVEL DE FERMAT S. P.

I munus quod tibi, Celsissime Princeps, offero non respuas, grati simul animi & obsequii quodam erga te, ac pietatis officio erga Parentem fungi videbor : dum in illius operum Mathemati-corum limine nomen statuo, quod injurias temporum & in-vidiæ morsus arcere possit. Quis enim unquam credat impro-bari quod tu semel probaveris, quem Arctoi sideris instar

The theorem that includes Fermat into our little Hall of Fame is that for a prime p and an integer a, $a^{p-1} - 1$ is divisible by p. He stated it in a letter to Frénicle on 18 October 1640: *Tout nombre premier mesure infailliblement une des puissance -1 de quelque progression que ce soit, et l'exposant de la dite puissance est sous-multiple du nombre premier donné -1.*[1] He forgot to mention that we have to disallow the geometric progression $a, a^2, a^3, \ldots$ if p divides a. We will call it and various generalizations "Fermat's little theorem" in this book; they play a crucial role in primality testing and the factorization of polynomials and integers (Chapters 14, 18, and 19). Leibniz rediscovered and proved this result in unpublished notes from 1680; see Notes 4.4. Euler (1732/33, 1747/48) was the first to publish a proof. He also derived conditions on the factors of Fermat numbers, which led him to the factor 641 of F_5.

Finally, there is Fermat's (in)famous remark in the margin near the eighth problem of Book II of Bachet's translation of Diophantus' *Arithmetic*, which deals with rational solutions of the equation $x^2 + y^2 = z^2$: *Cubum autem in duos cubos, aut quadratoquadratum in duos quadratoquadratos & generaliter nullam in infinitum ultra quadratum potestatem in duos eiusdem nominis fas est dividere; cuius rei demonstrationem mirabilem sane detexi. Hanc marginis exiguitas non*

---

[1] Every prime number divides invariably one of the powers -1 in any given geometric progression, and the exponent of this power is a divisor of the given prime number -1.

caperet.[2] A proof of this eluded mathematicians for over three centuries and inspired Kummer's theory of ideals and the construction of large parts of the edifice of *arithmetic algebraic geometry*, culminating in Wiles' proof of "Fermat's last theorem" via a special case of the Taniyama–Weil conjecture (Wiles 1995, Taylor & Wiles 1995; see van der Poorten 1996 for the mathematics and Singh 1997 for the story). The designation comes from the fact that after all of Fermat's claims had been proven, this remained open as the last one.

His son, Samuel de Fermat, published Diophant's Arithmetic with Fermat's annotations, and in 1679 the *Varia opera mathematica D. Petri de Fermat, Senatoris Tolosani.* His dedication to Ferdinand II. von Fürstenberg, featured on page 487, reads: *To His Highness Prince Ferdinand, Bishop of Paderborn, Coadiutor of Münster, Duke of Pyrmont, Free Baron of Fürstenberg. By Samuel de Fermat S. P. Motto: soft and strong.* Ferdinand II. (1626–1683) was a shining light of Paderborn science, student at the University of Paderborn from 1644 to 1646, erudite author of *Monumenta Paderbornensia* on the local history, correspondent with the leading philosophers and scientists of his times, and sponsor of the arts and architecture. His residence is shown in Figure 13.4. Fermat's dedication makes it plausible that he financed the *Varia opera.*

Samuel de Fermat includes a poem, whose title and first lines are:

De Principis eiusdem præclaro
Monumentorum Paderbornensium opere.

Dum Paderæ fontes æterno carmine Princeps
Aonij celebrat spes columenque chori,
Ut superat quæ sic ponit monumenta, suisque
Altius ipse aliud tollit ad astra modis![3]

---

[2] But it is impossible to divide a cube into two cubes, or a fourth power into two fourth powers, or generally any power beyond the squares into two like powers; I discovered a truly marvelous proof of this fact. The margin is too narrow to write it down.

[3] On the Prince's famous work *Monumenta Paderbornensia*: The Prince, hope and pillar of the chorus of the Muses, celebrates the sources of the Pader river with his eternal song. Just as he who builds such monuments towers high, he carries in his way [through his generosity] another work [Fermat's *Opera*] higher up to the stars!

Il est remarquable qu'on déduise ainsi du calcul intégral
une propriété essentielle des nombres premiers; mais
toutes les vérités mathématiques sont liées les unes aux autres,
et tous les moyens de les découvrir sont également admissibles.[1]

Adrien-Marie Legendre (1830)

Can I get a witness

The Rolling Stones (1964)

No mathematician can now write on demand a prime with,
say, 10 million digits, although one surely exists.

Stanisław Marcin Ulam (1964)

Such sentiments [half-credence in the supernatural] are seldom
thoroughly stifled unless by reference to the doctrine of chance, or, as
it is technically termed, the Calculus of Probabilities. Now this
Calculus is, in its essence, purely mathematical; and thus we have the
anomaly of the most rigidly exact in science applied to the shadow and
spirituality of the most intangible in speculation.

Edgar Allan Poe (1842)

"Du har sagt det där förut", sa Kollberg torrt.
"Det är rena gissningen."—"Sannolikhetsprincipen."[2]

Maj Sjöwall and Per Wahlöö (1967)

---

[1] It is remarkable that one should deduce in this way from integral calculus an essential property of the prime numbers; but all mathematical truths are connected to each other, and all means of discovering them are equally admissible.

[2] "You have said that before," Kollberg said drily. "It is pure guesswork."—"The principle of probability."

18

Primality testing

We want to know whether a given integer is prime or not. Certainly we can find out by factoring it. Can you think of any other way? Well, there is, and the major discovery in this area is that primality testing is much easier than factoring, at least to current knowledge. One can test integers with many thousands of digits, but factoring numbers with only 300 digits is in general not feasible.

In this chapter, we provide an efficient probabilistic algorithm to test primality; factorization is the subject of the next chapter. As an easy application, we can also find large prime numbers, as they are required in some modular algorithms and in modern cryptography. We conclude with brief discussions of other primality testing algorithms.

For numbers of a special form, such as the **Mersenne numbers** $M_n = 2^n - 1$, particularly efficient methods have been known since the last century. Indeed, throughout history the largest known prime has usually been a Mersenne prime. On 27 January 1998, 19 year old student Roland Clarkson discovered the 37th known Mersenne prime $M_{3021377}$, a number with 909526 decimal digits. This current world record (at the time of writing) is an achievement of GIMPS, the Great Internet Mersenne Prime Search, based on software by George Woltman and Scott Kurowski. It harnesses the spare power of thousands of computers (such as Clarkson's 200 MHz Pentium processor) all over the world, and consumes about a decade of CPU time each day. This new paradigm of *internet computing* started in the area of integer factorization, and may solve in the future very large instances of such easily distributed problems.

18.1. Multiplicative order of integers

An integer $N \in \mathbb{N}_{\geq 2}$ is a **prime number** if $N \mid ab$ implies that $N \mid a$ or $N \mid b$, or, equivalently, if $ab = N$ implies that $a \in \{1, -1\}$ or $b \in \{1, -1\}$, for all $a, b \in \mathbb{Z}$ (Section 25.2). The other integers $N \geq 2$ are **composite**. (The number 1 is neither prime nor composite, but a unit. In the ring $\mathbb{Z}$, -5 is a prime just as 5 is; see

Section 3.1 for a discussion of **associates**.) The prime numbers form the "building blocks" for all integers, according to the following basic fact.

FUNDAMENTAL THEOREM OF ARITHMETIC. Every positive integer can be written as a product of positive prime factors. This is unique up to the order of the factors. In other words, $\mathbb{Z}$ is a Unique Factorization Domain.

The idea of primality was known to the Pythagoreans (around 500 BC), and Book IX of Euclid's *Elements* contains his famous proof that there are infinitely many primes (see page 24).

This chapter deals mainly with testing whether a given integer N is prime or not. Can we do better than to try division by all integers up to $\sqrt{N}$, a method already known to Eratosthenes in the third century BC? Yes, indeed, there are efficient probabilistic algorithms that differentiate between prime and composite numbers, and as a result the set of prime numbers can be recognized in probabilistic polynomial time; more precisely, it is in the complexity class $\mathcal{ZPP}$ (see Section 25.8).

We recall the following facts. $\mathbb{Z}_N^\times = \{a \bmod N \in \mathbb{Z}_N : \gcd(a,N) = 1\}$ is the multiplicative group of units in $\mathbb{Z}_N = \mathbb{Z}/N\mathbb{Z}$. Remember that a unit in a ring is an element that has an inverse in the ring. The elements of $\mathbb{Z}_N^\times$ form a multiplicative group of cardinality $\varphi(N) = \#\mathbb{Z}_N^\times$; φ is **Euler's totient function**. If the prime factorization of N is $N = p_1^{e_1} \cdots p_r^{e_r}$, where $p_1, \ldots, p_r$ are distinct positive primes and $e_1, \ldots, e_r$ are positive integers, then the Chinese Remainder Theorem 5.3 says that $\mathbb{Z}_N \cong \mathbb{Z}_{p_1^{e_1}} \times \cdots \times \mathbb{Z}_{p_r^{e_r}}$ (a ring isomorphism), and that $\mathbb{Z}_N^\times \cong \mathbb{Z}_{p_1^{e_1}}^\times \times \cdots \times \mathbb{Z}_{p_r^{e_r}}^\times$ (a group isomorphism). If N is prime, then $\mathbb{Z}_N$ is a field, and $\mathbb{Z}_N^\times$ is a group of order $\varphi(N) = N - 1$. If $N = p^e$ is a prime power, then $\varphi(N) = p^{e-1}(p-1)$, and in general, $\varphi(N) = p_1^{e_1-1} \cdot (p_1 - 1) \cdots p_r^{e_r-1} \cdot (p_r - 1)$, by Corollary 5.6.

A central fact is **Fermat's little theorem** 4.9 which says that $a^{N-1} \equiv 1 \bmod N$ for a prime N and any $a \in \mathbb{Z}$ which is coprime to N. For coprime integers a, N we define the **order** $\mathrm{ord}_N(a)$ of a modulo N as the smallest integer $k \geq 1$ such that $a^k \equiv 1 \bmod N$. **Euler's theorem**, generalizing Fermat's, states that $a^{\varphi(N)} \equiv 1 \bmod N$, and is a consequence of Lagrange's theorem (Section 25.1). Besides these "upper bounds" on the order, we also need some "lower bounds".

LEMMA 18.1. *Let $N \in \mathbb{N}_{\geq 2}$.*

(i) *If $a \in \mathbb{Z}$ is coprime to N and $k \in \mathbb{N}$ with $a^k \equiv 1 \bmod N$, then $\mathrm{ord}_N(a)$ divides k. In particular, $\mathrm{ord}_N(a)$ divides $\varphi(N)$.*

(ii) *If p is prime, $e \in \mathbb{N}_{\geq 2}$, $N = p^e$, and $a = 1 + p^{e-1}$, then $\mathrm{ord}_N(a) = p$.*

PROOF. (i) Let $e = \mathrm{ord}_N(a)$ and divide k by e with remainder: $k = qe + r$ with $0 \leq r < e$. Then $a^r = a^{k-qe} = a^k \cdot (a^e)^{-q} \equiv 1 \bmod N$, and hence $r = 0$. By Euler's theorem, we have $a^{\varphi(N)} \equiv 1 \bmod N$, and (i) follows.

(ii) We have

$$a^p \equiv \sum_{0 \leq i \leq p} \binom{p}{i} p^{(e-1)i} \equiv 1 \bmod p^e.$$

By (i), $\mathrm{ord}_N(a)$ is either 1 or p, and since $a \not\equiv 1 \bmod N$, the claim follows. $\square$

If p is a prime, then in the language of Section 8.2, $a \in \mathbb{Z}$ is a primitive kth root of unity in $\mathbb{F}_p$ if and only if $p \nmid a$ and $\mathrm{ord}_p(a) = k$.

18.2. The Fermat test

From now on, we assume that $N \in \mathbb{N}_{\geq 3}$ is odd; testing even numbers for primality is rather easy. We recall that $a \,\mathrm{rem}\, N \in \mathbb{N}$ is the remainder of $a \in \mathbb{Z}$ on division by N, with $0 \leq a \,\mathrm{rem}\, N < N$. We often use it to represent $a \bmod N \in \mathbb{Z}_N$, but the two objects live in different domains. Fermat's little theorem furnishes the **Fermat test** for primality.

▬▬ ALGORITHM 18.2 Fermat test. ▬▬▬▬▬▬▬▬▬▬▬▬▬▬▬▬▬▬
Input: An odd integer $N \geq 3$.
Output: Either "composite" or "possibly prime".

1. choose $a \in \{2, \cdots, N-2\}$ uniformly at random

2. **call** the repeated squaring algorithm 4.8 to compute $b = a^{N-1} \,\mathrm{rem}\, N$

3. **if** $b \neq 1$ **then return** "composite" **else return** "possibly prime" ▬▬▬▬▬

If a and N are not coprime, then neither are b and N, and the algorithm correctly returns "composite". So we may assume that $\gcd(a, N) = 1$. Then by Fermat's little theorem, the answer is correct if the test replies "composite". If it replies "possibly prime", it may be right or it may be wrong. We have to understand when and why an error may occur. To this end, we consider the subgroup of

$$L_N = \{u \in \mathbb{Z}_N^\times : u^{N-1} = 1\}$$

of $\mathbb{Z}_N^\times$. Clearly L_N is a group, and Fermat's little theorem says that $L_N = \mathbb{Z}_N^\times$ if N is prime. If $L_N \neq \mathbb{Z}_N^\times$, then in fact $\#L_N \leq \frac{1}{2}\#\mathbb{Z}_N^\times$, since the size of a finite group is an integer multiple of the size of any of its subgroups, by Lagrange's theorem (Section 25.1). If the a chosen in step 1, taken modulo N, happens to be in $\mathbb{Z}_N^\times \setminus L_N$, then the test will answer "composite". Such an a, and also its residue class $a \bmod N$, is called a **Fermat witness** to the compositeness of N. Similarly, if $a \bmod N \in L_N$, then a (and also $a \bmod N$) is a **Fermat liar** for N.

If we know any Fermat witness, we are guaranteed that N is composite, although we still do not necessarily know a factor of N. The required computation is fairly

easy to do. We have come across a famous historical example on page 487: the first
five **Fermat numbers** $F_n = 2^{2^n} + 1$ are prime, for $n = 0, 1, 2, 3, 4$. Pierre Fermat
conjectured in August 1640 that all these numbers are prime, while he communicated his famous "little" theorem in a letter dated 18 October 1640. However,
$3^{2^{32}} \equiv 1\,461\,798\,105 \not\equiv 1 \bmod 2^{32} + 1$; therefore, by Fermat's little theorem, Fermat's conjecture is false. The required computation amounts to 32 multiplications
modulo the 10-digit number $2^{32} + 1$ (it takes a few milliseconds on a workstation).
We saw in Section 4.3 how Euler had found the factor 641 of F_5. It turns out that
for "most" composite N, most a's are Fermat witnesses. The impressive recent
progress in factorization of Fermat numbers is presented in Section 19.1.

It would be nice if this test were enough. However, it clearly fails if N is composite and $L_N = \mathbb{Z}_N^\times$. Are there such numbers? Indeed there are, and we define
the **Carmichael numbers** to be precisely those composite integers N for which
$L_N = \mathbb{Z}_N^\times$. In other words, they are the composite numbers without any Fermat
witnesses.

For the cost analysis, we recall the multiplication time $\mathsf{M}(n)$ for multiplying two
integers of length n (Definition 8.26). We can use $\mathsf{M}(n) \in O(n \log n \log \log n)$, but
the reader may also think of classical multiplication with $\mathsf{M}(n) \in O(n^2)$ (see inside
front cover).

▬▬ THEOREM 18.3. ▬▬▬▬▬▬▬▬▬▬▬▬▬▬▬▬▬▬▬▬▬▬▬▬▬▬▬▬▬▬▬▬▬▬▬▬

*If N is prime or a Carmichael number, then the Fermat test 18.2 returns "possibly
prime". If N is composite and not a Carmichael number, then it returns "composite" with probability at least $1/2$. The algorithm uses $O(\log N \cdot \mathsf{M}(\log N))$ word
operations.* ▬▬▬▬▬▬▬▬▬▬▬▬▬▬▬▬▬▬▬▬▬▬▬▬▬▬▬▬▬▬▬▬▬▬▬▬▬▬▬

PROOF. If $\gcd(a, N) > 1$, then also $\gcd(b, N) > 1$, and the test returns "composite", so that we only need to consider the cases where a and N are coprime. If N
is composite and not Carmichael, then $\#L_N \le \varphi(N)/2$, as noted above, so that at
least half of the possible choices for a in step 1 (coprime to N) are Fermat witnesses. Repeated squaring in step 2 takes $O(\log N)$ multiplications modulo N or
$O(\log N \mathsf{M}(\log N))$ word operations, and the bound on the running time follows. □

18.3. The strong pseudoprimality test

What to do with the challenge posed by the Carmichael numbers? Pomerance
(1990b) pleads: *Using the Fermat congruence is so simple, that it seems a shame
to give up on it just because there are a few counter-examples!*

We now resolve this shortcoming of the Fermat test in a drastic way: we actually
factor these seemingly difficult Carmichael numbers in random polynomial time.
In general, factoring integers is much harder than testing them for primality, and
so these numbers turn out to be quite harmless after all.

LEMMA 18.4. *Any Carmichael number is squarefree.*

PROOF. We take a prime number p and assume that it divides the Carmichael number N exactly $e \geq 2$ times. By the Chinese Remainder Theorem, there exists an $a \in \mathbb{Z}$ with $a \equiv 1 + p^{e-1} \bmod p^e$ and $a \equiv 1 \bmod N/p^e$. Then a has order p modulo p^e, by Lemma 18.1, and hence also modulo N. Since $a^{N-1} \equiv 1 \bmod N$, it follows that p divides $N-1$, by the same lemma. Since p also divides N, we have a contradiction, and the claim is proved. $\square$

Exercise 18.9 shows that N is a Carmichael number if and only if N is squarefree and $p-1$ divides $N-1$ for any prime factor p of N, and that Carmichael numbers are odd and have at least three prime factors. The first three Carmichael numbers are: $561 = 3 \cdot 11 \cdot 17, 1105 = 5 \cdot 13 \cdot 17$, and $1729 = 7 \cdot 13 \cdot 19$.

The following algorithm refines the Fermat test, and there is no input on which it systematically fails. If it is run on a Carmichael number, then it probably not only recognizes it as composite but in addition finds a proper factor of it.

═══ ALGORITHM 18.5 Strong pseudoprimality test. ═══════════════════
Input: An odd integer $N \geq 3$.
Output: Either "composite", or "probably prime", or a proper factor of N.

1. choose $a \in \{2, \ldots, N-2\}$ uniformly at random

2. $g \longleftarrow \gcd(a,N)$
   if $g > 1$ **then return** g

3. write $N - 1 = 2^k m$ with $k, m \in \mathbb{N}$, $k \geq 1$, and m odd
   call the repeated squaring algorithm 4.8 to compute $b_0 = a^m$ rem N
   if $b_0 = 1$ **then return** "probably prime"

4. **for** $1 \leq i \leq k$ **do** $b_i \longleftarrow b_{i-1}^2$ rem N

5. **if** $b_k = 1$ **then** $j \longleftarrow \min\{0 \leq i < k : b_{i+1} = 1\}$ **else return** "composite"

6. $g \longleftarrow \gcd(b_j + 1, N)$
   if $g = 1$ or $g = N$ **then return** "probably prime" **else return** g ═══════

═══ THEOREM 18.6. ═══
If N is prime, then Algorithm 18.5 returns "probably prime". If N is composite and not a Carmichael number, then the algorithms returns "composite" with probability at least $1/2$. If N is a Carmichael number, the algorithm returns a proper divisor of N with probability at least $1/2$. It uses $O(\log N \cdot \mathsf{M}(\log N))$ word operations. ═══════

PROOF. By induction, we have $b_i \equiv a^{2^i m} \bmod N$ for $0 \leq i \leq k$, and in particular $b_k \equiv a^{N-1} \bmod N$. If $b_{i-1} = 1$, then also $b_i = 1$, for any i. If N is composite and not Carmichael, then with probability at least $1/2$, a is a Fermat witness for N, $b_k \neq 1$, and the algorithm returns "composite" in step 5. We next assume that N is prime. Then $b_k = 1$. If $b_0 = 1$, then the algorithm correctly returns "probably prime" in step 3. Otherwise, we have $b_j \neq 1$ and $b_j^2 \equiv b_{j+1} = 1 \bmod N$ in step 6. By Lemma 25.4, the polynomial $x^2 - 1 \in \mathbb{Z}_N[x]$ has at most two zeroes. Hence the only square roots of 1 modulo N are 1 and -1, so that $b_j = N - 1$ and $g = N$, and the correct result is returned in step 6.

The last case to be considered is when N is a Carmichael number. We let P be the set of prime divisors of N. Since N is squarefree, we have $N = \prod_{p \in P} p$. We consider

$$I = \{i : 0 \leq i \leq k \text{ and } \forall u \in \mathbb{Z}_N^\times \ u^{2^i m} = 1\}.$$

Then $k \in I$, by the definition of Carmichael numbers, and $i + 1 \in I$ for any $i \in I$ with $i < k$. Let $p \in P$ and $a \in \mathbb{Z}$ be a nonsquare modulo p, so that $a^{(p-1)/2} \not\equiv 1 \bmod p$; such an a exists by Lemma 14.7. Since $a^{p-1} \equiv 1 \bmod p$, $\mathrm{ord}_p(a)$ divides $p - 1$; it does not divide $(p - 1)/2$, and hence $\mathrm{ord}_p(a)$ is even. Now m is odd, so that $a^m \not\equiv 1 \bmod p$. The Chinese Remainder Theorem provides a $u \in \mathbb{Z}_N^\times$ with $u^m \neq 1$. Therefore $0 \notin I$. Hence there exists some $l < k$ such that $l \notin I$ and $l + 1 \in I$. Now let

$$G = \{u \in \mathbb{Z}_N^\times : u^{2^l m} = \pm 1\} \subseteq \mathbb{Z}_N^\times.$$

This is a subgroup of $\mathbb{Z}_N^\times$, and we now show that $G \neq \mathbb{Z}_N^\times$. There exists some $p \in P$ and $b \in \mathbb{Z}$ coprime to p with $b^{2^l m} \not\equiv 1 \bmod p$, since otherwise we would have $l \in I$. We take some such p and b. The Chinese Remainder Theorem implies that there exists a $c \in \mathbb{Z}$ such that $c \equiv b \bmod p$ and $c \equiv 1 \bmod N/p$. Then $c \bmod N \in \mathbb{Z}_N^\times \setminus G$. Being a proper subgroup, G has at most $\# \mathbb{Z}_N^\times / 2 = \varphi(N)/2$ elements.

If a in step 1 is chosen so that $a \bmod N \in \mathbb{Z}_N^\times \setminus G$, then we claim that the algorithm will actually discover a proper divisor of N. The fact that $b_{l+1} \equiv a^{2^{l+1} m} \equiv 1 \bmod N$ implies that for all $p \in P$, also $b_{l+1} \equiv 1 \bmod p$. Again, the only square roots of 1 modulo p are 1 and -1, so that for each p, $a^{2^l m} \bmod p$ is either 1 or -1. Since $b_l \bmod N = a^{2^l m} \bmod N$ is neither 1 nor -1, both possibilities actually occur, we have $j = l$ in step 5, and

$$g = \gcd(b_l + 1, N) = \prod_{\substack{p \in P \\ a^{2^l m} \equiv -1 \bmod p}} p$$

is a proper divisor of N. The fact that $\#(\mathbb{Z}_N^\times \setminus G) \geq \varphi(N)/2$ implies the bound on the probability.

Steps 2 and 6 take $O(\mathsf{M}(\log N) \log\log N)$ word operations, as discussed at the end of Section 11.1, the cost of steps 3 and 4 is $O(\log N)$ multiplications modulo N or $O(\log N \, \mathsf{M}(\log N))$ word operations, and the time estimate follows. $\square$

If N is composite, then a number $a \in \{1,\ldots,N-1\}$, coprime to N, such that Algorithm 18.5 outputs "composite" or a proper factor of N is called a **strong witness** for the compositeness of N, and if "probably prime" is returned, it is a **strong liar**. We also use these two notions for the corresponding residue class $a \bmod N$. Every Fermat witness is a strong witness.

In order to push the error probability below some given positive ε, we can run the test independently $\lceil \log_2 \varepsilon^{-1} \rceil$ times and return "probably prime" if this is the result of each run, and otherwise "composite" or a factor.

In the proof of Theorem 18.3 and in step 2 of Algorithm 18.5, we have dealt separately with the case where $\gcd(a,N) > 1$. This is highly unlikely to happen when N is reasonably large.

What does it mean when a primality test returns "probably prime" on input N? Is N then "probably prime"? Of course not; N is either prime or it is not. If we have run the test 1001 times, say, then it means the following: if N is not prime, then an event has been witnessed whose probability is at most 2^{-1001}. If you fly in an airplane whose safety depends on the actual primality of such an "industrial-strength pseudo-prime", then this fact should not worry you unduly, since other things are much more likely to fail ;-)

Exercise 18.6 shows that with a small modification, both the Fermat test and the strong pseudoprimality test find the prime factor p when $N = p^e$ is a prime power. Exercise 18.12 shows how to modify the algorithm to find all prime factors of a Carmichael number (whose factors are in general not Carmichael numbers).

18.4. Finding primes

For our modular algorithms and in cryptography, one needs prime numbers satisfying certain specifications. For example, we may be given an integer n and require an n-bit prime. In this section, we provide the tools for a variety of such tasks, and the corollaries at the end give cost estimates for all our prime-consuming algorithms. In most (but not all) cases, this cost is negligible when compared to the overall time taken by the algorithms.

The famous **prime number theorem** in analytic number theory says approximately how many primes there are in an initial segment of the natural numbers. It may be stated in two equivalent ways, using the two functions

$$\pi(x) = \#\{p \in \mathbb{N} : p \leq x, p \text{ prime}\}, \qquad p_n = \text{the } n\text{th prime number,}$$

where $x \in \mathbb{R}_{>0}$ and $n \in \mathbb{N}_{>0}$ (so that $p_1 = 2$). Its proof is beyond the scope of this text.

▬▬ THEOREM 18.7 *Prime number theorem.* ▬▬▬▬▬▬▬▬▬▬▬▬▬▬▬▬▬▬▬▬▬▬

Let ln *denote the logarithm in base e. Then we have approximately*

$$\pi(x) \approx \frac{x}{\ln x}, \quad p_n \approx n \ln n,$$

and more precisely

$$\frac{x}{\ln x}\left(1 + \frac{1}{2\ln x}\right) \quad < \quad \pi(x) \quad < \quad \frac{x}{\ln x}\left(1 + \frac{3}{2\ln x}\right) \qquad \text{if } x \geq 59,$$

$$n\left(\ln n + \ln\ln n - \frac{3}{2}\right) \quad < \quad p_n \quad < \quad n\left(\ln n + \ln\ln n - \frac{1}{2}\right) \qquad \text{if } n \geq 20.$$

The first statement says that a random integer near x is prime with probability about $(\ln x)^{-1}$. If we choose random n-bit integers and test them for primality, we expect to find a prime with about $n \cdot \ln 2$ trials. Throughout this section, "ln" is the "natural" logarithm for the prime number theory, but we continue to use "log" in "O" estimates of running times, where the base is irrelevant.

In order to find a large prime p, say with $B < p \leq 2B$ for some given B, we simply test uniformly selected random numbers p in the range for primality and return the first number that passes k such tests, for some given k. On any composite number, the tests return "probably prime" with probability at most 2^{-k}. One might then want to conclude that the output is prime with probability at least $1 - 2^{-k}$. This is fallacious. Imagine that there were only few primes between B and $2B$, say just one. Then for small k one would be much more likely to receive a composite number than a prime. Thus the density of the primes enters the following result.

▬▬ THEOREM 18.8. ▬▬▬▬▬▬▬▬▬▬▬▬▬▬▬▬▬▬▬▬▬▬▬▬▬▬▬
Given positive integers B, k, the output of the above procedure is prime with probability at least $1 - 2^{-k+1} \ln B$. It uses an expected number of $O(k(\log^2 B)\mathsf{M}(\log B))$ word operations. ▬▬▬▬▬▬▬▬▬▬▬▬▬▬▬▬

PROOF. The probability space here is the set of all random choices within the procedure. By the prime number theorem, the set P of primes considered has

$$\#P = \pi(2B) - \pi(B) \geq \frac{B}{\ln B}\left(1 - \frac{3}{\ln B}\right) \geq \frac{B}{2\ln B} \tag{1}$$

elements, provided that $B \geq 6$ (Exercise 18.18). Thus a random integer between $B + 1$ and $2B$ is prime with probability at least

$$\frac{\#P}{B} \geq \frac{1}{2\ln B}.$$

We denote by C and T the events that the chosen random number is composite and that all k tests answer "probably prime", respectively. Then $\text{prob}(p \text{ prime}) \le \text{prob}(T)$, and, using conditional probabilities (Section 25.6), we have

$$(2\ln B)^{-1} \cdot \text{prob}_T(C) \le \text{prob}(p \text{ prime}) \cdot \text{prob}_T(C) \le \text{prob}(T) \cdot \text{prob}_T(C)$$

$$= \text{prob}(C \cap T) = \text{prob}(C) \cdot \text{prob}_C(T) \le \text{prob}_C(T) \le 2^{-k},$$

which implies the probability estimate. We expect to make at most $2\ln B$ choices. By Theorem 18.6, each choice costs $O(k\log B \cdot \mathsf{M}(\log B))$ word operations, and the claim follows for $B \ge 6$. If $B \in \{1,\dots,5\}$, then we modify the procedure to choose one of the primes $2,3,5$, or 7. $\square$

The procedure can be viewed as a computationally efficient version of **Bertrand's postulate** which says that there is always a prime between an integer and its double. The estimate (1) is too pessimistic for larger values of B; a more realistic assumption is $\#P \approx B/\ln B$.

In Section 6.9, we proved that a nonzero polynomial probably takes a nonzero value at a random point. We now give an integer version of this important tool for modular algorithms. Evaluating a polynomial at a point and taking an integer modulo a prime are analogous operations. If we rewrite "$f(u) = 0$" as "$f \equiv 0 \mod x - u$" in the case $n = 1$, the integer analog of Lemma 6.44 reads as follows.

LEMMA 18.9. *Let $P \subseteq \mathbb{N}$ be a finite nonempty set of prime numbers, $a = \min P$, and $M \in \mathbb{Z}$ with $0 \ne |M| \le C$. If p is chosen from P uniformly at random, then*

$$\text{prob}\{M \equiv 0 \mod p \colon p \in P\} \le \frac{\log_a C}{\#P}. \tag{2}$$

PROOF. There are at most $\log_a |M| \le \log_a C$ primes in P that divide M. $\square$

We are now in a position to provide one of the ingredients for the modular algorithms for the determinant (Section 5.5), gcds and the Extended Euclidean Algorithm (Chapter 6), root finding (Sections 14.5 and 15.6), and factorization (Chapters 15 and 16) in $\mathbb{Z}[x]$, and for cryptography: finding suitable primes. Table 18.1 summarizes the costs and requirements. The second last algorithm does not occur explicitly in Section 16.5; essentially, one has to replace the first four steps of Algorithm 16.22 by the first three steps of the big prime algorithm 15.2. For most algorithms, we see in the fourth column that the time for finding one or several small primes is much less than the time for finding a big prime; in practice, we would work with a precomputed list of small primes, as discussed below. However, also the remaining stages of small primes and prime power algorithms are faster than the corresponding stages of their big prime counterparts: in theory only by

	modular algorithm	prime requirements	prime finding	cost for algorithm
deter- minant	big prime §5.5 small primes 5.10	$p > 2n^{n/2}A^n$ $p_1,\dots,p_r < 2r\ln r$	$n^3\log^3 A$ $n\log A$	$n^4\log A$ $n^4\log A$
gcd	big prime 6.34 small primes 6.38	$p > \sqrt{n+1}\cdot 2^{n+1}A^2$ $p_1,\dots,p_r < 2r\ln r$	$n^3+\log^3 A$ $n\log A$	$n^2+n\log A$ $n^2+n\log A$
EEA	small primes 6.57	$p_1,\dots,p_r < 2r\ln r$	$n\log A$	$n^3\log A$
root finding	big prime 14.17 prime power §15.6	$p > 2n(A^2+A)$ $p < 2r\ln r$	$\log^3 A$ $n\log A$	$n^2\log A+n\log^2 A$ $n^2\log A$
factor- ization	big prime 16.22 prime power 16.22	$p > \sqrt{n+1}\cdot 2^{n+1}A^2$ $p < 2r\ln r$	$n^3+\log^3 A$ $n\log A$	$n^{10}+n^8\log^2 A$ $n^{10}+n^8\log^2 A$

TABLE 18.1: Costs and requirements of various modular algorithms on inputs of degree (or dimension) n and max-norm at most A. For all small prime and prime power algorithms, there is a parameter $r \in O(n\log(nA))$. For some big prime algorithms, we also have the requirement that p does not divide a certain subresultant, of word length $O(n\log(nA))$. The last column contains the running time for the remaining algorithm without the prime finding stage. All stated costs are with fast arithmetic and ignore logarithmic factors.

logarithmic factors, which do not show up in the last column of Table 18.1, but they are clearly visible in practice (see Section 6.13).

═══ THEOREM 18.10. ═══

(i) *There is a probabilistic algorithm which, with probability at least $3/4$, returns a prime p between $B+1$ and $2B$, for any positive integer $B \in \mathbb{N}$ of word length β. Moreover, if $M \in \mathbb{Z}$ is a nonzero number such that $6\ln|M| \le B$, then p is prime and p does not divide M with probability at least $1/2$. The algorithm takes $O(\beta^2 \cdot \mathsf{M}(\beta)\log\beta)$ word operations.*

(ii) *For $r \in \mathbb{N}$, we can compute the first r prime numbers $p_1 = 2,\dots,p_r \in \mathbb{N}$ deterministically at a cost of $O(r\log^2 r\log\log r)$ word operations, and each of them is less than $2r\ln r$ if $r \ge 2$.* ═══════════════════

PROOF.   (i) If $B \ge 6$, thenTheorem 18.8 with $k = 2 + \lceil\log_2\ln B\rceil$ gives the first claim. Using Lemma 18.9 and (1), we find that p divides M with probability at most

$$\frac{\log_B C}{\#P} \le \frac{\ln C \cdot 2\ln B}{\ln B \cdot B} \le \frac{1}{3}$$

if it is prime. Therefore the probability that p has the required properties is at least $\frac{3}{4}(1-\frac{1}{3}) = \frac{1}{2}$. If $B \in \{1,\dots,5\}$, then $|M| \le e^{B/6} < B$, so that none of the primes between $B+1$ and $2B$ divides M, and we may take one of $2,3,5$, or 7 for p.

(ii) We have $p_r < r(\ln r + \ln\ln r - 1/2) \le 2r\ln r$ for $r \ge 20$, by the prime number theorem 18.7. In fact, $p_r < 2r\ln r$ for all $r \ge 2$. We find our primes by the **sieve**

of Eratosthenes, as follows. We write down a list of all integers below $x = 2r \ln r$. Then we cross out all even numbers, all multiples of 3, all multiples of 5, and so on, for each prime less than $\sqrt{x}$. The remaining integers are not divisible by a prime less than $\sqrt{x}$, and hence they are prime. The cost is $\lfloor x/p \rfloor$ steps for each prime $p \leq \sqrt{x}$, altogether at most

$$x \sum_{\substack{p < \sqrt{x} \\ p \text{ prime}}} \frac{1}{p} \in O(x \log \log x)$$

steps, by equation (3.20) in Rosser & Schoenfeld (1962). We may implement a single step by setting a flag for "crossed out" and incrementing a counter by p, taking $O(\log x)$ word operations. We obtain a total cost of $O(x \log x \log \log x)$ word operations, and the claim follows from $\log x \in O(\log r)$. $\square$

Our first application is the big prime modular gcd algorithm 6.34.

━━ COROLLARY 18.11. ━━━━━━━━━━━━━━━━━━━━━━━━━━━━━━━━━━━━━

Let $n \in \mathbb{N}_{\geq 2}$, $f, g \in \mathbb{Z}[x]$ be primitive, with degrees at most n and max-norms at most A, $h = \gcd(f, g)$, $b = \gcd(\mathrm{lc}(f), \mathrm{lc}(g))$, $B = \lceil (n+1)^{1/2} 2^{n+1} bA \rceil$, and $\beta = \log B$. If $n \geq 5$ or $A \geq 5$, then we can find an integer p with $B < p \leq 2B$ such that, with probability at least $1/2$, p is prime and does not divide $\mathrm{res}(f/h, g/h)$. This algorithm uses $O(\beta^2 \mathsf{M}(\beta) \log \beta)$ or $O^{\sim}(n^3 + \log^3 A)$ word operations. ━━━

PROOF. We let $\sigma = \mathrm{res}(f/h, g/h)$, and have $|\sigma| \leq (n+1)^n A^{2n}$, by Theorem 6.35, and therefore $6 \ln |\sigma| \leq 12n \ln((n+1)A)$. Since $12n < 2^{n+1}$ and $\ln((n+1)A) < (n+1)^{1/2}A$ if $n \geq 5$, and

$$12n \ln((n+1)A) < (n+1)^{1/2} 2^{n+1} A \leq B$$

if $n = 2, 3, 4$, for all $A \geq 5$, we find $6 \ln |\sigma| \leq B$ in all cases, and the claims follow from Theorem 18.10 (i) and $\beta \in O(n + \log A)$. $\square$

It is satisfying to have a worst-case guarantee on the cost of prime generation, and to see yet another reason why the big prime modular algorithms are impractical in spite of their conceptual simplicity. In Figure 6.5 the big prime running times are quite erratic, but smooth when the cost of prime generation is suppressed. In small primes or prime power modular algorithms, the cost of obtaining primes is negligible.

The prime finding step in the factorization algorithms 15.2 (big prime) and 15.19 and 16.22 (prime power) in $\mathbb{Z}[x]$ is quite inexpensive.

━━ COROLLARY 18.12. ━━━
Let $f \in \mathbb{Z}[x]$ be squarefree of degree $n \geq 2$ and with max-norm $\|f\|_\infty = A$, $\gamma = 2n\ln((n+1)A)$, and suppose that $A \geq 5$ if $n \leq 4$.

(i) There is a probabilistic algorithm which, with probability at least $1/2$, outputs a prime p between $B+1$ and $2B$ and not dividing $\operatorname{res}(f, f')$, where $B = \lceil (n+1)^{1/2} 2^{n+1} | \operatorname{lc}(f) | A \rceil$. Then $\beta = \log B \in O(n + \log A)$, and the algorithm uses an expected number of $O(\beta^2 \mathsf{M}(\beta) \log \beta)$ or $O^\sim(n^3 + \log^3 A)$ word operations.

(ii) With $O(\gamma \log^2 \gamma \log\log \gamma)$ or $O^\sim(n \log A)$ word operations we can find (probabilistically) a prime p of word length in $O(\log \gamma)$ and such that $p \nmid \operatorname{res}(f, f')$ with probability at least $1/2$. ━━━━━━━━━━━━━━━━━━━━━━━━━━━━

PROOF. (i) We let $\sigma = \operatorname{res}(f, f')$ and $C = (n+1)^{2n} A^{2n-1}$. As in the proof of Corollary 18.11, we have $6 \ln C \leq 6\gamma \leq B$. Since $\|f'\|_\infty \leq nA$ and $0 < |\sigma| \leq C$ by Theorem 6.23, the claim follows from Theorem 18.10 (i).

(ii) We let σ and C be as in the proof of (i). Then Theorem 18.10 (ii) with $r = \lceil 2 \log_2 C \rceil \in O(\gamma)$ says that we can compute the first r primes, each less than $2r \ln r$, within the stated time bound. By the choice of r, at most half of these primes divide σ, and we choose one of them uniformly at random. □

With some more calculations using the prime number theorem one can shave off a logarithmic factor in the estimate of (ii) (Exercise 18.21). Similar improvements are possible for small primes modular determinant computation (Algorithm 5.10), small primes modular gcd computation (Algorithm 6.38), and the small primes modular EEA (Algorithm 6.57).

A software implementation of small primes or prime power modular algorithms should precompute a table of small primes, so that for most purposes only table look-up is needed. Rather than using the first primes, it is more efficient to take the largest single precision primes. As discussed at the beginning of Chapter 5 and in Section 8.3, it is advantageous in the small primes modular approach to choose $p_1, \ldots, p_r$ to be Fourier primes, so that $p_i - 1$ is divisible by some large power 2^t of 2, for all i. There are quantitative versions of Dirichlet's (1837) famous theorem on primes in arithmetic progressions that give asymptotic estimates, but even the best versions (Alford, Granville & Pomerance 1994, Bach & Sorenson 1996) are considerably less precise than the prime number theorem 18.7. For practical purposes, however, it is reasonable to assume that a random number $p \equiv 1 \bmod 2^t$ near x is prime with probability about $2/\ln x$. To find enough such primes, we consecutively test $2^t + 1, 2 \cdot 2^t + 1, 3 \cdot 2^t + 1, \ldots$ for primality until we have found r primes. This will be a precomputation stage. Exercise 18.19 estimates the number of single precision Fourier primes for 32-bit and 64-bit processors.

In our big prime algorithms for gcd computation and factorizations, it may happen that the number p given by Theorem 18.10 is not prime. If we stumble upon a nonzero element which is not invertible in our computation, then we recognize our p as composite and start all over again with a new one. However, it may happen that all computations go through even if p is composite. In the gcd case, it is possible to show that the output is nevertheless correct, but in the polynomial factoring algorithm, reducible polynomials may wrongly be declared irreducible. However, this only happens with probability at most $1/2$, by Theorem 18.10, and we may simply rerun the whole algorithm several times independently to make the error probability arbitrarily small. Or, preferably, we use the prime power factoring algorithm, which is faster and returns the complete factorization in any case.

18.5. The Solovay and Strassen test

The following two sections are not used in what follows and may be skipped at first reading. We do not give proofs.

The first probabilistic polynomial-time test for primality is due to Solovay & Strassen (1974, published 1977). The **Legendre symbol** is defined for $a, N \in \mathbb{Z}$ with N prime as

$$
\left(\frac{a}{N} \right) = \begin{cases} 1 & \text{if } \gcd(a, N) = 1 \text{ and } a \text{ is a square modulo } N, \\ -1 & \text{if } \gcd(a, N) = 1 \text{ and } a \text{ is not a square modulo } N, \\ 0 & \text{if } \gcd(a, N) \neq 1, \end{cases}
$$

A famous theorem of number theory, Gauß' **law of quadratic reciprocity**, says that for odd primes a, N the two symbols

$$
\left(\frac{a}{N} \right) \text{ and } \left(\frac{N}{a} \right)
$$

are equal unless and only unless both a and N are congruent to 3 modulo 4. The **Jacobi symbol** is the generalization to an arbitrary odd N. If $N = p_1^{e_1} \cdots p_r^{e_r}$ is its prime factorization, then it is defined as

$$
\left(\frac{a}{N} \right) = \left(\frac{a}{p_1} \right)^{e_1} \cdots \left(\frac{a}{p_r} \right)^{e_r}.
$$

This quantity can be computed by an efficient method, akin to the Euclidean Algorithm, without actually factoring N (Notes 18.5 and Exercise 18.23).

When N is a prime, then Lemma 14.7 implies that

$$
\left(\frac{a}{N} \right) \equiv a^{(N-1)/2} \bmod N \tag{3}
$$

for all $a \in \mathbb{Z}$. Solovay & Strassen (1977) prove that (3) is false for at least half of all a in $\{1, \ldots, N-1\}$ if N is composite and not a prime power. Their algorithm checks (3) for randomly chosen a; each test takes $O(\log N \cdot \mathsf{M}(\log N))$ word operations.

Although Berlekamp's (1970) probabilistic algorithm for factoring polynomials (Section 14.8) had been around for a while, it was the Solovay & Strassen (1977) result for integers that aroused widespread interest in the power of randomized algorithms. (Are numbers more intuitive to computer scientists than polynomials? The reader should by now—and even more so after reading Chapter 19—be convinced that polynomials are much easier objects than numbers.) See Notes 6.5.

Both the Solovay–Strassen and the strong pseudoprimality tests should properly be called **compositeness tests** because they show the set PRIMES of all prime numbers is in co-$\mathcal{RP}$ and its complement (without 0 and 1) COMPOSITES is in $\mathcal{RP}$, which is a (possibly proper) subset of $\mathcal{BPP}$ (Section 25.8), but the wrong terminology has stuck.

18.6. The complexity of primality testing

With $(\log N)^{O(\log\log\log N)}$ word operations, the **Jacobi sum test** by Adleman, Pomerance & Rumely (1983) holds the current world record on completely proven deterministic primality testing; see also Lenstra's (1982) report. This is pretty close to polynomial time, since $\ln\ln\ln N$ grows rather slowly; it is at most 4 for $N \leq 10^{10^{23}}$.

We recall the complexity classes

$$\mathcal{P} \subseteq \mathcal{ZPP} = \mathcal{RP} \cap \text{co-}\mathcal{RP} \begin{matrix} \subseteq\ \mathcal{RP}\ \subseteq \\ \subseteq \text{co-}\mathcal{RP}\ \subseteq \end{matrix} \mathcal{BPP} \subseteq \mathcal{NP} \cap \text{co-}\mathcal{NP} \subseteq \mathcal{NP}$$

from Section 25.8. The general idea is that the practically solvable problems (for large inputs) are those in $\mathcal{BPP}$, in this picture. COMPOSITES $\in \mathcal{NP}$ is trivial, Pratt (1975) proves that PRIMES $\in \mathcal{NP} \cap \text{co-}\mathcal{NP}$ (Exercise 18.27), and Lehmann's algorithm (Exercise 18.24) shows PRIMES $\in \mathcal{BPP}$. Solovay & Strassen's and the strong pseudoprimality tests put PRIMES in co-$\mathcal{RP}$, and a fairly complicated algorithm by Adleman & Huang (1992) proves that PRIMES $\in \mathcal{RP}$, hence PRIMES $\in \mathcal{ZPP}$. The big open question is whether PRIMES $\in \mathcal{P}$. In fact, PRIMES seems to be the only problem in $\mathcal{ZPP}$ that is not known to be in $\mathcal{P}$ (and under the Extended Riemann Hypothesis, even the latter is false, by Theorem 18.14 below).

Randomness vs. ERH. Probabilistic tests like the strong pseudoprimality test 18.5 and the Solovay–Strassen test cannot be literally implemented because there is no known efficient source of truly random numbers to be used in today's computers. However, these algorithms work fine in practice with *pseudorandom number generators*; the most popular ones are the linear congruential generators (see

Sections 17.2 and 20.1). Knuth (1998), Chapter 3, gives an extensive discussion of this topic. We can replace the assumption of randomness by the assumption of the Extended Riemann Hypothesis (ERH) (see Notes 18.4), based on the following theorem by Ankeny (1952).

━━━ THEOREM 18.13. ━━

Let $N \in \mathbb{N}$, and q be a prime dividing $N - 1$. Under the ERH, there exists a **qth nonresidue** $a \in \mathbb{N}$ modulo N (that is, a has no qth root modulo N), with $a \in O(\log^2 N)$. ━━━

Miller (1976) used Ankeny's theorem for $q = 2$ to prove the following result.

━━━ THEOREM 18.14. ━━

Assuming the ERH, for each composite N there exists a strong witness a with $a \in O(\log^2 N)$. ━━━

This theorem proves the existence of a deterministic algorithm for primality testing under the ERH, but does not allow the explicit statement of such an algorithm. Since the constant in the "O" is not specified, one would not know when to stop looking for a witness. Bach (1985) resolved this strange situation by showing that, under the ERH, there exists a strong witness $a \leq 2 \ln^2 N$. Thus, the assumption of the ERH produces a deterministic algorithm for primality testing which runs in polynomial time $O(\log^3 N \mathsf{M}(\log N))$.

Primality tests for special numbers. For some special integers of interest in number theory, particularly efficient primality tests have been designed. Pepin (1877) obtained the following primality test for the Fermat numbers $F_n = 2^{2^n} + 1$ (see page 487 and Section 18.2):

$$F_n \text{ prime} \iff 3^{(F_n - 1)/2} \equiv -1 \bmod F_n.$$

In fact, this is just the Solovay–Strassen test with $a = 3$ (Exercise 18.25). If p is a prime dividing F_n, then p is of the form $p = a \cdot 2^{n+2} + 1$ for some integer a (Exercise 18.26). Trying such divisors led to the large factor $5 \cdot 2^{1947} + 1$ of F_{1945}.

The **Mersenne numbers** are defined by $M_n = 2^n - 1$ for $n \geq 1$. The integer M_a is a nontrivial factor of M_{ab}, for $a, b \in \mathbb{N}$, and hence if M_n is prime, then so is n. There is a special test for these numbers, the *Lucas-Lehmer test* (Lucas (1878), Lehmer 1930, 1935). The test says that $2^n - 1$ is prime if and only if $l_{n-1} \equiv 0 \bmod 2^n - 1$, where l_i is recursively defined by $l_1 = 4$ and $l_i = l_{i-1}^2 - 2$ for $i \geq 1$.

Presently it is not known if there are infinitely many Fermat primes or infinitely many Mersenne primes. No new Fermat primes have been discovered since Fermat's time, while there are now 37 Mersenne primes known, as mentioned at the beginning of this chapter.

Williams & Dubner (1986) used a Lucas-Lehmer type test to prove the primality of the **repunit**

$$\frac{10^{1031} - 1}{9} =$$

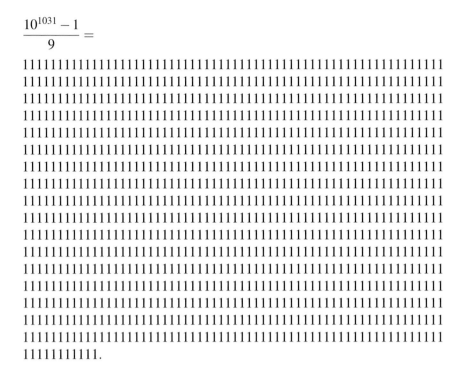

111111111111111111111111111111111111111111111111111111111111111111
111111111111111111111111111111111111111111111111111111111111111111
111111111111111111111111111111111111111111111111111111111111111111
111111111111111111111111111111111111111111111111111111111111111111
111111111111111111111111111111111111111111111111111111111111111111
111111111111111111111111111111111111111111111111111111111111111111
111111111111111111111111111111111111111111111111111111111111111111
111111111111111111111111111111111111111111111111111111111111111111
111111111111111111111111111111111111111111111111111111111111111111
111111111111111111111111111111111111111111111111111111111111111111
111111111111111111111111111111111111111111111111111111111111111111
111111111111111111111111111111111111111111111111111111111111111111
111111111111111111111111111111111111111111111111111111111111111111
111111111111111111111111111111111111111111111111111111111111111111
111111111111111111111111111111111111111111111111111111111111111111
111111111111111111111111111111111111111111111111111111111111111111
111111111111111111111111111111111111111111111111111111111111111111
1111111111.

Notes.   Good references for the material of this chapter are Knuth (1998), §4.5.4, Koblitz (1987a), Bach (1990), Lenstra & Lenstra (1990), Lenstra (1990), Adleman (1994), and Bach & Shallit (1996).

The word prime number (πρῶτος ἄριθμος) comes, according to Iamblichus, from the fact that in Eratosthenes' sieve (Section 18.4) they are the first to appear in the sequence of their multiples which have to be removed.

An integer is *perfect* if it equals the sum of all its proper divisors; $6 = 1 + 2 + 3$ is an example. Euclid proves in Proposition 36 of Book 9 of his *Elements* that $2^{n-1} M_n$ is perfect for any Mersenne prime M_n (Exercise 18.11); for $n = 2$ and 3 we obtain 6 and 28. The 37th Mersenne prime provides in this way the largest known perfect number (at the time of writing).

The idea of internet computing was pioneered by Silverman in the area of factoring integers (see Caron & Silverman 1988), and became popular with Lenstra & Manasse's (1990) article. The discovery of the 37th Mersenne prime is described on the web page http://www.mersenne.org/3021377.htm.

18.2. Carmichael numbers were introduced in the work of Carmichael (1909/10, 1912). Mahnke (1912/13) discusses Leibniz' proof of Fermat's little theorem (see Notes 4.4) and his attempts at a converse; Leibniz thought for a while that N is prime if $2^{N-1} \equiv 1 \bmod N$. In his discussion, Mahnke gives the defining property of Carmichael numbers, proves that neither a prime power nor a product of two primes is Carmichael, and gives five examples, including 561. He mentions a letter of Bachmann with similar results. Lenstra (1979b) proves that if $a^{N-1} \equiv 1 \bmod N$ for every prime $a < \ln^2 N$, then N is squarefree.

18.3. Miller (1976) proposed a deterministic version of the strong pseudoprimality test 18.5 and showed that it runs in polynomial time under the ERH (Theorem 18.6), and Rabin (1976, 1980a) suggested the probabilistic variant. Neither of the two algorithms looks for factors of Carmichael numbers. Earlier versions of the test were given by Dubois (1971) and Selfridge (not later than 1974, unpublished), but they did not reach a wide audience. Dubois suggests the strong pseudoprimality test with $a = 2, 3$, and 5. He is well aware that it may fail, and proposes to use $a = 7$ as well. See the end of these Notes for the smallest N on which this variant fails.

Bach, Miller & Shallit (1986) state a generalized version of Algorithm 18.5 for integer factorization, without actually mentioning the application to the Carmichael case. The fact that Carmichael numbers can be factored in random polynomial time seems to be folklore. Alford, Granville & Pomerance (1994) solved a long-standing open problem by proving that there are infinitely many Carmichael numbers.

For an odd composite integer N, the probability for a random $a \in \{1, \ldots, N-1\}$ with $\gcd(a, N) = 1$ to be a strong liar is at most $1/2$, by the proof of Theorem 18.6. Rabin (1980a), Monier (1980), and Atkin & Larson (1982) have shown the smaller bound $1/4$. To generate random primes, suppose that we fix n and k, choose n-bit odd numbers uniformly at random, subject them to k strong pseudoprimality tests, and return the first one that passes all these tests. We call $p_{n,k}$ the probability that a composite number is returned. Damgård, Landrock & Pomerance (1993) deal with the subtleties of estimating $p_{n,k}$, as noted before Theorem 18.8, and prove several estimates, for example:

$$p_{600,1} \leq 2^{-75}, \quad p_{n,k} < \frac{1}{7} n^{15/4} 2^{-n/2-2k} \text{ if } 4k \geq n \geq 21.$$

All reasonably small numbers have small strong witnesses: Pomerance, Selfridge & Wagstaff (1980) prove that for all composite $N \leq 25 \times 10^9$ (except for $N = 3\,215\,031\,751$), at least one of 2, 3, 5, and 7 is a strong witness. Pinch (1993) describes erroneous results of primality tests implemented in some computer algebra systems.

18.4. The prime number theorem is a central result in number theory, and has a long and distinguished history. Proofs of the asymptotic version stated first in Theorem 18.7 are in many texts, for example Hardy & Wright (1985). The precise version stated in Theorem 18.7 is from Rosser & Schoenfeld (1962).

An early attempt at the prime number theorem was by Legendre (1798), and Gauss (1849) said that he found the estimate around 1792. Chebyshev (1849, 1852) proved that $\pi(x)$ is asymptotically $x/\ln x$, up to a constant factor, and de la Vallée Poussin (1896) and Hadamard (1896) proved that $\pi(x) = x/\ln x + o(x/\ln x)$. A better approximation is given by the **logarithmic integral** $\pi(x) \approx \mathrm{Li}(x) = \int_2^x dt/\ln t$.

A vital tool in modern prime number theory is **Riemann's** (1859) **zeta function** $\zeta(s)$, a meromorphic function on the complex plane. It is obtained by analytic continuation of

$$\zeta(s) = \prod_{p \text{ prime}} (1 - p^{-s})^{-1} = \sum_{n \geq 1} n^{-s},$$

which is defined when $\Re s > 1$, and which already Euler used. Riemann made his famous conjecture, the **Riemann Hypothesis**, that all zeroes s of ζ lie on the **critical line**

$\Re s = 1/2$: [...] *und es ist sehr wahrscheinlich, dass alle Wurzeln* [von $\zeta(\frac{1}{2} + it)$] *reell sind. Hiervon wäre allerdings ein strenger Beweis zu wünschen; ich habe indess die Aufsuchung desselben nach einigen flüchtigen vergeblichen Versuchen vorläufig bei Seite gelassen, da er für den nächsten Zweck meiner Untersuchung entbehrlich schien.*[1] A proof of this conjecture, still elusive after over 130 years, would imply dramatic improvements in the estimates for the error term in the prime number theorem. Clever methods have been devised to calculate billions of roots of the zeta function (van de Lune, te Riele & Winter 1986, Odlyzko & Schönhage 1988, Odlyzko 1995c); fast arithmetic is a must for such high-performance calculations.

Already Legendre (1798) had used a logarithmic integral, but he was well aware that he had no proof of his (incorrect) formula. He set the task solved in this chapter: *Il serait à désirer, pour la perfection de la théorie des nombres, qu'on trouvât une méthode praticable au moyen de laquelle on pût décider assez promptement si un nombre donné est premier ou s'il ne l'est pas.*[2] Did he already feel that there is a computational difference between testing primality and factoring?

The zeta function has been generalized from integers to algebraic number fields. The conjecture that all those generalizations have their zeroes on the critical line is called the Extended Riemann Hypothesis. For several algorithms, the estimates of their running time (or their proofs of correctness) rely on the ERH; see Notes 14.9 and Section 18.6.

Pritchard (1983, 1987) and Sorenson (1998) give several more efficient versions of the sieve of Eratosthenes.

18.5. We heard the "unless and only unless" from Hendrik Lenstra. The "iff" was coined by Halmos (see Halmos 1985, page 403), and Conway invented comic imitations like "unlesss".

Monier (1980) compares the two tests by Solovay & Strassen (1977) and by Miller and Rabin. Eisenstein (1844) and Lebesgue (1847) present algorithms for the Jacobi symbol. They are analyzed in Shallit (1990), and efficient methods are given by Bach & Shallit (1996), §5.9, and Meyer & Sorenson (1998).

18.6. Cohen & Hendrik Lenstra (1984) and Cohen & Arjen Lenstra (1987) implemented the Jacobi sum test. See Bach & Shallit (1996) for details on Pepin's test, and Hardy & Wright (1985), §2.5, for the example F_5. In fact, Pepin used 5 instead of 3 as his witness. It is widely conjectured that no $F_n > F_4$ is prime, but Wagstaff (1983) has conjectured that

$$\#\{p < x \mid M_p \text{ is prime}\} \approx \frac{e^\gamma}{\ln 2} \ln\ln x \approx 2.57 \ln\ln x,$$

where $\gamma = 0.5772156649\ldots$ is Euler's constant. In particular, this would imply that there are infinitely many Mersenne primes. The term "Mersenne number" was apparently coined by Rouse Ball in 1892 (see Ball & Coxeter 1974).

Further notes. Hendrik Lenstra's (1982, 1984) **cyclotomy primality test** combines Jacobi sums with a generalization of Lucas-Lehmer tests in cyclotomic ring extensions. Implementations and improvements on this method were done by Bosma & van der Hulst (1990)

---

[1] [...] and it is very probable that all roots [of $\zeta(\frac{1}{2} + it)$] are real. A rigorous proof of this would be desirable; I have, however, left aside the quest for one after several brief and unsuccessful attempts, since it seemed dispensable for the immediate goal of my investigation.

[2] It would be desirable for the perfection of number theory to find a practical method by which one should be able to decide fairly quickly whether a given number is prime or not.

in their two-man thesis, and by Mihăilescu (1989, 1998a) in his one-man thesis. Mihăilescu (1998b) points out the connections between various tests, and his software proved primality of $2^{10\,000} + 177$—a record at its time. This method is likely to gain in importance in the near future.

The compositeness tests discussed in this chapter perform some computations in the multiplicative group of units modulo N. The basic idea of the **elliptic curve test** is to use different types of groups. Lenstra (1987) introduced the elliptic curve method for factoring integers (Section 19.7); Goldwasser & Kilian (1986) (see also Kilian 1990) combined an approach by Pratt (1975) that showed PRIMES$\in \mathcal{NP}$ (Exercise 18.27) with this new technique. The advantage is not being tied to a single group like $\mathbb{Z}_N^\times$, but to have many groups at one's disposal. The primality test of Goldwasser & Kilian runs in expected polynomial time under an unproved assumption, called Cramér's conjecture, about prime numbers in small intervals. (Granville (1995) tells the story how, to everybody's surprise, some other predictions implied by Cramér's model turned out to be false.) Atkin improved this approach by using elliptic curves with an additional structure called "complex multiplication". Atkin & Morain (1993) and Morain (1998) discuss the method and implementations. An interesting feature is that it produces **witnesses of primality** which are much easier to check than it is to execute the whole algorithm again.

Exercises.

18.1 Show that $a^2 + b^2 \equiv 0, 1$, or 2 modulo 4 for all $a, b \in \mathbb{Z}$.

18.2 Compute $2^{1\,000\,005} \bmod 55$. Hint: This needs virtually no calculation.

18.3 Which of the two integers $10^{200} + 349$ and $10^{200} + 357$ is probably prime and which is certainly composite? You may use a computer algebra system to find this out, but you should not use routines like `isprime` or `ifactor`. Warning: not every exponentiation routine is suited for solving this task.

18.4[*] You are to determine precisely the error probability of the Fermat test in a special case. Let $p \neq q$ be primes with $p \equiv q \equiv 3 \bmod 4$ and $\gcd(p - 1, q - 1) = 2$, and $N = pq$.

(i) Show that $\sigma : u \longmapsto u^{(N-1)/2}$ is a group isomorphism of $\mathbb{Z}_p^\times$. Hint: Exercise 14.11.

(ii) Prove that $\{u^{N-1} : u \in \mathbb{Z}_p^\times\} = \{u^2 : u \in \mathbb{Z}_p^\times\}$ and $\text{prob}(a^{N-1} \equiv 1 \bmod p) = 2/(p-1)$ for a uniform random element $a \in \{1, \dots, p-1\}$.

(iii) Calculate the probability that the Fermat test outputs "possibly prime" on input N, assuming that a is chosen from $\{1 \leq c < N : \gcd(c, N) = 1\}$ uniformly at random in step 1. Compare your result numerically to the estimate from Theorem 18.3 for $p = 79$ and $q = 83$.

18.5[*] (i) Find all Fermat liars for $N = 15$.

(ii) Show that if p and $2p - 1$ are both prime and $N = p(2p - 1)$, then 50% of the elements in $\mathbb{Z}_N^\times$ are Fermat liars, namely all those which are squares modulo $2p - 1$.

18.6 (Lenstra, Lenstra, Manasse & Pollard 1993) Let N be composite.

(i) Let $a \in \{1, \dots, N-1\}$ with $\gcd(a, N) = 1$ be a Fermat witness and $g = \gcd(a^{N-1} - 1, N)$. Prove that N is not a prime power if $g = 1$.

(ii) State and prove a similar criterion when a is a strong witness.

18.7 Prove that for $N = 3\,215\,031\,751$, the smallest strong witness is 11.

18.8 Find a 20 decimal digit prime. Explain how you obtained it and why you believe it is prime. You may find functions such as MAPLE's `isprime` useful.

18.9 Let $N \in \mathbb{N}_{>3}$. Prove:

(i) If N is a Carmichael number, then $p - 1$ divides $N - 1$ for all prime divisors p of N. Hint: CRT and Exercise 8.16.

(ii) N is prime or a Carmichael number if and only if it is squarefree and (i) holds.

(iii) A Carmichael number is odd and has at least three distinct prime divisors.

(iv) Which of the following integers are Carmichael numbers: 561, 663, 867, 935, 1105, 1482, 1547, 1729, 2077, 2465, 2647, 2821, 172081? You may use the integer factoring routine of your favorite computer algebra system.

18.10* (i) Find all Carmichael numbers of the form $3pq$, where $p \neq q$ are primes.

(ii) Find all Carmichael numbers of the form $5pq$, where $p \neq q$ are primes.

(iii) Show that for any fixed prime number r there are only finitely many Carmichael numbers of the form rpq, with distinct primes p, q.

18.11* For $N \in \mathbb{N}_{\geq 2}$, we denote by $D(N) = \{1 \leq d < N : d \mid N\}$ the set of proper divisors of N.

(i) Let $n \in \mathbb{N}$ be such that $M_n = 2^n - 1$ is a Mersenne prime. Show that $P_n = 2^{n-1} M_n$ is a **perfect number**, so that

$$\sum_{d \in D(P_n)} d = P_n.$$

(These are the only even perfect numbers, and it is unknown whether there are odd perfect numbers.)

(ii) Assume that $p_1 = 6m + 1$, $p_2 = 12m + 1$, and $p_3 = 18m + 1$ are primes, for some $m \in \mathbb{N}_{\geq 1}$. Prove that $p_1 p_2 p_3$ is a Carmichael number. (The smallest example is $1729 = (6+1)(12+1)(18+1)$, where $m = 1$. Can you find other examples? $1729 = 1 + 12^3 = 9^3 + 10^3$ is Hardy and Ramanujan's famous **taxi-cab number**, the smallest integer which is the sum of two cubes in two different ways; see Hardy 1937, page 147.)

(iii) Let $D(P_n) = \{d_1, d_2, \ldots, d_{2n-1}\}$, $m \in \mathbb{N}_{\geq 1}$, $p_i = d_i P_n m + 1$ for $1 \leq i < 2n$, and $N = p_1 \cdots p_{2n-1}$. Show that $p_i - 1$ divides $N - 1$ for $1 \leq i < 2n$, and conclude that N is a Carmichael number if $p_1, \ldots, p_{2n-1}$ are prime. (Part (ii) is the special case $n = 2$.)

18.12* (i) Modify Algorithm 18.5 so as to find all prime factors of a Carmichael number N, and show that the modified algorithm takes an expected number of $O(\log^2 N \cdot \mathsf{M}(\log N))$ word operations.

(ii) Generalize your algorithm from (i) so that it can factor a squarefree number N if a multiple m of $\lambda(N)$ (see Exercise 18.13) is known. Prove the same time bound as for (i) if $\log m \in O(\log N)$. (A more general algorithm is in Bach, Miller & Shallit 1986).

18.13 Let $N > 1$ be an odd integer with prime factorization $N = p_1^{e_1} \cdots p_r^{e_r}$. The **Carmichael function** $\lambda(N)$ is defined as the least common multiple of $\varphi(p_1^{e_1}), \ldots, \varphi(p_r^{e_r})$, where φ is Euler's totient function.

(i) Prove that $a^{\lambda(N)} = 1$ for all $a \in \mathbb{Z}_N^\times$.

(ii) Prove that $a^{N-1} = 1$ for all $a \in \mathbb{Z}_N^\times$ if and only if $\lambda(N) \mid N - 1$. Hint: Exercise 18.9.

18.14* Let $N > 1$ be an odd integer, $\lambda(N)$ as in Exercise 18.13, and $C_N = \{a \in \mathbb{Z}_N^\times : a^{\lambda(N)/2} = \pm 1\}$.

(i) Prove that C_N is a multiplicative subgroup of $\mathbb{Z}_N^\times$.

(ii) Show that if $N = p^e$ for some $e \geq 1$ and some prime p, then $C_N = \mathbb{Z}_N^\times$. Hint: Exercise 9.40.

(iii) Prove the converse of (ii). Hint: CRT.

(iv) Recall that N is a perfect power if $N = m^k$ for some integers $m, k > 1$. Discuss whether the following is a good primality testing algorithm: First check whether N is a perfect power. If it is not, then output "probably prime" if $a^{\lambda(N)/2} = \pm 1$ for a randomly chosen $a \in \mathbb{Z}_N^\times$, and return "composite" otherwise.

18.15 Let $p \in \mathbb{N}$ be an odd prime.

(i) Prove that no square in $\mathbb{F}_p^\times$ is a generator of that group.

(ii) If $p = 2^{2^n} + 1$ is a Fermat prime, for some $n \in \mathbb{N}$, then show that any nonsquare in $\mathbb{F}_p^\times$ is a generator of that group. Hint: Exercise 8.16.

18.16 Let $r, s \in \mathbb{N}$ such that $p = r2^s + 1$ is prime.

(i) Let $a \in \mathbb{N}$ be a nonsquare modulo p. Prove that $a^r \bmod p$ is a primitive 2^sth root of unity in $\mathbb{F}_p^\times$. Hint: Exercise 8.15.

(ii) Design a probabilistic algorithm that on input r, s computes a primitive 2^sth root of unity in $\mathbb{F}_p^\times$ (the algorithm need not check whether p is prime), and prove that it uses an expected number of $O(\log p \cdot \mathsf{M}(\log p))$ word operations.

(iii) Using a computer algebra system, find all primes p between 2^{31} and 2^{32} such that $p - 1$ is divisible by 2^{27}, and find a primitive 2^{27}th root of unity modulo each such prime. Prove that 27 is the largest exponent for which three such primes exist.

18.17 Show that for each positive integer n, there exists a positive integer a such that $a, a+1, a+2, \ldots, a+n$ are all composite.

18.18 (i) Prove that $\pi(2x) - \pi(x) > x/2\ln x$ if $x \ge e^6$. Hint: Prime number theorem.

(ii) Write a program which checks that the claim from (i) is indeed true for $x \ge 6$.

(iii) How many primes between 2^{k-1} and 2^k are there at least for $k = 32$ and $k = 64$?

(iv) Assuming that $n \approx \log_2 B$ in the small primes modular determinant algorithm 5.10, for which values of n are k-bit primes sufficient for $k = 32$ and $k = 64$?

18.19 Let k and s be integers with $0 < s < k$. A **single precision Fourier prime** is a prime p with $2^{k-1} < p < 2^k$ and $p \equiv 1 \bmod 2^s$. For simplicity, you may assume that the probability for a random number of the form $1 + q2^s$ between 2^{k-1} and 2^k to be prime is $2/(k-1)\ln 2$, as discussed at the end of Section 18.4.

(i) For $k = 32$ and $k = 64$ and $1 \le s < k$, estimate the number of single precision Fourier primes and tabulate the estimates. Compare them to the actual number of such primes for $k - 8 \le s < k$.

(ii) Consider the small primes modular multiplication algorithm in $\mathbb{Z}[x]$ from Section 8.4. Use your estimates from (i) to answer the following question for processors with word size $k = 32$ and $k = 64$. Assuming that you want to multiply polynomials of degree less than 2^{s-1} with 2^{s-1}-bit coefficients by that method using single precision Fourier primes, what is the maximal possible value of s?

18.20* The following method improves the cost in Theorem 18.8 by a logarithmic factor, by first testing for small prime factors. We use the fact that the number of integers up to x having no prime factor less or equal to y is asymptotically at most $x/\ln y$ (see Tenenbaum (1995), Theorem III.6.3).

Given B and k as for Theorem 18.8, we set $\beta = \ln B$ and let $r \in \mathbb{N}$ be a parameter. We compute the first r primes $p_1, \ldots, p_r$. Then we choose integers $p \in \{B+1, \ldots, 2B\}$ uniformly at random, and if $\gcd(a, p_i) = 1$ for all i, we run k strong pseudoprimality tests on p. We return the first p that is always pronounced "probably prime". Prove:

(i) The expected cost for all gcd's is $O(r\log^2 r\log\log r + \beta^2 r\log r)$.

(ii) The output is prime with probability (over the random choices) at least $1 - 2^{-k+1}\beta/\ln p_r$.

(iii) With $r = \beta$, $k \ge \ln \beta$, and $\mathsf{M}(\beta) \ge \beta\log_2\beta$, the analog of Theorem 18.8 is valid with success probability as in (ii) and cost $O(k\beta^2\mathsf{M}(\beta)/\log\beta)$.

18.21* You are to improve the time estimates for some small primes and prime power modular algorithms over $\mathbb{Z}$ by logarithmic factors. The function $\vartheta(x) = \sum_{p \le x} \ln p$, with p running over the primes, will be useful. We have $\vartheta(x) \approx x$, and Rosser & Schoenfeld (1962) show more precisely that

$$x\left(1 - \frac{1}{\ln x}\right) < \vartheta(x) < x\left(1 + \frac{1}{2\ln x}\right) \quad \text{if } x \ge 41.$$

(i) The small primes modular determinant algorithm 5.10 and the small primes modular EEA 6.57 only require that we find a collection of primes $p_1, \ldots, p_r \leq x$ such that their product exceeds a given bound $C \in \mathbb{R}_{>0}$, and we took the first $r \approx \log_2 C$ primes for simplicity (Theorems 5.12 and 6.58), so that $x = p_r \approx (\log_2 C) \ln \log_2 C$. But in fact, $\vartheta(x) \geq \ln C$ is sufficient, which leads to the choice $x \approx \ln C$, by the above, so that $r = \pi(x) \approx \ln C / \ln \ln C$. Work out the details and show that the cost of Algorithms 5.10 and 6.57 drops to $O(n^4 \log^2(nB))$ and $O(n^4 \log^2(nA))$ word operations, respectively.

(ii) In Corollary 18.12, the requirement is slightly different: we need r primes such that the product of each $r/2$ of them exceeds the discriminant bound C. Thus we may take $x \approx \ln C$ and $r = 2\pi(x) \approx 2 \ln C / \ln \ln C$. Use this to improve the cost estimate of Corollary 18.12 (ii) to $O(\gamma \log \gamma \log \log \gamma)$ word operations.

18.22 Let $p \in \mathbb{N}$ be an odd prime.

(i) Prove that 4 divides $p - 1$ if -1 is a square modulo p. Hint: Lagrange's theorem.

(ii) Prove the converse of (i). Hint: Consider $a^{(p-1)/4}$ for a nonsquare $a \in \mathbb{F}_p^\times$.

(iii) Conclude that the Legendre symbol $\left(\frac{-1}{p}\right)$ is 1 if and only if $p \equiv 1 \bmod 4$.

18.23* (i) Show that the Jacobi symbol is multiplicative with respect to both arguments:

$$\left(\frac{ab}{N}\right) = \left(\frac{a}{N}\right)\left(\frac{b}{N}\right), \qquad \left(\frac{a}{MN}\right) = \left(\frac{a}{M}\right)\left(\frac{a}{N}\right)$$

for all $a, b, M, N \in \mathbb{N}_{>0}$ with $M, N \geq 3$ odd.

(ii) Prove that the law of quadratic reciprocity also holds for the Jacobi symbol: If $a, N \in \mathbb{N}$ are coprime and odd, then $\left(\frac{a}{N}\right)$ and $\left(\frac{N}{a}\right)$ are equal unless and only unless $a \equiv N \equiv 3 \bmod 4$.

(iii) A special case of the law of quadratic reciprocity is that $\left(\frac{2}{N}\right) = 1$ if and only if $N \equiv \pm 1 \bmod 8$ for an odd prime $N \in \mathbb{N}$. Prove that this also holds for the Jacobi symbol, where $N \geq 3$ is an arbitrary odd integer.

(iv) Show that $\left(\frac{a}{N}\right) = \left(\frac{a \text{ rem } N}{N}\right)$ for all $a, N \in \mathbb{N}_{\geq 1}$ with $N \geq 3$ odd.

(v) Write an efficient algorithm that, given an odd integer $N > 1$ and $a \in \{1, \ldots, N-1\}$, computes the Jacobi symbol $\left(\frac{a}{N}\right)$, and analyze its cost.

18.24* (Lehmann 1982) Let $N \in \mathbb{N}_{\geq 3}$ be odd, $\sigma \colon \mathbb{Z}_N^\times \longrightarrow \mathbb{Z}_N^\times$ the power map $\sigma(a) = a^{(N-1)/2}$, and $T = \mathrm{im}(\sigma) \subseteq \mathbb{Z}_N^\times$.

(i) Show that $T = \{1, -1\}$ if N is prime.

(ii) Prove that $T \neq \{1, -1\}$ if N is not a prime power. Hint: Assume that $-1 \in T$ and apply the Chinese Remainder Theorem.

(iii) Show that $T \neq \{1, -1\}$ if $N = p^e$ for a prime $p \in \mathbb{N}$ and $e \in \mathbb{N}_{\geq 2}$. Hint: Lemma 18.1.

(iv) Prove that N is a Carmichael number if $T = \{1\}$.

(v) Consider the following algorithm.

▬▬▬ ALGORITHM 18.15 Lehmann's primality test. ▬▬▬▬▬▬▬▬▬▬▬▬▬▬▬▬
Input: An odd integer $N \geq 3$ and a parameter $k \in \mathbb{N}$.
Output: Either "probably composite" or "probably prime".

1. **for** $1 \leq i \leq k$ **do**

2.   choose $a_i \in \{1, \ldots, N-1\}$ uniformly at random

3.   **call** the repeated squaring algorithm 4.8 to compute $b_i = a_i^{(N-1)/2}$ rem N.

4. **if** $\{b_1, \ldots, b_k\} \neq \{1, -1\}$ **then return** "probably composite" **else return** "probably prime"

▬▬▬▬▬▬▬▬▬▬▬▬▬▬▬▬▬▬▬▬▬▬▬▬▬▬▬▬▬▬▬▬▬▬▬▬▬▬▬

Prove that the algorithm outputs "probably prime" with probability at least $1 - 2^{1-k}$ if N is prime, and that it outputs "probably composite" with probability at least $1 - 2^{-k}$ if N is composite.

(vi) Prove that Lehmann's algorithm can be executed with $O(k \log N \cdot M(\log N))$ word operations.

(vii) Discuss the following modification of step 4: if $b_i = -1$ for $1 \le i \le k$, then the algorithm should return "probably prime" as well.

(viii) For each of the composite numbers $N = 343$, 561, 667, and 841, compute T and determine exactly the error probability of Lehmann's algorithm for $k = 10$ (you may assume that $\gcd(a_i, N) = 1$ for all i). Compare your results to the estimate from (v).

18.25* Let $F_n = 2^{2^n} + 1$ be the nth Fermat number, for $n \in \mathbb{N}$.

(i) Assume that F_n is prime. Show that 3 and 7 are nonsquares modulo F_n if $n \ge 1$ and that 5 is a nonsquare modulo F_n if $n \ge 2$. Hint: Exercise 18.23.

(ii) Conclude that for $n \ge 1$, Pepin's (1877) test works correctly: F_n is prime if and only if $3^{(F_n - 1)/2} \equiv -1 \mod F_n$.

(iii) Show that Pepin's test can be performed with $O(2^n M(2^n))$ word operations.

18.26* Let $n \in \mathbb{N}_{\ge 2}$, $F_n = 2^{2^n} + 1$ the nth Fermat number, and $p \in \mathbb{N}$ a prime divisor of F_n. Prove that $2^{n+2} \mid p - 1$. Hint: Lagrange's theorem and Exercise 18.23.

18.27* (Pratt 1975) Let $N \in \mathbb{N}_{\ge 2}$.

(i) Prove that the following are equivalent for $u \in \mathbb{Z}_N$:

○ $u \in \mathbb{Z}_N^\times$ and $\mathrm{ord}(u) = N - 1$,

○ $u^{N-1} = 1$ and $u^{(N-1)/p} \ne 1$ for all prime divisors p of $N - 1$.

Hint: Proceed as in Exercise 8.16. We will call an $u \in \mathbb{Z}_N$ with these properties a **Pratt witness** for (the primality of) N.

(ii) Prove that N is prime if and only if it has a Pratt witness.

Now let N be prime. A **Pratt certificate** C for the primality of N is defined recursively as follows:

○ $C = (2, 1)$ for $N = 2$,

○ $C = (N, u; p_1, e_1, \ldots, p_r, e_r; C_1, \ldots, C_r)$ if $N \ge 3$, such that

  – u is a Pratt witness for N,

  – $p_1 < \cdots < p_r \in \mathbb{N}_{\ge 2}$ are primes, $e_1, \ldots, e_r \in \mathbb{N}_{\ge 0}$, and $N - 1 = p_1^{e_1} \cdots p_r^{e_r}$ is the prime factorization of $N - 1$,

  – For all i, C_i is a Pratt certificate for the primality of p_i.

For example, here are all Pratt certificates for the primality of 7:

$$\left(7, 3; 2, 1, 3, 1; (\mathbf{2}, 1), (\mathbf{3}, 2; 2, 1; (\mathbf{2}, 1)) \right), \quad \left(7, 5; 2, 1, 3, 1; (\mathbf{2}, 1), (\mathbf{3}, 2; 2, 1; (\mathbf{2}, 1)) \right).$$

(iii) Compute a Pratt certificate for each of the three primes 19, 23, and 31. Illustrate the recursive structure of the certificates in form of a tree. How many has each of the three primes in total?

(iv) Prove that each Pratt certificate for N can be checked in time $(\log N)^{O(1)}$. Conclude that PRIMES$\in$ co-$\mathcal{NP}$.

Research problem.

18.28 Find out whether prime numbers can be recognized in deterministic polynomial time. (According to Miller's result, it is sufficient to prove the ERH ;-).)

Problema, numeros primos a compositis dignoscendi,
hosque in factores suos primos resolvendi, ad gravissima
ac utilissima totius arithmeticae pertinere [...] tam notum est,
ut de hac re copiose loqui superfluum foret. [...] Praetereaque
scientiae dignitas requirere videtur, ut omnia subsidia ad solutionem
problematis tam elegantis ac celebris sedulo excolantur.[1]

Carl Friedrich Gauß (1801)

ANTON FELKEL hatte [die Faktorentafel ...] bis zu zwei Millionen in
der Handschrift vollendet [...] ; allein was davon in Wien auf
öffentliche Kosten bereits gedruckt war, wurde, weil sich keine Käufer
fanden, im Türkenkriege zu Patronen verbraucht![2]

Carl Friedrich Gauß (1812)

Factoring is the resolving of a composite number into its factors,
and is performed by division.

Daniel W. Fish (1874)

L'équation $x^2 - y^2 = N$, est de la plus grande importance
dans les questions de factorisation.

Maurice Kraïtchik (1926)

They made another calculation: how long it would take
to complete the job. The answer: Seven years.
They persuaded the professor to set the project aside.

Richard Phillips Feynman (1984)

---

[1] The problem of distinguishing prime numbers from composite numbers and of resolving the latter into their prime factors is so well known to be one of the most important and useful in arithmetic [...] that it is superfluous to speak at length about this matter. [...] Further, the dignity of the science itself seems to require that every possible means be explored for the solution of such an elegant and celebrated problem.

[2] Anton Felkel [...] had completed the manuscript of his table [of factors of integers] up to two million [...] ; the parts that had been printed in Vienna with a government grant did not sell and were, unfortunately, used to make cartridges in the war against the Turks!

19

Factoring integers

In this chapter, we present several of the algorithms listed in Table 19.1 to factor an integer N of length n into its prime divisors. The running time of Lenstra's algorithm actually depends not on n, but mainly on the size of the second largest prime factor of N. Some of the timing analyses are only heuristic, not rigorously proven. We note that the input size is $n \approx \log_2 N / 64$ words.

method	year	time
trial division	$-\infty$	$O^\sim(2^{n/2})$
Pollard's $p - 1$ method	1974	$O^\sim(2^{n/4})$
Pollard's ρ method	1975	$O^\sim(2^{n/4})$
Pollard's and Strassen's method	1976	$O^\sim(2^{n/4})$
Morrison's and Brillhart's continued fractions	1975	$\exp(O^\sim(n^{1/2}))$
Dixon's random squares	1981	$\exp(O^\sim(n^{1/2}))$
Lenstra's elliptic curves	1987	$\exp(O^\sim(n^{1/2}))$
number field sieve	1990	$\exp(O^\sim(n^{1/3}))$

TABLE 19.1: Some algorithms to factor an integer of length n.

The reader will become convinced that a fair amount of mathematical ingenuity has been spent on this problem, and that modern methods can attack surprisingly large numbers. But in comparison to the striking success in factoring polynomials (say, of degree 200 000 over $\mathbb{F}_2$), such 150-digit numbers are still disappointingly small. This is a manifestation of the practical relevance of polynomial time.

In Chapter 20, we will see how this disappointment has been turned around to major progress in another area: the assumed difficulty of factoring is important for the security of some cryptosystems.

19.1. Factorization challenges

A driving force and benchmark for the development of integer factoring algorithms is the **Cunningham project**. Cunningham & Woodall (1925) published a table of factorizations of $b^n \pm 1$ for nonsquare b with $2 \leq b \leq 12$. The book by Brillhart,

Lehmer, Selfridge, Tuckerman & Wagstaff (1988) contains substantial extensions of these tables, and Sam Wagstaff regularly keeps the world up to date with a newsletter on progress and the "most wanted" factorizations. At the ftp directory `ftp.ox.ac.uk/pub/math/cunningham/`, Paul Leyland maintains a list of currently known factorizations of $b^n \pm 1$.

If it were easy to factor large integers, then cryptosystems like RSA (Section 20.2) would be insecure. A company marketing these security products posed the *RSA challenge* of factoring certain integers. An implementation of the number field sieve distributed over the world wide web factored in 1996 the 130-digit RSA challenge into its two prime factors, each with 65 decimal digits (Cowie, Dodson, Elkenbracht-Huizing, Lenstra, Montgomery & Zayer 1996).

Another challenge for a new algorithm or implementation is to factor one of the Cunningham numbers. The number field sieve (see Notes 19.7), gained instant fame when it was used to factor the ninth Fermat number $F_9 = 2^{2^9} + 1$ (Section 18.2).

n	Factorization	Method	Discovery
5	$p_3 \cdot p_7$		Euler (1732/33, 1747/48)
6	$p_6 \cdot p_{14}$	unknown	Landry (1880); see Williams (1993)
7	$p_{17} \cdot p_{22}$	cont. fractions	Morrison & Brillhart (1971)
8	$p_{16} \cdot p_{62}$	Pollard ρ	Brent & Pollard (1981)
9	$p_7 \cdot p_{49} \cdot p_{99}$	number field sieve	Lenstra *et al.* (1990)
10	$p_8 \cdot p_{10} \cdot p_{40} \cdot p_{252}$	elliptic curves	Brent (1995)
11	$p_6 \cdot p_6' \cdot p_{21} \cdot p_{22} \cdot p_{564}$	elliptic curves	Brent (1988)

TABLE 19.2: Factorization of Fermat numbers F_n.

The elliptic curve method has been successful in finding some of the "most wanted" factorizations of the Cunningham project, in particular for some Fermat numbers. Table 19.2 shows the history of factorizations of Fermat numbers F_n; p_k stands of a prime number with k decimal digits. Richard Brent (1999) reports on two factorizations that he calculated:

$$F_{10} = 45\,592\,577 \cdot 6\,487\,031\,809 \cdot$$
$$4\,659\,775\,785\,220\,018\,543\,264\,560\,743\,076\,778\,192\,897 \cdot p_{252},$$
$$F_{11} = 319\,489 \cdot 974\,849 \cdot 167\,988\,556\,341\,760\,475\,137 \cdot 3\,560\,841\,906\,445\,833\,920\,513 \cdot p_{564},$$

He factored the 617-digit number F_{11} in 1988, and F_{10} (with 309 decimal digits) in 1995; the former was easier for his elliptic curve software because its second-largest prime divisor has 22 digits vs. 40 digits for F_{10} and it is this second-largest divisor that determines the running time of the elliptic curve algorithm. Numbers of this size are typically outside the reach of modern factorization software. The next Fermat number factors as

$$F_{12} = 114\,689 \cdot 26\,017\,793 \cdot 63\,766\,529 \cdot 190\,274\,191\,361 \cdot 1\,256\,132\,134\,125\,569 \cdot c,$$

where c is a composite integer with 1187 digits. These factorizations require a careful implementation and a slew of special insights and tricks, devised by the people working in the area.

In Wagstaff's Cunningham list dated 9 February 1998, the top "most wanted" factorization was that of the composite number N which equals $2^{569} - 1$ divided by its known 23-digit prime factor:

$$2^{599} - 1 = 16\,659\,379\,034\,607\,403\,556\,537 \cdot N. \tag{1}$$

N has 159 decimal digits. Alas, these challenges are sometimes short-lived: the list from 23 March 1998 already reported on Paul Zimmermann's factorization of N, into prime factors with 45 and 114 digits, using the elliptic curve method.

In order to factor an integer N, one will first remove all "small" prime factors, say below 10^6, by taking gcd's with the product of several of these; see also Exercise 19.5. So we may assume N to be odd, and also composite, which can be ascertained by some probabilistic primality test (Chapter 18). Some algorithms assume in addition that N is not a perfect power, so that we first use the algorithm in Section 9.5 to check whether N is an rth power for some integer r, and replace N by its rth root for the largest possible r (Exercise 9.44). Exercise 18.6 describes how the strong primality test 18.5 can be modified so as to recognize prime powers as well. If successful, most algorithms return one nontrivial divisor d of N, and to obtain the complete factorization of N, the whole procedure—including primality and perfect power test—is applied recursively to d and N/d. Figure 19.3 illustrates the whole process. We only discuss probabilistic algorithms, which guarantee the primality of the returned factors with high probability. Some applications require a rigorous proof of their primality. Such a certificate may be computed by one of the methods mentioned briefly in Section 18.6.

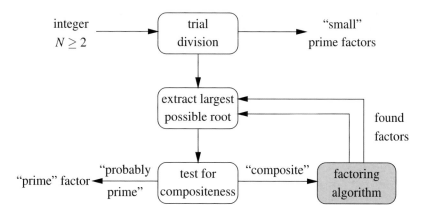

FIGURE 19.3: Factoring an integer into primes.

19.2. Trial division

The following is the simplest factoring algorithm.

ALGORITHM 19.1 Trial division.
Input: $N \in \mathbb{N}_{\geq 3}$, neither a prime nor a perfect power, and $b \in \mathbb{N}$.
Output: The smallest prime factor of N if it is less than b, and otherwise "failure".

1. **for** $p = 2, 3, \ldots, b$ **do**

2.   **if** $p \mid N$ **then return** p

3. **return** "failure"

To find all prime factors, we divide out p as often as possible and continue as illustrated in Figure 19.3. When calling the algorithm again (with some larger value of b in case of failure), we may of course use that the input has no prime factors below p. This procedure will terminate when p is the second largest prime factor of N.

For $N \in \mathbb{N}$, we let $S_1(N)$ denote the largest prime divisor of N, and $S_2(N)$ the second largest prime divisor of N. Thus $S_2(N) < N^{1/2}$. The number of steps required by trial division is $S_2(N)(\log N)^{O(1)}$. For random integers N,

$$\mathrm{prob}(S_1(N) > N^{0.85}) \approx 0.20, \quad \mathrm{prob}(S_2(N) > N^{0.30}) \approx 0.20.$$

Thus, the number of steps needed for the trial division algorithm is $O^{\sim}(N^{0.30})$ "most of the time".

19.3. Pollard's and Strassen's method

We denote by $a \longmapsto \bar{a}$ the reduction of integers modulo N. Let $1 \leq c \leq \sqrt{N}$, $F = (x+1)(x+2)\ldots(x+c) \in \mathbb{Z}[x]$, and $f = \bar{F} \in \mathbb{Z}_N[x]$. Then

$$\overline{c^2!} = \prod_{0 \leq i < c} f(\overline{ic}).$$

The following algorithm uses a "baby step/giant step" strategy.

ALGORITHM 19.2 Pollard's and Strassen's integer factoring algorithm.
Input: $N \in \mathbb{N}_{\geq 3}$, neither a prime nor a perfect power, and $b \in \mathbb{N}$.
Output: The smallest prime factor of N if it is less than b, or otherwise "failure".

1. $c \longleftarrow \lceil b^{1/2} \rceil$
   call Algorithm 10.3 to compute the coefficients of $f = \prod_{1 \leq j \leq c} (x + \bar{j}) \in \mathbb{Z}_N[x]$

2. **call** the fast multipoint evaluation algorithm 10.7 to compute $g_i \in \{0, \dots, N-1\}$ such that $g_i \bmod N = f(\overline{ic})$ for $0 \le i < c$

3. **if** $\gcd(g_i, N) = 1$ for $0 \le i < c$ **then return** "failure"
$k \longleftarrow \min\{0 \le i < c : \gcd(g_i, N) > 1\}$

4. **return** $\min\{kc + 1 \le d \le kc + c : d \mid N\}$

We recall the multiplication time M (see inside front cover).

THEOREM 19.3.

Algorithm 19.2 works correctly and uses $O(\mathsf{M}(b^{1/2})\mathsf{M}(\log N)(\log b + \log\log N))$ word operations and space for $O(b^{1/2} \log N)$ words.

PROOF. For $0 \le i < c$, a prime divisor p of N divides $F(ic)$, and hence also $\gcd(g_i, N) = \gcd(F(ic) \text{ rem } N, N)$, if and only if p divides some number in the interval $\{ic + 1, \dots, ic + c\}$, and the correctness follows.

By Lemma 10.4 and Corollary 10.8, the cost for steps 1 and 2 is $O(\mathsf{M}(c) \log c)$ additions and multiplications in $\mathbb{Z}_N$. Step 3 takes $O(c\,\mathsf{M}(\log N) \log\log N)$ word operations, as noted in the end of Section 11.1, and step 4 takes $O(c\,\mathsf{M}(\log N))$ word operations, by Theorem 9.8. The cost for one addition or multiplication in $\mathbb{Z}_N$ is $O(\mathsf{M}(\log N))$, by Corollary 9.9, and we get a total cost of $O(\mathsf{M}(b^{1/2})\mathsf{M}(\log N) \cdot (\log b + \log\log N))$. We have to store $O(b^{1/2})$ integers of length $O(\log N)$. $\square$

If we run Algorithm 19.2 for $b = 2^i$ and $i = 1, 2, \dots$, then we have factored N completely as soon as $b > S_2(N)$. This leads to the following result.

COROLLARY 19.4.

Using Algorithm 19.2, we can completely factor N with

$$O\left(\mathsf{M}(S_2(N)^{1/2})\mathsf{M}(\log N) \log N\right) \text{ or } O^{\sim}(N^{1/4})$$

word operations and space $O^{\sim}(N^{1/4})$.

19.4. Pollard's rho method

This probabilistic method is by Pollard (1975). Its time bounds are "heuristic" and have not been rigorously established. The idea is as follows. We choose some function $f : \mathbb{Z}_N \longrightarrow \mathbb{Z}_N$ and a starting value $x_0 \in \mathbb{Z}_N$, and recursively define $x_i \in \mathbb{Z}_N$ by $x_i = f(x_{i-1})$ for all $i > 0$. We hope that $x_0, x_1, x_2, \dots$ behave like a sequence of independent random elements in $\mathbb{Z}_N$. If p is an (unknown) prime divisor of p, then we will have a collision modulo p if there are two integers t, l with $l > 0$

and $x_t \equiv x_{t+l} \bmod p$. If N is not a prime power and q is a different prime divisor of N, and the x_i's are random residues modulo N, then $x_i \bmod p$ and $x_i \bmod q$ are independent random variables, by the Chinese Remainder Theorem. Thus it is very likely that $x_t \not\equiv x_{t+l} \bmod q$, and $\gcd(x_{t+l} - x_l, N)$ is a nontrivial factor of N.

The first question now is: how "small" can we expect t and l to be? We certainly have $t + l \leq p$, and the following analysis shows that the expected value is only $O(\sqrt{p})$ for a *random* sequence $(x_i)_{i \in \mathbb{N}}$. The problem is known as the **birthday problem:** Assuming peoples' birthdays occur randomly, how many people do we need to get together before we have probability at least $1/2$ for at least two people to have the same birthday? Surprising answer: only 23 are sufficient. In fact, with 23 or more people at a party, the probability of two coinciding birthdays is at least 50.7%.

THEOREM 19.5 *Birthday problem.*
We consider random choices, with replacement, among p labeled balls. The expected number of choices until a collision occurs is $O(\sqrt{p})$.

PROOF. Let $s \geq 2$ be the number of choices until a collision occurs. This is a random variable. For $j \geq 2$, we have

$$\mathrm{prob}(s \geq j) = \frac{1}{p^{j-1}} \prod_{1 \leq i < j} (p - (i-1)) = \prod_{1 \leq i < j} \left(1 - \frac{i-1}{p}\right)$$

$$\leq \prod_{1 \leq i < j} e^{-(i-1)/p} = e^{-(j-1)(j-2)/2p} \leq e^{-(j-2)^2/2p},$$

where we have used $1 - x \leq e^{-x}$. It follows that

$$\mathcal{E}(s) = \sum_{j \geq 2} \mathrm{prob}(s \geq j) \leq \sum_{j=0}^{\infty} e^{-j^2/2p} \leq 1 + \int_0^\infty e^{-x^2/2p}\,dx$$

$$\leq 1 + \sqrt{2p} \int_0^\infty e^{-x^2}\,dx = 1 + \sqrt{\frac{p\pi}{2}},$$

since $\int_0^\infty e^{-x^2}\,dx = \sqrt{\pi}/2$, by Exercise 19.6. $\square$

Floyd's cycle detection trick. Given an integer $x_0 \in \{0, \ldots, p-1\}$ and a function $f \colon \{0, \ldots, p-1\} \longrightarrow \{0, \ldots, p-1\}$, we examine the sequence $x_0, x_1, \ldots$ defined by $x_{i+1} = f(x_i)$ for $i \geq 0$. This is an infinite sequence from a finite set, so that at some point the values repeat. This results in a cycle of some length $l > 0$ such that $x_i = x_{i+l}$ for all $i \geq t$, for some $t \in \mathbb{N}$. We may assume that l and t are minimal with that property. In Figure 19.4, we see an example with $t = 3$ and $l = 7$.

An obvious method to find $i \neq j$ such that $x_i = x_j$ is to write down the sequence until a value repeats itself, but this requires space $O(t + l)$. The following algorithm

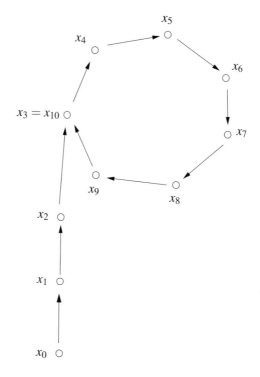

FIGURE 19.4: Pollard's ρ method.

uses only constant space. The idea of Floyd's 1-step/2-step cycle detection method is to use a second sequence $(y_i)_{i\in\mathbb{N}}$ that iterates f with double speed, so that $y_i = x_{2i}$ for all i, and to store only the current values of x_i and y_i. Intuitively, it should be clear that the "faster" sequence "overtakes" the slower one for some i, and then we have $x_{2i} = y_i = x_i$.

▬▬ ALGORITHM 19.6 Floyd's cycle detection trick. ▬▬▬▬▬▬▬▬▬
Input: $x_0 \in \{0,\ldots,p-1\}$ and $f\colon \{0,\ldots,p-1\} \longrightarrow \{0,\ldots,p-1\}$, as above.
Output: An index $i > 0$ such that $x_i = x_{2i}$.

1. $y_0 \longleftarrow x_0, \quad i \longleftarrow 0$

2. **repeat** $i \longleftarrow i+1, \quad x_i \longleftarrow f(x_{i-1}), \quad y_i \longleftarrow f(f(y_{i-1}))$
   until $x_i = y_i$

3. **return** i ▬▬▬▬▬▬▬▬▬▬▬▬▬▬▬▬▬▬▬▬▬

The following lemma says that the number of steps until the first collision $x_i = y_i$ in Floyd's method occurs is at most the number of steps until the first collision $x_i = x_j$ with $i < j$ happens.

LEMMA 19.7. *With t and l as above, Algorithm 19.6 halts after at most $t + l$ steps.*

PROOF. Since $y_{2i} = x_i$ for all i, we have $x_i = y_i$ if and only if $i \geq t$ and $l \mid (2i - i) = i$, and the smallest positive such index is $i = t + (-t \text{ rem } l) < t + l$ if $t > 0$, and $i = l$ if $t = 0$. $\square$

We now describe Pollard's ρ method for factoring N. It generates a sequence $x_0, x_1, \ldots \in \{0 \ldots N - 1\}$. We pick x_0 at random and define $x_{i+1} \in \{0, \ldots, N - 1\}$ by $x_{i+1} = f(x_i) = x_i^2 + 1 \text{ rem } N$. The choice of this iteration function is black magic, but linear functions do not work, and higher degree polynomials are more costly to evaluate, and one cannot prove more about them than about $x^2 + 1$.

Let p be the smallest prime dividing N. Then we have $x_{i+1} \equiv x_i^2 + 1 \bmod p$ for $i \geq 0$. The birthday problem and heuristic reasoning which says that the x_i's "look" random imply that we can expect a collision mod p after $O(\sqrt{p})$ steps. This duplicate can be detected by using Floyd's cycle detection trick.

ALGORITHM 19.8 Pollard's ρ method.
Input: $N \in \mathbb{N}_{\geq 3}$, neither a prime nor a perfect power.
Output: Either a proper divisor of N, or "failure".

1. pick $x_0 \in \{0, \ldots, N - 1\}$ at random, $y_0 \longleftarrow x_0$, $i \longleftarrow 0$

2. **repeat**

3. $i \longleftarrow i + 1$, $x_i \longleftarrow x_{i-1}^2 + 1 \text{ rem } N$, $y_i \longleftarrow (y_{i-1}^2 + 1)^2 + 1 \text{ rem } N$

4. $g \longleftarrow \gcd(x_i - y_i, N)$
        if $1 < g < N$ **then return** g
        else if $g = N$ **then return** "failure"

THEOREM 19.9.
Let $N \in \mathbb{N}$ be composite, p its smallest prime factor, and $f(x) = x^2 + 1$. *Under the assumption that the sequence $(f^i(x_0))_{i \in \mathbb{N}}$ behaves modulo p like a random sequence, the expected running time of Pollard's algorithm for finding the smallest prime factor p of N is $O(\sqrt{p}\, \mathsf{M}(\log N) \log\log N)$. By applying the algorithm recursively, N can be completely factored in expected time $S_2(N)^{1/2} O^{\sim}(\log^2 N)$, or $O^{\sim}(N^{1/4})$.*

EXAMPLE 19.10. We want to factor $N = 82\,123$. Starting with $x_0 = 631$, we find the following sequence:

i	$x_i \bmod N$	$x_i \bmod 41$
0	631	16
1	69 670	11
2	28 986	40
3	69 907	2
4	13 166	5
5	64 027	26

i	$x_i \bmod N$	$x_i \bmod 41$
6	40 816	21
7	80 802	32
8	20 459	0
9	71 874	1
10	6685	2

The iteration modulo 41 is illustrated in Figure 19.4; the algorithm's name derives from the similarity to the Greek letter ρ. It leads to the factor $\gcd(x_3 - x_{10}, N) = 41$.

When we execute the algorithm, only the values modulo N are known; the values modulo 41 are included for our understanding. The algorithm calculates in tandem x_i and $y_i = x_{2i}$ and performs the gcd test each time. We have $t = 3$, $l = 7$, and $t + (-t \text{ rem } l) = 7$, and in fact, after seven 2-steps the algorithm catches up with the 1-steps:

i	$x_i \bmod N$	$x_i \bmod 41$	$y_i \bmod N$	$y_i \bmod 41$	$\gcd(x_i - y_i, N)$
0	631	16	631	16	1
1	69 670	11	28 986	40	1
2	28 986	40	13 166	5	1
3	69 907	2	40 816	21	1
4	13 166	5	20 459	0	1
5	64 027	26	6685	2	1
6	40 816	21	75 835	26	1
7	80 802	32	17 539	32	41

The factorization $N = 41 \cdot 2003$ is found as $\gcd(x_7 - y_7, N) = 41$. Of course the sequence also repeats modulo 2003, and in fact $x_{38} \equiv 4430 \equiv x_{143} \bmod N$. If this repetition occurred simultaneously with the one modulo 41, we would not find a factor: an "unlucky" x_0. ◇

19.5. Dixon's random squares method

In this section, we present Dixon's (1981) method of using random squares for factoring an odd integer N that is not a prime power. It was the first method proven to be faster than $\exp(\varepsilon \cdot \log N)$ for any $\varepsilon > 0$. Our explanation of Dixon's method proceeds in four stages. We first describe the idea of the algorithm, including an example, and then state the algorithm, with an unspecified parameter B. The crux then is to show that sufficiently many random numbers computed in the algorithm are smooth, that is, they have only prime factors below B. From this, we can determine the best value for B and complete the analysis.

We begin by observing that the equations

$$N = s^2 - t^2 = (s+t)(s-t),$$
$$N = a \cdot b = \left(\frac{a+b}{2}\right)^2 - \left(\frac{a-b}{2}\right)^2$$

describe a bijection between factorizations of N and representations of N as a difference of two squares. This immediately suggests a crude factorization algorithm: for $t = \lceil\sqrt{N}\rceil, \lceil\sqrt{N}\rceil + 1, \ldots$, check whether $t^2 - N$ is a perfect square. If we find such a square, then we can factor N. This algorithm will work well if $N = ab$ with $|a-b|$ small, since then the running time is dependent on $|a-b|$. This was already clear to Fermat; he took $N = 2\,027\,651\,281$, so that $\sqrt{N} \approx 45\,029$, and found

$$N = 45\,041^2 - 1020^2 = 46\,061 \cdot 44\,021.$$

A modification is to choose some integer $k \ll N$, to let $t = \lceil\sqrt{kN}\rceil, \lceil\sqrt{kN}\rceil + 1, \ldots$, and then to check if $t^2 - kN$ is a perfect square. If $t^2 - kN = s^2$, then $\gcd(s+t, N)$ is a factor of N, hopefully nontrivial, so that $s \not\equiv \pm t \bmod N$.

Actually, finding a relation $s^2 \equiv t^2 \bmod N$ in this way is unlikely for large N. The basic idea of the random squares method is illustrated in the following example.

EXAMPLE 19.11. Let $N = 2183$. Suppose that we have found the system of congruences

$$453^2 \equiv 7 \bmod N, \quad 1014^2 \equiv 3 \bmod N, \quad 209^2 \equiv 21 \bmod N.$$

Then we obtain $(453 \cdot 1014 \cdot 209)^2 \equiv 21^2 \bmod N$, or $687^2 \equiv 21^2 \bmod N$. This yields the factors $37 = \gcd(687 - 21, N)$ and $59 = \gcd(687 + 21, N)$; in fact $N = 37 \cdot 59$ is the prime factorization of N. $\diamond$

The above example suggests a systematic approach: choose b at random and hope that $b^2 \operatorname{rem} N$ is a product of small primes. When enough have been found, we will get a congruence $s^2 \equiv t^2 \bmod N$. We now describe this approach in detail.

We take as our **factor base** the prime numbers $p_1, p_2, \ldots, p_h$ up to B, for some parameter $B \in \mathbb{R}_{>0}$. A number b is a **B-number** if the integer $b^2 \operatorname{rem} N$ (the remainder of b^2 on division by N) is a product of these primes. Thus, in Example 19.11, the integers 453, 1014, and 209 are B-numbers, for any $B \geq 7$ and $N = 2183$. A variant of the algorithm allows $p_0 = -1$ in the factor base and considers the least absolute residue a of $b \in \mathbb{Z}$, defined by $b \equiv a \bmod N$ and $-N/2 < a \leq N/2$; we do not pursue this here.

For every B-number b, we write $b^2 \equiv p_1^{\alpha_1} p_2^{\alpha_2} \cdots p_h^{\alpha_h} \bmod N$, with $\alpha_1, \ldots, \alpha_h \in \mathbb{N}$, and associate with b the binary exponent vector

$$\varepsilon = (\alpha_1 \bmod 2, \alpha_2 \bmod 2, \ldots, \alpha_h \bmod 2) \in \mathbb{F}_2^h. \tag{2}$$

Now suppose that we have $b_1, b_2, \ldots, b_l$ such that $\varepsilon_1 + \varepsilon_2 + \cdots + \varepsilon_l = 0$ in $\mathbb{F}_2^h$. Writing $b_i^2 \equiv \prod_{1 \le j \le h} p_j^{\alpha_{ij}} \bmod N$, we see that

$$\left(\prod_{1 \le i \le l} b_i \right)^2 \equiv \prod_{1 \le j \le h} p_j^{\sum_{1 \le i \le l} \alpha_{ij}} = \prod_{1 \le j \le h} p_j^{2\gamma_j} = \left(\prod_{1 \le j \le h} p_j^{\gamma_j} \right)^2 \bmod N,$$

where $\gamma_j = \frac{1}{2} \sum_{1 \le i \le l} \alpha_{ij} \in \mathbb{N}$ for all j. This gives the desired congruence $s^2 \equiv t^2 \bmod N$, where

$$s = \prod_{1 \le i \le l} b_i, \quad t = \prod_{1 \le j \le h} p_j^{\gamma_j}. \qquad (3)$$

Note that we have to generate no more than $h + 1$ B-numbers, so that we may always take $l \le h + 1$, since any set of $h + 1$ vectors in $\mathbb{F}_2^h$ is linearly dependent over $\mathbb{F}_2$.

Having obtained $s^2 \equiv t^2 \bmod N$, we hope that $s \not\equiv \pm t \bmod N$. If N is not a prime power and has $r \ge 2$ distinct prime factors, then the Chinese Remainder Theorem 5.3 implies that every square in $\mathbb{Z}_N^\times$ has exactly 2^r square roots in $\mathbb{Z}_N$. Therefore, if s is a random square root of t^2 we have

$$\mathrm{prob}\{s \equiv \pm t \bmod N\} = \frac{2}{2^r} \le \frac{1}{2}.$$

In Example 19.11, with $B = \{2, 3, 5, 7\}$, we have $\varepsilon_1 = (0,0,0,1)$, $\varepsilon_2 = (0,1,0,0)$, $\varepsilon_3 = (0,1,0,1)$ and $\varepsilon_1 + \varepsilon_2 + \varepsilon_3 = 0$ in $\mathbb{F}_2^4$. Furthermore $\gamma_1 = \gamma_3 = 0$, $\gamma_2 = \gamma_4 = 1$, $s = 453 \cdot 1014 \cdot 209$, and $t = 2^0 \cdot 3^1 \cdot 5^0 \cdot 7^1$.

Here is the resulting algorithm.

ALGORITHM 19.12 Dixon's random squares method. ▬▬▬
Input: An odd integer $N \ge 3$, neither a prime nor a perfect power, and $B \in \mathbb{R}_{>0}$.
Output: Either a proper divisor of N, or "failure".

1. compute all primes $p_1, p_2, \ldots, p_h$ up to B
   if p_i divides N for some $i \in \{1, \ldots, h\}$ **then return** p_i

2. $A \longleftarrow \emptyset$ { initialize the set of B-numbers }
   repeat

3.   choose a uniform random number $b \in \{2, \ldots, N-2\}$
          $g \longleftarrow \gcd(b, N)$,   **if** $g > 1$ **then return** g

4. $a \longleftarrow b^2$ rem N
          { factor a over $\{p_1, \ldots, p_h\}$ }
          for $i = 1, \ldots, h$ **do**

5.   { determine multiplicity of p_i in a }

$\alpha_i \longleftarrow 0$

while p_i divides a **do** $a \longleftarrow \dfrac{a}{p_i}$, $\alpha_i \longleftarrow \alpha_i + 1$

6.   **if** $a = 1$ **then** $\alpha \longleftarrow (\alpha_1, \ldots, \alpha_h)$, $A \longleftarrow A \cup \{(b, \alpha)\}$

7. **until** $\#A = h + 1$

8. find distinct pairs $(b_1, \alpha^{(1)}), \ldots, (b_l, \alpha^{(l)}) \in A$ with $\alpha^{(1)} + \cdots + \alpha^{(l)} \equiv 0 \bmod 2$ in $\mathbb{F}_2^h$, for some $l \geq 1$, by solving an $(h+1) \times h$ system of linear equations over $\mathbb{F}_2$

9. $(\gamma_1, \ldots, \gamma_h) \longleftarrow \dfrac{1}{2}(\alpha^{(1)} + \cdots + \alpha^{(l)})$

$s \longleftarrow \displaystyle\prod_{1 \leq i \leq l} b_i, \quad t \longleftarrow \prod_{1 \leq j \leq h} p_j^{\gamma_j}, \quad g \longleftarrow \gcd(s+t, N)$

if $g < N$ **then return** g **else return** "failure"

We let $n = \log N$. Using the sieve of Eratosthenes, the cost for setting up the factor base in step 1 is $O(h \log^2 h \log\log h)$ word operations, by Theorem 18.10, and the cost for checking divisibility is $O(h \cdot \mathsf{M}(n))$. The cost for one iteration of the loop 2 is $O(\mathsf{M}(n) \log n)$ word operations for the gcd, $O(\mathsf{M}(n))$ word operations to compute b^2 rem N, and $O((h+n)\mathsf{M}(n))$ operations for trial division by all primes $p_1, \ldots, p_h$ to check smoothness. (The check can actually be performed faster with a modification of the Pollard and Strassen algorithm 19.2.) If k is the number of iterations of the loop 2, then the total cost of the loop is $O(k(h+n)\mathsf{M}(n))$ word operations. The cost of solving the system of linear equations over $\mathbb{F}_2$ in step 8 is $O(h^3)$ word operations. The cost of all other steps is dominated by these estimates, and we obtain a total cost of

$$O(h^3 + k(h+n)\mathsf{M}(n)) \tag{4}$$

word operations.

In practice, the numbers b are chosen randomly in the vicinity of $\sqrt{N}$, because b^2 rem N is then only about $O(\sqrt{N})$ and more likely to have all prime factors less than B than an arbitrary number up to N. For our arguments below, however, we need the assumption that the b's are uniform random numbers between 1 and $N-1$.

Our goal now is to estimate the expected number k of iterations, and to determine the right choice for B, given just N. For given $x, y \in \mathbb{R}_{>2}$, we let

$$\begin{aligned} \Psi(x, y) &= \{a \in \mathbb{N} \colon 1 \leq a \leq x, \forall p \text{ prime } p \mid a \Longrightarrow p \leq y\}, \\ \psi(x, y) &= \#\Psi(x, y). \end{aligned} \tag{5}$$

The numbers in $\Psi(x, y)$, all of whose prime factors are not greater than y, are called **y-smooth**. We have

$$b \text{ is a } B\text{-number} \iff b^2 \text{ rem } N \in \Psi(N, B).$$

Clearly the crux of the problem is to choose B wisely: if B is too small, then B-numbers are rare and take a long time to find, and if B is too large, then it takes a long time to test a prospective B-number, and the linear system is large.

As a warmup exercise, we estimate roughly the probability that a random integer $a \in \{1, \ldots, x\}$ is y-smooth, with $y = B$. We put $u = \ln(x)/\ln(y)$, so that $y = x^{1/u}$, and $v = \lfloor u \rfloor$, and let $(a_1, a_2, \ldots, a_v) \in \{p_1, \ldots, p_h\}^v$ and $a = a_1 a_2 \cdots a_v$. (ln is the natural logarithm.) Then $a \leq B^v \leq y^u = x$, hence $a \in \Psi(x, y)$. Each a comes from at most $v!$ vectors in $\{p_1, \ldots, p_h\}^v$, and hence we have the approximate inequalities

$$\psi(x, y) \geq \frac{h^v}{v!} \geq \left(\frac{h}{v}\right)^v \gtrsim \left(\frac{y}{\ln y}\right)^v \cdot v^{-v} \approx \left(\frac{y}{\ln y}\right)^u \cdot u^{-u} = x(u \ln y)^{-u},$$

by the prime number theorem 18.7 which says that $h \approx y/\ln y$. So for a random positive integer $a \leq x$, we have

$$\text{prob}\{a \text{ is } y\text{-smooth}\} = \frac{\psi(x, y)}{x} \gtrsim (u \ln y)^{-u}.$$

We state without proof that for reasonably small u, the true order of this probability, called **Dickman's ρ-function**, is u^{-u} for large enough y. Although we will not use this fact, it is comforting to know that our coarse estimate is not too far off.

━━━ THEOREM 19.13. ━━━

Let $u \colon \mathbb{N} \longrightarrow \mathbb{R}_{>1}$ be an increasing function with $u(x) \in O(\log x / \log\log x)$. Then the probability that a random integer in $\{1, \ldots, \lfloor x \rfloor\}$ is $x^{1/u}$-smooth satisfies

$$\frac{\psi(x, x^{1/u})}{x} = u^{-u(1 + o(1))}.$$

Here, $o(1)$ is shorthand for a function which tends to zero as u approaches infinity. The above estimates apply to random values a. We now prove a similar result about b^2 rem N for random values b. Then the expected number of trials necessary to find a single B-number is at most $(u \ln y)^u$ (or, in fact, at most u^u). A different argument is in Exercise 19.10.

LEMMA 19.14. *Suppose that N is not divisible by any of $p_1, \ldots, p_h$, and $r \in \mathbb{N}$ with $p_h^{2r} \leq N$. Then*

$$\#\{b \in \mathbb{N} \colon 1 \leq b < N \text{ and } b^2 \text{ rem } N \in \Psi(N, p_h)\} \geq \frac{h^{2r}}{(2r)!}. \tag{6}$$

PROOF. The idea of the proof is to adapt our warmup strategy to this situation. So we consider power products b of $p_1, \ldots, p_h$ with exactly r factors. The square of such a b is smooth, and therefore b is clearly in the set S on the left hand side of (6). But there are not enough of these numbers. It would be sufficient if the product of any two b's, rather than just the squares, was actually a square modulo N. This looks implausible at first. But consider a prime factor q of N. Modulo q, half of the numbers are squares (Lemma 14.7), and we have not only "square $\cdot$ square $=$ square", but also "nonsquare $\cdot$ nonsquare $=$ square". The same actually holds modulo a power of q. The proof will produce sufficiently many numbers in S by partitioning the set of all b's as above according to their square/nonsquare character modulo all the prime factors of N. Then when we take two b's that are distinct but have the same character, their product will actually be a square modulo all q's, and therefore modulo N. The following proof makes this precise. For a first understanding, the reader may want to assume that $N = q_1 q_2$ is the product of two distinct primes.

To begin the proof, we let $N = q_1^{l_1} \cdots q_t^{l_t}$ be the prime factorization of N. The **quadratic character** $\chi_i = \chi_{q_i^{l_i}}$ on $\mathbb{Z}_{q_i^{l_i}}^{\times}$ is defined as follows:

$$\chi_i(a \bmod q_i^{l_i}) = \begin{cases} 1 & \text{if } \exists b \in \mathbb{N} \, a \equiv b^2 \bmod q_i^{l_i}, \\ -1 & \text{otherwise.} \end{cases}$$

Relatives of this character have played a role (implicitly) in equal-degree factorization (Section 14.3) and primality testing (Chapter 18), then called the Jacobi symbol. The map χ_i is a group homomorphism. Putting all these characters together, we get

$$\chi \colon \mathbb{Z}_N^{\times} \longrightarrow \{1, -1\}^t = G,$$
$$a \bmod N \longmapsto \left(\chi_1(a \bmod q_1^{l_1}), \ldots, \chi_t(a \bmod q_t^{l_t}) \right).$$

We let

$$Q = \{a \in \mathbb{N} \colon 1 \leq a < N, \ \gcd(a, N) = 1, \text{ and } \exists b \in \mathbb{N} \, a \equiv b^2 \bmod N\}$$

be the set of (invertible) squares modulo N. Since a number is a square modulo N if and only if it is modulo each $q_i^{l_i}$, by the Chinese Remainder Theorem 5.3, we have

$$a \in Q \iff \chi(a \bmod N) = (1, \ldots, 1)$$

for $1 \leq a < N$. Furthermore, an invertible square modulo $q_i^{l_i}$ has precisely two square roots, and, again by the Chinese Remainder Theorem, any $a \in Q$ has precisely 2^t square roots modulo N (Exercise 9.40).

We denote by S the set in (6). For $x \in \mathbb{R}$ and $s \in \mathbb{N}$, we let

$$T_s(x) = \{a \in \mathbb{N} \colon a \leq x \text{ and } \exists e_1, \ldots, e_h \in \mathbb{N} \, a = p_1^{e_1} \cdots p_h^{e_h} \text{ and } e_1 + \cdots + e_h = s\}$$

be the set of p_h-smooth integers below x with exactly s (not necessarily distinct) prime factors. By assumption, we have $a \bmod N \in \mathbb{Z}_N^\times$ for all $a \in T_s(x)$. Now we partition $T_r(\sqrt{N})$ into 2^t sets U_g for $g \in G$:

$$U_g = \{a \in T_r(\sqrt{N}) : \chi(a \bmod N) = g\}.$$

We denote by V the image of the multiplication map

$$\mu: \bigcup_{g \in G} (U_g \times U_g) \longrightarrow \mathbb{N}$$

with $\mu(b,c) = bc \text{ rem } N$. Since $\chi(bc \bmod N) = (1,\ldots,1)$ for all $b,c \in U_g$ and $g \in G$, we have $V \subseteq Q$. Furthermore, $V \subseteq T_{2r}(N)$, so that $V \subseteq T_{2r}(N) \cap Q$.

Every element in $T_{2r}(N) \cap Q$ has exactly 2^t square roots, and these are all in S, so that $\#S \geq 2^t \cdot \#(T_{2r}(N) \cap Q)$. How many elements $(b,c) \in \bigcup_{g \in G} U_g \times U_g$ are mapped by μ to the same $a \in V$? Since $b,c \leq \sqrt{N}$ and $bc \equiv a \bmod N$, we then actually have $bc = a$. Thus we have to split the $2r$ prime factors of a into two halves to make up b and c, and there are at most $\binom{2r}{r} = (2r)!/(r!)^2$ ways of doing this. Thus

$$\#V \cdot (2r)!/(r!)^2 \geq \#(\bigcup_{g \in G} U_g \times U_g) = \sum_{g \in G} (\#U_g)^2.$$

Putting things together, we have

$$\#S \geq 2^t \cdot \#(T_{2r}(N) \cap Q) \geq 2^t \cdot \#V \geq 2^t \sum_{g \in G} (\#U_g)^2 \frac{(r!)^2}{(2r)!}.$$

The Cauchy-Schwarz inequality (Exercise 16.10) says that for any two vectors $x = (x_1,\ldots,x_n), y = (y_1,\ldots,y_n) \in \mathbb{R}^n$ we have

$$\sum_{1 \leq i \leq n} x_i^2 \cdot \sum_{1 \leq i \leq n} y_i^2 = \|x\|_2^2 \cdot \|y\|_2^2 \geq x \star y^2 = \left(\sum_{1 \leq i \leq n} x_i y_i \right)^2.$$

We apply this to $n = 2^t = \#G$, $x_g = 1$ and $y_g = \#U_g$ for $g \in G$, to obtain

$$2^t \cdot \sum_{g \in G} (\#U_g)^2 \geq \left(\sum_{g \in G} \#U_g \right)^2 = \left(\#T_r(\sqrt{N}) \right)^2.$$

Since $p_h^r \leq \sqrt{N}$, an element of $T_r(\sqrt{N})$ corresponds to a choice of exactly r primes up to p_h, with repetitions. Thus

$$\#T_r(\sqrt{N}) = \binom{h+r-1}{r} \geq \frac{h^r}{r!}.$$

Finally, we find

$$\#S \geq \frac{2^t (r!)^2}{(2r)!} \sum_{g \in G} (\#U_g)^2 \geq \frac{(r!)^2}{(2r)!} \left(\#T_r(\sqrt{N}) \right)^2 \geq \frac{h^{2r}}{(2r)!}. \quad \square$$

Step 1 of Algorithm 19.12 guarantees that N is not divisible by any of the primes $p_1, \ldots, p_h$. Then the expected number of trials to find a single B-number is at most

$$\left(\frac{\#\{B\text{-numbers}\}}{N} \right)^{-1} = \frac{N}{\#\{B\text{-numbers}\}} \le \frac{N(2r)!}{h^{2r}}$$

for any r with $p_h^{2r} \le N$, by Lemma 19.14. We now fix $r \in \mathbb{N}$ and let $n = \ln N$ and $B = N^{1/2r}$, so that $\ln B = n/2r$. By the prime number theorem 18.7, we have $h = \pi(B) > B/\ln(B)$ if $B \ge 59$. Using the rough estimate $(2r)! \le (2r)^{2r}$, we find that the expected number k of trials is at most

$$\frac{N}{h^{2r}}(2r)! < \frac{N(\ln B)^{2r}}{B^{2r}}(2r)^{2r} = n^{2r}.$$

Plugging this into (4) and using $h < B$, we obtain a total cost of

$$O^{\sim}(B^3 + Bn^{2r+2}) \tag{7}$$

word operations. Ignoring the factor n^2 and equating the logarithms of the two summands $B^3 = e^{3n/2r}$ and $Bn^{2r} = e^{n/2r + 2r\ln n}$ gives $3n/2r \approx n/2r + 2r\ln n$ or

$$r = \left\lceil \sqrt{\frac{n}{2\ln n}} \right\rceil, \tag{8}$$

and then $B \le e^{\sqrt{n(\ln n)/2}}$. We define

$$L(N) = e^{\sqrt{\ln N \ln \ln N}}, \tag{9}$$

and obtain the following result by substituting (8) in (7).

──── THEOREM 19.15. ────
Dixon's random squares method factors an integer N with an expected number of $O^{\sim}(L(N)^{\sqrt{9/2}})$ word operations. ────

Variants of this algorithm are used for factoring large integers, and many practical improvements to it have been made. We only mention two. The first one notes that, since a number below N has at most $\log_2 N$ factors, each exponent vector (2) has at most $\log_2 N$ nonzero entries, the matrix of the linear system in step 8 is sparse, and we can use a variant of Wiedemann's algorithm (Section 12.4) to solve it in $O^{\sim}(h^2)$ steps. In fact, Wiedemann (1986) invented his algorithm specifically for this approach. Plugging this into (7) and choosing $2r \approx \sqrt{n/\ln n}$ decreases the cost to $O^{\sim}(L(N)^2)$ operations.

The second important practical improvement, due to Pomerance (1982, 1985), is to use a sieving method—reminiscent of Eratosthenes' sieve to generate prime numbers—which does not test individual numbers b as above, but rather generates whole series of B-numbers. The amortized cost for a single smoothness test reduces to about $4\log_2\log_2 B$ additions of numbers up to $\log_2 B$. This is called the **quadratic sieve**.

The space requirement for these algorithms is $h\log_2 h$ bits to store the factor base, and roughly the same for the linear algebra, since the matrix has h sparse rows, and Wiedemann's algorithm can be executed in the same space.

19.6. Pollard's $p-1$ method

This algorithm is a useful introduction to the elliptic curve method in the next section. We wish to factor the integer N and assume that N has a prime factor p such that $p-1$ is smooth. Specifically, we assume that all prime powers l^e dividing $p-1$ are such that $l^e \leq B$ for some suitably chosen parameter B. The algorithm is as follows.

▬▬ ALGORITHM 19.16 Pollard's $p-1$ method. ▬▬▬▬▬▬▬▬▬▬▬▬▬▬
Input: Positive integers $N \geq 3$ and B.
Output: Either a proper divisor of N, or "failure".

1. $k \longleftarrow \text{lcm}\{i : 2 \leq i \leq B\}$

2. choose $a \in \{2,..,N-2\}$ uniformly at random

3. $b \longleftarrow a^k \bmod N, \quad d \longleftarrow \gcd(b-1,N)$

4. **if** $1 < d < N$ **then return** d **else return** "failure" ▬▬▬▬▬▬▬▬▬▬

We hope that d is a nontrivial divisor of N. Under the above assumption it is certainly true that $a^k \equiv 1 \bmod p$ since $p-1 \mid k$. This guarantees that $d > 1$. In order to have $d < N$ it is sufficient that N have another prime factor q such that $a^k \not\equiv 1 \bmod q$.

Another way to view the above method is as follows. We begin by choosing a group G (in this case $G = \mathbb{Z}_N^\times$) and we hope that the size of the group "G mod p" is smooth. Then we choose k as a multiple of the order of G mod p and $a \in G$ at random, and hope that a^k is the unit element modulo p and is not the unit element modulo q. In Section 19.7 below, G mod p will be an elliptic curve over $\mathbb{F}_p$.

19.7. Lenstra's elliptic curve method

In this section, we present Lenstra's (1987) method for factoring integers using elliptic curves. Its running time is expressed by the same function L as for the random squares method, but instead of $L(N)$ we have $L(p)$, where p is the second largest prime factor of N. Thus it is faster than Dixon's method when $N = pq$ is the product of two primes of substantially different sizes, say 50 and 100 digits. In Section 19.1, we have highlighted some of the successes of this method.

Elliptic Curves.   The basic approach in the elliptic curve method to factor N is as follows. One prescribes a certain sequence of computations modulo N. A division by $w \in \mathbb{Z}$ in this sequence can only be executed if $\gcd(w, N) = 1$. Thus at each division step, we either continue the computation or we are lucky—$\gcd(w, N)$ is not trivial and we have found a divisor of N. This is sometimes called the **pretend field technique**. Calculating a multiple of a random point on a random elliptic curve leads to such a sequence of computations. What makes this work is that we will be lucky with reasonably large probability.

The elliptic curve factoring method corresponds to choosing randomly a group G from a set of elliptic curve groups. Lenstra (1987) showed that with large enough probability at least one curve will have smooth order.

We start by defining elliptic curves and stating some of their properties. They inhabit the realm of *algebraic geometry*, one of the richest and deepest areas of mathematics. In this text, we cannot but scratch the surface of this beautiful theory. We have to rely on several results whose proof is beyond the scope of this text.

DEFINITION 19.17. *Let F be a field of characteristic different from 2 and 3, and $x^3 + ax + b \in F[x]$ squarefree. Then*

$$E = \{(u,v) \in F^2 : v^2 = u^3 + au + b\} \cup \{\mathcal{O}\} \subseteq F^2 \cup \{\mathcal{O}\}$$

*is an **elliptic curve** over F. Here $\mathcal{O}$ denotes the "point at infinity" on E.*

There are other—equivalent—ways of defining and presenting elliptic curves. The above is called the **Weierstraß equation** for E, and a and b are its **Weierstraß coefficients**. The polynomial $x^3 + ax + b$ is squarefree if and only if $4a^3 + 27b^2 \neq 0$ (Exercise 19.14).

EXAMPLE 19.18. $x^3 - x = x(x-1)(x+1)$ is squarefree if char $F \neq 2$. The corresponding elliptic curve, together with other examples of elliptic curves, is drawn in Figure 19.5 for $F = \mathbb{R}$. $\Diamond$

The reader may imagine that $\mathcal{O}$ lies beyond the horizon in the direction of the y-axis (up *and* down), and that any two vertical lines "intersect" at $\mathcal{O}$. Projective geometry provides a rigorous framework for these notions.

An elliptic curve E is **nonsingular** (or smooth) in the geometric sense, as follows. Let $f = y^2 - (x^3 + ax + b) \in F[x,y]$, so that $E = \{f = 0\} \cup \{\mathcal{O}\}$. For

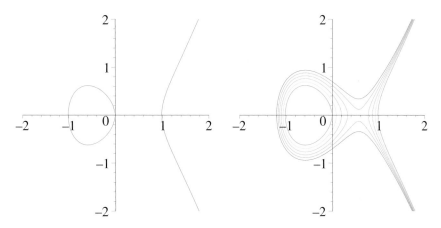

FIGURE 19.5: The elliptic curve $y^2 = x^3 - x$ over the real numbers (left diagram), and the elliptic curves $y^2 = x^3 - x + b$ for $b = 0, 1/10, 2/10, 3/10, 4/10, 5/10$.

$(u,v) \in E \setminus \{\mathcal{O}\}$, we have

$$\left(\frac{\partial f}{\partial x}(u,v), \frac{\partial f}{\partial y}(u,v) \right) = (-3u^2 - a, 2v),$$

which is $(0,0)$ (meaning that (u,v) is singular on E) if and only if $u = (-a/3)^{1/2}$ and $v = 0$. But then $u^3 + au + b = v^2$ implies that $4a^3 + 27b^2 = 0$, which contradicts our choice of E.

For $F = \mathbb{C}$, any line which intersects E does this in exactly three points, if multiplicities are counted properly. This is a special case of Bézout's theorem (Section 6.4). Let $L = \{(u,v) \in F^2 : v = ru + s\}$ be a line, for some $r, s \in F$. Then

$$L \cap E = \{(u,v) \in F^2 : (ru + s)^2 = u^3 + au + b\}.$$

Since a, b, r, s are all fixed, this is a cubic equation for u. In the case of a vertical line $L = \{(u,v) : v \in F\}$, where $u \in F$ is fixed, one of the points is $\mathcal{O}$.

The group structure.   The fundamental property that makes elliptic curves interesting for factorization is that they have a group structure in a natural way. We define the group operation as follows. The negative of a point $P = (u,v) \in E$ is its mirror image $-P = (u,-v)$ upon reflection at the x-axis, and $-\mathcal{O} = \mathcal{O}$. When we intersect the line through P and Q with E, we get three points, say $\{P, Q, S\}$. Then

$$R = P + Q = -S$$

(Figure 19.6). Special cases are:

(i) $Q = P$. We take the tangent line at P. Since E is smooth, the tangent is always well defined.

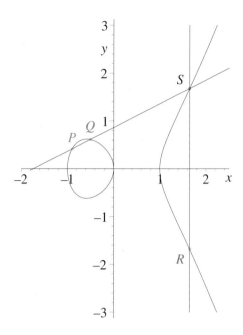

FIGURE 19.6: Adding two points P with $x = -0.9$ (red) and Q with $x = -0.5$ (green) on the elliptic curve $y^2 = x^3 - x$. The point $R = P + Q$ (blue) is the negative of the intersection point S (black) of the two lines with the curve.

(ii) $Q = \mathcal{O}$. We take the vertical line through P:

$$P + \mathcal{O} = -(-P) = P$$

(iii) $Q = -P$. We take again the vertical line through P and Q and obtain

$$P + (-P) = -\mathcal{O} = \mathcal{O}.$$

It turns out that these definitions make E into a commutative group. The second special case above shows that $\mathcal{O}$ is the neutral element of E, and the third case says that the inverse of a point P is its negative $-P$. As usual, for $k \in \mathbb{Z}$ and $P \in E$ we will write kP for adding P (respectively $-P$ if $k < 0$) k times ($-k$ times if $k < 0$) to itself, and $0P = \mathcal{O}$.

We now derive the rational expressions for addition on an elliptic curve E. Suppose that $P = (x_1, y_1)$, $Q = (x_2, y_2)$, and $x_1 \neq x_2$. Then $R = (x_3, y_3) = P + Q \in E \setminus \{\mathcal{O}\}$. The line through P and Q has the equation $y = \alpha x + \beta$, where $\alpha = (y_2 - y_1)/(x_2 - x_1)$ and $\beta = y_1 - \alpha x_1$. Let $S = (x_3, -y_3)$ be the third intersection point of this line with the curve. Then $(\alpha x_3 + \beta)^2 = x_3^3 + ax_3 + b$. Since x_1, x_2 are the two other roots of the cubic equation $(u^3 + au + b) - (\alpha u + \beta)^2 = 0$, we have $x_1 + x_2 + x_3 = \alpha^2$. It follows that

$$x_3 = \left(\frac{y_2 - y_1}{x_2 - x_1} \right)^2 - x_1 - x_2, \quad y_3 = -y_1 + \frac{y_2 - y_1}{x_2 - x_1} \cdot (x_1 - x_3). \qquad (10)$$

Thus, the coefficients of the sum of two distinct points are given by rational functions of the input coefficients. We note that these formulas do not explicitly use the Weierstraß coefficients of E, which are determined in fact by the two points on it. A similar formula holds for doubling a point (where $R = 2P$, $x_1 = x_2$, and $y_1 = y_2$; see Exercise 19.15): we have

$$x_3 = \left(\frac{3x_1^2 + a}{2y_1} \right)^2 - 2x_1, \quad y_3 = -y_1 + \frac{3x_1^2 + a}{2y_1} \cdot (x_1 - x_3), \tag{11}$$

if $y_1 \neq 0$, and $2P = \mathcal{O}$ if $y_1 = 0$.

The curve E with this operation is a commutative group. We have already checked all required properties, except associativity. The latter is not hard to check on a computer algebra system (Exercise 19.17).

The size of an elliptic curve. Our intuition so far has been based on the real numbers. But for the intended application we have to consider elliptic curves over finite fields. Our first task is to determine the size of such an elliptic curve, that is, to estimate the number of points on it. The following estimate is easy and crude.

THEOREM 19.19.

Let E be an elliptic curve over the finite field $\mathbb{F}_q$ of characteristic greater than three. Then $\#E \leq 2q + 1$.

PROOF. For each of the q possible values for u, there are at most two possible values for v such that $v^2 = u^3 + au + b$, corresponding to the two square roots of $u^3 + au + b$. Adding the point at infinity gives the required estimate. □

One reason to think that this is a crude estimate is that, pretending that the value of $u^3 + au + b$ varies randomly as u ranges over $\mathbb{F}_q$, we should expect that for about half of the u's there would be two solutions v for the equation, and no solution for the other half. In other words, $u^3 + au + b$ should be a square about half of the time. Random elements have this property by Lemma 14.7. More formally, we consider the **quadratic character** $\chi : \mathbb{F}_q^\times \longrightarrow \{1, 0, -1\}$ defined by

$$\chi(c) = \begin{cases} 1 & \text{if } c \text{ is a square}, \\ 0 & \text{if } c = 0, \\ -1 & \text{otherwise}. \end{cases}$$

For q prime, $\chi(c) = \left(\frac{c}{q} \right)$ is the Legendre symbol (Section 18.6), and for all $v \in \mathbb{F}_q$,

$$\#\{v \in \mathbb{F}_q : v^2 = c\} = 1 + \chi(c).$$

From this we conclude that

$$\#E = 1 + \sum_{u \in \mathbb{F}_q} (1 + \chi(u^3 + au + b)) = q + 1 + \sum_{u \in \mathbb{F}_q} \chi(u^3 + au + b).$$

If $\chi(u^3 + au + b)$ was a uniformly distributed random variable, then the sum would behave like a random walk on the line. After q steps of such a random walk, we expect to be about $\sqrt{q}$ steps away from the origin (Exercise 19.18). Of course this is not at all a random process, but the analogy provides some intuitive motivation for the following result.

THEOREM 19.20 Hasse's bound.
If E is an elliptic curve over the finite field $\mathbb{F}_q$, then $|\#E - (q + 1)| \le 2\sqrt{q}$.

EXAMPLE 19.21. Let $q = 7$. By the Hasse bound, each elliptic curve E over $\mathbb{F}_7$ has $|\#E - 8| \le 2\sqrt{7}$, so that $3 \le \#E \le 13$. Table 19.7 gives the orders of all 42 elliptic curves over $\mathbb{F}_7$.

n	3	4	5	6	7	8	9	10	11	12	13
$\#\{E : \#E = n\}$	1	4	3	6	4	6	4	6	3	4	1

TABLE 19.7: Frequencies of the orders of all elliptic curves E over $\mathbb{F}_7$.

If we take the curve E from Example 19.18 given by $y^2 = x^3 - x$, we can count the points by hand and determine that it contains exactly the eight points

$$(0,0), (1,0), (4,2), (4,5), (5,1), (5,6), (6,0), \mathcal{O}.$$

This group is generated by the two elements $(4,2)$ of order 4 and $(0,0)$ of order 2, and hence is isomorphic to $\mathbb{Z}_4 \times \mathbb{Z}_2$.

Another example is the curve E^* with the equation $y^2 = x^3 + x$, comprising the eight points

$$(0,0), (1,3), (1,4), (3,3), (3,4), (5,2), (5,5), \mathcal{O}.$$

E^* is cyclic and generated, for example, by $(3,3)$. Figure 19.8 illustrates the group structures of E and E^*. $\diamond$

As in any finite group, $(\#E) \cdot P = \mathcal{O}$ for any $P \in E$, by Lagrange's theorem. The order d of P is the smallest positive integer so that $dP = \mathcal{O}$; d is a divisor of $\#E$.

The elliptic curve algorithm.   We first describe Lenstra's algorithm to factor N, and then prove some of its properties.

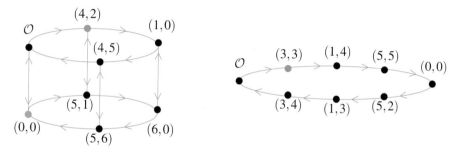

FIGURE 19.8: Structure of the elliptic curve groups E (left) and E^* (right) from Example 19.21. E is generated by $(4,2)$ (red) and $(0,0)$ (green), and E^* is generated by $(3,3)$ (red). There is a colored arrow from a point P to a point Q if $Q-P$ is the generator of that color.

ALGORITHM 19.22 Lenstra's elliptic curve factoring method.

Input: $N \in \mathbb{N}$ composite, not a perfect power of an integer, and not divisible by 2 or 3, a bound B on the primes in the base, and a guessed upper bound C for the smallest prime factor of N.

Output: Either a nontrivial divisor of N, or "failure".

1. choose randomly $(a,u,v) \in \{0,\dots,N-1\}^3$
   $b \longleftarrow v^2 - u^3 - au, \quad g \longleftarrow \gcd(4a^3 + 27b^2, N)$
   if $1 < g < N$ **then return** g **else if** $g = N$ **then return** "failure"

2. let E be the "elliptic curve" over $\mathbb{Z}_N$ with Weierstraß coefficients a,b
   compute all primes $p_1 = 2 < \cdots < p_h$ less or equal to B
   $P \longleftarrow (u,v), \quad Q \longleftarrow P, \quad t \longleftarrow 1$

3. **for** $1 \leq i \leq h$ **do**
   $\qquad e_i \longleftarrow \lfloor \log_{p_i}(C + 2\sqrt{C} + 1) \rfloor$
   $\qquad$ **for** $0 \leq j < e_i$ **do**
   $\qquad\qquad \{$ Loop invariants: $t = p_i^j \prod_{1 \leq r < i} p_r^{e_r}$ and $Q = tP \}$

4. $\qquad\qquad$ try to compute $p_i Q$ in E, using the formulas (10) and (11) and "repeated doubling"
   $\qquad\qquad$ **if** some denominator $w \in \{1,\dots,N-1\}$ which is not invertible modulo N shows up during the computation
   $\qquad\qquad$ **then return** $\gcd(w,N)$
   $\qquad\qquad$ **else** $Q \longleftarrow p_i Q, \quad t \longleftarrow p_i t$

5. **return** "failure"

The "elliptic curve" in step 2 is in quotes because the proper definition for a composite N is more complicated. All we need here is that for each prime factor p of N, $E \bmod p$ is an elliptic curve in the proper sense. In particular, the equations

(10) and (11) do *not* make E into a group. This is plausible since some denominator might be nonzero but not invertible, so that the expressions might not be well-defined modulo N. The point is that, until a divisor is found, they give the group structure on the reduction E_p modulo any prime divisor p of N.

We are going to show that successful termination eventually occurs if N has a prime factor below C. (The order of computation, from smaller to larger prime factors, might not be essential for the validity of the algorithm, but is required in the proof given below.)

Let p be a prime divisor of N. Then p does not divide $4a^3 + 27b^2$, since otherwise the choice is (successfully or unsuccessfully) abandoned in step 1. We denote by E_p the reduction of E modulo p, that is, the elliptic curve over $\mathbb{Z}_p$ with Weierstraß coefficients a, b modulo p. To $P \in E$ corresponds $P_p \in E_p$, just by reducing the coefficients modulo p. Moreover, we let $\mathcal{O}_p$, the point at infinity on E_p, correspond to the point at infinity $\mathcal{O}$ of E. Then $P_p \neq \mathcal{O}_p$ for all $P \in E \setminus \{0\}$, and hence

$$P_p = \mathcal{O}_p \text{ if and only if } P = \mathcal{O}. \tag{12}$$

Then, until the divisor p is found (so that $p \mid \gcd(w, N)$ in step 4), the computation in the algorithm can be considered as implementing arithmetic on E_p in the sense that each partial result $Q = tP$ on E gives, modulo p, the partial result $Q_p = tP_p$ on E_p; in other words, $tP_p = (tP)_p$. The lucky event that provides a factorization occurs when we reach a multiple of the order of P_p on E_p but not of P_q on E_q, for two prime divisors p, q of N. We had a similar situation in Pollard's $p - 1$ method, with the elliptic curve replaced by the group of units.

LEMMA 19.23. *Suppose that (E, P) is chosen, p, q are distinct prime divisors of N, l is the largest prime factor of the order of P_p in the group E_p, $p \leq C$, $\#E_p$ is B-smooth, and $l \nmid \#E_q$. Then the algorithm factors N.*

PROOF. We let $k = \prod_{1 \leq r \leq h} p_r^{e_r}$, with e_r as in step 3 for $1 \leq r \leq h$. The loop invariants are easily checked by induction on i and j. Since $\#E_p$ is B-smooth and $p \leq C$, the Hasse bound implies that $\#E_p \mid k$. Let d be the order of P_p in E_p. Then $d \mid \#E_p$, and hence $l \leq B$ and $d \mid k$. Let $p_i = l$ and e be the exponent of l in d, so that $1 \leq e \leq e_i$. When $j = e - 1$, then

$$t = l^{e-1} \prod_{1 \leq r < i} p_r^{e_r} \text{ and } Q = tP$$

holds before step 4, $t \not\equiv 0 \bmod d$, and $lt \equiv 0 \bmod d$. It follows that $Q_p = tP_p \neq \mathcal{O}_p$, and $lQ_p = ltP_p = \mathcal{O}_p$. Therefore, if the algorithm ever succeeded in computing lQ, the result could only be $\mathcal{O}$. We show that in fact it terminates by finding a divisor before reaching this situation.

Assume to the contrary that $lQ = \mathcal{O}$ is computed in step 4 by the algorithm. Since this computation also implements arithmetic on E_q, we have computed $lQ_q = (ltP)_q = \mathcal{O}_q$. But then, since l does not divide $\#E_q$ or the order of P_q, the point $Q_q = tP_q$ is already $\mathcal{O}_q$. It then follows that $Q = \mathcal{O}$ by (12) and hence $Q_p = \mathcal{O}_p$, a contradiction. □

We now turn to the analysis of the probability that the assumptions in this lemma are satisfied. We note that $\mathrm{prob}(l \nmid \#E_q)$ is almost 1 (see Notes 19.7), so we only consider the probability of the randomly chosen parameters to produce an elliptic curve E_p with $\#E_p$ being B-smooth. This is basically settled by the following result of Lenstra's, whose proof is outside the scope of this text.

▬▬ THEOREM 19.24. ▬▬

Let p be prime, $S \subseteq \mathbb{N}$ with $S \subseteq (p+1-\sqrt{p}, p+1+\sqrt{p})$, and $a, b \in \mathbb{F}_p$ chosen at random. Let

$$E_p = \{(u,v) : v^2 = u^3 + au + b\} \cup \{\mathcal{O}\}$$

be an elliptic curve over $\mathbb{F}_p$. Then there is a positive constant $c \in \mathbb{R}$ such that

$$\mathrm{prob}\{\#E_p \in S\} \geq \frac{c\#S}{\sqrt{p}\log p}.$$

We note that S is taken from the middle half of the range given by the Hasse bound; we have $S \subseteq \{6,7,8,9,10\}$ for $p = 7$. Thus the sizes of elliptic curves are roughly equally distributed in this middle half. Taking the set of B-smooth numbers for S and using Lemma 19.23, we have the following consequence.

▬▬ COROLLARY 19.25. ▬▬

Let $p \leq C$ be a prime divisor of N, and

$$\begin{aligned}
\sigma &= \#\{B\text{-smooth numbers in } (p+1-\sqrt{p}, p+1+\sqrt{p})\} \\
&= \psi(p+1+\sqrt{p}, B) - \psi(p+1-\sqrt{p}, B),
\end{aligned}$$

where ψ is the "number of smooth numbers" function defined in (5). Then the number M of triples $(a,u,v) \in \{0, \ldots, N-1\}^3$ for which the algorithm factors N satisfies

$$\frac{M}{N^3} \geq \frac{c_1 \sigma}{\sqrt{p}\log p}$$

for some constant $c_1 \in \mathbb{R}_{>0}$. ▬▬

How many trials of the algorithm are necessary for successful factoring with high probability? We let $s = \sigma/(2\sqrt{p})$ denote the probability for a random number in the range $(p+1-\sqrt{p}, p+1+\sqrt{p})$ to be B-smooth. If we run the algorithm repeatedly, say m times, then the failure probability is at most

$$\left(1 - \frac{M}{N^3}\right)^m \leq \left(1 - \frac{sc_1}{\ln p}\right)^m \leq \left(1 - \frac{sc_1}{\ln C}\right)^m \leq e^{-msc_1/\ln C},$$

for some constant c_1. To make this reasonably small, we take $m = c_2 \ln C/(sc_1)$ for some small constant c_2.

One addition or doubling according to (10) and (11) takes a constant number of arithmetic operations modulo N, and the time for one execution of step 4 is $O(\log p_i)$ operations modulo N. (It is amusing to note that the formula for addition is cheaper in this representation than the formula for doubling, requiring only two vs. three multiplications modulo N, plus one division and some additions.) Thus the overall cost of the algorithm is $O(Be_i \log p_i)$ or $O(B \log C)$ operations modulo N, and the number of arithmetic operations modulo N for m executions is

$$O(m \cdot B \log C) \text{ or } O(m \cdot B \log N). \tag{13}$$

Increasing B makes σ and s larger, hence m smaller, so that there is a trade-off in this time estimate. To choose B optimally, we would like to use a smoothness result like Theorem 19.13, but for random numbers from a small interval. Unfortunately, no proof of the following is known.

CONJECTURE 19.26. *For positive real numbers x, u, and an integer d chosen uniformly at random from the interval $(x - \sqrt{x}, x + \sqrt{x})$, we have*

$$\text{prob } \{d \text{ is } x^{1/u}\text{-smooth}\} = u^{-u(1+o(1))}.$$

For a rough estimate of the cost, we take $u = \ln p/\ln B$, so that $B = p^{1/u}$. Ignoring the term $o(1)$, the conjecture says that s is about u^{-u} and m about $\ln C \cdot u^u$. We want to minimize the factor mB in (13). Its logarithm is about

$$\ln(u^u) + \ln B = \frac{\ln p}{\ln B} \cdot \ln\left(\frac{\ln p}{\ln B}\right) + \ln B. \tag{14}$$

Setting

$$B = e^{\sqrt{(\ln p \cdot \ln\ln p)/2}} = L(p)^{1/\sqrt{2}}, \tag{15}$$

with the function L defined in (9), we have

$$\frac{\ln p}{\ln B} = \frac{\sqrt{2}\ln p}{(\ln p \cdot \ln\ln p)^{1/2}} = \left(\frac{2\ln p}{\ln\ln p}\right)^{1/2}.$$

The right hand side in (14) is, when $\ln\ln p \geq 2$, at most

$$\left(\frac{2\ln p}{\ln\ln p}\right)^{1/2} \cdot \frac{1}{2}\ln\ln p + \ln B = \sqrt{2}(\ln p \cdot \ln\ln p)^{1/2}.$$

Thus the number of word operations is, assuming the conjecture, $e^{(\sqrt{2}+o(1))\sqrt{\ln p \cdot \ln\ln p}}$ or

$$L(p)^{\sqrt{2}+o(1)}.$$

We note that $L(p)^{\sqrt{2}} \leq L(N)$ for any $p \leq N^{1/2}$. In an implementation, we do not know p and have to guess good values for B and C; the algorithm works well if there is a prime factor $p \leq C$ for which (15) holds approximately. One usually guesses a "small" initial value of C, determines B according to (15) with p replaced by C, and doubles the value of C in case the algorithm does not produce a factor. In the complete factorization of N, the second largest prime factor p will usually require the major portion of the effort. The particular strength of the elliptic curve method is that it profits from the presence of prime factors that are much smaller than $N^{1/2}$; Section 19.1 tells some of the success stories.

Notes. **19.1.** Table 19.2 is from Brent (1999).

19.2. The estimates for random integers are from Knuth & Trabb Pardo (1976).

19.3. Algorithm 19.2 is from Strassen (1976). An algorithm using a similar method was earlier given by Pollard (1974). It yields the same asymptotic result, but is quite a bit more complicated.

19.4. The assumption in Pollard's ρ method that x^2+1 is random is annoying, but attempts at a rigorous analysis have so far been largely unsuccessful; see Bach (1991) for the best result to date. Brent (1980) gives an improvement of Pollard's method. Brent & Pollard (1981) used it to factor F_8. Knuth (1998) attributes the cycle detection method to Floyd.

19.5. The simple observation that $s^2 - t^2 = (s+t)(s-t)$ leads to a description of all **Pythagorean triples** $(x,y,z) \in \mathbb{N}^3$ with $x^2 + y^2 = z^2$; see Exercise 19.8. A method for factoring integers based on congruent squares is designed in Kraïtchik (1926), Chapter 16. Theorem 19.13 is from Canfield, Erdős & Pomerance (1983). The approach via Lemma 19.14 (and its proof) are in Schnorr (1982). Charlie Rackoff has proposed a variant (Exercise 19.10). Pomerance (1982) gives an improvement of Dixon's method using $O^{\sim}(L(N)^{\sqrt{5/2}})$ word operations.

An important variant of the quadratic sieve, the **multiple polynomial quadratic sieve**, is practically useful for distributed computation on a network of workstations (Caron & Silverman 1988). See Silverman (1987) and Pomerance (1990b) for an overview.

19.6. The $p-1$ method is from Pollard (1974).

19.7. Elliptic curves and the role of the "point at infinity" are best understood in the framework of projective geometry. The **projective plane** $\mathbb{P}^2$ over F consists of all triples $(u : v : w)$ with $u,v,w \in F^3$, not all zero, where we identify two such triples if they are multiples of each other. We may also regard $(u : v : w)$ as the line in F^3 through (u,v,w) and the origin. The projective curve in $\mathbb{P}^2$ corresponding to an elliptic curve E given by

$y^2 = x^3 + ax + b$ is

$$\tilde{E} = \{(U : V : W) \in \mathbb{P}^2 : V^2 W = U^3 + aUW^2 + bW^3\},$$

and $E \cap F^2$ is in correspondence with the **affine part** $\tilde{E} \cap \{W \neq 0\} = \tilde{E} \cap \{W = 1\}$ via the substitution $u = U/W, v = V/W$. The intersection with the **line at infinity** is

$$\tilde{E} \cap \{W = 0\} = \{(U : V : W) \in \mathbb{P}^2 : W = U = 0\} = \{(0 : 1 : 0)\} = \{\mathcal{O}\}.$$

The choice of 1 for the second coordinate is arbitrary.

In order to get a better feeling for the required algebraic geometry, the reader is advised to consult Lenstra's (1987) article and, although maybe not in depth, one of the texts in algebraic geometry, such as Chapters 1 and 4 of Hartshorne (1977), Fulton (1969), Brieskorn & Knörrer (1986), Section VI.1 of Koblitz (1987a), or the detailed books by Silverman (1986) and Cox (1989).

Over the complex numbers, an elliptic curve is a one-dimensional curve and hence a two-dimensional real surface that looks like a torus. You can think of the real picture as being the intersection of such a torus with a plane (in four dimensions).

In general, one invariant of complex curves is the **genus** g. In the real surface representation, g is the number of *holes*. If $E \subseteq \mathbb{C}^2$ is a nonsingular planar curve defined by an irreducible polynomial of degree d (and also nonsingular at infinity), then $g = (d-1)(d-2)/2$. For an elliptic curve, we have $d = 3$ and $g = 1$. Also, $g = 0$ if and only if the curve is isomorphic to the projective line $\mathbb{P}^1$, which is defined analogously to the projective plane. (An example is the parabola given by $y = x^2$.)

No curve of genus ≥ 2 is a group with a rational operation. Of course any curve (and any set) can be made into a group, since a group of the same cardinality exists, and one can translate the group operations via a bijection. However, the above says that if we want to express the group operation by rational functions in the coordinates, as done in Section 19.7 for elliptic curves, then this is impossible for genus ≥ 2.

Manin (1956) and Chahal (1995) present proofs of Hasse's (1933) bound 19.20 that use only "elementary" methods. This bound had been conjectured by Emil Artin in 1923. It is a special case of the famous **Weil bound**, which says that $|\#X - (q+1)| \leq 2g\sqrt{q}$ for a nonsingular projective algebraic curve X over $\mathbb{F}_q$ of genus g. A variant of Weil's bound, also valid for singular curves, is given in Bach (1996).

An elliptic curve group over a finite field is either cyclic or a direct product of two cyclic groups, as illustrated in Figure 19.8 (see Silverman 1986).

A fixed prime number ℓ divides a random number with probability about $1/\ell$. In view of Theorem 19.24, one might expect that ℓ divides $\#E$, where E is a random elliptic curve over a finite prime field $\mathbb{F}_p$, with probability about $1/\ell$ as well. This is false, however. Lenstra (1987) shows that the probability tends to $1/(\ell - 1)$ and $\ell/(\ell^2 - 1)$ as p tends to infinity over the primes with $p \not\equiv 1 \bmod \ell$ and $p \equiv 1 \bmod \ell$, respectively.

Further notes. We list some other integer factorization algorithms. The $p + 1$ **method** by Guy (1975) and Williams (1982) and the $\Phi_k(p)$ **method** by Bach & Shallit (1988) are generalizations of Pollard's (1975) $p - 1$ method. ($\Phi_k \in \mathbb{Z}[x]$ is the kth cyclotomic polynomial; see Section 14.10). These methods work well if N has a prime factor with the property that $\Phi_k(p)$ is smooth.

The **continued fraction method** by Morrison & Brillhart (1971, 1975) is a different approach to generating B-numbers, where the continued fraction expansion (Section 4.6) of $\sqrt{N}$ is used to get the b's. By a heuristic argument, their algorithm should use $L(N)^{O(1)}$ steps, thus predating Dixon's result, but this was not proven rigorously. (They factored F_7 and introduced several other important ideas, such as using a factor base and linear algebra modulo 2 to find squares.) Already Lehmer & Powers (1931) had used this expansion to find two squares that are congruent modulo N. Pomerance (1982) exhibits variants that use $L(N)^{\sqrt{3/2}+o(1)}$ word operations, under some unproven hypotheses. Further discussions are in Pomerance & Wagstaff (1983) and Williams & Wunderlich (1987). The origins of this method can already be found in Legendre (1785), § XV. (In the Berkeley library copy that we consulted, D. H. Lehmer has corrected a calculation error of Legendre's.)

The **number field sieve** by Lenstra, Lenstra, Manasse & Pollard (1990) runs in time $\exp(O(\sqrt[3]{\log N (\log\log N)^2}))$. It was the first general asymptotic progress (in terms of the order of the exponent) since Dixon's (1981) random squares method. Lenstra & Lenstra (1993) give a status report. The original approach was designed for numbers of a special form (as they occur in the Cunningham project), but newer versions apply to arbitrary numbers; see Dodson & Lenstra (1995) and Cowie, Dodson, Elkenbracht-Huizing, Lenstra, Montgomery & Zayer (1996) about their efficiency.

As we have seen, the analyses of several factoring algorithms rely on unproven conjectures. The current world records on *rigorously* proven upper bounds on integer factoring algorithms are Pollard's and Strassen's $O^{\sim}(N^{1/4})$ for deterministic methods and $L(N)^{1+o(1)}$, due to Lenstra & Pomerance (1992), for probabilistic algorithms.

Exercises.

19.1$^{\longrightarrow}$ Prove that the 128-digit factor N of $2^{569}-1$ defined in (1) is composite.

19.2* (Lenstra 1990) Consider the following special polynomial factorization task: input is a prime p and $f \in \mathbb{F}_p[x]$ of degree n and dividing $x^p - x$, so that all monic irreducible factors of f in $\mathbb{F}_p[x]$ are linear and distinct. Adapt the Pollard and Strassen method to find a deterministic algorithm for factoring f with $O^{\sim}(n\sqrt{p})$ operations in $\mathbb{F}_p$ if $p^2 > n$.

19.3 Factor the integer $N = 23\,802\,996\,783\,967$ using Pollard's ρ method, and also with the Pollard and Strassen method.

19.4 Let p be a prime. For a sequence $u = (u_i)_{i\in\mathbb{N}} \in \mathbb{Z}_p^{\mathbb{N}}$ let $S(u) = \min\{i \in \mathbb{N} : \exists j < i \; u_j = u_i\}$ be the least index with a collision.

(i) For any $u_0 \in \mathbb{Z}_p$, we define a sequence $u = (u_i)_{i\in\mathbb{N}} \in \mathbb{Z}_p^{\mathbb{N}}$ by $u_i = u_{i-1}^2 + 1$ if $i \geq 1$, as in Pollard's algorithm 19.8. Determine the mean value (over the choices of u_0) of $S(u)$ for $p = 167$ and $p = 179$ by trying all possible initial values of u_0. Compare your result with the estimated expected value of $S(u)$ for random sequences from the proof of Theorem 19.5.

(ii) Determine the mean value of $T(u) = \min\{i \in \mathbb{N}_{>0} : u_i = u_{2i}\}$, with u and p as in (i), for all possible values of u_0. Compare to your results of (i).

19.5 (Guy 1975) Let $x_0 = 2$ and $x_i = x_{i-1}^2 + 1$ for $i \geq 1$. For $p \in \mathbb{N}$, we let $e(p) = \min\{i \in \mathbb{N}_{\geq 1} : x_i \equiv x_{2i} \bmod p\}$.

(i) Calculate $e(p)$ for the primes $p \leq 11$.

(ii) Calculate $e(p)$ for the primes $p \leq 10^6$. You should find $e(p) \leq 3680$ for all these p. (Guy (1975) notes that $e(p)$ seems to grow like $(p \ln p)^{1/2}$.)

(iii) Let N be a number to be factored, run Pollard's ρ method on it with initial value $x_0 = 2$, and assume that $\gcd(x_i - x_{2i}, N) = 1$ for $0 \leq i \leq k$. Show that $e(p) > k$ for all prime divisors p of N.

(iv) Conclude that if the gcd in (iii) is trivial for 3680 steps, then N has no factor up to 10^6.

19.6 Prove that

$$\left(\int_{-\infty}^{\infty} e^{-x^2} dx \right)^2 = \pi. \tag{16}$$

Hint: Write (16) as a two-dimensional integral, and use the substitution $(x, y) = (r\cos\varphi, r\sin\varphi)$.

19.7$\longrightarrow$ Factor the number N from Exercise 19.3 using Dixon's random squares method with all primes less than $B = 40$ as your factor base.

19.8 Three integers $(x, y, z) \in \mathbb{N}^3$ form a **Pythagorean triple** if $x^2 + y^2 = z^2$, and a **primitive Pythagorean triple** if furthermore $\gcd(x, y, z) = 1$.

(i) Show that any Pythagorean triple is of the form $(\lambda x, \lambda y, \lambda z)$ for a primitive Pythagorean triple (x, y, z) and some $\lambda \in \mathbb{N}$.

(ii) Let $s, t \in \mathbb{N}$ be coprime with $s > t$ and st even. Show that $(s^2 - t^2, 2st, s^2 + t^2)$ is a primitive Pythagorean triple.

(iii) Let (x, y, z) be a primitive Pythagorean triple. Show that z is odd and either x or y is odd, but not both. Hint: Calculate modulo 4. Assume that x is odd. Prove that $(z+x)/2$ and $(z-x)/2$ are coprime squares, not both odd, and conclude that (x, y, z) is of the form as in (ii).

(iv) Use (ii) and (iii) to generate all primitive Pythagorean triples (x, y, z) with $z \le 100$.

19.9 What is the relation between $n^{1+o(1)}$ and $O^{\sim}(n)$?

19.10** In Lemma 19.14, we proved that the numbers a^2 rem N for random a are smooth sufficiently often. We can avoid the use of this lemma by the following modifications to Dixon's random squares algorithm 19.12, as proposed by Charlie Rackoff.

    ◦ In step 1: $u \longleftarrow (\ln N)/\ln p_h, \quad \tau \longleftarrow \lambda u^u$ with a small constant λ, say $\lambda = 10$
          choose $y \in \{1, \ldots, N-1\}$ at random, $\quad g \longleftarrow \gcd(y, N), \quad$ **if** $1 < g < N$ **then return** g
    ◦ In step 4: $a \longleftarrow b^2 y$ rem N
    ◦ In step 7: **until** $\#A = \tau$
    ◦ In step 8: l must be even
    ◦ In step 9: $s \longleftarrow y^{l/2} \prod_{1 \le i \le l} b_i$

We denote by $\sigma = \psi(N, p_h)/\varphi(N)$ the probability for $x \in \{1, \ldots, N-1\}$ with $\gcd(x, N) = 1$ to be B-smooth. Thus σ is about τ^{-1}. We let $N = q_1^{l_1} \cdots q_t^{l_t}$ be the prime factorization of N, with pairwise different primes $q_1, \ldots, q_t$. For each $i \le t$, there are exactly $(q_i - 1)q_i^{l_i - 1}/2$ squares modulo $q_i^{l_i}$, and the same number of nonsquares. In a somewhat audacious notation we write $+S_i \subset \mathbb{Z}_{q^{l_i}}^{\times}$ for the set of squares, and $-S \subset \mathbb{Z}_{q^{l_i}}^{\times}$ for the nonsquares.

Then the Chinese Remainder Theorem gives a decomposition

$$\mathbb{Z}_N^{\times} \cong \bigcup_{\varepsilon_1, \ldots, \varepsilon_t \in \pm} \varepsilon_1 S_1 \times \varepsilon_2 S_2 \times \cdots \times \varepsilon_t S_t = \bigcup_{\varepsilon \in \pm^t} T_{\varepsilon}$$

of $\mathbb{Z}_N^{\times}$ into 2^t subsets T_{ε} of equal size.

If $y \in T_{\varepsilon}$, then also all a computed in step 4 are in T_{ε}. If T_{ε} has its fair share of B-smooth numbers, namely about $\sigma \cdot \#T_{\varepsilon}$ many, then the algorithm will work well with that choice of y. However, we do not know that the smooth numbers are equally distributed over the 2^t sets T_{ε}. So the first question is to show that a reasonable fraction of all y's is sufficiently good.

(i) Let $A = \bigcup_{i \in I} B_i$ be a partition of a finite set A into disjoint subsets of equal size $k = \#A/\#I$, $C \subseteq A$, and $s = \#C/\#A$. Then for at least $s \cdot \#I/2$ indices $i \in I$ we have $\#(B_i \cap C) \ge sk/2$.

(ii) Show that for a fraction at least $\sigma/2$ of the $\varepsilon \in \pm^t$, T_{ε} contains a fraction at least $\sigma/2$ of B-smooth numbers. Hint: Apply (i) to $A = \mathbb{Z}_N^{\times}$, C the B-smooth numbers, so that $s = \sigma$, and the partition into the subsets T_{ε}.

(iii) Analyze the success probability and the running time of the algorithm described above.

19.11 Check that the curve $E = \{(x,y) \in \mathbb{F}_7^2 : y^2 = x^3 + x + 3\}$ over $\mathbb{F}_7$ is nonsingular. Compute all points on it, and verify that it is cyclic and generated by $(4,1)$.

19.12 Show that $-P = (x, -y)$ is in fact the inverse of $P = (x,y)$ with respect to the addition on an elliptic curve E.

19.13 Let E be an elliptic curve and $P, Q \in E$. Explain why $P + Q = S$, where S is the third inter-section point of E with the line through P and Q (see Figure 19.6), is not a group operation.

19.14 Let F be a field and $f = x^3 + ax + b \in F[x]$.

(i) Check that $r = \mathrm{res}(f, f') = 4a^3 + 27b^2$.

(ii) Conclude that f is squarefree if and only if $r \neq 0$.

(iii) For which values of b does $y^2 = x^3 - x + b$ not define an elliptic curve over $F = \mathbb{R}$? Plot the curves for all these values.

19.15 Let $E = \{(x,y) \in F^2 : y^2 = x^3 + ax + b\}$ be an elliptic curve over a field F and $P = (x_1, y_1) \in E$. Determine the equation of the tangent to E through P (distinguish the two cases $y_1 = 0$ and $y_1 \neq 0$), and prove that the doubling formula (11) realizes the geometric description using the tangent line.

19.16 Show that an elliptic curve E has at most three points P of order 2, for which $P \neq \mathcal{O}$ and $2P = \mathcal{O}$.

19.17$^{\longrightarrow}$ You are to check associativity of the addition we defined on an elliptic curve E.

(i) Write a procedure add to calculate the sum of two distinct points, using (10).

(ii) Check that for three points P, Q, R,

$$\mathrm{ass} = \mathrm{add}(\mathrm{add}(P,Q),R) - \mathrm{add}(P,\mathrm{add}(Q,R))$$

is not zero.

(iii) What has gone wrong in (ii)? We have not used that the three points lie on the same curve. Cal-culate the Weierstraß coefficients a, b from P and Q, set $f = y_3^2 - (x_3^3 + ax_3 + b)$, where $R = (x_3, y_3)$, and check that $\mathrm{ass} \equiv 0 \bmod f$. (You may have to simplify and take numerators at the appropriate place.)

(iv) We now have associativity at three "generic" points P, Q, R. Check associativity when one of them is $\mathcal{O}$.

(v) It remains to check the cases where two points coincide, say $P = Q$ or $P + Q = R$, so that (10) is not applicable. You have two ways of doing this: writing a little program for these cases, or arguing by continuity. The latter requires some algebraic geometry.

19.18** (i) Prove that $\sum_{0 \leq k < n} \binom{2n}{k} = (4^n - \binom{2n}{n})/2$ and $\sum_{0 \leq k < n} \binom{2n-1}{k} = 4^{n-1}$, for all posit-ive integers n.

(ii) Let $n \in \mathbb{N}_{>0}$, X_i for $1 \leq i \leq 2n$ be a collection of independent random variables which take on each of the two values 1 and -1 with probability $1/2$, and $X = \sum_{1 \leq i \leq 2n} X_i$ be a random walk of length $2n$. Prove that $\mathrm{prob}(X = 2(n-k)) = \mathrm{prob}(X = -2(n-k)) = \binom{2n}{k} 4^{-n}$ for $0 \leq k \leq n$.

(iii) Show that $\mathcal{E}(X) = 0$ and $\mathcal{E}(|X|) = 2n \binom{2n}{n} 4^{-n}$.

(iv) Use Stirling's formula $n! \in \sqrt{2\pi n}(n/e)^n (1 + O(n^{-1}))$ to show that $\mathcal{E}(X) \in 2\pi^{-1/2} n^{1/2} + O(n^{-1/2})$.

(v) Prove the same formulas as in (iii) when there are $2n - 1$ instead of $2n$ random variables.

19.19$^{\longrightarrow}$ Program Lenstra's algorithm 19.22, and use it to factor the number N from Exercise 19.3 with $B = 40$ and $C = 12\,000$.

Real mathematics has no effects on war. No one has yet discovered any
warlike purpose to be served by the theory of numbers or relativity;
and it seems very unlikely that anyone will do so for many years.

Godfrey Harold Hardy (1940)

Die reine Zahlentheorie ist dasjenige Gebiet der Mathematik,
das bisher noch nie Anwendung gefunden hat.[1]

David Hilbert (1930)

It would not be an exaggeration to state that *abstract* cryptography
is *identical* with abstract mathematics.

Abraham Adrian Albert (1941)

Give me problems, give me work, give me the most
abstruse cryptogram, or the most intricate analysis,
and I am in my own proper atmosphere.

Sir Arthur Conan Doyle (1890)

"Right. So I have a translation key and you have a signature key and all
the communication from you to me needs both
those keys to encode and decode it properly. But if I want
to send a message back, I can't use those same keys—
I need *my* signature key and *your* translation key."
"And Joe has a different translation key and when I send
him a message I have to use *his* key. And that's how
everybody is approaching this, and doing it that way has
the kinds of problems we're sitting here to solve."

Philip Friedman (1996)

The KGB, more than other foreign-intelligence agencies,
still depended on one-time-pad cipher systems.
These were unbreakable, even in a theoretical sense,
unless the code sequence itself were compromised.

Tom Clancy (1988)

---

[1] Pure number theory is that part of mathematics for which up to now no application has ever been found.

20

Application: Public key cryptography

This chapter presents one of the most interesting applications of the ideas from complexity theory and the algorithms from computer algebra: modern cryptography. After an introduction to the problem, we present six cryptographic algorithms: the famous RSA scheme, the Diffie-Hellman key exchange, two cryptosystems by ElGamalElGacryp and by Rabin, and systems based on elliptic curves and short vectors in lattices.

It is satisfying to see how many of the computer algebra methods discussed in this text, certainly designed without this application in mind, have been useful for cryptography.

20.1. Cryptosystems

The scenario in this chapter is as follows. Bob wants to send a message to Alice in such a way that an eavesdropper Eve[1] listening to the transmission channel cannot understand the message. This is done by enciphering the message so that only Alice, possessing the right **key**, can decipher it, but Eve, having no access to the key, has no chance to recover the message.

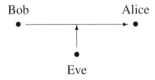

The following are some of the ciphers that have been used in history.

- ○ The **Caesar cipher**, which simply permutes the alphabet. The classical Caesar cipher used the cyclic shift by three letters $A \longmapsto D$, $B \longmapsto E$, $C \longmapsto F$, ..., $Y \longmapsto B$, $Z \longmapsto C$. For example, the word "CAESAR" is then enciphered as "FDHVDU". This cryptosystem is trivial to break: there are only 26 possibilities to try out. More generally, one can use any of the $26! \approx 4 \cdot 10^{26}$ per-

---

[1] Alice, Bob, and Eve are the leading characters of modern cryptography.

mutations of a 26-letter alphabet. The key in this simple cryptosystem is the permutation; its inverse is used to decipher an encrypted message. However, if the eavesdropper knows in what language the original message was and thus knows the (approximate) probabilities for individual letters to occur in an average text, she may easily recover the message without knowledge of the key by performing a frequency analysis—provided the message is long enough. Thus this cipher is a convenient but highly insecure method.

○ The **one-time pad**, which works as follows. To encipher a message of length n over the usual alphabet with 26 elements, a random sequence of n letters is chosen as a key and added letterwise modulo 26 to the message. The recipient then deciphers the encrypted message by subtracting the key letterwise. For example, if the message is "CAESAR", the key is "DOHXLG", and we identify the letters A,...,Z with the numbers $0, \ldots, 25$, then the ciphertext is "FOLPLX".

The one-time pad is the only known provably secure cryptosystem (in an information theoretic sense), but has the disadvantage that the keys are of the same length as the message (keys cannot be reused without loss of security). It is an inconvenient but highly secure method.

In a more practical variant, a **pseudorandom number generator** is used to generate keys. Both Alice and Bob then use the same kind of generator parameterized by a **seed**, so that the two generators produce the same sequence when the same seed is used. Popular examples of such generators are the linear congruential generators.

However, we have seen in Section 17.2 that linear congruential generators are badly suited for cryptographical purposes since they are vulnerable to so-called "short vector" attacks. Today there are other types of pseudorandom number generators where no such attacks are known. In fact, several of the cryptosystems we are about to describe can be modified to work as pseudorandom generators. The variant of the one-time pad using pseudorandom number generators is no longer provably secure; its security heavily depends on the hardness of determining the elements of the pseudorandom sequence without knowledge of the seed.

In World War II, the German Wehrmacht[2] and Marine[3] used an enciphering machine called ENIGMA. This was a mechanical device where the keys were on cylinders; the underlying cipher was somewhat similar to the Caesar cipher but vastly more complicated. Its breaking by a British intelligence group at Bletchley Park under the famous computer scientist Alan Turing was vital for the Allied victory in the North Atlantic submarine war.

The main customers for cryptosystems used to be the military and secret services. Today, these systems are employed for all kinds of secure electronic data

---

[2] army
[3] navy

processing and communication like passwords, point-of-sale registers, banking machines, electronic cash, and internet commerce.

All of the classical cryptosystems are **symmetric** in the sense that the same key is used for both enciphering and deciphering, or at least the decryption key is easy (which means in polynomial time) to infer from the encryption key. A problem with this approach is that the number of keys grows quadratically with the number of parties if each party needs to communicate with each other party.

In classical cryptography, there never was a clear mathematical understanding of what "difficult to break" means; one could only take it to mean "the tricks that I know are not sufficient to break it". The security of a cryptosystem depends on the eavesdropper's cryptanalytic skills and her knowledge about the system. In the age of Caesar, it may have been reasonable to assume that the cryptanalyst has only a limited amount of computing power and that the encryption method may be kept secret from her. In the 20th century however, designers of cryptosystems, both classical and public key, have to take into account that potential eavesdroppers have high mathematical intelligence, access to supercomputers, complete knowledge about the encryption method except the keys, or can even channel in arbitrary parts of plaintext so that they have many plaintext/ciphertext pairs encrypted with the current key at their disposal.

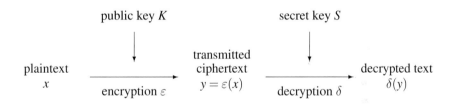

FIGURE 20.1: A public key cryptosystem.

Diffie & Hellman (1976) made a revolutionary proposal which has since then been known as **public key cryptography**. The idea is to have two different keys K and S for encryption and decryption, respectively, such that both encryption and decryption are "easy", but decryption without knowledge of S is "hard". Here "easy" means polynomial time, preferably almost linear or quadratic time in the message length. Figure 20.1 illustrates the situation. The name "public key cryptography" comes from the fact that the encryption key K may be publicly available. Since we want $x = \delta(y) = \delta(\varepsilon(x))$, δ is an inverse of ε. A function that is "easy" but its inverse is "hard" to compute without additional knowledge, like the encryption function in a public key cryptosystem, is called a **trapdoor function**. The keys K and S are called **public key** and **secret key** (or private key), respectively. With such an **asymmetric cryptosystem**, n public-secret key pairs are sufficient to permit secure communication among any two of n parties.

A cryptosystem is certainly broken when the secret key is easy to find, but an appropriate notion of breaking a code is much more generous: a system is considered broken if there exists a Boolean predicate $B(x)$—say, the parity of x if x is an integer—and a polynomial-time probabilistic algorithm which takes $y = \varepsilon(x)$ as input and has a slightly better capability of predicting $B(x)$ than a random guess. Otherwise, the system is **semantically secure**; this is only possible for probabilistic encryption schemes, and the precise definition is a bit tricky.

There are several possibilities to make precise what "hard" means. Here is a list of some, ordered in increasing desirability.

- The inventor of the cryptosystem does not know of any polynomial time algorithm.

- Nobody knows of a polynomial time algorithm.

- Whoever breaks the system will probably in turn have solved a well-studied "hard" problem.

- Whoever breaks the system has in turn solved a well-studied "hard" problem.

- Whoever breaks the system has in turn solved an $\mathcal{NP}$–complete problem (Section 25.8).

- There is provably no (probabilistic) polynomial-time algorithm, as we have stipulated above.

At present, nobody knows of a cryptosystem fulfilling any of the last three requirements. However, it was a major conceptual breakthrough of the Diffie & Hellman proposal that the hitherto elusive notion of a "hard-to-break cipher" should be studied within the well-established framework of computational complexity.

Some of the modern proposals for cryptosystems have already been broken. Merkle & Hellman (1978) suggested a cryptosystem based on the **subset sum problem**. This system and several variants were broken using a basis reduction algorithm (Section 17.1). Another cipher proposed by Cade in 1985 (see Cade 1987) was based on the assumed hardness of the functional decomposition problem for polynomials: Given a polynomial f over a field F of degree n, compute nonconstant polynomials $g, h \in F[x]$ (if they exist) such that $f = g \circ h = g(h)$. The system was broken by Kozen & Landau (1989), who gave an algorithm for the problem with running time $O(n^3)$. Beyond our fairly simple scenario, modern cryptography studies many other tasks: electronic signatures and authentication of messages, multi-party communication, electronic cash, etc.

We now present some modern public key cryptosystems.

20.2. The RSA cryptosystem

We have already introduced in Section 1.2 this famous system, which is named after its inventors Rivest, Shamir & Adleman (1978) and is based on the assumed hardness of factoring integers. The idea is that Alice randomly chooses two large (say 150-digit) primes $p \neq q$, and sets $N = pq$. Anybody who can factor N can break the system; ideally, we would also like the converse to be true, since numbers N with more than about 160 decimal digits seem out of the range of current integer factorization software (see the Notes and Chapter 19). Messages are encoded as sequences of elements of $\mathbb{Z}_N = \{0, \ldots, N-1\}$. If, for example, we use the standard alphabet $\Sigma = \{A, \ldots, Z\}$ of cardinality $\#\Sigma = 26$, then messages of up to $212 = \lfloor \log_{26} 10^{300} \rfloor$ letters can be uniquely represented by a single element of $\mathbb{Z}_N$, using the 26-adic representation. For example, the message "CAESAR" is encoded as

$$2 \cdot 26^0 + 0 \cdot 26^1 + 4 \cdot 26^2 + 18 \cdot 26^3 + 0 \cdot 26^4 + 17 \cdot 26^5 = 202\,302\,466 \in \mathbb{Z}_N.$$

If Alice wants to receive messages from Bob, she chooses $e \in \{2, \ldots, \varphi(N) - 2\}$ with $\gcd(e, \varphi(N)) = 1$ at random, where φ is Euler's totient function (Section 4.2) and $\varphi(N) = \#\mathbb{Z}_N^\times = (p-1)(q-1)$. (She can also fix e, say $e = 3$.) Then she computes $d \in \{2, \ldots, \varphi(N) - 2\}$ with $de \equiv 1 \bmod \varphi(N)$, using the Extended Euclidean Algorithm (Theorem 4.1), publishes the pair $K = (N, e)$ as her public key, and keeps her secret key $S = (N, d)$ as well as p, q secret (the latter may even be discarded). The encryption and decryption functions $\varepsilon, \delta \colon \mathbb{Z}_N^\times \longrightarrow \mathbb{Z}_N^\times$ are defined by $\varepsilon(x) = x^e$ and $\delta(y) = y^d$. To send a message $x \in \mathbb{Z}_N^\times$ to Alice, Bob looks up her public key, computes $y = \varepsilon(x)$, and sends this to Alice, who computes $\delta(y)$, using her secret key. Then, with $u \in \mathbb{Z}$ such that $de - 1 = u \cdot \varphi(N)$, we have

$$(\delta \circ \varepsilon)(x) = \delta(x^e) = x^{de} = x^{1 + u \cdot \varphi(N)} = x(x^{\varphi(N)})^u \equiv x \bmod N,$$

since $x^{\varphi(N)} = 1$ by Euler's theorem (Section 18.1). Although the latter is only valid if $\gcd(x, N) = 1$, actually $(\delta \circ \varepsilon)(x) = x$ is true for all x (Exercise 20.5). However, values of x that are not coprime to N lead to the factorization of N and thus to a break of the cryptosystem. Fortunately, if p and q are large and we assume that many or all messages x are likely to occur, then this will practically never happen.

We recall that a **polynomial-time reduction** from one problem X to another one Y is a polynomial-time algorithm for X making calls to a subroutine for Y. If polynomial-time reductions exist in both directions, then X and Y are **polynomial-time equivalent** (see Section 25.8). The following theorem is proven in Exercise 20.6.

THEOREM 20.1.

The following three problems are polynomial-time equivalent:

   (i) *factoring N,*

   (ii) *computing $\varphi(N)$,*

   (iii) *computing $d \in \mathbb{N}$ with $de \equiv 1 \bmod \varphi(N)$ from $K = (N, e)$.*

Unfortunately, the theorem does *not* say that breaking the system means that one can factor integers efficiently, since there might be a successful attack that does not compute the secret key at all.

The RSA scheme can also be used for **authentication**, where the sender of a message has to prove that he actually is the originator. This is also called a **digital signature**. If Bob wants to send a signed message x to Alice, he computes $y = \delta(x)$ using his own secret key, and sends this to Alice, who looks up Bob's public key and recovers $x = \varepsilon(y)$. Since only Bob is assumed to know his secret key, no forger would have been able to produce y, and Alice is convinced that the message originated from Bob. Instead of the whole message x, Bob might just sign a short digest of x obtained with a cryptographic hash function.

The authentication scheme may even be used in conjunction with the encryption scheme to ensure privacy. If ε_A, δ_A and ε_B, δ_B are Alice's and Bob's encryption and decryption functions, respectively, and Bob wants to send a signed message x to Alice that no one else can decipher, he computes $y = \varepsilon_A(\delta_B(x))$, and sends this to Alice, who first decrypts $\delta_A(y) = \delta_B(x)$ and then $x = \varepsilon_B(\delta_A(y))$, at the same time assuring herself that the message originates from Bob.

20.3. The Diffie–Hellman key exchange protocol

Diffie & Hellman (1976) presented this scheme for two parties to agree upon a common key for future communication with a symmetric cryptosystem rather than a public key cryptosystem. An example might be the seed of a pseudorandom generator to be used for a one-time pad. Let $q \in \mathbb{N}$ be a "large" prime power (say with about 1000 bits) and g be a generator of $\mathbb{F}_q^\times$, the multiplicative group of the finite field $\mathbb{F}_q$ (Section 25.4). Then $\mathbb{F}_q^\times$ is isomorphic to the cyclic (additive) group $\mathbb{Z}_{q-1}$, via $g^i \longleftrightarrow i$. The protocol works as follows.

1. Alice and Bob agree on q and g, which may be public.

2. Alice secretly chooses $a \in \mathbb{Z}_{q-1}$ at random, computes $u = g^a \in \mathbb{F}_q^\times$, and sends u to Bob.

3. Bob secretly chooses $b \in \mathbb{Z}_{q-1}$ at random, computes $v = g^b \in \mathbb{F}_q^\times$, and sends v to Alice.

4. Alice computes $g^{ab} = v^a$.

5. Bob computes $g^{ab} = u^b$.

Now both parties may use g^{ab} as a common key for further communication with a symmetric cryptosystem. In this context, the following two problems play a central role.

PROBLEM 20.2. *(Diffie-Hellman Problem, DH) Given $g^a, g^b \in \mathbb{F}_q^\times$, compute g^{ab}.*

PROBLEM 20.3. *(Discrete Logarithm Problem, DL) Given $g^a \in \mathbb{F}_q^\times$, compute a.*

It is conjectured that DL is a "hard" problem. The fastest algorithms for DL have the same subexponential running times as for factoring integers, and DL seems unlikely to be $\mathcal{NP}$-complete. An eavesdropper knowing q, g and the transmitted u, v but not a or b has to solve DH to find out g^{ab}, which in turn is polynomial-time reducible to DL. It is, however, not clear whether DL is polynomial-time reducible to DH.

The currently best estimate for the computation of discrete logarithms in $\mathbb{F}_q^\times$ is $\exp(O(\sqrt[3]{n \log^2 n}))$ word operations, where $n \approx \log_2 q$ is the binary length of a description for an element of $\mathbb{F}_q$ (Gordon 1993). A cryptosystem using $q = 2^{1013}$ was marketed, and $\exp(\sqrt[3]{1\,013 \log_2^2 1013}) > 1.6 \cdot 10^{20}$; a machine performing one calculation per nanosecond takes about 500 years to achieve this number.

20.4. The ElGamal cryptosystem

As before, $\mathbb{F}_q^\times$ is a "large" finite field with q elements, and g is a generator of $\mathbb{F}_q^\times$. To receive messages from Bob, Alice randomly chooses $S = b \in \mathbb{Z}_{q-1}$ as her secret key and publishes $K = (q, g, g^b)$. If Bob wants to send a message x to Alice, he looks up her public key, randomly chooses $k \in \mathbb{Z}_{q-1}$, computes g^k and xg^{kb}, and sends $y = (u, v) = (g^k, xg^{kb})$ to Alice, who computes the original message as $x = v/u^b$. Computing x from y without knowing S is polynomial-time equivalent to the Diffie-Hellman Problem.

A practical problem in implementing the Diffie-Hellman scheme or the ElGamal system is that exponentiation in $\mathbb{F}_q^\times$ is theoretically easy ($O(n^3)$ word operations for $q = 2^n$ using classical arithmetic), but not fast enough to achieve high throughput. One can, however, achieve time $O^\sim(n^2)$.

20.5. Rabin's cryptosystem

This is based on the hardness of computing square roots modulo $N = pq$, where p, q are two "large" primes as in the RSA scheme. The factorization of N can be reduced to the computation of square roots, as follows. Choose some $x \in \mathbb{Z}_N$ and compute $y = \sqrt{x^2}$. Then $x^2 \equiv y^2 \bmod N$, or equivalently, $pq = N \mid (x+y)(x-y)$. If $x \not\equiv \pm y \bmod N$, then this gives us the factorization of N. This is the main idea for Dixon's random squares algorithm in Section 19.5.

Thus to send a message x to Alice, Bob uses her public key N, and sends $y \equiv x^2 \bmod N$. Alice can compute the two square roots each of y modulo p and q, by equal-degree factorization (Section 14.3), and combine them via the Chinese

Remainder Algorithm. There are various tricks to deal with the choice among the four different answers computed by Alice.

However, the system's use as a signature scheme is vulnerable to an **active attack**: if Eve chooses a random x and gets Alice to sign a message $y \equiv x^2 \bmod N$, by returning a square root z of y modulo N, then with probability $1/2$, $\gcd(x - z, N)$ will be a proper factor of N. The system is not considered secure for this reason.

20.6. Elliptic curve systems

These work similarly to the ElGamal system, except that the multiplicative group $\mathbb{F}_q^\times$ is replaced by the additive group of an elliptic curve E over $\mathbb{F}_q$ (see Section 19.7). The curve is public, and so is a point P on E. Let n be the order of P in E. Alice chooses $a \in \{2, \ldots, n-2\}$ at random and publishes aP. When Bob wants to send her the message $(m_1, m_2) \in \mathbb{F}_q^2$, with $m_1, m_2 \in \mathbb{F}_q$, he chooses a random k, computes $kP = (r_1, r_2)$ and $k \cdot aP = (s_1, s_2)$ in $\mathbb{F}_q^2$, and sends $(y_1, y_2, y_3, y_4) = (r_1, r_2, s_1 m_1, s_2 m_2) \in \mathbb{F}_q^4$ to Alice. She then computes $a \cdot (r_1, r_2) = a \cdot kP = (s_1, s_2)$ and retrieves Bob's message as $(m_1, m_2) = (s_1^{-1} y_3, s_2^{-1} y_4)$.

An implementation of such a system over $\mathbb{F}_{2^{155}}$ is commercially available (Agnew, Mullin & Vanstone 1993). Using a VLSI chip rated at 40 MHz, they estimate an encryption rate of about 60 kbits/sec.

20.7. Short vector cryptosystems

Starting in 1996, Miklos Ajtai initiated a new type of cryptosystem. At the time of writing, it is too early to gauge its impact; it clearly presents major progress and has been heralded as "marking an important day for cryptography" (Goldreich, Goldwasser & Halevi 1997).

Ajtai began by solving an important complexity-theoretic question. If we have found a way of using a computationally difficult problem—such as factoring integers, subset sums, or the discrete logarithm—for cryptographic purposes, the following difficulty arises. Complexity is always measured in terms of "worst-case" inputs, so that it is conceivable that the problem is hard for some but maybe fairly rare inputs and easy on "most" inputs. Although this phenomenon does not seem to happen in general, one has to be careful about this issue. Ajtai showed that the problem of finding shortest vectors in lattices (Chapter 16) is "$\mathcal{NP}$-hard", and that it is as hard on average as in the worst case.

Ajtai actually showed this for the type of lattice that corresponds to simultaneous Diophantine approximations (Section 17.3). Len Adleman had in 1995 reduced—under some reasonable but unproven assumptions—the factorization of integers to simultaneous approximation of $\sqrt{\log p}$ for the small primes p. Van Emde Boas (1980) had shown that finding a shortest vector in the max-norm is $\mathcal{NP}$-hard. But it had remained an open question whether this is true for the Euclidean norm $\| \cdot \|_2$, as considered in Chapter 16.

Ajtai & Dwork (1996) describe a public-key cryptosystem whose security is based on the difficulty of finding a shortest vector in a certain type of lattice. The type of lattice is different from that described above, but both have the property that a shortest vector v is unique in the sense that any vector w in the lattice with $\|w\| \leq n^c \|v\|$ is parallel to v, for a choosable constant c.

The important new feature of this system is that Ajtai & Dwork (1996) show that breaking it for random messages is as difficult as in the worst case.

Notes. **20.1.** Koblitz (1987a) and Stinson (1995) are good introductions to algebraic public-key cryptography. The state of the art in 1990 is described in Pomerance (1990a). See Denning (1982), Stinson (1995), and Menezes, van Oorschot & Vanstone (1997) for general cryptography, and Diffie (1988) for the early history of public keys.

The one-time pad is in Vernam (1926). Cryptographically strong pseudorandom number generators, whose prediction is thought to be computationally hard, are discussed in Lagarias (1990). An algorithm with time $O^{\sim}(n)$ for functional decomposition is in von zur Gathen (1990a, 1990b); see Exercise 20.3.

20.2. The security of individual bits in the RSA scheme has been discussed by several researchers; see Näslund (1998) and Håstad & Näslund (1998) for references and the latest results. It is generally hard to predict, and even harder to predict the future. Nevertheless, Odlyzko (1995b) extrapolates past progress and concludes that 1500 to 10000 bits are needed for a number (used in a cryptosystem) to be safe against factoring attempts.

20.3. McCurley (1990) gives an overview on discrete logarithm algorithms. Maurer & Wolf (1999) reduce DL to DH in some special cases.

20.4. ElGamal (1985) gives his cryptosystem. Fast exponentiation in finite fields $\mathbb{F}_{2^n}$ can be achieved using Gauß periods, normal bases, and fast arithmetic (Gao, von zur Gathen & Panario 1995, 1998, von zur Gathen & Nöcker 1997).

20.6. Public key cryptosystems based on elliptic curves were invented by Miller (1986) and Koblitz (1987b). Menezes (1993) presents a comprehensive treatment.

20.7. Ajtai (1996) presents the shortest vector problem which is hard on average, and Ajtai (1997) shows "$\mathcal{NP}$-hardness". This is under probabilistic polynomial-time reductions rather than the usual deterministic reduction for standard $\mathcal{NP}$-hardness. As long as $\mathcal{BPP} \neq \mathcal{NP}$ is considered about as likely as $\mathcal{P} \neq \mathcal{NP}$, this difference does not matter much. Goldreich, Goldwasser & Halevi (1997) give a material improvement to the Ajtai & Dwork cryptosystem.

Exercises.

20.1 As in Section 20.1, we identify the letters $A, B, C, \ldots, Z$ with the elements $0, 1, 2, \ldots, 25$ of $\mathbb{Z}_{26}$.

(i) The word "OAYBGFQD" is the result of an encryption with a Caesar cipher, which maps each letter $x \in \mathbb{Z}_{26}$ to $x + k$, where $k \in \mathbb{Z}_{26}$ is the key. What are the cleartext and the key?

(ii) The word "MLSELVY" is the ciphertext after encryption with the one-time pad using the key "IAMAKEY". Find the cleartext.

20.2$\overset{\rightarrow}{}$ This exercise is about a variant of the following password encryption scheme suggested by Purdy (1974), before the advent of public-key cryptography (Diffie & Hellman 1976). Let $p = 2^{64} - 59$, which is the largest prime below our processor's assumed word length 2^{64}, encode a 13-letter password w^* over the 26-letter alphabet $\{A, B, \ldots, Z\}$ as a number w using 26-adic notation, and consider $w \in \mathbb{F}_p$. This makes sense, since $26^{13} < p$. Then w is encrypted as $f(w) \in \mathbb{F}_p$, where

$$f = x^{2^{24}+17} + a_1 x^{2^{24}+3} + a_2 x^3 + a_3 x^2 + a_4 x + a_5 \in \mathbb{F}_p[x],$$

for some specific values $a_1, \ldots, a_5 \in \mathbb{F}_p$. The pairs (login-name, f(password)) are stored in a public file. When a user logs on and types in her password w^*, $f(w)$ is calculated and checked against the entry in the file.

(i) Let $a_1 = 2$, $a_2 = 37$, $a_3 = -42$, $a_4 = 15$, $a_5 = 7$, and $w^* = $ RUMPELSTILTZK. Calculate w and $f(w)$.

(ii) How many arithmetic operations in $\mathbb{F}_p$ are used to calculate $f(w)$ from w?

(iii) Let $v \in \mathbb{F}_p$. The core of the algorithm in Exercise 14.20, which calculates $\{w \in \mathbb{F}_p : f(w) = v\}$, is the computation of x^p rem f. Extrapolating the timings from Figure 9.10, you may assume that one multiplication modulo f can be done in about one hour. Since f is sparse, the reduction modulo f is inexpensive. How long does the computation of x^p rem f take approximately? What do you conclude about the security of this system (on today's computers)?

20.3* (Kozen & Landau 1989, von zur Gathen 1990a) Let F be a field and $f \in F[x]$ of degree n. A **functional decomposition** of f is given by two polynomials $g, h \in F[x]$ of degrees at least two such that $f = g \circ h = g(h)$. If no such decomposition exists, then f is **indecomposable**. Obviously a necessary condition for the existence of a decomposition is that n be composite.

(i) Let $f = g \circ h$ be a functional decomposition and $c, d \in F$ with $c \neq 0$. Show that $f = g(cx+d) \circ (h-d)/c$ is also a functional decomposition. Find a functional decomposition $f/\text{lc}(f) = g^* \circ h^*$ into monic polynomials $g^*, h^* \in F[x]$, with the same degrees as g, h, and such that $h^*(0) = 0$. We call such a decomposition **normal**.

(ii) Let $f = g \circ h$ be a normal decomposition, $r = \deg g$, $s = \deg h$, and $f^* = \text{rev}(f) = x^n f(x^{-1})$ and $h^* = \text{rev}(h) = x^s h(x^{-1})$ the reversals of f and h, respectively. Prove that $f^* \equiv (h^*)^r \mod x^s$.

(iii) Let $f = g_1 \circ h_1$ be another normal decomposition with $r = \deg g_1$ and $s = \deg h_1$. Prove that $h = h_1$ and $g = g_1$. Hint: Uniqueness of Newton iteration (Theorem 9.27).

(iv) Consider the following algorithm, which works even over rings.
▬▬▬ ALGORITHM 20.4 Functional decomposition of polynomials. ▬▬▬▬▬▬▬▬▬▬▬▬▬▬▬▬▬
Input: A monic polynomial $f \in R[x]$ of degree $n > 3$ and a nontrivial divisor r of n, where R is a ring (commutative, with 1) of characteristic coprime to r.
Output: Either a normal decomposition $f = g \circ h$ with $g, h \in R[x]$ and $\deg g = r$, or "no such decomposition".

1. $f^* \longleftarrow \text{rev}(f)$, $s \longleftarrow n/r$
   { compute rth root of f^* via Newton iteration }
   call the Newton iteration algorithm 9.22 to compute $h^* \in R[x]$ of degree less than s with $h^*(0) = 1$ and $(h^*)^r \equiv f^* \mod x^s$
   $h \longleftarrow x^s h^*(x^{-1})$

2. **call** Algorithm 9.14 to compute the h-adic expansion $f = h^r + g_{r-1}h^{r-1} + \cdots + g_1 h + g_0$ of f, with $g_{r-1}, \ldots, g_0 \in R[x]$ of degrees less than s

3. **if** $g_i \in R$ for all i **then return** $g = x^r + \sum_{0 \leq i < r} g_i x^i$ and h
   else return "no such decomposition" ▬▬▬▬▬▬▬▬▬▬▬▬▬▬▬▬▬▬▬▬▬▬▬▬▬

Prove that the algorithm works correctly, and show that it takes $O(\mathsf{M}(n) \log r)$ additions and multiplications in R. What goes wrong if $\gcd(r, \text{char} R) > 1$?

(v) Apply the algorithm to find a decomposition of $f = x^6 + x^5 + 2x^4 + 3x^3 + 3x^2 + x + 1 \in \mathbb{F}_5[x]$.

20.4 Let $N = 8051 = 97 \cdot 83$.

(i) The public key in a RSA cryptosystem is $K = (N, e) = (8051, 3149)$. Find the corresponding secret key $S = (N, d)$.

(ii) A message x has been encrypted using K, and the resulting ciphertext is 694. What is x?

20.5 Let $p, q \in \mathbb{N}$ be distinct primes, $N = pq$, $K = (N, e)$ the public key, and $S = (N, d)$ the secret key in a RSA cryptosystem, such that $d, e \in \mathbb{N}$ satisfy $de \equiv 1 \bmod \varphi(N)$.

(i) In Section 20.2, we have assumed that messages x to be encrypted are coprime to N. Prove that the RSA scheme also works if this condition is violated. Hint: Chinese Remainder Theorem.

(ii) Show that the intruder Eve, who has intercepted the ciphertext $\varepsilon(x)$ but does not know the secret key S, can easily break the system if x is not coprime to N.

20.6* In this exercise, you are to prove Theorem 20.1. So let $N = pq$ for two distinct primes $p, q \in \mathbb{N}$.

(i) Show how to compute p, q from the knowledge of N and $\varphi(N)$. Hint: Consider the quadratic polynomial $(x - p)(x - q) \in \mathbb{Z}[x]$.

(ii) Suppose that you are given a black box which on input $e \in \mathbb{N}$ decides whether it is coprime to $\varphi(N)$, and if so, returns $d \in \{1, \ldots, \varphi(N) - 1\}$ such that $de \equiv 1 \bmod \varphi(N)$. Give an algorithm using this black box which computes $\varphi(N)$ in time $(\log N)^{O(1)}$. Hint: Find a "small" e coprime to $\varphi(N)$.

20.7$\longrightarrow$ (i) Program a procedure key_generate that generates a pair (K, S) of keys for the RSA cryptosystem, such that $K = (N, e)$ is the public key, $S = (N, d)$ is the secret key, N is the product of two random 100 bit prime numbers, $e \in \{2, \ldots \varphi(N) - 2\}$ is chosen uniformly at random, and $d \in \{2, \ldots, \varphi(N) - 2\}$ satisfies $de \equiv 1 \bmod \varphi(N)$.

(ii) Design a coding for short strings of English words with at most 30 letters, including punctuation marks, parentheses, and blanks, as integers between 0 and $N - 1$, and write corresponding procedures encode and decode.

(iii) Write a procedure crypt for encrypting and decrypting with the RSA cryptosystem. Its arguments should be a number in $\mathbb{Z}_N$ and a key.

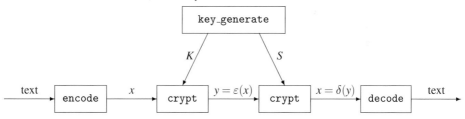

(iv) Check your programs with sample messages of your choice, and produce some timings.

Research problems.

20.8 Reduce (in probabilistic polynomial time) factoring integers to breaking RSA (or some other cryptosystem).

20.9 Reduce DL to DH in polynomial time.

Part V
Hilbert

David Hilbert (1862–1943) grew up in Königsberg, then capital of East Prussia and now Kaliningrad in Russia, in an upper middle-class family; his father was a judge. The town had been home to the philosopher Immanuel Kant, to Leonard Euler, whose solution to the riddle of how to cross its seven bridges across the river Pregel without re-using one became a starting point for graph theory and topology, and to C. G. J. Jacobi.

After an unimpressive school career, he studied at the university to graduate with his doctoral thesis on invariant theory in 1885. He worked in this area until 1893, proving among other things the *Hilbert basis theorem* saying that any ideal in a polynomial ring (in finitely many variables over a field) is finitely generated (Theorem 21.23), and introducing the *Hilbert function* of algebraic varieties.

Two further results from his "multivariate polynomial phase" are relevant to the subject matter of this text: firstly *Hilbert's Nullstellensatz*[1] (1890), which says that if a polynomial g vanishes on the set of common roots of some multivariate polynomials $f_1, \ldots, f_s$ over $\mathbb{C}$, then some power g^e is in the ideal $\langle f_1, \ldots, f_s \rangle$ (see Section 21.7). Secondly, *Hilbert's irreducibility theorem* (1892), stating that for an irreducible polynomial $f \in \mathbb{Q}[x, y]$, the univariate polynomial $f(x, a) \in \mathbb{Q}[x]$ is irreducible for "most" $a \in \mathbb{Z}$. This sounds useful for reducing bivariate to univariate factorization. Unfortunately, no efficient versions of "most" are known, but, fortunately, such versions are known for reducing from many to two variables (Section 16.6).

Hilbert became a professor at the university of Göttingen in 1895. Under his leadership and that of Felix Klein, its fame, established by Gauß, as a center for mathematics kept growing. Among their famous colleagues were Hermann Minkowski, Ernst Zermelo, Constantin Carathéodory, Emmy Noether, Hermann Weyl, Carl Runge, Richard Courant, Edmund Landau, Alexander Ostrowski, Carl Ludwig Siegel, and Bartel van der Waerden, who based his *Modern Algebra* (1930b, 1931) on Emmy Noether's Göttingen lectures.

Hilbert's *Zahlbericht*[2], commissioned by the *Deutsche Mathematiker-Vereinigung*[3], gave a rich overview of the state of algebraic number theory and led him to a vast and elegant generalization of Gauß' quadratic reciprocity law and to the *Hilbert class field theory*.

His next area of work culminated in the booklet *Grundlagen der Geometrie*[4], where he laid down the basic properties that a "nice" system of axioms should have: soundness, completeness, and independence.

[1] Nullstelle = root
[2] Report on [the theory of] numbers
[3] German Mathematical Society
[4] Foundations of Geometry

Then came what turned out to be his most influential "work": his talk on August 8, 1900, at the International Congress of Mathematicians in Paris (Hilbert 1900). He began with: *Wer von uns würde nicht gern den Schleier lüften, unter dem die Zukunft verborgen liegt, um einen Blick zu werfen auf die bevorstehenden Fortschritte unserer Wissenschaft und in die Geheimnisse ihrer Entwicklung während der künftigen Jahrhunderte!*[5], and ended with the list of the 23 *Hilbert problems*. As intended, this set of problems shaped the mathematics of the next century, and those who contributed to a solution would be said to belong to the "honors class" of mathematicians.

Hilbert liked lecturing, and excelled at it. He usually prepared only an outline of his lecture and filled in the details in front of the students—so he got stuck and confused everybody at times, but "a third of his lectures were superb". He was *Doktorvater* to the impressive number of 69 doctoral students, and this *Hilbert school* spread his approach to mathematics around the world.

Hilbert could be funny and entertaining at social events, loved dancing, and was a successful charmer of the ladies. His unprejudiced and liberal thinking led to a clash with the German authorities when he refused to sign, at the beginning of World War I, a declaration supporting the Kaiser and his government. At the beginning of the next German catastrophe, the Nazis forced in 1933 almost all Jewish professors out of their positions (and brutally worse was to come). Constance Reid (1970) relates in her wonderful biography how the Nazi minister of education said to Hilbert at a banquet in 1933 that mathematical life in

[5] Who of us would not be glad to lift the veil behind which the future lies hidden, to cast a glance at the next advances of our science and at the secrets of its development during future centuries!

Göttingen probably had not suffered from being freed of Jewish influence. Hilbert's reply: *Jelitten? Das hat nicht jelitten, das jibt es nicht mehr.*[6]

After work on the Dirichlet Principle, Waring's Problem, the transcendence of e and π, integral equations, Hilbert spaces (*spectral theory*), calculus of variations, and a less successful attempt at laying the foundations of modern physics, Hilbert returned to logic and the foundations of mathematics in the 1920s. The 19th century philosopher Emil du Bois-Reymond had pointed to the limits of our understanding of nature: *ignoramus et ignorabimus*[7]. Hilbert was strongly opposed to this scepticism (*in der Mathematik gibt es kein ignorabimus*[8]) and set himself the goal of formalizing mathematics in a symbolic way, as pioneered by Gottlob Frege, and Bertrand Russell and Alfred North Whitehead. Alas, Hilbert's program was proved to be infeasible on this point by Kurt Gödel and Alan Turing; see Section 14.6 for the interesting juxtaposition of Hilbert's belief and a precocious undecidability result in polynomial factorization by van der Waerden. Although that particular goal of Hilbert's turned out to be unattainable, the ideas he introduced into proof theory and symbolic logic are alive and well today; see Section 24.1 for a small example. In fact, modern programming languages realize, in some sense, Hilbert's program of formalizing mathematics and science.

In the last decade of Hilbert's life, his health—including his mental facilities—deteriorated, and he led a secluded life. He died in February 1943, of the long-term effects of a fall. By then, the war had his country in its grip, and only a miserable procession of a dozen people accompanied the great mathematician on his last trip.

---

[6] Suffered? It did not suffer, it does not exist any more.
[7] we do not know and we shall not know
[8] in mathematics there is no ignorabimus [quoted from his 1900 lecture.]

Tant que l'Algèbre et la Géométrie ont été séparées, leurs progrès
ont été lents et leurs usages bornés; mais lorsque ces deux sciences
se sont réunies, elles se sont prêté des forces mutuelles
et ont marché ensemble d'un pas rapide vers la perfection.[1]

Joseph Louis Lagrange (1795)

À la vérité le travail qu'il faudra faire pour trouver
ce diviseur, sera de nature, dans plusieurs cas,
à rebuter le Calculateur le plus intrépide. [...] Dans un travail
aussi long que l'est souvent celui de l'élimination,
il n'est pas inutile de multiplier les méthodes
sur lesquelles les Calculateurs peuvent porter leur choix.[2]

Étienne Bézout (1764)

The theory of modular systems is very incomplete and offers
a wide field for research. The object of the algebraic theory is
to discover those general properties of a module [polynomial ideal]
which will afford a means of answering the question
whether a given polynomial is a member of a given module or not.
Such a question in its simpler aspect is of importance in Geometry
and in its general aspect is of importance in Algebra.

Francis Sowerby Macaulay (1916)

---

[1] As long as algebra and geometry proceeded separately, their progress was slow and their application limited; but when these two sciences joined forces, they mutually strengthened each other, and marched together at a rapid pace toward perfection.

[2] Actually the effort required to find this divisor will, in several cases, be so large as to discourage the most intrepid Computer. [...] In an undertaking that is as hard as elimination often is, it is not useless to multiply the methods between which Computers can make their choice.

21

Gröbner bases

In this chapter, we present an important algorithmic approach to dealing with polynomials in several variables. Hironaka (1964) introduced in his work on resolution of singularities over $\mathbb{C}$—for which he received the Fields medal, the "Nobel prize" in mathematics—a special type of basis for polynomial ideals, called "standard basis". Bruno Buchberger (1965) invented them independently in his Ph. D. thesis, and named them **Gröbner bases** after his thesis advisor Wolfgang Gröbner. They are a vital tool in modern computational algebraic geometry.

We start with two examples, one from robotics and one illustrating "automatic" proofs of theorems in geometry. We then introduce the basic notions of orders on monomials and the resulting division algorithm. Next come two important theorems, by Dickson and by Hilbert, that guarantee finite bases for certain ideals. Then we can define Gröbner bases and Buchberger's algorithm to compute them.

The end of this chapter presents two "geometric" applications: implicitization of algebraic varieties and solution of systems of polynomial equations. While these fall naturally into the realm of manipulating polynomials, the examples in Sections 24.1 and 24.2 below are less expected: logical proof systems and analysis of parallel processes. We cannot even mention numerous other applications, for example, in tiling problems and term rewriting. We finish with some facts—without proof—on the cost of computing Gröbner bases.

21.1. Polynomial ideals

We begin with two examples that illustrate the kind of problems that can be solved with the help of Gröbner bases.

EXAMPLE 21.1. Figure 21.1 shows a very simple robot, one-armed with two joints. The arm is fixed at one end with a joint to a point (say, the origin of the Cartesian plane), and has another joint in the middle. The distance between the two joints is 2, the joint between the two arms is in position (x, y), and the distance from the second joint to the endpoint, at position (z, w), is 1. Furthermore, there

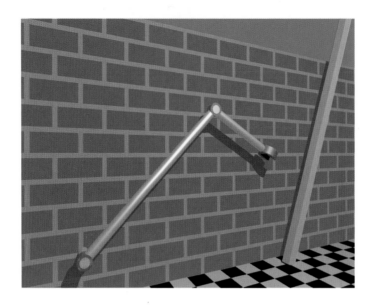

FIGURE 21.1: A two-segment robot.

is a line $L = \{(u, \lambda u + \mu) : u \in \mathbb{R}\}$ with some fixed parameters $\lambda, \mu \in \mathbb{R}$. A simple question is: can the robot reach the line? The possible positions $(x, y, z, w) \in \mathbb{R}^4$ of the robot are characterized by the algebraic equations

$$x^2 + y^2 = 4 \text{ and } (z - x)^2 + (w - y)^2 = 1, \tag{1}$$

and an answer to the question is either a quadruple (x, y, z, w) satisfying (1) and the additional equation $w = \lambda z + \mu$, or a proof that no such quadruple exists. $\diamond$

EXAMPLE 21.2. A well-known geometric theorem says that the three medians of a triangle intersect at one point, the center of gravity of the triangle, and that the intersection point trisects each median (Figure 21.2). We now formulate this as a problem about multivariate polynomials. Since the assumptions and the conclusion of the theorem are invariant under translation, rotation, and scaling, we may assume that two of the vertices of the triangle are $A = (0,0)$ and $B = (1,0)$, and the third point is $C = (x, y)$, with arbitrary $x, y \in \mathbb{R}$. Then the midpoints of the three edges BC, AC, and AB are $P = ((x+1)/2, y/2)$, $Q = (x/2, y/2)$, and $R = (1/2, 0)$, respectively. We let $S = (u, v)$ be the intersection point of the two medians AP and BQ. (If $y = 0$, then these two lines coincide.) The condition that S lies on AP is equivalent to saying that AS and AP have the same slope, so that

$$\frac{u}{v} = \frac{x+1}{y},$$

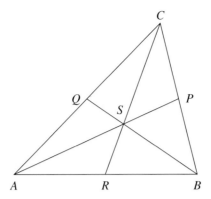

FIGURE 21.2: The three medians AP, BQ, and CR of a triangle ABC intersect at the center of gravity S.

or, after clearing denominators,

$$f_1 = uy - v(x+1) = 0.$$

Similarly, the condition that S lies on BQ can be expressed as

$$f_2 = (u-1)y - v(x-2) = 0.$$

The claims now are that S also lies on the third median CR, or

$$g_1 = -2(u-x)y - (v-y)(1-2x) = -2uy - (v-y) + 2vx = 0,$$

and that S trisects each of the three medians, so that

$$(u,v) = AS = 2SP = (x+1-2u, y-2v),$$
$$(u-1,v) = BS = 2SQ = (x-2u, y-2v),$$
$$(u-x,v-y) = CS = 2SR = (2u-1, 2v),$$

or equivalently,

$$g_2 = 3u - x - 1 = 0 \text{ and } g_3 = 3v - y = 0.$$

A short computation shows that $g_1 = -f_1 - f_2$, so that $g_1 = 0$ follows from $f_1 = f_2 = 0$, which establishes that the three medians intersect indeed in S. We will continue this example in Section 21.6. $\diamond$

Let F be a field, $R = F[x_1, \ldots, x_n]$ a polynomial ring in n variables over F, and $f_1, \ldots, f_s \in R$. The polynomials $f_1, \ldots, f_s$ **generate** (or form a **basis** of) the ideal

$$I = \langle f_1, \ldots, f_s \rangle = \left\{ \sum_{1 \leq i \leq s} q_i f_i : q_i \in R \right\}$$

(not to be confused with the *sequence* $(f_1, \ldots, f_s)$), and

$$V(I) = \{u \in F^n : f(u) = 0 \text{ for all } f \in I\} = \{u \in F^n : f_1(u) = \cdots = f_s(u) = 0\}$$

is the **variety of I**. We also write $V(f_1, \ldots, f_s)$ instead of $V(\langle f_1, \ldots, f_s \rangle)$ for short. Interesting questions about I include:

o Is $V(I) \neq \emptyset$?

o How "big" is $V(I)$?

o Ideal membership problem: given $f \in R$, is $f \in I$?

o Triviality: Is $I = R$?

EXAMPLE 21.2 (continued). In Example 21.2, we have seen that

$$f_3 = -f_1 - f_2 \in \langle f_1, f_2 \rangle \subseteq \mathbb{R}[u, v, x, y],$$

and used this to prove that $V(f_1, f_2) \subseteq V(f_3)$.

The other conclusion of the theorem is that S trisects each median, so that $AS = 2SP$, $BS = 2SQ$, and $CS = 2SR$, or equivalently,

$$\begin{pmatrix} u - (x + 1 - 2u) \\ v - (y - 2v) \end{pmatrix} = \begin{pmatrix} u - 1 - (x - 2u) \\ v - (y - 2v) \end{pmatrix} = \begin{pmatrix} u - x - (1 - 2u) \\ v - y + 2v \end{pmatrix} = \begin{pmatrix} 0 \\ 0 \end{pmatrix},$$

which boils down to

$$f_4 = 3u - x - 1 = 0 \text{ and } f_5 = 3v - y = 0.$$

If we can show that also $f_4, f_5 \in V(f_1, f_2)$, then this concludes the proof of the theorem. $\diamond$

EXAMPLE 21.3. (i) Let $f_1 = x^2 + y^2 - 1$ and $f_2 = y - 2$ in $R = \mathbb{R}[x, y]$, and $I = \langle f_1, f_2 \rangle$. Then

$$V(I) = \{(u, v) \in \mathbb{R}^2 : u^2 + v^2 - 1 = v - 2 = 0\} = \{(u, 2) \in \mathbb{R}^2 : u^2 = -3\} = \emptyset$$

is the intersection of the circle $V(x^2 + y^2 - 1)$ with the line $V(y - 2)$ (see Figure 21.3), which is empty over $\mathbb{R}$. If we regard f_1, f_2 as polynomials in $\mathbb{C}[x, y]$ and consider their variety over the complex numbers, then

$$V(I) = \{(u, 2) \in \mathbb{C}^2 : u^2 = -3\} = \{(\sqrt{3}i, 2), (-\sqrt{3}i, 2)\}$$

consists of two points, where $i = \sqrt{-1} \in \mathbb{C}$.

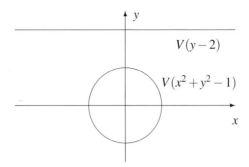

FIGURE 21.3: A circle and a line in $\mathbb{R}^2$.

(ii) Let $f = (y^2+6)(x-1) - y(x^2+1)$, $g = (x^2+6)(y-1) - x(y^2+1)$, $h = (x-5/2)^2 + (y-5/2)^2 - 1/2$ in $\mathbb{C}[x,y]$, and $I = \langle f, g \rangle$. We have seen in Example 6.41 that $V(I)$, the intersection of the two plane curves $V(f)$ and $V(g)$, consists of the six points

$$V(I) = \left\{ (2,2), (2,3), (3,2), (3,3), \left(\frac{1 \pm \sqrt{15}i}{2}, \frac{1 \mp \sqrt{15}i}{2} \right) \right\} \subseteq \mathbb{C}^2. \qquad (2)$$

A short calculation shows that $h = -f - g \in I$, and hence h vanishes at all points of $V(I)$ as well. Figure 6.3 shows the three curves $V(f)$, $V(g)$, $V(h)$, and their four real intersection points.

Now let $h^* = x^2+y^2-5x-5y+11 \in \mathbb{C}[x,y]$. Then $V(h^*) \cap \mathbb{R}$ is a circle centered at $(5/2, 5/2)$ with a bigger radius than that of $V(h)$, and it contains none of the points in $V(I)$. Thus h^* does not belong to I. In fact, we have $-f - g - h^* = 1$ in $\mathbb{C}[x,y]$, and hence $\langle f, g, h^* \rangle = \mathbb{C}[x,y]$ and $V(f,g,h^*) = \emptyset$. Indeed, any common root of f, g, h would also be a "root" of 1. Hilbert's famous **Nullstellensatz** (see Section 21.7) states that such a certificate always exists: when J is an ideal with $V(J) = \emptyset$, then $1 \in J$. This is true over $\mathbb{C}$, and any algebraically closed field, but, as (i) shows, not over $\mathbb{R}$. ◇

The structure of these varieties is the subject of *algebraic geometry*, a deep mathematical theory whose most recent success is the solution of the 350–year old Fermat problem (page 488). We give a few pointers to the recent exciting work in *computational algebraic geometry* at the end of this chapter. A **Gröbner basis** of I is a special "basis" for I, in which these questions are easy to answer. Everything is easy in the case $n = 1$: Since $F[x]$ is a Euclidean domain (Chapter 3), we have

$$\langle f_1, \ldots, f_s \rangle = \langle \gcd(f_1, \ldots, f_s) \rangle \qquad (3)$$

(Exercise 21.3), so that we may assume $s = 1$. Now we let $f, g \in F[x]$ and divide f by g with remainder, yielding $q, r \in F[x]$ with $f = qg + r$ and $\deg r < \deg g$. Then

$$f \in \langle g \rangle \iff r = 0, \qquad (4)$$

and $V(g) = \{u_1, \ldots, u_s\}$ if $x - u_1, \ldots, x - u_d$ are the distinct linear factors of g in $F[x]$. Equation (3) is no longer true in the case of two variables or more. For example, $\gcd(x, y) = 1$ in $F[x, y]$, but $\langle x, y \rangle$ is different from $\langle 1 \rangle = F[x, y]$ (Exercise 21.1). Much of the effort of Gröbner bases goes into restoring some of these apparently lost properties, such as division with remainder.

21.2. Monomial orders and multivariate division with remainder

We introduce an analog of division with remainder in the case of many variables. In order to do that, we have to say what the "leading term" of a polynomial should be in the general case.

A **partial order** $<$ on a set S is an irreflexive and transitive relation, so that

$$\text{not } (\alpha < \alpha) \text{ and } \alpha < \beta < \gamma \Longrightarrow \alpha < \gamma \text{ for all } \alpha, \beta, \gamma \in S.$$

These conditions imply that $<$ is asymmetric: $((\alpha < \beta) \text{ and } (\beta < \alpha))$ is always false (Exercise 21.7). A partial order is a **total order** (or simply order) if either $\alpha = \beta$ or $\alpha < \beta$ or $\beta < \alpha$, for all $\alpha, \beta \in S$, and is a **well-order** if in addition every nonempty subset of S has a least element. If $<$ is a partial order, we write $\alpha \leq \beta$ if $\alpha < \beta$ or $\alpha = \beta$, and $\alpha > \beta$ or $\alpha \geq \beta$ if $\beta < \alpha$ or $\beta \leq \alpha$, respectively. For example, the familiar orders $<$ on $\mathbb{N}, \mathbb{Z}, \mathbb{Q}, \mathbb{R}$ are total, but only the first one is a well-order. The inclusion $\subseteq$ on the set $2^{\mathbb{N}}$ of subsets of $\mathbb{N}$ is a partial order, but not total.

We identify the vector $\alpha = (\alpha_1, \ldots, \alpha_n) \in \mathbb{N}^n$ with the monomial

$$x^\alpha = x_1^{\alpha_1} \cdots x_n^{\alpha_n} \in R.$$

DEFINITION 21.4. *A **monomial order** in $R = F[x_1, \ldots, x_n]$ is a relation $\prec$ on $\mathbb{N}^n$ such that*

(i) $\prec$ is a total order,

(ii) $\alpha \prec \beta \Longrightarrow \alpha + \gamma \prec \beta + \gamma$ for all $\alpha, \beta, \gamma \in \mathbb{N}^n$,

(iii) $\prec$ is a well-order.

Under the above identification, this gives an order on the monomials in R. If $n = 1$, for example, the natural order on $\mathbb{N} = \mathbb{N}^1$ is a monomial order, and the corresponding univariate monomials are ordered by their degree.

If (i) holds, then (iii) is equivalent to the condition that there be no infinite descending chain $\alpha_1 \succ \alpha_2 \succ \alpha_3 \succ \cdots$ in $\mathbb{N}^n$.

EXAMPLE 21.5. Here are three standard examples of monomial orders:

(i) **Lexicographic order**:

$$\alpha \prec_{\text{lex}} \beta \iff \text{the leftmost nonzero entry in } \alpha - \beta \text{ is negative.}$$

For example, if $n = 3$, $\alpha_1 = (0,4,0)$, $\alpha_2 = (1,1,2)$, $\alpha_3 = (1,2,1)$, and $\alpha_4 = (3,0,0)$, then $\alpha_1 \prec_{\text{lex}} \alpha_2 \prec_{\text{lex}} \alpha_3 \prec_{\text{lex}} \alpha_4$.

(ii) **Graded lexicographic order**: Let $\alpha = (\alpha_1, \ldots, \alpha_n), \beta = (\beta_1, \ldots, \beta_n) \in \mathbb{N}^n$. Then

$$\alpha \prec_{\text{grlex}} \beta \iff \sum_{1 \leq i \leq n} \alpha_i < \sum_{1 \leq i \leq n} \beta_i \text{ or } \left(\sum_{1 \leq i \leq n} \alpha_i = \sum_{1 \leq i \leq n} \beta_i \text{ and } \alpha \prec_{\text{lex}} \beta \right).$$

With $\alpha_1, \ldots, \alpha_4$ as above, we have $\alpha_4 \prec_{\text{grlex}} \alpha_1 \prec_{\text{grlex}} \alpha_2 \prec_{\text{grlex}} \alpha_3$.

(iii) **Graded reverse lexicographic order**:

$$\alpha \prec_{\text{grevlex}} \beta \iff \sum_{1 \leq i \leq n} \alpha_i < \sum_{1 \leq i \leq n} \beta_i \text{ or } \left(\sum_{1 \leq i \leq n} \alpha_i = \sum_{1 \leq i \leq n} \beta_i \text{ and the} \right.$$

$$\left. \text{rightmost nonzero entry in } \alpha - \beta \in \mathbb{Z}^n \text{ is positive} \right).$$

Then $\alpha_4 \prec_{\text{grevlex}} \alpha_2 \prec_{\text{grevlex}} \alpha_3 \prec_{\text{grevlex}} \alpha_1$, with $\alpha_1, \ldots, \alpha_4$ as before. $\diamond$

In all three examples, the variables (that is, the monomials of degree one) are ordered as $x_1 \succ x_2 \succ \ldots \succ x_{n-1} \succ x_n$. "Graded" refers to the fact that the total degree $\sum \alpha_i$ is the main criterion. In the case $n = 1$, we have $\prec_{\text{lex}} = \prec_{\text{grlex}} = \prec_{\text{grevlex}}$.

Once we have a monomial order on R, we can sort terms of a polynomial according to $\prec$.

EXAMPLE 21.5 (continued). Let $f = 4xyz^2 + 4x^3 - 5y^4 + 7xy^2z \in \mathbb{Q}[x,y,z]$ (we always identify x, y, z with x_1, x_2, x_3). Then the orders of f with respect to $\prec_{\text{lex}}$, $\prec_{\text{grlex}}$, and $\prec_{\text{grevlex}}$ are: $4x^3 + 7xy^2z + 4xyz^2 - 5y^4$, $7xy^2z + 4xyz^2 - 5y^4 + 4x^3$, and $-5y^4 + 7xy^2z + 4xyz^2 + 4x^3$, respectively. $\diamond$

THEOREM 21.6.

$\prec_{\text{lex}}$, $\prec_{\text{grlex}}$, *and* $\prec_{\text{grevlex}}$, *are monomial orders.*

PROOF. The proof is a simple check; we give some details only for $\prec_{\text{grevlex}}$. We omit the verification that $\prec_{\text{grevlex}}$ is a partial order. For each $\alpha, \beta \in \mathbb{N}^n$ with $\alpha \neq \beta$, we have either $\sum_{1 \leq i \leq n} \alpha_i < \sum_{1 \leq i \leq n} \beta_i$, or $\sum_{1 \leq i \leq n} \beta_i < \sum_{1 \leq i \leq n} \alpha_i$, or $\sum_{1 \leq i \leq n} \alpha_i = \sum_{1 \leq i \leq n} \beta_i$, and in the last case either the rightmost nonzero entry in $\alpha - \beta$ is positive or the rightmost nonzero entry in $\beta - \alpha$ is positive. Thus $\prec_{\text{grevlex}}$ is total.

For condition (ii), we have

$$\sum_{1 \leq i \leq n} \alpha_i < \sum_{1 \leq i \leq n} \beta_i \iff \sum_{1 \leq i \leq n} (\alpha_i + \gamma_i) < \sum_i (\beta_i + \gamma_i),$$

and similarly for "$=$", and $\alpha - \beta = (\alpha + \gamma) - (\beta + \gamma)$. For condition (iii), if $S \subseteq \mathbb{N}^n$ is nonempty and $T \subseteq S$ the set of monomials of smallest total degree in S, then T is finite (since for any $m \in \mathbb{N}$ there are only finitely many monomials of total degree m) and $\min T = \min S$. $\square$

The antilexicographic order $\prec_{\mathrm{alex}}$ on $\mathbb{N}^2$, with $\alpha \prec_{\mathrm{alex}} \beta \iff \beta \prec_{\mathrm{lex}} \alpha$, is an example where condition (iii) is violated: $S = \mathbb{N} \times \{0\}$ has no smallest element, since $(0,0) \succ_{\mathrm{alex}} (1,0) \succ_{\mathrm{alex}} (2,0) \succ_{\mathrm{alex}} \cdots$.

DEFINITION 21.7. *Let $f = \sum_{\alpha \in \mathbb{N}^n} c_\alpha x^\alpha \in R$ be a nonzero polynomial with all $c_\alpha \in F$ (only finitely many nonzero), and $\prec$ a monomial order.*

(i) *Each $c_\alpha x^\alpha$ with $c_\alpha \neq 0$ is a **term** of f.*

(ii) *The **multidegree** of f is $\mathrm{mdeg}(f) = \max_\prec \{\alpha \in \mathbb{N}^n : c_\alpha \neq 0\}$, where $\max_\prec$ is the maximum with respect to $\prec$.*

(iii) *The **leading coefficient** of f is $\mathrm{lc}(f) = c_{\mathrm{mdeg}(f)} \in F \setminus \{0\}$.*

(iv) *The **leading monomial** of f is $\mathrm{lm}(f) = x^{\mathrm{mdeg}(f)} \in R$.*

(v) *The **leading term** of f is $\mathrm{lt}(f) = \mathrm{lc}(f) \cdot \mathrm{lm}(f) \in R$.*

EXAMPLE 21.5 (continued). To illustrate these notions, we take the polynomial $f = 4xyz^2 + 4x^3 - 5y^4 + 7xy^2z \in \mathbb{Q}[x,y,z]$ and the three orders from Example 21.5.

	$\prec_{\mathrm{lex}}$	$\prec_{\mathrm{grlex}}$	$\prec_{\mathrm{grevlex}}$
$\mathrm{mdeg}(f)$	$(3,0,0)$	$(1,2,1)$	$(0,4,0)$
$\mathrm{lc}(f)$	4	7	-5
$\mathrm{lm}(f)$	x^3	xy^2z	y^4
$\mathrm{lt}(f)$	$4x^3$	$7xy^2z$	$-5y^4$	$\diamond$

If we wanted to extend these definitions to the zero polynomial, we would formally adjoin the element $-\infty$ to $\mathbb{N}^n$ and let $\mathrm{lt}(0) = \mathrm{lm}(0) = \mathrm{lc}(0) = 0$ and $\mathrm{mdeg}(0) = -\infty$, with the obvious interpretation. Also, $\alpha \preccurlyeq \beta$ means that $\alpha \prec \beta$ or $\alpha = \beta$.

The following lemma is proved in Exercise 21.11.

LEMMA 21.8. *Let $\prec$ be a monomial order on R, and $f, g \in R \setminus \{0\}$.*

(i) $\mathrm{mdeg}(fg) = \mathrm{mdeg}(f) + \mathrm{mdeg}(g)$.

(ii) *If $f + g \neq 0$ then $\mathrm{mdeg}(f + g) \preccurlyeq \max\{\mathrm{mdeg}(f), \mathrm{mdeg}(g)\}$, with equality if $\mathrm{mdeg}(f) \neq \mathrm{mdeg}(g)$.*

Our next goal is an algorithm for division with remainder in R. Given polynomials $f, f_1, \ldots, f_s \in R$, we want to write $f = q_1 f_1 + \ldots + q_s f_s + r$ with $q_1, \ldots, q_s, r$ in R. Before stating the algorithm formally, we give some examples.

EXAMPLE 21.9. Let $\prec = \prec_{\text{lex}}$, $f = xy^2 + 1$, $f_1 = xy + 1$, $f_2 = y + 1$.

	$xy + 1$	$y + 1$
$xy^2 + 1$	y	
$-(xy^2 + y)$		
$-y + 1$		-1
$-(-y - 1)$		
2		

	$xy + 1$	$y + 1$
$xy^2 + 1$		xy
$-(xy^2 + xy)$		
$-xy + 1$		$-x$
$-(-xy - x)$		
$x + 1$		

In the left hand table, division is performed as in the univariate case, with the difference that we have two divisors instead of one. The quotient of the two leading terms that we get in each step is recorded in the column below the respective divisor. In the last line, 2 is not divisible by the leading term of f_1 or f_2, and the process stops. Hence $f = y \cdot f_1 - 1 \cdot f_2 + 2$. Note that there is some non-determinism here because we might as well have chosen f_2 instead of f_1 in the first step; this is illustrated in the right hand table, where we find that $f = 0 \cdot f_1 + (xy - x) \cdot f_2 + (x + 1)$, and no term in $x + 1$ is divisible by $\text{lc}(f_1)$ or $\text{lc}(f_2)$. ◇

EXAMPLE 21.10. Let $\prec = \prec_{\text{lex}}$, $f = x^2 y + xy^2 + y^2$, $f_1 = xy - 1$, $f_2 = y^2 - 1$.

	$xy - 1$	$y^2 - 1$	remainder
$x^2 y + xy^2 + y^2$	x		
$-(x^2 y - x)$			
$xy^2 + x + y^2$	y		
$-(xy^2 - y)$			
$x + y^2 + y$			x
$-x$			
$y^2 + y$		1	
$-(y^2 - 1)$			
$y + 1$			

Here, a phenomenon occurs that cannot happen in the univariate case. In the third step, the leading term x is not divisible by the leading term of f_1 or f_2 and is moved to the remainder column. Afterwards, the division may continue further, and the result is $f = (x + y) \cdot f_1 + 1 \cdot f_2 + (x + y + 1)$. ◇

▬▬ ALGORITHM 21.11 Multivariate division with remainder. ▬▬▬▬▬▬▬▬▬▬▬▬▬
Input: Nonzero polynomials $f, f_1, \ldots, f_s \in R = F[x_1, \ldots, x_n]$, where F is a field, and a monomial order $\prec$ on R.
Output: $q_1, \ldots, q_s, r \in R$ such that $f = q_1 f_1 + \cdots + q_s f_s + r$ and no monomial in r is divisible by any of $\text{lt}(f_1), \ldots, \text{lt}(f_s)$.

1. $r \longleftarrow 0$, $\quad p \longleftarrow f$
   for $i = 1, \ldots, s$ **do** $q_i \longleftarrow 0$

2. **while** $p \neq 0$ **do**

3.   **if** $\mathrm{lt}(f_i)$ divides $\mathrm{lt}(p)$ for some $i \in \{1,\dots,s\}$

        then choose some such i, $q_i \longleftarrow q_i + \dfrac{\mathrm{lt}(p)}{\mathrm{lt}(f_i)}$, $p \longleftarrow p - \dfrac{\mathrm{lt}(p)}{\mathrm{lt}(f_i)} f_i$

        else $r \longleftarrow r + \mathrm{lt}(p)$, $p \longleftarrow p - \mathrm{lt}(p)$

4. **return** $q_1,\dots,q_s,r$.

The following theorem implies the correctness of the algorithm and is proven in Exercise 21.12.

THEOREM 21.12.

Each time the algorithm passes through step 3, the following invariants hold.

  (i) $\mathrm{mdeg}(p) \preccurlyeq \mathrm{mdeg}(f)$ *and* $f = p + q_1 f_1 + \cdots + q_s f_s + r$,

  (ii) $q_i \neq 0 \Longrightarrow \mathrm{mdeg}(q_i f_i) \preccurlyeq \mathrm{mdeg}(f)$ *for* $1 \leq i \leq s$,

 (iii) *no term in r is divisible by any* $\mathrm{lt}(f_i)$.

This kind of division with remainder need not be unique: there may be a choice for the value of i in step 3 when the leading term of f is divisible by more than one $\mathrm{lt}(f_i)$. We have already encountered this in Example 21.9, and here is another one.

EXAMPLE 21.10 (continued). If we choose f_2 instead of f_1 in the second step of Example 21.10, we get

	$xy - 1$	$y^2 - 1$	remainder
$x^2 y + xy^2 + y^2$	x		
$-(xy^2 - x)$			
$xy^2 + x + y^2$		x	
$-(xy^2 - x)$			
$2x + y^2$			$2x$
$-2x$			
y^2		1	
$-(y^2 - 1)$			
1			

and $f = x \cdot f_1 + (x+1) \cdot f_2 + (2x+1)$. $\diamond$

If we make Algorithm 21.11 deterministic by always choosing the smallest possible i in step 3, then the **quotients** $q_1,\dots,q_s$, and the **remainder** r, for which we write

$$r = f \ \mathrm{rem} \ (f_1,\dots,f_s), \tag{5}$$

are uniquely determined. For $s = 1$, division with remainder solves the ideal membership problem: $f \in \langle f_1 \rangle$ holds if and only if the remainder is zero. This fails in general for $s \geq 2$, as the following example shows.

EXAMPLE 21.13. We divide $f = xy^2 - x$ by $f_1 = xy + 1$ and $f_2 = y^2 - 1$:

$$
\begin{array}{c|cc}
 & xy+1 & y^2-1 \\
\hline
xy^2 - x & y & \\
-(xy^2 + y) & & \\
\hline
-x - y & &
\end{array}
$$

so that $f = y \cdot f_1 + 0 \cdot f_2 + (-x - y)$. But on the other hand, $f = 0 \cdot f_1 + x \cdot f_2 + 0$, which shows that $f \in \langle f_1, f_2 \rangle$. ◇

Our goal is now to find a special basis of an arbitrary ideal such that the remainder on division by that basis is unique and thus gives the correct answer to the ideal membership problem, as in (4) for $n = 1$. At first sight, it is not clear whether such a type of basis exists at all.

21.3. Monomial ideals and Hilbert's basis theorem

DEFINITION 21.14. *A **monomial ideal** $I \subseteq R$ is an ideal generated by monomials in R, so that there exists a subset $A \subseteq \mathbb{N}^n$ with*

$$ I = \langle x^A \rangle = \langle \{x^\alpha : \alpha \in A\} \rangle. $$

LEMMA 21.15. *Let $I = \langle x^A \rangle \subseteq R$ be a monomial ideal, and $\beta \in \mathbb{N}^n$. Then*

$$ x^\beta \in I \quad \Longleftrightarrow \quad \exists \alpha \in A \quad x^\alpha \mid x^\beta. $$

PROOF. "$\Longleftarrow$" is clear. Conversely, let $\alpha_1, \ldots, \alpha_s \in A$ and $q_1, \ldots, q_s \in R$ such that $x^\beta = \sum_i q_i x^{\alpha_i}$. Each monomial on the right hand side is divisible by some x^α with $\alpha \in A$, and hence so is the monomial on the left hand side. □

LEMMA 21.16. *Let $I \subseteq R$ be a monomial ideal and $f \in R$. Then the following are equivalent:*

(i) *$f \in I$,*

(ii) *each term of f is in I,*

(iii) *f is an F-linear combination of monomials in I.*

PROOF. (i) $\Longrightarrow$ (ii): As in the proof of Lemma 21.15, a representation $f = \sum_i q_i x^{\alpha_i}$ implies that each monomial of f is divisible by some x^γ, with $\gamma \in A$. The implications (ii) $\Longrightarrow$ (iii) $\Longrightarrow$ (i) are clear, and, in fact, hold for any ideal I. $\square$

For example, if $I = \langle x^3, x^2 y \rangle \subseteq \mathbb{Q}[x, y]$, then the lemma shows that $3x^4 + 5x^2 y^3 \in I$ and $2x^4 y + 7x^2 \notin I$. The implication (i) $\Longrightarrow$ (ii) is false for some ideals, as shown in Example 21.21 below.

COROLLARY 21.17.
Two monomial ideals are identical if and only if they contain the same monomials.

THEOREM 21.18 *Dickson's lemma.*
Every monomial ideal is generated by a finite set of monomials. More precisely, for every $A \subseteq \mathbb{N}^n$ there exists a finite subset $B \subseteq A$ such that $\langle x^A \rangle = \langle x^B \rangle$.

PROOF. Except for its last sentence, our proof is purely combinatorial, without any algebra. The claim is trivial if $A = \emptyset$, and we may assume that A is nonempty. We define a relation "$\leq$" on $\mathbb{N}^n$ by

$$\alpha \leq \beta \iff \alpha_i \leq \beta_i \text{ for } 1 \leq i \leq n,$$

for all $\alpha = (\alpha_1, \ldots, \alpha_n)$ and $\beta = (\beta_1, \ldots, \beta_n)$ in $\mathbb{N}^n$, so that $\alpha \leq \beta$ if and only if $x^\alpha \mid x^\beta$. As usual, we write $\alpha < \beta$ if $\alpha \leq \beta$ and $\alpha \neq \beta$. Then $<$ is a partial order on $\mathbb{N}^n$ which is not total if $n \geq 2$ (for example, we have neither $(1, 0) < (0, 1)$ nor $(1, 0) > (0, 1)$). We now let $B = \{\alpha \in A : \forall \beta \in A \; \beta \not< \alpha\}$ be the set of minimal elements of A with respect to $\leq$, and claim that B is a finite subset of A and

$$\text{for each } \alpha \in A \text{ there exists some } \beta \in B \text{ with } \beta \leq \alpha. \tag{6}$$

For any $\alpha \in \mathbb{N}^n$ there are only finitely many $\beta \in \mathbb{N}^n$ with $\beta \leq \alpha$ (Exercise 21.13), and hence there is no infinite descending chain of elements $\alpha^{(1)} > \alpha^{(2)} > \alpha^{(3)} > \cdots$ in $\mathbb{N}^n$. In particular, for any $\alpha \in A$ there is some minimal element $\beta \in B$ such that $\beta \leq \alpha$.

It remains to show that B is finite, which we prove by induction on n. If $n = 1$, then $<$ is a total order, and B consists of the unique smallest element of A. If $n \geq 2$, we let $A^* = \{(\alpha_1, \ldots, \alpha_{n-1}) \in \mathbb{N}^{n-1} : \exists \alpha_n \in \mathbb{N} \; (\alpha_1, \ldots, \alpha_n) \in A\}$. By the induction hypothesis, the set B^* of minimal elements of A^* is finite. For each $\beta = (\beta_1, \ldots, \beta_{n-1}) \in B^*$, we choose some $b_\beta \in \mathbb{N}$ such that $(\beta_1, \ldots, \beta_{n-1}, b_\beta) \in A$, and let $b = \max\{b_\beta : \beta \in B^*\}$. We claim that every $(\alpha_1, \ldots, \alpha_n) \in B$ has $\alpha_n \leq b$. Let $\alpha = (\alpha_1, \ldots, \alpha_n) \in A$. Then there exists some minimal element $\beta = (\beta_1, \ldots, \beta_{n-1}) \in B^*$ of A^* such that $\beta \leq (\alpha_1, \ldots, \alpha_{n-1})$. If $\alpha_n > b$, then

$$(\beta_1, \ldots, \beta_{n-1}, b_\beta) \leq (\beta_1, \ldots, \beta_{n-1}, b) < \alpha,$$

and α is not minimal. This proves the claim, and similarly we also find that all other coordinates of minimal elements are bounded, which implies that there are only finitely many of them.

Now (6) and the fact that $\alpha \le \beta \iff x^\alpha \mid x^\beta$ imply that $x^A \subseteq \langle x^B \rangle$, whence $\langle x^A \rangle \subseteq \langle x^B \rangle$, and the reverse inclusion follows trivially from $B \subseteq A$. $\square$

EXAMPLE 21.19. Let $n = 2$ and $A = \{(\alpha_1, \alpha_2) \in \mathbb{N}^2 : 6\alpha_2 = \alpha_1^2 - 7\alpha_1 + 18\}$. Then the set of minimal elements is $B = \{(0,3),(1,2),(3,1)\}$, as can be seen from Figure 21.4, and hence $\langle x^A \rangle = \langle y^3, xy^2, x^3y \rangle$. $\diamond$

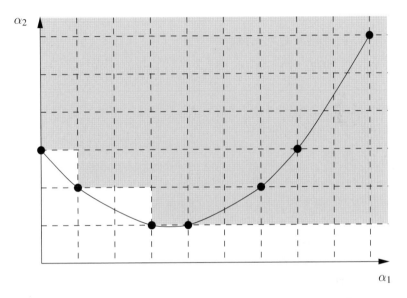

FIGURE 21.4: The monomial ideal $I = \langle x^A \rangle$, where $A = \{(\alpha_1, \alpha_2) \in \mathbb{N}^2 : f(\alpha_1, \alpha_2) = 0\}$ and $f(\alpha_1, \alpha_2) = 6\alpha_2 - \alpha_1^2 + 7\alpha_1 - 18$. The elements of A are marked by a $\bullet$, the black curve is the set of all *real* (α_1, α_2) such that $f(\alpha_1, \alpha_2) = 0$, and a monomial x^α is contained in I if and only if α lies in the grey area.

COROLLARY 21.20.

Let $\prec$ be a total order on $\mathbb{N}^n$ such that

$$\forall \alpha, \beta, \gamma \in \mathbb{N} \quad \alpha \prec \beta \implies \alpha + \gamma \prec \beta + \gamma.$$

Then $\prec$ is a well-order if and only if $\alpha \not\prec 0$ for all $\alpha \in \mathbb{N}^n$.

PROOF. We only prove "$\impliedby$"; the reverse implication is Exercise 21.8. Let $A \subseteq \mathbb{N}^n$ be nonempty, and $I = \langle x^A \rangle \subseteq R$. Then I is finitely generated, by Dickson's lemma, and

$$\exists \alpha_1, \dots, \alpha_s \in A \quad I = \langle x^{\alpha_1}, \dots, x^{\alpha_s} \rangle.$$

We order them so that $\alpha_1 \prec \alpha_2 \prec \cdots \prec \alpha_s$, and claim that $\min_\prec A = \alpha_1$. Let $\alpha \in A$ be arbitrary. Since $x^\alpha \in I$, by Lemma 21.15 there exist $i \leq s$ and $\gamma \in \mathbb{N}^n$ with $\alpha = \alpha_i + \gamma$. Thus $\alpha = \alpha_i + \gamma \succcurlyeq \alpha_1 + \gamma \succcurlyeq \alpha_1 + 0 = \alpha_1$, and hence $\alpha_1 = \min_\prec A$. $\square$

Thus we can replace the condition (iii) in the definition of monomial orders by

(iii)' $\forall \alpha \in \mathbb{N}^n \quad \alpha \succcurlyeq 0.$

For any subset $G \subseteq R$ different from $\emptyset$ and $\{0\}$, we let $\mathrm{lt}(G) = \{\mathrm{lt}(g) : g \in G\}$. If $I \subseteq R$ is an ideal, then there is a finite subset $G \subseteq I$ such that $\langle \mathrm{lt}(G) \rangle = \langle \mathrm{lt}(I) \rangle$, by Dickson's lemma. However, it can happen that a finite set G generates I but $\langle \mathrm{lt}(G) \rangle \subsetneqq \langle \mathrm{lt}(I) \rangle$, as in the following example.

EXAMPLE 21.21. Let $g = x^3 - 2xy, h = x^2y - 2y^2 + x \in \mathbb{Q}[x,y]$, $\prec = \prec_{\text{grlex}}$, $G = \{g,h\}$, and $I = \langle G \rangle$. Then $x^2 = -y \cdot g + x \cdot h$ and $x^2 \in \langle \mathrm{lt}(I) \rangle$ but $x^2 \notin \langle \mathrm{lt}(G) \rangle = \langle x^3, x^2y \rangle$. $\diamond$

LEMMA 21.22. *Let I be an ideal in $R = F[x_1, \ldots, x_n]$. If $G \subseteq I$ is a finite subset such that $\langle \mathrm{lt}(G) \rangle = \langle \mathrm{lt}(I) \rangle$, then $\langle G \rangle = I$.*

PROOF. Let $G = \{g_1, \ldots, g_s\}$. If f is an arbitrary polynomial in I, then division with remainder yields $f = q_1 g_1 + \cdots + q_s g_s + r$, with $q_1, \ldots, q_s, r \in R$, such that either $r = 0$ or no term of r is divisible by the leading term of any g_i. But $r = f - q_1 g_1 - \cdots - q_s g_s \in I$, and hence $\mathrm{lt}(r) \in \mathrm{lt}(I) \subseteq \langle \mathrm{lt}(g_1), \ldots, \mathrm{lt}(g_s) \rangle$. This together with Lemma 21.15 implies that $r = 0$. Thus $f \in \langle g_1, \ldots, g_s \rangle = \langle G \rangle$. $\square$

Together with Dickson's lemma, applied to $\langle \mathrm{lt}(I) \rangle$, and the fact that the zero ideal $\{0\}$ is generated by the zero polynomial, we obtain the following famous result.

THEOREM 21.23 *Hilbert's basis theorem.*
Every ideal I in $R = F[x_1, \ldots, x_n]$ is finitely generated. More precisely, there exists a finite subset $G \subseteq I$ such that $\langle G \rangle = I$ and $\langle \mathrm{lt}(G) \rangle = \langle \mathrm{lt}(I) \rangle$.

An immediate consequence is the following corollary.

COROLLARY 21.24 *Ascending chain condition.*
Let $I_1 \subseteq I_2 \subseteq I_3 \subseteq \ldots$ be an ascending chain of ideals in R. Then the chain stabilizes, so that $I_n = I_{n+1} = I_{n+2} = \cdots$ for some $n \in \mathbb{N}$.

PROOF. Let $I = \bigcup_{j \geq 1} I_j$. Then I is an ideal, which is finitely generated, by Hilbert's basis theorem, say $I = \langle g_1, \ldots, g_s \rangle$. With $n = \min\{j \geq 1 : g_1, \ldots, g_s \in I_j\}$, we then have $I_n = I_{n+1} = \cdots = I$. $\square$

In general, a ring satisfying the ascending chain condition is called **Noetherian**, after Emmy Noether. Thus $F[x_1, \ldots, x_n]$ is Noetherian if F is a field.

21.4. Gröbner bases and S-polynomials

Hilbert's basis theorem motivates the following definition.

DEFINITION 21.25. *Let $\prec$ be a monomial order and $I \subseteq R$ an ideal. A finite set $G \subseteq I$ is a **Gröbner basis** for I with respect to $\prec$ if $\langle \mathrm{lt}(G) \rangle = \langle \mathrm{lt}(I) \rangle$.*

Lemma 21.22 says that any Gröbner basis G for I is in fact a basis of I in the ring theoretic sense, which means that $\langle G \rangle = I$. With the convention that $\langle \rangle = \langle \emptyset \rangle = \{0\}$, Hilbert's basis theorem implies the following.

COROLLARY 21.26.
Every ideal I in $R = F[x_1, \ldots, x_n]$ has a Gröbner basis.

In Example 21.21, G is not a Gröbner basis for I, but $\{g, h, x^2, 2xy, -2y^2 + x\}$ is, as we will see below.

We now want to show that division with remainder by a Gröbner basis is a valid ideal membership test. Throughout this section, we assume some monomial order on R.

LEMMA 21.27. *Let G be a Gröbner basis for an ideal $I \subseteq R$, and $f \in R$. Then there is a unique polynomial $r \in R$ with*

(i) $f - r \in I$,

(ii) *no term of r is divisible by any monomial in $\mathrm{lt}(G)$.*

PROOF. Existence follows from Theorem 21.12. For the uniqueness, we suppose that $f = h_1 + r_1 = h_2 + r_2$ with $h_1, h_2 \in I$ and no term of r_1 or r_2 divisible by any of $\mathrm{lt}(G)$. Then $r_1 - r_2 = h_2 - h_1 \in I$, and $\mathrm{lt}(r_1 - r_2)$ is divisible by some $\mathrm{lt}(g)$ with $g \in G$, by Lemma 21.15. Hence $r_1 - r_2 = 0$. $\square$

Thus the remainder r on division of f by G does not depend on the order in which we divide by the elements of G. Extending the notation (5), we then write

$$f \text{ rem } G = r \in R.$$

The next result follows immediately from the lemma.

▬▬ THEOREM 21.28. ▬▬▬▬▬▬▬▬▬▬▬▬▬▬▬▬▬▬▬▬▬▬▬▬▬▬▬▬
Let G be a Gröbner basis for the ideal $I \subseteq R$ with respect to a monomial order $\prec$, and $f \in R$. Then $f \in I$ if and only if f rem $G = 0$. ▬▬▬▬▬▬▬▬▬▬▬

This property of G is equivalent to being a Gröbner basis (Exercise 21.17). It solves the ideal membership problem: all we have to do in order to test whether $f \in I$ is to divide f by G.

However, the proof of Hilbert's basis theorem is not constructive: it does not tell us how to compute a Gröbner basis for an ideal I from a given basis G. We now solve this computational problem, so that we obtain an effective version of Hilbert's basis theorem. In order to construct a Gröbner basis, we investigate how G can fail to be a Gröbner basis. One possible reason is that a linear combination $ax^{\alpha}g + bx^{\beta}h$ of two polynomials $g, h \in G$ with $a, b \in F$ and $\alpha, \beta \in \mathbb{N}^n$ may yield a polynomial whose leading term is not divisible by any of $\mathrm{lt}(G)$, by cancellation of leading terms. In Example 21.21, we had $(-y) \cdot g + x \cdot h = x^2$, and $\mathrm{lt}(x^2) = x^2$ is not divisible by any of $\mathrm{lt}(G) = \{x^3, x^2 y\}$.

DEFINITION 21.29. *Let $g, h \in R$ be nonzero, $\alpha = (\alpha_1, \ldots, \alpha_n) = \mathrm{mdeg}(g)$, $\beta = (\beta_1, \ldots, \beta_n) = \mathrm{mdeg}(h)$, and $\gamma = (\max\{\alpha_1, \beta_1\}, \ldots, \max\{\alpha_n, \beta_n\})$. The **S-polynomial** of g and h is*

$$S(g, h) = \frac{x^{\gamma}}{\mathrm{lt}(g)} g - \frac{x^{\gamma}}{\mathrm{lt}(h)} h \in R. \tag{7}$$

Clearly $S(h, g) = -S(g, h)$, and since $x^{\gamma}/\mathrm{lt}(g), x^{\gamma}/\mathrm{lt}(h) \in R$, we have $S(g, h) \in \langle g, h \rangle$. In Example 21.21, we have $\alpha = (3, 0)$, $\beta = (2, 1)$, $\gamma = (3, 1)$, and

$$S(g, h) = \frac{x^3 y}{x^3} g - \frac{x^3 y}{x^2 y} h = -x^2.$$

The following lemma says that when cancellation of leading terms occurs in a linear combination of polynomials in G, it necessarily comes from S-polynomials.

LEMMA 21.30. *Let $g_1, \ldots, g_s \in R$, $\alpha_1, \ldots, \alpha_s \in \mathbb{N}^n$, $c_1, \ldots, c_s \in F \setminus \{0\}$,*

$$f = \sum_{1 \leq i \leq s} c_i x^{\alpha_i} g_i \in R, \tag{8}$$

and $\delta \in \mathbb{N}^n$ such that $\alpha_i + \mathrm{mdeg}(g_i) = \delta$ for $1 \leq i \leq s$, and $\mathrm{mdeg}(f) \prec \delta$. (This expresses the assumption that the leading terms cancel.) Then $x^{\gamma_{ij}}$ divides x^{δ} for $1 \leq i < j \leq s$, where $x^{\gamma_{ij}} = \mathrm{lcm}(\mathrm{lm}(g_i), \mathrm{lm}(g_j))$, and there are $c_{ij} \in F$ such that

$$f = \sum_{1 \leq i < j \leq s} c_{ij} x^{\delta - \gamma_{ij}} S(g_i, g_j) \tag{9}$$

and $\mathrm{mdeg}(x^{\delta - \gamma_{ij}} S(g_i, g_j)) \prec \delta$ for all $1 \leq i < j \leq s$.

PROOF. By multiplying each c_i with $\mathrm{lc}(g_i)$ if necessary, we may assume that $\mathrm{lc}(g_i) = 1$ and $\mathrm{lt}(g_i) = \mathrm{lm}(g_i) = x^{\mathrm{mdeg}(g_i)}$ for all i. Let $1 \le i < j \le s$. The monomial $x^\delta = x^{\alpha_i} \mathrm{lm}(g_i) = x^{\alpha_j} \mathrm{lm}(g_j)$ is a common multiple of $\mathrm{lm}(g_i)$ and $\mathrm{lm}(g_j)$, so that $x^{\gamma_{ij}} \mid x^\delta$. Now

$$S(g_i, g_j) = \frac{x^{\gamma_{ij}}}{\mathrm{lt}(g_i)} g_i - \frac{x^{\gamma_{ij}}}{\mathrm{lt}(g_j)} g_j,$$

and hence $\mathrm{mdeg}(S(g_i, g_j)) \prec \gamma_{ij}$, by Lemma 21.8. Since the leading terms in (7) cancel, we have

$$\mathrm{mdeg}(x^{\delta - \gamma_{ij}} S(g_i, g_j)) = \delta - \gamma_{ij} + \mathrm{mdeg}(S(g_i, g_j)) \prec \delta - \gamma_{ij} + \gamma_{ij} = \delta.$$

We prove (9) by induction on s. If $s = 1$, then no cancellation can occur, and the claim is vacuously true. If $s \ge 2$, then

$$
\begin{aligned}
g &= f - c_1 x^{\delta - \gamma_{12}} S(g_1, g_2) \\
&= c_1 x^{\alpha_1} g_1 + c_2 x^{\alpha_2} g_2 + \sum_{3 \le i \le s} c_i x^{\alpha_i} g_i - c_1 x^{\delta - \gamma_{12}} \left(\frac{x^{\gamma_{12}}}{\mathrm{lt}(g_1)} g_1 - \frac{x^{\gamma_{12}}}{\mathrm{lt}(g_2)} g_2 \right) \\
&= c_1 (x^{\alpha_1} - x^{\delta - \mathrm{mdeg}(g_1)}) g_1 + (c_2 x^{\alpha_2} + c_1 x^{\delta - \mathrm{mdeg}(g_2)}) g_2 + \sum_{3 \le i \le s} c_i x^{\alpha_i} g_i \\
&= (c_1 + c_2) x^{\alpha_2} g_2 + \sum_{3 \le i \le s} c_i x^{\alpha_i} g_i,
\end{aligned}
$$

where we use that $\alpha_1 + \mathrm{mdeg}(g_1) = \delta = \alpha_2 + \mathrm{mdeg}(g_2)$ in the last equation. Now Lemma 21.8 says that $\mathrm{mdeg}(g) \prec \max_\prec \{\mathrm{mdeg}(f), \mathrm{mdeg}(x^{\delta - \gamma_{12}} S(g_1, g_2))\} \prec \delta$, and hence g is again of the form (8), with a sum of length $s - 1$ if $c_1 + c_2 \ne 0$ and of length $s - 2$ otherwise. The induction hypothesis implies that

$$g = \sum_{2 \le i < j \le s} c_{ij} x^{\delta - \gamma_{ij}} S(g_i, g_j),$$

with some $c_{ij} \in F$ for $2 \le i < j \le s$; we have $g = 0$ if $s = 2$. If we let $c_{12} = c_1$ and $c_{1j} = 0$ for $3 \le j \le s$, then

$$f = g + c_1 x^{\delta - \gamma_{12}} S(g_1, g_2) = \sum_{1 \le i < j \le s} c_{ij} x^{\delta - \gamma_{ij}} S(g_i, g_j). \quad \square$$

The following theorem gives us an easy test for Gröbner bases.

▬ THEOREM 21.31. ▬▬▬▬▬▬▬▬▬▬▬▬▬▬▬▬▬▬▬▬▬▬▬▬▬▬▬▬
A finite set $G = \{g_1, \dots, g_s\} \subseteq R$ is a Gröbner basis of the ideal $\langle G \rangle$ if and only if

$$S(g_i, g_j) \ \mathrm{rem} \ (g_1, \dots, g_s) = 0 \ \text{for} \ 1 \le i < j \le s. \tag{10}$$

PROOF. "$\Longrightarrow$" follows from Theorem 21.28, since $S(g_i,g_j) \in I = \langle G \rangle$ for all i,j. For the reverse direction, we let $f \in I \setminus \{0\}$, and have to show that $\mathrm{lt}(f) \in \langle \mathrm{lt}(G) \rangle$. We write

$$f = \sum_{1 \le i \le s} q_i g_i, \quad \delta = \max_{\prec}\{\mathrm{mdeg}(q_i g_i) : 1 \le i \le s\}, \tag{11}$$

with all $q_i \in R$. Then $\mathrm{mdeg}(f) \preccurlyeq \delta$. If strict inequality holds, then some cancellation of leading terms occurs in (11), and

$$f^* = \sum_{\substack{1 \le i \le s \\ \mathrm{mdeg}(q_i g_i) = \delta}} \mathrm{lt}(q_i) g_i$$

is of the form (8). We can write f^* as an F-linear combination of polynomials of the form $x^{\alpha_{ij}} S(g_i, g_j)$, with $\alpha_{ij} \in \mathbb{N}^n$ such that $\alpha_{ij} + \mathrm{mdeg}(S(g_i, g_j)) \prec \delta$ for all i, j, by Lemma 21.30, and then divide by $(g_1, \ldots, g_s)$ with remainder. Since the remainder of $S(g_i, g_j)$ on division by $(g_1, \ldots, g_s)$ is zero, we get $q_i^* \in R$ for $1 \le i \le s$ with $f^* = \sum_{1 \le i \le s} q_i^* g_i$, and Theorem 21.12 (ii) implies that $\max_{\prec}\{\mathrm{mdeg}(q_i^* g_i) : 1 \le i \le s\} \prec \delta$. Now both $f - f^*$ and f^* have a representation of the form (11) with a smaller value of δ, and so has f.

Continuing this replacement process if necessary (it terminates because of the well-order property), we find $q_i \in R$ for $1 \le i \le s$ with (11) and $\mathrm{mdeg}(f) = \delta$, and hence $\mathrm{mdeg}(f) = \mathrm{mdeg}(q_i g_i)$ for at least one index i. Then

$$\mathrm{lt}(f) = \sum_{\substack{1 \le i \le s \\ \mathrm{mdeg}(q_i g_i) = \delta}} \mathrm{lt}(q_i) \cdot \mathrm{lt}(g_i) \in \langle \mathrm{lt}(G) \rangle. \quad \square$$

EXAMPLE 21.32. The **twisted cubic** $C = V(G)$ is the curve in F^3 given by $G = \{y - x^2, z - x^3\}$, so that $C = \{(a, a^2, a^3) : a \in F\} \subseteq F^3$. In $\mathbb{R}^3$, C is the intersection of the two cylindrical surfaces $V(y - x^2)$ and $V(z - x^3)$, as illustrated in Figure 21.5. G is a Gröbner basis for $I = \langle G \rangle$ with respect to the lexicographic order and $y \succ z \succ x$, by Theorem 21.31, since

$$\begin{aligned} S(y - x^2, z - x^3) &= z(y - x^2) - y(z - x^3) = yx^3 - zx^2 \\ &= x^3(y - x^2) + (-x^2)(z - x^3) + 0. \quad \Diamond \end{aligned}$$

21.5. Buchberger's algorithm

We now describe a method for computing a Gröbner basis, and start by looking at Example 21.21. The basic idea is that, whenever (10) is violated, we add the offending S-polynomial to our basis. Let $\prec = \prec_{\mathrm{grlex}}$ with $y \prec x$, $f_1 = x^3 - 2xy$, and $f_2 = x^2 y - 2y^2 + x \in \mathbb{Q}[x, y]$. $G = \{f_1, f_2\}$ is not a Gröbner basis since $S(f_1, f_2) = -x^2$ and $\mathrm{lt}(S(f_1, f_2)) = -x^2 \notin \langle x^3, x^2 y \rangle = \langle \mathrm{lt}(G) \rangle$. Now we include $f_3 = S(f_1, f_2) \mathrm{\ rem\ } (f_1, f_2) = -x^2$ in our basis, and $S(f_1, f_2) \mathrm{\ rem\ } (f_1, f_2, f_3) = 0$.

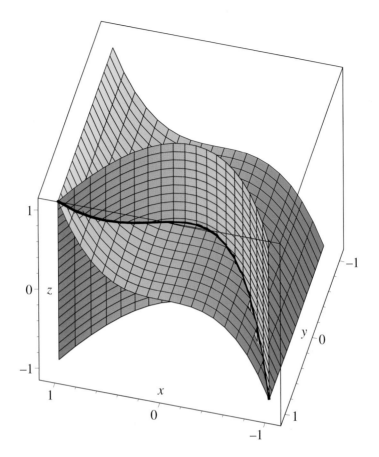

FIGURE 21.5: The twisted cubic (black) in $\mathbb{R}^3$.

Next,

$$S(f_1, f_3) = 1 \cdot f_1 - (-x) \cdot f_3 = -2xy,$$
$$S(f_1, f_3) \text{ rem } (f_1, f_2, f_3) = -2xy = f_4,$$

which is adjoined to our basis, so that $S(f_1, f_3) \text{ rem } (f_1, \ldots, f_4) = 0$. Now

$$S(f_1, f_4) = y \cdot f_1 - (-\frac{1}{2}x^2) \cdot f_4 = -2xy^2 = y \cdot f_4,$$

so that $S(f_1, f_4) \text{ rem } (f_1, \ldots, f_4) = 0$, and

$$S(f_2, f_3) = 1 \cdot f_2 - (-y)f_3 = -2y^2 + x.$$

After adjoining $f_5 = S(f_2, f_3) \text{ rem } (f_1, \ldots, f_4) = -2y^2 + x$, we check that

$$S(f_i, f_j) \text{ rem } (f_1, \ldots, f_5) = 0 \text{ for } 1 \le i < j \le 5,$$

and $\{f_1, \ldots, f_5\}$ is a Gröbner basis.

We now present a simplified version of Buchberger's (1965) algorithm.

▬▬▬ ALGORITHM 21.33 Gröbner basis computation. ▬▬▬▬▬▬▬▬▬▬▬▬▬▬▬
Input: $f_1, \ldots, f_s \in R = F[x_1, \ldots, x_n]$, and a monomial order $\prec$.
Output: A Gröbner basis $G \subseteq R$ for the ideal $I = \langle f_1, \ldots, f_s \rangle$ with respect to $\prec$,
with $f_1, \ldots, f_s \in G$.

1. $G \longleftarrow \{f_1, \ldots, f_s\}$

2. **repeat**

3. $S \longleftarrow \emptyset$
         order the elements of G somehow as $g_1, \ldots, g_t$
         for $1 \le i < j \le t$ **do**

4. $r \longleftarrow S(g_i, g_j)$ rem $(g_1, \ldots, g_t)$
                  if $r \neq 0$ **then** $S \longleftarrow S \cup \{r\}$

5.   **if** $S = \emptyset$ **then return** G **else** $G \longleftarrow G \cup S$ ▬▬▬▬▬▬▬▬▬▬▬▬

▬▬▬ THEOREM 21.34. ▬▬▬▬▬▬▬▬▬▬▬▬▬▬▬▬▬▬▬▬▬▬▬▬▬▬▬
Algorithm 21.33 works correctly as specified. ▬▬▬▬▬▬▬▬▬▬▬▬▬▬▬

PROOF. First we show the correctness assuming that the procedure terminates. At
any stage of the algorithm, the set G in step 2 is a basis of I and $f_1, \ldots, f_s \in G$,
since this is true initially and only elements of I, namely the remainders of S-
polynomials of $g_i, g_j \in I$ on division by elements of I, are added to G during the
algorithm. If the algorithm terminates, the remainders of all the S-polynomials on
division by G are zero, and G is a Gröbner basis by Theorem 21.31.

It remains to show that the algorithm terminates. If G and G^* correspond to
successive passes through step 2, then $G^* \supseteq G$ and $\langle \mathrm{lt}(G^*) \rangle \supseteq \langle \mathrm{lt}(G) \rangle$. Hence the
ideals $\langle \mathrm{lt}(G) \rangle$ in successive passes through step 2 form an ascending chain, which
stabilizes by the ascending chain condition of Corollary 21.24. Thus, after a finite
number of steps we have $\langle \mathrm{lt}(G^*) \rangle = \langle \mathrm{lt}(G) \rangle$. We claim that then $G = G^*$. So let
$g, h \in G$, and $r = S(g, h)$ rem G. Then $r \in G^*$ and either $r = 0$ or $\mathrm{lt}(r) \in \langle \mathrm{lt}(G^*) \rangle = \langle \mathrm{lt}(G) \rangle$, and from the definition of the remainder we conclude that $r = 0$. $\square$

▬▬▬ COROLLARY 21.35. ▬▬▬▬▬▬▬▬▬▬▬▬▬▬▬▬▬▬▬▬▬▬▬▬▬▬
The following problems are solvable using Gröbner bases:

(i) *ideal membership testing via division with remainder,*

(ii) *ideal containment testing,*

(iii) *ideal equality testing.* ▬▬▬▬▬▬▬▬▬▬▬▬▬▬▬▬▬▬▬▬▬▬▬

In general, the Gröbner basis computed by Buchberger's algorithm is neither minimal nor unique. One can, however, manipulate it so that both properties hold.

LEMMA 21.36. *If G is a Gröbner basis of $I \subseteq R$, $g \in G$, and $\mathrm{lt}(g) \in \langle \mathrm{lt}(G \setminus \{g\}) \rangle$, then $G \setminus \{g\}$ is a Gröbner basis of I.*

PROOF. Exercise 21.18. □

DEFINITION 21.37. *A subset $G \subseteq R$ is a **minimal** Gröbner basis for $I = \langle G \rangle$ if it is a Gröbner basis for I and for all $g \in G$*

(i) $\mathrm{lc}(g) = 1$,

(ii) $\mathrm{lt}(g) \notin \langle \mathrm{lt}(G \setminus \{g\}) \rangle$.

*An element g of a Gröbner basis G is **reduced with respect to G** if no monomial of g is in $\langle \mathrm{lt}(G \setminus \{g\}) \rangle$. A minimal Gröbner basis G for $I \subseteq R$ is **reduced** if all its elements are reduced with respect to G.*

THEOREM 21.38.
Every ideal has a unique reduced Gröbner basis.

PROOF. We first show the existence. Repeatedly applying Lemma 21.36 if necessary, we may start with a minimal Gröbner basis $G = \{g_1, \dots, g_s\}$. For $1 \le i \le s$, we then set

$$h_i = g_i \text{ rem } \{h_1, \dots, h_{i-1}, g_{i+1}, \dots, g_s\}.$$

Induction on i proves that $\mathrm{lt}(g_j) = \mathrm{lt}(h_j)$ and h_j is reduced with respect to $G_i = \{h_1, \dots, h_i, g_{i+1}, \dots, g_s\}$ for $0 \le j \le i \le s$, and finally $G_s = \{h_1, \dots, h_s\}$ is a reduced Gröbner basis.

Now suppose that G and G^* are reduced Gröbner bases of I. We claim that $\mathrm{lt}(G) = \mathrm{lt}(G^*)$. For $g \in \mathrm{lt}(G) \subseteq \langle \mathrm{lt}(G) \rangle = \mathrm{lt}(I) = \langle \mathrm{lt}(G^*) \rangle$, there is some $g^* \in G^*$ such that $\mathrm{lt}(g^*) \mid \mathrm{lt}(g)$, by Lemma 21.15. By a symmetric argument, there exists a $g^* \in G$ such that $\mathrm{lt}(g^*) \mid \mathrm{lt}(g^*)$. Since G is minimal, we have $\mathrm{lt}(g) = \mathrm{lt}(g^*) = \mathrm{lt}(g^*) \in \mathrm{lt}(G^*)$, and $\mathrm{lt}(G) \subseteq \mathrm{lt}(G^*)$. Similarly, $\mathrm{lt}(G^*) \subseteq \mathrm{lt}(G)$, which proves the claim.

For a given $g \in G$, let $g^* \in G^*$ be such that $\mathrm{lt}(g) = \mathrm{lt}(g^*)$. Both G and G^* are reduced, and hence no monomial in $g - g^* \in I$ is divisible by any element of $\mathrm{lt}(G) = \mathrm{lt}(G^*)$. Thus $g - g^* = g - g^* \text{ rem } G = 0$ since $g - g^* \in I$, whence $g \in G^*$, $G \subseteq G^*$, and by a symmetric argument, also $G^* \subseteq G$. □

At the beginning of this section, we saw how several polynomials may have to be added to form a Gröbner basis. How many? In Section 21.7, we will learn the rather devastating answer: sometimes doubly exponentially many, and their degrees may be doubly exponentially large (in the number of variables). It is not easy to say how many steps Buchberger's algorithm takes, but for such huge outputs it uses at least exponential space.

Both Gaussian elimination and Euclid's algorithm for gcds in $F[x]$ are special cases of Buchberger's algorithm (see Exercise 21.24 for the former).

21.6. Geometric applications

Algebra provides a powerful language which can express a wide range of problems. Then a general–purpose solution strategy like Gröbner bases is available for the solution of these problems. Of course, this approach has its limitations, for example, with regards to efficiency. We now give two sample applications from geometry. In Chapter 24, we will exhibit two computer science questions whose geometric formulation is not obvious (but easy to produce, once we set our mind on it), and a larger example from chemistry.

Automatic geometric theorem proving. Geometric theorems can often be formulated in terms of polynomial equations. We have seen this for the theorem about the center of gravity of a triangle in Example 21.2, where the hypotheses yielded two polynomials $f_1, f_2 \in \mathbb{R}[u, v, x, y]$, the conclusions three further polynomials $g_1, g_2, g_3 \in \mathbb{R}[u, v, x, y]$, and the theorem is equivalent to "$f_1 = f_2 = 0 \Longrightarrow g_1 = g_2 = g_3 = 0$". In general, we obtain a set of hypothesis polynomials $f_1, \ldots, f_s$ in $R = \mathbb{R}[x_1, \ldots, x_n]$ and one (or several) conclusion polynomials $g \in R$, and the theorem is true if and only if $V(f_1, \ldots, f_s) \subseteq V(g)$. In particular, we can prove the theorem by showing that $g \in \langle f_1, \ldots, f_s \rangle$.

In Example 21.2, we have already done this for $g = g_1$, so let us try Gröbner bases on g_2 and g_3. We start by computing a Gröbner basis for the ideal $I = \langle f_1, f_2 \rangle$ with respect to $\preceq = \preceq_{\mathrm{lex}}$ and $u \succ v \succ x \succ y$. We have

$$f_1 = uy - vx - v, \quad f_2 = uy - vx + 2v - y$$

with respect to this monomial order,

$$S(f_1, f_2) = f_1 - f_2 = -3v + y = -g_3, \quad -g_3 \text{ rem } (f_1, f_2) = -g_3.$$

After adding g_3 to our basis, it turns out that

$$
\begin{aligned}
S(f_1, g_3) \text{ rem } (f_1, f_2, g_3) &= -uy^2 - 3v^2x - 3v^2 \text{ rem } (f_1, f_2, g_3) = 0, \\
S(f_1, f_2) \text{ rem } (f_1, f_2, g_3) &= -uy^2 - 3v^2x + 6v^2 - 3vy \text{ rem } (f_1, f_2, g_3) = 0,
\end{aligned}
$$

and $\{f_1, f_2, g_3\}$ is a Gröbner basis. By Lemma 21.36, we may discard f_2, and using the process from the proof of Theorem 21.38 for reducing, we obtain

$$f_3 = f_1 \text{ rem } g_3 = uy - \frac{1}{3}xy - \frac{1}{3}y, \quad g_3 \text{ rem } f_3 = g_3,$$

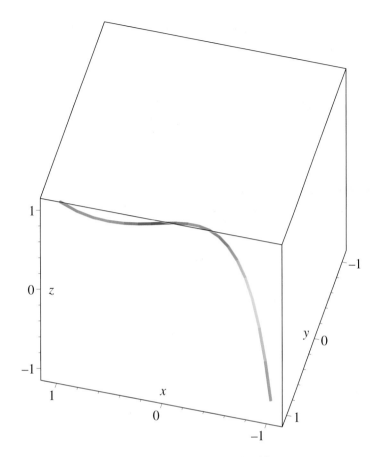

FIGURE 21.6: The twisted cubic.

and $G = \{uy - \frac{1}{3}xy - \frac{1}{3}y, v - \frac{1}{3}y\}$ is the unique reduced Gröbner basis of I with respect to $\prec$.

We know already that $g_3 \in I$, but division with remainder yields g_2 rem $G = g_2 \neq 0$, and Theorem 21.28 implies that $g_2 \notin I$. On the other hand, $f_3 = \frac{1}{3}yg_2$ belongs to I, and hence the theorem about the center of gravity is true if $y \neq 0$. (See Notes 21.6 for the degenerate case $y = 0$.)

Implicitization. Let $f_1, \ldots, f_n \in F[t_1, \ldots, t_m]$, and suppose that the affine algebraic variety $V \subseteq F^n$ is given in parametrized form by

$$
\begin{aligned}
x_1 &= f_1(t_1, \ldots, t_m), \\
&\vdots \\
x_n &= f_n(t_1, \ldots, t_m),
\end{aligned}
$$

so that V is "explicitly" described as $V = \{a \in F^n \colon \exists b \in F^m \ a = (f_1(b), \ldots, f_n(b))\}$. The task is now to find polynomials $g_1, \ldots, g_s \in F[x_1, \ldots, x_n]$ such that V has the "implicit" representation $V = V(I)$, where $I = \langle g_1, \ldots, g_s \rangle$. (More precisely, $V(I)$ will equal the "closure" of V.)

EXAMPLE 21.32 (continued). The twisted cubic C from Example 21.32 can be parametrized by

$$x = t, \quad y = t^2, \quad z = t^3.$$

An implicitization for C is $g_1 = y - x^2, g_2 = z - x^3$. The curve is illustrated in Figures 21.5 and 21.6 on pages 583 and 587, respectively. The latter corresponds to the explicit representation of C (the plot was generated by letting the parameter t run through the interval $[-1, 1]$), while the former depicts the implicit form as the intersection of the two surfaces defined by g_1 and g_2; this picture is somehow more informative. $\diamond$

EXAMPLE 21.39. Let $V \subseteq F^3$ be parametrized by $x = t^2, y = t^3, z = t^4$. Then an implicitization for V is $g_1 = z - x^2, g_2 = y^2 - x^3$. $\diamond$

To solve the implicitization problem, we consider $J = \langle x_1 - f_1, \ldots, x_n - f_n \rangle \subseteq F[t_1, \ldots, t_m, x_1, \ldots, x_n]$, order the variables so that $t_1 \succ \cdots \succ t_m \succ x_1 \succ \cdots \succ x_n$, and compute a Gröbner basis G for J with respect to $\prec = \prec_{\text{lex}}$. Then some $g \in G$ will depend only on $x_1, \ldots, x_n$. These are candidates for the g_i's.

In Examples 21.32 and 21.39, the reduced Gröbner bases for J with respect to $t \succ z \succ y \succ x$ are $\{t - x, z - x^3, y - x^2\}$ and $\{t^2 - x, ty - x^2, tx - y, z - x^2, y^2 - x^3\}$, respectively.

This approach always works over an infinite field, in the sense that the variety in F^n defined by the polynomials in $G \cap F[x_1, \ldots, x_n]$ is the smallest variety containing the image of the parametrization (see Cox, Little & O'Shea 1997, §3.3).

Solving systems of polynomial equations. This is the most natural application of Gröbner bases, and they were originally invented for this. In general, we have polynomials $f_1, \ldots, f_m \in F[x_1, \ldots, x_n]$ and want to answer questions about the corresponding affine variety $V = \{a \in F^n : f_1(a) = \cdots = f_m(a) = 0\}$. Examples of such questions are: Is $V \neq \emptyset$? If so, please find a point on V. Given another polynomial $g \in F[x_1, \ldots, x_n]$, is $g(a) = 0$ for all $a \in V$?

One of the simplest situations occurs when V is **zero-dimensional**, so that it consists only of finitely many isolated points. An example is the intersection of two plane curves. We saw in Section 6.8 how to use resultants for this problem: one first finds a polynomial $r \in F[x]$ in one variable which the x-coordinates of all intersection points satisfy, computes all roots of r, and then has to solve, for each root, the original bivariate equations (or their gcd). As mentioned, this resultant approach has a (nontrivial) generalization to higher dimensions.

Gröbner bases provide an alternative approach. For a zero–dimensional problem, the Gröbner basis with respect to lexicographic order $\prec = \prec_{lex}$ and $x_1 \prec \cdots \prec x_n$ will often include some polynomials only containing x_1, some only with x_1, x_2, and so on. These can then be solved by back substitution: first for x_1, then for x_2, and so on.

Application areas such as robot kinematics and motion planning provide many such interesting geometric problems. We now look at a simple example: the intersection of two plane curves. A more elaborate application in chemistry is discussed in Section 24.4.

We let $f = (y^2 + 6)(x - 1) - y(x^2 + 1)$ and $g = (x^2 + 6)(y - 1) - x(y^2 + 1) = f(y, x)$ in $\mathbb{C}[x, y]$, as in Example 21.3 (ii), and use Gröbner bases to determine all intersection points of the two plane curves $V(f)$ and $V(g)$, or equivalently, all common roots of the system of polynomial equations $f = g = 0$. We start by computing the reduced Gröbner basis G of $I = \langle f, g \rangle$ with respect to the lexicographic order $\prec = \prec_{lex}$ and $x \prec y$. We find that G consists of f, g, and the three polynomials

$$h = -f - g = x^2 - 5x + y^2 - 5y + 12, \quad p = y^2x - 5yx + 6x + y^3 - 6y^2 + 11y - 6,$$

$$q = y^4 - 6y^3 + 15y^2 - 26y + 24.$$

The last polynomial contains only the variable y, and we determine all its roots symbolically by factoring it over $\mathbb{Q}$. Using one of the algorithms from Part III, we obtain $q = (y - 2)(y - 3)(y^2 - y + 4)$, and hence

$$V(q) = \left\{ 2, 3, \frac{1 \pm \sqrt{15}i}{2} \right\}.$$

It remains to determine which of these partial solutions extend to a solution in $V(h, p, q) = V(I)$. Substituting $y = 2$ in h and p, we find that $p(x, 2)$ vanishes identically, and from the solutions of the univariate equation

$$h(x, 2) = x^2 - 5x + 6 = (x - 2)(x - 3) = 0,$$

for x, we find the two common zeroes $(3, 2)$ and $(3, 3)$ of f and g in $\mathbb{C}^2$. The other four intersection points from (2) can be obtained in a similar fashion, by substituting $y = 2$ or $y = (1 \pm \sqrt{15}i)/2$ in $h = p = 0$ and solving for x.

21.7. The complexity of computing Gröbner bases

For over thirty years after its publication in 1965, the cost of computing Gröbner bases remained a mystery. In this section, we briefly recount its solution by Mayr and his collaborators, and some remaining open questions. The limited space of this text prevents us from giving any details.

Experiments with implementations almost invariably ran into the dreaded phenomenon of **intermediate expression swell**. Starting out with a few polynomials of low degree and with small coefficients, the systems produce huge numbers of polynomials with very large degrees and enormous coefficients. In fact, the solution tells us that this is so by necessity, at least in the worst case. This should be contrasted with the situation for Euclid's algorithm in $\mathbb{Q}[x]$, where also intermediate expression swell was empirically observed, but then kept under control, using subresultants and clever algorithmic variations (Chapter 6).

We need some notions from complexity theory, as explained in Section 25.8. We have "feasible" classes like $\mathcal{P}$ and $\mathcal{BPP}$, the infeasible $\mathcal{NP}$-complete problems (assuming $\mathcal{P} \neq \mathcal{NP}$), and much "higher up" the class $\mathcal{EXPSPACE}$ of problems that can be solved using exponential space. The $\mathcal{EXPSPACE}$-complete problems are exceedingly difficult; they typically use doubly exponential time $2^{2^{O(n)}}$, for some inputs of size n at least.

We write IM for the polynomial ideal membership problem over $\mathbb{Q}$. Already Mayr & Meyer (1982) had shown that IM is $\mathcal{EXPSPACE}$-hard for general ideals. Mayr (1989, 1992) proved that IM is in $\mathcal{EXPSPACE}$, and thus $\mathcal{EXPSPACE}$-complete. Since Theorem 21.28 provides a reduction from IM to computing a Gröbner basis, the (decision version of the) latter problem is also $\mathcal{EXPSPACE}$-hard. The question was finally settled by Mayr (1989) and Kühnle & Mayr (1996), who gave an exponential space algorithm for computing a (reduced) Gröbner basis.

▬▬ THEOREM 21.40. ▬▬▬
The problem of finding a reduced Gröbner basis is $\mathcal{EXPSPACE}$-complete. ▬▬

The same results hold for **binomial ideals** (generated by binomials $x^\alpha - x^\beta$), and for some other types of fields besides $\mathbb{Q}$. Bürgisser (1998) proved that over any infinite field, the ideal membership problem requires exponential parallel time. For homogeneous ideals (generated by polynomials f each of whose terms has total degree $\deg f$), Mayr (1995) proved that IM is $\mathcal{PSPACE}$-complete, while computing a Gröbner basis is $\mathcal{EXPSPACE}$-complete.

The upper bounds mentioned make use of estimates of certain degrees. Ideal membership was first proven to be decidable by Hilbert (1890). Hermann (1926) gave a constructive method to represent any $f \in \langle f_1, \ldots, f_s \rangle$ as a linear combination

$$f = \sum_{1 \leq i \leq s} q_i f_i. \tag{12}$$

She gave a doubly exponential bound on the degrees of these q_i's; see also Mayr & Meyer (1982). In fact the degrees of the polynomials in a reduced Gröbner basis for $\langle f_1, \ldots, f_s \rangle \subseteq F[x_1, \ldots, x_n]$ are at most

$$2\left(\frac{d^2}{2} + d\right)^{2^{n-1}}, \tag{13}$$

when $\deg f_i \leq d$ for all i. This bound does not depend on the number of polynomials nor on their coefficients, depends polynomially on the degree, and doubly exponentially on the number of variables.

On the other hand, there exist ideals every Gröbner basis of which contains at least $2^{2^{cn}}$ elements and elements of degree at least $2^{2^{c^*n}}$, for some positive constants $c, c^* \in \mathbb{R}$.

If an ideal is such that the degrees in its reduced Gröbner basis come close to the doubly exponential bound (13), one might think that the output cannot even be written down in exponential space, and similarly for the certificate (12) of ideal membership. However, the model of space-bounded computations is such that one may take doubly exponential time to write a result of doubly exponential length on a special output tape, all the while using only singly exponential work space (Section 25.8).

Hilbert's famous **Nullstellensatz** says the following. If F is algebraically closed (say, $F = \mathbb{C}$), $f, f_1, \ldots, f_s \in F[x_1, \ldots, x_n]$, and $f(a) = 0$ for all $a \in F^n$ with $f_1(a) = \cdots = f_s(a) = 0$, then there exists $e \in \mathbb{N}$ with $f^e \in \langle f_1, \ldots, f_s \rangle$. In particular, the variety $V(f_1, \ldots, f_s)$ is empty if and only if $1 \in \langle f_1, \ldots, f_s \rangle$. If this is the case, then 1 will appear in any Gröbner basis of $f_1, \ldots, f_s$. This provides a test of whether $V(f_1, \ldots, f_s)$ is empty. For this particular instance of IM better results are available: one can always choose e and the degrees in (12) to be simply exponential, and this implies that the problem is in $\mathcal{PSPACE}$.

The worst-case cost of Buchberger's algorithm is still unknown today, but the important result of Theorem 21.40 completely settles the question of the "best" worst-case cost of any algorithm for Gröbner bases, and provides a lower bound for Buchberger's. It gives rise to the pessimistic view that these methods for polynomial ideals are not useful in practice, except for rather small cases.

However, it is not the full story. The inputs used for the lower bound are more combinatorial than geometric in nature, while most of the problems that people try to solve derive from geometric tasks. The algorithm of Kühnle & Mayr (1996) uses essentially the same time for all polynomials of a given degree and number of variables and thus is uniformly impractical, while one might hope that "natural" geometric problems are easier to solve than "combinatorial" ones.

Notes.   **21.1.** The papers in Eisenbud & Robbiano (1993) present the state of the art at that time. A good reference for this chapter is Cox, Little & O'Shea (1997), which we have followed closely in our exposition. Cox, Little & O'Shea (1998) discuss more advanced topics.

21.3. With the passage of time, the proof of Hilbert's basis theorem has become quite simple. But his 1890 paper was a milestone, solving this long–standing open question, and furthermore introducing the Hilbert function of an ideal and showing that invariant rings are finitely generated.

21.5. Buchberger (1965,1970,1976,1985,1987) explains his Gröbner basis method, gives many references, and puts it in the context of more general questions about grammars and term writing systems. Two further important contributions of Bruno Buchberger are the founding of the Journal of Symbolic Computation in 1985 and of the Research Institute for Symbolic Computation (RISC) in Linz, Austria.

21.6. Buchberger & Winkler (1998) contains a variety of tutorials on applications of Gröbner bases.

With slight modifications, the approach described in the text works for a rich class of geometric theorems (see Cox, Little & O'Shea 1997, §6.4, and Wu 1994).

We found that $g_2 \in I$ and $yg_2 \in I$. Thus we may conclude that $g_2(x,y) = 0$ if $(x,y) \in V(I)$ and $y \neq 0$. This can be phrased as an ideal membership property via *Rabinowitsch's trick* (1930) of adding $1 - yz$ to I, where z is a new indeterminate. This ensures that the value of y is nonzero, and $g_2 = g_2 \cdot (1 - yz) + 3z \cdot f_3 \in \langle f_1, f_2, 1 - yz \rangle$.

The reverse question of transforming an implicit representation of a variety into an explicit one has in general no solution; it can be solved only for the "rational varieties" of genus zero. However, it can be solved "near a smooth point" in general, if we allow appropriate power series for the f_i's, as in the implicit function theorem of calculus. The state of the art about algorithms on parametric varieties is presented in the twelve articles of a Special Issue of the *Journal of Symbolic Computation* (Hoffman, Sendra & Winkler 1997).

It can be shown that for zero-dimensional ideals $I \in F[x_1, \ldots, x_n]$, so that $V(I)$ is finite, a Gröbner basis with respect to lexicographic order $x_1 \prec x_2 \prec \cdots \prec x_n$ always contains a "triangular" subset $g_1, \ldots, g_n$, such that $g_i \in F[x_1, \ldots, x_i]$ and $\mathrm{lm}(g_i)$ is a power of x_i, for $1 \leq i \leq n$ (see, for example, Becker & Weispfenning (1993), Theorem 6.54, or Cox, Little & O'Shea (1997), §3.1 and 3.2).

21.7. Yap (1991) gave an improvement of Mayr & Meyer's result. Brownawell (1987) and Kollár (1988) proved that one can always choose the Nullstellensatz exponent e to be simply exponential; see also Amoroso (1989). Caniglia, Galligo & Heintz (1989), Lakshman (1990), and Berenstein & Yger (1990) showed that in some important cases the q_i's in (12) have only singly exponential degree: for zero-dimensional varieties, and for complete intersections.

Giusti (1984), Möller & Mora (1984), Bayer & Stillman (1988), and Dubé (1990) proved upper bounds for the elements of a reduced Gröbner basis; (13) is from the latter paper. Huynh (1986) showed the lower bound on the number and degrees of polynomials in Gröbner bases. Mayr (1997) gives a survey of complexity results, more references, and discusses applications such as those in Section 24.2.

Bayer & Stillman (1988) considered an invariant m associated to any multivariate ideal, called the *Castelnuovo-Mumford regularity*. This number seems to be fairly small for many natural geometric problems, but is exponential in the number of variables for the combinatorial problems of Mayr & Meyer (1982). Furthermore, Bayer & Stillman prove that, after a generic change of coordinates, the polynomials in a Gröbner basis with respect to the graded reverse lexicographic order $\prec_{\mathrm{grevlex}}$ have degree at most m. This gives rise to a bit of hope that the method might be able to deal successfully with interesting geometric problems, and to a practical recommendation in favor of $\prec_{\mathrm{grevlex}}$.

Almost all computer algebra systems contain some routines for Gröbner bases; Dave Bayer's system MACAULAY focuses particularly on this problem, and SINGULAR is another powerful package in this area. The research projects POSSO and FRISCO of the European Community have produced substantial software and a library of benchmark problems. Efficient algorithms and software are a highly active area of research. Three topics of particular interest (at the time of writing) are modular algorithms (Traverso 1988), selection strategies for S-polynomials (Giovini, Mora, Niesi, Robbiano & Traverso 1991), and conversion between Gröbner bases with respect to different orders (Faugère, Gianni, Lazard & Mora 1993).

Finally, we mention that there are other methods of dealing with certain geometric problems, based on cylindrical algebraic decomposition (Collins 1975), elimination theory, also using arithmetic circuits as a data structure (Chistov & Grigor'ev 1984, Caniglia, Galligo & Heintz 1988, Fitchas, Galligo & Morgenstern 1990, Giusti & Heintz 1991), u-resultants (Macaulay 1902, 1916, 1922, Canny 1987), and characteristic sets (Ritt 1950, Wu 1994, Gallo & Mishra 1991).

The important subject of *computational real algebraic geometry* started with Tarski (1948). Major progress was made by Collins (1975), and later by Ben-Or, Kozen & Reif (1986), Fitchas, Galligo & Morgenstern (1987), Grigor'ev (1988), Canny (1988), Renegar (1992a, 1992b, 1992c), and others. See the surveys of Heintz, Recio & Roy (1991) and Renegar (1991) for references and applications; our cyclohexane example in Section 24.4 can be viewed as such an application.

Exercises.

21.1 Let F be a field and x,y indeterminates. Prove that the two ideals $\langle x,y \rangle$ and $\langle \gcd(x,y) \rangle$ in $F[x,y]$ are distinct, and conclude that $F[x,y]$ is not Euclidean. Hint: Exercise 3.17.

21.2 Let F be a field. Prove that the ideals $I = \langle x + xy, y + xy, x^2, y^2 \rangle$ and $J = \langle x,y \rangle$ in $F[x,y]$ are identical. Your proof should also work if $\operatorname{char} F = 2$. Hint: It is sufficient to prove that the generators of each ideal belong to the other ideal.

21.3 Prove (3). Hint: Theorem 4.11.

21.4* Besides the usual Cartesian coordinates (u,v) with $u,v \in \mathbb{R}$, we represent the points of the plane by polar coordinates (r, φ) with $r \in \mathbb{R}$ and $0 \le \varphi < 2\pi$. This representation is not unique; for example, when $\varphi < \pi$ then (r, φ) and $(-r, \varphi + \pi)$ represent the same point. We obtain the polar coordinates from the Cartesian ones by the formulas $u = r\cos\varphi$, and $v = r\sin\varphi$. Now consider the curve $C = \{(r, \varphi) : 0 \le \varphi < 2\pi \text{ and } r = \sin 2\varphi\} \subseteq \mathbb{R}^2$, and let $I = \langle (x^2 + y^2)^3 - 4x^2 y^2 \rangle \subseteq \mathbb{R}[x,y]$.
  (i) Create a plot of C.
  (ii) Using the addition formulas for sine and cosine, show that $C \subseteq V(I)$.
  (iii) Prove that also the reverse inclusion $V(I) \subseteq C$ holds (be careful with the signs).

21.5* Let F be a field and $n \in \mathbb{N}$. For a subset $M \subseteq F^n$, we define the **ideal of** M by

$$\mathbf{I}(M) = \{f \in F[x_1, \dots, x_n] : f(u) = 0 \text{ for all } u \in M\}.$$

  (i) Show that $\mathbf{I}(M)$ is in fact an ideal.
  (ii) Prove that $N \subseteq M \Longrightarrow \mathbf{I}(N) \supseteq \mathbf{I}(M)$ and $V(\mathbf{I}(M)) \supseteq M$ for all $M, N \subseteq F^n$.
  (iii) Prove that $\mathbf{I}(M)$ is **radical**, which means that $f^m \in I$ implies $f \in I$ for all $m \in \mathbb{N}$ and $f \in F[x_1, \dots, x_n]$.
  (iv) Let $P = (u,v) \in F^2$ be an arbitrary point. Determine polynomials $f_1, f_2 \in F[x,y]$ such that $\mathbf{I}(\{P\}) = \langle f_1, f_2 \rangle$. Find a set $M \subseteq F^2$ such that $\mathbf{I}(M) = \langle x,y \rangle$.
  (v) Determine $\mathbf{I}(\varnothing)$ and $\mathbf{I}(F^n)$. Hint: Start with $n = 1$.
  (vi) Let $M = \{(u,0) \in \mathbb{R}^2 : 0 \le u \le 1\} \subseteq \mathbb{R}^2$, and find a polynomial $f \in \mathbb{R}[x,y]$ with $\mathbf{I}(M) = \langle f \rangle$.

21.6 Let $f = 2x^4 y^2 z - 6x^4 yz^2 + 4xy^4 z^2 - 3xy^2 z^4 + x^2 y^4 z - 5x^2 yz^4$ in $\mathbb{Q}[x,y,z]$.
  (i) Determine the order of the monomials in f for the three monomial orders $\prec_{\text{lex}}$, $\prec_{\text{grlex}}$, and $\prec_{\text{grevlex}}$, with $x \succ y \succ z$ in all cases.
  (ii) For each of the three monomial orders from (i), determine $\operatorname{mdeg}(f)$, $\operatorname{lc}(f)$, $\operatorname{lm}(f)$, and $\operatorname{lt}(f)$

21.7 Let $<$ be an order on a set S. Prove that $\alpha < \beta$ implies $\beta \not< \alpha$ for all $\alpha, \beta \in S$.

21.8 Show that $0 = (0, \ldots, 0) \in \mathbb{N}^n$ is the smallest element with respect to a monomial order $\prec$: $0 = \min_\prec \mathbb{N}^n$.

21.9$\longrightarrow$ (i) Prove that $\prec_{\text{lex}}$ is a monomial order.

(ii) Let $\prec$ be a total order on R, not necessarily a well–order. Prove that the graded variant of $\prec$ defined by

$$\alpha \prec_{\text{gr}} \beta \iff \sum_{1 \le i \le n} \alpha_i < \sum_{1 \le i \le n} \beta_i \text{ or } \left(\sum_{1 \le i \le n} \alpha_i = \sum_{1 \le i \le n} \beta_i \text{ and } \alpha \prec \beta \right)$$

is a monomial order, and conclude that so is $\prec_{\text{grlex}}$.

21.10 How many monomials in variables $x_1, \ldots, x_n$ have total degree m?

21.11 Prove Lemma 21.8.

21.12 Prove Theorem 21.12.

21.13 Let $n \in \mathbb{N}$ and $\alpha = (\alpha_1, \ldots, \alpha_n) \in \mathbb{N}^n$. Determine the number of elements $\beta = (\beta_1, \ldots, \beta_n) \in \mathbb{N}^n$ such that $\beta_i \le \alpha_i$ for $1 \le i \le n$.

21.14 Show that the set B from the proof of Dickson's lemma is the smallest subset of A (with respect to inclusion) such that $\langle x^B \rangle = \langle x^A \rangle$.

21.15 Show that for each $n \in \mathbb{N}$ there exists a monomial ideal $I \subseteq \mathbb{Q}[x, y]$ such that every basis of I has at least n elements.

21.16 Show that G from Example 21.32 is not a Gröbner basis with respect to $\prec_{\text{lex}}$ and $x \succ y \succ z$.

21.17 Let F be a field, $R = F[x_1, \ldots, x_n]$, and $f_1, \ldots, f_s \in R$. Prove that $\{f_1, \ldots, f_s\}$ is a Gröbner basis if $f \text{ rem } (f_1, \ldots, f_s) = 0$ for all $f \in I = \langle f_1, \ldots, f_s \rangle$.

21.18 Prove Lemma 21.36.

21.19 Let G be a Gröbner basis for the ideal $I \subseteq F[x_1, \ldots, x_n]$, where F is a field. Prove that $1 \in I$ if and only if G contains a nonzero constant from F. Conclude that $G = \{1\}$ if $1 \in I$ and G is reduced.

21.20 (i) Compute a Gröbner basis for the ideal $I = \langle x^2 + y - 1, xy - x \rangle \subseteq \mathbb{Q}[x, y]$ with respect to $\prec = \prec_{\text{lex}}$ and $x \succ y$, using Buchberger's algorithm. If your basis is not minimal, then use Lemma 21.18 to compute a minimal one.

(ii) Which of the following polynomials belong to I: $f_1 = x^2 + y^2 - y$, $f_2 = 3xy^2 - 4xy + x + 1$?

21.21 Which of the following finite subsets of $\mathbb{Q}[x, y, z]$ are Gröbner bases with respect to $\prec = \prec_{\text{lex}}$? Which are minimal or even reduced?

(i) $\{x + y, y^2 - 1\}$ for $x \succ y$,

(ii) $\{y + x, y^2 - 1\}$ for $y \succ x$,

(iii) $\{x^2 + y^2 - 1, xy - 1, x + y^3 - y\}$ for $x \succ y$,

(iv) $\{xyz - 1, x - y, y^2z - 1\}$ for $x \succ y \succ z$.

21.22 Let F be a field and $\{f_1, \ldots, f_s\}$ and $\{g_1, \ldots, g_t\}$ in $R = F[x_1, \ldots, x_n]$ be minimal Gröbner bases of the same ideal $I \subseteq R$, with $f_1 \prec \cdots \prec f_s$ and $g_1 \prec \cdots \prec g_t$. Prove that $s = t$ and $\text{lt}(f_i) = \text{lt}(g_i)$ for all i.

21.23$\longrightarrow$ Compute a Gröbner basis for

$$\langle f_1 = x^2y - 2yz + 1, f_2 = xy^2 - z^2 + 2x, f_3 = y^2z - x^2 + 5 \rangle \subseteq \mathbb{Q}[x, y, z],$$

using $\prec = \prec_{\text{grlex}}$ with $x \prec y \prec z$. Compare your output to the Gröbner basis that MAPLE computes with a different order.

21.24* Let F be a field, $n \in \mathbb{N}$, and $A = (a_{ij})_{1 \le i,j \le n} \in F^{n \times n}$ a square matrix. Moreover, let $G_A = \{\sum_{1 \le j \le n} a_{ij} x_j : 1 \le i \le n\} \subseteq F[x_1, \ldots, x_n]$ be the set of linear polynomials corresponding to the rows of A and $I_A = \langle G_A \rangle$. Then $V(G_A) = V(I_A)$ is equal to $\ker A$, the set of solutions $v \in F^n$ of the linear system $Av = 0$. Prove:

(i) $I_{LA} = I_A$ if $L \in F^{n \times n}$ is nonsingular.

(ii) Assume that there exists a nonsingular matrix $L \in F^{n \times n}$ such that

$$U = LA = \begin{pmatrix} I_r & V \\ 0 & 0 \end{pmatrix},$$

where r is the rank of A, I_r is the $r \times r$ identity matrix, and $V \in F^{r \times (n-r)}$ (this means that no pivot search is necessary when applying Gaussian elimination to A). Prove that G_U is a reduced Gröbner basis of I_A with respect to any monomial order $\prec$ such that $x_1 \succ x_2 \succ \cdots \succ x_n$.

(iii) What is the reduced Gröbner basis of I_A if A is nonsingular, with respect to an arbitrary monomial order?

21.25* You are to solve the following nonlinear optimization problem: Determine all maxima and minima of the polynomial $f = x^2 y - 2xy + y + 1$ on the unit circle $S = \{(u, v) \in \mathbb{R}^2 : g(u, v) = 0\}$, where $g = x^2 + y^2 - 1$. In numerical analysis, such a problem is solved with the aid of **Lagrange multipliers**: if $\nabla f = (f_x, f_y, f_z)$ and $\nabla g = (g_x, g_y, g_z)$ are the Jacobians of f and g, respectively, where $f_x = \partial f / \partial x$ and f_y, f_z, g_x, g_y, g_x are defined analogously, then the equality $\nabla f = \lambda \nabla g$ holds at a local maximum or minimum of f on S for some $\lambda \in \mathbb{R}$.

(i) Set up the system of polynomial equations

$$g = 0 \text{ and } \nabla f - z \nabla g = 0, \tag{14}$$

where z is another indeterminate.

(ii) Let $I \subseteq \mathbb{Q}[x, y, z]$ be the ideal generated by the equations in (14). Compute a Gröbner basis G of I with respect to $\prec = \prec_{\text{lex}}$ and $z \succ x \succ y$.

(iii) Solve the system of polynomial equations corresponding to G, which is equivalent to (14), by back substitution. Check that all solutions are in fact solutions of (14). Which are the absolute maxima and minima of f on the unit circle?

(iv) Generate a plot of the values of f on S.

21.26 Find an example over $\mathbb{F}_5$ (which is not algebraically closed) where the statement of Hilbert's Nullstellensatz is false.

21.27 Prove Hilbert's Nullstellensatz for univariate polynomials over $\mathbb{C}$.

Schönheit, höre ich Sie da fragen; entfliehen nicht die Grazien,
wo Integrale ihre Hälse recken.[1]

Ludwig Boltzmann (1887)

Es dürfte richtig sein, zu sagen, daß die Begriffe Differentialquotient
und Integral, deren Usprung jedenfalls bis auf Archimedes zurückgeht,
dem Wesen der Sache nach durch die Untersuchungen von Kepler,
Descartes, Cavalieri, Fermat und Wallis in die Wissenschaft
eingeführt worden sind. [...] Sie hatten noch nicht bemerkt,
daß Differentiation und Integration *inverse* Operationen sind.
Diese kapitale Entdeckung gehört Newton und Leibniz.[2]

Marius Sophus Lie (1895)

Common integration is only the *memory of differentiation*
[...] the artifices by which it [integration] is effected, are changes,
not from the unknown to the known, but from the forms
in which memory will not serve us to those in which it will.

Augustus De Morgan (1844)

He who can digest a second or third Fluxion,
a second or third Difference, need not, methinks,
be squeamish about any Point in Divinity.

George Berkeley (1734)

The Integration of Quantities seems to merit farther labour and
research; and no doubt this important and abstruse branch will, by and
by, obtain due consideration, and we shall have important
simplifications of, and additions to, our already large stock of
knowledge.

William Shanks (1853)

---

[1] Beauty, I hear you ask; do not the Graces flee where integrals stretch forth their necks?

[2] It may be said that the notions of differential quotient and integral, whose origin certainly goes back to Archimedes, were essentially introduced into science by the investigations of Kepler, Descartes, Cavalieri, Fermat, and Wallis. [...] They had not yet noticed that differentiation and integration are *inverse* operations; this capital discovery belongs to Newton and Leibniz.

22

Symbolic integration

The basic task in this chapter is, given an "expression" f, say $f \in F(x)$, where F is a field, to compute the indefinite integral $\int f = \int f(x)dx$, that is, another "expression" (possibly in a larger domain) g with $g' = f$, where $'$ denotes differentiation with respect to the variable x. "Expressions" are usually built from rational functions and "elementary functions" such as sin, cos, exp, log, etc. (Since it is more common, we denote the natural (base e) logarithm by "log" instead of "ln" in this chapter.) Such integrals need not exist: Liouville's (1835) theorem implies that $\exp(x^2)$ has no integral involving only rational functions, sin, cos, exp, and log.

A practical approach to the symbolic integration problem is to use a plethora of formulas for special functions, tricks from basic calculus like substitutions and integration by parts, and table lookups. There are projects that load the whole contents of existing printed integral tables into computer algebra systems, using optical character recognition, and modern computer algebra systems can solve practically all integration exercises in calculus textbooks. In the following, we discuss a systematic algorithm, restricted, however, to the case of rational functions as integrands. This approach can be extended—with plenty of new ideas and techniques—to more general functions, but we do not pursue this topic further.

22.1. Differential algebra

A remarkable fact about symbolic integration is that the theory can be set up in a purely algebraic way, without any use of limit processes. We are familiar with this approach from Chapter 9, where we used a formal Taylor expansion for Newton iteration.

DEFINITION 22.1. *We let R be an integral domain of characteristic zero, and $D: R \longrightarrow R$ such that the following hold for all $f, g \in R$.*

> *(i)* $D(f+g) = D(f) + D(g)$,

> *(ii)* $D(fg) = D(f)g + fD(g)$ *(Leibniz rule).*

Then D is called a **differential operator** (or derivation, or derivative), and (R,D) is a **differential algebra** (or **differential field**, if R is in fact a field).

The set $R_0 = \{c \in R : D(c) = 0\}$ is the **ring of constants** of (R,D). If $f, g \in R$ are such that $D(f) = g$, then we say that f is an **integral** of g and write $f = \int g$.

The notation $f = \int g$ is merely a relation and not a function since, as in calculus, we may add an arbitrary constant $c \in R_0$ to f to get another integral of g.

LEMMA 22.2. *In a differential algebra* (R,D), *the usual properties hold for all* $f, g \in R$:

(i) $D(1) = 0$,

(ii) D *is* R_0–*linear*: $D(af + bg) = aD(f) + bD(g)$ *for* $a, b \in R_0$,

(iii) $D\left(\dfrac{f}{g}\right) = \dfrac{D(f)g - fD(g)}{g^2}$ *if* g *is a unit,*

(iv) $D(f^n) = nf^{n-1}D(f)$,

(v) $\int(fD(g)) = fg - \int(D(f)g)$ *(integration by parts).*

See Exercise 22.2 for a proof.

EXAMPLE 22.3.   (i) $D(a) = 0$ for all $a \in R$. This is the **trivial derivative** on R, with $R_0 = R$.

(ii) $R = \mathbb{Q}(x)$, $D(x) = 1$, and $D(a) = 0$ for all $a \in \mathbb{Q}$. This gives the usual derivative: $D(\sum_i f_i x^i) = \sum_i i f_i x^{i-1}$ when all f_i are rational numbers. Here, $R_0 = \mathbb{Q}$ (Exercise 22.4), and polynomials are easily integrated as

$$\int \sum_i f_i x^i = \sum_i \frac{f_i}{i+1} x^{i+1}. \quad \Diamond$$

In what follows, we write f' instead of $D(f)$ for the usual derivative on $F(x)$, where F is a field of characteristic zero.

LEMMA 22.4. *The rational function* $1/x \in \mathbb{Q}(x)$ *has no rational integral:*

$$\forall f \in \mathbb{Q}(x) \quad f' \neq \frac{1}{x}.$$

See Exercise 22.5 for a proof. The lemma motivates the need for domain extensions when looking for integrals: the usual derivation on $\mathbb{Q}(x)$ is not surjective, so that we need logarithms.

DEFINITION 22.5. *Let (K,D) be a differential field, $F \subseteq K$ a subfield, $\vartheta \in K$, and $u \in F$ with $D(\vartheta) = D(u)/u$. Then we write $\vartheta = \log u$ (this is in general a relation, not a function, since we may add an arbitrary constant to ϑ and get another integral of $D(u)/u$), and say that ϑ is **logarithmic over F**.*

EXAMPLE 22.6. (i) We let $u = x \in F = \mathbb{Q}(x)$, $K = \mathbb{Q}(x, \vartheta)$ and $\vartheta' = u'/u = 1/x$, so that $\vartheta = \log x$. Then $\displaystyle\int \frac{1}{x} = \log x$.

(ii) Similarly, $\displaystyle\int \frac{1}{x^2 - 2} = \frac{\sqrt{2}}{4} \log(x - \sqrt{2}) - \frac{\sqrt{2}}{4} \log(x + \sqrt{2})$ in the differential field $\mathbb{Q}(\sqrt{2})(x, \log(x - \sqrt{2}), \log(x + \sqrt{2}))$.

(iii) $\displaystyle\int \frac{1}{x^3 + x} = \log x - \frac{1}{2} \log(x + i) - \frac{1}{2} \log(x - i) = \log x - \frac{1}{2} \log((x + i)(x - i))$

$$= \log x - \frac{1}{2} \log(x^2 + 1) \in \mathbb{Q}(x, \log x, \log(x^2 + 1)). \diamond$$

22.2. Hermite's method

Let F be a field of characteristic zero, $f, g \in F[x]$ nonzero and coprime, and suppose that we want to compute $\int (f/g)$. The idea is to find first $a, b, c, d \in F[x]$ with

$$\int \frac{f}{g} = \frac{c}{d} + \int \frac{a}{b}, \tag{1}$$

$\deg a < \deg b$, and b squarefree. The rational function c/d is called the **rational part**, $\int (a/b)$ the **logarithmic part** of the integral; we deal with the latter in the next section.

First, the polynomial part is separated from f/g by performing one division with remainder. This yields $q, h \in F[x]$ with $f = qg + h$ and $\deg h < \deg g$, so that $f/g = q + h/g$, and h/g is a proper rational function. Integration of the polynomial q is of course trivial.

We compute the squarefree decomposition of g, that is, $g_1, \ldots, g_m \in F[x]$ monic, squarefree and pairwise coprime with $g_m \neq 1$ and $g = g_1 g_2^2 \cdots g_m^m$ (Section 14.6). Next, we calculate the corresponding partial fraction decomposition

$$\frac{h}{g} = \sum_{1 \leq i \leq m} \sum_{1 \leq j \leq i} \frac{h_{ij}}{g_i^j}, \tag{2}$$

with all $h_{ij} \in F[x]$ of smaller degree than g_i (see Section 5.11).

Now comes the Hermite reduction process. Let $i \in \{1, \ldots, m\}$. We reduce $\int h_{ij}/g_i^j$ to a sum of a rational function plus an integral of the same form, but with the index j lowered by 1, from $j = i$ down to $j = 2$. Using that $\gcd(g_i, g_i') = 1$

since g_i is squarefree, we can compute $s, t \in F[x]$ such that $sg_i + tg'_i = h_{ij}$ and $\deg s, \deg t < \deg g_i$, by Theorem 4.10. Then

$$
\begin{aligned}
\int \frac{h_{ij}}{g_i^j} &= \int \frac{s}{g_i^{j-1}} + \int \frac{t \cdot g'_i}{g_i^j} = \int \frac{s}{g_i^{j-1}} + \frac{-t}{(j-1)g_i^{j-1}} + \int \frac{t'}{(j-1)g_i^{j-1}} \\
&= \int \frac{s + t'/(j-1)}{g_i^{j-1}} + \frac{-t}{(j-1)g_i^{j-1}},
\end{aligned}
\tag{3}
$$

using integration by parts. Adding $s + t'/(j-1)$ to $h_{i,j-1}$ and proceeding recursively leads to the following theorem. We use the multiplication time M as described on the inside front cover.

━━ THEOREM 22.7 Hermite reduction. ━━━━━━━━━━━━━━━━━━━━━━━━
The problem of integrating rational functions over a field F of characteristic zero can be reduced to integrating rational functions with squarefree denominator in softly linear time. More specifically, for nonzero polynomials $f, g \in F[x]$ of degree at most n, we can compute polynomials $q, c, d, a_1, \ldots, a_m \in F[x]$ and squarefree and pairwise coprime polynomials $g_1, \ldots, g_m \in F[x]$ such that

$$
\frac{f}{g} = q + \left(\frac{c}{d}\right)' + \frac{a_1}{g_1} + \cdots + \frac{a_m}{g_m},
$$

$\deg q \leq n$, $\deg c < \deg d < n$, $\deg a_i < \deg g_i$ *for all* i, *and* $\sum_{1 \leq i \leq m} \deg g_i < n$, *using* $O(\mathsf{M}(n) \log n)$ *operations in F*. ━━━━━━━━━━━━━━━━━━━━━

PROOF. Splitting off the polynomial part is one division with remainder, taking $O(\mathsf{M}(n))$ operations in F. The squarefree decomposition of g can be computed using $O(\mathsf{M}(n) \log n)$ operations, by Theorem 14.23. Using fast Chinese remaindering (Section 10.3), the partial fraction decomposition (2) can again be computed with $O(\mathsf{M}(n) \log n)$ arithmetic operations (Exercise 10.18). Let $d_i = \deg g_i$ for all i. To analyze the cost of Hermite reduction, let $1 \leq j \leq i \leq m$. Then one Hermite step (3) takes $O(\mathsf{M}(d_i) \log d_i)$ operations for computing s and t, plus $O(d_i)$ operations for updating $h_{i,j-1}$, in total $O(i\mathsf{M}(d_i) \log d_i)$ operations per g_i. Now

$$
\sum_{1 \leq i \leq m} i\mathsf{M}(d_i) \log d_i \leq (\log n)\mathsf{M}\left(\sum_{1 \leq i \leq m} id_i\right) \leq \mathsf{M}(n) \log n,
$$

since $\sum_{1 \leq i \leq m} id_i = \deg g \leq n$, and the claim follows. ☐

It is sufficient to use the fast Extended Euclidean Algorithm only once per g_i to compute $s^*, t^* \in F[x]$ such that $s^* g_i + t^* g'_i = 1$, and then for each j the polynomials s, t can be obtained from s^*, t^* and h_{ij} as described in Section 4.5, using only

$O(\mathsf{M}(d_i))$ arithmetic operations. This does not affect the asymptotic time bound but is a practical improvement.

A different approach, due to Horowitz (1971), is the method of undetermined coefficients. Splitting off the polynomial part if necessary, we may assume that $\deg f < \deg g$. All denominators arising via (3) outside an integral divide the product $g_2 g_3^2 \cdots g_m^{m-1}$, and hence so does the denominator d in (1). Thus we may take the latter polynomial as d, the squarefree part (Section 14.6) of g as b, and plug a of degree $\deg b - 1$ and c of degree $\deg g - \deg b - 1$ with unknown coefficients into (1). This yields a linear system of equations for the coefficients of a and c, which has a coefficient matrix with at most n rows and columns, and it can be solved in time $O(n^3)$ using Gaussian elimination. Hermite reduction, however, is asymptotically faster by nearly two orders of magnitude.

22.3. The method of Rothstein and Trager

It remains to compute $\int (a/b)$ for nonzero coprime polynomials $a, b \in F[x]$ with b squarefree. Many calculus texts provide the following solution. Let K be the splitting field of b over F, that is, the smallest algebraic field extension of F containing all roots of b. Then $b = \prod_{1 \le k \le n}(x - \lambda_k)$, with distinct $\lambda_1, \ldots, \lambda_n \in K$. There exist $c_1, \ldots, c_n \in K$ such that $a/b = \sum_{1 \le k \le n} c_k/(x - \lambda_k)$ is the partial fraction decomposition of the rational function a/b, and the integral is

$$\int \frac{a}{b} = \sum_{1 \le k \le n} c_k \log(x - \lambda_k) \in K(x, \log(x - \lambda_1), \ldots, \log(x - \lambda_n)).$$

EXAMPLE 22.6 (continued). The integral in (iii) has been expressed without any algebraic extension of the field of constants $\mathbb{Q}$, while it is not clear how to do that with the integral in (ii). In fact, from what we will prove below, it is impossible to write the latter integral as a sum of logarithms with rational arguments. ◇

This example shows that it may be unwise to compute the integral using the complete partial fraction decomposition. The following method computes the integral with as small an algebraic extension of the field of constants as possible.

▬▬ THEOREM 22.8 *Rothstein's and Trager's integration algorithm.* ▬▬
Let $a, b \in F[x]$ be coprime with $\deg a < \deg b = n$, and b monic and squarefree. If E is an algebraic extension of F, $c_1, \ldots, c_l \in E \setminus \{0\}$ are pairwise distinct, and $v_1, \ldots, v_l \in E[x] \setminus E$ are monic, squarefree, and pairwise coprime, then the following are equivalent:

(i) $\displaystyle \int \frac{a}{b} = \sum_{1 \le i \le l} c_i \log v_i.$

(ii) *The polynomial $r = \mathrm{res}_x(b, a - yb') \in F[y]$ splits over E in linear factors, $c_1, \ldots, c_l$ are precisely the distinct roots of r, and $v_i = \gcd(b, a - c_i b')$ for $1 \leq i \leq l$. Here, res_x denotes the resultant with respect to the variable x (Chapter 6).*

PROOF. (i) $\Longrightarrow$ (ii): Differentiating (i) yields

$$\frac{a}{b} = \sum_{1 \leq i \leq l} c_i \frac{v_i'}{v_i},$$

or equivalently,

$$a \cdot \prod_{1 \leq j \leq l} v_j = b \cdot \sum_{1 \leq i \leq l} c_i u_i v_i',$$

where $u_i = \prod_{1 \leq j \leq l, \, j \neq i} v_j$. We claim that $b = \prod_{1 \leq j \leq l} v_j$ and $a = \sum_{1 \leq i \leq l} c_i u_i v_i'$.

Since a and b are coprime, b divides $\prod_{1 \leq j \leq l} v_j$. On the other hand, v_j divides $b \sum_{1 \leq i \leq l} c_i u_i v_i'$ and $v_j \mid u_i$ for $i \neq j$, whence $v_j \mid b \cdot c_j u_j v_j'$. But $c_j \in E$ is nonzero, $\gcd(v_j, u_j) = 1$, and $\gcd(v_j, v_j') = 1$, so that $v_j \mid b$ for $1 \leq j \leq l$. By the relative primality of the v_j, we also have $\prod_j v_j \mid b$. This implies that $b = \prod_{1 \leq j \leq l} v_j$, since b and all the v_j are monic, and $a = \sum c_i u_i v_i'$, as claimed.

Now Lemma 14.22 yields

$$\gcd(b, a - cb') = \begin{cases} v_j & \text{if } c = c_j \text{ for some } j \in \{1, \ldots, l\}, \\ 1 & \text{otherwise,} \end{cases}$$

and for any $c \in E$

$$c \in \{c_1, \ldots, c_l\} \iff \gcd(b, a - cb') \neq 1 \iff \mathrm{res}_x(b, a - cb') = 0 \iff r(c) = 0,$$

by Lemma 6.25. Thus r splits over E, and $\{c_1, \ldots, c_l\}$ are precisely the distinct roots of r.

(ii) $\Longrightarrow$ (i): Let K be the splitting field of b over E, and $\lambda_1, \ldots, \lambda_n \in K$ pairwise distinct with $b = \prod_{1 \leq k \leq n}(x - \lambda_k)$. Since b is squarefree, $b'(\lambda_k) \neq 0$ for $1 \leq k \leq n$. For $c \in K$, we have

$$
\begin{aligned}
r(c) = 0 \quad &\iff \quad \mathrm{res}_x(b, a - cb') = 0 \iff \gcd(b, a - cb') \neq 1 \\
&\iff \quad \exists k \in \{1, \ldots, n\} \quad (a - cb')(\lambda_k) = 0 \\
&\iff \quad \exists k \in \{1, \ldots, n\} \quad c = \frac{a(\lambda_k)}{b'(\lambda_k)}.
\end{aligned}
$$

We write $d_k = a(\lambda_k)/b'(\lambda_k) \in K$ for $1 \leq k \leq n$. Then every root c_j of r is equal to d_k for some $k \in \{1, \ldots, n\}$, and conversely every d_k is a root of r, so that $\{c_1, \ldots, c_l\} = \{d_1, \ldots, d_n\}$. In particular, we have $l \leq n$. The values $d_1, \ldots, d_n$ need not be distinct.

We now claim that v_j has precisely those λ_k as zeroes where $d_k = c_j$. Let $\sigma \colon \{1,\ldots,n\} \longrightarrow \{1,\ldots,l\}$ be such that $d_k = c_{\sigma(k)}$ for all k. Then σ is surjective,

$$(a - c_{\sigma(k)}b')(\lambda_k) = (a - d_k b')(\lambda_k) = 0$$

for $1 \le k \le n$, and $v_{\sigma(k)}(\lambda_k) = 0$ since $(x - \lambda_k)$ divides $\gcd(b, a - c_{\sigma(k)}b') = v_{\sigma(k)}$. Conversely, if $v_j(\lambda_k) = 0$ for some j, then also $(a - c_j b')(\lambda_k) = 0$, so that $c_j = d_k$ and $j = \sigma(k)$. Thus

$$v_j = \prod_{1 \le k \le n,\ \sigma(k)=j} (x - \lambda_k),$$

and $b = \prod_{1 \le j \le l} v_j$.

Now let $u_i = \prod_{1 \le j \le l,\ j \ne i} v_j$ for $1 \le i \le l$, as before. Then

$$\begin{aligned}
\left(\sum_{1 \le i \le l} c_i u_i v_i' \right)(\lambda_k) &= (c_{\sigma(k)} u_{\sigma(k)} v_{\sigma(k)}')(\lambda_k) = c_{\sigma(k)} \left(\sum_{1 \le i \le l} u_i v_i' \right)(\lambda_k) \\
&= d_k b'(\lambda_k) = a(\lambda_k)
\end{aligned}$$

for $1 \le k \le n$. Both a and $\sum_{1 \le i \le l} c_i u_i v_i'$ have degrees less than n and interpolate the same values at the n points $\lambda_1, \ldots, \lambda_n$, and thus are equal. Hence

$$\left(\sum_{1 \le i \le l} c_i \log v_i \right)' = \sum_{1 \le i \le l} c_i \frac{v_i'}{v_i} = \frac{1}{b} \cdot \sum_{1 \le i \le l} c_i u_i v_i' = \frac{a}{b}. \quad \square$$

EXAMPLE 22.6 (continued). Let $a = 1$ and $b = x^3 + x$, as in Example 22.6 (iii). Then

$$\begin{aligned}
r &= \operatorname{res}_x(x^3 + x, 1 - y(3x^2 + 1)) = \det \begin{pmatrix} 1 & 0 & -3y & 0 & 0 \\ 0 & 1 & 0 & -3y & 0 \\ 1 & 0 & -y+1 & 0 & -3y \\ 0 & 1 & 0 & -y+1 & 0 \\ 0 & 0 & 0 & 0 & -y+1 \end{pmatrix} \\
&= -4y^3 + 3y + 1 = -(2y+1)^2(y-1),
\end{aligned}$$

and its zeroes are $c_1 = -1/2$ and $c_2 = 1$. Thus

$$\begin{aligned}
v_1 &= \gcd(x^3 + x, 1 + \tfrac{1}{2}(3x^2 + 1)) = \gcd\left(x^3 + x, \tfrac{3}{2}(x^2 + 1)\right) = x^2 + 1, \\
v_2 &= \gcd(x^3 + x, 1 - (3x^2 + 1)) = \gcd(x^3 + x, -3x^2) = x.
\end{aligned}$$

Now $u_1 = b/v_1 = x$, $u_2 = b/v_2 = x^2 + 1$, and we check that $v_1 v_2 = b$,

$$c_1 u_1 v_1' + c_2 u_2 v_2' = -\tfrac{1}{2}x \cdot 2x + 1 \cdot (x^2 + 1) \cdot 1 = 1 = a,$$

and therefore in fact $(-\tfrac{1}{2}\log(x^2 + 1) + \log x)' = 1/(x^3 + x)$, as in Example 22.6. $\Diamond$

We have derived the following integration algorithm for rational functions.

▨▨▨ ALGORITHM 22.9 Symbolic integration of rational functions. ▨▨▨▨▨▨▨
Input: $f, g \in F[x]$ coprime, where F is a field of characteristic zero and $g \neq 0$
monic.
Output: $\int \dfrac{f}{g}$.

1. $h \longleftarrow f \text{ rem } g, \quad \sum_i q_i x^i \longleftarrow f \text{ quo } g, \quad U \longleftarrow \sum_i \dfrac{q_i}{i+1} x^{i+1}$

2. **call** Yun's algorithm 14.21 to compute the squarefree decomposition $g = \displaystyle\prod_{1 \leq i \leq m} g_i^i$ of g

3. compute the partial fraction decomposition $\dfrac{h}{g} = \displaystyle\sum_{1 \leq i \leq m} \sum_{1 \leq j \leq i} \dfrac{h_{ij}}{g_i^j}$, with $h_{ij} \in$
   $F[x]$ such that $\deg h_{ij} < \deg g_i$ for $1 \leq j \leq i \leq m$

4. { Hermite reduction }
   $V \longleftarrow 0$
   for $i = 2, \ldots, m$ **do**
       for $j = i, i-1, \ldots, 2$ **do**
           compute $s, t \in F[x]$ such that $sg_i + tg_i' = h_{ij}$ and $\deg s, \deg t <$
           $\deg g_i$ using Theorem 4.10
   $$V \longleftarrow V - \dfrac{t}{(j-1)g_i^{j-1}}, \quad h_{i,j-1} \longleftarrow h_{i,j-1} + s + \dfrac{t'}{j-1}$$

5. $W \longleftarrow 0$
   for $k = 1, \ldots, m$ **do**

6.   { Rothstein and Trager method }
       $a \longleftarrow h_{k1}, \quad b \longleftarrow g_k, \quad r \longleftarrow \text{res}_x(b, a - yb')$
       compute the distinct monic irreducible factors $r_1, \ldots, r_l \in F[y]$ of r
       for $i = 1, \ldots, l$ **do**
           $\gamma_i \longleftarrow y \bmod r_i$
           compute $v_i \in F[x, y]$ with $\deg_y v_i < \deg_y r_i$ and $v_i(x, \gamma_i) =$
           $\gcd(b, a - \gamma_i b') \in (F[y]/\langle r_i \rangle)[x]$
           $W \longleftarrow W + \displaystyle\sum_{r_i(\gamma)=0} \gamma \log v_i(x, \gamma)$

7. **return** $U + V + W$ ▨▨▨▨▨▨▨▨▨▨▨▨▨▨▨▨▨▨

Updating V in step 4 may be done by bringing $V - t/((j-1)g_i^{j-1})$ to a common
denominator. Usually, however, it is more desirable to concatenate the summands

symbolically, without actually computing the sum. This also applies to the updating of W in step 6, and then the integral is returned as a formal sum of several "small" rational functions and logarithms in step 7. Many computer algebra systems handle it that way, and the user must explicitly direct the system to bring the integral to a common denominator after calling the symbolic integration engine.

A similar remark applies to the sum over all zeroes γ of r_i in step 6. This can be left as is, without further evaluation (for example, by using the RootOf construct in MAPLE). Alternatively, we can compute a "primitive element" β (not related to the primitive elements of Chapter 18) for the splitting field $K = F(\beta)$ of r_i (or even r) over F, express all roots of r_i as polynomials in β, and calculate modulo the minimal polynomial of β. This is a topic on its own; we have touched on it in Section 6.8 where we used resultants to compute the minimal polynomial of the sum of two algebraic numbers. In general, however, the splitting field of r_i has degree $(\deg r_i)!$ over F, and it may be more convenient to avoid it in practice.

EXAMPLE 22.6 (continued). Let $f = 1$ and $g = x^2 - 2$, as in Example 22.6 (ii). Then $g = g_1$ is squarefree, and nothing happens in steps 1 through 4. In step 6, we have $m = 1$, $a = f$, $b = g$, and

$$r = \operatorname{res}_x(x^2 - 2, 1 - y \cdot 2x) = \det \begin{pmatrix} 1 & -2y & 0 \\ 0 & 1 & -2y \\ -2 & 0 & 1 \end{pmatrix} = -8y^2 + 1.$$

This polynomial is irreducible in $\mathbb{Q}[x]$, so that $l = 1$, and with $\gamma_1 = y \bmod r$ (representing $1/2\sqrt{2}$ or $-1/2\sqrt{2}$), we obtain $a - \gamma_1 b' = -2\gamma_1 x + 1 = -2\gamma_1 (x - 4\gamma_1)$ since $8\gamma_1^2 = 1$. The Euclidean Algorithm over $(\mathbb{Q}[y]/\langle r \rangle)$ for b and $a - \gamma_1 b'$ computes $x^2 - 2 = (x + 4\gamma_1)(x - 4\gamma_1)$. Thus $v_1 = x - 4y$, $W = \sum_{r(\gamma)=0} \gamma \log(x - 4\gamma)$, and if we plug in the two zeroes $\pm 1/2\sqrt{2} \in \mathbb{R}$ of r for γ, we arrive at the same result as in Example 22.6. ◇

━━━ THEOREM 22.10. ━━━━━━━━━━━━━━━━━━
Algorithm 22.9 works correctly as specified. If f and g are of degree at most n, its running time is $O(\mathsf{M}(n)^2 \log n)$ or $O^\sim(n^2)$ operations in F, plus the cost for factoring all resultants r in step 6, whose degrees sum to at most n. ━━━━

PROOF. Correctness follows from the discussion preceding Theorem 22.7 and from Theorem 22.8.

By Theorem 22.7, steps 1 through 4 take $O(\mathsf{M}(n) \log n)$ operations. Let $k \in \{1, \ldots, m\}$ and $d_k = \deg g_k$. Exercise 6.12 implies that $\deg r = d_k$, and the cost for computing r is $O(d_k \mathsf{M}(d_k) \log d_k)$, by Corollary 11.18. Let $F_i = F[y]/\langle r_i \rangle$ for $1 \le i \le l$. Computing $\gcd(b, a - \gamma_i b') \in F_i[x]$ takes $O(\mathsf{M}(d_k) \log d_k)$ additions and multiplications and at most d_k inversions in F_i, by Corollary 11.6, or

$O(\mathsf{M}(d_k)\log d_k \cdot \mathsf{M}(\deg r_i))$ operations in F. Since $\sum_{1\le i\le l}\deg r_j \le \deg r = d_k$, the total cost for one execution of step 6 is $O(\mathsf{M}(d_k)^2 \log d_k)$. Now $\sum_{1\le k\le m} d_k \le n$, and the overall cost for the loop 5 is $O(\mathsf{M}(n)^2 \log n)$ operations in F. This dominates the cost for the other steps, and the claim follows. $\square$

Notes. Historically, the foundations of symbolic integration were laid by Joseph Liouville (1833a, 1833b, 1835). Ritt (1948) invented the notion of a differential algebra, which is the appropriate framework for the integration problem. A more general method was presented by Risch (1969, 1970), and variants of his algorithm are implemented today in almost any computer algebra system. They employ suitably modified versions of Hermite's and Rothstein's and Trager's methods.

Richardson (1968) and Caviness (1970) showed that a sufficiently general version of the integration problem is unsolvable. Already when we just consider real functions built up from the constant 1, a single variable, the four arithmetic operations, and the sine function, then determining whether the definite integral (from $-\infty$ to ∞) of such an expression exists is undecidable, and similarly for the existence of indefinite integrals as we considered in this chapter (Matiyasevich 1993, §9.4).

In spite of this fundamental limitation, symbolic integration and, more generally, the symbolic solution of ordinary differential equations, is a highly active area of research. Among its goals are algorithms for a wider range of problems, and better algorithms for special types of problems. Bronstein (1997) gives a nice overview.

22.1. A project for OCR-reading integral tables is described in Berman & Fateman (1994).
22.2. Ostrogradsky (1845) shows that for coprime $f, g \in F[x]$ with $\deg f < \deg g$, there exist unique polynomials $a, c \in F[x]$ such that (1) holds, $\deg a < \deg b$, and $\deg c < \deg d$, where b is the squarefree part of g and $d = g/b$, and presents an algorithm for computing a and c. The algorithm described in Section 22.2 is from Hermite (1872). Theorem 22.7 appears in Yun (1977a). Gerhard (1999) gives fast modular algorithms for Hermite reduction.
22.3. Theorem 22.8 is from Rothstein (1976, 1977) and Trager (1976). Lazard & Rioboo (1990) and Trager (unpublished) discuss an alternative of step 6 of Algorithm 22.9 which avoids computing gcds over algebraic extensions of F by computing all remainders of the Euclidean Algorithm for b and $a - yb'$ in $F(y)[x]$ and plugging all γ_j for y into the remainders of suitable degree. This is advantageous when classical arithmetic is used.

In step 6 of Algorithm 22.9, $v_i(x,\gamma) = \gcd(b, a - \gamma b')$ is computed for only one *generic* root $\gamma = \gamma_i$ of r_i. But the coefficients of this gcd are polynomial expressions in γ_i, so that any embedding of $F[y]/\langle r_i\rangle$ into a splitting field K of r over F which maps γ_i to some root $\gamma^* \in K$ of r also maps $v_i(x,\gamma_i)$ to $v_i(x,\gamma^*)$. Thus the gcd for one yields the gcd for all roots of R. In Example 22.6, the splitting field of $r = r_1$ over $\mathbb{Q}$ is $K = \mathbb{Q}(\sqrt{2})$, and we have two embeddings of $\mathbb{Q}[y]/\langle r\rangle$ into K, given by $\gamma_1 \longmapsto 1/2\sqrt{2}$ and $\gamma_1 \longmapsto -1/2\sqrt{2}$, which map the generic gcd $x - 4\gamma_1$ to $x - 4/2\sqrt{2} = x - \sqrt{2}$ and $x + 4/2\sqrt{2} = x + \sqrt{2}$, respectively.

Exercises.

22.1 Let (R,D) be a differential algebra. Show that R_0 is in fact a subring of R, and a subfield if R is a field.

22.2 Prove Lemma 22.2.

22.3 Show that $\mathbb{Q}$ has only the trivial derivative.

22.4 Let $'$ denote the usual derivative on $\mathbb{Q}(x)$. Prove *without* using arguments from calculus that $f' = 0 \Longrightarrow f \in \mathbb{Q}$ holds for all $f \in \mathbb{Q}(x)$. Hint: Prove the claim first for polynomials $f \in \mathbb{Q}[x]$.

22.5* Let F be a field of characteristic zero, and $a, b, c, d \in F[x]$ nonzero polynomials such that $(c/d)' = (a/b)$.

(i) Prove that $\deg a - \deg b \leq \deg c - \deg d - 1$, with equality if and only if $\deg c \neq \deg d$. Give an example where equality does not hold. Conclude that $\deg a - \deg b = -1$ is impossible.

(ii) Let $p \in F[x]$ be irreducible and $v_p(a) = e \in \mathbb{N}$ if $p^e \mid a$ and $p^{e+1} \nmid a$ (this is the negative logarithm of the p-adic value of a, as in Example 9.31 (iii)), and similarly $v_p(b)$, $v_p(c)$, $v_p(d)$. Prove that $v_p(a) - v_p(b) \leq v_p(c) - v_p(d) - 1$, with equality if and only if $v_p(c) \neq v_p(d)$. Give an example where equality does not hold. Conclude that $v_p(a) - v_p(b) = -1$ is impossible and that b is not squarefree if $\gcd(a,b) = 1$.

22.6* You are to show that e^{x^2} has no integral of the form $g \cdot e^{x^2}$ with a rational function $g \in \mathbb{R}(x)$.

(i) Suppose to the contrary that such a g exists. Derive a first order differential equation $g' + sg = t$ for g, with polynomials $s, t \in \mathbb{R}[x]$.

(ii) Now assume that $g = u/v$ with coprime $u, v \in \mathbb{R}[x]$ and v monic. Prove that $v = 1$.

(iii) Compare degrees on both sides of the equation $u' + su = t$, and conclude that no polynomial $u \in \mathbb{R}[x]$ satisfies it.

22.7* Let F be a field of characteristic zero and $f, g \in F[x]$ nonzero polynomials with g monic.

(i) Prove that the decomposition (1) is unique (up to adding a constant to c/d) when we stipulate that b is the (monic) squarefree part of g, $d = f/b$, and $\deg a < \deg b$. Hint: Use Exercise 22.5 (ii).

(ii) Show that a decomposition (1) always exists uniquely if $g = bd$ for monic polynomials $b, d \in F[x]$ such that $b \mid d$ and every irreducible factor of d divides b, and $\deg a < \deg b$. Give an example where such a decomposition does not exist if we drop the requirement that every irreducible factor of d divides b.

22.8* This exercise discusses a variant of Hermite reduction, due to Mack (1975) (see also Bronstein 1997, §2.2). Let F be a field of characteristic zero and $g, h \in F[x]$ nonzero such that $n = \deg g > \deg h$ and g is monic.

(i) Let $g = g_1 g_2^2 \cdots g_m^m$ be the squarefree decomposition of g, with all $g_i \in F[x]$ monic, pairwise coprime, and $g_m \neq 1$. Moreover, let $g^* = g/g_1$, $b = g_2 \cdots g_m$ be the squarefree part of g^*, and $d = g_2 g_3^2 \cdots g_m^{m-1} = g^*/b$. Now $\gcd(g_1, g^*) = 1$, and we have the partial fraction decomposition

$$\frac{h}{g} = \frac{h_1}{g_1} + \frac{h^*}{g^*},$$

with unique $h_1, h^* \in F[x]$ such that $\deg h_1 < \deg g_1$ and $\deg h^* < \deg g^*$. The first fraction has a squarefree denominator; it contributes to the logarithmic part of $\int (h/g)$.

Prove that d divides bd' and that $\gcd(bd'/d, b) = 1$. Thus there exist $s, t \in F[x]$ of smaller degree than b such that $s(bd'/d) + tb = h^*$. Use this to write

$$\frac{h^*}{g^*} = \left(\frac{u}{d}\right)' + \frac{v}{d},$$

with $u, v \in F[x]$ of smaller degree than d, and determine u and v.

(ii) Use (i) iteratively to split $\int (h/g)$ into its rational and logarithmic parts, and show that this takes $O(mM(n)\log n)$ operations in F.

(iii) Analyze both the Hermite reduction as described in Section 22.2 and Mack's variant when using classical polynomial arithmetic, and compare your results.

22.9 What is the leading coefficient of the resultant r in Theorem 22.8? Hint: Prove that it is the constant coefficient of $\mathrm{res}_x(ay - b', b)$.

22.10$\longrightarrow$ Trace Algorithm 22.9 on computing the integral of

$$f = \frac{x^9}{x^7 + 3x^6 - 5x^5 - 23x^4 - 8x^3 + 40x^2 + 48x + 16} \in \mathbb{Q}(x).$$

Summa cum laude.[1]

A sum to trick th' arithmetic.

Rudyard Kipling (1893)

Some merely took refuge in the mathematics, chains of difficult
calculations using symbols as stepping stones on a march through fog.

James Gleick (1992)

As an algorist Euler has never been surpassed, and probably never
even closely approached, unless perhaps by Jacobi. An algorist
is a mathematician who devises "algorithms" (or "algorisms")
for the solution of problems of special kinds [...] There is no uniform
mode of procedure—algorists, like facile rhymesters, are born,
not made. It is fashionable today to despise the 'mere algorist';
yet, when a truly great one like the Hindu Ramanujan
arrives unexpectedly out of nowhere, even expert analysts
hail him as a gift from Heaven [...] An algorist is a 'formalist'
who loves beautiful formulas for their own sake.

Eric Temple Bell (1937)

Sometimes when studying his work I have wondered how much
Ramanujan could have done if he had had MACSYMA or
SCRATCHPAD or some other symbolic algebra package. More often
I get the feeling that he was such a brilliant, clever, and intuitive
computer himself that he really did not need them.

George E. Andrews (1986)

---

[1] Sum with praise ;-)

23

Symbolic summation

The task that we address in this chapter is, given an "expression" $g(n)$ depending on n, to find an "expression" $f(n)$ such that

$$f(n) = \sum_{0 \leq k < n} g(k),$$

or, more generally, a closed form for the sum $\sum_{a \leq k < b} g(k)$ for arbitrary nonnegative integers $a \leq b$. We will explain later what kind of expressions we consider; for the time being, the reader may imagine univariate rational functions over a field of characteristic zero.

We first solve the summation problem for polynomials, and introduce much of the notation used later. After a digression about harmonic numbers, we discuss hypergeometric terms and their summation. Section 24.3 gives a brief outlook on further extensions, where computer algebra systems have had remarkable success in giving short proofs of seemingly difficult problems. In contrast to the rest of this book, we omit cost analyses.

23.1. Polynomial summation

Most computer algebra systems can handle tasks like these:

$$\sum_{0 \leq k < n} k = \frac{n(n-1)}{2},$$

$$\sum_{0 \leq k < n} k^2 = \frac{n(n-1)(2n-1)}{6},$$

$$\sum_{0 \leq k < n} k^3 = \frac{n^2(n-1)^2}{4},$$

$$\sum_{0 \leq k < n} k^4 = \frac{n(n-1)(2n-1)(3n^2-3n-1)}{30},$$

$$\sum_{0\le k<n} c^k = \frac{c^n - 1}{c - 1} \text{ if } c \neq 1,$$

$$\sum_{0\le k\le n} \binom{n}{k} = (1+1)^n = 2^n, \tag{1}$$

$$\sum_{0\le k\le n} (-1)^k \binom{n}{k} = (1-1)^n = 0 \text{ if } n > 0. \tag{2}$$

The last two summations are of a different type than the others, in that the upper bound n also occurs in the summand. In this chapter, we will only consider summations where this is not the case; this is called **indefinite summation**.

A useful tool for symbolic summation is the **difference operator** Δ. It associates to an expression f an expression Δf, defined by $(\Delta f)(n) = f(n+1) - f(n)$. It has the following properties:

○ Linearity: $\Delta(af + bg) = a\Delta f + b\Delta g$ for expressions f, g and constants a, b in F,

○ Product rule: $\Delta(fg) = f\Delta g + g\Delta f - \Delta f \cdot \Delta g$ for expressions f, g.

In particular, Δf is a rational function if f is. We will see below, however, that the converse is false in general. Related operators are the **shift operator** E, with $(Ef)(n) = f(n+1)$, and its powers $(E^k f)(n) = f(n+k)$ for $k \in \mathbb{Z}$. We have the operator identity $\Delta = E - I$, where $I = E^0$ is the identity operator.

The following lemma gives the connection between the difference operator and symbolic summation.

LEMMA 23.1. *If f, g are expressions such that $g = \Delta f$, then*

$$\sum_{a\le k<b} g(k) = f(b) - f(a)$$

for all $a, b \in \mathbb{N}$ with $a \le b$.

PROOF.

$$\sum_{a\le k<b} g(k) = \sum_{a\le k<b} \left(f(k+1) - f(k) \right) = \sum_{a\le k<b} f(k+1) - \sum_{a\le k<b} f(k)$$

$$= \sum_{a<k\le b} f(k) - \sum_{a\le k<b} f(k) = f(b) - f(a). \ \square$$

This effect of cancellation of consecutive summands is called **telescoping**. The lemma shows that the **symbolic summation problem** can be reformulated as follows: Given an expression g, find another expression f such that $\Delta f = g$. We also write $f = \Sigma g$ for such an expression, noting that Σ is not really a function but a binary relation, since $\Delta(f+c) = \Delta f + \Delta c = \Delta f = g$ for any expression with $\Delta c = 0$, for example, a constant $c \in F$. Thus Δ is a left inverse of Σ: $\Delta(\Sigma f) = f$ for all expressions f. Depending on the class of expressions we consider, there may be nonconstant periodic expressions which are annihilated by Δ, such as $\sin(2n\pi)$. Lemma 23.3 below implies that the rational functions c with $\Delta c = 0$ are precisely the constants.

Symbolic summation is the discrete analog of symbolic integration. The role of the (formal) derivative $D = d/dx$ is played by the difference operator Δ, which is some kind of analog to the limit

$$(Df)(x) = \lim_{h \to 0} \frac{f(x+h) - f(x)}{h}$$

when only positive integral values for h are allowed. The expression Σg corresponds to the indefinite integral $\int g(x)dx$, and Lemma 23.1 is the analog of the fundamental theorem of calculus:

$$g = Df = \frac{d}{dx}f \implies \int_a^b g(x)dx = f(b) - f(a).$$

We have seen that the product rule is somewhat different from the Leibniz rule. What about the analog of

$$D(x^m) = mx^{m-1} \tag{3}$$

for $m \in \mathbb{N}$? For $m = 3$, for example, we have

$$\Delta(n^3) = (n+1)^3 - n^3 = 3n^2 + 3n + 1,$$

so that (3) does not hold with Δ instead of D. The following notions restore (3) for the difference operator.

DEFINITION 23.2. *For a polynomial $f \in F[x]$ and $m \in \mathbb{N}$, we define the mth* **falling factorial** *by*

$$f^{\underline{m}} = f(x)f(x-1)\cdots f(x+m-1) = f \cdot E^{-1}f \cdot E^{-2}f \cdots E^{-m+1}f.$$

In particular, we have

$$x^{\underline{m}} = x(x-1)\cdots(x-m+1),$$

which is a monic polynomial of degree m. Similarly, we also have the mth **rising factorial**

$$f^{\overline{m}} = f(x)f(x+1)\cdots f(x+m-1) = E^{m-1}f^{\underline{m}}.$$

For $m = 0$, we let $f^{\underline{0}} = f^{\overline{0}} = 1$.

The similarity with the definition of $m! = m(m-1)(m-2)\cdots 1$ gives rise to the name *factorial*, and in fact $m! = x^{\underline{m}}(m) = x^{\overline{m}}(1)$. It is possible to extend the definition also to negative values of m; see Exercise 23.10.

LEMMA 23.3. *The shift operator E^k for $k \in \mathbb{Z}$ is an automorphism of $F(x)$ leaving each element of F fixed, with inverse E^{-k}. The following relations hold for all $\rho, \sigma \in F(x)$, $f, g \in F[x]$, and $m \in \mathbb{N}$.*

(i) $E^k(\rho \pm \sigma) = E^k\rho \pm E^k\sigma$, $E^k(\rho \cdot \sigma) = E^k\rho \cdot E^k\sigma$, $E^k(\rho/\sigma) = E^k\rho/E^k\sigma$,

(ii) $E^k(f^{\underline{m}}) = (E^k f)^{\underline{m}}$, $E^k(f^{\overline{m}}) = (E^k f)^{\overline{m}}$,

(iii) $\gcd(E^k f, E^k g) = E^k \gcd(f, g)$,

(iv) *f is irreducible $\Longleftrightarrow$ $E^k f$ is irreducible,*

(v) $\deg(E^k f) = \deg f$,

(vi) $\rho = E\rho \Longleftrightarrow \rho \in F$.

PROOF. Statements (i)–(v) and (vi) "$\Longleftarrow$" are clear. We first prove (vi) "$\Longrightarrow$" when $\rho = \sum_{0 \le i \le n} f_i x^i \in F[x]$ is a polynomial, with $f_n \ne 0$ and $n > 0$. Then the coefficient of x^{n-1} in $E\rho = f_n(x+1)^n + f_{n-1}(x+1)^{n-1} + \sum_{0 \le i \le n-2} f_i(x+1)^i$ is $nf_n + f_{n-1}$, and in ρ it is f_{n-1}. Since F has characteristic zero, $nf_n \ne 0$, and $E\rho \ne \rho$.

Now we let $\rho = f/g$, with coprime $f, g \in F[x]$ and $\deg g > 1$, and assume that $E\rho = \rho$, or equivalently, $g \cdot Ef = f \cdot Eg$. Then $g \mid Eg$, by the relative primality of f and g. Since the degrees and the leading coefficients of g and Eg agree, we have $g = Eg$, and hence $g \in F$, by what we have already shown. This is a contradiction to $\deg g > 1$ and concludes the proof. $\square$

By (ii) of the above lemma, it is unambiguous to write $E^k f^{\underline{m}}$ and $E^k f^{\overline{m}}$. Now we calculate

$$
\begin{aligned}
\Delta(x^{\underline{m}}) &= Ex^{\underline{m}} - x^{\underline{m}} = (x+1)^{\underline{m}} - x^{\underline{m}} \\
&= (x+1)x(x-1)\cdots(x-m+2) - x(x-1)\cdots(x-m+2)(x-m+1) \\
&= \left((x+1) - (x-m+1)\right)x^{\underline{m-1}} = mx^{\underline{m-1}}
\end{aligned}
$$

for all $m \in \mathbb{N}$, and this is the discrete analog of (3). Thus $\Sigma x^{\underline{m}} = x^{\underline{m+1}}/(m+1)$ and

$$
\sum_{0 \le k < n} k^{\underline{m}} = \frac{n^{\underline{m+1}}}{m+1}
$$

for all $m, n \in \mathbb{N}$, by Lemma 23.1. We are somewhat abusing our notation here in that we write $k^{\underline{m}}$ instead of $x^{\underline{m}}(k)$ for $k \in \mathbb{N}$.

By expressing the ordinary powers x^m as a linear combination of falling factorials, we can solve the summation problem for arbitrary polynomials, as in the following example.

EXAMPLE 23.4.

$$\sum_{0 \le k < n} k = \sum_{0 \le k < n} k^{\underline{1}} = \frac{n^{\underline{2}}}{2} = \frac{n(n-1)}{2},$$

$$\sum_{0 \le k < n} k^2 = \sum_{0 \le k < n} (k^{\underline{2}} + k^{\underline{1}}) = \frac{n^{\underline{3}}}{3} + \frac{n^{\underline{2}}}{2} = \frac{n(n-1)(n-2)}{3} + \frac{n(n-1)}{2}$$

$$= \frac{n(n-1)(2n-1)}{6},$$

$$\sum_{0 \le k < n} k^3 = \sum_{0 \le k < n} (k^{\underline{3}} + 3k^{\underline{2}} + k^{\underline{1}}) = \frac{n^{\underline{4}}}{4} + n^{\underline{3}} + \frac{n^{\underline{2}}}{2} = \frac{n^2(n-1)^2}{4}.$$

These sums are in accordance with the first three examples at the beginning of the chapter. $\diamond$

Since for each $m \in \mathbb{N}$ both $x^m, \ldots, x^2, x, 1$ and $x^{\underline{m}}, \ldots, x^{\underline{2}}, x, 1$ are $\mathbb{Q}$-bases of the vector space of polynomials in $\mathbb{Q}[x]$ of degree at most m, we can write

$$x^m = \sum_{0 \le i \le m} \left\{ {m \atop i} \right\} x^{\underline{i}} \tag{4}$$

with rational numbers $\left\{ {m \atop i} \right\}$ for $0 \le i \le m$. Then

$$x^m = x \cdot x^{m-1} = \sum_{0 \le i < m} \left\{ {m-1 \atop i} \right\} x \cdot x^{\underline{i}}$$

$$= \sum_{0 \le i < m} \left\{ {m-1 \atop i} \right\} x^{\underline{i+1}} + \sum_{0 \le i < m} \left\{ {m-1 \atop i} \right\} i \cdot x^{\underline{i}}$$

$$= x^{\underline{m}} + \sum_{1 \le i < m} \left(\left\{ {m-1 \atop i-1} \right\} + i \left\{ {m-1 \atop i} \right\} \right) x^{\underline{i}}$$

for $m > 1$, where we have used that $x^{\underline{i+1}} = x^{\underline{i}}(x-i)$ in the second line. Comparing coefficients of $x^{\underline{i}}$ in the last line and in (4), we find that the $\left\{ {m \atop i} \right\}$ satisfy the recursion formula

$$\left\{ {m \atop i} \right\} = \left\{ {m-1 \atop i-1} \right\} + i \left\{ {m-1 \atop i} \right\} \tag{5}$$

for $m \ge i > 0$, with the boundary conditions

$$\left\{ {m \atop i} \right\} = 0 \text{ if } i > m, \quad \left\{ {m \atop 0} \right\} = 0 \text{ for } m \ge 1, \quad \left\{ {0 \atop 0} \right\} = 1.$$

In particular, $\left\{ {m \atop i} \right\}$ is a nonnegative integer for $0 \le i \le m$.

The numbers $\left\{{m \atop i}\right\}$ have a combinatorial interpretation: they count the number of partitions of the set $\{1,\ldots,m\}$ into i nonempty subsets and are known as the **Stirling numbers of the second kind**. For example, the partitions of $\{1,\ldots,4\}$ into two nonempty subsets are

$$\{1\}\{2,3,4\},\quad \{2\}\{1,3,4\},\quad \{3\}\{1,2,4\},\quad \{4\}\{1,2,3\},$$
$$\{1,2\}\{3,4\},\quad \{1,3\}\{2,4\},\quad \{1,4\}\{2,3\},$$

and hence $\left\{{4 \atop 2}\right\} = 7$. Obviously $\left\{{m \atop 1}\right\} = \left\{{m \atop m}\right\} = 1$ for $m \geq 1$. The combinatorial interpretation of the recursion formula (5) is that there are $\left\{{m-1 \atop i-1}\right\}$ possibilities for m to be in a subset of its own and $i \cdot \left\{{m-1 \atop i}\right\}$ possibilities to adjoin m to one of the i subsets of a partition of $\{1,\ldots,m-1\}$ into i nonempty subsets.

The representation (4) for $m = 1,\ldots,5$ is:

$$
\begin{aligned}
x^1 &= x^{\underline{1}}, \\
x^2 &= x^{\underline{2}} + x^{\underline{1}}, \\
x^3 &= x^{\underline{3}} + 3x^{\underline{2}} + x^{\underline{1}}, \\
x^4 &= x^{\underline{4}} + 6x^{\underline{3}} + 7x^{\underline{2}} + x^{\underline{1}}, \\
x^5 &= x^{\underline{5}} + 10x^{\underline{4}} + 25x^{\underline{3}} + 15x^{\underline{2}} + x^{\underline{1}}.
\end{aligned}
$$

If $g = \sum_{0 \leq m \leq d} g_m x^m \in F[x]$ is an arbitrary polynomial of degree d, we get

$$
\begin{aligned}
\Sigma g &= \Sigma\left(\sum_{0 \leq m \leq d} g_m \sum_{0 \leq i \leq m} \left\{{m \atop i}\right\} x^{\underline{i}}\right) = \sum_{0 \leq i \leq m \leq d} g_m \left\{{m \atop i}\right\} \Sigma x^{\underline{i}} \\
&= \sum_{0 \leq i \leq m \leq d} g_m \left\{{m \atop i}\right\} \frac{x^{\underline{i+1}}}{i+1},
\end{aligned}
$$

(6)

and hence

$$\sum_{0 \leq k < n} g(k) = \sum_{0 \leq i \leq m \leq d} g_m \left\{{m \atop i}\right\} \frac{n^{\underline{i+1}}}{i+1}.$$

In particular, Σg is a polynomial of degree $d+1$, in analogy with symbolic integration. This completely solves the summation problem for polynomials. For a different approach using Bernoulli numbers, see Exercise 23.8.

23.2. Harmonic numbers

In the case of symbolic integration, we have seen that the rational function $1/x$ in $F(x)$ has no rational integral. Something similar happens when summing $1/x$:

$$\sum_{1 \leq k \leq n} \frac{1}{k} = 1 + \frac{1}{2} + \cdots + \frac{1}{n} = H_n.$$

The rational number H_n is called the nth **harmonic number**, since it is the nth partial sum of the (divergent!) harmonic series $\sum_{k\geq 1} 1/k$. The following lemma implies that the harmonic numbers cannot be represented by a rational function.

LEMMA 23.5. *There is no rational function $\rho \in F(x)$ with $\Delta\rho = 1/x$.*

PROOF. We assume the contrary, namely that there exist coprime polynomials $f,g \in F[x]$ of degrees m and n, respectively, such that

$$\frac{1}{x} = \Delta\left(\frac{f}{g}\right) = \frac{Ef}{Eg} - \frac{f}{g} = \frac{g \cdot Ef - f \cdot Eg}{g \cdot Eg}$$

in $F(x)$, or, equivalently,

$$g \cdot Eg = x(g \cdot Ef - f \cdot Eg) \tag{7}$$

in $F[x]$. It is clear that g is not constant, and hence $m + n \geq 1$. The coefficient of x^{m+n} in $g \cdot Ef - f \cdot Eg = g\Delta f - f\Delta g$ is zero, and the coefficient of x^{m+n-1} is $(m-n)\,\mathrm{lc}(f)$. Comparing degrees on the two sides of (7), we obtain

$$
\begin{aligned}
m = n &\iff \deg(g \cdot Eg) = m + n\\
&\iff \deg(x(g \cdot Ef - f \cdot Eg)) = m + n\\
&\iff m \neq n.
\end{aligned}
$$

This contradiction proves the claim. $\square$

Generalizations of this lemma are in Exercises 23.12 and 23.28. The harmonic numbers are the discrete analog of the natural logarithm $\ln x$, and in fact

$$H_n \in \ln n + \gamma + \frac{1}{2n} + O\left(\frac{1}{n^2}\right),$$

where $\gamma = \lim_{n \to \infty}(H_n - \ln n) = 0.5772156649\ldots$ is **Euler's constant**. Table 23.1 shows the values of H_n, $\ln n$, and their difference for increasing values of n.

n	H_n	$\ln n$	$H_n - \ln n$	$n(H_n - \ln n - \gamma)$
10	2.9289682540	2.3025850930	0.6263831610	0.4916749607
100	5.1873775176	4.6051701860	0.5822073316	0.4991666750
1000	7.4854708606	6.9077552790	0.5777155816	0.4999166667
10 000	9.7876060360	9.2103403720	0.5772656640	0.4999916667
100 000	12.0901461299	11.5129254650	0.5772206649	0.4999991667
1 000 000	14.3927267229	13.8155105579	0.5772161650	0.4999999167

TABLE 23.1: The difference between H_n and $\ln n$.

One can also prove that there is no rational function representing the sum

$$\sum_{1 \leq k \leq n} \frac{1}{k^j}$$

for $j = 2, 3, \ldots$ (Exercise 23.28). The corresponding infinite series is the famous **Riemann zeta function** $\zeta(j) = \sum_{k \geq 1} k^{-j}$, which converges for $j \geq 2$ (in fact, for any complex $j \in \mathbb{C}$ with $\Re j > 1$). This function plays a fundamental role in analytic number theory (Notes 18.4). For $j = 2$, its value is

$$\zeta(2) = \sum_{k \geq 1} \frac{1}{k^2} = \frac{\pi^2}{6}.$$

We have come across this number in Chapter 3, where we found its inverse to be the probability that two random integers have a nontrivial gcd.

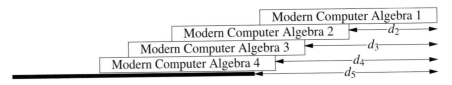

FIGURE 23.2: A tower of books on a table.

The following example gives a physical interpretation of the harmonic numbers. Suppose that we have a collection of books, all of equal size and equal weight and with the center of gravity in the middle, and want to build a tower of them at the edge of a table with a horizontal overhang as far as possible so that the tower does not fall over (see Figure 23.2). We assume for simplicity that each book has length 2, and denote the distance between the right edges of book 1 and book i (counted from the top) by d_i. The book on top of the tower does not fall down if the vertical projection of its gravity center hits the second book, so the maximal possible value for d_2 is 1. The second book does not produce a collapse if the common center of gravity of the upper two books is vertically above book 3, and so on. In general, d_i is the horizontal distance between the common gravity center of books 1 through $i-1$ and the right edge of book 1, which leads to the recursive formula

$$(i-1)d_i = (d_1 + 1) + \cdots + (d_{i-1} + 1), \tag{8}$$

since the center of gravity of k objects of equal weight whose respective centers of gravity are at position $p_1, \ldots, p_k$ is at position $(p_1 + \cdots + p_k)/k$. We get rid of the dependence on all previous values in (8) by subtracting the recursion formulas for i and $i-1$:

$$(i-1)d_i - (i-2)d_{i-1} = d_{i-1} + 1.$$

After rearranging terms and unfolding the recurrence, we obtain

$$d_i = d_{i-1} + \frac{1}{i-1} = d_1 + 1 + \frac{1}{2} + \cdots + \frac{1}{i-1} = H_{i-1},$$

if $i \geq 2$, since $d_1 = 0$. The first values are $d_2 = 1$, $d_3 = 3/2$, $d_4 = 11/6$, $d_5 = 25/12$, so that 4 is the minimal number of books in a tower whose top book is horizontally completely beyond the table (try this at home!). Since H_n is unbounded, one can in principle reach any horizontal distance from the table, but the logarithmic growth of H_n necessitates exponentially many books. For example, with $1\,000\,000$ books, the overhang is ≈ 14.39 (don't try this at home!).

Now that we have seen the discrete analog of the logarithm, what is the analog of the exponential function? Its characteristic differential equation is $De^x = e^x$. The corresponding identity $\Delta f = f$ implies that $f(x+1) = 2f(x)$, and we check that $f = 2^x$ does the job. More generally,

$$\Delta c^x = c^{x+1} - c^x = (c-1)c^x$$

for all constants $c \in F$, and hence $\Sigma c^x = c^x/(c-1)$ if $c \neq 1$. In the version

$$\sum_{0 \leq k < n} c^k = \frac{c^n}{c-1} - \frac{c^0}{c-1} = \frac{c^n - 1}{c-1},$$

we recognize the familiar formula for the geometric sum.

Here is a summary of the analogies between integration and summation.

$g = Df$	$g = \Delta f$	
$f = \int g$	$f = \Sigma g$	
$f(b) - f(a) = \int_a^b g(x)dx$	$f(b) - f(a) = \displaystyle\sum_{a \leq k < b} g(k)$	
$Dx^m = mx^{m-1}$	$\Delta x^{\underline{m}} = mx^{\underline{m-1}}$	for $m \in \mathbb{Z}$
$\displaystyle\int x^m dx = \frac{x^{m+1}}{m+1}$	$\displaystyle\Sigma x^{\underline{m}} = \frac{x^{\underline{m+1}}}{m+1}$	for $m \in \mathbb{Z} \setminus \{-1\}$
$\displaystyle\int_1^n x^{-1} dx = \ln n$	$\displaystyle\sum_{1 \leq k \leq n} k^{-1} = H_n$	
$\displaystyle\int c^x dx = \frac{c^x}{\ln c}$	$\displaystyle\Sigma c^x = \frac{c^x}{c-1}$	for $c \neq 1$

23.3. Greatest factorial factorization

In this section, we discuss a representation of polynomials related to the squarefree decomposition from Section 14.6. As the latter does for symbolic integration, this **greatest factorial factorization** will play a crucial role for symbolic summation in Section 23.4. The aim is to write a monic polynomial $f \in F[x]$ uniquely as a product $f = f_1^{\underline{1}} f_2^{\underline{2}} \cdots f_m^{\underline{m}}$, with $f_1, \ldots, f_m \in F[x]$.

EXAMPLE 23.6. To write

$$f = x^5 + 2x^4 - x^3 - 2x^2 = (x-1)x^2(x+1)(x+2) \in \mathbb{Q}[x]$$

as a product of falling factorials, we have (among others) the following possibilities:

$$f = x^{\underline{1}}(x+2)^{\underline{4}} = x^{\underline{2}}(x+2)^{\underline{3}} = (x^2+2x)^{\underline{1}}(x+1)^{\underline{3}} = f^{\underline{1}}. \diamond$$

Intuitively, the first factorization in the above example is "maximal" in the sense that we have extracted the "greatest" possible falling factorial. An informal algorithm for its computation would be to look for the largest $m \in \mathbb{N}$ such that $g^{\underline{m}} \mid f$ for some nonconstant $g \in F[x]$, divide $g^{\underline{m}}$ out, and proceed recursively.

DEFINITION 23.7. *Let* $f, f_1, \ldots, f_m \in F[x]$ *and* f *monic. Then* $(f_1, \ldots, f_m)$ *is called a **greatest factorial factorization (gff)** of* f *if the following hold.*

(F1) $f = f_1^{\underline{1}} \cdots f_m^{\underline{m}}$,

(F2) $f_1, \ldots, f_m$ *are monic and* $f_m \neq 1$,

(F3) $\gcd(f_i^{\underline{i}}, E f_j) = 1$ *for* $1 \leq i \leq j \leq m$,

(F4) $\gcd(f_i^{\underline{i}}, E^{-j} f_j) = 1$ *for* $1 \leq i \leq j \leq m$.

The definition formalizes the maximality condition indicated above: (F3) states that the falling factorial $f_j^{\underline{j}} = f_j \cdot E^{-1} f_j \cdots E^{-j+1} f_j$ cannot be extended to the left (if $g = \gcd(f_i^{\underline{i}}, E f_j) \neq 1$, then $g^{\underline{j+1}}$ is a falling factorial of length $j+1$ dividing f), and (F4) means that it cannot be extended to the right.

In the example, only the first sequence $(x, 1, 1, x+2)$ is a greatest factorial factorization. For $(1, x, x+2)$, condition (F4) is violated since $\gcd(x^2, E^{-3}(x+2)) = x-1$, so that $(x+2)^{\underline{3}}$ may be extended to the right by $(x-1)$ to get $(x+2)^{\underline{4}}$. The factorization $(x^2+2x, 1, x+1)$ fails to satisfy (F3) for $i = 1$ and $j = 3$, since $(x+1)^{\underline{3}}$ may be extended to the left by the factor $x+2$ of x^2+2x, and (f) violates both (F3) and (F4) for $i = j = 1$.

EXAMPLE 23.8. The monic irreducible factors of the polynomial

$$f = x(x-1)^3(x-2)^2(x-4)^2(x-5) \in F[x]$$

are all integral shifts of x. Figure 23.3 illustrates the shift structure of f. A bullet at point $(i, j) \in \mathbb{N}^2$ indicates that $E^{-i}x^j = (x-i)^j$ divides f. A gff of f can be read off this figure by collecting maximal horizontal chains and packing together chains of equal length (shaded equally in Figure 23.3). Thus $(x^2-5x+4, x^2-5x+4, x) = ((x-1)(x-4), (x-1)(x-4), x)$ is a gff of f. $\diamond$

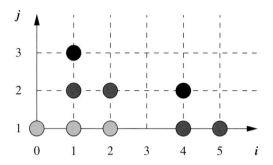

FIGURE 23.3: The shift structure of $x(x-1)^3(x-2)^2(x-4)^2(x-5)$.

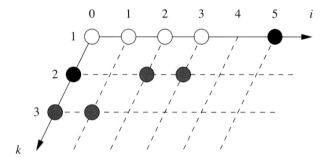

FIGURE 23.4: The shift structure of f from Example 23.9.

This example also shows that—in contrast to the squarefree decomposition—the $f_1,\ldots,f_m$ need not be pairwise coprime.

EXAMPLE 23.9. We let

$$f = x(x-1)(x-2)(x-3)(x-5)(x-\frac{1}{3})(x-\frac{7}{3})(x-\frac{10}{3})(x-\frac{2}{3})(x-\frac{5}{3}) \in F[x].$$

Then f is squarefree, and all monic irreducible factors of f are shifts of exactly one of the three polynomials $p_1 = x$, $p_2 = x - 1/3$, and $p_3 = x - 2/3$. Figure 23.4 illustrates the shift structure of f. A bullet at point $(i,k) \in \mathbb{N}^2$ indicates that $E^{-i}p_k$ divides f. Again, collecting maximal horizontal chains easily leads to a gff of f, which is

$$\left(x^2 - \frac{16}{3}x + \frac{5}{3}, x^2 - 3x + \frac{14}{9}, 1, x\right) = \left((x-\frac{1}{3})(x-5), (x-\frac{7}{3})(x-\frac{2}{3}), 1, x\right). \diamond$$

Examples 23.8 and 23.9 illustrate two extreme cases. The general situation is three-dimensional: If we partition the monic irreducible factors of a polynomial $f \in F[x]$ into **shift-equivalence classes** $\Pi_1,\ldots,\Pi_l$ and determine the unique representative $p_k \in \Pi_k$ for each k so that all other elements of Π_k are of the form $E^{-i}p_k$

for some $i \in \mathbb{N}$, then the full information about the shift structure of f can be read off the set of ordered triples $S = \{(i,j,k) \in \mathbb{N}^3 : E^{-i}p_k^j \mid f\}$. In Example 23.8, we have only one shift-equivalence class $\Pi_1 = \{x, x-1, x-2, x-4, x-5\}$ and $p_1 = x$. In Example 23.9, we have the three classes $\Pi_1 = \{x, x-1, x-2, x-3, x-5\}$, $\Pi_2 = \{x-1/3, x-7/3, x-10/3\}$, and $\Pi_3 = \{x-2/3, x-5/3\}$, and all multiplicities are 1. It is easy to find a gff of f knowing S: As in the examples, we look for maximal chains "in the i-direction" and combine all chains of equal length.

The examples suggest that the gff is unique, and the following lemma confirms this.

LEMMA 23.10. *A nonzero monic polynomial* $f \in F[x]$ *has at most one gff.*

PROOF. If $f = 1$, then the empty sequence is the only gff of f, by (F1), and we now assume that $\deg f > 0$. We suppose that $(f_1, \ldots, f_m)$ and $(g_1, \ldots, g_n)$ are both greatest factorial factorizations of f, and show by induction on $\deg f$ that they are equal. Let $p \in F[x]$ be an irreducible factor of f_m. We will show that $p \mid g_m$. To this end, we let $k \in \{1, \ldots, n\}$ be maximal such that $\gcd(p^m, g_k^k) \neq 1$. Then there exists some $i \in \{-m+1, \ldots, k-1\}$ with $p \mid E^{-i}g_k$.

If $i > 0$, then $Ep \mid E^{-i+1}g_k \mid f$, which is impossible by (F3) for $(f_1, \ldots, f_m)$, and we conclude that $i \leq 0$. If $i < 0$, then $E^{i+1}p$ divides f, and hence $E^{i+1}p \mid g_j^j$ for some $j \in \{1, \ldots, k\}$, by the maximality of k. Thus $E^{i+1}p \mid \gcd(g_j^j, Eg_k)$, contradicting (F3) for $(g_1, \ldots, g_n)$, which implies that $i = 0$ and $p \mid g_k$. In (9) and (10), the situations $i > 0$ and $i < 0$, respectively, are illustrated; arrows indicate divisibility.

$$
\begin{array}{ccccccc}
 & & p & E^{-1}p & E^{-2}p & \cdots & \\
 & & \downarrow & \downarrow & \downarrow & & \\
g_k & E^{-1}g_k & \cdots & E^{-i+1}g_k & E^{-i}g_k & E^{-i-1}g_k & E^{-i-2}g_k & \cdots
\end{array}
\tag{9}
$$

$$
\begin{array}{ccccccc}
p & E^{-1}p & \cdots & E^{i+1}p & E^{i}p & E^{i-1}p & E^{i-2}p & \cdots \\
 & & & & \downarrow & \downarrow & \downarrow & \\
 & & & & g_k & E^{-1}g_k & E^{-2}g_k & \cdots
\end{array}
\tag{10}
$$

If $k < m$, then $E^{-k}p$ divides f, and by the maximality of k, $E^{-k}p \mid \gcd(g_j^j, E^{-k}g_k)$ for some $j \in \{1, \ldots, k\}$; as illustrated in (11).

$$
\begin{array}{ccccccc}
p & E^{-1}p & \cdots & E^{-k+1}p & E^{-k}p & \cdots & E^{-m+1}p \\
\downarrow & \downarrow & & & \downarrow & & \\
g_k & E^{-1}g_k & \cdots & E^{-k+1}g_k & & &
\end{array}
\tag{11}
$$

This contradiction to (F4) for $(g_1, \ldots, g_n)$ proves that $m \leq k \leq n$. By symmetry, we also have $n \leq m$, hence $m = k = n$ and $p \mid g_m$. After shortening tails if necessary, $(f_1, \ldots, f_m/p)$ and $(g_1, \ldots, g_m/p)$ are both greatest factorial factorizations of f/p^m, and we conclude that $f_i = g_i$ for $1 \leq i \leq m$ by induction on the degree of f. $\square$

If $(f_1, \ldots, f_m)$ is a gff of f, we write $\mathrm{gff}(f) = (f_1, \ldots, f_m)$. For $f = 1$, we set $\mathrm{gff}(f) = ()$, the empty sequence.

DEFINITION 23.11. *The **shift gcd** of f is* $\mathrm{gcdE}(f) = \gcd(f, Ef)$.

The following lemma not only proves that a gff always exists, but also leads to an algorithm for its computation similar to the algorithm for computing the squarefree decomposition (Section 14.6).

━━ THEOREM 23.12 *Fundamental lemma about gff.* ━━━━━━━
Every nonzero monic polynomial $f \in F[x]$ has a unique gff, and it can be recursively computed as $\mathrm{gff}(f) = (f_1, f_2, \ldots, f_m)$ if f is nonconstant, where

$$\mathrm{gff}(\mathrm{gcdE}(f)) = (f_2, \ldots, f_m) \text{ and } f_1 = \frac{f}{f_2^2 \cdots f_m^m}. \tag{12}$$

PROOF. Uniqueness was proven in Lemma 23.10. For the existence, we proceed by induction on $\deg f$. If $f = 1$, then by definition $\mathrm{gff}(f) = ()$, and we may assume that $\deg f > 0$. Then $g = \mathrm{gcdE}(f)$ has strictly smaller degree than f, since $f = Ef$ if and only if f is constant, by Lemma 23.3. If $g = 1$, then $\mathrm{gff}(f) = (f)$ (it is easily checked that (F1) through (F4) hold).

If g is nonconstant, then by induction there are $m \in \mathbb{N}_{\geq 2}$ and nonconstant monic $g_1, \ldots, g_{m-1} \in F[x]$ such that

$$\mathrm{gff}(g) = (g_1, \ldots, g_{m-1}) \text{ and } \mathrm{gff}(\mathrm{gcdE}(g)) = (g_2, \ldots, g_{m-1}).$$

Thus

$$(E^{-1}g_1) \cdots (E^{-m+1}g_{m-1}) = E^{-1}\frac{g}{\mathrm{gcdE}(g)} = \frac{E^{-1}g}{\gcd(g, E^{-1}g)} = \frac{\mathrm{lcm}(g, E^{-1}g)}{g}.$$

Now both g and $E^{-1}g$ divide f, by the definition of gcdE, and hence

$$(E^{-1}g_1) \cdots (E^{-m+1}g_{m-1}) = \frac{\mathrm{lcm}(g, E^{-1}g)}{g} \Big| \frac{f}{g}. \tag{13}$$

This proves that f_1 in (12) is indeed a polynomial. If we now let $f_{i+1} = g_i$ for $1 \leq i < m$ and $f_1 \in F[x]$ as in (12), then (F1) and (F2) are satisfied for $(f_1, \ldots, f_m)$.

To show (F3) for $(f_1, \ldots, f_m)$, let $1 \leq i \leq j \leq m$. If $i \geq 2$, then property (F3) for $(g_1, \ldots, g_{m-1})$ implies that $\gcd(f_i^{i-1}, Ef_j) = \gcd(g_{i-1}^{i-1}, Eg_{j-1}) = 1$. Now $E^{-i+1}f_i = E^{-i+1}g_{i-1}$ divides f/g, by (13), and Ef_j divides $E(f_1 \cdots f_m) = (Ef)/g$, and since

f/g and $(Ef)/g$ are coprime, so are $E^{-i+1}f_i$ and Ef_j. Thus (F3) holds if $i \geq 2$. For $i = 1$, we have that $f_1 \mid f/g$ and $Ef_j \mid (Ef)/g$, and again $\gcd(f/g, (Ef)/g) = 1$ implies that $\gcd(f_1, Ef_j) = 1$. This concludes the proof of (F3).

The proof of (F4) is similar, see Exercise 23.16. □

In Example 23.6, we have $Ef = x(x+1)^2(x+2)(x+3)$, and

$$\gcd E(f) = x(x+1)(x+2) = (x+2)^3,$$

so that $\mathrm{gff}(\gcd E(f)) = (1, 1, x+2)$, in accordance with the previous lemma.

If $f = g_1^1 g_2^2 \cdots g_k^k$ is the squarefree decomposition of f, with monic squarefree and pairwise coprime polynomials $g_1, \ldots, g_k \in F[x]$, then $\gcd(f, f') = g_2^1 \cdots g_k^{k-1}$ (Section 14.6). The fundamental lemma is the discrete analog of this statement, since $\gcd(f, Ef) = \gcd(f, (Ef) - f) = \gcd(f, \Delta f)$. As in the case of squarefree factorization, the gff of a polynomial f can be computed without factoring f completely, only by performing essentially gcd calculations.

▬▬ ALGORITHM 23.13 Computation of the gff. ▬▬▬▬▬▬▬▬▬▬▬▬▬
Input: A monic polynomial $f \in F[x]$.
Output: $\mathrm{gff}(f)$.

1. **if** $f = 1$ **then return** ()

2. **call** the algorithm recursively to compute $(g_1, \ldots, g_{m-1}) = \mathrm{gff}(\gcd E(f))$

3. **for** $i = 1, \ldots, m-1$ **do** $f_{i+1} \longleftarrow g_i$,
$$f_1 \longleftarrow \frac{f}{\gcd E(f) \cdot (E^{-1} g_1) \cdots (E^{-m+1} g_{m-1})}$$

4. **return** $(f_1, \ldots, f_m)$ ▬▬▬▬▬▬▬▬▬▬▬▬▬▬▬▬▬▬▬

▬▬ THEOREM 23.14. ▬▬▬▬▬▬▬▬▬▬▬▬▬▬▬▬▬▬▬▬▬▬▬▬▬
Algorithm 23.13 works correctly as specified and uses $O(n \cdot \mathsf{M}(n) \log n)$ operations in F, where $n = \deg f$. ▬▬▬▬▬▬▬▬▬▬▬▬▬▬▬▬▬▬▬

PROOF. Correctness follows from the fundamental lemma. The recursion depth of the algorithm is at most n. The cost for one iteration of the algorithm is $O(\mathsf{M}(n) \log n)$, and the claim follows. □

23.4. Hypergeometric summation: Gosper's algorithm

In Section 23.1, we have solved the summation problem for polynomials. In the following, we will solve the summation problem for a much larger class of expressions, including rational functions, exponentials, factorials, and binomial coefficients. As before, F will denote a field of characteristic zero throughout.

DEFINITION 23.15. A **difference field** is a field K together with an automorphism E of K. The **field of constants** C_K of K is the fixed field of E: $C_K = \{f \in K : Ef = f\}$.

Our most important example of a difference field is the field $F(x)$ of rational functions, with E being the shift operator $Ef = f(x+1)$, as before, and Lemma 23.3 implies that $C_{F(x)} = F$. Another example is the difference field $\mathbb{Q}(2^x)$ with $E(2^x) = 2^{x+1} = 2 \cdot 2^x$.

DEFINITION 23.16. Let K be a subfield of the difference field L with automorphism E. An element $f \in L \setminus \{0\}$ is **hypergeometric over** K if the **term ratio** Ef/f belongs to the smaller field K.

EXAMPLE 23.17.   (i) Every nonzero rational function in $F(x)$ is hypergeometric over $F(x)$ with respect to the shift operator $Ex = x+1$.

(ii) The element $f = 2^x \in \mathbb{Q}(x, 2^x)$, with $Ex = x+1$ and $E(2^x) = 2 \cdot 2^x$, is hypergeometric over $F(x)$ (in fact, even over F), with term ratio $Ef/f = 2$.

(iii) Let $L = \mathbb{R}(x, \Gamma)$, where Γ is the **gamma function** (see Notes 23.1 and Exercise 23.5). This is a continuous function on $\mathbb{R}_{>0}$ which satisfies $\Gamma(1) = 1$ and the functional equation $\Gamma(x+1) = x\Gamma(x)$. Thus $\Gamma(n+1) = n!$ for all $n \in \mathbb{N}$ and Γ "interpolates" the factorial at real values. If we let E act as the shift operator $E\Gamma = \Gamma(x+1)$, then Γ is hypergeometric over $\mathbb{R}(x)$, with term ratio $E\Gamma/\Gamma = x \in \mathbb{R}(x)$.

(iv) We let $L = \mathbb{R}(x, f)$, where

$$f = \binom{n}{x} = \frac{\Gamma(n+1)}{\Gamma(x+1)\Gamma(n-x+1)}$$

extends the familiar binomial coefficient $\binom{n}{k}$ for $n, k \in \mathbb{N}$ to arbitrary real numbers in the lower argument. (The gamma function has simple poles at all nonpositive integers, and the convention $1/\Gamma(x) = 0$ for $-x \in \mathbb{N}$ makes the binomial coefficient zero for integer values of x outside $\{0, \ldots, n\}$, as it should be.) We compute the term ratio

$$\frac{Ef}{f} = \frac{\binom{n}{x+1}}{\binom{n}{x}} = \frac{\Gamma(n+1)\Gamma(x+1)\Gamma(n-x+1)}{\Gamma(x+2)\Gamma(n-x)\Gamma(n)} = \frac{-x+n}{x+1} \in \mathbb{R}(x),$$

and conclude that binomial coefficients are hypergeometric over $\mathbb{R}(x)$ with respect to their lower argument. (In fact, n might even be another indeterminate, and then the binomial coefficient is hypergeometric over $\mathbb{R}(x, n)$.) A similar computation shows that binomial coefficients are also hypergeometric over $\mathbb{R}(x)$ with respect to the upper argument. $\diamond$

In what follows, we will say "hypergeometric" for short if we mean "hypergeo-metric over $F(x)$", and E always is the shift operator on $F(x)$. Also, we will ig-nore questions of convergence and poles completely, simply regarding the gamma function and the binomial coefficients as formal indeterminates subject to the addi-tional (purely algebraic) properties $E\Gamma = x\Gamma$ and $E(\binom{n}{x}) = (-x+n)/(x+1) \cdot \binom{n}{x}$, keeping in mind that—as for rational functions—we should only evaluate them at points or sum them over ranges where they are well-defined.

The **hypergeometric summation problem** is, given a nonzero hypergeometric term g, to determine another hypergeometric term f such that $\Delta f = Ef - f = g$, where $\Delta = E - I$ is the difference operator, or to assert (correctly) that no such term exists. Since g is hypergeometric if g itself is a rational function, a method to solve the hypergeometric summation problem will in particular provide a solution for the summation of rational functions. However, Example 23.17 shows that the range of problems that fall into the hypergeometric category is much larger.

Suppose that we are given a nonzero hypergeometric term g, together with its term ratio $\sigma = Eg/g \in F(x)$. If f is another hypergeometric term with term ratio $\rho = Ef/f \in F(x)$ such that $g = \Delta f$, then $g = Ef - f = (\rho - 1)f$, which implies that $f = \tau g$, where $\tau = 1/(\rho - 1) \in F(x)$ (we have $\rho \neq 1$, for otherwise $g = 0$). In other words: if $f = \Sigma g$ is hypergeometric, then f is a rational multiple of g and already belongs to the same difference field as g.

So let us assume that $f = \tau g$ for a rational function $\tau \in F(x)$. Then

$$\Delta f = Ef - f = E\tau \cdot Eg - \tau g = (E\tau \cdot \sigma - \tau)g,$$

and this is equal to g if and only if τ solves the difference equation

$$E\tau \cdot \sigma - \tau = 1 \text{ in } F(x). \tag{14}$$

We note that only rational functions occur in (14); we have eliminated all hy-pergeometric terms and reduced the original hypergeometric summation problem to a purely rational question.

If we write $\sigma = a/b$ with coprime polynomials $a, b \in F[x]$, $b \neq 0$ monic, and similarly $\tau = u/v$ with coprime $u, v \in F[x]$, $v \neq 0$ monic, and multiply up denom-inators in (14), we arrive at the equivalent polynomial condition

$$a \cdot v \cdot Eu - b \cdot u \cdot Ev = b \cdot v \cdot Ev. \tag{15}$$

Conversely, we see that any polynomial solution $u, v \in F[x]$ of the above equa-tion for the given $a, b \in F[x]$ yields a solution to our hypergeometric summation problem by setting

$$f = \frac{u}{v}g. \tag{16}$$

In order to solve (15), we try to find a suitable denominator polynomial v or a multiple of it. We define $v_0, v_1 \in F[x]$ by $v = v_0 \cdot \gcd E(v)$ and $Ev = v_1 \cdot \gcd E(v)$, so that v_0, v_1 are coprime. Dividing (15) by $\gcd E(v)$ yields

$$a \cdot v_0 \cdot Eu - b \cdot u \cdot v_1 = b \cdot v_0 \cdot v_1 \cdot \gcd E(v). \tag{17}$$

Since v_0 divides $a \cdot v_0 \cdot Eu$ and the right hand side of (17), it divides $b \cdot u \cdot v_1$. But $\gcd(u, v_0)$ divides $\gcd(u, v) = 1 = \gcd(v_1, v_0)$, and hence $v_0 \mid b$. Similarly, $v_1 \mid a$.

Let $\mathrm{gff}(v) = (h_1, \ldots, h_m)$ be the greatest factorial factorization of v. Then

$$
\begin{aligned}
v_0 &= \frac{h_1^1 h_2^2 \cdots h_m^m}{h_2^1 \cdots h_m^{m-1}} = h_1 \cdot (E^{-1} h_2) \cdots (E^{-m+1} h_m) \mid b, \\
v_1 &= \frac{(Eh_1)^1 (Eh_2)^2 \cdots (Eh_m)^m}{h_2^1 \cdots h_m^{m-1}} = (Eh_1)(Eh_2) \cdots (Eh_m) \mid a,
\end{aligned}
\tag{18}
$$

by the fundamental lemma 23.12. Thus h_i divides $E^{-1}a$ and $E^{i-1}b$ for $1 \le i \le m$. If $v \ne 1$, then $1 \ne h_m \mid \gcd(E^{-1}a, E^{m-1}b) = E^{-1}\gcd(a(x), b(x+m))$. Therefore $\gcd(a(x), b(x+m)) \ne 1$, or, equivalently, $R(m) = 0$, where $R = \mathrm{res}_x(a(x), b(x+y))$ in $F[y]$, by Lemma 6.25. This leads to the following algorithm for computing a multiple of v.

▬ ALGORITHM 23.18 Multiple of summation denominator. ▬
Input: Relatively prime polynomials $a, b \in F[x]$ with $b \ne 0$ monic.
Output: A monic polynomial $V \in F[x]$ such that (15) for some coprime $u, v \in F[x]$ implies that $v \mid V$.

1. $R \longleftarrow \mathrm{res}_x(a(x), b(x+y))$, $\quad d \longleftarrow \max\{k \in \mathbb{N} : k = 0 \text{ or } R(k) = 0\}$
   if $d = 0$ **then return** 1

2. **for** $i = 1, \ldots, d$ **do** $H_i \longleftarrow \gcd(E^{-1}a, E^{i-1}b)$

3. **return** $H_1^1 \cdots H_d^d$ ▬

▬ THEOREM 23.19. ▬
Algorithm 23.18 works correctly as specified. In particular, if u, v are coprime polynomials in $F[x]$, with $v \ne 0$ monic, solving (15), and $\mathrm{gff}(v) = (h_1, \ldots, h_m)$, then $m \le d$ and $h_i \mid H_i$ for $1 \le i \le m$. ▬

PROOF. There is nothing to prove if $v = 1$, and we assume that $\deg v \ge 1$. Then the discussion preceding the algorithm implies that $m \ge 1$ is a positive integer zero of the resultant R in step 1, whence $d \ge m$, and that $h_i \mid H_i$ for $1 \le i \le m$. Finally,

$$v = h_1^1 \cdots h_m^m \mid H_1^1 \cdots H_m^m H_{m+1}^{m+1} \cdots H_d^d \mid V. \quad \square$$

Gosper's (1978) algorithm computes a multiple of v which sometimes has smaller degree than the multiple computed above. Furthermore, it runs often faster than Algorithm 23.18, as shown in Example 23.21 below.

━━ ALGORITHM 23.20 Gosper's multiple of summation denominator. ━━
Input: Relatively prime polynomials $a, b \in F[x]$ with $b \neq 0$ monic.
Output: A monic polynomial $V \in F[x]$ with the property that if v is the denominator of a solution to (15), then $v \mid V$.

1. $R \longleftarrow \text{res}_x(a(x), b(x+y))$, $d \longleftarrow \max\{k \in \mathbb{N} : k = 0 \text{ or } R(k) = 0\}$
    if $d = 0$ **then return** 1

2. $a_0 \longleftarrow a$, $b_0 \longleftarrow b$
    for $i = 1, \ldots, d$ **do**
    $$H_i \longleftarrow \gcd(E^{-1}a_{i-1}, E^{i-1}b_{i-1}), \quad a_i \longleftarrow \frac{a_{i-1}}{EH_i}, \quad b_i \longleftarrow \frac{b_{i-1}}{E^{-i+1}H_i}$$

3. **return** $H_1^1 \cdots H_d^d$ ━━━━━━━━━━━━

In practice, the algorithm may be stopped as soon as $a_i = 1$ or $b_i = 1$ for some $i < d$, since then $H_j = 1$ for $i < j \leq d$. Moreover, it is sufficient to perform the loop in step 2 only for those i that are roots of the resultant R.

EXAMPLE 23.21. Let $a = x + 2$ and $b = x(x+1) = x^2 + x$ in $F[x]$. Then both Algorithms 23.18 and 23.20 compute

$$R = \text{res}_x(x+2, x^2 + 2xy + y^2 + x + y) = \det \begin{pmatrix} 1 & 0 & 1 \\ 2 & 1 & 2y+1 \\ 0 & 2 & y^2 + y \end{pmatrix}$$

$$= (y^2 + y) - 2(2y+1) + 4 = (y-1)(y-2),$$

whence $d = 2$. In step 2 of Algorithm 23.18, we now have

$$\begin{aligned} H_1 &= \gcd(E^{-1}a, b) = \gcd(x+1, x^2 + x) = x + 1, \\ H_2 &= \gcd(E^{-1}a, Eb) = \gcd(x+1, x^2 + 3x + 2) = x + 1, \end{aligned}$$

and finally $V = H_1^1 H_2^2 = x(x+1)^2$ in step 3.

On the other hand, in step 2 of Algorithm 23.20, we compute

$$\begin{aligned} a_0 &= a = x + 2, \quad b_0 = b = x^2 + x, \\ H_1 &= \gcd(E^{-1}a_0, b_0) = \gcd(x+1, x^2 + x) = x + 1, \\ a_1 &= \frac{a_0}{EH_1} = 1, \quad b_1 = \frac{b_0}{H_1} = x. \end{aligned}$$

Here the algorithm stops and returns $V = H_1^1 = x + 1$ in step 3. $\Diamond$

Let $a, b \in F[x]$ be nonzero monic polynomials that split over some extension field K of F into linear factors $a = \prod_{1 \leq i \leq m}(x - \alpha_i)$ and $b = \prod_{1 \leq j \leq n}(x - \beta_j)$, and $R = \mathrm{res}_x(a(x), b(x+y)) \in F[y]$, as in step 1 of Algorithms 23.18 and 23.20. For any $\gamma \in K$, we have

$$
\begin{aligned}
R(\gamma) = 0 \;&\Longleftrightarrow\; \mathrm{res}_x(a(x), b(x+\gamma)) = 0 \text{ in } K \\
&\Longleftrightarrow\; \gcd(a(x), b(x+\gamma)) \neq 1 \text{ in } K[x] \\
&\Longleftrightarrow\; a(x) \text{ and } b(x+\gamma) = \prod_{1 \leq j \leq n}(x - \beta_j + \gamma) \text{ have a common zero} \\
&\Longleftrightarrow\; \gamma = \beta_j - \alpha_i \text{ for some } i \in \{1, \dots, m\} \text{ and } j \in \{1, \dots, n\}.
\end{aligned}
$$

Thus the roots of R are exactly the distances between the roots of a and b. We have already used this in Section 6.8 to find the minimal polynomial of the sum of two algebraic numbers. In particular, if the value d computed in step 1 of Algorithms 23.18 and 23.20 is nonzero, then it is the maximal positive integer distance between a root of a and a root of b. Thus for computing d, we may replace a and b by their squarefree parts.

EXAMPLE 23.22. Let $g = x \cdot \Gamma(x+1)$, so that $g(k) = k \cdot k!$ for $k \in \mathbb{N}$. Then the term ratio is

$$
\sigma = \frac{(x+1)\Gamma(x+2)}{x\Gamma(x+1)} = \frac{(x+1)^2}{x} \in F(x),
$$

and hence $a = (x+1)^2$ and $b = x$. In step 1 of Algorithms 23.18 and 23.20, we compute

$$
R = \mathrm{res}_x(x^2 + 2x + 1, x + y) = \det\begin{pmatrix} 1 & 1 & 0 \\ 2 & y & 1 \\ 1 & 0 & y \end{pmatrix} = y^2 - 2y + 1 = (y-1)^2,
$$

whence $d = 1$. Thus the maximal positive integer distance between a zero of a and a zero of b is 1, which can also be seen directly in this example. In fact, if replace a by its squarefree part $a^* = x + 1$, then the smaller resultant

$$
\mathrm{res}_x(a^*(x), b(x+y)) = \mathrm{res}_x(x+1, x+y) = \det\begin{pmatrix} 1 & 1 \\ 1 & y \end{pmatrix} = y - 1
$$

leads to the same value $d = 1$.

In step 2 of Algorithm 23.18, we now compute

$$
H_1 = \gcd(E^{-1}a, b) = \gcd(x^2, x) = x.
$$

(Algorithm 23.20 computes the same value for H_1), and the denominator v of a solution u/v of (15) divides $V = H_1^1 = x$—provided that such a solution exists. $\diamond$

Exercise 23.27 gives an upper bound on d, and the following example shows that this bound is almost sharp, and that the value of d may be exponentially large in the input length.

EXAMPLE 23.23. We let $g = (x^2 + nx)^{-1} \in \mathbb{Q}(x)$, with a parameter $n \in \mathbb{N}_{\geq 1}$. Its term ratio is

$$\frac{Eg}{g} = \frac{x(x+n)}{(x+1)(x+n+1)},$$

so that the input to Algorithm 23.18 is $a = x(x+n)$ and $b = (x+1)(x+n+1)$. Then $d = n - 1$ in step 1, $H_i = \gcd(a(x-1), b(x+i-1)) = 1$ for $1 \leq i < n-1$, and $H_{n-1} = \gcd(a(x-1), b(x+n-2)) = (x+n-1)$, so that $V = (x+n-1)^{\underline{n-1}} = (x+1)^{n-1}$. (Algorithm 23.20 computes the same result.) Its degree is exponential in the size of a and b, which is about $\log_{2^{64}} n$ words. $\diamond$

At this point, we have computed a monic multiple V of v. If we find $U \in F[x]$ such that

$$a \cdot V \cdot EU - b \cdot EV \cdot U = b \cdot V \cdot EV, \tag{19}$$

then $\tau = U/V \in F(x)$ is a solution of (14), and $f = Ug/V$ solves the hypergeometric summation problem. Conversely, if $\tau = u/v$, with u, v coprime and $v \neq 0$ monic, satisfies (14), then $U = uV/v$ is a solution of (19).

Dividing both sides by $h = \gcd(a \cdot V, b \cdot EV) \in F[x]$, we arrive at the equivalent equation

$$r \cdot EU - s \cdot U = t, \tag{20}$$

where $r = a \cdot V/h$, $s = b \cdot EV/h$ is monic, and $t = s \cdot V$. (In fact, we can also get rid of the factor s on the right hand side; see Exercise 23.26.) In Example 23.22, (19) reads

$$x(x+1)^2 \cdot EU - x(x+1) \cdot U = x^2(x+1),$$

or equivalently, $(x+1)EU - U = x$, after dividing by $h = x(x+1)$, so that $r = x+1$ and $s = 1$.

In order to solve (20) for U, it is sufficient to have an upper bound on the degree of U, since then (20) is equivalent to a system of linear equations in the coefficients of U. Such a bound is provided by the following lemma.

LEMMA 23.24. *Let* $r = r_m x^m + r_{m-1} x^{m-1} + \cdots + r_0$, $s = x^n + s_{n-1} x^{n-1} + \cdots + s_0$, t, *and* $U = U_e x^e + \cdots + U_0$ *be nonzero polynomials in* $F[x]$, *with nonzero* $r_m, U_e \in F$ *(where we set* $r_{m-1} = 0$ *if* $m = 0$, *and similarly* $s_{n-1} = 0$ *if* $n = 0$*), such that (20) holds. Furthermore, let* $\delta = s_{n-1} - r_{m-1} \in F$. *Then*

(i) $\deg U = e = \begin{cases} \deg t - \deg(r - s) & \text{if } \deg(r-s) \geq \deg(r+s), \\ 1 + \deg t - \deg r & \text{if } \deg(r-s) < \deg(r+s) \text{ and } \delta \notin \mathbb{N}, \\ 1 + \deg t - \deg r \text{ or } \delta & \text{if } \deg(r-s) < \deg(r+s) \text{ and } \delta \in \mathbb{N}. \end{cases}$

In the last case, we have $\delta \neq 1 + \deg t - \deg r$.

(ii) If $\deg(r-s) \geq \deg(r+s)$ or $\delta \notin \mathbb{N}$, then (20) has as most one polynomial solution $U \in F[x]$.

PROOF. We rewrite (20) in the equivalent form

$$\frac{r-s}{2}(EU+U) + \frac{r+s}{2}(EU-U) = t. \tag{21}$$

Then $\deg(EU+U) = e > \deg(EU-U)$.

(i) We compare degrees on both sides of (21). If $\deg(r-s) \geq \deg(r+s)$, then $\deg(r-s) + e = \deg t$, and we assume now that $\deg(r-s) < \deg(r+s)$. Then $m = \deg r = \deg s = n$, $r_m = 1$, and the left hand side of (21) has degree at most $m+e-1$. If $m = n = 0$, then $\delta = 0$, (20) reads $\Delta U = t$, and we conclude that $\deg U = 1 + \deg t = 1 + \deg t - \deg r$, by Section 23.1. Otherwise, if $m = n \geq 1$, then the coefficient of x^{m+e-1} in (21) equals

$$(r_{m-1} - s_{m-1} + e)U_e = (e - \delta)U_e \in F.$$

Since $U_e \neq 0$, the degree is strictly less than $m+e-1$ if and only if $e = \delta$. Thus either $m+e-1 = \deg t$ and $e \neq \delta$, or $m+e-1 > \deg t$ and $e = \delta \in \mathbb{N}$.

(ii) If $U, U^* \in F[x]$ are both solutions of (21), their difference $\overline{U} = U - U^*$ satisfies

$$\frac{r-s}{2}(E\overline{U}+\overline{U}) - \frac{r+s}{2}(E\overline{U}-\overline{U}) = 0.$$

By the same reasoning as for (i), this equation can only hold for a nonzero $\overline{U} \in F[x]$ if $\deg(r-s) < \deg(r+s)$ and $\deg \overline{U} = \delta \in \mathbb{N}$. $\square$

In any case, we can (almost) determine $\deg U$ from the known polynomials r, s, and $t = s \cdot V$. If the value e from Lemma 23.24 is a nonnegative integer, we set up the system of linear equations equivalent to (20) and solve it for the unknown coefficients of U. Then $\tau = U/V \in F(x)$ satisfies (14), and we get a solution to our hypergeometric summation problem as in (16). If, however, e is negative or $\delta = \deg t - \deg r + 1$ in the last case of the above lemma or the linear system is unsolvable, then we know that (14) has no rational solution $\tau \in F(x)$, and no hypergeometric term f with $\Delta f = g$ exists. Here is the complete algorithm.

▬▬ ALGORITHM 23.25 Gosper's algorithm for hypergeometric summation. ▬▬
Input: Nonzero coprime polynomials $a, b \in F[x]$, with b monic, where F is a field of characteristic zero.
Output: Coprime polynomials $u, v \in F[x]$, with v monic, satisfying (15), if such polynomials exists, otherwise "unsolvable".

1. **call** Algorithm 23.20 with input a, b, yielding a monic multiple $V \in F[x]$ of the denominator.

2. $g \longleftarrow \gcd(a \cdot V, b \cdot EV), \quad r \longleftarrow \dfrac{a \cdot V}{g}, \quad s \longleftarrow \dfrac{b \cdot EV}{g}, \quad t \longleftarrow s \cdot V$

3. $m \longleftarrow \deg r, \quad \delta \longleftarrow s_{m-1} - r_{m-1}$
   if $\deg(r-s) \geq \deg(r+s)$ **then** $e \longleftarrow \deg t - \deg(r-s)$
   else if $\delta \notin \mathbb{N}$ **then** $e \longleftarrow 1 - m + \deg t$
   else if $\delta = 1 - m + \deg t$ **then return** "unsolvable"
   else $e \longleftarrow \max\{1 - m + \deg t, \delta\}$

4. **if** $e < 0$ **then return** "unsolvable"

5. solve the linear system corresponding to (20) for the unknown coefficients
   $U_0, \ldots, U_e \in F$ of U of degree at most e
   if the system is unsolvable **then return** "unsolvable"
   else $U \longleftarrow U_e x^e + \cdots + U_1 x + U_0$

6. **return** $\dfrac{U}{\gcd(U,V)}$ and $\dfrac{V}{\gcd(U,V)}$ ▬▬▬▬▬▬▬▬▬▬▬▬

The solution space of the linear system in step 5 is either empty, or has precisely one element, or is one-dimensional. In the latter case, we preferably take a solution leading to a numerator U of smallest degree. The coefficient matrix of the linear system is triangular, so that the system is particularly easy to solve without Gaussian elimination, simply by back substitution, taking $O(e^2)$ operations in F. At most one diagonal element is zero, and this occurs only if $\deg(r-s) < \deg(r+s)$.

Exercise 23.26 shows that we may even obtain $\gcd(r,t) = \gcd(s,t) = 1$ in step 2, by appropriately dividing out common factors, and perform steps 3 through 5 for a divisor of U. This may further reduce the size of the linear system in step 5.

We conclude this section with a series of examples.

EXAMPLE 23.22 (continued). We obtain the equation $(x+1)EU - U = x$, or, equivalently, $x(EU - U)/2 + (x+2)(EU + U)/2 = x$. Thus $r = x+1$, $s = 1$, $t = x$, $\deg(r-s) = \deg x = 1 = \deg(x+2) = \deg(r+s)$, and $\deg U = \deg t - \deg(r-s) = 1 - 1 = 0$. Hence if the equation is solvable for U, then $U = U_0 \in F$ is a constant polynomial, and by comparing coefficients on both sides, we see that $U = 1$ does the job. This shows that $f = Ug/V = \Gamma(x+1)$ is a hypergeometric solution of the summation problem $\Delta f = g$ (indeed we check that $\Gamma(x+2) - \Gamma(x+1) = x \cdot \Gamma(x+1)$), and we obtain the formula

$$\sum_{0 \leq k < n} k \cdot k! = \sum_{0 \leq k < n} g(k) = f(n) - f(0) = n! - 1. \ \diamond$$

EXAMPLE 23.23 (continued). We have $h = \gcd(a \cdot V, b \cdot EV) = (x+1)^{\overline{n}}$, and equation (20) reads

$$x \cdot EU - (x+n+1) \cdot U = (x+n+1)(x+1)^{\overline{n-1}}, \qquad (22)$$

with $r = x$, $s = x + n + 1$, and $t = (x + n + 1)(x + 1)^{\overline{n-1}}$. Then

$$\deg(r - s) = \deg(-n - 1) = 0 < 1 = \deg(2x + n + 1) = \deg(r + s)$$

and $\delta = n + 1$. We are in the last case of Lemma 23.24 and find $e = \max\{n, n+1\} = n+1$ in step 3 of Algorithm 23.25. If $n = 2$, for example, we let $U = U_3 x^3 + U_2 x^2 + U_1 x + U_0$, with undetermined coefficients U_3, U_2, U_1, U_0. Plugging this into (22), we see that the coefficients of x^4 and x^3 cancel, as expected, and comparing coefficients of x^2, x and 1 on both sides, we arrive at the linear system

$$3U_3 - U_2 = 1, \quad U_3 + U_2 - 2U_1 = 4, \quad 3U_0 = 3,$$

whose solutions are $U_3 = \lambda$, $U_2 = 3\lambda - 1$, $U_1 = 2\lambda - 5/2$, and $U_0 = 1$, for an arbitrary choice of $\lambda \in F$. Taking $\lambda = 0$ yields the solution $U = -(x^2 + \frac{5}{2}x + 1)$ of smallest degree, and in fact

$$f = \frac{U}{V}g = -\frac{x^2 + \frac{5}{2}x + 1}{(x^2 + 2x)(x + 1)} = -\frac{x + \frac{1}{2}}{x(x + 1)}$$

satisfies $\Delta f = g$. Exercise 23.13 shows that for an arbitrary positive integer n, $U = -\frac{1}{n}(x + n)(x^{\overline{n}})'$ solves (22), where $'$ denotes the formal derivative, and that $\Delta(-(x^{\overline{n}})'/nx^{\overline{n}}) = 1/(x^2 + nx)$. $\diamond$

EXAMPLE 23.26. Let $g = 1/x \in F(x)$. Then $\sigma = Eg/g = x/(x + 1)$, and $a = x$, $b = x + 1$. We compute $R = \operatorname{res}_x(x, x + y + 1) = y + 1$ in step 1 of Algorithms 23.20 and 23.18, and hence $d = 0$ and $V = 1$. Plugging this into (20), we obtain

$$x \cdot EU - (x + 1)U = (x + 1).$$

We have $r = x$, $s = t = x + 1$, $\deg(r - s) = 0 < 1 = \deg(r + s)$, and $1 + \deg t - \deg r = 1 = \delta$. By Lemma 23.24 (i), last case, equation (20) has no solution U, and we conclude that $\Sigma(1/x)$ is not hypergeometric. This generalizes Lemma 23.5. $\diamond$

The following example shows that in the last case of Lemma 23.24 (i), both choices for e may lead to a solution of the hypergeometric summation problem.

EXAMPLE 23.27. This is another nonrational hypergeometric summation that we can do. For a fixed $n \in \mathbb{N}_{\geq 1}$, we want to determine

$$\sum_{0 \leq k < m} (-1)^k \binom{n}{k}. \tag{23}$$

We know, of course, that the sum is 0 for $m > n$, by the binomial theorem, but sometimes such sums also occur with the upper summation bound being smaller than n. The term ratio of the summand $g = (-1)^x \binom{n}{x}$ is

$$\sigma = \frac{Eg}{g} = \frac{(-1)^{x+1}\binom{n}{x+1}}{(-1)^x\binom{n}{x}} = \frac{x-n}{x+1},$$

and hence $a = x - n$ and $b = x + 1$. (The reader being concerned about what $(-1)^x$ might mean for $x \notin \mathbb{Z}$ may replace it by $e^{i\pi x}$.) The first step of Algorithms 23.18 and 23.20 computes

$$R = \mathrm{res}_x(x-n, x+y+1) = y+n+1,$$

so that $d = 0$ and $V = 1$. Equation (20) then is

$$(x-n)EU - (x+1)U = x+1, \tag{24}$$

and we have $r = x - n$, $s = t = x + 1$, $\deg(r-s) = 0 < 1 = \deg(r+s)$, and $\delta = n + 1$. We are in the last case of Lemma 23.24, and hence $e = 1 + \deg t - \deg r = 1$ or $e = \delta = n + 1$. The lemma does not tell us which choice to make, so we try $e = 1$ first, since it looks easier. With $U = U_1 x + U_0$, (24) is

$$\begin{aligned}
x+1 &= (x-n)(U_1(x+1) + U_0) - (x+1)(U_1 x + U_0) \\
&= (-n)U_1 x + (-nU_1 - (n+1)U_0),
\end{aligned}$$

and the linear system

$$1 = -nU_1, \quad 1 = -nU_1 - (n+1)U_0$$

has the unique solution $U_1 = -1/n$ and $U_0 = 0$. Thus $\tau = U/V = -x/n$,

$$\Sigma(-1)^x \binom{n}{x} = \tau \cdot (-1)^x \binom{n}{x} = -\frac{x}{n}(-1)^x \binom{n}{x} = (-1)^{x-1}\binom{n-1}{x-1},$$

and consequently

$$\begin{aligned}
\sum_{0 \le k < m}(-1)^k \binom{n}{k} &= 1 + \sum_{1 \le k < m}(-1)^k \binom{n}{k} \\
&= 1 + (-1)^{m-1}\binom{n-1}{m-1} - (-1)^0 \binom{n-1}{0} \\
&= (-1)^{m-1}\binom{n-1}{m-1}
\end{aligned}$$

for all $m \in \mathbb{N}$. In particular, the sum is 0 if we plug in $m > n$, as it should be.

Now let us try $e = \delta = n + 1$. If a solution $U^* \in F[x]$ of (24) of degree $n + 1$ exists, then the difference $\overline{U} = U^* - U$ solves the homogeneous equation

$$(x - n)E\overline{U} - (x + 1)\overline{U} = 0,$$

and vice versa. Inspection shows that $\overline{U} = x^{\underline{n+1}}$ is a solution of the homogeneous equation, and hence $U^* = U + \overline{U} = x^{\underline{n+1}} - x/n$ is a solution of (24) of degree $n + 1$. Now $\overline{U} = \Gamma(x+1)/\Gamma(x-n)$, and hence

$$E(\overline{U}g) = E\overline{U} \cdot Eg = \frac{(x+1)\Gamma(x+1)}{(x-n)\Gamma(x-n)} \cdot \sigma g = \overline{U}g,$$

or equivalently, $\Delta(\overline{U}g) = 0$, which means that $\overline{U}g$ is a new "constant". In particular, $\overline{U}g$ vanishes at all integers since it vanishes at zero, and we may ignore it if we are only interested in summing g for integral values of x.

The above derivation is essentially still valid if n is an indeterminate, that is, if we want to solve the summation problem over the field $F(n)$ of rational functions in n with coefficients in F. One exception is that then $\delta = n + 1 \notin \mathbb{N}$, and hence the case $e = \delta$ need not be considered at all. Moreover, $(-1)^{m-1}\binom{n-1}{m-1}$ is nonzero as a polynomial in n for all integers $m \geq 1$, but has $0, \dots, m-2$ as zeroes.

Exercise 23.21 shows that the summation problem (23) has no hypergeometric solution if we omit the factor $(-1)^x$. $\diamond$

Notes.   An excellent reference for much of this chapter is Graham, Knuth & Patashnik (1994); the book tower example is from this text. It also contains useful information about binomial coefficients, Bernoulli numbers, Euler numbers, and Stirling numbers, including lots of pretty sums involving them.

The whole theory of differencing, summing, and solving difference (or recurrence) equations in a symbolic fashion has already been treated in classics like Boole (1860) and Jordan (1965, first edition 1939). The solution of differential equations by discretization has been a driving force for studying "difference calculus" and solving difference equations numerically.

23.1. Von zur Gathen & Gerhard (1997) analyze several algorithms for computing $Ef = f(x + 1)$ for a polynomial $f \in \mathbb{Z}[x]$.

There is a common framework which covers the similarity between the two equalities $Dx^n = nx^{n-1}$ and $\Delta x^{\underline{n}} = nx^{\underline{n-1}}$ for $n \in \mathbb{N}$, the *umbral calculus*. It studies linear operators on the vector space $F[x]$ of polynomials over a field F. If T is such a linear operator with the additional properties that T commutes with the differential operator D and $\deg(Tf) = \deg f - 1$ for all nonzero $f \in F[x]$, then there is a unique sequence $f_0 = 1, f_1, f_2, \dots \in F[x]$ of polynomials such that $\deg f_n = n$, $Tf_n = nf_{n-1}$, and $f_n(0) = 0$ for all $n \geq 1$, the sequence **associated** to T. Thus $f_n = x^n$ is associated to D and $f_n = x^{\underline{n}}$ is associated to Δ. All associated sequences satisfy a binomial theorem

$$f_n(x+y) = \sum_{0 \leq k \leq n} \binom{n}{k} f_k(x) f_{n-k}(y)$$

(this is clear for $f_n = x^n$, and Exercise 23.9 proves it for the falling factorials); in fact, this property is equivalent to being an associated sequence. The origins of the umbral calculus date back to the middle of the 19th century, and Gian-Carlo Rota put it on a rigorous formal basis in the 1970s. An excellent reference is Roman (1984).

The **gamma function** is defined by $\Gamma(x) = \int_0^\infty e^{-t} t^{x-1} dt$ for all $x \in \mathbb{R}_{\geq 0}$. It satisfies the functional equation $\Gamma(x+1) = x\Gamma(x)$ for all $x \geq 1$, and since $\Gamma(1) = 1$, we have in particular $\Gamma(n+1) = n!$ for all $n \in \mathbb{N}$ (Exercise 23.5). By analytic continuation, the gamma function can be extended to a meromorphic function on the complex plane with simple poles at the nonpositive integers $0, -1, -2, -3, \ldots$. This leads to a more general definition of (falling and rising) factorials and binomial coefficients, via $x^{\overline{n}} = \Gamma(x+n)/\Gamma(x)$ for arbitrary complex numbers x and n with $x + n \notin -\mathbb{N}$.

The rising factorial is also called the Pochhammer symbol and written as $(x)_m$.

The formula for summing a polynomial goes back to Stirling (1730), where also the Stirling numbers (of both kinds) are defined. Vandermonde introduced $x^{\underline{n}}$ in 1772. Knuth (1993) explains Johann Faulhaber's (1631) methods for summation of powers, yielding much more beautiful expressions than the ones we give. A true renaissance man.

23.3. The definition of the gff, as well as Theorem 23.12 and Algorithm 23.13, are from Paule (1995). We have adopted the graphical representation of the shift structure from Pirastu (1992).

23.4. Hypergeometric terms inherit their name from **hypergeometric series**, which are power series over $\mathbb{C}$ with hypergeometric coefficients in the sense of Definition 23.16: a series $f = \sum_{k \geq 0} f_k x^k / k! \in \mathbb{C}[[z]]$ is hypergeometric if

$$f_k = \frac{a_1^{\overline{k}} \cdots a_m^{\overline{k}}}{b_1^{\overline{k}} \cdots b_n^{\overline{k}}}$$

for all $k \in \mathbb{N}$, where the upper parameters $a_1, \ldots, a_m \in \mathbb{C}$ may be arbitrary and the lower parameters $b_1, \ldots, b_n \in \mathbb{C}$ must not lie in $-\mathbb{N}$. Hypergeometric series have a distinguished history in calculus, and many familiar series such as

$$\exp(z) = \sum_{k \geq 0} \frac{z^k}{k!}, \quad \frac{1}{(1-z)^a} = \sum_{k \geq 0} a^{\overline{k}} \frac{z^k}{k!}, \quad \ln \frac{1}{1-z} = z \sum_{k \geq 0} \frac{1^{\overline{k}} 1^{\overline{k}}}{2^{\overline{k}}} \frac{z^k}{k!}$$

are in fact hypergeometric, including the second example for $a = 1$: the geometric series. Hypergeometric series with two upper parameters and one lower parameter were first studied by Euler, Gauß, and Pfaff.

Algorithm 23.20, Lemma 23.24, and Algorithm 23.25 are due to Gosper (1978); see also Graham, Knuth & Patashnik (1994), §5.7. Our presentation follows Paule (1995).

In view of the fact that the values of d and δ may be exponentially large in the input size, as in Examples 23.23 and Exercise 23.24, it would be interesting to know what asymptotically fast methods can achieve in this area; a first step was taken by von zur Gathen & Gerhard (1997).

If Gosper's algorithm is applied to a rational function $g = p/q$, with nonzero $p, q \in F[x]$, then $\deg(r - s) < \deg(r + s)$ in Lemma 23.24. Lisoněk, Paule & Strehl (1993) prove that in this situation the case $\deg U = \delta$ occurs if and only if g is a proper rational function, so that $\deg p < \deg q$. Moreover, they show that if Σg exists, then (20) has a unique solution

$U \in F[x]$ of degree $1 + \deg t - \deg r$, so that the case $\deg U = \delta$ in Lemma 23.24 (i) need not be considered.

Further notes. The early work of Abramov (1971), Moenck (1977b), Gosper (1978), and Karr (1981, 1985) was influential for symbolic summation. Lafon (1983) gives an overview of the state in the early 1980s, and Paule (1995) and Paule & Strehl (1995) review the methods and some recent developments from a modern point of view.

An exciting development was started by Zeilberger's (1990a, 1990b, 1991) solution of the definite hypergeometric summation problem (the two sums (1) and (2) are of that type). It provided rather surprising computer-aided verifications of well-known identities, such as the Rogers-Ramanujan formula, the Pfaff-Saalschütz identity, Dixon's theorem, Apéry's formula, and similar proofs of new identities. We will briefly discuss this in Section 24.3; see also Notes 24.3.

Exercises.

23.1 Give an example of functions $f, g: \mathbb{R} \longrightarrow \mathbb{R}$ such that $f(k+1) - f(k) = g(k)$ for all $k \in \mathbb{Z}$ but $\Delta f \neq g$.

23.2 Let ∇ be the "backward" difference operator, with $\nabla f = f - E^{-1}f = \Delta E^{-1}f$. Prove the following identities for all $m \in \mathbb{N}$.
  (i) $x^{\overline{m}} = (x+m-1)^{\underline{m}} = (-1)^m(-x)^{\underline{m}}$,
  (ii) $\Delta x^{\overline{m}} = m \cdot E x^{\overline{m-1}}$,
  (iii) $\nabla x^{\overline{m}} = m x^{\overline{m-1}}$.

23.3 (i) Show that $\Delta f \cdot g - f \cdot \Delta g = E f \cdot g - f \cdot E g$.
  (ii) The product rule for the difference operator Δ can be written as
$$\Delta(f \cdot g) = f \cdot \Delta g + E g \cdot \Delta f = E f \cdot \Delta g + g \cdot \Delta f.$$
Find and prove a quotient rule for Δ expressing $\Delta(f/g)$ in terms of $f, \Delta f, g, \Delta g$, and $E g$.
  (iii) Prove that $\Delta f^{\underline{m}} = \left(E f - E^{1-m} f\right) \cdot f^{\underline{m-1}}$ for all $m \in \mathbb{N}$.

23.4* Let F be a field of characteristic zero. For an arbitrary $h \in F$, we define the **h-shift operator** E^h by $E^h f = f(x+h)$ (if $h \in \mathbb{Z}$, then this coincides with the usual definition as hth power of E), and similarly $\Delta_h = E^h - I$.
  (i) Show that $\sum_{0 \leq k < n} g(a+kh) = f(a+nh) - f(a)$ for all $n \in \mathbb{N}$ and $a \in F$ if $\Delta_h f = g$.
  (ii) Prove the operator identities $\Delta_h^k = \sum_{0 \leq i \leq k}(-1)^{k-i}\binom{k}{i}E^{ih}$ and $\Delta_k = \Delta \sum_{0 \leq i < k} E^i$ for $k \in \mathbb{N}$.
  (iii) Let $f \in F[x]$ of degree less than n. Prove that f has the **Newton expansion**
$$f = \sum_{0 \leq i < n} \frac{(\Delta_h^i f)(0)}{i!} x(x-h)\cdots(x-ih+h),$$
and relate this to the Taylor expansion of f around 0, and also to Newton interpolation (Exercise 5.11) at the equidistant points $u_j = jh$ for $0 \leq i < n$.
  (iv) Conclude that $i!\left\{{m \atop i}\right\} = (\Delta^i x^m)(0)$ for $0 \leq i \leq m$.

23.5 (i) Show that $\Gamma(x) = \int_0^\infty e^{-t}t^{x-1}dt$ converges for all $x \in \mathbb{R}_{>0}$.
  (ii) Prove the functional equation $\Gamma(x+1) = x\Gamma(x)$ for all $x \in \mathbb{R}_{\geq 1}$. Hint: Integration by parts.
  (iii) Show that $\Gamma(1) = 1$, and conclude that $\Gamma(n+1) = n!$ for all $n \in \mathbb{N}$.

23.6 Show that $\left\{{m \atop m-1}\right\} = \binom{m}{2}$ and $\left\{{m \atop 2}\right\} = 2^{m-1} - 1$ for $m \geq 1$.

23.7* Let $\left[\begin{smallmatrix} n \\ k \end{smallmatrix}\right]$ denote the number of permutations on $\{1,\dots,n\}$ with exactly k cycles, for all non-negative integers. These numbers are the **Stirling numbers of the first kind**. We have the boundary conditions $\left[\begin{smallmatrix} 0 \\ 0 \end{smallmatrix}\right] = 1$, $\left[\begin{smallmatrix} n \\ 0 \end{smallmatrix}\right] = 0$ if $n > 0$, and $\left[\begin{smallmatrix} n \\ k \end{smallmatrix}\right] = 0$ if $k > n$.

(i) Give all permutations on $\{1,\dots,n\}$ having k cycles, for $1 \leq k \leq n \leq 4$.

(ii) Prove that $\left[\begin{smallmatrix} n \\ n \end{smallmatrix}\right] = 1$, $\left[\begin{smallmatrix} n \\ n-1 \end{smallmatrix}\right] = \binom{n}{2}$, and $\left[\begin{smallmatrix} n \\ 1 \end{smallmatrix}\right] = (n-1)!$ for all $n \in \mathbb{N}_{>0}$.

(iii) Find and prove a recursion formula for $\left[\begin{smallmatrix} n \\ k \end{smallmatrix}\right]$ for $1 \leq k \leq n$. Hint: Distinguish the two cases whether n is a fixed point (a cycle of length 1) or not.

(iv) Prove that $x^{\underline{m}} = \sum_{0 \leq i \leq m} (-1)^{m-i} \left[\begin{smallmatrix} m \\ i \end{smallmatrix}\right] x^i$ for $m \in \mathbb{N}$. What is the corresponding formula for $x^{\overline{m}}$?

(v) Conclude that

$$\sum_{i \leq m \leq n} (-1)^{m-i} \left[\begin{matrix} m \\ i \end{matrix}\right] \left\{\begin{matrix} n \\ m \end{matrix}\right\} = \delta_{n-i} = \sum_{i \leq m \leq n} (-1)^{n-m} \left\{\begin{matrix} m \\ i \end{matrix}\right\} \left[\begin{matrix} n \\ m \end{matrix}\right]$$

for all $i, n \in \mathbb{N}$ such that $i \leq n$, where δ_{n-i} is 1 if $n = i$ and 0 otherwise.

23.8* For $n \in \mathbb{N}$, the nth **Bernoulli number** $B_n \in \mathbb{Q}$ is recursively defined by $B_0 = 1$ and

$$\sum_{0 \leq i \leq n} \binom{n+1}{i} B_i = 0 \text{ for } n \in \mathbb{N}_{>1},$$

and the nth **Bernoulli polynomial** is

$$S_n = \frac{1}{n+1} \sum_{1 \leq k \leq n+1} \binom{n+1}{k} B_{n+1-k} x^k \in \mathbb{Q}[x].$$

(i) Compute the S_n for $0 \leq n \leq 4$.

(ii) For nonnegative integers $c \leq b \leq a$, prove the identity

$$\binom{a}{b}\binom{b}{c} = \binom{a}{c}\binom{a-c}{b-c}.$$

(iii) Prove that $\Delta S_n = x^n$ for all $n \in \mathbb{N}$. Hint: Use (ii). Conclude that $\sum_{0 \leq k < m} k^n = S_n(m)$ for all $m \in \mathbb{N}$.

(iv) Conclude from Exercise 23.7 that

$$\frac{B_{n+1-k}}{n+1} \binom{n+1}{k} = \sum_{j-1 \leq i \leq n+1} \frac{(-1)^{i+1-j}}{i+1} \left\{\begin{matrix} n \\ i \end{matrix}\right\} \left[\begin{matrix} i+1 \\ j \end{matrix}\right]$$

holds for all $k, n \in \mathbb{N}$ such that $k \leq n+1$.

23.9* (i) Give a combinatorial proof of **Vandermonde's convolution**

$$\sum_{0 \leq i \leq m} \binom{r}{i}\binom{s}{m-i} = \binom{r+s}{m} \tag{25}$$

for integers r, s, m with $1 \leq m \leq r+s$ by counting in two different ways the number of possibilities to choose m persons among r women and s men.

(ii) Give a different proof of (25) by comparing coefficients of z^m on both sides of the (formal) power series equality

$$\frac{1}{(1-z)^r} \cdot \frac{1}{(1-z)^s} = \frac{1}{(1-z)^{r+s}}$$

in $\mathbb{Q}[[z]]$.

(iii) Show that for each $m \in \mathbb{N}_{\geq 1}$, (25) becomes an equality in the polynomial ring $\mathbb{Z}[x,y]$ if we formally replace r, s by indeterminates x, y. Hint: Lemma 6.44.

(iv) Conclude that the falling factorials satisfy the binomial theorem

$$\sum_{0\le i\le m} \binom{m}{i} x^{\underline{i}} y^{\underline{m-i}} = (x+y)^{\underline{m}}.$$

What about the rising factorials?

23.10 (i) Prove that the falling factorials satisfy the identity

$$x^{\underline{m+n}} = x^{\underline{m}}(x-m)^{\underline{n}} = x^{\underline{m}} E^{-m} x^{\underline{n}}, \tag{26}$$

For $m, n \in \mathbb{N}$ (This corresponds to the power law $x^{m+n} = x^m x^n$ for the ordinary powers.)

(ii) We take (26) as definition for $x^{\underline{m}}$ when $m = -n$ is negative. Prove that (26) and $\Delta x^{\underline{m}} = m x^{\underline{m-1}}$ hold for all $m, n \in \mathbb{Z}$.

23.11 Compute closed forms for the following sums and verify your results for $n = 1, 2$.

(i) $\displaystyle\sum_{0\le k<n} (k^3 - 3k^2 + 2k + 5)$,

(ii) $\displaystyle\sum_{0\le k<n} k2^k$. Hint: Think of integration by parts.

23.12 This exercise generalizes Lemma 23.5. Let F be a field. For a rational function $\rho = f/g$ in $F(x)$, with nonzero $f, g \in F(x)$, we let $\deg(\rho) = \deg f - \deg g$. Prove that $\deg(\Delta\rho) \le \deg\rho - 1$ holds for all $\rho \in F(x)$ such that $\Delta\rho \ne 0$, with equality if and only if $\deg\rho \ne 0$. Conclude that if $\sigma \in F(x)$ has $\deg\sigma = -1$, then there is no rational function $\rho \in F(x)$ such that $\Delta\rho = \sigma$.

23.13 Let F be a field of characteristic 0.

(i) Prove that the usual differential operator D and the difference operator Δ on $F(x)$ commute, so that $D(\Delta\rho) = \Delta(D\rho)$ for all $\rho \in F(x)$.

(ii) For $m \in \mathbb{N}$, the mth **polygamma function** is defined as $\Psi_m(x) = D^m \ln \Gamma(x)$ for $x \in \mathbb{C}$, where Γ is the gamma function from Exercise 23.5. Prove that $\Sigma x^{-m} = (-1)^{m-1} \Psi_m/(m-1)!$ for all nonzero $m \in \mathbb{N}$.

(iii) For $d \in \mathbb{N}_{>0}$, use (ii) to prove that $\Sigma(x^2 + dx)^{-1} = -D(x^{\underline{d}})/dx^{\underline{d}}$. Hint: Partial fraction decomposition.

23.14 Let F be a field. Prove that the relation $\sim$ on the polynomial ring $F[x]$ defined by

$$f \equiv g \iff f = E^i g \text{ for some } i \in \mathbb{Z}$$

is an equivalence relation.

23.15 What is the gff of the following polynomials?
(i) $x^2(x+1)(x+2)^3(x+3)^4$, (ii) $x^{\underline{3}}(x+1)^2(x+3)^{\underline{4}}$.

23.16 Complete the proof of Theorem 23.12.

23.17* This exercise discusses the analog of Hermite reduction, using the gff. Let F be a field of characteristic zero, $f, g \in F[x]$ nonzero, and $\text{gff}(g) = g_1^{\underline{1}} \cdots g_m^{\underline{m}}$, with monic $g_1, \ldots, g_m \in F[x]$ and $g_m \ne 1$. For simplicity, we assume that $\deg f < \deg g$ and that g is **saturated**, which means that $\gcd(g_i, E^k g_j) \ne 1$ implies $i = j$ and $k = 0$, for all $1 \le i, j \le m$ and $k \in \mathbb{Z}$. The following analog of Hermite reduction is due to Moenck (1977b) and Pirastu (1992).

(i) Prove that there exist $h_{ij} \in F[x]$ of degree less than $j \deg g_i$ for $1 \le i \le m$ such that we have the "partial fraction decomposition"

$$\frac{f}{g} = \sum_{1\le j\le i\le m} \frac{h_{ij}}{g_i^{\underline{j}}}.$$

(ii) Show that there are polynomials $s,t \in F[x]$ of degree less than $\deg g_i$ such that $sE^{-j+1}g_i + t \cdot (g_i - E^{-j+1}g_i) = h_{ij}$. Using the product rule, conclude that

$$\frac{h_{ij}}{g_i^j} = \Delta\left(\frac{t}{g_i^{j-1}}\right) + \frac{s - Et}{g_i^{j-1}}.$$

(iii) Let $b = g_1 \cdots g_m$ and $d = E^{-1}(g/b)$. Conclude that there exist polynomials $a, c \in F[x]$ with $\deg a < \deg b$ and $\deg c < \deg d$ such that

$$\frac{f}{g} = \Delta\left(\frac{c}{d}\right) + \frac{a}{b}.$$

23.18 Which of the following expressions are hypergeometric, which are not? Compute the term ratios.

(i) $\left(\dfrac{(x+1)^2}{3}\right)$,   (ii) $(x+1)2^{x^2}$,   (iii) $(-1)^{x^2}\Gamma(x+1)$.

23.19 Prove that hypergeometric terms are closed under multiplication and division but not under addition.

23.20 Trace Algorithm 23.25 on computing $\Sigma x^{\overline{2}}$, and compare its result to the one that you obtain from Section 23.1.

23.21 Let $n \in \mathbb{N}_{\geq 1}$. Prove that there is no hypergeometric expression f such that $\Delta f = \binom{n}{x}$.

23.22 Decide whether the following hypergeometric expressions have hypergeometric sums, and if so, compute them.

(i) $\dfrac{3x+1}{x+1}\left(\dfrac{2x}{x}\right)$,   (ii) $(2x+1)2^x\Gamma(x+1)$,   (iii) $2^x\left(\dfrac{100}{x}\right)$.

23.23 Fix $n \in \mathbb{N}$, and show that the indefinite sum $\Sigma(-1)^x\binom{n}{x}^2$ is hypergeometric, while $\Sigma\binom{n}{x}^2$ is not.

23.24$\longrightarrow$ (Gerhard 1998) Let $n \in \mathbb{N}_{\geq 2}$ and

$$g = \frac{2^{4x}}{\left(\dfrac{n+x}{x}\right)^2\left(\dfrac{2n+2x}{n+x}\right)^2}.$$

(i) Show that the term ratio of g is

$$\sigma = \frac{Eg}{g} = \frac{(x+1)^2}{\left(x+\dfrac{2n+1}{2}\right)^2} = \frac{x^2+2x+1}{x^2+(2n+1)x+\dfrac{(2n+1)^2}{4}}. \tag{27}$$

(ii) The numerator and denominator in (i) are $a = x^2+2x+1$ and $b = x^2+(2n+1)x+(2n+1)^2/4$. Show that both Algorithms 23.20 and 23.18 return the denominator $V = 1$.

(iii) Equation (20) now reads $a \cdot EU - b \cdot u = b$. Prove that the solution $U \in \mathbb{Q}[x]$ has degree $\delta = 2n-1$ if it exists.

(iv) Show that the linear operator $L = aE - b \colon \mathbb{Q}[x] \longrightarrow \mathbb{Q}[x]$, with $Lf = a \cdot Ef - b \cdot f$, maps the $2n$-dimensional vector space $W \subseteq F[x]$ of all polynomials of degree less than $2n$ to itself, and conclude that there is a unique polynomial $U \in \mathbb{Q}[x]$ with $LU = a \cdot EU - b \cdot U = b$.

(v) Compute U for $n = 6$.

23.25 Let K be a difference field with automorphism E, y an indeterminate, $a,b,c,d \in K$ such that $ad \neq bc$, and $\sigma = (ay+b)/(cy+d) \in K(y)$. Prove that there is a unique automorphism E^* of $K(y)$ extending E such that $E^*y = \sigma$. For what choices of a,b,c,d is y hypergeometric over K?

23.26 Let F be a field of characteristic zero and $r, s, t, U \in F[x]$ such that $r \cdot EU - s \cdot U = t$ and $\gcd(r, s) = 1$. Suppose that $\deg \gcd(r, t) \geq 1$, and reduce this difference equation for U to a difference equation for a proper divisor U^* of U, with coefficients r^*, s^*, t^* of degrees no larger than those of r, s, t. Answer the same question when $\deg \gcd(s, t) \geq 1$.

23.27 Let $a, b \in \mathbb{Z}[x]$ be nonzero with max-norm $\|a\|_\infty, \|b\|_\infty \leq B \in \mathbb{N}$. Prove that $d \leq 4B$, where d is the value computed in step 1 of Algorithms 23.18 and 23.20. Hint: Exercise 6.23.

23.28* (Abramov 1971) Let F be a field of characteristic zero and $\rho = f/g \in F(x)$ a rational function, with coprime $f, g \in F[x]$ and $\deg f > 0$. The **dispersion** of ρ is defined as

$$\mathrm{dis}(\rho) = \max\{k \in \mathbb{N} \colon \gcd(g, E^k g) \neq 1\}.$$

(i) Prove that $\mathrm{dis}(\Delta \rho) = \mathrm{dis}(\rho) + 1$.

(ii) Conclude that there is no rational function $\rho \in F(x)$ such that $\Delta \rho = x^{-m}$, for any $m \in \mathbb{N}_{\geq 1}$. (Exercise 23.13 gives a "closed form" for Σx^{-m}.)

23.29* Let F be a field of characteristic zero and $a, b \in F[x]$ with $b \neq 0$ monic.

(i) Use Algorithm 23.20 to prove that there exist polynomials $r, s, v \in F[x]$ with s, v nonzero and monic such that

$$\frac{a}{b} = \frac{r}{Es} \cdot \frac{Ev}{v}, \quad \gcd(r, E^i s) = 1 \text{ for } i \in \mathbb{N}_{>0}. \tag{28}$$

(ii) Show how to obtain from an arbitrary representation (28) one where $\gcd(r, v) = \gcd(s, v) = 1$ (hint: Exercise 23.26), and prove that it is unique. It is called the **Gosper-Petkovšek representation** of a/b, after its inventors Gosper (1978) and Petkovšek (1992).

(iii) Prove that there exist unique polynomials $r, s, u, v \in F[x]$ such that s, u, v are monic and non-constant,

$$\frac{a}{b} = \frac{r}{s} \cdot \frac{u}{Eu} \cdot \frac{Ev}{v}, \quad \gcd(r, E^i s) = 1 \text{ for } i \in \mathbb{Z}, \tag{29}$$

and $\gcd(r, Eu) = \gcd(r, v) = \gcd(s, u) = \gcd(s, Ev) = \gcd(u, v) = 1$. We call this the **extended Gosper-Petkovšek representation** of a/b.

(iv) Prove that there is a rational function $c/d \in F(x)$, with $d \neq 0$, such that $\Delta(c/d) = a/b$ if and only if $r = s = 1$ in (29).

(v) Compute the extended Gosper-Petkovšek representation of the rational function

$$\frac{x^4 + 4x^3 + 3x^2}{x^6 + 7x^4 + 5x^5 + x^3 - 2x^2 - 4x - 8} \in \mathbb{Q}(x).$$

It is no paradox to say that in our most theoretical moods
we may be nearest to our most practical applications.
Alfred North Whitehead (1911)

L'algèbre est généreuse, elle donne souvent plus qu'on lui demande.[1]
Jean le Rond D'Alembert ()

I will, however, mention an unexpected circumstance,
as it illustrates, in a striking manner, the connection between
remote inquiries in mathematics, and as it may furnish a lesson
to those who are rashly inclined to undervalue the more
recondite speculations of pure analysis, from an erroneous idea
of their inapplicability to practical matters.
Charles Babbage (1822)

Many identities in combinatorics are still out of the range of
computers, but even if one day they would all be computerizable,
that would by no means render them obsolete,
since the *ideas* behind the human proofs are often
much more important than the theorems that are being proved.
Marko Petkovšek, Herbert S. Wilf, and Doron Zeilberger (1996)

---

[1] Algebra is generous, she often gives more than is asked of her.

24

Applications

24.1. Gröbner proof systems

This application from mathematical logic shows how very general situations can be coded in polynomial ideals, and then our techniques applied to them.

A **proof system** in logic consists of **axioms** and **inference rules**. By applying these rules repeatedly, starting with the axioms, one obtains the **theorems** provable in the system. The set of all these theorems is the **theory** of the system. As an example, we can take as axioms the basic facts about real numbers, expressible with $0, 1, +, *, =, <$, such as

$$\forall x \, \exists y \; y < x,$$

as inference rules the usual ones, such as

$$\frac{x < y, \, z < w}{x + z < y + w}$$

which is to be read as: "if $x < y$ and $z < w$ are provable, then so is $x + z < y + w$", and then one obtains as provable theorems the theory of the real numbers.

We only deal with **propositional calculus**, a much simpler object, where we only have variables that may assume the values **true** or **false**, and the logical connectives $\neg$ (not), $\vee$ (or), $\wedge$ (and), $\longrightarrow$ (implies). There are no quantifiers. An example of an axiom is

$$x \vee \neg x,$$

and of two inference rules

$$\frac{x, \, x \longrightarrow y}{y}, \qquad \frac{x, \, \neg x}{\textbf{false}}. \tag{1}$$

In a typical formulation of propositional proof systems, one proves that a certain set of formulas, such as

$$S = \{x_1, \, x_1 \longrightarrow x_2, \, x_2 \longrightarrow x_3, \, x_3 \longrightarrow x_4, \, \neg x_4\}, \tag{2}$$

641

is **unsatisfiable**, that is, it is impossible to make all formulas in S simultaneously **true** by giving truth values **true** or **false** to its variables.

A **refutation** of S is a derivation of the simplest contradiction **false** by using repeatedly formulas from S, axioms, and inference rules. In (2), we can derive x_2 from x_1, $x_1 \longrightarrow x_2$, and the first rule in (1), and then similarly x_3, and x_4, and finally **false** from x_4, $\neg x_4$, and the second rule in (1).

There are several propositional proof systems, among them tableaux, resolution, Horn clause resolution, the Davis-Putnam procedure, Frege-Hilbert proofs, and Gentzen systems. Two measures of such a system are of interest: How long is a shortest refutation of a given unsatisfiable set of formulas? How hard is it to find a "short" refutation, if one exists?

The **pigeonhole principle** states that, for any $n \in \mathbb{N}$, it is not possible to fit $n+1$ pigeons into n pigeonholes without a collision. (Animal rights supporters, worried about the well-being of pigeons stuffed into dreary holes, may prefer the German term *Dirichlets Schubfachprinzip*[1].) To express this as a propositional formula, we let x_{ij} stand for "pigeon i is in pigeonhole j". Then the principle for $n = 2$ says that

$$PHP_2 = \{x_{11} \vee x_{12},\, x_{21} \vee x_{22},\, x_{31} \vee x_{32},$$

$$\neg x_{11} \vee \neg x_{21},\, \neg x_{11} \vee \neg x_{31},\, \neg x_{21} \vee \neg x_{31},\, \neg x_{12} \vee \neg x_{22},\, \neg x_{12} \vee \neg x_{32},\, \neg x_{22} \vee \neg x_{32}\}$$

is unsatisfiable. PHP_n has length about $n^3 \log_2 n$ in general. A famous result by Haken (1985) is that any resolution proof of PHP_n has exponential length at least 2^{cn} for some positive constant $c \in \mathbb{R}$. This is an active area of research, and we cannot but scratch the surface.

Propositional proof systems occur in several areas of computer science. For example, back-tracking algorithms can be formulated as such systems, and in artificial intelligence, logic programming languages such as Prolog employ them as a method of computation and as a means of representing knowledge.

Algebra is a powerful tool that can express many things, and we now describe how it can be used to build a propositional proof system. We fix a field F, usually $F = \mathbb{F}_2$. To each Boolean variable x we associate a variable $\tilde{x}$ over F. We use the (somewhat unusual) correspondence

$$\text{true} \longleftrightarrow 0, \quad \text{false} \longleftrightarrow 1$$

between Boolean values and field elements.

The polynomial $\tilde{x}^2 - \tilde{x}$ expresses the fact that $\tilde{x}$ can only take the values 0 or 1. The Boolean connectives are translated as follows: if φ and ψ are formulas, with corresponding polynomials $\tilde{\varphi}$ and $\tilde{\psi}$, then

$$\neg \varphi \longleftrightarrow 1 - \tilde{\varphi}; \quad \varphi \vee \psi \longleftrightarrow \tilde{\varphi}\tilde{\psi}; \quad \varphi \wedge \psi \longleftrightarrow 1 - (1 - \tilde{\varphi})(1 - \tilde{\psi}).$$

---

[1] Dirichlet's drawer principle. The English "pigeonhole" is actually an office mail box.

In this way, to every propositional formula φ in $x_1, \ldots, x_n$ there corresponds a polynomial $\widetilde{\varphi} \in F[\widetilde{x}_1, \ldots, \widetilde{x}_n] = R$. For example, if φ is $x \longrightarrow y$, which is logically equivalent to $\neg x \vee y$, then $\widetilde{\varphi} = (1 - \widetilde{x})\widetilde{y}$. An algebraic derivation makes use of the axioms

$$\widetilde{x}_1^2 - \widetilde{x}_1, \ldots, \widetilde{x}_n^2 - \widetilde{x}_n \in R, \tag{3}$$

and the rules of inference are that if one has $f, g \in R$ already, $a, b \in F$ and $1 \leq i \leq n$, then one can derive

$$af + bg \text{ and } \widetilde{x}_i f.$$

To derive a formula ψ from a set $S = \{\varphi_1, \ldots, \varphi_s\}$ of formulas, one may apply these rules to the axioms and to $\widetilde{\varphi}_1, \ldots, \widetilde{\varphi}_s \in R$ to derive $\widetilde{\psi} \in R$. In other words, we consider the ideal

$$I = \langle \widetilde{x}_1^2 - \widetilde{x}_1, \ldots, \widetilde{x}_n^2 - \widetilde{x}_n, \widetilde{\varphi}_1, \ldots, \widetilde{\varphi}_s \rangle \subseteq R.$$

The **Nullstellensatz proof system** asks to derive 1, that is, to prove that $1 \in I$, according to these rules, in order to refute S. Corresponding to (2), we have

$$I = \langle \widetilde{x}_1^2 - \widetilde{x}_1, \widetilde{x}_2^2 - \widetilde{x}_2, \widetilde{x}_3^2 - \widetilde{x}_3, \widetilde{x}_4^2 - \widetilde{x}_4,$$

$$\widetilde{x}_1, (1 - \widetilde{x}_1)\widetilde{x}_2, (1 - \widetilde{x}_2)\widetilde{x}_3, (1 - \widetilde{x}_3)\widetilde{x}_4, (1 - \widetilde{x}_4)\rangle \subseteq F[\widetilde{x}_1, \widetilde{x}_2, \widetilde{x}_3, \widetilde{x}_4], \tag{4}$$

and a refutation of S is

$$\widetilde{x}_2 = (1 - \widetilde{x}_1)\widetilde{x}_2 + \widetilde{x}_2 \cdot \widetilde{x}_1, \quad \widetilde{x}_3 = (1 - \widetilde{x}_2)\widetilde{x}_3 + \widetilde{x}_3 \cdot \widetilde{x}_2,$$

$$\widetilde{x}_4 = (1 - \widetilde{x}_3)\widetilde{x}_4 + \widetilde{x}_4 \cdot \widetilde{x}_3, \quad 1 = \widetilde{x}_4 + (1 - \widetilde{x}_4) \in I.$$

The **Gröbner proof system**, introduced by Clegg, Edmonds & Impagliazzo (1996), computes the reduced Gröbner basis G of I and then checks whether $G = \{1\}$, thus testing whether $1 \in I$ (Exercise 21.19). For the ideal in (4), MAPLE's gbasis command produces $G = \{1\}$, immediately showing that $1 \in I$. Clegg *et al.* prove that their Gröbner proof system can simulate others efficiently, such as Horn clause resolution, and thus is at least not worse than these, in an appropriate sense. They also show that in some cases, this system is better than others. The details are not too difficult, but beyond the scope of this text.

24.2. Petri nets

This section shows how algebraic methods—Gröbner bases in this case—can be put to use for another apparently remote problem: the analysis of parallel processes. A widely used model is **Petri nets**, introduced by Petri (1962). Rather than give a formal definition, we content ourselves with an example. Figure 24.1 shows a Petri net. It is a weighted bipartite directed graph, with **places** $s_1, s_2, s_3,$

transitions t_1, t_2, t_3, and weights on the edges. All weights are 1, except weight 2 from s_3 to t_3. Furthermore, a **marking** M of the net assigns to each place s_i a non-negative integer $M(s_i)$, the number of **tokens** on that node. Such a marked Petri net can be used to describe a state of a system of processes.

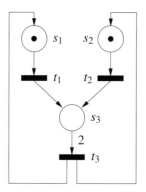

FIGURE 24.1: A marked Petri net.

The dynamics of the system correspond to a **firing** of some of the transitions in the Petri net. Each participating transition receives tokens from its input places and sends tokens to its output places; the number of tokens equals the edge weight. Three consecutive firings of the net in Figure 24.1 are given in Figure 24.2. The first two could be exchanged or even combined into one firing. Only the marking changes in a firing.

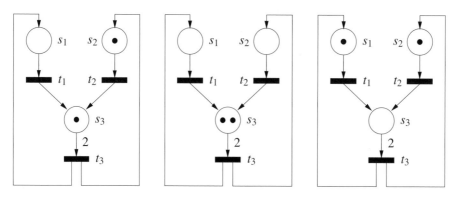

FIGURE 24.2: The Petri net from Figure 24.1 after one, two, and three firings, respectively.

A Petri net is **reversible** if for each firing there is a sequence of firings that form the reverse of the given one. This is illustrated in Figure 24.2, where the last two firings reverse the first one. The **reachability problem** for (reversible) Petri nets is, given two markings M and M^* of the same net, to decide whether M^* can be obtained from M by a sequence of firings. If the Petri net is reversible, then M^* is reachable from M if and only if M is reachable from M^*.

What does this have to do with algebra? We choose a field F, variables $x_1,\ldots,x_n$ corresponding to the n places, and consider the ideal generated by polynomials $f_1,\ldots,f_m \in F[x_1,\ldots,x_n]$ corresponding to the m transitions, as illustrated now for Figure 24.1:

$$f_1 = x_3 - x_1, \quad f_2 = x_3 - x_2, \quad f_3 = x_1 x_2 - x_3^2. \tag{5}$$

Such an ideal, generated by binomials, is called a **binomial ideal**. It is interesting that its reduced Gröbner basis consists again of binomials. It is now possible to decide the reachability problem for reversible Petri nets by means of Gröbner bases: Let M and M^* be two markings. Then the binomial

$$x_1^{M^*(s_1)} \cdots x_n^{M^*(s_n)} - x_1^{M(s_1)} \cdots x_n^{M(s_n)}$$

is in the ideal generated by $f_1,\ldots,f_m$ if and only if M and M^* are reachable from each other.

In our example, the two markings given by $M(s_1) = M(s_2) = 1$, $M(s_3) = 0$ and $M^*(s_1) = 0$, $M^*(s_2) = M^*(s_3) = 1$, corresponding to Figure 24.1 and the leftmost marking in Figure 24.2, respectively, are reachable from each other, and in fact the polynomial

$$x_2 x_3 - x_1 x_2 = x_2 \cdot f_1$$

is in the ideal $\langle f_1, f_2, f_3 \rangle \subseteq F[x_1, x_2, x_3]$.

24.3. Proving identities and analysis of algorithms

We will briefly discuss how the symbolic summation algorithms from Chapter 23 can be used to prove combinatorial identities. As an example, we take a summation problem that shows up in the analysis of a variant of our modular gcd algorithm 6.36. We can only roughly sketch the ideas and refer to the literature for details (see Notes 24.3).

Given $a, b \in F[x, y]$, where F is a sufficiently large field and a, b are primitive with respect to x, Algorithm 6.36 chooses a set $S \subseteq F$ of evaluation points, computes $v_u = \gcd(a(x, u), b(y, u))$ for all $u \in S$, and recovers $c = \gcd(a, b) \in F[x, y]$ by interpolation. We have seen that some evaluation points u may be "unlucky", so that $\gcd(\mathrm{lc}_x(a), \mathrm{lc}_x(b))$ vanishes at $y = u$ or $\deg_x v_u > \deg_x c$, which happens if and only if u is a root of a certain subresultant $\sigma \in F[y]$ of a and b. Thus the total number of unlucky points is at most $\deg_y \sigma$. The number of "lucky" points sufficient to recover the gcd by interpolation is $s = 2\max\{\deg_y a, \deg_y b\} + 1$, which in general is much smaller than $\deg_y \sigma$. Theorem 6.37 analyzes this algorithm.

In practice, however, we would successively choose points u from a fixed subset $U \subseteq F$ of (sufficiently large) cardinality n uniformly at random and discard unlucky choices until we have found exactly s lucky points. To analyze this variant, we are interested in the expected number of choices until s lucky points are found. We model this by the following random experiment. An urn contains w white and $n-w$ black balls, for integers $0 < w \le n$. The white and black balls represent the lucky and unlucky points in U, respectively. We repeatedly draw balls, without replacement, and let the random variable T denote the number of trials until we have first found precisely s white balls, where $0 \le s \le w$. Moreover, we consider random variables $X_1, \ldots, X_n$, where X_k counts the number of white balls obtained after k trials. Then the X_k have a hypergeometric distribution

$$\text{prob}(X_k = s) = \frac{\binom{w}{s}\binom{n-w}{k-s}}{\binom{n}{k}},$$

since there are $\binom{w}{s}$ possibilities to choose s white balls, $\binom{n-w}{k-s}$ possibilities to obtain $k-s$ black balls, and the total number of choices is $\binom{n}{k}$. If $k < s$, then we have $\text{prob}(X_k = s) = 0$. Using conditional probabilities, we find

$$
\begin{aligned}
p_k &= \text{prob}(T = k) = \text{prob}(X_k = s \text{ and } X_{k-1} = s-1)\\
&= \text{prob}_{X_{k-1}=s-1}(X_k = s) \cdot \text{prob}(X_{k-1} = s-1)\\
&= \frac{w-s+1}{n-k+1} \frac{\binom{w}{s-1}\binom{n-w}{k-s}}{\binom{n}{k-1}},
\end{aligned}
$$

$$
k p_k = \frac{(w-s+1)\binom{w}{s-1}\binom{n-w}{k-s}}{\frac{n-k+1}{k}\binom{n}{k-1}} = s\frac{\binom{w}{s}\binom{n-w}{k-s}}{\binom{n}{k}} = s\frac{\binom{k}{s}\binom{n-k}{w-s}}{\binom{n}{w}}.
$$

We claim that the expected number $\mathcal{E}(T) = \sum_{0 \le k \le n} k p_k$ of trials is

$$
\sum_{0 \le k \le n} k p_k = \frac{(n+1)s}{w+1}, \tag{6}
$$

(this is quite close to the expected value ns/w for drawing *with replacement*) and let

$$
g(n,k) = \frac{k p_k(w+1)}{(n+1)s} = \frac{\binom{k}{s}\binom{n-k}{w-s}}{\frac{n+1}{w+1}\binom{n}{w}} = \frac{\binom{k}{s}\binom{n-k}{w-s}}{\binom{n+1}{w+1}}. \tag{7}
$$

for $0 \le k \le n$. If we define $S(n) = \sum_{0 \le k \le n} g(n,k) = \sum_{k \in \mathbb{Z}} g(n,k)$, then the claim (6) is equivalent to $S(n) = 1$ for all $n \in \mathbb{N}$ with $n \ge w$. It is easy to check that the hypergeometric term $f(n,k)$ defined by

$$f(n,k) = -\frac{(k-n-1)(k-s)}{(n+2)(k-n-1+w-s)}g(n,k) \tag{8}$$

satisfies

$$f(n,k+1) - f(n,k) = g(n+1,k) - g(n,k) \tag{9}$$

for all $n \geq w$ and $k \in \mathbb{Z}$ (after dividing both sides in (9) by $g(n,k)$, only rational functions in n and k remain). Thus

$$S(n+1) - S(n) = \sum_{k \in \mathbb{Z}} g(n+1,k) - \sum_{k \in \mathbb{Z}} g(n,k) = \sum_{k \in \mathbb{Z}} (f(n,k+1) - f(n,k)) = 0$$

for all $n \geq w$, so that indeed $S(n) = S(n-1) = \cdots = S(w) = 1$ (by (7), the only nonvanishing summand in $S(w) = \sum_{0 \leq k \leq w} g(w,k)$ is $g(w,s) = 1$), and the claim is proved.

But where does the magic term f in (8) come from? We consider s,w to be indeterminates, let x and y be two other indeterminates over $\mathbb{Q}$, and see that (9), with n and k replaced by y and x, respectively, is just an *indefinite* summation problem with respect to the variable x over the field $\mathbb{Q}(s,w,y)$ of rational functions in s,w,y, namely $\Delta f^* = g^*$, where $f^*(x) = f(y,x)$ and $g^*(x) = g(y+1,x) - g(y,x)$, and we can apply the hypergeometric summation algorithm 23.25. In our example, we have

$$g(y+1,x) - g(y,x) = \binom{x}{s}\left(\frac{\binom{y-x+1}{w-s}}{\binom{y+2}{w+1}} - \frac{\binom{y-x}{w-s}}{\binom{y+1}{w+1}}\right)$$

$$= \left(\frac{(y+1-w)(x-y-1)}{(y+2)(x-y+w-s-1)} - 1\right)\frac{\binom{x}{s}\binom{y-x}{w-s}}{\binom{y+1}{w+1}}$$

$$= -\frac{(w+1)x - (s+1)y + w - 2s - 1}{(y+2)(x-y+w-s-1)}g(y,x), \tag{10}$$

which is hypergeometric in x. Its term ratio is

$$\sigma = \frac{g(y+1,x+1) - g(y,x+1)}{g(y+1,x) - g(y,x)}$$

$$= \frac{(x+1)(x-y+w-s-1)\Big((w+1)x - (s+1)y + 2w - 2s\Big)}{(x-s+1)(x-y)\Big((w+1)x - (s+1)y + w - 2s - 1\Big)},$$

and we apply Algorithm 23.20 with the polynomials

$$a = (x+1)(x-y+w-s-1)\Big((w+1)x-(s+1)y+2w-2s\Big),$$

$$b = (x-s+1)(x-y)\Big((w+1)x-(s+1)y+w-2s-1\Big)$$

in $\mathbb{Q}(s,w,y)[x]$ as input. Then the algorithm computes $V = (w+1)x-(s+1)y+w-2s-1$, and the solution of the difference equation for the numerator is $U = (x-y-1)(x-s)$. Using (10), we obtain

$$f(y,x) = \frac{U}{V}(g(y+1,x)-g(y,x)) = -\frac{(x-y-1)(x-s)}{(y+2)(x-y-1+w-s)}g(y,x),$$

so that $f(n,k)$ is precisely as in (8), and we are done.

The procedure as described above has provided us with a **proof certificate**, namely f, or more precisely, the rational function

$$\frac{f(n,k)}{g(n,k)} = \frac{(2k-3n-3)k^2}{2(k-n-1)^2(2n+1)},$$

which enabled us to verify the correctness of (6) *independently* of the above computations, by simply checking the validity of (9). In the example, it may be easier to prove (6) directly by induction (Exercise 24.3). A variant of the above procedure can even *find* the right hand side in (6), given only the summand kp_k.

The above approach, due to Herbert Wilf and Doron Zeilberger, works for a certain class of bivariate hypergeometric summands. In this way a large variety of combinatorial identities involving sums over binomial coefficients, with (6) being only a rather trivial special case, can be automatically proved, and proof certificates similar to f in (9) such that $f(n,k)/g(n,k)$ is a rational function can be generated. If a closed form for the sum is not known in advance, then Zeilberger's method finds one if it exists, or otherwise at least a recursion formula. For example, the method finds routinely the second order recurrence

$$(n+2)^3 a(n+2) - (34n^3+153n^2+231n+117)a(n+1) + (n+1)^3 a(n) = 0$$

for the **Apéry numbers**

$$a(n) = \sum_{0 \le k \le n} \binom{n}{k}^2 \binom{n+k}{k}^2 \quad \text{for } n \in \mathbb{N},$$

which played an important role in Roger Apéry's sensational proof that $\zeta(3)$ is irrational. The ideas can also be extended to more than two variables, nested sums, definite integrals, and q-hypergeometric sums: a prominent example is a machine-generated proof for the identity

$$\sum_{0 \leq k \leq n} \frac{q^{k^2}}{(1-q) \cdots (1-q^k) \cdot (1-q) \cdots (1-q^{n-k})}$$

$$= \sum_{-n \leq k \leq n} \frac{(-1)^k q^{(5k^2-k)/2}}{(1-q) \cdots (1-q^{n-k}) \cdot (1-q) \cdots (1-q^{n+k})}, \qquad (11)$$

whose limit for $n \longrightarrow \infty$ is the first Rogers-Ramanujan identity.

24.4. Cyclohexane revisited

In this last section, we return to the problem from the first section to determine all spatial conformations of cyclohexane and show how computer algebra is used to obtain the solution indicated in Section 1.1. This will make use of some of the tools that we have discussed in the book.

We have six vectors $a_1, \ldots, a_6 \in \mathbb{R}^3$ that represent the bonds between carbon atoms (Figure 24.3) and satisfy

$$\begin{aligned}
a_1 \star a_1 = a_2 \star a_2 = \cdots = a_6 \star a_6 &= 1, \\
a_1 \star a_2 = a_2 \star a_3 = \cdots = a_6 \star a_1 &= \frac{1}{3}, \\
a_1 + a_2 + \cdots + a_6 &= 0,
\end{aligned} \qquad (12)$$

where $\star$ is the inner product. These conditions express the convention that each bond has unit length, the angle α between two successive (oriented) bonds has $\cos \alpha = 1/3$, and that the structure is cyclic. We now let $S_{ij} = a_i \star a_j$ for $1 \leq i, j \leq 6$. Under the conditions (12), S_{ij} is the cosine of the angle between a_i and a_j. Since

$$S_{i1} + \cdots + S_{i6} = a_i \star a_1 + \cdots + a_i \star a_6 = a_i \star (a_1 + \cdots + a_6) \qquad (13)$$

for all i, (12) implies that

$$\begin{aligned}
S_{ij} &= S_{ji} \text{ for } 1 \leq i < j \leq 6, \\
S_{11} = S_{22} = \cdots = S_{66} &= 1, \\
S_{12} = S_{23} = \cdots = S_{61} &= \frac{1}{3}, \\
S_{i1} + S_{i2} + \cdots + S_{i6} &= 0 \text{ for } 1 \leq i \leq 6
\end{aligned} \qquad (14)$$

The advantage of (14) over (12) is that all equations are linear. We have $33 = 15 + 6 + 6 + 6$ linear equations in 36 variables. It turns out that these equations are linearly independent, so that the solution space has $36 - 33 = 3$ dimensions. Calculating by hand, we plug the first three lines into the last six equations and

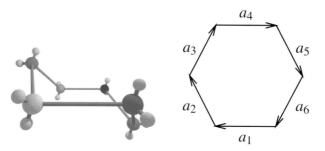

FIGURE 24.3: A "chair" conformation of cyclohexane, and the orientation we give to the bonds $a_1, \ldots, a_6$.

arrange the indices so that only S_{ij}'s with $i < j$ appear. All 36 values are then expressed as linear functions of the nine unknowns

$$S_{13}, S_{14}, S_{15}, S_{24}, S_{25}, S_{26}, S_{35}, S_{36}, S_{46},$$

and the remaining six equations between these can be written as

$$
\begin{aligned}
S_{13} + S_{14} + S_{15} = S_{14} + S_{24} + S_{46} &= \\
S_{13} + S_{35} + S_{36} = S_{26} + S_{36} + S_{46} &= \qquad\qquad (15) \\
S_{15} + S_{25} + S_{35} = S_{24} + S_{25} + S_{26} &= -\frac{5}{3},
\end{aligned}
$$

which in turn is equivalent to

$$
\begin{aligned}
S_{24} = S_{15}, \qquad S_{26} = S_{35}, \qquad S_{46} = S_{13}, \\
S_{14} = -S_{13} - S_{15} - \frac{5}{3}, \ S_{25} = -S_{15} - S_{35} - \frac{5}{3}, \ S_{36} = -S_{13} - S_{35} - \frac{5}{3}
\end{aligned}
\qquad (16)
$$

(for example, by adding the first two lines in (15) and subtracting the third from it, we obtain $2S_{13} = 2S_{46}$). Thus all S_{ij} are linear expressions in the three unknowns S_{13}, S_{35}, and S_{15}, each of them either a constant (1 or $1/3$), or an unknown, or as in the last line of (16). The three unknowns correspond precisely to the possible rotations around the bonds a_2, a_4, and a_6. We have now moved from ordinary three-space in which the a_i's live (and where the six a_i's really form a point in $\mathbb{R}^{18}$) to the configuration space as parametrized by $(S_{13}, S_{35}, S_{15}) \in \mathbb{R}^3$.

In the computer algebra system MAPLE V.5, the above calculation goes as follows:

```
with(linalg):
G := matrix(['['S[i,j]' $ 'j'=1..6]' $ 'i'=1..6]);
```

```
for i from 1 to 6 do
  S[i,i] := 1:
od:
for i from 1 to 5 do
  S[i,i+1] := 1/3:
od:
S[1,6] := 1/3:
for i from 2 to 6 do
  for j from 1 to i-1 do
    S[i,j] := S[j,i]:
  od:
od:
eq := {'S[i,1]+S[i,2]+S[i,3]+S[i,4]+S[i,5]+S[i,6]=0' $
       'i'=1..6}:
sol := solve(eq, {S[1,4],S[2,4],S[2,5],S[2,6],S[3,6],S[4,6]});
G := matrix([['subs(sol, S[i,j])' $ 'j'=1..6]' $ 'i'=1..6]);
```

$$
G := \begin{bmatrix}
S_{1,1} & S_{1,2} & S_{1,3} & S_{1,4} & S_{1,5} & S_{1,6} \\
S_{2,1} & S_{2,2} & S_{2,3} & S_{2,4} & S_{2,5} & S_{2,6} \\
S_{3,1} & S_{3,2} & S_{3,3} & S_{3,4} & S_{3,5} & S_{3,6} \\
S_{4,1} & S_{4,2} & S_{4,3} & S_{4,4} & S_{4,5} & S_{4,6} \\
S_{5,1} & S_{5,2} & S_{5,3} & S_{5,4} & S_{5,5} & S_{5,6} \\
S_{6,1} & S_{6,2} & S_{6,3} & S_{6,4} & S_{6,5} & S_{6,6}
\end{bmatrix}
$$

$$
sol := \{ S_{1,4} = -\frac{5}{3} - S_{1,3} - S_{1,5}, \ S_{2,5} = -S_{1,5} - S_{3,5} - \frac{5}{3},
$$
$$
S_{3,6} = -S_{1,3} - \frac{5}{3} - S_{3,5}, \ S_{4,6} = S_{1,3}, \ S_{2,6} = S_{3,5}, \ S_{2,4} = S_{1,5} \}
$$

$$
G := \begin{bmatrix}
1, \dfrac{1}{3}, S_{1,3}, -\dfrac{5}{3} - S_{1,3} - S_{1,5}, S_{1,5}, \dfrac{1}{3} \\[2mm]
\dfrac{1}{3}, 1, \dfrac{1}{3}, S_{1,5}, -S_{1,5} - S_{3,5} - \dfrac{5}{3}, S_{3,5} \\[2mm]
S_{1,3}, \dfrac{1}{3}, 1, \dfrac{1}{3}, S_{3,5}, -S_{1,3} - \dfrac{5}{3} - S_{3,5} \\[2mm]
-\dfrac{5}{3} - S_{1,3} - S_{1,5}, S_{1,5}, \dfrac{1}{3}, 1, \dfrac{1}{3}, S_{1,3} \\[2mm]
S_{1,5}, -S_{1,5} - S_{3,5} - \dfrac{5}{3}, S_{3,5}, \dfrac{1}{3}, 1, \dfrac{1}{3} \\[2mm]
\dfrac{1}{3}, S_{3,5}, -S_{1,3} - \dfrac{5}{3} - S_{3,5}, S_{1,3}, \dfrac{1}{3}, 1
\end{bmatrix}
$$

We have included MAPLE's results here. The MAPLE code can be downloaded from the book's web page http://www-math.uni-paderborn.de/mca/, and the reader is encouraged to run this code herself or to modify it so that it runs under her computer algebra system, if that is different from MAPLE.

In the transition from the vectors a_i to the inner products S_{ij} we have lost one central piece of information: the dimension of the space in which the a_i's live. Mathematically (but not chemically) the S_{ij} might just as well be the inner products of some a_i's in $\mathbb{R}^{10}$ or so. In fact, if we consider science-fiction cyclohexane in six (or more) dimensions, then (14) describes precisely all its conformations. (Actually, some inequalities also have to hold; these are explained later.)

Back to the real world! We have to reintroduce the information that chemistry (unlike mathematics and computer science) lives in three dimensions only. In $\mathbb{R}^3$, any four vectors are linearly dependent, and hence a solution to (14) can be realized in three-space if and only if any four of $a_1, \ldots, a_6$ are linearly dependent. In order to express this in terms of the S_{ij}, we introduce the abbreviations $x = S_{13}$, $y = S_{35}$, and $z = S_{15}$, and consider the **Gramian matrix** (Section 25.5)

$$G = G_{a_1,\ldots,a_6} = (a_i \star a_j)_{1 \le i,j \le 6} = (S_{ij})_{1 \le i,j \le 6}$$

$$= \begin{pmatrix} 1 & \frac{1}{3} & x & v_y & z & \frac{1}{3} \\ \frac{1}{3} & 1 & \frac{1}{3} & z & v_x & y \\ x & \frac{1}{3} & 1 & \frac{1}{3} & y & v_z \\ v_y & z & \frac{1}{3} & 1 & \frac{1}{3} & x \\ z & v_x & y & \frac{1}{3} & 1 & \frac{1}{3} \\ \frac{1}{3} & y & v_z & x & \frac{1}{3} & 1 \end{pmatrix} \in \mathbb{R}^6 \qquad (17)$$

of $a_1, \ldots, a_6$, where v_x is an abbreviation for $-y - z - 5/3$, and similarly for v_y, v_z. Exercise 24.4 shows that the Gramian matrix of a sequence of vectors is nonsingular (so that its determinant is nonzero) if and only if the vectors are linearly independent. Thus the three-dimensionality condition is equivalent to the fact that for any subset $T \subseteq \{1, \ldots, 6\}$ of cardinality 4, the Gramian matrix $G_{a_i : i \in T}$ of $(a_i : i \in T)$, which is a 4×4 submatrix of G, is singular, that is,

$$\forall T \subseteq \{1, \ldots, 6\} \quad \#T = 4 \Longrightarrow \det(G_{a_i : i \in T}) = 0. \qquad (18)$$

Among the $\binom{6}{4} = 15$ submatrices of this kind, there are only nine distinct ones, since the matrix G is invariant under the exchange of rows and columns $1, 2, 3$ with $4, 5, 6$, which corresponds to a vertical and horizontal swap of the 3×3 blocks indicated in (17).

We now have arrived at a system of nine equations in the three indeterminates x, y, z, expressing the fact that the subdeterminants of G corresponding to the 9 subsets $\{1, 2, 3, 4\}$, $\{1, 2, 3, 5\}$, $\{1, 2, 3, 6\}$, $\{1, 2, 4, 5\}$, $\{1, 2, 4, 6\}$, $\{1, 2, 5, 6\}$, $\{1, 3, 4, 6\}$, $\{1, 3, 5, 6\}$, and $\{2, 3, 5, 6\}$ vanish. For example, the subdeterminant belonging to the subset $\{1,2,3,6\}$ is

$$g_1 = \det G_{a_1,a_2,a_3,a_6} = \det \begin{pmatrix} 1 & \frac{1}{3} & x & \frac{1}{3} \\ \frac{1}{3} & 1 & \frac{1}{3} & y \\ x & \frac{1}{3} & 1 & -x-y-\frac{5}{3} \\ \frac{1}{3} & y & -x-y-\frac{5}{3} & 1 \end{pmatrix} \tag{19}$$

$$= \frac{1}{9}(9x^2y^2 + 6x^2y + 6xy^2 - 23x^2 - 20xy - 23y^2 - 34x - 34y - 15).$$

We let $F \subseteq \mathbb{Q}[x,y,z]$ be the set of those nine subdeterminants, regarded as polynomials in the three variables x,y,z, and $I = \langle F \rangle$ the ideal in $\mathbb{Q}[x,y,z]$ generated by the polynomials in F. Here is the MAPLE code to compute F.

```
S[1,3] := x:
S[3,5] := y:
S[1,5] := z:
A := {1,2,3,4,5,6}:
F := {}:
for i from 2 to 6 do
  for j from 1 to i-1 do
    T := convert(A minus {i,j}, list):
    F := F union {det(submatrix(G, T, T))}:
  od:
od:
```

The `convert` command transforms the set $A \setminus \{i,j\}$ into a list, the data format required for the second and third arguments of the `submatrix` command.

As noted above, any assignment of specific real values for the inner products S_{ij} for $1 \le i,j \le 6$ coming from a conformation of the cyclohexane molecule in three-space yields a common zero of the polynomials in F, and hence a zero of all polynomials in I. More precisely, we have

$$\{(S_{13},S_{35},S_{15}) \in \mathbb{R}^3 : \exists S_{11},S_{12},\ldots,S_{66} \text{ such that (14) and (18) hold}\} = V(I).$$

We first look at a two-dimensional image of our situation. We are lucky: the set F already contains exactly one polynomial in x and y only, namely g_1 from (19). It will turn out that its zero set $X = V(g_1)$, shown in Figure 24.4, is the projection of $V(F)$ onto the x,y-plane, and that with two exceptions, over each point of X lies exactly one point of $V(F)$.

The polynomial g_1 is quadratic both in x and y and of total degree four, and for a specific value $u \in \mathbb{R}$, we can determine $v \in \mathbb{R}$ such that $(u,v) \in V(g_1)$ by solving $g_1(u,v) = 0$:

$$v = \frac{-3u^2 + 10u + 17 \pm \sqrt{8(27u^4 + 48u^3 - 24u^2 - 44u - 7)}}{9u^2 + 6u - 23}, \tag{20}$$

as provided by MAPLE's command

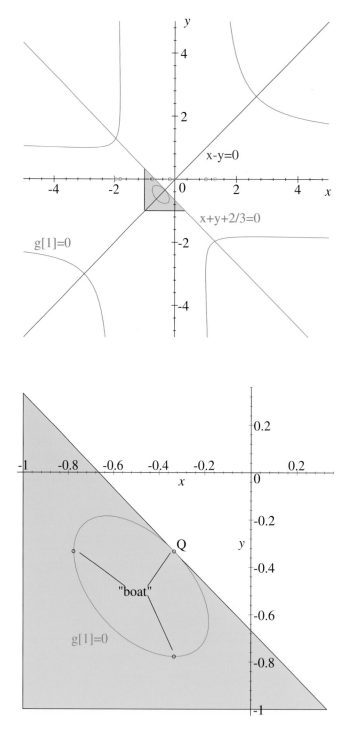

FIGURE 24.4: Projections of $V(F)$ and $V(F) \cap A$ onto the x, y plane.

```
g[1] := det(submatrix(G, [1,2,3,6], [1,2,3,6]))
solve(g[1], y)
```

If the denominator in (20) does not vanish, then this equation has 0, 1, or 2 real solutions $v \in \mathbb{R}$, depending on whether the discriminant

$$\frac{32}{81}(27u^4 + 48u^3 - 24u^2 - 44u - 7)$$

of g_1 (see Example 6.18) is negative, zero, or positive. The latter happens when

$$u < -1 - \frac{\sqrt{6}}{3} \text{ or } -\frac{7}{9} < u < -1 + \frac{\sqrt{6}}{3} \text{ or } 1 < u, \tag{21}$$

and single solutions occur for

$$u \in \{-1 \pm \frac{\sqrt{6}}{3}, -\frac{7}{9}, 1\} \approx \{-1.8165, -0.1835, -0.7778, 1\} \tag{22}$$

(the pink points in Figure 24.4), as certified by the MAPLE command

```
factor(discrim(g[1], y));
```

For $u = (-1 \pm 2\sqrt{6})/3 \approx -0.3333 \pm 1.6330$ (the light blue points in Figure 24.4), the coefficient of y^2 in g_1, which equals the denominator in (20), vanishes, and there is a unique $v \in \mathbb{R}$ such that $g_1(u, v) = 0$, namely

$$v = \frac{23u^2 + 34u + 15}{6u^2 - 20u - 34} = \frac{-1 \mp 2\sqrt{6}}{3}. \tag{23}$$

Figure 24.4 shows a plot of X and of a magnification of the central piece of X, which will turn out to be the only piece relevant for our cyclohexane problem. (The yellow triangle is explained below.) The points $(-1/3, -1/3)$, $(-1/3, -7/9)$, and $(-7/9, -1/3)$ marked in Figure 24.4 are the projections of the three "boat" points in Figure 1.5 on page 13.

What is the precise connection between X and $V(F)$? Since $g_1 \in F$, for any $(u, v, w) \in V(F)$, we have $g_1(u, v) = 0$, and thus the whole projection of $V(F)$ is contained in X. Conversely, if $(u, v) \in X$, can we find a $w \in \mathbb{R}$ such that (u, v, w) is a common zero of the other eight polynomials in F? All of them have degree two in z, and it would be nice if we could somehow eliminate the occurrences of z^2. We take a close look, and find that the two polynomials

$$\begin{aligned}
g_2(x,y,z) &= \det G_{a_2,a_3,a_5,a_6} \\
&= \frac{1}{9}(9x^2y^2 + 18x^2yz + 9x^2z^2 + 18xy^2z + 18xyz^2 + 9y^2z^2 + 30x^2y \\
&\quad + 30x^2z + 60xy^2 + 120xyz + 30xz^2 + 60y^2z + 30yz^2 + 16x^2 \\
&\quad + 118xy + 98xz + 36y^2 + 118yz + 16z^2 + 50x + 60y + 50z + 21), \\
g_3(x,y,z) &= \det G_{a_1,a_3,a_4,a_6} = g_2(y,x,z)
\end{aligned}$$

have the same leading coefficient $(9x^2 + 18xy + 9y^2 + 30x + 30y + 16)/9$ with respect to the variable z. Thus

$$
\begin{aligned}
g_4 &= g_3 - g_2 = \frac{10}{9}(3x^2y + 3x^2z - 3xy^2 - 3y^2z + 2x^2 + 2xz - 2y^2 - 2yz + x - y) \\
&= \frac{10}{9}(x - y)(3xy + 3xz + 3yz + 2x + 2y + 2z + 1)
\end{aligned}
$$

is a linear polynomial in z, and any common zero of the nine polynomials in F is also a zero of g_4. Thus for an arbitrary point $(u, v) \in X$ with $u \neq v$, we may determine a unique $w \in \mathbb{R}$ from the equation $g_4(u, v, w) = 0$, namely

$$
w = -\frac{3uv + 2u + 2v + 1}{3u + 3v + 2}. \tag{24}
$$

It remains to verify that then in fact $g(u, v, w) = 0$ for all $g \in F$. It is sufficient to show that the polynomial

$$
(3x + 3y + 2)^2 \cdot g\left(x, y, -\frac{3xy + 2x + 2y + 1}{3x + 3y + 2}\right)
$$

is a multiple of g. This is certified by MAPLE's reply to the commands

```
g[2] := det(submatrix(G, [2,3,5,6], [2,3,5,6]));
g[3] := det(submatrix(G, [1,3,4,6], [1,3,4,6]));
g[4] := factor(g[3] - g[2]);
w := solve(g[4], z);
'rem(numer(subs(z = w, F[i])), g[1], x)' $ 'i' = 1..nops(F);
```

There are four points (u, v) in X with $u = v$, namely

$$
(-3, -3), \quad Q = \left(-\frac{1}{3}, -\frac{1}{3}\right), \quad \left(1 \pm \frac{2}{3}\sqrt{6}, 1 \pm \frac{2}{3}\sqrt{6}\right), \tag{25}
$$

as provided by

```
factor(subs(y = x, g[1]));
```

The plane curve X contains no line and has degree four, and any line in the plane intersects X in at most four points, counting multiplicities, by the famous **theorem of Bézout**; see Section 6.8. We have found those four points for our special line $x = y$ (see Figure 24.4). We have to check separately—by using other polynomials from F—that they yield the six points

$$
\begin{aligned}
&(-3, -3, -3), \quad (-3, -3, 1), \quad C = \left(-\frac{1}{3}, -\frac{1}{3}, -\frac{1}{3}\right), \quad \left(-\frac{1}{3}, -\frac{1}{3}, -\frac{7}{9}\right), \\
&\left(1 + \frac{2}{3}\sqrt{6}, 1 + \frac{2}{3}\sqrt{6}, -1 - \frac{1}{3}\sqrt{6}\right), \quad \left(1 - \frac{2}{3}\sqrt{6}, 1 - \frac{2}{3}\sqrt{6}, -1 + \frac{1}{3}\sqrt{6}\right)
\end{aligned}
\tag{26}
$$

in $V(F)$; the point C corresponds to the isolated "chair" conformation.

Oops! We have overlooked something: division by zero. We have to investigate separately the case where the denominator in (24) vanishes, namely when $3u + 3v + 2 = 0$. Which points on X satisfy this equation?

```
factor(subs(y = - x - 2/3, g[1]));
```

gives three values for u, and substituting each of them in the equation $v = -u - 2/3$ yields the three intersection points

$$\left(-\frac{1}{3}, -\frac{1}{3}\right), \quad \left(\frac{-1+2\sqrt{6}}{3}, \frac{-1-2\sqrt{6}}{3}\right), \quad \left(\frac{-1-2\sqrt{6}}{3}, \frac{-1+2\sqrt{6}}{3}\right) \quad (27)$$

of the line $V(3x + 3y + 2)$ with X (see Figure 24.4). The first one is the point Q from above, which lies on the central piece and is actually a "double point" of the intersection. The slope of the tangent to X at a point (u, v) is

$$\left(-\frac{\partial g_1/\partial x}{\partial g_1/\partial y}\right)(u, v) = -\frac{18uv^2 + 12uv + 6v^2 - 46u - 20v - 34}{18u^2v + 6u^2 + 12uv - 20u - 46v - 34},$$

and its value at $Q = (-1/3, -1/3)$ is -1. The line has the same slope, and so it is the tangent at Q to X. We have already seen that there are precisely two points of $V(F)$ lying over Q. In the vicinity of the other two intersection points, the z-coordinate grows unboundedly, and there are no points of $V(F)$ lying above them.

Putting things together, we have found the following. In order to determine all solutions $S_{11}, S_{12}, \ldots, S_{66}$ of (14) and (18), we can proceed as follows. We pick a point $P = (u, v, w) \in V(F)$, set $S_{13} = u$, $S_{35} = v$, $S_{15} = w$, and solve for the remaining S_{ij} via (14) and (16). To find $P \in V(F)$, we pick a real number u as in (21) or (22), determine v according to (20) or (23) (so that $(u, v) \in X$), and w by (24) if (u, v) equals none of the points in (25) and (27); otherwise, P is one of the six points in (26). We obtain similar solutions, with the roles of three coordinates permuted, when we apply the MAPLE command `solve` directly to the original nine equations in F.

Finally, another constraint comes into play that we have ignored so far. Each S_{ij} is the cosine of an angle, and hence lies between -1 and 1. These inequalities, applied to S_{14}, S_{25}, S_{36}, and using (16), show that all our physical solutions lie in the polytope

$$A = \{(u, v, w) \in [-1, 1]^3 : u + v \leq -\frac{2}{3}, \ u + w \leq -\frac{2}{3}, \ v + w \leq -\frac{2}{3}\},$$

The projection of A onto the first two coordinates is the yellow triangle in Figure 24.4. Thus neither the point $(-3, -3, -3)$ nor the outlying branches of X contribute physical solutions, but $C = (-1/3, -1/3, -1/3)$ (the "chair") and $-7/9 \leq u \leq -1 + \sqrt{6}/3$ do, leading precisely to the points in $V(F) \cap A$.

From the point of view of computer algebra, this completely solves the problem, except that we would also have to calculate actual $a_1, \ldots, a_6$ from $S_{11}, S_{12}, \ldots, S_{66}$ (Exercise 24.6).

We now indicate how Gröbner bases lead to a somewhat more systematic way of solving our problem than the above ad hoc approach. It may seem that this is a bit of overkill, but the reader may imagine that the solution "by hand" is no longer feasible for cycloheptane (seven carbon atoms), where 35 polynomial equations in seven unknowns have to be solved, while Gröbner bases still work.

We take the lexicographical order with $z \succ y \succ x$. In MAPLE, the commands

```
with(Groebner):
B := gbasis(F, plex(z, y, x));
```

provide in a few seconds the reduced Gröbner basis B of $V(F)$ consisting of the four polynomials

$$
\begin{aligned}
f_1 &= 9g_1 = 9x^2y^2 + 6x^2y + 6xy^2 - 23x^2 - 20xy - 23y^2 - 34x - 34y - 15, \\
f_2 &= 27x^4y + 27x^4z + 18x^4 + 108x^3y + 108x^3z + 18x^2y + 18x^2z \\
&\quad - 284x^2 - 212xy - 212xz - 400x - 69y - 69z - 102. \\
f_3 &= -9x^3y - 9x^3z - 6x^3 - 9x^2y - 9x^2z + 18x^2 + 41xy + 41xz + 20yz \\
&\quad + 54x + 21y + 21z + 18, \\
f_4 &= 9x^2z^2 + 6x^2z + 6xz^2 - 23x^2 - 20xz - 23z^2 - 34x - 34z - 15.
\end{aligned}
$$

(Depending on your specific MAPLE version, the polynomials may appear in a different order. While in our definition each polynomial in a reduced Gröbner basis is monic, MAPLE computes the primitive integer multiples.) What is "nice" about this new basis? In f_2 and f_3, the variables y and z occur only linearly. This makes it easy to eliminate (at least one of) them, and does not occur in any of the original equations. (Alternatively, the resultant method of Section 6.8 allows one to eliminate even a variable occurring with high degree.) Moreover, f_1 and f_4 have two variables only. This is no surprise, since—up to a multiplicative constant—they equal (19) and $\det G_{a_1,a_2,a_3,a_4}$, respectively.

It is not hard to show that the set F of all 4×4 subdeterminants of G—and hence the ideal I—is invariant under an arbitrary permutation of the variables x, y, z. This symmetry is only partially reflected in the Gröbner basis: f_4 is f_1 with z substituted for y, and f_2 and f_3 are symmetric with respect to y and z. Hence our basis B is invariant under the exchange of y and z.

Since B is a basis for I, we have $V(f_1, f_2, f_3, f_4) = V(I)$, so that we only need to look at the solutions of $f_1 = f_2 = f_3 = f_4 = 0$. MAPLE's command

```
B := factor(B);
```

shows that f_1, f_3 and f_4 are irreducible over $\mathbb{Q}$. For f_1, for example, this follows from the facts that f_1 is primitive with respect to x, so that it has no nonconstant factor in $\mathbb{Q}[y]$, and that $f_1(x,2) = 25(x^2 - 2x - 7)$ is irreducible. The polynomial f_2 factors as $f_2 = (x+3)(3x+1)f_5$, where

$$f_5 = 9x^2y + 9x^2z + 6x^2 + 6xy + 6xz - 20x - 23y - 23z - 34.$$

The first two factors can be found by computing contents with respect to y or z, and f_5 is irreducible because it is primitive with respect to x, so that it contains no nonconstant factor in $\mathbb{Q}[y,z]$, and since $f_5(x,0,0) = 2(3x^2 - 10x - 17)$ is irreducible. Since a point in $\mathbb{R}^3$ is a root of a polynomial $f = gh$ if and only if it is either a root of g or a root of h (or of both), we have $V(I) = V(I_1) \cup V(I_2) \cup V(I_3)$, where

$$I_1 = \langle f_1, f_3, f_4, x+3 \rangle, \quad I_2 = \langle f_1, f_3, f_4, 3x+1 \rangle, \quad I_3 = \langle f_1, f_3, f_4, f_5 \rangle.$$

The MAPLE commands

```
F1 := {B[1],B[3],B[4],op(1,B[2])}:
F2 := {B[1],B[3],B[4],op(2,B[2])}:
F3 := {B[1],B[3],B[4],op(3,B[2])}:
B1 := gbasis(F1, plex(z, y, x));
B2 := gbasis(F2, plex(z, y, x));
B3 := gbasis(F3, plex(z, y, x));
```

compute the reduced Gröbner bases for the three new ideals with respect to the lexicographic order and $z \succ y \succ x$. The op command in the first line extracts the first operand x+3 of its second argument B[2], and analogously in the following two lines. We obtain

$$\begin{aligned}
B_1 &= \{z^2 + 2z - 3, yz + 3y + 3z + 9, y^2 + 2y - 3, x+3\}, \\
B_2 &= \{27z^2 + 30z + 7, 9yz + 3y + 3z + 1, 27y^2 + 30y + 7, 3x+1\}, \\
B_3 &= \{f_1, f_5, f_6\},
\end{aligned}$$
(28)

where

$$f_6 = 3xy + 3xz + 3yz + 2x + 2y + 2z + 1.$$

All polynomials in B_1 and B_2 are products of linear factors; for example, the second one in B_1 is $yz + 3y + 3z + 9 = (y+3)(z+3)$. The solutions of B_1 and B_2 are easily determined:

$$\begin{aligned}
V(I_1) &= \{(-3,-3,-3),(-3,1,-3),(-3,-3,1)\}, \\
V(I_2) &= \{(-\frac{1}{3},-\frac{1}{3},-\frac{1}{3}),(-\frac{1}{3},-\frac{7}{9},-\frac{1}{3}),(-\frac{1}{3},-\frac{1}{3},-\frac{7}{9})\},
\end{aligned}$$

as furnished by

```
V1 := solve({op(B1)});
V2 := solve({op(B2)});
```

The following three MAPLE lines verify that of the six points in $V(I_1)$ and $V(I_2)$, all but $(-3, -3, -3)$ and $C = (-1/3, -1/3, -1/3)$ are also contained in $V(I_3)$.

```
for v in V1 do
   subs(v, B3);
od;
for v in V2 do
   subs(v, B3);
od;
```

It now remains to understand $V(I_3)$. The output of the following command reveals that the three polynomials in (28) are irreducible over $\mathbb{Q}$.

```
factor(B3);
```

We note that $f_6 = 9g_4/(x-y)$, and proceeding as in our ad-hoc approach, we can show that over each point of $X = V(f_1)$ lies precisely one point of $V(I_3)$, and hence $V(F)$ is the disjoint union of $V(I_3)$ and two isolated points $(-3, -3, -3)$ and $C = (-1/3, -1/3, -1/3)$.

Figure 1.5 on page 13 gives a three-dimensional plot of $E = V(I_3) \cap A$. We did not proceed as described above to produce this plot, but instead took the equation $f_5(u, v, w) = 0$ to obtain the third coordinate

$$w = \frac{-9u^2v - 6u^2 - 6uv + 20u + 23v + 23}{9u^2 + 6u - 23} \tag{29}$$

from a point $(u, v) \in X$, since the denominator $9u^2 + 6u - 23$ is nonzero inside the yellow triangle (Exercise 24.5), which makes the numerical computations more stable than using (24). E is not an algebraic curve, but only one of several real connected components of the algebraic curve $V(I_3)$. Since E is described by algebraic equations and inequalities, it is **semialgebraic**. It can be shown that the points of E describe precisely the flexible conformations of cyclohexane, namely those which can be obtained from a "boat" conformation by rotations around the bonds, but we will not do this here.

When you have generated the MAPLE plot in Figure 1.5 on your system, you can click on it and rotate it. We did this, and from one direction it looked as if the curve were nearly a circle lying in a plane perpendicular to the diagonal vector $(1, 1, 1)$. We knew that this could not be exactly true, plotted the value of $u + v + w + 13/9$ on E, and found that this value is always between -0.0051 and 0. It would be interesting to know if this has any chemical significance.

We have now completed the three steps indicated at the beginning of Section 1.1: modeling, solving the model, and interpreting. These steps are not straightforward, and we used some ad hoc tricks. Our strategy can be summarized as follows: we expressed the solutions as roots of polynomial equations, computed Gröbner bases, and factored our polynomials whenever possible. A factorization splits the problem into smaller subproblems; each of these is better manageable than the big problem. The bottleneck in this approach is typically the Gröbner basis computation.

Notes. **24.1.** We refer the reader to Krajíček (1995), Urquhart (1995), Pitassi (1997), and Beame & Pitassi (1998) for excellent surveys of the state of the art in proof systems. The Nullstellensatz proof system was introduced by Beame, Impagliazzo, Krajíček, Pitassi & Pudlák (1996). Gröbner proof systems are an active area of research; see Buss, Impagliazzo, Krajíček, Pudlák, Razborov & Sgall (1996/97) and Razborov (1998); they are also called *polynomial calculus systems*. A central measure of the complexity of such a system is the degree of the polynomials that occur. The pigeonhole principle for $n = 100$ is stated in Schwenter (1636), 53. Auffgab.

24.2. Peterson (1981) and Reisig (1985) give general introductions to Petri nets. Our algebraic description of Petri nets follows Mayr (1992). Further results about the reachability problem for Petri nets and connections to finitely presented commutative semigroups and vector addition systems are given in Mayr (1995). The fact about binomial ideals is due to Eisenbud & Sturmfels (1996).

Mayr (1984) solved a long-standing open problem by showing that reachability for Petri nets is decidable. His algorithm is not primitive recursive, but the best proven lower bound for reachability is $\mathcal{EXPSPACE}$-hardness. In fact, reachability for reversible Petri nets is $\mathcal{EXPSPACE}$-complete.

24.3. See also Notes 23.4. The *method of creative telescoping* for proving hypergeometric identities was pioneered by Doron Zeilberger (1990a, 1990b, 1991), who has his computers publish papers (Ekhad 1990, Ekhad & Tre 1990) ("And how many papers did your workstation publish?"), and Herbert Wilf (Wilf & Zeilberger 1990, 1992), and started a debate about the price of mathematical theorems (Zeilberger 1993, Andrews 1994). Wilf and Zeilberger received the 1998 Leroy P. Steele Prize for a Seminal Contribution to Research, as reported in the April 1998 issue of the *Notices of the AMS*. We refer the reader to the well-written book of Petkovšek, Wilf & Zeilberger (1996) for further reading on the method.

Our proof of (6) actually uses *WZ-pairs*, as invented by Wilf & Zeilberger (1990); see also Wilf (1994), §4.4. Van der Poorten (1978) gives an overview of Apéry's proof. Paule's (1994) computer-generated proof of (11) can be verified using only high-school algebra.

For the analysis of algorithms, it is often sufficient to have only an *asymptotic* approximation for a sum such as (6), in particular in those cases where (provably) no closed form exists. There is a powerful general tool, *generating functions*, which together with singularity analysis from complex analysis provides a standard means to obtain such asymptotic expansions (Flajolet & Odlyzko 1990, Vitter & Flajolet 1990, Flajolet, Salvy & Zimmermann 1991, Odlyzko 1995a). The software package $\Lambda\Upsilon\Omega$ (Flajolet, Salvy & Zimmermann 1989a, 1989b, Salvy 1991, Zimmermann 1991) automates this process; the code can be downloaded from `ftp://ftp.inria.fr/INRIA/Projects/algo/programs/luo/`. Sedgewick & Flajolet (1996) is a very readable textbook in this area.

24.4. Most introductory texts on organic chemistry discuss the cyclohexane conformations; see for example Wade (1995). Sachse (1890, 1892) first postulated the existence
of infinitely many flexible and a single rigid conformation of cyclohexane. Oosterhoff
(1949) and Hazebroek & Oosterhoff (1951), whose goal was to determine the potential energy of cyclohexane conformations, pioneered the approach given here, based on the inner
products. Levelt (1997) applied computer algebra to the problem, actually to cycloheptane;
our presentation is based on Levelt's work. Levelt cautions: *Does it matter to the chemists?
The answer is "NO!". In our model the geometry rules: the 'building blocks' are rigid; in
chemistry energy rules and nothing is rigid. Distances between carbon molecules may
vary, just as angles between bonds. The molecule is viewed as a conglomerate of atoms
kept together by the various forces between the constituents. The geometry of the molecule
is the result of the balance of the forces. The chemist's flexible model is the opposite of
the rigid one in this* [model]. Of course, one might now take the formulas for the potential
energy and process them with computer algebra tools; we do not know whether something
really useful comes out of that.

In their important paper, Gō & Scheraga (1970) found that for a cyclic molecule with
$n \geq 6$ carbon atoms, the solution space of possible conformations is $(n-6)$-dimensional in
the generic case. This does not apply to cyclohexane, where $n = 6$ and we have seen that the
solution space contains a one-dimensional component. For more recent contributions and
references, see Havel & Najfeld (1995) and Emiris & Mourrain (1999). The cyclohexane
problem is closely related to the well-studied $6R$ inverse kinematics problem from robotics;
see Parsons & Canny (1994) for references and an overview on related problems.

MOLGEN is a general purpose computer chemistry system (Benecke, Grund, Hohberger,
Kerber, Laue & Wieland 1995).

The two equations (24) and (29) are equivalent since

$$-(3xy + 2x + 2y + 1) \cdot h = 27g_1 + (3x + 3y + 2) \cdot g$$

in $\mathbb{Q}[x, y, z]$, where

$$g = -9x^2y - 6x^2 - 6xy + 20x + 23y + 34, \quad h = 9x^2 + 6x - 23,$$

so that both equations determine the same value of w whenever $(u, v) \in X = V(g_1)$ and
both are defined.

Exercises.

24.1$^{\longrightarrow}$ Refute PHP_2 with both the Nullstellensatz and the Gröbner proof system.

24.2 Prove that the Petri net in Figure 24.1 is not reversible. Hint: Consider the marking $M(s_1) = 2$,
$M(s_2) = M(s_3) = 0$.

24.3* Prove (6) for all $n \geq w$ by induction on n.

24.4* Let V be a vector space over a field F and $\star: V \times V \longrightarrow F$ an inner product on V. For a finite
sequence $a_1, \ldots, a_n \in V$ of vectors, let $G = (a_i \star a_j) \in F^{n \times n}$ be the Gramian matrix of $a_1, \ldots, a_n$.

  (i) Show that $\det G = 0$ if and only if $a_1, \ldots, a_n$ are linearly dependent.

  (ii) Conclude that the rank of G is equal to the rank of $\{a_1, \ldots, a_n\}$.

24.5　(i) Show that the set

$$B = \{(u,v) \in [-1,1]^2 : u+v \leq -\frac{2}{3}\} \subseteq \mathbb{R}^2$$

(the yellow triangle in Figure 24.4) is the projection of A onto the x,y-plane.

　(ii) Show that the denominator of (29) does not vanish on B.

24.6$^{\longrightarrow}$　Take an arbitrary point (u,v) on the curve in Figure 24.4 and compute the coordinates of a corresponding conformation $a_1, a_2, \ldots, a_6$. To constrain the degrees of freedom arising from the possibility of rotating the whole structure in space, you may assume that $a_1 = (1,0,0)$ and the third coordinate of a_2 is zero. (Note: this is a lengthy calculation.) Since u,v,w represent cosines of angles and $\cos\alpha = \cos(2\pi - \alpha)$ for all angles α, to each point $(u,v,w) \in E$ there correspond up to four conformations which are mirror images of each other.

24.7$^{\longrightarrow}$　Buy six plumbing knees at your local hardware store, and find out their angle α. Then perform the whole calculation with $\cos\alpha$ instead of $1/3$. Plot the ellipse-like curve as in Figure 24.4, find a point on it, and construct physically the corresponding conformation with your plumbing materials.

24.8$^{\longrightarrow}$　Redo the cyclohexane computations after making the substitutions $x^* = 3x+1$, $y^* = 3y+1$, $z^* = 3z+1$ in (17).

C'est icy un livre de bonne foy, lecteur.[1]

Michel Eysquem Seigneur de Montaigne (1580)

Quis leget haec?[2]

Aules Persius Flaccus (c. 62 AD)

Der Schreibende selbst weiß freilich nie so recht,
ob er ein bloßer Spinner ist oder ein exemplarischer Mensch.[3]

Markus Werner (1984)

Non difficile nobis foret hoc Caput multis aliis observationibus
locupletare, nisi limites, intra quos restringi oportet,
vetarent. Iis qui ulterius progredi amant,
haec principia viam saltem addigitare poterunt.[4]

Carl Friedrich Gauß (1798)

---

[1]　This book is written in good faith, reader.
[2]　Who would read this stuff?
[3]　The writer himself is never quite sure whether he is plain nuts or a model of virtue.
[4]　It would not be difficult for us to enrich this chapter with many other observations, but the limits within which it is proper to remain forbid this. These principles will at least be able to indicate the direction to those who like to progress further.

Appendix

Elementary, my dear Watson.[1]

Sherlock Holmes (1929)

We may always depend upon it that algebra, which cannot be
translated into good English and sound common sense, is bad algebra.

William Kingdon Clifford (1885)

Angling may be said to be so like the Mathematicks,
that it can never be fully learnt.

Izaak Walton (1653)

At Kent he was curious about computer science
but in just the introductory course Math 10 061
in Merrill Hall the math got to be too much for him.

John Updike (1981)

At the mathematical school, the proposition and demonstration were
fairly written on a thin wafer, with ink composed of a cephalic tincture.
This the student was to swallow upon a fasting stomach, and for three
days following eat nothing but bread and water. As the wafer digested,
the tincture mounted to his brain, bearing the proposition along with it.

Jonathan Swift (1726)

---

[1] Popularly but erroneously attributed to Sir Arthur Conan Doyle.

25

Fundamental concepts

This appendix presents some of the basic notions used throughout the text, for the reader's reference. By necessity, this is kept rather short and without proofs; we indicate, however, reference texts where these can be found. The reader is required to either have previous acquaintance with the material or be willing to read up on it. Our presentation is too concise for self-study; its purpose is to fix the language and point the reader to those areas, if any, where she needs brushing up.

The first five sections deal with algebra: groups, rings, polynomials and fields, finite fields, and linear algebra. Then we discuss finite probability spaces. After this mathematical background come some fundamentals from computer science: O-notation and a modicum of complexity theory.

25.1. Groups

The material of the first three sections can be found in any basic algebra text, such as Hungerford (1990) or the latest edition of van der Waerden's (1930b, 1931) classic on *Modern Algebra*.

DEFINITION 25.1. *A **group** is a nonempty set G with a binary operation $\cdot : G \times G \longrightarrow G$ satisfying*

○ *Associativity:* $\forall a, b, c \in G \quad (a \cdot b) \cdot c = a \cdot (b \cdot c)$,
○ *Identity:* $\exists 1 \in G \; \forall a \in G \quad a \cdot 1 = 1 \cdot a = a$,
○ *Inverse:* $\forall a \in G \; \exists a^{-1} \in G \quad a \cdot a^{-1} = a^{-1} \cdot a = 1$.

The group is denoted by $(G; \cdot, 1, ^{-1})$, but usually just the set name G is sufficient.

It is usual, for convenience of notation, to omit the symbol $\cdot$ from products. Thus $a \cdot b$ becomes the simpler ab. We will also frequently need to distinguish between two group operations. The alternate notation $+$ for $\cdot$, 0 for 1 and $-a$ instead of a^{-1} is used. The first representation is called a **multiplicative group** and the new one is called an **additive group**, denoted by $(G; +, 0, -)$.

Familiar examples are the additive groups of $\mathbb{Z}$, $\mathbb{Q}$, $\mathbb{R}$, and $\mathbb{C}$, the multiplicative groups of $\mathbb{Q} \setminus \{0\}$, $\mathbb{R} \setminus \{0\}$, and $\mathbb{C} \setminus \{0\}$, and for any $n \in \mathbb{N}$, the additive group $\mathbb{Z}_n = \{0, 1, 2, \ldots, n-1\}$ with addition modulo n and the multiplicative group $\mathbb{Z}_n^{\times} = \{1 \leq a < n : \gcd(a, n) = 1\}$ with multiplication modulo n.

A nonempty subset H of a group G is called a **subgroup** of G if it is closed under multiplication and inversion, that is, if $ab \in H$ and $a^{-1} \in H$ for all $a, b \in H$. A subset S of a group G **generates** the set $\langle S \rangle \subseteq G$ consisting of all finite products of elements in S and their inverses. If $S = \{g_1, \ldots, g_s\}$ is finite, then we also write $\langle g_1, \ldots, g_s \rangle$ instead of $\langle \{g_1, \ldots, g_s\} \rangle$. $\langle S \rangle$ is the smallest (with respect to inclusion) subgroup of G containing S. For $G = \mathbb{Z}_{12} = \{0, 1, 2, 3, 4, 5, 6, 7, 8, 9, 10, 11\}$ with addition mod 12, $S = \{3, 8\}$ generates G. In fact, $\mathbb{Z}_{12}$ has a generating set consisting of just one generator, namely $S = \{1\}$. If there is an element $g \in G$ that generates the entire group $G = \langle g \rangle$, then the group is called **cyclic**, and g a **generator** of G. Each of the four elements $1, 5, 7$, and 11 generates $\mathbb{Z}_{12}$. The additive group of $\mathbb{R}$ has no finite generating set.

For a finite set A, $\#A$ is its cardinality, that is, the number of elements in it. The number of elements in a finite group is its **order** $\#G$. If G is a finite group and $H \subseteq G$ is a subgroup, then **Lagrange's theorem** says that $\#G = \#H \cdot \#(G : H)$, where $G : H = \{gH : g \in G\}$ is the set of **right cosets** of H. In particular, $\#H$ is a divisor of $\#G$.

The **order** $\mathrm{ord}(g)$ of an element $g \in G$ is the order of $\langle g \rangle$, the cyclic subgroup generated by g, or equivalently, the smallest positive integer n such that $g^n = 1$. It divides any other integer k with $g^k = 1$. An immediate consequence of Lagrange's theorem is that $\mathrm{ord}(g)$ divides $\#G$, and $g^{\#G} = 1$ for all $g \in G$. Special cases are Fermat's little theorem 4.9 and Euler's theorem (Section 18.1).

Most groups occurring in this text are **commutative** (or Abelian), satisfying the additional property

○ Commutativity: $\forall a, b \in G \; ab = ba$.

The integers under addition form a commutative group, while the invertible $n \times n$ matrices over $\mathbb{R}$ are a noncommutative group under multiplication if $n \geq 2$. Every cyclic group is commutative, but not vice versa: $\mathbb{Z}_{12}^{\times}$ is commutative but not cyclic.

A **group homomorphism** is a map $\varphi: G \longrightarrow H$ between two (multiplicative) groups G and H that respects the group operation: $\varphi(g_1 g_2) = \varphi(g_1) \varphi(g_2)$ for all $g_1, g_2 \in G$. A map $\varphi: A \longrightarrow B$ between two sets A and B is **injective** (or one-to-one) if $\varphi(a_1) = \varphi(a_2)$ implies $a_1 = a_2$ for all $a_1, a_2 \in A$; φ is **surjective** (or onto) if for all $b \in B$ there exists some $a \in A$ such that $\varphi(a) = b$. If φ is both injective and surjective, then it is **bijective**. A bijective group homomorphism $\varphi: G \longrightarrow H$ is called an **isomorphism** between G and H; then G and H are **isomorphic** and we write $G \cong H$. As far as group theory is concerned, G and H are instantiations of the same object. A group homomorphism $f: G \longrightarrow H$ is an isomorphism if and only if there exists a group homomorphism $\psi: H \longrightarrow G$ so that $\varphi \circ \psi = \mathrm{id}_H$ and $\psi \circ \varphi = \mathrm{id}_G$, where $\circ$ is the composition of maps.

The **kernel** of a group homomorphism $\varphi: G \longrightarrow H$ is $\ker \varphi = \{g \in G : \varphi(g) = 1\} \subseteq G$, and the **image** of φ is $\varphi(G) = \{\varphi(g) : g \in G\} \subseteq H$. The homomorphism φ is injective if and only if $\ker \varphi = \{1\}$. If $K = \ker \varphi$ is the kernel of φ, then $G : K$, the set of right cosets of K, forms again a group by letting $(gK)(g^*K) = (gg^*)K$ for any $g, g^* \in G$. This group is called the **factor group** of G modulo K and denoted by G/K. The **homomorphism theorem for groups** states that $G/K = G/\ker \varphi$ is isomorphic to $\varphi(G)$; and thus $\#G = \#\ker \varphi \cdot \#\varphi(G)$ if these are all finite.

Given two groups G and H, a new group $G \times H$—called the **direct product**—is constructed by setting $G \times H = \{(g, h) : g \in G, h \in H\}$, and defining multiplication by $(g_1, h_1) \cdot (g_2, h_2) = (g_1 g_2, h_1 h_2)$ for $g_1, g_2 \in G$ and $h_1, h_2 \in H$. (What is the identity element of $G \times H$, and what is the inverse of some (g, h)?)

For $n \in \mathbb{N}_{>1}$, the **symmetric group** S_n consists of all **permutations** of the elements $\{1,\ldots,n\}$:

$$S_n = \{\sigma:\{1,\ldots,n\} \longrightarrow \{1,\ldots,n\}: \sigma \text{ bijective}\};$$

the group operation is the composition $\circ$ of maps. This group has $\#S_n = n!$ elements and is not commutative if $n \geq 3$.

25.2. Rings

A ring is an algebraic structure with two operations, as follows.

DEFINITION 25.2. *A **ring** is a set R with two binary operations* $\cdot, + : R \times R \longrightarrow R$ *satisfying*

 ○ *R together with* $+$ *is a commutative group with identity 0,*
 ○ $\cdot$ *is associative,*
 ○ *R has an identity element 1 for* $\cdot$,
 ○ *Distributivity:* $\forall a,b,c \in R \quad a(b+c) = (ab)+(ac)$ *and* $(b+c)a = (ba)+(ca)$.

*The ring is **commutative** if furthermore* $\cdot$ *is commutative. One sometimes drops the requirement that an identity element 1 exist.*

Familiar examples are $\mathbb{Z}$, $\mathbb{Q}$, $\mathbb{R}$, and $\mathbb{C}$, with the usual addition and multiplication, and, for all $n \in \mathbb{N}_{>0}$, $\mathbb{Z}_n$ with addition and multiplication modulo n, and the set $\mathbb{R}^{n \times n}$ of all $n \times n$ matrices with real entries, with matrix addition and matrix multiplication. All these examples, except the matrices, form a commutative ring. Matrix rings briefly occur in Chapter 12.

> In this book, all rings are **commutative with 1** unless otherwise stated.

A **ring homomorphism** from a ring R to a ring S is a map φ such that $\varphi(r_1 + r_2) = \varphi(r_1) + \varphi(r_2)$, $\varphi(r_1 r_2) = \varphi(r_1)\varphi(r_2)$ for all $r_1, r_2 \in R$, and $\varphi(0_R) = 0_S$ and $\varphi(1_R) = 1_S$. φ is an **isomorphism** if it is also bijective, and then R and S are isomorphic: $R \cong S$. (We have a small ambiguity here, in that two rings might be isomorphic as groups with the operation $+$, but not as rings, for example, $\mathbb{R} \times \mathbb{R}$ and $\mathbb{C}$.) Thus a ring homomorphism is a homomorphism for both the additive and the multiplicative structure. Again isomorphic rings are considered to be essentially the same structure.

A **right ideal** I is a subset of the ring R satisfying

 ○ $\forall a,b \in I \quad a+b \in I$,
 ○ $\forall a \in I, r \in R \quad ar \in I$.

When R is commutative, this is called an **ideal**. (Question: is every ideal a ring?) As an example, in $\mathbb{Z}$ the numbers that are divisible by 12 form the ideal

$$I = \{\ldots, -24, -12, 0, 12, 24, \ldots\} = \{12r: r \in \mathbb{Z}\} = 12\mathbb{Z}.$$

In general, we write

$$\langle a_1, \ldots, a_s \rangle = a_1 R + \cdots + a_s R = \{a_1 r_1 + \cdots + a_s r_s: r_1, \ldots, r_s \in R\}$$

for the **ideal generated by** $a_1, \ldots, a_s$, and say that $a_1, \ldots, a_s$ is a **basis** of that ideal. In particular, $\langle a \rangle = aR = \{ar : r \in R\}$ is the principal ideal generated by $a \in R$. We note an ambiguity inherent in the notation $\langle a \rangle$, as exemplified by $12\mathbb{Z} = \text{``}\langle 12 \rangle\text{''} \neq 12\mathbb{Q} = \mathbb{Q}$.

Suppose that $I \subseteq R$ is an ideal, and $r, s \in R$. We say that r and s are **congruent modulo** I (written as "$r \equiv s \bmod I$") if $r - s \in I$. As an example, with $R = \mathbb{Z}$, we have $14 \equiv 2$ mod $12\mathbb{Z}$, which we also write as $14 \equiv 2$ mod 12. If $a, b \in R$, we write $a \mid b$ ("a divides b") if there exists some $r \in R$ with $ar = b$, and $a \nmid b$ otherwise.

For $r \in R$, the set $r \bmod I = r + I = \{r + a : a \in I\} \subseteq R$ is a **residue class modulo** I or a coset of the ideal I. (Note the distinction between the congruence relation modulo I, as in $14 \equiv 2$ mod $12\mathbb{Z}$, where the "mod" belongs to the $\equiv$ sign, and the residue class modulo I, as in 2 mod $12\mathbb{Z}$.) We have the following equivalences:

$$r \bmod I = s \bmod I \iff r - s \in I \iff r \equiv s \bmod I$$

for all $r, s \in R$. The set $R/I = \{r \bmod i : r \in R\}$ of all residue classes modulo I is again a ring if we define the ring operations by $(r \bmod I) + (s \bmod I) = (r + s) \bmod I$ and $(r \bmod I) \cdot (s \bmod I) = (rs) \bmod I$. It is called the **residue class ring** (or factor ring) **of** R **modulo** I. We have the **canonical ring homomorphism** $\varphi : R \longrightarrow R/I$ mapping $r \in R$ to its residue class $r \bmod I$. For instance, if $R = \mathbb{Z}$ and $I = 12\mathbb{Z}$, then $R/I = \mathbb{Z}/12\mathbb{Z} = \{0 \bmod 12\mathbb{Z}, 1 \bmod 12\mathbb{Z}, 2 \bmod 12\mathbb{Z}, \ldots, 11 \bmod 12\mathbb{Z}\}$, and $\varphi(14) = 14 \bmod 12\mathbb{Z} = 2 \bmod 12\mathbb{Z}$. We will also write $2 \bmod 12$, or even simply 2, for $2 \bmod 12\mathbb{Z}$, thus identifying the residue class ring $\mathbb{Z}/12\mathbb{Z}$ with $\mathbb{Z}_{12} = \{0, 1, 2, \ldots, 11\}$.

More generally, a set of elements $S \subseteq R$ is a **system of representatives** for I if for all $a \in R$ there exists exactly one $b \in S$ such that $a \equiv b \bmod I$. For example, $\{0, 1, 2, \ldots, 11\}$ is a system of representatives for $I = 12\mathbb{Z}$; another one is $\{-5, -4, \ldots, 4, 5, 6\}$. There are many other such systems. A system of representatives can be made into a ring again, by using multiplication and addition modulo I, and then $S \cong R/I$.

As for groups, there is also a **homomorphism theorem** for rings. If R and S are rings, $\varphi : R \longrightarrow S$ is a ring homomorphism, and $I = \ker \varphi = \{r \in R : \varphi(r) = 0\} \subseteq R$ is the **kernel** of φ, then I is an ideal of R, and R/I is isomorphic to the subring $\varphi(R) = \{\varphi(r) : r \in R\}$ of S, the **image** of φ.

If R and S are rings, then the ring $R \times S = \{(r, s) : r \in R, s \in S\}$ is the **direct product** of R and S. The ring operations are defined componentwise: $(r_1, s_1) + (r_2, s_2) = (r_1 + r_2, s_1 + s_2)$ and $(r_1, s_1) \cdot (r_2, s_2) = (r_1 r_2, s_1 s_2)$ for all $r_1, r_2 \in R$ and $s_1, s_2 \in S$.

We can add more and more properties to rings, to get domains in which more interesting things can be done, for instance computing greatest common divisors or factoring. The first restriction is to consider **integral domains**, which are nontrivial commutative rings without nonzero zero divisors. Here, nontrivial means that 1 and 0 are distinct, and a **zero divisor** is an element $a \in R$ for which there is a nonzero element $b \in R$ such that $ab = 0$. (Is $\mathbb{Z}_{12}$ or $\mathbb{Z}_7$ an integral domain?) Thus 0 is a zero divisor in any ring. In an integral domain we have the useful fact that if $a \neq 0$ and $ab = ac$ then $b = c$, known as the **cancellation law**.

For the ring of integers, we have two further interesting properties.

○ Division property: $\forall a, b \in \mathbb{Z}, b \neq 0, \exists! q, r \in \mathbb{Z} \quad a = qb + r$ and $0 \leq r < |b|$.
○ Unique factorization: Every integer greater than 1 has an (essentially) unique factorization as a product of primes.

These properties generalize to other rings. To talk about the division property we need an extra function to satisfy the role played by the absolute value in the integer case. An integral domain R is called a **Euclidean domain** if there is a **Euclidean function** $d: R \longrightarrow$ $\mathbb{N} \cup \{-\infty\}$ satisfying the division property for all $a, b \in R$: If $b \neq 0$ then there exist $q, r \in R$ satisfying $a = qb + r$ and $d(r) < d(b)$ (Section 3.1). Such a q is called a **quotient** and r is called a **remainder**. They need not be unique. (Is there a Euclidean function on $\mathbb{Z} \times \mathbb{Z}$?)

A **greatest common divisor** (gcd) of two elements a, b in an integral domain R is an element $c \in R$ such that $c \mid a$ and $c \mid b$ and any other common divisor of a and b divides c. Two elements $a, b \in R$ are **coprime** (or relatively prime) if $\gcd(a, b) = 1$. Greatest common divisors need not be unique: for example, both -2 and 2 are gcd's of 4 and 6 in $R = \mathbb{Z}$. The slightly tricky issue of choosing between several possible "gcd's" is discussed in Section 3.1. The Euclidean Algorithm for computing greatest common divisors and the Chinese Remainder Algorithm (Chapters 3 and 5) work in Euclidean domains.

For unique factorization, we need some more concepts. A **unit** u in an integral domain R is an element with a multiplicative inverse, so that there exists a $v \in R$ with $uv = 1$. The set $R^{\times}$ of units of R is a group under multiplication. Thus $\mathbb{Z}^{\times} = \{-1, 1\}$. An element a is an **associate** of an element b if there is a unit u such that $a = ub$. We write $a \sim b$ if a is an associate of b. This is an **equivalence relation**: we have $a \sim a$ (reflexivity), $a \sim b \iff b \sim a$ (symmetry), and $a \sim b \sim c \implies a \sim c$ (transitivity), for all $a, b, c \in R$. In $\mathbb{Z}$, $+4$ and -4 are associates. A nonzero nonunit p in an integral domain R is **reducible** if there are nonunits $a, b \in R$ such that $p = ab$, otherwise p is **irreducible**. Units are neither reducible nor irreducible. A nonzero nonunit $p \in R$ is **prime** if $p \mid (ab)$ implies $p \mid a$ or $p \mid b$ for all $a, b \in R$. R is a **Unique Factorization Domain (UFD)** (or a factorial ring) if every nonzero nonunit $a \in R$ can be written as a product of irreducible elements in a unique way up to reordering and multiplication by units. For example, $R = \mathbb{Z}$ is a UFD, and $12 = 2 \cdot 2 \cdot 3 = (-3) \cdot 2 \cdot (-2)$ are both decompositions of 12 into irreducibles. (What are the units of the ring $\mathbb{Z} \times \mathbb{Z}$? Factor $(18, 27)$ in $\mathbb{Z} \times \mathbb{Z}$ and figure out how many different ways there are to factor it when associates are not considered the same.)

Greatest common divisors need not exist in arbitrary integral domains (we will see an example below), but they always exist in UFDs. Similarly, "prime" and "irreducible" are not necessarily equivalent notions in arbitrary integral domains (see below). Primes are always irreducible, and the converse is true if any two nonzero ring elements have a gcd, in particular, in a UFD.

Algebraic number fields furnish interesting examples illustrating some ring properties. We consider imaginary quadratic fields $\mathbb{Q}(\sqrt{d}) = \mathbb{Q} + \mathbb{Q}\sqrt{d} = \{b + c\sqrt{d} : b, c \in \mathbb{Q}\} \subseteq \mathbb{C}$, where $d \in \mathbb{Z}$ is negative and squarefree. Then $R = \mathcal{O}_d$, the **ring of algebraic integers** in $\mathbb{Q}(\sqrt{d})$, equals

$$\mathcal{O}_d = \begin{cases} \mathbb{Z}[\sqrt{d}] = \mathbb{Z} + \mathbb{Z}\sqrt{d} & \text{if } d \equiv 2, 3 \bmod 4, \\ \mathbb{Z}[\frac{1+\sqrt{d}}{2}] = \mathbb{Z} + \mathbb{Z}\frac{1+\sqrt{d}}{2} & \text{if } d \equiv 1 \bmod 4. \end{cases}$$

The ring $\mathbb{Z}[i]$ of **Gaussian integers** is the special case where $d = -1$. The **norm** $N: R \longrightarrow \mathbb{Z}$ is defined by $N(a) = a\bar{a} = |a|^2 = b^2 + c^2$, where $\bar{a}$ denotes the complex conjugate of $a = b + ic$, with $b, c \in \mathbb{R}$, and takes only nonnegative values. This norm is a Euclidean function on R if and only if $d \in \{-1, -2, -3, -7, -11\}$, and these are the only cases where R is Euclidean at all. Furthermore, R is a Unique Factorization Domain if and only if R is Euclidean or $d \in \{-19, -43, -67, -163\}$.

There exist integral domains that are not even UFDs. The classical example (from Dirichlet's (1863) *Zahlentheorie*, page 451) is $R = \mathcal{O}_{-5} = \mathbb{Z} + \mathbb{Z}\sqrt{-5}$, the ring of algebraic integers of $\mathbb{Q}(\sqrt{-5})$. In this ring,

$$(1+\sqrt{-5})\cdot(1-\sqrt{-5}) = 6 = 2\cdot 3$$

are two essentially different decompositions of 6 into irreducibles. To see this, we first convince ourselves that $2, 3$, and $1\pm\sqrt{-5}$ are all irreducible.

Let us assume that $1+\sqrt{-5} = bc$ for some $b, c \in R$. By the multiplicativity of the norm, we have $6 = N(1+\sqrt{-5}) = N(b)N(c)$. The units of R are exactly the elements of norm 1, that is $1, -1 \in R$. But $N(\alpha + \beta\sqrt{-5}) = \alpha^2 + 5\beta^2$ is congruent to $0, 1$, or 4 modulo 5 for any $\alpha, \beta \in \mathbb{Z}$. Thus $N(b) \in \{2, 3\}$ is impossible, and either b or c is a unit, so that $1+\sqrt{-5}$ is irreducible. The proof for $1-\sqrt{-5}$, 2, and 3 goes analogously.

It remains to show that none of $1\pm\sqrt{-5}$ is associate to 2 or 3. But $N(2) = 4$ and $N(3) = 9$ are both different from $N(1\pm\sqrt{-5}) = 6$, and associate elements have the same norm. This also shows that irreducibles are not necessarily prime in arbitrary integral domains: 2 is irreducible and divides $(1+\sqrt{-5})(1-\sqrt{-5})$ in R, but divides none of the factors; hence 2 is not prime. Moreover, 6 and $2+2\sqrt{-5}$ have no gcd in $\mathcal{O}_{-5}$.

The following theorem summarizes some properties of integral domains that are equivalent to being a UFD.

THEOREM 25.3.
For an integral domain R, the following are equivalent.

(i) *R is a UFD.*

(ii) *Any nonzero nonunit in R can be written as a product of primes.*

(iii) *Any nonzero nonunit in R can be written as a product of irreducibles, and any irreducible in R is prime.*

(iv) *Any nonzero nonunit in R can be written as a product of irreducibles, and any two nonzero elements of R have a gcd in R.*

In particular, since gcd's exist in Euclidean domains (Chapter 3), every Euclidean domain is a UFD. The reverse is false in general, as we have seen above: $\mathcal{O}_{-19}$ is a UFD but not a Euclidean domain. Other examples are in Exercises 3.17 and 21.1.

25.3. Polynomials and fields

Given a ring R, the ring of univariate **polynomials** over R is the set S of vectors $a = (a_0, a_1, \ldots)$ with entries from R, where all but a finite number of the a_i's are zero, and where addition and multiplication are defined by $(a_0, a_1, \ldots) + (b_0, b_1, \ldots) = (a_0 + b_0, a_1 + b_1, \ldots)$ and $(a_0, a_1, \ldots)\cdot(b_0, b_1, \ldots) = (c_0, c_1, \ldots)$, with $c_n = \sum_{i=0}^n a_i b_{n-i}$. The **degree** $\deg a$ of a nonzero polynomial a is the largest integer n such that $a_n \neq 0$. Its **leading coefficient** $\mathrm{lc}(a)$ is a_n, and a is **monic** if $\mathrm{lc}(a) = 1$. It is convenient to define the degree of the zero polynomial as $-\infty$. It is more usual to denote the polynomial $(a_0, a_1, a_2, \ldots)$ by $a_n x^n + \cdots + a_2 x^2 + a_1 x + a_0$ when $a_k = 0$ for all $k > n$. Here the **indeterminate** x is just a placeholder, and we then write $S = R[x]$. The ring of **power series** is defined similarly but without the restriction that only a finite number of terms be nonzero, and denoted by $R[[x]]$.

We also use polynomials in two or more variables. $R[x][y]$ consists of univariate polynomials in y with coefficients in $R[x]$, but by collecting powers of x, we may as well consider its elements as univariate polynomials in x with coefficients in $R[y]$. To reflect this symmetry, we use the notation $R[x, y]$, and more generally $R[x_1, \ldots, x_n]$. We denote the degree and the leading coefficient of such a **multivariate polynomial** a with respect to the variable x_i by $\deg_{x_i} a$ and $\mathrm{lc}_{x_i}(a)$, respectively. The **total degree** of a multivariate monomial $x_1^{e_1} \cdots x_n^{e_n}$ is $e_1 + \cdots + e_n$, and the total degree of $a \neq 0$ is the maximal total degree of its monomials.

If R is a commutative ring or an integral domain, then so is $R[x]$. Gauß' famous theorem 6.8 shows that $R[x]$ is a UFD if R is. We might hope that the same holds for Euclidean domains. However, the division property goes away (say, in $\mathbb{Z}[x]$, as can be seen when you try to divide $x^2 + 3$ by $3x + 1$). The division property holds if the leading coefficient of b is a unit of R (Section 2.4).

If R is integral, then the units of $R[x]$ are simply the units of R, where we use the natural identification of R with polynomials of degree 0. Irreducibles are a bit trickier. For instance, $x^2 + 1$ is irreducible in $\mathbb{Z}[x]$ and $\mathbb{Z}_3[x]$, but in $\mathbb{Z}_5[x]$, $x^2 + 1 = (x+2)(x-2)$.

The following lemma states an important property of polynomials over integral domains.

LEMMA 25.4. *Let R be a ring (commutative, with 1) and $f \in R[x]$.*

(i) *For any $u \in R$, we have $f(u) = 0$ if and only if $(x - u) \mid f$.*

(ii) *If R is an integral domain and $f \neq 0$, then f has at most $\deg f$ many roots in R.*

Claim (ii) is not true in general rings: $f = x^2 \in \mathbb{Z}_{16}[x]$ has the four roots $0, 4, 8$, and 12.

For $m \in \mathbb{Z}$, the canonical ring homomorphism $\varphi \colon \mathbb{Z} \longrightarrow \mathbb{Z}_m$ can be applied to each coefficient of a polynomial; this yields a homomorphism $\mathbb{Z}[x] \longrightarrow \mathbb{Z}_m[x]$ that is usually also denoted by φ. Its kernel is $m \cdot \mathbb{Z}[x]$, the ideal of polynomials with all coefficients divisible by m. When u is an element of a ring R, then the **evaluation homomorphism** $\varepsilon \colon R[x] \longrightarrow R$ takes a polynomial $f \in R[x]$ to $\varepsilon(f) = f(u) \in R$. Its kernel is $\langle x - u \rangle$, by Lemma 25.4 (i), and the homomorphism theorem for rings shows that $R[x]/\langle x - u \rangle \cong \mathrm{im}\,\varepsilon = R$.

More generally, we have the canonical homomorphism $R[x] \longrightarrow R[x]/\langle m \rangle$ for any m in $R[x]$. If m is nonconstant and monic, then the polynomials $f \in R[x]$ of degree less than $\deg m$ form a system of representatives for $\langle m \rangle$, and hence they form the factor ring $R[x]/\langle m \rangle$, with addition and multiplication modulo m. When computing in $R[x]/\langle m \rangle$, one usually takes these representatives. The evaluation homomorphism ε is the special case $m = x - u$.

If R and S are rings, $\varphi \colon R \longrightarrow S$ is a ring homomorphism, $f \in R[x_1, \ldots, x_n]$ a polynomial in n variables, and $r_1, \ldots, r_n$ are elements of R, then

$$\varphi(f(r_1, \ldots, r_n)) = \varphi(f)(\varphi(r_1), \ldots, \varphi(r_n)),$$

where $\varphi(f) \in S[x_1, \ldots, x_n]$ is obtained from f by applying φ to the coefficients. Similarly, if I is an ideal of R, f is as above, and $r_1, \ldots, r_n, r_1^*, \ldots, r_n^*$ are elements of R satisfying $r_i \equiv r_i^* \bmod I$ for $1 \leq i \leq n$, then $f(r_1, \ldots, r_n) \equiv f(r_1^*, \ldots, r_n^*) \bmod I$. (Check this!) We say that ring homomorphisms and congruences **commute** with polynomial expressions. This is the basis for **modular arithmetic** (Section 4.1).

A **field** is an integral domain in which every nonzero element is a unit, that is, it has a multiplicative inverse. Familiar examples are the fields $\mathbb{Q}$ of the rational numbers, the field $\mathbb{R}$ of the real numbers, and the field $\mathbb{C}$ of the complex numbers. We have $\mathbb{Q} \subseteq \mathbb{R} \subseteq \mathbb{C}$. The polynomial ring $F[x]$ over a field F is Euclidean.

The number of elements in a field or ring is called its order. The above fields all have infinite order, however, there are fields of finite order too. Among them are the fields $\mathbb{Z}_p$, where p is a prime. The existence of the inverse of a nonzero element a in $\mathbb{Z}_p$ follows from the fact that for $1 \le a < p$, the Extended Euclidean Algorithm 3.6 computes $s, t \in \mathbb{Z}$ such that $1 = as + pt \equiv as$ mod p. Finite fields will be discussed in the next section.

If we consider the ring $\mathbb{Z}_3 \times \mathbb{Z}_3$ of order 9, then its multiplicative identity is $(1,1)$, and $(1,1) + (1,1) + (1,1) = (0,0)$. This leads us to define the **characteristic** char R of a ring or field R to be the minimum number of times the identity element can be added to itself to get 0. In the case where this can never produce zero, the ring or field is said to have characteristic zero. $\mathbb{Q}$, $\mathbb{R}$, and $\mathbb{C}$ are fields of characteristic zero, and the characteristic of $\mathbb{Z}_p$ is p.

If R is an integral domain, then $K = \{a/b : a, b \in R, b \ne 0\}$ is the **field of fractions** of R. For example, $\mathbb{Q}$ is the field of fractions of $\mathbb{Z}$, and $F(x)$, the set of **rational functions** in x with coefficients in the field F, is the field of fractions of the polynomial ring $F[x]$.

If a field F is contained in another field E, then we say that E is an **extension field** of F and F is a **subfield** of E. For instance, $\mathbb{C}$ is an extension field of $\mathbb{R}$, and $\mathbb{R}$ is an extension field of $\mathbb{Q}$. E is a vector space over F (see Section 25.5). An element $\alpha \in E$ is **algebraic** over F if it is the root of a polynomial $f \in F[x] : f(\alpha) = 0$ (or equivalently, if the F-subspace of E generated by $1, \alpha, \alpha^2, \ldots$ is finite dimensional). Thus all elements of F are algebraic over F, and $i = \sqrt{-1} \in \mathbb{C}$ is algebraic over $\mathbb{Q}$ and $\mathbb{R}$ (taking $f = x^2 + 1$). Elements that are not algebraic are called **transcendental**. For example, π and e are transcendental over $\mathbb{Q}$ (see Notes 4.6). If all elements of E are algebraic over F, then we say that E is an **algebraic extension** of F. For example, $\mathbb{C}$ is an algebraic extension of $\mathbb{R}$, but not of $\mathbb{Q}$. If the dimension of E as a vector space over F is finite, then we say that E is a **finite extension** of F. The dimension is denoted by $[E : F]$, also called the **degree** of E over F. All finite extensions are algebraic. If $F \subseteq E \subseteq K$ are finite extensions, we have the **degree formula** $[K : F] = [K : E] \cdot [E : F]$.

If $\alpha \in E$ is algebraic over F, then the set $I = \{f \in F[x] : f(\alpha) = 0\}$ of all polynomials with coefficients in F that have α as a root is an ideal in $F[x]$. Since $F[x]$ is a Euclidean domain, every ideal in $F[x]$ is generated by a single element, namely the unique nonzero monic polynomial m_α of least degree in I, so that $I = \langle m_\alpha \rangle$. It is called the **minimal polynomial** of α. The minimal polynomial m_α is irreducible, since otherwise there would be a divisor of m_α of smaller degree that has α as a root. Since m_α generates I, all other polynomials having α as a root are divisible by m_α, and it is the only monic polynomial with that property. The **degree** of α over F is deg m_α. If $F(\alpha) \subseteq E$ denotes the smallest subfield of E containing F and α, then deg $m_\alpha = [F(\alpha) : F]$. For example, if $E = \mathbb{C}$, $F = \mathbb{R}$, and $\alpha = i$, then $m_i = x^2 + 1$, $\mathbb{R}(i) = \mathbb{C}$, and $[\mathbb{C} : \mathbb{R}] = 2$.

We may construct an algebraic field extension of a field F by taking $E = F[x]/\langle f \rangle$ for an irreducible polynomial $f \in F[x]$. Since $F[x]$ is Euclidean, the Extended Euclidean Algorithm 3.6 computes $s, t \in F[x]$ with $1 = as + ft \equiv as$ mod f for all nonzero $a \in F[x]$ with deg $a < \deg f$. This shows that all nonzero elements of E are invertible, and E is an extension field of F if we identify F with the set of constant polynomials in E; in fact, it is an algebraic extension. The polynomial $f \in F[x]$ has $\alpha = (x$ mod $f) \in E$ as a root

(Lemma 4.4); actually, it is the minimal polynomial of α. If $\deg f = n$, then the elements $\alpha^{n-1}, \ldots, \alpha^2, \alpha, 1 \in E$ are a basis of E over F. Thus $E = F(\alpha)$ and $[E : F] = n$.

On the other hand, if E is any extension field of F and $\alpha \in E$ is algebraic over F, with minimal polynomial $f \in F[x]$, then $F(\alpha)$, the smallest subfield of E containing F and α, is isomorphic to $F[x]/\langle f \rangle$. This follows from the homomorphism theorem for rings, since the homomorphism $F[x] \longrightarrow E$ which evaluates at α has kernel $\langle f \rangle$ and image $F(\alpha)$. For example, $\mathbb{R}[x]/\langle x^2 + 1 \rangle$ and $\mathbb{C}$ are isomorphic fields, under an isomorphism that associates $x \bmod (x^2 + 1)$ to i.

An algebraic field extension E of a field F is the **splitting field** of a nonconstant polynomial $f \in F[x]$ if f splits into linear factors over E, but not over any proper subfield of E. A field F is **algebraically closed** if and only if every nonconstant polynomial $f \in F[x]$ has a root in F; then f has $\deg f$ many roots, counting multiplicities. The **fundamental theorem of algebra** says that the field $\mathbb{C}$ of complex numbers has this property.

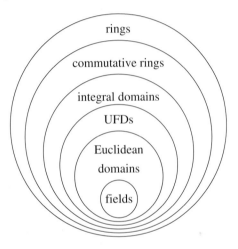

FIGURE 25.1: The hierarchy of rings.

Figure 25.1 illustrates the classes of rings that we have discussed so far and their containment relations.

25.4. Finite fields

The reader can find the following facts and techniques about finite fields, and all she ever wants to know about this topic, in the "bible of finite fields" by Lidl & Niederreiter (1997).

We have already dealt with the finite fields $\mathbb{Z}_p = \mathbb{Z}/\langle p \rangle$, where p is a prime. These, together with $\mathbb{Q}$, are the **prime fields**; every field contains exactly one (isomorphic copy) of these. What other finite fields are there? If $f \in \mathbb{Z}_p[y]$ is an irreducible polynomial of degree n, then $\mathbb{Z}_p[y]/\langle f \rangle$ is an algebraic field extension of $\mathbb{Z}_p$ of degree n. It is a vector space of dimension n over $\mathbb{Z}_p$; hence it has p^n elements. A basis for $\mathbb{Z}_p[y]/\langle f \rangle$ over $\mathbb{Z}_p$ is $\{y^{n-1} \bmod f, \ldots, y \bmod f, 1 \bmod f\}$.

For every prime power $q = p^n$, there exists a field with q elements. All such fields are (non-canonically) isomorphic to each other, and we write $\mathbb{F}_q$ for any of them. In particular, $\mathbb{F}_p = \mathbb{Z}_p$ for a prime p, but it is important to remember that $\mathbb{F}_{p^n} \not\cong \mathbb{Z}_{p^n}$ for $n \geq 2$.

On the other hand, every finite field has p^n elements, for some prime p and $n \geq 1$, and is isomorphic to $\mathbb{Z}_p[y]/\langle f \rangle$ for some irreducible polynomial $f \in \mathbb{Z}_p[y]$ of degree n. The characteristic of $\mathbb{F}_{p^n}$ is p.

Fermat's little theorem 4.9 says that $a^{p-1} = 1$ for a prime p and all $a \in \mathbb{F}_p^\times$, hence $a^p = a$ for all $a \in \mathbb{F}_p$. This holds in arbitrary finite fields.

THEOREM 25.5 *Fermat's little theorem.*
Let q be a prime power. For all $a \in \mathbb{F}_q$, we have $a^q = a$, thus $a^{q-1} = 1$ if $a \neq 0$, and

$$x^q - x = \prod_{a \in \mathbb{F}_q} (x - a) \text{ in } \mathbb{F}_q[x].$$

PROOF. Lagrange's theorem implies that each element g of a group with m elements satisfies $g^m = 1$. The unit group $\mathbb{F}_q^\times = \mathbb{F}_q \setminus \{0\}$ has $q - 1$ elements, so that $a^{q-1} = 1$ for all nonzero $a \in \mathbb{F}_q$, and $a^q = a$ for all $a \in \mathbb{F}_q$. Thus $x - a$ divides $x^q - x$ for all $a \in \mathbb{F}_q$, and since $\gcd(x - a, x - b) = 1$ for $a \neq b$, we have that $\prod_{a \in \mathbb{F}_q}(x - a)$ divides $x^q - x$. Both polynomials are monic and have degree q, and hence they are equal. $\square$

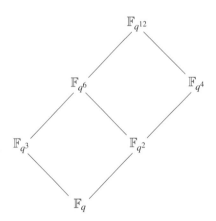

FIGURE 25.2: The subfield lattice of $\mathbb{F}_{q^{12}}$.

If a finite field $\mathbb{F}_{q^m}$ is contained in another finite field $\mathbb{F}_{q^n}$, then $\mathbb{F}_{q^n}$ is a vector space over $\mathbb{F}_{q^m}$, and in particular the number of elements $\#\mathbb{F}_{q^n} = q^n$ is a power of $\#\mathbb{F}_{q^m} = q^m$, or equivalently, $m \mid n$. Conversely, if $m \mid n$, then $\mathbb{F}_{q^n}$ is an extension field of (an isomorphic copy of) $\mathbb{F}_{q^m}$, namely the set of all roots of $x^{q^m} - x$ in $\mathbb{F}_{q^n}$. For example, $\mathbb{F}_4$ is a subfield of $\mathbb{F}_{16}$, but $\mathbb{F}_8$ is not, despite the fact that $8 \mid 16$. Figure 25.2 shows the lattice of all subfields of $\mathbb{F}_{q^{12}}$ corresponding to the lattice of divisors of 12; a field is contained in another one if there is a path from the latter down to the former. (A different notion of "lattice" is used in Chapter 16.)

The order of the multiplicative group $\mathbb{F}_q^\times$ is $q - 1$. Fermat's little theorem implies that $\text{ord}(a) \mid q - 1$ for all $a \in \mathbb{F}_q^\times$. An element $a \in \mathbb{F}_q^\times$ is **primitive** if it generates the group $\mathbb{F}_q^\times$, or equivalently, if its order is $q - 1$. $\mathbb{F}_q^\times$ contains a primitive element, so that $\mathbb{F}_q^\times$ is cyclic

(Exercise 8.16). More generally, $\mathbb{F}_q$ contains an element of order n if and only if $n \mid q - 1$ (Lemma 8.8).

A ring R containing $\mathbb{F}_p$ is called an $\mathbb{F}_p$-**algebra**. A fundamental property is that for any commutative $\mathbb{F}_p$-algebra R, elements $a, b \in R$, and $i \in \mathbb{N}$, we have

$$(a+b)^{p^i} = a^{p^i} + b^{p^i}.$$

This is proved by induction on i; for $i = 1$, all binomial coefficients in the expansion of the left-hand power are divisible by p, and hence 0 in R. Let $\mathbb{F}_{q^n}$ be an extension field of $\mathbb{F}_q$. The map

$$\varphi: \begin{cases} \mathbb{F}_{q^n} & \longrightarrow & \mathbb{F}_{q^n} \\ \alpha & \longmapsto & \alpha^q \end{cases}$$

is an automorphism of the finite field $\mathbb{F}_{q^n}$, called the **Frobenius automorphism**. The following hold for all $\alpha, \beta \in \mathbb{F}_{q^n}$:

$$\begin{aligned} (\alpha + \beta)^q = \alpha^q + \beta^q, \quad (\alpha\beta)^q = \alpha^q \beta^q, \\ \alpha^q = \alpha \iff \alpha \in \mathbb{F}_q. \end{aligned} \tag{1}$$

The last property, an immediate consequence of Fermat's little theorem, says in the language of Galois theory that $\mathbb{F}_q$ is the fixed field of φ.

Similarly, in any $\mathbb{F}_q$-algebra R, we have the **Frobenius endomorphism**

$$\varphi: \begin{cases} R & \longrightarrow & R \\ \alpha & \longmapsto & \alpha^q \end{cases} \tag{2}$$

Of particular importance is the case $R = \mathbb{F}_q[x]$, which also shows that φ is not surjective in general.

If $f \in \mathbb{F}_q[x]$ is irreducible of degree n and $\alpha \in \mathbb{F}_{q^n} \cong \mathbb{F}_q[x]/\langle f \rangle$ is a root of f, then $f(\alpha^q) = f(\alpha)^q = 0$, so that α^q is also a root of f. More generally, the roots of f in $\mathbb{F}_{q^n}$ are precisely the n **conjugates** $\alpha, \alpha^q, \alpha^{q^2}, \dots, \alpha^{q^{n-1}}$ of α.

In computer algebra, both the finite fields $\mathbb{F}_{p^n}$ and the finite commutative rings $\mathbb{Z}_{p^n}$, each with p^n elements, play a role. If $n \geq 2$, then these are non-isomorphic objects, since the former is a field while the latter has nonzero zero divisors. Another difference is that char $\mathbb{F}_{p^n} = p$ and its additive group is isomorphic to $\mathbb{Z}_p^n$, while char $\mathbb{Z}_{p^n} = p^n$ and its additive group is cyclic.

25.5. Linear algebra

We present the basic concepts of linear algebra, mainly to fix the language. This material is too condensed to be understood on its own; previous instruction in linear algebra is an indispensable prerequisite for this book. Among the good textbooks in this area is Strang (1980).

The central objects in linear algebra are **vector spaces** over a field F. These are commutative groups $(V, +)$ with a **scalar multiplication** $\cdot$ by elements of F satisfying the following properties:

○ $\lambda \cdot (v + w) = \lambda \cdot v + \lambda \cdot w,$

○ $(\lambda + \mu) \cdot v = \lambda \cdot v + \mu \cdot v,$

○ $\lambda \cdot (\mu \cdot v) = (\lambda \mu) \cdot v,$

for all $\lambda, \mu \in F$ and $v, w \in V$. We will write λv instead of $\lambda \cdot v$ for short. The elements of V are called **vectors**, those of F **scalars**. The most popular example of a vector space is F^n for some $n \in \mathbb{N}$, whose elements are n-tuples $(a_1, \ldots, a_n)$ of elements $a_1, \ldots, a_n \in F$, with componentwise addition and scalar multiplication.

A subset U of a vector space V is a **subspace** of V if it is closed under addition and scalar multiplication, so that $u + v$ and λv are again in U for all $u, v \in U$ and $\lambda \in F$. A finite sequence $v_1, \ldots, v_n \in V$ of vectors is called **linearly dependent** if there exist scalars $\lambda_1, \ldots, \lambda_n \in F$, not all zero, such that $\lambda_1 v_1 + \cdots + \lambda_n v_n = 0$. Otherwise, $v_1, \ldots, v_n$ are **linearly independent**. The subspace **generated** by the vectors $v_1, \ldots, v_n \in V$ is the set of all linear combinations $\langle v_1, \ldots, v_n \rangle = \{\lambda_1 v_1 + \cdots + \lambda_n v_n : \lambda_1, \ldots, \lambda_n \in F\}$. A vector space V is **finite-dimensional** if it is generated by finitely many vectors. A finite sequence $(v_1, \ldots, v_n)$ of elements of V is a **basis** of V if the vectors are linearly independent and $\langle v_1, \ldots, v_n \rangle = V$. A central theorem in linear algebra is that any finitely generated vector space V has a finite basis (and any generating sequence contains one), and that all bases have the same number of elements, called the **dimension** $\dim V$ of V. For example, $\dim F^3 = 3$, and a basis is given by the three unit vectors $(1, 0, 0)$, $(0, 1, 0)$, and $(0, 0, 1)$. More generally, we have $\dim F^n = n$ for all $n \in \mathbb{N}_{>0}$. With respect to a basis $(v_1, \ldots, v_n)$ of V, every vector v has a unique representation $v = \lambda_1 v_1 + \cdots + \lambda_n v_n$ as a linear combination of the basis elements, with **coordinates** $\lambda_1, \ldots, \lambda_n \in F$.

A map $f: V \longrightarrow W$ between two vector spaces over the same field F is **(F-)linear** or a **homomorphism** if $f(v_1 + v_2) = f(v_1) + f(v_2)$ and $f(\lambda v_1) = \lambda f(v_1)$ for all $\lambda \in F$ and $v_1, v_2 \in V$. The notions **endo-**, **iso-**, and **automorphism** are defined similarly as for groups. V and W are **isomorphic** if there exists an isomorphism between them. If V and W are finite-dimensional, then they are isomorphic if and only if $\dim V = \dim W$. The **image** $\mathrm{im}\, f = \{f(v) : v \in V\}$ of a homomorphism $f: V \longrightarrow W$ is a subspace of W, and the **kernel** $\ker f = \{v \in V : f(v) = 0\}$ is a subspace of V. As for groups, f is injective if and only if $\ker f = \{0\}$, and f is surjective if and only if $\mathrm{im}\, f = W$. An equivalent of Lagrange's theorem is the **dimension formula** for homomorphisms:

$$\dim \ker f + \dim \mathrm{im}\, f = \dim V, \tag{3}$$

if V is finitely generated.

If V and W are vector spaces over F with bases $v_1, \ldots, v_n$ and $w_1, \ldots, w_m$, respectively, then to a homomorphism $f: V \longrightarrow W$ corresponds the $m \times n$ **matrix** $A = (a_{ij})_{\substack{1 \leq i \leq m \\ 1 \leq j \leq n}} \in F^{m \times n}$ defined by

$$f(v_i) = a_{1i} w_1 + \cdots + a_{mi} w_m, \tag{4}$$

and then

$$A \begin{pmatrix} \lambda_1 \\ \vdots \\ \lambda_n \end{pmatrix} = \begin{pmatrix} \mu_1 \\ \vdots \\ \mu_m \end{pmatrix} \iff f(\lambda_1 v_1 + \cdots + \lambda_n v_n) = \mu_1 w_1 + \cdots + \mu_m w_m$$

for arbitrary $\lambda_i, \mu_j \in F$. Conversely, for any matrix $A \in F^{m \times n}$, (4) defines a homomorphism $f: V \longrightarrow W$, and the kernel and image of A are defined to be those of f. The **rank** of A is

$\dim(\operatorname{im} A)$, or equivalently, the maximal number of linearly independent columns (or rows) of A. Composition of homomorphisms corresponds to multiplication of matrices.

A square matrix $A = (A_{ij})_{1 \le i,j \le n} \in F^{n \times n}$ is **nonsingular** (or invertible) if there exists a matrix $B \in F^{n \times n}$ such that $AB = I_n$, where I_n is the $n \times n$ unit matrix. Otherwise, A is **singular**. We write A^{-1} for B. The matrix A is nonsingular if and only if the endomorphism $y \longmapsto Ay$ of F^n is an automorphism, which holds if and only if the rank of A is n. The set of all nonsingular $n \times n$ matrices forms a group with respect to matrix multiplication.

An $n \times n$ matrix $A = (a_{ij})_{1 \le i,j \le n} \in F^{n \times n}$ is a **permutation matrix** if there is a permutation $\sigma \in S_n$ such that for all i, j, we have $a_{ij} = 1$ if $j = \sigma(i)$ and $a_{ij} = 0$ otherwise. The set of all permutation matrices in $\mathbb{R}^{n \times n}$ is a finite subgroup of the multiplicative group of invertible $n \times n$ matrices which is isomorphic to S_n.

A **system of linear equations** over F has the form

$$\begin{aligned}
a_{11}y_1 + a_{12}y_2 + \cdots + a_{1n}y_n &= b_1, \\
a_{21}y_1 + a_{22}y_2 + \cdots + a_{2n}y_n &= b_2, \\
&\ \ \vdots \\
a_{m1}y_1 + a_{m2}y_2 + \cdots + a_{mn}y_n &= b_m,
\end{aligned}$$

where $a_{11}, a_{12}, \ldots, a_{mn}, b_1, \ldots, b_m \in F$ are given and $y_1, \ldots, y_n \in F$ are sought. The matrix $A = (a_{ij}) \in F^{m \times n}$ is the **coefficient matrix** and the vector $b = (b_1, \ldots, b_m)^T \in F^m$ the **right hand side** of the system, where ^{T} denotes transposition. The system may then be written more briefly as $Ay = b$, where $y = (y_1, \ldots, y_n)^T$ is the vector of indeterminates. The **solution space** $\{y \in F^n : Ay = b\}$ of the linear system is either empty or a coset (in the sense of additive groups) $v + \ker A$ of the subspace $\ker A = \{y \in F^n : Ay = 0\}$, where $v \in F^n$ is any particular solution. In the language of homomorphisms, $\{y \in F^n : Ay = b\}$ is the preimage of b under the homomorphism $f : F^n \longrightarrow F^m$ given by $f(y) = Ay$.

The famous **Gaussian elimination** algorithm provides a means for solving linear systems (and many other computational problems in linear algebra). Given a matrix $A \in F^{m \times n}$, Gaussian elimination computes an invertible matrix $L \in F^{m \times m}$ and a permutation matrix $P \in F^{n \times n}$ such that $U = LAP$ is of block form

$$U = \begin{pmatrix} I_r & V \\ 0 & 0 \end{pmatrix}$$

where r is the rank of A, I_r the $r \times r$ identity matrix, and $V \in F^{r \times (n-r)}$. If $m = n$, then the procedure takes $O(n^3)$ arithmetic operations in F. A basis of $\ker A$ is $(Pv_1, \ldots, Pv_{n-r})$, where v_i is the ith column of the block matrix $\begin{pmatrix} -V \\ I_{n-r} \end{pmatrix} \in F^{n \times (n-r)}$. If $b \in F^m$ is an arbitrary right hand side, then $Ay = b$ is solvable if and only if the lower $m - r$ coefficients of Lb are zero. In that case, we let $v \in F^n$ be the vector whose upper r coefficients are those of Lb and whose lower $n - r$ ones are zero, and then Pv is a particular solution of the linear system. In case we start with an invertible $n \times n$ matrix A, then U is the identity matrix, and $A^{-1} = PL$.

The **determinant** of a square matrix $A = (A_{ij})_{1 \le i,j \le n} \in F^{n \times n}$ is

$$\det A = \sum_{\sigma \in S_n} (-1)^{\operatorname{sgn} \sigma} a_{1\sigma(1)} \cdots a_{n\sigma(n)} \in F,$$

where sgn $\sigma = \#\{1 \leq i < j \leq n: \sigma(i) > \sigma(j)\}$ is the number of inversions of the permutation σ of $\{1,\ldots,n\}$. The determinant is multiplicative, so that $\det(AB) = \det A \cdot \det B$ for all $A, B \in F^{n \times n}$, changes sign when two rows (or columns) are exchanged, and is invariant under addition of a multiple of one row (or column) to another one. Moreover,

$$\det A = 0 \iff A \text{ is singular.}$$

Let $i, n \in \mathbb{N}$ with $1 \leq i \leq n$, $A \in F^{n \times n}$ be a square matrix, $a_1, \ldots, a_n \in F$ the entries of the ith row of A, and $A_j \in F^{(n-1) \times (n-1)}$ the matrix resulting from A by deleting row i and column j, for $1 \leq j \leq n$. Then

$$\det A = \sum_{1 \leq j \leq n} (-1)^{i+j} a_j \det A_j;$$

this is called **Laplace expansion** (or expansion into cofactors) along the ith row. Of course, this also holds when the roles of rows and columns are exchanged.

For computing determinants, this is not useful. It is more efficient to use a variant of Gaussian elimination which produces a matrix $L \in F^{n \times n}$ with $\det L = 1$ and a permutation matrix $P \in F^{n \times n}$, which has $\det P = \pm 1$, such that $U = LAP$ is upper triangular, and then $\det A = \det L^{-1} \det U \det P^{-1} = \pm \det U$ is—up to sign—equal to the product of the diagonal elements of U. This follows from repeated use of Laplace expansion.

If $A \in F^{n \times n}$ is nonsingular, then the linear system $Ay = b$ has a *unique* solution $y \in F^n$ for any right hand side $b \in F^n$, namely $y = A^{-1}b$. The following theorem is an important theoretical application of determinants; it is not useful for the practical solution of nonsingular systems of linear equations.

THEOREM 25.6 *Cramer's rule.*
Let $A \in F^{n \times n}$ be nonsingular and $b \in F^n$. Then the coefficients of the unique solution $y = (y_1, \ldots, y_n)^T \in F^n$ of the linear system $Ay = b$ are given by

$$y_i = \frac{\det A_i}{\det A},$$

where $A_i \in F^{n \times n}$ is the matrix A with the ith column replaced by b.

The **characteristic polynomial** χ_A of a square matrix $A \in F^{n \times n}$ is $\chi_A = \det(A - xI)$ in $F[x]$. It has degree n, and its zeroes (over an algebraic closure of F) are precisely the **eigenvalues** of A, that is, the scalar values $\lambda \in F$ such that $Av = \lambda v$ for some nonzero $v \in F^n$. We have $\det A = \chi_A(0)$. If $f = \sum_{0 \leq i \leq m} f_i x^i \in F[x]$ is any polynomial, then we may plug in A for the indeterminate x and obtain $f(A) = \sum_{0 \leq i \leq m} f_i A^i \in F^{n \times n}$. The set $\text{Ann}(A) = \{f \in F[x]: f(A) = 0\}$ is an ideal in $F[x]$ and has a unique nonzero monic generator $m_A \in F[x]$, the **minimal polynomial** of A. The **Cayley–Hamilton theorem** says that $\chi_A(A) = 0$ and m_A divides χ_A.

For any real number $q > 0$, we have the **q-norm** $\|\cdot\|_q$ on the vector space $\mathbb{C}^n$ defined by

$$\|a\|_q = \left(\sum_{1 \leq i \leq n} |a_i|^q \right)^{1/q}.$$

for $a = (a_1, \ldots, a_n) \in \mathbb{C}^n$. We also have the **max-norm** (or ∞-norm)

$$\|a\|_\infty = \max_{1 \leq i \leq n} |a_i| = \lim_{q \longrightarrow \infty} \|a\|_q.$$

All these norms for $q > 0$ (including $q = \infty$) satisfy

○ $\|a\|_q \geq 0$, with equality if and only if $a = 0$ (positive definiteness),

○ $\|a + b\|_q \leq \|a\|_q + \|b\|_q$ (triangle inequality),

○ $\|\lambda a\| = |\lambda| \cdot \|a\|$ (homogeneity),

for all $a, b \in \mathbb{C}^n$ and $\lambda \in \mathbb{C}$. The norms are related by

$$\|a\|_p \leq \|a\|_q \leq n^{1/q} \|a\|_p$$

for all $a \in \mathbb{C}^n$ and $p > q$. Besides the max-norm, the most important norms are the 1-norm $\|a\|_1 = \sum_{1 \leq i \leq n} |a_i|$ and the 2-norm (or **Euclidean norm**) $\|a\|_2 = (\sum_{1 \leq i \leq n} |a_i|^2)^{1/2}$. We have the following relations between these three norms:

$$\|a\|_\infty \leq \|a\|_2 \leq \sqrt{n} \|a\|_\infty, \quad \|a\|_2 \leq \|a\|_1 \leq n \|a\|_\infty. \tag{5}$$

These norms carry over in a natural way to univariate polynomials with complex coefficients: for $f = \sum_{0 \leq i \leq n} f_i x^i \in \mathbb{C}[x]$, we write $\|f\|_q$ for the q-norm of the coefficient vector $(f_0, \ldots, f_n) \in \mathbb{C}^{n+1}$.

A map $\star: V \times V \longrightarrow F$, where V is a vector space over a field F, is called an **inner product** on V if

○ $v \star v = 0 \iff v = 0$,

○ $u \star v = v \star u$,

○ $(\lambda u + \mu v) \star w = \lambda(u \star w) + \mu(v \star w)$

hold for all $u, v, w \in V$ and $\lambda, \mu \in F$. (Not all vector spaces have such an inner product; for example, $\mathbb{F}_2^2$ does not.) Two vectors $v, w \in V$ are **orthogonal** (with respect to $\star$) if $v \star w = 0$. The most important example of an inner product on $\mathbb{R}^n$ is $(x_1, \ldots, x_n) \star (y_1, \ldots, y_n) = x_1 y_1 + \cdots + x_n y_n$, and we have $v \star v = \|v\|_2^2$ for all $v \in \mathbb{R}^n$. For a sequence $v_1, \ldots, v_n \in V$ of vectors, $G = (v_i \star v_j)_{1 \leq i, j \leq n} \in F^{n \times n}$ is the **Gramian matrix** of $v_1, \ldots, v_n$, and $\det G$ is their **Gramian determinant**. The vectors $v_1, \ldots, v_n \in V$ are linearly dependent if and only if their Gramian determinant vanishes. (Exercise 24.4).

A basis $(v_1, \ldots, v_n)$ of a vector space V is **orthogonal** with respect to an inner product $\star$ if its vectors are pairwise orthogonal, so that their Gramian matrix is a diagonal matrix. The **Gram-Schmidt orthogonalization procedure**, described in Chapter 16, transforms an arbitrary basis into an orthogonal one.

25.6. Finite probability spaces

An introduction to this material is in Chapter 8 of Graham, Knuth & Patashnik (1994), and Feller (1971) is a classical reference.

A **finite probability space** is a finite set U with a **probability function** $P: U \longrightarrow [0, 1]$ such that $\sum_{u \in U} P(u) = 1$. For example, if we think of rolling a fair die, then $U =$

$\{1,2,3,4,5,6\}$ and $P(u) = 1/6$ for all $u \in U$ gives a finite probability space describing the possible outcomes of the experiment. When $P(u) = 1/\#U$ for all u, as in the example, we say that P is a **uniform** probability function.

An **event** is a subset $A \subseteq U$, and the probability of A is $P(A) = \sum_{u \in A} P(u)$. In the above example, the probability of the event "odd roll" $A = \{1,3,5\}$ is $1/2$. We have $P(\emptyset) = 0$, $P(U \setminus A) = 1 - P(A)$, and $P(A \cup B) = P(A) + P(B) - P(A \cap B)$ for all $A, B \subseteq U$. In particular, $P(A \cup B) = P(A) + P(B)$ if A and B are disjoint. We usually write prob(A) for $P(A)$.

The **conditional probability** $P_B(A) = P(A \cap B)/P(B)$ for two events A, B with $P(B) \neq 0$ is the probability of A under the condition that also B happens. This makes (B, P_B) into a finite probability space. The events A and B are **independent** if $P(A \cap B) = P(A)P(B)$. In that case, we have $P_B(A) = P(A)$ if $P(B) \neq 0$. In the above example, the two events $A = \{u \in U : u \text{ is odd}\} = \{1,3,5\}$ and $B = \{u \in U : u \leq 2\} = \{1,2\}$ are independent, while A and $C = \{u \in U : u \leq 3\} = \{1,2,3\}$ are not. Intuitively, if two events are independent, then the occurrence of one of them has no impact on the probability of the other one to happen.

A **random variable** X on a finite probability space (U, P) is a function $X : U \longrightarrow \mathbb{R}$. The **expected value** (or mean value, or average) of X is

$$\mathcal{E}(X) = \sum_{u \in U} X(u) \cdot P(u) = \sum_{x \in X(U)} x \cdot P(X = x),$$

where $X = x$ is shorthand for the event $X^{-1}(x) = \{u \in U : X(u) = x\}$. If $X(u) = u$ in our running example, then the expected value of X is

$$\mathcal{E}(X) = \sum_{1 \leq i \leq 6} i \cdot \frac{1}{6} = \frac{21}{6} = 3.5.$$

If $Y : U \longrightarrow \mathbb{R}$ is another random variable and $a, b \in \mathbb{R}$, then $\mathcal{E}(aX + bY) = a\mathcal{E}(X) + b\mathcal{E}(Y)$, so that the expected value is linear. The **variance** of a random variable X is var$(X) = \mathcal{E}((X - \mathcal{E}(X))^2)$, and the **standard deviation** of X is $\sigma(X) = \text{var}(X)^{1/2}$. It expresses by how much the actual value of X differs from its mean value on average. The function $P_X : \mathbb{R} \longrightarrow [0,1]$ defined by $P_X(x) = P(X = x) = P(\{u \in U : X(u) = x\})$ is called the **probability distribution** of the random variable X, and $(X(U), P_X)$ is again a finite probability space. Two random variables X and Y are **independent** if $P((X = x) \cap (Y = y)) = P(X = x)P(Y = y)$ (so that the events $X = x$ and $Y = y$ are independent) for all $x, y \in \mathbb{R}$. Similarly, n random variables $X_1, \ldots, X_n$ are independent if for any $x_1, \ldots, x_n \in \mathbb{R}$ and $I \subseteq \{1, \ldots, n\}$, the probability that $X_i = x_i$ for all $i \in I$ equals $\prod_{i \in I} P(X_i = x_i)$.

Given two finite probability spaces (U_1, P_1) and (U_2, P_2), we may form their **direct product** $(U_1 \times U_2, P_1 \cdot P_2)$ by letting $(P_1 \cdot P_2)(u_1, u_2) = P_1(u_1) \cdot P_2(u_2)$. If X_i is a random variable on U_i and π_i denotes the projection of $U_1 \times U_2$ to U_i for $i = 1, 2$, then $X_1 \circ \pi_1$ and $X_2 \circ \pi_2$ are independent random variables. We have the nth power (U^n, P^n) of (U, P) with $P^n(u_1, \ldots, u_n) = P(u_1) \cdots P(u_n)$, and if X is a random variable on U, then the n random variables $X_i = X \circ \pi_i$ on U^n defined by

$$X_i(u_1, \ldots, u_n) = X(u_i) \tag{6}$$

are independent and have the same probability distribution.

For example, we consider the third power (U^3, P^3) of the experiment "rolling a die". Thus, for example, $P^3(1,2,3) = 6^{-3}$. Let X be the random variable counting the result of a roll of one die. The average sum of three rolls is

$$\mathcal{E}(Y) = \mathcal{E}(X_1) + \mathcal{E}(X_2) + \mathcal{E}(X_3) = 3\mathcal{E}(X) = 10.5,$$

where $Y = X_1 + X_2 + X_3$ and X_i is the result of die number i for $i = 1, 2, 3$. More generally, if $X_1, \ldots, X_n$ are as in (6), then $\mathcal{E}(X_1 + \cdots + X_n) = n\mathcal{E}(X)$.

Let (U, P) be a finite probability space, $A \subseteq U$ an event, $p = P(A) > 0$ and $q = 1 - P(A)$, and X the random variable indicating whether A has occurred or not, so that $X(u) = 1$ if $u \in A$ and $X(u) = 0$ otherwise. Such an X is called a **Bernoulli random variable**. We are only interested in whether the outcomes of our random experiment are in A or not. Suppose that we repeat the experiment (say, rolling dice) potentially infinitely often and want to know the expected number of trials until $X = 1$ happens (say, a 6 occurs) for the first time. Each new trial is independent of the previous ones, and intuitively we expect to need about $1/p$ trials (that is, six rolls). We will now see that this is in fact the case.

In order to avoid infinite probability spaces, we model this situation by considering the probability space (U^n, P^n) for some $n \in \mathbb{N}$ and random variables X_i for $1 \le i \le n$ as in (6). (Later, we will let n tend to infinity.) Then $P(X_i = 1) = p$ and $P(X_i = 0) = q$ for all i and $X_1, \ldots, X_n$ are independent. Now let $Y^{(n)}$ be the random variable counting the first occurrence of $X_i = 1$. Thus $Y^{(n)} = i$ if and only if $X_1 = X_2 = \cdots = X_{i-1} = 0$ and $X_i = 1$ for $1 \le i \le n$, and $Y^{(n)} = n+1$ if $X_i = 1$ never happens, that is, if $X_1 = X_2 = \cdots = X_n = 0$. Then

$$P(Y^{(n)} = i) = P(X_1 = 0)P(X_2 = 0) \cdots P(X_{i-1} = 0)P(X_i = 1) = q^{i-1}p$$

for $1 \le i \le n$ (this is called a **geometric distribution**),

$$P(Y^{(n)} = n+1) = P(X_1 = 0)P(X_2 = 0) \cdots P(X_n = 0) = q^n,$$

and hence

$$\mathcal{E}(Y^{(n)}) = \sum_{1 \le i \le n+1} i \cdot P(Y^{(n)} = i) = (n+1)q^n + \sum_{1 \le i \le n} iq^{i-1}p.$$

Now

$$p \sum_{1 \le i \le n} iq^{i-1} = (1-q) \sum_{1 \le i \le n} iq^{i-1} = -nq^n + \sum_{0 \le i < n} q^i = -nq^n + \frac{1 - q^n}{1 - q},$$

by the formula for the geometric sum, and we obtain

$$\mathcal{E}(Y^{(n)}) = (n+1)q^n - nq^n + \frac{1 - q^n}{1 - q} = -\frac{q^{n+1}}{1 - q} + \frac{1}{p}.$$

Finally, $\lim_{n \to \infty} \mathcal{E}(Y^{(n)}) = 1/p$, as expected, since $|q| < 1$ implies that $\lim_{n \to \infty} q^{n+1} = 0$. As an example, the waiting time for a 6 to be rolled with a fair die is close to $1/(1/6) = 6$. More precisely, the value of $\mathcal{E}(Y^{(n)})$ with $p = 1/6$ is the expected number of rolls until a 6 shows up, if that happens with no more than n rolls, and counting $n+1$ if no 6 shows up at all. This value gets close to 6 when n is large; the difference $q^{n+1}/(1 - q)$ is about 0.13 for $n = 20$ and about $0.6 \cdot 10^{-7}$ for $n = 100$.

The probability that we need at least $k \le n$ trials until A happens for the first time is

$$P(Y^{(n)} \ge k) = P(X_1 = 0) \cdots P(X_{k-1} = 0) = q^{k-1}$$

for $k \ge 1$, independent of n. It is exponentially decreasing with k. For example, the probability that we need at least 10 rolls until a 6 occurs is $(5/6)^9 \approx 19.38\%$.

25.7. "Big Oh" notation

We only give a brief introduction; extensive discussions are in Graham, Knuth & Patashnik (1994), Chapter 9, and Brassard & Bratley (1996), Chapter 2.

In many situations in algorithmics it is convenient to express the cost of an algorithm only "up to a constant factor". What is needed is not the *exact* cost for increasing input sizes but merely the "rate of growth". We say for example that the familiar multiplication algorithm for $n \times n$ matrices over a field "is an n^3 algorithm", which means that the number $f(n)$ of field operations needed to multiply two $n \times n$ matrices is less than $c \cdot n^3$ for all $n \in \mathbb{N}$, where c is a real constant that we are not really interested in. This "sloppiness" can be formalized by means of the "big Oh" notation.

DEFINITION 25.7.　　(i) *A partial function $f: \mathbb{N} \longrightarrow \mathbb{R}$, that is, one that need not be defined for all $n \in \mathbb{N}$, is called **eventually positive** if there is a constant $N \in \mathbb{N}$ such that $f(n)$ is defined and strictly positive for all $n \geq N$.*

(ii) *Let $g: \mathbb{N} \longrightarrow \mathbb{R}$ be eventually positive. Then $O(g)$ is the set of all eventually positive functions $f: \mathbb{N} \longrightarrow \mathbb{R}$ for which there exist $N, c \in \mathbb{N}$ such that $f(n)$ and $g(n)$ are defined and $f(n) \leq cg(n)$ for all $n \geq N$.*

If $f(n)$ denotes the cost for matrix multiplication as above and $g(n) = n^3$, we may write $f \in O(g)$. In the literature, one often finds $f = O(g)$ or $f(n) = O(n^3)$ for this. The equal sign then has unusual properties: if $g(n) = n^3$ and $h(n) = n^4$, then $g = O(h)$ and $h = O(h)$, but we do not want to conclude that $g = h$.

A slight abuse of notation is that we often write, for example, $n^3 \in O(n^4)$. For each $n \in \mathbb{N}$, n^3 is just a number and the O-notation makes little sense for single numbers. What is meant is that $g \in O(h)$, with g, h as above. Similarly, we may write $f(n) \in O(n^3)$, or $f \in O(n^3)$. There is a notation to avoid this abuse, called the λ-calculus, but it is somewhat clumsy and we do not use it.

For example, if $f: \mathbb{N} \longrightarrow \mathbb{R}$ with $f(n) = 3n^4 - 300n + 1$, then $f(n) \in O(n^4)$, and also $f(n) \in O(n^5)$ ("O" does not imply "as accurate as possible"), but $f \notin O(n^3)$. An eventually positive function h satisfies $h(n) \in O(1)$ if and only if h is bounded from above. We have $f \in O(f)$, and $f \in O(g)$ and $g \in O(h)$ imply that $f \in O(h)$, for all eventually positive functions f, g, h.

Often the O is used in a more extended form, where it may appear *anywhere* on the right hand side. For instance, $f(n) \in g(n) + O(h(n))$ is shorthand for $f(n) = g(n) + k(n)$ with some $k \in O(h)$, or more briefly $f - g \in O(h)$. Similarly, $f(n) \in g(n) \cdot O(h(n))$ if $(f/g) \in O(h)$, $f(n) \in g(n)^{O(h(n))}$ if $f(n) = g(n)^{k(n)}$ for some $k \in O(h)$, and more generally $f(n) \in g(n, O(h(n)))$ if $f(n) = g(n, k(n))$ for some $k \in O(h)$. If $f, g: \mathbb{N} \longrightarrow \mathbb{R}$ are eventually positive, then

○ $c \cdot O(f) = O(f)$ for any $c \in \mathbb{R}_{>0}$,

○ $O(f) + O(g) = O(f + g) = O(\max(f, g))$, where max is the pointwise maximum,

○ $O(f) \cdot O(g) = O(f \cdot g) = f \cdot O(g)$,

○ $O(f)^m = O(f^m)$ for any $m \in \mathbb{R}_{>0}$, where f^m denotes the function for which $f^m(n) = f(n)^m$ (and not $\underbrace{f(f(\cdots f(n) \cdots)))}_{m}$), and

○ $f(n) \in g(n)^{O(1)} \iff f$ is bounded by a polynomial in g.

All equations are equations of sets, so for example $O(f) + O(g)$ is shorthand for the set $\{h + k : h \in O(f) \text{ and } k \in O(g)\}$.

We use logarithms in O-expressions without explicit reference to a base, and the reader may always think of some fixed base such as 2 or e.

Be cautious with exponentiation of O! At first glance, you might consider $e^{O(f)} = O(e^f)$ to be valid. But we have $e^{2n} \in e^{O(n)}$, and yet $e^{2n} = (e^n)^2 \notin O(e^n)$. The constant hidden within the "O" *does* influence the rate of growth when it occurs as an exponent.

We often also use the O-notation for functions g of two or three arguments, in the following sense. A partial function $g : \mathbb{N} \times \mathbb{N} \longrightarrow \mathbb{R}$ is eventually positive if there is a constant $N \in \mathbb{N}$ such that $g(m,n)$ is defined and positive for all $m,n \geq N$. For such a function g, $O(g)$ is the set of all eventually positive functions $f : \mathbb{N} \times \mathbb{N} \longrightarrow \mathbb{R}$ for which there exist $N, c \in \mathbb{N}$ such that $f(m,n), g(m,n)$ are defined and $f(m,n) \leq cg(m,n)$ for all $m,n \geq N$, and similarly for ternary functions.

In some situations, the "O" carries still too much information. For instance, the fast algorithm for multiplying two integers of length n uses $O(n \log n \log \log n)$ word operations (Section 8.3), and hence is, up to logarithmic factors, essentially a linear algorithm like the addition algorithm for n-word integers.

DEFINITION 25.8. *Let $f, g : \mathbb{N} \longrightarrow \mathbb{R}$ be eventually positive. Then we write $f \in O^{\sim}(g)$ (pronounced "f in soft Oh of g"), if $f(n) \in g(n)(\log_2(3 + g(n)))^{O(1)}$, or equivalently, if there are constants $N, c \in \mathbb{N}$ such that $f(n) \leq g(n)(\log_2(3 + g(n)))^c$ for all $n \geq N$. (The addition of 3 makes the $\log_2$ eventually greater than 1.)*

Thus $n \log n \log \log n \in O^{\sim}(n)$, and all the ugly log-factors are swallowed by the "soft Oh". We use terminology like "quadratic time" for $O(n^2)$, and "softly linear time" for $O^{\sim}(n)$.

25.8. Complexity theory

Excellent introductions to this rich theory are Sipser (1997), Papadimitriou (1993), and Wegener (1987). The notions are fairly intricate in their full generality, and to acquire ease of manipulating them requires substantial exposure to them, which is not provided by this précis. Algebraic complexity theory is briefly mentioned in Section 12.1.

A **decision problem** $X \subseteq I$ is a subset of a set I of **instances**. As an example, $X = \text{PRIMES} = \{x \in \mathbb{N} : x \text{ is prime}\} \subseteq I = \mathbb{N}$. The complexity class $\mathcal{P}$ ("polynomial time") consists of those X for which there exists a Turing machine (an idealized binary computer "hard-wired" to a particular program) which correctly accepts (if $x \in X$) or rejects (if $x \in I \setminus X$) any $x \in I$ in a number of steps that is polynomial in the input length $\lambda(x)$; such a machine is called a polynomial-time Turing machine. As an example, the binary representation of a nonzero integer $x \in \mathbb{N}$ has length $\lambda(x) = 1 + \lfloor \log_2 x \rfloor$.

The randomized complexity class $\mathcal{BPP}$ ("bounded-error probabilistic polynomial time") consists of those decision problems X for which there exists a polynomial-time Turing machine which, given an instance $x \in I$ of X and a random bit string of length polynomial in $\lambda(x)$, does the following. If $x \in X$, then with probability at least $2/3$ it accepts x. If $x \notin X$, then with probability at least $2/3$ it rejects x. Such a machine is called a **two-sided Monte Carlo Turing machine**. A standard trick is to run such an algorithm k times, for an odd integer k, and accept if and only if most of the runs accept; then an element in X gets accepted with probability at least

$$1 - 3^{-k} \sum_{0 \le i < k/2} \binom{k}{i} 2^i > 1 - 3^{-k} 2^{k/2} \sum_{0 \le i < k/2} \binom{k}{i} > 1 - \left(\frac{2\sqrt{2}}{3} \right)^k,$$

and the same bound holds for the rejection probability of an $x \in I \setminus X$. Furthermore, $X \in \mathcal{BPP}$ if and only if its complement $I \setminus X$ is in $\mathcal{BPP}$.

The complexity class $\mathcal{RP}$ ("random polynomial time") consists of those decision problems X for which there exists a polynomial-time Turing machine which, given an instance $x \in I$ of X and a random bit string of length polynomial in $\lambda(x)$, does the following. If $x \in X$, then it accepts x with probability at least $1/2$, while if $x \notin X$, then it always rejects x. The difference to the definition of $\mathcal{BPP}$ is that a $\mathcal{BPP}$ machine is allowed to make mistakes both in accepting instances not in X and in rejecting instances in X, while an $\mathcal{RP}$ machine is not allowed to accept instances not in X. A standard trick is to run such an algorithm k times and accept if and only if one of the runs accepts; then an element in X will be accepted with probability at least $1 - 2^{-k}$. Furthermore, we define co-$\mathcal{RP}$ to consist of those problems X whose complement $I \setminus X$ is in $\mathcal{RP}$. An $\mathcal{RP}$ Turing machine is also called a **one-sided Monte Carlo Turing machine**.

The class $\mathcal{ZPP} = \mathcal{RP} \cap \text{co-}\mathcal{RP}$ ("zero-error probabilistic polynomial time") consists of those problems for which probabilistic polynomial-time algorithms exist that always give the right answer; their running time is a random variable with a certain mean t (polynomial in the input length) and exponential decay: $\text{prob}(\text{time} \ge at) \le 2^{-a}$. The only two problems in this class that are not known to be already in $\mathcal{P}$ are treated extensively in this text: PRIMES and (the decision version of) factoring polynomials over finite fields. A $\mathcal{ZPP}$ Turing machine is also called a **Las Vegas Turing machine**. We have $\mathcal{P} \subseteq \mathcal{ZPP}$, since every deterministic algorithm is also a probabilistic one (that just does not use any random bits).

The class $\mathcal{NP}$ ("non-deterministic polynomial time"), introduced by Cook (1971) and Karp (1972), comprises those problems X that have a non-deterministic polynomial-time solution, so that there exists a deterministic polynomial-time Turing machine M such that for all $x \in I$ we have $x \in X$ if and only if there exists a bit string y of length polynomial in $\lambda(x)$ such that M accepts (x, y). ("Non-deterministic" does *not* mean "not deterministic"; taking the empty string for y shows that $\mathcal{P} \subseteq \mathcal{NP}$.) The only known simulations of M on a realistic computer try all exponentially many possibilities for y, and it is the most important open problem in theoretical computer science to prove Cook's hypothesis that $\mathcal{P} \ne \mathcal{NP}$. The class co-$\mathcal{NP}$ consists of those X for which $I \setminus X \in \mathcal{NP}$.

A **(Turing-)reduction** from a problem X to a problem Y is a deterministic polynomial-time algorithm (Turing machine) for X that may use an (unspecified) subroutine for deciding membership in Y. If such a reduction exists, then X is **(polynomial-time) reducible** to Y; this implies that X is not harder to solve than Y (in the sense of polynomial time). If also Y is reducible to X, then they are **(polynomial-time) equivalent**.

A decision problem X is $\mathcal{C}$-**hard** for a complexity class $\mathcal{C}$ if every problem in $\mathcal{C}$ is reducible to it, and $\mathcal{C}$-**complete** if in addition $X \in \mathcal{C}$. The $\mathcal{C}$-complete problems are the "hardest" ones in $\mathcal{C}$. Cook's hypothesis implies that the $\mathcal{NP}$-**complete** problems cannot be solved in polynomial time. His first example were satisfiable formulas of propositional calculus (see Section 24.1), and the subset sum problems of Section 17.1 are also $\mathcal{NP}$-complete. The classic by Garey & Johnson (1979) lists over 1000 such problems.

For the classes $\mathcal{EXPTIME}$ and $\mathcal{EXPEXPTIME}$, one allows the algorithms to take exponential and doubly-exponential time, respectively, that is,

$$\text{time } 2^{n^{O(1)}} \text{ and } 2^{2^{n^{O(1)}}}, \text{ respectively,}$$

on inputs of length n. Such algorithms can be run in practice only for rather small values of n.

In **space bounded** complexity classes, one limits the number of memory cells used by algorithms. The read-only input cells and the write-only output cells are not counted, but only the essential work cells. This leads to the classes $\mathcal{PSPACE}$ and $\mathcal{EXPSPACE}$, with polynomially and exponentially bounded work space, respectively.

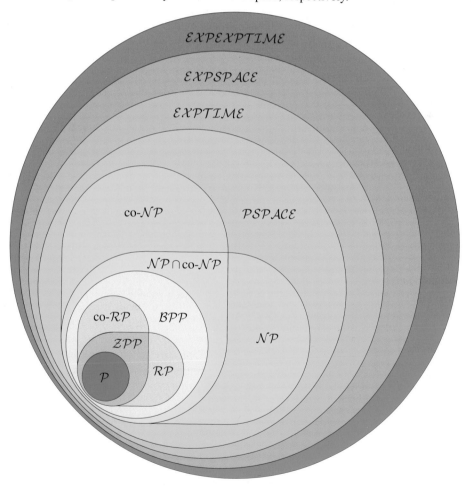

FIGURE 25.3: Containment relations between various complexity classes.

The relations between the complexity classes described above are illustrated in the "complexity onion" of Figure 25.3. The feasible problems, for which algorithms exist that can handle inputs up to a "reasonable" size, are those in $\mathcal{BPP}$ and smaller classes. (This statement has to be taken with a grain of salt.) The first two thirds of this book (up to Chapter 18) deal with such problems. Sometimes an effort is required to show that they are in $\mathcal{ZPP}$ (for PRIMES and polynomial factorization over finite fields) or $\mathcal{P}$ (Gaussian elimination over $\mathbb{Q}$), and sometimes they are clearly in $\mathcal{P}$ and our effort goes into reducing the time from $O(n^2)$ to $O^\sim(n)$, say (for multiplication, division with remainder, etc.). The later chapters treat problems that are not known to be in $\mathcal{BPP}$. For their solutions, there are reasonably small inputs (say, a 400-digit integer to be factored) for which all known methods take more time than is feasible in practice. But still, experience so far gives rise to the hope that improved algorithms (and hardware) will increase the range of interesting solvable problems further and further.

Notes. **25.2.** Proposition 30 in Book 7 of Euclid's *Elements* shows that prime numbers are irreducible. Gauss (1863c) showed that $\mathbb{Q}[i]$ and $\mathbb{Q}[\sqrt{-3}]$ are Euclidean. Hendrik Lenstra (1979a, 1980a, 1980b) studied Euclidean number fields in detail, and Lemmermeyer (1995) provides an exhaustive discussion.

25.3. Gauss (1863a), article 243, proved Lemma 25.4 (ii) for $R = \mathbb{Z}_p$, where p is a prime.

25.4. Galois (1830) laid the foundations of the theory of finite fields. They are often called Galois fields, and GF(q) is a common notation for our $\mathbb{F}_q$.

25.5. See Notes 5.5 for Gauß' elimination procedure. Laplace (1772), chapter IV, gives his determinant expansion; it is also in Bézout (1764), pages 293 ff. Cramer (1750), Appendice N° I, page 658, states his rule.

25.7. The "big Oh" notation was introduced by Paul Bachmann and Edmund Landau in number theory at the turn of the century, and popularized in computer science by Don Knuth (1970). Von zur Gathen (1985) and Babai, Luks & Seress (1988) invented the "soft Oh" notation.

25.8. Ulam used a randomized method to estimate the success probability in the card game *solitaire* and apparently coined the term *Monte Carlo*. Babai (1979) invented the designation *Las Vegas* algorithm. See Notes 6.5.

Exercises for this section can be found on the book's web page.

Sources of illustrations

Page 12: Désirée von zur Gathen twisting a plastic model of cyclohexane.

Page 21: First page of Euclid's *Elements*, printed 1482 by Erhard Ratdolt in Venice. University Library, Basel. Reproduced with kind permission.

Page 23: Miniature from the manuscript *Agrimensorum* on Roman land surveyors, 6th century AD. Possibly represents Euclid. Courtesy Herzog–August–Bibliothek, manuscript 2403, Wolfenbüttel.

Page 205: Portrait of Isaac Newton by Sir Godfrey Kneller, 1689. Courtesy of the Trustees of the Portsmouth Estates.

Page 207: One pound UK banknote (in circulation until 1988) depicting Isaac Newton. Reproduced with kind permission of the Bank of England.

Pages 341 ff.: Schloß Neuhaus in Paderborn. Residence of Bishop Ferdinand von Fürstenberg (see page 487).

Page 347: Portrait of Carl Friedrich Gauß. Oil painting by Gottlieb Biermann (1824–1908), a copy made in 1887 of a portrait executed by Christian Albrecht Jensen (1792–1870) in 1840. Lecture Hall in the Sternwarte (observatory), Göttingen. Reproduced with kind permission of the Universitäts-Sternwarte Göttingen.

Page 349: German 10 DM banknote, using a mirror-image of the portrait on page 347. Designed by Reinhold Gerstetter. In circulation since 16 April 1991. Reproduced with kind permission of Deutsche Bundesbank.

Page 485: Marble statue of Pierre Fermat with muse, by Théophile Barrau, 1898. Inscription: *Fermat. Inventeur du calcul différentiel. 1585[sic!]–1665*. Salle des illustres, Capitole, Toulouse.

Page 486: Engraving of Pierre Fermat by François Poilly. From *Varia Opera*, Toulouse, 1679.

Page 487: Dedication by Samuel Fermat to Ferdinand von Fürstenberg, Bishop of Paderborn, in the *Varia Opera*, Toulouse, 1679.

Page 559: Portrait of David Hilbert. Lecture Hall in the Mathematisches Institut, Universität Göttingen. Reproduced with kind permission of Mathematisches Institut der Georg-August-Universität, Göttingen.

Page 561: Signed photograph of David Hilbert. Apparently taken by the photographer August Schmidt. This was one in a series of popular postcards *Portraits Göttinger Professoren. Hrsg. von der Göttinger Freien Studentenschaft. Nr. 13*. Acquired by the library in 1915. Courtesy Niedersächsische Staats- und Universitätsbibliothek, Göttingen.

All photographs except those on pages 23, 205, and 561 ⓒ1999 by Joachim von zur Gathen.

Sources of quotations

Introduction (page 0): **William Shakespeare** (1564–1616), *King Henry VIII*, 1.1.123. *The Works*, Jacob Tonson, London, 1709, vol. 4, p. 1725. **Lord Francis Bacon** (1561–1626), *Essays*, Of Studies, 1597. Reprinted by Henry Altemus Company, Philadelphia PA, c. 1900, p. 201. **Anonymous referee**, *Bulletin des sciences mathématiques Férussac* **3** (1825), p. 77. **Isaac Newton** (1642–1727), *Universal Arithmetick: or, A Treatise of Arithmetical Composition and Resolution*, translated by the late Mr. Raphson and revised and corrected by Mr. Cunn, London, 1728, Preface *To The Reader*. Translation of *Arithmetica Universalis, sive de compositione et resolutione arithmetica liber*, 1707. Reprinted in: Derek T. Whiteside, *The mathematical works of Isaac Newton*, vol. 2, Johnson Reprint Co, New York, 1967, pp. 4–5. **Ghiyāth al-Dīn Jamshīd ben Masʿūd ben Maḥmūd al-Kāshī** (c. 1390–c. 1448), مفتاح الحساب (*miftāḥ al-ḥisābi, The key to computing*), written in 1427. Manuscript copied in 1645, now in the Preußische Staatsbibliothek, Berlin, edited by Luckey (1951), p. 128, lines 15–17.

Chapter 1 (page 8): **Paul Theroux** (*1941), *The Mosquito Coast*. Hamish (Hamilton) Ltd, 1981. **Napoléon I. Bonaparte** (1769–1821). *Correspondance de Napoléon*, t. 24, p. 131, letter 19 028, 1 August 1812, Vitebsk, to Laplace. Imprimerie Royale, Paris, 1868. **Augusta Ada Lovelace** (1815–1852), Sketch of the Analytical Engine Invented by Charles Babbage, Esq., by L. F. Menabrea (translated and with notes by "A. A. L."). *Taylor's Scientific Memoirs* **3** (1843), Article XXIX, 666–731. Reprinted in *Babbage's Calculating Engines*, E. and F. N. Spon, London, 1889, 4–50, p. 23. Reprinted in The Charles Babbage Institute Reprint Series for the History of Computing, vol. II, Tomash Publishers, Los Angeles/San Francisco CA, 1982. **Robert Ludlum** (*1927), *Apocalypse Watch*, Bantam paperback, 1996, ch. 8, p. 135. Reprinted with kind permission of Bantam Books, a divison of Bantam, Doubleday, Dell Publishing Group, Inc., New York. **Eric Temple Bell** (1883–1960), *Men of Mathematics I*, ch. 1: Introduction, Penguin Books, 1937, p. 2.

Chapter 2 (page 26): **Leopold Kronecker** (1823–1891), Vortrag bei der Berliner Naturforscher-Versammlung, 1886. Quoted by H. Weber, *Leopold Kronecker*, Jahresberichte der Deutschen Mathematiker Vereinigung **2** (1891/92), p. 19. Also quoted by David Hilbert, Neubegründung der Mathematik, *Abhandlungen aus dem Mathematischen Seminar der Hamburger Universität* **1** (1922), p. 161. **Lewis Carroll** (Rev. Charles Lutwidge Dodgson) (1832–1898), *Alice's Adventures in Wonderland*, Macmillan and Co., London, 1865, Ch. 9: The mock turtle's story. Reprinted by Avon, The Heritage Press, 1969. **Isaac Newton** (1642–1727), *Universal Arithmetick: or, A Treatise of Arithmetical Composition and Resolution*, translated by the late Mr. Raphson and revised and corrected by Mr. Cunn, London, 1728, p. 1. Translation of *Arithmetica Universalis, sive de compositione et resolutione arithmetica liber*, 1707. Reprinted in: Derek T. Whiteside, *The mathematical works of Isaac Newton*, vol. 2, Johnson Reprint Co, New York, 1967, pp. 6–7. **Stanisław Marcin Ulam** (1909–1984), Computers, *Scientific American*, September 1964, 203–216. Reprinted with kind permission. Also reprinted in *Science, Computers, and People*, Birkhäuser, Boston, 1986, p. 43. **Marcus Tullius Cicero** (106–43 BC), *Tusculanae Disputationes*, Liber primus, II.5. *Opera Omnia*, Lugdunus, Sumptibus Sybillæ à Porta, 1588, vol. 4, p. 165. **Robert Louis Stevenson** (1850–1894), *The Master of Ballantrae*, Collins, London and Glasgow, 1889, p. 51. **State of California**, Instructions for Form 540 NR, California Nonresident or Part-Year Resident Income Tax Return, 1996, p. 3.

Chapter 3 (page 42): **Godfrey Harold Hardy** (1877–1947), *A Mathematician's Apology*, Cambridge University Press, 1940, ch. 8, p. 21. **Robert Recorde** (c. 1510–1558), *The Whetstone of Witte*, The seconde parte of Arithmetike, London, 1557. **Murray Gell-Mann** (*1929), *The Quark and the Jaguar*, Abacus, London, 1994, ch. 9: What is fundamental, p. 109. Reprinted with kind permission from Little, Brown, London. **Robert Boyle** (1627–1691), *Some Considerations touching the Usefulness of Experimental Natural Philosophy*, vol. 2, *The Usefulness of Mathematicks to Natural Philosophy*; Oxford, 1671. *The Works*, ed. by Thomas Birch, vol. 3, London, 1772, p. 426. **Augustus De Morgan** (1806–1871), *Smith's Dictionary of Greek and Roman Biography and Mythology*, London, 1902, Article "Eucleides".

Chapter 4 (page 62): **Novalis** (Friedrich Leopold Freiherr von Hardenberg) (1772–1801), *Materialien zur Encyclopädie*. In: *Schriften*, hrsg. Ernst Heilbronn, Teil 2, Georg Reimer, Berlin, 1901, p. 549. **Karl Theodor Wilhelm Weierstraß** (1815–1897), letter to Sonja Kowalevski, 27 August 1883. See Gustav Magnus Mittag-Leffler: Une page de la vie de Weierstrass, *Compte rendu du deuxième congrès international des mathématiciens* (Paris, 1900), Gauthiers-Villars, Paris, 1902, p. 149. **David Hume** (1711–1776), *A Treatise of Human Nature*, John Noon, London, 1739, Part III: Of Knowledge and Probability, Sect. I: Of Knowledge. **Augustus De Morgan** (1806–1871), *Elements of Algebra*, London, 1837, Preface. **Abū Jaʿfar Muḥammad ben Mūsā al-Khwārizmī** (c. 780–c. 850), الكتاب المختصر في حساب الجبر و المقابلة (*al-kitāb al-mukhtaṣiri fī ḥisābi al-jabri wā al-muqābalati, The concise book on computing by moving and reducing terms*), often called *Algebra*, c. 825, marginal note to p. ٥١ (51) and pp. 299–300 of Rosen's (1831) edition. Manuscript in the Bodleian Library at Oxford, UK, transcribed in 1342, edited by Frederic Rosen.

Chapter 5 (page 88): **Eric Temple Bell** (1883–1960), *Men of Mathematics I*, ch. 2: Modern minds in ancient bodies, Penguin Books, 1937, p. 33. **James Joseph Sylvester** (1814–1897), Proof of the Fundamental Theorem of Invariants, *Philosophical Magazine* (1878), p. 186. *Collected Mathematical Papers*, vol. 3, p. 126. **Gottfried Wilhelm Freiherr von Leibniz** (1646–1716), Untitled and unpublished manuscript, Hannover Library. From: *Gottfried Wilhelm Leibniz, Opera philosophica*, ed. Johann Eduard Erdmann, 1840, XI. De scientia universali seu calculo philosophico (title by Erdmann). Reprint Scientia Verlag, Aalen, 1974, p. 84. **Augustus De Morgan** (1806–1871), *Study and Difficulties of Mathematics*, Society for the Diffusion of Useful Knowledge, 1831, chap. 12, On the Study of Algebra. Fourth Reprint Edition, Open Court Publishing Company, La Salle IL, 1943, p. 176.

Chapter 6 (page 130): **Godfrey Harold Hardy** (1877–1947), *A Mathematician's Apology*, Cambridge University Press, 1940, ch. 10, p. 25. **David Hilbert** (1862–1943), Mathematische Probleme, *Nachrichten von der Königlichen Gesellschaft der Wissenschaften zu Göttingen* (1900), 253–297. *Archiv für Mathematik und Physik*, 3. *Reihe* **1** (1901), 44–63 and 213–237. *Gesammelte Abhandlungen*, Springer Verlag, 1970, 290–329, p. 294. Reprinted with kind permission. **Johann Wolfgang von Goethe** (1749–1832), *Wilhelm Meisters Wanderjahre*, Zweites Buch; Betrachtungen im Sinne der Wanderer: Kunst, Ethisches, Natur. **Thomas Edward Lawrence** (1888–1935), *Seven Pillars of Wisdom*, George Doran Publishing Co., 1926. Book III: A railway diversion, ch. XXXIII. Reprint by Anchor Books, Doubleday, New York, 1991, p. 192.

Chapter 7 (page 196): **Oliver Cromwell** (1599–1658), Letter C (= 100), to Richard Mayor, father of Cromwell's daughter-in-law, written off Milford Haven, 13th August 1649. In: Thomas Carlyle, *Oliver Cromwell's Letters and Speeches*, vol. II, Chapman and Hall, London, 1845, p. 41. **John Locke** (1632–1704), *An Essay concerning Humane Understanding: in Four Books*, Thomas Basset, London, 1690, Bk. 4: Of Knowledge and Opinion, chap. 3: Of the extent of human knowledge, sect. 18. **John Cougar Mellencamp** (*1951), CD *Big Daddy*, J. M.'s Question, Mercury Records, Copyright © Full Keel Music Co. Rights for Germany, Austria, Switzerland and Eastern Europe except Lithuania, Latvia, and Estonia by Heinz Funke Musikverlag GmbH, Berlin. Reprinted with kind permission of Heinz Funke Musikverlag GmbH, Berlin. **Michael Crichton** (*1942), *The Lost World*. Ballantine Books, Random House, Inc., New York, 1996, ch. *Raptor*, pp. 82–83. **Immanuel Kant** (1724–1804), *Über Pädagogik* (A. Von der physischen Erziehung). Notes on his lectures on pedagogy between 1776 and 1787, published 1803 by Friedrich Theodor Rink. *Werke*, hrsg. Karl Rosenkranz und Friedrich Wilhelm Schubert, Band 9, Leopold Voss, Leipzig, 1838, 367–439, p. 409.

Chapter 8 (page 208): **Richard Phillips Feynman** (1918–1988), *Surely You're Joking, Mr. Feynman. Adventures of a Curious Character*. With Ralph Leighton. W. W. Norton Inc., 1984. Paperback: Vintage, 1992,

p. 100. Reprinted with kind permission of W. W. Norton & Company. Inc., New York. **John le Carré** (David John Moore Cornwell) (* 1931), *The Russia House*, Hodder & Stoughton, 1989, ch. 8, p. 160. Reprinted by kind permission of David Higham Associates Limited, London. **Arnold Schönhage** (*1935), Andreas F. W. Grotefeld, Ekkehard Vetter, *Fast Algorithms: A Multitape Turing Machine Implementation*, BI-Wissenschaftsverlag, Mannheim, 1994, p. 284. ⓒ Spektrum Akademischer Verlag, Heidelberg. Reprinted with kind permission. **Ernst Mach** (1836–1916), *Populär-wissenschaftliche Vorlesungen*. Barth, Leipzig, 1896. 13. Vorlesung: Die ökonomische Natur der physikalischen Forschung, 217–244, pp. 228–229. Reprinted by Böhlau Verlag Wien, Köln, Graz 1987. English translation by McCormack, *Popular Scientific Lectures*, Open Court Publishing Company, La Salle IL, 1895.

Chapter 9 (page 242): **Isaac Newton** (1642–1727), Saying attributed to Newton. **Robert Edler von Musil** (1880–1942), *Der mathematische Mensch*, 1913. *Gesammelte Werke*, Band II, hrsg. Adolf Frisé, Rowohlt, 1978, p. 1006. Copyright ⓒ 1978 by Rowohlt Verlag GmbH, Reinbek. Reprinted with kind permission. **Carl Friedrich Gauß** (1777–1855), Announcement of *Theoria residuorum biquadraticorum, Commentatio secunda; Göttingische Gelehrte Anzeigen* (1831). *Werke* **II**, Königliche Gesellschaft der Wissenschaften, Göttingen, 1863, 165–178, pp. 177–178. Reprinted by Georg Olms Verlag, Hildesheim New York, 1973. **Alfred North Whitehead** (1861–1947), *An Introduction to Mathematics*, Ch. 5: The Symbolism of Mathematics, Oxford University Press, 1911, pp. 39–40. Reprinted by kind permission of Oxford University Press, New York. **Abū Jaʿfar Muḥammad ben Mūsā al-Khwārizmī** (c. 780–c. 850), *Algorithmi de numero Indorum*, often called *Arithmetic*, c. 830. 13th century Latin manuscript from the library of the Hispanic Society of America, New York. It is probably a copy of a 12th century Latin translation of al-Khwārizmī's book كتاب حساب الاعداد الهندي (*kitāb hisābi al-aʿdādi al-hindī, A book on computing with the Indian numbers*) on arithmetic whose original is lost. It was written after his *Algebra*. This recently discovered manuscript was edited by Folkerts (1997). Quote from end of Chapter 7, Plate 8 (f. 20v) and p. 70. Crossley & Henry (1990) translate the text of the other surviving manuscript, at Cambridge.

Chapter 10 (page 278): **James William Cooley** (*1926), The Re-Discovery of the Fast Fourier Transform Algorithm, *Mikrochimica Acta* (Wien) **3** (1987), 33–45. Reprinted with kind permission of Springer-Verlag, Wien. **Voltaire** (François-Marie Arouet) (1694–1778), *Questions sur l'Encyclopédie*, Article "Imagination", 1771. Reprinted in *Dictionnaire de la pensée de Voltaire par lui-même*, Éditions Complexe, 1994, p. 604. **Pierre Simon Laplace** (1749–1827), *Théorie analytique des probabilités*, Courcier, Paris, 1812. *Œuvres*, Paris, 1847, t. 7, p. 131. **James Joseph Sylvester** (1814–1897), On the explicit values of Sturm's quotients, *Philosophical Magazine* **6** (1853), 293–296. *Mathematical Papers*, vol. 1, p. 637–640.

Chapter 11 (page 294): **Leslie Gabriel Valiant** (*1949), *Circuits of the Mind*, Oxford University Press, 1994, p. ix. Copyright ⓒ 1994 by Oxford University Press. Reprinted with kind permission of Oxford University Press, Inc. **Charles Babbage** (1792–1871), *Passages from the Life of a Philosopher*, Chapter VIII: Of the Analytical Engine. Reprinted in *Babbage's Calculating Engines*, E. and F. N. Spon, London, 1889, 154–283, p. 167. Reprinted in The Charles Babbage Institute Reprint Series for the History of Computing, vol. II, Tomash Publishers, Los Angeles/San Francisco CA, 1982. **Plato** (c. 428–c. 347 BC), Πολιτεια (*Republic*), Book 7, chap. 8.

Chapter 12 (page 312): **Иосиф Семенович Иохвидов**, *Ганкелевы и теплицевы матрицы и формы*, §18. Обращение теплицевых и ганкелевых матриц, Наука, 1974, p. 171. English translation by G. Philipp A. Thijsse: I. S. Iohvidov, *Hankel and Toeplitz Matrices and Forms*, §18. Inversion of Toeplitz and Hankel matrices, Birkhäuser, Basel, 1982, p. 147. Reprinted with kind permission of Birkhäuser Verlag AG, Basel, Switzerland. **James Joseph Sylvester** (1814–1897), On the relation between the minor determinants of linearly equivalent quadratic functions, *Philosophical Magazine* **1** (1851), 295–305, p. 300. *Collected Mathematical Papers* **1**, 241–250, pp. 246–247. **René Descartes** (1596–1650), *Discours de la Méthode*, troisième partie, 1637.

Chapter 13 (page 334): **Emil Luckhardt**, German version of the *Internationale*. Original French version 1871 by Eugène Pottier (Paris), music 1888 by Pierre-Chrétien Degeyter (Lille, 1848–1932). **Jean Baptiste Joseph Fourier** (1768–1830), *Théorie Analytique de la Chaleur*, Firmin Didot Frères, Paris, 1822. Discours Préliminaire, p. xxii. **Felix Klein** (1849–1925), *Elementarmathematik vom höheren Standpunkte aus*, Band II, Springer, Leipzig, 1909. Also: Grundlehren der Mathematik **15**, 1925, Springer, Berlin, p. 206. ⓒ Springer-Verlag, Heidelberg. Reprinted with kind permission. **Johann Wolfgang von Goethe** (1749–1832), *Maximen und Reflexionen*, Aus dem Nachlass, Sechste Abtheilung, No. 1279. **Mark Twain** (Samuel Longhorne Clemens) (1835–1910), *A Tramp Abroad*, Vol. 2, Appendix D: The awful German language. Harper & Brothers Publishers, New York and London, 1897.

Chapter 14 (page 352): **Zhuojun Liu** and **Paul Shyh-Horng Wang**, Height as a Coefficient Bound for Univariate Polynomial Factors, Part I, *SIGSAM Bulletin* **28**(2) (1994), ACM Press, 20–27. Reprinted with kind permission of ACM Publications. **Maurice Borisovitch Kraïtchik** (1882–1957), *Théorie des Nombres*, Tome II, Gauthier-Villars et Cie., Paris, 1926, Avant-propos, pp. iii–iv. **Évariste Galois** (1811–1832), Sur la théorie des nombres, *Bulletin des sciences mathématiques Férussac* **13** (1830), 428–435. See Galois (1830). **Hermann Hankel** (1839–1873), *Die Entwicklung der Mathematik in den letzten Jahrhunderten*, 2. Auflage, Fues'sche Sortiment Buchhandlung Tübingen, 1885, p. 25. **Tom Clancy** (*1947), *Debt of Honor*, G. P. Putnam's Sons, New York, 1994, ch. 44 … from one who knows the score …, p. 687.

Chapter 15 (page 406): **Charles Davies**, *University Algebra*, Barnes & Co., New York, 1867, p. 41. **Pierre Simon Laplace** (1749–1827), *Théorie analytique des probabilités*, Courcier, Paris, 1812. *Œuvres*, Paris, 1847, t. 7, p. 156.

Chapter 16 (page 446): **Joseph Liouville** (1809–1882), *Œuvres mathématiques d'Évariste Galois*, *Journal de mathématiques pures et appliquées* **9** (1846), 381–444, p. 382. **Sue Taylor Grafton** (*1940), *"A" is for Alibi*, Bantam Books, 1987, ch. 9, p. 71. Holt, Rinehart & Winston 1982. **Philip Friedman**, *Inadmissible Evidence*, Ivy Books, published by Ballantine Books, 1992, ch. 22, p. 224. ⓒ Random House, Inc., New York. Reprinted with kind permission.

Chapter 17 (page 476): **Voltaire** (François-Marie Arouet) (1694–1778), *Questions sur l'Encyclopédie*, Article "Géométrie", 1771. Reprinted in *Dictionnaire de la pensée de Voltaire par lui-même*, Éditions Complexe, 1994, p. 479. **Napoléon I. Bonaparte** (1769–1821). *Correspondance de Napoléon*, t. 2, letter 1231, 15 frimaire 5 = 5 December 1796, to Lalande. Imprimerie Royale, Paris, 1868. **Robert Recorde** (c. 1510–1558), *The Whetstone of Witte*, London, 1557.

Chapter 18 (page 490): **Adrien-Marie Legendre** (1752–1833), *Théorie des nombres*, Firmin Didot Frères, Paris, 1830. 4ᵉ édition, Hermann, Paris, 1900, p. 70. **The Rolling Stones**, UK: LP *The Rolling Stones*, 26 April 1964; USA: LP *England's Newest Hit Makers*, 1964. Composers: Eddie Holland/Lamont Dozier/Brian Holland. **Stanisław Marcin Ulam** (1909–1984), Computers, *Scientific American*, September 1964, 203–216, p. 207. Reprinted with kind permission. Also reprinted in *Science, Computers, and People*, Birkhäuser, Boston, 1986, p. 48. **Edgar Allan Poe** (1809–1849), The Mystery of Marie Rogêt. Snowden's *Ladies' Companion*, November and December 1842 and February 1843, pp. 15–20, 93–99, 162–167. *Collected Works*, ed. Thomas Ollive Mabbott, Harvard University Press, Cambridge MA, 1978, 723–774. **Maj Sjöwall** (*1935) and **Per Wahlöö** (1926–1975), *Mannen på balkongen*, ch. 24, P. A. Norstedt & Söner, 1967. English translation: *The Man On The Balcony*, Random House, New York, 1968.

Chapter 19 (page 514): **Carl Friedrich Gauß** (1777–1855), *Disquisitiones Arithmeticae*, Duae methodi numerorum factores investigandi. Article 329, p. 401. **Carl Friedrich Gauß**, Review of Ladislaus Chernac, *Cribrum Arithmeticum*, 1811, in *Göttingische Gelehrte Anzeigen* (1812). *Werke* **II**, Königliche Gesellschaft der Wissenschaften, Göttingen, 1863, p. 182. Reprinted by Georg Olms Verlag, Hildesheim New York, 1973. **Daniel W. Fish**, *The Complete Arithmetic*, ch. *Factoring*, §162. Ivison, Blakeman, Taylor & Co, New York and Chicago, 1874, p. 81. **Maurice Borisovitch Kraïtchik** (1882–1957), *Théorie des nombres*, Tome II, Gauthier-Villars et Cie., Paris, 1926, chap. XII, p. 144. **Richard Phillips Feynman** (1918–1988), *Surely You're Joking, Mr. Feynman. Adventures of a Curious Character*. With Ralph Leighton. W. W. Norton Inc., 1984. Paperback: Vintage, 1992, p. 77. Reprinted with kind permission of W. W. Norton & Company. Inc., New York.

Chapter 20 (page 546): **Godfrey Harold Hardy** (1877–1947), *A Mathematician's Apology*, Cambridge University Press, 1940, ch. 28, p. 80. **David Hilbert** (1862–1943), Naturerkennen und Logik, *Naturwissenschaften* (1930), 959–963. *Gesammelte Abhandlungen*, Springer-Verlag 1970, Teil 3, 378–387, p. 386. ⓒ Springer-Verlag, Heidelberg. Reprinted with kind permission. **Abraham Adrian Albert** (1905–1972), Some Mathematical Aspects of Cryptography, Invited address, AMS Meeting in Manhattan KS on 22 November 1941. *Collected Mathematical Papers* **2**, AMS, Providence RI, 1993, 903–920. Reprinted with kind permission of American Mathematical Society. **Sir Arthur Conan Doyle** (1859–1930), The Sign of the Four; or, The Problem of the Sholtos, *Lippincott's Magazine*, February 1890. Also *The Sign of Four*, Chapter 1, Spencer Blackett, London, 1890. **Philip Friedman**, *Grand Jury*, ch. 14, Ivy Books, Random House, Inc., New York, 1996. **Tom Clancy** (*1947), *The Cardinal of the Kremlin*, ch. 18: Advantages, Harper Collins Publisher, London, 1988.

Chapter 21 (page 564): **Joseph Louis Lagrange** (1736–1813), *Leçons élémentaires sur les Mathématiques*, Leçon Cinquième: Sur l'usage des courbes dans la solution des Problèmes, École Polytechnique, Paris, 1795. *Journal de l'École Polytechnique*, VIIᵉ et VIIIᵉ cahiers, tome 2, 1812. *Œuvres*, publiées par J.-A. Serret, Gauthiers-Villars, Paris, 1877, t. 7, 183–288, p. 271. **Étienne Bézout** (1739–1783), Recherches sur le degré des équations résultantes de l'évanouissement des inconnus, *Histoire de l'académie royale des sciences*, 1764, 288–338, pp. 290–291. **Francis Sowerby Macaulay** (1862–1937), *The Algebraic Theory of Modular Systems*, Introduction, Cambridge University Press, 1916, p. 2.

Chapter 22 (page 596): **Ludwig Boltzmann** (1844–1906), *Gustav Robert Kirchhoff*, Festrede, Graz, 15.11. 1887. Reprinted in: Ludwig Boltzmann, *Populäre Schriften*, eingeleitet und ausgewählt von Engelbert Broda, Friedr. Vieweg & Sohn, Braunschweig/Wiesbaden, 1979, 47–53, p. 50. Reprinted with kind permission of Friedr. Vieweg & Sohn, Wiesbaden. **Marius Sophus Lie** (1842–1899), Zur allgemeinen Theorie der partiellen Differentialgleichungen beliebiger Ordnung, *Leipziger Berichte* **47** (1895), Math.-phys. Classe, 53–128, p. 53. *Gesammelte Abhandlungen*, herausgegeben durch Friedrich Engel und Poul Heegaard, B. G. Teubner, Leipzig, 1929, vol. 4, p. 320. **Augustus De Morgan** (1806–1871), On Divergent Series, and various Points of Analysis connected with them. *Transactions of the Cambridge Philosophical Society* **8** (1844), 182–203, p. 188. **George Berkeley** (1684–1753), *The Analyst*, J. Tonson, London, 1734, sect. 7. **William Shanks** (1812–1882), *Contributions to Mathematics, comprising chiefly the Rectification of the Circle to 607 places of decimals*, G. Bell, London, 1853, p. vi. Excerpt reprinted in Berggren, Borwein & Borwein (1997), 147–161.

Chapter 23 (page 608): **Joseph Rudyard Kipling** (1865–1936), To the True Romance, In *Many Inventions*, MacMillan, London, 1893. **James Gleick** (*1954), *Genius: The life and science of Richard Feynman*, Vintage

Books, Random House, Inc., New York, 1992, Prologue, p. 7. © Random House, Inc., New York. Reprinted with kind permission. **Eric Temple Bell** (1883–1960), *Men of Mathematics I*, ch. 9: Analysis incarnate (Euler), Penguin Books, 1937, p. 152. **George Eyre Andrews** (*1938), *q-series: Their Development and Application in Analysis, Number Theory, Combinatorics, Physics, and Computer Algebra*, AMS Regional Conference Series in Mathematics **66**, American Mathematical Society, 1986, p. 87. Reprinted with kind permission of the American Mathematical Society.

Chapter 24 (page 640): **Alfred North Whitehead** (1861–1947), *An Introduction to Mathematics*, Oxford University Press, 1911, p. 71. Reprinted with kind permission. **Jean le Rond D'Alembert** (1717–1783), Quoted in Edward Kasner, The present problems of geometry, *Bulletin of the American Mathematical Society* **11** (1905), 283–314, p. 285. **Charles Babbage** (1792–1871), On the Theoretical Principles of the Machinery for Calculating Tables, Letter to Dr. Brewster, 6 November, 1822. Appeared in *Brewster's Journal of Science*. Reprinted in *Babbage's Calculating Engines*, E. and F. N. Spon, London, 1889, 216–219, p. 218. Reprinted in The Charles Babbage Institute Reprint Series for the History of Computing, vol. II, Tomash Publishers, Los Angeles/San Francisco CA, 1982. **Marko Petkovšek, Herbert Saul Wilf**, and **Doron Zeilberger**, *A=B*, A K Peters, Natick MA, 1996, ch. 9, p. 193. Reprinted with kind permission.

End of Chapter 24 (page 663): **Michel Eysquem Seigneur de Montaigne** (1533–1592), *Essais*, Au Lecteur, Bordeaux, 1580. **Aules Persius Flaccus** (34–62 AD), *Satura prima*, line 2. Published posthumously. **Markus Werner**, *Zündels Abgang*, Residenz Verlag, 1984, p. 30. © 1984 Residenz Verlag, Salzburg und Wien. Reprinted with kind permission. **Carl Friedrich Gauß** (1777–1855), Disquisitiones generales de congruentiis. Analysis residuorum caput octavum. Article 367. *Werke* **II**, Handschriftlicher Nachlass, Königliche Gesellschaft der Wissenschaften, Göttingen, 1863, 212–242. Reprinted by Georg Olms Verlag, Hildesheim New York, 1973. Published posthumously, see page 348.

Chapter 25 (page 666): **Sherlock Holmes**' most famous words do not occur in the writing of Sir Arthur Conan Doyle (1859–1930). The actor Clifford Hardman (Clive) Brook (1887–1974) said them in his title role in the first talking film *The Return of Sherlock Holmes* about the famous sleuth. Garrett Ford (1898–1945) and Basil Dean wrote the screenplay, Basil Dean directed the movie of 79 minutes' length, Paramount Famous Players Lasky Corporation produced it, and it was released on 18 October 1929. **William Kingdon Clifford** (1845–1879), *The Common Sense of the Exact Sciences*, London, 1885 (appeared posthumously), chap. 1, sect. 7, p. 20. **Izaak Walton** (1593–1683), *The Compleat Angler*, Richard Marriot, London, 1653. Dedication to all readers. p. xvii. **John Updike** (*1932), *Rabbit is Rich*, Fawcett Crest, New York, published by Ballantine Books, Random House, Inc., 1982, ch. IV, p. 301. © Random House, Inc., New York. Reprinted with kind permission. **Jonathan Swift** (1667–1745), *Lemuel Gulliver, Travels into Several Remote Nations of the World*, Part III: A voyage to Laputa, Balribarbi, Glubbdubdrib, Luggnag, and Japan. Ch. V: The grand academy of Lagado, London, 1726.

References (page 698): **Novalis** (Friedrich Leopold Freiherr von Hardenberg) (1772–1801), Mathematische Fragmente. In *Schriften*, hrsg. Richard Samuel, vol. 3, Verlag W. Kohlhammer, Stuttgart, 1983, Handschrift Nr. 241, p. 594. **Eugenio Beltrami** (1835–1900), Foreword to A. Clebsch's *Commemorazione di Giulio Plücker*, *Giornale di matematiche* **11** (1873), Napoli, 153–179, p. 153. **Bartel Leendert van der Waerden** (1903–1996), *Ontwakende wetenschap*, Een woord vooraf. P. Noordhoff N.V., Groningen, 1950, English translation by Arnold Dresden: *Science awakening*, Oxford University Press, 1961. **Raymond Chandler** (1888–1959), *The Simple Art of Murder, An Essay*, Houghton Mifflin, 1950. Copyright © 1950 by Raymond Chandler, © renewed 1978 by Helga Greene. Reprinted by kind permission of Houghton Mifflin Co. All rights reserved.

End of index (page 754): **Al-Qur'an**, Surah 27 an-naml (The ants), 76. **Joseph Liouville** (1809–1882), Œuvres mathématiques d'Évariste Galois, *Journal de mathématiques pures et appliquées* **9** (1846), 381–444, p. 381. **René Descartes** (1596–1650), *Les Principes de la Philosophie, écrits en latin par René Descartes, et traduits en français par un de ses amis*, Henri le Gras, Paris, 1647. Translation by abbé Picot. *Œuvres philosophiques*, tome III, ed. Ferdinand Alquié, Garnier Frères, Paris, 1973, 86–525, p. 525. **Francis Sowerby Macaulay** (1862–1937), *The Algebraic Theory of Modular Systems*, Preface, Cambridge University Press, 1916, p. xiv. **Robert Recorde** (c. 1510–1558), *The Whetstone of Witte*, The preface. London, 1557. **Douglas Noël Adams** (*1952), *The Restaurant at the End of the Universe*, Pan Books, London, 1980. UK and Commonwealth copyright © Serious Productions Ltd 1980. Copyright for the rest of the universe © Completely Unexpected Productions 1980. Reprinted with kind permission of The Crown Publishing Group, New York, of Macmillan Publishers, London, and of Ed Victor Ltd, London.

Moritz' (1914) compilation is a rich source of mathematical quotations.

List of algorithms

List of figures and tables

Wer ein mathematisches Buch nicht mit Andacht ergreift
und es, wie Gottes Wort, ließt, der versteht es nicht.[1]

Novalis (1799)

I giovani [...] imparino [...] ad educarsi di buon'ora
sui capolavori dei grandi maestri, anzichè isterilire
l'ingegno in perpetue esercitazioni da scuola.[2]

Eugenio Beltrami (1873)

Het is niet alleen veel leerrijker, het geeft ook veel meer genot de
klassieke schrijvers zelf te lezen. [...] Daarom zeg ik mijn lezers
met nadruk: geloof niets op mijn woord, maar kijk alles na![3]

Bartel Leendert van der Waerden (1950)

Even Einstein couldn't get very far if three hundred treatises
of the higher physics were published every year.

Raymond Chandler (1950)

References

The numbers in brackets at the end of a reference are the pages on which it is cited. Names of authors and titles are usually given in the same form as on the article or book.

S. A. ABRAMOV (1971), On the summation of rational functions. *Zhurnal vȳcislitel'noi Matematiki i matematicheskoi Fiziki* **11**(4), 1071–1075. English translation in U.S.S.R. Computational Mathematics and Mathematical Physics, 324–330. [635, 639]

L. M. ADLEMAN (1983), On breaking generalized knapsack public key cryptosystems. In *Proceedings of the Fifteenth Annual ACM Symposium on the Theory of Computing*, Boston MA, ACM Press, 402–412. [483]

LEONARD M. ADLEMAN (1994), Algorithmic Number Theory—The Complexity Contribution. In *Proceedings of the 35th Annual IEEE Symposium on Foundations of Computer Science*, Santa Fe NM, ed. SHAFI GOLDWASSER, IEEE Computer Society Press, Los Alamitos CA, 88–113. [506]

LEONARD M. ADLEMAN and MING-DEH A. HUANG (1992), *Primality Testing and Abelian Varieties Over Finite Fields*. Lecture Notes in Mathematics **1512**, Springer-Verlag, Berlin. [504]

LEONARD M. ADLEMAN and HENDRIK W. LENSTRA, JR. (1986), Finding Irreducible Polynomials over Finite Fields. In *Proceedings of the Eighteenth Annual ACM Symposium on the Theory of Computing*, Berkeley CA, ACM Press, 350–355. [397]

LEONARD M. ADLEMAN, CARL POMERANCE, and ROBERT S. RUMELY (1983), On distinguishing prime numbers from composite numbers. *Annals of Mathematics* **117**, 173–206. [504]

G. B. AGNEW, R. C. MULLIN, and S. A. VANSTONE (1993), An Implementation of Elliptic Curve Cryptosystems Over $F_{2^{155}}$. *IEEE Journal on Selected Areas in Communications* **11**(5), 804–813. [554]

ALFRED V. AHO, JOHN E. HOPCROFT, and JEFFREY D. ULLMAN (1974), *The Design and Analysis of Computer Algorithms*. Addison-Wesley, Reading MA. [272, 310]

M. AJTAI (1996), Generating Hard Instances of Lattice Problems. *Electronic Colloquium on Computational Complexity* TR96-007. 29 pages. [555]

M. AJTAI (1997), The Shortest Vector Problem in L_2 is $\mathcal{NP}$-hard for Randomized Reductions. *Electronic Colloquium on Computational Complexity* TR97-047. 33 pages. [555]

[1] He who does not take a mathematical book with reverence and reads it like God's word, does not understand it.

[2] Students [...] should learn [...] to study at an early stage the main works of the great masters instead of making their minds sterile through the everlasting exercises of college.

[3] It is not only more instructive but also more fun to read the classical authors themselves [...] Therefore I implore my readers: do not believe anything I say, verify everything!

MIKLOS AJTAI and CYNTHIA DWORK (1996), A Public-Key Cryptosystem with Worst-Case/Average-Case Equivalence. *Electronic Colloquium on Computational Complexity* TR96-065. 50 pages. [555]

ANDRES ALBANESE, JOHANNES BLÖMER, JEFF EDMONDS, MICHAEL LUBY, and MADHU SUDAN (1994), Priority Encoding Transmission. In *Proceedings of the 35th Annual IEEE Symposium on Foundations of Computer Science*, Santa Fe NM, ed. SHAFI GOLDWASSER, IEEE Computer Society Press, Los Alamitos CA, 604–612. [203]

W. R. ALFORD, ANDREW GRANVILLE, and CARL POMERANCE (1994), There are infinitely many Carmichael numbers. *Annals of Mathematics* **140**, 703–722. [502, 507]

NOGA ALON, JEFF EDMONDS, and MICHAEL LUBY (1995), Linear Time Erasure Codes With Nearly Optimal Recovery. In *Proceedings of the 36th Annual IEEE Symposium on Foundations of Computer Science*, Milwaukee WI, IEEE Computer Society Press, Los Alamitos CA, 512–519. [203]

FRANCESCO AMOROSO (1989), Tests d'appartenance d'après un théorème de Kollár. *Comptes Rendus de l'Académie des Sciences Paris, série I* **309**, 691–694. [592]

GEORGE E. ANDREWS (1994), The Death of Proof? Semi-Rigorous Mathematics? You've Got to Be Kidding! *The Mathematical Intelligencer* **16**(4), 16–18. [661]

N. C. ANKENY (1952), The least quadratic non residue. *Annals of Mathematics* **55**(1), 65–72. [505]

ANONYMOUS (1835), Wie sich die Division mit Zahlen erleichtern und zugleich sicherer ausführen läßt, als auf die gewöhnliche Weise. *Journal für die Reine und Angewandte Mathematik* **13**(3), 209–218. [39]

ANDREAS ANTONIOU (1979), *Digital filters: analysis and design.* McGraw-Hill electrical engineering series: Communications and information theory section, McGraw-Hill, New York. [330]

TOM M. APOSTOL (1983), A Proof that Euler Missed: Evaluating $\zeta(2)$ the Easy Way. *The Mathematical Intelligencer* **5**(3), 59–60. Reprinted in Berggren, Borwein & Borwein (1997), 456–457. [57]

ARCHIMEDES (c. 250 BC), Κύκλου μέτρησις (Measurement of a circle). In *Opera Omnia*, vol. I, ed. I. L. HEIBERG, 231–243. B. G. Teubner, Stuttgart, Germany, 1910. Reprinted 1972. [76]

A. ARWIN (1918), Über Kongruenzen von dem fünften und höheren Graden nach einem Primzahlmodulus. *Arkiv för matematik, astronomi och fysik* **14**(7), 1–46. [393]

C. A. ASMUTH and G. R. BLAKLEY (1982), Pooling, splitting and restituting information to overcome total failure of some channels of communication. In *Proceedings 1982 Symposium on Security and Privacy*, IEEE Computer Society Press, Los Alamitos CA, 156–159. [122]

A. O. L. ATKIN and R. G. LARSON (1982), On a primality test of Solovay and Strassen. *SIAM Journal on Computing* **11**(4), 789–791. [507]

A. O. L. ATKIN and F. MORAIN (1993), Elliptic curves and primality proving. *Mathematics of Computation* **61**(203), 29–68. [509]

L. BABAI (1979), *Monte Carlo algorithms in graph isomorphism testing.* Technical Report 79-10, Département de Mathématique et Statistique, Université de Montréal. [187, 688]

LÁSZLÓ BABAI, EUGENE M. LUKS, and ÁKOS SERESS (1988), Fast Management of Permutation Groups. In *Proceedings of the 29th Annual IEEE Symposium on Foundations of Computer Science*, White Plains NY, IEEE Computer Society Press, Washington DC, 272–282. [688]

E. BACH (1985), *Analytic Methods in the Analysis and Design of Number Theoretic Algorithms.* MIT Press. [505]

ERIC BACH (1990), Number-theoretic algorithms. *Annual Review of Computer Science* **4**, 119–172. [506]

ERIC BACH (1991), Toward a Theory of Pollard's Rho-Method. *Information and Computation* **90**(2), 139–155. [541]

ERIC BACH (1996), Weil Bounds for Singular Curves. *Applicable Algebra in Engineering, Communication and Computing* **7**, 289–298. [542]

ERIC BACH, JOACHIM VON ZUR GATHEN, and HENDRIK W. LENSTRA, JR. (1998), Deterministic Factorization of Polynomials Over Special Finite Fields. Preprint. [397]

ERIC BACH, GARY MILLER, and JEFFREY SHALLIT (1986), Sums of divisors, perfect numbers and factoring. *SIAM Journal on Computing* **15**(4), 1143–1154. [507, 510]

ERIC BACH and JEFFREY SHALLIT (1988), Factoring with cyclotomic polynomials. *Mathematics of Computation* **52**(185), 201–219. [542]

ERIC BACH and JEFFREY SHALLIT (1996), *Algorithmic Number Theory, Vol.1: Efficient Algorithms.* MIT Press, Cambridge MA. [55, 396, 506, 508]

ERIC BACH and JONATHAN SORENSON (1993), Sieve algorithms for perfect power testing. *Algorithmica* **9**, 313–328. [272]

ERIC BACH and JONATHAN SORENSON (1996), Explicit bounds for primes in residue classes. *Mathematics of Computation* **65**(216), 1717–1735. [502]

JOHANN SEBASTIAN BACH (1722), *Das Wohltemperierte Klavier.* BWV 846–893, Part I appeared in 1722, Part II in 1738. [79]

CLAUDE GASPAR BACHET DE MÉZIRIAC (1612), *Problèmes plaisans et délectables, qui se font par les nombres.* Pierre Rigaud, Lyon. [55]

DAVID H. BAILEY, KING LEE, and HORST D. SIMON (1990), Using Strassen's Algorithm to Accelerate the Solution of Linear Systems. *The Journal of Supercomputing* **4**(4), 357–371. [2, 315]

GEORGE A. BAKER, JR. and PETER GRAVES-MORRIS (1996), *Padé Approximants*. Encyclopedia of Mathematics and its Applications **59**, Cambridge University Press, Cambridge, UK, 2nd edition. First edition published in two volumes by Addison-Wesley, Reading MA, 1982. [123]

W. W. ROUSE BALL and H. S. M. COXETER (1974), *Mathematical Recreations & Essays*. University of Toronto Press, Toronto, 12th edition. 1st edition in 1892. [508]

ERWIN H. BAREISS (1968), Sylvester's Identity and Multistep Integer-Preserving Gaussian Elimination. *Mathematics of Computation* **22**, 565–578. [123]

WALTER BAUR and VOLKER STRASSEN (1983), The complexity of partial derivatives. *Theoretical Computer Science* **22**, 317–330. [330]

DAVID BAYER and MICHAEL STILLMAN (1988), On the complexity of computing syzygies. *Journal of Symbolic Computation* **6**, 135–147. [592]

PAUL W. BEAME, RUSSELL IMPAGLIAZZO, JAN KRAJÍČEK, TONIANN PITASSI, and PAVEL PUDLÁK (1996), Lower bounds on Hilbert's Nullstellensatz and propositional proofs. *Proceedings of the London Mathematical Society* **3**, 1–26. [661]

PAUL BEAME and TONIANN PITASSI (1998), Propositional Proof Complexity: Past, Present, and Future. *Bulletin of the European Association for Theoretical Computer Science* **65**, 66–89. [661]

THOMAS BECKER and VOLKER WEISPFENNING (1993), *Gröbner Bases—A Computational Approach to Commutative Algebra*. Graduate Texts in Mathematics **141**, Springer-Verlag, New York. [592]

ERIC TEMPLE BELL (1937), *Men of Mathematics*. Penguin Books Ltd., Harmondsworth, Middlesex. [207, 689, 690, 693]

CHRISTOF BENECKE, ROLAND GRUND, REINHARD HOHBERGER, ADALBERT KERBER, REINHARD LAUE, and THOMAS WIELAND (1995), MOLGEN, a computer algebra system for the generation of molecular graphs. In *Computer Algebra in Science and Engineering*, Bielefeld, Germany, August 1994, eds. J. FLEISCHER, J. GRABMEIER, F. W. HEHL, and W. KÜCHLIN, World Scientific, Singapore, 260–272. [662]

M. BEN-OR (1981), Probabilistic algorithms in finite fields. In *Proceedings of the 22nd Annual IEEE Symposium on Foundations of Computer Science*, Nashville TN, 394–398. [396]

M. BEN-OR, D. KOZEN, and J. REIF (1986), The complexity of elementary algebra and geometry. *Journal of Computer and System Sciences* **32**, 251–264. [593]

MICHAEL BEN-OR and PRASOON TIWARI (1988), A Deterministic Algorithm For Sparse Multivariate Polynomial Interpolation. *Proceedings of the Twentieth Annual ACM Symposium on the Theory of Computing*, Chicago IL, 301–309. [472]

CARLOS A. BERENSTEIN and ALAIN YGER (1990), Bounds for the Degrees in the Division Problem. *Michigan Mathematical Journal* **37**, 25–43. [592]

LENNART BERGGREN, JONATHAN BORWEIN, and PETER BORWEIN, *Pi: A Source Book*. Springer-Verlag, New York. [83, 692, 699, 701, 711, 713, 715, 722, 724]

E. R. BERLEKAMP (1967), Factoring polynomials over finite fields. *Bell System Technical Journal* **46**, 1853–1859. [377, 393, 395, 437]

E. R. BERLEKAMP (1970), Factoring Polynomials Over Large Finite Fields. *Mathematics of Computation* **24**(11), 713–735. [187, 377, 381, 393, 394, 395, 396, 437, 440, 504]

ELWYN R. BERLEKAMP (1984), *Algebraic Coding Theory*. Aegean Park Press. First edition McGraw Hill, New York, 1968. [203, 441]

ELWYN R. BERLEKAMP, ROBERT J. MCELIECE, and HENK C. A. VAN TILBORG (1978), On the Inherent Intractability of Certain Coding Problems. *IEEE Transactions on Information Theory* **IT-24**(3), 384–386. [203]

BENJAMIN P. BERMAN and RICHARD J. FATEMAN (1994), Optical character recognition for typeset mathematics. In *Proceedings of the 1994 International Symposium on Symbolic and Algebraic Computation ISSAC '94*, Oxford, UK, eds. J. VON ZUR GATHEN and M. GIESBRECHT, ACM Press, 348–353. [606]

DANIEL J. BERNSTEIN (1997), Multidigit multiplication for mathematicians. Preprint, http://pobox.com/~djb/papers/m3.dvi. [235]

DANIEL J. BERNSTEIN (1998a), Composing Power Series Over a Finite Ring in Essentially Linear Time. *Journal of Symbolic Computation* **26**(3), 339–341. [330]

DANIEL J. BERNSTEIN (1998b), Detecting perfect powers in essentially linear time. *Mathematics of Computation* **67**(223), 1253–1283. [272]

P. BÉZIER (1970), *Emploi des Machines à Commande Numérique*. Masson & Cie, Paris. English translation: *Numerical Control*, John Wiley & Sons, 1972. [128]

ÉTIENNE BÉZOUT (1764), Recherches sur le degré des équations résultantes de l'évanouissement des inconnues. *Histoire de l'académie royale des sciences*, 288–338. Summary 88–91. [186, 688, 692]

J. BINET (1841), Recherches sur la théorie des nombres entiers et sur la résolution de l'équation indéterminée du premier degré qui n'admet que des solutions entières. *Journal de Mathématiques Pures et Appliquées* **6**, 449–494. [56]

ENRICO BOMBIERI and ALFRED J. VAN DER POORTEN (1995), Continued fractions of algebraic numbers. In *Computational Algebra and Number Theory*, eds. WIEB BOSMA and ALF VAN DER POORTEN, Kluwer Academic Publishers, 137–155. [82]

GEORGE BOOLE (1860), *Calculus of finite differences*. Chelsea Publishing Co., New York. 5th edition 1970. [633]

A. BORODIN and R. MOENCK (1974), Fast Modular Transforms. *Journal of Computer and System Sciences* **8**(3), 366–386. [272, 290]

A. BORODIN and I. MUNRO (1975), *The Computational Complexity of Algebraic and Numeric Problems*. Theory of computation series **1**, American Elsevier Publishing Company, New York. [290]

ALLAN BORODIN and PRASOON TIWARI (1990), On the Decidability of Sparse Univariate Polynomial Interpolation. In *Proceedings of the Twenty-second Annual ACM Symposium on the Theory of Computing*, Baltimore MD, ACM Press, 535–545. [472]

J. M. BORWEIN, P. B. BORWEIN, and D. H. BAILEY (1989), Ramanujan, Modular Equations, and Approximations to Pi or How to Compute One Billion Digits of Pi. *The American Mathematical Monthly* **96**(3), 201–219. Reprinted in Berggren, Borwein & Borwein (1997), 623–641. [76]

R. C. BOSE and D. K. RAY-CHAUDHURI (1960), On A Class of Error Correcting Binary Group Codes. *Information and Control* **3**, 68–79. [203]

WIEB BOSMA and MARC-PAUL VAN DER HULST (1990), Faster primality testing. In *Advances in Cryptology: Proceedings of EUROCRYPT 1989*, Houthalen, Belgium, eds. J. J. QUISQUATER and J. VANDEWALLE. Lecture Notes in Computer Science **434**, Springer-Verlag, 652–656. [508]

JOAN BOYAR (1989), Inferring Sequences Produced by Pseudo-Random Number Generators. *Journal of the ACM* **36**(1), 129–141. [479]

GILLES BRASSARD and PAUL BRATLEY (1996), *Fundamentals of Algorithmics*. Prentice-Hall, Inc., Englewood Cliffs NJ. First published as *Algorithmics - Theory & Pretice*, 1988. [39, 684]

A. BRAUER (1939), On addition chains. *Bulletin of the American Mathematical Society* **45**, 736–739.

RICHARD P. BRENT (1980), An improved Monte Carlo factorization algorithm. *BIT* **20**, 176–184. [541]

R. P. BRENT (1989), Factorization of the eleventh Fermat number (preliminary report). *AMS Abstracts* **10**, 89T-11-73. [516]

RICHARD P. BRENT (1999), Factorization of the tenth Fermat number. *Mathematics of Computation* **68**(225), 429–451. [516, 541]

RICHARD P. BRENT, FRED G. GUSTAVSON, and DAVID Y. Y. YUN (1980), Fast Solution of Toeplitz Systems of Equations and Computation of Padé Approximants. *Journal of Algorithms* **1**, 259–295. [310]

R. P. BRENT and H. T. KUNG (1978), Fast Algorithms for Manipulating Formal Power Series. *Journal of the ACM* **25**(4), 581–595. [330, 331]

RICHARD P. BRENT and JOHN M. POLLARD (1981), Factorization of the Eighth Fermat Number. *Mathematics of Computation* **36**(154), 627–630. Preliminary announcement in *AMS Abstracts* **1** (1980), 565. [516, 541]

ERNEST F. BRICKELL (1984), Solving low density knapsacks. In *Advances in Cryptology: Proceedings of CRYPTO 1983*, Plenum Press, New York, 25–37. [483]

ERNEST F. BRICKELL (1985), Breaking iterated knapsacks. In *Advances in Cryptology: Proceedings of CRYPTO 1984*, Santa Barbara CA. Lecture Notes in Computer Science **196**, Springer-Verlag, 342–358. [483]

EGBERT BRIESKORN and HORST KNÖRRER (1986), *Plane Algebraic Curves*. Birkhäuser Verlag, Basel. [542]

JOHN BRILLHART, D. H. LEHMER, J. L. SELFRIDGE, BRYANT TUCKERMAN, and S. S. WAGSTAFF, JR. (1988), *Factorizations of $b^n \pm 1$, $b = 2, 3, 5, 6, 7, 10, 11, 12$ up to high powers*. Contemporary Mathematics **22**, American Mathematical Society, Providence RI, 2nd edition. [515]

MANUEL BRONSTEIN (1997), *Symbolic Integration I—Transcendental Functions*. Algorithms and Computation in Mathematics **1**, Springer-Verlag, Berlin Heidelberg. [606, 607]

W. S. BROWN (1971), On Euclid's Algorithm and the Computation of Polynomial Greatest Common Divisors. *Journal of the ACM* **18**(4), 478–504. [55, 187, 188]

W. S. BROWN (1978), The Subresultant PRS Algorithm. *ACM Transactions on Mathematical Software* **4**(3), 237–249. [188]

W. S. BROWN and J. F. TRAUB (1971), On Euclid's Algorithm and the Theory of Subresultants. *Journal of the ACM* **18**(4), 505–514. [188, 310]

W. DALE BROWNAWELL (1987), Bounds for the degrees in the Nullstellensatz. *Annals of Mathematics* **126**, 577–591. [592]

BRUNO BUCHBERGER (1965), *Ein Algorithmus zum Auffinden der Basiselemente des Restklassenringes nach einem nulldimensionalen Polynomideal*. PhD thesis, Philosophische Fakultät an der Leopold-Franzens-Universität, Innsbruck, Austria. [565, 583, 591]

B. BUCHBERGER (1970), Ein algorithmisches Kriterium für die Lösbarkeit eines algebraischen Gleichungssystems. *aequationes mathematicae* **4**(3), 271–272 and 374–383. English translation by Michael Abramson and Robert Lumbert in Buchberger & Winkler (1998), 535–545. [591]

B. BUCHBERGER (1976), A theoretical basis for the reduction of polynomials to canonical forms. *ACM SIGSAM Bulletin* **10**(3), 19–29. [591]

B. BUCHBERGER (1985), Gröbner Bases: An Algorithmic Method in Polynomial Ideal Theory. In *Multidimensional Systems Theory*, ed. N. K. BOSE, Mathematics and Its Applications, chapter 6, 184–232. D. Reidel Publishing Company, Dordrecht. [591]

BRUNO BUCHBERGER (1987), History and basic features of the critical–pair/completion procedure. *Journal of Symbolic Computation* **3**, 3–38. [591]

BRUNO BUCHBERGER and FRANZ WINKLER, *Gröbner Bases and Applications*. London Mathematical Society Lecture Note Series **251**, Cambridge University Press, Cambridge, UK. [592, 702]

JAMES R. BUNCH and JOHN E. HOPCROFT (1974), Triangular Factorization and Inversion by Fast Matrix Multiplication. *Mathematics of Computation* **28**(125), 231–236. [330]

PETER BÜRGISSER (1998), On the Parallel Complexity of the Polynomial Ideal Membership Problem. *Journal of Complexity* **14**, 176–189. [590]

P. BÜRGISSER, M. CLAUSEN, and M. A. SHOKROLLAHI (1996), *Algebraic Complexity Theory*. Grundlehren der mathematischen Wissenschaften **315**, Springer-Verlag. [81, 210, 272, 316, 330]

S. BUSS, R. IMPAGLIAZZO, J. KRAJÍČEK, P. PUDLÁK, A. A. RAZBOROV, and J. SGALL (1996/97), Proof complexity in algebraic systems and bounded depth Frege systems with modular counting. *computational complexity* **6**(3), 256–298. [661]

M. C. R. BUTLER (1954), On the reducibility of polynomials over a finite field. *Quarterly Journal of Mathematics Oxford* **5**(2), 102–107. [395]

JOHN J. CADE (1987), A modification of a broken public-key cipher. In *Advances in Cryptology: Proceedings of CRYPTO 1986*, Santa Barbara CA, ed. A. M. ODLYZKO. Lecture Notes in Computer Science **263**, Springer-Verlag, 64–83. [550]

PAUL CAMION (1980), Un algorithme de construction des idempotents primitifs d'idéaux d'algèbres sur $\mathbb{F}_q$. *Comptes Rendus de l'Académie des Sciences Paris* **291**, 479–482. [395]

PAUL CAMION (1981), Factorisation des polynômes de $\mathbb{F}_q$. *Revue du CETHEDEC* **18**, 1–17. [394]

PAUL CAMION (1982), Un algorithme de construction des idempotents primitifs d'idéaux d'algèbres sur $\mathbb{F}_q$. *Annals of Discrete Mathematics* **12**, 55–63. [394]

PAUL F. CAMION (1983), Improving an Algorithm for Factoring Polynomials over a Finite Field and Constructing Large Irreducible Polynomials. *IEEE Transactions on Information Theory* **IT-29**(3), 378–385. [394]

E. R. CANFIELD, PAUL ERDŐS, and CARL POMERANCE (1983), On a problem of Oppenheim concerning 'Factorisatio Numerorum'. *Journal of Number Theory* **17**, 1–28. [541]

LÉANDRO CANIGLIA, ANDRÉ GALLIGO, and JOOS HEINTZ (1988), Borne simple exponentielle pour les degrés dans le théorème des zéros sur un corps de caractéristique quelconque. *Comptes Rendus de l'Académie des Sciences Paris, série I* **307**, 255–258. [593]

LEANDRO CANIGLIA, ANDRÉ GALLIGO, and JOOS HEINTZ (1989), Some new effectivity bounds in computational geometry. In *Algebraic Algorithms and Error-Correcting Codes: AAECC-6*, Rome, Italy, 1988, ed. T. MORA, Lecture Notes in Computer Science **357**, 131–152. Springer-Verlag. [592]

JOHN CANNY (1987), A New Algebraic Method for Robot Motion Planning and Real Geometry. In *Proceedings of the 28th Annual IEEE Symposium on Foundations of Computer Science*, Los Angeles CA, IEEE Computer Society Press, Washington DC, 39–48. [593]

JOHN F. CANNY (1988), *The Complexity of Robot Motion Planning*. ACM Doctoral Dissertation Award 1987, MIT Press, Cambridge MA. [593]

DAVID G. CANTOR (1989), On Arithmetical Algorithms over Finite Fields. *Journal of Combinatorial Theory, Series A* **50**, 285–300. [265, 266, 267, 269, 272]

DAVID G. CANTOR and ERICH KALTOFEN (1991), On fast multiplication of polynomials over arbitrary algebras. *Acta Informatica* **28**, 693–701. [232, 234]

DAVID G. CANTOR and HANS ZASSENHAUS (1981), A New Algorithm for Factoring Polynomials Over Finite Fields. *Mathematics of Computation* **36**(154), 587–592. [381, 393]

R. D. CARMICHAEL (1909/10), Note on a new number theory function. *Bulletin of the American Mathematical Society* **16**, 232–238. [506]

R. D. CARMICHAEL (1912), On composite numbers P which satisfy the Fermat congruence $a^{P-1} \equiv 1 \mod P$. *The American Mathematical Monthly* **19**, 22–27. [506]

THOMAS R. CARON and ROBERT D. SILVERMAN (1988), Parallel implementation of the quadratic sieve. *The Journal of Supercomputing* **1**, 273–290. [506, 541]

PAUL DE FAGET DE CASTELJAU (1985), *Shape mathematics and CAD*. Hermes Publishing, Paris. [128]

PIETRO ANTONIO CATALDI (1513), *Trattato del modo brevissimo di trouare la radice quadra delli numeri*. Bartolomeo Cochi, Bologna. [82]

AUGUSTIN CAUCHY (1821), Sur la formule de Lagrange relative à l'interpolation. In *Cours d'analyse de l'École Royale Polytechnique (Analyse algébrique)*, Note V. Imprimerie royale Debure frères, Paris. *Œuvres Complètes*, IIe série, tome III, Gauthier-Villars, Paris, 1897, 429–433. [123]

AUGUSTIN CAUCHY (1840), Mémoire sur l'élimination d'une variable entre deux équations algébriques. In *Exercices d'analyse et de physique mathématique, tome 1er*. Bachelier, Paris. *Œuvres Complètes*, IIe série, tome 11. Gauthier-Villars, Paris, 1913, 466–509. [186]

AUGUSTIN CAUCHY (1841), Mémoire sur diverses formules relatives à l'Algèbre et à la théorie des nombres. *Comptes Rendus de l'Académie des Sciences Paris* **12**, p. 813 ff. *Œuvres Complètes*, Ire série, tome 6, Gauthier-Villars, Paris, 1888, 113–146. [122]

AUGUSTIN CAUCHY (1847), Mémoire sur les racines des équivalences correspondantes à des modules quelconques premiers ou non premiers, et sur les avantages que présente l'emploi de ces racines dans la théorie des nombres. *Comptes Rendus de l'Académie des Sciences Paris* **25**, p. 37 ff. *Œuvres Complètes*, Ire série, tome 10, Gauthier-Villars, Paris, 1897, 324–333. [272]

B. F. CAVINESS (1970), On Canonical Forms and Simplification. *Journal of the Association for Computing Machinery* **17**(2), 385–396. [606]

ARTHUR CAYLEY (1848), On the theory of elimination. *The Cambridge and Dublin Mathematical Journal* **3**, 116–120. Also *Cambridge Mathematical Journal* **7**. [186]

MIGUEL DE CERVANTES SAAVEDRA (1615), *El ingenioso cavallero Don Quixote de la Mancha, segunda parte*. Francisco de Robles, Madrid. [82]

JASBIR S. CHAHAL (1995), Manin's Proof of the Hasse Inequality Revisited. *Nieuw Archief voor Wiskunde, Vierde serie* **13**(2), 219–232. [542]

BRUCE W. CHAR, KEITH O. GEDDES, and GASTON H. GONNET (1989), GCDHEU: Heuristic Polynomial GCD Algorithm Based On Integer GCD Computation. *Journal of Symbolic Computation* **7**, 31–48. Extended Abstract in *Proceedings of EUROSAM '84*, ed. JOHN FITCH, Lecture Notes in Computer Science **174**, Springer-Verlag, 285–296. [191]

N. CHEBOTAREV (N. Tschebotareff) (1926), Die Bestimmung der Dichtigkeit einer Menge von Primzahlen, welche zu einer gegebenen Substitutionsklasse gehören. *Mathematische Annalen* **95**, 191–228. [415, 440]

П. Л. ЧЕБЫШЕВ (P. L. CHEBYSHEV) (1849), Объ опредѣленіи числа простыхъ чиселъ не превосходящихъ данной велигины. (Sur la fonction qui détermine la totalité des nombres premiers inférieurs à une limite donnée). *Mémoires présentés à l'Académie Impériale des sciences de St.-Pétersbourg par divers savants* **6**, 141–157. *Journal de Mathématiques Pures et Appliquées, I série* **17** (1852), 341–365. *Œuvres I*, eds. A. MARKOFF and N. SONIN, reprint by Chelsea Publishing Co., New York, 26–48. [507]

P. L. CHEBYSHEV (1852), Mémoire sur les nombres premiers. *Journal de Mathématiques Pures et Appliquées, I série* **17**, 366–390. *Mémoires présentées à l'Académie Impériale des sciences de St.-Pétersbourg par divers savants* **6** (1854), 17–33. *Œuvres I*, eds. A. MARKOFF and N. SONIN, reprint by Chelsea Publishing Co., New York, 49–70. [507]

ZHI-ZHONG CHEN and MING-YANG KAO (1997), Reducing Randomness via Irrational Numbers. In *Proceedings of the Twenty-ninth Annual ACM Symposium on the Theory of Computing*, El Paso TX, ACM Press, 200–209. [187]

A. L. CHISTOV (1990), Efficient Factoring Polynomials over Local Fields and Its Applications. In *Proceedings of the International Congress of Mathematicians 1990*, Kyoto, Japan, vol. II, 1509–1519. Springer-Verlag. [441]

A. L. CHISTOV and D. YU. GRIGOR'EV (1984), Complexity of quantifier elimination in the theory of algebraically closed fields. In *Proceedings of the 11th International Symposium Mathematical Foundations of Computer Science 1984*, Praha, Czechoslovakia. Lecture Notes in Computer Science **176**, Springer-Verlag, Berlin, 17–31. [593]

BENNY CHOR and RONALD L. RIVEST (1988), A knapsack–type public key cryptosystem based on arithmetic in finite fields. *IEEE Transactions on Information Theory* **IT-34**(5), 901–909. *Advances in Cryptology: Proceedings of CRYPTO 1984*, Santa Barbara CA, Lecture Notes in Computer Science **196**, Springer-Verlag, New York, 1985, 54–65. [483]

C.-C. CHOU, Y.-F. DENG, G. LI, and Y. WANG (1995), Parallelizing Strassen's Method for Matrix Multiplication on Distributed-Memory MIMD Architectures. *Computers and Mathematics with Applications* **30**(2), 49–69. [330]

MICHAEL CLAUSEN, ANDREAS DRESS, JOHANNES GRABMEIER, and MAREK KARPINSKI (1991), On Zero–Testing and Interpolation of k-Sparse Multivariate Polynomials over Finite Fields. *Theoretical Computer Science* **84**, 151–164. [472]

MATTHEW CLEGG, JEFFREY EDMONDS, and RUSSELL IMPAGLIAZZO (1996), Using the Groebner basis algorithm to find proofs of unsatisfiability. In *Proceedings of the Twenty-eighth Annual ACM Symposium on the Theory of Computing*, Philadelphia PA, ACM Press, 174–183. [643]

H. COHEN and A. K. LENSTRA (1987), Implementation of a New Primality Test. *Mathematics of Computation* **48**(177), 103–121. [508]

H. COHEN and H. W. LENSTRA, JR. (1984), Primality Testing and Jacobi Sums. *Mathematics of Computation* **42**(165), 297–330. [508]

G. E. COLLINS (1966), Polynomial remainder sequences and determinants. *The American Mathematical Monthly* **73**, 708–712. [186, 188]

GEORGE E. COLLINS (1967), Subresultants and Reduced Polynomial Remainder Sequences. *Journal of the ACM* **14**(1), 128–142. [186, 188, 310]

G. E. COLLINS (1973), Computer algebra of polynomials and rational functions. *The American Mathematical Monthly* **80**, 725–55. [188]

G. E. COLLINS (1975), *Quantifier elimination for real closed fields by cylindrical algebraic decomposition.* Lecture Notes in Computer Science **33**, Springer-Verlag. [593]

G. E. COLLINS (1979), Factoring univariate integral polynomials in polynomial average time. In *Proceedings of EUROSAM '79*, Marseille, France. Lecture Notes in Computer Science **72**, 317–329. [430, 440]

GEORGE E. COLLINS and MARK J. ENCARNACIÓN (1996), Improved Techniques for Factoring Univariate Polynomials. *Journal of Symbolic Computation* **21**, 313–327. [440]

S. A. COOK (1966), *On the minimum computation time of functions.* Doctoral Thesis, Harvard University, Cambridge MA. [234, 272]

STEPHEN A. COOK (1971), The Complexity of Theorem–Proving Procedures. In *Proceedings of the Third Annual ACM Symposium on the Theory of Computing*, Shaker Heights OH, ACM Press, 151–158. [686]

JAMES W. COOLEY (1987), The Re–Discovery of the Fast Fourier Transform Algorithm. *Mikrochimica Acta* **3**, 33–45. [234, 691]

JAMES W. COOLEY (1990), How the FFT Gained Acceptance. In *A History of Scientific Computing*, ed. STEPHEN G. NASH, ACM Press, New York, and Addison-Wesley, Reading MA, 133–140. [234]

JAMES W. COOLEY and JOHN W. TUKEY (1965), An Algorithm for the Machine Calculation of Complex Fourier Series. *Mathematics of Computation* **19**, 297–301. [220, 234]

GENE COOPERMAN, SANDRA FEISEL, JOACHIM VON ZUR GATHEN, and GEORGE HAVAS (1998), Gcd of many integers. Preprint. [187]

D. COPPERSMITH (1993), Solving Linear Equations Over $GF(2)$: Block Lanczos Algorithm. *Linear Algebra and its Applications* **192**, 33–60. [331]

DON COPPERSMITH (1994), Solving homogeneous linear equations over GF(2) via block Wiedemann algorithm. *Mathematics of Computation* **62**(205), 333–350. [330]

DON COPPERSMITH and SHMUEL WINOGRAD (1990), Matrix Multiplication via Arithmetic Progressions. *Journal of Symbolic Computation* **9**, 251–280. [330, 396]

THOMAS H. CORMEN, CHARLES E. LEISERSON, and RONALD L. RIVEST (1990), *Introduction to Algorithms.* MIT Press, Cambridge MA. [39, 344]

JAMES COWIE, BRUCE DODSON, R. MARIJE ELKENBRACHT-HUIZING, ARJEN K. LENSTRA, PETER L. MONTGOMERY, and JÖRG ZAYER (1996), A World Wide Number Field Sieve Factoring Record: On to 512 Bits. In *Advances in Cryptology—ASIACRYPT '96*. Lecture Notes in Computer Science **1163**, Springer-Verlag, 382–394. [516, 543]

DAVID A. COX (1989), *Primes of the Form $x^2 + ny^2$: Fermat, Class Field Theory, and Complex Multiplication.* John Wiley & Sons, New York. [542]

DAVID COX, JOHN LITTLE, and DONAL O'SHEA (1997), *Ideals, Varieties, and Algorithms: An Introduction to Computational Algebraic Geometry and Commutative Algebra.* Undergraduate Texts in Mathematics, Springer-Verlag, New York, 2nd edition. First edition 1992. [588, 591, 592]

DAVID COX, JOHN LITTLE, and DONAL O'SHEA (1998), *Using Algebraic Geometry.* Graduate Texts in Mathematics **185**, Springer-Verlag, New York. [591]

GABRIEL CRAMER (1750), *Introduction a l'analyse des lignes courbes algébriques.* Frères Cramer & Cl. Philibert, Genève. [187, 688]

JOHN N. CROSSLEY and ALAN S. HENRY (1990), Thus Spake al-Khwārizmī: A Translation of the Text of Cambridge University Library Ms. Ii.vi.5. *Historia Mathematica* **17**, 103–131. [691]

ALLAN J. C. CUNNINGHAM and H. J. WOODALL (1925), *Factorization of $(y^n \mp 1)$, y = 2, 3, 5, 6, 7, 10, 11, 12 up to high powers (n).* Francis Hodgson, London. [515]

IVAN DAMGÅRD, PETER LANDROCK, and CARL POMERANCE (1993), Average case error estimates for the strong probable prime test. *Mathematics of Computation* **61**(203), 177–194. [507]

PIERRE DÈBES (1996), Hilbert subsets and s-integral points. *Manuscripta Mathematica* **89**, 107–137. [471]

RICHARD A. DEMILLO and RICHARD J. LIPTON (1978), A probabilistic remark on algebraic program testing. *Information Processing Letters* **7**(4), 193–195. [81, 187]

DOROTHY ELIZABETH ROBLING DENNING (1982), *Cryptography and Data Security.* Addison-Wesley, Reading MA. Reprinted with corrections, January 1983. [555]

ANGEL DÍAZ and ERICH KALTOFEN (1995), On Computing Greatest Common Divisors with Polynomials Given By Black Boxes for Their Evaluations. In *Proceedings of the 1995 International Symposium on*

Symbolic and Algebraic Computation ISSAC '95, Montreal, Canada, ed. A. H. M. LEVELT, ACM Press, 232–239. [187]

ANGEL DÍAZ and ERICH KALTOFEN (1998), FOXBOX: A System for Manipulating Symbolic Objects in Black Box Representation. In *Proceedings of the 1998 International Symposium on Symbolic and Algebraic Computation ISSAC '98*, Rostock, Germany, ed. OLIVER GLOOR, ACM Press, 30–37. [472]

WHITFIELD DIFFIE (1988), The First Ten Years of Public-Key Cryptography. *Proceedings of the IEEE* **76**(5), 560–577. [555]

WHITFIELD DIFFIE and MARTIN E. HELLMAN (1976), New directions in cryptography. *IEEE Transactions on Information Theory* **IT-22**(6), 644–654. [477, 549, 550, 552, 556]

G. LEJEUNE DIRICHLET (1837), Beweis des Satzes, dass jede unbegrenzte arithmetische Progression, deren erstes Glied und Differenz ganze Zahlen ohne gemeinschaftlichen Factor sind, unendlich viele Primzahlen enthält. *Abhandlungen der Königlich Preussischen Akademie der Wissenschaften*, 45–81. *Werke*, Erster Band, ed. L. KRONECKER, 1889, 315–342. Reprint by Chelsea Publishing Co., 1969. [502]

G. LEJEUNE DIRICHLET (1842), Verallgemeinerung eines Satzes aus der Lehre von den Kettenbrüchen nebst einigen Anwendungen auf die Theorie der Zahlen. *Bericht über die Verhandlungen der Königlich Preussischen Akademie der Wissenschaften*, 93–95. *Werke*, Erster Band, ed. L. KRONECKER, 1889, 635–638. Reprint by Chelsea Publishing Co., 1969. [480, 483]

G. LEJEUNE DIRICHLET (1849), Über die Bestimmung der mittleren Werthe in der Zahlentheorie. *Abhandlungen der Königlich Preussischen Akademie der Wissenschaften*, 69–83. *Werke*, Zweiter Band, ed. L. KRONECKER, 1897, 51–66. Reprint by Chelsea Publishing Co., 1969. [57]

P. G. LEJEUNE DIRICHLET (1863), *Vorlesungen über Zahlentheorie*, herausgegeben von R. DEDEKIND, Erste Auflage, Braunschweig. Corrected reprint, Chelsea Publishing Co., New York, 1968. [671]

JOHN D. DIXON (1981), Asymptotically Fast Factorization of Integers. *Mathematics of Computation* **36**(153), 255–260. [515, 523, 543]

BRUCE DODSON and ARJEN K. LENSTRA (1995), NFS with Four Large Primes: An Explosive Experiment. In *Advances in Cryptology: Proceedings of CRYPTO 1995*, Santa Barbara CA, ed. DON COPPERSMITH. Lecture Notes in Computer Science **963**, Springer-Verlag, 372–385. [543]

JEAN LOUIS DORNSTETTER (1987), On the Equivalence Between Berlekamp's and Euclid's Algorithms. *IEEE Transactions on Information Theory* **IT-33**(3), 428–431. [203]

THOMAS W. DUBÉ (1990), The structure of polynomial ideals and Gröbner bases. *SIAM Journal on Computing* **19**(4), 750–773. [592]

RAYMOND DUBOIS (1971), *Utilisation d'un théorème de Fermat à la découverte des nombres premiers et notes sur les nombres de Fibonacci*. Albert Blanchard, Paris. [507]

ATHANASE DUPRÉ (1846), Sur le nombre des divisions à effectuer pour obtenir le plus grand commun diviseur entre deux nombres entiers. *Journal de Mathématiques Pures et Appliquées* **11**, 41–64. [56]

WAYNE EBERLY and ERICH KALTOFEN (1997), On Randomized Lanczos Algorithms. In *Proceedings of the 1997 International Symposium on Symbolic and Algebraic Computation ISSAC '97*, Maui HI, ed. WOLFGANG W. KÜCHLIN, ACM Press, 176–183. [331]

JACK EDMONDS (1967), Systems of Distinct Representatives and Linear Algebra. *Journal of Research of the National Bureau of Standards* **71B**(4), 241–245. [123]

D. EISENBUD and L. ROBBIANO (1993), eds., *Computational algebraic geometry and commutative algebra*. Symposia Mathematica **34**, Cambridge University Press, Cambridge, UK. [591]

D. EISENBUD and B. STURMFELS (1996), Binomial ideals. *Duke Mathematical Journal* **84**(1), 1–45. [661]

G. EISENSTEIN (1844), Einfacher Algorithmus zur Bestimmung des Werthes von $\left(\frac{a}{b}\right)$. *Journal für die Reine und Angewandte Mathematik* **27**(4), 317–318. [508]

SHALOSH B. EKHAD (1990), A Very Short Proof of Dixon's Theorem. *Journal of Combinatorial Theory, Series A* **54**, 141–142. [661]

SHALOSH B. EKHAD and SOL TRE (1990), A Purely Verification Proof of the First Rogers–Ramanujan Identity. *Journal of Combinatorial Theory, Series A* **54**, 309–311. [661]

PETER VAN EMDE BOAS (1980), *Another $\mathcal{NP}$-complete partition problem and the complexity of computing short vectors in a lattice*. Technical Report 81-04, Department of Mathematics, University of Amsterdam. [554]

IOANNIS Z. EMIRIS and BERNARD MOURRAIN (1999), Computer Algebra Methods for Studying and Computing Molecular Conformations. *Algorithmica*. Special Issue on Algorithms for Computational Biology, to appear. [662]

LEONHARD EULER (1732/33), Observationes de theoremate quodam Fermatiano aliisque ad numeros primos spectantibus. *Commentarii Academiae Scientiarum Imperialis Petropolitanae* **6**, 103–107. Eneström 26. *Opera Omnia*, ser. 1, vol. 2, B. G. Teubner, Leipzig, 1915, 1–5. [70, 81, 487, 516]

LEONHARD EULER (1734/35a), Solutio problematis arithmetici de inveniendo numero qui per datos numeros divisus relinquat data residua. *Commentarii Academiae Scientiarum Imperialis Petropolitanae* **7**, 46–66. Eneström 36. *Opera Omnia*, ser. 1, vol. 2, B. G. Teubner, Leipzig, 1915, 18–32. [122]

LEONHARD EULER (1734/35b), De summis serierum reciprocarum. *Commentarii Academiae Scientiarum Petropolitanae* **7**, 123–134. Eneström 41. *Opera Omnia*, ser. 1, vol. 14, B. G. Teubner, Leipzig, 1925, 73–86. [57]

LEONHARD EULER (1736a), *Mechanica sive motus scientia analytice exposita, Tomus I.* Typographia Academia Scientiarum, Petropolis. *Opera Omnia*, ser. 2, vol. 1, B. G. Teubner, Leipzig, 1912. [83]

LEONHARD EULER (1736b), Theorematum quorundam ad numeros primos spectantium demonstratio. *Commentarii Academiae Scientiarum Imperalis Petropolitanae* **8**, 1741, 141–146. Eneström 54. *Opera Omnia*, ser. 1, vol. 2, B. G. Teubner, Leipzig, 1915, 33–37. [81]

LEONHARD EULER (1737), De fractionibus continuis dissertatio. *Commentarii Academiae Scientiarum Imperalis Petropolitanae* **9**, 1744, 98–137. Eneström 71. *Opera Omnia*, ser. 1, vol. 14, B. G. Teubner, Leipzig, 1925, 187–215. [82, 84]

LEONHARD EULER (1743), Démonstration de la somme de cette suite $1 + \frac{1}{4} + \frac{1}{9} + \frac{1}{16} + \frac{1}{25} + \frac{1}{36} +$ etc. *Journal littéraire d'Allemagne, de Suisse et du Nord (La Haye)* **2**, 115–127. *Bibliotheca Mathematica, Serie 3*, **8** 1907–1908, 54–60. Eneström 63. *Opera Omnia*, ser. 1, vol. 14, 177–186. [57]

LEONHARD EULER (1747/48), Theoremata circa divisores numerorum. *Novi Commentarii Academiae Scientiarum Imperalis Petropolitanae* **1**, 20–48. Summarium ibidem, 35–37. Eneström 134. *Opera Omnia*, ser. 1, vol. 2, B. G. Teubner, Leipzig, 1915, 62–85. [122, 487, 516]

LEONHARD EULER (1748a), *Introductio in analysin infinitorum, tomus primus et secundus.* M.-M. Bousquet, Lausanne. *Opera Omnia*, ser. 1, vol. 8 and 9. Teubner, Leipzig, 1922/1945. [55, 83, 123]

LEONHARD EULER (1748b), Sur une contradiction apparente dans la doctrine des lignes courbes. *Mémoires de l'Académie des Sciences de Berlin* **4**, 1750, 219–233. Eneström 147. *Opera Omnia*, ser. 1, vol. 26, Orell Füssli, Zürich, 1953, 34–45. [187]

LEONHARD EULER (1748c), Démonstration sur le nombre des points où deux lignes des ordres quelconques peuvent se couper. *Mémoires de l'Académie des Sciences de Berlin* **4**, 1750, 234–248. Eneström 148. *Opera Omnia*, ser. 1, vol. 26, Orell Füssli, Zürich, 1953, 46–59. [186, 187]

LEONHARD EULER (1754/55), Demonstratio theorematis Fermatiani omnem numerum sive integrum sive fractum esse summam quatuor pauciorumve quadratorum. *Novi Commentarii Academiae Scientiarum Imperalis Petropolitanae* **5**, 13–58. Summarium ibidem 6–7. Eneström 242. *Opera Omnia*, ser. 1, vol. 1, B. G. Teubner, Leipzig, 1915, 339–372. [394]

LEONHARD EULER (1758/59), Theoremata circa residua ex divisione potestatum relicta. *Novi Commentarii Academiae Scientiarum Imperalis Petropolitanae* **7**, 49–82. Eneström 262. *Opera Omnia*, ser. 1, vol. 2, B. G. Teubner, Leipzig, 1915, 493–518. [70, 394]

LEONHARD EULER (1760/61), Theoremata arithmetica nova methodo demonstrata. *Novi Commentarii Academiae Scientiarum Imperalis Petropolitanae* **8**, 74–104. Summarium ibidem 15–18. Eneström 271. *Opera Omnia*, ser. 1, vol. 2, B. G. Teubner, Leipzig, 1915, 531–555. [122]

LEONHARD EULER (1762/63), Specimen algorithmi singularis. *Novi Commentarii Academiae Scientiarum Imperalis Petropolitanae* **9**, 1764, 53–69. Summarium ibidem 10–13. Eneström 281. *Opera Omnia*, ser. 1, vol. 15, B. G. Teubner, Leipzig, 1927, 31–49. [82]

LEONHARD EULER (1764), Nouvelle méthode d'éliminer les quantités inconnues des équations. *Mémoires de l'Académie des Sciences de Berlin* **20**, 1766, 91–104. Eneström 310. *Opera Omnia*, ser. 1, vol. 6, B. G. Teubner, Leipzig, 1921, 197–211. [186, 187]

LEONHARD EULER (1783), De eximio methodi interpolationum in serierum doctrina. *Opuscula analytica* **1**, 157–210. Eneström 555. *Opera Omnia*, ser. 1, vol. 15, Teubner, Leipzig, 1927, 435–497. [125]

SERGEI EVDOKIMOV (1994), Factorization of Polynomials over Finite Fields in Subexponential Time under GRH. In *Proceedings of the First International ANTS Symposium.* Lecture Notes in Computer Science **877**, 209–219. [397]

ROBERT M. FANO (1949), *The transmission of information.* Technical Report 65, M.I.T., Research Laboratory of Electronics. [291]

ROBERT M. FANO (1961), *Transmission of Information.* MIT Press. [291]

J. C. FAUGÈRE, P. GIANNI, D. LAZARD, and T. MORA (1993), Efficient computation of zero-dimensional Gröbner bases by change of ordering. *Journal of Symbolic Computation* **16**, 329–344. [593]

W. FELLER (1971), *An Introduction to Probability Theory and its Applications.* John Wiley & Sons, 2nd edition. [681]

CHARLES M. FIDUCCIA (1972a), Polynomial evaluation via the division algorithm: the fast Fourier transform revisited. In *Proceedings of the Fourth Annual ACM Symposium on the Theory of Computing,* Denver CO, ACM Press, 88–93. [290]

CHARLES M. FIDUCCIA (1972b), On obtaining upper bounds on the complexity of matrix multiplication. In *Complexity of computer computations,* eds. RAYMOND E. MILLER and JAMES W. THATCHER, 31–40. Plenum Press, New York. [330]

CHARLES M. FIDUCCIA (1973), *On the Algebraic Complexity of Matrix Multiplication.* PhD thesis, Brown University, Providence RI. [330]

P.-J. E. FINCK (1841), *Traité élémentaire d'arithmétique à l'usage des candidats aux écoles spéciales.* Derivaux, Strasbourg. [56]

NOAÏ FITCHAS, ANDRÉ GALLIGO, and JACQUES MORGENSTERN (1987), *Algorithmes rapides en séquentiel et en parallèle pour l'élimination de quantificateurs en géometrie élémentaire.* Séminaire Structures Ordonnées, U. E. R. de Mathématiques, Université de Paris VII. [593]

NOAÏ FITCHAS, ANDRÉ GALLIGO, and JACQUES MORGENSTERN (1990), Precise sequential and parallel complexity bounds for quantifier elimination over algebraically closed fields. *Journal of Pure and Applied Algebra* **67**, 1–14. [593]

PHILIPPE FLAJOLET, XAVIER GOURDON, and DANIEL PANARIO (1996), Random Polynomials and Polynomial Factorization. In *Proceedings of the 23rd International Colloquium on Automata, Languages and Programming ICALP 1996*, Paderborn, Germany, eds. F. MEYER AUF DER HEIDE and B. MONIEN. Lecture Notes in Computer Science **1099**, Springer-Verlag, 232–243. INRIA Rapport de Recherche No 3370, March 1998, 28 pages. [394]

PHILIPPE FLAJOLET and ANDREW ODLYZKO (1990), Singularity analysis of generating functions. *SIAM Journal on Discrete Mathematics* **3**(2), 216–240. [661]

P. FLAJOLET, B. SALVY, and P. ZIMMERMANN (1989a), Lambda–Upsilon–Omega: An Assistant Algorithms Analyzer. In *Algebraic Algorithms and Error-Correcting Codes: AAECC-6*, Rome, Italy, 1988, ed. T. MORA. Lecture Notes in Computer Science **357**, Springer-Verlag, 201–212. [661]

PHILIPPE FLAJOLET, BRUNO SALVY, and PAUL ZIMMERMANN (1989b), *Lambda–Upsilon–Omega—The 1989 CookBook.* Rapport de Recherche 1073, INRIA. 116 pages. [661]

PHILIPPE FLAJOLET, BRUNO SALVY, and PAUL ZIMMERMANN (1991), Automatic average-case analysis of algorithms. *Theoretical Computer Science* **79**, 37–109. [661]

MENSO FOLKERTS (1997), *Die älteste lateinische Schrift über das indische Rechnen nach al-Ḫwārizmī.* Abhandlungen der Bayerischen Akademie der Wissenschaften, Philosophisch-historische Klasse, neue Folge **113**, Verlag der Bayerischen Akademie der Wissenschaften, München. C. H. Beck'sche Verlagsbuchhandlung, München. [272, 691]

JEAN BAPTISTE JOSEPH FOURIER (1822), *Théorie Analytique de la Chaleur.* Firmin Didot, Paris. [234, 691]

TIMOTHY S. FREEMAN, GREGORY M. IMIRZIAN, ERICH KALTOFEN, and LAKSHMAN YAGATI (1988), *Dagwood:* a system for manipulating polynomials given by straight-line programs. *ACM Transactions on Mathematical Software* **14**(3), 218–240. [472]

RŪSIŅŠ FREIVALDS (1977), Probabilistic machines can use less running time. In *Information Processing 77—Proceedings of IFIP Congress 77*, ed. B. GILCHRIST, North-Holland, Amsterdam, 839–842. [81]

ALAN M. FRIEZE, JOHAN HASTAD, RAVI KANNAN, JEFFREY C. LAGARIAS, and ADI SHAMIR (1988), Reconstructing truncated integer variables satisfying linear congruences. *SIAM Journal on Computing* **17**(2), 262–280. [479]

FERDINAND GEORG FROBENIUS (1881), Über Relationen zwischen den Näherungsbrüchen von Potenzreihen. *Journal für die Reine und Angewandte Mathematik* **90**, 1–17. *Gesammelte Abhandlungen*, Band 2, herausgegeben von J.-P. SERRE, Springer-Verlag, Berlin, 1968, 47–63. [123, 186]

G. FROBENIUS (1896), Über Beziehungen zwischen den Primidealen eines algebraischen Körpers und den Substitutionen seiner Gruppe. *Sitzungsberichte der Königlich Preussischen Akademie der Wissenschaften, Berlin*, 689–702. [415, 440]

A. FRÖHLICH and J. C. SHEPHERDSON (1955–56), Effective procedures in field theory. *Philosophical Transactions of the Royal Society of London* **248**, 407–432. [395]

W. FULTON (1969), *Algebraic Curves.* W. A. Benjamin, Inc., New York. [542]

G. GALLO and B. MISHRA (1991), Wu-Ritt Characteristic sets and Their Complexity. In *Discrete and Computational Geometry: Papers from the DIMACS Special Year*, eds. JACOB E. GOODMAN, RICHARD POLLACK, and WILLIAM STEIGER. DIMACS Series in Discrete Mathematics and Theoretical Computer Science **6**, American Mathematical Society and ACM, 111–136. [593]

É. GALOIS (1830), Sur la théorie des nombres. *Bulletin des sciences mathématiques Férussac* **13**, 428–435. See also *Journal de Mathématiques Pures et Appliquées* **11** (1846), 398–407, and *Écrits et mémoires d'Évariste Galois*, eds. ROBERT BOURGNE and J.-P. AZRA, Gauthier-Villars, Paris, 1962, 112–128. [187, 393, 396, 688, 691]

T. ELGAMAL (1985), A Public Key Cryptosystem and a Signature Scheme Based on Discrete Logarithms. *IEEE Transactions on Information Theory* **IT-31**(4), 469–472. [555]

SHUHONG GAO and JOACHIM VON ZUR GATHEN (1994), Berlekamp's and Niederreiter's Polynomial Factorization Algorithms. In *Finite Fields: Theory, Applications and Algorithms*, eds. G. L. MULLEN and P. J.-S. SHIUE. Contemporary Mathematics **168**, American Mathematical Society, 101–115. [395]

SHUHONG GAO, JOACHIM VON ZUR GATHEN, and DANIEL PANARIO (1995), Gauss periods and fast exponentiation in finite fields. In *Proceedings of LATIN '95*, Valparaíso, Chile. Lecture Notes in Computer Science **911**, Springer-Verlag, 311–322. [81, 555]

SHUHONG GAO, JOACHIM VON ZUR GATHEN, and DANIEL PANARIO (1998), Gauss periods: orders and cryptographical applications. *Mathematics of Computation* **67**(221), 343–352. [81, 555]

SHUHONG GAO and DANIEL PANARIO (1997), Tests and Constructions of Irreducible Polynomials over Finite Fields. In *Foundations of Computational Mathematics*, eds. FELIPE CUCKER and MICHAEL SHUB, 346–361. Springer Verlag. [394, 396]

MICHAEL R. GAREY and DAVID S. JOHNSON (1979), *Computers and Intractability: A Guide to the Theory of NP-Completeness*. Freeman, San Francisco CA. [483, 687]

HARVEY L. GARNER (1959), The Residue Number System. *IRE Transactions on Electronic Computers*, 140–147. [123]

JOACHIM VON ZUR GATHEN (1984a), Hensel and Newton methods in valuation rings. *Mathematics of Computation* **42**(166), 637–661. [395, 441, 471, 474]

JOACHIM VON ZUR GATHEN (1984b), Parallel algorithms for algebraic problems. *SIAM Journal on Computing* **13**(4), 802–824. [186, 188]

JOACHIM VON ZUR GATHEN (1985), Irreducibility of Multivariate Polynomials. *Journal of Computer and System Sciences* **31**(2), 225–264. [441, 471, 472, 688]

JOACHIM VON ZUR GATHEN (1986), Representations and parallel computations for rational functions. *SIAM Journal on Computing* **15**(2), 432–452. [122]

JOACHIM VON ZUR GATHEN (1987), Factoring polynomials and primitive elements for special primes. *Theoretical Computer Science* **52**, 77–89. [396]

JOACHIM VON ZUR GATHEN (1988), Algebraic complexity theory. *Annual Review of Computer Science* **3**, 317–347. [330]

JOACHIM VON ZUR GATHEN (1990a), Functional Decomposition of Polynomials: the Tame Case. *Journal of Symbolic Computation* **9**, 281–299. [272, 555, 556]

JOACHIM VON ZUR GATHEN (1990b), Functional Decomposition of Polynomials: the Wild Case. *Journal of Symbolic Computation* **10**, 437–452. [555]

JOACHIM VON ZUR GATHEN (1991a), Tests for permutation polynomials. *SIAM Journal on Computing* **20**(3), 591–602. [471]

JOACHIM VON ZUR GATHEN (1991b), Values of polynomials over finite fields. *Bulletin of the Australian Mathematic Society* **43**, 141–146. [400]

JOACHIM VON ZUR GATHEN and JÜRGEN GERHARD (1996), Arithmetic and Factorization of Polynomials over $\mathbb{F}_2$. In *Proceedings of the 1996 International Symposium on Symbolic and Algebraic Computation ISSAC '96*, Zürich, Switzerland, ed. LAKSHMAN Y. N., ACM Press, 1–9. Technical report tr-rsfb-96-018, University of Paderborn, Germany, 1996, 43 pages, http://www-math.uni-paderborn.de/~aggathen/Publications/polyfactTR.ps. [265, 272, 441]

JOACHIM VON ZUR GATHEN and JÜRGEN GERHARD (1997), Fast Algorithms for Taylor Shifts and Certain Difference Equations. In *Proceedings of the 1997 International Symposium on Symbolic and Algebraic Computation ISSAC '97*, Maui HI, ed. WOLFGANG W. KÜCHLIN, ACM Press, 40–47. [633, 634]

JOACHIM VON ZUR GATHEN and SILKE HARTLIEB (1998), Factoring Modular Polynomials. *Journal of Symbolic Computation* **26**(5), 583–606. [441]

JOACHIM VON ZUR GATHEN and ERICH KALTOFEN (1985), Factoring Sparse Multivariate Polynomials. *Journal of Computer and System Sciences* **31**(2), 265–287. [471]

JOACHIM VON ZUR GATHEN, MAREK KARPINSKI, and IGOR E. SHPARLINSKI (1996), Counting curves and their projections. *computational complexity* **6**, 64–99. Extended Abstract in *Proceedings of the Twenty-fifth Annual ACM Symposium on the Theory of Computing*, San Diego CA, ACM Press, 1993, 805–812. [187]

JOACHIM VON ZUR GATHEN and MICHAEL NÖCKER (1997), Exponentiation in Finite Fields: Theory and Practice. In *Applied Algebra, Algebraic Algorithms and Error-Correcting Codes: AAECC-12*, Toulouse, France, eds. TEO MORA and HAROLD MATTSON. Lecture Notes in Computer Science **1255**, Springer-Verlag, 88–113. [81, 555]

JOACHIM VON ZUR GATHEN and DANIEL PANARIO (1999), Factoring polynomials over finite fields: a survey. *Journal of Symbolic Computation*. To appear. [394]

JOACHIM VON ZUR GATHEN and VICTOR SHOUP (1992), Computing Frobenius maps and factoring polynomials. *computational complexity* **2**, 187–224. [381, 394, 395, 441]

CARL FRIEDRICH GAUSS (1801), *Disquisitiones Arithmeticae*. Gerh. Fleischer Iun., Leipzig. English translation by ARTHUR A. CLARKE, Springer-Verlag, New York, 1986. [122, 348, 471, 692]

CARL FRIEDRICH GAUSS (1809), *Theoria motus corporum coelestium in sectionibus conicis solem ambientium*. Perthes and Besser, Hamburg. *Werke* **VII**, Königliche Gesellschaft der Wissenschaften, Göttingen, 1906, 1–261. Reprinted by Georg Olms Verlag, Hildesheim New York, 1973. [123]

CARL FRIEDRICH GAUSS (1810), Disquisitio de elementis ellipticis Palladis. *Commentationes societatis regiae scientarium Gottingensis recentiores* **1** (1811). *Werke* **VI**, Königliche Gesellschaft der Wissenschaften, Göttingen, 1874, 1–24. Reprinted by Georg Olms Verlag, Hildesheim New York, 1973. [123]

CARL FRIEDRICH GAUSS (1849), Brief an Encke, 24. Dezember 1849. In *Werke* **II**, Handschriftlicher Nachlass, 444–447. Königliche Gesellschaft der Wissenschaften, Göttingen, 1863. Reprinted by Georg Olms Verlag, Hildesheim New York, 1973. [507]

CARL FRIEDRICH GAUSS (1863a), Solutio congruentiae $X^m - 1 \equiv 0$. Analysis residuorum. Caput sextum. Pars prior. In *Werke* **II**, Handschriftlicher Nachlass, ed. R. DEDEKIND, 199–211. Königliche Gesellschaft der Wissenschaften, Göttingen. Reprinted by Georg Olms Verlag, Hildesheim New York, 1973. [393, 440, 688]

CARL FRIEDRICH GAUSS (1863b), Disquisitiones generales de congruentiis. Analysis residuorum caput octavum. In *Werke* **II**, Handschriftlicher Nachlass, ed. R. DEDEKIND, 212–242. Königliche Gesellschaft der Wissenschaften, Göttingen. Reprinted by Georg Olms Verlag, Hildesheim New York, 1973. [55, 186, 349, 393, 394, 396, 440]

CARL FRIEDRICH GAUSS (1863c), Zur Theorie der complexen Zahlen. In *Werke* **II**, Handschriftlicher Nachlass, 387–398. Königliche Gesellschaft der Wissenschaften, Göttingen. Reprinted by Georg Olms Verlag, Hildesheim New York, 1973. [688]

CARL FRIEDRICH GAUSS (1866), Theoria interpolationis methodo nova tractata. In *Werke* **III**, Nachlass, 265–330. Königliche Gesellschaft der Wissenschaften, Göttingen. Reprinted by Georg Olms Verlag, Hildesheim New York, 1973. [234]

LEOPOLD GEGENBAUER (1884), Asymptotische Gesetze der Zahlentheorie. *Denkschriften der kaiserlichen Akademie der Wissenschaften Wien* **49**, 37–80. [57]

W. M. GENTLEMAN and G. SANDE (1966), Fast Fourier transforms—for fun and profit. In *Proceedings of the fall joint computer conference, San Francisco CA*. AFIPS conference proceedings **29**, Spartan books, Washington DC, 563–578. [234]

FRANÇOIS GENUYS (1958), Dix mille décimales de π. *Chiffres* **1**, 17–22. [76]

JÜRGEN GERHARD (1998), High degree solutions of low degree equations. In *Proceedings of the 1998 International Symposium on Symbolic and Algebraic Computation ISSAC '98*, Rostock, Germany, ed. OLIVER GLOOR, ACM Press, 284–289. [638]

JÜRGEN GERHARD (1999), Fast modular algorithms for squarefree factorization and Hermite integration. Submitted. [445, 606]

M. GIESBRECHT, A. LOBO, and B. D. SAUNDERS (1998), Certifying Inconsistency of Sparse Linear Systems. In *Proceedings of the 1998 International Symposium on Symbolic and Algebraic Computation ISSAC '98*, Rostock, Germany, ed. OLIVER GLOOR, ACM Press, 113–119. [331]

JOHN GILL (1977), Computational complexity of probabilistic Turing machines. *SIAM Journal on Computing* **6**(4), 675–695. [187]

ALESSANDRO GIOVINI, TEO MORA, GIANFRANCO NIESI, LORENZO ROBBIANO, and CARLO TRAVERSO (1991), "One sugar cube, please" or Selection strategies in the Buchberger algorithm. In *Proceedings of the 1991 International Symposium on Symbolic and Algebraic Computation ISSAC '91*, Bonn, Germany, ed. STEPHEN M. WATT, ACM Press, 49–54. [593]

M. GIUSTI (1984), Some effectivity problems in polynomial ideal theory. In *Proceedings of EUROSAM '84*, Cambridge, UK, ed. JOHN FITCH, Lecture Notes in Computer Science **174**, 159–171. Springer-Verlag. [592]

MARC GIUSTI and JOOS HEINTZ (1991), Algorithmes – disons rapides – pour la décomposition d'une variété algébrique en composantes irréductibles et équidimensionnelles. In *Proceedings of Effective Methods in Algebraic Geometry MEGA '90*, eds. TEO MORA and CARLO TRAVERSO. Progress in Mathematics **94**, Birkhäuser Verlag, Basel, 169–193. [593]

NOBUHIRO GŌ and HAROLD A. SCHERAGA (1970), Ring Closure and Local Conformational Deformations of Chain Molecules. *Macromolecules* **3**(2), 178–187. [662]

ODED GOLDREICH, SHAFI GOLDWASSER, and SHAI HALEVI (1997), Eliminating Decryption Errors in the Ajtai-Dwork Cryptosystem. *Electronic Colloquium on Computational Complexity* TR97-018. 6 pages. [554, 555]

HERMANN H. GOLDSTINE (1977), *A History of Numerical Analysis from the 16th through the 19th Century*. Studies in the History of Mathematics and Physical Sciences **2**, Springer-Verlag. [272]

S. GOLDWASSER and J. KILIAN (1986), Almost All Primes Can be Quickly Certified. In *Proceedings of the Eighteenth Annual ACM Symposium on the Theory of Computing*, Berkeley CA, ACM Press, 316–329. [509]

R. M. F. GOODMAN and A. J. MCAULEY (1984), A New Trapdoor Knapsack Public Key Cryptosystem. In *Advances in Cryptology: Proceedings of EUROCRYPT 1984*, Paris, France, eds. T. BETH, N. COT, and I. INGEMARSSON. Lecture Notes in Computer Science **209**, Springer-Verlag, Berlin, 150–158. [483]

PAUL GORDAN (1885), *Vorlesungen über Invariantentheorie—Erster Band: Determinanten*. B. G. Teubner, Leipzig. Herausgegeben von Dr. GEORG KERSCHENSTEINER. [188, 310]

DANIEL M. GORDON (1993), Discrete logarithms in $GF(p)$ using the number field sieve. *SIAM Journal on Discrete Mathematics* **6**(1), 124–138. [553]

R. WILLIAM GOSPER, JR. (1978), Decision procedure for indefinite hypergeometric summation. *Proceedings of the National Academy of Sciences of the USA* **75**(1), 40–42. [626, 634, 635, 639]

R. GÖTTFERT (1994), An acceleration of the Niederreiter factorization algorithm in characteristic 2. *Mathematics of Computation* **62**(206), 831–839. [395]

XAVIER GOURDON (1996), *Combinatoire, Algorithmique et Géométrie des Polynômes*. PhD thesis, École Polytechnique, Paris. [394]

R. L. GRAHAM, D. E. KNUTH, and O. PATASHNIK (1994), *Concrete Mathematics*. Addison-Wesley, Reading MA, 2nd edition. First edition 1989. [633, 634, 681, 684]

J. P. GRAM (1883), Ueber die Entwickelung reeller Functionen in Reihen mittelst der Methode der kleinsten Quadrate. *Journal für die Reine und Angewandte Mathematik* **94**, 41–73. [470]

ANDREW GRANVILLE (1990), Bounding the Coefficients of a Divisor of a Given Polynomial. *Monatshefte für Mathematik* **109**, 271–277. [187]

ANDREW GRANVILLE (1995), Harald Cramér and the Distribution of Prime Numbers. *Scandinavian Actuarial Journal* **1**, 12–28. [509]

D. YU. GRIGOR'EV (1988), Complexity of deciding Tarski algebra. *Journal of Symbolic Computation* **4**(1/2). [593]

DIMA YU. GRIGORIEV, MAREK KARPINSKI, and MICHAEL F. SINGER (1990), Fast parallel algorithms for sparse multivariate polynomial interpolation over finite fields. *SIAM Journal on Computing* **19**(6), 1059–1063. [472]

DIMA GRIGORIEV, MAREK KARPINSKI, and MICHAEL F. SINGER (1994), Computational complexity of sparse rational interpolation. *SIAM Journal on Computing* **23**(1), 1–11. [472]

H. F. DE GROOTE (1987), *Lectures on the Complexity of Bilinear Problems*. Lecture Notes in Computer Science **245**, Springer-Verlag. [330]

MARTIN GRÖTSCHEL, LÁSZLÓ LOVÁSZ, and ALEXANDER SCHRIJVER (1993), *Geometric Algorithms and Combinatorial Optimization*. Algorithms and Combinatorics **2**, Springer-Verlag, Berlin, Heidelberg, 2nd edition. First edition 1988. [470]

L. J. GUIBAS and A. M. ODLYZKO (1980), Long Repetitive Patterns in Random Sequences. *Zeitschrift für Wahrscheinlichkeitstheorie und verwandte Gebiete* **53**, 241–262. [194]

RICHARD K. GUY (1975), How to factor a number. In *Proceedings of the Fifth Manitoba Conference on Numerical Mathematics*, 49–89. [542, 543]

WALTER HABICHT (1948), Eine Verallgemeinerung des Sturmschen Wurzelzählverfahrens. *Commentarii Mathematici Helvetici* **21**, 99–116. [188]

J. HADAMARD (1893), Résolution d'une question relative aux déterminants. *Bulletin des Sciences Mathématiques* **17**, 240–246. [470]

J. HADAMARD (1896), Sur la distribution des zéros de la fonction $\zeta(s)$ et ses conséquences arithmétiques. *Bulletin de la Société mathématique de France* **24**, 199–220. [507]

ARMIN HAKEN (1985), The intractability of resolution. *Theoretical Computer Science* **39**, 297–308. [642]

PAUL R. HALMOS (1985), *I want to be a mathematician*. Springer-Verlag. [508]

JOHN H. HALTON (1970), A retrospective and prospective survey of the Monte Carlo method. *SIAM Review* **12**(1), 1–63. [187]

RICHARD W. HAMMING (1986), *Coding and Information Theory*. Prentice-Hall, Inc., Englewood Cliffs NJ, 2nd edition. First edition 1980. [292]

G. H. HARDY (1937), The Indian Mathematician Ramanujan. *The American Mathematical Monthly* **44**, 137–155. *Collected Papers*, volume VII, Clarendon Press, Oxford, 1979, 612–630. [510]

GODFREY HAROLD HARDY (1940), *A mathematician's apology*. Cambridge University Press, Cambridge, UK. [24, 690, 692]

G. H. HARDY and E. M. WRIGHT (1985), *An introduction to the theory of numbers*. Clarendon Press, Oxford, 5th edition. First edition 1938. [57, 396, 507, 508]

ROBIN HARTSHORNE (1977), *Algebraic Geometry*. Graduate Texts in Mathematics **52**, Springer-Verlag, New York. [542]

M. W. HASKELL (1891/92), Note on resultants. *Bulletin of the New York Mathematical Society* **1**, 223–224. [310]

HELMUT HASSE (1933), Beweis des Analogons der Riemannschen Vermutung für die Artinschen und F. K. Schmidtschen Kongruenzzetafunktionen in gewissen elliptischen Fällen. Vorläufige Mitteilung. *Nachrichten von der Gesellschaft der Wissenschaften zu Göttingen, Mathematisch-Physikalische Klasse* **42**, 253–262. [542]

JOHAN HÅSTAD and MATS NÄSLUND (1998), The Security of Individual RSA Bits. In *Proceedings of the 39th Annual IEEE Symposium on Foundations of Computer Science*, Palo Alto CA, IEEE Computer Society Press, Los Alamitos CA, 510–519. [555]

TIMOTHY F. HAVEL and IGOR NAJFELD (1995), A new system of equations, based on geometric algebra, for the ring closure in cyclic molecules. In *Computer Algebra in Science and Engineering*, Bielefeld,

Germany, August 1994, eds. J. FLEISCHER, J. GRABMEIER, F. W. HEHL, and W. KÜCHLIN, World Scientific, Singapore, 243–259. [662]

P. HAZEBROEK and L. J. OOSTERHOFF (1951), The isomers of cyclohexane. *Discussions of the Faraday Society* **10**, 88–93. [662]

THOMAS L. HEATH (1925), *The thirteen books of Euclid's elements*, vol. 1. Dover Publications, Inc., New York, Second edition. First edition 1908. [22, 23]

MICHAEL T. HEIDEMAN, DON H. JOHNSON, and C. SIDNEY BURRUS (1984), Gauss and the history of the Fast Fourier Transform. *IEEE ASSP Magazine*, 14–21. [234]

JOOS HEINTZ, TOMAS RECIO, and MARIE-FRANÇOISE ROY (1991), Algorithms in Real Algebraic Geometry and Applications to Computational Geometry. In *Discrete and Computational Geometry: Papers from the DIMACS Special Year*, eds. JACOB E. GOODMAN, RICHARD POLLACK, and WILLIAM STEIGER. DIMACS Series in Discrete Mathematics and Theoretical Computer Science **6**, American Mathematical Society and ACM, 137–163. [593]

JOOS HEINTZ and MALTE SIEVEKING (1981), Absolute Primality of Polynomials is Decidable in Random Polynomial Time in the Number of Variables. In *Proceedings of the 8th International Colloquium on Automata, Languages and Programming ICALP 1981*, Acre ('Akko), Israel. Lecture Notes in Computer Science **115**, Springer-Verlag, 16–27. [471]

KURT HENSEL (1918), Eine neue Theorie der algebraischen Zahlen. *Mathematische Zeitschift* **2**, 433–452. [418, 440]

GRETE HERMANN (1926), Die Frage der endlich vielen Schritte in der Theorie der Polynomideale. *Mathematische Annalen* **95**, 736–788. [590]

C. HERMITE (1872), Sur l'intégration des fractions rationnelles. *Annales de Mathématiques, 2ème série* **11**, 145–148. [606]

NICHOLAS J. HIGHAM (1990), Exploiting Fast Matrix Multiplication Within the Level 3 BLAS. *ACM Transactions on Mathematical Software* **16**(4), 352–368. [315]

DAVID HILBERT (1890), Ueber die Theorie der algebraischen Formen. *Mathematische Annalen* **36**, 473–534. [560, 590, 591]

DAVID HILBERT (1892), Ueber die Irreducibilität ganzer rationaler Functionen mit ganzzahligen Coefficienten. *Journal für die Reine und Angewandte Mathematik* **110**, 104–129. [469, 560]

DAVID HILBERT (1893), Ueber die Transcendenz der Zahlen e und π. *Mathematische Annalen* **43**, 216–219. *Nachrichten von der Königlichen Gesellschaft der Wissenschaften und der Georg-Augusts-Universität zu Göttingen* **2** (1893), 113–116. Reprinted in Berggren, Borwein & Borwein (1997), 226–229. [83]

DAVID HILBERT (1900), Mathematische Probleme. *Nachrichten von der Königlichen Gesellschaft der Wissenschaften zu Göttingen*, 253–297. *Archiv für Mathematik und Physik, 3. Reihe* **1** (1901), 44–63 and 213–237. English translation: Mathematical Problems, *Bulletin of the American Mathematical Society* **8** (1902), 437–479. [561, 690]

DAVID HILBERT (1930), Probleme der Grundlegung der Mathematik. *Mathematische Annalen* **102**, 1–9. [395]

HEISUKE HIRONAKA (1964), Resolution of singularities of an algebraic variety over a field of characteristic zero. *Annals of Mathematics* **79**(1), I: 109–203, II: 205–326. [565]

A. HOCQUENGHEM (1959), Codes correcteurs d'erreurs. *Chiffres* **2**, 147–156. [203]

JORIS VAN DER HOEVEN (1997), Lazy Multiplication of Formal Power Series. In *Proceedings of the 1997 International Symposium on Symbolic and Algebraic Computation ISSAC '97*, Maui HI, ed. WOLFGANG W. KÜCHLIN, ACM Press, 17–20. [444]

C. M. HOFFMAN, J. R. SENDRA, and F. WINKLER (1997), eds., Parametric Algebraic Curves and Applications. Special Issue of the *Journal of Symbolic Computation* **23**(2/3). [592]

D. G. HOFFMAN, D. A. LEONARD, C. C. LINDNER, K. T. PHELPS, C. A. RODGER, and J. R. WALL (1991), *Coding Theory: The Essentials*. Marcel Dekker, Inc., New York. [203]

ELLIS HOROWITZ (1971), Algorithms for partial fraction decomposition and rational function integration. In *Proceedings 2nd ACM Symposium on Symbolic and Algebraic Manipulation*, Los Angeles CA, ed. S. R. PETRICK, ACM Press, 441–457. [601]

ELLIS HOROWITZ (1972), A fast method for interpolation using preconditioning. *Information Processing Letters* **1**, 157–163. [290]

MING-DEH A. HUANG (1985), Riemann Hypothesis and Finding Roots over Finite Fields. In *Proceedings of the Seventeenth Annual ACM Symposium on the Theory of Computing*, Providence RI, ACM Press, 121–130. [397]

MING-DEH HUANG and YIU-CHUNG WONG (1998), Extended Hilbert Irreducibility and its Applications. In *Proceedings of the 9th Annual ACM-SIAM Symposium on Discrete Algorithms SODA '98*, 50–58. [472]

XIAOHAN HUANG and VICTOR Y. PAN (1998), Fast Rectangular Matrix Multiplication and Applications. *Journal of Complexity* **14**, 257–299. [330, 381, 395, 396]

D. HUFFMAN (1952), A method for the construction of minimum redundancy codes. In *Proceedings IRE 40*, 1098–1101. [291, 344]

CHRISTIANUS HUGENIUS (1703), Descriptio Automati Planetarii. In *Opuscula postuma, quae continent dioptricam. Commentarios de vitris figurandis. Dissertationem de corona & parheliis. Tractatum de motu/de vi centrifuga. Descriptionem automati planetarii*. Cornelius Boutesteyn, Leiden. [82]

THOMAS W. HUNGERFORD (1990), *Abstract Algebra: An Introduction*. Saunders College Publishing, Philadelphia PA. [667]

A. HURWITZ (1891), Über die angenäherte Darstellung der Irrationalzahlen durch rationale Brüche. *Mathematische Annalen* **39**, 279–284. [82]

DUNG T. HUYNH (1986), A Superexponential Lower Bound for Gröbner Bases and Church-Rosser Commutative Thue Systems. *Information and Control* **68**(1–3), 196–206. [592]

KARL-HEINZ INDLEKOFER and ANTAL JÁRAI (1996), Largest known twin primes. *Mathematics of Computation* **65**(213), 427–428. [234]

KARL-HEINZ INDLEKOFER and ANTAL JÁRAI (1998), Largest known twin primes and Sophie Germain primes. Preprint, 8 pages. [209, 234]

C. G. J. JACOBI (1836), De eliminatione variabilis e duabus aequationibus algebraicis. *Journal für die Reine und Angewandte Mathematik* **15**, 101–124. [186]

C. G. J. JACOBI (1846), Über die Darstellung einer Reihe gegebner Werthe durch eine gebrochne rationale Function. *Journal für die Reine und Angewandte Mathematik* **30**, 127–156. [123, 186]

WILLIAM JONES (1706), *Synopsis Palmariorum Matheseos: or, a New Introduction to the Mathematics*, London. [83]

CHARLES JORDAN (1965), *Calculus of finite differences*. Chelsea Publishing Co., New York. First edition Röttig and Romwalter, Sopron, Hungary, 1939. [633]

NORBERT KAJLER and NEIL SOIFFER (1998), A Survey of User Interfaces for Computer Algebra Systems. *Journal of Symbolic Computation* **25**, 127–159. [19]

K. KALORKOTI (1993), Inverting polynomials and formal power series. *SIAM Journal on Computing* **22**(3), 552–559. [272]

E. KALTOFEN (1982), Factorization of Polynomials. In *Computer Algebra, Symbolic and Algebraic Computation*, eds. B. BUCHBERGER, G. E. COLLINS, and R. LOOS, 95–113. Springer-Verlag, New York, 2nd edition. [394]

ERICH KALTOFEN (1983), On the Complexity of Finding Short Vectors in Integer Lattices. In *Proceedings of EUROCAL 1983*, London, UK. Lecture Notes in Computer Science **162**, Springer-Verlag, Berlin/New York, 236–244. [471]

ERICH KALTOFEN (1985a), Polynomial-time reductions from multivariate to bi- and univariate integral polynomial factorization. *SIAM Journal on Computing* **14**(2), 469–489. [471]

ERICH KALTOFEN (1985b), Effective Hilbert Irreducibility. *Journal of Computer and System Sciences* **66**, 123–137. [472]

E. KALTOFEN (1989), Factorization of Polynomials Given by Straight-Line Programs. In *Randomness and Computation*, ed. S. MICALI, JAI Press, Greenwich CT, 375–412. [469, 471]

E. KALTOFEN (1990), Polynomial factorization 1982–1986. In *Computers in Mathematics*, eds. D. V. CHUDNOVSKY and R. D. JENKS, Marcel Dekker, Inc., New York, 285–309. [394]

E. KALTOFEN (1992), Polynomial Factorization 1987–1991. In *Proceedings of LATIN '92*, São Paulo, Brazil, ed. I. SIMON. Lecture Notes in Computer Science **583**, Springer-Verlag, 294–313. [394]

ERICH KALTOFEN (1995a), Effective Noether Irreducibility Forms and Applications. *Journal of Computer and System Sciences* **50**(2), 274–295. [472]

ERICH KALTOFEN (1995b), Analysis of Coppersmith's block Wiedemann algorithm for the parallel solution of sparse linear systems. *Mathematics of Computation* **64**(210), 777–806. [330]

ERICH KALTOFEN (1998), Challenges of Symbolic Computation—My Favourite Open Problems. With an Appendix by ROBERT M. CORLESS and DAVID J. JEFFREY. Preprint. [330]

ERICH KALTOFEN and LAKSHMAN YAGATI (1988), Improved Sparse Multivariate Polynomial Interpolation Algorithms. In *Proceedings of the 1988 International Symposium on Symbolic and Algebraic Computation ISSAC '88*, Rome, Italy, ed. P. GIANNI. Lecture Notes in Computer Science **358**, Springer-Verlag, 467–474. [472]

E. KALTOFEN and A. LOBO (1994), Factoring High-Degree Polynomials by the Black Box Berlekamp Algorithm. In *Proceedings of the 1994 International Symposium on Symbolic and Algebraic Computation ISSAC '94*, Oxford, UK, eds. J. VON ZUR GATHEN and M. GIESBRECHT, ACM Press, 90–98. [380]

ERICH KALTOFEN, DAVID R. MUSSER, and B. DAVID SAUNDERS (1983), A generalized class of polynomials that are hard to factor. *SIAM Journal on Computing* **12**(3), 473–483. [440]

ERICH KALTOFEN and HEINRICH ROLLETSCHEK (1989), Computing greatest common divisors and factorizations in quadratic number fields. *Mathematics of Computation* **53**(188), 697–720. [123]

ERICH KALTOFEN and B. DAVID SAUNDERS (1991), On Wiedemann's Method of Solving Sparse Linear Systems. In *Algebraic Algorithms and Error-Correcting Codes: AAECC-10*, San Juan de Puerto Rico. Lecture Notes in Computer Science **539**, Springer-Verlag, 29–38. [318, 328, 329, 380]

ERICH KALTOFEN and VICTOR SHOUP (1997), Fast Polynomial Factorization Over High Algebraic Extensions of Finite Fields. In *Proceedings of the 1997 International Symposium on Symbolic and Algebraic Computation ISSAC '97*, Maui HI, ed. WOLFGANG W. KÜCHLIN, ACM Press, 184–188. [396]

ERICH KALTOFEN and VICTOR SHOUP (1998), Subquadratic-Time Factoring of Polynomials over Finite Fields. *Mathematics of Computation* **67**(223), 1179–1197. [377, 380, 381, 395, 396]

ERICH KALTOFEN and BARRY M. TRAGER (1990), Computing with Polynomials Given By Black Boxes for Their Evaluations: Greatest Common Divisors, Factorization, Separation of Numerators and Denominators. *Journal of Symbolic Computation* **9**, 301–320. [470, 472]

MICHAEL KAMINSKI, DAVID G. KIRKPATRICK, and NADER H. BSHOUTY (1988), Addition Requirements for Matrix and Transposed Matrix Products. *Journal of Algorithms* **9**, 354–364. [330]

YASUMASA KANADA (1988), Vectorization of Multiple-Precision Arithmetic Program and $201,326,000$ Decimal Digits of π Calculation. In *Supercomputing '88, volume II: Science and Applications*, 117–128. Reprinted in Berggren, Borwein & Borwein (1997), 576–587. [235]

RAVI KANNAN (1987), Algorithmic geometry of numbers. *Annual Review of Computer Science* **2**, 231–267. [470]

А. КАРАЦУБА и Ю. ОФМАН (1962), Умножение многозначных чисел на автоматах. *Доклады Академий Наук СССР* **145**, 293–294. A. KARATSUBA and YU. OFMAN, Multiplication of multidigit numbers on automata, Soviet Physics–Doklady **7** (1963), 595–596. [211, 232]

RICHARD M. KARP (1972), Reducibility among combinatorial problems. In *Complexity of computer computations*, eds. RAYMOND E. MILLER and JAMES W. THATCHER, 85–103. Plenum Press, New York. [483, 686]

MICHAEL KARR (1981), Summation in Finite Terms. *Journal of the ACM* **28**(2), 305–350. [635]

MICHAEL KARR (1985), Theory of Summation in Finite Terms. *Journal of Symbolic Computation* **1**, 303–315. [635]

WALTER KELLER-GEHRIG (1985), Fast algorithms for the characteristic polynomial. *Theoretical Computer Science* **36**, 309–317. [330]

H. KEMPFERT (1969), On the Factorization of Polynomials. *Journal of Number Theory* **1**, 116–120. [393, 440]

JOE KILIAN (1990), *Uses of Randomness in Algorithms and Protocols*. An ACM Distinguished Doctoral Dissertation, MIT Press, Cambridge MA. [509]

ARNOLD KNOPFMACHER (1995), Enumerating basic properties of polynomials over a finite field. *South African Journal of Science* **91**, 10–11. [394]

ARNOLD KNOPFMACHER and JOHN KNOPFMACHER (1993), Counting irreducible factors of polynomials over a finite field. *Discrete Mathematics* **112**, 103–118. [394]

ARNOLD KNOPFMACHER and RICHARD WARLIMONT (1995), Distinct degree factorizations for polynomials over a finite field. *Transactions of the American Mathematical Society* **347**(6), 2235–2243. [394]

DONALD E. KNUTH (1970), The analysis of algorithms. In *Proceedings of the International Congress of Mathematicians 1970*, Nice, France, vol. 3, 269–274. [310, 688]

DONALD E. KNUTH (1993), Johann Faulhaber and sums of powers. *Mathematics of Computation* **61**(203), 277–294. [634]

DONALD E. KNUTH (1997), *The Art of Computer Programming, vol. 1, Fundamental Algorithms*. Addison-Wesley, Reading MA, 3rd edition. First edition 1969. [292]

DONALD E. KNUTH (1998), *The Art of Computer Programming, vol. 2, Seminumerical Algorithms*. Addison-Wesley, Reading MA, 3rd edition. First edition 1969. [23, 38, 55, 57, 81, 82, 234, 272, 393, 479, 505, 506, 541]

DONALD E. KNUTH and LUIS TRABB PARDO (1976), Analysis of a simple factorization algorithm. *Theoretical Computer Science* **3**, 321–348. [541]

NEAL KOBLITZ (1987a), *A Course in Number Theory and Cryptography*. Graduate Texts in Mathematics **114**, Springer-Verlag, New York. [506, 542, 555]

NEAL KOBLITZ (1987b), Elliptic Curve Cryptosystems. *Mathematics of Computation* **48**(177), 203–209. [555]

JÁNOS KOLLÁR (1988), Sharp effective Nullstellensatz. *Journal of the American Mathematical Society* **1**(4), 963–975. [592]

DEXTER KOZEN and SUSAN LANDAU (1989), Polynomial Decomposition Algorithms. *Journal of Symbolic Computation* **7**, 445–456. [550, 556]

LEON G. KRAFT, JR. (1949), *A Device for Quantizing, Grouping, and Coding Amplitude Modulated Pulses*. M.Sc. thesis, Electrical Engineering Department, M.I.T. [291]

M. KRAÏTCHIK (1926), *Théorie des Nombres*, vol. II. Gauthier-Villars, Paris. [541, 691, 692]

J. KRAJÍČEK (1995), *Bounded arithmetic, propositional logic and complexity theory*. Encyclopedia of Mathematics and its Applications **60**, Cambridge University Press, Cambridge, UK. [661]

L. KRONECKER (1873), Die verschiedenen Sturmschen Reihen und ihre gegenseitigen Beziehungen. *Monatsberichte der Königlich Preussischen Akademie der Wissenschaften, Berlin*, 117–154. [186]

L. KRONECKER (1878), Sturmsche Functionen. *Monatsberichte der Königlich Preussischen Akademie der Wissenschaften, Berlin*, 95–121. [186]

L. KRONECKER (1881a), Zur Theorie der Elimination einer Variabeln aus zwei algebraischen Gleichungen. *Monatsberichte der Königlich Preussischen Akademie der Wissenschaften, Berlin*, 535–600. [123, 128, 330]

L. KRONECKER (1881b), Auszug aus einem Briefe des Herrn Kronecker an E. Schering. *Nachrichten der Akademie der Wissenschaften, Göttingen*, 271–279. [186]

L. KRONECKER (1882), Grundzüge einer arithmetischen Theorie der algebraischen Grössen. *Journal für die Reine und Angewandte Mathematik* **92**, 1–122. *Werke*, Zweiter Band, ed. K. HENSEL, Leipzig, 1897, reprinted by Chelsea Publishing Co., New York, 1968, 237–387. [235, 440]

LEOPOLD KRONECKER (1883), Die Zerlegung der ganzen Grössen eines natürlichen Rationalitäts-Bereichs in ihre irreductibeln Factoren. *Journal für die Reine und Angewandte Mathematik* **94**, 344–348. *Werke*, Zweiter Band, ed. K. HENSEL, Leipzig, 1897, 409–416. Reprint by Chelsea Publishing Co., New York, 1968. [440]

А. Н. КРЫЛОВ (A. N. KRYLOV) (1931), О численном решении уравнения, которым в технических вопросах определятся частоты малых колебаний материальных систем (On numerical solutions which determine the frequencies of small oscillations of material systems in technical problems). *Известия Академии Наук СССР, Отделение Математических и естественных наук (Bulletin de l'académie des sciences de l'URSS, Classe des sciences mathématiques et naturelles)* **4**, 491–539. [330]

Y. H. KU and XIAOGUANG SUN (1992), The Chinese Remainder Theorem. *Journal of the Franklin Institute* **329**, 93–97. [122]

KLAUS KÜHNLE and ERNST W. MAYR (1996), Exponential Space Computation of Gröbner Bases. In *Proceedings of the 1996 International Symposium on Symbolic and Algebraic Computation ISSAC '96*, Zürich, Switzerland, ed. LAKSHMAN Y. N., ACM Press, 63–71. [590, 591]

H. T. KUNG (1974), On Computing Reciprocals of Power Series. *Numerische Mathematik* **22**, 341–348. [272]

J. C. LAFON (1983), Summation in Finite Terms. In *Computer Algebra, Symbolic and Algebraic Computation*, eds. B. BUCHBERGER, G. E. COLLINS, and R. LOOS, 71–77. Springer-Verlag, New York, 2nd edition. [635]

J. C. LAGARIAS (1982a), Best simultaneous Diophantine approximations. I. Growth rates of best approximation denominators. *Transactions of the American Mathematical Society* **272**(2), 545–554. [483]

J. C. LAGARIAS (1982b), Best simultaneous Diophantine approximations. II. Behavior of consecutive best approximations. *Pacific Journal of Mathematics* **102**(1), 61–88. [483]

J. C. LAGARIAS (1985), The computational complexity of simultaneous Diophantine approximation problems. *SIAM Journal on Computing* **14**(1), 196–209. [480, 483]

J. C. LAGARIAS (1990), Pseudorandom Number Generators in Cryptography and Number Theory. In *Cryptology and Computational Number Theory*, ed. CARL POMERANCE. Proceedings of Symposia in Applied Mathematics **42**, American Mathematical Society, 115–143. [483, 555]

J. C. LAGARIAS and A. M. ODLYZKO (1977), Effective Versions of the Chebotarev Density Theorem. In *Algebraic Number Fields*, ed. A. FRÖHLICH, 409–464. Academic Press, London. [416]

J. C. LAGARIAS and A. M. ODLYZKO (1985), Solving Low-Density Subset Sum Problems. *Journal of the ACM* **32**(1), 229–246. [483]

JOSEPH LOUIS DE LAGRANGE (1759), Recherches sur la méthode de maximis et minimis. *Miscellanea Taurinensi* **1**. *Œuvres*, publiées par J.-A. SERRET, vol. 1, 1868, Gauthier-Villars, Paris, 1–16. [123]

JOSEPH LOUIS DE LAGRANGE (1769), Sur la résolution des équations numériques. *Mémoires de l'Académie des Sciences et Belles-Lettres de Berlin* **23**. *Œuvres*, publiées par J.-A. SERRET, vol. 2, 1868, Gauthier-Villars, Paris, 539–578. [394]

JOSEPH LOUIS DE LAGRANGE (1770a), Additions au mémoire sur la résolution des équations numériques. *Mémoires de l'Académie des Sciences et Belles-Lettres de Berlin* **24**. *Œuvres*, publiées par J.-A. SERRET, vol. 2, 1868, Gauthier-Villars, Paris, 581–652. [82]

JOSEPH LOUIS DE LAGRANGE (1770b), Nouvelle méthode pour résoudre les problèmes indéterminés en nombres entiers. *Mémoires de l'Académie des Sciences et Belles-Lettres de Berlin* **24**. *Œuvres*, publiées par J.-A. SERRET, vol. 2, 1868, Gauthier-Villars, Paris, 655–726. [122]

JOSEPH LOUIS DE LAGRANGE (1795), Sur l'usage des courbes dans la solution des Problèmes. In *Leçons élémentaires sur les mathématiques*, Leçon cinquième. École Polytechnique, Paris. *Œuvres*, publiées par J.-A. SERRET, vol. 7, 1877, Gauthier-Villars, Paris, 271–287. [122, 692]

JOSEPH LOUIS DE LAGRANGE (1798), Additions aux éléments d'algèbre d'Euler. Analyse indéterminée. In LEONHARD EULER, *Éléments d'algèbre*, St. Petersburg. *Œuvres*, publiées par J.-A. SERRET, vol. 7, 1877, Gauthier-Villars, Paris, 5–180. [82, 84]

LAKSHMAN Y. N. (1990), On the Complexity of Computing a Gröbner Basis for the Radical of a Zero Dimensional Ideal. In *Proceedings of the Twenty-second Annual ACM Symposium on the Theory of Computing*, Baltimore MD, ACM Press, 555–563. [592]

B. A. LAMACCHIA and A. M. ODLYZKO (1990), Solving large sparse linear systems over finite fields. In *Advances in Cryptology: Proceedings of CRYPTO 1990*, Santa Barbara CA. Lecture Notes in Computer Science **537**, Springer-Verlag, Berlin and New York, 109–133. [330]

LARRY A. LAMBE (1997), ed., Special Issue on Applications of Symbolic Computation to Research and Education. *Journal of Symbolic Computation* **23**(5/6). [19]

LARRY A. LAMBE and DAVID E. RADFORD (1997), *Introduction to the Quantum Yang-Baxter Equation and Quantum Groups: An Algebraic Approach*. Mathematics and its Applications **423**, Kluwer Academic Publishers, Dordrecht. [19]

LAMBERT (1761), Mémoire sur Quelques Propriétés Remarquables des Quantités Transcendentes Circulaires et Logarithmiques. *Histoire de l'Académie Royale des Sciences et des Belles-Lettres de Berlin* **17**, 265–322. Reprint of pages 265–276 in Berggren, Borwein & Borwein (1997), 129–140. [75]

GABRIEL LAMÉ (1844), Note sur la limite du nombre des divisions dans la recherche du plus grand commun diviseur entre deux nombres entiers. *Comptes Rendus de l'Académie des Sciences Paris* **19**, 867–870. [55]

C. LANCZOS (1952), Solutions of systems of linear equations by minimized iterations. *Journal of Research of the National Bureau of Standards* **49**, 33–53. [330]

E. LANDAU (1905), Sur quelques théorèmes de M. Petrovitch relatifs aux zéros des fonctions analytiques. *Bulletin de la Société de France* **33**, 251–261. [154]

F. LANDRY (1880), Note sur la décomposition du nombre $2^{64} + 1$ (Extrait). *Comptes Rendus de l'Académie des Sciences Paris* **91**, p. 138. [516]

SERGE LANG (1983), *Fundamentals of Diophantine Geometry*. Springer-Verlag, New York. [471]

DE LA PLACE (1772), Recherches sur le calcul intégral et sur le système du monde. *Mémoires de l'Académie Royale des Sciences* **II**. *Œuvres complètes de Laplace publiées sous les auspices de l'académie des sciences*, vol. 8, Gauthier-Villars, Paris, 1791, 367–501. [688]

D. LAZARD and R. RIOBOO (1990), Integration of Rational Functions: Rational Computation of the Logarithmic Part. *Journal of Symbolic Computation* **9**, 113–115. [606]

V.-A. LEBESGUE (1847), Sur le symbole $\left(\frac{a}{b}\right)$ et quelques-unes de ses applications. *Journal de Mathématiques Pures et Appliquées* **12**, 497–517. [508]

A. M. LEGENDRE (1785), Recherches d'analyse indéterminée. *Mémoires de l'Académie Royale des Sciences*, 465–559. [187, 393, 395, 440, 443, 543]

A. M. LE GENDRE (1798), *Essai sur la théorie des nombres*. Duprat, Paris. [394, 507, 508, 692]

D. J. LEHMANN (1982), On primality tests. *SIAM Journal on Computing* **11**, 374–375. [512]

D. H. LEHMER (1930), An extended theory of Lucas' functions. *Annals of Mathematics, Series II* **31**, 419–448. [505]

D. H. LEHMER (1935), On Lucas's test for the primality of Mersenne's numbers. *Journal of the London Mathematical Society* **10**, 162–165. [505]

D. H. LEHMER (1938), Euclid's algorithm for large numbers. *The American Mathematical Monthly* **45**, 227–233. [310]

D. H. LEHMER and R. E. POWERS (1931), On factoring large numbers. *Bulletin of the American Mathematical Society* **37**, 770–776. [543]

GOTTFRIED WILHELM LEIBNIZ (1683), Draft letter to Tschirnhaus. In *Der Briefwechsel von Gottfried Wilhelm Leibniz mit Mathematikern, Erster Band*, ed. C. I. GERHARDT, 446–450. Mayer & Müller, Berlin, 1899. Reprinted by Georg Olms Verlag, Hildesheim, 1987. [186]

GOTTFRIED WILHELM LEIBNIZ (1700), Nova algebrae promotio. Undated manuscript, c. 1700. In *Mathematische Schriften*, vol. 7, ed. C. I. GERHARDT, 1863, 154–189. Reprinted by Georg Olms Verlag, Hildesheim, 1971. [81]

GOTTFRIED WILHELM LEIBNIZ (1701), Initia mathematica. De ratione et proportione. Undated manuscript, c. 1701. In *Mathematische Schriften*, vol. 7, ed. C. I. GERHARDT, 1863, 40–49. Reprinted by Georg Olms Verlag, Hildesheim, 1971. [82]

FRANZ LEMMERMEYER (1995), The Euclidean algorithm in algebraic number fields. *Expositiones Mathematicae* **13**, 385–416. [688]

ARJEN K. LENSTRA (1984), Factoring Polynomials over Algebraic Number Fields. In *Proceedings of the 11th International Symposium Mathematical Foundations of Computer Science 1984*, Praha, Czechoslovakia. Lecture Notes in Computer Science **176**, 389–396. [440]

ARJEN K. LENSTRA (1987), Factoring multivariate polynomials over algebraic number fields. *SIAM Journal on Computing* **16**, 591–598. [440]

ARJEN K. LENSTRA (1990), Primality Testing. In *Cryptology and Computational Number Theory*, ed. CARL POMERANCE. Proceedings of Symposia in Applied Mathematics **42**, American Mathematical Society, 13–25. [506]

ARJEN K. LENSTRA and HENDRIK W. LENSTRA, JR. (1990), Algorithms in Number Theory. In *Handbook of Theoretical Computer Science*, vol. A, ed. J. VAN LEEUWEN, 673–715. Elsevier Science Publishers B.V., Amsterdam, and The MIT Press, Cambridge MA. [506]

ARJEN K. LENSTRA and HENDRIK W. LENSTRA, JR. (1993), eds., *The development of the number field sieve*. Lecture Notes in Mathematics **1554**, Springer-Verlag, Berlin. [543]

ARJEN K. LENSTRA, HENDRIK W. LENSTRA, JR., and L. LOVÁSZ (1982), Factoring Polynomials with Rational Coefficients. *Mathematische Annalen* **261**, 515–534. [448, 471, 480]

ARJEN K. LENSTRA, HENDRIK W. LENSTRA, JR., M. S. MANASSE, and J. M. POLLARD (1990), The number field sieve. In *Proceedings of the Twenty-second Annual ACM Symposium on the Theory of Computing*, Baltimore MD, ACM Press, 564–572. [543]

ARJEN K. LENSTRA, HENDRIK W. LENSTRA, JR., M. S. MANASSE, and J. M. POLLARD (1993), The factorization of the ninth Fermat number. *Mathematics of Computation* **61**(203), 319–349. [509, 516]

A. K. LENSTRA and M. S. MANASSE (1990), Factoring by electronic mail. In *Advances in Cryptology: Proceedings of EUROCRYPT 1989*, Houthalen, Belgium. Lecture Notes in Computer Science **434**, Springer-Verlag, Berlin, 355–371. [506]

HENDRIK W. LENSTRA, JR. (1979a), Euclidean Number Fields 1. *The Mathematical Intelligencer* **2**(1), 6–15. [688]

HENDRIK W. LENSTRA, JR. (1979b), Miller's primality test. *Information Processing Letters* **8**(2), 86–88. [507]

HENDRIK W. LENSTRA, JR. (1980a), Euclidean Number Fields 2. *The Mathematical Intelligencer* **2**(2), 73–77. [688]

HENDRIK W. LENSTRA, JR. (1980b), Euclidean Number Fields 3. *The Mathematical Intelligencer* **2**(2), 99–103. [688]

H. W. LENSTRA, JR. (1982), Primality testing. In *Computational Methods in Number Theory*, Part 1, eds. H. W. LENSTRA, JR. and R. TIJDEMAN, Mathematical Centre Tracts **154**, 55–77. Mathematisch Centrum, Amsterdam. [504, 508]

H. W. LENSTRA, JR. (1984), Galois theory and primality testing. In *Orders and their Applications*, eds. I. REINER and K. W. ROGGENKAMP, Lecture Notes in Mathematics **1142**, 169–189. Springer-Verlag. [508]

H. W. LENSTRA, JR. (1987), Factoring integers with elliptic curves. *Annals of Mathematics* **126**, 649–673. [509, 515, 531, 532, 539, 542]

H. W. LENSTRA, JR. (1990), Algorithms for finite fields. In *Number theory and cryptography*, ed. J. H. LOXTON, London Mathematical Society Lecture Notes **154**, 76–85. Cambridge University Press, Cambridge, UK. [543]

H. W. LENSTRA, JR. (1991), Finding isomorphisms between finite fields. *Mathematics of Computation* **56**(193), 329–347. [394]

H. W. LENSTRA, JR. and CARL POMERANCE (1992), A rigorous time bound for factoring integers. *Journal of the American Mathematical Society* **5**(3), 483–516. [543]

A. H. M. LEVELT (1997), The cycloheptane molecule – a challenge to computer algebra. Invited lecture given at the 1997 International Symposium on Symbolic and Algebraic Computation ISSAC '97, Maui HI. [662]

DANIEL LEWIN and SALIL VADHAN (1998), Checking Polynomial Identities over any Field: Towards a Derandomization? In *Proceedings of the Thirtieth Annual ACM Symposium on the Theory of Computing*, Dallas TX, ACM Press, 438–447. [187]

T. LICKTEIG (1987), The computational complexity of division in quadratic extension fields. *SIAM Journal on Computing* **16**, 278–311.

THOMAS LICKTEIG and MARIE-FRANÇOISE ROY (1997), Cauchy Index Computation. *Calcolo* **33**, 331–357. [173, 188, 310]

RUDOLF LIDL and HARALD NIEDERREITER (1997), *Finite Fields*. Encyclopedia of Mathematics and its Applications **20**, Cambridge University Press, Cambridge, UK, 2nd edition. First published by Addison-Wesley, Reading MA, 1983. [396, 675]

F. LINDEMANN (1882), Über die Zahl π. *Mathematische Annalen* **20**, 213–225. [75]

J. H. VAN LINT (1982), *Introduction to Coding Theory*. Graduate Texts in Mathematics **86**, Springer-Verlag, New York. [203]

JOSEPH LIOUVILLE (1833a), Sur la détermination des Intégrales dont la valeur est algébrique. *Journal de l'École Polytechnique* **14**, Premier Mémoire: 124–148, Second Mémoire: 149–193. [606]

JOSEPH LIOUVILLE (1833b), Note sur la détermination des intégrales dont la valeur est algébrique. *Journal für die Reine und Angewandte Mathematik* **10**, 347–359. Errata **11** (1834), 406. [606]

JOSEPH LIOUVILLE (1835), Mémoire sur l'intégration d'une classe de fonctions transcendantes. *Journal für die Reine und Angewandte Mathematik* **13**(2), 93–118. [597, 606]

JOHN D. LIPSON (1971), Chinese remainder and interpolation algorithms. In *Proceedings 2nd ACM Symposium on Symbolic and Algebraic Manipulation*, Los Angeles CA, ed. S. R. PETRICK, ACM Press, 372–391. [290]

JOHN D. LIPSON (1981), *Elements of Algebra and Algebraic Computing*. Addison-Wesley, Reading MA. [235]

PETR LISONĚK, PETER PAULE, and VOLKER STREHL (1993), Improvement of the degree setting in Gosper's algorithm. *Journal of Symbolic Computation* **16**, 243–258. [634]

DANIEL B. LLOYD (1964), Factorization of the general polynomial by means of its homomorphic congruential functions. *The American Mathematical Monthly* **71**, 863–870. [394]

DANIEL B. LLOYD and HARRY REMMERS (1966), Polynomial factor tables over finite fields. *Mathematical Algorithms* **1**, 85–99. [394]

RÜDIGER LOOS (1983), Computing rational zeroes of integral polynomials by *p*-adic expansion. *SIAM Journal on Computing* **12**(2), 286–293. [441]

S. C. LU and L. N. LEE (1979), A simple and effective public-key cryptosystem. *COMSAT Technical Review* **9**(1), 15–24. [483]

EDOUARD LUCAS (1878), Théorie des fonctions numériques simplement périodiques. *American Journal of Mathematics* **1**, I: 184–240, II: 289–321. [505]

PAUL LUCKEY (1951), *Die Rechenkunst bei Ǧamšīd b. Masʿūd al-Kāšī*. Abhandlungen für die Kunde des Morgenlandes, XXXI,1, Kommissionsverlag Franz Steiner GmbH, Wiesbaden. Herausgegeben von der Deutschen Morgenländischen Gesellschaft. [689]

P. LUCKEY (1953), *Der Lehrbrief über den Kreisumfang (Ar-risāla al-muḥīṭīya) von Ǧamšīd B. Masʿūd Al-Kāšī*. Abhandlungen der Deutschen Akademie der Wissenschaften zu Berlin, Klasse für Mathematik und allgemeine Naturwissenschaften **6**, Akademie-Verlag, Berlin. [83]

J. VAN DE LUNE, H. J. J. TE RIELE, and D. T. WINTER (1986), On the Zeros of the Riemann Zeta Function in the Critical Strip. IV. *Mathematics of Computation* **46**(174), 667–681. [508]

KEJU MA and JOACHIM VON ZUR GATHEN (1990), Analysis of Euclidean Algorithms for Polynomials over Finite Fields. *Journal of Symbolic Computation* **9**, 429–455. [57]

F. S. MACAULAY (1902), Some formulæ in elimination. *Proceedings of the London Mathematical Society* **35**, 3–27. [186, 593]

F. S. MACAULAY (1916), *The algebraic theory of modular systems.* Cambridge University Press, Cambridge, UK. Reissued 1994. [186, 593, 692, 693]

F. S. MACAULAY (1922), Note on the resultant of a number of polynomials of the same degree. *Proceedings of the London Mathematical Society, Second Series* **21**, 14–21. [186, 593]

D. MACK (1975), *On rational integration.* Technical Report UCP-38, Department of Computer Science, University of Utah. [607]

COLIN MACLAURIN (1742), *A treatise of fluxions.* 2 volumes, Edinburgh. 2nd ed., London, 1801; French translation Paris, 1749. [272]

F. J. MACWILLIAMS and N. J. A. SLOANE (1977), *The Theory of Error-Correcting Codes.* Mathematical Library **16**, North-Holland, Amsterdam. [203]

DIETRICH MAHNKE (1912/13), Leibniz auf der Suche nach einer allgemeinen Primzahlgleichung. *Bibliotheca Mathematica, Serie 3*, **13**, 29–61. [81, 506]

BENOÎT B. MANDELBROT (1977), *The fractral geometry of nature.* Freeman. [263]

Ю. И. МАНИН (1956), О сравнениях третьей степени по простому модулю. *Известия Академий Наук СССР, Серия Математическая* **20**, 673–678. YU. I. MANIN, On cubic congruences to a prime modulus, *American Mathematical Society Translations*, Series 2, **13** (1960), 1–7. [542]

J. L. MASSEY (1965), Step by step decoding of the Bose-Chaudhuri-Hocquenghem codes. *IEEE Transactions on Information Theory* **IT-11**, 580–585. [203]

Ю. В. МАТИЯСЕВИЧ (1970), Диофантовость перечислимих множеств. *Доклады Академий Наук СССР* **191**(2), 279–282. YU. V. MATIYASEVICH, Enumerable sets are Diophantine, *Soviet Mathematics Doklady* **11**(2), 354–358. [81]

ЮРИЙ В. МАТИЯСЕВИЧ (1993), *Десятая проблема Гильберта.* Наука, Moscow. YURI V. MATIYASEVICH, Hilbert's Tenth Problem, Foundations of Computing Series, The MIT Press, Cambridge MA, 1993. [82, 606]

UELI M. MAURER and STEFAN WOLF (1999), The Relationship Between Breaking the Diffie-Hellman Protocol and Computing Discrete Logarithms. *SIAM Journal on Computing.* To appear. [555]

ERNST W. MAYR (1984), An algorithm for the general Petri net reachability problem. *SIAM Journal on Computing* **13**(3), 441–460. [661]

ERNST MAYR (1989), Membership in Polynomial Ideals over *Q* Is Exponential Space Complete. In *Proceedings of the 6th Annual Symposium on Theoretical Aspects of Computer Science STACS '89,* Paderborn, Germany, eds. B. MONIEN and R. CORI. Lecture Notes in Computer Science **349**, Springer-Verlag, 400–406. [590]

ERNST W. MAYR (1992), Polynomial ideals and applications. *Festschrift zum 300jährigen Bestehen der Gesellschaft, Mitteilungen der Mathematischen Gesellschaft in Hamburg* **12**(4), 1207–1215. [590, 661]

ERNST W. MAYR (1995), On Polynomial Ideals, Their Complexity, and Applications. In *Proceedings of the 10th International Conference on Fundamentals of Computation Theory FCT '95,* Dresden, Germany, ed. HORST REICHEL. Lecture Notes in Computer Science **965**, Springer-Verlag, 89–105. [590, 661]

ERNST W. MAYR (1997), Some complexity results for polynomial ideals. *Journal of Complexity* **13**, 303–325. [592]

ERNST W. MAYR and ALBERT R. MEYER (1982), The Complexity of the Word Problems for Commutative Semigroups and Polynomial Ideals. *Advances in Mathematics* **46**, 305–329. [590, 592]

KEVIN S. MCCURLEY (1990), The Discrete Logarithm Problem. In *Cryptology and Computational Number Theory*, ed. CARL POMERANCE. Proceedings of Symposia in Applied Mathematics **42**, American Mathematical Society, 49–74. [555]

ROBERT J. MCELIECE (1969), Factorization of Polynomials over Finite Fields. *Mathematics of Computation* **23**, 861–867. [394]

ALFRED MENEZES (1993), *Elliptic curve public key cryptosystems*. Kluwer Academic Publishers, Boston MA. [555]

ALFRED J. MENEZES, PAUL C. VAN OORSCHOT, and SCOTT A. VANSTONE (1997), *Handbook of Applied Cryptography*. CRC Press, Boca Raton FL. [555]

RALPH C. MERKLE and MARTIN E. HELLMAN (1978), Hiding information and signatures in trapdoor knapsacks. *IEEE Transactions on Information Theory* **IT-24**(5), 525–530. [477, 478, 483, 550]

MARIN MERSENNE (1636), *Harmonie universelle contenant la théorie et la pratique de la musique*. Sebastien Cramoisy, Paris. Reprinted by Centre National de la Recherche Scientifique, Paris, 1975. [79]

F. MERTENS (1897), Über eine zahlentheoretische Function. *Sitzungsberichte der Akademie der Wissenschaften, Wien, Mathematisch-Naturwissenschaftliche Classe* **106**, 761–830. [482]

NICHOLAS METROPOLIS and S. ULAM (1949), The Monte Carlo Method. *Journal of the American Statistical Association* **44**, 335–341. [187]

SHAWNA MEYER EIKENBERRY and JONATHAN P. SORENSON (1998), Efficient algorithms for computing the Jacobi symbol. *Journal of Symbolic Computation* **26**(4), 509–523. [508]

M. MIGNOTTE (1974), An Inequality About Factors of Polynomials. *Mathematics of Computation* **28**(128), 1153–1157. [187]

M. MIGNOTTE (1982), Some Useful Bounds. In *Computer Algebra, Symbolic and Algebraic Computation*, eds. B. BUCHBERGER, G. E. COLLINS, and R. LOOS, 259–263. Springer-Verlag, New York, 2nd edition. [187]

MAURICE MIGNOTTE (1988), An Inequality about Irreducible Factors of Integer Polynomials. *Journal of Number Theory* **30**, 156–166. [187]

MAURICE MIGNOTTE (1989), *Mathématiques pour le calcul formel*. Presses Universitaires de France, Paris. English translation: *Mathematics for Computer Algebra*, Springer-Verlag, New York, 1992. [187]

MAURICE MIGNOTTE and PHILIPPE GLESSER (1994), On the Smallest Divisor of a Polynomial. *Journal of Symbolic Computation* **17**, 277–282. [187]

MAURICE MIGNOTTE and C. SCHNORR (1988), Calcul des racines d-ièmes dans un corps fini. *Comptes Rendus de l'Académie des Sciences Paris* **290**, 205–206. [396]

PREDA MIHĂILESCU (1989), A Primality Test using Cyclotomic Extensions. In *Algebraic Algorithms and Error-Correcting Codes: AAECC-6*, Rome, Italy, 1988, ed. T. MORA. Lecture Notes in Computer Science **357**, Springer-Verlag, 310–323. [509]

PREDA MIHĂILESCU (1998a), *Cyclotomy of Rings & Primality Testing*. PhD thesis, Swiss Federal Institute of Technology, Zürich, Switzerland. [509]

PREDA MIHĂILESCU (1998b), Cyclotomy Primality Proving—Recent Developments. In *Algorithmic Number Theory, Proceedings ANTS-III*, Portland OR, ed. J. P. BUHLER. Lecture Notes in Computer Science **1423**, Springer-Verlag, 95–110. [509]

GARY L. MILLER (1976), Riemann's Hypothesis and Tests for Primality. *Journal of Computer and System Sciences* **13**, 300–317. [505, 507]

VICTOR S. MILLER (1986), Use of Elliptic Curves in Cryptography. In *Advances in Cryptology: Proceedings of CRYPTO 1985*, Santa Barbara CA, ed. HUGH C. WILLIAMS. Lecture Notes in Computer Science **218**, Springer-Verlag, Berlin, 417–426. [555]

H. MINKOWSKI (1910), *Geometrie der Zahlen*. B. G. Teubner, Leipzig. [470]

R. T. MOENCK (1973), Fast computation of gcd's. In *Proceedings of the Fifth Annual ACM Symposium on the Theory of Computing*, Austin TX, ACM Press, 142–151. [310]

ROBERT T. MOENCK (1976), Practical Fast Polynomial Multiplication. In *Proceedings of the 1976 ACM Symposium on Symbolic and Algebraic Computation ISSAC '76*, Yorktown Heights NY, ed. R. D. JENKS, ACM Press, 136–148. [235]

ROBERT T. MOENCK (1977a), On the Efficiency of Algorithms for Polynomial Factoring. *Mathematics of Computation* **31**(137), 235–250. [396]

ROBERT MOENCK (1977b), On computing closed forms for summation. In *Proceedings of the 1977 MACSYMA Users Conference*, Berkeley CA, NASA, Washington DC, 225–236. [635, 637]

R. MOENCK and A. BORODIN (1972), Fast modular transform via division. In *Proceedings of the 13th Annual IEEE Symposium on Switching and Automata Theory*, Yorktown Heights NY, IEEE Press, New York, 90–96. [290]

H. MICHAEL MÖLLER and FERDINANDO MORA (1984), Upper and lower bounds for the degree of Gröbner bases. In *Proceedings of EUROSAM '84*, Cambridge, UK, ed. JOHN FITCH. Lecture Notes in Computer Science **174**, Springer-Verlag, New York, 172–183. [592]

LOUIS MONIER (1980), Evaluation and comparison of two efficient probabilistic primality testing algorithms. *Theoretical Computer Science* **12**, 97–108. [507, 508]

PETER L. MONTGOMERY (1985), Modular Multiplication Without Trial Division. *Mathematics of Computation* **44**(170), 519–521. [273]

PETER. L. MONTGOMERY (1991), Factorization of $X^{216091} + X + 1$ mod 2—A problem of Herb Doughty. Manuscript. [266]

PETER LAWRENCE MONTGOMERY (1992), *An FFT Extension of the Elliptic Curve Method of Factorization.* PhD thesis, University of California, Los Angeles CA. ftp://ftp.cwi.nl/pub/pmontgom/ucladissertation.psl.gz. [272, 292]

PETER L. MONTGOMERY (1995), A Block Lanczos Algorithm for Finding Dependencies over GF(2). In *Advances in Cryptology: Proceedings of EUROCRYPT 1995*, Saint-Malo, France, eds. LOUIS C. GUILLOU and JEAN-JACQUES QUISQUATER. Lecture Notes in Computer Science **921**, Springer-Verlag, 106–120. [331]

F. MORAIN (1998), Primality Proving Using Elliptic Curves: An Update. In *Algorithmic Number Theory, Proceedings ANTS-III*, Portland OR, ed. J. P. BUHLER. Lecture Notes in Computer Science **1423**, Springer-Verlag, 111–127. [509]

ROBERT EDOUARD MORITZ (1914), *Memorabilia Mathematica.* The Mathematical Association of America. [693]

MICHAEL A. MORRISON and JOHN BRILLHART (1971), The factorization of F_7. *Bulletin of the American Mathematical Society* **77**(2), p. 264. [516, 542]

MICHAEL A. MORRISON and JOHN BRILLHART (1975), A Method of Factoring and the Factorization of F_7. *Mathematics of Computation* **29**(129), 183–205. [515, 542]

JOEL MOSES and DAVID Y. Y. YUN (1973), The EZGCD Algorithm. In *Proceedings of the ACM National Conference*, Atlanta GA, 159–166. [187, 441]

RAJEEV MOTWANI and PRABHAKAR RAGHAVAN (1995), *Randomized Algorithms.* Cambridge University Press, Cambridge, UK. [81, 187]

THOM MULDERS (1997), A note on subresultants and the Lazard/Rioboo/Trager formula in rational function integration. *Journal of Symbolic Computation* **24**(1), 45–50. [188]

R. C. MULLIN, I. M. ONYSZCHUK, S. A. VANSTONE, and R. M. WILSON (1989), Optimal normal bases in GF(p^n). *Discrete Applied Mathematics* **22**, 149–161. [81]

DAVID R. MUSSER (1971), *Algorithms for Polynomial Factorization.* PhD thesis, Computer Science Department, University of Wisconsin. Technical Report #134, 174 pages. [440]

MATS NÄSLUND (1998), *Bit Extraction, Hard-Core Predicates, and the Bit Security of RSA.* PhD thesis, Department of Numerical Analysis and Computing Science, Kungl Tekniska Högskolan (Royal Institute of Technology), Stockholm. [555]

ISAAC NEWTON (1707), *Arithmetica Universalis, sive de compositione et resolutione arithmetica liber.* J. Senex, London. English translation as *Universal Arithmetick: or, A Treatise on Arithmetical composition and Resolution*, translated by the late Mr. Raphson and revised and corrected by Mr. Cunn, London, 1728. Reprinted in: DEREK T. WHITESIDE, *The mathematical works of Isaac Newton*, Johnson Reprint Co, New York, 1967, p. 4 ff. [55, 191, 689, 690]

ISAAC NEWTON (1710), Quadrature of Curves. In *Lexicon Technicum. Or, an Universal Dictionary of Arts and Sciences*, vol. 2, John Harris. Reprinted in: DEREK T. WHITESIDE, *The mathematical works of Isaac Newton*, vol. 1, Johnson Reprint Co, New York, 1967. [272]

THOMAS R. NICELY (1996), Enumeration to 10^{14} of the Twin Primes and Brun's Constant. *Virginia Journal of Science* **46**(3), 195–204. [76]

H. NIEDERREITER (1986), Knapsack-type cryptosystems and algebraic coding theory. *Problems of Control and Information Theory* **15**, 159–166. [483]

HARALD NIEDERREITER (1993a), A New Efficient Factorization Algorithm for Polynomials over Small Finite Fields. *Applied Algebra in Engineering, Communication and Computing* **4**, 81–87. [395]

H. NIEDERREITER (1993b), Factorization of Polynomials and Some Linear Algebra Problems over Finite Fields. *Linear Algebra and its Applications* **192**, 301–328. [395]

HARALD NIEDERREITER (1994a), Factoring polynomials over finite fields using differential equations and normal bases. *Mathematics of Computation* **62**(206), 819–830. [395]

HARALD NIEDERREITER (1994b), New deterministic factorization algorithms for polynomials over finite fields. In *Finite fields: theory, applications and algorithms*, eds. G. L. MULLEN and P. J.-S. SHIUE. Contemporary Mathematics **168**, American Mathematical Society, 251–268. [395]

HARALD NIEDERREITER and RAINER GÖTTFERT (1993), Factorization of Polynomials over Finite Fields and Characteristic Sequences. *Journal of Symbolic Computation* **16**, 401–412. [395]

HARALD NIEDERREITER and RAINER GÖTTFERT (1995), On a new factorization algorithm for polynomials over finite fields. *Mathematics of Computation* **64**(209), 347–353. [395]

A. M. ODLYZKO (1990), The Rise and Fall of Knapsack Cryptosystems. In *Cryptology and Computational Number Theory*, ed. CARL POMERANCE. Proceedings of Symposia in Applied Mathematics **42**, American Mathematical Society, 75–88. [471, 483]

A. M. ODLYZKO (1995a), Asymptotic Enumeration Methods. In *Handbook of Combinatorics*, eds. R. GRAHAM, M. GRÖTSCHEL, and L. LOVÁSZ. Elsevier Science Publishers B.V., Amsterdam, and The MIT Press, Cambridge MA. [661]

ANDREW M. ODLYZKO (1995b), The Future of Integer Factorization. *CryptoBytes* **1**(2), 5–12. [555]

ANDREW M. ODLYZKO (1995c), Analytic computations in number theory. In *Mathematics of Computation 1943–1993: A Half-Century of Computational Mathematics*, ed. WALTER GAUTSCHI. Proceedings of Symposia in Applied Mathematics **48**, American Mathematical Society, 451–463. [508]

A. M. ODLYZKO and H. J. J. TE RIELE (1985), Disproof of the Mertens conjecture. *Journal für die Reine und Angewandte Mathematik* **357**, 138–160. [482]

A. M. ODLYZKO and A. SCHÖNHAGE (1988), Fast algorithms for multiple evaluations of the Riemann zeta function. *Transactions of the American Mathematical Society* **309**(2), 797–809. [508]

JOSEPH OESTERLÉ (1979), Versions effectives du théorème de Chebotarev sous l'hypothèse de Riemann généralisée. *Société Mathématique de France, Astérisque* **61**, 165–167. [417]

H. ONG, C. P. SCHNORR, and A. SHAMIR (1984), An efficient signature scheme based on quadratic equations. In *Proceedings of the Sixteenth Annual ACM Symposium on the Theory of Computing*, Washington DC, ACM Press, 208–216. [483]

LUITZEN JOHANNES OOSTERHOFF (1949), *Restricted free rotation and cyclic molecules*. PhD thesis, Rijksuniversiteit te Leiden. [662]

ALAN V. OPPENHEIM and RONALD W. SCHAFER (1975), *Digital Signal Processing*. Prentice-Hall, Inc., Englewood Cliffs NJ. [344]

ALAN V. OPPENHEIM, ALAN S. WILLSKY, and IAN T. YOUNG (1983), *Signals and Systems*. Prentice-Hall signal processing series, Prentice-Hall, Inc., Englewood Cliffs NJ. [344]

M. OSTROGRADSKY (1845), De l'intégration des fractions rationnelles. *Bulletin de la classe physico-mathématique de l'Académie Impériale des Sciences de Saint-Pétersbourg* **4**(82/83), 145–167. [606]

H. PADÉ (1892), Sur la représentation approchée d'une fonction par des fractions rationnelles. *Annales Scientifiques de l'Ecole Normale Supérieure, 3e série* **9**, Supplément S3-S93. [123]

В. Я. ПАН (1966), О способах вычисления значении многочленов. *Успехи Математических Наук* **21**(1(127)), 103–134. V. YA. PAN, Methods of computing values of polynomials, *Russian Mathematical Surveys* **21** (1966), 105–136. [290]

V. YA. PAN (1984), *How to multiply matrices faster*. Lecture Notes in Computer Science **179**, Springer-Verlag, New York. [330]

VICTOR Y. PAN (1997), Faster Solution of the Key Equation for Decoding BCH Error-Correcting Codes. In *Proceedings of the Twenty-ninth Annual ACM Symposium on the Theory of Computing*, El Paso TX, ACM Press, 168–175. [310]

DANIEL NELSON PANARIO RODRIGUEZ (1997), *Combinatorial and Algebraic Aspects of Polynomials over Finite Fields*. PhD thesis, Department of Computer Science, University of Toronto. Technical Report 306/97, 154 pages. [394]

DANIEL PANARIO, XAVIER GOURDON, and PHILIPPE FLAJOLET (1998), An Analytic Approach to Smooth Polynomials over Finite Fields. In *Algorithmic Number Theory, Proceedings ANTS-III*, Portland OR, ed. J. P. BUHLER. Lecture Notes in Computer Science **1423**, Springer-Verlag, 226–236. [394]

DANIEL PANARIO and BRUCE RICHMOND (1998), Analysis of Ben-Or's Polynomial Irreducibility Test. *Random Structures and Algorithms* **13**(3/4), 439–456. [394, 396]

DANIEL PANARIO and ALFREDO VIOLA (1998), Analysis of Rabin's polynomial irreducibility test. In *Proceedings of LATIN '98*, Campinas, Brazil, eds. CLÁUDIO L. LUCCHESI and ARNALDO V. MOURA. Lecture Notes in Computer Science **1380**, Springer-Verlag, 1–10. [394, 396]

CHRISTOS H. PAPADIMITRIOU (1993), *Computational complexity*. Addison-Wesley, Reading MA. [685]

DAVID PARSONS and JOHN CANNY (1994), Geometric Problems in Molecular Biology and Robotics. In *Proceedings 2nd International Conference on Intelligent Systems for Molecular Biology*, Palo Alto CA, 322–330. [662]

PETER PAULE (1994), Short and Easy Computer Proofs of the Rogers-Ramanujan Identities and of Identities of Similar Type. *The Electronic Journal of Combinatorics* **1**(# R10). 9 pages. [661]

PETER PAULE (1995), Greatest Factorial Factorization and Symbolic Summation. *Journal of Symbolic Computation* **20**, 235–268. [634, 635]

PETER PAULE and VOLKER STREHL (1995), Symbolic summation — some recent developments. In *Computer Algebra in Science and Engineering*, Bielefeld, Germany, August 1994, eds. J. FLEISCHER, J. GRABMEIER, F. W. HEHL, and W. KÜCHLIN, World Scientific, Singapore, 138–162. [635]

HEINZ-OTTO PEITGEN, HARTMUT JÜRGENS, and DIETMAR SAUPE (1992), *Chaos and Fractals: New Frontiers of Sience.* Springer-Verlag, New York. [263]

WILLIAM B. PENNEBAKER and JOAN C. MITCHELL (1993), *JPEG still image data compression standard.* Van Nostrand Reinhold, New York. [344]

PEPIN (1877), Sur la formule $2^{2^n} + 1$. *Comptes Rendus des Séances de l'Académie des Sciences, Paris* **85**, 329–331. [505, 513]

OSKAR PERRON (1929), *Die Lehre von den Kettenbrüchen.* 2nd edition. Reprinted by Chelsea Publishing Co., New York. [82]

JAMES L. PETERSON (1981), *Petri net theory and the modeling of systems.* Prentice-Hall, Inc., Englewood Cliffs NJ. [661]

MARKO PETKOVŠEK (1992), Hypergeometric solutions of linear recurrences with polynomial coefficients. *Journal of Symbolic Computation* **14**, 243–264. [639]

MARKO PETKOVŠEK, HERBERT S. WILF, and DORON ZEILBERGER (1996), *A=B.* A K Peters, Wellesley MA. [661, 693]

KAREL PETR (1937), Über die Reduzibilität eines Polynoms mit ganzzahligen Koeffizienten nach einem Primzahlmodul. *Časopis pro pěstování matematiky a fysiky* **66**, 85–94. [377, 395]

C. A. PETRI (1962), *Kommunikation mit Automaten.* PhD thesis, Universität Bonn. [643]

R. G. E. PINCH (1993), Some Primality Testing Algorithms. *Notices of the American Mathematical Society* **40**(9), 1203–1210. [507]

R. PIRASTU (1992), *Algorithmen zur Summation rationaler Funktionen.* Diplomarbeit, Universität Erlangen-Nürnberg, Germany. [634, 637]

TONIANN PITASSI (1997), Algebraic Propositional Proof Systems. In *Descriptive Complexity and Finite Models: Proceedings of a DIMACS Workshop, January 14–17, 1996,* Princeton NJ, eds. NEIL IMMERMAN and PHOKION G. KOLAITIS. DIMACS Series in Discrete Mathematics and Theoretical Computer Science **31**, American Mathematical Society, Providence RI, 215–244. [661]

H. C. POCKLINGTON (1917), The Direct Solution of the Quadratic and Cubic Binomial Congruences with Prime Moduli. *Proceedings of the Cambridge Philosophical Society* **19**, 57–59. [81, 187]

J. M. POLLARD (1971), The Fast Fourier Transform in a Finite Field. *Mathematics of Computation* **25**(114), 365–374. [235, 266]

J. M. POLLARD (1974), Theorems on factorization and primality testing. *Proceedings of the Cambridge Philosophical Society* **76**, 521–528. [515, 541]

J. M. POLLARD (1975), A Monte Carlo method for factorization. *BIT* **15**, 331–334. [515, 519, 542]

C. POMERANCE (1982), Analysis and comparison of some integer factoring algorithms. In *Computational Methods in Number Theory,* Part 1, eds. H. W. LENSTRA, JR. and R. TIJDEMAN, Mathematical Centre Tracts **154**, 89–139. Mathematisch Centrum, Amsterdam. [530, 541, 543]

CARL POMERANCE (1985), The quadratic sieve factoring algorithm. In *Advances in Cryptology: Proceedings of EUROCRYPT 1984,* Paris, France, eds. T. BETH, N. COT, and I. INGEMARSSON. Lecture Notes in Computer Science **209**, Springer-Verlag, Berlin, 169–182. [530]

CARL POMERANCE (1990a), ed., *Cryptology and Computational Number Theory.* Proceedings of Symposia in Applied Mathematics **42**, American Mathematical Society. [555]

CARL POMERANCE (1990b), Factoring. In *Cryptology and Computational Number Theory,* ed. CARL POMERANCE. Proceedings of Symposia in Applied Mathematics **42**, American Mathematical Society, 27–47. [494, 541]

C. POMERANCE, J. L. SELFRIDGE, and S. S. WAGSTAFF, JR. (1980), The pseudoprimes to $25 \cdot 10^9$. *Mathematics of Computation* **35**, 1003–1025. [507]

CARL POMERANCE and S. S. WAGSTAFF, JR. (1983), Implementation of the continued fraction integer factoring algorithm. *Congressus Numerantium* **37**, 99–118. [543]

ALFRED VAN DER POORTEN (1978), A proof that Euler missed ... Apéry's proof of the irrationality of $\zeta(3)$. *The Mathematical Intelligencer* **1**, 195–203. [661]

ALF VAN DER POORTEN (1996), *Notes on Fermat's Last Theorem.* Canadian Mathematical Society series of monographs and advanced texts, John Wiley & Sons, New York. [488]

EUGENE PRANGE (1959), *An algorism for factoring $X^n - 1$ over a finite field.* Technical Report AFCRC-TN-59-775, Air Force Cambridge Research Center, Bedford MA. [394, 405]

VAUGHAN R. PRATT (1975), Every prime has a succinct certificate. *SIAM Journal on Computing* **4**(3), 214–220. [504, 509, 513]

PAUL PRITCHARD (1983), Fast Compact Prime Number Sieves (among Others). *Journal of Algorithms* **4**, 332–344. [508]

PAUL PRITCHARD (1987), Linear prime-number sieves: a family tree. *Science of Computer Programming* **9**, 17–35. [508]

GEORGE B. PURDY (1974), A high-security log-in procedure. *Communications of the ACM* **17**(8), 442–445. [556]

MICHAEL O. RABIN (1976), Probabilistic algorithms. In *Algorithms and Complexity*, ed. J. F. TRAUB,
    Academic Press, New York, 21–39. [507]
MICHAEL O. RABIN (1980a), Probabilistic Algorithms for Testing Primality. *Journal of Number Theory* **12**,
    128–138. [507]
MICHAEL O. RABIN (1980b), Probabilistic algorithms in finite fields. *SIAM Journal on Computing* **9**(2),
    273–280. [396, 399]
MICHAEL O. RABIN (1989), Efficient Dispersal of Information for Security, Load Balancing, and Fault
    Tolerance. *Journal of the ACM* **36**(2), 335–348. [122, 203]
J. L. RABINOWITSCH (1930), Zum Hilbertschen Nullstellensatz. *Mathematische Annalen* **102**, p. 520. [592]
BARTOLOMÉ RAMOS (1482), *De musica tractatus*. Bologna. [79]
JOSEPH RAPHSON (1690), *Analysis Æquationum universalis seu Ad Æquationes algebraicas Resolvendas
    methodus generalis, et expedita, ex nova infinitarum serierum doctrina deducta ac demonstrata*. Abel
    Swalle, London. [207]
ALEXANDER A. RAZBOROV (1998), Lower bounds for the polynomial calculus. *computational
    complexity* **7**(4), 291–324. [661]
CONSTANCE REID (1970), *Hilbert*. Springer-Verlag, Heidelberg, 1st edition. Third Printing 1978. [561]
DANIEL REISCHERT (1995), *Schnelle Multiplikation von Polynomen über GF(2) und Anwendungen*.
    Diplomarbeit, Institut für Informatik II, Rheinische Friedrich-Wilhelm-Universität Bonn, Germany. [265]
DANIEL REISCHERT (1997), Asymptotically Fast Computation of Subresultants. In *Proceedings of the 1997
    International Symposium on Symbolic and Algebraic Computation ISSAC '97*, Maui HI, ed.
    WOLFGANG W. KÜCHLIN, ACM Press, 233–240. [310]
WOLFGANG REISIG (1985), *Petri Nets: An Introduction*. EATCS Monographs on Theoretical Computer
    Science **4**, Springer-Verlag, Berlin. Translation of the German edition *Petrinetze: eine Einführung*,
    Springer-Verlag, 1982. [661]
GEORGE W. REITWIESNER (1950), An ENIAC Determination of π and e to more than 2000 Decimal Places.
    Mathematical Tables and other Aids to Computation **4**, 11–15. Reprinted in Berggren, Borwein &
    Borwein (1997), 277–281. [76]
JAMES RENEGAR (1991), Recent Progress on the Complexity of the Decision Problem for the Reals. In
    Discrete and Computational Geometry: Papers from the DIMACS Special Year, eds. JACOB E.
    GOODMAN, RICHARD POLLACK, and WILLIAM STEIGER. DIMACS Series in Discrete Mathematics
    and Theoretical Computer Science **6**, American Mathematical Society and ACM, 287–308. [593]
JAMES RENEGAR (1992a), On the Computational Complexity of the First-order Theory of the Reals. Part I:
    Introduction. Preliminaries. The Geometry of Semi-algebraic Sets. The Decision Problem for the
    Existential Theory of the Reals. *Journal of Symbolic Computation* **13**(3), 255–299. [593]
JAMES RENEGAR (1992b), On the Computational Complexity of the First-order Theory of the Reals. Part II:
    The General Decision Problem. Preliminaries for Quantifier Elimination. *Journal of Symbolic
    Computation* **13**(3), 301–327. [593]
JAMES RENEGAR (1992c), On the Computational Complexity of the First-order Theory of the Reals. Part III:
    Quantifier Elimination. *Journal of Symbolic Computation* **13**(3), 329–352. [593]
REYNAUD (1824), *Traité d'arithmétique à l'usage des élèves qui se destinent à l'École Polytechnique à l'école
    spéciale militaire et à l'école de marine*. Courcier, Paris, 12th edition. [56]
DANIEL RICHARDSON (1968), Some undecidable problems involving elementary functions of a real variable.
    Journal of Symbolic Logic **33**(4), 514–520. [606]
GEORG FRIEDRICH BERNHARD RIEMANN (1859), Ueber die Anzahl der Primzahlen unter einer gegebenen
    Grösse. *Monatsberichte der Berliner Akademie*, 145–153. *Gesammelte Mathematische Werke*, ed.
    HEINRICH WEBER, Teubner Verlag, Leipzig, 1892, 177-185. [507]
ROBERT H. RISCH (1969), The problem of integration in finite terms. *Transactions of the American
    Mathematical Society* **139**, 167–189. [606]
ROBERT H. RISCH (1970), The solution of the problem of integration in finite terms. *Bulletin of the American
    Mathematical Society* **76**(3), 605–608. [606]
J. F. RITT (1948), *Integration in Finite Terms*. Columbia University Press, New York. [606]
JOSEPH FELS RITT (1950), *Differential Algebra*. American Mathematical Society, Providence RI. Reprint by
    Dover Publications, Inc., New York, 1966. [593]
R. L. RIVEST, A. SHAMIR, and L. M. ADLEMAN (1978), A Method for Obtaining Digital Signatures and
    Public-Key Cryptosystems. *Communications of the ACM* **21**(2), 120–126. [550]
STEVEN ROMAN (1984), *The umbral calculus*. Pure and applied mathematics **111**, Academic Press,
    Orlando FL. [634]
LAJOS RÓNYAI (1988), Factoring Polynomials over Finite Fields. *Journal of Algorithms* **9**, 391–400. [397]
LAJOS RÓNYAI (1989), Galois groups and factoring over finite fields. In *Proceedings of the 30th Annual IEEE
    Symposium on Foundations of Computer Science*, Research Triangle Park NC, IEEE Computer Society
    Press, Los Alamitos CA, 99–104. [397]

FREDERIC ROSEN (1831), *The Algebra of Mohammed ben Musa*. Oriental Translation Fund, London. Reprint by Georg Olms Verlag, Hildesheim, 1986. [690]

J. BARKLEY ROSSER and LOWELL SCHOENFELD (1962), Approximate formulas for some functions of prime numbers. *Illinois Journal of Mathematics* **6**, 64–94. [501, 507, 511]

MICHAEL ROTHSTEIN (1976), *Aspects of symbolic integration and simplification of exponential and primitive functions*. PhD thesis, University of Wisconsin-Madison. [606]

MICHAEL ROTHSTEIN (1977), A new algorithm for the integration of exponential and logarithmic functions. In *Proceedings of the 1977 MACSYMA Users Conference*, Berkeley CA, NASA, Washington DC, 263–274. [606]

H. SACHSE (1890), Ueber die geometrischen Isomerien der Hexamethylenderivate. *Berichte der Deutschen Chemischen Gesellschaft* **23**, 1363–1370. [662]

H. SACHSE (1892), Über die Konfigurationen der Polymethylenringe. *Zeitschrift für physikalische Chemie* **10**, 203–241. [662]

BRUNO SALVY (1991), *Asymptotique automatique et fonctions génératrices*. PhD thesis, École Polytechnique, Paris. [661]

ERHARD SCHMIDT (1907), Zur Theorie der linearen und nichtlinearen Integralgleichungen, I. Teil: Entwicklung willkürlicher Funktionen nach Systemen vorgeschriebener. *Mathematische Annalen*, 433–476. Reprint of Erhard Schmidt's Dissertation, Göttingen, 1905. [470]

C. P. SCHNORR (1982), Refined Analysis and Improvements on Some Factoring Algorithms. *Journal of Algorithms* **3**, 101–127. [541]

C. P. SCHNORR (1987), A hierarchy of polynomial time lattice basis reduction algorithms. *Theoretical Computer Science* **53**, 201–224. [471]

C. P. SCHNORR (1988), A More Efficient Algorithm for Lattice Basis Reduction. *Journal of Algorithms* **9**, 47–62. [471]

C. P. SCHNORR and M. EUCHNER (1991), Lattice Basis Reduction: Improved Practical Algorithms and Solving Subset Sum Problems. In *Proceedings of the 8th International Conference on Fundamentals of Computation Theory 1991*, Gosen, Germany, ed. LOTHAR BUDACH. Lecture Notes in Computer Science **529**, Springer-Verlag, 68–85. [471]

A. SCHÖNHAGE (1966), Multiplikation großer Zahlen. *Computing* **1**, 182–196. [234]

A. SCHÖNHAGE (1971), Schnelle Berechnung von Kettenbruchentwicklungen. *Acta Informatica* **1**, 139–144. [310]

A. SCHÖNHAGE (1977), Schnelle Multiplikation von Polynomen über Körpern der Charakteristik 2. *Acta Informatica* **7**, 395–398. [232, 234, 240]

ARNOLD SCHÖNHAGE (1984), Factorization of univariate integer polynomials by Diophantine approximation and an improved basis reduction algorithm. In *Proceedings of the 11th International Colloquium on Automata, Languages and Programming ICALP 1984*, Antwerp, Belgium. Lecture Notes in Computer Science **172**, Springer-Verlag, 436–447. [471]

ARNOLD SCHÖNHAGE (1985), Quasi-GCD Computations. *Journal of Complexity* **1**, 118–137. [191]

A. SCHÖNHAGE (1988), Probabilistic Computation of Integer Polynomial GCDs. *Journal of Algorithms* **9**, 365–371. [191]

ARNOLD SCHÖNHAGE, ANDREAS F. W. GROTEFELD, and EKKEHART VETTER (1994), *Fast Algorithms – A Multitape Turing Machine Implementation*. BI Wissenschaftsverlag, Mannheim. [265, 691]

A. SCHÖNHAGE and V. STRASSEN (1971), Schnelle Multiplikation großer Zahlen. *Computing* **7**, 281–292. [209, 210, 230, 232, 234, 241, 269]

FRIEDRICH THEODOR VON SCHUBERT (1793), De inventione divisorum. *Nova Acta Academiae Scientiarum Imperalis Petropolitanae* **11**, 172–182. [440]

J. T. SCHWARTZ (1980), Fast Probabilistic Algorithms for Verification of Polynomial Identities. *Journal of the ACM* **27**(4), 701–717. [187, 310]

ŠTEFAN SCHWARZ (1939), Contribution à la réductibilité des polynômes dans la théorie des congruences. *Věstník Královské České Společnosti Nauk, Třída Matemat.-Př Ročník Praha*, 1–7. [395]

ŠTEFAN SCHWARZ (1940), Sur le nombre des racines et des facteurs irréductibles d'une congruence donnée. *Časopis pro pěstování matematiky a fysiky* **69**, 128–145. [395]

ŠTEFAN SCHWARZ (1956), On the reducibility of polynomials over a finite field. *Quarterly Journal of Mathematics Oxford* **7**(2), 110–124. [395]

ШТЕФАН ШВАРЦ (ŠTEFAN SCHWARZ) (1960), Об одном классе многочленов над конечным телом (On a class of polynomials over a finite field). *Matematicko-Fyzikálny Časopis* **10**, 68–80. [395]

ШТЕФАН ШВАРЦ (ŠTEFAN SCHWARZ) (1961), О числе неприводимых факторов данного многочлена над конечным полем (On the number of irreducible factors of a polynomial over a finite field). *Чехословацкий математический журнал* (Czechoslovak Mathematical Journal) **11**(86), 213–225. [395]

DANIEL SCHWENTER (1636), *Deliciæ Physico-Mathematiæ*. Jeremias Dümler, Nürnberg. Reprint by Keip Verlag, Frankfurt am Main, 1991. [56, 122, 661]

ROBERT SEDGEWICK and PHILIPPE FLAJOLET (1996), *An Introduction to the Analysis of Algorithms.*
    Addison-Wesley, Reading MA. [661]

J.-A. SERRET (1866), *Cours d'algèbre supérieure.* Gauthier-Villars, Paris, 3rd edition. [393]

JEFFREY SHALLIT (1990), On the Worst Case of Three Algorithms for Computing the Jacobi Symbol. *Journal
    of Symbolic Computation* **10**, 593–610. [508]

JEFFREY SHALLIT (1994), Origins of the Analysis of the Euclidean Algorithm. *Historia Mathematica* **21**,
    401–419. [56]

ADI SHAMIR (1979), How to Share a Secret. *Communications of the ACM* **22**(11), 612–613. [122]

ADI SHAMIR (1984), A polynomial-time algorithm for breaking the basic Merkle-Hellman cryptosystem. *IEEE
    Transactions on Information Theory* **IT-30**(5), 699–704. [477, 483]

A. SHAMIR (1993), On the Generation of Polynomials which are Hard to Factor. In *Proceedings of the
    Twenty-fifth Annual ACM Symposium on the Theory of Computing*, San Diego CA, ACM Press,
    796–804. [443]

ADI SHAMIR and RICHARD E. ZIPPEL (1980), On the Security of the Merkle-Hellman Cryptographic Scheme.
    IEEE Transactions on Information Theory **IT-26**(3), 339–340. [483]

DANIEL SHANKS and JOHN W. WRENCH, JR. (1962), Calculation of π to 100,000 Decimals. *Mathematics of
    Computation* **16**, 76–99. [76]

WILLIAM SHANKS (1853), *Contributions to Mathematics Comprising Chiefly the Rectification of the Circle to
    607 Places of Decimals.* G. Bell, London. Excerpt reprinted in Berggren, Borwein & Borwein (1997),
    147–161. [76, 83, 692]

C. E. SHANNON (1948), A Mathematical Theory of Communication. *Bell System Technical Journal* **27**,
    379–423 and 623–656. Reprinted in CLAUDE E. SHANNON and WARREN WEAVER, *The mathematical
    theory of communication*, University of Illinois Press, Urbana IL, 1949. [197, 203, 291]

SHEN KANGSHENG (1988), Historical Development of the Chinese Remainder Theorem. *Archive of the
    History of Exact Sciences* **38**, 285–305. [122]

L. A. SHEPP and S. P. LLOYD (1966), Ordered cycle lengths in a random permutation. *Transactions of the
    American Mathematical Society* **121**, 340–357. [396]

VICTOR SHOUP (1991), *Topics in the theory of computation.* Lecture Notes for CSC 2429, Spring term,
    Department of Computer Science, University of Toronto. [194]

VICTOR SHOUP (1994), Fast Construction of Irreducible Polynomials over Finite Fields. *Journal of Symbolic
    Computation* **17**, 371–391. [396]

VICTOR SHOUP (1995), A New Polynomial Factorization Algorithm and its Implementation. *Journal of
    Symbolic Computation* **20**, 363–397. [234, 265, 437]

IGOR E. SHPARLINSKI (1992), *Computational and Algorithmic Problems in Finite Fields.* Mathematics and its
    applications **88**, Kluwer Academic Publishers. [394]

IGOR E. SHPARLINSKI (1999), *Finite Fields: Theory and Computation.* Kluwer Academic Publishers. [394]

M. SIEVEKING (1972), An Algorithm for Division of Powerseries. *Computing* **10**, 153–156. [272]

JOSEPH H. SILVERMAN (1986), *The Arithmetic of Elliptic Curves.* Graduate Texts in Mathematics **106**,
    Springer-Verlag, New York. [542]

ROBERT D. SILVERMAN (1987), The Multiple Polynomial Quadratic Sieve. *Mathematics of
    Computation* **48**(177), 329–339. [541]

SIMON SINGH (1997), *Fermat's Enigma: The epic quest to solve the world's greatest mathematical problem.*
    Anchor Books, New York. [488]

MICHAEL SIPSER (1997), *Introduction to the Theory of Computation.* PWS Publishing Company, Boston MA.
    [81, 685]

A. O. SLISENKO (1981), Complexity problems in computational theory. Успехи Математически Наук
    (*Uspekhi Matematicheski Nauk*) **36**(6), 21–103. *Russian Mathematical Surveys* **36** (1981), 23–125. [394]

R. SOLOVAY and V. STRASSEN (1977), A fast Monte-Carlo test for primality. *SIAM Journal on
    Computing* **6**(1), 84–85. Erratum in **7** (1978), p. 118. [187, 503, 504, 508]

JONATHAN P. SORENSON (1998), Trading Time for Space in Prime Number Sieves. In *Algorithmic Number
    Theory, Proceedings ANTS-III*, Portland OR, ed. J. P. BUHLER. Lecture Notes in Computer
    Science **1423**, Springer-Verlag, 179–195. [508]

В. Г. СПРИНДЖУК (1981), Диофантовы уравнения с неизвестными простыми числами.
    Труды Математического института АН СССР **158**, 180–196. V. G. SPRINDZHUK,
    Diophantine equations with unknown prime numbers, Proc. Steklov Institute of Mathematics **158** (1983),
    197–214. [471]

V. G. SPRINDŽUK (1983), Arithmetic specializations in polynomials. *Journal für die Reine und Angewandte
    Mathematik* **340**, 26–52. [471]

P. STEVENHAGEN and H. W. LENSTRA, JR. (1996), Chebotarëv and his density theorem. *The Mathematical
    Intelligencer* **18**(2), 26–37. [415]

SIMON STEVIN (1585), *De Thiende.* Christoffel Plantijn, Leyden. Übersetzt und erläutert von HELMUTH
    GERICKE und KURT VOGEL, Akademische Verlagsgesellschaft, Frankfurt am Main, 1965. [39]

DOUGLAS R. STINSON (1995), *Cryptography, Theory and Practice*. CRC Press Inc., Boca Raton FL. [555]

JAMES STIRLING (1730), *Methodus Differentialis: sive Tractatus de Summatione et Interpolatione Serierum Infinitarum*. Gul. Bowyer, London. Translated into English with the Author's Approbation By FRANCIS HOLLIDAY, Master of the Grammar Free-School at Haughton-Park near Retford, Nottinghamshire, London, 1749. [634]

ARNE STORJOHANN (1996), *Faster Algorithms for Integer Lattice Basis Reduction*. Technical Report 249, Eidgenössische Technische Hochschule Zürich. 24 pages. [471]

ARNE STORJOHANN and GEORGE LABAHN (1996), Asymptotically Fast Computation of Hermite Normal Forms of Integer Matrices. In *Proceedings of the 1996 International Symposium on Symbolic and Algebraic Computation ISSAC '96*, Zürich, Switzerland, ed. LAKSHMAN Y. N., ACM Press, 259–266. [473]

GILBERT STRANG (1980), *Linear Algebra and Its Applications*. Academic Press, New York, second edition. [677]

VOLKER STRASSEN (1969), Gaussian Elimination is not Optimal. *Numerische Mathematik* **13**, 354–356. [313, 315, 330]

V. STRASSEN (1972), Berechnung und Programm. I. *Acta Informatica* **1**, 320–335. [471]

VOLKER STRASSEN (1973a), Vermeidung von Divisionen. *Journal für die Reine und Angewandte Mathematik* **264**, 182–202. [272, 330, 471]

V. STRASSEN (1973b), Berechnung und Programm. II. *Acta Informatica* **2**, 64–79. [471]

VOLKER STRASSEN (1976), Einige Resultate über Berechnungskomplexität. *Jahresberichte der DMV* **78**, 1–8. [515, 541]

V. STRASSEN (1983), The computational complexity of continued fractions. *SIAM Journal on Computing* **12**(1), 1–27. [303, 310]

VOLKER STRASSEN (1984), Algebraische Berechnungskomplexität. In *Perspectives in Mathematics, Anniversary of Oberwolfach 1984*. Birkhäuser Verlag, Basel. [330]

VOLKER STRASSEN (1990), Algebraic Complexity Theory. In *Handbook of Theoretical Computer Science*, vol. A, ed. J. VAN LEEUWEN, 633–672. Elsevier Science Publishers B.V., Amsterdam, and The MIT Press, Cambridge MA. [330]

C. STURM (1835), Mémoire sur la résolution des équations numériques. *Mémoires présentés par divers savants à l'Académie des Sciences de l'Institut de France* **6**, 273–318. [87]

A. SVOBODA and M. VALACH (1955), Operátorové obvody (Operational Circuits). *Stroje na Zpracování Informací, Sborník III, Nakl. ČSAV*. [123]

A. SVOBODA and M. VALACH (1957), Rational Numerical System of Residual Classes. *Stroje na Zpracování Informací, Sborník V, Nakl. ČSAV*, 9–37. [123]

J. J. SYLVESTER (1840), A method of determining by mere inspection the derivatives from two equations of any degree. *Philosophical Magazine* **16**, 132–135. *Mathematical Papers* **1**, Chelsea Publishing Co., New York, 1973, 54–57. [186]

J. J. SYLVESTER (1853), On the explicit values of Sturm's quotients. *Philosophical Magazine* **VI**, 293–296. *Mathematical Papers* **1**, Chelsea Publishing Co., New York, 1973, 637–640. [186, 691]

J. J. SYLVESTER (1881), On the resultant of two congruences. *Johns Hopkins University Circulars* **1**, p. 131. *Mathematical Papers* **3**, Chelsea Publishing Co., New York, 1973, p. 475. [186]

NICHOLAS S. SZABÓ and RICHARD I. TANAKA (1967), *Residue arithmetic and its applications to computer technology*. McGraw-Hill, New York. [123]

ALFRED TARSKI (1948), *A decision method for elementary algebra and geometry*. The Rand Corporation, Santa Monica CA, 2nd edition. Project Rand, R-109. [593]

BROOK TAYLOR (1715), *Methodus Incrementorum Directa & Inversa*. Gul. Innys, London. [272]

RICHARD TAYLOR and ANDREW WILES (1995), Ring-theoretic properties of certain Hecke algebras. *Annals of Mathematics* **141**, 553–572. [488]

GÉRALD TENENBAUM (1995), *Introduction to analytic and probabilistic number theory*. Cambridge studies in advanced mathematics **46**, Cambridge University Press, Cambridge, UK. [511]

A. THUE (1902), Et par andtydninger til en talteoretisk methode. *Videnskabers Selskab Forhandlinger Christiana* **7**. [123]

А. Л. ТООМ (1963), О сложности схемы из функциональных элементов, реализующей умножение целых чисел. *Доклады Академий Наук СССР* **150**(3), 496–498. A. L. TOOM, The complexity of a scheme of functional elements realizing the multiplication of integers, *Soviet Mathematics Doklady* **4** (1963), 714–716. [234]

BARRY M. TRAGER (1976), Algebraic Factoring and Rational Function Integration. In *Proceedings of the 1976 ACM Symposium on Symbolic and Algebraic Computation ISSAC '76*, Yorktown Heights NY, ed. R. D. JENKS, ACM Press, 219–226. [441, 606]

CARLO TRAVERSO (1988), Gröbner trace algorithms. In *Proceedings of the 1988 International Symposium on Symbolic and Algebraic Computation ISSAC '88*, Rome, Italy, ed. P. GIANNI. Lecture Notes in Computer Science **358**, Springer-Verlag, Berlin, 125–138. [593]

A. M. TURING (1937), On computable numbers, with an application to the Entscheidungsproblem. *Proceedings of the London Mathematical Society, Second Series*, **42**, 230–265, and **43**, 544–546. [395]

ALASDAIR URQUHART (1995), The complexity of propositional proofs. *The Bulletin of Symbolic Logic* **1**(4), 425–467. [661]

GIOVANNI VACCA (1894), Intorno alla prima dimostrazione di un teorema di Fermat. *Bibliotheca Mathematica, Serie 2*, **8**, 46–48. [81]

CH.-J. DE LA VALLÉE POUSSIN (1896), Recherches analytiques sur la théorie des nombres premiers. *Annales de la Société Scientifique de Bruxelles* **20**, 183–256 and 281–397. [507]

R. C. VAUGHAN (1974), Bounds for the coefficients of cyclotomic polynomials. *Michigan Mathematical Journal* **21**, 289–295. [187]

G. S. VERNAM (1926), Cipher Printing Telegraph Systems. *Journal of the American Institute of Electrical Engineers* **45**, 109–115. [555]

G. VILLARD (1997), Further Analysis of Coppersmith's Block Wiedemann Algorithm for the Solution of Sparse Linear Systems. In *Proceedings of the 1997 International Symposium on Symbolic and Algebraic Computation ISSAC '97*, Maui HI, ed. WOLFGANG W. KÜCHLIN, ACM Press, 32–39. [330]

J. S. VITTER and PH. FLAJOLET (1990), Average-case analysis of algorithms and data structures. In *Handbook of Theoretical Computer Science*, vol. A, ed. J. VAN LEEUWEN, 431–524. Elsevier Science Publishers B.V., Amsterdam, and The MIT Press, Cambridge MA. [661]

L. G. WADE, JR. (1995), *Organic Chemistry*. Prentice-Hall, Inc., Englewood Cliffs NJ, 3rd edition. [662]

BARTEL L. VAN DER WAERDEN (1930a), Eine Bemerkung über die Unzerlegbarkeit von Polynomen. *Mathematische Annalen* **102**, 738–739. [395]

B. L. VAN DER WAERDEN (1930b), *Moderne Algebra, Erster Teil*. Die Grundlehren der mathematischen Wissenschaften in Einzeldarstellungen **33**, Julius Springer, Berlin. English translation: *Algebra, Volume I.*, Springer Verlag, 1991. [560, 667]

BARTEL L. VAN DER WAERDEN (1931), *Moderne Algebra, Zweiter Teil*. Die Grundlehren der mathematischen Wissenschaften in Einzeldarstellungen **34**, Julius Springer, Berlin. English translation: *Algebra, Volume II.*, Springer Verlag, 1991. [327, 560, 667]

B. L. VAN DER WAERDEN (1933/34), Die Seltenheit der Gleichungen mit Affekt. *Mathematische Annalen* **109**, 13–16. [440]

B. L. VAN DER WAERDEN (1938), Eine Bemerkung zur numerischen Berechnung von Determinanten und Inversen von Matrizen. *Jahresberichte der DMV* **48**, 29–30. [330]

SAMUEL S. WAGSTAFF, JR. (1983), Divisors of Mersenne numbers. *Mathematics of Computation* **40**(161), 385–397. [508]

GREGORY K. WALLACE (1991), The JPEG Still Picture Compression Standard. *Communications of the ACM* **34**(4), 30–44. [344]

D. WAN (1993), A *p*-adic lifting lemma and its applications to permutation polynomials. In *Proceedings 1992 Conference on Finite Fields, Coding Theory, and Advances in Communications and Computing*, eds. G. L. MULLEN and P. J.-S. SHIUE. Lecture Notes in Pure an Applied Mathematics **141**, Marcel Dekker, Inc., 209–216. [400]

EDWARD WARING (1770), *Meditationes Algebraicæ*. J. Woodyer, Cambridge, England, second edition. English translation by DENNIS WEEKS, American Mathematical Society, 1991. [272]

EDWARD WARING (1779), Problems concerning Interpolations. *Philosophical Transactions of the Royal Society of London* **69**(7), 59–67. [122]

STEPHEN M. WATT and HANS J. STETTER (1998), eds., Symbolic-Numeric Algebra for Polynomials. Special Issue of the *Journal of Symbolic Computation* **26**(6). [39]

INGO WEGENER (1987), *The Complexity of Boolean Functions*. Wiley-Teubner Series in Computer Science, B. G. Teubner, Stuttgart, and John Wiley & Sons. [685]

B. M. M. DE WEGER (1989), *Algorithms for Diophantine equations*. CWI Tract no. 65, Centrum voor Wiskunde en Informatica, Amsterdam. 212 pages. [471]

ANDRÉ WEIL (1984), *Number theory: An approach through history; From Hammurapi to Legendre*. Birkhäuser Verlag. xxi+375 pages. [487]

ANDREAS WERCKMEISTER (1691), *Musicalische Temperatur*. Theodorus Philippus Calvisius, Franckfurt und Leipzig. First edition 1686/87. Reprint edited by GUIDO BIMBERG and RÜDIGER PFEIFFER, Denkmäler der Musik in Mitteldeutschland: Ser. 2., Documenta theoretica musicae; Bd. 1: Werckmeister-Studien. Verlag Die Blaue Eule, Essen, 1996. [79]

DOUGLAS H. WIEDEMANN (1986), Solving Sparse Linear Equations Over Finite Fields. *IEEE Transactions on Information Theory* **IT-32**(1), 54–62. [318, 323, 328, 329, 333, 530]

ANDREW WILES (1995), Modular elliptic curves and Fermat's Last Theorem. *Annals of Mathematics* **142**, 443–551. [488]

HERBERT S. WILF (1994), *generatingfunctionology*. Academic Press, 2nd edition. First edition 1990. [440, 661]

HERBERT S. WILF and DORON ZEILBERGER (1990), Rational functions certify combinatorial identities. *Journal of the American Mathematical Society* **3**(1), 147–158. [661]

HERBERT S. WILF and DORON ZEILBERGER (1992), An algorithmic proof theory for hypergeometric (ordinary and "q") multisum/integral identities. *Inventiones Mathematicae* **108**, 575–633. [661]

MICHAEL WILLETT (1978), Factoring polynomials over a finite field. *SIAM Journal on Applied Mathematics* **35**, 333–337. [394]

H. C. WILLIAMS (1982), A $p+1$ Method of Factoring. *Mathematics of Computation* **39**(159), 225–234. [542]

H. C. WILLIAMS (1993), How was F_6 factored? *Mathematics of Computation* **61**(203), 463–474. [516]

H. C. WILLIAMS and HARVEY DUBNER (1986), The primality of R1031. *Mathematics of Computation* **47**(176), 703–711. [505]

H. C. WILLIAMS and M. C. WUNDERLICH (1987), On the Parallel Generation of the Residues for the Continued Fraction Factoring Algorithm. *Mathematics of Computation* **48**(177), 405–423. [543]

LELAND H. WILLIAMS (1961), Algebra of Polynomials in Several Variables for a Digital Computer. *Journal of the ACM* **8**, 29–40. [18]

S. WINOGRAD (1971), On Multiplication of 2×2 matrices. *Linear Algebra and its Applications* **4**, 381–388. [330]

WEN-TSÜN WU (1994), *Mechanical Theorem Proving in Geometries: Basic Principles.* Springer-Verlag, New York. English translation by XIAOFAN JIN and DONGMING WANG. Originally published as "Basic Principles of Mechanical Theorem Proving in Geometry" in Chinese language by Science Press, Beijing, 1984. [592, 593]

CHEE K. YAP (1991), A New Lower Bound Construction for Commutative Thue Systems with Applications. *Journal of Symbolic Computation* **12**, 1–27. [592]

DAVID Y. Y. YUN (1976), On Square-free Decomposition Algorithms. In *Proceedings of the 1976 ACM Symposium on Symbolic and Algebraic Computation ISSAC '76,* Yorktown Heights NY, ed. R. D. JENKS, ACM Press, 26–35. [394, 441]

DAVID Y. Y. YUN (1977a), Fast algorithm for rational function integration. In *Information Processing 77—Proceedings of the IFIP Congress 77,* ed. B. GILCHRIST, North-Holland, Amsterdam, 493–498. [606]

DAVID Y. Y. YUN (1977b), On the equivalence of polynomial gcd and squarefree factorization problems. In *Proceedings of the 1977 MACSYMA Users Conference,* Berkeley CA, NASA, Washington DC, 65–70. [401]

HANS ZASSENHAUS (1969), On Hensel Factorization, I. *Journal of Number Theory* **1**, 291–311. [393, 418, 440, 441]

DORON ZEILBERGER (1990a), A holonomic systems approach to special function identities. *Journal of Computational and Applied Mathematics* **32**, 321–368. [635, 661]

DORON ZEILBERGER (1990b), A fast algorithm for proving terminating hypergeometric identities. *Discrete Mathematics* **80**, 207–211. [635, 661]

DORON ZEILBERGER (1991), The Method of Creative Telescoping. *Journal of Symbolic Computation* **11**, 195–204. [635, 661]

DORON ZEILBERGER (1993), Theorems for a Price: Tomorrow's Semi-Rigorous Mathematical Culture. *Notices of the American Mathematical Society* **40**(8), 978–981. [661]

PAUL ZIMMERMANN (1991), *Séries génératrices et analyse automatique d'algorithmes.* PhD thesis, École Polytechnique, Paris. [661]

PHILIP R. ZIMMERMANN (1996), *The Official PGP User's Guide.* MIT Press. [16]

RICHARD ZIPPEL (1979), Probabilistic Algorithms for sparse Polynomials. In *Proceedings of EUROSAM '79,* Marseille, France. Lecture Notes in Computer Science **72**, Springer-Verlag, 216–226. [187, 472]

RICHARD ZIPPEL (1993), *Effective polynomial computation.* Kluwer Academic Publishers, Boston MA. [192]

List of notation

$\mathbb{N}, \mathbb{N}_{>n}$	set of nonnegative integers, set of integers greater than $n \in \mathbb{N}$
$\mathbb{Z}$	ring of integers
$\mathbb{Q}, \mathbb{Q}_{>0}$	field of rational numbers, set of positive rational numbers
$\mathbb{R}, \mathbb{R}_{>r}$	field of real numbers, set of real numbers greater than $r \in \mathbb{R}$
$\mathbb{C}$	field of complex numbers
$\emptyset$	empty set
$A \cup B$	union of the sets A and B
$A \cap B$	intersection of the sets A and B
$A \setminus B$	set-theoretic difference of A and B
$A \times B$	Cartesian product of the sets A and B
A^n	vectors of length $n \in \mathbb{N}$ over the set A
$A^{\mathbb{N}}$	countably infinite sequences over the set A, page 318
$\#A$	cardinality (number of elements) of the set A
$\langle A \rangle$	subgroup, ideal, or subspace generated by the elements of A, pages 668, 670, 678
$A \cong B$	A and B are isomorphic groups or rings, pages 668, 669
$R^\times$	group of units of the ring R, page 671
$R[x]$	ring of polynomials in the variable x over the ring R, page 672
$R[x_1, \ldots, x_n]$	ring of polynomials in n variables over the ring R, page 673
$R[[x]]$	ring of power series in the variable x over the ring R, page 672
$R^{n \times m}$	ring of $n \times m$ matrices over the ring R for $n, m \in \mathbb{N}$
R/I	residue class ring of the ring R modulo the ideal $I \subseteq R$, page 670
$F(x)$	field of rational functions in the variable x over the field F, page 674
$F((x))$	field of Laurent series in the variable x over the field F, page 84
$\exp x$	exponential function, e^x for $x \in \mathbb{R}$
$\ln x$	natural (base e) logarithm of $x \in \mathbb{R}_{>0}$
$\log x$	binary (base 2) logarithm of $x \in \mathbb{R}_{>0}$
$\Re a$	real part of $a \in \mathbb{C}$
$\Im a$	imaginary part of $a \in \mathbb{C}$
$|a|$	absolute value of $a \in \mathbb{C}$
$\mathrm{sgn}(a)$	sign of $a \in \mathbb{R}$
$\lfloor a \rfloor$	greatest integer less or equal to $a \in \mathbb{R}$
$\lceil a \rceil$	smallest integer greater or equal to $a \in \mathbb{R}$
$\lceil a \rfloor$	nearest integer to $a \in \mathbb{R}$, $\lfloor a + 1/2 \rfloor$, page 452
$\|a\|_1$	1-norm of a vector or polynomial a, page 681
$\|a\|_2$	Euclidean norm of a vector or a polynomial a, page 681
$\|a\|_\infty$	max-norm of a vector or polynomial a, page 681
$a \star b$	inner product of vectors a and b, page 681
$a \mid b$	a divides b, $\exists c \; b = ac$
$a \nmid b$	a does not divide b
f'	formal derivative of the polynomial or rational function f, page 252
$\partial f / \partial x$	formal derivative of the multivariate polynomial f with respect to x
$f^{\overline{m}}$	mth rising factorial power for $m \in \mathbb{Z}$, $f \cdot Ef \cdots E^{m-1}f$ if $m \in \mathbb{N}$, page 610
$f^{\underline{m}}$	mth falling factorial power for $m \in \mathbb{Z}$, $f \cdot E^{-1}f \cdots E^{1-m}f$ if $m \in \mathbb{N}$, page 611
$\binom{n}{k}$	binomial coefficient for $n, k \in \mathbb{N}$
$\left[\begin{matrix} n \\ k \end{matrix} \right]$	Stirling number of the first kind for $n, k \in \mathbb{N}$, page 636
$\left\{ \begin{matrix} n \\ k \end{matrix} \right\}$	Stirling number of the second kind for $n, k \in \mathbb{N}$, page 614
$[q_1, q_2, \ldots, q_n]$	continued fraction $q_1 + 1/(q_2 + 1/(\cdots + 1/q_n) \cdots)$, page 73
$I(n, q)$	number of monic irreducible polynomials of degree n in $\mathbb{F}_q[x]$, page 384
$S(f, g)$	S-polynomial of multivariate polynomials f and g, page 580
$\longleftarrow$	assignment in algorithm
$*, **, \longrightarrow$	ranking of exercises: medium, difficult, lengthy (no mark = easy)
$\square$	end of proof
$\diamond$	end of example

Index

A page number is underlined (for example: <u>667</u>) when it represents the definition or the main source of information about the index entry. For several key words that appear frequently only ranges of pages or the most important occurrences are indexed.

¹ وَ مَا مِنْ غَآئِبَةٍ فِى ٱلسَّمَآءِ وَ ٱلْأَرْضِ إِلَّا فِى كِتَبٍ مُّبِينٍ
The Holy Qur°an (732)

Les bons élèves font la gloire du maître.[2]
Joseph Liouville (1846)

Je prie les lecteurs de n'ajouter point du tout de foi
à tout ce qu'ils trouveront ici écrit, mais seulement de l'examiner
et n'en recevoir que ce que la force et l'évidence de la raison
les pourra contraindre de croire.[3]
René Descartes (1647)

The subject is full of pitfalls. I have pointed out
some mistakes made by others, but have no doubt
that I have made new ones. It may be expected that any errors
will be discovered and eliminated in due course.
Francis Sowerby Macaulay (1916)

Wherfore I trust thei that be learned, and happen to reade
this worke, wil beare the moare with me, if thei finde any thyng,
that thei doe mislike: Wherein if thei will use this curtesie,
either by writynge to admonishe me thereof, either
theim selfes to sette forthe a moare perfecter woorke,
I will thynke them praise worthie.
Robert Recorde (1557)

There is a theory which states that if ever anyone discovers exactly
what the Universe is for and why it is here, it will instantly disappear
and be replaced by something even more bizarre and inexplicable.
There is another theory which states that this has already happened.
Douglas Adams (1980)

---

¹ There is nothing hidden in heaven or on earth that is not in a clear book.
² Good students are the teacher's glory.
³ I ask the readers to put no faith at all in anything they find written here, but just to examine it and to accept only whatever the strength and evidence of reason may oblige them to believe.